실수 없는 수능 듣기 만점 공략!

Listening

수능 듣기 실전 모의고사 35회 + 5회

저자 및 연구진

저자
Jason Lee

연세대학교 영어교육 석사
Jason Lee Academy 대표
www.jasonlee.co.kr
jasonlee@jasonlee.co.kr

연구
Jason Lee Academy 연구원

연구실장: 김희선
Ryan DeLaney 수석연구원: University of Southern Indiana/University of Cambridge(CELTA)
서지연 연구원: 한국외대 영어과(卒)
박주현 연구원: 고려대 영어교육 석사
박성우 연구원: 연세대 영어영문학 석사
백재민 연구원: 연세대 영어영문학 석사
박동준 연구원: 서울대 경영학과(卒)
박국일 연구원: Boston University(卒)
이민령 연구원: 고려대 경영학과
Taylor Lagieski 연구원: University of Montana/ University of Cambridge(CELTA)

감수
양유리 선생님: 연세대 영어교육 석사, 양천고 교사
김세리 선생님: 연세대 영어교육 석사, 화곡중 교사

평가
김동원(성균관대) 김정호(인제의대) 김효중(육군사관학교) 박찬슬(서울대) 이승혁(경희대)
이우진(제주의대) 이종식(서울시립대) 임재훈(연세대) 장정우(美미시간주립대) 조원우(연세대)
최진명(서울대) 탁우령(고려대) 황인찬(서울대)

수능직방 Listening Combined / 종합편

지은이 Jason Lee
펴낸이 최회영
영문교열 윤은지, Eric Williams
펴낸곳 (주)웅진컴퍼스
등록번호 제22-2943호
등록일자 2006년 6월 16일
주소 서울특별시 서초구 강남대로39길 15-10 한라비발디스튜디오193 3층
전화 (02)3471-0096
홈페이지 http://www.wjcompass.com

ISBN 978-89-6697-899-1

15 14 13 12 11 10 9 8
25 24 23 22

Printed in Korea

이 책을 내며

최근 수능 영어는 많은 변화를 겪고 있습니다. 2013학년도까지 15년간 기본 틀을 유지하며 난이도만 조절해 오던 데서 벗어나 2014학년도에 갑자기 수준별 시험(A·B형)으로 출제되더니 2015학년도부터는 A·B형 구분을 없애고 다시 단일형으로 바뀌었습니다. 급기야 2018학년도 수능 시험부터는 절대평가로 바뀌게 되었습니다. **급변하는 대입 영어 정책에 수험생과 학부모의 마음이 무거운 상황에서, 수능 영어 어떻게 준비해야 할까요?**

'최적의 수능 대비'와 '실질적인 영어 실력 향상'이 동시에 가능한 교재로서 불철주야 연구와 노력을 다하여 **수능직방 Voca 시리즈**에 이어 이번에 **수능직방 Listening 시리즈**를 출간하게 되었습니다. 그 특징은 다음과 같습니다.

첫째, 평가원의 최신 수능 개편안 및 출제 방침, 그리고 수능 연계 EBS 교재를 활용한 출제 경향까지 과학적으로 철저히 분석·반영하였습니다. 즉, 코퍼스 언어학에 기반을 둔 Jason Lee Academy는 이번 수능직방 Listening 개발 과정에서도 고유의 특허 기술을 활용하여 수능·평가원 모의고사의 어휘 수준과 문장 수, 선택지 길이와 한 문장에서의 최대 어휘 수까지 분석·반영하였습니다.

둘째, EBS 수능 연계 교재 및 최근 7년간의 시·도 교육청 모의고사 듣기 평가에서 정답률이 낮았던 문항들(60% 이하)을 엄선하여 비슷한 난이도로 재구성하였습니다.

셋째, 모든 문제와 지문은 수능·평가원 출제 경험이 있는 학교 선생님들의 조언과 감수를 거쳐 최신 수능이 요구하는 기준을 만족시키도록 구성되었고, 앞으로 출제 가능성이 없는 유형은 배제하였습니다.

넷째, 학생 개인별 맞춤 학습, 완전학습이 가능하도록 3종의 음원(문제풀이용, 문항별, 실전보다 빠른 듣기용 MP3 음원)과 무료 Mobile App을 제공합니다.

다섯째, 실제 원어민의 대화, 담화에 가깝게 구성하여 수능 시험을 준비하면서 살아있는 영어(Real English) 실력까지 갖출 수 있습니다. 국내 유명 어학원과 학교에서 강의 경력이 풍부한 원어민 선생님들이 교재 기획·개발 전 과정에 참여하였기 때문입니다.

저희 Jason Lee Academy 연구진과 웅진컴퍼스 모두의 열정과 노력이 여러분의 수능 만점과 영어 실력 향상이라는 결실로 이어지리라 확신합니다.

강남 Jason Lee Academy에서

Jason Lee

수능 출제 경향 분석 및 대비 전략

수능 듣기의 역사

수능 영어에서 가장 큰 변화를 겪은 영역은 단언컨대 듣기 영역입니다. 1994학년 1차 수능 8문항을 시작으로 1996학년에 10문항, 1997학년 17문항으로 늘어났고, 1998학년 수능부터 2013학년까지 15년간은 거의 비슷한 유형과 포맷을 유지하였습니다. 하지만 2014학년 6월 평가원 모의고사부터 '외국어 영역'에서 '영어 영역'으로 이름도 바뀌고 A형, B형으로 수준별 시험을 치르게 되면서 수능 영어 시험에 많은 변화가 나타났습니다. 그중 듣기 영역이 문항 수와 구성 면에서 가장 큰 변화가 있었습니다. 17문항에서 22문항으로 증가하여, 듣기 비중이 기존 약 37.78%에서 약 48.89%로 대폭 상승하였습니다. TOEIC과 TEPS 등의 시험과 매우 유사한 '짧은 대화 응답'과 '한 지문 두 문항' 등과 같은 신유형이 나타났습니다. 하지만 야심 차게 시작된 수준별 시험은 난이도 조절 실패 등의 이유로 2014학년 수능이 처음이자 마지막 시험이 되었고 2015학년부터 다시 듣기 문항 수도 기존 17문항으로 돌아가게 되었습니다. 다만, 2014학년의 22문항 체제에서 문제 유형은 그대로 유지하되, 중복 유형을 줄여 17문항으로 만든 점은 주목할 만한 대목입니다.

NEW 통합형 수능 영어 듣기 출제 경향 분석 및 학습 전략

우리가 준비해야 하는 수능 영어 듣기는 크게 4가지, 세부적으로는 총 15가지 유형으로 구성되어 있습니다.

1. 대의 파악 (2014학년 5문항 → 2015학년 이후 3문항)

대화 · 담화를 듣고 전체적인 내용을 이해하거나 추론하는 능력을 측정합니다.

① 대화 · 담화 목적
② 대화 · 주제/요지
③ 대화 · 담화자 주장/의견
④ 대화자 심정/관계, 대화 장소 → 관계의 비중이 압도적으로 높음

학습 전략

◈ 대화 도입부를 들으면서 대화/담화가 일어나는 상황, 장소, 대화자 간의 관계를 유추해 본다.
◈ 대화자가 반복, 강조하는 핵심 단어 · 표현에 집중한다.
◈ 너무 광범위하거나 지엽적인 선택지는 피한다.

2. 세부 사항 (2014학년 9문항 → 2015학년 이후 7문항)

대화 · 담화의 핵심적 내용과 전개 방식에 비추어 제시된 특정 정보를 가급적 정확하고 신속하게 파악할 수 있는 능력을 측정합니다. 직접적으로 제시된 정보를 구체적인 사항에 초점을 맞추어 정확하게 파악하는 연습이 필요합니다.

① 그림 내용 일치/불일치 → 대부분 불일치 문제
② 한 일/할 일/부탁한 일
③ 5W1H 세부사항 → 6하 원칙 중 주로 '이유'를 묻는 유형으로 출제
④ 숫자 관련 정보 → 고난도 문항으로 출제
⑤ 대화 언급/불언급
⑥ 담화 내용 일치/불일치 → 주로 불일치로 출제
⑦ 도표 내용 일치/불일치

학습 전략

◈ 평소 들으며 내용을 메모하는 연습을 하자.
◈ 계산 문제는 넓은 공간에 식을 세우고 복잡한 식은 대화가 끝난 후 계산한다.
◈ 내용 일치/불일치 문제는 선택지 순서대로 나오기 때문에, 선택지를 미리 봐놓고 줄을 그어가며 푼다.

3. **간접 말하기 (2014학년 6문항 → 2015학년 이후 5문항)**

실제 일상생활에서 흔히 발생할 수 있는 의사소통 상황과 관련된 듣기 자료를 통해 이해한 바를 가상의 말하기 상황에 적용할 수 있는 능력을 측정합니다.

① 짧은 대화 응답
② 대화 응답
③ 담화 응답

학습 전략

◈ 교과서 주요 의사소통 기능 표현을 미리 익혀두자.
◈ 미리 선택지의 내용을 읽고 무슨 내용인지 파악한다. (대화/담화를 듣고 난 후 선택지 내용을 읽으면, 시간에 쫓겨 다음 문제까지 영향을 받기 때문이다.)
◈ 선택지의 내용을 두 개 이상 모르면, 과감히 그 문제는 건너뛰고 다음 문제에 집중하자.

4. **복합 (2014학년 2문항 → 2015학년 이후 2문항)**

하나의 대화 · 담화문을 통해서 주로 전체적인 흐름 파악과 세부적인 내용 파악 능력을 동시에 측정하고자 출제합니다.

① 하나의 대화 · 담화문 2문항

학습 전략

◈ 대화/담화가 시작되기 전에, 문제와 선택지를 반드시 미리 읽어놔야 한다.
◈ 들으면서 본인만 알 수 있도록 최대한 간결하게 메모하는 습관을 평소 들여놔야 한다.
◈ 세부적인 내용은 처음에 놓쳤더라도 두 번째에서 만회할 기회가 있다. 포기하지 말자.
◈ 상위권의 경우, 한 번 들을 때 두 문제를 정확하게 맞힐 수 있도록 집중한다. 그래야 시간을 아껴서 독해에 더 투자할 수 있다.

수능 영어 듣기 만점 전략

1. **평소 매일 꾸준히 듣는 연습이 필요합니다.**
노력에 비해 당장 실력이 늘지 않는 듯해도, 영어 실력은 결국 계단식으로 향상된다는 것을 기억하세요.

2. **안 들리는 원인을 파악하여 보완하세요.**
자신이 자주 틀리는 문제 유형, 모르는 어휘, 취약점을 파악해서 보완하세요. 받아쓰기(Dictation) 및 오답 노트 작성이 도움이 됩니다.

3. **들으면서 메모하는 연습을 해 보세요.**
문장 전체를 꼼꼼히 받아 적기는 사실 쉽지 않은 일입니다. 따라서 나만의 전략을 세워 평소 최대한 간결히 메모하는 습관을 들여야 합니다. 예를 들어, Studying English를 받아 적어야 한다면 다 적는 것이 아니라 Stu~g Eng~ 처럼 본인만이 알아볼 수 있도록, 기호 또는 축약 등의 방법을 이용하면 유용합니다.

4. **실제 수능보다 빠른 속도로 듣는 연습을 하세요.**
실제 시험 당일에는 심리적으로 위축되고 긴장한 탓에 자칫 속도가 빠르지 않음에도 불구하고 순간적으로 놓칠 수가 있습니다. 따라서 평소 실제 수능보다 빠른 속도의 대화/담화문을 긴장감을 유지하며 듣는 연습을 하세요. 실전 감각을 키울 수 있습니다.

BONUS TIP

평가원 공식 발표에 따르면, 2014학년도 수준별 영어 A형을 끝으로 **'지도를 활용한 길 찾기' 문항은 더는 출제되지 않습니다.** 또한, 1997학년도 수능부터 2013학년도 수능까지 13번으로 출제되었던 **'그림 상황에 맞는 대화를 고르기' 문제도 신수능에서는 더 이상 찾아보기 어렵습니다.**

구성과 특징

{ Step 1 }

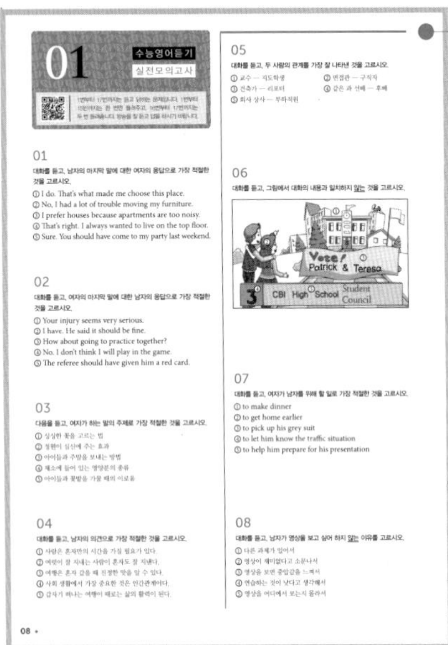

100% 수능 실전 모의고사

▶ 수능 최신 출제 경향 반영: 평가원에서 제시한 수능 출제 방침과 수능 개편안을 최고의 연구 · 집필진이 철저히 분석, 반영하여 **문항유형 및 배치, 어휘의 난이도와 script 길이까지 실전과 100% 동일**하게 구성하였습니다.

▶ 바로 듣는 바로 푸는 QR Code 수록: **언제 어디서나 자투리 시간에도 듣기 학습이 가능합니다.**

{ Step 2 }

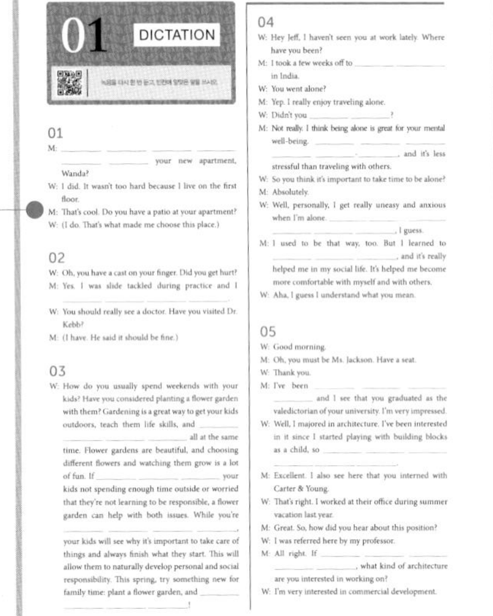

Dictation (받아쓰기)

▶ Lexical Chunk(의미 단위)별로 빈칸 구성: **정답을 찾는 데 꼭 필요한 핵심 어구 및 수능 필수 어휘를 듣고 받아쓰는 연습**을 통해, 해당 표현을 완전히 자신의 것으로 소화할 수 있고 수능 출제 포인트가 어디에 있는 지까지 파악하게 되어, 결국 수능 고득점으로 이어집니다.

▶ 문항별 MP3 음원 제공: 자신이 틀린 문제, 다시 듣고 싶은 표현만 빠르게 찾아 학습할 수 있도록 문항별로 구분해둔 파일도 제공합니다.

{ Step 3 }

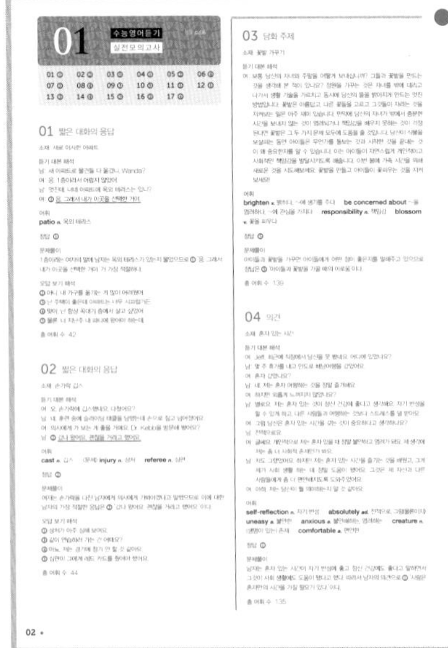

친절한 정답 및 해설

▶ **친절하고 상세한 정답 및 해설, 해석과 소재와 핵심 어휘까지 빠짐없이 수록**: 학습자 스스로 꼼꼼히 복습이 가능하도록 구성하였습니다.

▶ **평가원 지침에 따라 분류한 수능 듣기 문제 유형도 문항별로** 친절히 표기해 놓았습니다. 자신이 자주 틀리는 문제 유형이 무엇인지 파악하고 부족한 점을 보완하는 데에 도움이 될 것입니다.

완전학습을 위한 무료 제공

* **용도별 MP3 음원 3종 (문제풀이용, 빠른 듣기용, 문항별)**
  www.wjcompass.com/sjlistening
* **수능직방 Listening 전용 Mobile App 제공**
  Apple App Store / Google Play Store 접속 후, '수직리스닝'을 검색하세요.

목차

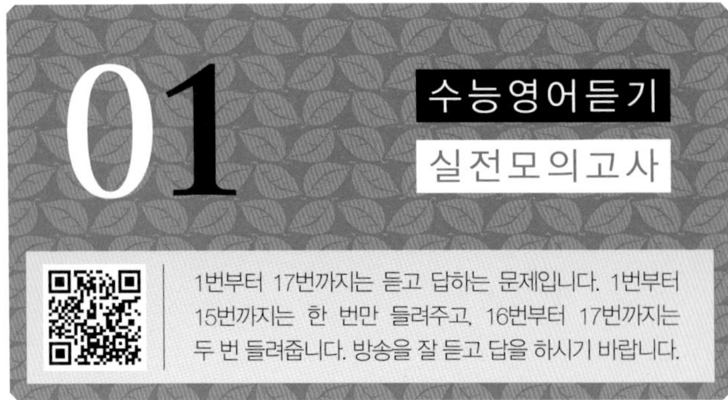

01

대화를 듣고, 남자의 마지막 말에 대한 여자의 응답으로 가장 적절한 것을 고르시오.

① I do. That's what made me choose this place.
② No, I had a lot of trouble moving my furniture.
③ I prefer houses because apartments are too noisy.
④ That's right. I always wanted to live on the top floor.
⑤ Sure. You should have come to my party last weekend.

02

대화를 듣고, 여자의 마지막 말에 대한 남자의 응답으로 가장 적절한 것을 고르시오.

① Your injury seems very serious.
② I have. He said it should be fine.
③ How about going to practice together?
④ No. I don't think I will play in the game.
⑤ The referee should have given him a red card.

03

다음을 듣고, 여자가 하는 말의 주제로 가장 적절한 것을 고르시오.

① 싱싱한 꽃을 고르는 법
② 정원이 심신에 주는 효과
③ 아이들과 주말을 보내는 방법
④ 채소에 들어 있는 영양분의 종류
⑤ 아이들과 꽃밭을 가꿀 때의 이로움

04

대화를 듣고, 남자의 의견으로 가장 적절한 것을 고르시오.

① 사람은 혼자만의 시간을 가질 필요가 있다.
② 여럿이 잘 지내는 사람이 혼자도 잘 지낸다.
③ 여행은 혼자 갔을 때 진정한 맛을 알 수 있다.
④ 사회 생활에서 가장 중요한 것은 인간관계이다.
⑤ 갑자기 떠나는 여행이 때로는 삶의 활력이 된다.

05

대화를 듣고, 두 사람의 관계를 가장 잘 나타낸 것을 고르시오.

① 교수 — 지도학생
② 면접관 — 구직자
③ 건축가 — 리포터
④ 같은 과 선배 — 후배
⑤ 회사 상사 — 부하직원

06

대화를 듣고, 그림에서 대화의 내용과 일치하지 않는 것을 고르시오.

07

대화를 듣고, 여자가 남자를 위해 할 일로 가장 적절한 것을 고르시오.

① to make dinner
② to get home earlier
③ to pick up his grey suit
④ to let him know the traffic situation
⑤ to help him prepare for his presentation

08

대화를 듣고, 남자가 영상을 보고 싶어 하지 않는 이유를 고르시오.

① 다른 과제가 있어서
② 영상이 재미없다고 소문나서
③ 영상을 보면 중압감을 느껴서
④ 연습하는 것이 낫다고 생각해서
⑤ 영상을 어디에서 보는지 몰라서

09

대화를 듣고, 여자가 지불할 금액을 고르시오.

① $20 ② $25 ③ $27 ④ $30 ⑤ $33

10

대화를 듣고, 건물에 관해 두 사람이 언급하지 않은 것을 고르시오.

① 겉모습 ② 주소 ③ 용도
④ 층수 ⑤ 건축 년도

11

Big Bear Resale Services에 관한 다음 내용을 듣고, 일치하지 않는 것을 고르시오.

① 고객들이 원치 않는 물건을 팔아준다.
② 20년 동안 운영해 왔다.
③ 골동품 가게, 폐품 처리장과 일을 한다.
④ 직접 와서 사진을 찍어서 웹사이트에 올려준다.
⑤ 픽업과 배달 서비스는 유료이다.

12

다음 표를 보면서 대화를 듣고, 두 사람이 선택할 동아리를 고르시오.

Jeremy's Academy English Clubs

	Club Name	Meeting Schedule	Activities	Number of Members
①	Great Storytellers	Wed. 5:00 p.m.	Reading & Listening	20
②	Global Leaders	Fri. 5:30 p.m.	Speaking & Writing	20
③	Drama Addicts	Mon. 4:30 p.m.	Reading & Acting	15
④	Better on Paper	Tue. 4:30 p.m.	Reading & Writing	10
⑤	Real Debaters	Fri. 3:00 p.m.	Speaking & Debating	10

13

대화를 듣고, 여자의 마지막 말에 대한 남자의 응답으로 가장 적절한 것을 고르시오.

Man: ______________________________

① I should cancel the meeting.
② I think you need to see a doctor.
③ Thank you so much. I owe you one.
④ I already copied all of the information.
⑤ Okay, great. Get some help from Craig.

14

대화를 듣고, 남자의 마지막 말에 대한 여자의 응답으로 가장 적절한 것을 고르시오.

Woman: ______________________________

① I'm sorry, but you can't. My phone is broken.
② Sure. Playing computer games helps me relax.
③ No problem. That's what friendship is all about.
④ You're right. Everyone has different preferences.
⑤ You should probably find a different game to play.

15

다음 상황 설명을 듣고, Taylor가 기차역 직원에게 할 말로 가장 적절한 것을 고르시오.

Taylor: ______________________________

① I had a great visit with my friend here in New York.
② Can you tell me how to get to my train platform?
③ Is there any other place I can get my ticket?
④ This is the nicest train station I've ever seen.
⑤ I'd like one ticket for Minneapolis, please.

[16-17] 다음을 듣고, 물음에 답하시오.

16

여자가 하는 말의 주제로 가장 적절한 것은?

① Different types of social networking
② Community involvement through the co-op
③ Organizational methods using social networking
④ Attending upcoming social events in the community
⑤ Benefits of joining community involvement programs

17

여자가 언급한 social media의 하나로 언급되지 않은 것은?

① Twitter ② KakaoTalk ③ Facebook
④ Instagram ⑤ YouTube

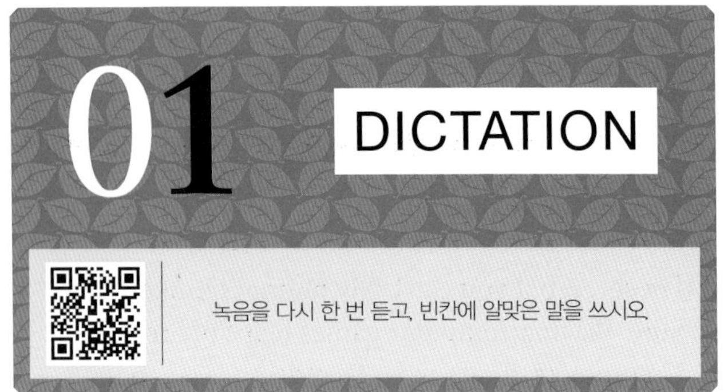

01

M: ________ ________ ________ ________ ________ ________ your new apartment, Wanda?

W: I did. It wasn't too hard because I live on the first floor.

M: That's cool. Do you have a patio at your apartment?

W: (I do. That's what made me choose this place.)

02

W: Oh, you have a cast on your finger. Did you get hurt?

M: Yes. I was slide tackled during practice and I ________ ________ ________ ________.

W: You should really see a doctor. Have you visited Dr. Kebb?

M: (I have. He said it should be fine.)

03

W: How do you usually spend weekends with your kids? Have you considered planting a flower garden with them? Gardening is a great way to get your kids outdoors, teach them life skills, and ________ ________ ________ ________ all at the same time. Flower gardens are beautiful, and choosing different flowers and watching them grow is a lot of fun. If ________ ________ ________ your kids not spending enough time outside or worried that they're not learning to be responsible, a flower garden can help with both issues. While you're ________ ________ ________ ________, your kids will see why it's important to take care of things and always finish what they start. This will allow them to naturally develop personal and social responsibility. This spring, try something new for family time: plant a flower garden, and ________ ________ ________ ________!

04

W: Hey Jeff, I haven't seen you at work lately. Where have you been?

M: I took a few weeks off to ________ ________ in India.

W: You went alone?

M: Yep. I really enjoy traveling alone.

W: Didn't you ________ ________?

M: Not really. I think being alone is great for your mental well-being. ________ ________ ________ ________ ________-________, and it's less stressful than traveling with others.

W: So you think it's important to take time to be alone?

M: Absolutely.

W: Well, personally, I get really uneasy and anxious when I'm alone. ________ ________ ________ ________ ________ ________, I guess.

M: I used to be that way, too. But I learned to ________ ________ ________, and it's really helped me in my social life. It's helped me become more comfortable with myself and with others.

W: Aha, I guess I understand what you mean.

05

W: Good morning.

M: Oh, you must be Ms. Jackson. Have a seat.

W: Thank you.

M: I've been ________ ________ ________ ________ and I see that you graduated as the valedictorian of your university. I'm very impressed.

W: Well, I majored in architecture. I've been interested in it since I started playing with building blocks as a child, so ________ ________ ________ ________ ________ ________.

M: Excellent. I also see here that you interned with Carter & Young.

W: That's right. I worked at their office during summer vacation last year.

M: Great. So, how did you hear about this position?

W: I was referred here by my professor.

M: All right. If ________ ________ ________ ________ ________, what kind of architecture are you interested in working on?

W: I'm very interested in commercial development.

M: It seems like ________ ________ ________ ________ ________ ________ ________ ________ ________.

W: I appreciate you saying that.

06

W: Hey, Patrick!

M: Hi, Teresa. What are you up to?

W: I've almost finished our campaign poster.

M: Great! Did you find a good picture of the school to use in the background?

W: I did, and I used that picture of us pointing as the foreground.

M: It looks great. I also like the banner you drew next to us.

W: I couldn't ________ ________ ________ ________ ________ campaign slogans, though. Sorry.

M: That's all right. By the way, I don't think that the candidate number looks good on the right side.

W: Now that you mention it, it probably ________ ________ ________ ________ ________ ________. How about our school's name and the position we're running for at the bottom?

M: I think that's fine. You've done a great job, Teresa.

W: Thanks. Remember, we need to start the election campaign by 8:30 tomorrow morning.

M: All right. I'll be there ________ ________ ________ ________ ________ ________. Thanks again.

07

[Cell phone rings.]

W: Hey, honey. Are you ________ ________ ________ ________?

M: Yes, but the road is really crowded. I wonder ________ ________ ________ ________ ________.

W: Has there been an accident or something?

M: I'm not sure what's going on. You can have dinner without me if you're hungry.

W: All right. When do you think you'll be home?

M: I really don't know. But can you ________ ________ ________ ________?

W: Of course. What's up?

M: Can you stop by the dry cleaner's and pick up my grey suit? I want to wear it tomorrow for my big presentation.

W: Sure, I'll go over there and get it now.

M: Thanks so much, sweetie. ________ ________ ________ ________ ________ ________ so you just need to pick it up. I hope I can make it home soon.

W: Okay, honey. See you when you get here.

08

W: Hey, Tommy. Have you watched any videos of ________ ________ ________ ________ ________?

M: Not yet. But I've heard he's amazing.

W: You heard right. Everyone on the Internet ________ ________ ________ ________ ________. Would you like to see some highlights?

M: Hmm. . . I don't think I should.

W: Why not? Wouldn't you like to see why he's so good?

M: I'd rather wait until ________ ________ ________ ________.

W: But wouldn't you be more prepared for the game if you watched some video?

M: I think practice is a better way to prepare.

W: That's what a lot of the other players said. They said ________ ________ ________ ________ ________ ________ ________ ________.

M: They're right. Watching videos is a waste of time. My time would be better spent in the gym than the living room.

09

M: Thanks for calling Brother's Pizza. ________ ________ ________ ________ ________?

W: Yeah, I'd like a large triple-cheese pizza. How much will that be?

M: One large special-topping pizza is normally $25, but today is Customer Appreciation Day, so you can get any large pizza for the price of a ________-________ ________.

W: Oh, great. ________ ________ ________, I'd like to add an order of chicken wings.

M: Sure. Will that be all for you today?

W: Yeah, that's all.

M: Okay. The pizza is $20 and the chicken wings are $10 so your total today comes to $30.

W: __________ __________ __________ __________ __________ __________ __________ for this order?

M: Yes, of course. Is it a coupon from our website?

W: Yeah. It's for 10% off.

M: Just give it to the delivery man when he comes.

10

M: Hey, what's that you're looking at on your computer?

W: Just some pictures from my summer vacation to London. Would you like to see them?

M: Sure. *[Pause]* This building is interesting. __________ __________ __________ __________ __________.

W: That's right. Londoners have nicknamed it "The Gherkin" because it looks like a gherkin, a small pickle.

M: What's its real name?

W: 30 Saint Mary Axe. __________ __________ __________.

M: What's inside it?

W: Well, it's located in the financial district of London, so __________ __________ __________ __________ __________ __________, along with several restaurants.

M: How tall is it?

W: I think it's around 180 meters tall. __________ __________-__________ __________ __________.

M: Did you go inside?

W: I did. I have pictures of the interior. Would you like to see them?

11

M: Is your house __________ __________ __________ __________ __________ __________ you don't need? Do you have old TVs, refrigerators, or computers sitting around collecting dust? Well, Big Bear Resale Services is just the place for you. We've been in the business of __________ __________ __________ __________ for 20 years. We work with the best antique shops, scrapyards, and private buyers to assure you'll get the most money __________ __________ __________, __________ __________. All you have to do is pick up the phone and call us. We'll come to your place, appraise your old goods, photograph them, and post the photos on our website in order to __________ __________ __________ __________. Then we'll pick your items up and __________ __________ __________ __________. Call Big Bear Resale Services today!

12

W: Hi, Aaron. I'm thinking about joining an afterschool English club.

M: Mr. Baek __________ __________ __________ __________ __________ __________ __________, too.

W: Hey, let's join one together then. I'm kind of new to the school and you're pretty much my only friend.

M: That's a great idea. He gave me this schedule. What about this club? I've always wanted to try out acting.

W: I really want to join that one, too, but I have piano lessons after school on Mondays. What about the debate club? I've always been interested in arguing.

M: __________ __________ __________ __________ __________ that lets us read a lot. I don't really care much for speaking or debating.

W: Well, I guess __________ __________ __________ __________ __________ __________ __________ __________. Which one should we choose?

M: It looks like this one has a lot more members. Let's join that.

W: Yeah, that way I have a better chance of making new friends.

M: Exactly. I'll sign us up.

13

W: __________ __________ __________ __________ __________ __________ __________ __________?

M: Have you seen Craig?

W: Craig? He called me earlier today and said he was sick, so he wasn't coming in.

M: Are you serious? He's called in sick three times this month.

W: I guess he's been quite ill for a few weeks now. Is there a problem?

M: He and I are supposed to meet our business partners today, and he's the one ________ ________ ________ ________.

W: Oh, no. Really?

M: ________ ________ ________ ________ ________ sometimes. Anyway, have you seen the handouts he had prepared for the meeting?

W: What did they look like?

M: They had a lot of information and data ________ ________ ________ ________ and sales rankings for the last quarter.

W: ________ ________ ________ ________ ________, and if I find them I'll bring them to you.

M: (Thank you so much. I owe you one.)

14

M: Hey, Carol. I see that you're playing that new *Candy Stomp* game on your phone.

W: Yeah. My friend James recommended that ________ ________ ________ ________.

M: I've really wanted to try it, too. ________ ________ ________ ________ ________ ________ when you're finished?

W: No problem. I'll give it to you in a few minutes.

M: Awesome. Hey, have you ever played *Battle of the Clans*? It's pretty fun.

W: I did once, but I thought it was boring.

M: Really? It's so popular.

W: Well, it was a little ________ ________ ________ ________ ________. I enjoy simple games.

M: I don't think it's complicated at all. Even my little cousin can play it.

W: I couldn't get into it. I guess I'm just not like everyone else.

M: Well, ________ ________ ________ ________ ________ ________ ________, can they?

W: (You're right. Everyone has different preferences.)

15

W: After visiting his friend in New York City, Taylor is on his way to Grand Central Station to take a train back to his hometown, Minneapolis. ________ ________ ________ ________ ________ ________ ________ ________ is much more congested than he thought it would be, and the taxi is driving very slowly. Taylor is afraid that he's going to ________ ________ ________ ________ ________. When he arrives at the station, he sees that he has twenty minutes ________ ________ ________ ________. The ticket line is very long. He sees a station worker and wants to ask him ________ ________ ________ ________ ________ where he can buy his ticket. In this situation, what would Taylor most likely say to the station worker?

Taylor: (Is there any other place I can get my ticket?)

16-17

W: Good afternoon, everyone. I'm sure you all know about the social events our city has to offer, but do you know about the co-op? Our city's co-op is very important to our community. It's open daily so that members can trade fresh produce and recipe ideas as well as ________ ________ ________ ________, such as fund raisers and volunteer projects. This allows members of the community to join together ________ ________ ________ ________. You might wonder how you can join the co-op and participate. Well, ________ ________ ________ ________ ________ ________, such as Twitter and KakaoTalk, to communicate with one another and promote upcoming events. We also have a Facebook page and occasionally run online campaigns to raise money. You can also check our YouTube page to see what kind of projects we've done in the past. ________ ________ ________ ________ ________ ________ ________ your fellow community members by joining the co-op. Thank you for your time.

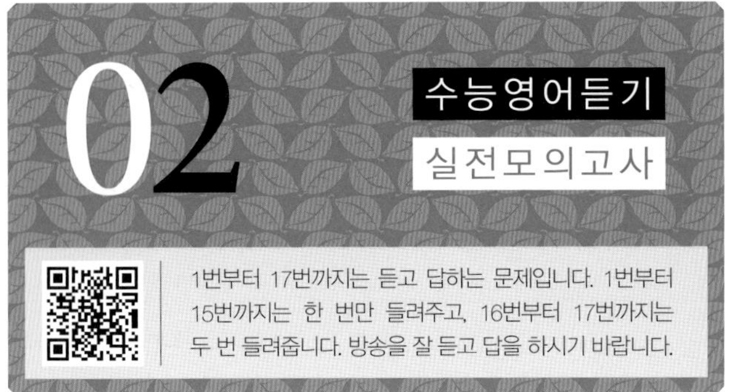

01

대화를 듣고, 남자의 마지막 말에 대한 여자의 응답으로 가장 적절한 것을 고르시오.

① I'm studying to be a nurse.
② No. I haven't been home yet.
③ You should go to the hospital.
④ Yes. I saw the doctor this morning.
⑤ Sounds good. I hope I get better soon.

02

대화를 듣고, 여자의 마지막 말에 대한 남자의 응답으로 가장 적절한 것을 고르시오.

① I'll keep on watching it, then.
② You should continue watching it.
③ I've never watched that TV show before.
④ I'd like to borrow it when you're finished.
⑤ You can watch it on TV on Saturday nights.

03

다음을 듣고, 남자가 하는 말의 목적으로 가장 적절한 것을 고르시오.

① 공원 내 이용시설을 알려주려고
② 캠핑장 이용 수칙을 안내하려고
③ 환경 보호의 중요성을 강조하려고
④ 위험 야생 동물 신고를 촉구하려고
⑤ 소지 불가한 물품 목록을 공지하려고

04

대화를 듣고, 두 사람이 하는 말의 주제로 가장 적절한 것을 고르시오.

① 명상을 하는 방법
② 명상의 긍정적 효과
③ 기분 전환 방법의 소개
④ 팟캐스트에서 강의 듣는 법
⑤ 운동이 우리 몸에 주는 이점

05

대화를 듣고, 두 사람의 관계를 가장 잘 나타낸 것을 고르시오.

① director — actress
② art director — judge
③ boss — office worker
④ customer — hairdresser
⑤ personal trainer — model

06

대화를 듣고, 그림에서 대화의 내용과 일치하지 않는 것을 고르시오.

07

대화를 듣고, 여자가 남자를 위해 할 일로 가장 적절한 것을 고르시오.

① 아이 돌보기
② 거실 재배치하기
③ 공항으로 마중 가기
④ 시내 관광 계획 짜기
⑤ 고객에게 식사 대접하기

08

대화를 듣고, 남자가 여자를 찾아온 이유를 고르시오.

① 경기 시간 변경을 알리려고
② 상대 팀에 관해 알아보려고
③ 새 유니폼 구매를 요청하려고
④ 주문한 유니폼의 색상을 확인하려고
⑤ 신임 지도 교사에게 인사를 드리려고

09

대화를 듣고, 남자가 지불할 금액을 고르시오.

① $45 ② $54 ③ $55 ④ $60 ⑤ $64

10

대화를 듣고, 자원봉사 활동에 관해 언급하지 않은 것을 고르시오.

① 자원봉사 할 사람
② 자원봉사 할 장소
③ 자원봉사 활동 내용
④ 자원봉사 시작 방법
⑤ 자원봉사 하게 될 시간

11

과학 박람회에 관한 다음 내용을 듣고, 일치하지 않는 것을 고르시오.

① 첫 번째 라운드에서 25명이 선발되었다.
② 최종 라운드의 아이디어는 실제 생활과 관련이 있고 유용해야 한다.
③ 최종 라운드는 5월 22일부터 2주 동안 열릴 것이다.
④ 사용한 재료의 수와 종류는 평가에 반영되지 않는다.
⑤ 수상자의 작품은 특허권을 얻을 수 있다.

12

다음 표를 보면서 대화를 듣고, 여자가 선택한 에어컨을 고르시오.

Air Conditioners

	Window Unit	Remote Control	Cooling Power (BTU)	Oscillation	Price
①	X	O	8,000	X	$240
②	O	X	5,000	X	$215
③	X	O	5,000	O	$260
④	X	X	8,000	O	$230
⑤	X	X	8,000	O	$275

13

대화를 듣고, 여자의 마지막 말에 대한 남자의 응답으로 가장 적절한 것을 고르시오.

Man: ______________________

① Don't worry about it. I can do it alone.
② Congratulations on making it into the show.
③ Cheer up! You'll have another chance next year.
④ No problem. I'll give you a call when I'm finished.
⑤ It's all right. You really don't need to apologize to me.

14

대화를 듣고, 남자의 마지막 말에 대한 여자의 응답으로 가장 적절한 것을 고르시오.

Woman: ______________________

① Relax. You shouldn't be so hard on yourself.
② It's great that you're following your dreams.
③ You should audition for some movies.
④ We should watch the movie together.
⑤ You should consider a new career.

15

다음 상황 설명을 듣고, Jayden이 Lucy에게 할 말로 가장 적절한 것을 고르시오.

Jayden: Lucy, ______________________

① make sure to tell me if you need my help.
② I hope that you do really well in the magic club.
③ I need you to handle your responsibilities for this project.
④ you should make an effort to balance school and home life.
⑤ why don't we take a break for a while if it's too much work?

[16-17] 다음을 듣고, 물음에 답하시오.

16

여자가 하는 말의 주제로 가장 적절한 것은?

① Combining professional education with liberal arts
② Employment opportunities for liberal arts majors
③ Reasons for decreasing interest in liberal arts
④ The impact of liberal arts on humanity
⑤ The benefits of studying liberal arts

17

언급된 과목이 아닌 것은?

① philosophy ② education ③ history
④ languages ⑤ mathematics

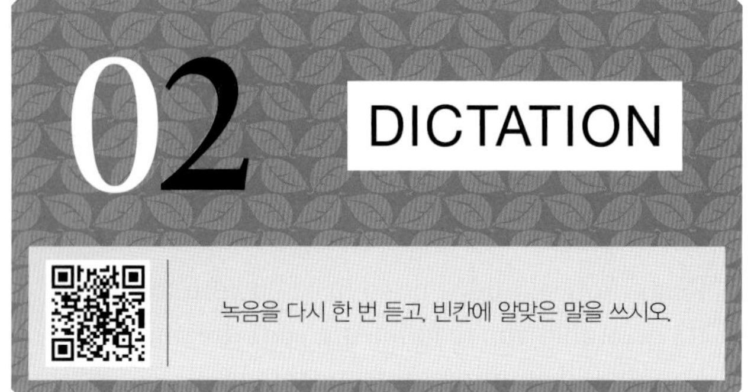

01

M: Hello, Lilly. You don't look so well. You look really tired.

W: I'm all right. I've just ________ ________ ________ ________ ________ ________ ________ all day.

M: That sounds awful. ________ ________ ________ ________ ________ ________ ________?

W: (Yes. I saw the doctor this morning.)

02

W: I heard that you're watching one of my favorite TV series.

M: Is it really one of your favorites? I'm only on the second episode. ________ ________ ________ ________.

W: Yeah. ________ ________ ________ ________ ________, but it gets really interesting later.

M: (I'll keep on watching it, then.)

03

M: Hi. Welcome to Walker Mountain State Park Campground. I'm park ranger Frank Reynolds, and I'd like to discuss the rules we expect you to follow here at the state park. Due to pollutants in soap and other cleaning goods, we ask that you only shower and ________ ________ ________ ________ ________ ________. We also ask that you tend to your campfires and extinguish them before midnight. Fireworks are ________ ________ ________ ________. As you can imagine, untended campfires and fireworks can cause forest fires, which will ________ ________ ________ ________ ________ ________ ________ ________ ________. ________ ________ ________ ________ ________ ________ a park ranger if you witness anyone violating these rules. Thank you for listening and we hope that you enjoy your time here at Walker Mountain State Park.

04

W: Hi, Chase. What are you listening to?

M: Hey, Hailey. I'm listening to a ________ ________ ________.

W: Meditation, huh? I've never tried it.

M: I'm learning a lot from the podcast. Did you know that you can benefit from meditation ________ ________ ________ ________ ________? For example, it boosts your energy.

W: That's interesting. So if I get tired in the afternoon, it will help if I meditate.

M: That's right. They're also talking about how meditation can help you sleep at night and relieve stress.

W: Really? That must be why people who meditate are always in such a great mood.

M: Could be. They also said that meditation can improve your health and ________ ________ ________.

W: So ________ ________ ________ ________ ________ ________?

M: Yeah, it's great for your overall health.

W: I guess I should start meditating.

M: I think I'm going to start, too.

05

M: Cindy, how's it going with trying to memorize your lines?

W: Very well, Mr. Reynolds.

M: I hope you can do it quickly. We don't have a lot of time.

W: Well, ________ ________ ________ ________ ________, and I just got the script this morning.

M: I understand. But we only have the space ________ ________ ________ ________, and we need to work on your intonation.

W: All right, let's start now. I think I'm ready.

M: Great. Come in stage left and ________ ________ ________ ________ from there.

W: Okay. *[Pause]* "In delivering my son from me, I bury a second husband." How was that?

M: Good. Now, ________ ________ ________ ________ ________ from stage right.

W: All right. *[Pause]* "In delivering my son from me, I bury a second husband." ________ ________ ________ ________?

M: It did, actually. It seems more natural.

W: Great. I'm so excited for opening night!

M: I'm glad to hear that. I know you'll do a great job.

06

M: This place is pretty amazing, isn't it?

W: Yeah, I'm having a great time. But it's pretty cold, don't you think?

M: Well, ________ ________ ________ ________ ________ ________. Look, back near those icicles. That's a very peculiar ice sculpture back there.

W: You mean the one with the monkey riding the animal?

M: Yeah. What kind of animal do you think it is that he's riding?

W: It looks like a pig. Anyway, I can't believe they ________ ________ ________ ________ ________ ________ ________.

M: Yeah. It looks really neat. Do you want to check out the inside?

W: Well, I'm having a lot of fun on this seesaw right now.

M: I'm not. You're a lot bigger than me, so ________ ________ ________ ________ ________ ________.

W: You're right. ________ ________ ________ ________ ________, it's not a lot of fun to be on the bottom all the time.

M: Yeah. So, how about we go over to the castle?

07

W: Sweetheart, can you help me ________ ________ ________ this Friday?

M: I'm afraid I can't. Can we do it next Friday?

W: Did something come up?

M: Yes. I have an important client coming in from LA, and ________ ________ ________ ________ ________ over the weekend.

W: Will you be busy all weekend?

M: I'm not sure. She's arriving Friday morning, and ________ ________ ________ ________ ________ ________ at the airport.

W: Do you need to ________ ________ ________ ________ with her?

M: She wants to take a tour of the city, so I have to show her around.

W: Well, why don't you invite her to dinner, ________ ________ ________ ________ ________?

M: That sounds great. Can you cook something French for us?

W: Okay. I'll go grocery shopping on Thursday, then.

08

M: Hi there, Mrs. Temmel.

W: Good morning, John. Come in. What can I do for you?

M: I need to talk about the basketball team.

W: What about it?

M: Well, you know we bought new team uniforms last season.

W: I remember. They were really ________ ________ ________ ________ ________ ________.

M: Right, but ________ ________ ________ ________ ________ ________ is using the same colors on their uniforms.

W: You mean Mound High School?

M: Yes. I saw some of their students wearing them the other day.

W: Okay, so are you suggesting we buy new uniforms again?

M: I am. That way, we can use different uniforms for different matches.

W: All right, let me talk with the principal and ________ ________ ________ ________.

M: I'd really appreciate that, Mrs. Temmel. Please let me know what you guys decide.

09

W: Good morning. What can I do for you today?

M: Hi. I'm looking to ________ ________ ________ ________ ________ for the day.

W: Great. Well, we have 50cc scooters and 125cc motorbikes.

M: I see. ________ ________ ________ ________?

W: The motorbikes are $30 a day. The scooters usually cost you $25, but we're ________ ________ ________-________ ________, so you get an additional 10% off.

M: Awesome! I don't think we'll be driving them very far, so we'll just take two scooters, please.

W: Great. Do you need to rent helmets as well?

M: Of course. I'd like to be safe while riding. How much are they?

W: Helmets are $5 a day. They're not included ________ ________ ________.

M: I see. Well, I guess we'll take two scooters and two helmets, then.

W: All right. We'll get them ready for you.

10

W: Good morning, everyone. I'm Terry Loggins, and I'm here to take any questions you might have about volunteering in your community.

M: Hi, Terry. I've been wanting to get my kids ________ ________ ________ for some time now.

W: What type of volunteer work did you have in mind?

M: Well, they're both still in middle school, so they really can't do too much.

W: Oh, there are still positions available. They could help out at soup kitchens or retirement homes, or they could help single moms and senior citizens ________ ________ ________ ________ ________ such as mowing the lawn or taking out the trash.

M: Those are some really great recommendations. ________ ________ ________ ________ ________?

W: Just stop by your city hall. They should have ________ ________ ________ ________ ________ ________ ________.

M: That sounds easy enough.

W: It is easy, and it'll mean a lot to those you help!

11

W: We've just finished the first round of the science fair, and there are 25 students who have made it through the preliminaries ________ ________ ________ ________ ________ ________.

All of the students who qualified for the final round submitted ideas that are ________ ________ ________ ________ in today's world. ________ ________ ________ ________ ________ ________ two weeks from today, on May 22nd, in the Student Center's Event Hall. This time, students will make working models of their ideas. They will be judged not only on whether or not they can make their ideas work, but also on ________ ________ ________ ________ ________ ________ ________ was used to make them. The grand-prize winner will receive $5,000 toward obtaining a patent and producing an actual prototype of the idea.

12

M: Hello. What can I help you with today?

W: Hello. I'm looking for an air conditioner for my new apartment.

M: All right. How about this one? It's a window unit and it has a lower power rating, so ________ ________ ________ ________ ________ ________ ________ ________.

W: Oh, I'm not looking for a window unit.

M: Okay. Well, these are quite popular these days. ________ ________ ________ ________ ________ ________.

W: I don't think I need a remote. I would like an AC that's more powerful, though.

M: Okay. Do you want one that oscillates, as well?

W: Absolutely.

M: That narrows your choices down to these two. ________ ________ ________ ________?

W: ________ ________ ________ ________ ________ ________ $250, if possible.

M: Then this one is perfect for you.

W: Great. I'll take it.

13

M: Laura, you don't look so well. Are you all right?

W: I'm fine. __________ __________ __________ __________ __________.

M: Come on. You can tell me anything. What's the matter?

W: Well, you know how I tried out for the school's talent show last week?

M: Yeah, I remember. You spent hours working on your juggling act.

W: Right. So, I checked the bulletin board today, and I didn't make it into the show.

M: Really? How is that even possible? You're great.

W: I thought __________ __________ __________ __________. I didn't make any mistakes at all.

M: I understand your frustration. __________ __________ __________ __________ __________ __________ when I tried out for the drama club.

W: It's just so heartbreaking. __________ __________ __________ __________.

M: (Cheer up! You'll have another chance next year.)

14

M: Hi. I think we've met before. Isn't your name Jamie?

W: Yes, I'm Jamie. You're Ricky, from my high school, right? It's been a long time.

M: It sure has. The last time I saw you was at graduation, I think. That's been almost eight years!

W: Wow! It's hard to believe it's been that long. So, what've you been up to?

M: I've been living in Los Angeles for the past few years. I've been trying to __________ __________ __________ __________ __________ as an actor.

W: Really? __________ __________ __________ __________ __________ __________?

M: Just one as a vampire in a commercial for heartburn medication.

W: Oh, I know that commercial! It's __________ __________ __________ __________. It's so funny.

M: Thanks, but I was really hoping to get into a Hollywood feature. I have some auditions next week.

W: (It's great that you're following your dreams.)

15

M: Lucy and Jayden are students at the local high school. This semester they are taking a science class together. The students in the class were assigned team projects. Lucy and Jayden are working as a team and __________ __________ __________ __________ __________ __________. The problem is that Lucy has joined the magic club and needs to attend practices often. Therefore, she can't __________ __________ __________ __________ __________. In the beginning, Jayden understands Lucy's situation. But he __________ __________ __________ __________ when she continues to put off her responsibilities. Jayden wants to talk to Lucy about this. What should he say to her in this situation?

Jayden: Lucy, (I need you to handle your responsibilities for this project.)

16-17

W: Universities and colleges all around the country have been experiencing __________ __________ __________ __________ __________ __________ __________ __________. Many influential members of our great nation believe that the liberal arts are useless. They encourage students to study other subjects because they might lead to a better job. Let's take a minute to consider whether or not liberal arts are useful. __________ __________ __________ __________ __________ __________ future jobs by providing them with an invaluable set of skills that no other subjects offer. Studying philosophy, history, and languages __________ __________ __________ __________ __________ that are essential for survival in the real world and could not be obtained from subjects like mathematics. These problem-solving skills help create a __________ -__________ __________. I urge you to rethink your position on liberal arts. Consider signing up for classes that will, in many ways, make you a better person.

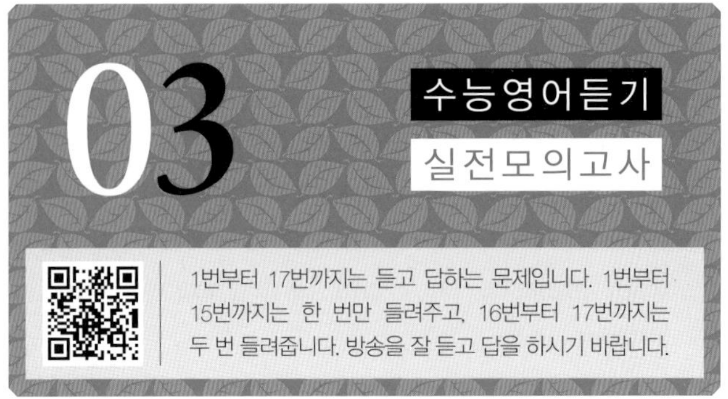

01

대화를 듣고, 여자의 마지막 말에 대한 남자의 응답으로 가장 적절한 것을 고르시오.

① Well, let's look at the weather.
② Yeah, me too. I'm really excited.
③ I'll come by your house in the evening.
④ Oh, that's fine. We can do it another time.
⑤ I think we should study more for our test.

02

대화를 듣고, 남자의 마지막 말에 대한 여자의 응답으로 가장 적절한 것을 고르시오.

① No. I did it on my own.
② Perhaps by next Monday.
③ Sure. Let me do it for you.
④ I like chemistry more than physics.
⑤ Yes. They'll leave in a couple of days.

03

다음을 듣고, 남자가 하는 말의 요지로 가장 적절한 것을 고르시오.

① 스포츠 활동은 학업에 지장을 준다.
② 여자가 남자보다 학업 성적이 우수하다.
③ 지나친 스포츠 활동은 학생들의 건강을 해친다.
④ 학생들의 스포츠 활동은 학업 이상의 것을 줄 수 있다.
⑤ 학교는 학생들을 위한 운동기구와 프로그램을 마련해야 한다.

04

대화를 듣고, 여자의 의견으로 가장 적절한 것을 고르시오.

① 아이들도 간단한 음식은 만들 줄 알아야 한다.
② 음식을 가리지 말고 골고루 먹어야 한다.
③ 자신의 방은 항상 깨끗이 정리해야 한다.
④ 바쁠 때는 패스트푸드를 먹을 수 있다.
⑤ 건강을 위해 정크푸드를 삼가야 한다.

05

대화를 듣고, 두 사람의 관계를 가장 잘 나타낸 것을 고르시오.

① 학부모 — 교사
② 승무원 — 승객
③ 상사 — 부하직원
④ 학생 — 지도교사
⑤ 아동전문가 — 고객

06

대화를 듣고, 그림에서 대화의 내용과 일치하지 않는 것을 고르시오.

07

대화를 듣고, 여자가 남자에게 부탁한 일로 가장 적절한 것을 고르시오.

① to get party decorations
② to help start a book club
③ to reserve enough tables
④ to give a call to close friends
⑤ to give her directions to the party

08

대화를 듣고, 여자가 음반을 사러 갈 수 없는 이유를 고르시오.

① 가족여행 준비를 해야 해서
② 다른 친구와 약속이 있어서
③ 저녁 식사 준비를 도와야 해서
④ 버스 터미널에 마중을 나가야 해서
⑤ 엄마가 청소하는 것을 도와야 해서

09

대화를 듣고, 남자가 지불할 금액을 고르시오.

① $73 ② $80 ③ $87 ④ $89 ⑤ $107

10

대화를 듣고, 음악 캠프에 관해 두 사람이 언급하지 않은 것을 고르시오.

① 캠프 시기 ② 캠프 기간 ③ 캠프 위치
④ 셔틀버스 운행 ⑤ 나이 제한

11

실험에 관한 다음 내용을 듣고, 일치하지 않는 것을 고르시오.

① 8살에서 10살 사이의 영국 학생들이 참가했다.
② 쌍방향 책상은 학생들의 공감능력 향상을 보기 위한 실험이다.
③ DeskTouch는 기술을 통해 학습 효과를 높이도록 고안되었다.
④ 스마트폰이나 iPad처럼 기기를 터치하는 것에 반응한다.
⑤ 모든 책상은 중앙 책상과 쌍방향으로 연결되어 있다.

12

다음 표를 보면서 대화를 듣고, 두 사람이 선택할 게스트 하우스를 고르시오.

	Name	Rate per Night	Location	Hot Tub
①	Bright Chalet	$65	Mountainside	Yes
②	Sky Chalet	$60	Mountainside	No
③	Gold Chalet	$50	Mountainside	Yes
④	Royal Chalet	$70	In Town	Yes
⑤	Star Chalet	$50	In Town	No

13

대화를 듣고, 여자의 마지막 말에 대한 남자의 응답으로 가장 적절한 것을 고르시오.

Man: ________________

① It's all right. I bought a new sleeping bag.
② I really appreciate your recommendations.
③ Do you think I can borrow his hiking boots?
④ That would be great. I really need to save money.
⑤ That's awesome. He seemed like he really had fun.

14

대화를 듣고, 남자의 마지막 말에 대한 여자의 응답으로 가장 적절한 것을 고르시오.

Woman: ________________

① Yeah, I really enjoy red wine with dinner.
② I think it's your turn to cook dinner for me.
③ Sorry, but we don't have time to drink it now.
④ All right. Just don't drink it in the living room.
⑤ Don't worry. I won't get any wine on your carpet.

15

다음 상황 설명을 듣고, Linda가 Mike에게 할 말로 가장 적절한 것을 고르시오.

Linda: ________________

① It could be colder up there than you think.
② Please be safe and camp only in areas where it's permitted.
③ You should wash your jacket before you leave. It's really dirty.
④ You can't leave the house until you've finished washing your clothes.
⑤ Climbing mountains is fun, but it can be dangerous. Please be careful.

[16-17] 다음을 듣고, 물음에 답하시오.

16

남자가 하는 말의 목적으로 가장 적절한 것은?

① to bring people with like minds together
② to show appreciation for the artists' help
③ to provide advice on how to buy artwork
④ to promote innovation in the art industry
⑤ to help creators receive funding for projects

17

프로젝트 분야로 언급되지 않은 것은?

① 영화 ② 패션 ③ 발명품
④ 만화 ⑤ 출판

01

W: I'm so happy now that final exams are finished.

M: So am I. Do you want to ________ ________ ________ ________ with me this weekend?

W: That sounds lovely, but I already have ________ ________ ________ ________ ________.

M: (Oh, that's fine. We can do it another time.)

02

M: Clara, don't you think the physics assignment is ________ ________ ________ ________?

W: It was quite difficult, but I was able to finish it last night.

M: You must be joking! Your parents ________ ________ ________ ________, right?

W: (No. I did it on my own.)

03

M: You would think that participating in high school athletic programs would ________ ________ ________ ________ ________ a student's grades. However, recent research shows that, in general, students who play sports do better in school than those who don't. Exercise has a positive effect on learning, memory, and concentration, which can ________ ________ ________ ________ ________ in the classroom. The effects of participating in sports sometimes ________ ________ ________ ________, as student athletes also learn valuable lessons about other skills that are important in life, such as teamwork and goal-setting. Working with coaches, trainers, and teammates to ________ ________ and achieve other goals teaches students skills that are important to success and so can help them throughout their lives.

04

W: Tom, what's going on in here?

M: What are you talking about, Mom?

W: This place is ________ ________. Look at all of this garbage!

M: Yeah, you're right. Sorry about that, Mom. I'll ________ ________ ________ now.

W: And look at what caused the mess. There are fast food bags, junk food boxes, soda cans, and candy wrappers all over the place. You didn't eat all of that, did you?

M: I did. I was so hungry.

W: But all of this stuff is really bad for you. None of it is healthy at all.

M: Well, you never ________ ________ ________ ________ ________, so every once in a while I eat a lot of it when you're not home.

W: I don't want you to eat that stuff because I ________ ________ ________ ________.

M: I understand. I'll try not to eat junk food anymore.

W: Just remember how important your health is.

05

M: How about this weather?

W: It's awful, isn't it? The forecast says it's supposed to be rainy all week.

M: Are we still going to work outside today?

W: No. I have some work for you to do in the office.

M: That's great. ________ ________ ________ ________ ________ if I work outside.

W: There's something I've been meaning to talk to you about, Frank.

M: Sure. What is it?

W: Well, you ________ ________ ________ ________ ________ lately. Is everything all right?

M: Honestly, my son has been having a lot of difficulties at school, and ________ ________ at home. I'm really worried about him.

W: I can understand. I have two children myself. But, you know, kids will be kids. You just have to let them develop naturally.

M: Thanks for the advice, Mrs. Stark. What is it you need me to do today?

W: I'd like you to ________ ________ ________.

06

M: What's that you're working on, Sandra?

W: It's __________ __________ __________ my new band. We have a show coming up next week.

M: It looks pretty cool. So your band is called Bastion?

W: That's right. I wrote our name __________ __________ __________ __________ __________. I also drew some skulls next to it.

M: I see that. I guess you're a rock 'n' roll band. That's a pretty cool guitar you drew on the left side.

W: Yeah, that's my guitar: a Bender P-159.

M: It looks like you put a picture of yourself on the right. Where's your guitar?

W: Well, I couldn't find a picture of me with my guitar so I chose one where I'm not holding it.

M: Cool. You wrote the date and the venue __________ __________ __________, huh?

W: That's right. We're playing at the Denton Shelter House at 9 p.m. on the 27th.

M: Awesome. I might __________ __________ __________ __________.

07

W: Hi, Oliver! You made it just in time!

M: Really? What's going on?

W: I was just __________ __________ __________ __________ __________ Elena's birthday this weekend.

M: Oh, nice. Will it be a surprise party?

W: No. I think we'll just __________ __________ __________ __________ __________ __________ get together at Joe's Crab Shack.

M: Sounds good. I know she's wanted to go there for a while.

W: I was thinking of inviting all of our good friends.

M: I like that idea. What can I do to help?

W: __________ __________ __________ __________ to the party store and picking up balloons and "Happy Birthday" signs?

M: Of course. I'll head over there __________ __________.

W: Awesome. This is going to be a great party.

M: Yeah, I'm really excited!

08

W: Hey, Julian. What's up?

M: Not too much. I'm just reading this music review in the school newspaper.

W: That's cool. What album is it?

M: Kenny North's new album, *Graduate School*. __________ __________ __________ __________ __________?

W: Of course. A lot of people are talking about it these days.

M: Yeah, I'm thinking about buying it. Do you want to come over and listen to it with me after school?

W: I'd love to, but I really can't. I __________ __________ __________ __________ __________ after school today.

M: Really? Why?

W: My brother's __________ __________ __________ __________ to visit.

M: So you need to pick him up from the bus station?

W: My dad is going to pick him up. I have to __________ __________ __________ __________ __________ __________.

M: I see. Well, I hope you have a great time catching up with your brother.

09

W: Welcome to Jenna's Butcher Shop. What can I do for you?

M: I'm looking for some steaks.

W: Steaks, huh? What kind of steaks do you want?

M: Well, I'm __________ __________ __________ tomorrow with my parents-in-law, so I'd like something that would impress them.

W: Well, we're having a sale on premium T-bone steaks. __________ __________ __________ $20 a steak.

M: That sounds amazing. I'll take four, please.

W: No problem. __________ __________ __________ __________ baked potatoes. Would you like a bag?

M: Sure. How much are they?

W: They're usually $9 a bag, but you seem like a loyal customer, so I'll give them to you for $7.

M: That's great. I'll take one bag of potatoes, then.

W: All right. So, we have four premium T-bones and a bag of potatoes. __________ __________ __________ __________?

M: I believe that's it. Here's my card.

10

[Telephone rings.]

W: Hello?

M: Hi, Stacy. This is Dominic. Is Russell around? My son is really wanting to play with him today.

W: Oh, Russell isn't here. He's at music camp today.

M: Music camp, huh?

W: Yeah. The local orchestra holds one every summer. The students get to practice with professional musicians.

M: ________ ________ ________. Where is it?

W: It's at the auditorium, right across from the library.

M: I see. Do they still have any spots available?

W: They do. I just signed Russell up yesterday, and they still had several left. They also have a shuttle bus that picks the students up.

M: That's great. Do they have any ________ ________?

W: It's for kids age ten and up. You can find all the information on the orchestra's website.

M: Nice! I'll check it out. I think my son would love to join.

11

M: Since 2009, eight- to ten-year-old students across Britain have been involved in a very cool experiment: to see if replacing pencils, paper, and even calculators with hi-tech interactive desks would help ________ ________ ________ ________! The project was created by Britain's Dunham University and SinergyCom. The hi-tech desks, called DeskTouch, are just one of several research projects ________ ________ ________ learning through technology. They've been fitted with software that responds to one's touch, much like a smartphone or iPad. All of the desks ________ ________ ________ ________ ________ from which the teacher can create and send math problems to the students and then check them afterwards.

12

W: Hey sweetheart, you know that Billy finishes up school in less than a month, right?

M: Yeah. He's ________ ________ about his summer vacation. I've been thinking that we should do something special this year.

W: What did you have in mind?

M: Well, you know how I've said that I've always wanted to go to The Smoky Mountains?

W: Yeah. We ________ ________ ________ ________ ________ ________.

M: Right. So I've been searching the Internet, and I found this list of chalets in the mountains. Tell me what you think.

W: Well, I don't think we should spend more than $60 a night.

M: Yeah. I'd prefer to stay on the mountain, though. The towns there look so touristy.

W: I agree. I guess that leaves these two, then.

M: Hmm. . . let's go for the one that has a hot tub. ________ ________ ________.

W: Sure. Go ahead and book it.

13

W: Hey, Eddie. You look busy. Should I come back another time?

M: I'm just finishing up here. I'm almost ________ ________ ________ ________ ________ to Nepal.

W: That's exciting. Did you buy everything I recommended?

M: I did. Thanks for the recommendations. I bought a new pair of boots and a tent.

W: That's great. Oh my! Is this your sleeping bag? I think it's too thin. ________ ________ ________ ________.

M: I think you're right, but sleeping bags are expensive. I ________ ________ ________ ________ a new one.

W: Hmm. . . I think I might be able to help.

M: Really? Do you have one I can borrow?

W: Well, my father has one that he never uses. I'll see if he'll ________ ________ ________ ________.

M: (That would be great. I really need to save money.)

14

W: Hey, thanks for coming. Welcome to my new apartment.

M: I'm sorry I'm late. I had to __________ __________ __________ __________.

W: Wine, huh? It isn't red wine, is it?

M: It is. Don't you like red wine?

W: I do. But I just __________ __________ __________ __________ __________ in my living room. I don't want you to spill any on it.

M: Don't worry about it. I'll be extra careful.

W: I'm not sure if I trust you. Remember when we ate spaghetti together and you got sauce all over your white shirt?

M: That was a one-time mistake. You're __________ __________.

W: I'd really feel more comfortable if you didn't drink it. I want to keep this apartment spotless.

M: If that's how you feel, I'll __________ __________ __________ __________ __________.

W: (All right. Just don't drink it in the living room.)

15

W: Mike, a high school student, is planning on spending the weekend with his friends. They've __________ __________ __________ __________ in the mountains. However, Mike's mom, Linda, is worried about her son. She's been camping in the late summer and knows that it can get quite cold in the mountains. She __________ __________ __________ __________ __________ __________ __________, but he refuses. He thinks that wearing a winter jacket in the summer is ridiculous and doesn't want to __________ __________ __________ __________. Linda isn't sure if he'll need the jacket or not, but she wants to try to convince Mike to take it __________ __________ __________. In this situation, what would Linda most likely say to Mike?

Linda: (It could be colder up there than you think.)

16-17

M: Crowd funding has become a great way for people around the world to __________ __________ for their artistic endeavors. Many creative people have ideas that they would love to put into practice, but lack the money necessary to make that happen. That's where our program, Donation Station, comes in. Donation Station connects artists and other creative people to investors who believe in their projects. To get started, all you need to do is __________ __________ __________ on the Donation Station website and describe your project. If investors like it, they can send you the funds you need to __________ __________ __________ __________. Do you have a great idea for a movie, but lack the money to produce it? Donation Station can help. Perhaps you have a new fashion design or a useful invention, or maybe you need help publishing a book. Donation Station realizes that creativity is essential for our society and helps advance the whole world. That's why we try to help make your dreams reality. Sign up right now at our website to __________ __________ __________ __________ __________ __________.

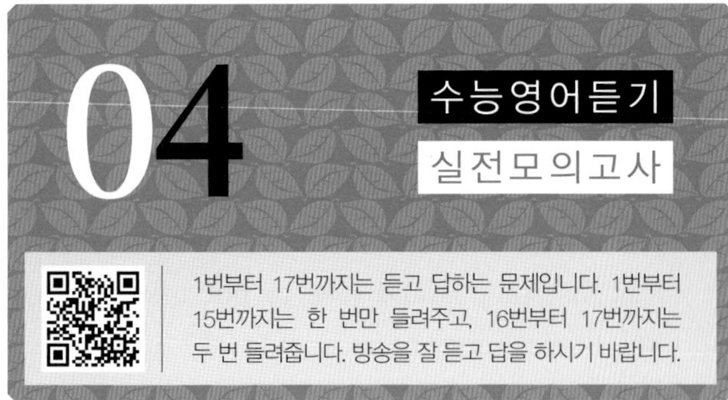

01

대화를 듣고, 여자의 마지막 말에 대한 남자의 응답으로 가장 적절한 것을 고르시오.

① Your lessons have really helped me.
② That's okay. You just need to practice.
③ I'll come by your house at around noon.
④ I'm happy to share my music collection with you.
⑤ Hold on! You need to tune the guitar before playing it.

02

대화를 듣고, 남자의 마지막 말에 대한 여자의 응답으로 가장 적절한 것을 고르시오.

① Okay. I guess the tip isn't included in the bill.
② Sounds good to me. How about I cook for you?
③ I didn't really care for the pasta at that restaurant.
④ Sure. That way you won't have to go to the grocery store.
⑤ All right. I heard about a new Mexican restaurant down the street.

03

다음을 듣고, 여자가 하는 말의 목적으로 가장 적절한 것을 고르시오.

① 팬들의 적극적인 응원을 부탁하려고
② 공식 웹사이트의 개설을 안내하려고
③ 팬들의 의견 제안 방식의 변경을 공지하려고
④ 경기장과 시설의 보수 공사 계획을 알려주려고
⑤ 효과적인 팬들의 의견 제안 방법을 추천 받으려고

04

대화를 듣고, 두 사람이 하는 말의 주제로 가장 적절한 것을 고르시오.

① 한국의 다양한 미신
② 돌잔치에서 지켜야 할 예절
③ 한국 돌잔치의 특별한 전통
④ 돌잔치 문화의 지나친 상업화
⑤ 한국 부모들의 자녀에 대한 큰 사랑

05

대화를 듣고, 두 사람의 관계를 가장 잘 나타낸 것을 고르시오.

① 선배 — 후배
② 교사 — 학부모
③ 교수 — 회사 직원
④ 입사 지원자 — 면접관
⑤ 인사팀 담당자 — 학생

06

대화를 듣고, 그림에서 남자가 선택한 차량을 고르시오.

07

대화를 듣고, 여자가 남자를 위해 할 일로 가장 적절한 것을 고르시오.

① 여행 경험 들려주기
② 웹 사이트 읽어주기
③ 일본어 강좌 소개해주기
④ 가볼 만한 곳 추천해주기
⑤ 호텔 예약 방법 알려주기

08

대화를 듣고, 남자가 늦게 귀가하는 이유를 고르시오.

① 오랜만에 만난 친구와 이야기가 길어져서
② 휴대폰이 고장 났는데 수리가 오래 걸려서
③ 스쿨버스가 고장이 나서 대중교통을 이용하느라
④ 사고가 났는데 친구가 다쳐서 같이 병원에 가느라
⑤ 길이 통제되고 주변 교통수단을 이용할 수 없어서

09

대화를 듣고, 여자가 지불할 금액을 고르시오.

① $30 ② $44 ③ $50 ④ $54 ⑤ $60

10

대화를 듣고, 여자가 본 영화에 관해 두 사람이 언급하지 않은 것을 고르시오.

① 영화 제목 ② 영화 주제 ③ 영화 길이
④ 관람 소감 ⑤ 상영관 위치

11

컴퓨터 게임 대회에 관한 다음 내용을 듣고, 일치하지 않는 것을 고르시오.

① 다음 주말에 개최된다.
② 두 가지 전략 게임을 한다.
③ 컴퓨터를 상대로 하는 게임도 있다.
④ 이 대회에 아마추어는 참가가 불가능하다.
⑤ 참가 신청서 제출 마감은 1월 7일까지이다.

12

다음 표를 보면서 대화를 듣고, 두 사람이 선택한 기부 내용을 고르시오.

Make a Difference Charity

	Option	Category	Project	Donation Amount
①	A	Overseas	Disaster Relief	$200
②	B	Overseas	Medical Care	$250
③	C	Overseas	Disaster Relief	$350
④	D	Domestic	Education	$100
⑤	E	Domestic	Medical Care	$200

13

대화를 듣고, 여자의 마지막 말에 대한 남자의 응답으로 가장 적절한 것을 고르시오.

Man: ______________________

① New York is beautiful this time of year.
② I'm sorry to hear you had such bad luck.
③ It's nice that the police were able to find it.
④ You should arrive at the airport an hour early.
⑤ I should be more careful the next time I travel.

14

대화를 듣고, 남자의 마지막 말에 대한 여자의 응답으로 가장 적절한 것을 고르시오.

Woman: ______________________

① Well, I'm thinking of donating money to this website.
② Right. Killing elephants is illegal in many countries.
③ Why don't we check out the elephants at the zoo?
④ No problem. You can borrow this documentary.
⑤ People shouldn't hunt elephants for ivory.

15

다음 상황 설명을 듣고, Jane이 Tim에게 할 말로 가장 적절한 것을 고르시오.

Jane: Tim, ______________________

① your workout and dieting habits are not healthy.
② your diet and exercise routine is working well.
③ you still seem to be out of shape.
④ you need to work out more.
⑤ you have to study harder.

[16-17] 다음을 듣고, 물음에 답하시오.

16

남자가 하는 말의 목적으로 가장 적절한 것은?

① to provide some advice on mountain biking
② to persuade others to take up mountain biking
③ to identify the health benefits of mountain biking
④ to explain reasons why mountain biking is popular
⑤ to warn of potential dangers during mountain biking

17

남자가 언급하지 않은 것은?

① 헬멧 ② 물 ③ 날씨
④ 지도 ⑤ 여벌 옷

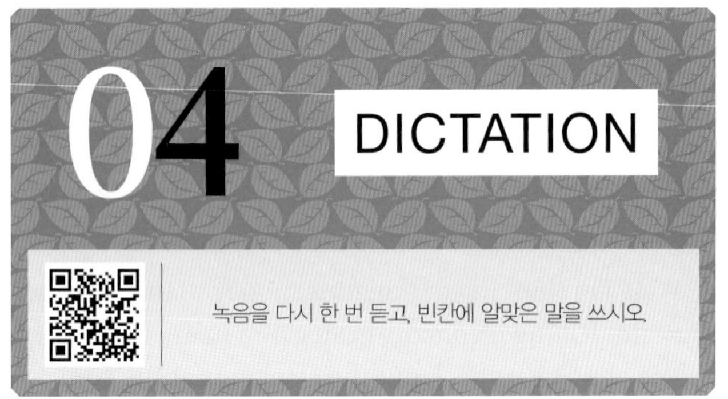

01

W: Daniel, you're becoming a really _____ _____ _____.

M: _____ _____ _____ _____ _____. Have you ever tried playing an instrument?

W: I love music, but I don't have any musical ability.

M: (That's okay. You just need to practice.)

02

M: I'm getting hungry. What would you like to eat?

W: I'm not sure. Do you want to _____ _____ _____ _____ again?

M: We're _____ _____ _____ _____ eating out. Let's eat at home tonight.

W: (Sounds good to me. How about I cook for you?)

03

W: Good morning, fans. I understand some of you have suggestions about the new stadium and its facilities. _____ _____ _____ _____ _____ _____ you've dropped in the box that we put up in the stadium several months ago. However, we've decided to make this process easier by _____ _____ _____ _____ _____ _____. This will allow you to do it from anywhere at any time. It's so simple. Just go to the official website, _____ _____ _____ "_____" _____, type your suggestion into the box provided, and click "Submit." This new system also _____ _____ _____ _____ _____ to your suggestions in a timely manner. Thank you for your time.

04

W: Jimmy, I have a party invitation for you.

M: Wow, your son's first birthday. How exciting!

W: Yeah. Can you make it to the party?

M: In Busan? Of course! And I heard there's a _____ _____ _____ _____ a child's first birthday.

W: Yes, there is. At its first birthday party, a baby chooses from one of several _____ _____ _____.

M: So, does the item the baby chooses predict his or her future?

W: That's right. For instance, if my son chooses a pencil, we believe it means he'll have a _____ _____ _____.

M: I see. What else can the baby choose from?

W: Well, if he chooses money then he'll be wealthy. If he chooses a spool of thread, it means he'll have a long life.

M: That makes sense. I'm really looking forward to your baby's party!

05

[Telephone rings.]

W: Hello?

M: Hi, Aria. This is Walter.

W: Hello, Walter. How is everything?

M: Great, thanks. I just wanted to take some time to thank you for recommending the two interns that are working with us now. We really _____ _____ _____ _____ _____ _____.

W: Great! I'm glad to hear that hiring my students has worked out so well for you.

M: _____ _____ _____ _____ _____ that I'm actually calling to ask if you have any other students you could recommend.

W: Sure. Which department needs interns?

M: We have _____ _____ _____ _____ _____.

W: I see. I think I know the perfect students for those positions. I'll notify them after class next week.

M: Great. Please _____ _____ _____ _____ _____ and have them call me directly.

W: Will do, Walter.

M: Thank you.

06

W: Hi. Welcome to Isaac's Rent-a-Car. What can I do for you today?

M: Hello. I have a reservation to pick up a vehicle this afternoon. My name is Robert Clay.

W: Just a second. Okay, I have your reservation right here, Mr. Clay. ________ ________ ________ ________ ________ ________ and tell me which car you'd like.

M: ________, ________ ________ ________ ________ ________ ________-________ ________. I'm traveling alone.

W: I see. How about the convertible, then? It's sporty, so it's fun for people driving alone.

M: Well, the air is quite smoggy today. I don't want to ________ ________ ________ ________ ________ ________.

W: Okay. I guess that narrows it down to these two.

M: Hmm. I don't want a gray car. Gray is a bit of ________ ________ ________.

W: Uh-huh. Well, I suppose this one is the best fit for you then.

M: Looks good. I'll take it. Here's my credit card.

07

W: Hey, what are you up to?

M: I'm searching the Internet for a hotel room for my vacation.

W: That's cool. ________ ________ ________ ________?

M: Tokyo. Have you ever been?

W: Tokyo? Yeah, I've been. I stayed at the Tokyo Palace Hotel. It was wonderful.

M: I looked at rooms there, but they're far too expensive for me.

W: I see. Well, you should check out ________ ________ ________ ________ ________ ________. It's called *tokyodeals.com*.

M: Cool. Let me check it out. *[Pause]* Oh, here it is. But I think ________ ________ ________ ________ ________ to me.

W: Why's that?

M: The website is in Japanese. I can't read Japanese at all. Can you?

W: Sure. I studied Japanese in college. Want me to help you?

M: That would be awesome! Thanks for your help.

08

[Telephone rings.]

W: Hello?

M: Hey, Mom. It's Tom.

W: Where have you been, Tom? ________ ________ ________ ________ ________ ________ an hour ago. It's seven o'clock.

M: ________ ________ ________ ________ earlier. I even had to borrow someone's phone to call you now.

W: Okay. So you're not home now, and you're calling me, which means you won't be home soon. What's the matter?

M: Didn't you hear that ________ ________ ________ ________ ________ in front of the park?

W: No. Are you all right?

M: Yeah, I'm okay. I was on the other side of the park when it happened.

W: So why haven't you come home yet?

M: Because the police and fire department have blocked the roads around the park. Traffic's really bad, and the subway ________ ________ ________ ________ ________ ________ ________ ________ ________.

W: That's awful news. Did you have dinner?

M: I had some fruit and a little salad a while ago. I'm okay.

W: All right. Take care. I'll see you later.

M: Okay, Mom. See you soon.

09

M: Hi. Welcome to Franklin University's Arts Center. What can I do for you today?

W: Hello. I'd like tickets for two adults and two children, please.

M: No problem. *[Keyboard typing sound]* That'll be $44.

W: Do these tickets __________ __________ __________ the Harmony Blues show?

M: I'm sorry, but they don't. Tickets to that performance cost an additional $4 a person.

W: I see. What is the cost per ticket, then, __________ __________ __________?

M: They're $18 for adults and $12 for children.

W: Okay. I'd like to get those tickets for two adults and two children. Oh! I almost forgot about these coupons I have for 10% off. Here they are.

M: *[Pause]* I'm sorry, but __________ __________ __________ __________ __________ the performance tickets.

W: Oh. Well, that's all right. Here's my card.

M: Thank you, ma'am.

10

W: Hey Pablo, have you ever seen the documentary *An Unfortunate Fact*?

M: I haven't. What's it about?

W: It's about climate change. It discusses the dangers that __________ __________ __________.

M: Hmm. . . I think I've heard about it. I really like science documentaries. How was it?

W: It was __________ __________ __________-__________. It made me think hard about the future of the world.

M: Was it a long documentary?

W: It was about two hours. __________ __________ __________ __________, but if you like science documentaries, I'm sure you'll enjoy it.

M: I'd love to see it, but I don't think I'll have time this weekend. Do you think __________ __________ __________ __________ __________ __________ next weekend?

W: I have no idea. You could check their websites for information.

M: Yeah, all right. I look forward to talking with you more about it once I've seen it.

11

M: Good afternoon, gamers! My name is Nimbus, and __________ __________ __________ __________ at the PC Playground next weekend. These contests are for players of real-time strategy games. We'll be playing two different games in our contests: *Suncraft* and *League of Heroes*. In the *Suncraft* contest, you will play side-by-side with professional *Suncraft* players. For the *League of Heroes* contest, players will be grouped into random teams and compete against computer AI __________ __________ __________ __________. For these contests, we will only accept amateurs. __________ __________ __________ __________ __________ __________. To apply, visit our website at *www.PCPlayg.co* and submit your application before January 7th. We wish you all the best of luck and __________ __________ __________ __________ __________ __________.

12

W: Hey sweetheart, I think I've found the charity that I'd like to donate to this year.

M: Great! Is it another children's charity?

W: Not this time. It helps people of all ages. It's called *Make a Difference*, and we can choose to help __________ __________ __________ __________ or here in our own country.

M: Well, didn't we __________ __________ __________ __________ __________ __________ last year? I think this year we should help people overseas.

W: Me, too. I've been watching the news a lot lately, and I think that we should donate money to victims of that terrible tsunami.

M: It does look awful, doesn't it? __________ __________ __________ __________ __________ __________ __________.

W: All right. So, how much do you think we should donate?

M: I don't think that we can afford anything more than $300.

W: Then that leaves us with this option.

M: Good! It feels great to use our money to help others.

13

M: Hey, Samantha. Did you enjoy your trip to New York?

W: I don't think it __________ __________ __________ __________ __________.

M: Really? That's a shame. What went wrong?

W: Pretty much everything. When I got to New York, the airline had lost my baggage. It took three days for them to find it.

M: That's awful, but I know how you feel. __________ __________ __________ __________ __________ __________ when I went to Rome.

W: Oh, that was just the start of it. While I was sitting at a cafe enjoying my coffee, someone stole my briefcase.

M: Really? That's unfortunate.

W: Unfortunate? I was infuriated! And the police couldn't help me. But __________ __________ __________ __________ __________ __________.

M: You __________ __________ __________ __________, right?

W: Nope. My flight back to Seattle __________ __________ __________ __________ __________. Then when I went to claim my luggage, it was missing again.

M: (I'm sorry to hear you had such bad luck.)

14

M: Hey Brittney, what's that you're looking at?

W: Oh, I'm searching online for ways to save the elephants.

M: You want to help elephants, huh?

W: Yeah. __________ __________ __________ __________ with kind hearts. __________ __________ __________ __________ __________.

M: That's interesting. I never knew that.

W: It's the truth. But there are a lot of poachers out there that hunt elephants for their ivory.

M: Still? I thought people __________ __________ __________ __________ __________. How many elephants are killed each year just for their tusks?

W: As many as 40,000 a year, some experts say.

M: That's terrible. What do people want the ivory for?

W: It can be used to make collectible figurines, billiard balls, and traditional medicines.

M: That's so sad. What can we do to help?

W: (Well, I'm thinking of donating money to this website.)

15

M: Jane's son, Tim, a middle school student, is really concerned about __________ __________ __________ __________ __________ __________. Jane knows that it's good to be aware of your health, but she thinks Tim takes it too far. She has noticed that he's been going to the gym for hours a day and __________ __________ __________ __________ __________. This concerns her because he seems to be getting too skinny. He looks unhealthy. But Tim thinks that he needs to lose more weight. Jane thinks he's becoming obsessed, and she worries it's going to lead to a serious health problem. She wants to try to __________ __________ __________ __________ __________ __________ __________ __________ __________ __________. What would Jane most likely say to Tim in this situation?

Jane: Tim, (your workout and dieting habits are not healthy.)

16-17

M: Good morning, everyone. Today, we're going to talk about mountain biking. As you know, mountain biking is a great way to exercise. It's also a nice way to __________ __________ __________ __________ __________. But while it may be fun and beneficial to your well-being, it's also very dangerous. Be sure to __________ __________ __________ __________ __________ before your next trip. First of all, please __________ __________ __________ __________. Always, and I mean always, wear a helmet. Protecting your head is crucial when mountain biking. Another very important thing to consider is water. Mountain biking is physically exhausting, so __________ __________ __________ __________ __________ __________. You'll also want to check the weather before going out on the mountain. You wouldn't want to get stranded in the rain. And lastly, bring a map and compass. That way, if you get lost, you can find your way back down. Keep these tips in mind on your next mountain biking trip.

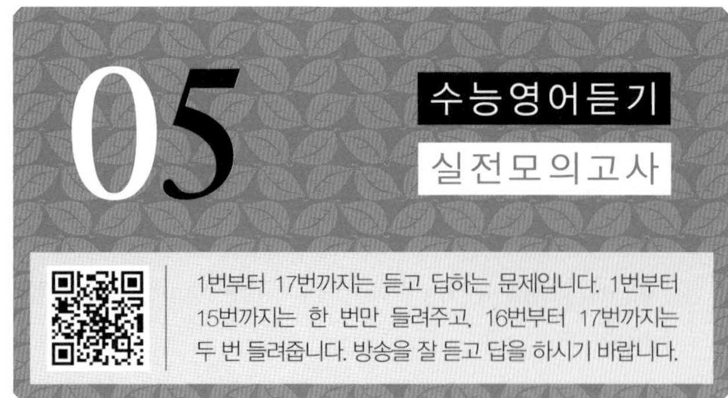

01

대화를 듣고, 여자의 마지막 말에 대한 남자의 응답으로 가장 적절한 것을 고르시오.

① That's fine. I'll pay with my credit card.
② Well, then I need to get my money back.
③ It looks like you were really overcharged.
④ I apologize. There has been a misunderstanding.
⑤ We can give you a 5% discount on your next purchase.

02

대화를 듣고, 남자의 마지막 말에 대한 여자의 응답으로 가장 적절한 것을 고르시오.

① I look forward to interviewing him tonight.
② It's important to be thoroughly prepared.
③ You should bring some flowers.
④ She will graduate next year.
⑤ I think getting a job is.

03

다음을 듣고, 남자가 하는 말의 주제로 가장 적절한 것을 고르시오.

① 컴퓨터 보안 프로그램의 중요성
② 온라인상 개인정보 도용 방지 요령
③ 웹사이트 비밀번호 분실 예방 방법
④ 온라인 개인 정보 유출의 피해 사례
⑤ 전자상거래의 개인 정보 유출 위험성

04

대화를 듣고, 여자의 의견으로 가장 적절한 것을 고르시오.

① 수업 시간에 필기를 빠짐없이 해야 한다.
② 휴대폰으로 인터넷 하는 시간을 줄여야 한다.
③ 성적 향상이 높은 친구의 방법을 따라야 한다.
④ 성적에 대한 지나친 스트레스를 경계해야 한다.
⑤ 방해요소를 제거하여 학습 집중력을 높여야 한다.

05

대화를 듣고, 두 사람의 관계를 가장 잘 나타낸 것을 고르시오.

① 의사 — 환자
② 사장 — 비서
③ 영화배우 — 매니저
④ 투숙객 — 호텔 직원
⑤ 관광 가이드 — 관광객

06

대화를 듣고, 그림에서 대화의 내용과 일치하지 않는 것을 고르시오.

07

대화를 듣고, 남자가 여자를 위해 할 일로 가장 적절한 것을 고르시오.

① 집안을 정리해 주기
② 자전거 주문해 주기
③ 택배 확인해주기
④ 간식 사다 주기
⑤ 설거지 해 주기

08

대화를 듣고, 여자가 공항에 마중 나갈 수 없는 이유를 고르시오.

① 회사에 갑자기 급한 일이 생겨서
② 집에 손님이 오기로 되어 있어서
③ 비행기 도착 시간이 너무 늦어서
④ 기념품 목록을 작성해 줘야 해서
⑤ 딸을 피아노 레슨에 데려가야 해서

09

대화를 듣고, 남자가 지불한 금액을 고르시오.

① $15 ② $20 ③ $27 ④ $36 ⑤ $40

10

대화를 듣고, 수업에 관해 두 사람이 언급하지 않은 것을 고르시오.

① 수업 과목 ② 수업 장소 ③ 수업 횟수
④ 수업 요일 ⑤ 수업료

11

Johnny Bahama's Sea Tours에 관한 다음 내용을 듣고, 일치하지 않는 것을 고르시오.

① 하는 내내 가이드가 있다.
② 하루에 네 번 투어가 있다.
③ 체력적으로 힘든 활동이다.
④ 구명조끼를 착용해야 한다.
⑤ 예약은 전화로도 가능하다.

12

다음 표를 보면서 대화를 듣고, 두 사람이 선택한 프로그램을 고르시오.

Upton Library Summer Program Schedule

	Program	Days	Time	Activities	Fee
①	Reading	Mon. ~ Wed.	16:00 ~ 17:00	Reading	$20
②	Reading	Thu. & Fri.	15:00 ~ 16:30	Active Reading	$30
③	Writing	Wed. & Thu.	16:00 ~ 17:30	Creative Writing	$40
④	Writing	Thu. & Fri.	17:00 ~ 19:00	Nonfiction Writing	$50
⑤	Art	Wed. ~ Fri.	16:00 ~ 17:30	Painting	$60

13

대화를 듣고, 여자의 마지막 말에 대한 남자의 응답으로 가장 적절한 것을 고르시오.

Man: ______________________________

① I don't want him to join any school clubs.
② I'd like to know how to teach students better.
③ I'll tell him to be at school on time from now on.
④ I feel relieved to hear he behaves so well in school.
⑤ I think I should advise him to be active in your class.

14

대화를 듣고, 남자의 마지막 말에 대한 여자의 응답으로 가장 적절한 것을 고르시오.

Woman: ______________________________

① I'm not too busy now, so I can come with you to see him.
② That's a shame, but I'm sure he'll understand the situation.
③ I'm sure you can pass the exam, since you've worked so hard.
④ That's right, but he must be too busy to go camping with you.
⑤ The assignments should be submitted by email to the teachers.

15

다음 상황 설명을 듣고, Carl이 정비사에게 할 말로 가장 적절한 것을 고르시오.

Carl: ______________________________

① I think that I should get a second opinion.
② How much is it going to cost to fix my car?
③ I don't think I have any spark plugs in my car.
④ How long will it take to change the spark plugs?
⑤ That's great! I was worried that it was a serious problem.

[16-17] 다음을 듣고, 물음에 답하시오.

16

남자가 하는 말의 주제로 가장 적절한 것은?

① to inform people of a new herbal supplement
② to provide tips on improving memory and brain function
③ to suggest a supplement proven to help Alzheimer's patients
④ to remind people of the dangers of taking herbal supplements
⑤ to help people recognize the warning signs of Alzheimer's disease

17

Ginkgo biloba에 관한 내용과 일치하지 않는 것은?

① 독일에서 쓰이는 예방법이다.
② 독일 외 다른 나라에선 쓰지 않는다.
③ 뇌활동과 기억력 회복에 도움을 준다.
④ 뇌로 가는 혈액의 순환을 증가시켜준다.
⑤ 복용 20분 내에도 효과가 나타날 수 있다.

01

W: Where did you get the postcards? Were they expensive?

M: I picked them up ________ ________ ________ ________. I got the whole set for $10.

W: Really? I bought the same cards yesterday for $15 in town.

M: (It looks like you were really overcharged.)

02

M: Next Monday, my daughter is going to ________ ________ ________, but I have a job interview at the same time.

W: But you can't do both.

M: I know. Which do you think is more important?

W: (I think getting a job is.)

03

M: Due to recent technological advances, people are spending more and more time on the Internet. As many of you may know, this has led to the rise of online predators that are looking to steal your personal information. I'm here today to offer some tips on ________ ________ ________ ________ ________ ________. For one thing, it's very important to change the passwords of your online accounts regularly. Furthermore, you should use unique ________ ________ ________ ________ ________ ________. These passwords should contain numbers, letters, and special characters, such as asterisks or punctuation. You should ________ ________ ________ ________ ________ ________. Be careful when inputting your information ________ ________ ________. Finally, when using a public computer, be sure to log out completely. Close the browser when you're finished.

04

M: Tiffany, you're really ________ ________ ________ ________ ________. You've also been participating more often.

W: It's funny you've noticed, but yes I have.

M: How are you doing it? You were struggling so much earlier in the semester.

W: I've been trying to read the textbooks before class at home and ________ ________ ________ ________.

M: How can I improve my concentration and interest when I study, like you have?

W: It's quite simple, actually. Just get rid of all of the things that can be a distraction.

M: You mean I should turn off my TV and stop browsing the Internet?

W: Well, everything is ________ ________ ________. But you should make time to study, and only study during that time.

M: That makes sense. Sometimes I like to study with the TV on, but I find it to be really distracting.

W: I'm sure you can improve in class if you just get rid of the things that are distracting you.

05

W: Good morning, Boris. How are you feeling today?

M: A lot better, thanks. I'm really enjoying my time here at the resort. It's a lot more comfortable than the last place we stayed.

W: I'm glad you like it. The view from ________ ________ ________ ________, right?

M: It's lovely. I really don't want to leave.

W: Well, what would you like for breakfast? I can have room service send up steak and eggs if you'd like.

M: That sounds great. So, ________ ________ ________ ________ for today? Is that magazine shoot today or tomorrow?

W: That's tomorrow. You have a television interview at the local station today.

M: I see. Thanks, Diane. I really appreciate all of your help. By the way, ________ ________ ________ ________ ________?

W: Next Monday. Our set manager ________ ________ ________ ________ ________ to prepare.

M: That sounds great. Thanks again.

06

W: Hello, Jayden. What are you using the computer for?

M: I'm working on a new design for our website. Check it out.

W: It's looking a lot nicer. I really like the ________ ________ ________ ________ ________ ________.

M: Thanks. I wanted to make it more user-friendly.

W: I like the picture of the soccer player on the top, too. Is that a link to the players' biographies underneath it?

M: It sure is. I thought it would be nice for the fans to learn more about the players.

W: What is that picture?

M: It's a picture of the player of the month. He's ________ ________ ________ ________.

W: How about the video under the picture?

M: That's a video of some of the highlights of the year so far.

W: How about ________ ________ ________ ________ ________ ________?

M: There's one at the bottom of the page.

07

[Telephone rings.]

W: Hello?

M: Hi, darling. ________ ________ ________ ________ ________ ________?

W: Not yet. I just finished my work. I'll leave the office in five minutes. Did you have dinner yet?

M: Yeah, Richard and I had hamburgers. Oh, a large box came for you in the mail today. What's in it?

W: That must be Richard's new coat. ________ ________ ________ ________ ________ on the Internet the other day.

M: Ah, I see.

W: So, I've had a really long day. I think I'll be ________ ________ ________ ________ ________ ________ when I get home. Will you take care of them?

M: Sure. I'll do them with Richard.

W: That's great. I'll ________ ________ ________ ________ ________ and pick up some dessert for you guys on the way home.

M: That sounds nice.

W: Is there anything specific you'd like?

M: Some chocolate and maybe some ice cream. I'll see you when you get here.

08

[Cell phone rings.]

M: Hello?

W: Hey, sweetheart. How was your presentation?

M: It went really well. My clients seemed very impressed.

W: That's great. Are you going to make it home today?

M: Yep. I ________ ________ ________ for this afternoon.

W: Awesome. The kids will be so excited to see you. ________ ________ ________ ________ ________.

M: Yeah, I'm really excited to get home so I can be with the family. Do you think you can pick me up at the airport?

W: Maybe. What time does your flight arrive?

M: It lands at 4:45.

W: Oh. Well, I don't think I'll be able to get there until later. I have to ________ ________ ________ ________ ________ ________ at 5.

M: No problem. I'll ________ ________ ________.

W: Sorry, sweetheart. Oh, could you ________ ________ ________ ________ ________ ________ on your way back?

M: Sure. See you tonight.

09

W: Good evening. What can I do for you?

M: Hello. I'd like tickets to the play for my wife and myself, please.

W: Well, sir, ________ ________ ________ ________. The only seats left are in Section C or in Section F on the balcony.

M: I guess one of those will be fine. How much are they?

W: The Section C tickets are $20 and the Section F tickets are $15.

M: Why are the tickets in Section C so much more expensive?

W: ________ ________ ________ ________ in Section C, sir.

M: I guess I'll take two tickets in Section C, then. Do you offer any discounts?

W: ________ ________ ________ ________ ________ ________ 65 can receive a 10% discount.

M: I'm 67, and my wife turned 65 last month. Here's my credit card and our IDs.

W: Very well, sir. Here are your tickets. You can enter through the door on your right. Enjoy the play.

M: Thank you.

10

W: Hey Felix, I heard that you're trying to ________ ________ ________ ________ by tutoring.

M: I am. Do you know anyone who's looking for a tutor?

W: Well, my little sister is ________ ________ ________ and could really use some help.

M: What kind of math does your sister need help with?

W: ________ ________ ________ ________ at the moment.

M: Oh, no problem. How often would she be able to meet?

W: Twice a week. Tuesdays and Thursdays would probably be best.

M: Okay. How long should the lessons be?

W: I think if it's twice a week, an hour-long lesson should be enough.

M: All right. And how much is your mom ________ ________ ________?

W: She said $40 a lesson seems fair, but you might be able to negotiate with her.

M: No, that's great. Why don't you give your mom my phone number and have her call me? That way we can work out the rest of the details.

W: Sure. No problem.

11

W: Have you ever wondered what it would be like to swim with dolphins, fish, and other marine life? Join Johnny Bahama's Sea Tours, where you can experience ________ ________ ________ ________ ________. Oh, you've never snorkeled before? That's no problem. We have ________ ________ ________ ________ ________ ________ ________ ________ of the way. We offer daily tours at 9 a.m., 1 p.m., and 4 p.m. Due to the physically demanding nature of the activity, only snorkelers age fifteen and older are allowed on these tours. We also ask that all snorkelers ________ ________ ________ ________ at all times. You can make reservations at your hotel lobby or by calling 110-555-7570 between the hours of 7 a.m. and 6 p.m. Thank you for listening and have a wonderful stay here on our beautiful island.

12

M: Hey sweetheart, the library is offering some summer programs for children. I think ________ ________ ________ ________ ________ one of them.

W: That sounds great. Do you have any information on them?

M: Sure. Here's the flyer they gave me.

W: *[Pause]* Leslie has swimming lessons on Mondays, so she ________ ________ ________ ________ on that day.

M: Yeah. She also has summer camp every day until three o'clock, right?

W: Right. So we need to find a program that starts after 3:30.

M: All right. Well, I ________ ________ ________ ________ ________ an artist, so maybe we can put her in one of the other classes.

W: Yeah. That narrows our choices down to these two.

M: All right. I think $50 is a bit much, don't you?

W: I agree. I guess we should enroll her in this program, then.

M: I'll go over to the library tomorrow and ________ ________ ________.

13

M: Hi, Ms. Swanson. I'm Daniel Hoult, Edward's father.

W: Oh, Mr. Hoult. It's a pleasure to meet you. Come in, please.

M: Thank you. How is my son doing in school?

W: Well, Edward ________ ________ ________ ________.

M: Is that so?

W: Yes. He's always smiling, and he tries to actively participate in class.

M: Isn't he a little aggressive, though?

W: No. He sometimes gets overly excited with his friends, but he ________ ________ ________ ________ ________ ________.

M: He gets irritated rather easily at home.

W: Well, students are often very different at home than at school.

M: You mean the other students are the same way?

W: Yes, Mr. Hoult. Edward's just fine here. He ________ ________ ________ ________ ________ everything.

M: (I feel relieved to hear he behaves so well in school.)

14

M: Jenny, how was your hiking trip over the weekend? You went with your family, right?

W: Actually, my father and I were alone this time, and it was ________ ________ ________ ________ ________!

M: Just you and your father?

W: Yes. We talked about a lot of things. I felt grown-up and ________ ________ ________ ________.

M: I bet you did. I miss my father a lot. He's been away for a year.

W: He's in Dubai, right? ________ ________ ________ ________ ________ during winter vacation?

M: He asked me to come, but I don't have time. I have to attend the winter pre-college program.

W: Oh. I heard that the ________-________ ________ ________ ________ ________.

M: Yes, it is. There are a lot of assignments and reading. I feel bad that I won't be able to visit him, though.

W: (That's a shame, but I'm sure he'll understand the situation.)

15

W: On the way to work, Carl begins to have car trouble. He ________ ________ ________ ________ ________ and explains that his car sometimes stalls when it's idling. The mechanic has a look at his car and discovers that he needs to change the spark plugs. Fortunately for Carl, this is a rather simple and cheap solution, so he instructs the mechanic to go ahead and change the plugs. Carl ________ ________ ________ ________ ________ ________ ________, so he wants to ask the mechanic ________ ________ ________ ________ ________ ________. In this situation, what would Carl most likely say to the mechanic?

Carl: (How long will it take to change the spark plugs?)

16-17

M: Alzheimer's disease is ________ ________ ________ ________ ________ in today's world. It's an awful disease that negatively affects a person's language, comprehension, memory, and thought processes. The disease most often affects the elderly, but Alzheimer's has been known to strike adults as young as 40. Through much research, doctors are now very confident that the disease can be prevented. ________ ________ ________ ________ in Germany is treatment with ginkgo biloba. The popular herbal supplement has been used for years in China and other countries in order to improve the circulatory system as well as increase brain function. Clinical studies have shown its ability to restore memory and ________ ________ ________ to the brain. It's so potent, in fact, that the effects of the supplement can be detected within 20 minutes of use. ________ ________ ________ ________ ________ ________, Alzheimer's patients may see dramatic improvements.

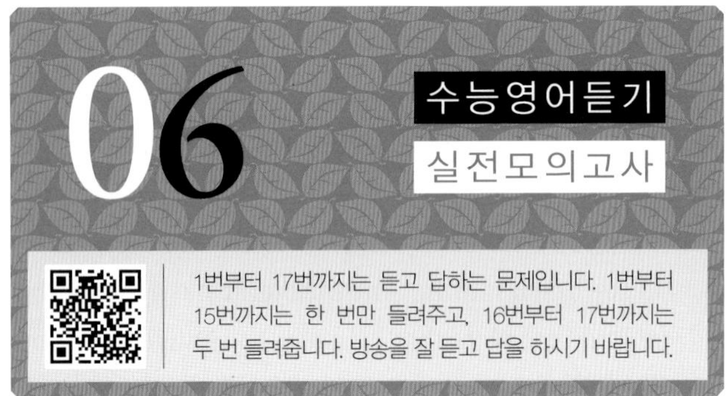

01

대화를 듣고, 남자의 마지막 말에 대한 여자의 응답으로 가장 적절한 것을 고르시오.

① Yeah. What a perfect way to spend a summer evening.
② Are you going to make your famous chicken salad?
③ Why don't you invite everyone to the party?
④ Just bring some snacks. It's not a big deal.
⑤ Do you need any help baking the pie?

02

대화를 듣고, 여자의 마지막 말에 대한 남자의 응답으로 가장 적절한 것을 고르시오.

① A penny for your thoughts.
② It looks like I only have coins.
③ The arcade is only two blocks away.
④ A ten-dollar bill, a five, and the rest in coins.
⑤ Do you know where I can find a change machine?

03

다음을 듣고, 여자가 하는 말의 목적으로 가장 적절한 것을 고르시오.

① 재난대책본부 견학 내용을 안내하려고
② 증가하는 자연 재해의 심각성을 알리려고
③ 교내 토네이도 대비 훈련에 대해 안내하려고
④ 단체 이동시 질서 유지의 중요성을 알리려고
⑤ 재난대처를 위해 지역 사회의 협력을 촉구하려고

04

대화를 듣고, 매출 증가를 위한 남자의 의견으로 가장 적절한 것을 고르시오.

① 주변에 다른 음식점과 협력해야 한다.
② 음식을 만들 재료를 싸게 구입해야 한다.
③ Blackbeans보다 싼 가격에 메뉴를 제공해야 한다.
④ Blackbeans보다 광고를 크고 확실하게 해야 한다.
⑤ Blackbeans에서 제공하지 않는 메뉴를 제공해야 한다.

05

대화를 듣고, 두 사람의 관계를 가장 잘 나타낸 것을 고르시오.

① 작가 — 편집자
② 기자 — 조각가
③ 사진작가 — 모델
④ 꽃가게 주인 — 고객
⑤ 카페 주인 — 배우

06

대화를 듣고, 그림에서 대화의 내용과 일치하지 않는 것을 고르시오.

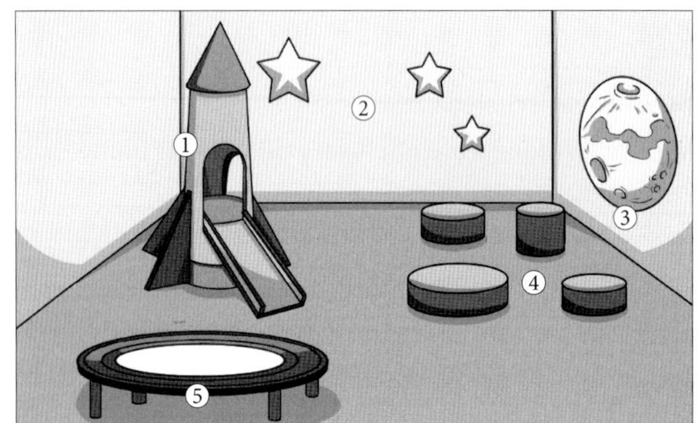

07

대화를 듣고, 여자가 남자를 위해 할 일로 가장 적절한 것을 고르시오.

① 도서 목록 만들어 보내 주기
② 남자가 읽을 책 추천해주기
③ 여름방학 때 함께 책 읽기
④ 학생들에게 책 읽어 주기
⑤ 서재의 책 정리 도와주기

08

대화를 듣고, 남자가 학교에 갈 수 없는 이유를 고르시오.

① 남동생을 돌봐야 해서
② 늦게까지 일해야 해서
③ 출장 준비를 해야 해서
④ 저녁 식사를 준비해야 해서
⑤ 과학 전시회를 준비해야 해서

09

대화를 듣고, 여자가 지불할 총 금액을 고르시오.

① \$180 ② \$200 ③ \$225 ④ \$250 ⑤ \$271

10

대화를 듣고, 겨울철 호주 여행에 관해 두 사람이 언급하지 않은 것을 고르시오.

① 관광객 수 ② 물가 ③ 교통수단
④ 날씨 ⑤ 낮의 길이

11

Sloth에 관한 다음 내용을 듣고, 일치하지 않는 것을 고르시오.

① 하루에 18시간 잠을 잔다.
② 나무 높은 곳에서 쉰다.
③ 땅에서 먹이를 찾는다.
④ 포식자들에게 취약하다.
⑤ 먹이를 많이 먹는다.

12

다음 표를 보면서 대화를 듣고, 여자가 선택한 제품을 고르시오.

2015 Zoo Used Car Sales

	Model	Year	Mileage	Price	Warranty
①	Cheetah	2008	20,200 miles	\$10,000	1 Year
②	Cheetah	2011	35,000 miles	\$12,000	6 Months
③	Cheetah	2014	26,000 miles	\$25,000	1 Year
④	Hawk	2009	70,500 miles	\$8,000	6 Months
⑤	Hawk	2013	45,000 miles	\$15,000	1 Year

13

대화를 듣고, 남자의 마지막 말에 대한 여자의 응답으로 가장 적절한 것을 고르시오.

Woman: ______________________________

① Any time. Remember to do it or you may be in trouble.
② You're right. I shouldn't have used the graph to begin with.
③ Don't worry. The graph gives all the information you'll need.
④ The graph actually came from another person in the office.
⑤ You're welcome. Tomorrow, we can hand in our reports together.

14

대화를 듣고, 여자의 마지막 말에 대한 남자의 응답으로 가장 적절한 것을 고르시오.

Man: ______________________________

① Which tablet would you recommend?
② I agree. You really need to buy a new tablet.
③ Which app do you use the most these days?
④ Yeah, it does. I think I need to cut down on my use.
⑤ The tablet was actually too expensive for my budget.

15

다음 상황 설명을 듣고, Dave가 Roy에게 할 말로 가장 적절한 것을 고르시오.

Dave: ______________________________

① Could you give me some advice about making friends?
② I really appreciate you helping me make new friends.
③ I don't think I'll be able to make the party today.
④ I'll see you during practice tomorrow, Roy.
⑤ I had a lot of close friends on my old team.

[16-17] 다음을 듣고, 물음에 답하시오.

16

남자가 하는 말의 주제로 가장 적절한 것은?

① Ways to be a clever consumer
② Where to find consumer reviews
③ How to write an effective shopping list
④ Reasons to be a more conscious shopper
⑤ Benefits of using coupons when shopping

17

남자가 언급한 것이 아닌 것은?

① 쇼핑 리스트 ② 웹 사이트 ③ 중고 거래
④ 영수증 ⑤ 스마트폰 앱

01

M: Hi, Amanda. What are you baking?

W: I'm going to __________ __________ __________ __________ tomorrow night's dessert.

M: That sounds great. Tomorrow is the outdoor barbeque dinner, right?

W: (Yeah. What a perfect way to spend a summer evening.)

02

W: It's finally the weekend. Let's go play some games at the arcade.

M: That sounds great, but __________ __________ __________ __________. Do you have change for a twenty-dollar bill?

W: I think so. __________ __________ __________ __________ __________?

M: (A ten-dollar bill, a five, and the rest in coins.)

03

[Chime bell rings.]

W: Good morning, students. This is your vice principal, Mrs. Lee. Tornado season is approaching, so the school is going to have a tornado drill after lunch today. Be sure to __________ __________ __________ __________ when the siren goes off. Please don't rush, and exit the room __________ __________ __________ __________. Your teachers will usher you into the basement, where you will receive instructions on __________ __________ __________ __________ __________ __________ __________ __________ __________ __________. Local firefighters will __________ __________ __________ to help with the procedure. The drill shouldn't take more than thirty minutes to complete. Please pay attention, as this drill is for your own safety. Thank you for your cooperation.

04

W: Justin, we need to sit down and talk about our cafe.

M: Sure. Is something wrong?

W: __________ __________ __________ __________ __________, as you know.

M: Yes, I know. __________ __________ __________ __________ since Blackbeans opened across the street.

W: Well, I was thinking we should __________ __________ __________.

M: Really? I don't think we should do that.

W: But it may be the only way to get our customers back into the cafe.

M: I think we should __________ __________ __________ __________ __________ that Blackbeans doesn't.

W: I really like that idea!

M: We need to remind people that __________ __________ __________ __________ __________. Should we place an ad about it?

W: Absolutely. I'll come up with a draft first thing tomorrow.

M: I think our logo and some pictures of all the items we offer that Blackbeans doesn't would make a perfect ad.

W: Great suggestion.

05

M: Hi, Ms. Sampson!

W: Hello, Steve. I appreciate you coming today.

M: Let's get started. So, this time you're __________ __________ __________ __________.

W: Yes, I am. This is the first time that I've decided to devote all my effort to the human face.

M: Are you enjoying yourself?

W: I really am. Actually, I'm now considering focusing all my work on the human body rather than abstract art.

M: That sounds exciting. I love the expression this model used for this sculpture. Is she someone you know?

W: Yes, she owns a coffee shop in my neighborhood. __________ __________ __________ __________ __________ __________, and she was more than happy to help out.

M: I see. Would you mind doing me a favor?

W: Of course. What is it?

M: I want to use a photo in our article. __________ __________ __________ __________ next to your favorite piece?

W: Sure.

06

M: It looks like you're almost ready to open up the daycare, Pam.

W: Yeah, we've __________ __________ __________ __________ __________ __________ __________ over the last couple of weeks. Check out the playroom.

M: It looks great. The rocket in the corner is awesome!

W: Yeah, I think it will be fun for the children to play on. I painted some stars on the back wall, too.

M: I see that, as well as the moon over on the right.

W: That's right. What do you think about __________ __________ __________?

M: It looks great. The cylinder chairs are quite space-like.

W: I thought so, too. And we've tried to make them different sizes.

M: The table __________ __________ __________ __________ __________ __________, though.

W: I agree. A square table in this room __________ __________ __________.

M: I'm sure the children won't care.

07

W: Hey, Mr. Smith. What are you up to?

M: Hello, Serena. I'm just looking up books.

W: What for?

M: I'm trying to find books that the students in my English class will find interesting. I'd like them to choose one to read over the summer.

W: Oh, so you're making a summer reading list. What books have you chosen so far?

M: I only have a couple. I'm going to need a lot more. It's hard to find books that __________ __________ __________ __________ __________.

W: I'm sure I can help. I read a lot __________ __________ __________ __________.

M: Really?

W: Sure. I can make a list of __________ __________ __________ __________ and email it to you.

M: That would be nice of you. Thanks for your help.

W: It's my pleasure. I hope you have a great summer vacation.

08

[Cell phone rings.]

W: Hello, Dad. What's up?

M: Hey, Elsa. Are you going home anytime soon?

W: I'm still at school. I don't know when I'll finish here.

M: I was wondering if you could pick up a couple of pizzas on your way home. __________ __________ __________ __________.

W: Well, I still have a bit of work to do here. The science fair starts tomorrow, you know.

M: Right. Now I remember. Are you planning on having dinner near the school?

W: Yeah, I'll __________ __________ __________ __________ at the diner next door.

M: All right. So, when are you going to head home?

W: Probably not until around eight o'clock. Is there any way you could come and pick me up?

M: I don't think I can. I'm working late tonight. Will you call your brother and tell him that __________ __________ __________ __________ __________ __________ __________ tonight?

W: Sure. I'll give him a call.

09

[Telephone rings.]

M: Thank you for calling Together Chicken. What can I do for you?

W: Hi. I'd like to __________ __________ __________ for tomorrow. We're going to need twenty orders of chicken for our club meeting.

M: No problem. What kind of chicken do you want?

W: Well, I think we're going to go with some garlic chicken and some smoked chicken.

M: All right. How many of each would you like?

W: We'll take ten orders of each. How much will it be?

M: Garlic chicken is $10 an order, and smoked chicken is $15.

W: Well, __________ __________ __________ __________ than I thought it would be.

M: Oh! I almost forgot. We offer a 10% discount on orders of ten or more chickens.

W: Oh, that's good. I'm going to need them delivered to Jason Bourne Academy at noon.

M: No problem. We'll send them over then.

10

M: Hey Maggie, what do you have going on this winter vacation? Any plans?

W: Well, __________ __________ __________ __________ __________, and I'm thinking about taking a trip to Cairns in Australia.

M: Hmm. . . I really don't think that's a very good idea.

W: Why not?

M: Well, first off, it's peak season, so __________ __________ __________ __________ __________.

W: Really?

M: For sure. And it's more expensive there during peak season.

W: I had no idea.

M: It's also really hot at that time of year because Australia is in the southern hemisphere. It'll be summer there.

W: Oh. I thought that it would be quite mild. I really hate the heat. Is there anything good about visiting Australia at that time of year?

M: Well, __________ __________ __________ __________ __________ __________, so you can get in more time at the beach.

W: That's nice, I guess. But maybe I should find somewhere else to go this winter.

11

M: Today, I'd like to talk about the sloth. The sloth is one of the sleepiest animals in the world! It sleeps 18 hours a day. Why would an animal sleep so much? Scientists believe that this is a way for the sloth to protect itself. It rests and sleeps high up in the trees, but the food it eats is located down on the ground below. Since the sloth is a very slow-moving animal, it is very __________ __________ __________ while it's on the ground looking for food. Over time, this sleepy animal has learned to live on very little food, so it only needs to spend a small amount of time hunting. This does not explain why the sloth sleeps so much, though. Possibly, sleeping helps it to __________ __________ __________. Or maybe it's just really lazy!

12

M: Good afternoon, ma'am. What can I do for you today?

W: Hi. I'm looking to buy a used car for my son.

M: __________ __________ __________ __________ __________ __________ __________?

W: Well, he likes fast cars so we've been looking at different sports cars.

M: Okay. I think __________ __________ __________ __________ __________ __________ __________ __________. *[Mouse clicking sound]* Here's a list of our used sports cars.

W: Hmm. . . I don't think we want a car that's more than five years old.

M: Well, the previous owner of __________ __________ __________ __________ __________ out of these five.

W: I understand that, but I'm looking for a newer car—one that has less than 50,000 miles on it.

M: Okay. How much are you looking to spend?

W: I don't want to spend more than $15,000.

M: Then we've narrowed it down to these two.

W: Great. I don't want to spend the extra money if something goes wrong, so I'll take the one __________ __________ __________ __________.

M: Okay. Let's go and take a look at it.

13

W: What are you working on?

M: I'm trying to finish my economics report. Did you get yours done?

W: I did. I turned it in yesterday.

M: You always finish so quickly. I hope I'll be able to ________ ________ ________ ________ ________.

W: Don't worry, you'll be fine. There's plenty of time. *[Pause]* I really like that graph. It looks great!

M: Thanks. I like it, too. I copied off of a website I found while doing my research.

W: Really? Did you ________ ________ ________ ________ ________ ________?

M: No, I didn't. Should I have?

W: Absolutely! You always need to ________ ________ when you're using someone else's work.

M: I didn't know it applied to the Internet, too. Thanks for letting me know.

W: (Any time. Remember to do it or you may be in trouble.)

14

W: Rudy, is that your new tablet? It looks really cool.

M: Thanks. I bought it last weekend.

W: Where did you buy it from?

M: I went to William's Electronics Mart.

W: ________ ________ ________ ________ ________ ________ ________ ________ ________?

M: Yeah, no problem. Here you go.

W: It's so neat. This must be the latest model. How do I get to the start menu?

M: Just push the round button ________ ________ ________ ________ ________ ________.

W: *[Pause]* Oh, okay. It looks like ________ ________ ________ ________ a lot of cool apps.

M: Yeah, I've actually been spending a lot of time on it since I bought it.

W: Do you use it every day?

M: Definitely. I would say I use it about four hours every day.

W: Really? Four hours? Doesn't that seem like a little too much?

M: (Yeah, it does. I think I need to cut down on my use.)

15

M: Dave recently transferred to a new baseball team. He's always had a hard time ________ ________ ________ ________ ________. After his first practice, the team manager, Roy, recommends having a party in the locker room. Roy thinks it'll be a great opportunity for Dave to get to know his teammates. Dave is ________ ________ ________ ________ ________, but, after some deliberation, he agrees to join the party. Dave develops a close friendship with some of his teammates during the party. He would like to let Roy know that he enjoyed the party and ________ ________ ________ ________ ________ ________.
In this situation, what would Dave most likely say to Roy?

Dave: (I really appreciate you helping me make new friends.)

16-17

M: Good morning, listeners. I'd like to talk to you today about how you can be a smarter shopper and spend your money wisely. Here are some tips you can use to become a keen consumer. First, consider the difference ________ ________ ________ ________ ________ ________ ________ ________. ________ ________ ________ ________ ________, and be sure to place those that are most important higher up on your shopping list. Second, do some product ________ ________ ________ ________ ________. There are several websites online that provide reviews and reports on a wide range of products, such as electronics, vehicles, and household appliances. Third, be conscious of the prices of what you buy and be sure to check your receipts to ________ ________ ________ ________ ________ ________. Finally, be sure to look for coupons and sales. You can search the Internet for deals. There are even applications for your smartphone that can provide coupons to save you money. Keep these tips in mind the next time you go shopping. Thank you for listening.

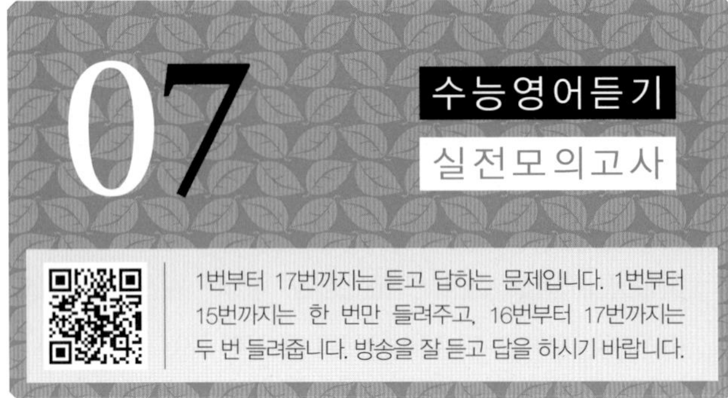

01

대화를 듣고, 남자의 마지막 말에 대한 여자의 응답으로 가장 적절한 것을 고르시오.

① No. I don't like the training facility.
② Thanks. I really needed this job.
③ Yes. They need more trainers.
④ I'm afraid I don't need a job.
⑤ Okay. I'll help you.

02

대화를 듣고, 여자의 마지막 말에 대한 남자의 응답으로 가장 적절한 것을 고르시오.

① He is almost two years old.
② His favorite food is chicken.
③ Children should eat healthy food.
④ Your son may have an allergy to milk.
⑤ I appreciate you taking care of my son.

03

다음을 듣고, 여자가 하는 말의 목적으로 가장 적절한 것을 고르시오.

① 헌혈증 기증을 부탁하려고
② 병문안 가기를 부탁하려고
③ 헌혈의 중요성을 강조하려고
④ 건강 검진 일정을 공지하려고
⑤ 학생의 수술 경과를 알리려고

04

대화를 듣고, 남자의 의견으로 가장 적절한 것을 고르시오.

① 휴대폰의 사용시간을 줄여라.
② 휴대폰의 다양한 기능을 익혀라.
③ 친구의 의견을 잘 듣고 존중하라.
④ 공공장소에서 휴대폰 사용을 자제해라.
⑤ 맹목적으로 최신 유행을 쫓으려고 하지 마라.

05

대화를 듣고, 두 사람이 대화하고 있는 장소로 가장 적절한 곳을 고르시오.

① 스키장　② 눈썰매장　③ 아이스링크
④ 야외 수영장　⑤ 농구 경기장

06

대화를 듣고, 그림에서 대화의 내용과 일치하지 않는 것을 고르시오.

07

대화를 듣고, 남자가 여자를 위해 한 일로 가장 적절한 것을 고르시오.

① 손상된 파일 복원해 주기
② 보고서 출력물 가져다 주기
③ 보고서 철자 오류 수정해 주기
④ 보고서에 수록할 자료 검색해 주기
⑤ 철자 검사 프로그램 사용법 알려주기

08

대화를 듣고, 여자가 주문을 취소하고자 하는 이유를 고르시오.

① 다른 상품을 잘못 주문해서
② 상품이 제때 도착하지 않아서
③ 오프라인이 훨씬 더 저렴해서
④ 배송지 주소를 잘못 입력해서
⑤ 주문한 것과 다른 상품이 도착해서

09

대화를 듣고, 남자가 지불할 금액을 고르시오.

① $40 ② $45 ③ $50 ④ $55 ⑤ $60

10

대화를 듣고, 보아뱀에 관해 두 사람이 언급하지 않은 것을 고르시오.

① 새끼 낳는 방법
② 새끼의 먹이
③ 알이 부화하는 장소
④ 낳는 새끼의 수
⑤ 새끼들의 허물 벗기

11

Eiffel Tower에 관한 다음 내용을 듣고, 일치하지 않는 것을 고르시오.

① 1887년에 건설을 시작해서 2년 후에 완성되었다.
② 관광객들이 접근할 수 있는 층은 총 세 개 층이다.
③ 전세계에서 가장 방문자가 많은 유료 기념물이다.
④ 첫째 층에서 둘째 층까지 계단이 300개가 넘는다.
⑤ 가장 위층까지 관광객들이 걸어서 이용할 수 있다.

12

다음 표를 보면서 대화를 듣고, 남자가 선택한 것을 고르시오.

	Location	Hotel Included	Price per Person
①	Honolulu, USA	X	$1,050
②	Las Vegas, USA	O	$750
③	Rio de Janeiro, Brazil	X	$900
④	Cancun, Mexico	O	$850
⑤	Kingston, Jamaica	O	$700

13

대화를 듣고, 남자의 마지막 말에 대한 여자의 응답으로 가장 적절한 것을 고르시오.

Woman: ____________________

① Bus rides are great for reflecting on your day.
② I think so, too. He should play with a safer one.
③ That's right. It's bad manners to speak loudly in public.
④ Sounds good. I really like listening to music on the bus.
⑤ I agree. I'll go ask the driver to turn the volume down a bit.

14

대화를 듣고, 여자의 마지막 말에 대한 남자의 응답으로 가장 적절한 것을 고르시오.

Man: ____________________

① I have never seen the kids have so much fun.
② I'm pretty good at designing haunted houses.
③ That's a great idea. It'll be exciting for the kids.
④ No problem. I'll let the parents know our plan.
⑤ That's a good plan. The kids love costume contests.

15

다음 상황 설명을 듣고, Aiden이 Mr. Lincoln에게 할 말로 가장 적절한 것을 고르시오.

Aiden: ____________________

① You should reconsider your priorities.
② When is the due date for this assignment?
③ Can we reschedule the meeting for a later date?
④ Is it okay if I keep these books for two more days?
⑤ Could you postpone the due date of my assignment?

[16-17] 다음을 듣고, 물음에 답하시오.

16

여자가 하는 말의 목적으로 가장 적절한 것은?

① to recommend Thai silk clothing
② to introduce Chatuchak Market in Bangkok
③ to describe the variety of souvenirs in Thailand
④ to discuss the importance of markets in Thai culture
⑤ to explain the size and popularity of Chatuchak Market

17

태국 비단에 대한 설명으로 언급하지 않은 것은?

① 값이 싸고 고품질이다.
② 전통 태국 의상에 사용된다.
③ 가장 많이 사는 기념품이다.
④ 여러 종류의 비단 제품이 있다.
⑤ 비단 스카프 가격은 40달러 이하이다.

01

M: Is it true that you started working at the ______ ______?

W: It's true. I started at the beginning of the month.

M: ______ ______ ______ ______ ______ ______ ______. Are they hiring anyone else?

W: (Yes. They need more trainers.)

02

W: I'm getting worried about my son. He suddenly turned red after breakfast.

M: I see. Let's ______ ______ ______ ______ ______. *[Pause]* What have you been feeding him?

W: Well, he had milk and bread this morning.

M: (Your son may have an allergy to milk.)

03

W: Good morning, everyone. This is your vice principal, Rebecca Smith. I think most of you know Helena Simson, one of your classmates. Her mother is in the hospital waiting to ______ ______-______ ______. I've just heard from Helena's homeroom teacher that her mother is supposed to have the surgery very soon. I've been informed that ______ ______ ______ ______ ______ ______ ______ ______ ______ for the surgery. I strongly believe it lies with us to help each other in times like this. So, if any of you want to donate blood to Helena's mother, please ______ ______ ______ ______ ______ ______ ______ ______. Your blood could save someone's life. Thank you for your heartwarming help on behalf of Helena and her mother.

04

W: Hey Dad, can I ask you a question?

M: Of course. What is it, dear?

W: I'd like to upgrade my cell phone.

M: What's the matter with the one you already have?

W: Nothing really, but I've had it for two years, and I'd like to get a new one.

M: Lizzy, if there's nothing wrong with the phone, why would you replace it?

W: Because it's old. It's not even a smartphone.

M: You know ______ ______ ______ ______ of a cell phone is to make calls. I'm a business man, and I don't even have a smartphone.

W: Please, Dad. You know that a cell phone is much more than a phone these days.

M: Maybe I'm not making myself clear. You shouldn't always feel the need to do something ______ ______ ______ ______ ______ ______.

W: Okay, Dad. I'll give it some more thought.

05

W: It's much more exciting than I expected.

M: Right. I used to go skating every winter when I was a kid.

W: Can we ______ ______ ______ for a minute, though? I'm feeling tired.

M: All right. Let's sit down for a while. Do you want me to get you something to drink?

W: Yes, a soda would be great. But isn't it difficult to buy something while wearing skates?

M: No. You don't need to go to the counter. You can call them and they'll bring your order for you.

W: That sounds good. I really want something to drink.

M: Me too. I didn't think ______ ______ ______ ______ ______. I thought it would be cold the whole time we were on the ice.

W: It's all because you didn't ______ ______ ______ ______ ______. Do you even remember how many laps we went around this ice rink?

M: I'm so sorry. I was so excited that I didn't even think about it.

06

M: Hannah, is this a picture of the play you acted in last semester?

W: It sure is. We worked so hard on that performance.

M: The tiger looks very realistic. Is the rabbit ________ ________ ________ ________ ________ his friend, the deer?

W: That's right. It's the Aesop's Fable about the tiger and the rabbit.

M: The set looks really cool.

W: Thanks. The drama club got together and designed it all. See the rocks in the background? I painted them.

M: Wow! You did a great job. That tree on the right side looks very realistic, too. It really gives the feeling of being in Africa.

W: Yeah, that's what we were going for.

M: Did you also ________ ________ ________?

W: No. We rented them from Fat Panda's Costume Shop.

M: I see. Well, it seems like ________ ________ ________ ________ ________ ________ ________ into this play.

07

M: Sophie, I heard you were writing a report on the Cold War.

W: Yes. You've been too busy to help me with it.

M: I'm sorry. But ________ ________ ________ ________ ________ today because I finished my own report.

W: Well, I've already finished writing it!

M: I know. ________ ________ ________ ________ ________ ________ ________, so I read it while you were at school.

W: Oh. Did you like it?

M: Yes, I did. Your ideas on the environmental problems of the Cold War were very interesting.

W: Thanks. I spent a lot of time researching that part.

M: But there were some spelling errors, so ________ ________ ________ ________ ________.

W: That was nice of you.

M: If you want, I'll teach you how to use the spell checker.

W: That's a good idea.

08

[Telephone rings.]

M: Good morning, this is Genie's Online Store.

W: Hi. I'm calling ________ ________ ________ a couple of books I ordered last week.

M: Sure. What's the problem? Were they damaged?

W: No. They were supposed to be here by Saturday, but it's already Monday and they're not here yet.

M: I see. I'll check your order. Can you please give me your seven-digit order number?

W: ________ ________ ________ ________ ________ ________ at the moment. My name is Ella Hanley. Does that help?

M: Yes. Please hold on for a minute while I check for you.

W: No problem.

M: *[Keyboard typing sound]* I apologize, but it looks like ________ ________ ________ ________. It should be there by Thursday.

W: Thursday, huh? That's unacceptable. ________ ________ ________ ________ ________ ________ on Wednesday.

M: I'm very sorry, ma'am.

W: Will you please cancel my order? I'll get them from the local bookstore.

09

[Telephone rings.]

W: Thank you for calling the Henderson Employment and Training Office. May I help you?

M: Hi. I saw a flyer about a career fair at the end of the month. I was wondering ________ ________ ________ ________ ________ ________.

W: Sure. We still have tickets.

M: Awesome. I need five of them. How much do they cost?

W: If you ________ ________ ________ ________, they cost $10. They're $20 at the door.

M: I see. Do you offer any group discounts?

W: I almost forgot—________ ________ ________ ________ ________. You can get a 10% discount for groups of 5 to 10, and a 20% discount if you buy more than 10 tickets.

M: That's awesome. So, a 10% discount for me. I'll buy them now, then.

W: No problem. If you have your __________ __________ __________ __________ __________, I can take your information now.

10

W: Good morning, Theo. Did you have a good weekend?

M: Yeah, it was all right. I didn't do anything special. I did __________ __________ __________ __________ __________ that I found interesting.

W: Really? What about reptiles?

M: Well, did you know that __________ __________ __________?

W: Of course. I thought that was common knowledge.

M: It is. But some species of snakes, such as the boa constrictor, give live birth.

W: No way. How do they do that?

M: __________ __________ __________ __________ __________ __________ __________ and once they hatch, they give birth.

W: That's incredible. How many babies can a boa have?

M: Anywhere from six to thirty-nine.

W: That's incredible. I had no idea.

M: It's true. Baby boas also __________ __________ __________ within ten days of being born.

W: Wow. Animals are truly amazing, huh?

11

W: Today, I'm going to talk to you about the Eiffel Tower. It's __________ __________ __________ __________ __________ __________ __________, but did you know that it was originally built as a watch tower? The tower's construction started in 1887 and was completed two years later. During its construction, the Eiffel Tower surpassed the Washington Monument to assume the title of __________ __________-__________ __________ in the world. The tower has three levels that visitors can access, and it is the most visited monument that requires an entry fee in the world. Visitors can ascend __________ __________ __________ __________ __________ to the first and second levels. The walk from ground level to the first level is over 300 steps, as is the walk from the first to the second level. The top level is __________ __________ __________ __________ __________ __________ __________.

12

W: Welcome to ABC Travel. What can I do for you today?

M: Hi. __________ __________ __________ __________ __________ __________ __________ for my business partners and me.

W: I'm sure I can help you with that. When are you planning on traveling?

M: We're looking at the last weekend of this month.

W: All right. Would you like to travel abroad or stay in the United States?

M: I'd like to go somewhere exotic, so how about somewhere outside of the United States?

W: Do you want your package to __________ __________ __________ __________?

M: Yes, please. I'd like it to be all-inclusive, if possible.

W: Sure. Let's see here. We have a destination that meets your criteria for only $850 per person.

M: __________ __________ __________ __________ __________ __________ __________ __________. I'm not looking to spend more than $750 per person.

W: That leaves us with one option.

M: I've always wanted to go there. Reserve four spots, please.

13

W: Hi, Stan!

M: Oh, hey Candace. I didn't know you take the bus home.

W: Well, I usually drive, but my car is in the shop this week. Anyway, __________ __________ __________ __________?

M: Oh no, this isn't the bus I take home. I'm actually going to the mall.

W: I'm sorry. You're going to fall?

M: No. I said that I'm going to the mall. There's a new toy that I want to pick up for my kid.

W: I see. The mall is really close to my place, so I know it very well.

M: I'm sorry, Candace, but I can't hear you too well. The music on this bus is incredibly loud.

W: Yeah, I hate it __________ __________ __________ __________ __________. When I ride the bus, I just want to __________ __________ __________ __________ __________ __________.

M: And why does he have to play heavy metal music? It's the worst.

W: (I agree. I'll go ask the driver to turn the volume down a bit.)

14

W: Hey Andrew, I need to talk to you about something.

M: Of course, Grace. What's up?

W: It's about the Halloween party. Have you __________ __________ __________ __________ __________?

M: Not yet. We should probably plan it together, don't you think?

W: Yeah, that would be perfect. I have some ideas for a couple of games and events.

M: All right. Well, last year the parents brought candy and we had a costume contest with the kids.

W: Don't you think that's __________ __________ __________ __________? Why don't we do something a little more special, like make a haunted house for them?

M: You mean you want to use the library __________ __________ __________ __________ __________ __________?

W: Exactly! We can call it the "haunted library" tour. Don't you think the kids would love it?

M: (That's a great idea. It'll be exciting for the kids.)

15

M: Aiden is the captain of his high school basketball team, which keeps him busy after school. He also __________ __________ __________ __________ __________ __________ at the school, such as the chess club, the movie club, and student government. When he isn't busy with these activities, he uses what little time he has to do his homework and study for exams. Aiden needs to read for an important assignment in Mr. Lincoln's class and won't be able to finish it __________ __________ __________. He would like to ask the teacher __________ __________ __________ __________ __________ __________ __________ __________ __________. In this situation, what would Aiden most likely say to Mr. Lincoln?

Aiden: (Could you postpone the due date of my assignment?)

16-17

W: Good morning, fellow classmates. I'd like to talk to you today about a very special market in Bangkok, the capital city of Thailand. Chatuchak Market is __________ __________ __________ __________ in the world. The market has more than 8,000 stalls and spans over 27 acres. More than 400,000 people visit the market every weekend. Visitors can enjoy local Thai food, buy souvenirs, shop for vintage sneakers, or even buy an exotic pet, such as a baby squirrel or a monkey. You can also buy something made of the cheap, high-quality silk that Thailand is famous for. This silk __________ __________ __________ __________ __________ __________. You can buy silk scarves, blankets, or neckties. __________ __________ where in the market you buy it, you can spend anywhere from $4 to $40 on a silk scarf. However, __________ __________ __________ __________ __________ __________ at Chatuchak Market. You can also buy purses, Muay Thai boxing shorts, jewelry, and ceramics. Now I'd like to show you some pictures I took of Chatuchak Market when I visited there last spring.

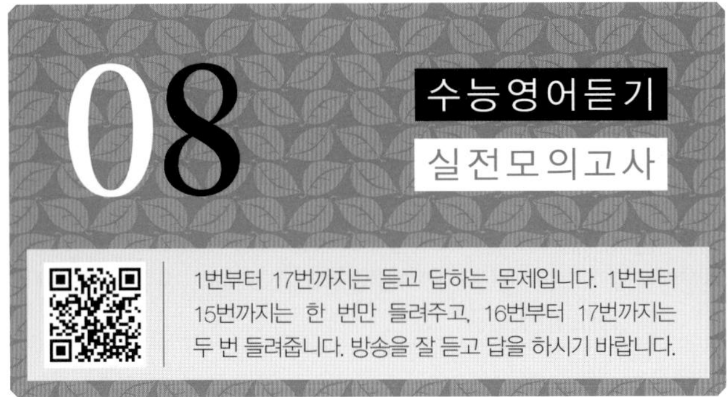

01

대화를 듣고, 남자의 마지막 말에 대한 여자의 응답으로 가장 적절한 것을 고르시오.

① Sorry, but I forgot to write it down.
② I'll send someone right over to help.
③ You can save 10% on your next rental.
④ It shows here that you reserved a sports car.
⑤ I'd like to change my reservation to a minivan.

02

대화를 듣고, 여자의 마지막 말에 대한 남자의 응답으로 가장 적절한 것을 고르시오.

① Why don't we check out the menu before we decide?
② I am not looking forward to meeting this weekend.
③ You go. I really need to complete this before 5 p.m.
④ I thought everything we had last time was great.
⑤ Do you have any advice on good dinner places?

03

다음을 듣고, 남자가 하는 말의 주제로 가장 적절한 것을 고르시오.

① 과다한 염분 섭취가 건강에 미치는 영향
② 피클 속 비타민K와 나트륨에 대한 오해
③ 피클이 함유하고 있는 영양성분
④ 고혈압을 예방하는 음식의 소개
⑤ 피클의 섭취와 건강과의 관계

04

대화를 듣고, 여자의 의견으로 가장 적절한 것을 고르시오.

① 컴퓨터 교체 주기가 점점 길어지고 있다.
② 최신 컴퓨터의 기능들을 많이 활용해야 한다.
③ 컴퓨터를 직접 고침으로써 수리비를 아껴야 한다.
④ 컴퓨터 구입에 있어 디자인 요소를 고려해야 한다.
⑤ 컴퓨터의 일부만 교체하고 가급적 버리지 말아야 한다.

05

대화를 듣고, 두 사람의 관계를 가장 잘 나타낸 것을 고르시오.

① 기자 — 편집장
② 학과장 — 학교직원
③ 신입회원 — 동아리장
④ 학생 — 진로 상담교사
⑤ 라디오 진행자 — 게스트

06

대화를 듣고, 그림에서 대화의 내용과 일치하지 않는 것을 고르시오.

07

대화를 듣고, 남자가 여자를 위해 할 일로 가장 적절한 것을 고르시오.

① 일 도와주기
② 함께 외출하기
③ 점심 주문하기
④ 커피 사다 주기
⑤ 보고서 대신 작성하기

08

대화를 듣고, 여자가 남자의 DVD를 가져오지 않은 이유를 고르시오.

① DVD를 분실해서
② 날짜를 잘못 알아서
③ 다른 장소에 들렀다 오게 돼서
④ 동생의 숙제를 도와주느라 잊어서
⑤ 자신의 발표 내용을 검토하느라 바빠서

09

대화를 듣고, 여자가 지불할 금액을 고르시오.

① $15 ② $17 ③ $45 ④ $47 ⑤ $60

10

대화를 듣고, 두 사람이 훈련 시설에 대해 언급하지 않은 것을 고르시오.

① 설계자 ② 건축 기간 ③ 완공 시기
④ 건축 비용 ⑤ 내부 시설

11

EcoBag에 관한 다음 내용을 듣고, 일치하지 않는 것을 고르시오.

① 전 세계 학교에 사회적 인식을 불러일으키기 위해 만들어졌다.
② 지퍼를 제외한 가방 전체가 재활용된 플라스틱으로 만들어졌다.
③ 가방의 끈과 손잡이는 튼튼하면서도 편안하고 가볍다.
④ 키가 자라서 가방이 작아지더라도 다시 재활용될 수 있다.
⑤ 한 개를 구입하면 회사가 다른 학생에게 한 개를 기부한다.

12

다음 표를 보면서 대화를 듣고, 두 사람이 선택할 기부 프로그램을 고르시오.

Guardian's Charity for Animals Donation Plan

	Option	Project	Payment frequency	Amount
①	A	Animal Shelter	One-Time	$75
②	B	Animal Shelter	Monthly	$10
③	C	Wild Sanctuary	Monthly	$5
④	D	Wild Sanctuary	Monthly	$20
⑤	E	Wild Sanctuary	One-Time	$50

13

대화를 듣고, 여자의 마지막 말에 대한 남자의 응답으로 가장 적절한 것을 고르시오.

Man: ______________________________

① Sorry, but only fans can vote.
② These are our mascot choices.
③ No. You can't participate in the event.
④ You have to sign up for the event early.
⑤ You're right. I'm going to buy one right now.

14

대화를 듣고, 남자의 마지막 말에 대한 여자의 응답으로 가장 적절한 것을 고르시오.

Woman: ______________________________

① I'll get you a souvenir from the science museum.
② I've really been looking forward to this field trip.
③ I visited the science museum when it opened.
④ The debate team has to compete on Friday.
⑤ It takes hard work to be part of any team.

15

다음 상황 설명을 듣고, Bill이 Martin에게 할 말로 가장 적절한 것을 고르시오.

Bill: Martin, ______________________________

① you should lead the way and I will follow you.
② I can always tell whether it's going to rain or not.
③ let's go running when we're sure that it won't rain.
④ always dry out your workout gear after you use it.
⑤ always be careful when riding your bike in bad weather.

[16-17] 다음을 듣고, 물음에 답하시오.

16

남자가 하는 말의 목적으로 가장 적절한 것은?

① 재활용 센터에 필요한 폐품을 모으기 위해
② 재활용 제품을 판매하는 회사를 홍보하려고
③ 재활용 제품 사용하기 운동에 참여를 유도하려고
④ 폐품을 재활용한 제품이 품질도 좋음을 알리려고
⑤ 폐품을 재활용한 제품 제작 아이디어를 공모하려고

17

언급된 물건이 아닌 것은?

① frames ② furniture ③ lamp shades
④ bookshelves ⑤ planters

01

[Telephone rings.]

M: Thank you for calling Bird's Car Rental. May I help you?

W: Yes. I was just calling to __________ __________ __________ I made online.

M: Sure. Do you have your reservation number?

W: (Sorry, but I forgot to write it down.)

02

W: Oh my! Look at the time. We should go eat soon.

M: In a minute. I just want to finish this last piece of work.

W: You can do that after lunch. __________ __________ __________ for some fresh air.

M: (You go. I really need to complete this before 5 p.m.)

03

M: Do you like hamburgers? Do you also like the pickles that are served with those hamburgers? Were you aware that pickles are actually quite healthy? That's right. Pickles not only taste great, but they are low in fat and calories as well. They are also a great source of Vitamin K, which __________ __________ __________ __________ __________ __________ by thickening the blood. Eating just half a pickle provides 17% of your daily requirement of Vitamin K. However, __________ __________ __________ __________, pickles can also __________ __________ __________ __________ because they are very high in sodium. You can fulfill over half of your daily sodium recommendation by eating just one whole pickle. Pickles can be enjoyed daily, but be sure not to eat too much.

04

W: Darling, my computer is having some issues. __________ __________ __________ __________.

M: Hmm. . . I suppose we can go shopping for a new computer this weekend.

W: I don't think we need to get a brand-new one. This one is pretty new.

M: These days technology changes so quickly that many people replace their computers __________ __________ __________ or so.

W: That's true. It just seems like such a waste. We can probably just replace the screen, right?

M: I guess so. But __________ __________ __________ __________ __________ __________ __________.

W: You're right, but other than the screen, __________ __________ __________ __________ __________ __________. I think I can use it for at least two more years.

M: Okay. If that's what you want.

W: We should try to get it fixed. I'll __________ __________ __________ the repair shop.

05

M: Good afternoon, Mrs. Towns.

W: Hi, Hugh. Have you put any more thought into what we talked about last week?

M: I have, and I think I've __________ __________ __________. I want to be a journalist.

W: A journalist, huh? What made you think of that?

M: Well, I've been watching a lot of video clips from Voice News. The work of the reporter seems so __________ __________ __________.

W: I see. Well, what kind of skills do you need to be a journalist?

M: You need to be naturally curious and __________ __________ __________ __________ __________ and investigating.

W: I see. I think that the local college has some great courses that would teach the skills that successful journalists need.

M: Really?

W: Yeah, I've heard great things. Also, you should __________ __________ __________ __________. I'm sure you can learn a lot about the process there.

M: Great idea. I appreciate all the advice, Mrs. Towns.
W: Anytime, Hugh.

06

M: What's this line all about, Dee?
W: They're waiting to take photos with their companions. Let's get in line.
M: All right. But don't you think this photo zone __________ __________ __________ __________?
W: Yeah, it's kind of silly, isn't it? Are we supposed to sit on the sofa? I'd rather stand.
M: Yeah, and __________ __________-__________ __________ __________ __________ __________. It looks old.
W: Look at the big flower next to the couch.
M: Is that a sunflower? It really doesn't match our prom's theme.
W: There are stars on the wall, too. It's like night and day in the same photo. What were they thinking?
M: I do like the poster on the wall. It kind of __________ __________ __________ __________ in high school.
W: I agree with you there.
M: All right, it's our turn. Be sure to smile!

07

M: Hey, Rachel! Are you __________ __________ __________ __________ __________ __________?
W: I want to, but I'm really busy today. What about you?
M: Yes. I have a break, so I'm going to get some food. Would you like me to __________ __________ __________ __________ __________?
W: It's really nice of you to ask, but actually working on this report is making me nervous. __________ __________ __________ __________ __________ __________.
M: Really? That's too bad. Well, how about some coffee then? Do you like Starbeans coffee?
W: Yeah, sure I do. I really love their vanilla lattes.
M: Okay, a vanilla latte it is. I'll be back in 30 minutes. Oh, what size would you like?
W: Wow, __________ __________ __________ __________ __________ __________. A tall-sized one is fine. Thank you so much!
M: Don't worry about it. I'll be back soon.

08

M: Hey, Carrie. What's up?
W: I'm just __________ __________ __________ __________ for Mr. DeWitt's class. I'm pretty stressed about it.
M: I can understand. So, did you remember to bring the DVD about Peru that I let you borrow?
W: Woops, I totally forgot. I'm really sorry, Conner. I can bring it to you tomorrow.
M: What? You forgot it again? I told you that I needed it for my presentation this afternoon.
W: I'm sorry. It just __________ __________ __________. I forgot to bring it because I was helping my brother with his math homework this morning.
M: You explanation __________ __________ __________ __________, Carrie.
W: I'm really sorry. I'll go home at lunch and get it for you.
M: All right. I'll meet you here at the end of the lunch period.
W: Okay. Sorry again. See you later.

09

W: Excuse me. I'd like to exchange these baby shoes for a different pair.
M: Why do you want to exchange them?
W: Actually, my friend bought these for my daughter in this shop, but we got the same shoes from another person a month ago.
M: Oh, I see. We have many kinds of shoes here. Do you see any that you like?
W: Let me see. . . Oh, these will __________ __________ __________ __________. The ribbon on the side of the shoes is so cute. How much are these?
M: They're $60.
W: How much more do I have to pay after the exchange, then?
M: The shoes you brought back were $45, so you only have to __________ __________ __________.
W: Okay. Here's my credit card. Oh, I also need a hairband for my daughter. __________ __________ __________ __________ __________ __________?
M: Yes, of course. __________ __________ __________ __________ __________ __________ __________. It's just $2.
W: Good. I'll take it, too.

10

W: Welcome to our facility, Dr. Fecc.

M: Hi, Ms. Johnson. It's great to finally meet you. This training facility is unbelievable.

W: We're very proud of our team's facility. Would you like a tour before we get to business?

M: I'd love a tour. Thanks. So, I heard that the EPL chose this facility as the best in the league last season.

W: That's true. It was ______ ______ ______-______ ______ Pete Parker.

M: Yeah, I've heard of him. Did it take a long time to complete?

W: It only took about two years. We were able to start training here last spring.

M: ______ ______ ______ ______ ______ ______ this place?

W: Well, where do I start? It has an Olympic-size swimming pool, a tennis court, a sauna, a steam room, ______ ______ ______ ______ ______ ______ ______.

M: That's amazing. Wait. . . you have a restaurant in here, too. This place is truly incredible.

11

M: This morning, I'd like to talk about a great new invention for the environment. It's called the EcoBag. As you probably assumed, it's an eco-friendly backpack. Amanda Stevens, a professor's daughter, created this great backpack to bring social awareness to schools around the world. EcoBag is ______ ______ ______ ______ ______ ______. Even the zippers are made this way. The straps and handle of the bag are made from a blend of recycled fabric and plastic so they are not only strong, but comfortable and lightweight. ______ ______ ______ ______ ______ ______ ______, it can be recycled. What's more, if you ______ ______ ______, the company will donate another bag to a student in need. So you see, the EcoBag is a great way to do your part by helping the environment and the needy.

12

M: Hey honey, what's that you're looking at?

W: It's a brochure for Guardian's Charity. They accept donations to help animals.

M: Right. That's a great program. Are you thinking about donating?

W: Well, what do you think? You do like helping animals, don't you?

M: Of course I do. Remember, how last year we ______ ______ ______-______ ______ to the local animal shelter? Let's try a different project this year.

W: All right. I read an article recently about wildlife sanctuaries and how they help ______ ______ ______ ______ return to their natural habitats.

M: That sounds interesting. I think we should make a ______ ______ ______ ______ ______.

W: That's a great idea. It's more affordable and more meaningful if we donate money month-by-month. How much do you think we should donate?

M: I don't think we can afford anything more than $10.

W: Okay. It looks like this option is ideal for us.

13

W: Hey, I have some exciting news! Our team is having an interesting event on their website.

M: Really? What is it?

W: They're calling it the "Choose Your Mascot" event and ______ ______ ______ during the next game.

M: I don't quite understand. Are they letting the fans choose what their mascot is going to be?

W: That's it. ______ ______ ______ ______ ______ ______ what the team mascot is.

M: And it will be any mascot the fans vote for?

W: Yep, ______ ______ ______ ______ ______ ______.

M: That's different. Can anyone participate in the event?

W: No. Only fans ______ ______ ______ ______ ______ can participate.

M: That's interesting. I want to help choose the next mascot.

W: Well, you're going to have to get a ticket for Saturday's game.

M: (You're right. I'm going to buy one right now.)

14

M: Hey, have you heard that plans for our field trip have changed?

W: No. I haven't heard anything about it.

M: Yeah. It's supposed to rain on Friday so we can't __________ __________ __________ __________ __________. We're going to the science museum instead.

W: That's a shame. But you must be happy. You went to the amusement park with your family last week, right?

M: Yeah, and I've really wanted to visit the science museum ever since it opened. __________ __________ __________ __________ __________ __________ __________ members of our science club.

W: Well, I can't go on the field trip this Friday.

M: Really? Why not?

W: __________ __________ __________ __________ to the debate team.

M: Really? I didn't know there was a debate on Friday.

W: There isn't, but we really need to prepare for next week's contest.

M: I see. You're really __________ __________ __________ __________.

W: (It takes hard work to be part of any team.)

15

W: Bill is watching TV in his house when he __________ __________ __________ from his friend, Martin. The two friends are usually quite active but haven't been able to get together in a few weeks because of the bad weather. This evening, Martin __________ __________ __________ __________ __________ __________. Bill really wants to __________ __________ __________ __________ __________ and get some exercise outside, but he's still worried about the weather. Last summer, he was out for a bike ride rather far from the city and __________ __________ __________ __________ __________ __________ __________. Because of that bad memory, he decides to __________ __________ __________. What would Bill likely say to Martin in this situation?

Bill: Martin, (let's go running when we're sure that it won't rain.)

16-17

M: Everyone knows that __________ __________ __________ is great for the environment, but is the quality as good as buying brand-new items? When you buy from Greenbacks, the answer is always "Yes." We collect discarded items and __________ __________ __________ __________ __________ that are both interesting and high in quality. We also offer very reasonable prices. Nothing in our inventory is more expensive than $100. We carry furniture made from discarded commercial wood, lamp shades made from old clothes, and bookshelves made from antique ladders. If you need new planters for spring, __________ __________ __________ __________ Greenbacks. We have repurposed many things, such as crates, boots, and jars, to give your garden a sharp, new look. All of our items are unique, so your purchases will make great conversation pieces. Check out our website at *www.greenbacksrepurpose.com* to join many others in the repurposing movement. __________ __________ __________ __________ __________ with Greenbacks.

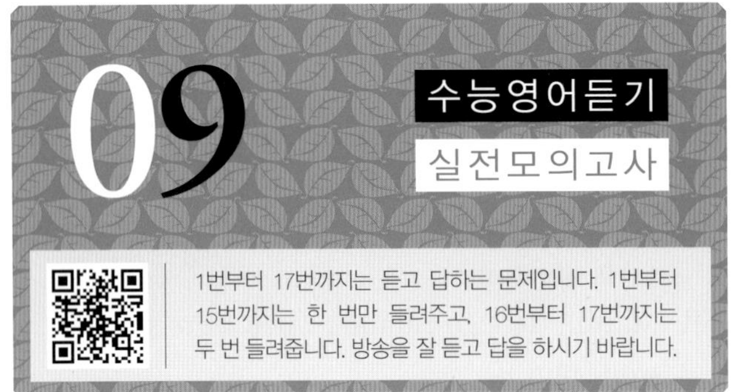

09 수능영어듣기 실전모의고사

1번부터 17번까지는 듣고 답하는 문제입니다. 1번부터 15번까지는 한 번만 들려주고, 16번부터 17번까지는 두 번 들려줍니다. 방송을 잘 듣고 답을 하시기 바랍니다.

01

대화를 듣고, 남자의 마지막 말에 대한 여자의 응답으로 가장 적절한 것을 고르시오.

① Sorry, but all sales are final in this store.
② We should be able to repair the screen next week.
③ I'm sorry, but we don't accept returns after 30 days.
④ You're going to need a receipt if you want a refund.
⑤ We have been having a lot of problems with this product.

02

대화를 듣고, 여자의 마지막 말에 대한 남자의 응답으로 가장 적절한 것을 고르시오.

① No problem. We will be departing shortly.
② That's great. This has really been a pleasant flight.
③ Yes. We sincerely apologize for the inconvenience.
④ That's right. We will be arriving to the airport on time.
⑤ Sorry for your troubles. I'll get you some water immediately.

03

다음을 듣고, 여자가 하는 말의 목적으로 가장 적절한 것을 고르시오.

① 보수공사로 인한 이용 통제를 공지하려고
② 안전사고에 대한 예방 교육을 실시하려고
③ 새로 단장한 커뮤니티 센터를 홍보하려고
④ 궂은 날씨로 인한 시설피해를 알려주려고
⑤ 학교행사 변경 내용과 장소를 안내하려고

04

대화를 듣고, 두 사람이 하는 말의 주제로 가장 적절한 것을 고르시오.

① 음악 감상이 운동에 주는 긍정적 효과
② 공원 내 조깅 전용 도로 설치의 필요성
③ 보행자를 위한 운전자의 배려 부족 현상
④ 헤드폰 끼고 음악 들으며 뛰는 것의 위험성
⑤ 공공장소에서 음악 들을 때 지켜야 할 매너

05

대화를 듣고, 두 사람의 관계를 가장 잘 나타낸 것을 고르시오.

① 상담사 — 구매자
② 기자 — 지역주민
③ 방송 작가 — 시청자
④ 영화 감독 — 연기자
⑤ 뉴스 진행자 — 프로듀서

06

대화를 듣고, 그림에서 대화의 내용과 일치하지 않는 것을 고르시오.

07

대화를 듣고, 남자가 여자에게 부탁한 일로 가장 적절한 것을 고르시오.

① to talk to Mr. Stevenson
② to sign up for her course
③ to supervise his new club
④ to participate in his new movie
⑤ to show him how to use a camera

08

대화를 듣고, 남자가 잠자리에 들지 못하는 이유를 고르시오.

① 친구와 전화 통화하느라
② 탄산음료를 너무 많이 마셔서
③ 친구들이 놀렸던 것이 속상해서
④ 내일 할 연설을 연습하고 싶어서
⑤ 내일 있을 시험 준비를 해야 해서

09

대화를 듣고, 여자가 지불할 금액을 고르시오.

① $70 ② $75 ③ $80 ④ $85 ⑤ $95

10

대화를 듣고, 연례 마라톤에 관해 두 사람이 언급하지 않은 것을 고르시오.

① 완주 거리 ② 당일 복장 ③ 현재 등록 인원
④ 수익금 사용처 ⑤ 완주 기념품

11

Miller Brody에 관한 다음 내용을 듣고, 일치하지 않는 것을 고르시오.

① 1920년 Tennessee에서 외아들로 태어났다.
② Minnesota 대학에서 박사 학위를 받았다.
③ 동료 교수들과 충돌 없이 잘 지냈다.
④ 재임기간 동안 많은 책을 출판했다.
⑤ 유럽에서 각국의 사람들을 만났다.

12

다음 표를 보면서 대화를 듣고, 두 사람이 선택할 관광지를 고르시오.

Madison Tourism

	Activity	Duration	Price	Hotel Pickup
①	River Zipline	2 hours	$90	No
②	Canoe Trip	5 hours	$70	Yes
③	Wine Tasting	4 hours	$50	Yes
④	Downtown Walking Tour	2.5 hours	$20	Yes
⑤	Butterfly Garden Tour	1 hour	$10	No

13

대화를 듣고, 여자의 마지막 말에 대한 남자의 응답으로 가장 적절한 것을 고르시오.

Man: ______________________________

① I told the usher to make them be quiet.
② I met the actor that played the main role.
③ I asked the usher if I could go to the toilet.
④ I'll never forget that amazing performance.
⑤ After watching the play, I complained to the theater.

14

대화를 듣고, 남자의 마지막 말에 대한 여자의 응답으로 가장 적절한 것을 고르시오.

Woman: ______________________________

① Okay, perfect. I'm very happy to help.
② We appreciate your donation. Thanks so much.
③ I'd rather not look at those pictures. They're so sad.
④ Thanks for the advice. I'll be sure to never do it again.
⑤ Just print your name, then sign here. That's all we need.

15

다음 상황 설명을 듣고, Katie가 Kenny에게 할 말로 가장 적절한 것을 고르시오.

Katie: ______________________________

① There are other movies we can choose.
② You won't get a reward for volunteering.
③ We already have enough people volunteering.
④ I'd like to help out by working at the orphanage.
⑤ It's very fun and I'm sure the children will love you.

[16-17] 다음을 듣고, 물음에 답하시오.

16

남자가 하는 말의 목적으로 가장 적절한 것은?

① 새로운 레스토랑을 홍보하려고
② 복합 쇼핑몰의 탄생을 알리려고
③ 세계 최대의 호텔을 소개하려고
④ 라스베가스 내의 관광법을 알려주려고
⑤ 세미나와 회의를 위한 장소를 추천하려고

17

매일 공연을 볼 수 있는 장소로 언급된 곳은?

① Area A ② Area B ③ Area C
④ Area D ⑤ Area E

01

M: Hi. I'd like to __________ __________ ____________.

W: I see. When did you purchase it?

M: Let me check the receipt. *[Pause]* It looks like I picked it up a little over a month ago.

W: (I'm sorry, but we don't accept returns after 30 days.)

02

W: Excuse me, sir. When will we land in Seattle?

M: We should be arriving in Seattle at around 7 p.m.

W: I see. So we're running a little bit __________ __________.

M: (Yes. We sincerely apologize for the inconvenience.)

03

[Bell rings.]

W: Good afternoon, everyone. Could I please have your attention? This is your principal, Mrs. Jones. __________ __________ __________ __________ __________ __________, the school's gym will be closed for construction for the next three weeks. Students must stay out of the gym __________ __________ __________ __________ __________. We apologize for the problems this closure will cause, but it is for the safety of the students. I assure you that __________ __________ __________ will be safer and much nicer when it reopens on February 22nd. Any activities that were scheduled to take place in the gym will be moved down the street to the community center. You can find __________ __________ on our website. Thank you for understanding our situation.

04

W: Hey, darling. I'm going to __________ __________ __________ __________ downtown.

M: Okay. Oh, I see you're bringing your headphones. Do you plan on listening to music during your run?

W: Of course. I just got the new Maroon 5 album. I'm looking forward to listening to it.

M: I don't think you should listen to music while you run.

W: Why not? Running is boring. Listening to music __________ __________ __________ __________.

M: If you wear your headphones, you won't be able to hear the passing traffic. It's dangerous.

W: Hmm. . . I never really considered that.

M: Yeah, it's important to __________ __________ __________ __________ __________ when you're outside. I wouldn't want you to get hurt.

W: I understand. I guess I'll listen to this album __________ __________ __________ __________.

M: I just want you to be careful, sweetheart.

05

W: Hey there, Sam. What are you holding?

M: Hi, Erica. Actually, these are __________ __________ __________ __________ __________.

W: Really?

M: Yes. Apparently some of our audience doesn't like our news content.

W: Sam, you're the one who wanted to make the local news more light-hearted.

M: I know, but I guess it's not working if we're disappointing our viewers.

W: So should I start reporting on more serious news?

M: Yeah, I guess so. __________ __________ __________ __________ __________ __________ so we can all discuss this matter?

W: That's a good idea. What should I do?

M: __________ __________ __________ __________ all of the staff and have everyone meet in the boardroom after lunch?

W: Okay, got it. But I would like to just say that I really enjoyed the way we were doing the news.

M: I know. Me, too. We'll talk about everything in the meeting.

06

W: Oh, my! What happened to your apartment, Alvin?

M: Wow! It looks like someone broke in and ________ ________ ________.

W: Yeah, whoever was in here broke your mirror.

M: ________ ________ ________ ________, too. This is terrible.

W: There's a bat by the table. That's probably what they used to smash everything.

M: I think you're right. I've never had this happen to me before. Why would someone do this to me?

W: Well, at least the tree hasn't been destroyed.

M: I don't think they took anything. I don't see anything missing. My books are just the way I left them on the floor.

W: I wonder how they got in.

M: Maybe they ________ ________ ________ my open window.

W: Probably. It doesn't look like they used the door.

07

W: Hello, Daryl. What can I do for you?

M: Well, Ms. Peterson, I'd like to ask you about something.

W: Sure, you know you can ask me anything.

M: Some friends and I are really ________ ________ ________ ________ and we want to know if we can start a movie club.

W: Well, first off, I think you should talk to Mr. Stevenson. He's the one ________ ________ ________ ________ ________.

M: Yeah, I talked to him. He said we need a teacher to supervise us.

W: Okay, so who were you thinking of?

M: We know ________ ________ ________ ________ in video production.

W: Oh, you knew that? So you want me to supervise your club?

M: We would really like that. Will you do it?

W: Of course I will. It actually ________ ________ ________ ________ ________ ________.

M: Thanks a lot, Ms. Peterson!

08

M: Hey, Mom. Do we have any coffee left?

W: I think so. Why?

M: I'm in the mood to have a cup.

W: It's far too late to drink coffee. It has a lot of caffeine in it, so it'll ________ ________ ________ ________ ________ ________.

M: Well, I kind of need the energy.

W: Why do you need to ________ ________ ________?

M: I have to ________ ________ ________ in Spanish class tomorrow, and I want to practice it.

W: I've heard you in your room practicing all week.

M: Yeah, I've actually been practicing since last week.

W: So ________ ________ ________ ________ ________ ________.

M: Well, I'm afraid that I'll make a mistake and everyone will laugh at me.

W: I see. Well, I don't think you have anything to worry about. If you make a mistake and everyone laughs, just laugh with them.

M: Okay. Thanks for the advice, Mom.

W: Anytime. Now get ready for bed.

09

M: Welcome to Chester Science Center. How may I help you?

W: Hi. I need tickets for two adults and one child, please.

M: Sure. It's $30 for an adult and $20 for a child.

W: All right. Do these tickets ________ ________ ________ ________ ________?

M: Well, they include all of the shows and main attractions, including the hands-on science show and the aquarium.

W: That's great. What about the planetarium? ________ ________ ________ in the ticket price?

M: It's not. However, you can purchase Science Center Plus tickets that include all of the shows and attractions as well as the planetarium and laser show.

W: All right. How much are those tickets?

M: They're ________ ________ ________ ________ ________ ________.

W: Sounds great. I'll take three of them.

M: Sure. Two adults and one child, right?

W: That's right. Here's my card.

10

M: Cathleen, did you know that they're __________ __________ __________ __________ on the 27th of this month?

W: Yeah, I did know that.

M: Well, do you want to join the race?

W: I'd like to, but it seems like 26 miles will be __________ __________ __________ __________ __________ __________.

M: Yeah, it is pretty far. But you don't have to run the whole thing. You can walk when you need to.

W: Really? That doesn't sound so bad.

M: There are a lot of people running it this year. Almost 2,000 have registered, according to the website.

W: Oh, my! That's a lot of people.

M: It's for a good cause, you know. The __________ __________ is $40, but the proceeds will be used to beautify the riverfront park.

W: I see.

M: You also get a t-shirt and your name on a plaque if you finish the run. We can do it together. I'll help you finish it.

W: All right. __________ __________ __________ __________ to think about it. I'll let you know before next week if I'm going to join or not.

11

W: Good morning, class. Today, I want to talk to you about an American psychologist named Miller Brody. He was born in 1920 in Tennessee, the only son of a hardworking businessman and a house wife. He graduated from the University of Minnesota in 1945 with __________ __________ __________ __________ and started teaching at the University of Montana the following year. He was handsome and fun so his students really loved him, though he was often __________ __________ __________ __________ __________ __________. Throughout his career, he published books that focused on the psychological impact that __________ __________ __________ __________ have on people. He went to Europe after marriage, where he held discussions with many scholars from different countries in hopes of discovering the origins of the social class system in America. Miller Brody __________ __________ from natural causes in 2002.

12

W: Hey, sweetheart. I found this pamphlet down in the lobby. It gives information on Madison's tourist attractions.

M: That's cool. We should find something to do tomorrow.

W: All right. Well, I'd like to __________ __________, but five hours is a little too long, don't you think?

M: Yeah. That's also too expensive. Let's find something that doesn't cost as much.

W: Okay. Well, we could check out the butterfly garden. I heard that it's beautiful this time of year.

M: We could check that out, but they don't __________ __________ __________ from the hotel.

W: Yeah, it would be a real pain to get out there.

M: You're right. Well, that __________ __________ __________ __________ __________. Which do you think will be more fun?

W: I think it'll be __________ __________ __________ __________ __________ __________ __________.

M: I agree. Let's check this one out, then.

13

W: Hey, Tom! Did you enjoy the play last night?

M: Well, the play itself was really good, but I didn't enjoy my time at the theater much.

W: Oh, I thought you were really excited to see that play. What happened?

M: Yeah, I was excited to see it because I love the actor that __________ __________ __________ __________. But I __________ __________ __________ __________ with a couple of people.

W: At the theater? What caused the argument?

M: They were sitting in my seats, and even after I pointed that out to them, they insisted that the seats were theirs.

W: It is __________ __________ when people do that!

M: That's not all. The usher came over to handle the situation and had a look at our tickets. After a closer look, it seems that the clerk had printed the wrong tickets for me, so ________ ________ ________ ________ ________ ________.

W: You must have been furious. What did you do in the end?

M: (After watching the play, I complained to the theater.)

14

W: Hey, Cameron. What does your picket sign say? "Stop animal testing"?

M: Oh, hi Ellie. Yeah, it's ________ ________ ________ ________ ________ ________ ________.

W: A lot of people I know are against that as well, but I'm not sure why.

M: Well, people shouldn't use animals to test products being developed for human use. These pictures show all kinds of terrible things being done to animals in testing labs.

W: Wow, I'm really shocked. I didn't know they treated them like that.

M: They can kill ________ ________ ________ a day just to research the effects of one product!

W: I think it's great that you're ________ ________ ________ ________ ________. Is it possible for me to make a donation?

M: That would be great, Ellie. Go to our website for all the information you need.

W: (Okay, perfect. I'll be happy to help.)

15

M: Kenny asks his friend Katie to go to see a new movie. Katie ________ ________ ________ because she has plans to help at the orphanage this afternoon. Kenny asks Katie why she volunteers and she tells him that helping others, especially children, is very rewarding for her. Kenny has considered volunteering because he also likes helping others. However, he doesn't know if he can ________ ________ ________ ________ because he doesn't think that he is good with children. Katie would really like for Kenny to join her at the orphanage and wants to ________ ________ ________ ________. In this situation, what would Katie most likely say to Kenny?

Katie: (It's very fun and I'm sure the children will love you.)

16-17

M: The Venetian Hotel in Las Vegas is a unique experience. Since it opened its doors in 1999, The Venetian has been the largest hotel in the world. Complete with more than 7,000 rooms, the hotel is ________ ________ ________ ________ ________. The restaurant complex, which offers a variety of food from around the world, can be found in Area A, which also houses the piano bar. Area B holds the casino, where patrons win big every night. In Area C, you can find a shopping mall featuring stores that carry designer brands such as Coach, Prada, and Louis Vuitton. Area D is home to The Venetian's entertainment district, where ________ ________ ________ ________ ________ ________ perform every day and night. You might see a circus, a magic show, watch Barbara Streisand sing, or see any of several other Vegas-style shows. Finally, there is Area E, the lobby and ballroom area. This area also commonly plays host to conventions and seminars. If you ever find yourself in Las Vegas, ________ ________ ________ ________ ________ ________ ________ in the world, The Venetian Hotel.

01

대화를 듣고, 남자의 마지막 말에 대한 여자의 응답으로 가장 적절한 것을 고르시오.

① Okay, I'll call the service center now.
② I'll make sure to take good care of it.
③ I think we should buy the same model.
④ We should try to save energy if possible.
⑤ Make sure he knows to come as soon as he can.

02

대화를 듣고, 여자의 마지막 말에 대한 남자의 응답으로 가장 적절한 것을 고르시오.

① Actually, I'm not sure if I need a car wash.
② No, not really. They do a great job.
③ I think so. They have no money.
④ I don't wash my car.
⑤ It's not my car.

03

다음을 듣고, 남자가 하는 말의 목적으로 가장 적절한 것을 고르시오.

① 아파트 주변 위험 시설을 안내하려고
② 애완동물 유기에 대한 폐해를 알리려고
③ 애완동물 돌보기 대행서비스를 홍보하려고
④ 아파트 내 치안 강화 활동에 동참하도록 격려하려고
⑤ 애완동물이 이웃에 피해를 끼치지 않도록 요청하려고

04

대화를 듣고, 여자의 의견으로 가장 적절한 것을 고르시오.

① 산에서 자신의 쓰레기를 다시 가지고 와야 한다.
② 산에 오를 때는 장비와 옷을 갖추어야 한다.
③ 산에서도 쓰레기 분리수거를 해야 한다.
④ 다양한 등산 코스 개발이 필요하다.
⑤ 산 위에 쓰레기통을 설치해야 한다.

05

대화를 듣고, 두 사람의 관계를 가장 잘 나타낸 것을 고르시오.

① 의사 — 환자
② 감독 — 배우
③ 농구감독 — 리포터
④ 교장 선생님 — 학생
⑤ 심리치료사 — 의뢰인

06

대화를 듣고, 그림에서 대화의 내용과 일치하지 않는 것을 고르시오.

07

대화를 듣고, 남자가 여자에게 부탁한 일로 가장 적절한 것을 고르시오.

① to give him a ride somewhere
② to lend him money for the bus
③ to check when his bus will arrive
④ to let him know where the bus stop is
⑤ to show him how to find an application

08

대화를 듣고, 남자가 요즘 조깅을 하지 않는 이유를 고르시오.

① 교통사고 부상 때문에
② 다른 운동이 좋아져서
③ 이사를 했기 때문에
④ 드럼 연습을 하느라
⑤ 시험 준비 때문에

09

대화를 듣고, 여자가 지불할 총 금액을 고르시오.

① $18 ② $20 ③ $22 ④ $24 ⑤ $26

10

대화를 듣고, 두 사람이 언급하지 않은 것을 고르시오.

① 여자가 주문했던 책의 권 수
② 여자가 주문했던 책의 종류
③ 잘못 배송된 책의 작가
④ 잘못 배송된 책의 처리 방법
⑤ 운송료 지급

11

학교공개 행사에 관한 다음 내용을 듣고, 일치하지 않는 것을 고르시오.

① 한 학기 동안 학생들이 만든 작품을 보여준다.
② 가족이나 친척을 데려오는 행사이다.
③ 3월 26일 수요일에 열린다.
④ 행사는 네 시간 동안 진행된다.
⑤ 선착순으로 입장한다.

12

다음 표를 보면서 대화를 듣고, 두 사람이 선택할 관광 스케줄을 고르시오.

Boat & Snorkeling Tours

	Option	Boat	Lunch	Goggles	Trek Fins
①	A	7 hours	Provided	Provided	Not Provided
②	B	6 hours	Not Provided	Provided	Provided
③	C	6 hours	Provided	Not Provided	Provided
④	D	5 hours	Not Provided	Not Provided	Provided
⑤	E	5 hours	Provided	Provided	Not Provided

13

대화를 듣고, 남자의 마지막 말에 대한 여자의 응답으로 가장 적절한 것을 고르시오.

Woman: ____________________

① You need to always be polite while on the phone.
② Okay, good. That way you won't miss my call.
③ I would prefer you took the subway home.
④ Be sure to talk softly on your cell phone.
⑤ You should shut off your phone.

14

대화를 듣고, 여자의 마지막 말에 대한 남자의 응답으로 가장 적절한 것을 고르시오.

Man: ____________________

① Yeah, there's no way for her to find a decent job.
② Yes, I always wanted her daughter to get a great job.
③ What a surprise! I haven't invited them to the party.
④ No need to worry. Alyssa found out you were concerned.
⑤ Yes. Now I understand that worrying only makes matters worse.

15

다음 상황 설명을 듣고, Rachel이 그녀의 아버지에게 할 말로 가장 적절한 것을 고르시오.

Rachel: ____________________

① Sorry about all of this, Dad.
② Calm down, Dad. It'll be okay.
③ Really? So shouldn't I ask her?
④ See, I knew she would help us!
⑤ Maybe we should have taken the bus.

[16-17] 다음을 듣고, 물음에 답하시오.

16

남자가 하는 말의 목적으로 가장 적절한 것은?

① to provide surveillance camera installation instructions
② to convince people to purchase surveillance cameras
③ to explain how surveillance cameras can prevent crime
④ to demonstrate the effectiveness of surveillance cameras
⑤ to propose a reduction in the number of surveillance cameras

17

감시 카메라가 설치된 곳으로 남자가 언급하지 않은 것은?

① 학교 ② 사무실 ③ 엘리베이터
④ 상점 ⑤ 자동차

01

M: Wow, it's so hot in here. Let's turn on the air conditioner, Amy.

W: It's not working properly. We can't use it until it's fixed.

M: Well, we should ________ ________ ________ as soon as possible then.

W: (Okay, I'll call the service center now.)

02

W: The weather is nice today.

M: Yeah, I'm going to wash my car.

W: How much does it cost to wash your car?

M: I usually ________ ________ ________ ________.

W: Really? Isn't that too expensive?

M: (No, not really. They do a great job.)

03

M: Over the last few weeks, we've received several complaints about neighborhood dogs barking late into the evening. These dogs have become ________ ________ ________ ________ ________ ________ ________, especially those who have to work early in the morning. It has ________ ________ ________ ________ ________, last night, a resident called the police, who came out to the neighborhood to deal with the problem. ________ ________ ________ ________ ________, we have also received several complaints that pet owners are not cleaning up after their pets. We at Greenville Apartments urge our residents to ________ ________ ________ ________ to keep our neighborhood clean and quiet. We appreciate your efforts.

04

W: Daniel, it's beautiful up here. The mountain air is so clean, and the views are amazing.

M: I agree. It's truly wonderful. But, I think ________ ________ ________ ________ ________ ________.

W: It's hard to leave, but it is getting dark. We should go soon.

M: First, where do you think I can ________ ________ ________ ________ ________ ________?

W: There doesn't seem to be any place to put it. Let's just take it with us.

M: Okay, but it would be so much easier if they'd put some trash cans up here.

W: Yeah, but then they'd have to hire someone to come ________ ________.

M: Well, without trash cans, people just throw their trash anywhere they want.

W: True, but if there was a trash can, it would fill up and then overflow and trash would ________ ________ ________ ________.

M: I suppose you're right.

W: I really don't think taking our trash with us is a big deal.

M: I guess it's not.

05

W: Excuse me, Mr. Wise, but ________ ________ ________ ________ ________?

M: Sure, Shelly. Come on in. What can I do for you?

W: I just wanted to apologize for my performance last night. I really ________ ________ ________ ________ ________ ________.

M: Yeah, you weren't as into the performance as you usually are. You made a lot of mistakes.

W: I know. I should have been more focused. I've just been really frustrated lately, and it's been ________ ________ ________ ________ ________ ________.

M: Frustrated about what?

W: Well, I'm falling behind in math class. I've been stressed out about that.

M: I see. Would you like me to replace you for a couple of shows so you can __________ __________ __________ __________?

W: No, it's fine. I've spoken to my teacher. She's agreed to let me retake the last exam.

M: All right. Well, forget about last night. Let's just focus on tomorrow's performance.

W: Okay. Thanks, Mr. Wise.

06

W: I love coming to town for the Spring Festival, Carl. It's so much fun!

M: Me, too. There's so much to do.

W: Absolutely. Let's get something to eat first.

M: Sure. But I need to go to the ATM to get some money.

W: That's perfect. __________ __________ __________ __________ __________ __________ __________ the bank.

M: Nice! What do you want to do after we eat?

W: Well, I always like riding the rides, especially that big wheel.

M: I don't think I can ride with you. __________ __________ __________ __________.

W: That's too bad. Well, I guess you can __________ __________ __________ __________ __________ __________. You can also listen to the band like those people over there.

M: There aren't any bands playing right now, unfortunately.

W: I'm sure you can find something to do while you wait.

M: Sure. Anyway, let's get something to eat!

07

W: Hello, Mr. Brown. It's nice to see you here. Are you waiting for a bus?

M: Yeah. Are you going somewhere, Laura?

W: I'm going home. I'm __________ __________ __________, too. Which one are you waiting for?

M: Number 52. I've been waiting for almost 10 minutes. Ah, do you have a smartphone with you?

W: Yes. Why do you ask?

M: I heard there's a __________ __________ __________. Can you let me know what time my bus will arrive?

W: Of course. Actually, I just installed that app on my phone this morning. Just a second. *[Pause]* Let's see. Here it says bus 52 __________ __________ __________ __________ about five minutes.

M: Oh, that's great. Thank you, Laura.

W: No problem. Oh, __________ __________ __________ __________. See you tomorrow, Mr. Brown.

08

W: Pardon me. Don't we know each other?

M: Cynthia! It's me, Mason!

W: Oh, my goodness, __________ __________ __________. How are you?

M: I'm doing really well. I don't think we've talked since you moved away.

W: I think you're right. Are you still playing music? You always loved the drums.

M: I am. I still really love to play.

W: What about jogging? I __________ __________ __________ __________ a lot.

M: I haven't jogged in a long time, actually.

W: Really? Why not?

M: __________ __________ __________ __________ __________ __________ __________ about a year ago. I can't really run at all.

W: That's terrible. I'm so sorry to hear that. I hope they caught the person that did it.

M: Yes, they did. He actually stopped the car and called the police himself. Anyway, I should be going.

W: Yeah, me too. Let's try to __________ __________ __________!

M: Of course.

09

M: Good morning, Ms. Smith.

W: Good morning, Mr. Baron. All your vegetables __________ __________ __________ today.

M: Yes. I'd especially recommend the onions and the carrots. They just arrived.

W: They do look really fresh. __________ __________ __________ __________?

M: The onions are $2 each, and the carrots are sold by the kilogram. One kilogram of carrots is $6.

W: Then, I'd like one kilogram of carrots and two onions, please.

M: Okay. __________ __________?

W: Yes, I need to buy some pumpkins and some potatoes to make soup.

M: Pumpkins are $5 each, and one kilogram of potatoes is $4.

W: I think two pumpkins and one kilogram of potatoes should be enough. Could I __________ __________ __________?

M: Yes, of course. I'll have someone bring them by in about two hours.

W: Great. Here's my credit card.

10

[Telephone rings.]

M: Shine On Top Bookstore. What can I do for you?

W: I __________ __________ __________ __________ and received them this morning, but there's a mistake with one of them.

M: Okay. May I have your name, please?

W: Yes. It's Rebecca Jackson.

M: Let me just pull up your purchase. *[Keyboard typing sound]* You ordered a collection of essays and a science textbook, right?

W: Yes. The problem is that the essay collection I received is __________ __________ __________ __________ __________.

M: Oh, I'm sorry about that. What's the title of the book you received?

W: It's *A Big Dream*. What I ordered was *Just a Dream* by John Thomas.

M: I __________ __________ __________ __________. We'll have the correct book shipped out to you right away.

W: What should I do with the book I have now?

M: Could you please return it to us by mail? We'll __________ __________ __________ __________.

W: Okay. I'll send it tomorrow.

11

W: Good afternoon, everyone. I'm Lilly Stevens, art director here at Maple's Academy. Today I'd like to announce a special open house event at our school. This event allows students to bring their families to the academy to __________ __________ __________ __________ they've created this semester. You can bring not only your parents, but also your __________, __________, __________ __________ __________. We will also host several activities, such as sculpting and tie-dyeing, that you may choose to participate in with your relatives. This open house event __________ __________ __________ __________ __________ in the activities center from 5 to 9 p.m. on Wednesday, March 26th. You will need to __________ __________ as there is only enough space to accommodate 100 guests. Please visit our website for more information.

12

W: Hey, sweetheart. What's that you're looking at?

M: It's a __________ __________ __________ __________ __________ __________ __________. I think we should do some snorkeling before we go home.

W: That's a great idea. Let's __________ __________ __________. I think it'll be a great experience for the kids. How about the seven-hour tour?

M: Seven hours is far too long for the kids to be on a boat. Don't you think __________ __________ __________ __________ __________?

W: You're probably right. Let's go for a shorter one, then.

M: All right. Do you think we should go on one of the tours that provides lunch?

W: I don't really think that's necessary. We bought a lot of food for our trip. I can make some sandwiches.

M: All right. So, we're obviously going to need goggles, unless we want to buy our own. What about trek fins? Do you think we'll need them?

W: Absolutely. Snorkeling is always __________ __________ __________ __________.

M: Okay. Well, I think we've found the perfect tour for us.

13

W: Are you __________ __________ __________ __________ __________ __________ __________ today between the Devils and the Rangers?

M: I sure am! I'm really excited for this game.
W: Did you get tickets yet?
M: Yes, of course.
W: What time will the game finish?
M: They usually end between 9:30 and 10:00 p.m.
W: Oh, really? I didn't know they lasted that long. I'll come __________ __________ __________.
M: That'd be great, Mom. Where should I meet you?
W: __________ __________ __________ __________ __________ when I arrive at the stadium.
M: All right, great. I'll be sure to have my cell phone with me.
W: Are you sure you'll be able to hear it ring? The stadium is so noisy.
M: I'll __________ __________ __________ __________ and put it in my front pocket so that I feel it when you call.
W: (Okay, good. That way you won't miss my call.)

14

W: Hello, dear. How was your time with all of your friends?
M: It was great. We __________ __________ __________ __________ and then went to the park.
W: That sounds like a lot of fun.
M: Yeah, it really was. We were all having such a good time that we wanted to keep it going, so __________ __________ __________ __________ __________ __________.
W: That was a great idea.
M: Oh, Lauren told me that her daughter landed a job in Phoenix.
W: That's nice. __________ __________ __________ __________? You've been so concerned about Alyssa getting a job.
M: Maybe a bit, but I know our Alyssa will find herself one soon.
W: You seem less worried about it than you were before.
M: Well, I just __________ __________ __________ __________ that there's nothing I can do about it.
W: You're right. There is no use worrying. It won't change anything.
M: (Yes. Now I understand that worrying only makes matters worse.)

15

W: Rachel and her father have been driving around the parking lot at the mall for 10 minutes. It's Saturday and the lot is nearly full. Rachel's father __________ __________ __________ __________. Rachel takes out one of her dolls and __________ __________ __________ __________ a parking space for them. Rachel's father asks what she's doing. She tells him that one of the characters in her favorite cartoon always says if you ever need help, you should ask a friend. Her father tries to explain that this is not the kind of help her cartoon was talking about, but Rachel insists. __________ __________ __________ __________, they see a spot open up in front of them. What would Rachel most likely say to her father?
Rachel: (See, I knew she would help us!)

16-17

M: Good evening, everyone. I'd like to take some time tonight to talk about closed-circuit television, or surveillance cameras for short. In this country, there are more than three million surveillance cameras __________ __________ __________ __________ __________. Some people believe that these cameras prevent crimes from being committed, as criminals are cautious around cameras. However, many of us feel that surveillance cameras can __________ __________. These cameras are everywhere: in our schools, offices, shops, and even our cars. While they might record potential criminals, they also record innocent passersby. There are even stories of people installing surveillance cameras to __________ __________ __________ __________ and other people. This conduct is clearly against the law, but is rarely punished. The police also seem to agree that we should reduce the number of surveillance cameras and increase the number of patrol officers. We should work together to __________ __________ __________ __________ __________ __________ in our city in order to __________ __________ __________ __________ __________.

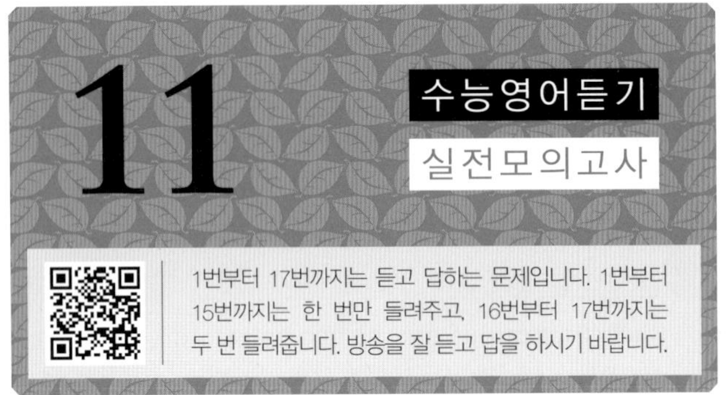

01

대화를 듣고, 남자의 마지막 말에 대한 여자의 응답으로 가장 적절한 것을 고르시오.

① No. This is too big for my house.
② I needed your advice before I bought it.
③ Sure. I'm going to hang the TV on the wall.
④ You have to clean the living room regularly.
⑤ I thought you said it was okay to buy a new TV.

02

대화를 듣고, 여자의 마지막 말에 대한 남자의 응답으로 가장 적절한 것을 고르시오.

① She must be proud of you for winning the prize.
② Yeah, the bakery sells delicious apple pies.
③ I'll make a special cake for your birthday.
④ I don't like alcoholic beverages.
⑤ Great. I'll bring some drinks.

03

다음을 듣고, 여자가 하는 말의 목적으로 가장 적절한 것을 고르시오.

① 연극 동아리의 모임 장소를 공지하려고
② 연극 동아리의 공연을 홍보하려고
③ 연극 동아리의 역사를 소개하려고
④ 연극 동아리 가입을 권유하려고
⑤ 연극 동아리 창단을 제안하려고

04

대화를 듣고, 두 사람이 하는 말의 주제로 가장 적절한 것을 고르시오.

① 다이어트에 효과적인 물
② 수돗물 공급 중단의 원인
③ 탄산수가 건강에 좋은 이유
④ 충분한 수분 섭취의 필요성
⑤ 과도한 탄산수 섭취의 문제점

05

대화를 듣고, 두 사람의 관계를 가장 잘 나타낸 것을 고르시오.

① 고객 — 부동산 중개업자
② 방문객 — 정원 관리사
③ 세입자 — 집주인
④ 투자가 — 금융설계사
⑤ 학부모 — 교사

06

대화를 듣고, 그림에서 대화의 내용과 일치하지 않는 것을 고르시오.

07

대화를 듣고, 남자가 여자를 위해 할 일로 가장 적절한 것을 고르시오.

① 밴드 리더의 전화번호 알려주기
② 밴드 공연 관람권 예매해 주기
③ 밴드 합주 연습실 제공해 주기
④ 밴드 오디션 참가 신청해 주기
⑤ 밴드 기타 연주자 구해 주기

08

대화를 듣고, 여자가 청바지를 자선단체에 기부하려는 이유를 고르시오.

① 키가 커지면서 바지가 맞지 않게 되어서
② 너무 많이 입었기 때문에 싫증이 나서
③ 자선단체에 물건을 보내고 싶어서
④ 유행에 뒤떨어지는 디자인이라서
⑤ 새로운 청바지를 선물 받아서

09

대화를 듣고, 남자가 지불할 금액을 고르시오.

① $30 ② $35 ③ $40 ④ $45 ⑤ $50

10

대화를 듣고, 컴퓨터 게임 토너먼트에 관해 두 사람이 언급하지 않은 것을 고르시오.

① 장소 ② 요일 ③ 대상 연령
④ 준비물 ⑤ 시작 시간

11

겨울 방학 캠프에 관한 다음 안내 방송을 듣고, 일치하지 않는 것을 고르시오.

① 자원봉사 학생들을 모집하고 있다.
② 캠프는 각각 12월과 1월에 실시된다.
③ 수업마다 다른 장소에서 캠프를 진행한다.
④ 자원봉사 신청서는 8월 31일까지 내야 한다.
⑤ 캠프 상담자들은 일주일에 3일 일해야 한다.

12

다음 표를 보면서 대화를 듣고, 여자가 구입할 CCTV를 고르시오.

CCTV Systems

	Model No.	Video Resolution	Infrared	Memory	Price
①	XT221	1280 x 480	X	32GB	$200
②	XT331	1920 x 1080	X	64GB	$350
③	S401	1280 x 480	O	32GB	$260
④	S501	1920 x 1080	X	32GB	$290
⑤	S502	1920 x 1080	O	64GB	$400

13

대화를 듣고, 남자의 마지막 말에 대한 여자의 응답으로 가장 적절한 것을 고르시오.

Woman: ______________________

① I'm not surprised. I knew you would like the movie.
② I don't understand why people like dinosaur movies.
③ I guess we should take a break and eat some snacks.
④ You're right, but I didn't know they were so interesting.
⑤ You will be scared if you watch another dinosaur movie.

14

대화를 듣고, 여자의 마지막 말에 대한 남자의 응답으로 가장 적절한 것을 고르시오.

Man: ______________________

① I think you should follow your dreams.
② I think I ought to major in accounting.
③ Really? I'll go there for help right now.
④ You should choose a major soon.
⑤ There aren't many jobs in art.

15

다음 상황 설명을 듣고, Morty가 카드 판매자에게 할 말로 가장 적절한 것을 고르시오.

Morty: ______________________

① Have you sent me the refund yet?
② Could I please purchase another set of cards?
③ How large is your collection of baseball cards?
④ I was wondering if you knew any other card dealers.
⑤ I haven't received the cards yet. Have you sent them?

[16-17] 다음을 듣고, 물음에 답하시오.

16

남자가 하는 말의 주제로 가장 적절한 것은?

① Ways to rescue mistreated animals
② Efforts to save endangered animals
③ Ways in which animals help humans
④ The role of animals in entertainment
⑤ Negative effects of using animals for help

17

언급된 동물이 아닌 것은?

① elephant ② deer ③ bear
④ dog ⑤ hog

01

M: Honey, did you buy this new TV?

W: Yes. Don't you remember? I told you we needed a better one with a clearer picture.

M: Yes, but why did you buy it ________ ________ ________ ________?

W: (I thought you said it was okay to buy a new TV.)

02

W: Robert, Helena's seventeenth birthday is ________ ________ ________ ________.

M: Oh, I nearly forgot. It's March 23rd. How about a surprise party for her?

W: Sounds great. Then I can prepare her favorite dish: apple pie.

M: (Great. I'll bring some drinks.)

03

W: Hello, I'm Grace Stamos, a junior journalism major. As freshmen, you've been here for about three months now. Are you enjoying your time here at the university? Is everything ________ ________ ________ ________ ________ ________? If you're looking to do more, you might think about ________ ________ ________ ________. The club has been a big part of the university for over 50 years, and many of our incoming freshmen ________ ________. Making new friends is easy ________ ________ ________ ________ ________, and you'll get to visit all the cool clubs and theaters in the city when you do your performances. I'm positive you'll find the club very enjoyable. If you would like to meet new people and ________ ________ ________ ________ ________ ________ ________ here, then join the Drama Club today!

04

M: Wow! It's such a hot day. Did you bring anything to drink, Katie?

W: Sure.

M: Thanks. *[Pause]* Wait, why did you bring soda?

W: That's sparkling water.

M: Sparkling water, huh? Why not regular water? This stuff ________ ________ ________ ________.

W: Well, sparkling water has benefits that you can't get from regular water. It's really ________ ________ ________ ________ ________.

M: I see. Why is that?

W: It suppresses your appetite, so that makes it great for dieting. Since I started drinking sparkling water, I've lost almost 4 kilograms.

M: That's incredible.

W: It's also a lot healthier than tap water in this area. I saw on the news that ________ ________ ________ ________ ________ for a few months.

M: I see. I guess I should start ________ ________ ________.

05

[Cell phone rings.]

M: Good morning, Ms. Tanner. This is Joseph Lancaster.

W: Mr. Lancaster, it's so nice to hear from you. Have you decided on a property?

M: Yes. My wife and I have decided to go with the Main Street property.

W: Ah, the two bedroom home with three bathrooms. It really is a wonderful property. It's ________ ________ ________ ________ ________ ________ ________.

M: Yes, we really love all the open space in the yard.

W: It's a perfect place for raising your kids. They'll have ________ ________ ________ ________ ________.

M: Yes, I agree. I was wondering if it would be all right to plant a small garden in the yard as well.

W: I'm sure it'll be fine. I've been working with the property owner for years.

M: Great. So when can I ________ ________ ________ ________ ________ ________?

W: Can you stop by the office this afternoon? The property owner will be here, too.

M: Sure. I'll come by at around 4 p.m.

06

M: Look, dear. I found this old picture in the attic.

W: Oh, my goodness. I haven't seen this picture in a very long time. That is the playground my father built for me and my brother, Tim, when we were younger.

M: So the little girl is you. You're __________ __________ __________ __________.

W: That's right. Wasn't I cute?

M: That man holding your hand __________ __________ __________ __________. He looks so young!

W: Well, he was. We all were!

M: The boy playing in the sand is Tim, right?

W: Yeah, he always liked to get dirty.

M: The slide looks like it was a lot of fun.

W: It was so much fun. All of the neighborhood kids __________ __________ __________ __________ __________ __________.

M: So, when was this photo taken?

W: When do you think?

M: Everything looks so green. I'm guessing it was taken in the summer.

W: Yeah, it was. Summers were always the best because we didn't have to go to school.

M: __________ __________ __________ __________ __________! It looks like you had an awesome summer.

W: I really did, thanks to my dad.

07

W: Oh, you're looking at an audition notice for a jazz band at a jazz cafe downtown. Are you interested in joining?

M: Not me. My sister is. She plays guitar in a jazz band.

W: Is her band going to __________ __________ __________ __________?

M: They want to. The problem is that their drummer broke his arm last week.

W: Oh, no! He won't be able to play the drums yet, then.

M: Yeah. So the band leader is trying to get a new drummer __________ __________ __________ __________.

W: Hmm. . . Do you think I could meet him?

M: Why? Do you play the drums?

W: Yes, I play a little. And I've been wanting to __________ __________ __________ for a long time.

M: Great! I'll ask my sister for his cell phone number and __________ __________ __________ soon.

W: Thanks. I hope I'm good enough to play with them.

08

M: Stacy, your jeans are on the floor. Will you pick them up, please?

W: Can I just leave them there for now, Brian? I'm __________ __________ __________ __________ later today.

M: Really? But they look new.

W: They are new, basically. I've only worn them a couple times.

M: Why are you giving them up? They seem to be really good quality.

W: I know, and I do like them, but I just can't wear them.

M: __________ __________ __________ __________? Why not?

W: They're too small for me.

M: Okay, but I thought __________ __________ __________ __________ __________. These days I see kids in really tight jeans all the time.

W: Yeah, but they're also too short for me.

M: Aha.

W: I bought those jeans last summer, and since then __________ __________ __________ almost two inches.

M: Well, I suppose we need to buy you some new jeans soon.

09

M: Hi. I'm looking to buy a new pair of headphones.

W: Sure. Do you have a particular brand or style in mind?

M: Well, I want something that's comfortable because I'll be wearing them __________ __________ __________.

W: All right. I think you'll really like this pair.

M: What can you tell me about them?

W: They're incredibly popular these days. They have ________ ________ ________ for comfort and use new technology for optimal sound.

M: That sounds great. How much do they run?

W: They retail for $50, but they're 10% off this week.

M: Awesome! I also found this coupon for $10 off on your website. Can I ________ ________ ________ ________ ________?

W: Absolutely. We can give you an additional $10 off the discounted price.

M: Nice. I'd like to ________ ________ ________ ________ ________.

W: Sure, no problem.

10

W: Sweetheart, how about taking Albert to the ________ ________ ________ tomorrow?

M: That sounds great! I saw a poster that said ________ ________ ________ at PC Playground Arena.

W: That's the place! They hold tournaments the last Saturday of every month.

M: Are you sure Albert would be interested in it? ________ ________ ________ ________ ________ ________ ________ first-person shooters.

W: I don't think so. I'm sure he'll enjoy it. It was actually his idea to go.

M: Okay. ________ ________ ________ ________ ________ ________ ________?

W: I'd say we should bring lunch, some snacks and drinks, and maybe our Ryan and Jason t-shirts so we can cheer them on.

M: That's quite a lot for an afternoon event. Do you think we should leave early?

W: I don't think we should leave too early. It starts at noon, so let's leave at around 11.

M: All right. ________ ________ ________ ________ ________ 11.

11

W: Attention, everyone. The New Poets Society is accepting applications from new students who are interested in poetry and art. There will be poetry camps during the winter vacation, and we would like to have as many student volunteers to ________ ________ ________ ________ as possible. Volunteer camp counselors are responsible for monitoring the younger students and modeling appropriate behavior and safety. Winter camps begin December 23rd and January 7th, and ________ ________ ________ ________ ________ at the Walker Art Center in Minneapolis. ________ ________ ________ ________ no later than August 31st. Camp counselors will be required to work at least eight hours a day, three days a week. If you would like any additional information on the winter camps, please visit us on the web at *www.winterpoets.com.*

12

W: Hey, Samuel. Didn't you buy a CCTV system for your house?

M: I did. Why?

W: Well, my husband and I are shopping for one, but I really don't know much about them. Can you help me?

M: Sure. Let me see that brochure. *[Pause]* Okay. You'll probably want to ________ ________ ________ ________ first.

W: Well, which one do you recommend?

M: I think ________ ________ ________ ________, ________ ________.

W: Okay. I'll go with the high resolution.

M: Do you think you'll ________ ________ ________ ________ ________ ________ ________?

W: The ones with infrared seem much more expensive. I don't really think I'll need it.

M: Okay. The next thing to consider is its storage capacity.

W: Well, I don't really think I'll need too much. What do you think?

M: I don't really use up much space on mine. I think 32GB should be enough space.

W: Great. I guess this is the one for me. Thanks for helping.

13

M: __________ __________ __________ __________ __________ the movie, Debra?

W: I loved it, Dad! Let's watch it again.

M: I knew you'd like it, but let's __________ __________ __________ and then watch something else.

W: I don't want to see anything else. Let's watch *Before Time* again!

M: We just saw that. Let's put in a different movie. Seriously. What about *Teddy Rex*? I heard that's a good one.

W: All right, but it'd better be __________ __________ __________ *Before Time*!

M: It's going to be even better. We'd better get it started soon __________ __________ __________ __________ __________.

W: I won't. Now put on *Teddy Rex*, Dad.

M: I'm quite surprised, Debra. You said that dinosaurs were scary just before we started watching *Before Time*.

W: (You're right, but I didn't know they were so interesting.)

14

M: Hey, Lynn. Do you know what you want to major in yet?

W: I do. I recently decided on online journalism. What about you?

M: I'm still undecided.

W: __________ __________ __________ __________ __________ accounting. You really __________ __________ __________ __________ numbers and managing money.

M: You're right. But I don't know if I want to work with numbers. I'm also interested in art and art history.

W: So you're not sure what to major in?

M: Yeah, I just don't know what to do.

W: Well, __________ __________ __________ __________ visit Ms. Marshall in the counseling center?

M: Why would I visit her? I don't have any behavioral problems.

W: Ms. Marshall can give you an aptitude test to see __________ __________ __________ __________. I think it will help you make a decision.

M: (Really? I'll go there for help right now.)

15

M: Morty likes to collect things. Baseball cards are his favorite thing to collect. A few weeks ago, Morty __________ __________ __________ __________ __________ on the Internet that offered 20 unopened packs of baseball cards for $20. He decided to jump on this deal, and immediately transferred the payment to the card dealer. After one week of waiting and checking the mailbox every day, the cards still hadn't arrived. He decided to __________ __________ __________, but the cards still didn't come. __________ __________ __________, and today he has decided to call the card dealer. After three rings, the dealer answers the phone. In this situation, what would Morty most likely say to the card dealer?

Morty: (I haven't received the cards yet. Have you sent them?)

16-17

M: Good morning, everyone. In our last class, we talked about how animals are often mistreated and used for entertainment and discussed the examples of elephants and bears in circuses. In today's class, I'd like to talk about how people use animals to help them __________ __________ __________ __________ __________. You may have seen our first animal in a shopping mall or walking down the street. This is a seeing-eye dog, and it __________ __________ __________ with their day-to-day lives. Seeing-eye dogs, usually golden retrievers, help their owners cross the street and __________ __________. These dogs also offer companionship and are generally very caring creatures. The next animal we're going to talk about is the truffle hog. People in North America and Europe use hogs to __________ __________ __________ __________ __________ __________ called truffles. Hogs have a great sense of smell and can identify truffles that are __________ __________ __________ __________ __________ __________. Hogs have a natural affinity to search for food underground, so they are perfect for this task.

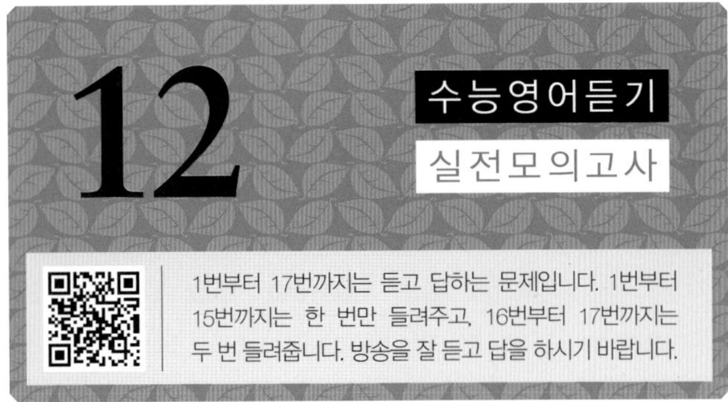

01

대화를 듣고, 여자의 마지막 말에 대한 남자의 응답으로 가장 적절한 것을 고르시오.

① You need to take a medical exam.
② You should fill out an application first.
③ Sure. The interviewer will see you now.
④ We scheduled an appointment for you yesterday.
⑤ We're busy right now, but we'll contact you next week.

02

대화를 듣고, 남자의 마지막 말에 대한 여자의 응답으로 가장 적절한 것을 고르시오.

① I agree with you. It's too expensive.
② I'd like to know what the present is.
③ You're right. Van Gogh is the best artist ever.
④ Do the tickets cost just $10? That's a real bargain.
⑤ I can't believe it! How did you know that I love his work?

03

다음을 듣고, 여자가 하는 말의 목적으로 가장 적절한 것을 고르시오.

① 건강 음료의 중독성을 설명하려고
② 경기력 향상 방법을 안내하려고
③ 건강에 좋은 식단을 권장하려고
④ 체력 유지의 중요성을 알리려고
⑤ 스포츠 음료를 홍보하려고

04

대화를 듣고, 두 사람이 하는 말의 주제로 가장 적절한 것을 고르시오.

① 머리를 맑게 해주는 식이요법
② 긴장감이 학습 효율에 미치는 영향
③ 시험으로 인한 긴장을 완화하는 방법
④ 학업 점수를 올릴 수 있는 공부 방법
⑤ 지나친 운동이 두뇌에 미치는 부정적 영향

05

대화를 듣고, 두 사람의 관계를 가장 잘 나타낸 것을 고르시오.

① 약사 — 환자
② 판매원 — 고객
③ 기자 — 기부자
④ 간호사 — 헌혈자
⑤ 변호사 — 의뢰인

06

대화를 듣고, 그림에서 대화의 내용과 일치하지 않는 것을 고르시오.

07

대화를 듣고, 여자가 할 일로 가장 적절한 것을 고르시오.

① 회의자료 복사하기
② 인력관리부서에 가기
③ 수정 테이프 구입하기
④ 인터넷 카페에 전화하기
⑤ 프린터 수리기사 기다리기

08

대화를 듣고, 여자가 해변에 갈 수 없는 이유를 고르시오.

① 과제를 해야 해서
② 몸이 좋지 않아서
③ 고향으로 가봐야 해서
④ 아르바이트를 해야 해서
⑤ 조별 과제 모임이 있어서

09

대화를 듣고, 새 고속도로 이용 시 단축될 시간과 고속도로 이용 요금을 바르게 짝지은 것을 고르시오.

	단축될 시간		고속도로 이용 요금		단축될 시간		고속도로 이용 요금
①	약 15분	—	$2	②	약 15분	—	$3
③	약 25분	—	$2	④	약 25분	—	$3
⑤	약 40분	—	$5				

10

대화를 듣고, 캠핑에 관해 두 사람이 언급하지 않은 것을 고르시오.

① 캠핑 가는 요일
② 남자가 여자에게 알려줄 일
③ 캠핑 가는 데 걸리는 시간
④ 캠핑에서 먹을 음식
⑤ 짐을 싸야 할 항목

11

Georgetown's Musical Mondays에 관한 다음 내용을 듣고, 일치하지 않는 것을 고르시오.

① 첫 행사는 4월 22일에 시작한다.
② 밴드의 리드보컬이 팬들과 만날 것이다.
③ 밴드의 공연은 6시부터 8시까지 있을 것이다.
④ 초등학생 이상의 어린이부터 입장할 수 있다.
⑤ 수익금은 Georgetown 예술문화협회에 전달될 것이다.

12

다음 표를 보면서 대화를 듣고, 두 사람이 선택한 자전거 강좌를 고르시오.

	Lesson	Instructor	Day	Years of Work Experience
①	A	Sally Fields (female)	Thursday & Friday	8
②	B	Tom Ford (male)	Monday & Wednesday	10
③	C	Wendy Fry (female)	Tuesday & Wednesday	5
④	D	Brenda Benson (female)	Monday & Friday	7
⑤	E	Steve Anderson (male)	Wednesday & Thursday	6

13

대화를 듣고, 남자의 마지막 말에 대한 여자의 응답으로 가장 적절한 것을 고르시오.

Woman : ______________________

① You've never gotten stage fright before.
② I'm sure. You've been practicing hard.
③ I couldn't have done it without you.
④ No. I'm too nervous to perform.
⑤ Okay. I should give it a try.

14

대화를 듣고, 여자의 마지막 말에 대한 남자의 응답으로 가장 적절한 것을 고르시오.

Man: ______________________

① Yes. I'll go back when my kids are a bit older.
② Actually, I wish I had never left America as a child.
③ Exactly. It would be hard to communicate overseas.
④ That's correct. Hard work made everything possible.
⑤ I really wanted to study abroad but couldn't afford it.

15

다음 상황 설명을 듣고, Greg이 Henry에게 할 말로 가장 적절한 것을 고르시오.

Greg: ______________________

① Emails are a great way to show your appreciation.
② It doesn't matter what they donated. It's the thought that counts.
③ I think that we should put together some gift baskets to show thanks.
④ I don't think that we should focus so much time on writing thank-you notes.
⑤ I think that handwritten thank-you notes are the best way to show appreciation.

[16-17] 다음을 듣고, 물음에 답하시오.

16

남자가 하는 말의 주제로 가장 적절한 것은?

① Tips on staying cool in hot weather
② What to do in emergency situations
③ How to save energy for the environment
④ Energy consumption of digital electronics
⑤ Dangers of overloading an electrical outlet

17

열을 발생시키는 전자제품으로 언급되지 않은 것은?

① 냉장고
② 전화기 충전기
③ 전자레인지
④ 커피메이커
⑤ 컴퓨터

01

W: Hi. I finished ________ ________ ________ ________. Is there anything else I need to do?

M: No, that's it. You're free to go.

W: I see. When will you call me to set up an interview?

M: (We're busy right now, but we'll contact you next week.)

02

M: Rosa, I've prepared something special for you. Would you like to know what it is?

W: Oh, yes please. Tell me quickly.

M: ________ ________ ________ ________ ________ the Van Gogh exhibition!

W: (I can't believe it! How did you know that I love his work?)

03

W: Hello, players. As you all know, sometimes it's hard to keep your energy levels up during a game. Playing sports naturally drains your energy. There is one thing you can do to help ________ ________ ________ ________—drink Rad CraCra. Rad CraCra helps keep you in the game. Its special mix of vitamins and minerals helps you ________ ________ ________ ________ ________ ________. It's cheap, too. One can of Rad CraCra only costs about a dollar, but it's all you need to ________ ________ ________ ________ ________ ________. It's a high-quality product that's about half the price of other sports drinks. Its effects even ________ ________ than those more expensive products. So, drink Rad CraCra anytime you need an extra boost.

04

W: Hey Joe, what's wrong? ________ ________ ________ ________.

M: Well, Mom, I'm very nervous about my English exam.

W: Calm down! You've been studying all week, so I'm sure you'll do great.

M: I'm just so worried. I can't ________ ________ anything else.

W: Have you tried doing some yoga or having a conversation with your friends?

M: I chatted on the phone with Molly, but it didn't really help. How do you relax when you're stressed?

W: I usually ________ ________ ________ ________ when I need to relax.

M: Do you think that will help? I think I'll get tired if I jog.

W: Exercising releases endorphins in your brain that help you think more clearly. I'm sure it'll make you feel better.

M: Yeah? Well, I'm going to try to jog ________ ________ ________ ________. Thanks for your help, Mom.

05

W: Good afternoon. ________ ________ ________ ________ ________?

M: I am, but I'm a bit nervous. This is the first time I've done it.

W: That's great! Welcome. ________ ________ ________ ________ ________ ________ ________ is fill out this form.

M: Sure. *[Pause]* Okay. I'm finished. What's the next step?

W: Now we need to prick your finger to check your blood type.

M: Sure. But I'm a little afraid of needles.

W: It will only hurt a bit. *[Pause]* All right, that's it. Are you currently on any medication?

M: Well, I ________ ________ ________ ________ ________ ________ a few days ago. Is that okay?

W: That shouldn't be a problem. Have a seat over here and roll up your sleeve, please.

M: I'm running a little late for a meeting. This won't take long, will it?

W: It usually takes about 20 minutes to give blood. We really appreciate your donation.

06

M: Check out this picture from my childhood, honey.

W: You were so cute back then. Look at you in your baseball uniform.

M: Yeah, I used to love baseball. I even wore my uniform in the winter. That's my first mitt.

W: Really? I see that you're holding a snowball in your left hand. ________ ________ ________-________ when you were young?

M: Yeah, I was ambidextrous when I was a child. I could never decide ________ ________ ________ ________.

W: I like the snowman you built. I guess you gave him your cap.

M: That's right. He's wearing my Ravens baseball cap. I'm wearing my Lions cap.

W: So I guess you were the pitcher and he was the batter, huh? He has your bat.

M: Yeah. I didn't have many friends growing up, so in the winter, I built my own.

W: ________ ________, sweetheart.

07

W: Hey, Bill. Do you have any whiteout?

M: I do. What do you need it for?

W: There's a mistake on this handout for today's partner meeting. I need to correct it.

M: I think you should ________ ________ ________ on your computer and print it again. Partner meetings are important.

W: I know. But ________ ________ ________ ________, and the meeting is in 30 minutes.

M: Yeah, I know. You'll need to go down to the human resources department and use theirs.

W: I need color copies, though. Theirs is only black and white.

M: Well, otherwise you'll have to wait until ________ ________ ________ ________ ________.

W: I can't wait that long. Do you think the Internet cafe down the road has a color printer?

M: I'm not sure, but I can ________ ________ ________ ________ and you can call them.

W: That would be great, Bill. Thanks for helping out.

M: No problem.

08

M: Hey, Sammie. How's everything at your new school?

W: It's all right. I'm starting to ________ ________ ________ ________ ________.

M: That's great. Hey, you remember Jeff, right? Well, we're going to the beach for the weekend.

W: That's cool. So, I guess he got back from his semester in Barcelona.

M: That's right. We're going to the beach to catch up and ________ ________ ________ ________. You should come with us.

W: I'd love to, but I don't think I can. I have a lot of homework to do.

M: School is ________ ________ ________ on the weekends, too?

W: Sometimes. This weekend is especially busy. I have a big chemistry report due on Monday, and an English exam on Tuesday.

M: Sounds like ________ ________ ________ ________.

W: You're right. I've been stressed out all week.

09

W: Honey, how about going to Grove Beach tomorrow?

M: Isn't it too far from here? ________ ________ ________ ________ ________ to get over the mountain on those curvy roads.

W: We don't have to go that way anymore. We can go on the new highway that opened last month.

M: Really? You mean we don't have to drive on ________ ________, ________ ________ ________?

W: Right. It only takes about 15 minutes to get over the mountain using the highway.

M: Wow, that's fantastic.

W: But it's not free. We have to pay for it.

M: How much is it?

W: Well, the government's original plan was to charge $5. But civil organizations requested that they __________ __________ __________.

M: So was it lowered?

W: Yeah, the government __________ __________ __________ $2 less than they originally planned.

M: Oh, great.

10

M: Darling, would you like to come camping with us next Saturday?

W: I don't know. I'm not sure I'll have fun there.

M: Sure you will. The lake is so pretty. I can teach you how to build a fire and set up a tent.

W: All right, I'll come. But you need to __________ __________ __________ __________ __________ __________ so I don't get bored.

M: Sure, sweetheart. The area we're going to __________ __________ __________ __________. You can look it up online if you like.

W: How far away is it from here?

M: It's about three and a half hours by car, but __________ __________ __________ __________ __________ is so beautiful.

W: That sounds nice, actually. So, what do we eat while we're up there?

M: We'll eat the fish that we catch, and of course we'll have other food too, like hot dogs and hamburgers.

W: All right. Do you need any help packing for the trip?

M: Nope! __________ __________ __________ __________ __________ __________. Your only job is to be my company!

11

M: Good morning, everyone. As you know, the weather is warming up, which means it's about time to kick off Georgetown's Musical Mondays by the river. The first event is __________ __________ next Monday, April 22nd at six o'clock. The famous blues band Back Section Action will be coming to perform at Riverside Park. The lead singer of the band will meet with fans after the show. The band will __________ __________ __________ at six o'clock and finish at around eight. As with all of our events, this is __________ __________-__________ __________, so bring your friends and the entire family. There will be a $5 fee __________ __________ __________, and all of the proceeds will go to the Georgetown Arts and Culture Society. Thank you for your time.

12

M: Hey sweetheart, I think that we should start teaching Adam how to ride his bike __________ __________ __________.

W: That's a great idea, but I don't think it's safe to do it around here. The streets are too busy.

M: Well, I found __________ __________ __________ __________ __________ at Freedom Park. These instructors specialize in teaching children to ride for the first time.

W: That's really cool.

M: I thought so, too. So, do you think we should hire a male or female instructor?

W: I think we should go with a woman. He really seems to prefer his female teachers at school.

M: Great. Well, he can't take the class with this one. He has baseball practice on Mondays.

W: Of the two that are left, I think we should go for the one __________ __________ __________.

M: I agree. It looks like we've found our instructor.

13

W: So Larry, __________ __________ __________ __________ __________ __________ __________ this year's talent show?

M: I'm not so sure.

W: Why not? You're great at juggling, and you've been working so hard at it.

M: I'm just worried that I'll make a mistake and everyone will laugh at me.

W: You need to be confident and believe in yourself, Larry. __________ __________ __________ __________ __________ __________ __________ when they perform in front of people.

M: Thanks for trying to help, Mom.
W: Well, are you going to __________ __________ __________ __________?
M: Hmm. . . I still don't know.
W: Come on! Show some confidence! It's not like you to be afraid!
M: After my disaster onstage last year, I'm not sure if I have it in me.
W: Relax. __________ __________ __________ __________ and everyone makes mistakes.
M: So, you think I'll do better this year?
W: (I'm sure. You've been practicing hard.)

14

W: Nicholas, I think I saw you in the city the other day. You were talking to a very attractive woman.
M: Ah, I remember that. I was talking to Clarice Heisenberg. She works for the family business. She handles all of our overseas accounts.
W: __________ __________ __________ __________ eavesdrop, but I couldn't help noticing that you were speaking in a different language.
M: Yes, Clarice is from Germany. She can speak English, but it's easier for her to speak German, and I like practicing.
W: __________ __________ __________ you spoke German.
M: Yes, I actually was born in Germany and lived there for 10 years as a child.
W: Really? I had no idea. Why did you live in Germany?
M: My father's business was based there.
W: That is so interesting. Will you ever __________ __________ __________ __________?
M: (Yes. I'll go back when my kids are a bit older.)

15

M: A severe tornado recently destroyed a neighboring town, so Greg and Henry held a charity event to __________ __________ __________ __________ __________. The event was a success because many caring individuals donated money and basic necessities like canned goods and bottled water. Greg and Henry delivered the goods to the victims, who __________ __________ __________ __________ the donations. Greg and Henry have decided that they would like to show thanks to those who donated. Henry thinks that __________ __________ __________ __________. Greg agrees that email would be convenient, but he feels that they should send handwritten notes because they are more personal and sincere. In this situation, what would Greg most likely say to Henry?
Greg: (I think that handwritten thank-you notes are the best way to show appreciation.)

16-17

M: This summer has been rather hot, hasn't it? In fact, the entire Earth is getting hotter and hotter because of global warming. If you want to __________ __________ __________ __________ __________ __________, wear proper clothing. Light colors reflect light, and with it heat, but dark colors absorb it. So wearing lighter colors will keep you cooler. You should also __________ __________ __________ __________ __________ __________ when you're not using them. For example, phone chargers don't need to be plugged in if the phone is not charging. Also, to stay cool, __________ __________ __________ __________ __________ with a clock. Microwaves and coffee makers are good examples of electronics with clocks that __________ __________ __________ __________ __________. Computers also generate a lot of heat, so you should shut down your computer if you're not using it. Lastly, stay downstairs if possible. A basement is always cooler than the rest of the house. Normally it's about five to ten degrees cooler than the other floors.

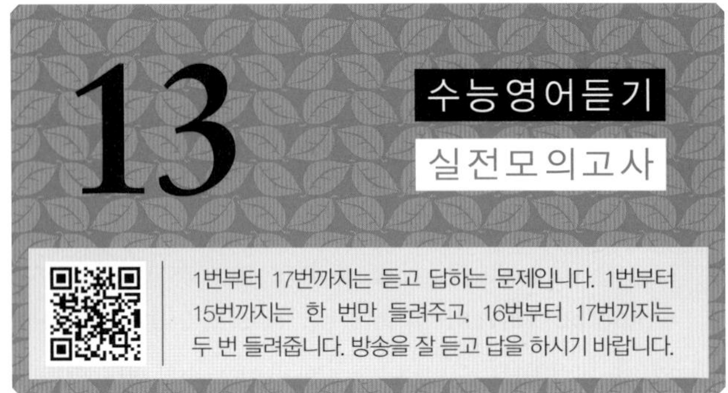

01

대화를 듣고, 여자의 마지막 말에 대한 남자의 응답으로 가장 적절한 것을 고르시오.

① Me, too. I like Chinese food a lot.
② Sounds good. Let's grab some popcorn.
③ I like romance movies more than action.
④ Well, I'd like to eat dinner after the movie.
⑤ Great idea. I know a nice restaurant nearby.

02

대화를 듣고, 남자의 마지막 말에 대한 여자의 응답으로 가장 적절한 것을 고르시오.

① She should be in her office. I'll introduce you two.
② If that's the case, you should find a new office.
③ My office is on the sixth floor of this building.
④ This isn't your office. Your office is over there.
⑤ The new team member seems like a great fit.

03

다음을 듣고, 여자가 하는 말의 목적으로 가장 적절한 것을 고르시오.

① 식습관 변화의 원인을 분석하려고
② 동물 실험 반대 운동을 소개하려고
③ 채식주의자가 되는 이유를 설명하려고
④ 육식 위주 식단의 부작용을 경고하려고
⑤ 종교적 신념과 음식과의 상관관계를 알리려고

04

대화를 듣고, 남자의 의견으로 가장 적절한 것을 고르시오.

① 블루레이 재생기의 사용법을 잘 숙지하고 사용해야 한다.
② TV 자막을 활용하면 효과적으로 외국어를 학습할 수 있다.
③ 미국 드라마 시청은 영어 청취력 향상에 매우 효과적인 방법이다.
④ 너무 빠른 속도의 외국어 TV 프로그램은 외국어 습득에 방해가 된다.
⑤ 청각 장애를 가진 사람들을 위해 자막이 있는 프로그램을 늘려야 한다.

05

대화를 듣고, 두 사람이 대화하고 있는 장소로 가장 적절한 곳을 고르시오.

① 세미나실　② 음반 매장　③ 악기 판매점
④ 종합 경기장　⑤ 밴드 대회장

06

대화를 듣고, 그림에서 대화의 내용과 일치하지 않는 것을 고르시오.

07

대화를 듣고, 여자가 남자에게 부탁한 일로 가장 적절한 것을 고르시오.

① to clean out the closets
② to prepare food for dinner
③ to call ahead to the restaurant
④ to feed the dogs before dinner
⑤ to turn off all the lights in the house

08

대화를 듣고, 남자가 내일 오토바이를 타러 갈 수 없는 이유를 고르시오.

① 출장 준비를 해야 해서
② 회사 일이 늦게 끝나서
③ 오토바이를 수리해야 해서
④ 가족 모임에 참석해야 해서
⑤ 여동생 이사를 도와줘야 해서

09

대화를 듣고, 두 사람이 공항을 향해 출발할 시각을 고르시오.

① 6시 ② 5시 ③ 5시 30분
④ 4시 30분 ⑤ 4시

10

대화를 듣고, 중고 판매점에 관해 두 사람이 언급하지 않은 것을 고르시오.

① 매장의 위치 ② 매장의 규모 ③ 폐점 시간
④ 할인 혜택 ⑤ 택배 서비스

11

Melon plant에 관한 다음 내용을 듣고, 일치하지 않는 것을 고르시오.

① 남아메리카의 남쪽 지역이 원산지이다.
② 오렌지색 꽃은 봄에 2주간 볼 수 있다.
③ 야생 꿀벌에 의해 수분이 이루어진다.
④ 열매는 달고 즙이 많아 사람이 먹을 수 있다.
⑤ 씨는 심한 화상 치료를 위한 연고로 만들어진다.

12

다음 표를 보면서 대화를 듣고, 두 사람이 구입할 태블릿 컴퓨터를 고르시오.

Tablet Computers

	Model	Price	Screen Size	Warranty
①	ZX-1	$169	7 inch	2 Years
②	ZX-2	$219	10 inch	2 Years
③	LV-101	$199	8 inch	1 Year
④	LVX-101	$279	10.4 inch	1 Year
⑤	Ai-6	$299	11 inch	1 Year

13

대화를 듣고, 여자의 마지막 말에 대한 남자의 응답으로 가장 적절한 것을 고르시오.

Man: ______________________

① That's incredible. Isn't technology amazing?
② You should get fitted for C-Braces right away.
③ I appreciate the advice. I'll get a new set of crutches.
④ That's right. I'm going to be able to walk again soon.
⑤ I heard that people with your condition can walk again.

14

대화를 듣고, 남자의 마지막 말에 대한 여자의 응답으로 가장 적절한 것을 고르시오.

Woman: ______________________

① I'm sure you can find a balanced solution.
② I need some help downloading this new game.
③ It's too expensive for kids to play sports these days.
④ Can you tell me the name of the baseball team he plays on?
⑤ I think you need newer hardware in order to play that game.

15

다음 상황 설명을 듣고, Michael이 아내에게 할 말로 가장 적절한 것을 고르시오.

Michael: ______________________

① I turned in the report last week.
② Let me know if I can help you with it.
③ The documents are on the kitchen table.
④ Will you bring the documents to my office?
⑤ Could you help me a bit with the report, please?

[16-17] 다음을 듣고, 물음에 답하시오.

16

여자가 하는 말의 목적으로 가장 적절한 것은?

① to explain how to effectively avoid mouth breathing
② to emphasize the delicacy of the respiratory organs
③ to highlight the importance of nose breathing
④ to explain the benefits of breathing filtered air
⑤ to describe several methods of breathing

17

Mouth breathing의 단점으로 언급되지 않은 것은?

① 불면증 유발 ② 폐에 불순물 유입
③ 질병 감염에 대한 취약성 ④ 폐에 찬 공기 유입
⑤ 호흡기 염증 유발

01

W: We've got some time before the movie starts. Let's have dinner.

M: Good. __________ __________. What are you in the mood for?

W: I'd like to eat Japanese food. What about you?

M: (Great idea. I know a nice restaurant nearby.)

02

M: So, I just started working here and I have no idea __________ __________ __________ __________.

W: __________ __________ __________ __________ the marketing manager, Sarah, about it.

M: Do you know where she is? I've never met her.

W: (She should be in her office. I'll introduce you two.)

03

W: In our last session, we learned that not eating meat is common in many religions, especially Buddhism and Hinduism. In today's session, I want to look at some other reasons for not eating meat and becoming a vegetarian. Many people choose vegetarianism because they __________ __________ __________ __________ __________ __________ __________ __________. They believe eating less animal meat and more fiber will __________ __________ __________ __________ __________ heart disease, cancer, and diabetes. Vegetarians also have ethical concerns. They don't like that certain animals, like cows and chickens, are fed different chemicals to make them bigger. There are also __________ __________ __________ __________ __________ __________ __________ __________ for any reason at all. Can you think of any other reasons for being a vegetarian? Please share your ideas with us.

04

W: Is that a Blu-ray player? It looks a little different.

M: It actually provides subtitles for people with hearing disabilities.

W: Really? That is a very interesting idea. I didn't know that technology was available.

M: Well, __________ __________ __________ __________ every TV show. But it works with most, and you can order more online.

W: But you don't have a __________ __________. Why do you have this machine?

M: Because we're __________ __________ __________ __________ live with us for a year, and I thought it would help her with her English skills.

W: That's very thoughtful of you, but how do you know she likes to watch TV?

M: We asked her in an email. She said she loves to watch American dramas, but the dialogue is sometimes so fast that she can't understand it.

W: Well, then this thing should really help her.

M: I hope so. It wasn't cheap.

05

W: Wow! This place is __________-__________. It's so loud!

M: Yeah, today is the last day of the competition. The final four bands are going to start playing soon.

W: Right. I didn't know it'd be this noisy and crowded in here.

M: It's a rock 'n' roll competition, Clara. Of course it's going to be noisy.

W: I thought so, but I didn't expect this. This is madness.

M: Yeah. It's incredible, isn't it? The annual Battle of the Bands competition __________ __________ __________ __________ in the past few years.

W: For sure. I guess the bands all saved their best songs for this performance, huh?

M: Yeah, my brother said that his band is going to __________ __________ __________, __________ __________ for the finals.

W: That makes a lot of sense.

M: I'm really looking forward to seeing him play.

W: Me, too.

06

M: Hey, Maro. What are you looking at?

W: It's a picture of my cat, Dubu, and me. Have a look.

M: *[Pause]* You look so young in this picture. ________ ________ ________ ________?

W: It must've been soon after I got Dubu. I used to wear glasses, you know.

M: I've never seen you wear them. I like Dubu's color. It's such a nice, solid grey.

W: Yeah. What do you think about the shirt?

M: I think it's kind of cheesy—I don't really like polka dots. Is that a heart pendant ________ ________ ________ ________ ________?

W: Yeah, I thought it was cute so I bought it for him. He's also playing with his favorite toy.

M: It's a ball, right?

W: That's right. I buy him new toys all the time, but ________ ________ ________ ________ ________.

M: That's cool. He seems like a nice cat.

07

W: Finally, we're finished cleaning the house.

M: Yeah, but it wasn't easy. I had no idea it would be such hard work.

W: ________ ________ ________ ________ it's really hot outside today, either.

M: But in the end, we did a great job. Everything looks much nicer.

W: I agree. Oh, look at the time. We ________ ________ ________. What should we make?

M: I don't want to make anything. Let's get out of the house and go somewhere for dinner. We deserve it.

W: Good idea. I don't want to ________ ________ ________ in the kitchen, since we just cleaned it.

M: That's right. I just want to relax and enjoy the rest of my day.

W: Will you ________ ________ ________ before we go? I want to wash up quickly for dinner.

M: Of course.

W: Thank you, dear.

08

W: Hey, Marcus. Is your motorcycle out of the shop yet?

M: Yeah, I got to ride it to work this morning. ________ ________ ________ ________ ________ ________. What do you say we go on a ride after work today?

W: I don't think I can. Let's go tomorrow afternoon.

M: Saturday afternoon? Why not tonight?

W: Well, you know how we have that big business trip next week? ________ ________ ________ ________ ________ ________ before I leave work today.

M: Oh. But I don't think I can go for a ride tomorrow.

W: Why not? Do you have something planned for the weekend?

M: Yeah, I have to meet my sister tomorrow morning.

W: What're you going to do?

M: She's moving into a new apartment, and she needs my help.

W: ________ ________. Anyway, I hope you enjoy spending time with your sister. We'll find some time to go riding soon.

M: Sounds good.

09

M: I can't believe it's already been a year since Marcia left.

W: I know it. I can't wait to catch up with her.

M: When does her flight arrive from Korea?

W: It should be here at 6 p.m.

M: Okay, then we should leave here at around five to make sure we ________ ________ ________ ________.

W: Yeah, but there's a lot of traffic these days because of road work. I think we need to leave earlier.

M: Okay, how about half an hour earlier?

W: Good idea. I'm going to go to the grocery store now and pick up some things for dinner tonight.

M: ________ ________ ________ ________ ________ ________ to leave?

W: Of course. See you then.

M: Okay, great. Make sure you're not late. Today is really important!

W: I know. ________ ________ ________ ________.

10

W: Hey Jason, did you buy the computer game for next month's competition?

M: Yeah, I picked it up at Big Panda's Resale Shop. It looks brand new, and I only paid $15 for it.

W: Really? That's __________ __________ __________ __________ __________ __________ __________ a new one. How far away is this shop?

M: It's right down the street, near the old high school.

W: So it's quite close.

M: It is. It's in a __________-__________ __________ that's full of used books, games, and movies.

W: Wow! That's quite big. I think I'll go down there and have a look for some games as well. What time does it close?

M: I think it closes at 10 p.m., but you should probably call first to make sure.

W: That's a good idea.

M: Oh! Also, if you show them your student ID, they'll __________ __________ __________ __________ __________ __________ __________.

W: That's awesome! I appreciate the help.

11

W: This morning, I'd like to talk about the melon plant. __________ __________ __________ southern regions of South America, and its orange blossoms can be seen at midnight every night for two weeks in the spring. __________ __________ __________ wild honey bees that inhabit the area. When pollinated, the blossoms appear to glow at night. The fruit which the plant produces is a special kind of melon found only in this specific area. Its taste is similar to watermelon or cantaloupe, very sweet and juicy. However, the fruit cannot be eaten because the bees that pollinate the melon plant are poisonous and __________ __________ __________ __________ __________ their poison in the plant. Even though the fruits cannot be eaten, their seeds __________ __________ __________ __________ __________ __________ used to treat severe sunburn.

12

M: Hey sweetie, I think it's about time we got a new tablet. The one we have is too old and slow.

W: I've noticed that, too. Have you found any that you like?

M: I have. I've made __________ __________ __________ __________ __________ __________. Take a look.

W: *[Pause]* I think this one looks all right. It's the cheapest, too.

M: Yeah, it's cheap. But it's not very big. It's actually smaller than the one we have.

W: Really? Well, this one has the biggest screen. It's also a really popular brand.

M: I've been thinking about that one. __________ __________ __________ __________ __________ __________ spending more than $250 on a tablet, though. Let's find something a bit cheaper.

W: All right. So that means that we should decide between these two. This one is more expensive, but __________ __________ __________ __________ __________.

M: Yeah, I think the longer warranty is important. If it breaks, we can replace it pretty easily.

W: All right. Let's get this one, then.

13

M: Hey, Lana. Where's your wheelchair?

W: I didn't bring it today.

M: So __________ __________ __________ now, then?

W: Nope. I don't need crutches either.

M: I see. So how are you going to get around? __________ __________ __________ __________ without help.

W: I can walk without a wheelchair or crutches now. I don't ever have to use them again.

M: What? That's impossible! You've been unable to walk your whole life!

W: I just got fitted for C-Braces.

M: What are C-Braces?

W: They're special, computer-controlled braces that I can attach to my legs and walk without any other help. They're a brand-new technology.

M: So you mean you're basically able to walk now?

W: That's right. I can __________ __________ __________ __________ __________ __________.

M: (That's incredible. Isn't technology amazing?)

14

W: What are you up to, George?

M: I'm downloading a new game on my computer.

W: Why are you downloading another new game?

M: Well, Teddy loves these educational games and they're free, so __________ __________ __________ __________ __________.

W: Don't you think he has enough games already?

M: I don't think so. He's at an age where he learns so fast.

W: I see. But if you download too many games, then __________ __________ __________ __________ and not want to go outside and play.

M: I'm not worried about that. We also __________ __________ __________ __________ gymnastics and baseball.

W: I think that's a good idea, but those activities are only twice a week. He can play games every day.

M: Yeah, I see your point. __________ __________ __________ __________ __________ __________ he can spend on the computer.

W: (I'm sure you can find a balanced solution.)

15

W: Michael has __________ __________ __________ __________ __________ __________ at work today. He submitted his last report a couple of days late because __________ __________ __________ __________ __________ __________. His boss wasn't happy with the delay, so he's very motivated to get this one in on time. Once he arrives at work, he __________ __________ __________ to take out the documents and finds that they're not there. He panics at first and doesn't know how to react. He calls his wife at home and she tells him he has left them on the kitchen table. He's glad that he hasn't lost the report, but __________ __________ __________ __________ __________ __________ __________ __________. In this situation, what would Michael most likely say to his wife?

Michael: (Will you bring the documents to my office?)

16-17

W: Good afternoon, everyone. I want to talk to you all today about how breathing properly can really benefit your overall health. First, you should breathe through your nose. Mouth breathing is more common, but using your nose is actually more natural and therefore healthier. __________ __________ __________ __________ __________ __________ against all of the impurities that can be found in the air we breathe. Mouth breathing doesn't purify the air at all, so things like dust and dirt don't get filtered out. This can __________ __________ __________ __________ __________ __________ __________ __________ or some other airborne illness. Breathing with your mouth also allows cold air to enter the lungs, which can __________ __________ __________ __________ __________ __________ __________. Breathing through your nose, however, __________ __________ __________ and gives you more energy. By filtering and keeping the air warm, the nasal passages only allow in air that is fit to enter the lungs. This means that all of the delicate organs that depend on air will work their best.

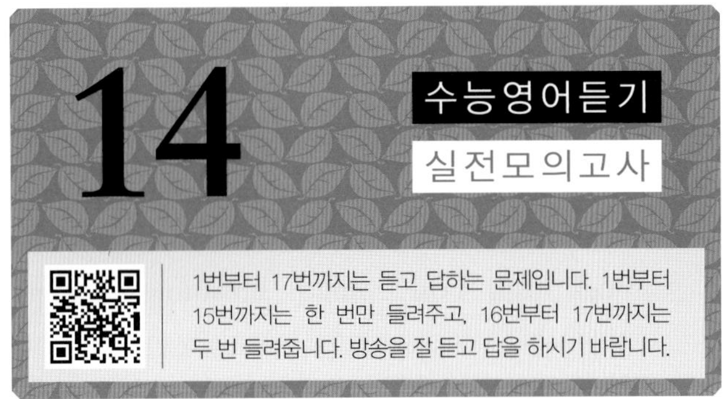

01

대화를 듣고, 남자의 마지막 말에 대한 여자의 응답으로 가장 적절한 것을 고르시오.

① I'm ready to go to the match.
② We should go see a movie instead.
③ We should leave tomorrow morning.
④ You forgot to turn in your homework.
⑤ It shouldn't take more than 15 minutes.

02

대화를 듣고, 여자의 마지막 말에 대한 남자의 응답으로 가장 적절한 것을 고르시오.

① Thanks for closing the windows.
② The weather is wonderful today.
③ You're right. I've been exercising often.
④ It's really rewarding to help other people.
⑤ I think I caught a cold from my classmate.

03

다음을 듣고, 남자가 하는 말의 목적으로 가장 적절한 것을 고르시오.

① 스포츠 광장에서 개최하는 프로그램을 소개하려고
② 공원 내 스포츠 광장 건립의 필요성을 강조하려고
③ 새로 개장한 스포츠 광장의 이용을 장려하려고
④ 공원 내 스포츠 광장 건립 계획에 반대하려고
⑤ 공원 시설에 대한 개선 및 보수를 촉구하려고

04

대화를 듣고, 두 사람이 하는 말의 주제로 가장 적절한 것을 고르시오.

① 다양한 민간요법의 재료
② 청결한 등산화의 중요성
③ 음식물 쓰레기 처리 방법
④ 바나나 껍질의 다양한 용도
⑤ 바나나를 주재료로 한 요리

05

대화를 듣고, 두 사람의 관계를 가장 잘 나타낸 것을 고르시오.

① 소설가 — 학생
② 평론가 — 기자
③ 영화감독 — 교사
④ 가수 — 공연 기획자
⑤ 영화관 직원 — 배우

06

대화를 듣고, 그림에서 대화의 내용과 일치하지 않는 것을 고르시오.

07

대화를 듣고, 여자가 남자에게 부탁한 일로 가장 적절한 것을 고르시오.

① 애완용 새 사주기
② 새집 만들어 주기
③ 새들한테 모이 주기
④ 새들이 많은 길 산책하기
⑤ 새들을 위해 같이 나무 심기

08

대화를 듣고, 남자가 콘서트에 갈 수 없는 이유를 고르시오.

① 표가 매진돼서
② 콘서트가 취소돼서
③ 어머니가 팔을 다쳐서
④ 상사 대신 출장을 가야 해서
⑤ 남동생의 결혼식에 참석해야 해서

09

대화를 듣고, 여자가 지불할 총 금액을 고르시오.

① $112 ② $116 ③ $120 ④ $132 ⑤ $140

10

대화를 듣고, 여드름 피부 관리 방법에 관해 여자가 언급하지 않은 것을 고르시오.

① 깨끗한 피부를 유지하기
② 여드름을 자극하지 않기
③ 여드름에 연고 바르기
④ 여드름을 짜지 말기
⑤ 기름진 음식 피하기

11

Maple syrup에 관한 다음 내용을 듣고, 일치하지 않는 것을 고르시오.

① 식민지화 이전부터 사용되었다.
② 주로 상처 치료에 널리 사용되었다.
③ 캐나다 퀘벡이 세계 최대 생산지이다.
④ 옥수수 시럽보다 영양분이 더 풍부하다.
⑤ 심장병을 예방하고 면역 체계를 강화한다.

12

다음 표를 보면서 대화를 듣고, 남자가 선택한 전자레인지를 고르시오.

Microwave Ovens

	Model	Price	Power (Watts)	Rotate	Size (Cubic feet)
①	A	$90	950	X	0.7
②	B	$130	950	O	0.9
③	C	$190	1200	O	0.9
④	D	$240	1200	X	1.2
⑤	E	$270	1200	O	1.2

13

대화를 듣고, 여자의 마지막 말에 대한 남자의 응답으로 가장 적절한 것을 고르시오.

Man: ______________________________

① French is more difficult than English.
② It seems that we should depend on theories.
③ They say fluency is more important than accuracy.
④ The theories emphasize the use of correct grammar.
⑤ They point out that theory and practice are different.

14

대화를 듣고, 남자의 마지막 말에 대한 여자의 응답으로 가장 적절한 것을 고르시오.

Woman: ______________________________

① I'll be sure that I invite her to the party.
② Sure. I can do that. I'd be happy to help.
③ Great. I'll take some pictures after lunch.
④ I made the collage and it looks really nice.
⑤ Sounds good. I'll be sure to bring some snacks.

15

다음 상황 설명을 듣고, Neil이 아내에게 할 말로 가장 적절한 것을 고르시오.

Neil: ______________________________

① I've always wanted to take a long trip like this.
② Now that I'm retired, I can go fishing whenever I want.
③ I really hope we can find something interesting to do.
④ I think we should go on a backpacking trip together.
⑤ I guess you're right. Traveling that long is too difficult for me.

[16-17] 다음을 듣고, 물음에 답하시오.

16

남자가 하는 말의 목적으로 가장 적절한 것은?

① to provide tricks on keeping fruit fresh
② to warn of the dangers of skipping breakfast
③ to recommend the best time of day to eat apples
④ to offer new and exciting ways to enjoy breakfast
⑤ to suggest eating fruit in the morning to benefit health

17

사과의 건강상 이점으로 언급되지 않은 것은?

① 비타민C의 공급원이다.
② 소화를 촉진시킨다.
③ 체중 관리에 좋다.
④ 뼈를 튼튼하게 한다.
⑤ 여러 가지 암을 예방한다.

01

M: Hey Mia, are you ready to go to the tennis match yet?

W: Almost. I just need to finish ________ ________ ________ ________ ________ on my math homework.

M: ________ ________ ________ do you think it will be?

W: (It shouldn't take more than 15 minutes.)

02

W: Hey Kevin, it's pretty cold in here. Let's close the windows.

M: I'm ________ ________ ________ ________ today.

W: What's the matter? ________ ________ ________ ________ ________ ________ this morning.

M: (I think I caught a cold from my classmate at school.)

03

M: Good evening, everyone. I'm Scott McGee, and I would like to talk to you all tonight about our city's plan to construct a sports arena at Central Park. I'm sure you can all agree that Central Park provides ________ ________ ________ ________ ________ ________ for everyone. We picnic there in the spring and summer, and we ________ ________ ________ ________ ________ ________ year-round. But if we allow the city to build the arena, we won't have space to do those things anymore. ________ ________ ________ ________ ________ ________ ________ ________ ________ ________ from people going to the arena for sports games and other events. I strongly believe that ________ ________ ________ ________ ________ ________ ________! I would like to think everyone here shares my opinion.

04

W: Don't throw that away, Cody.

M: Why not? It's just a banana peel.

W: There are ________ ________ ________ ________ ________.

M: Yeah, I've seen you make compost out of them for the garden. Is that what you're talking about?

W: Well, yes. But there are also many other uses for banana peels. For example, did you know you could use them to ________ ________ ________ and other itchy rashes?

M: That's interesting. So, you're going to ________ ________ ________ ________ ________ in case you get bitten by a bug?

W: Well, no. I was actually going to use that peel to polish my leather shoes.

M: Oh, maybe I'll use one to polish my shoes. What else are they good for?

W: If we put them outside the window, they'll attract birds and butterflies.

M: That's cool. Now I see why you ________ ________ ________ ________ ________ ________ ________.

05

[Telephone rings.]

W: Hello?

M: Hi, this is Ryan James. I just received your email, and I'd like to ________ ________ ________.

W: Really? That's good news. We really appreciate you taking time out of your busy schedule to visit our school.

M: Not a problem. ________ ________ ________ ________ ________ ________ at the graduation ceremony.

W: Great. ________ ________ ________ ________ ________ ________ to many of the students here at Henderson County High School.

M: Oh, I'm ecstatic to hear that from you.

W: Some of our students would love to speak to you in person. Is there any way you could ________ ________ ________-________-________ ________ ________ ________?

M: I don't see why not. I really respect my fans and love to hear from them, especially the young ones.

W: I'm sure they'll be excited to get to ________ ________ ________ ________.

06

M: I like what you did to your dorm room, Clara.

W: Thanks. It was pretty tough moving the desk and the bed.

M: Is that ________ ________ ________ on your bed?

W: Yeah, I've had it since I was young. His name is Geoffrey, and he's a giraffe.

M: Cool. Oh, nice map. Are the pins in it ________ ________ ________ ________ ________ ________?

W: That's right. I put the whiteboard next to it to write my schedule on. I'm really forgetful, you know.

M: I also like that lamp. ________ ________ ________ ________ the room well.

W: That was another gift I got from my grandmother.

M: That's a nice laptop on your desk. Did you bring it from home?

W: Yes, my father gave it to me ________ ________ ________ ________ ________.

M: Well, your room ________ ________ ________ ________ ________ than mine. I like it.

W: Oh? Now I'm curious to see your room.

07

W: I've always liked this trail, Dad.

M: I'm glad to hear that. It's always been one of my favorites, too.

W: I love seeing all of the pretty birds.

M: Yes, there are a lot of them out here.

W: Dad, ________ ________ ________ ________?

M: Birds live in the trees. They build bird homes called nests in the branches way up high.

W: Do birds ________ ________ ________ ________ ________ ________?

M: I'm not sure about that, sweetheart. I think there are birds that don't have houses, though.

W: Really? That's sad. Can we build houses for them?

M: If you ________ ________ ________ ________ ________ ________, then sure we can.

W: I really do, Dad. I want all birds to have nice homes.

M: All right. Then next weekend, we'll build some birdhouses and ________ ________ ________ ________ ________.

W: Great! Thanks, Dad.

08

W: Why are you ________ ________ ________ today, Jim?

M: You know I've been looking forward to Eric Benet's concert. He's my favorite singer.

W: Of course. You've been very excited. What's the matter?

M: ________ ________ ________ ________ I can't go to the concert.

W: Why not? ________ ________ ________?

M: No. I have to go to Shanghai for a meeting.

W: Wasn't ________ ________ ________ ________ ________ that meeting?

M: Yes, he was. But he broke his arm playing tennis last Sunday, so he can't go.

W: That's too bad. What are you going to do with your ticket?

M: I already gave it to my brother.

W: You mean the one who got married last year?

M: Yes. He was so happy about the ticket.

W: Good for him. ________ ________ ________ ________ ________ see Eric Benet someday, Jim.

09

M: Hi. Is there something I can help you with today?

W: I'm looking for some hiking boots. Can I ________ ________ ________ ________ those leather ones?

M: Those are actually men's shoes.

W: I know. I'm shopping for my teenage son. How much are they?

M: They were originally $100, but ________ ________ ________ ________ ________ for 20% off. They were very popular last season. I'm sure he'd like them.

W: I think so, too. I'll take a pair in size 9. Oh! I also need a couple of hiking poles for the two of us.

M: Sure. We have those in pink, purple, green, or blue.

W: I'll take one in purple and one in blue, please. How much are they?

M: They're $20 apiece.

W: Does that 20% discount __________ __________ __________ __________ __________ as well?

M: I'm sorry, but the discount only applies to the shoes.

W: That's all right. Here's my card.

10

M: Oh, no! There are so many pimples on my face.

W: It's just a little acne. It's totally normal to have that __________ __________ __________ __________ __________. By the time you're out of your teens, it will have gone away almost completely.

M: Yeah, I understand all of that. But I still don't like looking at all of these pimples.

W: It's not fun, I know.

M: What should I do about it?

W: Just be sure to keep your skin clean and clear and __________ __________ __________ __________ __________.

M: All right. I can do that.

W: When you see a pimple, you should resist __________ __________ __________ __________ __________.

M: Really? I want to get rid of them right away, though.

W: Most people do, but popping them only makes it worse.

M: Do certain foods cause acne?

W: If __________ __________ __________ __________, you should avoid greasy foods.

11

W: Today I'm going to tell you a little bit about the sweet treat that we call *maple syrup*. __________ __________ __________, the native peoples of North America collected this syrup by tapping into maple trees and collecting the liquid sap that seeped out. They found that maple syrup was a natural sweetener that could be included in many of their recipes. Today, Quebec, a province in Canada, is the world's largest producer of maple syrup. It produces about __________-__________ __________ __________ __________ __________. Compared to other sweeteners, such as cane sugar or corn syrup, maple syrup is __________ __________ __________ of important vitamins and nutrients. Many doctors believe that __________ __________ __________ __________ __________ __________ __________ each day can help prevent heart disease as well as __________ __________ __________ __________.

12

W: Hi. Is there something I can help you find?

M: Yes. I'm looking to buy a new microwave. What do you recommend?

W: Okay, have a look at this one.

M: __________ __________ __________ __________ __________ __________, given that it costs less than $100.

W: You might be right. What about this one? We just got this model in last week. It seems really popular.

M: It's visually appealing, but it has the same amount of power as the cheap one. I'm looking for a more powerful model.

W: Okay. This one is also quite popular, and it's just as new. It also came in last week.

M: What are __________ __________ __________ __________?

W: Well, it rotates, but it's pretty small. Its interior is only 0.9 cubic feet.

M: We heat up some pretty large dishes around my house so I think a larger one would probably be better.

W: Okay. How about this one?

M: It looks great. It rotates, and the interior looks bigger. Oh, the sticker on the panel says it's 1.2 cubic feet. I think I'll take this one.

W: Great. I'll help you load it into the cart, and you can take it to the front to check out.

13

W: Issac, how do you like our French teacher?

M: I think he's all right, but you don't really seem to like him.

W: I just think __________ __________ __________ __________ __________ and not enough basic grammar.

M: You don't like that?

W: I don't really like it because I think grammar is the most important part of __________ __________ __________ __________.

M: Are there any recent studies that support your idea?

W: Not really.

M: Well, why do you think so?

W: I mean, if you don't speak using __________ __________ __________, you'll sound funny.

M: __________ __________ __________ __________ on the basis of many recent theories of language education.

W: Really? What do those theories say?

M: (They say fluency is more important than accuracy.)

14

M: Hey Stacy, __________ __________ __________ __________ __________ this weekend?

W: I'm not sure yet. Why do you ask?

M: I'm __________ __________ __________ __________ __________ for Bruno. He's turning 30. I think he'd like it if you came.

W: That sounds great. I was wondering if he was going to have a party. I'm glad to come.

M: Cool. Well, I want everyone to be at my house by 5 o'clock.

W: That's perfect for me. Do you __________ __________ __________ __________ __________ __________ __________? I can pick up some snacks or something.

M: I think we'll have plenty of snacks. Just bring yourself.

W: Are you sure I can't __________ __________ __________ __________? Bruno is a great friend. I'd like to show him how much he means to us.

M: Well, in that case, there is something you can do for the party.

W: What is it?

M: Susie is making a collage with pictures of all of us at work. It would be great if you could help her choose some pictures.

W: (Sure. I can do that. I'd be happy to help.)

15

M: Neil, a successful lawyer, was __________ __________ __________ __________ for years. When he finally retired, he spent a lot of time fishing, drinking coffee at cafes, or exercising. __________ __________ __________ __________ __________ __________ __________ __________ and has decided that he should do something more interesting. He wants to travel through Southeast Asia for a few months. When Neil discusses his plans with his wife, she refuses to go with him, saying that __________ __________ __________ __________ for that long. __________ __________ __________ __________ __________ __________ to let him go alone because he may never get a chance to travel again. In this situation, what would Neil most likely say to his wife?

Neil: (I've always wanted to take a long trip like this.)

16-17

M: How often do you eat breakfast? Do you find yourself too busy to make time for the most important meal of the day? Next time you're in a hurry, __________ __________ __________ __________ __________ __________ __________ the door. Fruit is a great way to give you that much-needed morning boost. If you have to choose just one fruit, go for an apple. Apples are the healthiest fruit. You might remember hearing the old proverb, "__________ __________ __________ __________ __________ __________ __________ __________." Apples are packed with Vitamin C and __________ __________, __________ __________ __________ __________ __________ manage your weight. They're also great for __________ __________ __________ and lowering your cholesterol. Apples prevent heart disease and lung, breast, colon, and liver cancer. Apples have the nutritional benefits that'll help you lead a healthy life. Apples are easy to eat and require very little preparation time. So next time you're too busy for a full breakfast, __________ __________ __________.

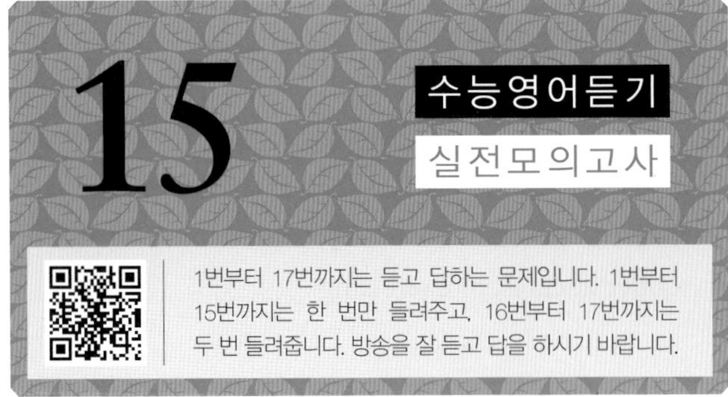

01

대화를 듣고, 여자의 마지막 말에 대한 남자의 응답으로 가장 적절한 것을 고르시오.

① I knew the shop would close eventually.
② I found out the clothes are good quality.
③ Yesterday you asked me what size I wear.
④ I shouldn't have put the box on the table.
⑤ You put the date on your phone to remember it.

02

대화를 듣고, 남자의 마지막 말에 대한 여자의 응답으로 가장 적절한 것을 고르시오.

① Thank you, but I bought a new calculator.
② You don't have to bring your lunch. It's free.
③ Please bring my science report when you come.
④ Let's meet somewhere else. The library is closed now.
⑤ I don't think we're going to use it. Just bring your textbook.

03

다음을 듣고, 남자가 하는 말의 목적으로 가장 적절한 것을 고르시오.

① 새로 개통된 지하철을 홍보하려고
② 지하철 탑승 시의 에티켓을 알려주려고
③ 도시 내 지하철의 필요성을 강조하려고
④ 지하철 공사 기금 마련을 위한 토론을 알리려고
⑤ 지하철 이용 시 불편한 점을 교통부에 항의하려고

04

대화를 듣고, 두 사람이 하는 말의 주제로 가장 적절한 것을 고르시오.

① 국립 공원 운영 자금에 대한 지원을 확대해야 하는 이유
② 국립 공원에서 애완동물에 대한 규정이 엄격한 이유
③ 국립 공원에서 애완동물 입장을 허용하는 이유
④ 국립 공원에서 야생동물에 대한 대처 방법
⑤ 국립 공원에서의 환경친화적인 캠핑 방법

05

대화를 듣고, 두 사람의 관계를 가장 잘 나타낸 것을 고르시오.

① 기자 — 평론가
② 할머니 — 손자
③ 요리사 — 식당 손님
④ 구직자 — 인사담당자
⑤ 심사위원 — 대회참가자

06

대화를 듣고, 그림에서 대화의 내용과 일치하지 않는 것을 고르시오.

07

대화를 듣고, 남자가 여자를 위해 할 일로 가장 적절한 것을 고르시오.

① 선물 사기
② 집안 청소 하기
③ 저녁 식사 준비하기
④ 크리스마스 계획 세우기
⑤ 공항으로 어머님 모시러 가기

08

대화를 듣고, 남자가 점심을 사무실에서 먹어야 하는 이유를 고르시오.

① 회의 시작 시간이 변경되어서
② 프레젠테이션 준비가 덜 되어서
③ 손님들이 일찍 올 것에 대비해서
④ 이메일을 확인할 시간이 필요해서
⑤ 드라이클리닝 맡긴 정장을 찾아야 해서

09

대화를 듣고, 여자가 받을 거스름돈의 액수를 고르시오.

① $15 ② $20 ③ $30 ④ $40 ⑤ $45

10

대화를 듣고, 아파트 임대에 관해 언급되지 않은 것을 고르시오.

① 위치 ② 가격 ③ 편의시설
④ 침실의 개수 ⑤ 선호하는 층

11

Berry Delicious Day에 관한 다음 내용을 듣고, 일치하지 않는 것을 고르시오.

① 행사는 토요일 오전 10시에 시작한다.
② 행사 당일에는 입장료 없이 무료로 입장할 수 있다.
③ 수확한 베리로 만든 파이로 어려운 사람들을 도울 수 있다.
④ 참가자는 활동을 위해 반바지를 입는 것이 좋다.
⑤ 애완동물을 데리고 오지 않는 것이 좋다.

12

다음 표를 보면서 대화를 듣고, 두 사람이 예약할 캠핑카를 고르시오.

RV Rental Options

	Model	Sleeping Capacity	Water Hookup	Stove & Refrigerator	Price per Day
①	Bronze	4	No	No	$140
②	Silver	5	No	Yes	$150
③	Gold	5	Yes	No	$160
④	Platinum	5	Yes	Yes	$180
⑤	Diamond	6	Yes	Yes	$200

13

대화를 듣고, 여자의 마지막 말에 대한 남자의 응답으로 가장 적절한 것을 고르시오.

Man: ______________________

① That's a good idea. I'll do that now.
② I gave Mrs. Garcia a key to the house.
③ We should have enough fish food to last.
④ Okay. I'll see if he can bring them to me.
⑤ Yeah. I've already turned on my cell phone.

14

대화를 듣고, 남자의 마지막 말에 대한 여자의 응답으로 가장 적절한 것을 고르시오.

Woman: ______________________

① The stadium doesn't open until one o'clock.
② Sure. I'll bring the materials to you as soon as I can.
③ Do you think I'll be able to cancel the presentation?
④ Not bad. When does the presentation need to be ready?
⑤ Okay. I'll give him a call and see if he can bring them to me.

15

다음 상황 설명을 듣고, Jason이 Ryan에게 할 말로 가장 적절한 것을 고르시오.

Jason: ______________________

① I really appreciate you being so kind to me.
② Let's get in there and try our best in this match.
③ Congratulations on winning the championship.
④ We couldn't have made it to the finals without you.
⑤ Aren't you happy that they canceled the championship?

[16-17] 다음을 듣고, 물음에 답하시오.

16

남자가 하는 말의 주제로 가장 적절한 것은?

① How people contribute to pollution
② Things to do to improve our air quality
③ The effects of pollution on the environment
④ The benefits of adopting energy-saving habits
⑤ Causes and solutions for environmental pollution

17

남자가 언급하지 않은 것은?

① to pick up garbage
② to recycle
③ to use solar energy
④ to use public transportation
⑤ to conserve energy

01

W: I've got a gift for you in this box. You'll never guess what it is!

M: Let me try to guess. Hmm. . . it's some kind of clothes, right?

W: Yes! __________ __________ __________ did you know that?

M: (Yesterday you asked me what size I wear.)

02

M: Helen, could you help me with my science report after school?

W: Of course. __________ __________ __________ __________ in the library?

M: Sounds good. Do I need to bring a calculator?

W: (I don't think we're going to use it. Just bring your textbook.)

03

M: Hello, everyone. Subways are __________ __________ __________ __________ __________-__________ __________ of transportation for our citizens. That's why we need a subway system that reaches more people and carries them to more destinations around the city. We have contacted the Department of Transportation, but at this time they don't think there is enough money to build a subway system that __________ __________ __________ __________ __________. It's our duty, however, to do what is best for our community, so we will be __________ __________ __________ __________ __________ __________ ways to raise money. This may include other social programs and services. Thanks to everyone here for taking the time to listen to my ideas.

04

M: I think I'll drive out to Yosemite National Park this weekend.

W: Really? That will be a great trip.

M: Do you know what the policies are on bringing pets into the park?

W: Actually, the national parks __________ __________ __________ __________ about pets.

M: Do they? But pets are supposed to be __________ __________ __________ __________. Why are the rules so strict?

W: Well, pets can harm smaller animals that inhabit the national parks.

M: Yeah, I guess you're right. I wouldn't want that.

W: The park's rules are also there __________ __________ __________ __________, you know.

M: How's that?

W: Well, there have been a number of cases where people's pets were attacked and sometimes killed by wild animals.

M: Oh my! Then I'll definitely __________ __________ __________ __________ __________ for this trip. Thanks for the information.

05

W: We really enjoyed your dish this evening. You really create some unique flavors.

M: Thanks. I've been experimenting with different combinations.

W: Where did you learn to __________ __________ __________ __________ __________? I've never seen anyone use that technique.

M: Well, I was raised by my grandmother, and I used to watch her in the kitchen. I learned everything I know from her.

W: She seems like a wonderful teacher. What were __________ __________ __________ __________ __________ __________?

M: I spent two years studying local flavors in southern Mexico. It really changed my perspective on the art.

W: You seem completely __________ __________ __________ __________. We're glad to have you here.

M: Thank you for giving me a chance.

W: We'd like to invite you to join us in __________ __________ __________ __________ __________ __________.

M: Really? Thank you for the opportunity.

06

W: Hey Spencer, why were you so late to the meeting this morning?

M: It's been a rough day for me. I've had so many problems.

W: Really? What happened?

M: Well, I left home really early so I could make it to the meeting on time, but there was __________ __________ __________ __________ __________.

W: I see. So they closed the road?

M: That's right. I wasn't really __________ __________, and I ran into a barrier that broke my window.

W: That's awful.

M: That's not all. My GPS couldn't __________ __________ __________, so I had to use a regular map.

W: I haven't seen one of those in years.

M: I got lost, so I had to ask a woman with a smartphone to help me.

W: Well, it's great that you can __________ __________ __________ __________ __________ __________.

M: I suppose you're right. I guess it could have been worse.

07

M: Sweetie, I'm home. What's up?

W: I just got a phone call from my mom. She's coming to visit for the holidays!

M: That's great!

W: Yes, I think so too. But __________ __________ __________ __________ __________ __________, and I didn't plan on her coming!

M: Sweetie, it's okay. Don't worry about that.

W: I still need to prepare the house, and I haven't even __________ __________ __________ __________ yet.

M: Let me help you. Should I work on the house or go shopping for a gift?

W: Well, since I know her tastes a little better than you, I think I should buy her gift.

M: Okay, __________ __________ __________. I'll try to get the house cleaned up a bit, then. When do you expect her to arrive?

W: Her flight arrives at 7 p.m., so I'll __________ __________ __________ __________ __________ __________ after work tomorrow.

M: Okay. That sounds good.

08

W: Good morning, Mr. Shepherd.

M: Hello, Paula. Did you get everything prepared for my meeting this evening?

W: I spent all last night working on it, but I finally finished your presentation.

M: That's great. Did you also __________ __________ __________ __________ __________ __________ __________ __________?

W: I did. It's in the closet in your office.

M: I really appreciate all the __________ __________ __________ __________ __________ __________. Now, let me take a look at the presentation.

W: I emailed it to you. Just check your inbox. Oh, by the way, the meeting __________ __________ __________ __________ for one o'clock.

M: What? That's too early. I won't have time to eat before the meeting.

W: Don't worry about it, sir. I've already __________ __________ for you. You can eat it here at the office.

M: Oh, great. Thanks.

09

M: Hi. Are you ready to check out?

W: Sure. I'm sorry about being a couple of minutes late.

M: That's no problem, ma'am.

W: That's good to know. The last place we stayed at __________ __________ __________ __________-__________ __________ __________ for checking out five minutes late.

M: Don't worry about it. It's no inconvenience to us if you're a couple of minutes late. Would you like me to __________ __________ __________ __________ __________?

W: No, thanks. I have the cash right here.

M: All right. It looks like your total comes to $120, and that ________ ________ ________.

W: Wait, what? You said that it was going to be $110 when we checked in yesterday.

M: That's the price of the room, but it shows here that ________ ________ ________ ________ last night.

W: I didn't realize that the movie we ordered was going to be so expensive. Here's $150.

M: All right. *[Pause]* Here's your change.

10

W: Honey, let's look in classified ads for an apartment. We have to decide on which one to rent ________ ________ ________ ________ ________ ________.

M: Right. Which area do you prefer, Demarest or Willington?

W: Actually I prefer Demarest, but the apartments there are generally a lot more expensive.

M: Then let's look at the Willington area. It's also quite ________ ________ ________ ________ ________ ________.

W: Okay. I think $2,000 a month is the most we can afford for rent.

M: I agree. What about the size? Don't you think we need at least three bedrooms?

W: Yes, you're right. The boys will want to have their own rooms.

M: They also want to live in an apartment that's above the 7th floor.

W: Same here. ________ ________ ________ ________ ________, the better the view will be.

M: Well, it won't be easy to find an apartment that ________ ________ ________ ________ ________.

11

M: Good morning, students. My name is Dustin Swift, and I'm speaking to you on behalf of Blue Mystic Berry Farm. I'd like to announce "Berry Delicious Day." Along with strawberries and blueberries, we'll also be allowing you to pick blackberries, raspberries, and boysenberries for you to harvest on Berry Delicious Day, which is this Saturday. The event begins at 10 a.m. and runs until 2 p.m. ________ ________ ________ ________, so tell your parents to bring the whole family. Some of the berries you pick will be used to make pies that will be sold to benefit the Homeless Shelter. Be sure to ________ ________. You should wear long-sleeved shirts and pants to ________ ________ ________ ________ the berry bushes. Some berries are harmful for pets, so we ask that you please ________ ________ ________ ________ ________. We hope to see you on Saturday here at Blue Mystic Berry Farm.

12

M: Hey, I've been looking at RV rentals for our camping trip this summer. I think we should make a reservation really soon.

W: Yeah, we should. We don't want to wait until it's too late.

M: Well, I found this company that ________ ________ ________ ________.

W: Let's have a look. *[Pause]* Since the whole family is going, we're going to need an RV that can sleep at least four people.

M: That's right. But maybe we should get one that's a bit bigger. I'd prefer one that sleeps at least five.

W: All right. Well, do we really need a water hookup?

M: It'll be much nicer if we have one. That way we can ________ ________.

W: All right. What about a stove and a refrigerator? We do most of our cooking outdoors.

M: I say we take that option. It's such a hassle to bring coolers to keep our food cold.

W: All right. That ________ ________ ________ to these two, then.

M: I don't think we need to spend the extra money. Let's go for the cheaper one.

W: Sounds good. Go ahead and make the reservation.

13

W: Hey sweetheart, we're going to be late. ________ ________ ________ ________?

M: I'm trying to hurry, but I think I've lost my cell phone.

W: I think I saw it on the couch earlier.
M: Ah, here it is. Okay, so is there anything else we need to take care of before we go?
W: Oh! Who's going to __________ __________ __________ while we're away?
M: Relax. Mrs. Garcia said that she'll take care of them.
W: Okay. We have to make sure to bring the tickets. __________ __________ __________ __________, right?
M: I didn't, but I have them saved on my cell phone.
W: Saved on your cell phone? Don't we have to print them out anymore?
M: Nope. I have the e-tickets right here. We just have to show them at the kiosk.
W: E-tickets, huh? __________ __________ __________ __________. Nevertheless, I think we should print them out just in case.
M: (That's a good idea. I'll do that now.)

14

[Cell phone rings.]
M: Hello?
W: Hey Charlie, this is Riley.
M: Hey, Riley. What's going on?
W: Well, __________ __________ __________ __________ __________ the EPL headquarters for the conference.
M: Are you ready to give your presentation about our new stadium?
W: I'm ready. But. . .
M: But what? Is there a problem?
W: Well, I seemed to have left all of the presentation materials on my desk in my office. __________ __________ __________ __________ __________ __________ bring them to me?
M: I wish I could help, but there's no way I can bring them. I'm not at the office right now.
W: Well, it's already noon and the meeting starts in an hour. If I went back to pick them up, there's no way I'd __________ __________ __________ __________ for the meeting.
M: That's __________ __________ __________. Give Kyle a call. He should be in the office.
W: (Okay. I'll give him a call and see if he can bring them to me.)

15

M: Ryan and Jason have just lost in the championship round of a tournament for players of the popular first-person shooter, *Counter Strike: GO*. Ryan made a couple of big mistakes early in the match; __________ __________ __________ __________ __________ __________ that they lost. Jason finds Ryan sitting outside on the sidewalk after the match. He notices that Ryan looks upset and __________ __________ __________. Jason is not upset at all. He's actually proud that they made it to the championship. He knows that Ryan __________ __________ __________ and that they were able to make it to the championship __________ __________ __________ __________ __________, and he wants to cheer Ryan up. In this situation, what would Jason most likely say to Ryan?
Jason: (We couldn't have made it to the finals without you.)

16-17

M: These days, humans are beginning to __________ __________ __________ __________ __________ __________. There are many factors that contribute to pollution. Some of them are natural, but most of them are man-made and preventable. To start with the obvious, people often pollute streets and waterways with litter. It's our duty to pick up after ourselves to help preserve and beautify our environment. Recycling is a great way to help the environment because it __________ __________ __________ __________ __________ __________ __________ __________ that goes into landfills. Personal vehicles also contribute significantly to air pollution. Therefore, riding bikes or __________ __________ __________ can help the environment. Power plants also pollute our air. If we cut down on our energy usage at home, we can cut down on emissions from power plants. We should be sure to use energy-efficient bulbs and __________ __________ __________-__________ __________. This will not only cut down on air pollution, but will also save us money.

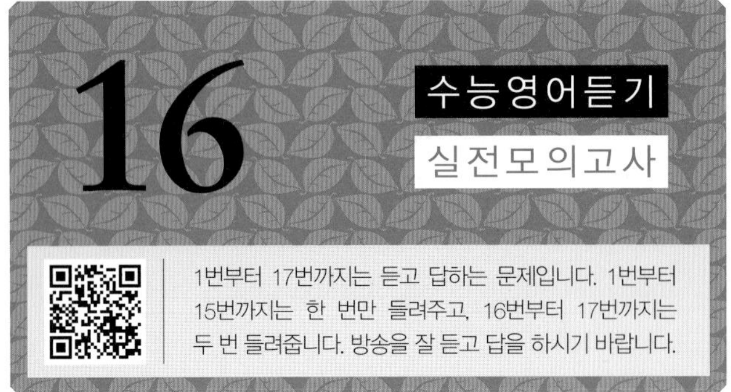

01

대화를 듣고, 남자의 마지막 말에 대한 여자의 응답으로 가장 적절한 것을 고르시오.

① Okay, please follow me there.
② I'm sorry. You'll have to wait in line.
③ *Wrong Number* is no longer showing.
④ Only balcony seating is available for that show.
⑤ No, that's not okay. You should speak to a manager.

02

대화를 듣고, 여자의 마지막 말에 대한 남자의 응답으로 가장 적절한 것을 고르시오.

① I heard the news about the environment this morning.
② I have spare coffee mugs. I can give you one.
③ Using a paper cup is so convenient.
④ You're wrong. I prefer tea to coffee.
⑤ I won't drink coffee from now on.

03

다음을 듣고, 여자가 하는 말의 목적으로 가장 적절한 것을 고르시오.

① 교내 식당의 메뉴 개선을 제안하려고
② 교내 식당의 시설 개선을 요청하려고
③ 학생들의 교내 식당 이용을 촉구하려고
④ 학교 시설에 대한 안전 점검을 요구하려고
⑤ 학생들의 학교 웹사이트 이용을 권장하려고

04

대화를 듣고, 두 사람이 하는 말의 주제로 가장 적절한 것을 고르시오.

① 휴대폰 구입 시 유의할 점
② 운전 중 휴대폰 사용의 위험성
③ 청소년들의 지나친 휴대폰 사용
④ 휴대폰 이용 시 헤드폰 사용방법
⑤ 휴대폰 사용이 건강에 미치는 영향

05

대화를 듣고, 여자의 심정으로 가장 적절한 것을 고르시오.

① embarrassed ② guilty ③ happy
④ relaxed ⑤ stressed

06

대화를 듣고, 그림에서 대화의 내용과 일치하지 않는 것을 고르시오.

07

대화를 듣고, 남자가 여자에게 부탁한 일로 가장 적절한 것을 고르시오.

① to make a reservation
② to purchase vitamins
③ to suggest gift ideas
④ to prepare dinner
⑤ to buy a card

08

대화를 듣고, 여자가 남편에게 화가 난 이유를 고르시오.

① 휴일인데 일하러 나가서
② 집을 너무 어질러 놓고 나가서
③ 행동하기 전에 너무 많은 생각을 해서
④ 가족 사진이 들어있는 USB를 잃어버려서
⑤ 자신의 USB 드라이브를 허락 없이 가져가서

09

대화를 듣고, 여자가 지불할 금액을 고르시오.

① $100 ② $105 ③ $110 ④ $120 ⑤ $125

10

대화를 듣고, The Prized Prince에 관해 두 사람이 언급하지 않은 것을 고르시오.

① 판매 부수 ② 저자 ③ 출판사
④ 장르 ⑤ 영화 제작 계획

11

Science Fair에 관한 다음 내용을 듣고, 일치하지 않는 것을 고르시오.

① 서너 명으로 구성된 팀 단위 프로젝트이다.
② 주제는 제한 없이 자유롭게 선택하면 된다.
③ 작동이 되는 모델은 만들 필요가 없다.
④ 지원서를 5월 5일까지 제출해야 한다.
⑤ 질문이 있으면 과학 선생님께 한다.

12

다음 표를 보면서 대화를 듣고, 남자가 선택할 바퀴를 고르시오.

Mackie Performance Wheels

	Model	Wheel Size (inches)	Color	Price
①	A	22	Mixed	$950
②	B	24	Mixed	$1,100
③	C	22	Black	$900
④	D	24	Black	$1,000
⑤	E	22	Black	$1,200

*wheel: (자동차) 바퀴(휠)

13

대화를 듣고, 여자의 마지막 말에 대한 남자의 응답으로 가장 적절한 것을 고르시오.

Man: ______________________________

① I'd take the military aptitude test if I were you.
② I think you should do what you're passionate about.
③ I haven't decided what kind of career I want to pursue.
④ It's really difficult to be a successful architect these days.
⑤ You'd better collect as many military strategy books as possible.

14

대화를 듣고, 남자의 마지막 말에 대한 여자의 응답으로 가장 적절한 것을 고르시오.

Woman: ______________________________

① Yes. The old phone can't run new apps.
② His phone works well, but it's not very stylish.
③ You're right, but I don't know which one is best.
④ Right. I never owned a smartphone when I was young.
⑤ Yeah, but he's usually complaining about how slow his phone is.

15

다음 상황 설명을 듣고, Nancy가 Maya에게 할 말로 가장 적절한 것을 고르시오.

Nancy: ______________________________

① You should join the weight-loss clinic.
② I know a lot about weight loss and nutrition.
③ Overeating can cause serious health problems.
④ If you're pregnant, then you'll naturally be eating more.
⑤ Have them choose a few items that fit into your nutrition goals.

[16-17] 다음을 듣고, 물음에 답하시오.

16

여자가 하는 말의 목적으로 가장 적절한 것은?

① 먼지가 우리 몸에 주는 악영향을 설명하려고
② 청소 대행 업체인 자신의 회사를 홍보하려고
③ 알레르기 유발 물질에 대해 경고하려고
④ 먼지를 줄이는 청소 요령을 알려주려고
⑤ 새로 나온 청소도구들을 소개하려고

17

여자가 언급하지 않은 것은?

① 진공청소기 사용하기 ② 베개와 쿠션 털기
③ 바닥 닦기 ④ 침구 세탁하기
⑤ 환기시키기

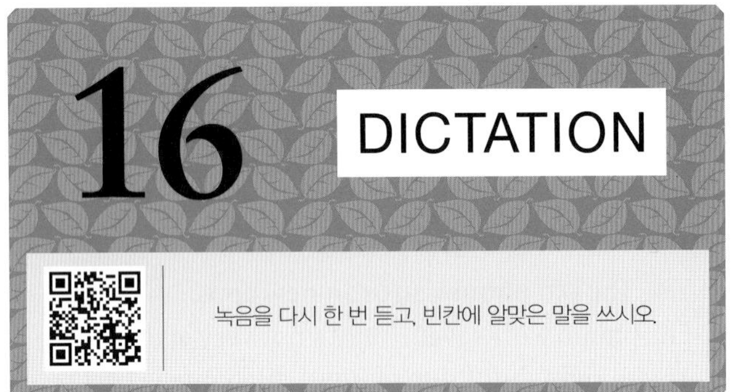

01

M: Hi, can I have two tickets for *Wrong Number*?

W: Sure. What time would you like to see the movie?

M: 7 p.m., please. Two adults __________ __________ __________ __________.

W: (Only balcony seating is available for that show.)

02

W: Oh, I see you're using your own coffee mug.

M: Yes. Using __________ __________ __________ is never good for the environment.

W: __________ __________ __________ __________. I think I should buy one for myself so that I can join you.

M: (I have spare coffee mugs. I can give you one.)

03

W: Good morning, students. Are you __________ __________ __________ __________ this afternoon? I would imagine you all say "Yes." Then, how do you feel about the cafeteria here at school? Do you think the facilities are nice? Probably not. There have been quite __________ __________ __________ __________ __________ __________ recently from a number of students. Some of them have even written messages on the school's website. I am one of those students. Unfortunately, I don't think the school is listening. Our cafeteria is giving our school a __________ __________. That reputation will continue to get worse if we don't improve the facilities. We need to __________ __________ __________ soon to ensure a better school life for all of us.

04

M: Whoa, my cell phone is really heating up.

W: You really shouldn't use it for so long.

M: What do you think about __________ __________ __________ __________ __________ __________ __________?

W: I know a lot of studies have shown that __________ __________ __________-__________ __________ __________ __________ can cause brain tumors.

M: I heard that on the radio the other day.

W: The electromagnetic waves are __________ __________ __________ __________. It's been shown in many studies.

M: I understand, but the reason I need to use my cell phone so often is for work.

W: Well, there are some ways to use it carefully. For instance, you should use earphones so that __________ __________ __________ __________ __________ __________ __________ __________.

M: All right, I'll start wearing my earphones more often.

W: There are other safety precautions you can take, too. You can look them up on the Internet.

05

M: Hey, Monica. How was the game?

W: Well, I can tell you this: I'm not going to watch another one anytime soon.

M: Why? I thought you really enjoyed football. Didn't your team do really well last year?

W: Yeah, they won the Super Bowl. But then the coach retired. They got a new one, and the team has been playing terribly!

M: Sounds like __________ __________ __________ __________ __________ this new coach.

W: I think the team is doing worse because of him.

M: Is he really that bad?

W: Well, just look at __________ __________ __________. We haven't won any away games this year.

M: Relax. I'm sure they will do better later in the season.

W: I hope so, but __________ __________ __________ __________. They lost to a team much weaker than them last week.

M: What about the game today?

W: They played one of the best teams in the league, so of course they lost.

06

W: This here is your office, Mr. Smith.

M: Wow! It's _____ _____ _____ _____ _____. Look out the window. What a wonderful view of the mountains!

W: It's lovely, isn't it? That's why we put the chair _____ _____ _____.

M: That's great. And I guess that's my new laptop on the desk.

W: It sure is. We just bought it last week. It should have everything you need already loaded onto it.

M: _____ _____ _____ _____ _____ _____ about that clock, though.

W: What do you mean?

M: Look at how big it is. And it's so distracting.

W: You're _____ _____ _____ _____ _____ _____, if you'd like.

M: How did you know I love coffee?

W: You look like a coffee drinker, Mr. Smith. I'm just kidding. All of our offices have an electric coffee pot in them. Anyway, welcome to our building.

M: Thank you very much.

07

M: Linda, _____ _____ _____ _____ _____ _____ for Dad's retirement party?

W: Yeah, I have a couple of choices in mind. The first is a new Mexican grill and the other is a Greek restaurant.

M: Well, you know Dad loves Greek food, so why don't we go to the Greek restaurant?

W: _____ _____ _____ _____.

M: Also, have you bought him a gift yet?

W: I haven't. Have you?

M: I haven't, either. We could buy a gift together. Maybe we could _____ _____ _____ _____ _____ _____ he likes.

W: That's a wonderful gift idea.

M: All right, great. I'll pick some up while I'm at work tomorrow. _____ _____ _____ _____ _____?

W: Sure. I know a great place.

M: Perfect. I'll see you tomorrow, then.

W: Okay. See you then.

08

W: Thanks for cleaning up the living room, Thomas.

M: No problem, Mom.

W: Hey, _____ _____ _____, have you seen my USB drive?

M: I don't think so. Why?

W: Well, I thought I _____ _____ _____ _____ _____ _____, but I can't seem to find it today.

M: Oh, right. I saw Dad pick it up.

W: Oh? Did he take it into the office?

M: Yes. He said that he needed it to get some files off of his coworker's computer.

W: Really? You're kidding me. He took off with my USB drive without asking first?

M: You mean _____ _____ _____?

W: Absolutely not. He knows that it has some of our family photos on it. It's really important to me.

M: Maybe he just forgot.

W: Sometimes I don't understand your father. _____ _____ _____ _____ _____ _____ _____.

M: Relax, Mom. I'm sure everything will be all right.

09

W: Hi. I'm looking to buy a new sweater for my son.

M: I'd love to help. How old is he?

W: He's 15. He usually wears an adult medium.

M: Great. Well, we have a couple of different materials to choose from. Would you _____ _____ _____ _____ _____ _____?

W: Well, what's the price difference?

M: The cotton sweater is $55, and the wool one _____ _____ _____ _____. The cotton one is really popular these days.

W: That's great. I'll take the cotton sweater, then. I want to buy him a pair of jeans.

M: Okay. These skinny jeans _____ _____ _____ _____ _____ the sweater. Their normal price is $50, but they're on sale for 10% off.

W: Does that discount apply to the sweater, too?

M: I'm sorry, but it only __________ __________ __________ __________.

W: That's fine. I'll take both anyway. Here's my card.

M: Great. Thank you.

10

M: Amy, are you already reading another book?

W: Yeah. I finished up the last one and started on this one this morning. It's called *The Prized Prince*.

M: I think I've heard of it. __________ __________ __________ __________ __________-__________ __________ recently?

W: That's right. It's sold over two million copies.

M: That's a lot. Why is it so popular?

W: Well, first of all, it was written by Steve Queen. He's really famous, you know.

M: Steve Queen, huh? So it must be __________ __________ __________.

W: Nope. He actually wrote a romance novel this time.

M: Oh, __________ __________ __________ __________ __________ __________ __________ romance novels. They're so boring.

W: This is a bit different from your average romance novel. I read online that they're going to make a movie out of it.

M: That's cool. In that case, I might __________ __________ __________ __________.

W: You should. I'll let you borrow it when I'm finished.

11

W: Good morning, everyone. I'd like to talk about this year's Science Fair. This year everyone will be working on a team, and you'll film your projects __________ __________ __________ __________. Your team will be made up of three or four classmates. Every team will __________ __________ __________ __________ from this year's science catalog. The topics include underwater breathing, race car design, the process of compacting trash, and the behavior of robot maids. Of course your projects do not have to be working models, but only proof of concept. Please __________ __________ __________, along with the names of all your team members and the topic you have chosen, by May 5th at 5 p.m. If you have any questions, please __________ __________ __________ __________. I am looking forward to seeing everyone's work.

12

W: What can we do for you today, sir?

M: I'm looking for some new wheels for my car. I don't like the factory ones that came with it when I bought it.

W: I see. It looks like __________ __________ __________ 22- or 24-inch wheels.

M: I'd like to ride a little low, so I think the 22-inch ones __________ __________ __________ __________.

W: All right. Would you prefer mixed or solid black rims?

M: Mixed is a little too fancy for me. I like black wheels. __________ __________.

W: All right. I think you'll love this model.

M: Those are cool! How much are they?

W: They're on sale this week for $1,200. That's after a 40% discount.

M: That's still a little too expensive for me. I'm looking to __________ __________ __________ __________ __________ __________.

W: All right. I suppose these are what you're looking for, then.

M: They're cheaper, but they look just as good. I'll take them.

13

M: Hey, Chloe. What are you up to?

W: I'm just looking at the results of the military aptitude test I took a couple of weeks ago.

M: Oh. __________ __________ __________ __________ __________ take a look?

W: Of course not.

M: *[Pause]* Wow! You got some impressive results. It says that you are great with __________ __________ __________ __________ __________. You'll be best as an architect or strategist.

W: Yeah, but I don't know if I like the results.

M: Really? Why not?

W: Well, my parents want me to __________ __________ __________, but I've always wanted to be a writer. I don't think I'm very good at writing now, but I've been practicing.
M: Well, it's always difficult to decide between what you want to do and what you're good at.
W: You're right. What would you do __________ __________ __________ __________?
M: (I think you should do what you're passionate about.)

14

M: Hey Mrs. Lewis, what are you doing on the computer?
W: Oh, hey Chris. I'm just looking for a new smartphone for my husband.
M: I see. Is his birthday coming up or something?
W: That's right. He __________ __________-__________ next month.
M: He must be really excited to get a new smartphone.
W: He doesn't know yet. But he's always complaining that __________ __________ __________ __________ __________ __________.
M: How old is it?
W: About four years old.
M: Yeah, __________ __________ __________ __________ __________ nowadays.
W: Right. He's having a lot of trouble __________ __________ __________ with his current phone, and he can't run some of the newer apps.
M: You should probably buy him one of the newest models. That way, it's sure to last a long time.
W: (You're right, but I don't know which one is best.)

15

W: Nancy is an employee at a weight-loss clinic. She's not a personal trainer, but she __________ __________ __________ __________ __________ __________ __________ at the clinic, so she is well-versed in nutrition and how to stay healthy. One afternoon, she __________ __________ __________ __________ __________ __________, Maya, in the hallway of her apartment building. Maya is carrying a bag of groceries. When she sees Nancy, she __________ __________ __________ __________ __________ __________ about the food she's bought. She says she's trying to buy healthy food, but she needs to buy for herself, her husband, and her son, and she __________ __________ __________ __________ __________ __________ __________ __________. What would Nancy most likely tell Maya in a situation like this?
Nancy: (Have them choose a few items that fit into your nutrition goals.)

16-17

W: Good afternoon, everyone. My name is Mary Anne Philips, and I am the lead nurse at the Big City Health Department. I'd like to talk to you briefly about allergens and, in particular, dust. Dust can have many __________ __________ __________, so we should strive to make our homes __________ __________ __________ __________. There are several methods of cleaning that can drastically reduce the amount of dust in your home. First of all, how often do you run your vacuum cleaner? I think you should do it __________ __________ __________ __________ __________. Second, beating your pillows and couch cushions out once a week also gets rid of dust. Mopping your floor often may seem like an inconvenience, but I can tell you that it's necessary to clean up the dirt and dust you might have missed while vacuuming. Finally, you should wash your bedding often, especially if you or someone you live with has allergies. __________ __________ __________ __________ __________ __________, and you'll be able to maintain a clean and healthy home. Thank you for your time.

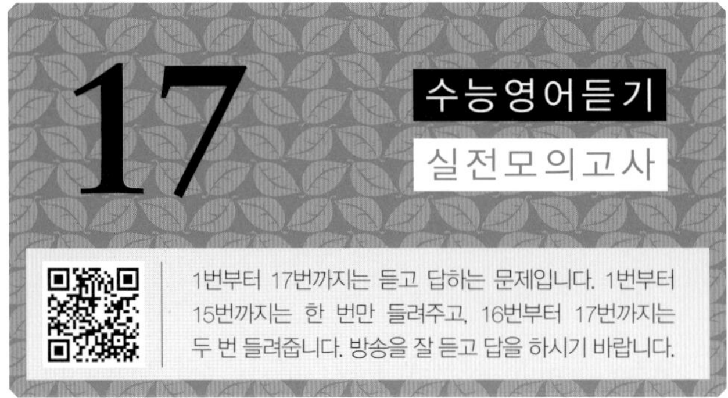

01

대화를 듣고, 여자의 마지막 말에 대한 남자의 응답으로 가장 적절한 것을 고르시오.

① I'm sorry, but we're sold out.
② You can have them tailored here.
③ I don't usually sell designer jeans.
④ Well, I can give you 10% off today.
⑤ Well, I'd like to see some other options.

02

대화를 듣고, 남자의 마지막 말에 대한 여자의 응답으로 가장 적절한 것을 고르시오.

① That's okay. I'll drive my car today.
② Is there a repair shop around here?
③ I guess I'll have to catch a taxi, then.
④ Oh, no! I think your car has a flat tire.
⑤ I need to stop by the grocery store first.

03

다음을 듣고, 여자가 하는 말의 목적으로 가장 적절한 것을 고르시오.

① 정기적인 건강 검진의 중요성을 알리려고
② 성공적인 심장병 치료 사례를 소개하려고
③ 심장병의 원인에 대해 설명하려고
④ 걷기 운동의 중요성을 알려주려고
⑤ 올바른 걷기 자세를 소개하려고

04

대화를 듣고, 남자의 의견으로 가장 적절한 것을 고르시오.

① 공무원들의 방만한 업무 행태를 개선해야 한다.
② 급커브 지역에 경고 표지판이나 전등을 설치해야 한다.
③ 운전자들은 과속하지 않고 신호를 잘 준수해야만 한다.
④ 낡고 훼손된 도로 교통 표지판을 모두 재정비 해야 한다.
⑤ 시에서 교통사고를 줄이기 위한 캠페인을 자주 벌여야 한다.

05

대화를 듣고, 두 사람의 관계를 가장 잘 나타낸 것을 고르시오.

① 집주인 — 수리공
② 건물주인 — 세입자
③ 건설업자 — 의뢰인
④ 건축 설계사 — 인부
⑤ 부동산 중개인 — 고객

06

대화를 듣고, 그림에서 대화의 내용과 일치하지 않는 것을 고르시오.

07

대화를 듣고, 여자가 할 일로 가장 적절한 것을 고르시오.

① 사진 찍기
② 입장권 사기
③ 지도 출력하기
④ 지도 받으러 가기
⑤ 주차 공간 찾아보기

08

대화를 듣고, 남자가 내일 학교에 일찍 오지 못하는 이유를 고르시오.

① 수학 숙제를 아침에 해야 하기 때문에
② 아침에 일찍 일어날 수가 없기 때문에
③ 등교 길에 Cup 카페에 들렀다 가야 하기 때문에
④ 아침에 엄마의 집안일을 도와드려야 하기 때문에
⑤ 걸어서 남동생을 학교에 바래다 줘야 하기 때문에

09

대화를 듣고, 여자가 지불할 금액을 고르시오.

① $60　② $100　③ $120　④ $140　⑤ $160

10

대화를 듣고, 여자가 학습에 대한 조언으로 언급하지 않은 것을 고르시오.

① 하루에 공부하는 시간　② 공부하는 장소
③ 수업을 듣는 태도　④ 사용하는 교재
⑤ 대학 진학 동기

11

The Reptile World Exhibit에 관한 다음 내용을 듣고, 일치하지 않는 것을 고르시오.

① 다양한 파충류들을 볼 수 있는 박람회이다.
② Mega Village 야생동물협회에서 개최한다.
③ 동물들에게 가까이 다가가서는 안 된다.
④ 무료 입장이지만 예약을 해야 한다.
⑤ 더 많은 정보는 홈페이지에 있다.

12

다음 표를 보면서 대화를 듣고, 남자가 빌릴 차를 고르시오.

Leicester Rental Cars

	Model	Type	Rental Price per Day	Capacity (Persons)	Number of Vehicles Available
①	Cube	Economy	50	4	1
②	Compact	Economy	55	4	2
③	Grandio	Family	60	5	2
④	Inistina	Family	65	7	0
⑤	Bentiz	Luxury	75	7	3

13

대화를 듣고, 여자의 마지막 말에 대한 남자의 응답으로 가장 적절한 것을 고르시오.

Man: ________________

① I'm sure everything will be fine in your new business.
② It's always nice to see my former employees succeed.
③ Work hard, but don't forget the important things in life.
④ It was great to see you. I'll stop by your office sometime.
④ You shouldn't exercise intensively for more than 3 hours.

14

대화를 듣고, 남자의 마지막 말에 대한 여자의 응답으로 가장 적절한 것을 고르시오.

Woman: ________________

① Sounds good. I hope they win!
② I'll cheer for your team with you.
③ Sure. I'll come over around 7 p.m.
④ Great. They may also come to cheer.
⑤ Actually, I'm really busy this weekend.

15

다음 상황 설명을 듣고, Candace가 Larry에게 할 말로 가장 적절한 것을 고르시오.

Candace: ________________

① If you have any problems, be sure to let me know.
② You should be more careful when you're running outside.
③ I don't think there's anything you can do to clean those papers.
④ Don't worry about it. There will be another bus in a few minutes.
⑤ I'm also responsible for this. I shouldn't have been using my phone.

[16-17] 다음을 듣고, 물음에 답하시오.

16

남자가 하는 말의 목적으로 가장 적절한 것은?

① 해외 자원봉사 단체를 홍보하려고
② 해외 자원봉사의 이점을 알려주려고
③ 해외 자원봉사의 종류를 소개하려고
④ 해외 자원봉사의 신청 방법을 설명하려고
⑤ 해외 자원봉사에 관한 수기를 공모하려고

17

언급된 해외 봉사 활동이 아닌 것은?

① 물 정화방법 가르치기
② 아기들 밥 먹이기
③ 집 짓기
④ 영어 가르치기
⑤ 아픈 아이들 돌보기

01

W: I really like these pants. How much are they?

M: Those are $100. They're designer jeans, _____ _____ _____ _____.

W: Oh, my. That price is a little high for me. _____ _____ _____ _____ _____ _____?

M: (Well, I can give you 10% off today.)

02

M: Get up, Annie! It's after ten! You're going to _____ _____ _____ _____!

W: Relax! It only takes twenty minutes to drive there.

M: Don't you remember? Your car is _____ _____ _____ _____.

W: (I guess I'll have to catch a taxi, then.)

03

W: How do you stay healthy? Do you exercise regularly? Do you go for walks? Were you aware of the _____ _____ _____ _____? In short, your life will be better if you walk more. I'd like to tell you the story of my friend Roger Williams, who _____ _____ _____ _____. He was told by several doctors that his disease could never be completely cured. _____ _____ _____, he no longer suffers from the disease at all. It was walking that helped him. He made walking a big part of his daily routine. Many other people will testify that walking has changed their lives for the better. Walking is _____ _____ _____ _____ _____ _____ _____ _____; it is necessary for everyone.

04

W: Hi, Mr. Anderson.

M: Thanks for meeting me this morning. I wanted to bring this road to your attention.

W: Yes, I can see why. It looks very dangerous.

M: It is dangerous. There aren't enough warning signs or lights _____ _____ _____ _____ _____ _____ _____ _____ _____ _____ _____.

W: Can you see the road from the house?

M: Yeah, I can. I can't tell you how many accidents I've seen.

W: Do you think they're occurring because people are driving too fast?

M: I do think people are driving too fast. I believe more warning signs will significantly _____ _____ _____ _____ _____.

W: Have you _____ _____ _____ _____ _____ _____ in the past?

M: I have, several times. But no one seems to care. They've never gotten back to me with a response.

W: I see. I'm going to _____ _____ _____ _____ _____ _____ _____ _____ as soon as I get to the office.

M: Really? That would be wonderful. Please tell them _____ _____ _____ _____ _____.

05

[Telephone rings.]

W: Hello. This is Brittney Smith.

M: Hi, Ms. Smith. This is Dominic Antonoff. You took me to several buildings yesterday, and I was wondering if I could ask you a few questions.

W: Hello, Mr. Antonoff. _____ _____ _____ _____ _____ _____?

M: That one on Water Street. Does it have a walk-in freezer?

W: Give me one second while I check that. *[Pause]* Yes, it does.

M: That's great. Oh, but does it have central heating and air conditioning?

W: It does. Is that a problem?

M: Hmm. . . _____ _____ _____ _____ _____. What about the building on 6th Street? Is it still available?

W: Yes, ________ ________ ________.
M: Would it be a problem if I remodeled the storefront?
W: I think that would be okay.
M: Great. And did you ask the owner if I could ________ ________ ________ ________ ________ ________ ________?
W: Yes, I asked him. He said that'd be okay.

06

W: Hey, Jay. How was your vacation?
M: It was great. My family really loved ________ ________ ________ ________ ________. Here. I have a photo.
W: *[Pause]* Cool. That's ________ ________ ________ ________ ________ ________ ________ ________?
M: It sure is. We stayed on the Big Island of Hawaii.
W: It looks like you all are really enjoying the view.
M: That's right. My wife and I enjoyed just relaxing at the resort. And those are my favorite sunglasses.
W: Nice. Are those ________ ________ ________ ________ ________ ________?
M: Yes. That's my son and daughter. They really enjoyed the weather there.
W: What kind of drink is that your wife is drinking? It looks fancy.
M: That's a Blue Hawaiian. It's a popular drink in Hawaii.
W: So, who took this picture?
M: My brother did. I wanted to ________ ________ ________ ________ ________ ________, but I lost it that day.
W: Isn't that it on the floor?
M: Oh, it is. ________ ________ ________ ________.

07

W: Sweetie, I can see a sign for Rain Valley Park over there.
M: Look at all of the people! ________ ________ ________ ________ ________ ________.
W: Yeah. Oh, the parking lot is over there!
M: Okay, great. We can park there and ________ ________ ________ ________ ________. Do you think it will take long to get there?
W: I think it will take about 20 minutes. Once we're down there, we can sit by the river.
M: Wow! There are so many cars.
W: Do you think we'll be able to find a parking space?
M: I'll find one. Don't worry about it. You should get out here and ________ ________ ________ ________ ________. I think the line is over there.
W: Okay, that's a good idea. Do you have the map I printed out?
M: I do. ________ ________ ________ ________. I'll be sure to bring it.
W: Great. I'll meet you ________ ________ ________ ________ ________ ________.

08

[Telephone rings.]
M: Hello?
W: Hey Mel, it's Katie.
M: Hey, Katie. What's up?
W: Not too much. So, ________ ________ ________ ________ ________ ________ ________ ________ Mr. Levine assigned today?
M: I just finished before you called.
W: I really don't understand math. ________ ________ ________ ________ ________ ________ ________ ________ with them?
M: Sure, no problem.
W: Great. Do you think you could come to school early tomorrow? We could meet, and you could help me with the questions then.
M: Hmm. . . I don't think I'll be able to come to school early tomorrow. I have to ________ ________ ________ ________ ________.
W: Why doesn't your mother take him?
M: Well, ________ ________ ________ ________ ________ tomorrow morning. I can help you now. How about we meet at Cafe Cup?
W: That sounds great. Thanks a lot.

09

M: Welcome to Seoul Art Center. What can I do for you?
W: I need to buy some tickets for my family for today's exhibition.
M: No problem. ________ ________ ________ ________ ________?

W: Well, I need them for my husband, my daughter, and myself, but my daughter is a high school student. So two adults and one student, I guess.

M: Very well. Adult tickets cost $60 each and a student ticket is $40. Your daughter has her student ID, right?

W: Yes, she does. Here it is.

M: Great. So, two adults and one student, right?

W: That's correct. Oh! I almost forgot that my daughter __________ __________ __________ __________ __________ __________. Can I still use it?

M: Let me check __________ __________ __________ __________.

W: It should be. She just got it last week.

M: *[Pause]* You're right. You can get your daughter's ticket for half price.

W: Excellent. Here's my card.

10

M: Can I speak with you for a minute, Ms. Whitman?

W: Yes, of course you can. What can I help you with?

M: My grades are still quite low, even though I've been studying much more.

W: Well, let's find the problem. __________ __________ __________ __________ __________ __________ __________?

M: I study at home until about midnight on weekdays, so I guess about four hours. But __________ __________ __________ __________ my siblings.

W: It's easy to be distracted when you're studying late at night. Why don't you try studying in the library?

M: You're right. I think I need to __________ __________ __________ __________.

W: Yes. You should also make sure the books you're using are the best.

M: Oh, I see.

W: Do you know why you want to go to university?

M: I guess I haven't thought too much about it.

W: I believe you'll get more from your studying if you have a clear idea of what you want to do.

M: Okay. Thanks a lot for the advice, Ms. Whitman.

11

M: Good afternoon, students. Would you like to come face-to-face with a cobra? Would you like to __________ __________ __________ __________ __________? If so, you should come out to the Reptile World Exhibit at Mega Village Fairgrounds this weekend. The exhibit will __________ __________ __________ __________ __________ __________, from geckos and iguanas to pythons and gators. The exhibit is presented by Mega Village Wildlife Association and __________ __________ __________ __________ __________ __________ and personal with some unique wildlife. It's very informative and educational. __________ __________ __________ __________, but we ask that you reserve your tickets ahead of time. Please visit the Mega Village Wildlife Association's website for more information. Thank you for listening.

12

W: What can I do for you, sir?

M: I'd like to __________ __________ __________ __________ __________ __________ __________. Would you recommend one?

W: All right. We have economy, family-sized, and luxury cars. How many people are there in your family?

M: There are four people, including me.

W: I think a family-sized or luxury one __________ __________ __________ __________ you.

M: What are the differences between those and the economy ones?

W: Besides the differences in rental price and gas mileage, economy cars don't have much space, so the four of you would feel pretty uncomfortable.

M: Well, we'll also need some space for luggage, so __________ __________ __________ __________ __________ __________ __________ __________ __________ __________ __________.

W: Why don't you rent a luxury one, then? It's spacious enough for seven people, so your family will feel quite comfortable.

M: But the rental price is too expensive for me. Oh, here's a family-sized one with the same capacity as the luxury one.

W: Sorry, sir. This model is not available at the moment. They're __________ __________ __________.

M: Then there is no other choice. I'll take that one.

13

W: Hi, Rodrick.

M: Oh, hey Karen. Long time no see.

W: For sure. You know, it's been about a year since I left your company. I really miss working there.

M: We miss you, too. Say, you look a bit different. Did you lose any weight?

W: I did. I've __________ __________ __________, and I've been doing this intense exercise routine.

M: That's great, but don't overdo it. I had a friend who __________ __________ __________ __________.

W: Don't worry. I'm being quite careful.

M: Okay. So, how's your new business coming along?

W: Well, it's __________ __________. I have so much work to do and not enough time to do it.

M: I understand. I also had a tough time when I first started my business.

W: I guess starting a business is always difficult. __________ __________ __________ __________ __________ for me?

M: (Work hard, but don't forget the important things in life.)

14

W: Did you get a chance to see the baseball game last night?

M: I did. __________ __________ __________! I was so happy Los Angeles beat Detroit.

W: I'm actually a Detroit fan, but the Los Angeles team played so well.

M: The pitcher for LA did an awesome job. __________ __________ __________ __________.

W: Yeah, he did. It looked like he hurt his arm __________ __________ __________ __________ __________ __________, __________.

M: I saw that, too. I expected to see a relief pitcher, but no one came out.

W: It was such a long game. Those players must have been so tired.

M: Yeah, it went thirteen innings. That's a long game!

W: It sure is.

M: When does Detroit play again?

W: Thursday night.

M: I'll come over and __________ __________ __________ __________ __________.

W: (Sounds good. I hope they win!)

15

M: Candace is a busy career woman. One day, she has an important business meeting, so she's writing an email on her phone while walking to the bus stop. A middle-aged man named Larry is out for his morning jog. __________ __________ __________ and stumbles into Candace, who drops some important papers onto the wet ground. Larry picks them up and tries to dry them off, but __________ __________. He is extremely apologetic and __________ __________ __________ __________ __________. Candace thinks that this is also her fault because she was distracted at the time of the accident. In this situation, what would Candace most likely say to Larry?

Candace: (I'm also responsible for this. I shouldn't have been using my phone.)

16-17

M: Hello, students. I'd like to talk to you today about our __________ __________ __________ __________. Volunteering abroad can be a challenging experience. You will undoubtedly face hardships, and you may have a difficult time adjusting. However, the experience is __________ __________ and will certainly change your perspective on the world. You'll learn where your priorities lie as you __________ __________ __________ __________. Your worldview will expand because living in a foreign land will change you. You'll adopt a new set of customs and rules. You'll try food that you've never even dreamed of, and __________ __________ __________ in a foreign language. Most importantly, you'll help those who need help. You may find yourself teaching Africans how to purify water, __________ __________ in India, building housing in Myanmar, or taking care of sick children in Indonesia. Volunteering abroad is truly a unique experience, and you'll definitely be a better person because of it.

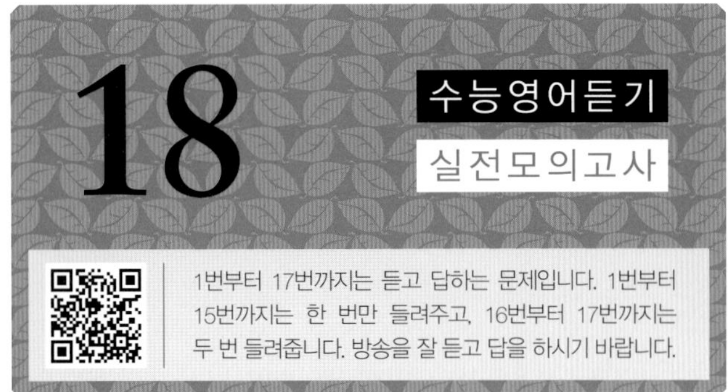

01

대화를 듣고, 남자의 마지막 말에 대한 여자의 응답으로 가장 적절한 것을 고르시오.

① Sure. I like trying foreign foods.
② Yes. It's only a five-minute walk.
③ No. I'm not very good at cooking.
④ I'm not sure. I've never eaten there.
⑤ Yes. It's going to be closed tomorrow.

02

대화를 듣고, 여자의 마지막 말에 대한 남자의 응답으로 가장 적절한 것을 고르시오.

① Thanks. I really need one in this weather.
② Yes, you should check tomorrow's weather.
③ That's all right. You can borrow my umbrella.
④ Usually, but I was in a big hurry this morning.
⑤ I'm glad that the weather will be nice tomorrow.

03

다음을 듣고, 남자가 하는 말의 목적으로 가장 적절한 것을 고르시오.

① 야외 활동 시 뇌우에 대처하는 방법을 알려주려고
② 뇌우로 인한 사고 대책반 신설을 촉구하려고
③ 뇌우 속 야외 활동의 자제를 촉구하려고
④ 재난 시 시설물 이용 방법을 설명하려고
⑤ 기상 변화 예측법에 대해 알려주려고

04

대화를 듣고, 두 사람이 하는 말의 주제로 가장 적절한 것을 고르시오.

① 다른 나라 친구와 불화가 생기는 이유
② 나라마다 다른 개인 위생의 인식 차이
③ 이탈리아 사람들의 인사 방법
④ 외국인 친구와 친해지는 방법
⑤ 정확한 언어 사용의 필요성

05

대화를 듣고, 두 사람의 관계를 가장 잘 나타낸 것을 고르시오.

① 환자 — 응급실 의사
② 관람객 — 박물관 직원
③ 관광객 — 관광 가이드
④ 승객 — 비행기 승무원
⑤ 보행자 — 교통 경찰관

06

대화를 듣고, 그림에서 대화의 내용과 일치하지 않는 것을 고르시오.

07

대화를 듣고, 남자가 여자를 위해 할 일로 가장 적절한 것을 고르시오.

① 공항으로 마중 나가기
② 여행 이야기 들려주기
③ 퀴즈 예상 문항 알려주기
④ 중국에서 만난 친구 소개해주기
⑤ 수업시간에 받은 자료 갖다 주기

08

대화를 듣고, 남자가 테니스 경기를 관람하지 못한 이유를 고르시오.

① 폭우로 경기가 취소돼서
② 경기 일정을 잘못 알아서
③ 테니스 경기를 안 좋아해서
④ 어머니의 가게를 대신 봐야 해서
⑤ 해야 할 공부와 숙제가 너무 많아서

09

대화를 듣고, 여자가 지불할 금액을 고르시오.

① $90 ② $100 ③ $110 ④ $120 ⑤ $130

10

대화를 듣고, 컴퓨터에 관해 두 사람이 언급하지 않은 것을 고르시오.

① 모니터 크기 ② 레이저 프린터 ③ 영상통화
④ 무료 백신 ⑤ 보증기간

11

The Great Tusk Concert에 관한 다음 내용을 듣고, 일치하지 않는 것을 고르시오.

① 세계 최대 동물 복지 단체가 후원한다.
② 유명 가수들과 배우들이 공연한다.
③ 행사 날짜는 6월 15일이다.
④ 수익금은 코끼리들을 위해 사용된다.
⑤ 홈페이지를 통해 표를 구매할 수 있다.

12

다음 표를 보면서 대화를 듣고, 두 사람이 선택한 RV캠프장을 고르시오.

Sunset Lake RV Park

	Campground	Water Hookup	Pets	Electricity	Fee
①	A	O	Allowed	X	$23
②	B	X	Allowed	O	$27
③	C	O	Allowed	O	$32
④	D	X	Prohibited	X	$20
⑤	E	O	Prohibited	O	$27

13

대화를 듣고, 남자의 마지막 말에 대한 여자의 응답으로 가장 적절한 것을 고르시오.

Woman: ______________________

① I don't think so. He should have called earlier.
② It's always nice to hear from you. Take care.
③ Sorry, but the news is too good to be true.
④ Actually, I don't know who that person is.
⑤ Of course. I'll be looking forward to it.

14

대화를 듣고, 여자의 마지막 말에 대한 남자의 응답으로 가장 적절한 것을 고르시오.

Man: ______________________

① I'm really glad that I asked you for help.
② I hope you get accepted to that university.
③ You should really ask your parents for advice.
④ If that's the case, that's the one you should go to.
⑤ You really learn a lot about yourself at university.

15

다음 상황 설명을 듣고, Valerie가 동물보호소 직원들에게 할 말로 가장 적절한 것을 고르시오.

Valerie: ______________________

① Please do not let any visitors into the animal shelter.
② We're struggling to get funding, so we'll have to close.
③ We shouldn't allow visitors to feed the animals human food.
④ We're going to have to buy more fresh food for the animals.
⑤ We need to make sure that the animals are eating the appropriate food.

[16-17] 다음을 듣고, 물음에 답하시오.

16

여자가 하는 말의 주제로 가장 적절한 것은?

① The effects of natural ingredients on skin
② Why we should always use sunscreen
③ The benefits of regular sunbathing
④ Alternatives to after-sun products
⑤ The best after-sun care products

17

여자가 언급하지 않은 것은?

① 찬물 ② 우유 ③ 식초
④ 알로에 ⑤ 오이

01

M: Hey Pat, have you been to that Sushi Safari restaurant yet?

W: I have. I went on ________ ________ ________. It's great!

M: I think ________ ________ ________ ________ ________ ________. Is it close to here?

W: (Yes. It's only a five-minute walk.)

02

W: Wade, ________ ________. What happened?

M: It's really coming down out there. I didn't think to bring an umbrella with me.

W: Yeah, that's tough. Don't you ________ ________ ________ ________ every day?

M: (Usually, but I was in a big hurry this morning.)

03

M: Almost everyone ________ ________ ________ ________ when the weather is nice. It's important to keep in mind that ________ ________ ________ ________ ________ ________ ________ rather quickly. You should know what to do in case this ever happens. If you ________ ________ ________ ________ ________ ________, you should seek shelter in a building or in your car. If those options aren't available, then you should find the lowest area around you and avoid open spaces. If you're in an open space and are taller than everything around you, you're at a higher risk of ________ ________ ________ ________. Always avoid trees and telephone poles. Follow this advice and you'll be prepared next time bad weather hits.

04

M: Are you all right? You seem worried.

W: Do you know Dimitri?

M: Sure. The Italian. He is a very friendly guy.

W: Yes, he is. And I like him. But have you noticed how he always has really bad breath?

M: Actually, I have. Does it upset you?

W: I think he's interesting and ________ ________ ________ ________ ________ ________, but his breath is unbearable.

M: Just relax. ________ ________ ________ ________ ________ ________ where he's from.

W: Is it? I've never been, so I have no idea.

M: Well, ideas about personal hygiene differ all over the world.

W: So these differences probably lead to social problems, right?

M: Yes, they do. It's important for everyone to try to understand that people are different.

W: ________ ________ ________ ________. I think Dimitri and I will get along better now.

M: I'm glad to hear it.

05

W: Excuse me, sir. Do you have a bandage on you?

M: Of course. I ________ ________ ________-________ ________ on all the tours I lead. What happened?

W: I tripped and scraped my knee on the museum steps.

M: Then you're going to need a big one. Give me a second. *[Pause]* Here you go.

W: Thanks. Also, I wanted to tell you that my husband and I are ________ ________ ________ ________ ________ ________ ________.

M: Awesome. ________ ________ ________ ________ to ensure that you have a great time.

W: So, when are we going to get to the cave?

M: We should be there at around one o'clock.

W: That's pretty soon. That cave has a lot of history, doesn't it?

M: That's right. During the mid-1800s, it was used as a hideout for Jesse James and his bandit gang.

W: That's so interesting. There's a lot of neat history around here, huh?

M: There is. This is a very historical area. It has a lot of natural beauty, too.

06

W: Wow! This band is really good, Joey!

M: Yeah, they're one of my favorite jazz bands. They're called Jazz Hands.

W: Interesting name. I love how they have a female violinist. She's wonderful.

M: _____ _____ _____ _____. The guitarist in the back is one of the best lead guitarists in the city.

W: _____ _____. It's cool that the lead singer plays guitar while he sings.

M: Yeah. I love the sound of his voice. _____ _____ _____ _____.

W: The piano player seems a bit out of place, though. He's sitting down while the rest of the band is standing.

M: Well, he's playing the piano. You can't really stand while you play it. You need to use the pedals.

W: Oh, right. Anyway, I'm really glad you brought me to this jazz club, Joey.

M: I'm really happy that you came with me.

07

[Cell phone rings.]

M: Hello?

W: Hi, Ted. This is Grace. How have you been?

M: Grace! Are you back?

W: Yes. The _____ _____ _____ _____ _____, so I flew back home last night.

M: Did you? Ms. Stone said you'd be back in school on Monday. How was China?

W: It was great. I feel much more confident when I speak to people in Chinese.

M: Great! We're all looking forward to talking with you about your time in China, especially the teachers.

W: I'd like to meet them as soon as possible, but I'm a bit worried since I've missed the first two weeks of class.

M: Right. . . We have two quizzes next week.

W: Really? _____ _____ _____ _____ _____ _____.

M: Well, I've got the handouts from the teachers. I'll bring them to you if you want.

W: Would you? That'd be great!

M: _____ _____ _____ _____?

08

W: Hey Davis, _____ _____ _____ _____?

M: I'm going over to my mom's flower shop. She needs to _____ _____ _____ at the post office, so I'm going to look after the store for her.

W: That's nice of you. Oh, you went to the tennis match last Sunday, right? How was it?

M: It was actually on Saturday, not Sunday.

W: Oh. Anyway, you must've had a great time. You love tennis.

M: I did go to the stadium, but the match was canceled.

W: Really? Why?

M: Thunderstorms. _____ _____ _____ _____ before it even started.

W: Oh, that's right! The weather was nasty on Saturday. That's too bad.

M: Yeah. I was really excited to go. I haven't had time to see a match this season with all the homework and studying I've had to do.

W: Yeah, I know the feeling. Sorry to hear you missed it.

09

W: Oh my! Are these antiques real?

M: They are. A few of the pieces were given to me by my grandmother.

W: Are those lamps over there expensive?

M: The lamp made of brass is $40, and _____ _____ _____ _____ _____ is $60.

W: I think the glass lamp is really nice, but _____ _____ _____ _____ _____ _____ _____.

M: I'll sell it to you for the price of the brass lamp if you really like it.

W: Wow, really? Okay, I'll take it! Also, how much are those lovely plates?

M: The bigger ones are $10 each, and the smaller ones are $5 each.

W: Okay, I'll take these two large plates.

M: Are there any other items ________ ________ ________ ________ ________?

W: I do really like that chair.

M: Yes, it's lovely, isn't it? Actually it's the last one. The others sold for $70, but I'd be happy to give you that one for $50.

W: Okay, wonderful. Thanks so much!

10

M: Hey, sweetheart. Your package arrived today.

W: That's great. ________ ________ ________ ________ ________ setting up this new computer.

M: It seems to be a lot bigger than our old computer.

W: It sure is. It's a lot faster, too. I purchased it as a set that included a 21-inch monitor and a laser printer.

M: It looks quite complicated. I wish I were ________ ________-________.

W: It's really easy, honey. I can teach you how to use it.

M: That's great. Can this computer run Cacao Chat? All of my coworkers have been talking about it.

W: Of course it can. You can also enjoy video calling for free.

M: That's cool. Did you ________ ________ ________ ________ it?

W: Yeah. If anything happens to it in the next two years, they'll come and fix it.

M: Well, ________ ________ ________ ________ ________ ________ ________ ________ in a safe place so we don't lose them.

W: Great idea.

11

M: Good morning, everyone. This is Ronnie Maroon with GBC News. I'm pleased to announce that ________ ________ ________ ________ ________ ________ in our lovely city. It's called The Great Tusk Concert, and it's sponsored by the Earth Wildlife Federation, the largest animal welfare organization in the world. The Great Tusk Concert will feature performances by ________ ________ ________ ________ ________ ________ music, movies, and television, and they're looking forward to bringing the community together for a spectacular evening. The event will be held on July 15th at the Metropolitan Opera House. The proceeds of this event will benefit elephants around the world that are ________ ________ ________ ________. For more information and to purchase tickets, visit the event's homepage at *www.thegreattuskconcert.com*.

12

W: Hey, sweetheart. ________ ________ ________ ________ ________?

M: I'm just checking our options for our RV trip next month. There are five campgrounds around the lake that we're going to.

W: That's cool. Can I help choose one?

M: Sure. So, what kinds of things do you think we need to consider as we choose?

W: Well, I think having a ________ ________ is pretty important.

M: I agree. Our RV has a shower, so we're going to need a water hookup if we want to use it.

W: Right. So we need to choose one of these three.

M: Okay. I guess we should probably rule out this one, ________ ________ ________ ________.

W: Yeah. I really want to take Baxter with us. I think he'll love the experience.

M: ________ ________ ________ ________ ________ these two.

W: Do you think we can make it for three days without electricity?

M: I think it's possible, but I'd rather have electricity just in case we need it.

W: All right. Well, I guess you should make a reservation for this campground.

13

M: You want to know what happened to me last night, Maria?

W: What happened?

M: Do you know who Dan is?
W: Of course. We played lacrosse together throughout high school, but then he moved to Texas __________ __________ __________ __________.
M: Right. Anyway, he sent me a Face Friend message last night.
W: Really? How's he doing?
M: I guess he's thinking of moving back here for work and was just reaching out to people he __________ __________ __________ __________ __________.
W: It would be great to see him. I wonder if he's changed much.
M: Well, __________ __________ __________ __________ __________. He will be in town in two weeks to look at apartments.
W: Wow! That's great news!
M: Yeah, __________ __________ __________ __________ __________ __________ __________ somewhere downtown. Do you want to join us?
W: (Of course. I'll be looking forward to it.)

14

M: Hey Leah, did you get into the university you wanted?
W: I did, Paul. In fact, __________ __________ __________ __________ __________ __________.
M: Two universities, huh? Well, have you decided which one you're going to yet?
W: They're both great schools. The main difference is that Upstate is a state-run university and Lakeside is private.
M: Yeah, they both have great reputations.
W: Right. I don't know how I'll ever choose between the two.
M: __________ __________ __________ __________. I know how you can decide, though.
W: How? I really need some advice.
M: __________ __________ __________. When it's in the air, you'll notice that there's a particular side you want it to land on.
W: I'll try it out. *[Pause]* You're right. When it was in the air, I was hoping for Upstate University.
M: (If that's the case, that's the one you should go to.)

15

M: Valerie recently started her own animal shelter and is very passionate about her work. She trains her staff so that she's sure __________ __________ __________ __________ __________ __________. She wants the staff to be especially careful what they feed the animals, as each species has __________ __________ __________. One day, she notices that some of the animals are getting sick. She looks in a cage and sees that a rescued raccoon is eating bird food. She's worried that if animals continue eating the wrong types of food, they could die. She __________ __________ __________ __________ __________ __________ __________ to address this issue. In this situation, what would Valerie most likely say to her staff?
Valerie: (We need to make sure that the animals are eating the appropriate food.)

16-17

W: Good morning, everyone. People have known for a long time about the damage the sun can do to your skin, but certain products, like "after-sun care," lead us to believe that __________ __________ __________ __________ __________. In fact, a lot of these so-called after-sun products can actually __________ __________ __________ __________ __________ __________ because their oil __________ __________ __________ __________ __________. So what can we do to really protect ourselves? How should we deal with sunburn? Simply keeping the skin cool will do the trick. You can immerse yourself in cool water or use vinegar. If you __________ __________ __________ __________ __________ and place it on your sunburn, the vinegar will __________ __________ __________ __________ __________ __________ __________. It's amazing, but it's also a little smelly. If you don't want to have to smell that smell, a layer of aloe vera or thinly sliced cucumber does the same thing.

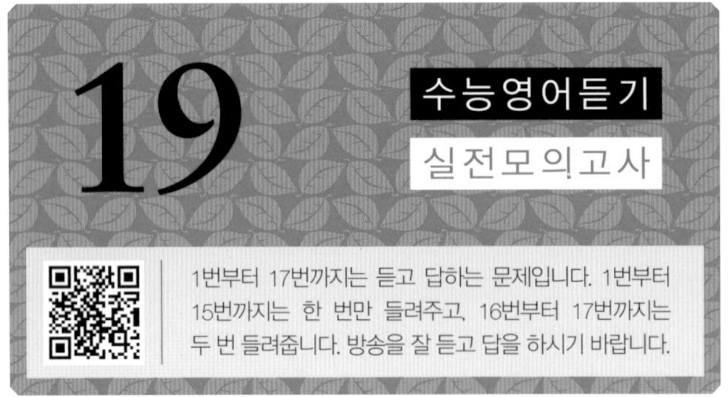

01

대화를 듣고, 여자의 마지막 말에 대한 남자의 응답으로 가장 적절한 것을 고르시오.

① The cafe is about an hour away.
② It should be ready in about 15 minutes.
③ Waffles with apple pie is a popular choice.
④ People say that potatoes are bad for your health.
⑤ I brought some up the other day from the market.

02

대화를 듣고, 남자의 마지막 말에 대한 여자의 응답으로 가장 적절한 것을 고르시오.

① Wow, I love Dragon Heart!
② I'm really busy this Saturday.
③ Sorry, but he said it's sold out.
④ I have two tickets for the concert.
⑤ You should definitely call him and ask.

03

다음을 듣고, 여자가 하는 말의 목적으로 가장 적절한 것을 고르시오.

① 인턴십 채용 절차를 공지하려고
② 로스쿨에 대한 전망을 분석하려고
③ 인턴십에 지원할 수 있는 자격을 알리려고
④ 법률 관련 실무 경험의 중요성을 알리려고
⑤ 로스쿨의 일부 문제점에 대한 개선을 요구하려고

04

대화를 듣고, 두 사람이 하는 말의 주제로 가장 적절한 것을 고르시오.

① 운동과 과학의 관계
② 맨발로 뛰기의 장점
③ 체중 감량을 위한 운동법
④ 달리기가 학습에 미치는 영향
⑤ 달리기 전용 신발 착용의 이점

05

대화를 듣고, 두 사람의 관계를 가장 잘 나타낸 것을 고르시오.

① 경찰관 — 운전자 ② 자동차 수리공 — 고객
③ 보험 판매원 — 보험 가입자 ④ 공장 관리자 — 기술자
⑤ 중고차 판매원 — 차 소유자

06

대화를 듣고, 그림에서 대화의 내용과 일치하지 않는 것을 고르시오.

07

대화를 듣고, 여자가 남자에게 부탁한 일로 가장 적절한 것을 고르시오.

① to get her cell phone
② to charge her cell phone
③ to keep an eye on her bag
④ to get her a phone charger
⑤ to take her to the bus station

08

대화를 듣고, 남자가 집에서 공부하려는 이유를 고르시오.

① 같이 공부하면 집중이 잘 안돼서
② 집에 있는 책상과 의자가 더 편해서
③ 카페에는 재미있는 할 거리가 많아서
④ 새로 생긴 카페에 사람이 너무 많아서
⑤ 카페 외부 공사로 인한 소음이 시끄러워서

09

대화를 듣고, 여자가 토네이도 발생 지역에 전달할 총 기부금액을 고르시오.

① $20 ② $50 ③ $75 ④ $90 ⑤ $95

10

대화를 듣고, 남자가 브로콜리의 건강상의 이점으로 언급하지 않은 것을 고르시오.

① 콜레스테롤 감소 ② 뼈 건강 증진 ③ 암 예방
④ 체중 감소 ⑤ 식욕 증진

11

Common raven에 관한 다음 내용을 듣고, 일치하지 않는 것을 고르시오.

① 주로 북반구에서 발견된다.
② 인간과 공존한 지는 오래되지 않았다.
③ 생존 성공의 결정적 요인은 식습관에 있다.
④ 여러 음식에서 영양 공급원을 잘 찾아낸다.
⑤ 많은 스포츠팀의 마스코트로 사용되어 왔다.

12

다음 표를 보면서 대화를 듣고, 두 사람이 함께 수강하기로 한 강좌를 고르시오.

Sports Center Summer Program Schedule

	Class	Instructor	Days & Time	Price	Age
①	Swimming (Beginner)	C. Williams	Tue./Thu., 6:00 ~ 7:00	$40	10+
②	Swimming (Advanced)	M. Hines	Mon./Thu., 8:00 ~ 9:00	$46	10+
③	Aerobics	M. Krupa	Wed./Fri., 19:00 ~ 20:00	$22	12+
④	Badminton	C. Paul	Mon./Wed., 16:00 ~ 17:00	$26	10+
⑤	Racquetball	L. James	Tue./Thu., 19:00 ~ 20:00	$26	13+

13

대화를 듣고, 여자의 마지막 말에 대한 남자의 응답으로 가장 적절한 것을 고르시오.

Man: ______________________

① Your dog has a very serious injury.
② Where do you think you lost your pet?
③ No, he'll be fine. Good luck in the contest.
④ Can you tell me why you decided to get a pet?
⑤ I'm sorry, but your pet can't join the pet contest.

14

대화를 듣고, 남자의 마지막 말에 대한 여자의 응답으로 가장 적절한 것을 고르시오.

Woman: ______________________

① That's a great idea, as long as you can afford it.
② I'm glad that you have a loyal customer base.
③ Do you think I could take out a small loan?
④ I'm sure that promotion helped out a little.
⑤ Advertisements are usually quite effective.

15

다음 상황 설명을 듣고, Casey가 Danny에게 할 말로 가장 적절한 것을 고르시오.

Casey: ______________________

① Let's take a helicopter tour of New York.
② That's all right. I'm sure we'll make the next helicopter.
③ That sounds interesting, but I'm not getting in a helicopter.
④ That sounds great. I've always wanted to see the canyon from above.
⑤ Let's check out the Grand Canyon Museum and get more information.

[16-17] 다음을 듣고, 물음에 답하시오.

16

남자가 하는 말의 주제로 가장 적절한 것은?

① The necessity of to-do lists
② How to organize your own desk
③ Tips for becoming more organized
④ Reasons to use calendars and planners
⑤ Advantages of using smartphone applications

17

언급된 항목이 아닌 것은?

① 달력 ② 일정 계획표 ③ 스마트폰
④ 시계 ⑤ 할 일 목록

01

W: I think I'm ready. ________ ________ ________ ________ ________?

M: Of course. What would you like this morning?

W: I'll have bacon and eggs with a side dish of baked potatoes. ________ ________ ________ ________ ________?

M: (It should be ready in about 15 minutes.)

02

M: I really want to go to the Dragon Heart concert at the Olympic Stadium this Saturday!

W: Yeah, me too. ________ ________ ________ ________ ________?

M: I'm not sure, but my friend, Kevin, ________ ________ ________ ________ ________.

W: (You should definitely call him and ask.)

03

W: Hello, everyone! I'd like to talk to you all today about an opportunity you won't want to miss. If anyone here is considering going to law school, the internship I want to share with you is a great way ________ ________ ________-________ ________. However, there are some things you need to be aware of. This particular internship is open to undergraduate and graduate students currently enrolled at our school. But, please ________ ________ ________ ________ the only undergraduates who ________ ________ ________ ________ ________ are those who are currently seniors. Candidates who are law students and have some exposure to the field will be given preference. Finally, applicants must be 28 years old or younger. If you would like to ________ ________ ________, ________ ________ ________ in law, please apply today.

04

W: Hey Cody, what are you up to?

M: I'm reading about ________ ________ ________ ________ ________.

W: I heard that a lot of people are trying that these days.

M: You're right. Some researchers believe that running barefoot can be great for your health.

W: What are the benefits?

M: Well, it can ________ ________ ________.

W: Really? How so?

M: When you run with shoes on, ________ ________ ________ ________ ________ ________ the shoe. Without shoes, you're able to spread your toes, which can give you more balance.

W: That's cool. Does it help with anything else?

M: It's great for the muscles in your legs. Most running shoes have a raised heel, so your Achilles tendon and calf muscles aren't exercised as much.

W: I see why so many people are starting to run barefoot. I might give it a shot.

M: I'm considering ________ ________ ________ ________.

05

M: Hi. What can we do for you?

W: Well, I got in an accident recently. Ever since then, the red lights on the dashboard have been flashing.

M: We'll ________ ________ ________ for you. Are you having any other problems?

W: Yeah. When I drive faster than 70 kilometers per hour, my car ________ ________ ________ ________ ________.

M: Hmm. . . it sounds like a problem with your tires.

W: My insurance should cover any of the repairs I need, right?

M: I'm afraid I don't know anything about that. You'll have to call them.

W: I'll give them a call after lunch. How long do you think the repairs will take?

M: Well, it depends on ________ ________ ________ ________ ________ ________ ________. I'll be able to tell you more after we have a look at it.

W: I have a couple of other ________ ________ ________ ________ ________ around the area. Is it okay if I come back later?

M: Sure, that's fine. Just leave your phone number. We'll call you once we've got a better idea of what's wrong with it.

W: Sounds good.

06

W: Hi, Peter. I'm sorry for being late. I've been very busy.

M: That's okay. I've got the campsite almost set up. What do you think of what I've done so far?

W: You did a great job. I like that you put the tent by the river.

M: Yeah, that way we can go swimming or fishing easily. It'll also be great to enjoy dinner just next to the water.

W: Ah, so that's why you put the table and chairs between the tent and the river. But where's the icebox? It should be ________ ________ ________.

M: Oh, I forgot about that. It's in the tent. ________ ________ ________ ________ and put it under the tree.

W: But then it'll be next to the fire. It's probably dangerous to have the fire so close to the tree, anyway.

M: ________ ________ ________. Let's put it out later and make a new one closer to the water. By the way, I hung the hammock between the trees. What do you think?

W: That's perfect. Good job!

07

W: Hey, Jeff. I'm really sorry I'm late.

M: I was seriously worried. I didn't think ________ ________ ________ ________ ________ ________. I tried to call, but you didn't answer your phone.

W: Well, I hopped in the taxi and ________ ________ ________ before I realized I'd left my cell phone at home and had to go back. Then there was ________ ________ ________ on the way here.

M: Yeah, it's always bad like that on Friday evenings.

W: I didn't know that. Hey, do you know if there's a convenience store around the bus station?

M: There's one right over there. Why?

W: Well, when I went back home to get my phone, ________ ________ ________ ________ ________ ________. I need to buy another one. Watch my bag, will you?

M: Sure. I'll wait here.

W: Thanks. It should only be a few minutes.

08

M: Hey Kate, ________ ________ ________ ________ ________ ________ tomorrow?

W: I don't think so. It looks like ________ ________ ________ ________ ________. How about you?

M: I've been studying in the cafe in the new Student Center.

W: Oh? How is it?

M: It's pretty cool. They have a few new restaurants, a recreation room with a ping-pong table, and a basketball court.

W: That's awesome. I might go play some ping-pong after the exam.

M: The new pizza shop they have there is really good, too.

W: Nice. What about having lunch there and studying together in the cafe, then?

M: I'd love to get lunch, but I think studying there is a bad idea.

W: Really? Why's that?

M: The terrace of the cafe ________ ________ ________ ________, so it's quite noisy.

W: I see. I guess I'll study at home then, too.

09

M: Good morning, Mrs. DeLaney. Are you busy? I need to talk to you about something.

W: Hey, Taylor. Come on in. What do you need?

M: I'm sure you heard about the tornadoes in Kentucky last week.

W: I did. It sounds awful. Many homes ________ ________ ________.

M: Well, a lot of the students got together to __________ __________ __________ __________ __________.

Everyone pitched in $3.

W: That's really nice of you. I'm sure it'll be helpful.

M: I hope so. Everyone seemed happy to help.

W: All twenty-five students donated? That's quite a bit of money.

M: Yeah, and here it is. I was wondering if you could send it to them __________ __________ __________.

W: I'd love to. I'll even donate $20 myself.

M: Thanks, Mrs. DeLaney. I really hope that this money helps.

W: I'm sure it will, Taylor.

10

M: I'm feeling great today. This new diet I just started is amazing. How about you? How're you doing?

W: Not as well as you. I guess I should try out your diet. What kinds of foods are you eating?

M: I'm eating a lot more vegetables. I'd recommend you do that, too. Broccoli is great for you.

W: Really? What are the health benefits of broccoli?

M: Well, first of all, __________ __________ __________ __________ __________ __________, which is great for lowering your cholesterol.

W: Okay. What else?

M: It's full of Vitamin C and Vitamin K, which __________ __________ __________ __________. It's also a great source of antioxidants that can help prevent cancer and keep you healthy.

W: That's great. I'd also like to lose a little bit of weight. Can broccoli help with that?

M: It sure can. Remember how I said broccoli is full of fiber? That means it makes you feel full __________ __________ __________ __________ __________.

W: Wow! I guess broccoli really is a super food!

11

M: The common raven, widely known as the northern raven, is a large black bird __________ __________ __________ __________ __________ __________.

It is the most common bird of its kind. In fact, from an evolutionary perspective, the species has been very successful. It __________ __________ __________ __________ for thousands of years, and in some areas has been so numerous that it was considered a pest. One crucial part of the raven's success comes from its diet. These birds are extremely versatile and opportunistic in __________ __________ __________ __________, feeding on rotting flesh, insects, cereal grains, berries, fruit, small animals, and food waste. They have also been considered a __________ __________ and have been used as a mascot for many different sports teams, including the National Football League's Baltimore Ravens.

12

W: Hey Garrett, I found this schedule for this summer's programs at the sports center. It made me think: we should get some exercise this summer. It'd be a shame to just __________ __________ __________ __________ __________ __________.

M: You're right. What classes are you looking at?

W: How about a swimming class? I want to become a better swimmer.

M: Actually, I have a phobia of water.

W: How about the aerobics class, then? I think it'll be fun.

M: That sounds all right, but we have book club meetings on Wednesday nights.

W: That's right. Well, I guess we only have these two choices then.

M: I like that they're pretty cheap. __________ __________ __________ __________ __________ more than $30.

W: So, which one is better for you?

M: Well, we can't take the class on Tuesdays and Thursdays. It's for older kids.

W: That's right. Let's __________ __________ __________ __________ __________, then.

M: Sounds like a plan.

13

M: Have a seat here, please. So, what's the matter with your dog?

W: Well, he can't walk properly.

M: Let me have a look at his feet. *[Pause]* Well, there's the problem. __________ __________ __________ __________ __________ __________ __________.

Do you know why?

W: I have no idea.
M: Fortunately, it's not that serious. The swelling should subside in about a week or so.
W: In a week? Actually, __________ __________ __________ __________ __________ __________ the Handsome Dog Contest next week.
M: You mean that contest hosted by The Dog Lovers' Club?
W: That's right. Do you think it's okay for him to __________ __________ __________ __________? I'm worried that he won't be able to.
M: Don't worry about it. Oh, so that's 9 days from now. Yes, he'll be completely fine by then.
W: That's good. I was really worried about him.
M: (No, he'll be fine. Good luck in the contest.)

14

W: Hi, Mr. Goodman. How is business at the store these days?
M: Actually, sales haven't been all that great lately.
W: That's too bad. The economy is in horrible shape nowadays.
M: Yeah. I need to do something about it soon.
W: How are you going to change the economy?
M: I can't change the economy, but I can change __________ __________ __________ __________ __________ in it.
W: So you mean like __________ __________ __________?
M: Well, I was thinking about putting out some coupons in the daily newspaper. I want to give people more for their money.
W: Well, that is very kind of you, but won't you still be losing money?
M: Yes, at first. But I think people will see that I'm trying to accommodate them __________ __________ __________ __________ __________, and that will help me __________ __________ __________ __________ __________.
W: (That's a great idea, as long as you can afford it.)

15

W: Casey lives in New York City, but she has decided to visit her friend Danny in Tucson, Arizona. Casey makes the long journey, and Danny is delighted to see her. He takes her on a tour of his city. __________ __________ __________ __________ __________, Casey tells Danny that she has always wanted to see the Grand Canyon. They set out to go to the Grand Canyon the next day and find a __________ __________ __________ __________ __________ __________. They stay there awhile, and then Danny suggests they take a helicopter ride around the canyon __________ __________ __________ __________ __________ __________. Casey, however, __________ __________ __________ __________ __________ and doesn't want to ride in a helicopter. In this situation, what would Casey most likely say to Danny?
Casey: (That sounds interesting, but I'm not getting in a helicopter.)

16-17

M: Do you frequently find yourself searching frantically for something on your messy desk? Have you missed meetings or appointments because you're just too unorganized? Well, I'm here today to offer some tips on __________ __________ __________ __________ __________ __________ __________ __________. First, organize your desk. Don't be a hoarder. Throw away things that you don't need or that are unimportant. Second, use a calendar, planner, or smartphone to __________ __________ __________ __________ __________. Calendars and planners are a bit outdated, but they can get you organized. Technology is your friend, and there are many apps that can help you organize your schedule. Third, __________ __________ __________ __________ __________ __________ __________ __________. To-do lists are a great way to organize your day, and there are many great smartphone applications that can help. Finally, __________ __________ __________ __________ __________ __________. Stop procrastinating and stick to a schedule. __________ __________ __________ for the items on your to-do list. Combine items to save time. If you follow these tips, I'm sure you'll lead a more organized and productive life.

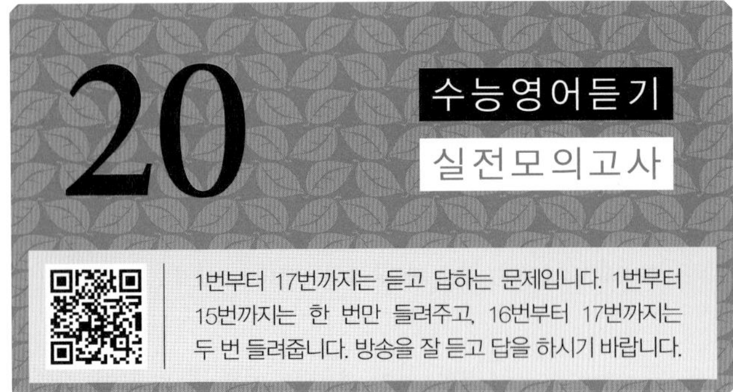

01

대화를 듣고, 남자의 마지막 말에 대한 여자의 응답으로 가장 적절한 것을 고르시오.

① Thanks for the suggestion.
② Yeah, I'm great at shooting.
③ That's okay. I don't really like basketball.
④ You should go to basketball practice today.
⑤ I thought you were interested in basketball.

02

대화를 듣고, 여자의 마지막 말에 대한 남자의 응답으로 가장 적절한 것을 고르시오.

① Help me become a better player.
② Play the instrument you're best at.
③ You shouldn't play the drum in the tryouts.
④ The marching band contest is this weekend.
⑤ Playing instruments is great for relieving stress.

03

다음을 듣고, 남자가 하는 말의 목적으로 가장 적절한 것을 고르시오.

① 팬 미팅 행사가 취소된 것을 사과하려고
② 유명 작가의 작품 세계를 설명하려고
③ 새로운 독립 영화 감독을 소개하려고
④ 영화 상영 시간의 변경을 알리려고
⑤ 영화표의 환불 절차를 안내하려고

04

대화를 듣고, 두 사람이 하는 말의 주제로 가장 적절한 것을 고르시오.

① 몸과 마음을 건강하게 유지하는 방법
② 현대인들이 운동을 하지 않는 이유
③ 건강 관련 정보를 얻는 요령
④ 건강한 식습관의 중요성
⑤ 운동의 장단기적 효과

05

대화를 듣고, 두 사람의 관계를 가장 잘 나타낸 것을 고르시오.

① photographer — film actress
② art collector — film director
③ reporter — interviewee
④ advertiser — editor
⑤ model — professor

06

대화를 듣고, 그림에서 대화의 내용과 일치하지 않는 것을 고르시오.

07

대화를 듣고, 이번 주 토요일에 남자가 할 일로 가장 적절한 것을 고르시오.

① 축제에 가기
② 시험 공부하기
③ 영화 보러 가기
④ 할머니 방문하기
⑤ 집 수리하는 것 돕기

08

대화를 듣고, 여자가 스터디 모임에 참석할 수 없는 이유를 고르시오.

① 화학 수업을 들어야 해서
② 수업 자료를 더 공부해야 해서
③ 아버지 생신 선물을 사야 해서
④ 부모님과 함께 외출하기로 해서
⑤ 다른 스터디 모임에 끼기로 해서

09

대화를 듣고, 남자가 지불할 금액을 고르시오.

① $20 ② $26 ③ $30 ④ $36 ⑤ $40

10

대화를 듣고, 공연 관람 에티켓에 관해 두 사람이 언급하지 않은 것을 고르시오.

① 휴대폰 무음으로 하기 ② 공연 중에 떠들지 않기
③ 앞 좌석 발로 차지 않기 ④ 공연 시간 지키기
⑤ 음료수 쏟지 않기

11

Maple 고등학교 에세이 대회에 관한 다음 내용을 듣고, 일치하지 않는 것을 고르시오.

① 에세이의 주제는 환경 보호에 대한 것이다.
② 제출은 학교에 직접 와서 해야 한다.
③ 4월 20일까지 제출해야 한다.
④ 2등과 3등의 상금 차이는 100달러이다.
⑤ 1등 수상작은 도시 신문에 실리게 될 것이다.

12

다음 표를 보면서 대화를 듣고, 두 사람이 딸을 위해 선택한 피아노 교습을 고르시오.

Piano Lessons for Kids

	Session	Time	Days
①	Mar.15 ~ Apr.5	5:00 ~ 6:30 p.m.	Mon. & Fri.
②	Mar.15 ~ Apr.5	6:30 ~ 8:00 p.m.	Tue. & Thur.
③	Mar.30 ~ Apr.15	5:00 ~ 6:30 p.m.	Tue. & Thur.
④	Mar.30 ~ Apr.15	5:00 ~ 6:30 p.m.	Mon. & Fri.
⑤	Mar.30 ~ Apr.15	6:30 ~ 8:00 p.m.	Mon. & Wed.

13

대화를 듣고, 여자의 마지막 말에 대한 남자의 응답으로 가장 적절한 것을 고르시오.

Man: ______________________

① You'd better look for another parking space upstairs.
② Is there any way I could use your bicycle for a moment?
③ You should always wear a helmet when you ride a bike.
④ Would you return this book when you go to the law building?
⑤ First, go and see whether the place you left it in is a designated area.

14

대화를 듣고, 남자의 마지막 말에 대한 여자의 응답으로 가장 적절한 것을 고르시오.

Woman: ______________________

① A balanced diet can help you get in shape.
② No way! It's not easy to do this program from home.
③ Of course you will. You can start with an easy routine.
④ That's fine. They don't have any classes for beginners.
⑤ No problem. You've gotten a lot stronger and healthier.

15

다음 상황 설명을 듣고, Bella가 Nathaniel에게 할 말로 가장 적절한 것을 고르시오.

Bella: Nathaniel, ______________________

① would you help me with my fundraiser?
② you should really start saving your money.
③ I'm sometimes let down by my closest friends.
④ why don't you want to support our good cause?
⑤ it's great that you made such a large contribution.

[16-17] 다음을 듣고, 물음에 답하시오.

16

남자가 하는 말의 주제로 가장 적절한 것은?

① Safety concerns when glamping
② Ways to relax in the great outdoors
③ A new camping trend called 'glamping'
④ How to avoid discomfort while camping
⑤ Positive effects of glamping on the environment

17

새로운 캠핑이 제공하는 것으로 언급되지 않은 것은?

① 텐트 ② 전기 ③ 샤워시설
④ 난방기기 ⑤ 화장실

01

M: Hey, Ava. What are you going to focus on today at basketball practice?

W: I need to ______ ______ ______ ______ ______.

M: You should work on shooting. I think it's more important.

W: (Thanks for the suggestion.)

02

W: Good morning, Max. So, ______ ______ ______ ______ ______ for the school's marching band.

M: That's great! ______ ______ ______ ______ ______ ______ ______?

W: I'll probably play a brass instrument, but I'm not sure which one.

M: (Play the instrument you're best at.)

03

M: Good evening, ladies and gentlemen. Thank you for coming to the Fourth Annual International Film Festival here at historic Wilma Theater. I know many of you are excited about ______ ______ ______ ______ ______ ______, *Moonset Monarchy*, by acclaimed director Mark Young. However, we're currently facing some ______ ______ ______ ______ ______ ______. The film was due to start momentarily, but as of now, we are postponing it for one hour. We ______ ______ ______ ______ ______ and are prepared to refund any tickets you have bought for this particular film. Thank you for your understanding.

04

W: Hey, Gilbert. What are you up to?

M: Hi, Mary. I just started listening to a new audio book about health.

W: Health? Is it about diets?

M: No, it's more about how to ______ ______ ______ ______ ______ ______.

W: That sounds really interesting.

M: We can do really simple things every day that will have significant effects in the long run. People want things right away, so they ignore ______ ______-______ ______ of the stuff they do and eat.

W: So, what's the first thing you would recommend doing to get on the right path toward a healthy mind and body?

M: The first thing we need to do is inventory our lives. Find out what we've got, and then figure out how much of it we need and ______ ______ ______ ______ ______.

W: And, this inventory should include not just material possessions but food, people, work, hobbies and pretty much everything we deal with on a daily basis, right?

M: Yes, precisely.

05

[Knock on the door]

M: Please come in.

W: Hello, Mr. Anderson. I was told you wanted to see me.

M: Yes, Stacy. I was ______ ______. Please have a seat and take a look at this layout.

W: Oh, I really like it!

M: Great. Now I need your help choosing a couple of shots we can use for the brochure.

W: These two are really nice. I think they best capture what the film is about.

M: I took shots that I thought best ______ ______ ______, since the article focuses on your acting.

W: I'm really excited to be working with you. Your pictures make me look great.

M: I'm happy you like my work. We should take a few more shots before ______ ______ ______ ______ ______ ______.

W: That sounds good. Can we do something with an action theme?

M: Sure. Come to the studio at three.

W: I __________ __________ __________ at four, so can we meet an hour earlier?

M: Of course.

06

W: Welcome to our school, Mr. Brown. Let me show you around.

M: Thanks. It's a pleasure to be working here. What's this room?

W: This is our teacher's lounge. It's where you can go between classes to relax and talk to the other teachers.

M: Wow, it seems quite nice. Is that a snack machine in the back?

W: It sure is. We also have two computers __________ __________ __________ __________ that you can use to access the Internet.

M: That's great. What's that on the table?

W: We sometimes have casual meetings in here, so we have two sofas and a phone on the table used to hold conference calls if we need to.

M: That's cool. What's __________ __________ __________ __________ next to the snack machine?

W: That's a poster for our upcoming Earth Day Fair. It __________ __________ __________ __________.

M: So the bulletin board announces upcoming events?

W: That's right. Sometimes we post other important information on there, so you should __________ __________ __________.

M: I see. What's the next stop on our tour?

W: We're going to the gym next.

07

W: How did you do on your test, Donald?

M: I'm not sure. I'll have my results by Wednesday of next week.

W: You studied hard, so I'm sure you'll __________ __________ __________ __________.

M: Thanks, Mom. By the way, can I go to the World Jazz Festival with my friends this Saturday?

W: Oh, no. Don't you remember what your father told you?

M: What's that?

W: Your father and I are __________ __________ __________ __________ __________. We really need your help.

M: Hmm. . . I guess I can't go. I'll go to the movies with them this Sunday instead.

W: Okay, but not on Sunday morning. We should __________ __________ __________ then. She's sick in bed.

M: Is it something serious?

W: No. She thinks it's just the flu.

M: __________ __________ __________! Don't worry, Mom. I'll meet my friends after visiting Grandma.

W: Thank you, Donald.

08

M: Hey, Claire. Are you all right? __________ __________ __________ __________ __________ __________.

W: I have a big chemistry test tomorrow, but I just don't understand the material. I think I might fail.

M: Cheer up. Ryan, Jason, Taylor, and I started a study group. You can join us.

W: I'd love to, but I don't want to be a bother. __________ __________ __________ __________.

M: Don't worry. I'm sure everyone would love to have you around.

W: I really appreciate it. I need all of the help I can get.

M: We're getting together tonight at 6. Can you make it?

W: Hmm. . . I really don't think I can. I'm supposed to __________ __________ __________ __________ __________ tonight. It's my father's birthday.

M: I see. Well, if you ever want to join us in the future, __________ __________ __________. Okay?

W: Thanks. I really appreciate it.

09

W: Hello. How may I help you?

M: Hi. How much is an Americano?

W: One is $5. But we're __________ __________ __________ this week. Americanos are buy one, get one free, so it's actually two for $5.

M: That's great. So I can get __________ __________ __________ __________ __________ __________. I'll have four Americanos, then.

W: Is there anything else I can get you today?

M: Yeah, actually it's my coworker's birthday today, so I'm thinking of __________ __________ __________ __________. How much for the devil's food cake?

W: That one is $20. __________ __________ __________ __________ __________ you can use?

M: I don't.

W: Well. I can give you one for 10% off your next purchase.

M: Thanks. Is it okay if I use my credit card?

10

W: Sweetheart, I don't think these are the right seats.

M: Of course they are. These are the seat numbers printed on our tickets.

W: Okay. I guess you're right. The play is about to start. Did you __________ __________ __________ __________ __________ __________?

M: Of course.

W: It's good that you're so considerate. Remember the last time we came to the theater? The couple behind us would not be quiet. __________ __________ __________ __________ __________, too.

M: Yeah, they had no manners. The usher had to come by three times to ask them to be silent.

W: Yeah, it was really annoying. It made it difficult to enjoy the performance. It didn't help that you __________ __________ __________ all over the floor and the people in front of us got their shoes wet and sticky.

M: __________ __________ __________. Anyway, the play is starting now.

W: Great. I hope it goes better than last time.

11

M: Good morning, students and faculty! I would like to announce the 20th Annual Maple High Essay Contest. __________ __________ __________ __________ __________ more and more these days, so this year we want to hear your ideas about how we can protect the environment. There is a 1,000-word limit on these essays, and __________ __________ __________ __________ via the school's homepage. For those of you planning on participating, __________ __________ __________ __________ __________ __________ April 20th. The top three essays will be announced at the end of the month, and prizes will be awarded. The first-place essay will receive $500. The second- and third-place essays will receive $200 and $100 respectively. __________ __________ __________ __________ __________, the first-place essay will also be published in the city newspaper. We encourage all of you to participate. More entries mean more ideas, and more ideas mean more help for the environment!

12

M: What are you doing, darling?

W: I'm looking at a leaflet on piano lessons for the kids. I think Susan needs to learn how to play the piano.

M: I agree with you. But does she have time to take any classes? __________ __________ __________ __________.

W: Don't worry about that. Her violin class is going to finish on March 29th, so she's free after that.

M: I see. Then how about the one that starts at 6:30 p.m.?

W: I think it would be better for her __________ __________ __________ __________ __________ __________.

M: True. Well, there are a couple of classes that start at 5 p.m. Which one is better?

W: It doesn't matter as long as it's not on Thursday. She has to __________ __________ __________ __________ __________ __________.

M: Okay, so there is only one class that she can take. When is the deadline for registration?

W: The leaflet says it is March 10th, so we should hurry before it fills up.

M: Oh, let's register right now.

13

M: You look upset, Nora. What's the matter?

W: I __________ __________ __________ __________ __________ this afternoon. It's very precious to me because my father bought it for me when I got into college.

M: What? The black one you always ride?
W: Yes.
M: What happened to it?
W: I parked it next to the law building.
M: Did you leave it ________ ________ ________ ________ ________ ________?
W: A designated bicycle parking area? What do you mean?
M: Oh, you didn't hear about the new regulation? On campus, you're only allowed to park bikes in designated areas.
W: So ________ ________ ________ ________ ________ because I parked it in the wrong place?
M: Could be.
W: How can I ________ ________ ________?
M: (First, go and see whether the place you left it in is a designated area.)

14

W: Hi, Louis! I never expected to see you here. What's up?
M: Hey, Francis. You were talking about your X-Cross exercise routine and got me curious.
W: I see. Are you looking to start?
M: I think so. You were telling me ________ ________ ________ ________ and how you're happier. I think I need that kind of change in my life.
W: Well, X-Cross does ________ ________ ________ ________ ________. It's also great for your mind.
M: Cool. I've been thinking I should get in shape. I've really let myself go these past few years.
W: Well, I think this program is perfect for you. Why don't you ________ ________ ________ ________?
M: I think I will. I'll ________ ________ today.
W: Nice! I'll help you get started.
M: Thanks. But, like I said, I'm not in very good shape. Do you think I'll do all right in the class?
W: (Of course you will. You can start with an easy routine.)

15

W: Last month, a massive earthquake hit Japan. Many people died, and others ________ ________ ________ ________ ________. Bella decided to hold a fundraiser to ________ ________ and collect other things that could help those affected by the disaster. Almost everyone in her life ________ ________ ________ to donate clothing, canned goods, and money. However, one of her closest friends, Nathaniel, ________ ________ ________ ________ ________ about helping the people who needed help. Later, Bella found out from a friend that Nathaniel actually donated all of his savings to a charity set up to ________ ________ ________ ________. This makes her feel good. What would Bella most likely say to Nathaniel when she sees him?
Bella: Nathaniel, (it's great that you made such a large contribution.)

16-17

M: Good afternoon, everyone. I'd like to talk to you today about recreational camping. In the early days of camping, many people used it as a way to be ________ ________ ________ ________ ________ ________. Others disliked camping because ________ ________ ________ ________ leaky tents, damp sleeping bags, and terrible food. These inconveniences brought about the birth of the camping car and the recreational vehicle. There's a new camping trend gaining popularity these days. It's called 'glamping'. The word is a combination of the words *glamour* and *camping*. When you go glamping, you don't have to ________ ________ ________ or set up a sleeping bag. You don't even have to build a fire. Glamping is a way to take in nature from a hut, a prebuilt tent, or a treehouse. You don't have to give up your daily luxuries to go glamping. This pastime is gaining popularity because it allows you to be in the countryside ________ ________ ________ ________ ________. Glamping provides electricity, showers, and even a toilet. It's also easy to cook meals on ________ ________ ________ ________ ________ ________ when you go glamping.

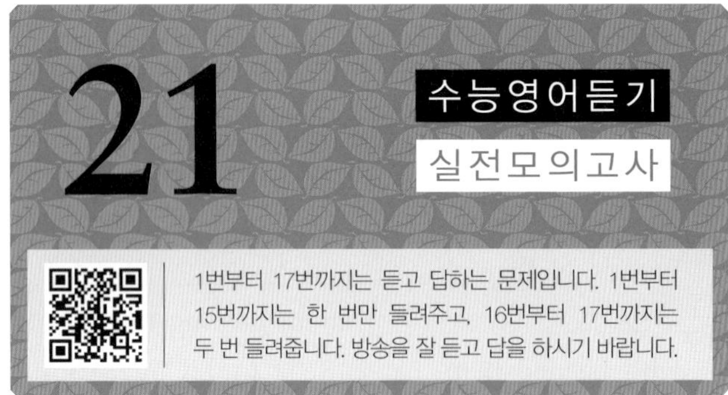

01

대화를 듣고, 남자의 마지막 말에 대한 여자의 응답으로 가장 적절한 것을 고르시오.

① Let's draw lines and start again.
② Could you bring something to draw?
③ I should have brought my umbrella today.
④ I guess we'll only be able to do indoor activities.
⑤ I heard that all the activities will finish after 6 p.m.

02

대화를 듣고, 여자의 마지막 말에 대한 남자의 응답으로 가장 적절한 것을 고르시오.

① That's why I always carry my camera.
② I don't really like the exhibits in this museum.
③ I'm truly sorry. I didn't notice it when I came in.
④ You should have brought your camera with you.
⑤ I didn't know there was a photography exhibition.

03

다음을 듣고, 여자가 하는 말의 목적으로 가장 적절한 것을 고르시오.

① 인터넷 설문 조사에 참여해줄 것을 권유하려고
② 인터넷 수강신청 방법을 학생들에게 설명하려고
③ 학생들의 과도한 인터넷 사용 자제를 당부하려고
④ 다음 학기 수강신청을 다시 해줄 것을 안내하려고
⑤ 학교 수강신청 사이트의 접속 장애 시간을 공지하려고

04

대화를 듣고, 두 사람이 하는 말의 주제로 가장 적절한 것을 고르시오.

① 상대팀의 축구 실력
② 축구 캠프 신청 절차
③ 자신감이 경기력에 미치는 영향
④ 경기 도중 부상에 대처하는 방법
⑤ 축구 경기력 향상을 위한 음료 소개

05

대화를 듣고, 두 사람의 관계를 가장 잘 나타낸 것을 고르시오.

① 꽃집 주인 — 점원
② 택배회사 직원 — 사장
③ 박물관 관장 — 큐레이터
④ 골동품 판매원 — 수집가
⑤ 이삿짐센터 직원 — 고객

06

대화를 듣고, 그림에서 대화의 내용과 일치하지 않는 것을 고르시오.

07

대화를 듣고, 남자가 여자를 위해 할 일로 가장 적절한 것을 고르시오.

① 병원 데려가기
② 숙제 도와주기
③ 알람 맞춰주기
④ 진통제 갖다 주기
⑤ 기분전환 시켜주기

08

대화를 듣고, 남자가 사무실 이사를 미룬 이유로 가장 적절한 것을 고르시오.

① 이사 업체에 사정이 생겨서
② 사무실이 아직 비지 않아서
③ 직원들의 스케줄이 맞지 않아서
④ 날씨가 좋지 않다는 예보가 있어서
⑤ 이사 전에 사무실 청소를 해야 해서

09

대화를 듣고, 여자가 지불할 총 금액을 고르시오.

① $90 ② $94 ③ $99 ④ $110 ⑤ $115

10

대화를 듣고, 현장학습에 관해 두 사람이 언급하지 않은 것을 고르시오.

① 활동 내용 ② 인원 ③ 날짜
④ 1인당 가격 ⑤ 당일 복장

11

Springfield Farmers' Market에 관한 다음 내용을 듣고, 일치하지 않는 것을 고르시오.

① Springfield Square에서 열린다.
② 신선한 유기농 농산물을 제공한다.
③ 다른 곳보다 가격이 더 저렴하다.
④ 매주 토요일과 일요일에 열린다.
⑤ 애완견은 데려올 수 없다.

12

다음 표를 보면서 대화를 듣고, 여자가 선택할 정수기를 고르시오.

Quality Water Purifier Rentals

	Ice	Hot Water	Energy Efficiency Rating	Monthly Rental Fee
①	Yes	Yes	1	$50
②	No	Yes	1	$40
③	Yes	No	1	$40
④	No	Yes	2	$30
⑤	No	No	2	$25

13

대화를 듣고, 여자의 마지막 말에 대한 남자의 응답으로 가장 적절한 것을 고르시오.

Man: ______________________________

① I really want to be a professor of journalism.
② Even though journalism is quite boring, I still love it.
③ I think that high-quality journalists are rare these days.
④ I want to change my major, but my father won't let me.
⑤ I'd major in what I was more interested in if I were you.

14

대화를 듣고, 남자의 마지막 말에 대한 여자의 응답으로 가장 적절한 것을 고르시오.

Woman: ______________________________

① Put everything in the garbage bin at school.
② You're right. I think everyone will be impressed.
③ No. I don't think it's that important to make it neater.
④ You can tell your teacher you've finished your project.
⑤ Try to find the most important message and make it clear.

15

다음 상황 설명을 듣고, Manny가 Katie에게 할 말로 가장 적절한 것을 고르시오.

Manny: ______________________________

① Can I take a look at your guidebook, please?
② Did you double-check all of our reservations?
③ Everything's going to be fine. Let's just have fun.
④ Do you know what hotel we're staying at tonight?
⑤ I can't believe we're going to Bangkok. I'm so excited.

[16-17] 다음을 듣고, 물음에 답하시오.

16

남자가 하는 말의 주제로 가장 적절한 것은?

① Negative effects of distraction on study
② Health problems related to distractions
③ Various methods to study more effectively
④ Benefits of setting goals and rewarding yourself
⑤ Benefits of studying in a comfortable environment

17

언급된 장소가 아닌 것은?

① 교실 ② 자신의 방 ③ 공원
④ 카페 ⑤ 도서관

01

M: Hey Kate, did you draw lines on the field for the sports day activities?

W: Not yet. The weather forecast says it's going to __________ __________ __________ __________ __________ that day.

M: Oh, no! What can we do?

W: (I guess we'll only be able to do indoor activities.)

02

W: I'm sorry, sir, but we have a __________ "__________ __________" __________ at this museum.

M: Really? No one told me that, and I didn't see any signs at the entrance.

W: There's a sign near the doorway that says *No Photography or Video Recording.*

M: (I'm truly sorry. I didn't notice it when I came in.)

03

W: Good afternoon, students. May I have your attention, please? We regret to inform you that everyone is going to have to __________ __________ __________ __________ __________ again. I know you all already completed your schedules yesterday; however, due to a problem with our registration site, we were unable to process some of the requests. Hopefully, all of our __________ __________ have been fixed and we can avoid problems like this in the future. Please sign up for your classes by the end of the day. We __________ __________ __________, and we're truly sorry for the inconvenience. Thank you.

04

W: Hey, Paul. I heard that you're going to join the FC APEC III soccer camp. Are you any good?

M: Not really.

W: How are you planning to __________ __________ __________ __________, then?

M: It shouldn't really be a problem. I'll drink some Rad CraCra every day.

W: How can Rad CraCra help you with your soccer skills?

M: It's got a special mixture of ingredients that can __________ __________ __________ __________ __________ I need. It can help me run faster, jump higher, and play longer.

W: Wow! I didn't know Rad CraCra was that powerful.

M: It also tastes great, and it's the __________ __________ __________ of FC APEC III.

W: Awesome! Rad CraCra is an amazing sports drink.

M: You're right! I never play soccer without it.

05

W: Hi. Please come in.

M: Wow. Look at this place! You have a lot of antique vases. Are you a collector?

W: I am. So, you guys offer __________ __________ __________ __________ __________ __________, right?

M: We sure do. We have containers specially designed to protect delicate items. It does cost an extra $150, though. When exactly are you moving out?

W: Not until next Sunday, but we'd like to get everything moved out a bit early. When are you available, and what's the cost?

M: We could __________ __________ __________ to your new place on Friday afternoon. From looking at everything you have, I'd say $900 would be fair.

W: That sounds perfect. Is there anything we should do in preparation?

M: Well, be sure to __________ __________ __________ __________ __________ and take them with you separately.

W: Sure. No Problem.

06

W: Hey sweetheart, I think I finally finished the design for the mural I'm going to paint in Colin's bedroom.

M: Cool. Let me see it.

정답 및 해설 p.106

W: Sure. _____ _____ _____ _____ _____ _____.

M: Well, the sun is pretty interesting. Those are some cool sunglasses, too.

W: Yeah. And the horse is eating grass from the ground.

M: That's cool. I guess that's an apple tree there. You did a great job drawing it.

W: Thanks. What do you think about the rabbits near the tree?

M: I think they look a little more like mice, but _____ _____ _____ _____ _____ _____ the wall. I like how the pig is playing in the mud.

W: Pigs love mud. You know, Colin also loves eagles, so I put one of those in the tree.

M: Neat. I'm sure he'll like it.

W: Well, I guess I should go to the art supply store and buy some paint.

M: Well, I'm really excited to see _____ _____ _____ _____.

W: Me too, sweetheart.

07

M: Hey, is everything okay? You look stressed.

W: I have a big test next week that I should have been preparing for, but _____ _____ _____ _____ _____ _____ _____ a lot instead of studying. I'm worried that I won't do well.

M: Don't worry about it too much. You'll do fine if you start studying today.

W: I appreciate you saying that. It makes me feel a bit better. But still, all of this anxiety is making me hot.

M: That's strange. Let me take your temperature to make sure you don't _____ _____ _____. *[Pause]* No, you're fine.

W: I want to take some pain medication anyway.

M: No, a pain pill won't help. If you want to be alert and able to study, you need to rest. You should _____ _____ _____.

W: I can't nap now. I haven't finished this assignment yet.

M: You really look like you need to sleep. _____ _____ _____ _____ _____. When you wake up, you'll be able to think more clearly and do better work.

W: Will you make sure to _____ _____ _____ _____ _____? I'm worried that if I fall asleep now, I'll sleep too long.

M: All right, I will. Now, go rest.

08

W: Good morning, Mr. Staller. We have everything ready to move to the new offices this weekend, right?

M: Didn't you hear? We're not moving in until next weekend.

W: Really? _____ _____ _____ _____ _____ _____?

M: I thought that it'd be best if we had the place thoroughly cleaned before we started over there.

W: Did you call the moving company to reschedule the move?

M: I did. _____ _____ _____ _____ the change of plans, though. They're actually going to be booked up next weekend.

W: Oh, no. What are we going to do if we can't find a moving company to replace them?

M: I'm not sure yet, but I thought about having the employees come in on Saturday to move everything out.

W: I really don't think they're going to like that.

M: You're probably right, but desperate times _____ _____ _____ _____.

09

M: Hi. How can I help you today?

W: I'm shopping for a backpack for my son.

M: Well, you've come at the perfect time. We're running our back-to-school sale, and we're _____ _____ _____ _____ 40% off.

W: Awesome! Well, what's popular these days?

M: Well, this Spikey brand backpack is a big seller. It's priced at $50, but it's currently on sale for 20% off.

W: That's reasonable. I'll take it.

M: Great! Is there anything else I can help you with?

W: Well, my daughter could probably use a new backpack too. How much is that pink one over there?

M: That one is generally $60, but it's 10% off right now.

W: __________ __________ __________ __________, but I'm sure she'll love it. I'll take it.

M: All right. We can also make the bags __________-__________, if you'd like.

W: How much does that cost?

M: It's an additional $5 per bag.

W: That's okay. They're fine the way they are.

10

[Telephone rings.]

M: Good afternoon, this is Tafford Orchard.

W: Hello, I'm Mrs. Fink, the biology teacher at Paulson High School. __________ __________ __________ __________ __________ bringing my students to the orchard on a field trip.

M: I'm glad to hear that, Mrs. Fink. We offer half-day and full-day programs for students.

W: __________ __________-__________ __________ would be more appropriate for our needs, I think. What are some of the activities that you all do in these programs?

M: If the weather's nice, we usually take students out to pick apples and make apple cider.

W: That seems like something they'd like. I'd be bringing around 25 students. Do you have any openings on September 26th?

M: Yes, our schedule is open __________ __________ __________ __________.

W: Excellent. I suppose I'd like to go ahead and make a reservation, then.

M: Okay. You said about 25 students on September 26th, correct?

W: That's right. And that's for Paulson High School.

M: All right. You'll need to provide lunch for your students and __________ __________ __________ __________ __________ __________.

W: Will do. Thanks for your help.

11

M: It's summer again, which means the return of the Springfield Farmers' Market. The market is located at Springfield Square and __________ __________ __________ __________ some of __________ __________ __________ __________ in the state. Why would you spend the extra money at the grocery store when you can buy directly from our local farmers for a fraction of the cost? Whether you're looking for watermelons, string beans, or fresh jams, our market has everything you need. We're __________ __________ __________ from noon until 7 p.m. and on Sundays from noon to 5. It's fun for the whole family. __________ __________ __________ __________ __________, so bring everyone down to the farmers' market this weekend.

12

M: Good evening, ma'am. What can I do for you?

W: Hi. I'm looking for a water purifier to rent for my office.

M: Well, you've come to the right place. We currently have five different models to choose from. I'll just need to __________ __________ __________ __________ __________ so we can find the perfect one for you.

W: That's fine. Ask away.

M: Okay. So, first off, what do you want this machine to do? Would you like it to make ice?

W: Well, that would be nice, but it doesn't have to. I do want it to make hot water, though.

M: All right. Now, as you might know, different purifiers use different amounts of energy. What kind of energy rating are you looking for?

W: We're an __________ __________ __________, so I think we should go with the best rating possible.

M: I see. A lower number means it's more efficient. Just one more question: how much are you looking to spend per month?

W: We decided that $40 per month is the most __________ __________ __________ __________.

M: Then this is the model for you.

W: Perfect. I'll take it. Thank you for all your help.

13

W: Hey, I heard that you decided to __________ __________ __________.

M: Yeah, I really want to be a journalist.

W: That's cool. I guess __________ __________ __________ __________?

M: That's right. I've loved writing since I was a child. Are you still going to major in anthropology?

W: No, I'm thinking about majoring in sociology.

M: __________ __________. You seemed pretty sure what you were going to major in the last time we talked.

W: Well, I realized I'm really interested in sociology as well. I don't know which one I want to study more.

M: What kind of job do you want when you graduate?

W: I really want to be a social worker, but my father says I should be an anthropology professor.

M: Ah. Isn't your father an anthropology professor?

W: Yeah. So which one do you think I should choose?

M: (I'd major in what I was more interested in if I were you.)

14

[Knocking sound]

M: Who's there?

W: Hey, Kevin. It's me.

M: Oh, hey Mom. Come on in. How's everything?

W: Not bad. What are you up to?

M: Just working on this project for science class. __________ __________ __________. Check it out.

W: *[Pause]* I'm not sure what I'm looking at here.

M: It's a battery made out of a potato. Pretty neat, huh?

W: Well, it is pretty interesting, but it seems a bit messy. There are wires everywhere. Can't you clean it up a little?

M: I know it's a bit complicated, but I __________ __________ __________ __________ __________ __________ __________ of how everything works. What do you think about the poster?

W: Well, when you're presenting something and trying to get others to understand, I think it's important to __________ __________ __________ __________ __________ __________.

M: Well, what do you think I should do, then?

W: (Try to find the most important message and make it clear.)

15

W: Manny and his girlfriend, Katie, __________ __________ __________ __________ through Southeast Asia. Neither of them had traveled abroad before, so they decided to prepare themselves rather than __________ __________ __________ __________ __________. Katie did most of the work to make arrangements. She found cheap accommodation and planned all of the routes. She also bought a Thai phrasebook so she could communicate with the locals. __________ __________ __________ __________ __________, they have finally arrived in Bangkok and are walking around The Grand Palace. Katie, however, is __________ __________ __________ __________ __________ and is trying to think of new things to do. Manny wants to tell Katie that she shouldn't worry about planning and instead should enjoy the trip. In this situation, what would Manny most likely say to Katie?

Manny: (Everything's going to be fine. Let's enjoy our trip.)

16-17

W: Good morning, everyone. With final exams coming up, I'd like to __________ __________ __________ __________ __________ __________ __________ effective study habits. Perhaps the first thing to consider when you study is finding the perfect place to concentrate. It needs to be quiet and comfortable, so it could be the classroom, your own room, a cafe, or the library. Second, it's important to __________ __________ when studying. Setting goals will help give you something to work towards as you study. You can also reward yourself with a treat when you reach the goals you have set for yourself. The third point I want to make is about resisting distraction. It's easy to __________ __________ by phones and other electronics these days, so make sure to __________ __________ __________ __________ __________, television, and other distracting devices before you start studying. Finally, recent studies have shown that some noises can be helpful for concentration. Droning noises, such as lights, white noise, rain, and the sounds of nature can help keep your mind sharp and relaxed. __________ __________ __________ __________ __________ while studying for next week's finals. Thank you for your time.

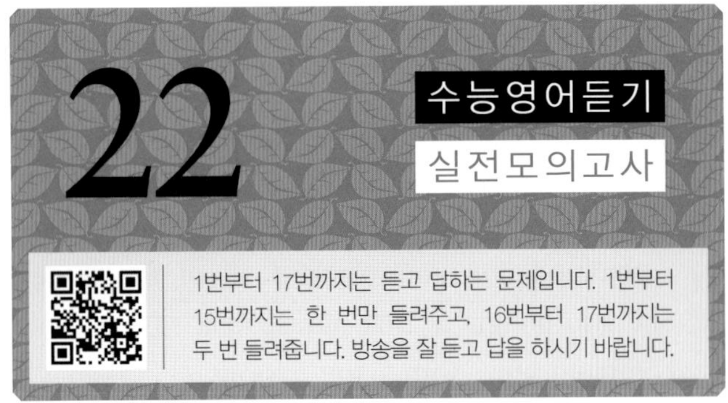

01

대화를 듣고, 남자의 마지막 말에 대한 여자의 응답으로 가장 적절한 것을 고르시오.

① I'll take hundreds and fifties, please.
② Would you like large or small bills?
③ I should exchange my money at the bank.
④ We don't allow you to exchange products here.
⑤ We can exchange it if you have the original receipt.

02

대화를 듣고, 여자의 마지막 말에 대한 남자의 응답으로 가장 적절한 것을 고르시오.

① I've never watched a documentary.
② It was certainly thought-provoking.
③ You can borrow it once I finish.
④ You know I haven't seen it yet.
⑤ I've read a few of his books.

03

다음을 듣고, 남자가 하는 말의 주제로 가장 적절한 것을 고르시오.

① 계절에 맞는 야외 운동법
② 날씨 변화에 따른 가구 배치법
③ 겨울에 몸을 따뜻하게 하는 방법
④ 일조량 부족으로 인한 우울증 대처법
⑤ 적절한 비타민 복용으로 활력 찾는 방법

04

대화를 듣고, 여자의 의견으로 가장 적절한 것을 고르시오.

① 야간에 차의 문단속을 철저히 하라.
② 차량 도난 신고는 가능한 한 빨리 해라.
③ 자동차에 경보장치를 반드시 설치하라.
④ 외출 시 집안에 전등을 하나 켜 두어라.
⑤ 경보장치보다는 밝고 좋은 곳에 주차하라.

05

대화를 듣고, 두 사람의 관계를 가장 잘 나타낸 것을 고르시오.

① 작가 — 성우
② 작곡가 — 리포터
③ 소설가 — 삽화가
④ 서점 주인 — 구직자
⑤ 도서 편집자 — 번역가

06

대화를 듣고, 그림에서 대화의 내용과 일치하지 않는 것을 고르시오.

07

대화를 듣고, 여자가 남자를 위해 할 일로 가장 적절한 것을 고르시오.

① 숙제 찾아주기
② 아침식사 챙겨주기
③ 선생님께 전화하기
④ 허가서 작성해주기
⑤ 학교에 태워다 주기

08

대화를 듣고, 남자가 기뻐하는 이유를 고르시오.

① 원하던 책을 사게 되어서
② 오디션 프로그램에 합격해서
③ 연락이 끊긴 친구에게 전화가 와서
④ 친한 친구가 TV에 출연하게 되어서
⑤ 오디션 프로그램을 방청하게 되어서

09

대화를 듣고, 두 사람이 지불할 총 금액을 고르시오.

① $29 ② $30 ③ $34 ④ $40 ⑤ $44

10

대화를 듣고, 신입 사원에 관해 두 사람이 언급하지 않은 것을 고르시오.

① 외국어 능력 ② 첫인상 ③ 전공
④ 자원봉사 이력 ⑤ 좌우명

11

Tarsier에 관한 다음 내용을 듣고, 일치하지 않는 것을 고르시오.

① 필리핀 군도의 남쪽 부근에 산다.
② 다 자란 안경원숭이는 어른 손바닥 크기이다.
③ 커다란 눈으로 유명하다.
④ 머리를 양쪽으로 180도 회전할 수 있다.
⑤ 낮에는 시력이 좋지만, 밤에는 잘 볼 수 없다.

12

다음 표를 보면서 대화를 듣고, 두 사람이 주문할 아기 침대를 고르시오.

Infant Cribs

	Model	Cage Height	Mattress Included	Material	Price
①	L-100	Low	No	Plastic	$120
②	M-100	Mid	Yes	Plastic	$140
③	M-200	Mid	Yes	Wood	$200
④	H-100	High	No	Wood	$180
⑤	H-200	High	Yes	Wood	$240

13

대화를 듣고, 남자의 마지막 말에 대한 여자의 응답으로 가장 적절한 것을 고르시오.

Woman: ______________________________

① They're charging way too much for admission.
② I'm glad that we decided to join the tour group.
③ I can see why so many people love Banksy's work.
④ It's rude to listen to audio while on an exhibition tour.
⑤ That way we can choose to listen to the explanation or not.

14

대화를 듣고, 여자의 마지막 말에 대한 남자의 응답으로 가장 적절한 것을 고르시오.

Man: ______________________________

① No problem. I'll get in touch and see if she has time.
② Sure. I'll look it over and get it back to you tomorrow.
③ That's fine, but I need to turn it in before this weekend.
④ It's great that you got a job with the school newspaper.
⑤ No, but I'll be sure to send you a copy of the school newspaper.

15

다음 상황 설명을 듣고, 교장 선생님이 Bill에게 할 말로 가장 적절한 것을 고르시오.

Mr. Thomas: Bill, ______________________________

① take a deep breath. You're going to do great.
② I'd like you to give the commencement speech.
③ I'm sure that you'll do great in your speech class.
④ congratulations on graduating from high school.
⑤ I'm sorry to hear that you won't be graduating this year.

[16-17] 다음을 듣고, 물음에 답하시오.

16

남자가 하는 말의 목적으로 가장 적절한 것은?

① 리조트의 새로운 시설들을 광고하려고
② 타지 음식 섭취의 위험을 알리려고
③ 다양한 해양 스포츠를 소개하려고
④ 세계 유명 맛집을 소개하려고
⑤ 좋은 휴양지를 홍보하려고

17

남자가 추천한 내용으로 언급되지 않은 것은?

① 스노클링 ② 채식 행사 ③ 음식 시식
④ 섬 방문 ⑤ 기념품 제작

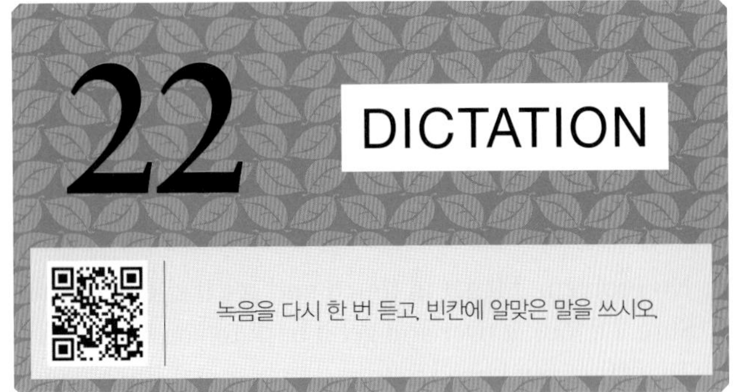

01

M: Hello. I have some leftover money that I'd like to exchange. __________ __________ __________ __________?

W: It's 119 yen to the dollar. How much are you looking to exchange?

M: I have 55,000 yen. Here you go.

W: (Would you like large or small bills?)

02

W: Conan, have you seen *Our History*, the new documentary on HBO?

M: Yeah, I watched it last night. It was really interesting to see __________ __________ __________ on the history of mankind.

W: I thought so, too. It really __________ __________ __________ __________ __________ __________ __________.

M: (It was certainly thought-provoking.)

03

M: Do you ever get moody or depressed during the winter season? If so, you might have what experts call "__________ __________." This condition is quite common, as the human body receives vitamins from sunlight. Experts now say that up to 50% of people worldwide __________ __________ __________ __________ __________. __________ __________ __________ __________ __________ of vitamin D, experts suggest spending between 10 and 15 minutes outside each day. You can also organize your house to allow more sunlight to enter. __________ __________ __________ __________ __________ __________, spending time under a bright light can also help.

04

M: Krista, do you have an alarm on your car?

W: I don't. Why do you ask?

M: __________ __________ __________ __________ __________ last night while I was out.

W: Oh, my. Did they take anything?

M: Luckily, there wasn't much to take. But they cut up my interior with knives. It seems like they just wanted to destroy property.

W: You must be pretty upset about that.

M: I am. That's why I'm thinking about __________ __________ __________ __________.

W: A good friend of mine had one and ended up taking it out because it would go off randomly. If people want to wreck your stuff, an alarm __________ __________ __________ __________ __________.

M: Yeah, I suppose you're right. What should I do, then?

W: Well, my advice is to always __________ __________ __________ __________ __________ __________-__________ __________ or a nice part of town. Even if the parking space isn't the most convenient, it's better than the alternative.

M: You think that'll work?

W: I do. That's what I do, and I've never had a problem.

M: Okay. I'll do that from now on.

05

M: Hello. You must be Amelia Hawkins.

W: That's me. You're the great Jeffrey Martin. It's a pleasure to meet you, Mr. Martin.

M: The pleasure is all mine. Please, call me Jeffrey.

W: All right, Jeffrey. It's really great to get the chance to work with someone so famous.

M: Thanks. I've heard a lot about you too, Amelia. You're a real __________ __________ __________ __________.

W: Well, thank you. It's taken a lot of hard work to get where I am.

M: I understand. Have you read any of my books?

W: I've read them all. They're amazing. I recommend them to everyone I meet.

M: __________ __________, but I couldn't have written any of them without my lovely wife, Lola. She inspired me and pushed me to write them. She also told me that I should __________ __________ __________.

W: That's where I come in, huh?

M: That's right. I'm excited to have such a talented and beautiful voice __________ __________ __________ __________ __________.

W: I'll try my best, Jeffrey.

06

W: Dad, would you look at this photo? This is the stage for the performance I'm working on for the school talent show.

M: Cool, __________ __________ __________ __________ __________. What is the calendar for? The one on the back wall.

W: It's to show the passing of time.

M: What about that __________ __________ __________ __________ __________?

W: Most of the characters will use the window to talk to people offstage.

M: Okay, that's a good idea. I really like the sofa and the coffee table on the right side of the stage.

W: Thanks. I really like the sofa as well.

M: I assume the actors will sit and talk there quite often?

W: Yes, exactly.

M: I see there's __________ __________ __________ __________ __________ __________ __________ of the stage. It balances the sofa, but it doesn't look very inviting.

W: That's what I was hoping for, Dad.

M: It looks like __________ __________ __________ __________ __________ __________ __________ __________. You did a good job.

W: I really appreciate that, Dad.

07

W: Peter, you're going to __________ __________ __________. Aren't you ready yet?

M: I'll be ready in a minute, Mom. I'm trying to __________ __________ __________ __________ for the field trip on Friday.

W: You gave it to me. Here you go.

M: This isn't the permission slip!

W: Well, I think I lost the original one, so __________ __________ __________ __________ __________.

M: I don't know if this will work, Mom.

W: It's okay. I'll give Mrs. Towns a call and explain.

M: Can you __________ __________ __________?

W: Okay. I'll call her now. You __________ __________ __________, though. Have a great day.

08

W: Where have you been, Alan?

M: I've been at the bookstore buying some books.

W: Is that all? Why do you look so happy?

M: Actually, I __________ __________ __________ __________ just a few minutes ago while I was on my back.

W: Oh? Who called?

M: You'd better sit down for this news. I __________ __________ __________ __________ __________ see the audition program *Rising Star K* live at the studio in Seoul.

W: Wow, I know you've really been wanting to see that. Congratulations!

M: Thanks, Beth. I applied to be a member of the studio audience about six months ago, but there was no response at all. I had almost given up, so I really wasn't __________ __________ __________ __________ __________.

W: That's amazing. I know how hard it is to get that chance. Some of my friends applied to do something like that __________ __________ __________ __________, but nobody ever got called back. You're so lucky. So when are you going?

M: Next Friday. God, this is so great. I still can't believe it!

W: I envy you so much.

09

M: Hey sweetheart, what movie did you choose?

W: It took me a while, but I finally decided on this one.

M: *Windsor's List*, huh? __________ __________ __________ __________ __________, but it's one of the greatest films of all time.

W: That's what I've heard. It was originally $30, but it's on sale for 50% off.

M: That's a great buy. What's that other movie you have?

W: Oh, this one? This is for Jake. It's called *The Light Crystal*. It's only $10.

M: I loved that movie when I was young. Oh, here's another version of it __________ __________ __________ __________ __________ __________.

W: That's cool. We should get that one. He really likes comics.

M: Yeah, but this one is __________ __________ __________ __________. It's $14.

W: That's still a great deal. Are you going to buy anything for yourself?

M: I can't find anything I want.

W: All right. Let's pay and go home.

10

W: Mr. Anderson, do you remember Randal Kim from the latest round of employee interviews?

M: Randal Kim? Ah, the one who __________ __________ __________?

W: Yes, that's the one. My initial impression of him was very strong.

M: What was the most impressive thing about him?

W: Besides his language skills, he was very confident in his ability to work as part of a team.

M: I agree with you there. When he was interviewed, he looked confident and __________ __________ __________ __________ __________ about contributing to the company.

W: One more thing that I liked about him was that he's done a lot of volunteer work for various organizations.

M: I saw that. He's done over 500 hours of volunteer work in Africa alone, __________ __________ __________ __________ __________ __________ __________ __________ __________. He says his motto is, "If it is to be, it is up to me."

W: I think he'll be a valuable addition to our team.

M: I think you're right.

11

W: Good afternoon, ladies and gentlemen. Today, I want to talk a bit about an extraordinary little animal called the tarsier. This little guy is found in the southern part of the Philippines archipelago, namely on the islands of Bohol and Mindanao. Tarsiers are very small mammals. A fully grown tarsier can fit in the palm of your hand. __________ __________ __________ __________ __________ __________ its huge eyes. These eyes are locked into position, but the tarsier can rotate its head 180 degrees in either direction. What's more is that their eyes __________ __________ __________ __________ __________ __________. When there is minimal light, their pupils will expand to almost the size of the entire eye, allowing it to __________ __________ __________ __________ __________ __________ __________ __________ __________ __________ as in broad daylight. Isn't that fascinating? To learn more about tarsiers, I suggest catching a flight to the Philippines to see them for yourselves.

12

M: Hey sweetheart, what are you doing on the Internet?

W: I'm looking at cribs for our baby. She'll be here really soon, you know.

M: That's right. We should start thinking about buying things for her room. Did you find anything good?

W: Well, I think we should buy one of these five. This company gets great reviews because __________ __________ __________-__________ __________.

M: Well, let me take a look. *[Pause]* I think we should __________ __________ __________ __________-__________ __________. That way we won't have to buy another one after she gets bigger.

W: Right. I think we should get one that includes a mattress as well. That way we won't have to buy one separately.

M: I agree.

W: What do you think about the material? Some of them are __________ __________ __________, and others are made of plastic.

M: I think we should get a wooden one. It'll look better in her room.

W: Okay, that narrows it down to these two. Which do you think is better?

M: We're __________ __________ __________ __________ __________, so let's go for the cheaper one.

W: Great. I'll go ahead and put in an order.

13

W: I can't believe we're finally here. I've been wanting to see some of Banksy's work for such a long time.

M: I can't believe he's __________ __________ __________ __________ in our city.

W: Let's go. I want to have plenty of time to look around before it closes.

M: We have to buy tickets first.

W: Okay. You know, $25 seems cheap for all the work he must've done.

M: Yeah, I'm sure __________ __________ __________ __________ __________.

W: Oh, look. There's a tour group that starts in a half hour. Should we wait and join that?

M: Well, if we join a group, we'll have to __________ __________ __________ __________. I'd rather take my time and enjoy the exhibition.

W: Really? I think it'd be interesting to learn more about the artist and his pieces.

M: Well, we can rent one of these __________ __________ __________. That seems interesting.

W: (That way we can choose to listen to the explanation or not.)

14

W: Hey, Mike. Are you busy? Do you have a couple of minutes?

M: I'm not too busy. What do you need?

W: Well, I've been trying to write this article for the school newspaper.

M: I always like reading your articles.

W: Yeah, I love writing. Anyway, I need someone to read over it and tell me what they think. I could use a bit of __________ __________.

M: But why would you want me to look over it?

W: Actually, I meant your sister. Didn't you say that she works for Kings and Queens Press?

M: She does, but she's __________ __________ __________ __________ __________ until next week.

W: Would it be possible for you to email it to her and __________ __________ __________ __________ __________ __________?

M: (No problem. I'll get in touch and see if she has time.)

15

W: Bill is a senior in high school and __________ __________ __________ __________ __________ __________ __________ his graduating class. He's very intelligent and has an outgoing personality. Because of his hard work and popularity, the school's principal, Mr. Thomas, asked Bill to speak during the graduation ceremony. Bill gladly __________ __________ __________ and has been working hard on his speech. While Bill is a great student and an all-around nice guy, __________ __________ __________ __________ __________. Before the ceremony, Mr. Thomas notices that Bill is very nervous and would like to give him some __________ __________ __________. In this situation, what would Mr. Thomas most likely say to Bill?

Mr. Thomas: Bill, (take a deep breath. You're going to do great.)

16-17

M: Are you tired of taking the same old boring vacation to the same old beach every year? Try something different this year. Take an exotic vacation to beautiful Phuket. Located in southern Thailand, Phuket is an island that __________ __________ __________ __________ as well as your budget. The island brings in __________ __________ __________ __________ __________ every year who take in the culture, the exquisite seafood, and the countless beach activities. With some of the whitest sand in the world, Phuket has amazing opportunities to scuba-dive and snorkel. The numerous festivals, such as the vegetarian festival, will __________ __________ __________ and open your mind. Try the famous dish called *sum tam*, which is a mixture of papaya, carrots, spices, and other delicacies. It's a flavor __________ __________ __________ __________. If you're a little more adventurous, take a trip to Phi Phi Island, which is known for its rich greenery and powdered beaches. You can visit the sets of movies filmed here, such as *Blue Lagoon* and *The Beach*. So, book your trip now and come on out to beautiful Phuket!

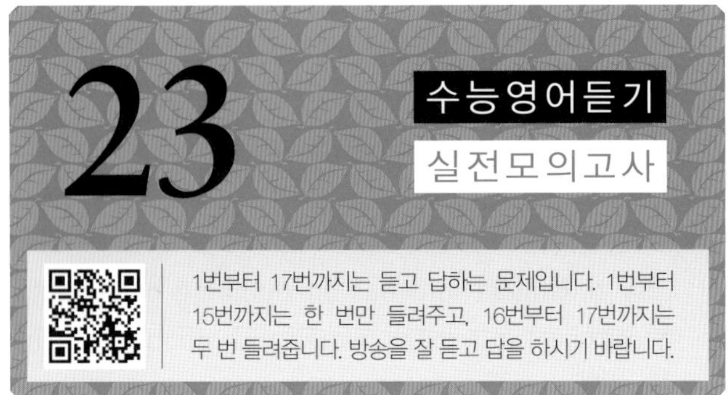

01

대화를 듣고, 여자의 마지막 말에 대한 남자의 응답으로 가장 적절한 것을 고르시오.

① Are you sure about that? Okay, let's find it together.
② I'm sorry. I lost your cell phone outside the house.
③ You don't have to feel guilty. It's all my fault.
④ Don't worry. You can look for it at school.
⑤ I don't remember when I had it last.

02

대화를 듣고, 남자의 마지막 말에 대한 여자의 응답으로 가장 적절한 것을 고르시오.

① No problem. I'm always happy to help.
② Of course. I'll make extra copies of the report.
③ I've finished the report and I'm printing it now.
④ I told you I needed reports on the new employees.
⑤ My mistake. I'll print the correct reports right now.

03

다음을 듣고, 남자가 하는 말의 목적으로 가장 적절한 것을 고르시오.

① 여름철을 건강하게 보내는 방법을 소개하려고
② 효율적인 에너지 종류에 대해 소개하려고
③ 지구 온난화의 심각성을 인식시키려고
④ 악천후에 대비하는 방법을 알려주려고
⑤ 전기 절약을 위한 방법을 알려주려고

04

대화를 듣고, 스페인어 교육에 관한 여자의 의견으로 가장 적절한 것을 고르시오.

① 모국어와 외국어의 습득방식은 다르다.
② 습득에 대한 동기가 가장 중요하다.
③ 듣기와 말하기로 시작해야 한다.
④ 발음은 어릴 때 습득해야 한다.
⑤ 다양한 책을 많이 읽혀야 한다.

05

대화를 듣고, 여자의 심정으로 가장 적절한 것을 고르시오.

① calm and graceful
② elated and energetic
③ nervous and anxious
④ proud and determined
⑤ envious and upset

06

다음을 듣고, 포스터에서 남자가 하는 말의 내용과 일치하지 않는 것을 고르시오.

07

대화를 듣고, 여자가 남자에게 부탁한 일을 고르시오.

① 가족 사진 찾아주기
② 참가 신청서 제출하기
③ 신청서 작성 도와주기
④ Katie를 학교에서 데려오기
⑤ 아시아 문화에 대해 알려주기

08

대화를 듣고, 남자가 버스 여행에 가지 못하는 이유를 고르시오.

① 일을 해야 해서
② 차멀미가 심해서
③ 표가 너무 비싸서
④ 날씨가 좋지 않아서
⑤ 버스를 예약하지 못해서

09

대화를 듣고, 여자가 남자에게 송금할 금액을 고르시오.

① $65 ② $80 ③ $85 ④ $105 ⑤ $165

10

대화를 듣고, 북극 대륙 빙하에 관해 두 사람이 언급하지 않은 것을 고르시오.

① 지구에서 빙하의 역할
② 해빙을 막기 위한 사람들의 노력
③ 해수면의 높이에 끼치는 영향
④ 빙하가 녹는 것을 막는 방법
⑤ 다른 의견을 가진 과학자들

11

Brittany Spikes에 관한 다음 내용을 듣고, 일치하지 않는 것을 고르시오.

① 전통적인 미국 가정에서 태어났다.
② 7살 때 노래와 춤을 훈련받기 시작했다.
③ 그녀는 Mickey Mouse Club에 처음 출연했다.
④ 20살에 Hollywood 영화감독과 결혼했다.
⑤ 지금은 가수 활동을 하지 않고 있다.

12

다음 표를 보면서 대화를 듣고, 두 사람이 예약할 숙소를 고르시오.

Guesthouses

	Name	Rate per Night	Location	Breakfast
①	Beach Guesthouse	$60	East Beach	X
②	East Guesthouse	$75	East Beach	O
③	Green Guesthouse	$55	Downtown Area	X
④	Rainbow Guesthouse	$65	Downtown Area	O
⑤	Seashore Guesthouse	$67	East Beach	O

13

대화를 듣고, 여자의 마지막 말에 대한 남자의 응답으로 가장 적절한 것을 고르시오.

Man: ______________________________

① You worked hard and you earned that degree.
② I need some advice on how to intern at a hospital.
③ He is one of the most popular doctors at the school.
③ My mother is working overseas, so she couldn't make it.
⑤ I'm truly grateful, and I owe you so much for all your help.

14

대화를 듣고, 남자의 마지막 말에 대한 여자의 응답으로 가장 적절한 것을 고르시오.

Woman: ______________________________

① Read this article. It's one of my favorites.
② That's fine. I can't wait to read your article.
③ I'm glad I've inspired you to become a writer.
④ I wish I could help you, but I'm not a journalist.
⑤ You really need to have it finished before tomorrow.

15

다음 상황 설명을 듣고, Craig이 Ms. Tate에게 할 말로 가장 적절한 것을 고르시오.

Craig: ______________________________

① Your tires are thin and should be replaced immediately.
② It's clear you don't take good care of your bicycle.
③ I'm going to make sure the brakes work properly.
④ It looks like you replaced your tires last year.
⑤ Your bike looks to be in great shape.

[16-17] 다음을 듣고, 물음에 답하시오.

16

여자가 하는 말의 주제로 가장 적절한 것은?

① How different sports strain feet
② The benefits of stretching before exercising
③ Why different sports require different styles of shoes
④ The importance of wearing shoes while playing sports
⑤ The advantages and disadvantages of high-top sneakers

17

언급된 운동이 아닌 것은?

① running ② tennis ③ soccer
④ badminton ⑤ basketball

01

W: Dad, where's my cell phone? I can't find it.

M: Didn't you ________ ________ ________ ________? Why don't you look in your backpack first?

W: I didn't take it to school today. It must be here somewhere.

M: (Are you sure about that? Okay, let's find it together.)

02

M: Ingrid, did you find those reports I wanted?

W: I did. I printed them out for you. Here you go.

M: Thanks. *[Pause]* Wait a second. I don't need ________ ________ ________ ________. I need the reports on the new employees.

W: (My mistake. I'll print the correct reports right now.)

03

M: Good afternoon, everyone. These days we're using too much coal, gas, and electricity ________ ________ ________ ________ ________ ________ ________. This summer, the most important issue is electricity. Because of global warming, summers are getting hotter and therefore we tend to use our air conditioners more often. However, this just adds to the problem. We need to seek out and practice ________ ________ ________ ________. If you're working in a place with abundant natural light, you should turn off the overhead lights. Also, wear short sleeves. Most businesses nowadays are adjusting their dress codes to ________ ________ ________ attire. Finally, instead of using the air conditioning, ________ ________ ________ windows to control the natural flow of air and use a fan if windows aren't available. Together we can make a difference in the environment and stay cool!

04

M: Ms. Hamilton, could you help me find a good Spanish book?

W: Sure. But why, Mr. Crowley? You're not a Spanish teacher.

M: My son Alfred has started to learn Spanish, and I'd like to help him study at home.

W: Okay. He is probably practicing his listening and speaking skills in class, right?

M: Yes, so I wanted to help him learn to read basic material in Spanish myself.

W: I think you should ________ ________ ________ ________ ________ ________ and speaking skills.

M: Really? But I thought reading was ________ ________ ________ ________ ________ ________ ________ ________.

W: Reading is important. But think about how your son learned to speak English. He started by listening and speaking.

M: You're right, but I think it's different now that he is older and ________ ________ ________ ________ ________.

W: Actually, you'll learn a second or even a third language faster if you study the same way you learned your native language.

M: I see. Thanks a lot for your advice. I'll give it some more thought.

05

M: Hey, Sandra. Are you getting ready for your business trip to New York tomorrow?

W: I'm ready to go, but ________, ________ ________ ________ ________ ________ ________ ________.

M: Really? I thought you were really excited to travel to a new city.

W: Yeah, of course I want to see New York. But I have a really important meeting and a presentation as soon as I get there.

M: You're going to do great. You're great with presentations.

W: I appreciate that. However, the clients are German so I need to do it in their language. I'm nervous that ________ ________ ________ ________ ________.

M: You'll be fine. They're aware that German isn't your first language, so even if you make a few mistakes it won't matter.

W: I understand that. I'm afraid because this is the most important presentation of my career. I need to do really well.

M: The most important thing is to relax. You're prepared for the meeting, so __________ __________ __________ __________ it for now and imagine you're headed to New York for a vacation.

W: Okay, I'll try. But it won't be easy.

06

M: Have you seen the new ad for the National Education Fund? The fund was created to give __________ __________ __________ __________ or children without families a way to pay for their education all the way through university. The title of the poster is *A Better Future for All*. In the center of the picture, there's a group of college graduates throwing their hats __________ __________ __________. On the bottom of the poster are three more pictures. On the left is a happy child coloring in a kindergarten class. In the middle is a group of girls eating together on a bench. And on the right there is a picture of two young professionals holding hands. __________ __________ __________ __________ __________ all the different types of people that can benefit from the National Education Fund.

07

M: Good morning, sweetheart. What are you up to?

W: I'm just __________ __________ __________ __________. It's for a homestay program at Katie's school.

M: A homestay program, huh? You mean like __________ __________ __________, right?

W: That's right. Katie's school is hosting several students from another country.

M: That sounds interesting. And you want to house one of the students here?

W: I'm hoping to. It'll be a great experience for Katie, and for us.

M: I agree. So, what country are these students from?

W: Two are from Korea, and one is from Taiwan. It'll be nice for Katie to __________ __________ __________ __________ __________ __________ Asian lifestyle and culture.

M: I'd like to learn more about their culture as well. What can I do to help?

W: Well, we're going to need a family photo to send out with the application. Can you find the photo we had taken for Christmas last year?

M: Sure. I think I know where it is.

W: Great. Thank you.

08

W: Hey Dylan, Lilly and I are __________ __________ __________ __________ __________ __________ __________ this weekend, and we were wondering if you wanted to join us.

M: That sounds great. I've been wanting to make it to the mountains this summer.

W: It's a long trip, though. __________ __________ __________ __________ __________?

M: I used to get sick on buses when I was young, but I'm fine now. How much are tickets?

W: Well, I got three tickets from a friend who had to change her plans, so you don't have to pay anything.

M: Awesome!

W: Yeah. And I was worried about the forecast, but it looks like the weather will be beautiful.

M: That's great. So, what time does the bus depart on Saturday?

W: Saturday? It's actually leaving on Friday at noon.

M: Really? Oh, no. I have to __________ __________ __________.

W: Oh, that's too bad. Lilly was really hoping you could come.

M: Well, maybe we can __________ __________ __________ __________ __________. Thanks for the invitation, though.

09

[Telephone rings.]

M: Hello, this is the ticket office.

W: Hi. I'm calling about buying a __________ __________ __________ __________ __________.

M: Sure. Are you interested in tickets for the LA Dodgers game or the Chicago Cubs one?

W: Both, actually. But how much are they?

M: The LA Dodgers tickets are $60 each, and the Chicago Cubs tickets are $80.

W: That's a bit pricier than I thought they would be. Are there any cheaper tickets?

M: I'm afraid not. These are the only tickets left for these games.

W: Fine, I'll just take one LA Dodgers ticket. I saw that you also sell the home team's banners. Do they come free with the tickets?

M: It's an extra $20 for the banner.

W: Okay, I guess I'll take the banner too. __________ __________ __________ __________ __________ __________?

M: Sorry, but shipping is an additional $5.

W: Okay. I'll transfer you the money as soon as I can.

10

W: Hey, Todd. Did you watch the documentary on the environment last night?

M: No, I missed it. What was the focus?

W: One of the main topics was the __________ __________ __________ __________ __________ __________.

M: Is it becoming a serious problem?

W: It is. You know, the ice caps act as a mirror which protects the Earth from overheating by reflecting the sun's rays.

M: Really? I didn't know that.

W: Yeah, most people don't. Since 2009, people have really __________ __________ __________ __________ __________ and trying to stop the melting.

M: That is really important, I suppose. Are they making progress?

W: Little by little, but they're still a long way off.

M: So, bigger problems may come from the melting?

W: Yes, exactly. It has a strong __________ __________ __________ __________ __________. Part of the problem is that it leads to __________ __________ __________ __________ __________ __________ of all the world's oceans, putting coastal cities around the world at risk of ending up underwater.

M: Oh, my. I've heard that most of the world's population lives on or near the coast.

W: Yes. However, some scientists believe the change is a part of a natural cycle. It's really hard to say who's right, but it's an important issue either way.

11

M: Good afternoon, everyone. I'd like to introduce one of the greatest performers of our time, Brittany Spikes. __________ __________ __________ to a traditional American family and named Bertha Beatrice. She started her vocal and dance training when she was seven. She first appeared on the Mickey Mouse Club, a children's talent show for up-and-coming young singers and dancers. She performed on the show until she was 16. During that time, she __________ __________ __________ __________ __________ for her flashy dance moves and winning smile. She married Hollywood movie director Albert Foster in May of 2001, when she was only 20 years old. Foster __________ __________ __________ __________ __________ the young performer and decided to get her into the music business. Today, Brittany __________ __________ __________ __________ and is delighting fans all around the world.

12

W: The school year is almost over. Amber's really excited about summer vacation.

M: I am too, actually. I think it would be nice to stay at a guesthouse nearby and just relax for a while.

W: That sounds wonderful.

M: Well, I've put together a list of guesthouses that I found on the Internet. How much do you think __________ __________ __________ __________ __________?

W: I think we should try to keep it under $70 a night if we can.

M: Okay, and among these locations, where would you most like to stay?

W: I'd like to __________ __________ __________ __________, if possible. It would be great if we could take our shoes off and walk around on a sandy beach.

M: All right. There are two guesthouses that seem to have everything we're looking for. Which one looks best to you?

W: Definitely the one that __________ __________. I don't want to do any cooking in the morning.

M: All right, great. I'll call them right now and make a reservation.

13

W: Congratulations __________ __________ __________, Dr. Nathan. I'm really proud of you.
M: I'm glad you could make it, Layla.
W: There's no way I'd miss my boyfriend's graduation.
M: I just really wish my mother could have been here, too.
W: It's too bad that she missed it.
M: At least all my friends from med school showed up.
W: __________ __________ __________ __________ meet them.
M: You know, Layla, I don't think I would be here if I hadn't met you.
W: Oh, come on! I didn't help you that much.
M: You really __________ __________ __________ __________ __________ __________.
W: Don't mention it, Nathan. It really wasn't that big of a deal.
M: (I'm truly grateful, and I owe you so much for all your help.)

14

W: Hey Ms. Collins, do you have a minute?
W: Sure, Aron. What do you need?
M: Well, you know that literary nonfiction project you assigned last week? Working on it __________ __________ __________. I think I want to be a journalist.
W: That's great. I've always loved reading your work.
M: Thanks. __________ __________ __________ __________ __________ or short stories, but I think writing nonfiction is interesting and fun. I'm having a problem in the nonfiction project, though.
W: Oh, what is that?
M: Well, I know that the article is only supposed to be 500 words, but I don't think I can shorten it that much.
W: So how many words have you written?
M: I've written almost 1,000 words. __________ __________ __________ __________?
W: (That's fine. I can't wait to read your article.)

15

M: Craig is a bicycle repairman. He is tuning up Ms. Tate's bike, which hasn't been tuned up in over a year and is not riding smoothly. He finds __________ __________ __________ __________ __________ __________ __________, pedals, and brakes. After he oils each of those parts, they operate more smoothly. He also discovers that the tread on the tires is worn quite thin, so the tires __________ __________ __________ __________. If Ms. Tate continues to ride on these tires, they __________ __________ __________ __________, which could cause an accident. Craig wants to __________ __________ __________ to Ms. Tate. In this situation, what would Craig most likely say to Ms. Tate?
Craig: (Your tires are thin and should be replaced immediately.)

16-17

W: Each day, you put a great deal of stress on your feet. It should come as no surprise that shoes are a very important factor in relieving some of this stress, especially for athletes. __________ __________ __________ can prevent serious injury while supporting your ankles and feet. Different sports will strain your feet in different ways. Therefore, you need to choose shoes that are sufficient to whatever activity you are participating in. For instance, if you are a long-distance runner, you need to choose shoes that cushion against the constant pounding while __________ __________ __________ __________ __________. On the other hand, tennis and badminton require a lot of movement from one side to the other. If you play these sports, you're going to want to look for shoes that support this kind of movement. In regards to basketball, you __________ __________ for jumping, running down the court, and reversing direction. That's why high-top shoes are necessary for basketball. As you can see, shoes vary a great deal from sport to sport. __________ __________ __________ __________ the next time you're shopping for athletic shoes.

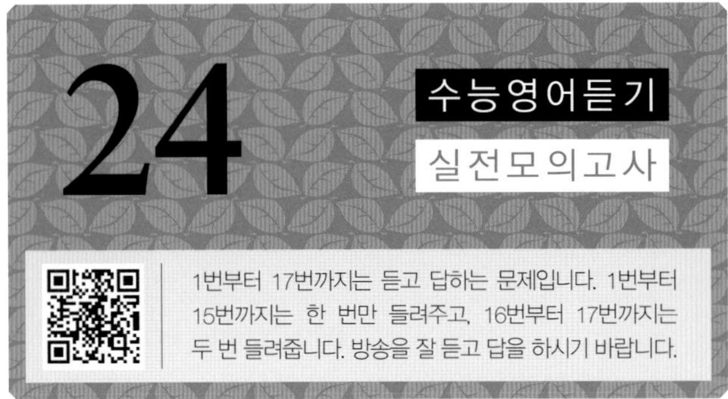

01

대화를 듣고, 남자의 마지막 말에 대한 여자의 응답으로 가장 적절한 것을 고르시오.

① It's a uPhone 6 with a black case.
② Well, I'm sure that I used it at work.
③ Don't worry. I'm sure you left it at home.
④ I thought so, too, but I already checked the bus.
⑤ I'll call your phone again to see if we can find it.

02

대화를 듣고, 여자의 마지막 말에 대한 남자의 응답으로 가장 적절한 것을 고르시오.

① I don't think so. It's not a useful example.
② If you say so, I'll use the same example.
③ I agree with you. This is a great report.
④ You're right. I'll correct it right now.
⑤ That's great. It really fits well here.

03

다음을 듣고, 여자가 하는 말의 목적으로 가장 적절한 것을 고르시오.

① 여름철 뱃놀이의 즐거움을 알려주려고
② 비상시 구명조끼의 사용법을 설명해 주려고
③ 배가 침몰할 때의 대처방법을 설명해 주려고
④ 안전한 뱃놀이를 위한 점검 항목들을 알려주려고
⑤ 여름철 물놀이 안전사고 예방교육에 대해 안내하려고

04

대화를 듣고, 남자의 의견으로 가장 적절한 것을 고르시오.

① 동물들은 훈련 받으면서 인간과 친밀해지고 교감하게 된다.
② 인간의 즐거움을 위해 동물을 훈련시키는 것은 옳지 않다.
③ 다치고 버려진 동물들에 대한 사람들의 배려가 필요하다.
④ 동물을 조련할 때 충분한 보상과 사랑을 주어야만 한다.
⑤ 동물 학대 및 유기에 대한 처벌을 보다 강화해야 한다.

05

대화를 듣고, 두 사람의 관계를 가장 잘 나타낸 것을 고르시오.

① 의사 — 간호사
② 경찰관 — 목격자
③ 영화 감독 — 배우
④ 구급 대원 — 신고자
⑤ 차량 정비사 — 고객

06

대화를 듣고, 그림에서 대화의 내용과 일치하지 <u>않는</u> 것을 고르시오.

07

대화를 듣고, 남자가 여자를 위해 할 일로 가장 적절한 것을 고르시오.

① 자동차 빌려주기
② 캠핑 같이 가주기
③ 세일 기간 알아봐주기
④ 상점까지 차로 태워다 주기
⑤ 캠핑용 휴대 스토브 골라 주기

08

대화를 듣고, 여자가 육상 경기에 나갈 수 <u>없는</u> 이유를 고르시오.

① 아버지가 다치셔서
② 넘어져 발을 다쳐서
③ 여동생을 돌봐야 해서
④ 부모님이 안 된다 하셔서
⑤ 할아버지 댁을 방문해야 해서

09

대화를 듣고, 남자가 지불할 금액을 고르시오.

① $30 ② $40 ③ $50 ④ $60 ⑤ $80

10

대화를 듣고, 봉사활동에 관해 두 사람이 언급하지 않은 것을 고르시오.

① 활동 내용 ② 봉사활동의 수혜자
③ 봉사 단체명 ④ 봉사해 온 기간
⑤ 봉사를 통해 얻는 이점

11

Artists in August 행사에 관한 다음 내용을 듣고, 일치하지 않는 것을 고르시오.

① 16년간 개최되었다.
② 지역 예술가를 홍보하는 행사이다.
③ 입장료는 무료이다.
④ 기부금을 받는다.
⑤ 사진 작품을 볼 수 있다.

12

다음 표를 보면서 대화를 듣고, 여자가 선택한 드럼 키트 모델을 고르시오.

River City Custom Drum Kits

	Model	Pieces	Custom Floor Tom	Price
①	A	3	X	$600
②	B	5	X	$660
③	C	5	O	$700
④	D	7	X	$760
⑤	E	7	O	$860

13

대화를 듣고, 여자의 마지막 말에 대한 남자의 응답으로 가장 적절한 것을 고르시오.

Man: ____________________

① You shouldn't leave work early to do yoga.
② Going to yoga every day must be pointless.
③ I really don't want to work overtime tonight.
④ I guess that's why you look so happy these days.
⑤ We should look for a place to practice yoga, then.

14

대화를 듣고, 남자의 마지막 말에 대한 여자의 응답으로 가장 적절한 것을 고르시오.

Woman: ____________________

① There's no need to worry. It won't rain that day.
② We really need to hurry. We have so much work.
③ We can finish the project before summer vacation.
④ Brilliant idea. I'm glad we're partners on this project.
⑤ Why would we do it in the gym? We can do it outside.

15

다음 상황 설명을 듣고, Pamela가 Malory에게 할 말로 가장 적절한 것을 고르시오.

Pamela: ____________________.

① Be careful when you talk to strangers on the phone.
② You should not play outside with your friends so often.
③ Finish your homework before you play computer games.
④ Being more active and outgoing can help you in your life.
⑤ Why don't you reduce the time you spend on the Internet?

[16-17] 다음을 듣고, 물음에 답하시오.

16

남자가 하는 말의 주제로 가장 적절한 것은?

① Tips for buying items for soccer
② Dangers of playing soccer at a park
③ Results of purchasing expensive items
④ The increasing popularity of the soccer camp
⑤ Various merits of playing soccer for teenagers

17

언급된 물건이 아닌 것은?

① 양말 ② 축구화 ③ 정강이 보호대
④ 반바지 ⑤ 축구공

01

M: Hey Lucy, I've been calling you for hours. We ______ ______ ______ ride the bus together.

W: Sorry about that. I lost my phone. I can't find it anywhere.

M: I've had that same problem before. Do you remember where you last had it?

W: (Well, I'm sure that I used it at work.)

02

W: I've finished going over your report, Edward.

M: How was it? Are there any problems with it, Ms. Jones?

W: There are no big mistakes. But it would be better to eliminate this example. ______ ______ ______ the topic.

M: (You're right. I'll correct it right now.)

03

W: Hello. My name is Jenny Brown, and I'm an officer of the Minnesota Department of Water Safety. Today, I would like to share a few tips that everyone should keep in mind to ensure a safe and clean summer on our lakes and rivers. While boating or sailing, there are a few essential items that ______ ______ ______ ______ ______ ______. For example, the number of life vests on the boat should ______ ______ ______ ______ ______ ______, and every vessel should be equipped with a working fire extinguisher, a horn or whistle, and a spotlight. In addition to having these things on board, you should always make sure that your vessel's lights ______ ______ ______ ______. Following these tips whenever you are on the water will make the lakes and rivers safer and more fun for everyone. If you would like to learn more about water safety, please visit our website at *www.MNwaterfun.gov.* Thank you for your time, and have a great summer.

04

W: I'm thinking about going to the circus this weekend. You should come with me. I love watching the bears and the elephants ______ ______.

M: Thanks for the offer. But I don't think what the circus does to those animals is ethical.

W: What do you mean? I think it's a way for people to admire the intelligence and work of animals.

M: I've been reading a lot about the abuse ______ ______ ______ ______ ______ ______ ______ ______. Some animals are trained by being punished.

W: That might be true, but I've also heard that the animals have close, loving relationships with their trainers.

M: Maybe, but they're also locked in small cages and ______ ______ ______ ______.

W: I see. Well, don't you think that circuses can be a good experience for the animals if the conditions are good?

M: I really don't think so. I think that it's terrible for the animals to be harmed in order to entertain others.

W: I understand. Maybe I should reconsider supporting the circus.

05

M: Hello. Are you the one who had the accident and was ______ ______ ______ ______?

W: Yes, that's me. I think it might be something serious. I can't seem to walk.

M: All right. Well, hold still and try not to move. What happened?

W: ______ ______ ______ ______ ______ on the sidewalk and hit me while I was walking.

M: That's terrible. Did you see what he looked like?

W: No, but I know he was wearing a helmet and a leather jacket.

M: Did you contact the police?

W: I didn't. I was in a daze.

M: I'll call them for you.

W: Thank you.

M: Anyway, I'm going to ________ ________ ________ ________ ________ to find out the extent of your injuries. First, I'm going to extend your leg like this. Does that hurt?

W: Ow! Yeah, it hurts.

M: Ma'am, I think you might have a broken leg. We're going to need to take you to the hospital to have it x-rayed.

06

W: Hey, Dad. Look at this poster I made for hallway safety at our school.

M: Looks pretty neat. What are those kids on the left doing?

W: They're playing with the sink, which is against the rules. Someone could slip in that puddle of water.

M: Who's the person wearing the sash?

W: That's the hallway monitor. They help ________ ________ ________, and students should always listen to them.

M: I see. Are those kids running in the hallway?

W: Yes, they are. I'm trying to show people ________ ________ ________ ________ ________ ________.

M: You're right. And it's also dangerous to leave doors open, huh?

W: Yeah. People can run into them and hurt themselves, so you should always keep them closed.

M: I like the round clock you put in the back. ________ ________ ________ ________.

W: Thanks, Dad. That's how all of the clocks in our school look.

M: Is it? Anyway, you did a great job.

07

W: Hey Charlie, it looks like Fat Panda Outfitters is having a big sale on outdoor gear.

M: I know. I stopped by there this morning and picked up a new pair of hiking boots. They have some great deals.

W: I'm going on a two-day hike next week, so I'm looking to ________ ________ ________ ________ ________.

M: You should get down there as soon as you can. There were a lot of people in the camping section.

W: I'll hurry, then. Oh, do you think I should buy a camp stove? It's my first hiking trip.

M: Well, you're probably going to need one to cook the food you bring. They're also ________ ________ ________ ________ and day trips to the mountains.

W: Okay. I guess I should buy one, then.

M: How are you going to get there? ________ ________ ________ ________ ________ ________.

W: That's a good point. I'm not sure.

M: I suppose I could ________ ________ ________ ________. Today's my day off, and I don't really have any plans for the rest of the day.

W: That'd be great. I really appreciate it. I'm a bit busy now, though. Can we go after about 20 minutes?

M: That's fine. Let me know when you're ready.

08

M: Hi, Laura. What can I do for you today?

W: Well, Mr. Baker, I wanted to tell you that I can't go to the track meet this weekend.

M: What do you mean you can't go? It's two days away. ________ ________ ________ ________ ________ now.

W: I'm really sorry. I know you need me, but my parents have to go to my grandparents' house this weekend. ________ ________ ________ ________ ________.

M: I see. Is everything all right?

W: My grandfather fell in the bathroom and broke his hip. He ________ ________, so he can't leave his house for a while.

M: That's terrible. I'm sorry to hear that. So you're going to your grandparents' house?

W: No. My parents are going alone. I need to ________ ________ ________ ________ ________ while they're away.

M: I understand. It's really a shame, but don't worry about it. We'll sure miss you. I hope your grandfather gets well soon.

W: Thanks, Mr. Baker.

09

[Telephone rings.]

W: Thank you for calling Beachwood Resort. May I help you?

M: Yes. I'd like to ________ ________ ________ ________ ________ a room. ________ ________ ________ ________ ________?

W: Well, it's $60 on the weekends and $40 during the week.

M: Then ________ ________ ________ ________ ________ ________ ________ next Saturday, please.

W: Sure. And what's your name, sir?

M: Dennis Reynolds. Oh, I'd also like to make a reservation for two in the restaurant for brunch.

W: Sure. That'll be an additional $10 per person.

M: That's fine. I also have a coupon here for 50% off. The coupon code is XT750.

W: Let me check on that for you. *[Keyboard typing sound]* I'm sorry, but that ________ ________ ________ to our rooms and not to the brunch.

M: That's fine. If I want to pay by card, should I give you the number now or can I wait until Saturday?

W: You can wait until Saturday if you'd like.

M: That's great. See you then.

10

W: Hey Louie, is now a good time for me to ask you some questions for that article I'm writing about your ________ ________ ________ ________?

M: Sure, Stacy. Ask away.

W: All right. What kind of things did you do as a volunteer?

M: Well, a lot of things. We helped ________ ________ ________ ________ ________, and I helped organize the staff.

W: I see. So how many houses did you help build?

M: We had a large team, so we were able to build 32 houses in two months.

W: That's great. Did the migrant workers move into the houses immediately?

M: Yes. They were ________ ________ ________ ________ ________, so they were quite excited to move into their new homes.

W: I bet they were. How long have you been doing this?

M: I've been working for this volunteer program since I was a freshman.

W: Really? So that's three years. Okay, one more question. What kind of benefits do you get from volunteering?

M: There are a lot of benefits, but most of all, I just like the feeling I get from helping others.

W: That's great. Thanks for your time, Louie.

11

M: Good afternoon, and welcome to our art gallery. I'm here to announce an upcoming event that I'm sure you'll be excited about. We here at the gallery would like to invite all of you to our annual Artists in August event. We have been holding this event ________ ________ ________ ________ ________ ________ ________. We do it to ________ ________ ________ and display their work in the gallery. Our city's artists are important to our community because they help beautify our parks and businesses as well as encourage creativity. Artists in August starts on August 17th this year and runs through the end of the month. ________ ________ ________ ________ is free. However, we recommend you ________ ________ ________ ________ to our foundation, which supports the local arts program. Please join us this year to see some of the area's finest paintings, drawings, and sculptures. Thank you for your time.

12

M: Good afternoon, ma'am. What can we do for you today?

W: I'm looking for a drum kit for my son's birthday. He wants to start a rock 'n' roll band.

M: All right. Well, we have five kits to choose from.

W: I'm not sure what's ________ ________ ________ ________ him. I was hoping you could help me with that.

M: Well, if he's going to be playing rock music, a three-piece kit won't be enough. You're going to want to look at the five- or seven-piece kits.

W: I see. He said something about wanting a kit that can ________ ________ ________ ________ ________.

M: Then he'll want a floor tom. We ________ ________ ________ ________. You're going to want to choose between these two sets.

W: All right. Hmm… I don't want to spend more than $800, so I think this one will have to do.

M: Okay. I'll get it ready for you to take home.

W: Thanks.

13

M: Did you get a new boyfriend or something, Heather?

W: Haha! No. What makes you say that?

M: It just seems that you're much happier and full of energy these days.

W: Really? Well, I have felt really good lately, but __________ __________ __________ __________ __________ __________ __________.

M: Has anything else changed, then?

W: I __________ __________ __________ recently. I've been going every night after work.

M: How long have you been practicing yoga?

W: Only about three months.

M: And it's not hard for you? I can't even touch my toes.

W: I had a hard time when I first started, but after a couple of weeks __________ __________ __________ __________ __________ __________ __________.

M: I heard that yoga also improves your cortisol levels, making it easier for you to __________ __________ __________.

W: I heard that, too. Anyway, I really love doing yoga every day. It gives me something to look forward to after work.

M: (I guess that's why you look so happy these days.)

14

W: __________ __________ __________ __________ __________ summer vacation. What about you, Henry?

M: I'm really looking forward to it. But I'm a bit concerned we won't be able to finish our science project by then.

W: Relax. We don't have too much left to do.

M: I guess you're right. Hey, have you checked the weather for this week?

W: Yeah, it's supposed to be rainy and windy all week.

M: Really? Then how will we finish our project? We need to do our experiments outside.

W: You're right! Well, it looks like there's only a 50% chance of rain on Wednesday.

M: Well, we should __________ __________ __________ __________ that it won't rain on Wednesday. But we __________ __________ __________ __________ __________ just in case.

W: Yeah. Do you have anything in mind?

M: We can probably use the gymnasium to do our experiments. Let's ask Mrs. Jones if that'll be okay.

W: (Brilliant idea. I'm glad we're partners on this project.)

15

W: Pamela went up to the school last night for parent-teacher conferences and met with her daughter's teacher. She was __________ __________ __________ __________ when the teacher told her that her daughter, Malory, is very shy and sensitive. The teacher said that Malory is a quiet child, who rarely runs at recess; she usually walks. Malory's teacher encouraged Pamela to try a few things to __________ __________ __________ __________ __________ __________ __________ and energetic. She also recommended some websites with suggestions for increasing children's activity levels. Pamela thanked the teacher for her advice and went straight home to __________ __________ __________ __________.
Tonight, when Pamela was busy making dinner, the phone rang. She asked Malory to answer the call. Malory refused to answer the phone because she was so shy. Worrying that her daughter might miss something important one day, she has decided to give some advice to her daughter. What would Pamela most likely say to Malory in this situation?

Pamela: (Being more active and outgoing can help you in your life.)

16-17

M: Good afternoon, team. Today, we're going to talk about equipment. When you go into a sporting goods store, you might __________ __________ __________ the massive amount of soccer equipment you can purchase. Everyone always asks me if they should purchase the most expensive goods. My answer is usually no. For example, there's no need to spend the extra money to buy those special space-age socks when the normal cheap ones work just as well. The most important items are, of course, the basic ones. You're going to need a pair of decent cleats, shin guards, socks, and a soccer ball. I believe that the most important item is a nice pair of cleats. You're going to want to make sure that they fit well and are durable enough to hold up for a long time. Another important item is your shin guards, as they are needed to __________ __________ __________ __________ __________. Remember, while the expensive items might look flashy and impress others, they're not really necessary for the game. I hope you have a great time at training camp.

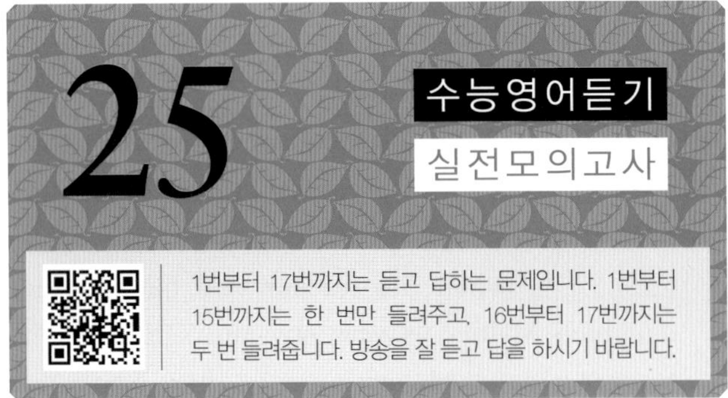

01

대화를 듣고, 여자의 마지막 말에 대한 남자의 응답으로 가장 적절한 것을 고르시오.

① I don't want to make a reservation just yet.
② Both of my kids have birthdays this month.
③ I hope to get a discount on the Disney tickets.
④ I've been meaning to talk to her about vacation.
⑤ Typically, we just go to the cabin and go fishing.

02

대화를 듣고, 남자의 마지막 말에 대한 여자의 응답으로 가장 적절한 것을 고르시오.

① About two kilometers away
② By taking the subway
③ Almost $100 each
④ About 15 minutes
⑤ Until about 9:30

03

다음을 듣고, 남자가 하는 말의 주제로 가장 적절한 것을 고르시오.

① 블로그 활성화를 위한 팁
② 블로그의 주제 선정 방법
③ 블로그 운영의 장점과 단점
④ 현대사회에서 블로그의 역할
⑤ 블로그를 통한 인간관계 형성법

04

대화를 듣고, 오락시설에 관한 여자의 의견으로 가장 적절한 것을 고르시오.

① 주말에는 예약 시스템의 운영을 중지해야 한다.
② 직원들은 고객 응대에 대한 교육을 받아야 한다.
③ 생일 파티 하는 팀들은 빨리 파티만 하고 나와야 한다.
④ 생일 파티 룸의 청결 상태 유지에 더 힘써야 한다.
⑤ 인원수에 따라 사용 시간을 다르게 줘야 한다.

05

대화를 듣고, 두 사람의 관계를 가장 잘 나타낸 것을 고르시오.

① 작가 — 리포터
② 기자 — 소설가
③ 감독 — 조명감독
④ 매니저 — 코디네이터
⑤ 배우 — 의상 디자이너

06

대화를 듣고, 그림에서 대화의 내용과 일치하지 않는 것을 고르시오.

07

대화를 듣고, 남자가 할 일로 가장 적절한 것을 고르시오.

① 도구 찾아오기
② 쓰레기 버려주기
③ 싱크대 청소하기
④ 고장 난 수도 고치기
⑤ 수돗물 필터 가져오기

08

대화를 듣고, 남자가 육상경기대회에 나가지 못하는 이유를 고르시오.

① 부상이 낫지 않아서
② 등록을 하지 못해서
③ 중간고사 기간과 겹쳐서
④ 부상 때문에 연습을 못해서
⑤ 인턴십 프로그램에 가입해서

09

대화를 듣고, 여자가 지불할 금액을 고르시오.

① $32 ② $40 ③ $48 ④ $52 ⑤ $54

10

대화를 듣고, 두 사람이 말하는 집에 관해 언급되지 않은 것을 고르시오.

① 침실과 화장실 개수 ② 인근 학교 유무
③ 대중교통 ④ 건축연도
⑤ 차고 유무

11

파쇄에 관한 다음 내용을 듣고, 일치하지 않는 것을 고르시오.

① 천연가스를 돌에서 추출하는 방법이다.
② 돌을 뭉쳐서 크게 만드는 방식을 이용한다.
③ 굉장히 쉽고 효율적인 방법이다.
④ 환경에 좋지 않은 영향을 끼친다.
⑤ 지진 활동의 원인으로도 의심된다.

12

다음 표를 보면서 대화를 듣고, 남자가 선택한 의사를 고르시오.

Find a Doctor

	Doctor	Specialty	Years of Experience	Clinic Location
①	Dr. Ryan Kebb	Allergies	12 Years	Henderson County
②	Dr. Jason Fecc	Eyes	12 Years	Union County
③	Dr. Maro Kim	Allergies	15 Years	Union County
④	Dr. Jeremy Paik	Eyes	15 Years	Henderson County
⑤	Dr. Sarah Tortclud	Allergies	10 Years	Henderson County

13

대화를 듣고, 남자의 마지막 말에 대한 여자의 응답으로 가장 적절한 것을 고르시오.

Woman: ______________________________

① Not everyone can get into the publishing class.
② Me, too. I'd like to photograph all of the students.
③ I'm sure he'd allow you have a pet in class if you ask.
④ You're right. It took them most of the semester to finish it.
⑤ Yes. Students can also bring in their pets to show the class.

14

대화를 듣고, 여자의 마지막 말에 대한 남자의 응답으로 가장 적절한 것을 고르시오.

Man: ______________________________

① Nothing in particular. I'm just being lazy.
② It's okay. I can help you study for your test.
③ How is everything going with your friends?
④ I agree. Social science is my favorite subject.
⑤ Okay, I'll do my best to improve the situation.

15

다음 상황 설명을 듣고, Betty가 John에게 할 말로 가장 적절한 것을 고르시오.

Betty: ______________________________

① Did you know that I can fix your old phone?
② I heard a nearby church has a lot of used phones.
③ You should've gotten a new phone a long time ago.
④ Why don't you give me the phone, and I'll donate it?
⑤ Can you do me a favor and throw away that old phone?

[16-17] 다음을 듣고, 물음에 답하시오.

16

Arts Center Benefit의 목적으로 가장 적절한 것은?

① to raise money to benefit the Arts Center
② to seek artist donations for the Arts Center auction
③ to exhibit the artwork of students at Franklin College
④ to seek support for the construction of a new Arts Center
⑤ to provide free campus tours to members of the art community

17

계획 중인 행사로 언급되지 않은 것은?

① 사진 전시회 ② 작품 경매 ③ 재즈 밴드 공연
④ 유명인사 초대 ⑤ 많은 먹거리

01

W: ________ ________ ________ ________ with the service at Hotel Disney.

M: I was actually considering taking my kids there this weekend. Do you have the number for their reservation line?

W: I sure do. Is there any special reason you're going?

M: (Both of my kids have birthdays this month.)

02

M: Oh! We're never going to ________ ________ ________ ________ ________ ________ ________.

W: I'm sorry, but I didn't think traffic would be this bad at this time of night.

M: Yeah, downtown is always bad on Friday nights. How much time before it starts?

W: (About 15 minutes)

03

M: Technology moves fast these days, and one of the fastest-growing advances is in blogging. Blogging is a great way to tell others about your life and your interests. It's also a lot of fun. However, there are several things you should remember if you want your blog ________ ________ ________ ________ the millions of others. First, you should make it look interesting. Choose an ________ ________ ________ ________ ________ for your blog. Second, keep it focused on one topic. Too many different topics are distracting and will cause you to lose readers. Finally, it's important to interact with your audience. You should ________ ________ ________ ________ ________ ________ ________ left by readers. If you keep these tips in mind, I'm sure you'll attract more visitors to your blog.

04

M: Hey, Cindy. Did your son have a good time at his birthday party last Saturday?

W: No, it was awful. I'm so upset with the staff at the entertainment center.

M: Oh my! What happened?

W: When we arrived, they told us we had to wait for 30 minutes—even though I ________ ________ ________!

M: Well, I'm sure they're very busy during the summer months.

W: That makes sense. But then once we were seated, they told us ________ ________ ________ ________-________ ________ ________!

M: Really? And two hours wasn't long enough for you?

W: No, it certainly wasn't. We had 15 kids to order for and get served so that they could eat. We also wanted them to have a chance to play games before we had cake and opened presents.

M: Well, they're probably trying to ________ ________ ________ ________ ________ ________.

W: Fine. But the time limit should be ________ ________ ________ ________ ________ ________ ________ ________.

M: So, did you talk to the management?

W: I did, but all they said was that it was company policy so there was nothing they could do. How rude!

05

M: Hey, Marie. I didn't think ________ ________ ________ ________ ________ ________.

W: Hey, Paul. I just had a quick talk with the director.

M: Oh. Are you ________ ________ ________ ________ again?

W: Yeah. Things didn't work out in Los Angeles.

M: I see. Have you ever done any modern work?

W: No. I've only done classics. So you're in *The Shape of Things*? What part are you playing?

M: I've ________ ________ ________ of Adam.

W: Wow, a leading role. That's pretty exciting. Congratulations.

M: Thanks, but it's pretty difficult to get everything just right.

W: I understand. I'm a bit nervous about my work, too. I know a lot about Shakespearean costumes, but not so much about modern fashion.

M: Well, you can watch the movie. I'm sure you can get some helpful tips from it.

W: You're right. I'm going to try to stay as __________ __________ __________ __________ __________ as I can. I'll work on them this weekend. Anyway, I should be going. See you at dress rehearsal.

M: Bye, Marie.

06

M: Hey Laura, what's that you're looking at on your phone?

W: It's a photo my grandfather took during summer vacation last year.

M: That's cool. Let me see.

W: Sure. Here you go.

M: You guys went camping, huh? I love the mountains and the clouds. It looks so peaceful and relaxing.

W: Yeah. We rented an RV and took it to Walker Mountain.

M: I see. Is that you there in the back?

W: Yeah. __________ __________ __________ __________ __________ __________ __________ __________, so I was watching music videos.

M: Who's that in the RV?

W: That's my uncle. He's reading a book.

M: What about the woman in front of the car?

W: That's my mother. She was running from a spider that she saw.

M: And those kids playing with the dog? Who are they?

W: Those are my cousins. They brought their dog along on the trip.

M: So I'm guessing the man __________ __________ __________ __________ __________ __________ RV is your father.

W: That's right. He wanted to go to the mountain to relax, but I think the rest of us __________ __________ __________.

07

W: Our tap water is starting to __________ __________ __________ __________, don't you think?

M: I guess so. It's probably about time to change the filter.

W: Do we have any other filters?

M: I'm pretty sure we do. It seems like I bought some __________ __________ __________ __________ __________.

W: Well, I guess we can change it anytime, then.

M: We might as well do it right now.

W: All right. I'll go get a filter.

M: I'll go get it. I don't think you'll be able to find it.

W: __________ __________ __________ __________ __________ __________.

M: I don't think I'll need them.

W: Okay. I guess __________ __________ __________ __________ __________.

M: Great. I'll be right back.

08

W: Hey Stan, how's your shoulder doing?

M: It's feeling a lot better, thanks.

W: Great! So __________ __________ __________ __________ __________ again?

M: Yeah. I practiced a bit yesterday. I'm almost as good as I was before the injury.

W: Nice. I'm really looking forward to seeing you compete in the track meet this weekend.

M: Unfortunately, I'm not going to be able to.

W: Why not? Is it because you couldn't practice __________ __________ __________ __________ __________?

M: No. Actually, I forgot to sign up for this weekend's meet.

W: Oh, no! I guess you were busy and __________ __________ __________ __________.

M: That's right. I was stressed about midterm exams and forgot all about it.

W: __________ __________ __________. I missed registration for the summer internship program. The deadline was last week.

M: Sorry to hear that. Maybe we should buy planners so we can be more organized.

09

M: Good afternoon, miss. What can I do for you today?

W: Hello. __________ __________ __________ __________ __________ sweets for a company picnic tomorrow afternoon. How much are the cookies?

M: They're $2 apiece, but everything in the store is 20% off right now because we're about to close.

W: That's great. I'll take 20 cookies, then. Also, do you have any pies left?

M: Sure. We __________ __________ __________ __________ __________ __________ this afternoon. They'll be perfect for your picnic.

W: How much __________ __________ __________ __________?

M: They're $10 each.

W: Great. I'll take two of them.

M: Is there anything else I can get for you?

W: I think that's it. I also have this coupon for 10% off that I'd like to use.

M: I'm sorry, but we can't accept any coupons on discounted items.

W: That makes sense. I'll __________ __________ __________ __________ __________, then.

M: All right. So, you're going to take 20 cookies and two chess pies at a 20% discount, right?

W: That's right. Here's my card.

10

W: This is a recent photo of the home you asked me about, Mr. Anderson.

M: Nice. I really like the big backyard.

W: Yes, it's really pretty. The house also has three bedrooms and three bathrooms, and a beautiful garden out front.

M: Where is it located? Is it in a nice area?

W: It is. The neighborhood is very clean and safe. __________ __________ __________ __________, __________.

M: I have two sons in middle school, so I'm glad to hear it's a good neighborhood. Are the schools nearby?

W: Yes. They're a short five-minute drive away. The house is on the school's bus route, as well.

M: That's wonderful. What about city buses or subways? __________ __________ __________ __________ __________ __________ __________?

W: Sure. The subway is about ten minutes away on foot.

M: Does the house have a garage? One car or two?

W: The house does __________ __________ __________ __________-__________ __________.

M: Great. Can we go take a look at the house now?

W: That shouldn't be a problem. Let me call the owner first __________ __________ __________.

11

W: One more thing, students. Before you leave, I'd like to talk to you for a moment about hydraulic fracking, or just 'fracking' for short. Fracking is a method for __________ __________ __________ __________ __________ using chemicals that break up rock that contains natural gas. The fracking method is very easy and quite __________-__________. However, there are certain environmental impacts associated with the process. For instance, fracking __________ __________ into the groundwater, which can __________ __________ __________ __________ __________. Fracking is also suspected of leading to seismic activity, such as earthquakes and tremors. We'll discuss fracking and its implications more in the next class.

12

M: My eyes are so itchy today. I guess __________ __________ __________ __________ __________ __________ again.

W: Yeah, __________ __________ __________ __________ in the spring, too. Why don't you see your allergist?

M: Well, I don't really have an allergist. Should I get one?

W: __________ __________ __________ __________ __________. Let's do a quick online search to find the right one for you. You don't need an eye doctor, right?

M: Yeah. My problem is with my allergies, so I don't think an eye doctor can help.

W: All right. This one has the most experience as an allergist. Why don't you call and __________ __________ __________ __________?

M: Okay. Wait a second! That doctor is all the way in Union County! It'll take me 45 minutes to get there.

W: I guess you're right. We should narrow our search to doctors in Henderson County. I guess these are the only two left.

M: All right. I'll go for the one that has more experience.

W: That'd be this one. I'll give you the phone number so you can make an appointment.

M: Great. Thanks for all of your help.

13

M: Hi, Chloe. What's that you're looking at?

W: Oh, hey Greg. It's __________ __________ __________ __________ __________ __________ __________ in our school.

M: A directory of animals? What for?

W: Well, our school actually has a lot of class pets. This shows all of the pets and what classrooms they're located in. Check it out.

M: That's cool. I didn't know the school had many pets. Who put this directory together?

W: Mr. Scott's publishing class assembled it, designed it, and printed it. Pretty neat, huh?

M: Yeah. So they did all of the work? Did they take the pictures of the pets, too?

W: Of course. They used Bailey's cell phone. The pictures ________ ________ ________ ________, huh?

M: Yes, they did. Wow, the sixth grade science teacher has a snake in his classroom? I had no idea.

W: ________ ________ ________ ________ ________, too. And did you know that Mr. Smith has a pet iguana?

M: Really? That's so cool. Anyway, it seems like the publishing class worked really hard on this pamphlet.

W: (You're right. It took them most of the semester to finish it.)

14

M: Hi, Ms. Diaz. I was told you wanted to see me?

W: Yes, Tom, I did. Why don't you have a seat?

M: Sure. *[Pause]* What did you want to see me about? Is everything all right?

W: Well, I'm becoming more and more ________ ________ ________ ________ in history. *[Mouse clicking sound]* Take a look at your most recent exam scores.

M: Hmm... Yeah, they don't look very good.

W: Right. But as you can see, your scores were going up until March. And then from there, ________ ________ ________ ________.

M: Yeah, I can see that.

W: Why do you think this is? Is everything all right at home?

M: *[Pause]* Well, to tell you the truth, I'm having some trouble with my friends and I haven't really ________ ________ ________ ________.

W: Well, Tom, you should work on figuring things out with your friends because I expect better scores ________ ________ ________ ________.

M: (Okay, I'll do my best to improve the situation.)

15

W: Betty goes to her friend John's house. While they're sitting in the living room having tea, Betty notices he has a new smartphone in his hand and an older one on the coffee table. He says he got the new smartphone because his old one wasn't very fast and didn't have enough memory. He says he's going to ________ ________ ________ ________ ________ ________ ________. Betty ________ ________ ________ ________ and that John just wanted a new phone. Either way, she doesn't think he should just throw it away. Betty ________ ________ ________ ________ ________ a local church that ________ ________ ________ ________ ________ ________ to give to people who need them but can't afford them. She wants to tell John that he should give the phone to charity. What would Betty most likely say to John in this situation?

Betty: (Why don't you give me the phone, and I'll donate it?)

16-17

M: Good afternoon students, parents, and fellow staff members. I'd like to ________ ________ ________ ________ ________ an incredible evening on our campus. The Tenth Annual Franklin College Arts Center Benefit will be held on the campus fairgrounds on Saturday, August 15th. As always, the purpose of the benefit will be to raise the funds needed to support the Arts Center and create new programs that benefit our students as well as our community. As you all know, ________ ________ ________ ________ ________ ________. It brings us together and ________ ________ ________ ________ ________ ________ unimaginable ways. The benefit allows the community to give back to our program. Every penny raised will benefit the FC Arts Center fund. There are many different events being planned. As usual, we'll have our photography exhibition, an auction of some of our prized artwork, live performances by our talented campus jazz band, and, of course, lots of food. If you'd like to reserve tickets for our event, or if you can't make it and would like to donate money to our cause, visit our campus website and ________ ________ ________ ________ ________ ________. Thanks for listening.

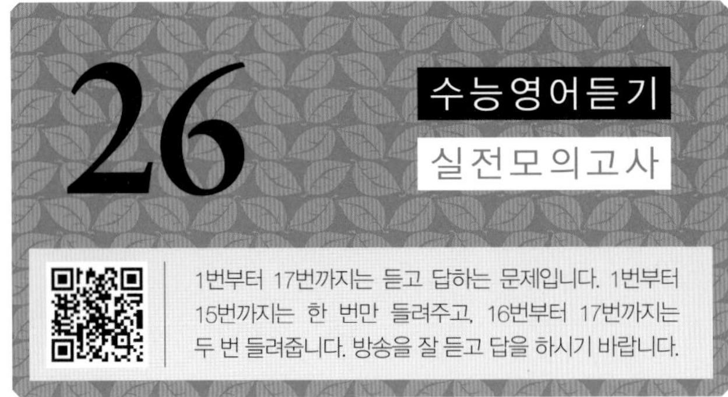

01

대화를 듣고, 남자의 마지막 말에 대한 여자의 응답으로 가장 적절한 것을 고르시오.

① I think I'm going to sell the tickets.
② That's too bad. We'll try later today.
③ I can't remember where I left the tickets.
④ Don't worry. I already bought the tickets.
⑤ I'm really sorry. I'll get tickets for tomorrow.

02

대화를 듣고, 여자의 마지막 말에 대한 남자의 응답으로 가장 적절한 것을 고르시오.

① I wish we had spent more time in the museum.
② I've had a great time, but I sure am getting tired.
③ The park closes at sunset, so you can take your time.
④ This is the first stop on the tour, so you should hurry.
⑤ I'm sorry, but we can't. The butterfly garden is closed.

03

다음을 듣고, 남자가 하는 말의 목적으로 가장 적절한 것을 고르시오.

① 자원봉사 단체의 활동을 홍보하려고
② 오늘의 토크쇼 초대 손님을 소개하려고
③ 올해의 인물 선정 행사에 표를 모으려고
④ 행사지원을 위한 자원봉사자를 모집하려고
⑤ 올해의 인물에 대한 조사 결과를 발표하려고

04

대화를 듣고, 두 사람이 하는 말의 주제로 가장 적절한 것을 고르시오.

① 자가용 통근의 주의점
② 걷기 운동의 긍정적 효과
③ 버스 안에서의 예절 지키기
④ 버스로 통학하는 것의 장점
⑤ 버스가 지하철보다 좋은 이유

05

대화를 듣고, 두 사람의 관계를 가장 잘 나타낸 것을 고르시오.

① 학생 — 지도교사
② 면접관 — 신입사원
③ 학부모 — 교장 선생님
④ 취업상담원 — 구직자
⑤ 컴퓨터 프로그래머 — 고객

06

대화를 듣고, 그림에서 여자가 산 시계를 고르시오.

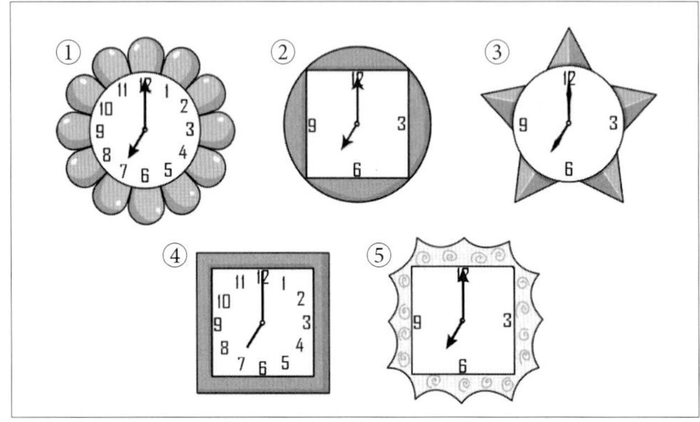

07

대화를 듣고, 남자가 할 일로 가장 적절한 것을 고르시오.

① 길 안내하기
② 책 주문하기
③ 책 가져다 주기
④ 컴퓨터로 책 찾아보기
⑤ 회원 카드 발급해 주기

08

대화를 듣고, 남자가 경기에 참가할 수 <u>없는</u> 이유를 고르시오.

① 연습량이 부족해서
② 병원에 입원해야 해서
③ 다른 팀으로 이적해서
④ 팀원과 심하게 다퉈서
⑤ 경기 중에 부상 당해서

09

대화를 듣고, 여자가 지불할 금액을 고르시오.

① $10 ② $15 ③ $20 ④ $24 ⑤ $30

10

대화를 듣고, 자선행사에 관해 두 사람이 언급하지 않은 것을 고르시오.

① 날짜 ② 슬로건 ③ 참가 방법
④ 장소 ⑤ 간식 제공 여부

11

Cherry Blossom Festival에 관한 다음 내용을 듣고, 일치하지 않는 것을 고르시오.

① 올해 네 번째로 열리는 축제이다.
② 축제는 매년 봄 같은 날짜에 열린다.
③ 아이들이 할 만한 활동도 계획되어 있다.
④ 주차를 하게 되면 입장료는 15달러이다.
⑤ 걸어서 입장하면 5달러만 내면 된다.

12

다음 표를 보면서 대화를 듣고, 여자가 구매할 중고 오토바이를 고르시오.

2016 Aladdin Used Motorcycle Sales

	Model	Year	Engine	Price
①	S-35	2007	300cc	$3,800
②	S-35	2009	400cc	$4,800
③	K-350	2005	250cc	$2,500
④	K-350	2008	350cc	$4,200
⑤	K-350	2010	350cc	$7,200

13

대화를 듣고, 여자의 마지막 말에 대한 남자의 응답으로 가장 적절한 것을 고르시오.

Man: ______________________

① I'm going to need a ride from the bus station.
② Well, we'll postpone dinner until you get here.
③ I think you should buy tickets for the earlier bus.
④ Great. I should be at the station at around 7 o'clock.
⑤ No problem. I'll book you a ticket on the earlier bus.

14

대화를 듣고, 남자의 마지막 말에 대한 여자의 응답으로 가장 적절한 것을 고르시오.

Woman: ______________________

① Sure. The doorman will be there to help soon.
② That's no problem. You don't have to change rooms.
③ You can take care of the additional fee at checkout, sir.
④ I'll be sure to turn off the light outside your window, sir.
⑤ Of course. The front desk will give you a wake-up call at 7 a.m.

15

다음 상황 설명을 듣고, Leah가 Brody에게 할 말로 가장 적절한 것을 고르시오.

Leah: ______________________

① You should explain the storyline in more detail.
② You should beta test the game more before you present.
③ It's important to consult your programming team every day.
④ You could benefit by having someone else present the game.
⑤ It's important to provide more visual examples in the presentation.

[16-17] 다음을 듣고, 물음에 답하시오.

16

남자가 하는 말의 주제로 가장 적절한 것은?

① Mental and physical benefits of outdoor activities
② Tips on being safe and having fun while camping
③ What to bring on your family camping trip
④ Dangers of getting lost while camping
⑤ How to give first aid while camping

17

남자가 언급하지 않은 것은?

① 여분의 옷 ② 충분한 음식 ③ 구급상자
④ 청소 ⑤ 랜턴

01

M: Honey, did you reserve tickets for today's baseball game?

W: Oh, that's right. I forgot. I'll do it now online.

M: I think it's too late. I saw online that ________ ________ ________ ________. You should have bought them sooner.

W: (I'm really sorry. I'll get tickets for tomorrow.)

02

W: This must be the butterfly garden I read about in the brochure.

M: That's right. It's also the end of our tour. ________ ________ ________ ________ ________, Mrs. Conn.

W: I did. Everything was beautiful. How long can I stay in the garden?

M: (The park closes at sunset, so you can take your time.)

03

M: Hi, everyone. I'm Michael Johnson. Thank you for joining us this morning for our program, "Student Volunteers." I'm sure all of you have taken, or at least know of, the survey ________ ________ ________ ________ ________ ________ ________ find out who is the most respected person in our country from the viewpoint of college students. Almost every year, the person chosen has been someone in a position of power, such as a successful entrepreneur or politician. But this year was quite different. College students voted for Amelia Henderson, someone who has been helping the less fortunate for many years. She has helped those in poor communities develop skills so they can find decent jobs. Her generosity and ambition has ________ ________ ________ ________ ________ ________ ________ ________. At this time, I would like to introduce Ms. Henderson, who we've invited here to speak with you all. She will share with us today why it's so important ________ ________ ________ ________ ________. Good morning, Ms. Henderson. Let me begin by saying ________ ________ ________ ________ to have you with us today.

04

M: Hey, Rachel.

W: Good morning, Mr. Turner. Do you always take the bus to school in the morning?

M: Not every morning. I take it a couple of times a month. What about you?

W: I take it every morning. My mother ________ ________ ________ ________ ________ ________ her car, but I prefer the bus.

M: Why's that?

W: ________ ________ ________ ________ ________ ________. Plus, because of expensive gas prices, it's also cheaper.

M: Well, that's quite thoughtful of you.

W: Well, I read that driving is ten times more expensive than taking the bus.

M: Is that right? That's a big difference.

W: It's also a great time for me to read the news and check my LookBook page on my smartphone.

M: I see. Well, I usually take the subway because ________ ________ ________ ________ ________ ________ ________ a little more.

W: I know what you mean. I really enjoy the short walk to my bus stop. It gives me the chance to think about my day. It's also great exercise.

M: That's a great way to think about it.

05

W: You must be Mr. Carter. How is everything going?

M: Well, honestly, I haven't been doing so well.

W: I'm sorry to hear that, but I'm here to help you ________ ________ ________ ________. Can you tell me anything about yourself that would be relevant?

M: I don't have any formal training, but I do know a lot about fixing motorcycles.

W: I see. What do you do when you have free time, Mr. Carter?

M: I spend a lot of time building computers and doing a little bit of networking.

W: I see. So you like computers?

M: That's right. I grew up with computers. They were my only friends when I was young.

W: That's great. ________ ________ ________ ________ ________ or around others?

M: ________ ________ ________ ________ ________. I'm a bit of an introvert.

W: I see. Well, it looks like there's an opening at Computers Plus for a technician. I think it'd be suitable for someone like you.

M: I agree. Thanks for your help.

06

M: Hi. What can I do for you today?

W: I'm looking for a new clock for my kitchen. ________ ________ ________ ________ ________ ________?

M: We only have these five in stock at this time. How about this flower one? It's designed for the kitchen.

W: It looks a bit cheesy for me. My kitchen is very modern.

M: I see. Well, in that case, what about this square one? It's elegant and simple.

W: I'd ________ ________ ________ ________ ________ than that, even. I'd like it to have just four numbers instead of all twelve.

M: All right, so we have these three left. I guess you don't want this one because it's star-shaped and probably wouldn't ________ ________ ________ ________.

W: Yeah, and the square sun clock is a bit too loud for me.

M: Well, I guess this one would be best for you.

W: I think you're right. ________ ________ ________ ________.

M: All right.

07

M: Good morning. What can I do for you?

W: I'm looking for *Chocalat*.

M: Well, you're going to want to check the candy aisle. It's ________ ________ ________.

W: Oh, I don't mean candy. I'm looking for the book by that name.

M: Ah, ________ ________ ________ ________. Do you know the author's name?

W: I'm not sure. I just know it's about a woman who opens up a chocolate shop in France.

M: Give me a minute and I'll search for it on the computer. *[Keyboard typing sound]* Okay, ________ ________ ________ ________ ________ ________ ________.

W: Great. How much is it?

M: It's $13.99. If you're a member of our rewards program, you can get 10% off.

W: Unfortunately, I'm not a member. I'll take the book anyway, though.

M: No problem. Let me go find it for you.

08

[Cell phone rings.]

W: Hey, Leo. You know, the team is pretty worried about you since you missed practice today.

M: Yeah, sorry I couldn't make it. Actually, what I called to talk to you about is the match tomorrow.

W: Oh, what's wrong?

M: Well, you're going to have to plan on me not playing tomorrow.

W: Really? But you're ________ ________ ________ ________ ________. We need you.

M: I'd love to play, but there's no way I'll be able to.

W: Are you going to tell me what happened?

M: Well, it's kind of embarrassing, but I was ________ ________ ________ ________ ________ and lost control and crashed into a wall.

W: That's awful! Are you okay?

M: I'm ________ ________ ________ ________ from the crash, but I feel all right. The doctors think that I should get x-rayed, though, and stay in the hospital overnight.

W: That's terrible news, but I guess ________ ________ ________ ________ ________ ________. I hope you heal up soon.

M: Thanks.

09

M: Hello, how can I help you?

W: I'd like to ________ ________ ________ ________ ________.

M: Okay, what would you like?

W: A supreme pizza and garlic bread combo and some extra dipping sauce.
M: Sure, but the extra sauce is a dollar more.
W: That's fine. And do you sell chicken?
M: Yes, we do. We have fried chicken and buffalo wings. They're $5 each.
W: Great. I'd like to add one of each to my order.
M: Will that be everything today?
W: Yeah, that's everything. How much is the total?
M: All together, the supreme pizza and garlic bread combo with extra sauce and two orders of chicken comes to $30. Will you be using any coupons this evening?
W: Yes, actually. I have a coupon for a 20% discount on orders over $30.
M: Okay, great. Oh, ________ ________ ________ ________ ________ if you're paying with a VISA credit or debit card.
W: Yes, I know. I have my VISA debit card.

10

W: What's that flyer you're looking at, Tommy?
M: It's for a charity event to ________ ________ ________ ________ ________. It's on October 13th.
W: That's this coming Saturday, right?
M: That's right. They even have a slogan. It's "________ ________ ________ to those without."
W: It seems that they could've ________ ________ ________ something more creative. Oh, this flyer says the event will be held at the new recreation center. Where is that?
M: It's right down the street. Do you know where the courthouse is? It's just across the street from that.
W: Ah, I've been wondering what that building is. I think we should join.
M: I agree. I always ________ ________ ________ ________ ________.
W: Me, too. And the advertisement says that they'll have free refreshments for the attendees.
M: Yep. Let's join and help the cause.

11

W: Good morning, ladies and gentlemen. Finally, spring has come again. Our cherry blossoms ________ ________ ________ ________! Take a deep breath of the fresh spring air and ________ ________ ________ ________ ________ all the beauty of the blossoms. ________ ________ ________ ________ ________ ________ ________ we will be hosting the Fourth Annual Cherry Blossom Festival! The festival dates change annually and this year will be April 20th through April 27th. We have some new activities planned for this year's festival, including more things for kids to enjoy! So get the whole family together and come out to enjoy our wonderful festival. There is so much to see and do that you'll wish you had more time! If you want to park your car on the festival grounds, the fee is $15, but if you choose to walk in, it's only $5. We look forward to seeing you soon!

12

M: Hello. May I help you?
W: Hi, I'm looking for a used motorcycle.
M: Do you ________ ________ ________ ________ ________ ________?
W: Yes. The S-35 and K-350 are my favorite models.
M: Okay. *[Mouse clicking sound]* Take a look at this list. We have five bikes available in those models.
W: Well, I don't want a motorcycle that's more than 10 years old.
M: The price of this K-350 is the cheapest of the five.
W: Nevertheless, I want one no more than 10 years old with an engine no bigger than 350cc.
M: All right. Can I ask ________ ________ ________ ________ ________ ________?
W: Less than $5,000.
M: That leaves you two choices.
W: Hmm. Although ________ ________ ________ ________ ________ ________, I want the bike with the bigger engine. It'll be faster than the other one.
M: Great! Excellent choice!

13

[Telephone rings.]
W: Hey, Dad.
M: Oh, hey Kaitlyn. Are you on your way?
W: Not yet, but I'm at the station.
M: Nice. So, when is your bus leaving?
W: It's scheduled to leave a little after 3 o'clock. I'm going to have a snack at the cafe while I wait.

M: I see. Do you think ________ ________ ________ ________ ________ ________ to have dinner with your grandparents at six?

W: I don't think so. It's Friday, so traffic is going to be really bad ________ ________ ________ ________ ________.

M: Why didn't you take the earlier bus?

W: I tried, but by the time I got to the station, all of the ________ ________ ________ ________.

M: Well, that's unfortunate. They're looking forward to seeing you.

W: Yeah, I'd really like to be there in time for dinner, but I'll probably arrive too late.

M: (Well, we'll postpone dinner until you get here.)

14

[Phone rings.]

W: This is the front desk. What can I do for you?

M: Hello. This is Dennis Reynolds in room 3D.

W: What can I do for you, Mr. Reynolds?

M: Listen, there's a street light outside my window. It's far too bright. ________ ________ ________ ________ ________ ________.

W: I'm sorry, Mr. Reynolds, but those lights have to ________ ________ ________ ________ ________.

M: I have to wake up early in the morning. I need to sleep. ________ ________ ________ ________.

W: Maybe I could switch you to a room on the other side of the building. Would that be okay?

M: I suppose that'll work.

W: Great. We'll put you in room 4B on the second floor.

M: Is there any way I could get someone to help me move my belongings?

W: (Sure. The doorman will be there to help soon.)

15

W: Brody has put the finishing touches on a presentation because he wants to promote a new game to a computer game company. He asks his good friend, Leah, if he could practice his presentation with her ________ ________ ________ ________ ________ ________ on it as well as some constructive feedback. They meet in a cafe, where he goes through his presentation. She likes the idea of the game, but thinks that his presentation has some problems. The story of the game seems too complicated, and he doesn't have enough screenshots. She notes that ________ ________ ________ ________ and not enough visual information will ________ ________ ________ ________ ________ ________. Brody wonders what he can do to improve the presentation, and asks Leah for advice. In this situation, what would Leah most likely say to Brody?

Leah: (It's important to provide more visual examples in the presentation.)

16-17

M: When living in the city, it might be hard to ________ ________ ________ ________ ________. However, many people have taken to the outdoors in order to escape their city lives. In particular, many hobbyists have taken up camping as their leisure activity of choice. Getting outdoors is great for your health, both mentally and physically. However, there are ________ ________ ________ ________ ________ when going on a camping trip. First of all, you're going to want to be sure to bring an extra set of clothes. This will keep you warm ________ ________ ________ ________ ________ ________ ________ or if you get your original clothes wet. Second, make sure to bring enough food to last for your whole trip. You might even want to pack extra food in case you get lost while hiking around your campsite. Third, be sure to pack a first-aid kit. As with all outdoor activities, camping can be dangerous. Also, be sure to clean up after yourself when leaving your campsite. It's important that we keep our environment clean. Finally, have fun. It's not a hobby if you don't enjoy it. With these tips in mind, you're sure to have a safe, fun time on your next camping trip.

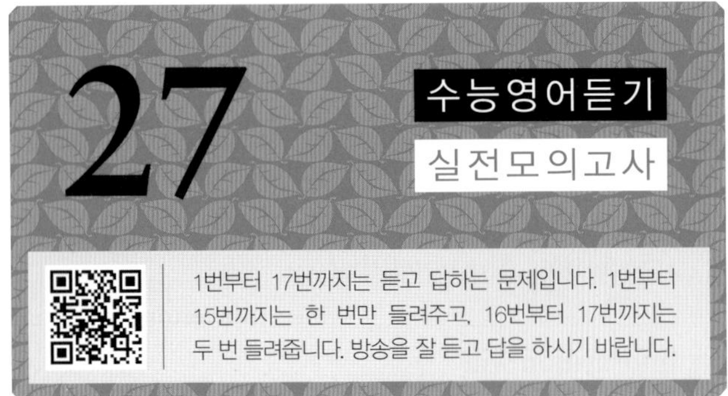

01

대화를 듣고, 여자의 마지막 말에 대한 남자의 응답으로 가장 적절한 것을 고르시오.

① There's an extra one in my car.
② I apologize for bothering you.
③ I'm not sure I understand.
④ I should prepare better.
⑤ Yes, you definitely will.

02

대화를 듣고, 남자의 마지막 말에 대한 여자의 응답으로 가장 적절한 것을 고르시오.

① That's okay. I already had dinner.
② There's none left. I ate it all last night.
③ All right. I know a great Italian restaurant.
④ Put the leftovers in the refrigerator, please.
⑤ I love pizza, but I don't think they sell it here.

03

다음을 듣고, 여자가 하는 말의 주제로 가장 적절한 것을 고르시오.

① 식초를 이용한 블랙베리의 신선도 유지법
② 세균을 없앨 수 있는 식기류 세척 요령
③ 신선한 블랙베리를 고르는 법
④ 과일에 세균이 많은 이유
⑤ 간편한 블랙베리 요리법

04

대화를 듣고, 남자의 의견으로 가장 적절한 것을 고르시오.

① 온라인에서 젊은이들의 은어 사용은 심각한 수준이다.
② 은어를 사용하면 매우 무례한 사람처럼 보일 수 있다.
③ 은어 사용을 통해 젊은 사람들과 가까워 질 수 있다.
④ 은어 사용은 젊은이들이 소속감을 갖도록 해준다.
⑤ 대중매체에서 은어의 사용을 자제해야 한다.

05

대화를 듣고, 두 사람의 관계를 가장 잘 나타낸 것을 고르시오.

① police officer — victim
② taxi driver — pedestrian
③ reporter — soccer coach
④ insurance agent — client
⑤ medical doctor — athlete

06

대화를 듣고, 그림에서 대화의 내용과 일치하지 않는 것을 고르시오.

07

대화를 듣고, 남자가 여자를 위해 할 일로 가장 적절한 것을 고르시오.

① to make survey questions
② to reserve two baseball tickets
③ to hand in her two term papers
④ to give advice about her book report
⑤ to ask people to complete the survey

08

대화를 듣고, 남자가 회의에 참석할 수 없는 이유를 고르시오.

① 사무실을 이전해야 해서
② 가족 모임이 잡혀 있어서
③ 촬영을 위한 출장을 가야 해서
④ 다른 다큐멘터리를 상영해야 해서
⑤ 아직 다큐멘터리 주제를 못 정해서

09

대화를 듣고, 여자가 지불할 총 금액을 고르시오.

① $60 ② $70 ③ $80 ④ $90 ⑤ $100

10

대화를 듣고, 남자가 사고 싶어 하는 정장에 관해 두 사람이 언급하지 않은 것을 고르시오.

① 매장 이름 ② 매장 위치 ③ 사이즈
④ 색상 ⑤ 가격

11

Bellington University에서 열릴 겨울 캠프에 관한 다음 내용을 듣고, 일치하지 않는 것을 고르시오.

① 캠프는 1월 2일부터 8일까지 열린다.
② 참가자들은 캠프 기간 동안 캠퍼스 내에서 생활한다.
③ 캠프 참가비는 무료이고 고등학생 누구나 참가 가능하다.
④ 미술이나 정보 통신 교사로부터 추천서를 받아야 한다.
⑤ 학교 홈페이지에서 지원서를 작성하면 된다.

12

다음 표를 보면서 대화를 듣고, 여자가 선택한 Flat Screen TV 모델을 고르시오.

Flat Screen TVs

	Model	Price	Brand	3D	Color
①	LD40	$570	LD	X	Silver
②	LD50	$630	LD	O	Black
③	S400	$510	Solo	X	Silver
④	S401	$540	Solo	O	Silver
⑤	S500	$570	Solo	O	Black

13

대화를 듣고, 여자의 마지막 말에 대한 남자의 응답으로 가장 적절한 것을 고르시오.

Man: ______________________

① I really don't want to get allergy shots.
② Yes. He can't go back to school until he is better.
③ He's not going to like that, but it'll help in the long run.
④ I think we should take him to the doctor for a checkup.
⑤ I'm happy that you're out of the hospital and back home.

14

대화를 듣고, 남자의 마지막 말에 대한 여자의 응답으로 가장 적절한 것을 고르시오.

Woman: ______________________

① Okay. I guess it's this fish's lucky day.
② We should go fishing together on Saturday.
③ If the water is too polluted, the fish will die.
④ I think Mom should use this one to make dinner.
⑤ I agree. The bigger fish are much harder to measure.

15

다음 상황 설명을 듣고, Peter가 Dr. Goldberg에게 할 말로 가장 적절한 것을 고르시오.

Peter: ______________________

① I don't think I can make a bigger roller coaster.
② I think I should rework some of the design flaws.
③ I really didn't expect to win the engineering contest.
④ I really enjoy studying engineering at this university.
⑤ Congratulations on winning the engineering contest.

[16-17] 다음을 듣고, 물음에 답하시오.

16

여자가 하는 말의 주제로 가장 적절한 것은?

① Defining characteristics of international English
② Changes in the English language throughout history
③ How English is becoming the international language
④ Differences in the English language among native speakers
⑤ Differences in pronunciation of American and British English

17

여자가 언급하지 않은 것은?

① 발음 ② 억양 ③ 강세
④ 어휘 ⑤ 철자

01

W: Wow! The temperature has really dropped. __________ __________ __________ __________.

M: You should have worn some warmer clothes. Do you want my coat?

W: No, that's all right. You'll be cold too without it.

M: (There's an extra one in my car.)

02

M: Hey, Lisa. You don't look so well. Is everything all right?

W: I had a really busy day at school, Dad. __________ __________. What's for dinner?

M: Well, I haven't prepared anything, but I think there's __________ __________ in the refrigerator.

W: (There's none left. I ate it all last night.)

03

W: It's springtime, which means it's almost time to enjoy fresh fruits like blackberries. I used to have problems with __________ __________ __________ __________, but then a friend showed me an easy way to maximize shelf life. Simply by using a solution of water and vinegar, you can greatly __________ __________ __________ of fresh berries. The process is so simple that anyone can do it. First, wash the berries in a mixture of equal parts vinegar and water. Let the berries soak for about five minutes while the vinegar does its work on the bacteria. Finally, just __________ __________ __________ __________ in the sink to rid them of any remaining vinegar. The secret is that the mixture has killed any bacteria that might eat away at the berries' freshness. __________ __________ __________ __________ is strong enough to kill the bacteria, but vinegar is still safe to use in the home and even to consume. Using this tip, you can keep berries fresh for weeks longer than you could otherwise.

04

M: Ms. May, are you okay? You look upset. What's the matter?

W: I feel as if I was a foreigner in my own land.

M: Why do you feel that way?

W: Well, I was on the subway this morning on my way here, and there was a group of young people sitting across from me. I didn't understand half of what they were talking about.

M: You mean they were using slang?

W: Exactly. I'm not sure what they were saying, but __________ __________ __________ __________ __________.

M: Yeah, I think many adults find that young people's language sounds impolite, but perhaps __________ __________ __________ __________ __________ __________ __________ they could get closer to the young people.

W: I don't understand.

M: They might see you as someone __________ __________ __________ __________ __________ if they hear you use their slang once in a while.

W: Oh, yeah. I get it.

M: Sometimes I ask my kids to teach me some of their slang, or I ask them about something I heard on TV.

W: I wasn't aware that you felt __________ __________ __________ __________ __________ was such a big deal.

M: I think it helps my relationship with them.

05

W: Phillip, can you hear me? Are you okay?

M: I think so. Ah, my neck. It really hurts.

W: Yeah. Don't move. We're going to __________ __________ __________ __________. So, do you remember what happened?

M: The last thing I remember, I was going for a pass and someone on the other team __________ __________ __________ __________. I fell on my shoulder, and my head hit the ground.

W: Do you remember anything after that?

M: I remember that I tried to walk, but I __________ __________. I think I fell back to the ground, maybe. I don't remember anything else until waking up here in the locker room.

W: I think you might have a concussion, Phillip.

M: Really? Is that bad?

W: Well, it's certainly not good. We're going to do some tests to see how serious it was.

M: Thank you. I really appreciate your help.

W: No problem. That's my job.

06

M: Hey Carrie, you did a great job preparing the table for the picnic.

W: Thanks, Bob. I'm worried ________ ________ ________ ________ ________ for everyone, though.

M: I'm sure it will be plenty. Anyway, I like how you decorated the table with flowers in the middle.

W: I picked them from the garden. I also made pasta for the vegetarians. I put it closest to the diners.

M: It looks delicious. I see that you also made chicken for us meat eaters.

W: That's right. Do you think that the corn is ________ ________ ________ ________ ________?

M: Yeah, maybe you should bring it closer to the front. Say, where are the drinks?

W: ________ ________ ________ ________ for the drinks.

M: I see. And it seems you put together a healthy dessert for the guests.

W: Yes. Fruit is great for picnics in the summertime and isn't ________ ________ ________ ________ or pie.

M: I agree. By the way, thanks for inviting me.

W: No problem, Bob. I'm glad you could come.

07

M: Hi, Catherine. I have two tickets to the baseball game this Friday. Would you like to go with me?

W: I'd love to, but I'm afraid I can't. I have two ________ ________ ________ ________ ________.

M: What are they? Can you go with me if I help you finish writing them?

W: Of course. One is a book report on a novel, and the other is an analysis report on how smartphones have ________ ________ ________ ________ ________.

M: How's your book report going?

W: I think it'll be done by tomorrow. The problem is the second report.

M: Have you ________ ________ ________ on the effects of the smartphone?

W: Yes, but I don't think it's possible to give it to enough people in such a short time. Could you help me with that?

M: Sure. ________ ________ ________ ________ ________ ________ ________. Then you'll go to the baseball game with me this Friday, right?

W: Yes, I promise. Thanks a million.

08

[Telephone rings.]

M: Hello? This is Dan Brown.

W: Good afternoon, Mr. Brown. This is Claudia from Global Media.

M: Hi, Claudia. What can I do for you today?

W: I talked to my bosses about the conversation that we had last week about you working with our company.

M: So you're calling to tell me you ________ ________ ________ ________ on the nature documentary, then?

W: That's right. We were wondering if you'd still be interested in producing it.

M: That'd be great. I'd love to.

W: Thank you. I'd like to ________ ________ ________ with you and the other producers we've lined up in the near future. Is Thursday at 7 p.m. okay with you?

M: I can't make it that day. ________ ________ ________ ________ ________ I've just finished up. How about Friday at noon?

W: I'm sorry, but one of the producers will be out of town on Friday and won't be back until the 14th.

M: Well, in that case, could you possibly have the meeting without me? You can brief me on it at a later date.

W: I think that'll work. I'll just need to confirm. Talk to you again soon, Mr. Brown.

09

M: Good afternoon. How can I help you today?

W: Hi. I'm looking for a pair of tennis rackets for my nephews. They're twins, and they have a birthday coming up.

M: Sure. How old are they going to be?

W: They'll be turning ten. Do you have anything for children that young?

M: Absolutely. __________ __________ __________ at this black racket. It's $70.

W: Wow! That's a bit too much.

M: Well, it's made of titanium alloy and __________ __________ __________ __________. What's your budget?

W: I'm looking to spend around $60 each.

M: If you absolutely won't go above that, then what about these aluminum rackets? The blue one is $20 __________ __________ __________ __________ __________ you just saw, and the red one is only $40.

W: They both like blue, so I think I'll get that one for both of them.

M: Great choice!

W: You take credit cards, right?

M: Absolutely. I'll walk you __________ __________ __________ __________ __________ __________.

10

M: Hey Mom, you know, I'm getting pretty excited about graduation.

W: Yeah, your father mentioned that this morning. He said you've been looking for a new suit.

M: I have, and I found a great one down at Bowtie Suits. You know where that is, right?

W: Of course. __________ __________ __________ __________ __________ on Fourth Street. What kind of suit have you found?

M: It's formal, but not too formal. The cut is great. I think __________ __________ __________ __________.

W: That sounds nice. Is it a black suit or a navy blue one?

M: It's a very dark navy blue. It almost __________ __________.

W: What's the price?

M: It's on sale for $300. Not too bad, huh?

W: That's a little more __________ __________ __________ __________. Let's go to the shop today. I want you to __________ __________ __________ for me.

M: Sure. When will you have time to take me?

W: Let's wait until your father comes home. We can all go together.

11

M: Good afternoon, everyone. I'd like to talk to you all about a new program we are offering at Bellington University this winter. Bellington University will offer a one-week camp focusing on acting and directing. The camp will be held from January 2nd to January 8th, and students who sign up will __________ __________ __________ __________ __________ __________. There is no fee to sign up, but the number of students allowed to participate is limited. Because of the limited space, only high school juniors and seniors who hold at least a B average __________ __________ __________ __________ __________. Also, for those eligible students who are interested, you must also __________ __________ __________ __________ __________ from your fine arts or communications teacher. You can sign up by __________ __________ __________ __________ on our school's homepage.

12

M: Good evening, ma'am. What can we do for you today?

W: Hi. I'm looking for a new TV. The one I have is really outdated. It's got tubes.

M: Wow. I haven't seen one of those in a while. Well, we have quite a variety of flat-screen TVs in stock. __________ __________ __________?

W: I don't want to __________ __________ __________ __________ __________ __________.

M: Is there a specific brand you have in mind?

W: I've read a lot of online reviews, and it seems that Solo makes great products.

M: They certainly do. We carry Solo at this location. Would you prefer one with 3D capabilities or without?

W: The reviews say that the 3D TVs are remarkable. I'd like one of those, if it's in my budget.

M: We have two that __________ __________ __________. They come in black or silver.

W: I'd __________ __________ __________ __________. That way it would match my cable box.

M: Great. If you wait right here, I'll go in the back and get one out of the stockroom.

W: That'd be wonderful. Thank you for your help.

13

M: Hey, sweetheart. Did you take Mike to the doctor?

W: I did. It seems like he has some serious issues with his stomach.

M: Is that right? I know he's been complaining a lot about __________ __________ __________ __________ __________.

W: Yeah, the doctor said that he might have food allergies. They're known to __________ __________ __________.

M: Wow! It never seemed to bother him when he was younger.

W: Well, the doctor said that sometimes people can get allergies later in life.

M: So what can we do now?

W: We need to watch what he eats. He should __________ __________ __________ __________ like rice and beans for now.

M: And he's going to do that for the rest of his life?

W: No, just until he gets an allergy test. The doctor __________ __________ as well.

M: (He's not going to like that, but it'll help in the long run.)

14

W: Hey Dad, why are you __________ __________ __________ __________?

M: Well, we don't want to keep the small ones.

W: Why not? We can still eat them.

M: Well, the small fish need more time to grow. There won't be any fish in the lake if we keep them all.

W: Can I help? I like playing with fish.

M: Sure. Pick up a fish and __________ __________ __________ __________ __________ __________.

W: How long should it be?

M: If it's under 25 centimeters, you should throw it back. It's actually __________ __________ __________ to keep any fish smaller than that.

W: Really? So __________ __________ __________ __________ __________ for keeping small fish?

M: That's right. Oh, you're going to have to let that one go. It's way too small.

W: (Okay. I guess it's this fish's lucky day.)

15

M: Peter is a physics major. His university opened up an engineering contest for students, and Peter decided to __________ __________ __________ __________ __________ to enter into the contest. After weeks of researching famous roller coasters around the world, he finally came up with an idea and built a finished product. Now at the contest, his model roller coaster has just finished up a strong performance and wowed the audience. The dean of the department, Dr. Goldberg, __________ __________ __________ and commends Peter for his effort. He informs Peter that other professors feel the same way, and so Peter is going to __________ __________ __________ __________ in the engineering contest. Peter is delighted by Dr. Goldberg's response and can't believe that he has been chosen as the contest's winner. In this situation, what would Peter most likely say to Dr. Goldberg?

Peter: (I really didn't expect to win the engineering contest.)

16-17

W: Good afternoon, everyone. Today, we're going to __________ __________ __________ __________ __________. According to a respected news authority based in London, there are around two billion people in the world who can speak English. In fact, there are about four times more non-native speakers of English than there are native English speakers. There are even __________ __________ __________ __________ for those who speak it as their first language. For instance, there are American English, Canadian English, British English, and Australian English. The differences between these are usually matters of pronunciation, intonation, and vocabulary. Oftentimes there are __________ __________ __________ __________ __________, especially between American English and British English. Words like *color* and *colour* or *favorite* and *favourite* are primary examples of these differences. Canadian English is __________ __________ __________ American and British English, but it definitely borrows more from the American side. To get a better idea of the differences in these native English countries, have a look at the handout I have provided. *[Pause]* Now, during our break I would like for each of you to think of other countries that speak the same language as one another and list any differences between them. Thanks for listening, everyone. We'll see you all after the break.

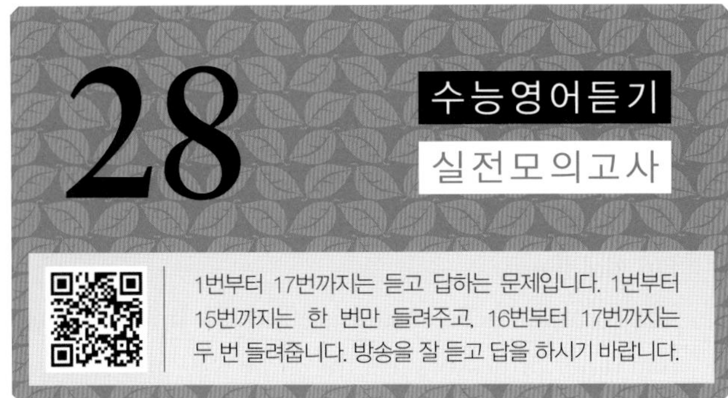

01

대화를 듣고, 여자의 마지막 말에 대한 남자의 응답으로 가장 적절한 것을 고르시오.

① You should be thankful that you've already performed.
② I thought my routine was better than the others.
③ Don't judge your ability based on other people.
④ My routine was really good compared to yours.
⑤ The show will start in just under an hour.

02

대화를 듣고, 남자의 마지막 말에 대한 여자의 응답으로 가장 적절한 것을 고르시오.

① All right. I'll just take some of the seashells with me.
② I'm having a hard time remembering that place.
③ Oh, now I see. I'll put them back right away.
④ That's great! I'll go get more to bring home.
⑤ I really hope we can visit here again soon.

03

다음을 듣고, 남자가 하는 말의 주제로 가장 적절한 것을 고르시오.

① 친환경적인 생활 습관
② 잘못된 환경 보호 운동
③ 대중교통 이용의 필요성
④ 전자제품의 효율성 문제
⑤ 삶의 질 향상을 위한 녹색주거공간

04

대화를 듣고, 새 도서관 건립에 관한 여자의 의견으로 가장 적절한 것을 고르시오.

① 새 도서관에 필요한 예산을 확보해야 한다.
② 신축 도서관의 건립 예정 위치를 바꿔야 한다.
③ 현 도서관의 전면부를 살려서 새로 지어야 한다.
④ 전통 양식 건물의 구조를 모방하여 설계해야 한다.
⑤ 현재 도서관은 역사적 건축물이므로 신축하면 안 된다.

05

대화를 듣고, 두 사람의 관계를 가장 잘 나타낸 것을 고르시오.

① 운전 연수 강사 — 수강생
② 주차 요원 — 건물 관리인
③ 보험회사 직원 — 차량 소유주
④ 자동차 정비사 — 정비 의뢰인
⑤ 자동차 판매원 — 자동차 구매자

06

대화를 듣고, 그림에서 대화의 내용과 일치하지 <u>않는</u> 것을 고르시오.

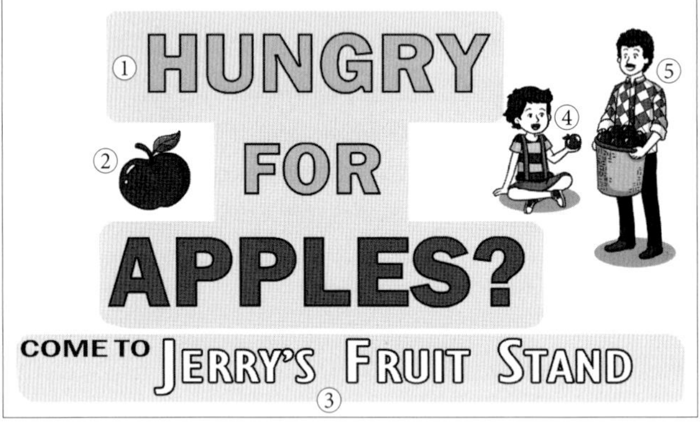

07

대화를 듣고, 여자가 할 일로 가장 적절한 것을 고르시오.

① 등산화 빌리기
② 준비 운동하기
③ 가방에서 물 빼기
④ 등산스틱 가져오기
⑤ 빠진 것 없는지 확인하기

08

대화를 듣고, 여자가 인터넷을 <u>끊은</u> 이유를 고르시오.

① 컴퓨터가 고장 나서
② 이용 요금이 비싸서
③ 성적이 많이 떨어져서
④ 수업 낙제가 우려되어서
⑤ 명의 도용이 걱정되어서

09

대화를 듣고, 남자가 지불할 총 금액을 고르시오.

① $280 ② $312 ③ $320 ④ $350 ⑤ $390

10

대화를 듣고, 신혼부부가 주의해야 할 재정적 조언으로 언급되지 않은 것을 고르시오.

① 저축 늘리기
② 소비 줄이기
③ 계좌 개설하기
④ 배우자의 계좌 개설하기
⑤ 보험 가입하기

11

Fantasy Film Festival에 관한 다음 내용을 듣고, 일치하지 않는 것을 고르시오.

① 2012년부터 매년 열리는 행사이다.
② 올해는 새로운 장소에서 열릴 것이다.
③ 입장권은 온라인으로만 구매 가능하다.
④ 축제 입장 가격은 1인당 60달러이다.
⑤ 10명 이상의 그룹은 할인받을 수 있다.

12

다음 표를 보면서 대화를 듣고, 여자가 선택할 프로그램을 고르시오.

Maro Hotel Special Activities

	Program	Time	Fee
①	Cooking Class	9:00 a.m. / 1:00 p.m.	Adults: $10 Children under 10: Free
②	Singing Lesson	10:00 a.m. / 2:00 p.m.	Adults: $10 Children under 10: $5
③	Dancing Class	10:00 a.m. / 3:00 p.m.	Adults: $5 Children under 10: Free
④	Yoga Class	11:00 a.m. / 12:00 p.m.	Free
⑤	Drawing Lesson	2:00 p.m. / 5:00 p.m.	Only Children under 10: Free

13

대화를 듣고, 여자의 마지막 말에 대한 남자의 응답으로 가장 적절한 것을 고르시오.

Man: ______________________________

① He should jump high off his right foot.
② I think you can block anything he shoots at you.
③ Don't worry. If you work hard, you can score on him.
④ I see what you mean. I think I can find a way to score on him.
⑤ I'm sorry, but I don't think you'll be able to win Saturday's match.

14

대화를 듣고, 남자의 마지막 말에 대한 여자의 응답으로 가장 적절한 것을 고르시오.

Woman: ______________________________

① So holding hands seems to lower stress in couples.
② I don't think they should show affection in public.
③ No wonder I get stressed when we hold hands.
④ It sounds like they had a nice afternoon.
⑤ They got married very recently.

15

다음 상황 설명을 듣고, Jason이 Ryan에게 할 말로 가장 적절한 것을 고르시오.

Jason: Ryan, ______________________________

① would you like to be my roommate?
② could you please be quieter during the week?
③ is it okay if I join one of your parties sometime?
④ will you teach me how to play that computer game?
⑤ how about playing in the computer game tournament?

[16-17] 다음을 듣고, 물음에 답하시오.

16

남자가 하는 말의 주제로 가장 적절한 것은?

① Tips for decreasing snoring
② Physiological causes of snoring
③ Natural ways to get rid of insomnia
④ How snoring affects your day-to-day life
⑤ Finding the most suitable sleeping position

17

피해야 할 것으로 언급되지 않은 것은?

① 비만 ② 수면제 ③ 유제품
④ 흡연 ⑤ 야식

01

W: Aiden, I'm really nervous. I don't know if I can do this.

M: Of course you can! You know all the moves, and ______ ______ ______ ______.

W: Yeah, but all of the other dancers did really awesome routines.

M: (Don't judge your ability based on other people.)

02

M: Lillian! You need to leave the shells on the beach. You can't ______ ______ ______ ______.

W: But there are so many. Why can't I just take a few?

M: Just imagine if everyone who came to the beach took "just a few."

W: (Oh, now I see. I'll put them back right away.)

03

M: It is becoming very important to ______ ______ ______ ______. In addition to the expense of energy, recent environmental problems caused by pollution have led many people around the country to a new, more conscientious way of life. There are some things you can do to help. For example, you should only use your car when it's absolutely necessary. When it's not, you should ______ ______ ______ ______ ______ ______ ______ of transportation, such as travel by bicycle, bus, or train. If you're not using an electronic device, be sure to unplug it. Your computers and televisions use power when they are plugged in even if they're not turned on. ______ ______ ______ ______ ______ of energy used when washing your laundry if you use cold water. Bring your own bags to the supermarket to reduce landfill waste, and try to avoid disposable items, such as paper cups or plates. ______ ______ ______ and join millions of others in going green.

04

W: Tom, have you heard about the city's plan to tear down the old library?

M: Yes, I did. But I also heard that they have plans to build a new library in its place.

W: It's really too bad. The current building is a ______ ______.

M: That's true, but ______ ______ ______ ______ ______ for all of the new material.

W: That's a good point. We need a new library. The old one is far too inconvenient.

M: Certainly. It's really hot in the summer and freezing in the winter.

W: A new building would definitely solve those problems, but they should at least save the front of the original building.

M: That's a really wonderful idea. The front of the building is so beautiful.

W: Yeah, and then we would have a modern building on the inside with an antique look on the outside.

M: Exactly. That way we can ______ ______ ______ ______ ______.

05

M: ______ ______ ______ ______, Mrs. Allen. Here's your key.

W: Thanks. Wait… This is just a remote. Where's the actual key?

M: All new Mondo cars come with a smart key. As long as this is in your pocket, you can unlock your car by pressing the button on the door handle.

W: Let's give it a try. *[Pause]* That's really cool, but how can I start the car?

M: As long as the smart key is in the car, all you have to do is press the *Start* button.

W: Wow! This is quite convenient. ______ ______ ______ ______.

M: Right! Also, you can never lock your keys in the car. If the key is in the car, the door won't lock.

W: That's great because I can get ______ ______ ______ ______. Is there anything else I should know?

M: I think that's it. Thanks again for buying from us. Don't hesitate to call us if you have any problems with the car.

W: Thanks for your help.

06

M: Hey Beth, check out this poster I made for the fruit stand at the farmers' market.

W: It looks great, Jerry. I like the slogan. "Hungry for apples?"

M: I thought that up myself.

W: I had no idea you were so creative. Is the apple on the left a drawing? It looks so real.

M: It took me a long time to draw that. What do you think of the name of our fruit stand? It isn't too boring, is it?

W: Well, it seems all right to me.

M: But "Jerry's Fruit Stand" seems so plain. I should ________ ________ ________ ________ ________.

W: It's fine. Maybe the font should be a little bigger, though. The slogan ________ ________ ________ ________ ________ on the poster.

M: You're right. I'll resize the fonts before I print it. I also drew a picture of my son holding some apples.

W: That's so cute. And the drawing of you carrying a basket full of apples ________ ________ ________ as well.

M: You think so? I think my head looks too big.

W: Not at all. This will be perfect for the fruit stand.

07

M: Hey, Lucy. I made it.

W: Hey, Bobby. Thanks for coming early. It's a great day for a hike, huh?

M: It sure is. I like your boots.

W: Thanks, but they're not mine. I borrowed them from my cousin.

M: That's cool. So, ________ ________ ________ ________ ________?

W: I'm ready, but I should warn you: it's been a while since I've been hiking.

M: That's all right. ________ ________ ________ ________. Let's make sure we have everything before we go.

W: I think I have everything I need. ________ ________ ________ ________ ________ ________ ________.

M: That's okay. We might need it. Did you bring your hiking sticks?

W: Oh, I guess I must've left them in the car. I'll go get them.

M: All right. I'll wait here.

08

M: Did you see the new Gamebox PC? It looks amazing.

W: Wow! It does look great! Look at the graphics!

M: I'd love to buy it, but I just got a new computer last year. I haven't paid it off yet.

W: Yeah, why would you buy a new PC when the one you have still works well?

M: You're right, but this new computer is just ________ ________ ________ ________. It could run all of the newest games.

W: You'll probably fail some of your classes, though. ________ ________ ________ ________.

M: Haha. Maybe you're right. Is that why you haven't upgraded your computer in so long?

W: Actually, I got rid of my Internet altogether. I'm afraid of getting my identity stolen.

M: I heard that it's getting riskier to use computers. I can't stay away, though. I love playing games.

W: Yeah, but ________ ________ ________ ________ ________ ________.

M: I understand ________ ________ ________ ________.

09

W: Hello. Welcome to Frank's Home Appliances. Is there anything I can help you with today?

M: Well, our washing machine just broke, so I'm looking for a new one.

W: All right. Well, we have a ________ ________ ________ ________ ________. How much are you looking to spend?

M: I'd like to spend less than $400.

W: Sure. Let's see what's in the clearance section. This one is nice. It was originally $500, but it has a little bit of cosmetic damage so we marked it down to $350.

M: Looks great. I'll take it.

W: Oh! And if you got a leaflet from our shop, there's a coupon for an additional 20% off.

M: Yeah, I saw that and I cut out the coupon. Here you go. Do you deliver?

W: We sure do. Delivery is free, but we do __________ __________ __________ __________. That's an additional $40.

M: Well, it's probably better that you install it. I don't know if I can.

W: Okay.

10

W: Jiho, now that you and Kate are getting married, you both need to be more careful about what you do financially.

M: Yes, I know. We have a responsibility to each other, and all of our decisions will impact more than just ourselves.

W: Exactly. You both should start __________ __________ __________ __________ __________, because you're definitely going to need it.

M: That's good advice. I'll open a savings account right away.

W: Good. And she should, too. Once you're married, your accounts will be shared.

M: She's a student right now, and __________ __________ __________ __________-__________, so she doesn't have much money to put into an account.

W: __________ __________ __________ __________ that will need to be paid? Or rent?

M: No, she doesn't.

W: Then she should be able to save most of what she makes, at least for a while, until you both are comfortable.

M: All right. I'll talk to her and see how she feels about it.

W: That's a good idea. I'm glad to hear it.

11

W: Good morning, everyone. __________ __________ __________ __________ __________ __________ of the annual Fantasy Film Festival. The Fantasy Film Festival has grown since 2012. Last year, we had to deny a lot of visitors entrance to the festival because our location was not big enough. Fortunately, we have found a new location that is much bigger but still __________ __________ __________ __________ __________ __________ locations used in years past. I can assure you that your friends and family will not be turned away, and a much larger audience will view your films. Because we're expecting more visitors than in the past, we have moved our ticket sales online. You can still get them at the box office, but it may be more convenient to buy them from our website: *www.fantasyfilms.com*. The price for a single admission ticket is $60, and __________ __________ __________ __________ __________ of ten or more.

12

M: This is the front desk. What can I do for you?

W: Hi. __________ __________ __________ about the rain today. We __________ __________ __________ __________ __________, but it looks like we'll be staying inside instead. I understand you have some activities here at the hotel that might keep us entertained.

M: Sure. We __________ __________ __________ __________ __________ the day.

W: Well, we're going to see a movie next door at 11 a.m. I think it runs for one hour and a half.

M: I see. Well, how about a cooking class? Today's lesson is how to make croissants.

W: That sounds interesting, but I really don't think my daughter would enjoy it much. __________ __________ __________ __________ __________.

M: Well, we offer two children's drawing lessons in the afternoon. Perhaps your daughter would be interested in that.

W: She might, but it's only for children, right? We're looking for something the whole family can enjoy.

M: All right. Well, there are a couple of other options. Does the cost of the activity matter?

W: Well, since it's our last day of vacation, we're running a little low on money. I don't want to spend more than $15 for my husband, my daughter, and myself.

M: I understand. Well, I have the perfect activity for you and your family.

13

W: What's up, captain?

M: Just watching some FC Barcelona videos. I don't know if we'll be able to beat them on Saturday.

W: Really? But your team is __________ __________ __________ __________ __________. I'm sure you'll be able to win.

M: Their goalie is much too strong. He can ________ ________ ________ ________ just about any ball ________ ________ him.

W: That might be so, but after you find his weakness, you'll ________ ________ ________ ________ ________ ________.

M: Hah! And what's his weakness?

W: If you look very carefully, you can see what part of the goal he has trouble defending.

M: *[Pause]* Well, I'm still not seeing anything.

W: Look at the way he moves his body. He's shifting his weight to his left side and jumping to his right.

M: You're right!

W: Now look again. He's doing a similar movement ________ ________ ________ ________ ________. If I were you, I'd shoot at the left corner.

M: (I see what you mean. I think I can find a way to score on him.)

14

W: What are you reading, dear?

M: This really interesting study ________ ________ ________.

W: A recent one?

M: Yep.

W: What kind of contact?

M: Things like holding hands and ________ ________ ________ ________ ________ married couples.

W: That sounds really interesting. Tell me more.

M: Well, the study focused on two groups of married couples. In one group, couples were asked to take a walk while holding hands.

W: So the other group took a walk without holding hands?

M: Exactly. After the walk, the couples sat down with the researchers and were asked to discuss ________ ________ ________ ________ ________ ________ ________ together after getting married.

W: What were the results?

M: The couples that spent the afternoon holding hands ________ ________ ________ ________ ________ than the other group while telling their stories.

W: (So holding hands seems to lower stress in couples.)

15

W: After winning a major FPS tournament, Jason finally ________ ________ ________ ________ buy a house. He found a place with two bedrooms and asked his friend, Ryan, to be his roommate. Everything was ________ ________ ________ ________. Jason enjoyed having someone to play computer games with, and Ryan liked living away from his parents. However, after Jason started studying in university, the ________ ________ ________ ________ ________. Now, Ryan stays up late playing games and sometimes has loud parties during the week. It's ________ ________ ________ ________ Jason, who has to study every night and wake up for class early every morning. Jason wants to talk about this noise problem with Ryan. In this situation, what would Jason most likely say to Ryan?

Jason: Ryan, (could you please be quieter during the week?)

16-17

M: Good morning, listeners. Have you or your loved one ever experienced ________ ________ ________ ________ due to snoring? Well, ________ ________ ________ ________ ________ ________ snoring can lead to poor sleep quality, tiredness during the day, health problems, and relationship problems with your partner. It really caused some problems for me in my thirties. My wife would complain about her sleepless nights due to my snoring. I started researching snoring and found some tips online that helped me stop. The first tip I followed was to lose weight. Being overweight can create fatty tissue in the back of your throat, which can lead to frequent, loud snoring. You should also ________ ________ ________ ________. They cause the muscles in the throat to relax, which interferes with breathing. Caffeine, dairy products, and late-night meals should also be avoided before bedtime. Finally, try sleeping on your side instead of your back. When you sleep on your back, ________ ________ ________ ________ ________ ________ ________. When you sleep on your side, it doesn't. If you follow all of these tips, I'm sure you'll make your partner and yourself happier.

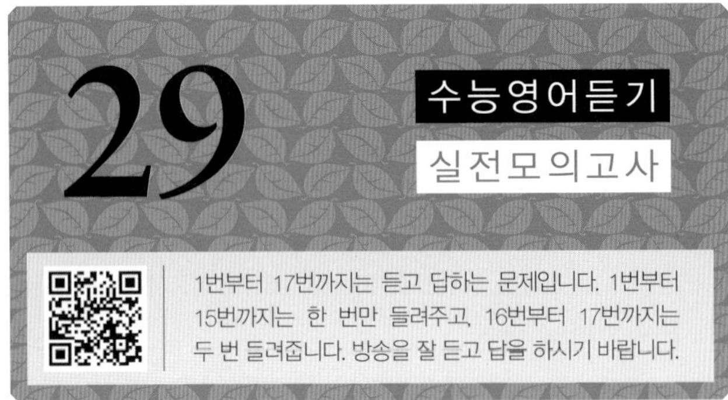

01

대화를 듣고, 남자의 마지막 말에 대한 여자의 응답으로 가장 적절한 것을 고르시오.

① I don't like eating at home.
② It'll be a while before I finish.
③ Sure. I'll help you finish the report.
④ That's fine. I'll wait until you're done.
⑤ The delivery man brought the food quickly.

02

대화를 듣고, 여자의 마지막 말에 대한 남자의 응답으로 가장 적절한 것을 고르시오.

① We have to sit in assigned seats.
② Sorry, but I have other plans tonight.
③ It's sold out, so there aren't any tickets left.
④ No problem. You can have these two tickets.
⑤ Let's get there early so we can sit near the front.

03

다음을 듣고, 남자가 하는 말의 요지로 가장 적절한 것을 고르시오.

① 직원들의 조기 출근 제도가 필요하다.
② 출퇴근용 통근버스의 수와 노선을 늘려야 한다.
③ 직원들의 근무환경 개선이 가장 시급한 문제이다.
④ 생산성 증대는 직원들의 자율성 보장에서 비롯된다.
⑤ 생산성을 증가시키는 재택근무 제도를 개발해야 한다.

04

대화를 듣고, 두 사람이 하는 말의 주제로 가장 적절한 것을 고르시오.

① 친한 친구 사이에서도 말을 가려서 해야 한다.
② 상대방의 동의를 구하지 않고 사진을 촬영해서는 안 된다.
③ 소셜 네트워킹 사이트에서 바르고 고운 말을 사용해야 한다.
④ 소셜 네트워킹 사이트에서 익명으로 남을 비방해서는 안 된다.
⑤ 소셜 네트워킹 사이트 이용 시 서로의 사생활 보호에 주의해야 한다.

05

대화를 듣고, 두 사람의 관계를 가장 잘 나타낸 것을 고르시오.

① 모델 — 매니저
② 호텔 직원 — 투숙객
③ 옷 가게 점원 — 고객
④ 여행 가이드 — 관광객
⑤ 비행기 승무원 — 승객

06

대화를 듣고, 그림에서 대화의 내용과 일치하지 않는 것을 고르시오.

07

대화를 듣고, 여자가 남자를 위해 할 일로 가장 적절한 것을 고르시오.

① 좋은 트레이너 소개시켜 주기
② 비타민과 영양보충제 주기
③ 영화 티켓 대신 예매하기
④ 영화 보고 커피 사주기
⑤ 남자와 함께 운동하기

08

대화를 듣고, 여자가 회계사가 된 이유를 고르시오.

① 학창 시절 매우 좋아했던 경제 선생님 때문에
② 대학 졸업 후 아버지의 조언을 받아들여서
③ 안정적이고 매력적인 직업이라 생각돼서
④ 대학교에서 인상 깊게 들은 강의 때문에
⑤ 원래 숫자 다루는 일을 좋아했기 때문에

09

대화를 듣고, 여자가 선물을 사기 위해 부담하기로 한 금액을 고르시오.

① $22 ② $24 ③ $26 ④ $48 ⑤ $60

10

대화를 듣고, 남자의 후원 활동에 관해 두 사람이 언급하지 않은 것을 고르시오.

① 동물을 입양한 지역
② 입양한 동물 이름
③ 후원해 온 기간
④ 입양하게 된 계기
⑤ 후원하는 방법

11

토네이도 대처법에 관한 다음 내용을 듣고, 일치하지 않는 것을 고르시오.

① 경보가 울리면 지하실로 대피한다.
② 수건이나 이불로 자신을 덮는다.
③ 창문에서 떨어져 있어야 한다.
④ 정전을 대비해서 휴대폰을 챙긴다.
⑤ 기상 상태를 주시한다.

12

다음 표를 보면서 대화를 듣고, 두 사람이 택한 관광 코스를 고르시오.

Bus Tour Guide

	Program	Time of Departure	Price	Location of Departure
①	Garden Tour	9:00 a.m. / 1:00 p.m. / 5:00 p.m.	$40	Central Station
②	Museum Tour	9:00 a.m. / 11:00 a.m. / 1:00 p.m.	$30	Central Station
③	Shopping Tour	9:30 a.m. / 12:30 p.m. / 3:30 p.m.	$20	West Terminal
④	City Tour	9:00 a.m. to 7:00 p.m. Every Hour	$50	Central Station
⑤	Castle Tour	10:00 a.m. (Once a Day)	$70	West Terminal

13

대화를 듣고, 여자의 마지막 말에 대한 남자의 응답으로 가장 적절한 것을 고르시오.

Man: ______________________________

① Let's test our rocket right now!
② Sorry. You should find a new partner.
③ I don't think we have enough supplies.
④ Let's use the Internet to get some ideas.
⑤ I think playing with rockets is dangerous.

14

대화를 듣고, 남자의 마지막 말에 대한 여자의 응답으로 가장 적절한 것을 고르시오.

Woman: ______________________________

① Maybe you still can, but for now you need to rest.
② I agree. You know your body better than anyone.
③ Yeah, I think you should consult another doctor.
④ Wow! I didn't know you were so good at tennis.
⑤ You should hurry. Otherwise you'll miss out.

15

다음 상황 설명을 듣고, Andrew가 사서에게 할 말로 가장 적절한 것을 고르시오.

Andrew: ______________________________

① I promise I'll return the DVD on time.
② It's late because I couldn't find the DVD.
③ I'd like to check this DVD out for longer, please.
④ I'd like to be a librarian in the future. Could you help me?
⑤ Someone stole the original DVD, so I bought a replacement.

[16-17] 다음을 듣고, 물음에 답하시오.

16

남자가 하는 말의 목적으로 가장 적절한 것은?

① to convince people to donate money
② to find a new job in a recruiting company
③ to recruit people with shipping experience
④ to talk about the benefits of working abroad
⑤ to discuss the challenges of working overseas

17

남자가 언급한 내용이 아닌 것은?

① He worked for a shipping company.
② He saw the Leaning Tower of Pisa.
③ He met lots of fascinating people.
④ He traveled the world with his friends.
⑤ He had lunch with the owner of a company.

01

M: Hey Stacy, it's getting late. _____ _____ _____ _____ _____ _____ and head home.

W: I can't tonight, Tyler. I really need to finish this report before tomorrow morning.

M: If you're almost finished, I can wait for you.

W: (It'll be a while before I finish.)

02

W: Hey George, my boss gave me two tickets to the basketball game tonight. _____ _____ _____ _____ _____.

M: Sure. That sounds great. _____ _____ _____ _____?

W: They're in the fan section, so we can sit anywhere.

M: (Let's get there early so we can sit near the front.)

03

M: Good morning, everyone. I would like to talk to you all today about _____ _____ _____ _____. In the past, _____ _____ _____ _____ _____ the employee coming to work in the morning and working all day under the close watch of his or her supervisor. But have you ever thought about the amount of time that's wasted commuting every morning, or how the stress of that commute could diminish the employee's energy before they even arrive at work? I'd like to see all of you employers develop a system that allows all or some of your employees to _____ _____ _____ _____ _____. By eliminating the stress brought on by the daily commute, you'll allow your employees to put more energy into their tasks. Allowing your employees to work at home will _____ _____ _____ _____ to you in the end.

04

M: Have you seen the photo of Daryl that Scott _____ _____ LookBook yesterday?

W: Yeah, I did see it.

M: Did you think it was funny?

W: Yes, it was quite humorous. But I think Daryl might be upset at Scott for posting it.

M: What do you mean?

W: Daryl looks very silly in the photo.

M: Oh, I understand. You think Daryl will be upset if he sees the photo and knows other people saw it. I suppose I would be angry, too.

W: Exactly. I just think Scott _____ _____ _____ Daryl if it was okay to post it.

M: I agree with you. Social networking sites like LookBook can be very useful for networking and _____ _____ _____ _____ _____ _____, but they can also compromise people's privacy.

W: Yeah. I really enjoyed those kinds of sites in the beginning, but soon I realized how quickly _____ _____ _____ _____.

M: Right. _____ _____ _____ _____ _____ when posting anything on social networking sites.

05

W: Good morning. I'm Lilly Jones. I'm sorry I'm late. _____ _____ _____ _____ by a couple of hours.

M: No problem, Mrs. Jones. Welcome to Alaska. I'm Joseph, but my friends call me Joey. I'll be your guide.

W: It's a pleasure to meet you, Joey. Have all the others already arrived?

M: Yes, the rest of the group has arrived. They're waiting in the lounge. You should probably _____ _____ _____ _____ in the restroom. Alaska isn't as warm as Florida.

W: Can't it wait until we get to the hotel?

M: I'd really recommend doing it now. We're going to stop by the traditional Inuit fish market before we go to the hotel. It's quite cold there.

W: All right, I guess that means I should change my clothes.

M: And by the way, there's been a change of plans. _____ _____ _____ _____ _____ _____ a lot of snow at the ski resort, so we're going to Denali National Park instead.

W: That's a shame, but it's okay. I've heard the park is beautiful.

M: I apologize nonetheless. Thank you for understanding.

06

M: Oh, isn't this a picture from one of your birthday parties?

W: It is. It was my seventh birthday. I remember because __________ __________ __________ __________ __________ all seven candles on the cake.

M: Are those your friends next to you in the picture?

W: Yes, that's Jessica and Tim. They were my best friends at the time. I wonder what they're doing now.

M: I love the birthday hats. All of you look adorable.

W: It's a really cute photo. You can see that all of the hats are a little different. My friends have stripes on theirs, and I have polka dots on mine.

M: I see that. You also have three balloons behind you.

W: Yes, my parents __________ __________ __________ __________ the room.

M: That's nice. __________ __________ __________ __________ __________ __________ Tim look delicious.

W: Actually, he ate one of the muffins just before we took this picture. I remember being very mad.

M: Really? In the picture you all look very happy.

07

W: Larry, do you have a minute?

M: I'm actually headed to the gym right now. I have a personal training appointment at noon.

W: Oh, that's right. I forgot. You have your personal training appointments every Monday and Wednesday, right? Do you like it?

M: Yeah, I really do. My trainer is very knowledgeable, and he __________ __________ __________ __________ __________.

W: That sounds great. __________ __________ __________ __________ __________ __________ __________? If you have time, we should go see the new *Iron Man* movie.

M: Well, I was planning on going to the health store to __________ __________ __________ __________ __________ __________.

W: Oh, I have a lot at home. In fact, depending on what kind you need, __________ __________ __________. You can come take a look, and I'll give you what you need.

M: Really? Wow, that'd be great. Then yeah, we can go to the movie.

W: Great. I actually won two free tickets at our office yesterday.

M: Perfect. We can watch the movie, then I'll come check out the supplements, and I'll treat you to coffee afterwards.

08

W: Hey, Paul. It's me, Lori Townsend. We went to school together at Markwell High School. Do you remember me?

M: Yes, of course. How's everything with you?

W: Everything is great. I just started a job as an accountant for Green Tree Financial. What about you?

M: I'm still in school. I'm __________ __________ __________ __________ at Transylvania University.

W: Is that right? What are you studying? Everyone thought you were going to be a big singer in high school.

M: Well, my interests have actually changed a bit since then. Now I'm studying political science.

W: That's awesome. Why did you choose political science?

M: Well, __________ __________ __________ __________ politics since the last election. What about you? Why did you become an accountant?

W: Do you remember our economics teacher in high school, Mrs. Lee?

M: Yeah, she was great. She was so charismatic and funny.

W: __________ __________ __________ __________. She and I became good friends after high school, and __________ __________ __________ __________ __________ __________.

M: Really? That's cool.

09

W: Hey, I just realized that Mom's birthday is this weekend.

M: I totally forgot! What do you think we should get her?

W: Well, I was at the mall earlier and I saw a necklace that I know she'll love.

M: Really? Is it expensive?

W: Not too bad. It's only $60 with a 20% discount.

M: __________ __________ __________ __________ __________. I only have $22. Is there anything we can buy that's cheaper than the necklace?

W: Well, I did see some earrings, but I really think she'll love the necklace.

M: But it's $48, right? I don't have enough money __________ __________ __________ __________ __________.

W: I guess you can give me your $22 and __________ __________ __________ __________ __________ __________.

M: Great. Thanks.

10

W: Hi, Max. What're you up to?

M: I'm just reading about this elephant I adopted in Africa. Look at this picture.

W: An elephant, huh? That's really cool. What's his name?

M: It's Chang.

W: So, you adopted him __________ __________ __________ __________ or something?

M: That's right. I recently watched a documentary about poaching and elephant abuse in Africa. __________ __________ __________ __________ __________ __________, so I decided that I'd do what I could to help.

W: That's nice of you. So what're you doing to help Chang?

M: Well, I found a wildlife sanctuary that takes care of these animals, and that's where he lives. I send them money every month.

W: How much do you send?

M: Well, I can send as much as I want, but it's usually not more than $30 a month. Would you like to __________ __________ __________ __________ __________?

W: It sounds great and all, but __________ __________ __________ __________ __________ at the moment.

M: That's all right. Maybe you can help when you have some money to spare.

11

M: Good afternoon, everyone. Thank you for coming to our town hall meeting. My name is Jerry Mills, and I'm the chief of the Milford Fire Department. As you know, __________ __________ __________ __________ __________. I'd like to go over some tips that will help you keep safe in the event of a tornado. First, when you hear a tornado siren, __________ __________ __________ __________ __________. If you don't have a basement, go into a bathroom and cover yourself with towels, blankets, or a mattress. Stay away from windows and sharp objects. Do not go outside during severe weather. It might be wise to keep a battery-powered radio handy __________ __________ __________ __________ __________ __________. That way you can stay current on the weather conditions. If you follow these helpful tips during a tornado, you can stay safe. Thank you for your time.

12

M: Oh, no. We missed the nine o'clock Garden Tour bus!

W: That's too bad. What time is the next one?

M: According to the tour schedule, they run every four hours. We can't wait that long.

W: Here's __________ __________ __________ __________ __________ __________. What do you think of this one?

M: Christine, did you already forget that we've been on that tour?

W: Oh, right. Then how about the tour that leaves at 10 o'clock? It's 9:10 now, so __________ __________ __________ __________ __________ to catch that one.

M: It costs too much. __________ __________ __________ __________ __________ more than $50 per person.

W: Okay. There's a tour that departs in 20 minutes. Let's take that one.

M: It leaves from West Terminal. It would take us at least 30 minutes to get there from here.

W: Then it looks like we have only one choice. I guess we'll have to wait a while for the next bus.

M: __________ __________ __________ __________ __________ by walking around Central Station.

W: Sounds like a plan.

13

W: Hey, Luke. Have you heard about the "Space Shooters" competition?

M: I haven't. What's that?

W: It's an event for __________ __________ __________ __________ __________.

M: So, what can you tell me about it?

W: Students have to work together to build a working miniature rocket to __________ __________ __________ __________ __________. It seems like something you'd be interested in.

M: You're right! I love making model rockets. My father and I used to build them all the time when I was younger.

W: Then you should be great at it! Would you like to be my partner?

M: That sounds great, but __________ __________ __________ __________ __________ __________ __________ __________. I don't know if __________ __________ __________ __________ the other students.

W: You'll be great! Let's do it together.

M: Hmm… Okay. We're a team. Where do you think we should start?

W: How about researching some rocket designs?

M: (Let's use the Internet to get some ideas.)

14

W: Owen, I was shocked to hear that you're in the hospital. Is everything all right?

M: I'm fine. I just hurt my knee playing tennis. Thanks for coming to see me though, Nora.

W: When I heard you were here, I downloaded some songs I thought you'd like. Let me send them to your phone. Maybe it'll help you keep from getting too bored.

M: __________ __________ __________ __________ __________.

W: So, how did you hurt your knee?

M: During practice this morning, I jumped up for the ball and it twisted as I landed.

W: Ouch! Is it serious?

M: No. The doctor said __________ __________ __________ __________ __________, but I should stay off of it for a couple of days.

W: Then you should listen to him and __________ __________ __________ __________ __________ __________.

M: But I need to continue my training if I want to compete in the tournament this coming fall.

W: I don't think that's such a good idea. If you hurt it more, you may never be able to play tennis again.

M: My doctor said the same thing. I really want to win that tournament, though.

W: (Maybe you still can, but for now you need to rest.)

15

W: Andrew checked out a DVD from the Hudson Public Library. However, when he was getting ready to return it a week later, he realized that __________ __________ __________. He believes that __________ __________ __________ __________ __________. However, the library's policy states that he should buy a new copy to replace the one that went missing. Andrew buys a new DVD from the department store, and takes it to the library. The librarian realizes that the DVD doesn't have a library sticker on it. She says that she can't check in the DVD and that Andrew must have __________ __________ __________. Andrew wants to explain himself. In this situation, what would Andrew most likely say to the librarian?

Andrew: (Someone stole the original DVD, so I bought a replacement.)

16-17

M: Good afternoon, ladies and gentlemen. My name is George Wondell, and I'm happy that you've joined me for my seminar here at the San Jose State Job Fair. I'd like to talk to you about __________ __________. Have you ever thought about the opportunities that come with working in another country? Let me tell you my story. After I graduated from high school, I went to a job fair much like this one. An international shipping company was hiring and took me on as a deckhand. This was my chance to see the world and __________ __________ __________. I got to travel to many beautiful and interesting places. I saw the Eiffel Tower, the Leaning Tower of Pisa, and many other famous landmarks. I also met a lot of interesting people along the way and made friends wherever I went. One day, I met a man who owned a company that recruits people from around the world to work __________ __________ __________ __________ __________. We had lunch, and I told him stories about my travels. He found them so interesting that he offered me a job speaking __________ __________ __________ __________ __________ at seminars and job fairs like this one. Working overseas was the experience of a lifetime. It opens doors and provides opportunities that you won't find anywhere else. If you'd like more information, please visit our booth. Thank you for listening.

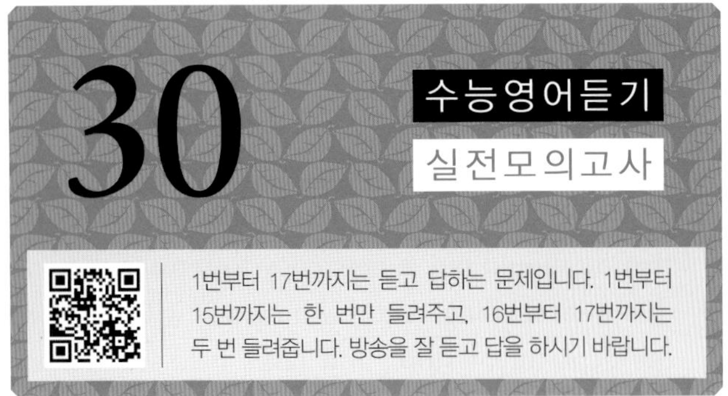

01

대화를 듣고, 여자의 마지막 말에 대한 남자의 응답으로 가장 적절한 것을 고르시오.

① Did you try to turn the headlights off?
② I think we should give them a call immediately.
③ I think so. Maybe you should answer the phone.
④ Leave your phone number and they'll call you later.
⑤ You're right. I think it's time to change the headlights.

02

대화를 듣고, 남자의 마지막 말에 대한 여자의 응답으로 가장 적절한 것을 고르시오.

① We need to buy another trash bin.
② I'm okay. The water is still too cold.
③ I appreciate all that you have done for us.
④ It only takes an hour to pick up the garbage.
⑤ Some people just don't care about the environment.

03

다음을 듣고, 남자가 하는 말의 목적으로 가장 적절한 것을 고르시오.

① 예술 축제 행사의 후원을 부탁하려고
② 예술 축제 행사의 개최 장소를 논의하려고
③ 예술 축제 행사의 기획 의도를 설명하려고
④ 예술 축제 개최를 위한 설문 참여를 부탁하려고
⑤ 예술 축제 행사를 위한 자원봉사자를 모집하려고

04

대화를 듣고, 두 사람이 하는 말의 주제로 가장 적절한 것을 고르시오.

① 방과후 운동이 아침운동보다 효과적인 이유
② 다양한 방과후 운동과목 신설의 필요성
③ 운동과 수업시간 집중력과의 상관관계
④ 학생들의 운동량을 늘리기 위한 방안
⑤ 운동 부족으로 인한 비만 학생 증가

05

대화를 듣고, 두 사람의 관계를 가장 잘 나타낸 것을 고르시오.

① customer — clerk
② journalist — cook
③ reporter — editor
④ photographer — model
⑤ interviewer — applicant

06

대화를 듣고, 그림에서 대화의 내용과 일치하지 않는 것을 고르시오.

07

대화를 듣고, 남자가 여자를 위해 할 일로 가장 적절한 것을 고르시오.

① 유리병 사기
② 집안일 도와주기
③ 차와 향신료 사기
④ 슈퍼마켓 함께 가기
⑤ 친구한테 병 받으러 가기

08

대화를 듣고, 남자가 어제 회의에 참석하지 못한 이유를 고르시오.

① 아내의 사무실에 들렀다 오느라
② 걸어오느라 시간이 많이 걸려서
③ 아내를 병원에 데려다 주느라
④ 넘어져서 다쳤기 때문에
⑤ 교통체증과 주차 때문에

09

대화를 듣고, 여자가 지불할 금액을 고르시오.

① $12 ② $16 ③ $21 ④ $22 ⑤ $25

10

대화를 듣고, 전시회에 관해 두 사람이 언급하지 않은 것을 고르시오.

① 전시회 주제 ② 전시회 기간
③ 장소 대여 비용 ④ 홍보 포스터
⑤ 정식 초대장

11

Ricardo's on the Boardwalk에 관한 다음 내용을 듣고, 일치하지 않는 것을 고르시오.

① 시내에서 5분 가량 떨어진 곳에 있다.
② 건물 완공에 거의 2년이 걸렸다.
③ 옥외에서는 호수 전망을 볼 수 있다.
④ 매일 평일 저녁에 재즈 공연이 있다.
⑤ 현지에서 재배된 식품만을 사용한다.

12

다음 표를 보면서 대화를 듣고, 남자가 선택한 축구화를 고르시오.

	Brands	Type	Material	Price
①	AP-101	Offensive	Cloth	$30
②	AP-102	Defensive	Plastic	$50
③	EC-201	All-Purpose	Cloth	$60
④	EC-202	All-Purpose	Plastic	$90
⑤	PE-300	All-Purpose	Plastic	$120

13

대화를 듣고, 여자의 마지막 말에 대한 남자의 응답으로 가장 적절한 것을 고르시오.

Man: ____________________

① Thanks for the tip. It's very helpful.
② This is my first time traveling to Thailand.
③ I finally got my flight confirmation to Bangkok.
④ I can get these souvenirs for much cheaper there.
⑤ That's a good idea. I've spent a lot of money here.

14

대화를 듣고, 남자의 마지막 말에 대한 여자의 응답으로 가장 적절한 것을 고르시오.

Woman: ____________________

① You're wrong. I really love eating desserts.
② Everybody loves to eat churros at an F1 race.
③ I don't want anything from the concession stand.
④ I think we should go to the F1 race this weekend.
⑤ No thanks. I don't want to eat anything that sweet.

15

다음 상황 설명을 듣고, Kristen이 Gavin에게 할 말로 가장 적절한 것을 고르시오.

Kristen: Gavin, ____________________

① the weather should be perfect for hiking tomorrow.
② you're going to need a set of dry clothes for our hike.
③ I've prepared some of your favorite snacks for our hike.
④ I think we should reschedule the hike for next weekend.
⑤ it will take longer to get to the top of the mountain in the rain.

[16-17] 다음을 듣고, 물음에 답하시오.

16

남자가 하는 말의 주제로 가장 적절한 것은?

① Benefits of cooking meals at home
② How to choose the freshest produce
③ Advice on how to save money on food
④ How to create delicious and healthy meals
⑤ Cheap and easy food recipes for busy people

17

남자가 언급한 식품이 아닌 것은?

① 즉석 요리 제품 ② 제철 농산물 ③ 통조림
④ 냉동식품 ⑤ 스파게티

01

W: Look, Dad. Someone left their headlights on. I don't see anyone else around the car.

M: I guess they __________ __________ __________ __________ __________. Is the door locked?

W: Yes. But here's their phone number.

M: (I think we should give them a call immediately.)

02

M: Mary, if you're hot, why don't you __________ __________ __________ __________ and put your feet in the water? It's nice and cool.

W: That sounds lovely. *[Pause]* Eww! Is that garbage floating in the water?

M: It is. I'll never understand how __________ __________ __________ __________ __________. It's so easy to just throw it away.

W: (Some people just don't care about the environment.)

03

M: Thank you all for coming to tonight's booster's meeting. The Boosters Board has an art festival planned for the spring of 2016, and we would like all of your help in making it a successful event. The art festival has been a great event for our school in the past, and we would like this year's event to be our most successful ever. We are looking for as much __________ __________ __________ __________ __________ as possible on matters like these: Should we __________ __________ __________ __________ __________ or elsewhere? Should we have live music? Should we invite other school districts to join or not? We would appreciate it if you would answer these questions and a few others that are on the questionnaires being passed out now. It won't take long to __________ __________ __________ __________, and all of your answers and opinions will be very useful. This is a community event, so we want to hear from all of you. Please __________ __________ __________ __________ __________ __________ when you've finished.

04

W: Mr. Baker, I don't think that students at our school are __________ __________ __________ __________ __________ __________.

M: I agree with that, but what can we do to help?

W: Maybe we should provide an extra exercise program.

M: You mean like an after-school class?

W: Well, I was actually thinking that we could do it in the mornings.

M: __________ __________ __________ __________ __________?

W: Before school starts in the morning, we can have students do some simple exercises in the courtyard.

M: That seems like a pretty good idea, but I don't think you'd want to make them tired before school even starts.

W: I've read that exercise in the morning actually has the opposite effect. It can help students with their focus and concentration.

M: Does it? Anyway, I've heard that some schools are __________ __________-__________ __________ to encourage students to be more active.

W: I think that's a great idea, too.

M: Well, __________ __________ __________ __________ __________ __________ __________ and see if they work.

05

W: Thanks for meeting with me, Mr. Gaines.

M: Thanks for having me.

W: I'd first like to congratulate you on Gaines' Eatery being named Austin's top restaurant of 2015.

M: Thanks. I appreciate it. But I couldn't __________ __________ __________ __________. The members of my crew are the real heroes.

W: So, Mr. Gaines, I have a few questions I'd like to ask you. First, when did you decide to get into the restaurant business?

M: Well, when I was young, my father owned a small bakery on Second Street. It was there that I really gained an appreciation for the business.

W: That's great. And what is the most difficult part of your job?

M: I sometimes ________ ________ ________ ________ ________ ________ during the dinner rush. It gets stressful, but my crew really helps ease the chaos.

W: What do you do in your free time?

M: The work never ends for me. When I'm not at work, I'm usually ________ ________ ________ and testing new methods.

W: It sounds like you take your work very seriously. Do you mind if we get a couple of photos of you ________ ________ ________ ________ ________?

M: Sure. No problem.

06

W: How's your advertisement coming along, Patrick?

M: I think I'm almost finished. Have a look.

W: I'm impressed. The slogan 'Need Energy?' ________ ________ ________ ________ ________ ________. The bold capital letters are so bright and full of energy.

M: That's what I was going for. I also put this arrow ________ ________ ________ ________ to show forward movement.

W: That's a great idea.

M: Also, to catch people's attention, I included a can of Rad CraCra with hands, and it's waving ________ ________ ________ ________ ________ ________.

W: That's a nice touch. I also like the soccer player kicking the ball.

M: That's Phil Phillips, the spokesmodel for the drink.

W: It's also cool that you put some ________ ________ ________ ________ ________. That's really important to some people these days.

07

[Telephone rings.]

M: Hello?

W: Hi, Bill. It's me.

M: Hi there, honey. What's going on?

W: ________ ________ ________ ________ you're still at the office.

M: I am still here, yes. I'll be leaving fairly soon, though.

W: Okay, that's great. Would you mind stopping by the supermarket ________ ________ ________ ________?

M: Sure. What do you need me to pick up?

W: Well, I helped out my friend Rachel yesterday with some errands she needed to take care of.

M: Yes. I remember you telling me about that.

W: She gave me a box of assorted teas and spices, and I need ________ ________ ________ ________ ________ ________ ________.

M: That was nice of her to give you a gift, and it's a great idea to put them in jars. What type of jars are you thinking about?

W: Just some small glass jars with screw-on lids. You know, ________ ________ ________ ________ ________-________.

M: All right, I got it. I'll give you a call again when I get to the supermarket.

08

M: Here you go, Amanda. I got you some tea.

W: Thanks a lot, Nathan. So, where were you yesterday? You ________ ________ ________.

M: I was late getting to work because my wife had an accident.

W: Oh my! Is everything okay?

M: Yes, everything is fine. She just slipped and fell in the bathroom.

W: That's terrible. I can see why you were late.

M: Well, that's not all. I decided to drive to work because I thought it would save time.

W: Oh. You usually ________ ________ ________ ________ ________, don't you?

M: Yeah, I do. I thought I could get to the office quicker if I drove, but ________ ________ ________ it takes longer because of ________ ________ ________ ________.

W: Yes, I know. I never drive because it takes so long to get here.

M: Well, since I'm new to the area, I ________ ________ ________ ________ ________ ________. I should have asked somebody.

W: It's all right. So your wife is okay?

M: Yeah, she just hurt her ankle. Thank god it was nothing more serious.

09

M: Good morning, Mrs. Crocker. What can I get for you today?

W: Well, I'm looking to make my famous cherry cake for a family reunion this afternoon.

M: All right. I have just what you need. These Washington cherries came in this morning. They're $6 a pound.
W: Perfect. I'll take two pounds. I think a pineapple would be great for the reunion, as well. How much are they running?
M: They're $10 a piece.
W: That's a bit too expensive. __________ __________ __________ __________ __________ __________ get half of one?
M: Sure. That's not a problem.
W: __________ __________ __________ __________ __________ of a full pineapple, right?
M: Well, it's actually $6 for half a pineapple, but since you're a regular customer, I'll give it to you for $5.
W: Thanks. I'd also like a gallon of lemonade.
M: It's $4 a gallon. But you can __________ __________ __________ __________ __________ if you spend more than $25.
W: That's all right. I'll just take the two pounds of cherries, half a pineapple, and a gallon of lemonade. __________ __________ __________ __________ __________, right?
M: Sure. Thank you, Mrs. Crocker.

10

W: Hey, Mr. Wise. I've been thinking what if we __________ __________ __________ for the photography contest this spring.
M: That's a great idea. We can show people in our town our students' hard work.
W: That's right. But we need to think of __________ __________ __________ __________ __________ __________. What do you think about nature photography?
M: That sounds good to me. Hey, I think we might be able to reserve some space in the exhibition room of the downtown library.
W: You think so? How much will it cost?
M: Well, I know some people on the library board. I think we might be able to __________ __________ __________ __________ __________. I'll check to see if it's available.
W: Great. I'll __________ __________ __________ __________ __________ so that we can promote the exhibit around town.
M: Good idea. What do you think about formal invitations for the parents?
W: I don't really think that'll be necessary. I think the posters and __________ __________ __________ __________ __________ __________.
M: I see. Well, I guess we should get to work.

11

M: This fall, we're bringing you the finest dining experiences the city has to offer. Ricardo's on the Boardwalk is the perfect restaurant for any dining situation. It's located on Scales Lake, situated __________ __________ __________ __________ __________. The construction of our magnificent restaurant has taken almost two years, but we're finally ready to open our doors. Our open-air dining room offers an incredible view of the lake, and our upstairs lounge houses local jazz talent __________ __________ __________ __________ __________ __________. You can enjoy a meal and drinks while listening to the best jazz the area has to offer. We also have a more family-friendly dining area to cater to your young ones. Our establishment employs only the finest chefs, and __________ __________ __________ __________ __________ __________. If you're looking for a memorable dining experience, look no further than Ricardo's on the Boardwalk, opening this fall.

12

W: Welcome to Owen Sports. What can I help you with today?
M: I'm looking for a new set of soccer cleats. Do you have any recommendations?
W: Here's a list of our products. Do you play defense or offense?
M: These cleats are actually for my son, and he likes to __________ __________ __________.
W: I see. Well, perhaps the all-purpose cleats would better suit him.
M: That sounds good. Would you recommend plastic or cloth?
W: I'd recommend the plastic ones. Plastic is __________ __________ __________, so they'll last longer.
M: All right. I'll take the plastic ones. So I have two options: the cheaper pair or the more expensive one.
W: Those are more expensive because they're new for this season.
M: I don't think my son will care if they're the newest model or not. I'll __________ __________ __________ __________ in size 5.

W: Great choice. I'll ring them up for you at the front register.

M: Sounds good. Thank you for your help.

13

W: Good morning, Stan. What's new?

M: Well, I'm trying to __________ __________ __________ to visit Thailand this summer.

W: Really? What part of Thailand are you going to? I went there last winter, you know.

M: Yeah, I'm going there because of what you said about it. Did you stay around Bangkok or did you make it to the beaches?

W: I stayed in Bangkok for a couple of days, and then I went to Phi Phi Island. You've got to get to the beaches. They're incredible.

M: Yeah, I don't think I'll care too much for the big city. __________ __________ __________ __________ __________ to give me about traveling there?

W: Well, you should haggle on prices everywhere you go.

M: Really? Is everything there expensive?

W: No. everything is quite cheap, but __________ __________ __________ __________ __________ __________. You can almost always bargain.

M: I see. So I should always argue about the price.

W: Yeah. Most of the time you can get souvenirs for about __________ __________ __________ __________ __________ they initially quote you.

M: (Thanks for the tip. It's very helpful.)

14

M: Are you excited to watch your first F1 race?

W: I'm really excited. Let's buy some snacks at the __________ __________ before we sit down.

M: Sure. I'm kind of __________ __________ __________ __________ __________ __________. Oh, look. They have cotton candy.

W: You like cotton candy? That's a snack for kids.

M: Maybe you're right, but this is an F1 race and cotton candy is a fun treat.

W: I guess so. I just think a grown man __________ __________ __________ __________ __________.

M: Okay. What about some churros? I love churros, too.

W: You've got to be kidding. Churros are __________ __________. Can't we get a couple of hotdogs and a hamburger, like normal people?

M: Oh, come on! Have a churro.

W: (No thanks. I don't want to eat anything that sweet.)

15

W: Kristen and her family are planning to __________ __________ __________ __________ __________ on Saturday. Her son, Gavin, is especially excited to go because he loves the outdoors. Kristen has been preparing for the hike all week, and she has even prepared some of Gavin's favorite snacks. However, Kristen __________ __________ __________ __________ on Friday night and realizes that it's calling for an 80% chance of rain. In fact, the forecast predicts that a series of storms will be in the area throughout the weekend. __________ __________ __________ __________ __________, the National Weather Service is urging people to stay in their homes. Kristen thinks that it'll be best if they __________ __________ __________ __________ __________ __________. In this situation, what would Kristen most likely say to Gavin?

Kristen: Gavin, (I think we should reschedule the hike for next weekend.)

16-17

M: Cooking every day can be costly and time-consuming. People these days are always on the go and don't have time to cook for themselves. I'm here to provide tips to save you money and time on food. First, buy food items in bulk. It's cheaper to buy items in bulk than it is to purchase them individually. Second, avoid brand names and buy store-brand goods. Brand-name products often contain the same ingredients as store-brand ones, but are much more expensive. Third, buy produce only when __________ __________ __________. Canned or frozen food can be substituted when produce is out of season and therefore expensive. Also, be sure to __________ __________ __________ __________ and sales. You can save a lot of money by using coupons and __________ __________ __________ __________. Finally, cook in bulk. I know it may be boring, but bringing your lunch to work every day will save you loads of money. For example, you can dedicate some time on Sunday night to cooking lunch for the week. Spaghetti is a great, cost-effective dish that can be reheated and eaten all week. Changing your lifestyle to save money can be difficult, but it's certainly worthwhile.

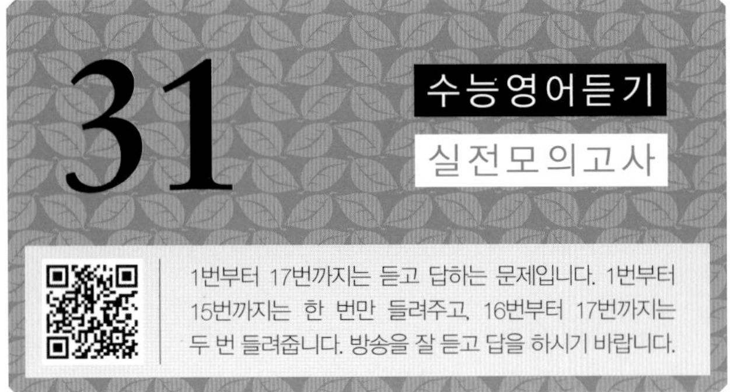

01

대화를 듣고, 여자의 마지막 말에 대한 남자의 응답으로 가장 적절한 것을 고르시오.

① Of course. I'm ready for the meeting now.
② I'm sorry, but I'm not sure how to get there.
③ Yes. Give me directions to your office, please.
④ No. I just got off at the wrong subway station.
⑤ The office is in the tall building across the street.

02

대화를 듣고, 남자의 마지막 말에 대한 여자의 응답으로 가장 적절한 것을 고르시오.

① You should take better care of your eyes.
② You don't have to get your eyes tested now.
③ You won't be able to break the habit that way.
④ You need to wait a while before you read a book.
⑤ You should consider using the computer more often.

03

다음을 듣고, 여자가 하는 말의 주제로 가장 적절한 것을 고르시오.

① 온라인 쇼핑의 부정적인 측면
② 온라인 쇼핑이 증가하게 된 원인
③ 믿을 만한 온라인 쇼핑 사이트 찾는 법
④ 오프라인 쇼핑과 온라인 쇼핑의 비교
⑤ 온라인 쇼핑의 판매 전략

04

대화를 듣고, 남자의 의견으로 가장 적절한 것을 고르시오.

① 자선 단체에서 파는 신발을 구입하라.
② 용도에 맞는 신발을 구입해서 신어라.
③ 새로 사지 말고 헌 신발을 수선해서 신어라.
④ 헌 신발을 버리지 말고 자선 단체에 기부하라.
⑤ 직접 상점에 가지 말고 인터넷 쇼핑몰을 이용하라.

05

대화를 듣고, 두 사람의 관계를 가장 잘 나타낸 것을 고르시오.

① 교수 — 학생
② 봉사자 — 리포터
③ 면접관 — 구직자
④ 사회자 — 출연자
⑤ 과학자 — 피실험자

06

대화를 듣고, 그림에서 대화의 내용과 일치하지 않는 것을 고르시오.

07

대화를 듣고, 남자가 할 일로 가장 적절한 것을 고르시오.

① 지구 온난화에 대해 조사하기
② 시 대회를 위한 야구 연습하기
③ 친구가 보고서 쓰는 것 도와주기
④ 도서관에 가서 영화 DVD 찾아보기
⑤ 지난주에 빌린 영화 DVD 반납하기

08

대화를 듣고, 남자가 일일 캠프 관리자로 일하는 이유를 고르시오.

① 다른 일보다 보수가 많은 편이라서
② 스트레스는 받지만 보람을 느껴서
③ 자연을 즐기며 일할 수 있어서
④ 아이들과 지내는 것이 좋아서
⑤ 근무 시간이 규칙적이라서

09

대화를 듣고, 남자가 지불할 총 금액을 고르시오.

① $48 ② $54 ③ $55 ④ $60 ⑤ $66

10

대화를 듣고, 섬에 관해 두 사람이 언급하지 않은 것을 고르시오.

① 위치 ② 날씨 ③ 숙박 비용
④ 현지 가이드 ⑤ 할 만한 것들

11

Mobile Device Photo Contest에 관한 다음 내용을 듣고, 일치하지 않는 것을 고르시오.

① 16세 이하의 아이들만 참가할 수 있다.
② 출품작은 세 주제 중 하나를 담아야 한다.
③ 우승자는 각 분야를 합쳐서 단 한 명이다.
④ 참가자는 부모님의 동의를 받아야만 한다.
⑤ 이번 주 목요일 정오부터 등록을 시작한다.

12

다음 표를 보면서 대화를 듣고, 두 사람이 주문할 공룡 장난감 모델을 고르시오.

Dinosaur Toys

	Type	Price	Material	Size
①	Tyrannosaurus Rex	$220	Plastic	Two Feet
②	Triceratops	$150	Plastic	Two Feet
③	Tyrannosaurus Rex	$150	Wood	Two Feet
④	Triceratops	$100	Wood	One Foot
⑤	Tyrannosaurus Rex	$150	Wood	One Foot

13

대화를 듣고, 여자의 마지막 말에 대한 남자의 응답으로 가장 적절한 것을 고르시오.

Man: ____________________

① How about joining our X-Fit club?
② Do you know any gyms that I can go to?
③ You look like you've lost some weight, too.
④ I think it's a lot better if you exercise alone.
⑤ You should be careful when exercising alone.

14

대화를 듣고, 남자의 마지막 말에 대한 여자의 응답으로 가장 적절한 것을 고르시오.

Woman: ____________________

① She must have helped you decide well.
② She suggested I try something different.
③ She considers the interest of all students.
④ She refused to help me find a new major.
⑤ She used to help students choose majors.

15

다음 상황 설명을 듣고, Katie가 Joseph에게 할 말로 가장 적절한 것을 고르시오.

Katie: ____________________

① Isn't there someone else you can help?
② I couldn't join the all-state choir competition.
③ I'm really excited about joining the talent show.
④ You should forget about including a musical act.
⑤ Could you give me a little time to think about it?

[16-17] 다음을 듣고, 물음에 답하시오.

16

여자가 하는 말의 목적으로 가장 적절한 것은?

① to repair couples' relationships through music
① to invite married couples to the music program
③ to promote conversation between a husband and wife
④ to teach the importance of healthy marital relationships
⑤ to introduce a topic of conversation for married couples

17

최근 실험에 언급된 부부들이 대화를 나누는 주당 평균 시간은?

① 6분 ② 14분 ③ 16분
④ 30분 ⑤ 1시간

01

W: Good afternoon. What can I do for you today?

M: Hi. I'm Thomas Moore. I ______ ______ ______ ______ ______ ______ ______. I'm sorry I'm late.

W: No problem, Mr. Moore. Was it difficult to find our office?

M: (No. I just got off at the wrong subway station.)

02

M: It's hard for me to see the words on the blackboard clearly.

W: Are you serious? ______ ______ ______ ______ ______ ______. What happened?

M: Lately I've gotten into the bad habit of playing computer games too much.

W: (You should take better care of your eyes.)

03

W: Did you know that you can shop for groceries online? Online grocery shopping has become quite popular in recent years. Buying online ______ ______ ______ ______ ______ ______ ______, tablets, or computers, which saves them the time it takes to go to the market. Shopping online can also save money. But beware—there are ______ ______ ______ ______. Most of the items are cheaper because they are stored in bulk in a warehouse instead of in a store, but the problem is that these warehouses are often left unattended and so there is little supervision of the goods. This could lead to ______ ______ ______ by infestation or improper storage methods. Some consumers have reported getting rotten fruit delivered to their homes. When they want to ______ ______ ______, all they can do is send an email and hope for a response. Buying online is a great way to ______ ______ ______ ______, but you should restrict the products you buy online to those that do not suffer negative consequences when they're neglected.

04

M: ______ ______ ______ ______, Amy?

W: I'm off to the mall to shop for some new sandals.

M: The sandals you have on now seem fine.

W: Actually, the soles are ______ ______ ______ ______.

M: Are you going to ______ ______ ______ after you buy new ones?

W: Probably. Why?

M: Instead of throwing them away, you should consider giving them to the Good Will Foundation. They'll give them to someone who needs them.

W: Really? But I don't know where the Good Will Foundation is located.

M: Don't worry about that. Just go to their website and look up the nearest donation center.

W: Do I need to repair my old shoes before I donate them?

M: Nope. They'll ______ ______ ______ ______ ______ ______ for you. They'll even repair the soles.

W: That's really cool. I'll definitely donate them after I buy new ones, then.

M: Great! I'm glad to hear it!

05

W: Thank you for joining our program, Professor Marsh.

M: Thanks for having me.

W: Well, let's ______ ______ ______ ______. First off, what do you think will be the next breakthrough technology?

M: Well, as you might be aware, power is a huge problem in our country. Not only is our current power infrastructure inefficient, but it's also polluting our air, land, and water.

W: That's right. You always hear about ______ ______ ______ ______ ______. It's even worse in less developed countries.

M: Right. We need to develop alternative energy sources and abandon our traditional methods.

W: What technology is ______ ______ ______ ______?

M: Solar cells. They're the future.

W: Do they have any benefit over other __________ __________ __________, like wind power or hydroelectric?

M: Absolutely. Most of the developed world has access to sunlight, but not everyone is close to a river, and even fewer can harness the wind. Solar power is also becoming a lot cheaper.

W: Well, there you have it, folks. Solar power is the future. Thank you for sharing, Professor Marsh.

M: No problem. I'm always happy to speak to your viewers.

06

M: Hey Rose, what's that you're looking at?

W: This? Oh, it's just a __________ __________ for the stadium's new cafe. Take a look.

M: It looks pretty fun. Is that a bakery in the back left?

W: Yeah. And next to that is a snack bar.

M: Those __________ __________ __________. And is that a DJ in the cafe?

W: Yeah, it is. It seems a little bit strange to have a DJ in a cafe, though. Don't you think?

M: I agree. This certainly doesn't seem like a normal cafe.

W: Yeah. They also have some entertainment for children outside of the cafe.

M: I see that. Is that a clown?

W: It looks like it. He's __________ __________ __________ __________ __________ there.

M: Yeah, I see the staff helping him prepare the balloons. It's a strange cafe, but I think it'll be a success.

W: I sure hope so. Its grand opening is just before this Sunday's concert.

07

M: Hey Rachel, could you help me with something?

W: Sure, Peter. What's up?

M: Well, __________ __________ __________ __________ __________, I wasn't in class on Thursday.

W: Right. You were playing baseball in the city tournament. How'd you all do?

M: We did great. We're __________ __________ __________ __________ __________ __________.

W: That's great. Your team is really talented this year. You all have been practicing hard. I bet you guys win it all.

M: I hope so. Anyway, did you finish your report on global warming for Mr. Smith's class?

W: I did. Have you finished yours?

M: Well, I'd like to work on it, but I can't seem to find the movie __________ __________ __________ __________ __________ __________.

W: Right. You're talking about *A Troublesome Fact*, right?

M: That's the one.

W: Have you checked the library? They must __________ __________ __________ __________ __________.

M: I didn't think about checking the library. I'll head over there right now.

08

W: Hey, what are you going to do this summer?

M: I was thinking of working at the school __________ __________ __________ __________ __________.

W: That sounds interesting.

M: I've been doing it every summer __________ __________ __________ __________ __________, actually.

W: Wow, I didn't know that. What's the job like?

M: It's pretty easy. I teach the kids and lead them in whatever fun things we have planned for the day.

W: Is it a fairly relaxed environment?

M: Yeah, it really is. The hours __________ __________ __________ __________ __________ __________ __________ __________ the activities, but everyone is really cool about staying late or arriving early. There's very little stress.

W: How about your pay?

M: It's average for a camp supervisor, but it's definitely __________ __________ __________ __________ __________. But I don't really care too much about the money.

W: Why have you been working there for so long?

M: It's really my ideal job. I get to be outside every day to __________ __________, and all of the work is very hands-on.

09

W: Well, that's it. __________ __________ __________ __________ __________.

M: Thank you so much. My hair looks much better. I'm going to look great at the company party tonight.

W: I __________ __________ __________ __________ __________.

M: That's good to hear. I'll be sure to recommend you to all of my friends.

W: Thank you. That'll be $25 for the haircut. Would you like to purchase any hair care products today?

M: Absolutely. I'll take some of your styling wax. How much is it?

W: The wax is $20. How about shampoo? Our aloe-infused shampoo is great for your hair type.

M: I'll take a bottle of that, too.

W: Great. It runs $15 a bottle. ________ ________ ________ ________ for you?

M: Yes. Hey, didn't you mention some kind of discount for first-time visitors?

W: Right. Since you're ________ ________-________ ________, you get a 10% discount on your total.

M: That's great. Here's my card.

10

M: Hey Sally, I'm thinking about taking a trip to somewhere warmer this winter. Do you have any suggestions?

W: Sure. There's ________ ________ ________ ________ ________ ________ ________ all the time called Tybee Island. I'm sure you'll love it.

M: Tybee Island? I've never heard of that. Where is it?

W: It's in Georgia, near Savannah.

M: I see. ________ ________ ________ ________ ________?

W: Well, that area of the country is very beautiful. The colonial-style houses are lovely, and the beach is quite stunning.

M: What's the weather like at that time of year?

W: It's not too hot, but it might be too cold to go swimming.

M: That's cool. I don't swim much anyway. How much do the hotels in the area usually run?

W: Well, you can ________ ________ ________ ________ for about 700 dollars a week. A three-bedroom condo would be perfect for your family, I think.

M: That sounds fair. I'd definitely like to tour some of the more historic places. Do they offer tours?

W: Absolutely. There are several history tours you can join. They ________ ________ ________ ________ you can take in the evening.

M: That sounds awesome. I'm going to start researching Tybee Island immediately.

11

M: We are proud to announce the entry dates for our world-famous Mobile Device Photo Contest. The idea is to give young people creative license with their smartphones or tablets. Contestants must be 16 years of age or younger to enter. ________ ________ ________ ________ and wish to participate should ________ ________ that fall into one of the following categories: architecture, nature, or commerce. We will choose ________ ________ ________ ________ ________ ________, and the winners will receive a cash prize of $500. Remember, each contestant must have ________ ________ ________ ________ to enter the contest. Online registration will open this Thursday at noon on our website: *www.mdphoto.com.* Entries must be submitted by October 15th, 2016.

12

M: Hey darling, what's that you're looking at?

W: I'm just browsing the Internet for a gift for Jake. You know his birthday is coming up, right?

M: Of course. What do you have in mind?

W: Well, ________ ________ ________ dinosaurs now, so I figured a toy triceratops would be cool. Look at this one. It's really cute.

M: Yeah, that might work, but he told me his favorite dinosaur is a tyrannosaurus rex.

W: I see. Well, I found a list of this website's top dinosaur toys. How much are we looking to spend?

M: I don't think ________ ________ ________ ________ ________ $200.

W: Okay. How about the material? I think we should get a wooden one. Plastic is ________ ________.

M: I think so, too. What size do you think we should get?

W: Well, I think that two feet is too big. Don't you?

M: I agree. Well, it looks like we've found the one we want. Go ahead and place the order.

W: All right. ________ ________ ________ ________ ________ before his birthday.

13

M: Hey, Laura. It's been a while. How's everything with you?

W: Everything's great. You look like you've changed a bit ________ ________ ________ ________ ________.

M: I have. I've ________ ________ ________ ________ weight from dieting and exercise.
W: That's cool. What kind of exercises are you doing?
M: I play soccer a bit, but I also do an X-Fit program ________ ________ ________ ________.
W: X-Fit? I was doing the Lunacy program at home, but I didn't like it.
M: That's one of those home video programs, huh? I tried one of those. I quit after three days.
W: So, what's so different about X-Fit?
M: Well, X-Fit is a routine you do with other people. We meet at a gym and do our routine.
W: I see. I guess exercising alone isn't very motivating.
M: Right. When you're with a group, ________ ________ ________ ________ ________ to try harder. It's really fun.
W: I think I should start exercising again, but I don't really want to do it alone.
M: (How about joining our X-Fit club?)

14

M: ________ ________ ________ ________ ________ ________, Sabrina. I don't know what I should do.
W: Really? I think your major is a lot more interesting than some of the other ones at the university.
M: I do the same things every day. I don't really learn much. I just don't think that computer science is for me.
W: Have you ________ ________ ________ ________ ________ about it?
M: No. She wasn't too helpful the last time I spoke to her. Plus, she's really busy speaking to new students because it's the ________ ________ ________ ________.
W: That may be true, but if you don't talk to her, you'll be stuck doing something you don't like ________ ________ ________ ________ ________ ________.
M: I don't want to waste her time. I'm not sure what other major I'd enjoy.
W: I think that's something your advisor can help you decide. I wasn't sure ________ ________ ________ ________ ________, but my advisor changed all of that.
M: Really? What did she do for you?
W: (She suggested I try something different.)

15

M: Joseph is ________ ________ ________ ________ ________ that takes place at the end of the school year. He has a magic act, a dancing act, and a juggling act, but he'd really like to find a musician to play in the show. He remembers that Katie was a finalist in last year's state choir competition. Joseph calls Katie and ________ ________ ________ ________. She declines his request because she's too busy preparing for her exams to practice. However, Joseph is persistent and keeps trying to ________ ________ ________ ________ ________ ________ ________. He tells her that she's the only person who can balance the show. Katie ________ ________ ________ ________, but can't make up her mind. In this situation, what would Katie most likely say to Joseph?
Katie: (Could you give me a little time to think about it?)

16-17

W: Good evening. This is *Sunday Evening Classics*, and I'm your host, Lauren Bell. Before we start tonight, I want to talk a little bit about married couples and communication. An experiment was conducted recently to calculate the ________ ________ ________ between a husband and wife, and the results might surprise you. The average person might assume that an average married couple would talk to each other quite often. But one psychologist found that couples speak far less than ________ ________ ________ ________. Keep in mind that the number I'm about to give you is for a week, not a day. It's sixteen minutes! Shocking, isn't it? If you consider yourself a part of an average couple, then try ________ ________ ________ ________ 14 minutes more per week to bring the total amount of time to 30 minutes of conversation. Then try to have 30 minutes of conversation every day. Will it help your relationship? We think so. ________ ________ ________ ________ or even just trivial conversation is very important for couples. So, in the interest of all the couples out there, I want to play *The Modern Love Song* by Scotty McGee. Enjoy!

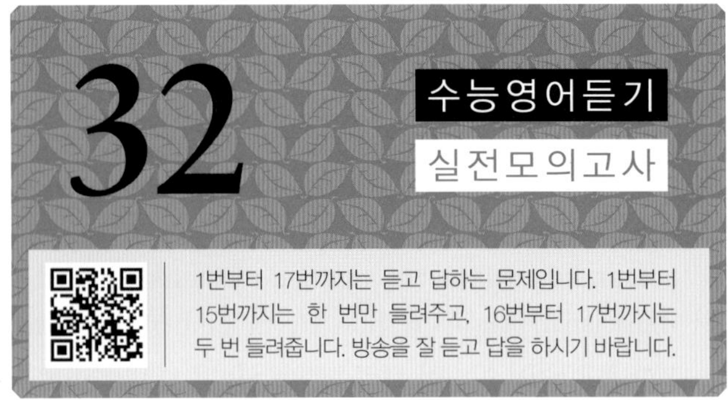

01

대화를 듣고, 남자의 마지막 말에 대한 여자의 응답으로 가장 적절한 것을 고르시오.

① All of his music was so inspiring.
② It's going to be at the state theater.
③ I appreciate the advice. Thank you.
④ Oh, I won't be able to make it then.
⑤ Make sure you take a lot of pictures.

02

대화를 듣고, 여자의 마지막 말에 대한 남자의 응답으로 가장 적절한 것을 고르시오.

① It should be less than $20.
② The price for admission is $10.
③ You should pay me back soon.
④ I think the gallery closes at 9 p.m.
⑤ I might be late because of bad traffic.

03

다음을 듣고, 남자가 하는 말의 주제로 가장 적절한 것을 고르시오.

① 창의성을 키우는 방법
② 뇌 활동을 자극하는 방법
③ 기분과 창의성의 상관관계
④ 지식이 창의성에 주는 영향
⑤ 뇌 활동을 활발히 하는 음식

04

대화를 듣고, 여자의 의견으로 가장 적절한 것을 고르시오.

① 아이에게 자신이 가지고 논 장난감을 정리하도록 해야 한다.
② 아이들은 장난감을 통해 또래와의 상호작용을 배워 나간다.
③ 아이들의 노는 방과 공부방을 따로 분리해 주어야 한다.
④ 장난감이 많으면 아이들의 자율성 강화에 도움이 된다.
⑤ 너무 많은 장난감은 아이들의 상상력에 방해가 된다.

05

대화를 듣고, 두 사람의 관계를 가장 잘 나타낸 것을 고르시오.

① 코치 — 골키퍼
② 기자 — 축구감독
③ 축구선수 — 축구팬
④ 물리치료사 — 운동선수
⑤ 경기 해설자 — 현장 진행자

06

대화를 듣고, 그림에서 대화의 내용과 일치하지 않는 것을 고르시오.

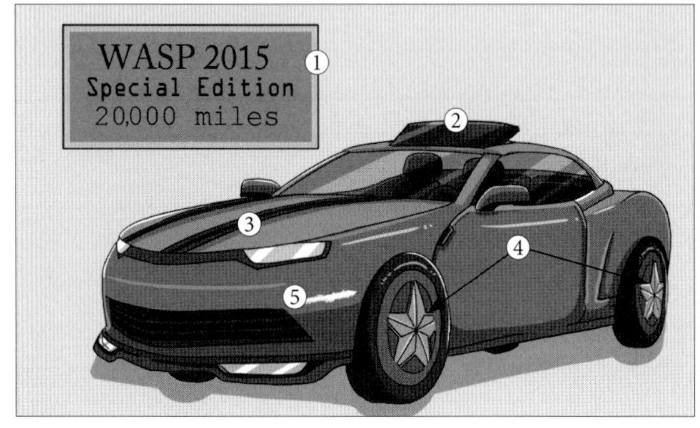

07

대화를 듣고, 여자가 남자에게 부탁한 일을 고르시오.

① 졸업 연설 후보자들의 지원서 받기
② 졸업 연설 후보자들과 대화하기
③ 졸업 연설 후보자 추천하기
④ 졸업 연설 후보자 추리기
⑤ 졸업 연설 대본 작성하기

08

대화를 듣고, 남자가 놀이공원에 갈 수 없는 이유를 고르시오.

① 딸의 여름캠프를 등록해야 해서
② 딸의 숙제를 도와주어야 해서
③ 회사 출장과 날짜가 겹쳐서
④ 가족 모임이 있어서
⑤ 부모님 생신이라서

09

대화를 듣고, 여자가 지불할 금액을 고르시오.

① $365 ② $405 ③ $450 ④ $500 ⑤ $550

10

대화를 듣고, 헌혈에 관해 두 사람이 언급하지 않은 것을 고르시오.

① 나이 ② 체중 ③ 혈액형
④ 맥박 ⑤ 체온

11

Franklin 대학교 '행진 악단 오디션'에 관한 다음 내용을 듣고, 일치하지 않는 것을 고르시오.

① 접수 날짜는 9월 25일에서 30일까지이다.
② 기성곡과 창작곡 모두 연주 가능하다.
③ 최소 10분간 연주를 해야 한다.
④ 연주할 곡의 악보도 첨부해야 한다.
⑤ 악단의 정원은 100명이다.

12

다음 표를 보면서 대화를 듣고, 남자가 선택한 파티를 고르시오.

Party Room Packages

	Party Packages	Maximum Number of Children	Time (minutes)	Price	Number of Large Pizzas
①	A	15	100	$220	2
②	B	15	90	$180	2
③	C	15	90	$170	1
④	D	15	70	$170	2
⑤	E	13	70	$160	1

13

대화를 듣고, 여자의 마지막 말에 대한 남자의 응답으로 가장 적절한 것을 고르시오.

Man: ______________________________

① You should have picked your son up earlier.
② It might be too dark for the students to study.
③ I'll see what I can do about keeping the lights on.
④ Don't worry. I'll have the lights repaired tomorrow.
⑤ Raymond should be more careful, so he doesn't get hurt.

14

대화를 듣고, 남자의 마지막 말에 대한 여자의 응답으로 가장 적절한 것을 고르시오.

Woman: ______________________________

① How much does this purse cost?
② You shouldn't waste old products.
③ I don't know how to make a purse.
④ I would, but I'm not very good with my hands.
⑤ My art teacher enjoys woodworking as a hobby.

15

다음 상황 설명을 듣고, Stella가 Clara에게 할 말로 가장 적절한 것을 고르시오.

Stella: ______________________________

① You shouldn't tell Grandpa you don't like his gift.
② I think that we should go and visit Grandpa soon.
③ Please don't tell Grandpa that I gave you this shirt.
④ This T-shirt is too small. Please send it back to Grandpa.
⑤ Will you take Grandpa to the store to exchange this shirt?

[16-17] 다음을 듣고, 물음에 답하시오.

16

여자가 하는 말의 목적으로 가장 적절한 것은?

① 저축의 필요성을 강조하려고
② 상품 판매 전략을 안내하려고
③ 돈을 절약하는 방법을 알려주려고
④ 새로운 온라인 쇼핑몰을 홍보하려고
⑤ 합리적 소비의 중요성을 설명하려고

17

여자가 언급하지 않은 것은?

① 대중교통 이용 ② 상점 평면도 의식
③ 온라인 쇼핑 이용 ④ 물 여과기 사용
⑤ 가계부 작성

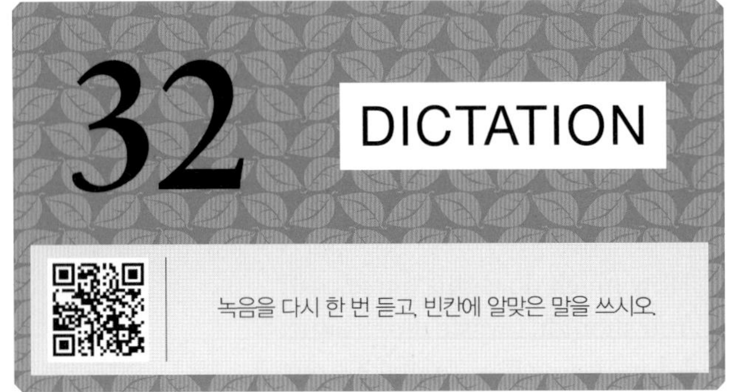

01

M: Aren't you a huge Elvis fan? Did you see that there's a new Elvis exhibition coming to town?

W: I did! I just read about it this morning. I'm really excited.

M: Yeah, I am too. __________ __________ __________ __________ __________ __________ __________ exactly?

W: (It's going to be at the state theater.)

02

W: Hi. I need to go to the art gallery downtown. How long will it take?

M: Well, __________ __________ __________ __________ __________ the traffic isn't so congested. It should take about a half hour.

W: That's not bad. Do you know how much it'll cost to take a taxi?

M: (It should be less than $20.)

03

M: Hi everyone, and good morning. I'd like to talk to you all today about a really interesting study that has just come out from the University of Minnesota. The study __________ __________ __________ __________ __________ happiness and creativity. The researchers took three groups of people and placed them in different scenarios. The first group was sent to an amusement park. The second group was sent to a theater to watch a horror movie, and the third group was sent to a pottery museum. After each group returned, the researchers __________ __________ __________ __________. As it turns out, the group of people who went to the amusement park did far better on the test than the other two groups. This result leads the researchers to believe that when we are happy, our brains can access more previously obtained knowledge and utilize this knowledge to create. Therefore, happy people are more creative because of their ability to __________ __________ __________ __________ and, out of them, form something new.

04

W: Hey, look at Tommy's playroom. His parents really bought him a lot of toys, huh?

M: Yeah. And you should see his bedroom. __________ __________ __________ __________ __________ in there.

W: I read an article about how fewer toys can help children develop different skills.

M: Really? I've never heard that before. I figured __________ __________ __________, __________ __________.

W: Well, some toys are great for helping children grow and learn, but too many can actually be harmful.

M: Hmm… I wonder why that is.

W: The article said that too many toys can really __________ __________ __________ __________.

M: Oh? How so?

W: Kids with fewer toys have to use their imagination more than kids with more toys. They have to be more creative when they're playing.

M: __________ __________ __________ __________ __________. I didn't really have too many toys growing up. I had to make my own toys or invent games instead.

05

W: Did you see the match between Liverpool and Manchester City on Saturday?

M: Yeah, I saw it.

W: What did you think of Liverpool?

M: They played great. They had a lot of __________ __________ __________ __________, but they __________ __________ __________ __________ __________.

W: Yeah. It was a very close game. __________ __________ __________ __________ __________ __________.

M: Yep. Manchester City managed to hold them off. Their goalie did an amazing job.

W: I agree. So, what kind of strategy are you going to use against Liverpool when you play them next week?

M: We're going to have to __________ __________ __________ to keep those shots away. We've also been reworking some of our offensive plays, so hopefully they'll produce some results.

W: We're excited to watch the match. Is there anything you'd like to say to the soccer fans watching this interview?

M: Thank you for all your support and for watching us grow in the league. We're looking forward to winning this next match.

W: We appreciate you taking the time to do this interview, Charlie. This is Susan Peters with BCC News signing off.

06

[Cell phone rings.]

M: Hey, Megan.

W: Sam? I was wondering if you could help me out with something.

M: Sure I can. What's up?

W: Well, I'm trying to sell my car and I thought using social media, like Twitter, would help get the word out.

M: Yeah, that's a great idea. I have a lot of followers on Twitter. You want me to ________ ________ ________ ________ ________ of your car?

W: That would be wonderful. The car is a Wasp 2015 Special Edition and has about 20,000 miles on it.

M: Does it have a sunroof?

W: Yes, the special edition comes standard with a sunroof.

M: I see. And are there any other features that are included with the special edition?

W: Yes, there are pinstripes along the sides.

M: Is that all?

W: It also has star-shaped wheels.

M: All right. Is there any damage to the car?

W: There's ________ ________ ________ ________ ________ ________ ________, but ________ ________ ________ ________ ________ my asking price. Other than that, I've taken good care of it and have all of the service records.

M: Okay, got it. I'll put the description up on Twitter right away.

W: Thanks a lot, Sam.

07

M: Hey, Amanda.

W: Hi, John. Come in, please.

M: I wanted to know if you needed any help deciding ________ ________ ________ ________ ________ ________ this year.

W: Yes, that would be great. I've narrowed it down to 15 candidates.

M: Okay. So what would you like me to do with these students?

W: I was hoping you could meet with them and just have a conversation with each one. I want you to find out ________ ________ ________ ________ ________ and what message they'd like to share with their classmates if they had the chance.

M: What should I do after meeting with them?

W: You and I will meet again, and I'd like for you to give me the details of what each student had to say along with your general impression of them.

M: All right, I can do that. But it may be difficult to meet with all of them because everyone's schedule is so different.

W: I think ________ ________ ________ ________ ________, John.

M: I appreciate your confidence in me. All right, ________ ________ ________.

W: Thanks, John. Let me know when you've finished so we can talk about it.

08

W: Hey Joe, where are you going?

M: ________ ________ ________ ________ the museum with my daughter. She's got an assignment about ancient Egypt that she has to do over summer vacation.

W: Homework over vacation, huh? That's rough. So, what else is she going to do this summer?

M: Well, we have her ________ ________ ________ ________ ________ at Lake Totanka. Why?

W: My boss gave me eight tickets to the Holidayland Amusement Park. I'm taking my family and was wondering if you wanted to join us.

M: That would be awesome. When are you going?

W: Next Sunday, the 20th.

M: Next Sunday, huh? Well, I'd love to, but we can't. We're going to my parents' house next weekend.

W: ________ ________ ________.

M: Yeah, we can't really reschedule because ________ ________ ________ ________ ________. It's going to be a pretty big party.

W: I see. Well, maybe some other time.

M: Sure. Thanks for the invitation.

09

M: How can I help you today?

W: I'm trying to decide on which monitor to buy.

M: Do you need one ________ ________ ________ ________ ________?

W: Well, what's the difference?

M: A professional monitor has an ultra-high-definition screen for areas like video editing and graphic design.

W: How about the one for general purposes? What are general purposes, anyway?

M: General purposes include emailing, word processing, and watching the occasional movie on your computer.

W: Okay. __________ __________ __________ graphic design or video production, but I'd still like a nice screen.

M: Of course. All of our monitors have really nice pictures, but you'll save some money by going with one of the general purpose monitors.

W: All right. How much are they?

M: The original price is $500, but __________ __________ __________ __________, so you'll get a 10% discount.

W: Wow, that's a good deal. Can I combine that with the coupon I got from your website?

M: Absolutely. That's why we have them.

W: That's great. So I get an additional __________ __________ __________ __________ __________ __________?

M: That's correct. I'll be right back with your monitor.

10

M: Hi. I've decided that I want to donate blood. This is my first time, though, so I'm a bit nervous.

W: That's okay. We'll __________ __________ __________ __________ __________. But I have a few questions I need to ask you. First, how old are you?

M: I'm 17. Is that going to be a problem?

W: Well, there is a limited age range we can allow, but it's between 16 and 69 years old, so you're fine.

M: Great. What other requirements do you have?

W: Men have to __________ __________ __________ __________ __________, and women have to be over 45 kilograms. It looks like you'll be fine there.

M: For sure. What else?

W: You should also have a steady resting pulse between 50 and 100 beats per minute. Also, __________ __________ __________ __________ __________?

M: I haven't. If I were sick, I couldn't give blood?

W: Right. You can't donate if your body temperature is above 37.5 degrees Celsius.

M: I see. I guess it's really important to be in good health __________ __________ __________ __________.

11

M: Good afternoon, students. The Franklin College marching band tryouts are coming up, and we're opening registration from the 10th to the 15th of September, __________ __________ __________ __________ __________ __________ from the 25th to the 30th. Any musician who would like to try out is welcome to play pieces that they've written or pieces published by others. We would like each contestant to play for at least 10 minutes. With your registration, you must also __________ __________ __________ __________ about your experience as well as the sheet music for the piece that you will play. Our professional judges will determine __________ __________ __________ __________ __________ __________. The band will be limited to 100 members. I hope that any of you who are interested in joining our award-winning marching band will register and try out. Thank you for listening.

12

W: Good afternoon, sir. What can I help you with?

M: Hi. I'm trying to __________ __________ __________ __________ my son's baseball team. Do you have any openings for Saturday afternoon?

W: Sure. It looks like we'll have something available at 2 p.m. We offer several different packages. Take a look at the brochure.

M: Well, there are 15 children on his team. Do all of the packages provide pizza?

W: They do. How long do you want to __________ __________ __________ __________? We have three options.

M: This is the last time they'll see each other, so I think a longer party would be nice.

W: You should probably book the room for either 90 or 100 minutes, then.

M: That sounds great, but I don't want to __________ __________ __________ __________ __________ __________.

W: Well, there are two different packages that will __________ __________ __________. One includes two large pizzas and drinks. The other comes with only one large pizza and drinks.

M: I think we'll go with the one with two pizzas.

W: All right, sir. __________ __________ __________ __________ __________ the party room at two o'clock on Saturday.

13

[Telephone rings.]

M: Good morning, St. Paul High School. This is Vice Principal Jones.

W: Hi, Mr. Jones. This is Grace Conroy, Raymond's mom. I'd like to talk to you for a minute about a problem on your campus.
M: Sure. What's the problem?
W: Well, I was picking my son up from the library last night and I noticed that it was ________ ________ ________ ________ ________ ________.
M: I'm sorry, but we usually turn off all of the campus lights after nine. ________ ________ ________ ________ ________ ________.
W: I understand. Conserving energy is important. But don't you think there's a safety concern here? Someone could fall and get hurt.
M: I didn't realize it was that big of an issue.
W: Also, lights might ________ ________ ________ ________.
M: (I'll see what I can do about keeping the lights on.)

14

M: Hey Amelia, I made something for you.
W: A purse? I've been wanting a new one. You didn't really make it yourself, did you?
M: Well, I did most of the work. My art teacher helped me a little bit. ________ ________ ________ ________ ________.
W: That's interesting. Did you ________ ________ ________ ________ ________ yourself?
M: Actually, I joined the Greenback Club at school. We learn how to repurpose old things.
W: That's really cool. What do you mean by "repurpose old things"?
M: We take old, unused things and use them to make new products—like this purse.
W: Sounds like an interesting club. This purse looks like it was hard to make.
M: Not really. In fact, most of our projects are really easy. In our next meeting, we're going to learn how to make drinking glasses ________ ________ ________ ________.
W: Sounds really cool. How do you do that?
M: The instructor will show us when we meet. You should come along.
W: (I would, but I'm not very good with my hands.)

15

M: A package has just arrived for Stella. It's from her grandfather, who Stella doesn't get the opportunity to see very often. After opening the package and reading the very touching note, Stella is delighted to see that her grandfather has sent her a Taylor Swift T-shirt. However, after ________ ________ ________, Stella realizes that the shirt is a bit too small for her. She considers sending it back to her grandfather and asking him to ________ ________ ________ ________ ________ ________. However, after some deliberation, she realizes that it wouldn't be easy for her grandfather to exchange the shirt and send her another. Instead, she ________ ________ ________ ________ ________ ________ ________, Clara. Clara also loves Taylor Swift and ________ ________ ________ ________ ________, but Stella doesn't want her grandfather to know that she gave it to her sister. In this situation, what would Stella most likely say to Clara?
Stella: (Please don't tell Grandpa that I gave you this shirt.)

16-17

W: Good evening, everyone. My name is Mary Anne Baker, and I work for Baker Financial. I'd like to talk to you today about ways you can save money in your day-to-day life. First of all, transportation can be expensive. If you ________ ________ ________ ________ ________ taking a taxi to work each day, you can save a lot of money by taking the bus or subway. Try to change your sleeping pattern so that you wake up earlier. Secondly, the floor plans of stores are set up to maximize what you buy. Have you ever wondered why the everyday goods that you need most, such as eggs and milk, are located in the back of the store? It's so that you walk through the store and see all of the other products on sale. Be conscious of these strategies and resist impulse purchases. Third, ________ ________ ________ ________ ________. Shopping online can save you money, as you can compare prices very easily and find the best deals. Finally, try to ________ ________ ________ ________. Instead of spending a dollar or two on water every day, invest in a water filter and fill a bottle before you leave the house. If you follow these simple tips, I'm sure you'll save money and live a more fulfilling life. Thanks for listening.

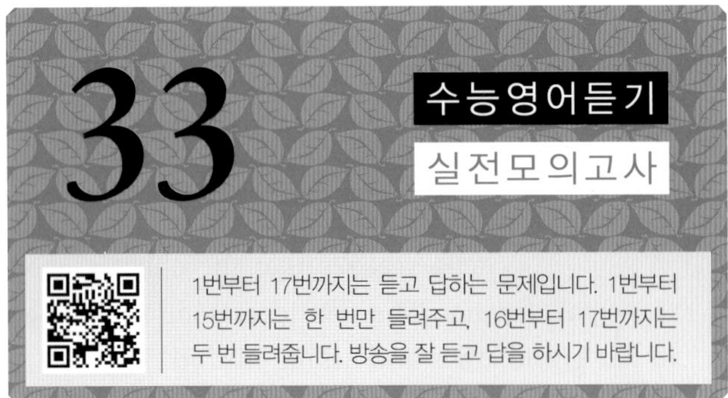

01

대화를 듣고, 여자의 마지막 말에 대한 남자의 응답으로 가장 적절한 것을 고르시오.

① The mattress is very stiff and uncomfortable.
② Actually, we don't have any rooms available.
③ I can't remember your room number.
④ I'd like to be connected to room 305.
⑤ Please leave your things with us.

02

대화를 듣고, 남자의 마지막 말에 대한 여자의 응답으로 가장 적절한 것을 고르시오.

① When are you going to leave?
② That's right. The festival is on Saturday.
③ Thanks a lot. I'm really excited about it.
④ We need to hurry. The party starts in 10 minutes.
⑤ That's a great idea. I think he'll appreciate the surprise.

03

다음을 듣고, 남자가 하는 말의 목적으로 가장 적절한 것을 고르시오.

① 의사결정에 필요한 지식을 소개하려고
② 학생들이 학교에서 하는 활동들을 알리려고
③ 전문 분야의 지식을 공유하도록 요청하려고
④ 경제적으로 힘든 학생들을 돕도록 부탁하려고
⑤ 경험을 통한 배경지식의 중요성을 강조하려고

04

대화를 듣고, 두 사람이 하는 말의 주제로 가장 적절한 것을 고르시오.

① 식품 안전 교육의 중요성
② 좋은 육류를 선택하는 기준
③ 영양성분 표시 라벨을 보는 법
④ 건강한 다이어트 식단 짜는 방법
⑤ 식료품 영양성분 표시제의 필요성

05

대화를 듣고, 두 사람의 관계를 가장 잘 나타낸 것을 고르시오.

① 간호사 — 환자 보호자
② 학부모 — 체육 교사
③ 학생 — 보건 교사
④ 구직자 — 면접관
⑤ 의사 — 환자

06

대화를 듣고, 그림에서 대화의 내용과 일치하지 않는 것을 고르시오.

07

대화를 듣고, 여자가 남자를 위해 할 일로 가장 적절한 것을 고르시오.

① 플래시 드라이브 사용법 알려주기
② 스마트폰으로 파일 전송해 주기
③ 더 좋은 제품 추천해주기
④ 사이트 주소 알려주기
⑤ 물건 대신 주문하기

08

대화를 듣고, 여자가 독서 클럽 모임에 참석할 수 없는 이유를 고르시오.

① 책을 잃어버려서
② 남편을 도와주어야 해서
③ 책을 다 읽고 갈 수 없어서
④ 중요한 발표를 준비해야 해서
⑤ 아들의 영어 선생님과 만나야 해서

09

대화를 듣고, 여자가 지불할 금액을 고르시오.

① $108 ② $117 ③ $130 ④ $135 ⑤ $150

10

대화를 듣고, Pear Computers 인턴 프로그램에 관해 두 사람이 언급하지 않은 것을 고르시오.

① 근무 장소 ② 지원 기한 ③ 지원 자격
④ 근무 기간 ⑤ 경비 지급

11

Environmental Edge Photography Contest에 관한 다음 내용을 듣고, 일치하지 않는 것을 고르시오.

① 전국의 학생들이 참여할 수 있다.
② 컬러 또는 흑백사진으로 제출 가능하다.
③ 이메일로 제출한 출품사진은 허용되지 않는다.
④ 우승자는 제출 마감일로부터 약 2주 후 발표된다.
⑤ 세 편의 우수사진을 선정하여 시상한다.

12

다음 표를 보면서 대화를 듣고, 두 사람이 살 냉장고를 고르시오.

Refrigerators on Sale

	Model	Price	Storage (liters)	Type	Warranty (years)
①	A	$1,300	1,000	Four-door	10
②	B	$1,000	950	Four-door	5
③	C	$900	800	Four-door	10
④	D	$800	800	Two-door	10
⑤	E	$600	650	Two-door	5

13

대화를 듣고, 여자의 마지막 말에 대한 남자의 응답으로 가장 적절한 것을 고르시오.

Man: ______________________

① Sure. I'd love to read your version.
② Don't consider the theme. Focus on content.
③ I think you'll really enjoy reading the original.
④ I'm going to need the author's permission first.
⑤ No. After you finish, you should write a review.

14

대화를 듣고, 남자의 마지막 말에 대한 여자의 응답으로 가장 적절한 것을 고르시오.

Woman: ______________________

① I think I should go see a doctor.
② We should plant some bamboo outside.
③ I'll go to the florist and buy some today.
④ You have to water the bamboo every day.
⑤ You should drink eight cups of water daily.

15

다음 상황 설명을 듣고, Paul이 담당자에게 할 말로 가장 적절한 것을 고르시오.

Paul: ______________________

① The problem is fixed. Thanks for all of your help.
② Thank you, but I already have an Internet provider.
③ Please send someone over to fix my Internet as soon as possible.
④ I'd like to know how I can become a customer service representative.
⑤ I'm sorry about your problem. We will send someone over to look at it.

[16-17] 다음을 듣고, 물음에 답하시오.

16

남자가 하는 말의 주제로 가장 적절한 것은?

① Parental roles in child health care
② Long-lasting impacts of childhood habits
③ Advantages of playing outside for children
④ Importance of close parent-child relationships
⑤ Activities to develop children's willingness to take risks

17

비타민 D와 관련된 질병으로 언급되지 않은 것은?

① 우울증 ② 심장병 ③ 당뇨병
④ 피부병 ⑤ 비만

01

W: Good morning, sir. How can I help you?
M: Well, ______ ______ ______ ______ ______ ______ ______ my room.
W: All right. So what exactly is the problem?
M: (The mattress is very stiff and uncomfortable.)

02

M: Hey, Julia. Did you hear the news? Owen is ______ ______ ______ Hong Kong next week.
W: I heard. I'm really excited to hear about his time there.
M: Let's go and meet him at the airport when he arrives.
W: (That's a great idea. I think he'll appreciate the surprise.)

03

M: Hi, everyone! Thank you all so much for continuing to show interest in our school. One of the things we really focus on is preparing and encouraging your children ______ ______ ______ ______ ______ ______ ______. So, now I want to introduce you all to one of our meaningful new programs. I'm sure most of you have heard the saying, "Knowledge is power." However, what's the point of having knowledge if it cannot be shared? Some of you here can ______ ______ ______. We want to encourage you to ______ ______ ______ ______ ______ ______ ______ ______. If you would like to participate and share with us, you can come to school next Wednesday. Sharing just a little of what you know can make a big difference in our students' lives.

04

W: I thought ______ ______ ______ ______ ______, Roy.
M: I am. Why do you ask?
W: Well, you just ordered that chicken salad with cheese and ranch dressing. If you're on a diet, the Asian salad would be a better choice.
M: Really? What's the difference?
W: Look at the nutritional information.
M: Ah, I see. The chicken salad has a lot more calories than the Asian salad. In fact, it has as many calories as a cheeseburger combo.
W: Right. It might seem healthy because it's a salad, but it's actually just as bad for you as a greasy sandwich.
M: I see. It's good that they have the information available for me to see. ______ ______ ______ ______ ______ on all food products. That way we can make better, healthier choices.
W: I agree. In some countries, ______ ______ ______ ______ on all food and drinks.
M: Really? I had no idea.
W: Yeah. For example, in the U.S., they have to include detailed information on meat. They even have to include the percentage of fat.
M: I wish our country would adopt the same policy. It'd make it easier for people like me to eat healthy.
W: Right. ______ ______ ______ ______ ______ ______ ______ ______ to see which one contained more fat, calories, or sodium.

05

M: Mrs. Tomlin, you asked to speak with me?
W: Yes, Alex. Come on in and have a seat. I just heard you had your appendix removed.
M: ______ ______ ______ ______ a couple of weeks ago. It was very sudden.
W: They are usually quite sudden. Are you feeling okay now?
M: I feel much better. It was a little scary when it happened, though.
W: Did you tell your P.E. teacher about it?
M: Yeah. He suggested ______ ______ ______ ______ for a week or two.
W: Are there any other problems you're dealing with?
M: Not really. I'm just nervous about my stomach area ever since the operation.
W: That's understandable. I think ______ ______ ______ ______ ______, but in the meantime just take it easy and relax.
M: Thanks for the advice. I'll definitely be doing more studying and less playing for the time being.

W: Well, perhaps that's a good thing. You'll be back outside playing in no time. Don't worry.

M: I appreciate your kindness. I should get back to class now.

06

M: Hey Katie, didn't you go to the Soccer Hall of Fame last weekend?

W: I did. Check out this picture that I took there.

M: Wow! ________ ________ ________ ________. Those posters on the wall are interesting. Why is the guy on the left wearing gloves and a different uniform?

W: Well, the goalkeeper always wears a different uniform so ________ ________ ________ ________ ________ ________ the other players.

M: Who's the player in the poster next to him? He looks very serious.

W: That's the legendary CF, or center forward, Conor James.

M: I see. Who is that guy taking a selfie with his smartphone?

W: That's my dad. He was really excited to ________ ________ ________ ________ ________. Behind him, there's a statue of a famous coach.

M: That's cool. I guess that must be your brother and mom on the right.

W: You're right. My little brother had to use the restroom. He really didn't enjoy the trip.

M: Well, it seems like your father was having a great time, at least.

07

W: Hey Aaron, do you have ________ ________ ________ ________ ________?

M: I do. If you have a flash drive handy, I can transfer them over to it.

W: I just bought one. Here you go.

M: Is this really a flash drive? It's a bit big, don't you think?

W: Yeah, it's new. On one end it has a regular USB plug, and on the other end it has a micro USB plug.

M: That's awesome. I guess that way you can ________ ________ ________ ________ ________ quite easily.

W: That's right. This is the first time I've used it, though.

M: It seems like it works great. It transferred all of the files very quickly. Is there anything else you need for the presentation?

W: I have everything we need. I think we'll be ready for tomorrow.

M: All right. Oh, by the way, where did you get that flash drive? I think I want to pick one up for myself.

W: I bought it online. I'll ________ ________ ________ ________ ________ for you.

M: That'd be great. Thanks.

08

M: Hey Susan, the book club meeting is tomorrow. Have you finished the book?

W: I haven't. What about you?

M: I finished it over the weekend. I couldn't put it down. It was so ________ ________ ________. I really think you're going to enjoy the ending.

W: I don't think ________ ________ ________ ________ ________ ________ ________. I think I left it on the train yesterday.

M: You can borrow my book if you'd like.

W: That'd be great. The meeting is at 8 tomorrow, right?

M: No, it actually starts at 6 this week.

W: Really? I'm not going ________ ________ ________ ________ ________ ________, then.

M: Why not? It's a pretty short book. I think you'll be able to finish it by then.

W: It's not that. I have a meeting with my son's English teacher tomorrow.

M: Can't your husband go?

W: He would, but ________ ________ ________ ________ ________ all week. He has an important presentation on Friday.

M: I see. Well, I'll tell everyone you said hello.

W: Thanks.

09

M: Welcome to the gift shop. ________ ________ ________ ________ ________ ________.

W: I did. What an amazing finish!

M: It sure was. What can I do for you today?

W: ________ ________ ________ ________ ________ ________.

M: We have all kinds of souvenirs, such as t-shirts, jerseys, hats, and bumper stickers.

W: How much for a jersey?

M: Well, the adult jerseys are $30 and the child-sized jerseys are $25.

W: All right. I guess ________ ________ ________ ________ ________ and two for children, please.

M: Sure. Is that all?
W: I think I'd like some hats as well. How much do they run?
M: They're $20 apiece.
W: Okay. I'll take two hats.
M: Great. If you still have your ticket stub, you can ______ ______ ______ ______ ______ ______.
W: Sure, it's right here.
M: So, we have two adult jerseys, two child jerseys, and two hats with a 10% discount off your total.
W: That's right. Here's my card.

10

W: Hey, did you see that they opened registration for the summer internship program at Pear Computers?
M: Really? I didn't know they were looking for interns.
W: Yeah. I thought that you'd be interested in it since you want to study computer science. It'd be a great opportunity for you.
M: Definitely. Do you know ______ ______ ______ ______ ______?
W: You'll be working in the labs at their company, so you'll have to spend the summer in California.
M: That sounds awesome. Do you think they'll accept me?
W: I think so. You're already quite ______ ______ ______ ______ ______, so you have the right qualifications.
M: Great! How long is the internship for?
W: They said that it's a two-month program.
M: Perfect. ______ ______ ______ ______ ______ this internship, right?
W: Right. You'll also have to ______ ______ ______ ______ ______ and travel costs.
M: Well, that is a drawback. But I think I'm interested anyway. I'm going to register as soon as I get home.

11

W: Good morning, students. I'd like to take some time to talk about the Environmental Edge Photography Contest. ______ ______ ______ ______ ______ ______, and students around the country are encouraged to participate. The theme of this year's contest is environmental awareness. Photo entries should ______ ______ ______ ______ highlight environmental issues. ______ ______ ______ ______ ______ ______, and in landscape orientation. All entries should be submitted to Mr. Lopez before May 15th. ______ ______ ______ ______ ______ ______. Environmental Edge will announce the winners of the contest on June 1st. The top three photos in the country will receive prizes. We know there is plenty of talent in our school, and we encourage you to participate. You can find more information ______ ______ ______ ______. Thank you for listening.

12

M: Look at this flyer, honey. There's a big sale on refrigerators this week.
W: Really? That's great, because we need to get a new one.
M: The flyer shows several models. How much do you think we should spend?
W: Well, I don't want to ______ ______ ______ ______ ______ ______.
M: All right. Then how about these models?
W: Hmm.... I'd like one with at least 700 liters of storage.
M: I agree. ______ ______ ______ ______ ______ would be good. That way all of our food would fit in easily. Should we get one with two doors or four?
W: I don't like two-door models. I think it's easier to ______ ______ in a four-door refrigerator.
M: Then there are two models we can choose from.
W: Oh, I think a warranty is pretty important, especially for appliances.
M: Okay. Then let's ______ ______ ______ ______ ______ ______ ______.
W: Great!

13

M: Rachel, did you finish watching *The Babbit*?
W: Yeah, Dad, I did. Why did you want me to watch it?
M: Didn't you like it?
W: It was okay. It had too much of a happy Hollywood ending for me, though.
M: It's quite different from the book, huh?
W: Yeah. The book had such a ______ ______ ______ ______. I thought that the movie would be the same.
M: I thought so, too. So, did you like the movie or the book better?

W: I really __________ __________ __________ __________ __________ __________. The original story was too dark, and the movie was so unrealistic and happy.

M: Well, what would make you like the story more?

W: I guess I'd like it to be a happier story throughout but not so unrealistic.

M: I think you should __________ __________ __________ __________, then.

W: What do you mean? You want me to __________ __________ __________?

M: (Sure. I'd love to read your version.)

14

W: Hey, Lenny. What's up?

M: Oh, hey Sam. Are you okay? You look pretty tired.

W: I'm fine, but I've been having a hard time sleeping the past couple of weeks. The weather makes the air in my room too dry.

M: I see. Well, you could get a humidifier. I also heard that keeping plants in your room can __________ __________ __________ __________ __________.

W: I'm pretty irresponsible, so I'll probably forget to water them and __________ __________ __________ __________.

M: Well, there are some plants that don't need that much attention. You could get some of those.

W: Really? Like what?

M: You can put bamboo in a jar of water and __________ __________ __________ __________ __________.

W: That seems easy enough.

M: Yeah. I have some bamboo plants in my room and I only have to water them when the jar is empty, which is about once a month.

W: I like the way bamboo looks, too.

M: I think bamboo would make __________ __________ __________ __________ __________ __________ __________. You should try it.

W: (I'll go to the florist and buy some today.)

15

M: Paul is working on an important assignment for his history class. However, while he's researching on his computer, the Internet goes out. He calls his Internet provider's customer service line to report the problem. He __________ __________ __________ __________ as it is late and there are no customer service representatives available. After a 15-minute wait, __________ __________ __________ __________ __________ __________ and tells Paul that he should try unplugging his modem and plugging it back in. He follows the representative's instructions, but it doesn't fix the problem. He __________ __________ __________ get his Internet fixed because his assignment is due tomorrow. In this situation, what would Paul most likely say to the customer service representative?

Paul: (Please send someone over to fix my Internet as soon as possible.)

16-17

M: Good afternoon, parents. I'd like to welcome you today to my seminar on children's health. My name is Dr. Jeffrey Day, and I've been a pediatrician for almost 30 years. Let's talk about children between the ages of 3 and 12. This age range is critical in the development of children. This is the timeframe within which __________ __________ __________ __________, become more physical, develop problem-solving skills, and __________ __________ __________ that will follow them for the rest of their lives. This is why I recommend that every parent urge their children to __________ __________ __________ __________ __________ __________. There are amazing benefits to playing outside. Children will have the chance to meet new friends and create lasting childhood relationships. They'll also build a sense of confidence by taking risks and playing outdoor games. Now, playing outside isn't always safe, but creating a willingness in a child to take risks and engage themselves in risky behaviors gives the child an opportunity to learn new skills and __________ __________ __________ __________. Lastly, playing outdoors provides children with vitamin D, which is essential to healthy development. This vitamin is known to help children battle depression, heart disease, diabetes, and obesity. So, please, I urge you parents to get your children outside. It'll be beneficial for you as well.

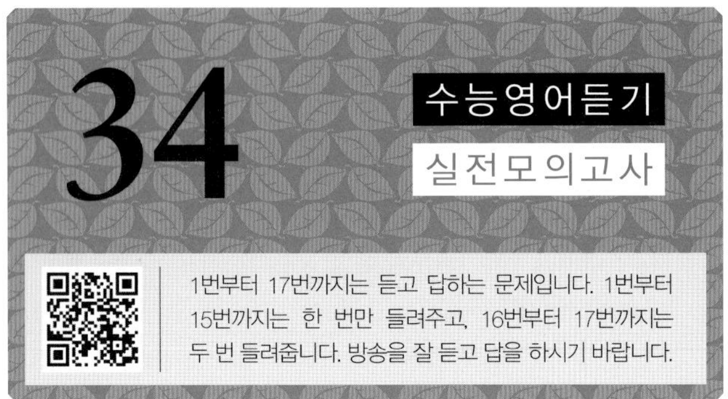

01

대화를 듣고, 남자의 마지막 말에 대한 여자의 응답으로 가장 적절한 것을 고르시오.

① I'll call the electric company and ask about the bill.
② I'll ask the repairman to look at our air conditioner.
③ Sure. Turn on the air conditioner when it's hot inside.
④ You shouldn't unplug appliances when you're using them.
⑤ Right. I guess we should turn it off when we leave the house.

02

대화를 듣고, 여자의 마지막 말에 대한 남자의 응답으로 가장 적절한 것을 고르시오.

① I agree. Let's order the book online.
② I know. That's why the book is easy to read.
③ Let's go to the library to check out the book.
④ I'll lend you my DVD. It's very interesting.
⑤ No. Once I finish reading this book, I'll watch the movie.

03

다음을 듣고, 여자가 하는 말의 주제로 가장 적절한 것을 고르시오.

① 인간관계 생성과 유지의 중요성
② 인간관계가 성공에 미치는 영향
③ 인간관계에 유사성이 미치는 영향
④ 인간관계에서 갈등을 해결하는 방법
⑤ 인종과 성별을 초월한 관계 형성의 필요성

04

대화를 듣고, 남자의 의견으로 가장 적절한 것을 고르시오.

① 출입문을 회전문으로 바꿔야 한다.
② 입구 쪽에 추가 난방기를 설치해야 한다.
③ 직원들에게 더 따뜻한 옷을 제공해야 한다.
④ 프런트 데스크에서 객실 온도를 체크해야 한다.
⑤ 에너지를 절약하기 위해 난방을 약하게 해야 한다.

05

대화를 듣고, 두 사람이 대화하고 있는 장소로 가장 적절한 곳을 고르시오.

① hospital
② restaurant
③ classroom
④ TV studio
⑤ grocery store

06

대화를 듣고, 그림에서 대화의 내용과 일치하지 않는 것을 고르시오.

07

대화를 듣고, 여자가 남자를 위해 할 일로 가장 적절한 것을 고르시오.

① 새 셔츠 사다 주기
② 야구경기 보러 오기
③ 친구에게 부탁해 주기
④ 학교로 셔츠 가져다 주기
⑤ 경기장에 아빠 모시고 오기

08

대화를 듣고, 남자가 화가 난 이유를 고르시오.

① 수집한 자료를 분실해서
② 발표 수업을 잘하지 못해서
③ 조원들이 모임에 나오지 않아서
④ 마음에 드는 배역을 맡지 못해서
⑤ 원하는 친구와 팀을 이루지 못해서

09

대화를 듣고, 여자가 지불할 금액을 고르시오.

① $70 ② $80 ③ $90 ④ $100 ⑤ $110

10

대화를 듣고, 인턴십 프로그램에 관해 두 사람이 언급하지 않은 것을 고르시오.

① 출시된 게임 ② 모집 인원
③ 모집 분야 ④ 남자의 지원 분야
⑤ 지원 자격

11

Campus tour에 관한 다음 내용을 듣고, 일치하지 않는 것을 고르시오.

① 학교 학생들이 안내한다.
② 학교 생활에 대해 알려준다.
③ 투어의 첫 부분은 1시에 시작한다.
④ 점심은 학교 식당에서 먹는다.
⑤ 학생회의 연극이 진행된다.

12

다음 표를 보면서 대화를 듣고, 여자가 선택할 프로그램을 고르시오.

Sustainable Living Programs

	Program	Organic Gardening (in groups)	Vegan Cooking (individually)	Lunch (provided)	Price
①	A	Yes	Yes	Yes	$50
②	B	Yes	Yes	No	$40
③	C	Yes	No	Yes	$30
④	D	No	Yes	Yes	$30
⑤	E	Yes	No	No	$25

13

대화를 듣고, 여자의 마지막 말에 대한 남자의 응답으로 가장 적절한 것을 고르시오.

Man: ______________________

① I'm not really sure why you need me to email it.
② No problem. I'll send the file as soon as it's ready.
③ You're welcome. I'll be sure to write your letter tonight.
④ I'm really sorry, but I think I've misplaced the document.
⑤ Sure. My email address is gwilson@northwestacademy.edu.

14

대화를 듣고, 남자의 마지막 말에 대한 여자의 응답으로 가장 적절한 것을 고르시오.

Woman: ______________________

① Of course. We need all the help we can get.
② We can find different volunteer work if you want.
③ You can teach me how to get along with children.
④ It's important to the children that you sing with them.
⑤ Playing games and singing helps them be more social.

15

다음 상황 설명을 듣고, Sarah가 Ryan에게 할 말로 가장 적절한 것을 고르시오.

Sarah: ______________________

① It's not easy to find a job in journalism these days.
② I thought it was your dream to work at Hush-Hush.
③ You shouldn't have accepted Courier Crossing's offer.
④ I don't do this work for the money. I do it because I really like it.
⑤ Good choice. Some things in life are more important than money.

[16-17] 다음을 듣고, 물음에 답하시오.

16

남자가 하는 말의 목적으로 가장 적절한 것은?

① to advertise for community businesses
② to promote the sale of Parents' Day kits
③ to introduce parents to members of the faculty
④ to inform parents of upcoming university events
⑤ to recruit volunteers to sell welcome kits to parents

17

쿠폰이 있는 곳으로 언급되지 않은 것은?

① 카페 ② 제과점 ③ 볼링장
④ 식당 ⑤ 수영장

01

M: Whoa! Look at our power bill for this month. It's almost $500.

W: Wow! That's far too expensive. I'll call the electric company. There must be some mistake.

M: I doubt they made a mistake. You know, we've been __________ __________ __________ __________ a lot this summer.

W: (Right. I guess we should turn it off when we leave the house.)

02

W: What are you doing, Liam? __________ __________ __________ __________ __________ __________.

M: I'm reading Yann Martel's *Life of Pi*. It is so interesting that I can't stop reading.

W: Did you see the movie first? It's a great movie.

M: (No. Once I finish reading this book, I'll watch the movie.)

03

W: Good morning, class. Last time, we discussed how important it is for us to create and __________ __________ and how that affects our overall success. In today's class, we'll talk about the truth in the old saying, "Birds of a feather flock together." As humans, we tend to __________ __________ __________ __________ __________. Most people make friends with people who are of the same age, race, or gender. Take your classmates, for example. You're much __________ __________ __________ __________ __________ with those classmates that you share certain characteristics with. Some of these characteristics might include your interests or hobbies. Now, of course these rules aren't across the board. Some people date or marry __________ __________ __________ __________. However, these relationships typically form out of shared values or education.

04

M: Sarah, what's the matter? Are you all right?

W: __________ __________ __________ __________ and a stuffy nose. I think I'm sick.

M: You should wear some warmer clothes.

W: You're right, I should. It gets quite cold in here.

M: I can relate. I've worked at a front desk before. I always hated the cold.

W: Yeah, the cold air always follows people in as they enter the building.

M: Perhaps if we __________ __________ __________, we can stop the cold from entering.

W: I don't think we need a new door. Wouldn't it __________ __________ __________ to just buy another heater?

M: No, a new door would be more effective. If we __________ __________ __________ __________ system, it'll greatly reduce the amount of cold air that enters the building.

W: Really? How does that work?

M: __________ __________ __________ __________ in the door and can't get in because the door is spinning.

W: That sounds great! I hope it works.

05

M: Welcome back, Dr. Delgado.

W: Thank you for having me. It's a pleasure to be here.

M: Great. Let's begin our program. First, I'd like you to give the audience a quick health tip.

W: Sure. You know, everyone is always on the go these days. That can be bad for your health.

M: Right. So what can someone who's always on the go do __________ __________ __________?

W: A good breakfast is the key to health. Breakfast is skipped more than any other meal. No one has time to make it. But with just a couple of basic ingredients, __________ __________ __________ __________ __________ __________.

M: What sort of ingredients are we talking about?

W: Protein shakes are a great way to get your day started. All you need is protein powder and milk.

M: What about fruit or other ingredients?

W: Good thinking. To __________ __________ __________ __________ __________ __________, you can add fruits such as bananas or strawberries. I like to add spinach to mine __________ __________ __________ __________.

M: Spinach in a shake, huh? That doesn't sound very tasty. I guess the nutrition is the point, right? Thank you, Dr. Delgado. We'll be back after the commercial break.

06

W: Hey Ryan, I just finished up the poster for the FPS World Championship. What do you think?

M: ________ ________ ________ ________! I like what you did with the title at the top. It looks like a banner.

W: Thanks. I also put the time and date on the left side.

M: I see that. Did we get a confirmation on that date and time?

W: We did. The gaming association confirmed it this morning.

M: Awesome. That gives us ________ ________ ________ ________ ________. I see that you left the box for the place blank.

W: Yeah. We're still ________ ________ ________ ________ ________ to have the event at the stadium, so it hasn't exactly been confirmed yet. How about the picture of you and Jason on the right?

M: Not my best picture, but I like how you put it together.

W: (laughs)

M: I also like the picture of the mascot, "Dinosaur", at the bottom. What's that it's saying?

W: It says, "________ ________ ________ ________!"

07

[Telephone rings.]

W: Hello?

M: Hey, Mom. Thank goodness you're home. I need your help with something.

W: What's the matter, Andrew?

M: I'm sure ________ ________ we have a big baseball game tonight?

W: Of course. Your father and I had ________ ________ ________ ________ ________ ________.

M: That's great, but I forgot my jersey at the house this morning.

W: Oh, Andrew. Why are you so forgetful? Do you have time to come get it after school?

M: I don't. We have a pre-game dinner after classes, and then we go straight to the field.

W: Is there anyone you know who can ________ ________ ________ ________ and pick it up for you?

M: Not that I know of. Everyone is pretty busy after school on Fridays. Would you please ________ ________ ________ ________ ________ for me?

W: Yes, I suppose I can do that.

M: Thank you so much, Mom.

W: No problem, honey. See you soon.

08

W: Daniel, you look so angry. What happened?

M: Never mind. ________ ________ ________ ________. I just feel tired.

W: Come on. Tell me ________ ________ ________ ________ and you'll feel better.

M: Well, Jeremy, Jane, Selena, and I were scheduled to meet to prepare for our presentation for English class this morning.

W: Oh, right. My group met yesterday to assign members their parts for the presentation.

M: We were also planning to divide up our presentation and start collecting materials for it.

W: So, ________ ________ ________ ________ ________?

M: Jeremy and Selena didn't show up.

W: Well, maybe they had a good reason.

M: Nope. They both said they just forgot about it. I'm so upset. How could they be so irresponsible?

W: Well, calm down. You still have lots of time to prepare for the presentation. I'm sure they're sorry.

M: Well, I'm not so sure. Anyway, I'm going to go home and rest for a while.

09

[Telephone rings.]

M: Walker Mountain Campgrounds. What can I do for you today?

W: Hi. My family is looking to come to your campground for our vacation next month. ________ ________ ________ ________?

M: It's $35, and that includes one vehicle spot.

W: Well, we're going to ________ ________ ________ ________ ________.

M: In that case, it'll be an additional $10 per night.

W: All right. I'd like to make a reservation for two nights, the 14th and 15th of August. My name is Minnie Martin.

M: All right, Mrs. Martin. Is there anything else I can do for you?

W: Oh, do you provide water and electricity at your campsites?

M: We do. However, __________ __________ __________ __________ water and electricity. Campsites with water hookups are an additional $5 per night, and ones with electricity are an additional $10 per night.

W: Okay. I don't think we'll need the water, but we'll __________ __________ __________ __________, please.

M: All right, two nights at a two-car campsite with electricity. I've made your reservation. We'll see you next month.

10

W: Hey Johnny, did you get my email?

M: I haven't checked it yet. What was it about?

W: There's a __________ __________ __________ at RD Games.

M: That's cool. They put out some great games.

W: That's right. They released *Counterclockwise* and *Super Doctor Brothers*.

M: Yeah, I love those games.

W: They're great. Anyway, they __________ __________ __________ __________ __________ __________, character design, and beta testing.

M: Awesome! I know a bit about programming, but I'd love to __________ __________ __________ __________. What kind of qualifications are they looking for?

W: Well, they're just looking for someone who has taken a couple of game design classes and has a love for creating fun and interesting games.

M: I've taken a few game design classes and, as you know, I really love gaming.

W: I think they'll take you on. You're quite popular around the gaming community.

M: I'll go apply right away. I appreciate you telling me about this.

11

W: Hello, everyone. I'm Mrs. Jones, the vice principal here at Williams Academy, and I'd like to welcome you to our prestigious school. Today, we're going to give potential students the chance to visit our campus and __________ __________ __________. Your guides are going to be students from the school who are going to __________ __________ __________ __________-__________ __________ of life at our establishment. They will also detail all of our educational programs and give you some history of the campus. The first part of the tour __________ __________ __________ __________. I'll meet you all at noon in our school's cafeteria for lunch. Then at one o'clock, we'll head to the auditorium, where our student council will __________ __________ __________. That will be followed by a short presentation. After the presentation, the student council will take any questions you might have about our school. I really hope you enjoy your day, and we thank you for coming.

12

M: Hey Brittney, didn't you say you __________ __________ __________ __________ __________ __________ this year?

W: I am. I think I'm going to become a vegan. Why?

M: Well, I found this flyer for some classes they're offering at the community college this summer. You should take one.

W: Really? That'd be great. *[Pause]* The organic gardening classes seem interesting.

M: Well, do you also want to learn how to cook vegan food?

W: That does sound cool. I get to __________ __________ __________ __________ __________ __________ in class, right?

M: That's right. You can also bring what you cook back home for me to try.

W: Awesome. I'll take that class as well, then.

M: Great. Then we're down to two programs you can take. Do you want them to provide you with lunch?

W: I don't really think that'll be necessary, since I'll be cooking there. I can eat the food I cook, right? It's also $10 cheaper.

M: All right. I think we found the perfect program for you.

13

W: Hi, Mr. Wilson.

M: Hey, Margaret. What's up?

W: Not a whole lot. I was just wondering if you finished up my __________ __________ __________. I need to turn in my university application __________ __________ __________ __________ __________ __________.

M: Right. I finished it up on Monday. It must be somewhere around here. Give me a minute.

W: Take your time.

M: *[Pause]* Oh, here it is. I spent a lot of time writing it. You were one of my favorite students, you know.

W: Thanks. It looks great, Mr. Wilson. Is there any way I can get the file?

M: Absolutely. Do you need it for backup or something?

W: Well, all of the university applications __________ __________ __________ these days. So I have to email it to them.

M: I can scan it so that you have a version with my signature.

W: That sounds great. Could you __________ __________ __________ __________ after you've scanned it?

M: Sure. Just write down your email address on this sheet of scrap paper.

W: All right. Thank you for all your help, Mr. Wilson.

M: (No problem. I'll send the file as soon as it's ready.)

14

M: Hey, Hailey. __________ __________ __________ __________ __________ today?

W: I had a great time. I played games and sang songs with all the children.

M: That's nice. But I really don't know how you can __________ __________ __________ __________ __________.

W: It's easy, really. Children are a lot of fun to be around.

M: I'd really love to __________ __________ __________ __________, but I don't know if I should.

W: Why not?

M: Well, I don't think that children like me.

W: Why do you think so? You're usually so kind and energetic.

M: I'm not a very good singer, and I don't think I __________ __________ __________ to play games with them. __________ __________ __________ __________ __________ __________ is make their lunch.

W: Well, I think you can volunteer to do that. Let's go together next time.

M: Do you really think I can be of help?

W: (Of course. We need all the help we can get.)

15

M: Ryan, a journalism student at Uptown University, will graduate at the end of this semester. He has been working hard to find a job after graduation and receives __________ __________ __________ __________ __________-__________ __________. The first offer is from Courier Crossing, a large newspaper in a big city. The other is from Hush-Hush, __________ __________ __________ __________. Courier Crossing offers him a great salary and job security, but it would force him to move away from his hometown. Hush-Hush has a much lower salary, but he won't have to leave his family and friends. __________ __________ __________, Ryan finally decides to accept the Hush-Hush offer. He meets his classmate Sarah in the hallway and tells her what he has decided. Sarah understands why Ryan made this decision and __________ __________ __________ __________ __________ __________. In this situation, what would Sarah most likely say to Ryan?

Sarah: (Good choice. Some things in life are more important than money.)

16-17

M: Good afternoon, parents. We'd like to welcome you to Franklin University's annual Parents' Day. Because you're parents of the students at this fine university, we are offering you the chance to buy our Parents' Day kits, which have been a tradition here at the university __________ __________ __________ __________ __________ 1927. In this kit, you'll find bumper stickers, pens, and key chains for you and your loved ones. Members of our student government have also baked homemade cookies for you to enjoy during this year's festivals. Our Parents' Day kits are created by student organizations and community businesses. On top of helping create these kits, these businesses have also put together a coupon booklet with a $200 value. In these booklets you'll find __________ __________ __________ Franklin City Cafe, Rainbow Bakery, Echo Lanes Bowling Alley, and The Downtown Diner. All of the proceeds for the Parents' Day kits are used to benefit campus-wide events such as Spring Fest and our annual Talent Contest. If you would like to __________ __________ __________ __________ __________ __________ __________ __________, come to the front desk of the visitor's center. Thank you for attending Parent's Day at our wonderful campus.

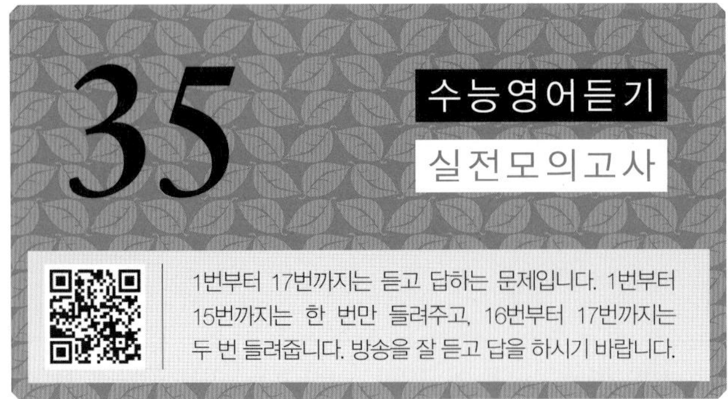

01

대화를 듣고, 여자의 마지막 말에 대한 남자의 응답으로 가장 적절한 것을 고르시오.

① That's nice! That way I can cancel my order.
② That's a great idea. Jane is a wonderful baker.
③ It really wouldn't be a problem if I baked a cake.
④ That's a good idea, but I've already chosen a cake.
⑤ It's really a shame that she can't make it to the banquet.

02

대화를 듣고, 남자의 마지막 말에 대한 여자의 응답으로 가장 적절한 것을 고르시오.

① Sorry, but Southback jackets are too expensive.
② I just washed it, so it's hanging up now.
③ I'll bring some extra gloves just in case.
④ You can borrow your dad's ski pants.
⑤ No, you shouldn't go skiing there.

03

다음을 듣고, 남자가 강의하는 내용의 주제로 가장 적절한 것을 고르시오.

① A lot of exercise can be unhealthy.
② Talk to a nutritionist about your diet.
③ Find ways to exercise in your daily life.
④ Diet and exercise at the same time.
⑤ Make time to exercise every day.

04

대화를 듣고, 여자의 의견으로 가장 적절한 것을 고르시오.

① 장난감에 대해 가지고 있는 성 고정관념을 없애야 한다.
② 건전한 장난감을 통해 창의성과 지능을 발달 시킬 수 있다.
③ 장난감을 고를 때 가장 중요하게 고려할 부분은 안전성이다.
④ 성에 맞는 장난감을 이용한 역할놀이는 사회성을 발달시킨다.
⑤ 아이들에게 고정관념을 심어줄 수 있는 장난감은 피해야 한다.

05

대화를 듣고, 두 사람이 대화하고 있는 장소로 가장 적절한 곳을 고르시오.

① 길거리 ② 박물관 ③ 음식점
④ 방송국 ⑤ 잡지사

06

대화를 듣고, 그림에서 대화의 내용과 일치하지 않는 것을 고르시오.

07

대화를 듣고, 여자가 남자를 위해 할 일로 가장 적절한 것을 고르시오.

① to show him around the city
② to help him find an apartment
③ to ask about on-campus housing
④ to clean the house before the party
⑤ to help him fill out his college application

08

대화를 듣고, 남자가 아침에 일찍 일어난 이유를 고르시오.

① 아침 식사를 하기 위해서
② 아빠와 하이킹을 가기 위해서
③ 친구와 영화를 보러 가기 위해서
④ 일찍 깨기로 한 자신과의 약속 때문에
⑤ 엄마한테 등산용 지팡이를 빌리기 위해서

09

대화를 듣고, 남자가 지불할 금액을 고르시오.

① $30 ② $40 ③ $45 ④ $50 ⑤ $60

10

대화를 듣고, 남자가 참여한 자원봉사 활동에 관해 두 사람이 언급하지 않은 것을 고르시오.

① 봉사 장소 ② 봉사 기간 ③ 주최 기관
④ 활동 내용 ⑤ 신청 방법

11

Field hockey에 관한 다음 내용을 듣고, 일치하지 않는 것을 고르시오.

① 캐나다와 미국에서 가장 인기 있는 운동이다.
② 인도와 파키스탄에서 전국민이 즐기는 스포츠이다.
③ 필드하키는 아이스하키와 거의 비슷하다.
④ 골키퍼는 몸의 어떤 부분으로든 공을 만질 수 있다.
⑤ 선수들은 스틱의 평평한 부분으로 공을 쳐야 한다.

12

다음 표를 보면서 대화를 듣고, 여자가 선택한 모델을 고르시오.

Bird Rental Cars

	Model	Type	Rental Fee (per day)	Capacity (persons)	Number of Vehicles Available
①	Magpie	Economy	60	4	3
②	Jay	Economy	65	4	2
③	Swift	Family	70	5	1
④	Raven	Luxury	75	7	0
⑤	Woodpecker	Minivan	80	7	2

13

대화를 듣고, 남자의 마지막 말에 대한 여자의 응답으로 가장 적절한 것을 고르시오.

Woman: ____________________

① This was a big help. Now I have an idea for a topic.
② I think you should focus on completing the graph.
③ You must have misinterpreted the assignment.
④ I don't understand what your report is about.
⑤ Sure. I'd love to help you with your project.

14

대화를 듣고, 여자의 마지막 말에 대한 남자의 응답으로 가장 적절한 것을 고르시오.

Man: ____________________

① Why don't you turn on the humidifier?
② You should see a doctor about your stuffy nose.
③ I can't seem to find the one that you want online.
④ You're right. Dry air is also very bad for your skin.
⑤ We can run the shower in the bathroom for a while.

15

다음 상황 설명을 듣고, Jack이 Charles에게 할 말로 가장 적절한 것을 고르시오.

Jack: ____________________

① I can't believe we actually won the game today!
② What's wrong with you? You let them score again!
③ You need to try harder. We're going to lose this game.
④ We all make mistakes. You're going to do fine in the game.
⑤ The season is almost over. Just play hard for one more game.

[16-17] 다음을 듣고, 물음에 답하시오.

16

남자가 하는 말의 주제로 가장 적절한 것은?

① How animals find their way back home
② Animal senses that aren't found in humans
③ Methods that animals use to identify their prey
④ Benefits of performing scientific research on animals
⑤ Animals that use electromagnetic fields for navigation

17

언급된 동물이 아닌 것은?

① 비둘기 ② 연어 ③ 박쥐
④ 바다거북 ⑤ 상어

35 DICTATION

녹음을 다시 한 번 듣고, 빈칸에 알맞은 말을 쓰시오.

01

W: Hey Evan, have you ________ ________ ________ the banquet this evening?

M: I've finished most of the preparations, but I can't decide on ________ ________ ________ ________ ________ ________.

W: Why don't you ask Jane? She said that she could help out.

M: (That's a great idea. Jane is a wonderful baker.)

02

M: Hey Mom, I'm ________ ________ with my friends tonight at Walker Mountain.

W: ________ ________ ________ ________ ________ ________ tonight. Be sure you take your scarf and beanie.

M: All right. I can't find my Southback jacket. Have you seen it?

W: (I just washed it, so it's hanging up now.)

03

M: Have you exercised today? Everyone knows that exercise is good for your health. But perhaps you feel like you're too busy and simply don't have the time or energy to get to a fitness center. So, what is someone like you to do? ________ ________ ________ ________ ________ ________ your gym. For instance, if you can, you should walk to the post office or grocery store instead of driving, or use a push lawn mower to cut the grass. ________ ________ ________ ________ people who stay active for most of the day will use 10 percent more energy than people who use a gym for 60 minutes a day but do not stay active otherwise. It's easier and better for ________ ________ ________ ________ ________ ________ ________. This also helps make weight loss goals easier to meet. So, what kinds of activities in your daily life could also be exercise?

04

M: Hey, Katie. Did you do your Christmas shopping yet?

W: I sure did. I bought a concert DVD for my father, a flowerpot for my mother, and some action figures for my cousin.

M: That's cool. I loved action figures when I was young. I'm sure he'll love them.

W: Why do you think my cousin is a boy?

M: You mean you bought action figures for your cousin who's a girl?

W: I did. She actually ________ ________ ________ ________ ________.

M: Hmm... I thought that only boys played with action figures. Girls play with dolls.

W: I thought so, too. I was confused about it at first, but after seeing how much she enjoys them I've really opened my mind up ________ ________ ________.

M: What are "gender stereotypes?"

W: It's what society ________ ________ ________ ________ ________ ________ ________. I think it's okay for boys to play with girls' toys and vice versa.

M: That's something that I've never thought about before.

W: I hadn't either, but my cousin really made me consider it.

05

W: Wow! This place is really busy. Is someone famous here? Look at all the cameramen.

M: I think they must be from the local news station.

W: What's so special about this place?

M: This place is very famous for its spaghetti. It's the owner's family's secret recipe. ________ ________ ________ ________ ________ his great grandmother.

W: Wow! So this place is pretty old, huh?

M: Yeah, it's been in the family for four generations. I heard it's almost 100 years old.

W: That's pretty incredible. I'm going to have to try that spaghetti.

M: I've heard such great things about it. Look! I think that's the owner over there, getting interviewed.

W: ________ ________ ________ ________ ________. He must be nervous.

M: ________ ________ ________ ________ if you were being interviewed?

06

W: Hey Taylor, what is that you're looking at?

M: It's a photo of the party room where we're going to welcome Ryan and Sarah to our facility. _______ _______ _______ _______ _______.

W: Cool. It's going to be a great time.

M: For sure. So, what do you think about the room?

W: It looks great. The banner on the back wall is huge!

M: Yeah, I thought it was going to be smaller, but I think it looks nice. What do you think of the balloon _______ _______ _______ _______?

W: I think it's a nice touch. I like that "Welcome" was written on it. Are the three tables on the left side for food?

M: No. We're not having a buffet. Those are for guests and Sarah's supporters.

W: So the table in the middle with the wine bottles must be for Sarah and Ryan.

M: That's right. I thought _______ _______ _______ _______ _______ _______ _______ in the center of the room.

W: I'm sure they'll love it. What's the podium under the balloon for?

M: That's for our guest speakers. Several of Sarah's friends and family members would like to speak to show their support.

W: That sounds lovely.

07

[Cell phone rings.]

W: Hello?

M: Hey, Alice. I am calling to share some good news with you.

W: Good news? Did you get into the college you wanted?

M: I did! I just got home and _______ _______ _______ _______ _______ in the mailbox from Princeton!

W: That is so wonderful. I never doubted it for a minute. Congratulations!

M: Thank you so much. Alice, I was wondering if you would help me with something.

W: Of course. How can I help?

M: Well, it's just that I don't have a lot of time and there are so many things I need to do before classes start and I can't seem to find a place to stay.

W: Would you like me to look at apartments for you?

M: That would be great. You've lived in the area for so long that I know _______ _______ _______ _______ _______.

W: Sure, it actually sounds like fun. _______ _______ _______ _______ _______ _______ _______ _______?

M: I'd like a one bedroom apartment. I'm not looking for anything too big, but I want more space than a studio.

W: All right, I'll call you back as soon as I've found a couple of good options for you.

M: You're the best. Thank you again for helping me out.

W: It's my pleasure.

08

M: Good morning, sis. What're you cooking?

W: I'm cooking an omelet. You're up early. I figured you'd be sleeping since _______ _______ _______ _______ _______ last night.

M: Yeah, I was out celebrating the end of the school year with my friends.

W: I'm sure you're tired. You should get some more sleep. It's the first day of summer vacation.

M: That'd be nice, but I promised Dad I'd _______ _______ _______ with him today.

W: Now I see why you got up so early.

M: You should come with us. _______ _______ _______ _______ _______ _______ _______ _______ sometimes. I don't know what to talk about with him.

W: I'd like to help and all, but I already have plans. I'm going to see a movie with Brandon.

M: Oh. No, that's fine. Hey, do you know where Mom is? I need to borrow her hiking sticks.

W: She ran to the grocery store, but she should be back soon.

M: All right. I guess I'll wait for her instead of looking myself.

09

W: Oh, hello. What can I do for you today?

M: Well, I want to buy a souvenir for my girlfriend. She was quite upset that she couldn't come on this trip with me.

W: I see. Well, _______ _______ _______ _______ _______ _______?

M: I want something that she can use every day, but something that _______ _______ _______.

W: How about this traditional Thai lantern? It's only $20.

M: I like it, but don't you think it's a little small? ________ ________ ________ ________ ________ ________?

W: That one is $40. It was handcrafted by tribesmen in the northern part of the country.

M: It's beautiful. Okay, I'll take the bigger lantern.

W: Sure. How about something for your mother or grandmother? They would like these traditional fans. They're only $5 each. Also, if you spend more than $45, I'll take 10% off your total.

M: They are nice. I'll take two of them. Is there any way you could giftwrap these?

W: I'm sorry, but ________ ________ ________ ________ ________ here.

M: No problem.

10

W: Hey, Kyle. How was your summer vacation?

M: It was great. I spent some time in Nepal as a volunteer.

W: That's awesome. How long did you stay?

M: 27 days.

W: Wow! ________ ________ ________ ________ ________ ________ ________.

M: Yeah, but I wish I could've stayed longer.

W: So, what kinds of things did you do there?

M: Well, as you know, ________ ________ ________ ________ ________ a few months ago. I helped take ________ ________ ________ ________ in the hospital and delivered food and water to the outskirts.

W: That's great. You must feel good about yourself. Were all the volunteers from America?

M: No, there was actually only one other American in our volunteer group. The rest came from all around the world.

W: I see. I might want to ________ ________ ________ ________ ________ ________. How do I go about applying?

M: I'll email you some information. You have to sign up on their website and choose what kind of volunteer program you want to participate in.

W: That sounds easy. Thanks.

11

M: Are you interested in unique sports? If so, then you should check out field hockey. Field hockey is played all around the world, but is less popular in Canada and the United States, ________ ________ ________ ________. However, field hockey is much more popular worldwide. In fact, it is the national sport of both India and Pakistan. Field hockey is almost identical to ice hockey, except that ________ ________ ________ ________ ________ ________ ________. During play, goalkeepers are the only players who are allowed to touch the ball with any part of their body, while field players must play the ball ________ ________ ________ ________ ________ ________ ________. This sport is a great alternative to ice hockey because it is much less expensive to start playing and you don't need a rink to play, ________ ________ ________ ________ ________ most of the world. If you're looking for something new to try, you should look for a field hockey club in your area!

12

M: Welcome to Bird Rental Cars. My name is Gabe. What can I do for you today?

W: Hi. I'd like to rent a car, please.

M: No problem. What kind of car would you like?

W: Well, we're going on a family vacation, so we're going to need something a bit big. There are five of us going on the trip.

M: Okay. In that case, you're going to want to take one bigger than ________ ________-________ ________.

W: We also have a lot of luggage. So we'll probably need one that's quite large.

M: I'd recommend taking one of our minivans, then. It has ample space and is very comfortable on long trips.

W: The minivan is a little pricey. What about a Raven? ________ ________ ________ ________ ________, and it's cheaper.

M: I'm sorry, but none of those are ________ ________ ________ ________.

W: Well, I guess I'll have to spend the extra money and take this one.

M: Great choice, ma'am.

13

M: Hey Lucy, did you finish the assignment that Mr. Miller gave us?

W: I didn't get a chance to work on it last night. It's a big assignment, and I have no idea __________ __________ __________.

M: You'd better start soon. It's due on Thursday, you know.

W: Yeah, I just don't know what to choose for my topic.

M: Take a look at my report. It's not finished, but maybe it can help you decide.

W: *[Pause]* This is really interesting. I didn't know that __________ __________ __________ __________ __________ __________ __________ __________ __________.

M: Yeah. I used a line graph to __________ __________ __________ __________ __________.

W: You did a great job with it. It must've taken you a while to organize all of the data.

M: Yeah, it did take a bit of work to choose my topic, but once I decided, it got a whole lot easier.

W: What did you do after you chose your topic?

M: I focused on finding as many sources of data as I could.

W: (This was a big help. Now I have an idea for a topic.)

14

M: Hey, sweetheart. I heard you coughing. Are you all right?

W: My throat is a bit dry. I think it's because of the weather.

M: Yeah, __________ __________ __________ __________ __________. I think our apartment is too dry.

W: Maybe __________ __________ __________ __________ __________.

M: I think so. I've been thinking about buying one for the last couple of weeks.

W: I looked at a couple when I was at the store earlier. I found one that I like.

M: Really? You should've bought it.

W: I didn't realize how badly we needed it.

M: I'll go to the store now and pick one up.

W: They must be closed by now. I bet we can find __________ __________ __________ __________ __________ __________.

M: Yeah, but if we order from the Internet, it'll take a couple of days to arrive. I'll stop by the store tomorrow and buy one.

W: But we're suffering now. What do we do until then?

M: (We can run the shower in the bathroom for a while.)

15

W: Charles and Jack have been chosen as co-captains of JLA's soccer team. The first game is coming up soon, and their team practices for about two hours every day. Charles is the team's goalie, but lately he __________ __________ __________ __________ __________ __________ __________ during practice. His team and his school are counting on him __________ __________ __________ __________ __________ __________ __________. Charles is __________ __________ __________ __________ __________ from his teammates and tells Jack that he wants to quit the team. Jack wants to reassure Charles that he'll do fine, and that nobody is perfect. In this situation, what would Jack most likely say to Charles?

Jack: (We all make mistakes. You're going to do fine in the game.)

16-17

M: I'd like to welcome you all to West Town Zoo. My name is Frank Berger, and I'm a zoologist. I'd like to talk to you today about senses in nature. Everyone knows that __________ __________ __________ __________ __________: sight, smell, touch, taste, and sound. What about animals? Do they have the same senses as humans? Some animals have stronger senses than humans, and some even have senses that humans don't have. Take the pigeon, for example. Pigeons are in tune with the Earth's magnetic fields. They can find their way home __________ __________ __________ __________ __________ __________ __________ __________. That's why the homing pigeon was used to send messages in the past. Salmon also use the __________ __________ __________ to find their way back to their birthplace to lay eggs. Sea turtles use a similar technique to return to the beaches where they were born. Some snakes, particularly vipers, have infrared vision, which they use to __________ __________ __________. Sharks can sense electricity from muscle contractions in their prey. The animal kingdom is truly magnificent. Let's take a look at some of these amazing animals.

MEMO

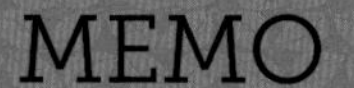

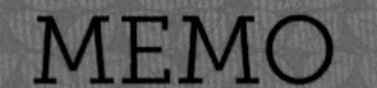

MEMO

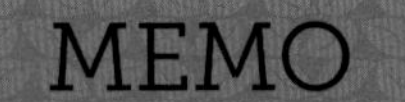

MEMO

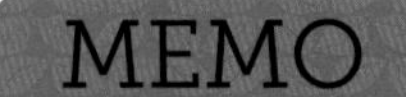

④ Yeah. It's really hard for me to kick my caffeine addiction.
⑤ Exactly. I think you should drink less cola and more water.

15. 다음 상황 설명을 듣고, Seha가 Laura에게 할 말로 가장 적절한 것을 고르시오.

Seha: ______________________________

① Don't worry. You'll do better next time.
② That's okay. I'll go home and get my charger.
③ That too bad. Why don't you buy a new one?
④ You can use mine. I'm not using it right now.
⑤ It's really nice of you to let me use your computer.

[16~17] 다음을 듣고, 물음에 답하시오.

16. 남자가 하는 말의 주제로 가장 적절한 것은?

① 즉각적인 보도의 중요성
② 최근 언론계에서 일어난 캠페인
③ 시대별 언론인들의 다양한 역할
④ 대중 매체에 대한 지역별 선호도
⑤ 보도에 사용되는 대중 매체의 변화

17. 언급된 매체가 아닌 것은?

① newspaper ② poster ③ radio
④ television ⑤ social media

⑤ Thanks for inviting me, but I've already had dinner.

3. 다음을 듣고, 남자가 하는 말의 목적으로 가장 적절한 것을 고르시오.

① 동파 발생 시 대처요령을 알려주려고
② 정전 사태 대비 훈련 계획을 알리려고
③ 교내에서의 에너지 절약 방법을 교육하려고
④ 동파 방지를 위해 창문을 닫고 다닐 것을 요청하려고
⑤ 난방을 위한 대체 에너지 개발의 필요성을 강조하려고

4. 대화를 듣고, 두 사람이 하는 말의 주제로 가장 적절한 것을 고르시오.

① 인터넷 사기를 피하는 방법
② 제품 사용 후기의 작성 요령
③ 가격비교 사이트 이용의 필요성
④ 품질 보증서를 보관해야 하는 이유
⑤ 중고거래에서 좋은 물건 고르는 법

5. 대화를 듣고, 두 사람이 대화하고 있는 장소로 가장 적절한 곳을 고르시오.

① supermarket ② culinary school
③ commercial kitchen ④ office building
⑤ coffee shop

8. 대화를 듣고, 여자가 아르바이트를 할 수 <u>없는</u> 이유를 고르시오.

① 건강상태가 좋지 않아서
② 학교 권투부에 가입해서
③ 부모님이 허락하시지 않아서
④ 지금 하는 일이 마음에 안 들어서
⑤ 스페인으로 수학여행을 가기 위해서

9. 대화를 듣고, 여자가 지불할 금액을 고르시오.

① $980 ② $1,020 ③ $1,050 ④ $1,110 ⑤ $1,120

10. 대화를 듣고, 전시회에 관해 두 사람이 언급하지 <u>않은</u> 것을 고르시오.

① 참가 예술가 수 ② 작품의 수
③ 시작하게 된 계기 ④ 기금마련의 목적
⑤ 전시 기간

11. Aspiring Writers Summer Camp에 관한 다음 내용을 듣고, 일치하지 <u>않는</u> 것을 고르시오.

① 캠프의 기간은 일주일이다.
② 글쓰기를 위한 다양한 프로그램이 있다.
③ 매년 초청 작가가 방문한다.
④ 한 달 전에 신청하면 할인을 받을 수 있다.
⑤ 신청서는 학교 홈페이지에서 받으면 된다.

③ No. I didn't take any pictures when I went there for Christmas.
④ Of course. I'll show you some of the ones we took on the farm.
⑤ Sure. I have a lot of photos of you from when you were a baby.

15. 다음 상황 설명을 듣고, Mike가 아빠에게 할 말로 가장 적절한 것을 고르시오.

Mike: Dad, ______________________

① I don't think you realize how much I worry about you.
② my friends really appreciate you letting me go out with them.
③ I'm really happy that we get to spend so much time together.
④ it's time that you treat me like an adult. I'm not a kid anymore.
⑤ how about you and Mom spend more time together on the weekends?

[16~17] 다음을 듣고, 물음에 답하시오.

16. 남자가 하는 말의 목적으로 가장 적절한 것은?

① to fight against animal testing for cosmetics
② to caution the public on the effects of poverty
③ to introduce new techniques of raising livestock
④ to explain the benefits of raising domesticated animals
⑤ to inform people about a way they can help the poor

17. 다음 중 소가 제공하는 것으로 언급되지 <u>않은</u> 것은?

① 우유 ② 치즈 ③ 비료
④ 고기 ⑤ 새끼

⑤ It looks like you can still book tickets for next weekend.

3. 다음을 듣고, 여자가 하는 말의 목적으로 가장 적절한 것을 고르시오.

① 운동의 중요성을 강조하려고
② 휘트니스 센터를 홍보하려고
③ 개인 트레이너 모집을 안내하려고
④ 휘트니스 센터의 이전을 알려주려고
⑤ 휘트니스 센터의 리모델링을 공지하려고

4. 대화를 듣고, 두 사람이 하는 말의 주제로 가장 적절한 것을 고르시오.

① 소셜 미디어 사이트의 효과적인 사용 방법
② 학생들 사이에서 소셜 미디어 사이트의 인기
③ 학생들의 소셜 미디어에 대한 중독의 심각성
④ 소셜 미디어 사이트가 학생들에게 끼치는 다양한 영향
⑤ 소셜 미디어 사이트가 학생들의 정서 발달에 끼치는 영향

5. 대화를 듣고, 두 사람의 관계를 가장 잘 나타낸 것을 고르시오.

① 인테리어 업자 — 고객
② 청소업체 사장 — 직원
③ 택배 회사 직원 — 의뢰인
④ 페인트 가게 주인 — 고객
⑤ 부동산 중개업자 — 건물주

8. 대화를 듣고, 여자가 도서관에 온 이유를 고르시오.

① 친구를 도와주기 위해서
② 역사책을 반납하기 위해서
③ 기말고사 공부를 하기 위해서
④ 보고서 작성을 하기 위해서
⑤ 조별 과제를 하기 위해

9. 대화를 듣고, 여자가 지불할 총 금액을 고르시오.

① $25 ② $40 ③ $51 ④ $61 ⑤ $70

10. 대화를 듣고, 팔라완 섬에 관해 두 사람이 언급하지 않은 것을 고르시오.

① 팔라완 섬의 문화
② 팔라완 섬의 날씨
③ 사람들이 팔라완 섬을 찾는 이유
④ 팔라완 섬을 처음 대중화시킨 사람들
⑤ 팔라완 섬에서 인기 있는 마을

11. Busan International Film Festival에 관한 다음 내용을 듣고, 일치하지 않는 것을 고르시오.

① 매년 부산 해운대에서 열린다.
② 1996년 9월 처음으로 개최되었다.
③ 주로 유럽의 저예산 영화들을 소개한다.
④ 젊은 사람들에게 호소력이 있다.
⑤ 2011년 영구적 장소로 옮겼다.

③ Staying up-to-date on my TV shows is more important than anything else.
④ I don't play many sports these days because of TV shows.
⑤ We can watch TV shows together if you'd like.

15. 다음 상황 설명을 듣고, Jane의 어머니가 Jane에게 할 말로 가장 적절한 것을 고르시오.

Jane's mother: Jane, ________________

① no one likes to be spoken poorly about when they're not around.
② why are you so negative towards everyone you meet at school?
③ why don't you stop hanging out with Olivia for a few weeks?
④ you need to look at all the options before choosing a club.
⑤ moving to a new school can make you feel lonely.

[16~17] 다음을 듣고, 물음에 답하시오.

16. 여자가 하는 말의 주제로 가장 적절한 것은?

① Benefits of eating vegetables regularly
② The dangers of eating processed foods
③ Foods that are harmful to a child's health
④ Tips to change your children's eating habits
⑤ Creative ways to spruce up a children's party

17. 언급된 음식이 아닌 것은?

① broccoli ② carrots ③ oatmeal
④ spinach ⑤ tomatoes

⑤ I haven't called anyone on my cell phone today.

3. 다음을 듣고, 남자가 하는 말의 요지로 가장 적절한 것을 고르시오.

① 가계부를 작성을 해야 한다.
② 환경 운동에 관심을 가져야 한다.
③ 환경친화적인 물건을 구입해야 한다.
④ 쓰레기 분리수거를 철저히 해야 한다.
⑤ 자신의 경제 능력에 맞게 쇼핑할 필요가 있다.

4. 대화를 듣고, 두 사람이 하는 말의 주제로 가장 적절한 것을 고르시오.

① 저널리즘 이해의 필요성
② 협동과제 참석에 관한 제안
③ 새로운 수업방식에 대한 대안
④ 사교기술 향상을 위한 방법
⑤ 인터뷰 숙제에 대한 조언

5. 대화를 듣고, 두 사람의 관계를 가장 잘 나타낸 것을 고르시오.

① 사장 — 비서 ② 세탁소 주인 — 고객
③ 식당 지배인 — 손님 ④ 패션모델 — 디자이너
⑤ 백화점 직원 — 수선공

8. 대화를 듣고, 여자가 학교를 휴학하려는 이유를 고르시오.

① 등록금을 내기 힘들어서
② 다른 공부를 해보고 싶어서
③ 가족이 이민을 가게 되어서
④ 해외로 봉사활동을 가기 위해
⑤ 해외 오지 여행을 하고 싶어서

9. 대화를 듣고, 여자가 지불할 금액을 고르시오.

① $10 ② $24 ③ $32 ④ $36 ⑤ $40

10. 대화를 듣고, speech contest에 관해 두 사람이 언급하지 않은 것을 고르시오.

① 개최 일자 ② 참가 자격 ③ 개최 장소
④ 신청 마감일 ⑤ 연설 제한시간

11. 미술관 견학 안내에 관한 다음 내용을 듣고, 일치하지 않는 것을 고르시오.

① 미술관을 견학 하는 동안 자녀와 함께 다녀라.
② 자녀 스스로 미술 작품을 즐기게 하라.
③ 자녀에게 작품에 대한 해석을 해 주지 마라.
④ 자녀에게 미술관의 투어가이드처럼 행동하게 하라.
⑤ 방문했을 때 최대한 많은 작품을 보여 주어라.

⑤ Yeah. I wish my father was as interested in soccer as yours is.

15. 다음 상황 설명을 듣고, Mrs. Towns가 James에게 할 말로 가장 적절한 것을 고르시오.

Mrs. Towns: ____________________

① I heard that you're very popular at this school.
② You should talk to your friends about your problems.
③ Why have you been missing so many classes these days?
④ I'm concerned about your behavior. Is everything all right?
⑤ I was wondering about extracurricular events at this school.

[16~17] 다음을 듣고, 물음에 답하시오.

16. 남자가 하는 말의 주제로 가장 적절한 것은?

① The symptoms of malaria sufferers
② The insect problem in tropical areas
③ The diseases passed on by mosquitoes
④ The medication used in malaria treatment
⑤ The methods to prevent mosquito infestation

17. ABCD 접근법에 관해 언급되지 <u>않은</u> 것은? [3점]

① 감염 위험에 대해 인식하기
② 모기 물림을 예방하기
③ 위험 지역은 방문하지 않기
④ 약 복용이 필요한지 확인하기
⑤ 유사증상이 있을 경우 즉시 진단 받기

⑤ You should always recycle old bottles.

3. 다음을 듣고, 남자가 하는 말의 목적으로 가장 적절한 것을 고르시오.

① 학생들의 학생회장 선거 투표를 촉구하려고
② 선거 관리에 필요한 자원봉사자를 모집하려고
③ 학생회장 선거의 투표율이 낮은 이유를 설명하려고
④ 학생회장 선거에 공식적인 출마를 선언하려고
⑤ 학생들에게 공정한 선거 운동을 장려하려고

4. 대화를 듣고, 두 사람이 하는 말의 주제로 가장 적절한 것을 고르시오.

① 등산 장비 구입 계획
② 추천할 만한 등산 코스
③ 등산 시 불을 피우는 요령
④ 안전한 등산을 위한 유의 사항
⑤ 등산 시 길을 잃었을 때 대처방안

5. 대화를 듣고, 두 사람의 관계를 가장 잘 나타낸 것을 고르시오.

① 피고 — 검사　② 앵커 — 기자
③ 검찰 — 특파원　④ 리포터 — 행인
⑤ 배심원 — 변호사

8. 대화를 듣고, 남자의 관심 진로 분야가 바뀐 이유를 고르시오.

① 선생님의 조언 때문에
② 즐겨보던 TV쇼 때문에
③ 인상 깊게 읽은 책 때문에
④ 경제전반에 관한 관심 때문에
⑤ 토론을 하면서 생각이 바뀌어서

9. 대화를 듣고, 남자가 지불할 금액을 고르시오.

① $500　② $540　③ $580　④ $600　⑤ $640

10. 대화를 듣고, 여자가 언급하지 않은 것을 고르시오.

① 지원동기　② 자격증 취득 시기
③ 근무 경력　④ 전 직장을 그만 둔 이유
⑤ 희망 보수

11. Angel Mounds Historic Park의 행사에 관한 다음 내용을 듣고, 일치하지 않는 것을 고르시오.

① 첫 번째 행사는 3월 마지막 주에 열릴 것이다.
② 원주민의 날 행사에서 투어는 4시간이 소요된다.
③ 원주민의 날 행사에서는 원주민 전통 음식을 먹어볼 수 있다.
④ 4월 17일에 열리는 행사는 어린이들을 위한 행사이다.
⑤ 어린이날 행사에서는 온 가족이 즐길 수 있는 행사가 많다.

④ I didn't care much for the topic, but the lecturer was really interesting.

⑤ I agree completely. I wish more people had the dedication that they have.

15. 다음 상황 설명을 듣고, Mike가 Mr. Smith에게 할 말로 가장 적절한 것을 고르시오.

Mike: Mr. Smith, ______________________________

① is everything going well for you at Jefferson Academy?

② what song are we going to perform for the festival?

③ I'm ready for our performance at the festival.

④ could you help me with the music routine?

⑤ I'd like to be in charge of the performance.

[16~17] 다음을 듣고, 물음에 답하시오.

16. 남자가 하는 말의 목적으로 가장 적절한 것은?

① 대입 추천서 작성을 위한 웹사이트 개통을 알리려고

② 온라인을 통한 대입 지원서 접수 방법을 공지하려고

③ 대입을 위한 상담 시 질문 사항들을 알려주려고

④ 대입에 필요한 서류의 작성요령을 설명하려고

⑤ 대입을 위한 추천서의 중요성을 알려주려고

17. 웹사이트에서 학생들이 할 수 있는 것으로 언급되지 않은 것은?

① 자기소개서 등록　② 선생님과 상담 예약

③ 자기소개서 샘플 참조　④ 지원 대학의 경쟁률 확인

⑤ 필요한 서류에 관한 정보 수집

④ You always give really good advice.
⑤ Sure, come back at around 3 p.m.

3. 다음을 듣고, 남자가 하는 말의 목적으로 가장 적절한 것을 고르시오.

① 천문대의 관측 프로그램에 대해 안내하려고
② 신설된 천문대의 개관행사를 소개하려고
③ 천문대 관람 시 질서유지를 부탁하려고
④ 천문대 안내원의 채용을 공고하려고
⑤ 천문대 오는 길을 안내해 주려고

4. 대화를 듣고, 두 사람이 하는 말의 주제로 가장 적절한 것을 고르시오.

① 성에 따른 생체 리듬 비교
② 생체 리듬이 서로 다른 이유
③ 생체 리듬에 따른 학습 능률
④ 집중력 향상에 좋은 수학 수업
⑤ 성적향상을 위한 시간 관리 방법

5. 대화를 듣고, 두 사람의 관계를 가장 잘 나타낸 것을 고르시오.

① 기자 — 배우　② 학생 — 교수
③ 승무원 — 승객　④ 여행객 — 럭비팀선수
⑤ 식당 종업원 — 손님

8. 대화를 듣고, 여자가 집에 가려고 하는 이유를 고르시오.

① 친구와 말다툼을 하게 되어서
② 동생을 집에 데려다 줘야 해서
③ 아빠의 부탁으로 동생을 돌보기 위해
④ 내일까지 마쳐야 할 학교 숙제가 있어서
⑤ 편의점에서 필요한 것을 사다 주기 위해

9. 대화를 듣고, 여자가 지불할 총 금액을 고르시오.

① $240　② $260　③ $300　④ $420　⑤ $450

10. 대화를 듣고, 총회의 일정에 관해 두 사람이 언급하지 않은 것을 고르시오.

① 부의장님의 연설　② 남자의 발표
③ 청중과의 대화　④ Paul Stevenson과의 회의
⑤ 점심식사

11. My Little Organics에 관한 다음 내용을 듣고, 일치하지 않는 것을 고르시오.

① 장갑은 참가자가 가져와야 한다.
② 강좌는 일주일에 네 차례 열린다.
③ 수강할 수 있는 연령에 제한이 있다.
④ 10명이 넘으면 강좌 예약을 해준다.
⑤ 수업료는 한 회당 15달러이다.

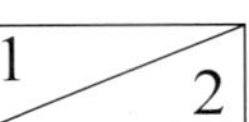

대학수학능력시험 대비 모의평가 1회

1

영어 영역

1번부터 17번까지는 듣고 답하는 문제입니다. 1번부터 15번까지는 한 번만 들려주고, 16번부터 17번까지는 두 번 들려줍니다. 방송을 잘 듣고 답을 하시기 바랍니다.

1. 대화를 듣고, 여자의 마지막 말에 대한 남자의 응답으로 가장 적절한 것을 고르시오.

① I really enjoyed the movie. I highly recommend it.
② You should see if you can check it out at the library.
③ No problem. I won't have time to watch it until Saturday.
④ You've already watched it. I didn't expect to get it back this fast.
⑤ I'm really sorry, but I need to keep the DVD for a couple more days.

2. 대화를 듣고, 남자의 마지막 말에 대한 여자의 응답으로 가장 적절한 것을 고르시오.

① Why don't you give me a hand with this?
② I actually have to go to a meeting now.
③ I was never very good at social studies.

6. 대화를 듣고, 그림에서 대화의 내용과 일치하지 <u>않는</u> 것을 고르시오.

7. 대화를 듣고, 남자가 여자에게 부탁한 일로 가장 적절한 것을 고르시오.

① to celebrate a holiday
② to put together a collage
③ to buy a new digital camera
④ to reserve the party room
⑤ to buy something special

12. 다음 표를 보면서 대화를 듣고, 두 사람이 선택할 서비스를 고르시오.

Office Cleaning Service

	Package	Window Cleaning	Floor Waxing	Thorough / Express	Cost (per floor)
①	A	X	O	Express	$200
②	B	X	O	Thorough	$300
③	C	O	O	Express	$400
④	D	O	X	Thorough	$400
⑤	E	O	O	Thorough	$500

13. 대화를 듣고, 여자의 마지막 말에 대한 남자의 응답으로 가장 적절한 것을 고르시오.

Man: ______________________________

① I think we should hurry because they'll close soon.
② We should finish up our work before we eat.
③ I'm trying not to eat anything after 8 p.m.
④ I think they're renovating the restaurant.
⑤ They have the best fish tacos in the city.

14. 대화를 듣고, 남자의 마지막 말에 대한 여자의 응답으로 가장 적절한 것을 고르시오.

Woman: ______________________________

① Put yourself in their shoes before you make any judgments.
② I'm not really interested in the forces behind decision-making.
③ What a disappointment. I'll never attend one of his lectures again.

대학수학능력시험 대비 모의평가 2회

영어 영역

1번부터 17번까지는 듣고 답하는 문제입니다. 1번부터 15번까지는 한 번만 들려주고, 16번부터 17번까지는 두 번 들려줍니다. 방송을 잘 듣고 답을 하시기 바랍니다.

1. 대화를 듣고, 여자의 마지막 말에 대한 남자의 응답으로 가장 적절한 것을 고르시오.

① Sure. I'll get them ready for you now.
② All right. I'll give them to you on Monday.
③ I haven't chosen a topic for the debate yet.
④ I don't really know too much about debate. Sorry.
⑤ No problem. You can go ahead and turn it in today.

2. 대화를 듣고, 남자의 마지막 말에 대한 여자의 응답으로 가장 적절한 것을 고르시오.

① I understand why you're so interested in this project.
② I'm going to use them to make some bird feeders.
③ Let's use them for your science project.
④ I'll throw away all of these old bottles.

6. 대화를 듣고, 그림에서 대화의 내용과 일치하지 <u>않는</u> 것을 고르시오.

7. 대화를 듣고, 남자가 할 일로 가장 적절한 것을 고르시오.

① 캠프 활동을 위한 준비물 사러 가기
② 캠프 활동을 위한 책 찾아보기
③ 영어공부를 위한 책 사러 가기
④ 대출한 도서 반납하기
⑤ 영어캠프 신청하기

영어 영역

12. 다음 표를 보면서 대화를 듣고, 여자가 수강할 강좌를 고르시오.

Film Editing Class

	Level	Teacher	Maximum Number	Time
①	Intermediate	Liam	20	Morning
②	Advanced A	Michael	10	Evening
③	Advanced B	Michael	10	Morning
④	Advanced C	Michael	15	Morning
⑤	Advanced D	Liam	15	Evening

13. 대화를 듣고, 여자의 마지막 말에 대한 남자의 응답으로 가장 적절한 것을 고르시오.

Man: ____________________

① She'll be glad to help you out with your novel.
② You're right. She should arrive to work on time.
③ Well, I don't think so. I don't really care for her novels.
④ I'll bring this to her attention and give her a warning.
⑤ I don't know. I think writing novels is very time consuming.

14. 대화를 듣고, 남자의 마지막 말에 대한 여자의 응답으로 가장 적절한 것을 고르시오.

Woman: ____________________

① Don't worry. I'm sure you can go to the next match.
② That's no problem. I can take your father to the match.
③ No. I was really surprised by how well they performed.
④ I'm worried that my father won't let me go to the match.

대학수학능력시험 대비 모의평가 3회

영어 영역

1번부터 17번까지는 듣고 답하는 문제입니다. 1번부터 15번까지는 한 번만 들려주고, 16번부터 17번까지는 두 번 들려줍니다. 방송을 잘 듣고 답을 하시기 바랍니다.

1. 대화를 듣고, 여자의 마지막 말에 대한 남자의 응답으로 가장 적절한 것을 고르시오.

① I enjoy joining clubs at school.
② Since I was in the fourth grade.
③ I'd like to join your writing club.
④ I used to write for about two hours a week.
⑤ I was better at writing in elementary school.

2. 대화를 듣고, 남자의 마지막 말에 대한 여자의 응답으로 가장 적절한 것을 고르시오.

① Can you find my cell phone?
② I've been cleaning the house all day.
③ You should call it and listen for the ring.
④ What kind of cell phone are you looking for?

6. 대화를 듣고, 그림에서 대화의 내용과 일치하지 <u>않는</u> 것을 고르시오.

7. 대화를 듣고, 여자가 남자를 위해 할 일로 가장 적절한 것을 고르시오.

① to meet an instructor
② to pay for a membership
③ to sign up for personal training
④ to assist him in choosing activities
⑤ to ask about annual sporting events

12. 다음 표를 보면서 대화를 듣고, 두 사람이 선택한 제품을 고르시오.

Toasters

	Model	Price	Capacity	Digital Display	Color
①	A	$49	2 Slices	X	Black
②	B	$69	4 Slices	X	White
③	C	$89	4 Slices	O	White
④	D	$119	6 Slices	X	Black
⑤	E	$149	6 Slices	O	Brushed Steel

13. 대화를 듣고, 남자의 마지막 말에 대한 여자의 응답으로 가장 적절한 것을 고르시오.

Woman: ______________________

① Great. I'm really looking forward to working here.
② I noticed that you studied journalism in university.
③ We think you'll be a perfect fit for this company.
④ I've published books for ESL BEST in the past.
⑤ I've always wanted to be an ESL teacher.

14. 대화를 듣고, 여자의 마지막 말에 대한 남자의 응답으로 가장 적절한 것을 고르시오.

Man: ______________________

① I forgot to do my homework last night, so I couldn't practice playing the piano.
② I might give that a try. There are a lot of TV shows I'd like to catch up on.

대학수학능력시험 대비 모의평가 4회

영어 영역

1번부터 17번까지는 듣고 답하는 문제입니다. 1번부터 15번까지는 한 번만 들려주고, 16번부터 17번까지는 두 번 들려줍니다. 방송을 잘 듣고 답을 하시기 바랍니다.

1. 대화를 듣고, 여자의 마지막 말에 대한 남자의 응답으로 가장 적절한 것을 고르시오.

① You will have another chance.
② I wish you could have seen it.
③ Wow, that's great! I don't believe it!
④ No problem. You can practice more.
⑤ Don't forget about your assignment.

2. 대화를 듣고, 남자의 마지막 말에 대한 여자의 응답으로 가장 적절한 것을 고르시오.

① I'd like to, but I can't. I have plans this weekend.
② Yeah. It wasn't easy getting tickets for the opera.
③ It's great that you and your wife will see the opera.
④ Don't worry about it. I know how to get to the theater.

6. 대화를 듣고, 그림에서 대화의 내용과 일치하지 <u>않는</u> 것을 고르시오.

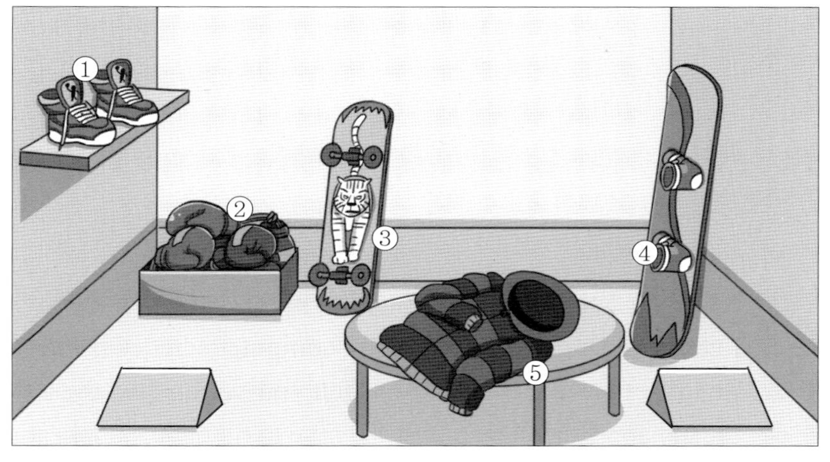

7. 대화를 듣고, 남자가 여자를 위해 할 일로 가장 적절한 것을 고르시오.

① 아들을 데려와 주기
② 워터 파크에 같이 가기
③ 여행을 위한 쇼핑 같이 하기
④ 크루즈 여행 예약하기
⑤ 보고서 작성 도와주기

12. 다음 표를 보면서 대화를 듣고, 여자가 선택한 스캐너 모델을 고르시오.

Scanner Rental Service

	Model \ Feature	Color Scan	Rental Fee per Month	Fax	Printer
①	TL-2	X	$25	O	X
②	TL-3	O	$27	X	O
③	D-3	O	$30	O	X
④	D-5	O	$32	X	O
⑤	D-7	O	$40	O	O

13. 대화를 듣고, 여자의 마지막 말에 대한 남자의 응답으로 가장 적절한 것을 고르시오.

Man: ____________________

① All right. I'll send my application in immediately, then.
② I guess you're right. I'll ask my computer science professor.
③ Thanks. Please let me know when you've finished the letter.
④ I really appreciate you taking the time to fill out the application.
⑤ That's not a problem. I'll finish writing it by the end of the week.

14. 대화를 듣고, 남자의 마지막 말에 대한 여자의 응답으로 가장 적절한 것을 고르시오.

Woman: ____________________

① Well, I don't really remember much from my time there.
② I've lost contact with all of my relatives in my hometown.

대학수학능력시험 대비 모의평가 5회

영어 영역

1번부터 17번까지는 듣고 답하는 문제입니다. 1번부터 15번까지는 한 번만 들려주고, 16번부터 17번까지는 두 번 들려줍니다. 방송을 잘 듣고 답을 하시기 바랍니다.

1. 대화를 듣고, 여자의 마지막 말에 대한 남자의 응답으로 가장 적절한 것을 고르시오.

① Why do I have to get up early?
② You know, the library is closed today.
③ Oh, you shouldn't have woken me up early.
④ Is that true? Then I need to get up and get ready.
⑤ I can't believe it. I think sixteen is old enough to go there alone.

2. 대화를 듣고, 남자의 마지막 말에 대한 여자의 응답으로 가장 적절한 것을 고르시오.

① Me, too. Fall is my favorite season.
② I think it's too cold to walk outside.
③ Thank you, but I think I'm busy next week.
④ Sounds great! That's just what I wanted to say.

6. 대화를 듣고, 그림에서 대화의 내용과 일치하지 않는 것을 고르시오.

7. 대화를 듣고, 여자가 남자를 위해 오후에 할 일로 가장 적절한 것을 고르시오.

① 시험공부 도와주기
② 병문안 같이 가주기
③ 수영 팀에 등록해주기
④ 병원에 차로 데려다 주기
⑤ 도서관에서 책 빌려다 주기

영어 영역

12. 다음 표를 보면서 대화를 듣고, 남자가 선택할 가방의 모델을 고르시오.

Rickshaw Bags

	Model	Size	Style	Material	Price
①	A	Small	Satchel	Waxed Canvas	$170
②	B	Small	Messenger	Waxed Canvas	$190
③	C	Small	Messenger	Leather	$210
④	D	Large	Satchel	Waxed Canvas	$220
⑤	E	Large	Messenger	Leather	$240

13. 대화를 듣고, 남자의 마지막 말에 대한 여자의 응답으로 가장 적절한 것을 고르시오.

Woman: ________________

① We should organize a school talent show.
② I don't think they should do it like that.
③ You can't go to the school's talent show.
④ Ribbons aren't as expensive as medals.
⑤ If that's the case, why not get medals?

14. 대화를 듣고, 여자의 마지막 말에 대한 남자의 응답으로 가장 적절한 것을 고르시오.

Man: ________________

① That's right. What brand do you usually drink?
② Right. Caffeine can help you be more productive.
③ Yes, I remember. Let's go out and have a couple of colas.

실수 없는 수능 듣기 만점 공략!

Listening

수능 듣기 실전 모의고사 35회 + 5회

정답 및 해설

목차

01 수능영어듣기 실전모의고사

본문 p.08

01 ①	02 ②	03 ⑤	04 ①	05 ②	06 ④
07 ③	08 ④	09 ③	10 ⑤	11 ⑤	12 ①
13 ③	14 ④	15 ③	16 ②	17 ④	

01 짧은 대화의 응답

소재 새로 이사한 아파트

듣기 대본 해석

남: 새 아파트로 물건들 다 옮겼니, Wanda?
여: 응. 1층이라서 어렵지 않았어.
남: 멋진데. 너네 아파트에 옥외 테라스는 있니?
여: ① 응. 그래서 내가 이곳을 선택한 거야.

어휘

patio ***n.*** 옥외 테라스

정답 ①

문제풀이

1층이라는 여자의 말에 남자는 옥외 테라스가 있는지 물었으므로 ① '응. 그래서 내가 이곳을 선택한 거야.'가 가장 적절하다.

오답 보기 해석

② 아니. 내 가구를 옮기는 게 많이 어려웠어.
③ 난 주택이 좋은데 아파트는 너무 시끄럽거든.
④ 맞아. 난 항상 꼭대기 층에서 살고 싶었어.
⑤ 물론. 너 지난주 내 파티에 왔어야 하는데.

총 어휘 수 42

02 짧은 대화의 응답

소재 손가락 깁스

듣기 대본 해석

여: 오, 손가락에 깁스했네요. 다쳤어요?
남: 네. 훈련 중에 슬라이딩 태클을 당했는데 손으로 짚고 넘어졌어요.
여: 의사에게 가 보는 게 좋을 거예요. Dr. Kebb을 방문해 봤어요?
남: ② 갔다 왔어요. 괜찮을 거라고 했어요.

어휘

cast ***n.*** 깁스 〈문제〉 **injury** ***n.*** 상처 **referee** ***n.*** 심판

정답 ②

문제풀이

여자는 손가락을 다친 남자에게 의사에게 가봐야겠다고 말했으므로 이에 대한 남자의 가장 적절한 응답은 ② '갔다 왔어요. 괜찮을 거라고 했어요.'이다.

오답 보기 해석

① 상처가 아주 심해 보여요.
③ 같이 연습하러 가는 건 어때요?
④ 아뇨. 저는 경기에 참가 안 할 것 같아요.
⑤ 심판이 그에게 레드 카드를 줬어야 했어요.

총 어휘 수 44

03 담화 주제

소재 꽃밭 가꾸기

듣기 대본 해석

여: 보통 당신의 자녀와 주말을 어떻게 보내십니까? 그들과 꽃밭을 만드는 것을 생각해 본 적이 있나요? 정원을 가꾸는 것은 자녀를 밖에 데리고 나가서 생활 기술을 가르치고 동시에 당신의 뜰을 밝아지게 만드는 멋진 방법입니다. 꽃밭은 아름답고, 다른 꽃들을 고르고 그것들이 자라는 것을 지켜보는 일은 아주 재미 있습니다. 만약에 당신의 자녀가 밖에서 충분한 시간을 보내지 않는 것이 염려되거나 책임감을 배우지 못하는 것이 걱정된다면 꽃밭은 그 두 가지 문제 모두에 도움을 줄 것입니다. 당신이 식물을 보살피는 동안 아이들은 무언가를 돌보는 것과 시작한 것을 끝내는 것이 왜 중요한지를 알 수 있습니다. 이는 아이들이 자연스럽게 개인적이고 사회적인 책임감을 발달시키도록 해줍니다. 이번 봄에 가족 시간을 위해 새로운 것을 시도해보세요. 꽃밭을 만들고 아이들이 꽃피우는 것을 지켜보세요!

어휘

brighten ***v.*** 밝히다, ~에 생기를 주다 **be concerned about** ~을 염려하다, ~에 관심을 가지다 **responsibility** ***n.*** 책임감 **blossom** ***v.*** 꽃을 피우다

정답 ⑤

문제풀이

아이들과 꽃밭을 가꾸면 아이들에게 어떤 점이 좋은지를 말해주고 있으므로 정답은 ⑤ '아이들과 꽃밭을 가꿀 때의 이로움'이다.

총 어휘 수 139

04 의견

소재 혼자 있는 시간

듣기 대본 해석

여: Jeff, 최근에 직장에서 당신을 못 봤네요. 어디에 있었나요?
남: 몇 주 휴가를 내고 인도로 배낭여행을 갔었어요.
여: 혼자 갔었나요?
남: 네. 저는 혼자 여행하는 것을 정말 즐겨해요.
여: 하지만 외롭게 느껴지지 않았나요?
남: 별로요. 저는 혼자 있는 것이 정신 건강에 좋다고 생각해요. 자기 반성을 할 수 있게 하고, 다른 사람들과 여행하는 것보다 스트레스를 덜 받아요.
여: 그럼 당신은 혼자 있는 시간을 갖는 것이 중요하다고 생각하나요?
남: 전적으로요.
여: 글쎄요. 개인적으로 저는 혼자 있을 때 정말 불안하고 염려가 돼요. 제 생각에 저는 좀 더 사회적 존재인가 봐요.
남: 저도 그랬었어요. 하지만 저는 혼자 있는 시간을 즐기는 것을 배웠고, 그게 제가 사회 생활 하는 데 정말 도움이 됐어요. 그것은 제 자신과 다른 사람들에게 좀 더 편안해지도록 도와주었어요.
여: 아하. 저는 당신이 뭘 의미하는지 알 것 같아요.

어휘

self-reflection ***n.*** 자기 반성 **absolutely** ***ad.*** 전적으로, 그럼(물론이지) **uneasy** ***a.*** 불안한 **anxious** ***a.*** 불안해하는, 염려하는 **creature** ***n.*** (생명이 있는) 존재 **comfortable** ***a.*** 편안한

정답 ①

문제풀이

남자는 혼자 있는 시간이 자기 반성에 좋고 정신 건강에도 좋다고 말하면서 그것이 사회 생활에도 도움이 됐다고 했다. 따라서 남자의 의견으로 ① '사람은 혼자만의 시간을 가질 필요가 있다.'이다.

총 어휘 수 135

05 대화자의 관계 파악

소재 구직자와의 인터뷰

듣기 대본 해석

여: 좋은 아침입니다.
남: Jackson씨군요. 앉으세요.
여: 감사합니다.
남: 당신의 자격증들을 살펴봤고 그리고 당신이 대학을 수석으로 졸업했다는 사실이 매우 인상 깊더군요.
여: 음, 저는 건축학을 전공했습니다. 저는 어릴 적 블록들을 가지고 놀기 시작한 후부터 그것에 관심을 갖고 있습니다. 그래서 저에겐 매우 자연스러운 일이지요.
남: 훌륭하군요. 또한 여기 보면 당신이 Carter & Young에서 인턴을 한 것으로 보이네요.
여: 네. 작년 여름방학 동안 그 사무실에서 일했습니다.
남: 좋습니다. 그럼, 저희 채용에 대해 어떻게 아셨죠?
여: 교수님께서 소개해 주셨습니다.
남: 알겠습니다. 만약 우리가 당신을 고용하기로 결정한다면, 어떤 종류의 건축에 관심을 갖고 계십니까?
여: 저는 상업 개발에 매우 관심이 많습니다.
남: 당신은 저희 회사에 잘 어울리는 것 같습니다.
여: 그렇게 말씀해 주시다니 감사합니다.

어휘

credential *n.* 자격증 **valedictorian *n.*** 졸업생 대표, 수석 졸업생 **architecture *n.*** 건축학 **hire *v.*** 고용하다 **commercial *a.*** 상업의

정답 ②

문제풀이

남자는 여자의 이력에 대한 질문을 하면서 채용에 대해 어떻게 알았는지 묻고 있고, 여자는 그에 알맞은 답을 하고 있으므로 면접하는 상황임을 알 수 있다. 따라서 정답은 ② '면접관 — 구직자'이다.

총 어휘 수 142

06 그림의 세부 내용 파악

소재 선거 포스터 제작

듣기 대본 해석

여: 안녕, Patrick!
남: 안녕, Teresa. 뭐하고 있니?
여: 나는 우리 선거 운동 포스터를 거의 끝냈어.
남: 대단해! 배경에 사용할 좋은 학교 사진 찾았어?
여: 응. 그리고 전경으로는 가리키고 있는 우리 사진을 사용했어.
남: 좋아 보인다. 우리 옆에 네가 그린 현수막도 마음에 들어.
여: 좋은 선거 운동 구호가 떠오르지 않았어. 미안해.
남: 괜찮아. 그런데 오른쪽에 있는 후보 번호가 좋아 보이지는 않는 듯해.
여: 네가 말하고 나서 보니, 그게 왼쪽에 있는 게 아마도 더 좋아 보이겠어. 하단에 우리 학교 이름과 우리가 출마한 직위는 어때?
남: 괜찮은 거 같아. 잘했어, Teresa.
여: 고마워. 기억해, 우리는 내일 아침 8시 30분까지 선거 캠페인을 시작해야 한다는 걸.
남: 알았어. 내가 늦어도 7시 30분까지는 거기 가 있을게. 고마워.

어휘

campaign *n.* 선거 운동, 캠페인 **slogan *n.*** 구호 **candidate *n.*** 후보 **election *n.*** 선거

정답 ④

문제풀이

남자가 후보 번호가 오른쪽에 있는 것이 좋아 보이지는 않는다고 한 것으로 보아 후보 번호는 오른쪽에 있어야 하나, 그림에서는 왼쪽에 있으므로 그림에서 대화 내용과 일치하지 않는 것은 ④번이다.

총 어휘 수 149

07 할 일

소재 남편의 양복 찾아다 주기

듣기 대본 해석

[휴대폰이 울린다.]

여: 여보, 집에 오는 중이에요?
남: 네. 그런데 도로가 매우 붐비네요. 무엇이 교통 체증을 유발하고 있는지 궁금하네요.
여: 사고 같은 게 난 거예요?
남: 어떻게 된 건지 잘 모르겠어요. 배고프면 나 없이 저녁 먹어요.
여: 좋아요. 언제 도착할 것 같아요?
남: 정말 모르겠어요. 부탁 좀 들어줄 수 있어요?
여: 물론이죠. 무슨 일인데요?
남: 세탁소에 들러서 내 회색 정장을 찾아줄래요? 내일 중요한 발표 때 그걸 입고 싶어서요.
여: 물론이죠. 지금 거기 가서 가져올게요.
남: 정말 고마워요, 여보. 내가 미리 돈은 냈으니까 그냥 가져오면 돼요. 곧 집에 도착할 수 있으면 좋겠네요.
여: 좋아요, 여보. 여기 오면 봐요.

어휘

on one's way ~ ~에 가는 중인 **presentation *n.*** 발표 **in advance** 미리

정답 ③

문제풀이

남편이 아내에게 양복점에서 자신의 회색 정장을 찾아달라고 부탁했으므로 정답은 ③ '회색 정장을 찾아오기'이다.

오답 보기 해석

① 저녁 만들기
② 집에 더 일찍 오기
④ 그에게 교통 상황 알려주기
⑤ 그의 발표 준비 도와주기

총 어휘 수 135

08 이유

소재 야구 경기 전 상대편 선수의 영상 보기

듣기 대본 해석

여: Tommy, 내일 상대팀 선발투수의 영상 본 적 있니?
남: 아직. 근데 진짜 놀랍다고 들었어.
여: 응, 맞아. 인터넷에서 모두 그에 대해서 난리야. 하이라이트 볼래?
남: 음... 보면 안 될 것 같아.
여: 왜? 왜 그렇게 잘하는지 보고 싶지 않아?
남: 그랑 경기할 때까지 기다리는 게 좋을 것 같아.
여: 근데 동영상 몇 개 보면 경기를 더 준비할 수 있지 않을까?
남: 훈련이 준비하는 더 좋은 방법인 것 같아.
여: 다른 선수들도 그 얘기 많이 했어. 동영상 보는 게 경기 준비에 도움이 안 된대.
남: 맞는 말이야. 동영상을 보는 건 시간 낭비야. 거실보다 체육관에서 시간을 보내는 게 더 좋을 것 같아.

어휘

starting pitcher (야구) 선발투수 **highlight *n.*** 하이라이트, 가장 흥미로운 부분 **prepare *v.*** 준비하다 **gym *n.*** 체육관

정답 ④

문제풀이

여자는 남자에게 야구 경기 전 상대팀 선수의 활약을 보여주는 동영상을 보라고 하지만 남자는 동영상을 보는 것보다 실제 연습하는 편이 더 나은 경기 준비라고 말하였으므로 정답은 ④ '연습하는 것이 낫다고 생각해서'이다.

총 어휘 수 128

09 숫자

소재 피자 주문

듣기 대본 해석

남: Brother's 피자에 전화 주셔서 감사합니다. 주문을 받을까요?

여: 네, 트리플 치즈 피자 라지로 주세요. 얼마가 될까요?

남: 스페셜토핑을 얹은 라지 사이즈는 보통 25달러지만 오늘은 고객 감사의 날이라 모든 라지 피자를 레귤러 사이즈 피자의 가격으로 사실 수 있습니다.

여: 아, 좋네요. 그러면 치킨윙 주문도 추가할게요.

남: 네. 이제 다 된 건가요?

여: 네, 그게 전부예요.

남: 좋아요. 피자는 20달러이고 치킨윙은 10달러, 전부 30달러가 되겠어요.

여: 이번 주문에서 쿠폰을 사용할 수 있나요?

남: 물론이죠. 쿠폰을 웹사이트에서 받으셨나요?

여: 네. 10퍼센트 할인이 되네요.

남: 배달원이 도착하면 그에게 건네주세요.

어휘

customer *n.* 고객

정답 ③

문제풀이

원래 라지 사이즈의 피자가 25달러인데 오늘이 고객 감사의 날이라서 레귤러 가격인 20달러이고, 10달러짜리 치킨윙을 추가했으므로 합이 30달러이다. 그리고 남자가 10퍼센트 할인 쿠폰을 사용할 수 있다고 말했으므로 여자는 27달러를 내게 된다. 따라서 정답은 ③ '$27'이다.

총 어휘 수 129

10 언급 유무

소재 흥미롭게 생긴 건물

듣기 대본 해석

남: 안녕. 컴퓨터로 무엇을 보고 있니?

여: 런던으로 여름 휴가 갔을 때 찍은 몇몇의 사진들이야. 한번 볼래?

남: 물론이지. *[잠시 후]* 이 건물 흥미롭네. 피클처럼 생겼네.

여: 맞아. 작은 피클인 오이 피클과 비슷해 보여서 런던 사람들은 그것을 "The Gherkin"이라고 불러.

남: 그것의 진짜 이름은 뭐니?

여: 30 Saint Mary Axe야. 그건 이 건물의 주소야.

남: 그 건물 안에는 뭐가 있니?

여: 음, 그것이 런던의 금융가에 위치하고 있어서, 많은 다른 금융 회사와 몇몇의 식당도 수용하고 있어.

남: 높이는 얼마인데?

여: 대략 180m 정도 된다고 생각해. 41층이나 돼.

남: 안에 들어 갔었니?

여: 응. 내부 사진을 찍었어. 사진 볼래?

어휘

gherkin *n.* 오이 피클 **address *n.*** 주소 **financial district** 금융가 **house *v.*** 수용하다 **along with** ~도 함께

정답 ⑤

문제풀이

건물의 겉모습, 주소, 용도, 층수에 관한 언급은 있지만 건축 년도에 관한 언급은 없으므로 정답은 ⑤ '건축 년도'이다.

총 어휘 수 118

11 내용 일치 · 불일치

소재 중고 물건 판매점

듣기 대본 해석

남: 여러분의 집은 필요 없는 물건들로 채워져 있나요? 먼지가 쌓여 있는 오래된 TV, 냉장고, 컴퓨터를 가지고 계신가요? 그럼, Big Bear Resale Services는 여러분께 딱 맞는 곳입니다. 저희는 20년 동안 고객들이 원하지 않는 물건들을 파는 사업을 해 왔습니다. 저희는 여러분의 오래된, 중고 물품으로부터 최상의 돈을 받을 수 있도록 최고의 골동품 가게, 폐품 처리장, 개인적인 구매자들과 일하고 있습니다. 여러분이 해야 할 일은 전화기를 들어서 저희에게 전화하는 것이 전부입니다. 저희는 여러분이 계신 곳에 가서 오래된 물건들을 살펴보고, 사진을 찍고, 관심이 있는 구매자를 찾기 위해 웹사이트에 사진을 올립니다. 그리고 나서 저희는 여러분의 물건들을 무료로 픽업하고 배달도 합니다. 오늘 Big Bear Resale Services에 전화주세요!

어휘

cluttered *a.* 어수선한, 필요 없는 **antique *n.*** 골동품 **scrapyard *n.*** 폐품 처리장 **assure *v.*** 장담하다, 확언하다 **appraise *v.*** 살피다, 뜯어보다 **buyer *n.*** 구매자

정답 ⑤

문제풀이

Big Bear Resale Services는 집에 있는 오래된 물건들을 팔아주는 곳으로 마지막 부분에서 물건을 픽업하고 배달하는 것도 무료로 해준다고 말했으므로 일치하지 않는 것은 ⑤ '픽업과 배달 서비스는 유료이다.'이다.

총 어휘 수 126

12 도표

소재 동아리 선택

듣기 대본 해석

여: Aaron, 안녕. 방과후 영어 동아리에 들어갈 생각이야.

남: 백 선생님께서도 나보고 계속 하나 들어가라 그러셔.

여: 그럼 같이 하나 들어가자. 전학 온 지 얼마 안 돼서 네가 거의 내 유일한 친구야.

남: 좋은 생각이야. 선생님께서 이 시간표 주셨어. 이 동아리는 어때? 난 항상 연기를 한번 해보고 싶었어.

여: 나도 그 동아리 진짜 듣고 싶은데 월요일에는 학교 끝나고 피아노 연습 가야 돼. 토론 동아리는 어때? 토론하는 게 항상 흥미로웠어.

남: 난 독서를 많이 할 수 있는 동아리가 좋을 것 같아. 말하기랑 토론하기에는 별로 관심 없어.

여: 음, 이제 남은 동아리가 두 개로 좁혀졌네. 어떤 것을 고를까?

남: 이 동아리가 회원이 더 많은가 보네. 가입하자.

여: 응, 그래야 내가 친구를 사귈 기회가 더 많으니까.

남: 그러니까. 내가 우리 둘을 가입해 놓을게.

어휘
afterschool *a.* 방과후 **debate** *n.* 토론 *v.* 토론하다 **option** *n.* 선택, 옵션 **sign up** 가입하다

정답 ①

문제풀이
연기 동아리인 ③번은 여자가 시간이 안 된다고 했고 남자는 토론과 말하기보다는 독서를 하고 싶다고 했으므로 남는 것은 ①번과 ④번이다. 이 둘 중에 회원이 더 많은 곳으로 하자고 했으므로 정답은 ①번이다.

총 어휘 수 154

13 긴 대화의 응답

소재 회의 준비

듣기 대본 해석
여: 뭔가 지금 급하신가 봐요?
남: Craig 봤어요?
여: Craig요? 아침 일찍 나한테 전화해서 아프다고 했는데, 그래서 그는 안 왔어요.
남: 정말이에요? 그는 이번 달에 세 번이나 아프다고 전화했었어요.
여: 그는 몇 주 동안 꽤 아픈 것 같았어요. 무슨 문제가 있나요?
남: 그와 저는 오늘 사업 동업자들과 만나기로 되어 있었고, 그가 그 회의를 소집한 사람이거든요.
여: 오, 정말이에요?
남: 그는 가끔 굉장히 무책임하네요. 어쨌든, 그가 회의를 위해 준비했던 유인물을 본 적 있나요?
여: 어떻게 생겼어요?
남: 지난 분기 동안 회사의 재정과 판매 순위에 관한 많은 정보와 데이터가 들어 있어요.
여: 제가 찾아보기 시작해보고, 찾으면 갖다 드릴게요.
남: ③ 고마워요. 제가 신세를 지네요.

어휘
in a hurry 서두르는 **call in sick** 아파서 결근한다고 전화하다
call a meeting 회의를 소집하다 **irresponsible** *a.* 무책임한
handout *n.* 유인물 **regarding** *prep.* ~에 관한 **finance** *n.* 재정

정답 ③

문제풀이
남자는 회의를 준비해야 하는데 Craig의 결근으로 여자가 회의 준비에 필요한 유인물을 찾아서 갖다 준다고 말했으므로 그에 대한 응답으로 가장 적절한 것은 ③ '고마워요. 제가 신세를 지네요.'이다.

오답 보기 해석
① 회의를 취소해야 해요.
② 당신 병원에 가봐야 할 것 같아요.
④ 저는 이미 정보를 모두 복사했어요.
⑤ 네, 좋아요. Craig한테 도움 좀 받아요.

총 어휘 수 141

14 긴 대화의 응답

소재 서로 다른 게임 선호도

듣기 대본 해석
남: 안녕, Carol. 너 휴대폰으로 새로운 Candy Stomp 게임을 하고 있구나.
여: 응, 내 친구 James가 한번 해보라고 추천해 줬어.
남: 나도 그거 정말 해보고 싶었는데, 네가 끝나면 내가 그것을 해봐도 괜찮을까?
여: 문제없어. 몇 분 후에 너에게 줄게.
남: 너무 좋아. 너 Battle of the Clans 해본 적 있어? 그거 꽤 재미있어.
여: 그거 한 번 해봤는데, 나는 지루하게 느꼈는데.
남: 정말? 그거 매우 인기 있는데.
여: 음, 내 취향에는 너무 복잡했어. 나는 단순한 게임을 좋아해.
남: 그거 그렇게 복잡하지는 않은 것 같은데. 심지어 내 어린 사촌도 하던걸.
여: 나는 거기에 집중할 수 없었어. 나는 다른 사람들 같지 않나 봐.
남: 음, 모든 사람이 같은 의견을 갖는 것은 아니니까, 그렇지?
여: ④ 네 말이 맞아. 모든 사람들이 다른 선호도를 갖지.

어휘
recommend *v.* 추천하다 **popular** *a.* 인기 있는 **complicated** *a.* 복잡한 **opinion** *n.* 의견 〈문제〉 **broken** *a.* 고장 난, 깨진
relax *v.* 긴장을 풀다, 진정하다 **preference** *n.* 선호도

정답 ④

문제풀이
남자가 말한 게임은 많은 사람들이 좋아하는 게임인데 여자는 좋아하지 않는다고 말하고 있는 상황이다. 마지막에 남자가 모든 사람이 같은 의견을 갖는 것은 아니라고 말하며 되물었으므로 여자의 적절한 대답은 ④ '네 말이 맞아. 모든 사람들이 다른 선호도를 갖지.'이다.

오답 보기 해석
① 미안한데, 넌 할 수 없어. 내 폰이 고장 났어.
② 물론이야. 컴퓨터 게임을 하는 것은 내가 긴장을 풀도록 도와줘.
③ 문제 없어. 그게 바로 우정이지.
⑤ 너는 다른 게임을 찾아야 할 것 같아.

총 어휘 수 135

15 상황에 적절한 말

소재 기차표 구매하기

듣기 대본 해석
여: 뉴욕시티에서 친구를 만난 후 Taylor는 고향인 Minneapolis로 돌아가는 기차를 타러 Grand Central 역으로 가고 있습니다. 역으로 가는 길이 생각보다 차가 너무 막히고 택시는 천천히 가고 있습니다. Taylor는 기차 시간에 늦을까 봐 걱정됩니다. 역에 도착하자 출발 시간까지 이십 분 남아 있는 것을 봅니다. 표를 사는 줄은 굉장히 깁니다. 그는 역무원을 발견하고 표를 살 수 있는 다른 곳이 있는지 물어보고 싶어합니다. 이러한 상황에서 Taylor가 역무원에게 할 말로 가장 적절한 것은 무엇일까요?
Taylor: ③ 표를 살 수 있는 다른 곳이 있나요?

어휘
congested *a.* 차가 막히는, 혼잡한 **departure** *n.* 출발, 떠남

정답 ③

문제풀이
Taylor는 기차역에 시간적인 여유 없이 도착했는데 표를 사기 위해 기다려야 하는 줄이 매우 긴 것을 발견하고, 역무원에게 다른 곳에서 표를 살 수 있는지 묻고자 한다. 이 상황에 Taylor가 할말로 가장 적절한 것은 ③ '표를 살 수 있는 다른 곳이 있나요?'이다.

오답 보기 해석
① 여기 뉴욕에서 친구와 즐거운 시간을 보냈어요.
② 기차 플랫폼으로 갈 수 있는 방법을 가르쳐 주시겠어요?
④ 이곳은 제가 본 기차역 중에서 가장 좋은 기차역이네요.
⑤ Minneapolis로 가는 표 한 장 주세요.

총 어휘 수 130

16 담화 주제 / 17 세부 내용 파악

소재 시에서 운영하는 조합 소개

듣기 대본 해석

여: 안녕하세요, 여러분. 저희 시에서 제공하는 사회적 행사에 대해 여러분 모두 아실 것이라 확신합니다만, 조합에 대해서는 아시나요? 저희 시의 조합은 우리 지역 공동체에 매우 중요합니다. 매일 열리기 때문에 회원들은 기금 마련, 자원봉사 프로젝트와 같은 지역사회 행사에 참여할 뿐 아니라, 신선한 농산물과 요리방법들을 교환할 수 있습니다. 조합은 공동체 내 회원들로 하여금 서로 돕는 데 참여하도록 하지요. 아마 여러분들께서는 어떻게 조합에 가입하고, 참여하는지 궁금해하실 수 있겠네요. 회원들은 서로 소통하고, 예정된 행사들을 홍보하는 데 Twitter와 KakaoTalk과 같은 여러 소셜 미디어 수단들을 활용한답니다. 또한 우리는 Facebook 페이지를 갖고 있고, 때때로 기금마련을 위해 온라인 캠페인을 운영합니다. 이전에 저희가 했던 프로젝트들이 어떤 종류가 있는지 보려면 YouTube에 가보셔도 되고요. 여러분이 조합에 가입함으로써 동료 지역사회 일원들과 함께 하길 촉구하는 바입니다. 시간 내주셔서 감사합니다.

어휘

co-op *n.* 조합 **produce** *n.* 농산물 **upcoming** *a.* 다가오는, 곧 있을

정답 16 ② 17 ④

문제풀이

16 여자는 조합 활동 내용에 대해 상세히 이야기하면서 조합에 참여하기를 유도하고 있으므로 정답은 ② '조합을 통한 지역사회 (행사) 참여'이다.

17 여자는 조합원들이 소통하고, 행사를 홍보하는 소셜 미디어로 Twitter, KakaoTalk, Facebook을 언급하였고, 이전 프로젝트를 보기 위해 YouTube 페이지를 볼 것을 권하였다. 언급되지 않은 것은 ④ 'Instagram'이다.

오답 보기 해석

16

① 소셜 네트워킹의 다른 유형들
③ 소셜 네트워킹을 이용한 조직적 방법
④ 곧 있을 지역사회 행사에 참여하는 것
⑤ 지역사회 프로그램에 참여하는 것의 이점

총 어휘 수 158

DICTATION ANSWERS

01 Did you get everything moved into

02 fell on my hand

03 brighten up your yard / you're concerned about / caring for the plants / watch your children blossom

04 go backpacking / feel lonely / It allows time for self-reflection / I'm more of a social creature / enjoy time alone

05 looking over your credentials / it comes quite naturally to me / we decide to hire you / you would be a great fit for our company

06 come up with any good / would look better on the left / by seven thirty at the latest

07 on your way home / what's causing the bad traffic / do me a favor / I paid for it in advance

08 the opposing team's starting pitcher / is going crazy about him / we play against him / watching videos doesn't help them prepare for games

09 May I take your order / regular-sized one / In that case / Is it possible to use a coupon

10 It looks like a pickle / That's its address / it houses many different financial companies / It's forty-one stories high

11 cluttered with a bunch of junk / selling your unwanted items / for your old, used stuff / find an interested buyer / deliver them for free

12 has been pushing me to join one / I'd rather join a club / we have it narrowed down to two options

13 Are you in a hurry for some reason / who called the meeting / He can be so irresponsible / regarding the company's finances / I'll start looking for them

14 I try it out / Do you mind if I play / too complicated for my taste / not everyone can have the same opinion

15 The traffic on the way to the station / be late for his train / before the train's departure / if there is another place

16-17 participate in community events / to help one another / members use several social media outlets / I urge you to become one with

02 수능영어듣기 실전모의고사

본문 p.14

01 ④	02 ①	03 ②	04 ②	05 ①	06 ⑤
07 ⑤	08 ③	09 ③	10 ⑤	11 ④	12 ④
13 ③	14 ②	15 ③	16 ⑤	17 ②	

01 짧은 대화의 응답

소재 컨디션이 좋지 않은 이유

듣기 대본 해석

남: 안녕, Lilly. 너 안 좋아 보여. 아주 피곤해 보이네.
여: 괜찮아. 하루 종일 두통이 있고 콧물이 날 뿐이야.
남: 심한 것 같아. 병원에 갔었니?
여: ④ 응. 오늘 아침에 의사를 만났어.

어휘

headache ***n.*** 두통 **runny nose** 콧물 **awful** ***a.*** 끔찍한, 엄청

정답 ④

문제풀이

병원에 다녀왔냐고 묻는 남자의 질문에 적절한 대답은 ④ '응. 오늘 아침에 의사를 만났어.'이다.

오답 보기 해석

① 나는 간호사가 되기 위해 공부하고 있어.
② 아니. 나 아직 집에 안 갔어.
③ 너는 병원에 가야 해.
⑤ 좋을 것 같아. 내가 곧 낫기를 원해.

총 어휘 수 42

02 짧은 대화의 응답

소재 TV 프로그램

듣기 대본 해석

여: 너 내가 제일 좋아하는 텔레비전 프로그램 보고 있다고 들었어.
남: 그거 네가 좋아하는 거였어? 난 두 번째 회까지만 봤어. 지금까진 재미없던데.
여: 맞아. 시작이 좀 지루하긴 한데 나중에 아주 재미있어져.
남: ① 그럼 계속 볼게.

어휘

boring ***a.*** 지루한, 재미없는

정답 ①

문제풀이

여자는 자신이 좋아하는 TV프로그램을 남자도 본다는 것을 알고, 시작은 지루하지만 나중에는 재미있어진다고 하였으므로, 남자가 이에 대해 할 말로 가장 적절한 것은 ① '그럼 계속 볼게.'이다.

오답 보기 해석

② 계속 봐봐.
③ 난 저 프로그램 한 번도 본 적 없어.
④ 너 다 보고 나한테 빌려줬으면 좋겠어.
⑤ 토요일 밤에 TV에서 하는 걸 볼 수 있어.

총 어휘 수 46

03 담화 목적

소재 캠핑장 이용 규칙

듣기 대본 해석

남: 안녕하세요. Walker Mountain State Park 캠핑장에 오신 것을 환영합니다. 저는 공원 관리원 Frank Reynolds이고 여기 주립 공원에서 지켜주셔야 할 규칙에 대해서 논하려고 합니다. 비누와 다른 세제용품에 있는 오염물질 때문에 지정된 곳에서만 샤워하고 설거지해주시기 바랍니다. 그리고 각 모닥불에 신경 쓰시고 자정 전에 꺼주시기 바랍니다. 불꽃놀이는 공원 부지 내에서 금지입니다. 아시다시피 방치된 모닥불과 불꽃은 야생동물들과 동료들을 위험에 빠트리는 산불을 일으킬 수 있습니다. 누군가가 이러한 규칙을 위반하는 것을 목격했을 경우 주저 없이 공원 경비원에게 알려주시기 바랍니다. 들어주셔서 감사하며 Walker Mountain State Park에서 즐거운 시간 보내시기 바랍니다.

어휘

discuss ***v.*** 상의하다, 논의하다 **pollutant** ***n.*** 오염물질 **designated** ***a.*** 지정된 **tend** ***v.*** ~에 신경 쓰다, 주의하다 **extinguish** ***v.*** 끄다, 없애다 **prohibited** ***a.*** 금지된 **premises** ***n.*** 부지, 지역, 구내 **untended** ***a.*** 방치된, 돌봄을 받지 않은 **hesitate** ***v.*** 망설이다, 주저하다 **violate** ***v.*** 위반하다, 어기다

정답 ②

문제풀이

남자는 주립공원 관리원으로서 공원 내 캠핑장 이용 규칙에 대해서 설명하고 있으므로 정답은 ② '캠핑장 이용 수칙을 안내하려고'이다.

총 어휘 수 128

04 대화 주제

소재 명상의 이점

듣기 대본 해석

여: 안녕, Chase. 너 뭐 듣고 있어?
남: 안녕, Hailey. 명상에 관한 팟캐스트를 듣고 있어.
여: 명상, 어? 나는 그거 시도해 본 적 없는데.
남: 팟캐스트에서 많은 걸 배우고 있어. 사람들은 여러 가지 방법으로 명상으로부터 좋은 점을 얻을 수 있다는 걸 아니? 예를 들면, 명상은 에너지를 북돋아 줘.
여: 흥미롭네. 그래서 만약에 내가 오후에 지쳤을 때 명상을 하면 도움이 되겠네.
남: 그럴 수 있지. 그들은 명상이 네가 밤에 잘 때 어떻게 도움을 주고 스트레스를 완화해 주는지에 대해서도 얘기하고 있어.
여: 정말? 그게 명상을 하는 사람들이 항상 그렇게 좋은 컨디션인 이유임에 틀림없어.
남: 맞아. 그들은 또 명상은 너의 건강을 증진시켜주고 정신을 선명하게 할 수 있다고도 말했어.
여: 그래서 명상이 정신적으로도 육체적으로도 좋은 거지?
남: 응. 너의 전체적인 건강에 좋아.
여: 나도 명상을 시작해야 한다고 생각해.
남: 나도 시작하려고 생각 중이야.

어휘

meditation ***n.*** 명상, 묵상 **benefit** ***v.*** 득을 보다, 유용하다 ***n.*** 이득 **boost** ***v.*** 북돋우다 **meditate** ***v.*** 명상하다 **relieve** ***v.*** 없애다, 완화하다 **sharpen** ***v.*** 분명하게 하다, 선명해지다 **beneficial** ***a.*** 유익한, 이로운 **mentally** ***ad.*** 정신적으로 **physically** ***ad.*** 육체적으로

정답 ②

문제풀이
남자가 팟캐스트를 통해 들은 명상에 관한 좋은 점을 여자에게 말해주고 있으므로 정답은 ② '명상의 긍정적 효과'이다.

총 어휘 수 139

05 대화자의 관계 파악

소재 연극 연기 지도

듣기 대본 해석
남: Cindy, 대사를 외우는 건 어떻게 되어 가고 있나요?
여: 매우 잘 되고 있어요, Reynolds씨.
남: 당신이 빨리 할 수 있길 바라요. 우리는 시간이 많지 않아요.
여: 음, 외울 건 많은데 저는 겨우 오늘 아침에 대본을 받았어요.
남: 나도 알아요. 그렇지만 우리는 한 시간 더 공간을 대여했을 뿐이고, 우린 연기 억양 연습을 해야 해요.
여: 그래요, 지금 시작해요. 준비된 것 같아요.
남: 좋아요. 무대 왼쪽으로 와서 거기서부터 첫 대사를 해 봐요.
여: 네. *[잠시 후]* "아들을 낳을 때, 나는 두 번째 남편을 묻었어요." 어땠나요?
남: 좋아요. 이제, 같은 대사를 무대 오른쪽에서 해봅시다.
여: 알았어요. *[잠시 후]* "아들을 낳을 때, 나는 두 번째 남편을 묻었어요." 이게 나은가요?
남: 사실 그래요. 더 자연스러운 것 같아요.
여: 좋아요. 저는 개막공연이 너무 기대 되네요!
남: 그렇게 들으니 나도 기뻐요. 당신이 멋지게 해낼 거라고 믿어요.

어휘
line ***n.*** 대사 **script** ***n.*** 대본 **deliver** ***v.*** (강연, 연기, 대사 등을) 하다

정답 ①

문제풀이
Line, script, stage, opening 등의 단어에서 연극배우와 연출자와의 대화임을 유추할 수 있으므로 정답은 ① '감독 — 여배우'이다.

오답 보기 해석
② 미술 감독 – 심사위원
③ 상사 – 사무실 직원
④ 고객 – 미용사
⑤ 개인 트레이너 – 모델

총 어휘 수 151

06 그림의 세부 내용 파악

소재 얼음으로 만든 놀이터

듣기 대본 해석
남: 여기 정말 놀라워, 그렇지 않아?
여: 응, 좋은 시간을 보내고 있지만 꽤 춥네, 그렇지 않아?
남: 음, 한겨울이잖아. 저 뒤편에 고드름들 좀 봐. 뒤쪽에 특이한 얼음 조각품이 있어.
여: 동물을 타고 있는 원숭이를 말하는 거니?
남: 응, 원숭이가 타고 있는 게 어떤 동물이라고 생각해?
여: 돼지 같아. 그건 그렇고, 나는 전체 성을 얼음으로 지었다는 것을 믿을 수 없어.
남: 그래, 정말 멋있어 보여. 성 안을 확인해 보고 싶어?
여: 음, 나 지금 이 시소를 타는 게 너무 재미있어.
남: 나는 아냐. 네가 나보다 훨씬 커서 나는 계속 위에만 있잖아.
여: 맞아. 네가 말하고 보니, 항상 아래에 있는 것도 그렇게 재미있지 않아.
남: 그래, 그럼 우리 성으로 가볼래?

어휘
icicle ***n.*** 고드름 **peculiar** ***a.*** 특이한, 이상한 **sculpture** ***n.*** 조각품
now that ~이므로, ~이기 때문에

정답 ⑤

문제풀이
여자가 자신이 아래에만 있다고 했는데 위에 올라가 있으므로 정답은 ⑤번이다.

총 어휘 수 151

07 할 일

소재 손님 접대

듣기 대본 해석
여: 여보, 이번 금요일에 침실 재배치 도와줄 수 있어요?
남: 아무래도 못할 것 같아요. 다음 주 금요일에 할 수 있을까요?
여: 무슨 일이 생겼어요?
남: 네. 중요한 고객이 LA에서 오셔서 이번 주말에는 그녀를 접대해야 해요.
여: 주말 내내 바쁠까요?
남: 정확히 모르겠어요. 금요일 아침에 그녀가 도착하면 내가 공항에 데리러 가야 해요.
여: 그녀와 하루 종일 같이 보내야 해요?
남: 그녀가 도시를 관광하고 싶어 해서 내가 구경시켜 줘야 해요.
여: 그럼, 그녀가 중요한 고객이라면 저녁 식사에 초대하는 게 어때요?
남: 좋은 생각이에요. 프랑스 요리를 좀 해줄 수 있어요?
여: 알겠어요. 그러면 목요일에 식료품 장을 봐야겠어요.

어휘
rearrange ***v.*** 재배치하다 **entertain** ***v.*** 접대하다
be supposed to V ~하기로 되어 있다

정답 ⑤

문제풀이
여자의 '그럼, 그녀가 중요한 고객이라면 저녁 식사에 초대하는 게 어때요?'에서 고객을 저녁식사에 초대했음을 알 수 있으므로 여자가 남자를 위해 할 일로 적절한 것은 ⑤ '고객에게 식사 대접하기'이다.

총 어휘 수 123

08 이유

소재 새 유니폼 구매 요청

듣기 대본 해석
남: 안녕하세요, Temmel 선생님.
여: 안녕, John. 들어오렴. 무엇을 도와줄까?
남: 농구팀에 대해 드릴 말씀이 있어요.
여: 뭔데?
남: 음, 지난 시즌에 저희가 새로운 팀 유니폼을 샀던 것 아시죠.
여: 기억해. 모든 선수들에게 인기가 있었잖니.
남: 맞아요, 하지만 문제는 저희 라이벌 팀이 그들의 유니폼에 같은 색깔을 사용하고 있다는 거예요.
여: Mound High School 말이니?
남: 네. 제가 일전에 그 학교 학생들이 입고 있는 것을 봤어요.
여: 알았어, 그래서 너는 우리가 새로운 유니폼을 다시 사야 한다고 제안하는 거니?
남: 네. 그러면 다른 경기에선 다른 유니폼을 사용할 수 있어요.
여: 그래, 교장 선생님과 이야기해 보고 어떻게 생각하시는지 볼게.
남: 정말 감사해요, Temmel 선생님. 결정하시는 대로 저한테 알려주세요.

어휘
rival *n.* 맞수, 경쟁자 **principal** *n.* 교장

정답 ③

문제풀이
남자는 작년에 농구부의 새 유니폼을 구매했지만, 라이벌 팀에서 같은 색의 유니폼을 입은 걸 보고 새로운 유니폼을 다시 사야 한다고 제안하고 있다. 따라서 정답은 ③ '새 유니폼 구매를 요청하려고'이다.

총 어휘 수 129

09 숫자

소재 스쿠터 대여하기

듣기 대본 해석
여: 안녕하세요. 무엇을 도와드릴까요?
남: 안녕하세요. 오늘 오토바이 몇 대 빌리려고 해요.
여: 알겠습니다. 일단 50cc 스쿠터랑 125cc 오토바이가 있어요.
남: 그렇군요. 가격 차이는요?
여: 오토바이는 하루당 30달러예요. 스쿠터는 보통 25달러인데, 비수기 행사 중이라 추가로 10퍼센트 할인해 드려요.
남: 좋은데요! 그렇게 멀리까지 몰지는 않을 것 같으니까 스쿠터 두 대로 할게요.
여: 알겠습니다. 헬멧도 필요하신가요?
남: 그럼요. 탈 때 안전한 게 좋아요. 얼마예요?
여: 헬멧은 하루당 5달러인데, 행사에 포함은 안 돼요.
남: 그렇군요. 그럼 스쿠터 두 대랑 헬멧 두 개로 할게요.
여: 알겠습니다. 준비해 드릴게요.

어휘
rent *v.* 빌리다 *n.* 임대료 **promotion** *n.* 홍보, 판촉 행사

정답 ③

문제풀이
처음에 남자가 오늘 하루 빌린다고 했고, 스쿠터 두 대라 하루에 50달러인데 10퍼센트 할인을 해준다고 했으므로 45달러이고, 헬멧 두 개 대여료는 10달러이므로 정답은 ③ '$55'이다.

총 어휘 수 133

10 언급 유무

소재 지역사회 자원봉사

듣기 대본 해석
여: 안녕하세요, 여러분. 제 이름은 Terry Loggins이고요. 저는 오늘 지역사회에서 자원봉사 하는 것에 대해 여러분이 가지고 있을 만한 질문을 듣고자 여기 왔어요.
남: 안녕하세요, Terry. 저는 제 아이들을 얼마 동안 자원봉사에 참가시키고 싶었어요.
여: 마음 속에 생각해 둔 자원봉사는 어떤 종류인가요?
남: 음, 그들은 아직 중학생이니 너무 많이 할 수는 없어요.
여: 오, 그래도 가능한 자리가 있어요. 그들은 무료급식소나 노인복지시설에서 도와줄 수 있겠네요. 아니면 그들은 싱글맘이나 나이든 분들이 잔디 깎기나 쓰레기 치우기 같은 일상의 일을 하는 것을 도와줄 수 있어요.
남: 정말 좋은 추천이네요. 제가 어떻게 시작하면 되죠?
여: 시청에 들르세요. 그들은 모든 가능한 자원봉사 자리에 대한 목록을 가지고 있을 거예요.
남: 충분히 쉬워 보이네요.
여: 그것은 쉽고, 당신이 도와주는 사람들에게 큰 의미가 있을 거예요!

어휘
community *n.* 지역사회 **volunteer work** 자원봉사
soup kitchen 무료급식소 **retirement home** 노인복지시설
senior citizen 고령자, 노인 **mow** *v.* (잔디를) 깎다
recommendation *n.* 추천 **city hall** 시청

정답 ⑤

문제풀이
대화에서 자원봉사 할 사람, 장소, 활동 내용, 시작 방법에 관해서는 언급되어 있지만 봉사하게 될 시간에 관해서는 언급되지 않았으므로 정답은 ⑤ '자원봉사하게 될 시간'이다.

총 어휘 수 144

11 내용 일치 · 불일치

소재 과학 박람회 소개

듣기 대본 해석
여: 우리는 과학 박람회의 첫 번째 라운드가 끝났고 학생들이 제출한 아이디어를 기초로 예선전을 통해 선발한 25명의 학생들이 있습니다. 마지막 라운드에 자격이 있는 모든 학생들은 오늘날의 세계에 관련이 있고 유용한 아이디어를 제출했습니다. 마지막 라운드는 5월 22일인 오늘부터 2주 동안 학생 센터 이벤트 홀에서 열릴 것입니다. 이번에는 학생들이 그들의 아이디어로 작동하는 모델을 만들 것입니다. 학생들은 아이디어가 작동할 수 있는지 뿐만 아니라 얼마나 많은 그리고 어떤 종류의 재료가 그것들을 만드는 데 사용되었는지에 따라 평가될 것입니다. 최우수 우승자는 특허권을 갖고 아이디어의 실제 원형을 제작하기 위해 5,000달러를 받게 될 것입니다.

어휘
preliminary *n.* 예선전 **submit** *v.* 제출하다 **qualify for** ~의 자격을 얻다 **relevant** *a.* 관련 있는, 적절한 **take place** 개최되다 **patent** *n.* 특허권

정답 ④

문제풀이
담화에서 학생들의 아이디어가 작동되는지 뿐만 아니라 사용한 재료의 수와 종류에 따라 평가된다고 했으므로 정답은 ④ '사용한 재료의 수와 종류는 평가에 반영되지 않는다.'이다.

총 어휘 수 127

12 도표

소재 에어컨 선택

듣기 대본 해석
남: 안녕하세요. 무엇을 도와드릴까요?
여: 안녕하세요. 새 아파트에 설치할 에어컨을 찾고 있어요.
남: 알겠습니다. 이 제품은 어때요? 창문에 다는 형식인데 전력 소요량이 낮아서 전기세를 꽤 아낄 수 있어요.
여: 아, 창문에 다는 건 별로 구입하고 싶지 않아요.
남: 알겠습니다. 음, 이 모델이 요즘 잘 팔려요. 리모컨도 함께 온답니다.
여: 리모컨 별로 필요 없을 것 같아요. 더 강력한 에어컨이면 좋겠어요.
남: 좋습니다. 풍향 조절 되는 모델을 원하세요?
여: 그럼요.
남: 그럼 이제 선택지가 두 모델로 줄어들었네요. 가격대는 어느 정도로 생각하고 계세요?
여: 가능하다면 250달러보다 적게 쓰고 싶네요.
남: 그럼 이 모델이 고객님께 딱 맞겠네요.
여: 좋네요. 이걸로 할게요.

어휘

power rating 전력 소요량, 전기요금률 **oscillate** ***v.*** 계속 오가다, 왔다 갔다 하다, 진동하다

정답 ④

문제풀이

여자가 창문에 달고 싶지 않다고 했으므로 ②번은 제외되고, 리모컨도 필요 없다고 했으므로 남는 것은 ④, ⑤번이다. ④번과 ⑤번은 파워는 같고 둘 다 풍향 조절이 되는데, 그 중에 가격이 250달러보다 싼 것을 원했으므로 정답은 ④번이다.

총 어휘 수 125

13 긴 대화의 응답

소재 교내 장기자랑 대회에서 탈락한 친구 위로하기

듣기 대본 해석

남: Laura, 너 상태가 안 좋아 보이는데, 괜찮니?
여: 괜찮아. 큰 문제는 아니야.
남: 말해봐. 나한텐 어떤 것도 말할 수 있잖아. 뭐가 문제야?
여: 음, 넌 내가 지난주 학교 장기자랑을 위해 얼마나 애썼는지 알지?
남: 응, 기억나. 저글링 공연에 몇 시간이나 들였잖아.
여: 맞아. 그래서 오늘 게시판을 확인해봤는데 장기자랑에서 탈락했어.
남: 정말? 어떻게 그럴 수가 있어? 잘하잖아.
여: 난 내 공연이 정말 완벽하다고 생각했어. 실수도 전혀 하지 않았고.
남: 네가 좌절한 거 이해해. 내가 연극부에 들어가려고 했을 때 나한테도 똑같은 일이 있었어.
여: 너무 속상해. 내 자신감이 완전히 무너졌어.
남: ③ 기운 내! 내년에 또 기회가 있을 거야.

어휘

bulletin board 게시판 **make it** 성공하다 **flawless** ***a.*** 완벽한, 나무랄 데 없는, 결점이 없는 **frustration** ***n.*** 좌절 **heartbreaking** ***a.*** 속상한, 가슴 아픈 **shot** ***a.*** 완전히 망가진 〈문제〉 **apologize** ***v.*** 사과하다

정답 ③

문제풀이

남자는 여자가 장기자랑에서 탈락했다는 소식을 듣고 위로하고 있다. 무척 속이 상하고 자신감이 무너졌다는 여자의 마지막 말에 남자의 응답으로 가장 적절한 것은 ③ '기운 내! 내년에 또 기회가 있을 거야.'이다.

오답 보기 해석

① 걱정 마. 나 혼자 할 수 있어.
② 쇼에 참여하게 된 걸 축하해.
④ 알겠어. 끝나면 전화할게.
⑤ 괜찮아. 나한테 사과할 필요 없어.

총 어휘 수 123

14 긴 대화의 응답

소재 오랜만에 만난 고교동창과의 대화

듣기 대본 해석

남: 안녕. 우리 전에 만난 것 같은데. 네 이름이 Jamie 아니었나?
여: 응, 맞아. 너 우리 고등학교 출신인 Ricky 맞지? 오랜만이네.
남: 응. 너를 마지막으로 본 게 졸업식인 것 같은데, 거의 8년이 되어가네!
여: 와! 그렇게 오래 됐다니 믿어지지 않네. 요즘 어때?
남: 지난 몇 년간 LA에서 살고 있어. 배우로 내 이름을 알리려고 노력 중이야.
여: 정말? 주요 배역을 맡은 적이 있어?
남: 단지 속 쓰림 약 광고에서 뱀파이어 역을 한 것 밖에 없어.
여: 오, 나 그 광고 알아! 내가 가장 좋아하는 것들 중 하나야. 정말 재미있던데.
남: 고마워. 하지만 난 정말 할리우드 영화를 하고 싶어. 다음 주에 오디션이 몇 개 있어.
여: ② 네가 꿈을 쫓는 건 훌륭해.

어휘

commercial ***n.*** 광고 **heartburn** ***n.*** (소화불량에 의한) 속 쓰림 **feature** ***n.*** (영화 등의) 인기 있는 프로그램, 주요 작품

정답 ②

문제풀이

남자와 여자는 고등학교 졸업 이후 약 8년 만에 만나 근황을 얘기하고 있다. 남자는 배우가 되는 꿈을 이루기 위해 다음 주에 오디션을 볼 예정이라고 말하였으므로 이에 대한 여자의 응답으로 가장 적절한 것은 ② '네가 꿈을 쫓는 건 훌륭해.'이다.

오답 보기 해석

① 진정해. 너 자신한테 그렇게 엄격하지 않는 게 좋아.
③ 너 영화 오디션 보는 게 좋겠다.
④ 우리 영화 같이 보는 게 좋겠다.
⑤ 새로운 직업을 고려하는 게 좋을 거야.

총 어휘 수 138

15 상황에 적절한 말

소재 과학 수업의 팀 과제

듣기 대본 해석

남: Lucy와 Jayden은 지역 고등학교 학생들입니다. 이번 학기에 그들은 과학 수업을 같이 듣고 있습니다. 그 수업의 학생들에게 팀 과제가 주어졌습니다. Lucy와 Jayden은 팀으로 작업하면서 책임량을 반으로 나눴습니다. 문제는 Lucy는 미술 동아리에 가입했고 연습에 자주 참석해야 한다는 것입니다. 따라서 그녀는 제 시간에 그녀의 과제를 끝내지 못합니다. 처음에 Jayden은 Lucy의 상황을 이해합니다. 그러나 그는 그녀가 자신의 책임을 자꾸 미루자 화가 나기 시작합니다. Jayden은 Lucy에게 이에 대해 말하고 싶습니다. 이런 상황에서 그는 그녀에게 무슨 말을 해야 할까요?
Jayden: Lucy, ③ 네가 이 과제에 대한 너의 책임을 다하길 바라.

어휘

assign ***v.*** (특별한 임무를) 하라고 하다(맡기다) **split** ***v.*** 나누다, 쪼개다 **responsibility** ***n.*** 책임 **put off** 미루다, 연기하다

정답 ③

문제풀이

팀 과제를 같이 하는데 친구가 자신이 맡은 부분을 하지 않아서 친구에게 화가 난 상황이다. 이럴 때는 친구에게 자기가 맡은 책임을 다하라고 말해주는 것이 가장 적절하므로 정답은 ③ '네가 이 과제에 대한 너의 책임을 다하길 바라.'이다.

오답 보기 해석

① 만약 네가 내 도움이 필요하면 꼭 말해줘.
② 나는 네가 미술 동아리에서 정말 잘 하길 바라.
④ 너는 학교와 집 생활의 균형을 맞추도록 노력해야 해.
⑤ 일이 너무 많다면 잠시 휴식을 취하는 게 어때?

총 어휘 수 116

16 담화 주제 / 17 세부 내용 파악

소재 교양과목 공부의 이점

듣기 대본 해석

여: 전국의 종합대학과 단과대학은 교양과목 프로그램에 대한 관심의 감소를 겪고 있습니다. 우리 나라의 영향력 있는 몇몇 인물들은 교양과목이 쓸모없다고 믿습니다. 그들은 더 좋은 직업으로 이끌 수 있기 때문에 다른 과목들을 공부하라고 학생들을 격려합니다. 교양과목이 유용한지 아닌지 잠깐 생각을 해보도록 합시다. 교양과목 강의는 다른 과목들이 줄 수 없는 아주 가치 있는 능력들을 줌으로써 미래의 직업을 위해 학생들을 준비시킵니다. 철학, 역사, 그리고 어학을 공부하는 것은 현실 세계에서의 생존에 필수적이고 수학 같은 과목들에서는 얻을 수 없는 학생들의 비판적 사고 능력을 길러 줍니다. 이러한 문제 해결 능력들은 다재 다능한 사람을 양성하는 데 도움을 줍니다. 교양과목에 대한 당신의 의견을 다시 한번 생각해 보시길 권고합니다. 여러 가지 방법으로 당신을 더 나은 사람으로 만들어줄 과목들을 신청하는 것을 고려하시기 바랍니다.

어휘

liberal arts 교양과목, 인문학 **influential** ***a.*** 영향력 있는 **subject** ***n.*** 과목, 주제 **invaluable** ***a.*** 매우 유용한, 귀중한 **critical thinking** 비판적 사고 **essential** ***a.*** 필수적인 **well-rounded** ***a.*** 다재 다능한 **sign up** ~을 등록하다, 신청하다

정답 16 ⑤ 17 ②

문제풀이

16 교양과목을 공부해서 얻을 수 있는 이점들을 이야기하고 있으므로 여자가 하는 말의 주제는 ⑤ '교양과목을 공부하는 것의 이점'이다.

17 여자는 철학, 역사, 어학, 수학은 언급했지만 교육학에 대한 언급은 하지 않으므로 정답은 ② '교육학'이다.

오답 보기 해석

16

① 교양과목과 전문적인 교육의 통합
② 교양과목 전공자들을 위한 취업 기회
③ 교양과목에 대한 관심 감소의 원인
④ 교양과목이 인류에 끼치는 영향

17

① 철학 ③ 역사 ④ 언어 ⑤ 수학

총 어휘 수 144

DICTATION ANSWERS

01 had a headache and a runny nose / Have you been to a doctor's office

02 It's boring so far / it starts a bit slow

03 wash your dishes in designated areas / prohibited within park premises / endanger our wildlife as well as your fellow campers / Do not hesitate to contact

04 podcast about meditation / in a variety of ways / sharpen your mind / it's beneficial both mentally and physically

05 there's a lot to memorize / rented for another hour / deliver your opening line / let's try the same line / Did that work better

06 it is the middle of winter / built that entire castle out of ice / I'm always stuck on the top / Now that you mention it

07 rearrange the bedroom / I have to entertain her / I'm supposed to pick her up / spend the whole day / if she's an important client

08 popular with all of the players / the problem is our rival team / see what he thinks

09 rent a couple of motorbikes / What's the price difference / running an off-season promotion / in the promotion

10 involved in volunteering / take care of daily matters / How do I get started / a listing of all available volunteer positions

11 based on the ideas they submitted / both relevant and useful / The final round will take place / how much and what kind of material

12 it'll save you quite a bit on electricity / They come with a remote control / What's your price range / I'd like to spend less than

13 It's really no big deal / my performance was flawless / The same thing happened to me / My confidence is shot

14 make a name for myself / Have you got any big parts / one of my favorites

15 have split the responsibilities in half / finish her work on time / begins to get upset

16-17 a decrease in interest in liberal arts programs / Liberal arts courses prepare students for / gives students critical thinking skills / well-rounded person

03 수능영어듣기 실전모의고사

본문 p.20

01 ④	02 ①	03 ④	04 ⑤	05 ③	06 ④
07 ①	08 ⑤	09 ③	10 ②	11 ②	12 ③
13 ④	14 ④	15 ①	16 ⑤	17 ④	

01 짧은 대화의 응답

소재 시험 이후의 계획

듣기 대본 해석

여: 기말고사가 끝나서 너무 행복해.
남: 나도 그래. 이번 주말에 나랑 소풍갈래?
여: 좋기는 한데, 나는 벌써 친척집에 방문할 계획이 있어.
남: ④ 아, 괜찮아. 우리는 다음에 갈 수 있잖아.

어휘

relative ***n.*** 친척

정답 ④

문제풀이

시험이 끝나고 주말에 소풍을 가자는 남자의 제안에 여자는 친척집 방문 계획이 있다고 말한다. 이에 대해 남자는 괜찮다며 다음에 갈 수 있다고 말하는 것이 자연스러우므로 정답은 ④ '아, 괜찮아. 우리는 다음에 갈 수 있잖아.'가 된다.

오답 보기 해석

① 글쎄, 날씨를 한번 보자.
② 그래 나도, 정말 신나.
③ 저녁에 너희 집에 들를게.
⑤ 우리는 시험 준비를 위해 공부를 좀 더 해야 해.

총 어휘 수 45

02 짧은 대화의 응답

소재 과제 완성하기

듣기 대본 해석

남: Clara, 물리 과제 완성하기에 너무 어렵다고 생각하지 않니?
여: 그것은 꽤 어려웠어. 하지만 난 어젯밤에 끝낼 수 있었어.
남: 농담이겠지! 분명히 너의 부모님께서 도와주셨을 거야, 그렇지?
여: ① 아니야, 내가 스스로 했어.

어휘

physics ***n.*** 물리학 **assignment** ***n.*** 과제 **complete** ***v.*** 완성하다 ***a.*** 완성된, 완료된 〈문제〉 **on one's own** 혼자서, 단독으로 **chemistry** ***n.*** 화학 **a couple of** 둘의, 몇 개의

정답 ①

문제풀이

과제를 부모님이 도와주셨을 거라고 말하는 남자의 말에 대한 대답으로 적절한 여자의 말은 ① '아니야, 내가 스스로 했어.'이다.

오답 보기 해석

② 아마도 다음주 월요일까지일거야.
③ 물론, 내가 해줄게.
④ 난 화학을 물리보다 좋아해.
⑤ 응, 그들은 며칠 뒤에 떠나.

총 어휘 수 43

03 요지

소재 학생들의 스포츠 활동

듣기 대본 해석

남: 여러분은 고등학교에서 체육 프로그램에 참여하는 것이 학생들의 성적에 부정적인 영향을 줄 것이라고 생각할 것입니다. 하지만, 최근의 연구에서, 일반적으로 운동을 하는 학생들이 하지 않는 학생들보다 학교에서 더 잘 생활한다고 보여줍니다. 운동은 학습, 기억, 집중에 긍정적인 영향을 주고, 그것은 교실에서 적극적인 학생들에게 이점을 줄 수 있습니다. 운동을 하는 학생들은 팀워크나 목표 설정과 같이 인생에서 가치 있는 다른 기술들에 대해서도 배우기 때문에 운동에 참여하는 효과는 때때로 학습적인 공부를 능가합니다. 경기에 이기고 다른 목표를 달성하기 위해서 코치, 트레이너, 팀원들과 노력하는 것은 학생들이 성공하는 데에 중요한 기술들을 가르쳐서 그들이 인생을 사는 동안 계속 그들에게 도움이 될 수 있습니다.

어휘

athletic ***a.*** 체육의, 경기의 **have an impact on** ~에 영향을 주다
advantage ***n.*** 이점 **go beyond** ~을 넘어서다, 능가하다

정답 ④

문제풀이

스포츠 활동이 학생들의 학업 성적과 인생을 사는 데 도움이 되는 이로움을 준다는 내용이므로 정답은 ④ '학생들의 스포츠 활동은 학업 이상의 것을 줄 수 있다.'이다.

총 어휘 수 118

04 의견

소재 정크푸드가 건강에 주는 영향

듣기 대본 해석

여: Tom, 여기서 대체 무슨 일이 일어난 거니?
남: 무슨 말씀이세요, 엄마?
여: 여기가 너무 지저분하잖니. 이 쓰레기들 좀 보렴!
남: 네, 맞아요. 죄송해요, 엄마. 제가 바로 치울게요.
여: 그리고 무엇이 지저분하게 했는지 보렴. 패스트푸드 봉지, 정크푸드 박스, 음료수 캔, 사탕 껍질들이 사방에 있구나. 네가 전부 먹은 건 아니지, 그렇지?
남: 제가 먹었어요. 너무 배가 고팠어요.
여: 하지만 이런 것들은 너한테 너무 안 좋아. 그것 중 어떤 것도 전혀 건강에 좋지 않아.
남: 네, 엄마는 저한테 정크푸드를 먹도록 절대 허락하지 않으시니까 엄마가 집에 안 계실 때 가끔 그것들을 많이 먹는 거예요.
여: 내가 너의 건강을 걱정하기 때문에 네가 그런 것들을 먹지 않았으면 하는 거야.
남: 저도 이해해요. 그리고 더 이상 정크푸드를 먹지 않도록 노력할게요.
여: 건강이 가장 중요하다는 것을 명심하렴.

어휘

messy ***a.*** 지저분한, 엉망인 **once in a while** 가끔, 때때로

정답 ⑤

문제풀이

엄마가 집을 비운 사이 많은 정크푸드를 먹은 아들에게 그것이 건강에 좋지 않다고 말하고 있는 상황이다. 따라서 ⑤ '건강을 위해 정크푸드를 삼가야 한다.'가 정답이다.

총 어휘 수 145

05 대화자의 관계 파악

소재 상사와 일상대화

듣기 대본 해석

남: 이런 날씨 어때요?
여: 끔찍해요, 그렇죠? 일기예보에 의하면 일주일 내내 비가 올 거라고 하네요.
남: 오늘도 여전히 야외에서 일해야 하나요?
여: 아니요. 당신은 사무실에서 할 일들이 있어요.
남: 잘 됐네요. 만약 야외에서 일하다 아플까 봐 걱정했거든요.
여: Frank, 당신에게 뭔가 줄곧 하려고 했던 말이 있어요.
남: 네. 무엇인가요?
여: 요즘 당신은 평소답지 않아요. 괜찮아요?
남: 솔직히 제 아들이 학교에서 많은 어려움을 겪고 있고 집에서는 쌀쌀맞거든요. 난 정말 그가 걱정돼요.
여: 이해해요. 저도 아이가 둘이 있거든요. 그런데 알다시피, 애들은 애들이죠. 아이들이 자연스럽게 성장하도록 놔두셔야 해요.
남: 조언 감사합니다 Stark씨. 제가 오늘 해야 할 일은 무엇이죠?
여: 이 서류들을 구분해주면 좋겠어요.

어휘

forecast ***n.*** 예보, 예측　**standoffish** ***a.*** 쌀쌀맞은

정답 ③

문제풀이

남자는 대화의 시작 부분에서 일을 어디서 해야 하는지 묻고 여자에게 아들에 대한 조언을 받았으며 마지막 부분에서 자신이 해야 할 일을 묻는 것으로 보아 두 사람의 관계는 ③ '상사 – 부하직원'임을 유추할 수 있다.

총 어휘 수 143

06 그림의 세부 내용 파악

소재 쇼를 위한 밴드의 전단지

듣기 대본 해석

남: Sandra, 무얼 하고 있니?
여: 내 새로운 밴드의 전단지야. 우리는 다음 주에 쇼가 있거든.
남: 오, 멋져 보인다. 그럼 너희 밴드 이름이 Bastion이구나.
여: 응, 우리 이름은 왼쪽 상단에 넣었어. 그리고 그것 옆에 해골도 그려 넣었지.
남: 그렇구나. 너희는 로큰롤 밴드 같아. 왼쪽에 그린 기타는 정말 멋진걸.
여: 응, 그건 내 기타인 Bender P-159야.
남: 네가 그림 오른쪽에 있는 것 같은데 네 기타는 어디 있니?
여: 내가 기타를 들고 있는 사진을 찾을 수가 없었어. 그래서 그것을 들고 있지 않은 사진을 선택했어.
남: 인상적이야. 날짜와 장소를 아래에 넣었구나?
여: 맞아. 우리는 27일 저녁 9시에 Denton Shelter House에서 연주할 거야.
남: 오, 멋지구나. 나도 가능하면 가고 싶네.

어휘

flyer ***n.*** 전단　**skull** ***n.*** 두개골, 해골　**venue** ***n.*** 장소

정답 ④

문제풀이

여자가 기타를 들고 있는 사진을 찾을 수가 없어서 기타를 들고 있지 않은 사진을 택했다고 했는데 그림에서는 기타를 어깨에 매고 있으므로 정답은 ④번이다.

총 어휘 수 148

07 부탁한 일

소재 생일파티 준비

듣기 대본 해석

여: 안녕, Oliver! 딱 맞춰 왔네!
남: 정말? 무슨 일이야?
여: 이번 주말 Elena의 생일파티를 위한 계획을 검토하려고.
남: 오, 좋아. 깜짝 파티를 할 거지?
여: 아니, 나는 우리가 Joe's Crab Shack에 가까운 친구 여러 명을 모이게 할 생각인데.
남: 좋아. 그녀가 한동안 거기 가고 싶어 했던 거 알아.
여: 나는 우리 친한 친구들 모두를 초대할까 생각 중이야.
남: 좋은 생각이야. 내가 도울 일은 없어?
여: 파티 상점에 가서 풍선이랑 "생일 축하" 표지를 사올래?
남: 물론, 바로 거기로 갈게.
여: 좋았어. 대단한 파티가 될 거야.
남: 그래, 정말 기대된다!

어휘

in time 시간 맞춰(늦지 않게)　**go over** 점검하다, 검토하다
a bunch of 다수의　〈문제〉 **reserve** ***v.*** 예약하다　**directions** ***n.*** 길 안내

정답 ①

문제풀이

Elena를 위해 생일파티를 계획하고 있다는 여자의 말에 남자가 자신이 도울 수 있는 일을 물었고, 여자는 파티 상점에 가서 풍선과 "생일 축하" 표지를 사달라고 부탁했으므로 여자가 남자에게 부탁한 일은 ① '파티 장식품 사기'이다.

오답 보기 해석

② 북클럽 시작하는 것 도와주기
③ 충분한 테이블 예약하기
④ 친한 친구들에게 전화하기
⑤ 그녀에게 파티 가는 길 알려주기

총 어휘 수 118

08 이유

소재 친구의 제안 거절하기

듣기 대본 해석

여: 안녕 Julian. 무슨 일이야?
남: 별거 아냐. 학교 신문에 나온 이 음악 평론을 읽고 있어.
여: 멋지다. 무슨 앨범이야?
남: Kenny North의 새 앨범 Graduate School이야. 들어본 적 있니?
여: 물론이지. 요즘 여러 사람들이 얘기하던데.
남: 응. 살까 생각 중이야. 학교 끝나고 가서 나하고 같이 들어볼래?
여: 그러고 싶은데 안 되겠네. 오늘은 학교 끝나고 집에 바로 가야 하거든.
남: 정말? 왜?
여: 남동생이 대학교에서 와.
남: 그럼 버스 터미널로 태우러 가야 하겠구나?
여: 아빠가 가실 거야. 난 엄마 집 청소 하시는 거 도와드려야 해.
남: 알겠어. 오빠랑 즐거운 시간 보내.

어휘

review ***n.*** (책, 영화 등에 대한) 평론, 비평　**pick ~ up** ~을 차로 데리러 가다

정답 ⑤

문제풀이
새 음반을 들으러 같이 가자는 남자의 제안에 여자는 남동생이 집에 와서 집안 청소를 도와야 한다며 거절하고 있으므로 정답은 ⑤ '엄마가 청소하는 것을 도와야 해서'이다.

총 어휘 수 135

09 숫자

소재 스테이크와 감자 구입하기

듣기 대본 해석
여: Jenna의 정육점에 오신 것을 환영합니다. 무엇을 도와드릴까요?
남: 스테이크 고기를 좀 찾고 있어요.
여: 스테이크요? 어떤 스테이크요?
남: 글쎄요, 내일 장인, 장모님을 모시고 바비큐 파티를 할건데 그들에게 잘 보일 수 있는 걸로 주세요.
여: 음, 고급 티본스테이크 세일을 하고 있어요. 스테이크당 20달러예요.
남: 좋을 것 같아요. 네 개 주세요.
여: 알겠습니다. 그건 구운 감자랑 정말 잘 어울려요. 한 봉지 드릴까요?
남: 네. 얼마예요?
여: 보통 봉지당 9달러인데 단골손님이신 것 같으니 7달러에 드릴게요.
남: 좋아요. 감자 한 봉지 가져갈게요.
여: 알겠습니다. 그럼 고급 티본스테이크 네 개랑 감자 한 봉지입니다. 더 필요한 것 있으세요?
남: 없는 것 같아요. 여기 신용카드요.

어휘
butcher shop ***n.*** 정육점 **barbecue** ***n.*** 바비큐 **in-law** ***n.*** 인척 ***a.*** 인척 관계의(특히 시부모, 장인과 장모) **premium** ***a.*** 고급의, 아주 높은

정답 ③

문제풀이
남자는 장인, 장모님에게 대접할 20달러짜리 스테이크 4개와 본래 9달러인데 7달러로 깎아준 감자 한 봉지를 샀으므로 정답은 ③ '$87'이다.

총 어휘 수 135

10 언급 유무

소재 음악 캠프

듣기 대본 해석
[전화벨이 울린다.]
여: 여보세요?
남: 안녕 Stacy. 저 Dominic이에요. Russell 있나요? 제 아들이 오늘 그 애와 진짜 놀고 싶어해요.
여: 오, Russell은 여기에 없어요. 오늘 그는 음악 캠프에 있어요.
남: 음악 캠프요?
여: 네, 지역 오케스트라에서 여름마다 개최해요. 학생들은 전문적인 음악가들과 연습하게 돼요.
남: 멋지네요. 캠프는 어디서 해요?
여: 도서관 바로 건너편에 있는 강당에서요.
남: 그렇군요. 아직 자리가 남아 있나요?
여: 네, 제가 어제 막 Russell을 등록시켰는데, 아직 몇 자리 남았었어요. 학생들을 태워 주는 셔틀버스도 있어요.
남: 멋지네요. 나이 제한이 있나요?
여: 10세 이상의 아이들을 위한 거예요. 오케스트라 웹 사이트에서 모든 정보를 찾을 수 있어요.
남: 좋아요! 확인해 볼게요. 제 아들이 가입하는 것을 좋아할 거예요.

어휘
awesome ***a.*** 굉장한, 멋진 **auditorium** ***n.*** 강당, 객석 **available** ***a.*** 이용 가능한 **sign ~ up** ~을 등록시키다 **restriction** ***n.*** 제한

정답 ②

문제풀이
음악 캠프의 시기와 위치, 셔틀버스 운행, 나이 제한에 관한 언급은 있지만 캠프 기간에 대한 언급은 없으므로 정답은 ② '캠프 기간'이다.

총 어휘 수 135

11 내용 일치 · 불일치

소재 최첨단 쌍방향 책상

듣기 대본 해석
남: 2009년 이후로 영국 전역에서 8살에서 10살 사이의 학생들이 매우 신선한 실험에 참가했습니다. 최첨단 쌍방향 책상으로 연필과 종이, 그리고 계산기를 대체하는 것이 학생들의 수학 실력을 향상시킬 수 있는지 알아보는 것이었습니다! 영국의 Dunham University와 SinergyCom이 이 프로젝트를 고안했습니다. DeskTouch라고 불리는 이 최첨단 책상은 기술을 통해 학습을 향상시키도록 의도된 여러 연구 프로젝트 중에 하나입니다. 이 책상은 스마트폰이나 iPad같은 기기처럼 터치에 반응하는 소프트웨어에 최적화 되어있습니다. 모든 책상은 선생님이 수학문제를 학생들에게 만들어 보내고 이후에 그것들을 확인할 수 있는 중앙 책상과 통신합니다.

어휘
involve ***v.*** 참가시키다 **enhance** ***v.*** 향상시키다 **respond** ***v.*** 반응하다 **afterwards** ***ad.*** 이후에

정답 ②

문제풀이
이 실험은 쌍방향 책상이 학생들의 수학 실력을 향상시킬 수 있는지 보기 위한 것이라고 했으므로 내용과 일치하지 않는 것은 ② '쌍방향 책상은 학생들의 공감능력 향상을 보기 위한 실험이다.'이다.

총 어휘 수 107

12 도표

소재 게스트 하우스 선택

듣기 대본 해석
여: 여보, Billy 학교 한 달도 안 남은 것 알지?
남: 응. 여름 방학 무척 기대하고 있더라. 올해는 좀 특별한 걸 할 생각이야.
여: 어떤 것을 생각하고 있는데?
남: 글쎄, 내가 Smoky 산맥에 항상 가고 싶다고 말한 거 알지?
여: 응. 신혼여행으로 거기 갈 뻔 했잖아.
남: 맞아. 그래서 인터넷을 보는데 그 산에 있는 오두막 목록을 찾았어. 어떤지 말해줘.
여: 음, 하룻밤에 60달러 넘게 쓰는 건 아니라고 생각해.
남: 응. 난 산에 머무르고 싶어. 거기 있는 도시는 관광객이 많을 거 같아.
여: 맞아. 그럼 두 개 남았네.
남: 흠... 온수욕조 있는 것으로 하자. 편안할 것 같아.
여: 그래. 어서 예약해.

어휘
honeymoon ***n.*** 신혼여행 **chalet** ***n.*** 샬레, 오두막 **touristy** ***a.*** 관광객이 많이 몰리는

정답 ③

문제풀이
하루에 60달러 넘게 쓰고 싶지는 않다고 했고, 산에 머무르고 싶다고 했으므로 남는 선택은 ②번과 ③번이다. 두 개중 온수욕조가 있는 것으로 하자고 했으므로 정답은 ③번이다.

총 어휘 수 142

13 긴 대화의 응답

소재 두꺼운 침낭 빌려주기

듣기 대본 해석
여: Eddie, 바빠 보이네. 다른 시간에 다시 올까?
남: 방금 마무리 중이었어. 네팔 여행을 위해 짐 싸는 것을 거의 끝냈어.
여: 좋네. 내가 추천한 것은 다 샀니?
남: 그래. 추천해줘서 고마워. 나는 새로운 부츠와 텐트를 샀어.
여: 멋지구나. 이런! 이게 너의 침낭이야? 너무 얇은 것 같은데. 밖에서 추위에 떨 거야.
남: 네 말이 맞지만 침낭이 너무 비싸. 새로운 것을 살 여유가 되지 않아.
여: 음... 내가 도움을 줄 수도 있겠다.
남: 정말? 내가 빌릴 침낭이라도 있니?
여: 음, 아버지께서 전혀 안 쓰시는 것이 있는데. 아버지께서 빌려주실지 내가 알아볼게.
남: ④ 그러면 좋겠다. 난 정말 돈을 아껴야 하거든.

어휘
sleeping bag 침낭 **freeze** ***v.*** 추워 죽을 지경이다, 얼다 **afford** ***v.*** (~을 사거나 할 금전적 · 시간적) 여유가 되다

정답 ④

문제풀이
침낭이 너무 비싸서 좀 더 두꺼운 침낭을 사지 못한 남자에게 여자는 아버지의 안 쓰는 침낭을 빌려줄 수 있도록 아버지께 여쭤본다고 하였으므로 이에 대한 남자의 응답으로 가장 적절한 것은 ④ '그러면 좋겠다. 난 정말 돈을 아껴야 하거든.'이다.

오답 보기 해석
① 괜찮아. 내가 새 침낭을 샀어.
② 추천해줘서 정말로 고마워.
③ 내가 그의 등산 부츠를 빌릴 수 있을까?
⑤ 굉장해. 그가 진짜로 즐거웠던 것 같더라.

총 어휘 수 128

14 긴 대화의 응답

소재 여자가 레드 와인을 반기지 않는 이유

듣기 대본 해석
여: 와줘서 고마워. 새로 이사한 아파트야.
남: 늦어서 미안해. 와인 사오느라.
여: 와인? 레드 와인은 아니지?
남: 맞는데. 레드 와인 싫어해?
여: 좋아해. 근데 거실에 최근에 이 하얀색 카펫 깔았단 말이야. 네가 여기에 흘리는 건 싫어.
남: 걱정 마. 각별히 조심할게.
여: 너 못 믿겠어. 우리 같이 스파게티 먹고 네 흰색 셔츠에 다 묻혔던 거 기억나?
남: 그건 딱 한 번 실수한 거였어. 너무 불합리해.
여: 네가 안 마시면 좀 더 마음이 편할 것 같아. 이 아파트 정말 깨끗하게 유지하고 싶어.
남: 정 그렇다면, 부엌으로 가지고 갈게.
여: ④ 알겠어. 거실에서만 마시지 마.

어휘
install ***v.*** 설치하다 **spill** ***v.*** 흘리다, 엎지르다 **unreasonable** ***a.*** 불합리한 **spotless** ***a.*** 티끌 하나 없는

정답 ④

문제풀이
여자는 남자가 사온 레드 와인이 자신이 최근 거실에 깐 하얀색 카펫을 더럽힐까 걱정하고 있다. 그러자 남자는 정 그렇다면 부엌으로 가지고 가겠다고 했는데, 이에 대해 가장 적절한 여자의 응답은 ④ '알겠어. 거실에서만 마시지 마.'이다.

오답 보기 해석
① 맞아, 저녁에 레드 와인 마시는 거 좋아해.
② 오늘은 네가 나한테 요리해 줄 차례인 것 같은데.
③ 미안한데 지금 마실 시간이 없어.
⑤ 걱정하지 마. 카펫에 와인 안 흘릴게.

총 어휘 수 134

15 상황에 적절한 말

소재 산으로 캠핑 가는 아들에게 재킷 챙겨주기

듣기 대본 해석
여: Mike는 고등학생인데 이번 주말에 그는 친구들과 함께 시간을 보낼 예정입니다. 그들은 산으로 캠핑을 가기로 결정했습니다. 하지만 Mike의 엄마인 Linda는 아들이 걱정됩니다. 그녀는 늦여름까지 캠핑을 해왔기 때문에 산이 꽤 추울 거라고 생각합니다. 그녀는 Mike에게 겨울 재킷을 가져가도록 충고하지만 그는 거절합니다. 그는 여름에 겨울 재킷을 입는 것이 우스꽝스럽다고 생각하고 엄마의 충고를 듣고 싶어 하지 않습니다. Linda는 그가 겨울 재킷이 필요한지 확실하지는 않지만 그녀는 만약을 위해 Mike가 겨울 재킷을 가져가도록 설득하려고 합니다. 이런 상황에서 Linda가 Mike에게 뭐라고 말할 것 같은가요?
Linda: ① 네가 생각하는 것보다 거기 위에는 더 추울지도 모른단다.

어휘
urge ***v.*** 충고하다 **ridiculous** ***a.*** 우스꽝스러운 **just in case** 만약을 위해서

정답 ①

문제풀이
산으로 캠핑을 가는 아들에게 엄마는 겨울 재킷을 가져가라고 하고, 아들은 여름에 겨울 재킷을 입는 것이 우스꽝스럽다고 생각하는 상황이다. 그럼에도 불구하고 만약의 경우를 대비해 재킷을 가져가라고 아들을 설득하고자 하는 상황에서 어머니인 Linda가 Mike에게 할 말은 ① '네가 생각하는 것보다 거기 위에는 더 추울지도 모른단다.'가 가장 적절하다.

오답 보기 해석
② 안전하게 지내고 허락된 곳에서만 캠핑을 하렴.
③ 떠나기 전 재킷을 빨고 가렴. 정말 더럽단다.
④ 네 옷들을 빨래하는 것을 끝내기 전까진 집을 떠날 수 없어.
⑤ 등산은 재미있지만 위험할 수 있어. 조심하렴.

총 어휘 수 124

16 담화 목적 / 17 세부 내용 파악

소재 예술 프로젝트에 대한 기금 마련

듣기 대본 해석

남: 크라우드 펀딩은 전 세계의 사람들이 그들의 예술적인 노력을 위한 자금을 모으는 멋진 방식이 되었습니다. 많은 창의적인 사람들이 실행시키고 싶은 아이디어들을 가지고 있지만 창작에 필요한 돈이 없습니다. 그것이 우리의 프로그램인 Donation Station이 관여하는 부분입니다. Donation Station은 예술가들과 창의적인 사람들을 그 프로젝트를 믿는 투자자들과 연결시켜 드립니다. 시작을 하기 위해서, Donation Station 웹사이트에서 프로필을 작성해 주시고, 당신의 프로젝트를 기술하시기만 하면 됩니다. 만약에 투자자가 그것을 좋아한다면, 그들은 당신에게 그 아이디어들이 생명력을 얻는 데 필요한 돈을 보내 줄 수 있습니다. 영화를 위한 좋은 아이디어가 있는데 그것을 제작할 돈이 부족합니까? Donation Station이 도움을 줄 수 있습니다. 아마도 당신은 새로운 패션 디자인이나 유용한 발명품을 가지고 있을 수도 있고, 아마도 책을 출판하는 데 도움이 필요할지도 모릅니다. Donation Station은 창의성이 우리 사회에서 필수적이고 전 세계가 발전하도록 도와준다는 것을 압니다. 그러한 이유로 우리는 당신의 꿈을 현실화하는 데에 도움을 주려는 것입니다. 당신의 아이디어가 순조롭게 시작되도록 지금 당장 저희 웹사이트에 가입하세요.

어휘

accumulate *v.* ~을 축적하다, 모으다 **endeavor** *n.* 노력
bring ~ to life ~에 활기(생기)를 불어넣다 **get ~ off the ground** ~을 순조롭게 출발(시작)하다

정답 16 ⑤ 17 ④

문제풀이

16 남자는 예술적 아이디어들이 현실화될 수 있도록 자금을 지원하는 웹사이트 Donation Station을 소개하고, 신청 방법 및 예술 분야의 예들을 말하고 있으므로 정답은 ⑤ '창작자들이 프로젝트에 관한 자금지원을 받도록 도움을 주기 위하여'이다.

17 남자는 영화, 새로운 패션 디자인, 유용한 발명품, 출판에 대해서는 언급하였으나 만화는 언급하지 않았으므로 정답은 ④ '만화'이다.

오답 보기 해석

16

① 비슷한 생각을 가진 사람들을 모으기 위하여
② 예술가들의 도움에 감사하기 위하여
③ 예술작품 사는 법을 조언하기 위하여
④ 예술산업의 혁신을 장려하기 위하여

총 어휘 수 181

DICTATION ANSWERS

01 go on a picnic / plans to visit my relatives

02 too hard to complete / helped you with it

03 have a negative impact on / give active students an advantage / go beyond academic studies / win games

04 so messy / clean it up / let me eat junk food / care about your health

05 I'm afraid I'll get sick / haven't been your usual self / he's standoffish / sort these documents

06 a flyer for / in the upper left corner / at the bottom / try to make it

07 going over my plans for / have a bunch of close friends / Would you mind running / right away

08 Have you heard of it / need to go straight home / coming in from college / help my mother clean the house

09 having a barbecue / They'll run you / They go great with / Anything else for you

10 That sounds awesome / age restrictions

11 improve their math skills / intended to enhance / communicate with a mother desk

12 getting excited / almost went there for our honeymoon / That sounds relaxing

13 done packing for my trip / You'll freeze out there / couldn't afford to buy / let you borrow it

14 pick up some wine / had this white carpet installed / being unreasonable / take it to the kitchen

15 decided to go camping / urges Mike to take a winter jacket / take his mom's advice / just in case

16-17 accumulate money / create a profile / bring it to life / get your ideas off the ground

04 수능영어듣기 실전모의고사

본문 p.26

01 ②	02 ②	03 ③	04 ③	05 ③	06 ③
07 ②	08 ⑤	09 ⑤	10 ⑤	11 ④	12 ①
13 ②	14 ①	15 ①	16 ①	17 ⑤	

01 짧은 대화의 응답

소재 음악적 능력

듣기 대본 해석

여: Daniel, 정말 훌륭한 기타리스트가 되어가고 있네요.
남: 그렇게 말해줘서 너무 감사해요. 악기를 연주해 본 적 있어요?
여: 나는 음악을 좋아하지만 음악적 능력은 전혀 없어요.
남: ② 괜찮아요. 연습만 하면 돼요.

어휘

appreciate ***v.*** 고마워하다 **instrument** ***n.*** 악기(= musical instrument), 기구, 도구 〈문제〉 **tune** ***v.*** (악기를) 조율하다

정답 ②

문제풀이

음악적 능력이 없다는 여자의 말에 대한 남자의 응답으로는 연습하면 된다고 대답하는 것이 적절하므로 정답은 ② '괜찮아요. 연습만 하면 돼요.'이다.

오답 보기 해석

① 당신의 레슨이 저한테 정말 도움 됐어요.
③ 내가 정오쯤에 당신 집에 들를게요.
④ 나는 당신과 내 음악 모음을 공유할 수 있어서 기뻐요.
⑤ 잠깐만요! 당신은 연주하기 전에 기타를 조율해야겠어요.

총 어휘 수 37

02 짧은 대화의 응답

소재 저녁식사 정하기

듣기 대본 해석

남: 배고파져요. 오늘 무엇을 먹고 싶어요?
여: 모르겠어요. 또 외식하고 싶어요?
남: 우리는 외식으로 너무 많은 비용을 썼어요. 오늘 저녁은 집에서 먹는 게 어때요?
여: ② 좋아요. 내가 당신을 위해 요리를 해주면 어떨까요?

어휘

〈문제〉 **bill** ***n.*** 계산서, 청구서 **care for** ~을 돌보다, 좋아하다

정답 ②

문제풀이

너무 자주 외식을 해서 오늘밤은 집에서 저녁 먹고 싶다는 남자의 말에 대한 여자의 응답으로 가장 적절한 것은 ② '좋아요. 내가 당신을 위해 요리를 해주면 어떨까요?'이다.

오답 보기 해석

① 네. 제 생각에는 팁이 계산서에 포함되지 않은 것 같아요.
③ 그 음식점의 파스타를 그다지 좋아하지 않았어요.
④ 물론이죠. 그러면 식료품점에 갈 필요가 없군요.
⑤ 맞아요. 길을 따라 가면 나오는 멕시코 음식점에 대해 들었어요.

총 어휘 수 43

03 담화 목적

소재 온라인상으로 팬들의 의견 받기

듣기 대본 해석

여: 안녕하세요 팬 여러분. 저는 팬 여러분들 중 몇 분께서 새로운 경기장과 시설에 관한 제안이 있다는 것을 들었습니다. 저희는 몇 개월 전에 경기장에 둔 상자 안에 팬 여러분들께서 넣어주신 제안들을 자세히 살펴보았습니다. 그러나, 우리는 이러한 과정을 여러분들께서 제안을 온라인 상에서 제출할 수 있도록 함으로써 더 쉽게 하기로 결정했습니다. 이는 팬 여러분들께서 언제, 어디서든지 할 수 있도록 할 것입니다. 이것은 꽤 간단합니다. 그냥 공식 웹사이트에 가셔서, "제안" 링크를 클릭하시고, 제공되는 상자 틀 안에 여러분의 제안을 입력하시고 "제출"을 클릭하세요. 이러한 새로운 시스템은 또한 여러분의 제안에 적시에 더 쉽게 응답하도록 해줍니다. 시간 내주셔서 감사합니다.

어휘

facility ***n.*** 시설 **sort through** ~을 자세히 살피다 **submit** ***n.*** (서류, 제안서 등을) 제출하다 **in a timely manner** 적시에, 시기 적절하게

정답 ③

문제풀이

이제까지는 팬들이 의견을 상자에 넣는 방식이었지만 이 과정을 더 쉽게 하기 위해서 온라인 상에서 하게 되었음을 알려주고 있다. 따라서 여자가 하는 말의 목적은 ③ '팬들의 의견 제안 방식의 변경을 공지하려고'이다.

총 어휘 수 110

04 대화 주제

소재 한국 돌잔치와 관련된 특별한 전통

듣기 대본 해석

여: Jimmy, 당신을 위한 파티 초대장이에요.
남: 와, 당신 아들의 첫 번째 생일이네요. 정말 기쁜 일이네요!
여: 네. 파티에 와 줄 수 있으세요?
남: 부산에서요? 물론이죠! 아기의 첫 번째 생일과 관련해 특별한 전통이 있다고 들었어요.
여: 네, 맞아요. 아기가 첫 번째 생일 파티에서 여러 가지 상징적인 물건들 중에 하나의 품목을 고르죠.
남: 그래서 아기가 선택하는 물건이 자신의 미래를 예측하나요?
여: 맞아요. 예를 들어, 제 아들이 연필을 고르면, 우리는 그것이 그가 학문 관련 직업으로 성공할 것이라고 믿어요.
남: 그렇군요. 아기가 무엇을 또 고를 수 있나요?
여: 음, 만약 아기가 돈을 선택하면 부자가 될 것이고, 실타래를 고르면 오래 살 것을 의미해요.
남: 일리 있네요. 당신 아기의 생일파티가 정말 기대되네요!

어휘

relating to ~과 관련된 **symbolic** ***a.*** 상징적인
academic career 학문 관련 직업 경력 **wealthy** ***a.*** 부유한
a spool of thread 실타래

정답 ③

문제풀이

아기의 돌잔치에서 아기가 물건을 선택하고 어떤 물건을 선택하는가에 따라 의미가 달라지는 한국의 독특한 전통을 말하고 있으므로 정답은 ③ '한국 돌잔치의 특별한 전통'이다.

총 어휘 수 133

05 대화자의 관계 파악

소재 교수님한테 학생 추천 받기

듣기 대본 해석

[전화벨이 울린다.]

여: 안녕하세요?

남: Aria, 안녕하세요. 저 Walter입니다.

여: 안녕하세요, Walter. 잘 지내시나요?

남: 네, 감사합니다. 지난번에 지금 저희와 일하고 있는 두 명의 인턴을 추천해 주셔서 정말 감사드린다는 말씀을 드리고 싶었어요. 우리는 그들이 열심히 일하고 헌신하는 것에 대해 정말로 높게 평가합니다.

여: 잘 됐군요! 제 학생들을 고용한 게 매우 도움이 되고 있다는 소식을 들으니 기뻐요.

남: 그들은 정말 잘 적응하고 있어요. 혹시 다른 학생들을 또 추천해주실 수 있는지 여쭤보려고 전화드렸습니다.

여: 물론이죠. 어떤 부서에서 필요하신가요?

남: 품질관리 일에 두 명이 필요합니다.

여: 알겠어요. 그 자리에 딱 맞는 학생들을 알고 있어요. 다음 주에 수업이 끝나고 그들에게 공지할게요.

남: 좋습니다. 그들에게 제 연락처를 주시고 제 번호로 바로 연락해 주길 바란다고 전해주십시오.

여: 그럴게요, Walter.

남: 감사합니다.

어휘

recommend ***v.*** 추천하다 **value** ***v.*** 평가하다, 존중하다, 소중히 하다 **dedication** ***n.*** 헌신, 전념

정답 ③

문제풀이

남자가 지난 번에 추천해준 두 명 학생이 일을 잘하고 있다면서 다른 학생들을 더 추천해줄 것을 부탁했고, 여자는 자신의 학생들이 잘하고 있다고 들으니 기쁘다며 다음 주 수업 후에 공지하겠다고 했으므로 둘 사이의 관계는 ③ '교수 – 회사 직원'으로 유추할 수 있다.

총 어휘 수 127

06 그림의 세부 내용 파악

소재 렌트할 자동차 선택

듣기 대본 해석

여: Isaac's Rent-a-Car에 오신 걸 환영합니다. 오늘 무엇을 도와드릴까요?

남: 안녕하세요. 오늘 오후에 차량을 가지고 가는 것을 예약했는데요, 제 이름은 Robert Clay입니다.

여: 잠시만요. 네, 바로 여기에 예약이 있네요, Clay씨. 저희 매장을 둘러보시고 어떤 차가 마음에 드시는지 말씀해 주세요.

남: 문이 네 개인 세단은 원하지 않아요. 혼자서 여행할 거예요.

여: 알겠습니다. 그럼 컨버터블은 어떠세요? 스포티해서 혼자 여행하는 분들에게 재미있습니다.

남: 오늘 날씨가 스모그가 많아요. 오염물질을 많이 들이마시고 싶지 않아요.

여: 네. 그럼 이 두 개로 좁혀지네요.

남: 음. 회색은 원치 않아요. 회색은 약간 우울한 색상이에요.

여: 음, 그럼 이게 가장 잘 맞을 것 같네요.

남: 좋네요. 그걸로 할게요. 여기 신용카드 있습니다.

어휘

smoggy ***a.*** 스모그가 많은 **inhale** ***v.*** 숨을 들이마시다 **pollution** ***n.*** 오염, 공해

정답 ③

문제풀이

문이 네 개인 세단과 지붕을 열 수 있는 컨버터블은 원치 않는다고 했으므로 ③, ⑤번이 남게 되고, 대화의 마지막 부분에서 회색은 원하지 않는다고 했으므로 정답은 ③번이다.

총 어휘 수 145

07 할 일

소재 외국어로 된 호텔 예약 사이트 내용 해석 부탁하기

듣기 대본 해석

여: 야, 뭐해?

남: 이번 휴가 때 묵을 호텔을 인터넷에서 찾아보고 있어.

여: 재미있겠다. 어디로 가는데?

남: 도쿄. 가 본 적 있어?

여: 도쿄? 가 본 적 있지. Tokyo Palace 호텔에서 묵었어. 정말 좋았어.

남: 거기 방들 찾아봤는데 나한테는 너무 비싸더라.

여: 그렇구나. 그럼 호텔 예약하려면 이 사이트를 들어가 봐. tokyodeals.com이야.

남: 좋아. 지금 확인해 봐야지. *[잠시 후]* 아, 여기 있긴 한데 나한테는 좀 쓸모가 없는 것 같아.

여: 왜?

남: 사이트가 일본어로 돼 있어. 나는 일본어 하나도 못 읽거든. 너는?

여: 물론이지. 대학에서 일본어를 공부했어. 내가 도와줄까?

남: 그럼 좋지! 도와줘서 고마워.

어휘

head ***v.*** ~로 가다, 향하다 **useless** ***a.*** 쓸모 없는

정답 ②

문제풀이

남자는 여자가 알려준 호텔 예약 사이트에 들어갔으나 일본어로 되어 있어 읽지 못하자 여자에게 일본어를 읽을 수 있는지 물었고 여자는 자신이 도와주겠다고 했다. 따라서 여자가 남자를 위해 할 일은 ② '웹 사이트 읽어주기'이다.

총 어휘 수 125

08 이유

소재 사고로 인한 교통 체증

듣기 대본 해석

[전화벨이 울린다.]

여: 여보세요?

남: 엄마, 저 Tom이에요.

여: 어디 갔었니, Tom? 한 시간 전에 집에 오기로 되어 있었잖아. 7시야.

남: 아까 제 휴대폰 배터리가 나갔어요. 심지어 엄마한테 전화하려고 지금 다른 사람의 휴대폰을 빌려야 했어요.

여: 그래, 네가 지금 집이 아니고 나한테 전화하고 있으니, 이것은 네가 금방 집에 오지 않는다는 의미구나. 무슨 일이니?

남: 공원 앞에서 큰 사고가 있었던 거 못 들으셨어요?

여: 아니. 넌 괜찮아?

남: 네, 전 괜찮아요. 사고가 났을 때 저는 공원의 반대편에 있었어요.

여: 그럼 너는 왜 아직 집에 오지 않은 거니?

남: 경찰과 소방서에서 공원 주변 길을 막았어요. 교통상황이 정말 안 좋고, 지하철은 남은 시간 동안 운행하지 않을 거예요.

여: 끔찍한 소식이구나. 저녁 먹었니?

남: 조금 전에 과일과 샐러드를 약간 먹었어요. 전 괜찮아요.

여: 그래, 그럼 조심하고 이따 보자.

남: 네, 엄마. 이따 봬요.

어휘

be supposed to V ~하기로 되어 있다 **operate** *v.* 운행하다 **awful** *a.* 끔찍한

정답 ⑤

문제풀이

남자는 공원 앞에서 난 큰 사고 때문에 경찰과 소방서에서 길을 막았고, 지하철도 운행하지 않았기 때문에 늦는다고 했으므로 정답은 ⑤ '길이 통제되고 주변 교통수단을 이용할 수 없어서'이다.

총 어휘 수 160

09 숫자

소재 예술 센터 표 구매하기

듣기 대본 해석

남: 안녕하세요. Franklin 대학교 예술 센터에 오신 것을 환영합니다. 무엇을 도와드릴까요?
여: 안녕하세요. 성인 두 명이랑 어린이 두 명 표 좀 살게요.
남: 알겠습니다. *[키보드 치는 소리]* 44달러입니다.
여: 이 표를 사면 Harmony Blues 공연도 관람할 수 있나요?
남: 죄송하지만 관람할 수 없어요. 공연 표는 1인당 추가로 4달러가 들어요.
여: 그렇군요. 그럼 공연을 포함하면 표 값은 얼마인가요?
남: 성인은 18달러이고 어린이는 12달러입니다.
여: 네. 그럼 그 표로 성인 두 명이랑 어린이 두 명 표 주세요. 아! 까먹을 뻔 했는데 10퍼센트 할인 쿠폰이 있어요. 여기요.
남: *[잠시 후]* 죄송하지만 이 할인은 공연이 포함된 표에는 적용되지가 않아요.
여: 오. 그럼, 알겠습니다. 여기 카드요.
남: 감사합니다.

어휘

admission *n.* 입장 **performance** *n.* 공연 **discount** *n.* 할인

정답 ⑤

문제풀이

공연을 포함한 표는 성인 두 장에 36달러, 어린이 두 장에 24달러이므로 정답은 ⑤ '$60'이다.

총 어휘 수 126

10 언급 유무

소재 다큐멘터리 소개하기

듣기 대본 해석

여: Pablo, An Unfortunate Fact라는 다큐멘터리 본 적 있니?
남: 아니. 뭐에 대한 건데?
여: 기후 변화에 관한 거야. 다음 세대에게 닥칠 위험들을 다뤄.
남: 흠... 들어본 적 있는 것 같아. 난 과학 다큐멘터리 아주 좋아해. 어땠어?
여: 정말 많은 걸 깨닫게 해주는 프로그램이었어. 우리 지구의 미래에 대해서 진지하게 생각을 하게 되더라.
남: 긴 다큐멘터리였어?
여: 거의 두 시간 정도 했어. 좀 지루할 때가 있지만 과학 다큐멘터리 좋아하면 재미있게 볼 수 있을 거야.
남: 정말 보고 싶은데 이번 주말에 시간이 없을 것 같아. 다음 주말에 아직도 상영 중일까?
여: 잘 모르겠어. 사이트에 들어가서 확인해 봐.
남: 아, 좋은 생각이야. 보고 나서 너랑 더 얘기해 보고 싶어.

어휘

climate *n.* 기후 **generation** *n.* 세대 **eye-opener** *n.* 눈을 뜨게 해주는(새로운 것을 깨닫게 해주는) 일 또는 경험

정답 ⑤

문제풀이

여자는 자신이 본 과학 다큐멘터리를 대화 소재로 꺼내면서 그것의 제목, 주제, 영화 길이, 관람 소감에 대해 이야기하고 있지만, 어디에서 상영 중인지는 언급하지 않았으므로 정답은 ⑤ '상영관 위치'이다.

총 어휘 수 140

11 내용 일치 · 불일치

소재 컴퓨터 게임 대회

듣기 대본 해석

남: 안녕하세요, 게이머 여러분! 저는 Nimbus이고요, 다음 주말에 PC Playground에서 2개의 대회를 개최할 겁니다. 이 대회들은 실시간 전략 게임 게이머들을 위한 것입니다. 이 대회들에서 두 가지 다른 게임을 할 건데요, Suncraft와 League of Heroes를 할 것입니다. Suncraft 대회에서는 Suncraft 프로게이머들과 함께 게임을 하게 될 것입니다. League of Heroes 대회에서는 참가자들이 무작위로 팀을 구성하게 될 것이고 컴퓨터 인공지능을 상대로 게임을 하는 스피드전이 이뤄질 것입니다. 이 대회들에서는 아마추어만 받아들입니다. 프로게이머는 참가가 불가능합니다. 신청을 하기 위해서는 저희 웹 사이트 www.PCPlayg.co를 방문해서 1월 7일 전에 신청서를 제출해 주시기 바랍니다. 모두에게 행운이 있기를 바라며 굉장한 이벤트를 기대해 주십시오.

어휘

host *v.* 주최하다 **strategy** *n.* 전략 **side-by-side** *ad.* 나란히 **random** *a.* 무작위의 **compete** *v.* 경쟁하다 **accept** *v.* 받아들이다, 수락하다 **amateur** *n.* 아마추어 **outstanding** *a.* 뛰어난

정답 ④

문제풀이

남자는 League of Heroes 대회에서는 프로게이머는 참가가 불가능하고 아마추어만 가능하다고 하였으므로 일치하지 않는 내용은 ④ '이 대회에 아마추어는 참가가 불가능하다.'이다.

총 어휘 수 118

12 도표

소재 기부 내용 선택

듣기 대본 해석

여: 여보, 올해 기부를 할 자선 단체를 찾은 것 같아.
남: 잘 됐네! 또 어린이 자선 단체야?
여: 이번엔 아냐. 모든 연령대의 사람들을 도와줘. Make a Difference라는 자선 단체인데 해외의 어려움에 처한 사람들이나 여기 우리 나라 사람들을 도와줄지를 고를 수 있어.
남: 근데 작년에 지역 자선 단체에 기부를 하지 않았어? 올해는 해외에 있는 사람들을 도와 주는 게 좋을 것 같아.
여: 나도 그렇게 생각해. 요즘 뉴스를 많이 보는데 그 끔찍한 쓰나미 피해자들을 돕는 데 기부하는 게 좋을 것 같아.
남: 너무 끔찍해 보였어, 그렇지? 우리가 도울 수 있는 건 해야지.
여: 맞아. 그럼 얼마 정도 기부해야 한다고 생각해?
남: 300달러 이상을 기부할 수는 없을 것 같아.
여: 그럼 남은 게 이거 밖에 없네.
남: 좋아! 우리의 돈으로 남을 도울 수 있다는 건 정말 기분 좋은 일이야.

어휘
charity *n.* 자선 단체　**donate** *v.* 기부하다　**overseas** *a. ad.* 해외의　**tsunami** *n.* 쓰나미　**afford** *v.* 여유(형편)가 되다　〈문제〉 **disaster** *n.* 재해　**relief** *n.* 경감, 완화

정답 ①

문제풀이
남자와 여자가 기부할 프로그램을 고르고 있다. 해외에 있는 사람들을 돕자고 했으므로 ①~③중에 골라야 하고 쓰나미 피해자를 돕고 싶다고 했으므로 ①, ③번이 남게 되는데 300달러 이상은 기부를 못한다고 했으므로 정답은 ①번이다.

총 어휘 수 149

13 긴 대화의 응답

소재 여행에서 있었던 불행한 일들

듣기 대본 해석
남: Samantha, 뉴욕은 잘 갔다 왔어?
여: 정말 최악이었어.
남: 정말? 그거 안됐네. 뭐가 문제였는데?
여: 거의 모든 게 다 문제였어. 뉴욕에 도착할 때 항공사가 내 짐을 분실했다고 했어. 찾는 데 3일이나 걸렸어.
남: 최악이다. 근데 네가 어떤 기분인지 알아. 내가 로마에 갔을 때도 같은 일이 일어났거든.
여: 오, 그건 시작에 불과해. 내가 카페에서 커피를 마시고 있을 때 누가 내 서류 가방을 훔쳐 갔어.
남: 진짜? 정말 운이 없다.
여: 운이 없다고? 정말 화가 났어! 경찰도 어떻게 도와줄 수 없더라고. 그런데 내 불운은 거기가 끝이 아니야.
남: 진심이야?
여: 응. 시애틀로 돌아가는 비행기가 2시간 지연됐어. 그리고 내가 다시 짐을 찾으러 갔을 때 또 분실했다는 거야.
남: ② 안 좋은 일(불운)이 생겼다니 정말 안됐다.

어휘
baggage *n.* (여행용) 짐　**infuriate** *v.* 격분시키다, 격노하게 하다　**delay** *v.* 미루다, 연기하다　**claim** *v.* (자기 권리나 재산이라고 여겨) 요구하다

정답 ②

문제풀이
여자는 뉴욕 여행에서 짐을 잃어버리고, 도둑을 맞는 등 여러 안 좋은 일에 대해 남자에게 이야기 했으므로 이에 대한 남자의 응답으로 가장 적절한 것은 ② '안 좋은 일(불운)이 생겼다니 정말 안됐다.'이다.

오답 보기 해석
① 뉴욕은 이때쯤 굉장히 아름다워.
③ 경찰들이 그걸 찾을 수 있어서 다행이야.
④ 한 시간 일찍 공항에 도착하는 게 좋아.
⑤ 난 다음에 여행갈 때 더 조심해야겠어.

총 어휘 수 149

14 긴 대화의 응답

소재 밀렵 당하는 코끼리를 돕는 방법

듣기 대본 해석
남: 안녕 Brittney. 너 보고 있는 것이 뭐니?
여: 아, 나는 온라인에서 코끼리를 지켜줄 방법을 검색하고 있어.
남: 너 코끼리를 돕는 것을 원하는구나, 그렇지?
여: 맞아. 코끼리들은 친절한 마음씨를 가진 감정적인 생명체야. 그들은 심지어 죽은 코끼리를 애도하기도 해.
남: 그거 흥미롭네. 나는 그것을 몰랐었어.
여: 그건 사실이야. 그런데 상아 때문에 코끼리를 사냥하는 밀렵꾼이 많잖아.
남: 아직도? 나는 사람들이 수십 년 전에 상아를 사용하는 것을 그만두었다고 생각했었어. 매년 얼마나 많은 코끼리들이 단지 그들의 상아 때문에 죽었을까?
여: 매년 40,000마리라고 몇몇의 전문가들이 그러더라.
남: 끔찍하네. 사람들은 코끼리의 상아가 무엇에 필요하지?
여: 상아는 수집용 입상이나, 당구공, 그리고 전통 약을 만드는 데 사용될 수 있어.
남: 너무 슬프구나. 도움을 위해서 우리가 무엇을 할 수 있을까?
여: ① 음, 이 웹사이트에 돈을 기부하려고 생각하고 있어.

어휘
save *v.* 안전하게 하다, 지키다　**being** *n.* 존재, 생명체　**mourn** *v.* 애도하다, 슬퍼하다　**poacher** *n.* 밀렵꾼　**ivory** *n.* 상아　**tusk** *n.* 엄니(상아)　**collectible** *a.* 수집할 수 있는, 모을 수 있는　**figurine** *n.* 작은 입상　**billiard ball** 당구공　**traditional** *a.* 전통의　**medicine** *n.* 약, 의학

정답 ①

문제풀이
밀렵 당하는 불쌍한 코끼리들을 위해 할 수 있는 일이 없는지 묻는 남자에게 여자가 해줄 응답은 ① '음, 이 웹사이트에 돈을 기부하려고 생각하고 있어.'가 적절하다.

오답 보기 해석
② 맞아. 많은 나라에서 코끼리를 죽이는 것은 불법이야.
③ 동물원에 있는 코끼리를 확인해 보는 것이 어때?
④ 문제 없어. 너는 이 다큐멘터리를 빌릴 수 있어.
⑤ 사람들은 상아를 얻기 위해 코끼리를 사냥해서는 안돼.

총 어휘 수 129

15 상황에 적절한 말

소재 아들의 운동과 다이어트에 대한 집착

듣기 대본 해석
남: Jane의 중학생인 아들 Tim은 운동과 몸매를 좋게 만드는 것에 매우 관심이 많습니다. Jane은 건강을 의식하는 것이 좋다는 것은 알지만, Tim이 너무 많이 한다고 생각합니다. 그녀는 그가 하루에 몇 시간씩 헬스장에 가고 살을 빼려고 식사를 거른다는 것을 알게 됩니다. 이는 그가 너무 말라 보여서 그녀가 걱정하게 합니다. 그는 건강하지 않아 보입니다. 하지만 Tim은 살을 더 뺄 필요가 있다고 생각합니다. Jane은 그가 점점 집착하게 되어서, 그것이 심각한 건강 문제를 일으킬까 봐 걱정합니다. 그녀는 그가 운동하는 것과 다이어트를 하는 것에 대해 생각하는 방식을 바꾸게끔 하고 싶습니다. 이 상황에서 Jane이 Tim에게 이 할 가장 적절한 말은 무엇일까요?
Jane: Tim, ① 너의 운동과 다이어트 습관은 건강에 좋지 않아.

어휘
be concerned about ~에 관심을 갖다, ~을 염려하다
stay in shape 몸매를 좋게 유지하다　**lose weight** 살을 빼다, 체중을 감량하다　**concern** *v.* ~을 걱정하게 만들다　**skinny** *a.* 마른　**obsessed** *a.* 사로잡힌, 집착하는　**lead to** ~에 이르다

정답 ①

문제풀이
Jane은 아들의 운동과 다이어트 습관이 큰 문제를 일으킬 수 있다고 걱정하고 있으므로 정답은 ① '너의 운동과 다이어트 습관은 건강에 좋지 않아.'가 가장 적절하다.

오답 보기 해석
② 너의 다이어트와 운동 요법은 효과가 좋구나.
③ 너는 여전히 건강이 안 좋아 보여(몸매가 엉망이야).
④ 너는 더 운동할 필요가 있어.
⑤ 너는 공부를 더 열심히 해야 해.

총 어휘 수 132

16 담화 목적 / 17 세부 내용 파악

소재 산악 자전거타기 시 주의점

듣기 대본 해석

남: 안녕하세요 여러분. 오늘 우리는 산악 자전거타기에 대해서 얘기해 보겠습니다. 아시다시피, 산악 자전거타기는 아주 좋은 운동 방법입니다. 그것은 또한 자연과 교감할 수 있는 훌륭한 방법입니다. 하지만 그것이 재미있고 건강에 도움이 될 수 있는 반면 위험하기도 합니다. 여러분의 다음 여행 전에 이런 것들을 꼭 명심하세요. 우선, 적절한 보호장비를 착용하세요. 항상 헬멧을 착용하세요. 산악 자전거를 탈 때 머리를 보호하는 것은 매우 중요합니다. 고려해야 할 또 다른 중요한 것은 물입니다. 산악 자전거타기는 신체적으로 매우 힘들기 때문에 충분한 물을 가져가는 것은 대단히 중요합니다. 산에 가기 전에 날씨도 확인해 봐야 합니다. 빗속에서 오도 가도 못하게 되기를 원치는 않을 것입니다. 그리고 마지막으로 지도와 나침반을 가져가세요. 그렇게 하면 만약 길을 잃었을 때 돌아 내려가는 길을 찾을 수 있습니다. 이러한 팁들을 다음 번에 산악 자전거를 탈 때 꼭 명심하세요.

어휘

take ~ into consideration ~을 고려하다 **proper** ***a.*** 적절한 **protective** ***a.*** 보호용의 **gear** ***n.*** 복장, 장비 **crucial** ***a.*** 중대한 **exhausting** ***a.*** 매우 힘든 **critical** ***a.*** 대단히 중요한, 비판적인 **compass** ***n.*** 나침반 〈문제〉 **persuade** ***v.*** 설득하다 **take up** 계속하다 **potential** ***a.*** 잠재적인

정답 16 ① 17 ⑤

문제풀이

16 남자는 산악 자전거를 탈 때 고려해야 할 몇 가지를 말해주고 있으므로 남자가 하는 말의 목적은 ① '산악 자전거에 관한 충고를 제공하기 위해'이다.

17 남자는 헬멧, 물, 지도와 나침반을 챙기라고 했고 날씨도 확인하라고 했지만 여벌 옷에 대한 언급은 하지 않았으므로 정답은 ⑤ '여벌 옷'이다.

오답 보기 해석

16
② 산악 자전거를 타도록 다른 사람들을 설득하기 위해
③ 산악 자전거의 건강상 이점을 확인하기 위해
④ 산악 자전거가 왜 인기 있는지에 관한 이유를 설명하기 위해
⑤ 산악 자전거를 타는 동안의 잠재적 위험에 대해 경고하기 위해

총 어휘 수 157

DICTATION ANSWERS

01 skilled guitar player / I appreciate you saying that

02 go out for dinner / spending too much money

03 We've been sorting through the suggestions / allowing you to submit suggestions online / click on the "Suggestions" link / makes it easier to respond

04 special tradition relating to / different symbolic objects / successful academic career

05 value their hard work and dedication / They're such a great fit / two openings in quality control / give them my contact information

06 Take a look at our lot / Well, I don't really want a four-door sedan / inhale too much of the pollution / a depressing color

07 Where are you heading / this website for booking a hotel / it'll be kind of useless

08 You were supposed to be home / My phone's battery died / there was a major accident / won't be operating for the rest of the day

09 include admission to / including the performance / the discount doesn't apply to

10 future generations face / a real eye-opener / It drags at points / it will still be in theaters

11 I'm hosting two contests / in a speed challenge / No professionals are allowed to enter / look forward to an outstanding event

12 people in need overseas / donate money to a local charity / We should do our part to help

13 could have gone any worse / The same thing happened to me / my bad luck continued beyond that / have to be joking / was delayed for two hours

14 They're very emotional beings / They even mourn their dead / stopped using ivory decades ago

15 working out and staying in shape / skipping meals to lose weight / change the way he thinks about working out and dieting

16-17 get in touch with nature / take these things into consideration / wear proper protective gear / bringing plenty of water is critical

05 수능영어듣기 실전모의고사

본문 p.32

01 ③	02 ⑤	03 ②	04 ⑤	05 ③	06 ①
07 ⑤	08 ⑤	09 ④	10 ②	11 ②	12 ③
13 ④	14 ②	15 ④	16 ③	17 ②	

01 짧은 대화의 응답

소재 물건 구매

듣기 대본 해석

여: 엽서 어디서 샀어요? 비싼가요?
남: 선물가게에서 샀어요. 전체 세트당 10달러예요.
여: 정말이요? 저는 어제 동네에서 같은 엽서를 15달러에 샀어요.
남: ③ 당신이 정말 바가지를 쓴 것 같군요.

어휘

〈문제〉 **overcharge** ***v.*** 바가지를 씌우다 **misunderstanding** ***n.*** 오해
purchase ***n.*** 구매 ***v.*** 구매하다

정답 ③

문제풀이

같은 엽서 세트를 5달러나 더 주고 산 여자에게 남자가 할 말은 ③ '당신이 정말 바가지를 쓴 것 같군요.'가 적절하다.

오답 보기 해석

① 괜찮아요. 저는 신용카드로 지불할게요.
② 음, 그렇다면 내 돈을 되돌려 받아야겠어요.
④ 사과할게요. 오해가 있었어요.
⑤ 다음 구매 시에 5퍼센트 할인을 해 드릴게요.

총 어휘 수 42

02 짧은 대화의 응답

소재 겹친 행사

듣기 대본 해석

남: 다음 월요일에 제 딸이 초등학교에 입학해요. 하지만 저는 동시에 구직 인터뷰가 있어요.
여: 둘 다 할 수는 없잖아요.
남: 알아요. 어떤 게 더 중요하다고 생각하세요?
여: ⑤ 제 생각엔 직업을 구하는 거요.

어휘

elementary school 초등학교 〈문제〉 **get a job** 직업을 구하다

정답 ⑤

문제풀이

남자가 딸의 초등학교 입학과 구직 인터뷰 중에 더 중요한 일이 어떤 것이라고 생각하는지 물었으므로 어떤 것이 더 중요하다는 대답이 와야 한다. 따라서 ⑤ '제 생각엔 직업을 구하는 거요.'가 적절하다.

오답 보기 해석

① 오늘 밤 그를 인터뷰 하는 것이 기대돼요.
② 철저하게 준비되는 것이 중요한 것 같아요.
③ 꽃을 좀 가져와야 해요.
④ 그녀는 내년에 졸업할 거예요.

총 어휘 수 40

03 담화 주제

소재 온라인상 개인정보 도용을 막기 위한 요령

듣기 대본 해석

남: 최근 기술의 발전으로 사람들은 점점 더 많은 시간을 인터넷을 하면서 보내고 있습니다. 많은 분들이 알다시피 이는 여러분의 개인정보를 훔치려고 하는 인터넷상 약탈자들을 증가시키고 있습니다. 저는 오늘 신원 도용을 막을 수 있는 방법들을 여러분께 설명해 드리려고 합니다. 우선 여러분의 온라인 계정의 비밀번호를 수시로 바꾸는 것은 매우 중요합니다. 더 나아가 계정마다 비밀번호를 다르게 해놓는 것이 좋습니다. 이 비밀번호들은 숫자, 글자, 그리고 별표나 구두점 같은 특수문자를 포함하는 것이 좋습니다. 그리고 피싱 사이트들도 경계해야 합니다. 의심스러운 사이트에 개인정보를 입력할 때는 항상 조심하십시오. 마지막으로 공용 컴퓨터를 사용할 때 완전히 로그아웃을 하고 작업이 끝나면 브라우저를 닫으십시오.

어휘

predator ***n.*** 포식자, 약탈자 **identity theft** 신원 도용
asterisk ***n.*** 별표 **punctuation** ***n.*** 구두점 **suspicious** ***a.*** 의심스러운

정답 ②

문제풀이

남자는 개인정보 도용을 막을 수 있는 방법으로 비밀번호 변경, 비밀번호를 만드는 요령, 주의해야 할 사이트, 공용 컴퓨터 사용시 로그아웃 등을 말하고 있으므로 주제로 가장 적절한 것은 ② '온라인상 개인정보 도용 방지 요령'이다.

총 어휘 수 127

04 의견

소재 방해물을 치움으로써 학습 효율을 높이는 방법

듣기 대본 해석

남: Tiffany, 너 요즘 성적도 오르고 있고 수업 참여도 활발하게 하고 있어.
여: 알아차린 게 신기한데 그래, 맞아.
남: 어떻게 하는 거야? 학기 초에는 굉장히 힘들어하고 있었잖아.
여: 나는 집에서 수업 전에 교과서를 읽고, 방해되는 것들로부터 거리를 두려고 노력해 왔어.
남: 내가 어떻게 하면 네가 한 것처럼 집중과 흥미를 향상시킬 수 있을까?
여: 사실 꽤 간단해. 방해될 만한 것들을 다 치우는 거야.
남: 그럼 텔레비전도 끄고 인터넷을 하지도 말라는 거야?
여: 뭐, 적당하면 괜찮아. 근데 공부할 시간을 만들고 그 시간에는 공부만 해야 해.
남: 그건 그렇네. 난 어떨 땐 텔레비전 켜둔 채로 공부하는데 사실 방해 되더라고.
여: 널 방해하는 것들을 처리하면 분명 성적이 더 오를 거야.

어휘

distraction ***n.*** 방해물 **in moderation** 알맞게, 적당히
improve ***v.*** 개선되다, 향상시키다

정답 ⑤

문제풀이

남자가 여자에게 어떻게 성적을 올리고 공부에 집중하게 되었는지를 묻자, 방해될 만한 것들을 치움으로써 공부에만 집중한다고 대답하였으므로 여자의 의견으로 가장 적절한 것은 ⑤ '방해요소를 제거하여 학습 집중력을 높여야 한다.'이다.

총 어휘 수 155

05 대화자의 관계 파악

소재 영화배우의 스케줄 체크

듣기 대본 해석

여: 좋은 아침이에요, Boris. 오늘은 좀 어때요?

남: 많이 좋아졌어요, 감사해요. 리조트에서 굉장히 즐거운 시간을 보내고 있어요. 저번에 묵었던 곳보다 훨씬 편하네요.

여: 맘에 드셔서 다행이네요. 발코니에서의 경치가 장관이죠?

남: 아름다워요. 정말 떠나기 싫어요.

여: 음, 그럼 아침은 뭐 드실래요? 원하신다면 룸 서비스로 스테이크와 계란을 가져오라고 할 수 있어요.

남: 좋은 생각이에요. 오늘은 어떤 스케줄이 있어요? 잡지 촬영이 오늘인가요 내일인가요?

여: 내일이에요. 오늘은 지역 방송사에서 텔레비전 인터뷰가 있어요.

남: 그렇군요. 고마워요, Diane. 항상 챙겨줘서 고마워하고 있어요. 그나저나 영화촬영은 언제 시작해요?

여: 다음 주 월요일에요. 세트장 매니저가 밤낮으로 준비하고 있어요.

남: 좋네요. 다시 한 번 고마워요.

어휘

balcony ***n.*** 발코니 **spectacular** ***a.*** 장관을 이루는, 극적인 **magazine** ***n.*** 잡지 **local** ***a.*** 지역의, 현지의 **station** ***n.*** 방송국, 역, 정류장 **around the clock** 24시간 내내, 밤낮으로

정답 ③

문제풀이

여자가 남자의 아침식사와 영화촬영 스케줄 등을 챙겨주는 것으로 보아 여자는 매니저, 남자는 영화배우임을 알 수 있으므로 정답은 ③ '영화배우 — 매니저'이다.

총 어휘 수 138

06 그림의 세부 내용 파악

소재 새로 만든 홈페이지 디자인

듣기 대본 해석

여: 안녕하세요, Jayden. 지금 컴퓨터로 뭘 하고 계세요?

남: 우리 홈페이지에 쓸 새로운 디자인을 만들고 있어요. 한번 봐요.

여: 훨씬 더 나아진 것 같네요. 새로운 색깔 조합이랑 레이아웃이 굉장히 마음에 드네요.

남: 고마워요. 사이트를 사용자에게 더 편리하게 만들고 싶었어요.

여: 나는 위쪽에 축구선수 사진도 좋아요. 그 아래에 저건 선수들 프로필로 연결되는 링크인가요?

남: 네, 맞아요. 팬들이 선수들에 대해 더 알 수 있게 하는 게 좋을 것 같더라고요.

여: 저 사진은 뭔가요?

남: 그것은 이달의 선수 사진이에요. 그는 모자를 거꾸로 쓰고 있어요.

여: 사진 밑에 있는 동영상은요?

남: 올해 여태까지의 하이라이트 몇 개를 보여주는 동영상이에요.

여: 팬들을 위한 게시판은요?

남: 페이지의 아래쪽에 하나 있어요.

어휘

color scheme 색채 배합 **biography** ***n.*** 전기, 프로필

정답 ①

문제풀이

위쪽에 축구선수 사진이 있다고 했는데 축구공 그림이 있으므로 일치하지 않는 것은 ①번이다.

총 어휘 수 138

07 할 일

소재 설거지 부탁

듣기 대본 해석

[전화벨이 울린다.]

여: 여보세요?

남: 안녕, 여보. 집에 오는 중이에요?

여: 아직이요. 방금 일을 마쳤어요. 5분 안에 퇴근할 거예요. 벌써 저녁 먹었어요?

남: 네, Richard랑 나는 햄버거를 먹었어요. 아, 오늘 당신한테 우편으로 큰 상자가 왔어요. 안에 뭐가 들었죠?

여: 그거 아마 Richard의 새 코트일 거예요. 며칠 전에 내가 인터넷에서 세일 중인 것을 발견했어요.

남: 아, 알았어요.

여: 그런데 나 오늘 엄청 긴 하루를 보냈어요. 내가 집에 갔을 때 설거지를 하기엔 너무 피곤할 것 같아요. 그것들 좀 해줄래요?

남: 물론이죠. 내가 Richard랑 할게요.

여: 좋아요. 내가 집에 가는 길에 식료품점에 잠깐 들려서 디저트를 사갈게요.

남: 좋아요.

여: 당신이 특별히 원하는 게 있나요?

남: 초콜릿이랑 아이스크림이면 괜찮아요. 집에 오면 봐요.

어휘

swing by 잠깐 들르다 **grocery store** 식품점, 슈퍼마켓 **on the(one's) way** (~으로) 가는 중에

정답 ⑤

문제풀이

여자는 오늘 긴 하루를 보냈다며 집에 가서 설거지를 못하겠다고 했고, 남자는 Richard와 함께 자신이 하겠다고 했으므로 남자가 여자를 위해 할 일은 ⑤ '설거지 해 주기'이다.

총 어휘 수 144

08 이유

소재 공항에 마중 나가지 못하는 이유

듣기 대본 해석

[휴대폰이 울린다.]

남: 여보세요?

여: 여보, 발표 어땠어?

남: 정말 잘 됐어. 나의 고객이 매우 인상 깊어했던 것 같아.

여: 잘 됐네. 오늘 집으로 올 거야?

남: 응, 오늘 오후 항공편을 예약했어.

여: 멋져. 아이들이 당신을 보면 굉장히 좋아할 거야. 너무 오랫동안 떠나 있었어.

남: 맞아, 집에 가서 가족과 함께 있게 되어 정말 신이 나. 공항에 나를 데리러 올 수 있어?

여: 아마도, 비행기가 몇 시에 도착해?

남: 4시 45분에 도착해.

여: 오, 음, 거기에 좀 늦게 도착할 수밖에 없을 것 같은데. 5시에 Alice를 피아노 레슨에 데려가야 해.

남: 문제없어. 택시타면 돼.

여: 미안해, 여보. 아, 당신이 돌아오는 길에 기념품 좀 사 올 수 있어?

남: 그럼. 오늘 밤에 봐.

어휘

make it home 집에 가다 **book** ***v.*** 예약하다 **flight** ***n.*** 항공편, 비행 **land** ***v.*** 착륙하다 **souvenir** ***n.*** 기념품, 선물

정답 ⑤

문제풀이
여자는 5시에 딸을 피아노 레슨에 데려가야 해서 비행기 도착시간에 공항에 도착할 수 있을 것 같지 않다고 말했으므로 여자가 공항에 마중 나갈 수 없는 이유는 ⑤ '딸을 피아노 레슨에 데려가야 해서'이다.

총 어휘 수 134

09 숫자

소재 연극 표 구입

듣기 대본 해석
여: 안녕하세요. 무엇을 도와드릴까요?
남: 안녕하세요. 저와 제 아내의 연극 표를 사고 싶습니다.
여: 음, 근데 지금 거의 매진입니다. 발코니에 위치한 C구역과 F구역에만 자리가 남았네요.
남: 그것들 중 하나라도 괜찮습니다. 얼마입니까?
여: C구역은 20달러이고 F구역은 15달러입니다.
남: 왜 C구역의 표가 더 비싸죠?
여: C구역이 시야가 더 좋습니다.
남: 그럼 C구역 표 두 장으로 할게요. 할인도 되나요?
여: 65세가 넘으신 고령자에게는 10퍼센트 할인을 해 드리고 있어요.
남: 저는 67살이고 제 아내는 지난 달에 65세가 됐습니다. 여기 신용카드랑 신분증이요.
여: 알겠습니다. 여기 표 받으세요. 오른쪽에 있는 문으로 입장하시면 됩니다. 즐거운 관람 되세요.
남: 감사합니다.

어휘
sold out (표가) 매진된

정답 ④

문제풀이
C구역 두 장이므로 40달러인데, 65세 이상 고령자 할인을 10퍼센트 받는다고 했으므로 남자가 지불해야 할 금액은 ④ '$36'이다.

총 어휘 수 150

10 언급 유무

소재 과외 수업

듣기 대본 해석
여: Felix, 과외 하면서 추가로 돈을 좀 벌려고 한다고 들었어.
남: 맞아. 누구 과외 선생님 찾는 사람 없어?
여: 음, 우리 여동생이 수학 때문에 좀 헤매고 있어서 도움이 필요할 것 같아.
남: 어떤 수학에서 도움이 필요한 건데?
여: 지금 고급 대수학 듣고 있어.
남: 오, 문제없어. 얼마나 자주 만날 수 있어?
여: 일주일에 두 번. 아마 화요일과 목요일이 가장 좋을 거야.
남: 응. 과외 시간은 얼마나 길어야 할까?
여: 일주일에 두 번이면, 한 시간이면 충분할 것 같아.
남: 그래. 어머님께서 얼마 정도 지불하실 생각이셔?
여: 한 수업 당 40달러면 괜찮을 것 같다고 하셨는데 상의해 볼 수 있을 거야.
남: 아니야. 그 정도면 괜찮아. 어머님께 내 휴대폰 번호 드리고 전화하시라고 하는 건 어때? 그럼 다른 더 자세한 얘기를 나눌 수 있잖아.
여: 그래. 알겠어.

어휘
tutoring ***n.*** 과외 **struggle** ***v.*** 허우적거리다, 버둥거리다
algebra ***n.*** 대수학 **negotiate** ***v.*** 협상하다

정답 ②

문제풀이
수업 과목(고급 대수학), 수업 횟수(일주일에 두 번), 수업 요일(화요일, 목요일), 수업료(40달러)는 언급했지만 수업 장소에 대해서는 언급하지 않았으므로 정답은 ② '수업 장소'이다.

총 어휘 수 156

11 내용 일치 · 불일치

소재 스노클링 투어

듣기 대본 해석
여: 돌고래, 물고기, 그리고 다른 바다 생물들과 수영하는 게 어떤 느낌일지 상상해 보신 적 있습니까? Johnny Bahama's 바다 투어에 참여해서 세계 최고의 스노클링 투어를 즐겨보세요. 오, 스노클링을 해본 적이 없으신가요? 문제 없습니다. 하는 내내 모든 과정을 여러분과 함께할 가이드들이 있습니다. 매일 아침 9시, 오후 1시, 오후 4시에 투어를 합니다. 스노클링은 체력적으로 힘든 활동이기 때문에 15세 이상인 분만 가능합니다. 그리고 모든 분들은 항상 구명조끼를 착용해 주시기 바랍니다. 호텔 로비나 아침 7시와 저녁 6시 사이에 110-555-7570으로 전화해서 예약하실 수 있습니다. 경청해 주셔서 감사드리고 이 아름다운 섬에서 좋은 시간 되시길 바랍니다.

어휘
marine ***a.*** 바다의, 해양의 **snorkeling** ***n.*** 스노클링 **demanding** ***a.*** 부담이 큰, 힘든

정답 ②

문제풀이
매일 아침 9시, 오후 1시, 오후 4시에 투어가 있다고 하였으므로, 하루에 총 세 번 투어가 있다. 따라서 일치하지 않는 것은 ② '하루에 네 번 투어가 있다.'이다.

총 어휘 수 133

12 도표

소재 딸의 도서관 여름 프로그램 선택

듣기 대본 해석
남: 여보, 도서관에서 어린이들을 위한 여름 프로그램을 개설한대요. 그 중 하나에 Leslie를 참가시킬 생각이에요.
여: 좋은 생각이네요. 그 프로그램에 대한 정보 있어요?
남: 물론이죠. 여기 받은 전단지에요.
여: *[잠시 후]* Leslie가 월요일에는 수영 수업 가야 돼서 그날 프로그램은 아무것도 못 들어요.
남: 맞아요. 매일 오후 3시까지 하는 여름 캠프도 있죠?
여: 그래요. 그러니까 3시 30분 이후에 시작하는 프로그램을 찾아야 해요.
남: 알겠어요. 근데 그 애는 별로 화가로서의 소질은 없는 것 같으니까 다른 프로그램을 찾아보죠.
여: 네. 이제 이 두 개로 좁혀졌네요.
남: 그렇군요. 50달러는 좀 비싼 것 같지 않아요?
여: 나도 그렇게 생각해요. 그럼 이 프로그램에 등록해야겠어요.
남: 내일 도서관 가서 등록할게요.

어휘
enroll ***v.*** 등록하다 **flyer** ***n.*** 전단지 **sign ~ up** ~을 등록시키다

정답 ③

문제풀이
월요일은 안 된다고 했고, 매일 오후 세시까지는 여름 캠프가 있어서 3시 30분 이후인 프로그램 중에서 선택해야 한다. 그림 말고 다른 프로그램을 찾자고 했으므로 ③번과 ④번이 남는다. 그 중에 50달러는 비싼 것 같으므로 다른 것을 선택하자고 했으므로 정답은 ③번이다.

총 어휘 수 142

13 긴 대화의 응답

소재 아들의 학교생활

듣기 대본 해석
남: Swanson씨, 안녕하세요. Edward의 아빠인 Daniel Hoult입니다.
여: 오, Hoult씨, 만나서 반가워요. 들어오세요.
남: 고마워요. 제 아들이 학교에서 어떻게 지내나요?
여: 음, Edward는 부지런한 학생이에요.
남: 정말입니까?
여: 네. 그는 항상 웃고 수업에 활발하게 참여하려고 노력해요.
남: 그런데 학교에서 약간 난폭하지는 않나요?
여: 아닙니다. 가끔 그의 친구들과 너무 흥분하긴 하지만 다른 학생들에게 피해를 주진 않아요.
남: 집에서는 다소 쉽게 짜증내거든요.
여: 음, 학생들은 종종 학교에서보다 집에서 매우 다르기도 해요.
남: 다른 학생들도 마찬가지라는 말씀이시죠?
여: 그렇습니다, Hoult씨. Edward는 여기에서 잘 하고 있어요. 그는 매사에 성실하게 최선을 다해요.
남: ④ 학교 생활을 정말 잘하고 있다니 안심이군요.

어휘
aggressive ***a.*** 난폭한, 공격적인 **get irritated** 짜증나다
genuinely ***ad.*** 진정으로, 성실하게

정답 ④

문제풀이
Edward의 아버지와 선생님의 대화 내용이다. 아들의 학교 생활을 걱정하는 아버지에게 여자는 Edward가 성실하게 최선을 다하는 학생이라고 말한다. 이에 적절한 대답은 ④ '학교 생활을 정말 잘하고 있다니 안심이군요.'이다.

오답 보기 해석
① 그가 어떤 학교 클럽에도 가입하지 않았으면 좋겠어요.
② 어떻게 학생들을 더 잘 가르칠 수 있는지 알고 싶네요.
③ 이제부터 학교에 제때 가라고 얘기할게요.
⑤ 수업에서 활동적으로 임하라고 충고해야 할 것 같아요.

총 어휘 수 126

14 긴 대화의 응답

소재 멀리 계신 아빠 방문

듣기 대본 해석
남: Jenny, 주말 동안 갔던 하이킹 여행 어땠어? 가족들과 함께 간 거야, 맞지?
여: 사실, 이번엔 아빠랑만 갔는데, 평생의 경험(일생일대의 경험)이었어!
남: 너랑 너희 아빠랑만?
여: 응. 우린 많은 이야기를 했지. 나는 다 컸고 내 인생에 책임을 져야 한다고 느꼈어.
남: 네가 그럴 거라고 생각해. 나도 우리 아빠가 많이 그리워. 아빠께서는 일 년 동안 멀리 가 계셔.
여: 두바이에 계시지, 맞지? 네가 겨울 방학 동안 아빠께 방문하는 게 어때?
남: 아빠도 나한테 오라고 하셨지만, 내가 시간이 없어. 겨울 대학진학 준비 프로그램에 참가해야 해.
여: 오, 대학진학 준비 프로그램이 아주 힘들다고 들었어.
남: 맞아. 숙제랑 읽기가 많아. 내가 아빠를 방문할 수 없어서 기분이 안 좋아.
여: ② 안됐지만 아빠가 상황을 이해하실 거라 믿어.

어휘
responsible for ~에 책임이 있는 **demanding** ***a.*** 부담이 큰, 힘든
〈문제〉 **that's a shame** 안됐군요, 유감이다

정답 ②

문제풀이
두바이에 계신 아빠가 보고 싶지만 겨울에 대학진학 준비 프로그램 참가로 방문을 못해서 기분이 좋지 않다고 말하는 남자에게 여자가 해줄 수 있는 말은 ② '안됐지만 아빠가 상황을 이해하실 거라 믿어.'가 가장 적절하다.

오답 보기 해석
① 지금은 많이 바쁘지 않아서 너랑 같이 그를 보러 갈 수 있어.
③ 네가 정말 열심히 해왔으니까 시험에 통과할 거라고 확신해.
④ 그렇긴 하지만 그는 너랑 캠핑 가기에는 너무 바쁘신 게 틀림없어.
⑤ 과제들은 선생님들께 이메일로 제출해야 해.

총 어휘 수 142

15 상황에 적절한 말

소재 문제가 생긴 차

듣기 대본 해석
여: 출근하는 길에 Carl의 차에 문제가 생깁니다. 그는 서비스 센터에 가서 공회전할 때 차가 가끔 시동이 꺼진다고 얘기합니다. 정비공은 자동차를 보고 점화 플러그를 교체해야 한다는 것을 알아냅니다. Carl에겐 다행히도 이는 꽤나 간단하고 저렴한 해결책이어서 그는 정비공에게 플러그를 교체할 것을 요구합니다. Carl은 시간이 많지 않아서 정비공에게 언제쯤 자동차 수리가 끝나는지 물어보고 싶어합니다. 이러한 상황에서 Carl이 정비공에게 뭐라고 말할까요?
Carl: ④ 점화 플러그를 교체하는 데 얼마나 걸릴까요?

어휘
stall ***v.*** (갑자기) 시동이 꺼지다 **idle** ***v.*** (엔진이) 공회전하다, 빈둥거리다 ***a.*** 게으른, 가동되지 않는 **spark plug** 점화 플러그 **mechanic** ***n.*** 정비공 〈문제〉 **get a second opinion** 다른 사람의 의견을 얻다

정답 ④

문제풀이
담화의 마지막 부분에서 Carl이 좀 바빠서 점화 플러그를 교체하는 데 얼마나 걸리는지 물어보고자 한다고 했으므로 정답은 ④ '점화 플러그를 교체하는 데 얼마나 걸릴까요?'이다.

오답 보기 해석
① 다른 정비공에게도 물어봐야 할 것 같아요.
② 차 수리하는 데 얼마 정도 들까요?
③ 차에 점화 플러그가 없는 것 같아요.
⑤ 좋네요! 심각한 문제일까 봐 걱정했어요.

총 어휘 수 111

16 담화 주제 / 17 세부 내용 파악

소재 치매 예방법

듣기 대본 해석
남: 치매는 오늘 날 세계에 점점 더 흔해지고 있습니다. 이는 사람의 언어능력, 이해능력, 기억력 그리고 사고 처리에 부정적으로 영향을 미치는 끔찍한 병입니다. 이 병은 보통 연세가 많으신 분들이 가장 영향을 많이 받지만,

치매는 40세만큼이나 젊은 성인들까지 걸리는 것으로 알려져 있습니다. 많은 연구를 통해서 의사들은 이제 이 병이 예방될 수 있다고 자신 있게 말합니다. 독일에서 쓰이는 예방법 중 하나는 은행잎 추출물을 사용한 치료법입니다. 이 유명한 약초는 순환계를 향상시킬 뿐만 아니라 뇌 기능을 상승시키기 위해서도 중국과 다른 나라들에서 수천 년 간 쓰여져 왔습니다. 임상 연구는 이 약초가 기억력을 회복하고 뇌로 가는 혈류량을 증가시키는 능력이 있음을 보여주었습니다. 사실 약초가 굉장히 강해서 복용 20분 내에 효과가 감지될 수 있습니다. 몇 개월 간 지속적으로 복용을 하면 치매 환자들은 큰 호전을 경험할 수 있을 것입니다.

어휘

Alzheimer's disease 치매 **prevalent *a.*** 일반적인, 흔한
comprehension *n.* 이해력 **preventative *a.*** 예방을 위한
measure *n.* 조치 **ginkgo biloba** 은행잎 추출물
circulatory system 순환계 **detect *v.*** 감지하다, 발견하다
dramatic *a.* 극적인, 인상적인

정답 16 ③ 17 ②

문제풀이

16 남자는 오늘날 치매가 점점 흔해지고 젊은 사람들에게까지 나타나고 있다고 말하면서 치매 치료에 도움을 주는 ginkgo biloba(은행잎 추출물)를 소개하고 있다. 따라서 남자가 하는 말의 주제는 ③ '치매 환자를 도와준다고 입증된 보조제를 제안하기 위해'이다.

17 독일에서 쓰이는 방법이지만 수천 년 전부터 중국과 다른 나라들에서도 쓰여 왔다고 했으므로 내용과 일치하지 않는 것은 ② '독일 외 다른 나라에선 쓰지 않는다.'이다

오답 보기 해석

16

① 사람들에게 새로운 약초 보조제에 대해 알리기 위해
② 기억력과 뇌활동 개선에 대한 조언을 주기 위해
④ 사람들에게 약초 복용의 위험성을 상기시키기 위해
⑤ 사람들이 치매 경고 증상을 인식하도록 돕기 위해

총 어휘 수 145

DICTATION ANSWERS

01 at the gift shop

02 enter elementary school

03 how you can prevent identity theft / passwords for each of your accounts / also be cautious of phishing websites / into suspicious websites

04 starting to excel in class / separate myself from distractions / okay in moderation

05 the balcony is spectacular / what's on the schedule / when do we start filming / is working around the clock

06 color scheme and the new layout / wearing his cap backward / a message board for the fans

07 Are you on your way home / I found it on sale / too tired to wash the dishes / swing by the grocery store

08 booked a flight / You've been gone so long / take Alice to her piano lesson / catch a taxi / pick up a couple of souvenirs

09 we're nearly sold out / The view is better / Senior citizens over the age of

10 earn some extra money / struggling in math / She's taking advanced algebra / willing to pay

11 the world's finest snorkeling tours / guides who will be with you every step / wear a life jacket

12 we should enroll Leslie in / can't attend any programs / don't think she's much of / sign her up

13 is a diligent student / never gives others a hard time / genuinely tries his best at

14 the experience of a lifetime / responsible for my life / Why don't you visit him / pre-college program is very demanding

15 pulls into a service station / is in a bit of a hurry / when his car will be fixed

16-17 becoming more and more prevalent / One preventative measure used / increase blood flow / After several months of steady use

06 수능영어듣기 실전모의고사

본문 p.38

01 ①	02 ④	03 ③	04 ⑤	05 ②	06 ⑤
07 ①	08 ②	09 ③	10 ③	11 ⑤	12 ⑤
13 ①	14 ④	15 ②	16 ①	17 ③	

01 짧은 대화의 응답

소재 야외 바비큐

듣기 대본 해석

남: 안녕, Amanda. 뭘 굽고 있어?

여: 내일 저녁 디저트를 위한 파이를 구울 거야.

남: 대단하네. 내일 야외 바비큐 저녁 식사야. 맞지?

여: ① 응. 여름 저녁을 보내는 데에 최고일 거야.

어휘

dessert ***n.*** 디저트 **outdoor** ***a.*** 야외의

정답 ①

문제풀이

남자가 내일 야외 바비큐 식사가 맞는지 확인 차 묻는 데 대해 맞다고 대답하는 답변이 가장 자연스럽다. 따라서 ① '응. 여름 저녁을 보내는 데에 최고일 거야.'가 정답이다.

오답 보기 해석

② 너의 그 유명한 치킨 샐러드를 만들 거니?
③ 모든 사람들을 파티에 초대하는 게 어때?
④ 스낵 좀 가져와. 그건 큰 일이 아니니까.
⑤ 파이 굽는 데 도움이 필요하니?

총 어휘 수 36

02 짧은 대화의 응답

소재 동전 바꾸기

듣기 대본 해석

여: 드디어 주말이다. 오락실에 가서 게임이나 하자.

남: 그거 좋겠다. 그런데 나 동전이 떨어졌어. 너 20달러 잔돈으로 가지고 있니?

여: 그럴 거야. 어떻게 줄까?

남: ④ 10달러 지폐 하나랑 5달러 지폐 하나, 그리고 나머지는 동전으로 줘.

어휘

change ***n.*** 동전, 잔돈 〈문제〉 **a penny for your thoughts**
[속담] 무엇을 멍하니 생각하고 있니

정답 ④

문제풀이

남자는 여자에게 잔돈이 있는지 물었고, 여자는 어떻게 바꿔줄지를 물었으므로 남자의 대답으로 적절한 것은 ④ '10달러 지폐 하나랑 5달러 지폐 하나, 그리고 나머지는 동전으로 줘.'이다.

오답 보기 해석

① 뭘 그리 멍하게 생각해.
② 난 동전만 있는 거 같아.
③ 오락실은 두 블록만 가면 돼.
⑤ 내가 어디서 잔돈으로 바꾸는 기계를 찾을 수 있는지 아니?

총 어휘 수 46

03 담화 목적

소재 교내 토네이도 대비 훈련 안내

듣기 대본 해석

[차임벨이 울린다.]

여: 안녕하세요 학생 여러분. 교감 선생인 Lee입니다. 토네이도가 많이 일어나는 철이 오고 있어서 오늘 점심을 먹은 후에 토네이도 대비 훈련을 실시할 예정입니다. 비상벨이 울릴 때 선생님의 지시에 따르도록 합시다. 서두르지 않으면서 질서 있게 방을 나가주시기 바랍니다. 선생님들께서 여러분을 지하실로 안내할 것이고 거기서 여러분은 토네이도가 일어날 경우 어떻게 자신을 보호해야 하는지 배우게 될 것입니다. 지역 소방관들도 참여하여 절차를 도와줄 것입니다. 대비 훈련은 마치는 데 30분 정도밖에 걸리지 않을 것입니다. 이 대비 훈련은 여러분의 안전을 위한 것이니 부디 집중해 주시기를 바랍니다. 협조해 주셔서 감사합니다.

어휘

drill ***n.*** 훈련 **instruction** ***n.*** 지도, 지시 **orderly** ***a.*** 질서 있는
usher ***v.*** 안내하다 **in the event of** 만약 ~하면, ~할 경우
in attendance 참석한 **procedure** ***n.*** 절차, 방법

정답 ③

문제풀이

토네이도가 자주 발생하는 철을 맞아 교내에서 실시되는 토네이도 대비 훈련에 대해 실시 시간, 절차, 소요 시간 등을 말하고 있는 것으로 보아 여자가 하는 말의 목적은 ③ '교내 토네이도 대비 훈련에 대해 안내하려고'이다.

총 어휘 수 112

04 의견

소재 카페 매출 신장 방안

듣기 대본 해석

여: Justin, 우리 앉아서 카페에 대해 얘기 좀 해요.

남: 네. 무슨 일 있어요?

여: 아시다시피, 우리는 이익을 내지 못하고 있어요.

남: 네, 저도 알아요. 길 건너편에 Blackbeans가 문을 연 후로 우린 계속 힘들었어요.

여: 음, 우리가 가격을 내려야 한다고 생각해요.

남: 정말이요? 저는 그래야 한다고 생각하지 않아요.

여: 그렇지만 우리 고객들을 카페로 다시 오게 하는 유일한 방법일 것 같아요.

남: 저는 우리는 제공하지만 Blackbeans에서는 제공하지 않는 메뉴에 집중해야 한다고 생각해요.

여: 그거 정말 좋은 생각이에요!

남: 우리가 더 좋은 다양한 메뉴를 제공한다고 사람들에게 알려야 해요. 그것에 관해 광고해야 될까요?

여: 물론이죠. 내일 초안을 바로 구상해볼게요.

남: Blackbeans에서는 제공하지 않고 우리가 제공하는 모든 메뉴들의 사진과 우리 로고면 완벽한 광고를 만들 수 있을 거예요.

여: 좋은 제안이에요.

어휘

suffer ***v.*** 악화되다, 시달리다, 고통 받다 **offer** ***v.*** 제공하다, 제안하다
remind ***v.*** 상기시키다, 다시 한번 알려주다 **variety** ***n.*** 여러 가지, 다양성

정답 ⑤

문제풀이

Blackbeans가 문을 연 후로 이익이 나지 않기 때문에 남자는 Blackbeans에서는 팔지 않는 메뉴에 집중하자고 말하고 있다. 따라서 답은 ⑤ 'Blackbeans에서 제공하지 않는 메뉴를 제공해야 한다.'이다.

총 어휘 수 136

05 대화자의 관계 파악

소재 조각가와의 인터뷰

듣기 대본 해석

남: 안녕하세요, Sampson씨!
여: 안녕하세요, Steve. 오늘 와주셔서 감사합니다.
남: 시작하겠습니다. 이번에 당신은 사람의 표정에 초점을 맞추고 있네요.
여: 네, 맞아요. 제가 사람의 표정에 혼신을 다하기로 정했던 것은 처음이에요.
남: 즐거웠나요?
여: 정말 즐거웠어요. 실제로, 이제 저는 추상적인 예술보다는 인간의 몸에 대한 작업에 집중해볼까 생각하고 있어요.
남: 재미있을 것 같네요. 저는 이 조각품의 이 모델 표정이 좋아요. 그녀는 당신이 아는 사람인가요?
여: 네, 그녀는 우리 이웃에 커피숍을 가지고 있어요. 저는 그녀에게 저를 위한 자세를 부탁했고 그녀는 기꺼이 도와줬어요.
남: 그렇군요. 부탁 하나 해도 될까요?
여: 물론이죠. 뭔데요?
남: 저희 기사에 사진을 싣고 싶습니다. 당신이 가장 좋아하는 작품 옆에 서 주시겠어요?
여: 물론이죠.

어휘

appreciate ***v.*** 고맙게 여기다 **expression** ***n.*** 표정 **devote** ***v.*** (시간 · 노력 · 돈을) 쏟다, 바치다, 기울이다 **abstract** ***a.*** 추상적인 **sculpture** ***n.*** 조각 **neighborhood** ***n.*** 이웃

정답 ②

문제풀이

대화에서 조각품이 나오고 어떤 것을 소재로 한 작업인지 이야기하고 있으므로 여자는 조각가이고, 대화의 마지막에 남자가 기사에 싣고 싶다고 하는 것으로 보아 남자는 여자를 취재하러 온 기자임을 알 수 있다. 따라서 정답은 ② '기자 ㅡ 조각가'이다.

총 어휘 수 140

06 그림의 세부 내용 파악

소재 어린이집 인테리어

듣기 대본 해석

남: 어린이집을 열 준비가 거의 된 것 같은데요, Pam.
여: 우리는 지난 몇 주 동안 많은 노력을 들였어요. 놀이방을 보세요.
남: 좋아 보여요. 구석이 있는 로켓은 굉장해요!
여: 네. 아이들이 거기서 놀기 재미있을 거예요. 뒤 벽에 별도 좀 그렸어요.
남: 그리고 오른쪽에 달도 보여요.
여: 맞아요. 좌석 배치는 어떤 것 같아요?
남: 잘된 것 같아요. 원통형 의자가 제법 우주 공간 같아요.
여: 나도 그렇게 생각했어요. 우리는 그것들의 크기를 다르게 하려고 노력했어요.
남: 하지만 탁자가 좀 부적절한 거 같네요.
여: 나도 그렇게 생각해요. 이 방에 사각 탁자는 어울리지 않아요.
남: 아이들은 상관없을 거예요.

어휘

arrangement ***n.*** 배열, 배치 **cylinder** ***n.*** 원통, 원기둥 **out of place** 어울리지 않는, 제 자리에 있지 않는 **square** ***a.*** 정사각형 모양의

정답 ⑤

문제풀이

대화의 마지막 부분에서 남자와 여자는 사각 탁자는 어울리지 않는다고 했는데 그림에서는 원형 탁자이므로 정답은 ⑤번이다.

총 어휘 수 132

07 할 일

소재 여자의 도움 제안

듣기 대본 해석

여: 안녕하세요 Smith 선생님. 뭐하세요?
남: 안녕, Serena. 책을 찾고 있어.
여: 무엇 때문에요?
남: 내 영어수업을 듣는 학생들이 재미있어 할 만한 책들을 찾고 있어. 학생들이 여름 동안 읽을 한 권을 선택했으면 하거든.
여: 아 여름 독서 목록을 만드시는 거군요. 지금까지 어떤 책들을 선택하셨어요?
남: 몇 개 밖에 안돼. 훨씬 더 많이 필요하지. 학생들이 흥미 있어 하는 책을 찾는 게 쉽지가 않네.
여: 제가 도와드릴 수 있을 것 같아요. 전 시간이 남을 때 책을 많이 읽거든요.
남: 정말이니?
여: 네. 제가 가장 좋아하는 것들을 목록으로 만들어서 이메일로 보내드릴 수 있어요.
남: 정말 친절하구나. 도와줘서 고마워.
여: 뭘요. 즐거운 여름방학 보내세요.

어휘

look up 찾아보다 **reading list** (추천) 도서 목록

정답 ①

문제풀이

남자가 학생들이 여름에 즐겁게 읽을 만한 책 찾기가 쉽지 않다고 하자, 여자는 남자에게 자신이 좋아하는 책 목록의 일부를 보내주겠다고 하였으므로 정답은 ① '도서 목록 만들어 보내 주기'이다.

총 어휘 수 132

08 이유

소재 집에 들어오는 시간

듣기 대본 해석

[휴대폰이 울린다.]
여: 여보세요, 아빠. 무슨 일이세요?
남: 안녕, Elsa. 집에 곧 오니?
여: 아직 학교에 있어요. 언제 끝날지 잘 모르겠어요.
남: 집에 오는 길에 피자 두서너 판 사올 수 있는지 궁금하구나. 남동생이 배가 고프단다.
여: 음, 아직 할 일이 남아있어요. 과학 전시회가 내일 있는 것 아시잖아요.
남: 맞다. 이제 기억이 나는구나. 저녁은 학교 근처에서 먹을 거니?
여: 네, 근처 작은 식당에서 간단히 먹을 거예요.
남: 알았다. 그럼 집에는 언제 올 것 같니?
여: 8시는 되어야 하지 않을까 싶어요. 저를 태우러 오실 수 있으세요?
남: 그러지 못할 것 같구나. 오늘 늦게까지 일해야 한단다. 남동생에게 전화해서 오늘 저녁은 스스로 챙겨먹으라고 얘기해주겠니?
여: 물론이죠. 제가 그에게 전화할게요.

어휘

be starving 배가 고파 죽을 지경이다 **grab a bite** 간단히 먹다

정답 ②

문제풀이

대화의 마지막 부분에서 여자가 자신을 데리러 올 수 있는지 물었는데, 남자는 늦게까지 일해야 해서 안 된다고 했으므로 정답은 ② '늦게까지 일해야 해서'이다.

총 어휘 수 144

09 숫자

소재 치킨 주문

듣기 대본 해석

[전화벨이 울린다.]

남: Together Chicken에 전화해 주셔서 감사합니다. 무엇을 도와드릴까요?

여: 안녕하세요. 내일 필요한 주문을 하려고요. 동아리 모임 때문에 치킨 20마리가 필요합니다.

남: 알겠습니다. 어떤 치킨으로 드릴까요?

여: 음, 갈릭 치킨과 훈제 치킨으로 할게요.

남: 네. 몇 마리씩 드릴까요?

여: 열 마리씩 살게요. 얼마예요?

남: 갈릭 치킨은 한 마리당 10달러이고 훈제 치킨은 15달러입니다.

여: 음, 제가 생각했던 것보다 좀 비싸네요.

남: 아! 깜박할 뻔 했네요. 치킨 열 마리 이상 주문할 시 10퍼센트 할인을 해 드리고 있어요.

여: 오, 좋네요! 오후 열두 시에 Jason Bourne Academy로 배달해 주세요.

남: 알겠습니다. 그때 배달해 드리겠습니다.

어휘

meeting ***n.*** 모임, 회의 **pricey** ***a.*** 비싼

정답 ③

문제풀이

여자는 10달러짜리 갈릭 치킨 열 마리와 15달러짜리 훈제 치킨 열 마리를 주문하였으므로 총액이 100달러+150달러=250달러인데, 열 마리 이상 구매하여 10퍼센트 할인을 받게 되었다. 그러므로 정답은 ③ '$225'이다.

총 어휘 수 137

10 언급 유무

소재 겨울철 호주 여행

듣기 대본 해석

남: 안녕 Maggie, 이번 겨울 방학에 뭐 할 거야? 계획 있어?

여: 음, 알아보고 있는 중인데 호주에 있는 Cairns로 여행 갈까 생각 중이야.

남: 음... 매우 좋은 생각은 아닌 것 같아.

여: 왜 안 되는데?

남: 음, 우선, 성수기이기 때문에 관광객들로 붐빌 거야.

여: 정말?

남: 확실해. 성수기에는 또한 거기가 더 많이 비싸.

여: 몰랐었어.

남: 호주가 남반구에 있기 때문에 그때 거기는 정말 덥기도 해. 거긴 여름 일거야.

여: 오, 나는 꽤 온화할 거라고 생각했는데. 나는 더위를 정말 싫어해. 그때 호주를 방문하는 것에 대해 좋은 점이 있을까?

남: 글쎄, 낮이 좀 더 길어서, 해변에서 좀 더 시간을 가질 수 있을 거야.

여: 그건 좋은 것 같네. 그런데 아마도 난 이번 겨울에 갈 다른 곳을 찾아야 할 것 같아.

어휘

look into ~을 조사하다, 주의 깊게 살피다 **first off** 우선
peak season 성수기 **be packed with** 붐비다, 북적거리다
hemisphere ***n.*** 반구

정답 ③

문제풀이

두 사람의 대화에서 겨울철 호주 여행시 관광객의 수, 물가, 날씨, 낮의 길이에 관한 언급은 있었지만 교통수단에 관한 언급은 없었으므로 정답은 ③ '교통수단'이다.

총 어휘 수 148

11 내용 일치 · 불일치

소재 잠을 많이 자는 나무늘보

듣기 대본 해석

남: 오늘, 저는 나무늘보에 대해 이야기하겠습니다. 나무늘보는 세계에서 가장 잠이 많은 동물 중 하나입니다! 나무늘보는 하루에 18시간을 잡니다. 왜 이 동물이 그렇게 잠을 많이 잘까요? 과학자들은 이것이 나무늘보가 스스로를 보호하는 방법이라고 생각합니다. 나무늘보는 나무 높은 곳에서 쉬고 잠을 자지만 먹는 먹이는 땅 아래에 있습니다. 나무늘보는 매우 천천히 움직이는 동물이기 때문에 땅에서 음식을 찾는 동안 포식자들에게 매우 취약합니다. 시간이 흐르면서 이 졸린 동물은 아주 적은 먹이로 사는 법을 배워서 사냥하는 데 적은 시간만 필요합니다. 그러나 이는 왜 나무늘보가 그렇게 잠을 많이 자는지 설명할 수 없습니다. 아마도 잠자는 것이 에너지를 아끼는 데 도움을 줄지도 모르죠. 아니 나무늘보가 정말 게으른 것일지도 모르고요!

어휘

sloth ***n.*** 나무늘보 **protect** ***v.*** 보호하다, 지키다 **vulnerable** ***a.*** 취약한 **predator** ***n.*** 포식자, 포식동물 **conserve** ***v.*** 아끼다, 보존하다

정답 ⑤

문제풀이

나무늘보는 아주 적은 먹이를 먹고 산다고 했으므로 일치하지 않는 것은 일치하지 않는 것은 ⑤번이다.

총 어휘 수 138

12 도표

소재 중고차 선택

듣기 대본 해석

남: 안녕하세요. 무엇을 도와드릴까요?

여: 안녕하세요. 아들을 위한 중고차를 찾고 있어요.

남: 찾고 계신 특정한 모델이 있나요?

여: 음, 그가 빠른 걸 좋아해서 스포츠카를 여러 대 둘러봤어요.

남: 그렇군요. 재고에 몇 대 있는 것 같아요. *[마우스 클릭 소리]* 우리가 갖고 있는 중고 스포츠카 목록이에요.

여: 흠... 5년 이상 된 차는 별로인 것 같아요.

남: 음, 근데 이 차의 전 주인은 이 다섯 개 중에서 운전을 가장 덜 했어요.

여: 저도 알지만, 50,000마일보다 적게 몰았던 좀 더 새 차를 찾고 있어요.

남: 알겠습니다. 가격은 얼마 정도 예상하세요?

여: $15,000 넘게 쓰고 싶진 않아요.

남: 그럼 이 두 가지로 좁혀졌네요.

여: 좋네요. 뭔가 잘못됐을 때 돈을 더 쓰고 싶지 않으니까 보증기간이 더 긴 걸로 할게요.

남: 알겠습니다. 가서 한번 살펴 보죠.

어휘

particular ***a.*** 특정한 **previous** ***a.*** 이전의 **warranty** ***n.*** 보증기간

정답 ⑤

문제풀이

여자는 5년 이하이고 50,000마일보다 적게 탔으며 15,000달러를 넘지 않는 것을 원하고 있으므로 ②번과 ⑤번이 남게 된다. 그 중에 보증기간이 긴 것으로 한다고 했으므로 정답은 ⑤번이다.

총 어휘 수 165

13 긴 대화의 응답

소재 출처 언급의 중요성

듣기 대본 해석

여: 뭐 하고 있어?

남: 경제학 리포트 마무리하려고. 너는 다 했어?

여: 응. 나는 어제 제출했어.

남: 너는 항상 빨리 끝내는구나. 나도 오늘 밤까지 리포트를 끝낼 수 있었으면 좋겠다.

여: 걱정 마. 너는 잘 할 거야. 시간 많잖아. *[잠시 후]* 저 그래프 정말 좋다. 멋져 보여!

남: 고마워. 나도 좋아. 내가 조사하면서 찾은 웹사이트에서 복사한 거야.

여: 정말? 네 자료출처에 사이트 목록을 작성했어?

남: 아니, 안 했는데. 해야 돼?

여: 당연하지! 네가 다른 사람의 자료를 사용할 때 출처를 항상 언급해야 해.

남: 나는 그게 인터넷에도 적용되는지 몰랐어. 알려줘서 고마워.

여: ① 언제든 괜찮아. 출처 언급을 기억하지 않으면 곤란하게 될 수도 있어.

어휘

source ***n.*** 원천, 자료, 출처 **cite** ***v.*** 인용하다 **apply to** ~에 적용되다 〈문제〉 **hand in** 제출하다

정답 ①

문제풀이

남자가 그래프를 인터넷 사이트에서 베꼈다고 하자 여자는 출처를 밝혔는지 물었고 남자에게 다른 사람의 자료를 사용할 때는 반드시 출처를 언급해야 함을 알려주었다. 남자가 거기에 대한 고마움을 표시했을 때 적절한 여자의 대답은 ① '언제든 괜찮아. 출처 언급을 기억하지 않으면 곤란하게 될 수도 있어.'이다.

오답 보기 해석

② 맞아. 난 우선 그 그래프를 사용하지 말았어야 했어.

③ 걱정 마. 이 그래프는 네가 필요할 모든 정보를 주고 있어

④ 그 그래프는 사실 사무실에 있는 다른 사람한테 있던 거야.

⑤ 천만에. 내일 우린 함께 우리의 보고서를 제출할 수 있어.

총 어휘 수 128

14 긴 대화의 응답

소재 태블릿 컴퓨터 장시간 사용

듣기 대본 해석

여: Rudy, 저게 너의 새 태블릿 컴퓨터니? 정말 좋아 보인다.

남: 고마워. 지난 주말에 샀어.

여: 어디서 샀니?

남: William's Electronics 마트에서 샀어.

여: 내가 사용해봐도 될까?

남: 물론이지. 해봐.

여: 정말 끝내준다. 이거 분명 최신 모델일 거야. 어떻게 시작메뉴로 가지?

남: 기기 밑에 있는 둥근 버튼을 누르기만 하면 돼.

여: *[잠시 후]* 오, 좋아. 너 많은 멋진 앱들을 다운받느라 바빴던 것 같네.

남: 맞아. 사실 산 뒤로 다운받느라 많은 시간을 보냈어.

여: 너 매일 사용하니?

남: 그럼. 매일 대략 4시간 정도 사용하지.

여: 정말? 4시간? 너무 오래 사용하는 것 아니야?

남: ④ 맞아. 그래. 사용 시간을 줄여야 할 것 같아.

어휘

neat ***a.*** 훌륭한 **bottom** ***n.*** 아래쪽 **device** ***n.*** 장치, 기구 〈문제〉 **cut down on** ~을 줄이다 **budget** ***n.*** 예산, 비용

정답 ④

문제풀이

여자는 새로 산 남자의 태블릿 컴퓨터에 대해 여러 가지 질문을 하고 남자가 하루에 4시간 사용한다는 말에 너무 오래 사용 하는 게 아닌지 묻고 있으므로 그에 적절한 정답은 ④ '맞아. 그래. 사용 시간을 줄여야 할 것 같아.'이다.

오답 보기 해석

① 어떤 태블릿 컴퓨터를 추천할래?

② 맞아. 너는 정말 새 태블릿 컴퓨터가 필요해.

③ 어떤 앱을 요즘 가장 많이 사용하니?

⑤ 그 태블릿 컴퓨터는 사실 내 예산으론 너무 비쌌어.

총 어휘 수 142

15 상황에 적절한 말

소재 새로운 팀에서 친구 만들기

듣기 대본 해석

남: Dave는 최근 새로운 야구팀으로 이적했습니다. 그는 항상 팀원들과 잘 지내지 못했어요. 첫 훈련 후에 팀 매니저인 Roy가 탈의실에서 파티를 할 것을 제안합니다. Roy는 이 파티가 Dave가 선수들과 친해질 수 있는 좋은 기회라고 생각합니다. Dave는 처음에 망설이지만 조금 생각하다가 파티에 가기로 합니다. Dave는 그 파티에서 몇몇 팀원들과 끈끈한 친구 관계를 만들었습니다. Dave는 Roy에게 자기가 파티를 즐겼고 새로운 팀에 잘 적응했다는 것을 알려주고 싶어합니다. 이러한 상황에서 Dave는 Roy에게 뭐라고 말할까요?

Dave: ② 새로운 친구를 만드는 것을 도와줘서 고마워요.

어휘

transfer ***v.*** 이적하다, 이동하다 **opportunity** ***n.*** 기회 **hesitant** ***a.*** 주저하는 **deliberation** ***n.*** 숙고, 숙의 **comfortable** ***a.*** 편한, 쾌적한

정답 ②

문제풀이

새로 이적한 팀에서 팀원들과 잘 지내지 못하는 Dave에게 매니저인 Roy는 탈의실 파티를 제안하고, Dave는 파티에서 몇몇의 팀원들과 우정을 쌓게 되어 고맙다는 인사를 하려는 상황이므로 ② '새로운 친구를 만드는 것을 도와줘서 고마워요.'가 정답이다.

오답 보기 해석

① 친구 사귀는 데에 조언 좀 해줄 수 있을까요?

③ 오늘 파티에 참석하지 못할 것 같아요.

④ 내일 훈련 때 만나요, Roy.

⑤ 저는 전의 팀에서 정말 친한 친구들이 많았어요.

총 어휘 수 120

16 담화 주제 / 17 세부 내용 파악

소재 보다 현명한 소비자가 되는 방법

듣기 대본 해석

남: 청취자 여러분 안녕하세요. 오늘 저는 여러분들에게 더 현명한 쇼핑객이 되는 법과 여러분의 돈을 현명하게 사용하는 법을 말하고 싶습니다. 예리한 소비자가 되기 위해서 여러분이 이용할 수 있는 몇 가지 요령이 여기 있습니다. 첫째, 여러분들이 필요로 하는 것과 원하는 것 사이에 차이를 고려하세요. 필요한 것들의 리스트를 만들고 가장 중요한 것들을 쇼핑 리스트에서 더 높은 위치에 (더 우선 순위에) 두는 것을 확실히 하세요. 둘째, 구매를 하기 전에 약간의 제품 조사를 하세요. 전자 제품, 자동차, 가전제품 같은 다양한 범위의 제품에 대한 후기들과 평판들을 제공하는 몇몇 웹사이트가 온라인

상에 있습니다. 셋째, 여러분들이 사는 것의 가격을 의식하고 여러분들이 적절하게 청구 되었는지 확신하기 위해 영수증을 확인하도록 하세요. 마지막으로, 쿠폰과 할인판매를 찾도록 하세요. 여러분들은 싼 거래를 인터넷에서 찾을 수 있습니다. 여러분들의 돈을 절약하는 쿠폰을 제공하는 스마트폰 앱도 있습니다. 다음에 여러분들이 쇼핑하러 가실 때 이러한 조언들을 명심하세요. 들어 주셔서 감사합니다.

어휘

keen ***a.*** 예리한, 날카로운 **necessities** ***n.*** 필수품 **review** ***n.*** 후기, 비평, 평론 **appliance** ***n.*** 기기 **be conscious of** ~을 자각하다, 알고 있다 **receipt** ***n.*** 영수증 **charge** ***v.*** 청구하다 **keep ~ in mind** ~을 명심하다

정답 16 ① 17 ③

문제풀이

16 남자는 더 현명한 쇼핑객이 되어 돈을 현명하게 사용하는 방법을 알려주고 있으므로 정답은 ① '보다 현명한 소비자가 되는 방법'이다.

17 남자는 쇼핑 리스트, 웹 사이트, 영수증, 스마트폰 앱에 대한 언급은 했지만 중고 거래에 관한 언급은 하지 않았으므로 정답은 ③ '중고 거래'이다.

오답 보기 해석

16

② 구매 후기를 찾을 수 있는 곳

③ 효과적인 쇼핑 리스트를 쓰는 방법

④ 더 의식 있는 쇼핑객이 되어야 하는 이유

⑤ 쇼핑할 때 쿠폰을 사용하는 것에 대한 이점

총 어휘 수 170

DICTATION ANSWERS

01 bake a pie for

02 I'm out of coins / How do you want it

03 follow your teacher's instructions / in an orderly fashion / how to protect yourself in the event of a tornado / be in attendance

04 We're not making a profit / We've been suffering ever / lower our prices / focus on what we offer / we offer a better variety

05 focusing on human expression / I asked her to pose for me / Would you mind standing

06 put a lot of work into it / the seating arrangement / seems a bit out of place / just doesn't fit

07 students are interested in reading / in my free time / some of my favorites

08 Your brother is starving / grab a quick bite / he's going to have to feed himself

09 place an order / that's a bit pricier

10 I've been looking into it / it'll be packed with tourists / the days are a bit longer

11 vulnerable to predators / conserve its energy

12 Are you interested in a particular model / we have a few of those in stock / this one drove the least / with the longer warranty

13 finish my report by tonight / list the site in your sources / cite sources

14 Do you mind if I give it a try / on the bottom of the device / you've been busy downloading

15 getting along with his teammates / hesitant to go at first / feels comfortable with his new team

16-17 between things you need and things you want / Make a list of necessities / research before making a purchase / make sure you were charged appropriately

07 수능영어듣기 실전모의고사

본문 p.44

01 ③	02 ④	03 ①	04 ⑤	05 ③	06 ⑤
07 ③	08 ②	09 ②	10 ②	11 ⑤	12 ⑤
13 ⑤	14 ③	15 ⑤	16 ②	17 ③	

01 짧은 대화의 응답

소재 트레이너 채용

듣기 대본 해석

남: 훈련 시설에서 일하기 시작했다는 말 사실이야?
여: 응. 이번 달 초에 시작했어.
남: 나 체육관에서 시간 보내는 거 좋아하는데. 다른 사람을 더 채용할 거래?
여: ③ 응. 트레이너 더 필요하대.

어휘

facility ***n.*** 시설, 기관 **hire** ***v.*** 고용하다

정답 ③

문제풀이

남자가 다른 사람을 채용할지를 물었으므로 적절한 대답은 ③ '응. 트레이너 더 필요하대.'이다.

오답 보기 해석

① 아니, 난 그 훈련 시설 안 좋아해.
② 고마워. 이 일이 진짜 필요했어.
④ 미안하지만 난 일자리가 필요 없어.
⑤ 알았어. 도와줄게.

총 어휘 수 38

02 짧은 대화의 응답

소재 우유에 대한 알레르기

듣기 대본 해석

여: 제 아들이 걱정돼요. 아침 식사 후에 갑자기 얼굴이 붉어졌어요.
남: 그렇군요. 어디 한 번 봅시다. *[잠시 후]* 그에게 무엇을 먹였나요?
여: 음, 그는 오늘 아침에 빵과 우유를 먹었어요.
남: ④ 당신의 아들은 우유 알레르기가 있을지도 몰라요.

어휘

turn red 얼굴이 붉게 변하다 **feed** ***v.*** ~에게 먹을 것을 주다
〈문제〉 **allergy** ***n.*** 알레르기

정답 ④

문제풀이

두 사람의 대화를 통해 두 사람은 의사와 아들을 데려온 엄마임을 알 수 있다. 엄마가 아이에게 빵과 우유를 먹였다고 했을 때 나올 수 있는 응답은 ④ '당신의 아들은 우유 알레르기가 있을지도 몰라요.'이다.

오답 보기 해석

① 그는 거의 2살이에요.
② 그의 가장 좋아하는 음식은 닭고기예요.
③ 아이들은 건강에 좋은 음식을 먹어야 해요.
⑤ 저의 아들을 돌봐주셔서 감사합니다.

총 어휘 수 42

03 담화 목적

소재 헌혈증 기증

듣기 대본 해석

여: 좋은 아침입니다, 여러분. 저는 교감인 Rebecca Smith입니다. 여러분 대부분이 학급 친구인 Helena Simson을 알고 있을 것이라 생각합니다. 그녀의 어머니가 위험성이 큰 수술을 앞두고 병원에 계십니다. 저는 방금 Helena의 담임 선생님으로부터 그녀의 어머니가 곧 수술하기로 되어 있다는 소식을 들었습니다. 저는 수술을 위해서 많은 양의 B형 혈액이 필요하다는 통지를 받았습니다. 이런 때에, 서로를 돕는 것은 우리에게 달려있다고 굳게 믿습니다. 그러니 만약 여러분 중 누구라도 Helena의 어머니에게 혈액을 기증하고 싶은 학생은 헌혈증을 제 사무실로 가져오기 바랍니다. 여러분의 피는 누군가의 목숨을 살릴 수도 있습니다. Helena와 그녀의 어머니를 대신해서 여러분의 따뜻한 도움에 감사드립니다.

어휘

vice principal 교감 **high-risk** ***a.*** 위험성이 큰 **surgery** ***n.*** 수술
on behalf of ~을 대신해서, ~을 대표하여

정답 ①

문제풀이

학급의 친구인 Helena의 어머니가 큰 수술을 앞두고 있는데 B형 혈액이 필요하니 헌혈증을 기증해 달라는 내용이므로 정답은 ①번이다.

총 어휘 수 123

04 의견

소재 새 휴대폰 구입

듣기 대본 해석

여: 아빠, 질문 하나 해도 되요?
남: 물론이지. 뭔데?
여: 제 휴대폰을 업그레이드하고 싶어요.
남: 네가 가지고 있는 휴대폰에 문제가 있니?
여: 그건 아닌데, 2년 동안 사용해서 새 것을 가지고 싶어서요.
남: Lizzy, 휴대폰에 문제가 없는데 왜 바꾸고 싶어하는 거지?
여: 그게 너무 오래 됐고 스마트폰도 아니잖아요.
남: 휴대폰의 가장 중요한 기능은 전화를 하는 것이라는 것을 알고 있잖아. 나는 사업가지만 스마트폰을 가지고 있지 않단다.
여: 제발요, 아빠. 요즘 휴대폰은 전화하는 것 이상이라는 것을 아시잖아요.
남: 내가 내 말을 잘 이해시키지 못했나 보다. 너는 단지 최신 유행이란 이유로 어떤 것을 필요하다고 느껴서는 안 되는 거야.
여: 네, 아빠. 제가 더 생각해 볼게요.

어휘

replace ***v.*** 바꾸다, 교체하다 **trend** ***n.*** 유행, 경향, 추세

정답 ⑤

문제풀이

휴대폰에 문제가 없는데 스마트폰으로 바꾸고 싶어하는 딸에게 아빠는 단지 최신 유행이라는 이유로 뭔가가 필요하다고 느껴서는 안 된다고 말해주고 있으므로 남자의 의견으로 가장 적절한 것은 ⑤ '맹목적으로 최신 유행을 쫓으려고 하지 마라.'이다.

총 어휘 수 138

05 장소 파악

소재 스케이트장에서의 대화

듣기 대본 해석

여: 내가 생각했던 것보다 더 재미있다.
남: 그렇지? 내가 어렸을 적에 매년 겨울에 스케이트 타러 갔었어.
여: 그런데 잠시 쉬면 안 될까? 너무 피곤해.
남: 알았어. 그럼 좀 앉아있자. 뭐 마실 것 좀 갖다 줄까?
여: 응. 소다음료가 좋을 것 같아. 근데 그 스케이트 신고 사러 가기 힘들지 않을까?
남: 아니, 카운터로 갈 필요 없어. 전화를 걸면 주문한 것을 갖다 줄 거야.
여: 잘됐다. 나 진짜 뭔가 마시고 싶거든.
남: 나도. 이렇게 땀이 많이 날 줄 몰랐어. 우리가 얼음 위에 있는 내내 추울 줄 알았어.
여: 그건 네가 안 쉬어서 그런 거잖아. 우리가 링크를 몇 번이나 돌았는지 알고 있니?
남: 미안해. 너무 재미있어서 쉬는 것을 까먹어서 그래.

어휘

order ***n.*** 주문 **sweat** ***v.*** 땀 흘리다 **lap** ***n.*** (경주 트랙의) 한 바퀴 **rink** ***n.*** 스케이트 링크

정답 ③

문제풀이

여자가 남자에게 스케이트를 신고 음료를 사러 가기 힘들지 않겠느냐고 물어봤고, 링크를 몇 바퀴나 돌았는지 물었으므로 장소는 ③ '아이스링크'이다.

총 어휘 수 156

06 그림의 세부 내용 파악

소재 연극 무대 디자인

듣기 대본 해석

남: Hannah, 이것이 네가 지난 학기에 공연했던 연극의 사진이지?
여: 맞아. 우리 그 공연에서 진짜 열심히 했었지.
남: 호랑이는 정말 진짜처럼 보여. 마치 토끼가 그의 친구 사슴을 붙잡고 있는 호랑이에게 놔달라고 빌고 있는 것 같은데?
여: 맞아. 호랑이와 토끼에 관한 이솝 우화야.
남: 세트가 정말 멋있어 보여.
여: 고마워. 연극부가 모두 모여서 그것을 전부 디자인했어. 배경에 바위들 보여? 내가 그것들을 칠했어.
남: 와! 잘했네. 오른편에 있는 저 나무도 진짜처럼 보여. 그것이 아프리카에 있는 것 같은 느낌을 주네.
여: 그래, 그게 우리가 원했던 거야.
남: 네가 의상도 디자인했어?
여: 아니. 의상은 Fat Panda's 의상샵에서 대여했어.
남: 그렇구나. 음, 이 연극에서 네가 정말 많이 애쓴 것 같아.

어휘

semester ***n.*** 학기 **performance** ***n.*** 공연 **beg** ***v.*** 애원하다 **costume** ***n.*** 의상

정답 ⑤

문제풀이

무대의 오른편에 나무가 있다고 했는데 꽃들이 있으므로 그림과 일치하지 않는 것은 ⑤번이다.

총 어휘 수 139

07 한 일

소재 보고서 철자 오류 수정

듣기 대본 해석

남: Sophie, 네가 냉전에 관한 보고서를 썼다고 들었어.
여: 응, 네가 너무 바빠서 날 도와줄 수 없었지.
남: 미안해. 그런데 내 보고서를 끝내서 오늘 시간이 생겼어.
여: 음, 이미 다 썼어!
남: 알아. 네가 데스크톱에 파일을 저장했길래 네가 학교에 있는 동안 내가 읽어봤어.
여: 오, 마음에 드니?
남: 응, 마음에 들어. 냉전의 환경적 문제에 관한 네 생각이 매우 흥미롭더라.
여: 고마워. 그 부분을 찾는 데 많은 시간을 들였거든.
남: 하지만 철자 오류가 조금 있어서 내가 수정했어.
여: 고마워.
남: 원한다면, 철자 검사 프로그램 사용법을 알려줄게.
여: 좋은 생각이야.

어휘

Cold War 냉전 **save** ***v.*** 저장하다 **correct** ***v.*** 정정하다, 바로잡다

정답 ③

문제풀이

남자는 여자를 위해 데스크톱에 저장되어 있던 보고서를 읽고 철자 오류를 수정해 주었으므로 남자가 여자를 위해 한 일은 ③ '보고서 철자 오류 수정해 주기'이다. 반면, ⑤ '철자 검사 프로그램 사용법 알려주기'는 한 일이 아니라 할 일이다.

총 어휘 수 125

08 이유

소재 제때 도착하지 않은 상품의 주문 취소하기

듣기 대본 해석

[전화벨이 울린다.]
남: 안녕하세요. Genie's 온라인 매장입니다.
여: 안녕하세요. 제가 지난주에 주문한 책 몇 권 때문에 연락 드렸습니다.
남: 네. 뭐가 문제입니까? 책에 손상이 있나요?
여: 아니요. 토요일까지 도착했어야 하는데 벌써 월요일이지만 아직 여기로 안 왔어요.
남: 그렇군요. 주문을 확인하겠습니다. 주문 번호 7자리를 불러주시겠어요?
여: 지금 주문 번호가 없어요. 제 이름은 Ella Hanley인데, 도움이 될까요?
남: 네. 확인하는 동안 조금만 기다려 주세요.
여: 알겠습니다.
남: *[키보드 치는 소리]* 죄송하지만 배송이 지연된 것 같습니다. 목요일까지는 도착할 겁니다.
여: 목요일이요? 그건 납득할 수 없네요. 수요일 수업 때 그 책들이 필요합니다.
남: 정말 죄송합니다.
여: 제 주문 취소해 주시겠어요? 동네 서점에서 살게요.

어휘

in regards to ~에 관해서 **damage** ***v.*** 훼손하다, 피해를 입히다 **digit** ***n.*** ~자리 숫자 **delay** ***v.*** 미루다, 연기하다 **unacceptable** ***a.*** 받아들일 수 없는 **cancel** ***v.*** 취소하다

정답 ②

문제풀이

여자는 지난주에 주문한 책이 도착하지 않자 전화를 걸어 확인한 결과 책이 필요한 수요일이 지나 목요일에 도착한다는 것을 알게 되었다. 따라서 여자가 주문을 취소하려는 이유는 ② '상품이 제때 도착하지 않아서'이다.

총 어휘 수 137

09 숫자

소재 진로 박람회 티켓 구입

듣기 대본 해석

[전화벨이 울린다.]

여: Henderson 고용 및 교육 사무실입니다. 도와드릴까요?

남: 안녕하세요. 제가 이번 달 말에 있는 진로 박람회에 관한 전단을 보았어요. 남은 표가 있는지 궁금해서요.

여: 네. 아직 표가 있습니다.

남: 좋네요. 저는 5장이 필요해요. 얼마인가요?

여: 미리 구매하신다면, 10달러입니다. 현장에서는 20달러입니다.

남: 알았어요. 단체 할인이 있나요?

여: 까먹을 뻔했네요. 저희는 단체 할인을 제공합니다. 5명에서 10명까지의 단체는 10퍼센트 할인을 받고 10장 이상의 표를 사시면 20퍼센트를 할인을 받으실 수 있습니다.

남: 너무 좋아요. 저는 10퍼센트 할인을 받을 수 있네요. 그럼 지금 살게요.

여: 문제 없어요. 신용카드나 직불카드가 지금 있으시면, 지금 당신의 정보를 좀 물을게요.

어휘

flyer ***n.*** 전단 **in advance** 미리 **at the door** 현장에서 **debit card** 직불카드 **handy** ***a.*** 유용한, 편리한, 사용하기 편한 곳에 있는

정답 ②

문제풀이

미리 구매하면 인당 10달러라고 했고 5장이 필요하다고 했으므로 50달러이다. 5명에서 10명까지는 10퍼센트 할인을 받는다고 했으므로 정답은 ② '$45'이다.

총 어휘 수 137

10 언급 유무

소재 보아뱀이 새끼를 낳는 방식

듣기 대본 해석

여: 안녕 Theo. 주말 잘 보냈어?

남: 응. 특별한 건 안 했어. 내가 관심 있게 여긴 파충류에 관한 짧은 다큐멘터리를 보긴 했어.

여: 정말? 파충류 어떤 점에 관한 건데?

남: 응. 너 파충류가 알을 낳는다는 건 알고 있었니?

여: 물론. 그런 건 상식이라고 생각했는데.

남: 그렇지. 하지만 뱀 중에서 몇몇 종은, 예를 들면 보아뱀 같은 건 살아있는 상태의 새끼를 낳아.

여: 말도 안 돼. 어떻게 그렇게 하지?

남: 뱃속에서 알을 품고 일단 부화하면 낳는 거지.

여: 믿을 수 없네. 보아뱀이 새끼를 몇 마리 낳아?

남: 6마리에서 39마리까지 새끼를 낳을 수 있어.

여: 믿을 수 없다. 전혀 몰랐어.

남: 사실이야. 보아 새끼들은 또한 태어난 지 10일 이내에 허물을 벗어.

여: 와, 동물들은 정말 놀랍다. 그렇지?

어휘

reptile ***n.*** 파충류 **common knowledge** 상식 **boa constrictor** 보아뱀 **incubate** ***v.*** (알을) 품다, 부화하다 **hatch** ***v.*** 부화하다 **shed** ***v.*** (옷을) 벗다, 없애다

정답 ②

문제풀이

보아뱀이 새끼 낳는 방법, 부화하는 장소, 낳는 새끼의 수, 새끼들의 허물 벗기에 대한 언급은 있지만 먹이에 대한 언급은 없으므로 정답은 ② '새끼의 먹이'이다.

총 어휘 수 127

11 내용 일치 · 불일치

소재 에펠탑 소개

듣기 대본 해석

여: 오늘은 에펠탑에 대해 말하겠습니다. 에펠탑은 세계에서 가장 잘 알려진 기념물 중 하나이지만, 원래 감시탑으로 지어졌다는 것을 아십니까? 그 탑의 건설은 1887년에 시작되었고 2년 후에 완성되었습니다. 에펠탑이 건설되는 동안, 그것은 세계에서 사람이 만든 가장 높은 구조물로 추정되는 워싱턴 기념비를 능가했습니다. 탑에는 관광객들이 이용할 수 있는 세 개의 층이 있고, 그것은 입장료를 받는 세계에서 가장 방문자가 많은 기념물입니다. 방문객들은 일층과 이층까지 계단이나 엘리베이터로 올라갈 수 있습니다. 첫 번째 층에서 두 번째 층으로 오르는 것처럼, 지상에서 첫 번째 층까지 300개가 넘는 계단이 있습니다. 마지막 층은 엘리베이터로만 대중들에게 입장 가능합니다.

어휘

recognized ***a.*** 알려진 **construction** ***n.*** 건설, 공사 **surpass** ***v.*** 능가하다, 뛰어넘다 **monument** ***n.*** 기념물 **assume** ***v.*** 추정하다 **access** ***v.*** 이용하다, 접근하다 **ascend** ***v.*** 올라가다 **accessible** ***a.*** 입장(이용) 가능한

정답 ⑤

문제풀이

에펠탑은 세 개의 층을 관광객이 이용할 수 있고 첫째 층과 둘째 층은 걷거나 엘리베이터를 이용할 수 있지만, 가장 위층은 엘리베이터로만 이용할 수 있다고 했으므로 정답은 ⑤ '가장 위층까지 관광객들이 걸어서 이용할 수 있다.'이다.

총 어휘 수 138

12 도표

소재 주말 휴가 예약

듣기 대본 해석

여: ABC여행사에 오신 것을 환영합니다. 오늘은 무엇을 도와드릴까요?

남: 안녕하세요. 저는 제 사업 파트너들과 저의 주말 휴가를 예약하고 싶어요.

여: 제가 도와드릴게요. 언제 여행을 가실 계획이에요?

남: 이번 달 마지막 주말에 가려고 해요.

여: 알겠어요. 해외로 여행하고 싶으세요, 미국 내에 머무르고 싶으세요?

남: 저는 이국적인 곳으로 가고 싶은데요. 미국 외 어딘가는 어떨까요?

여: 당신 패키지에 호텔을 포함시키고 싶으신가요?

남: 네, 그럼요. 가능하다면 일체의 경비가 포함되도록 하고 싶어요.

여: 물론이죠. 여기 좀 보세요. 1인당 단 850달러로 당신 조건을 만족시키는 목적지가 있어요.

남: 저희 비용 범위에서 좀 벗어나는군요. 저는 1인당 750달러 이상을 쓰지 않으려고 해요.

여: 그럼 하나의 선택만 남네요.

남: 저는 늘 거기 가길 원했어요. 4자리 예약해주세요.

어휘

getaway ***n.*** 휴가 **exotic** ***a.*** 외국의, 이국적인 **all-inclusive** ***a.*** 일체의 경비가 포함된 **destination** ***n.*** 목적지 **range** ***n.*** 범위

정답 ⑤

문제풀이

남자는 해외로 가길 원하므로 ③~⑤번이 남고, 호텔 등 일체의 경비가 포함된 여행을 원하므로 ④번과 ⑤번이 남는다. 둘 중 남자가 생각한 가격대에 맞는 것은 ⑤번이다.

총 어휘 수 148

13 긴 대화의 응답

소재 크게 음악을 틀어둔 버스 안

듣기 대본 해석

여: 안녕, Stan!

남: 안녕, Candace. 나는 네가 버스 타고 집에 가는 줄 몰랐어.

여: 음, 보통 운전해서 가는데, 이번 주에 나의 자동차가 정비소에 있어. 아무튼, 너도 집에 가는 길이야?

남: 오 아니 이건 우리 집에 가는 버스가 아니야. 나는 사실 쇼핑몰에 가고 있어.

여: 미안. 넘어지겠다고?

남: 아니. 나는 쇼핑몰에 가고 있다고 말했어. 아이를 위해 사고 싶은 새로운 장난감이 있거든.

여: 그렇구나. 그 쇼핑몰은 우리 집과 정말 가까워. 그래서 나는 거기를 매우 잘 알아.

남: Candace, 미안한데 잘 안 들려. 이 버스의 음악이 너무 시끄러워.

여: 그래. 나는 그들이 음악을 시끄럽게 켜 놓을 때가 너무 싫어. 내가 버스를 탈 때, 나는 단지 휴식을 취하고 하루에 대해 생각하기를 원해.

남: 왜 헤비메탈 음악을 틀어야 하지? 이건 최악이야.

여: ⑤ 동의해. 내가 가서 운전기사님에게 소리를 조금 낮추어 달라고 요청할게.

어휘

incredibly ***ad.*** 굉장히, 엄청나게 〈문제〉 **reflect** ***v.*** 깊이 생각하다, 반영하다 **in public** 사람들이 있는 데서

정답 ⑤

문제풀이

남자는 버스 내 음악이 너무 커서 여자의 말을 들을 수 없다고 했고, 최악이라고 얘기했으므로 이에 대한 여자의 응답으로 가장 적절한 것은 ⑤ '동의해. 내가 가서 운전기사님에게 소리를 조금 낮추어 달라고 요청할게.'이다.

오답 보기 해석

① 버스를 타는 것은 하루를 되돌아보는 데 아주 좋지.
② 나도 그렇게 생각해. 그는 더 안전한 것을 가지고 놀아야 해.
③ 맞아. 사람들이 있는 데서 크게 말하는 것은 예의가 아니야.
④ 좋네. 나 버스에서 음악 듣는 거 정말 좋아해.

총 어휘 수 159

14 긴 대화의 응답

소재 할로윈 파티 계획하기

듣기 대본 해석

여: 안녕 Andrew, 얘기 좀 하고 싶은데.

남: 물론, Grace. 무슨 일이야?

여: 할로윈 파티에 대한 거야. 준비는 다 한 거야?

남: 아직. 같이 계획하는 게 좋을 것 같아. 그렇게 생각하지 않니?

여: 응, 그게 좋을 것 같아. 나한테 몇몇 게임과 이벤트에 대한 생각이 있어.

남: 좋아. 작년에 부모님들이 사탕을 가져왔고 우리는 아이들과 의상 경연을 했지.

여: 그건 좀 평범한 것 같지 않아? 좀 더 특별한 걸 하는 게 어때? 예를 들면 유령의 집을 만드는 것처럼.

남: 네 말은 도서관을 이용해서 유령의 집을 만들고 싶다는 거야?

여: 정확해! "유령이 나오는 도서관 관광"이라고 부르면 되잖아. 아이들이 좋아할 것 같지 않아?

남: ③ 그거 좋은 생각이야. 아이들이 신나 할 거야.

어휘

arrangement ***n.*** 준비 **costume** ***n.*** 의상 **haunted** ***a.*** 유령이 나오는

정답 ③

문제풀이

두 사람은 할로윈 파티에 대해 계획하고 있는데 여자가 도서관을 유령의 집으로 만드는 것을 제안하고 있다. 이에 대한 남자의 응답으로 가장 적절한 것은 ③ '그거 좋은 생각이야. 아이들이 신나 할 거야.'이다.

오답 보기 해석

① 난 아이들이 그렇게 재미있어 하는 걸 본 적이 없어.
② 난 유령의 집 디자인을 꽤 잘해.
④ 문제 없어. 부모님들께 우리 계획을 알려드릴게.
⑤ 그거 좋은 계획이네. 아이들은 의상 경연을 좋아하잖아.

총 어휘 수 137

15 상황에 적절한 말

소재 숙제 제출 기한 연장

듣기 대본 해석

남: Aiden은 그의 고등학교 농구 팀의 주장인데, 그 때문에 방과 후에도 바쁩니다. 그는 또한 체스 동아리, 영화 동아리, 학생회 같은 학교에서의 다른 방과 후 활동에도 참여를 합니다. 그는 이런 활동들로 바쁘지 않은 얼마 안 되는 시간을 숙제와 시험공부에 사용합니다. Aiden은 Lincoln 선생님 수업의 중요한 과제를 위해 책을 읽어야 하는데, 내일 마감 전까지 끝내지 못할 것입니다. 그는 선생님께 과제 기간을 더 연장해 주실 수 있는지 물어보려고 합니다. 이러한 상황에서, Lincoln 선생님께 Aiden이 할 말로 가장 적절한 것은 무엇일까요?

Aiden: ⑤ 숙제의 제출기한을 연장해주실 수 있으세요?

어휘

take part in 참여하다 **extracurricular** ***a.*** 과외의 **assignment** ***n.*** 과제, 임무 **deadline** ***n.*** 기한, 마감시한 **extension** ***n.*** 연장, 확대 〈문제〉 **priority** ***n.*** 우선사항 **due date** 만기일 **postpone** ***v.*** 연기하다, 미루다

정답 ⑤

문제풀이

Aiden이 농구 팀 주장일과 여러 방과 후 활동으로 너무 바빠서 숙제를 마감 전까지 끝낼 수 없으므로 기한을 연장해 줄 수 있는지 물어야 하므로 ⑤ '숙제의 제출기한을 연장해주실 수 있으세요?'가 적절하다.

오답 보기 해석

① 우선사항을 다시 생각해 주셔야 합니다.
② 이 과제의 제출기한이 언제죠?
③ 회의를 더 뒤의 날짜로 다시 잡으실 수 있나요?
④ 이 책들을 이틀 더 가지고 있어도 될까요?

총 어휘 수 119

16 담화 목적 / 17 세부 내용 파악

소재 방콕의 주말 시장

듣기 대본 해석

여: 안녕하세요 학우 여러분. 저는 오늘 여러분께 태국의 수도인 방콕에 있는 아주 특별한 시장에 대해서 얘기드리고자 합니다. Chatuchak 시장은 세계에서 가장 큰 주말 시장입니다. 이 시장에는 27에이커에 걸쳐 있는 8,000개가 넘는 가판대가 있습니다. 400,000명이 넘는 사람들이 주말마다 이 시장을 방문합니다. 방문자들은 현지 태국 음식을 즐길 수 있고, 기념품을 사거나 빈티지 운동화도 사고, 새끼 다람쥐나 원숭이 같은 특이한 애완동물도 살 수 있습니다. 태국에서 유명하다는 저렴하면서도 고품질의 비단으로

만들어진 것 또한 살 수 있습니다. 그 비단은 태국 전통 의상에 쓰입니다. 비단 스카프, 담요, 그리고 넥타이도 살 수 있습니다. 시장의 어디에서 사느냐에 따라 비단 스카프를 4달러에서 40달러를 주고 살 수 있습니다. 그러나 비단만이 Chatuchak 시장에 있는 특별한 기념품이 아닙니다. 지갑도 살 수 있고, 무에타이 복싱 바지, 보석, 그리고 도자기도 살 수 있습니다. 이제 제가 지난 봄에 Chatuchak 시장을 방문했을 때 찍은 사진들을 보여드리겠습니다.

어휘

market ***n.*** 시장 **stall** ***n.*** 가판대 **souvenir** ***n.*** 기념품 **exotic** ***a.*** 이국적인 **specialty** ***n.*** 특징 **purse** ***n.*** 지갑 **ceramic** ***n.*** 도자기 〈문제〉 **popularity** ***n.*** 인기

정답 16 ② 17 ③

문제풀이

16 여자는 방콕에 있는 주말 시장 Chatuchak 시장의 규모, 방문자 수, 즐길거리, 쇼핑거리, 기념품 등을 말하고 있으므로 정답은 ② '방콕에 있는 Chatuchak 시장을 소개하려고'이다.

17 여자는 비단 제품의 우수한 품질, 용도, 제품 종류, 가격대에 대해 언급하였지만 가장 많이 사는 기념품이라고는 언급하지 않았으므로 정답은 ③ '가장 많이 사는 기념품이다.'이다

오답 보기 해석

16

① 태국 비단 옷을 추천하기 위해서

③ 태국의 여러 가지 기념품을 소개하기 위해서

④ 태국 문화에서 시장의 중요성을 설명하려고

⑤ Chatuchak 시장의 규모와 인기를 설명하려고

총 어휘 수 174

DICTATION ANSWERS

01 training facility / I enjoy spending time at the gym

02 take a look at him

03 have high-risk surgery / a large amount of type B blood is needed / bring your blood donor card to my office

04 the most important function / just because it's the latest trend

05 take a break / I could sweat this much / take a minute to rest

06 begging the tiger to release / design the costumes / you really put a lot of work

07 I've had some free time / You saved the file to the desktop / I corrected them for you

08 in regards to / I don't have my order number / shipping has been delayed / I need those books for class

09 if you had any tickets left / buy them in advance / we do offer group discounts / credit or debit card handy

10 catch a short documentary about reptiles / reptiles lay eggs / They actually incubate the eggs inside themselves / shed their skin

11 one of the world's most recognized monuments / tallest man-made structure / by stairs or by lift / only accessible to the public by lift

12 I'm looking to book a weekend getaway / include your hotel stay / That's a bit out of my price range

13 are you heading home / when they play loud music / relax and think about the day

14 made all of the arrangements / a little bit plain / to set up a haunted house

15 takes part in other extracurricular activities / before tomorrow's deadline / if he can get an extension on his assignment

16-17 the largest weekend market / is used in traditional Thai clothing / Depending on / silk isn't the only souvenir specialty

08 수능영어듣기 실전모의고사

본문 p.50

01 ①	02 ③	03 ⑤	04 ⑤	05 ④	06 ②
07 ④	08 ④	09 ②	10 ④	11 ②	12 ③
13 ⑤	14 ⑤	15 ③	16 ②	17 ①	

01 짧은 대화의 응답

소재 예약 확인

듣기 대본 해석

[전화벨이 울린다.]

남: Bird's Car Rental에 전화해 주셔서 감사합니다. 무엇을 도와드릴까요?

여: 네. 제가 온라인으로 한 예약을 확인하려고 전화드렸습니다.

남: 물론이죠. 예약 번호를 가지고 있나요?

여: ① 죄송하지만, 적어 두는 것을 잊었어요.

어휘

confirm ***v.*** ~을 확인하다 **reservation** ***n.*** 예약

정답 ①

문제풀이

여자는 예약을 확인하고 싶어서 전화를 걸었고 남자가 예약 번호를 알고 있는지 물었으므로 여자의 적절한 응답은 ① '죄송하지만, 적어 두는 것을 잊었어요.'이다.

오답 보기 해석

② 도와드릴 누군가를 바로 보낼게요.
③ 다음에 빌릴 때 10%를 할인 받을 수 있어요.
④ 당신이 스포츠카를 예약했다고 여기에 나와 있네요.
⑤ 제 예약을 미니밴으로 바꾸고 싶어요.

총 어휘 수 38

02 짧은 대화의 응답

소재 업무 중 식사

듣기 대본 해석

여: 이런! 시간 좀 봐요. 우리 먹으러 곧 가야 해요.

남: 잠시만요. 저는 일의 마지막 부분을 끝내고 싶어요.

여: 점심 먹고 할 수 있잖아요. 신선한 공기를 마시러 밖으로 나가요.

남: ③ 가세요. 저는 정말 오후 5시 전에 이것을 마쳐야만 해요.

어휘

〈문제〉 **look forward to** ~을 고대하다 **complete** ***v.*** 완료하다, 끝마치다

정답 ③

문제풀이

남자는 업무를 조금 더 해야 하는 상황이고 여자는 먹으러 나가자고 하고 있으므로 그 말에 대한 응답으로 ③ '가세요. 저는 정말 오후 5시 전에 이것을 마쳐야만 해요.'가 가장 적절하다.

오답 보기 해석

① 우리가 결정하기 전에 메뉴를 확인하는 게 어때요?
② 저는 이번 주말의 만남이 기대되지 않아요.
④ 저는 우리가 지난 번에 먹었던 모든 게 너무 좋았다고 생각했어요.
⑤ 좋은 저녁 식사 장소를 추천해 줄 수 있어요?

총 어휘 수 48

03 담화 주제

소재 피클과 건강

듣기 대본 해석

남: 여러분은 햄버거를 좋아하십니까? 햄버거와 같이 나오는 피클도 좋아하십니까? 여러분은 피클이 실제로 건강에 꽤 좋다는 것을 아십니까? 맞습니다. 피클은 맛도 좋을 뿐 아니라 지방과 칼로리도 낮습니다. 피클은 또한 상처 입은 후에 혈액을 진해지게 만들어서 몸의 회복을 돕는 비타민 K가 다량으로 함유되어 있습니다. 피클의 반만 먹어도 여러분이 하루에 필요한 비타민K의 17퍼센트가 공급됩니다. 그러나 피클의 나트륨 함량이 높기 때문에, 과도하게 먹으면 고혈압을 야기할 수도 있습니다. 피클 한 개를 다 먹으면 하루 나트륨 권장량의 절반 이상을 섭취하게 됩니다. 피클은 매일 즐기되 너무 많이 먹지 않도록 명심하십시오.

어휘

fat ***n.*** 지방 **recover** ***v.*** 회복되다 **injury** ***n.*** 부상 **thicken** ***v.*** (농도가) 진해지다 **requirement** ***n.*** 요구량 **in excess** 과도하게 **high blood pressure** 고혈압 **sodium** ***n.*** (화학) 나트륨 **fulfill** ***v.*** (의미, 약속 등을) 다하다, 수행하다 **recommendation** ***n.*** 권고(량), 추천

정답 ⑤

문제풀이

남자는 피클이 가지고 있는 영양분과 그것이 건강에 미치는 영향에 대해 설명하고 있으므로 정답은 ⑤ '피클의 섭취와 건강과의 관계'이다.

총 어휘 수 124

04 의견

소재 고장 난 컴퓨터 수리

듣기 대본 해석

여: 여보, 내 컴퓨터 이상해. 화면이 자꾸 깜박거려.

남: 흠... 그럼 이번 주말에 새 컴퓨터 사러 쇼핑 가자.

여: 새 것을 살 필요는 없을 것 같아. 이것도 꽤 새 거야.

남: 요즘에는 기술이 너무 빨리 발전해서 사람들은 거의 2년마다 컴퓨터를 바꿔.

여: 맞아. 근데 너무 낭비하는 것 같아. 화면만 바꾸면 되지 않을까?

남: 나도 그렇게 생각해. 근데 새 컴퓨터는 무척 얇고 빨라.

여: 당신 말이 맞는데, 근데 화면 외에는 이상한 게 없어. 아직 2년은 더 쓸 수 있을 것 같아.

남: 그래. 당신이 원한다면.

여: 우리 이걸 고치도록 해보자. 내가 그걸 수리점으로 가지고 갈게.

어휘

flicker ***v.*** 깜빡거리다 **replace** ***v.*** 교체하다 **sleek** ***a.*** 매끈한, (모양이) 날렵한

정답 ⑤

문제풀이

남자는 컴퓨터 화면이 깜빡거린다는 여자의 말에 컴퓨터를 새로 사자고 하지만 여자는 화면(모니터) 말고는 문제가 없다면서 버리지 말자고 한다. 이것으로 보아 여자의 의견은 ⑤ '컴퓨터의 일부만 교체하고 가급적 버리지 말아야 한다.'이다.

총 어휘 수 129

05 대화자의 관계 파악

소재 저널리스트가 되고 싶은 학생

듣기 대본 해석

남: 안녕하세요, Towns 선생님.
여: 안녕, Hugh. 우리가 지난주에 나눈 이야기에 대해 더 생각해 보았니?
남: 네. 결정을 내렸어요. 저널리스트가 되고 싶어요.
여: 저널리스트라고? 왜 그렇게 생각하니?
남: Voice News에서 많은 뉴스 클립들을 보아왔어요. 기자들의 일이 정말 흥미롭고 열정적인 것 같아요.
여: 그렇구나. 저널리스트가 되기 위해 어떤 종류의 기술들이 필요할 것 같니?
남: 자연스럽게 호기심도 많아야 하고 질문을 하거나 조사하는 것도 잘해야 할 것 같아요.
여: 그래. 내 생각에는 지역대학에 성공적인 저널리스트가 되기 위해 필요한 여러 기술들을 가르쳐주는 좋은 코스가 있을 것 같구나.
남: 정말이요?
여: 그래. 여러 좋은 점들을 들어왔어. 또한 네가 학교 신문부에 가입하는 게 좋을 것 같다. 너는 그곳에서 여러 과정에 대해 많이 배울 수 있을 거야.
남: 좋은 생각이네요. Towns 선생님, 조언해주셔서 감사합니다.
여: 언제든지 오렴, Hugh.

어휘

intense ***a.*** 열정적인, 강렬한, 극심한 **investigate** ***v.*** 조사하다

정답 ④

문제풀이

남자는 저널리스트가 되고 싶다면서 저널리스트가 되기 위한 조언을 구하고 있고, 여자는 도움이 될 만한 것들을 알려주고 있으므로 두 사람의 관계는 ④ '학생 – 진로 상담교사'임을 추측할 수 있다.

총 어휘 수 149

06 그림의 세부 내용 파악

소재 포토존

듣기 대본 해석

남: 이 줄은 다 뭐니, Dee?
여: 사람들이 같이 온 친구랑 사진을 찍기 위해 기다리고 있는 거야. 줄 서자.
남: 좋아. 하지만 이 포토존이 좀 촌스러운 것 같지 않니?
여: 응, 좀 유치하지? 우리 소파에 앉아야 하나? 난 서 있는 게 낫겠다.
남: 응. 그리고 원 모양 쿠션은 너무 누덕누덕하다. 오래 돼 보여.
여: 소파 옆에 큰 꽃 좀 봐.
남: 저거 해바라기인가? 우리 무도회 주제와는 정말 안 어울려.
여: 벽에는 별들도 있어. 같은 사진에 밤과 낮이 있는 것 같아. 뭘 생각한 거지?
남: 벽에 있는 포스터는 맘에 든다. 여기 고등학교에서 우리의 시간을 기념하고 있어.
여: 네 말이 맞는 것 같아.
남: 좋아. 우리 순서다. 웃어!

어휘

companion ***n.*** 동행, 친구, 짝 **cheesy** ***a.*** 질 낮은, 값싼, 촌스러운
ragged ***a.*** 누더기의, 다 찢어진 **prom** ***n.*** 무도회
commemorate ***v.*** 기념하다

정답 ②

문제풀이

남자가 소파에 원 모양의 쿠션이 있다고 했는데 그림에서는 하트 모양의 쿠션이 있으므로 정답은 ②번이다.

총 어휘 수 132

07 할 일

소재 커피 사다 주기

듣기 대본 해석

남: 안녕, Rachel! 점심 먹으러 갈 거야?
여: 그러고 싶지만 오늘은 너무 바빠. 너는 어때?
남: 응, 쉬는 시간이 있어서 뭐 좀 먹으러 가려고. 너 먹을 만한 음식을 좀 사올까?
여: 물어봐줘서 고맙지만 이 보고서를 작성하는 게 날 불안하게 해. 식욕이 전혀 없어.
남: 정말? 그거 참 안됐구나. 그럼 커피는 어때? 스타빈스 커피 좋아하니?
여: 응, 물론. 거기 바닐라 라떼 좋아해.
남: 좋아, 바닐라 라떼 하나로 하지. 30분 내로 돌아올게. 오, 어떤 사이즈가 좋을까?
여: 와, 넌 정말 친절해. Tall 사이즈가 좋겠어. 너무 고마워!
남: 괜찮아. 곧 돌아올게.

어휘

have a break 휴식을 취하다 **nervous** ***a.*** 초조해(불안해) 하는
appetite ***n.*** 식욕

정답 ④

문제풀이

남자가 너무 바빠 먹을 시간도 없고, 불안해서 식욕이 없다는 여자를 위해 커피를 사다 주겠다고 하였으므로 정답은 ④ '커피 사다 주기'이다.

총 어휘 수 134

08 이유

소재 친구에게 빌린 DVD

듣기 대본 해석

남: 안녕, Carrie. 무슨 일이니?
여: DeWitt 선생님 수업 때 발표할 내용을 검토하고 있어. 꽤나 스트레스 받네.
남: 이해해. 근데, 너 지난번 내가 빌려줬던 페루에 관한 DVD 갖고 왔니?
여: 어머나, 완전히 잊고 있었네. 정말 미안해 Conner. 내일 갖고 올게.
남: 뭐라고? 또 잊었다고? 내가 오늘 오후 내 발표를 위해 필요하다고 말했었잖아.
여: 미안해. 깜빡 잊었어. 오늘 아침에 내 남동생 수학 숙제를 도와주느라고 갖고 오는 걸 잊었어.
남: 네 설명이 문제를 해결해 주지는 못해, Carrie.
여: 정말 미안해. 점심시간에 집에 가서 갖다 줄게.
남: 알겠어. 점심시간 끝날 무렵 여기에서 기다릴게.
여: 응. 다시 한번 미안해. 이따 봐.

어휘

presentation ***n.*** 발표 **slip one's mind** (깜빡) 잊어 버리다

정답 ④

문제풀이

대화의 중간 부분에서 여자는 아침에 동생의 수학 숙제를 도와주느라 DVD 가져오는 것을 깜빡 잊었다고 했으므로 정답은 ④ '동생의 숙제를 도와주느라 잊어서'이다.

총 어휘 수 132

09 숫자

소재 아기 신발 교환

듣기 대본 해석

여: 실례합니다. 이 아기용 신발을 다른 것으로 교환하고 싶습니다.
남: 왜 교환하시려고요?
여: 실은, 친구가 이것을 이 매장에서 제 딸을 위해 사준 것인데, 한 달 전에 또 다른 사람으로부터 똑같은 신발을 받았습니다.
남: 오, 알겠습니다. 여기 다양한 종류의 신발이 있습니다. 마음에 드는 것이 보입니까?
여: 좀 보죠... 오, 이게 제 딸에게 잘 어울릴 것 같네요. 신발 옆의 리본이 아주 귀엽네요. 이건 얼마죠?
남: 60달러입니다.
여: 그러면, 교환 후에 제가 얼마를 더 지불해야 하죠?
남: 손님이 다시 가져오신 신발은 45달러였으므로 나머지만 지불하시면 됩니다.
여: 알겠습니다. 여기 제 신용카드입니다. 오, 우리 딸 머리띠도 하나 필요합니다. 하나 고르도록 도와주실래요?
남: 예, 물론이지요. 이것이 여기서 가장 잘 나가는 것들 중 하나입니다. 2달러밖에 안 합니다.
여: 좋아요. 그것도 살게요.

어휘

exchange ***v.*** 교환하다 **look good on** ~에게 어울리다

정답 ②

문제풀이

새로 사려고 하는 신발이 교환을 위해 가져간 신발보다 15달러가 비싸고, 2달러짜리 머리띠를 산다고 했으므로 여자가 지불할 금액은 ② '$17'이다.

총 어휘 수 155

10 언급 유무

소재 최신 훈련 시설

듣기 대본 해석

여: 저희 시설에 오신 것을 환영합니다, Fecc 박사님.
남: 안녕하세요, Johnson 씨. 당신을 드디어 만나게 되어서 좋습니다. 이 훈련 시설은 믿을 수가 없군요.
여: 저희 팀의 시설이 매우 자랑스러워요. 일 얘기를 시작하기 전에 둘러 보시겠어요?
남: 둘러보고 싶군요. 고마워요. 그런데, 지난 시즌 리그에서 EPL이 이 시설을 최고로 뽑았다고 들었어요.
여: 사실이에요. 세계적으로 유명한 트레이너인 Pete Parker가 설계했어요.
남: 네, 그에 대해 들은 적 있어요. 완성하는 데 오래 걸렸나요?
여: 2년 정도밖에 안 걸렸어요. 저희는 지난 봄에 여기서 훈련을 시작할 수 있었어요.
남: 여기에 어떤 종류의 편의시설이 있죠?
여: 음, 어디부터 시작할까요? 올림픽 사이즈의 수영장, 테니스 코트, 사우나, 한증실, 여러 가지가 계속 있답니다.
남: 놀라워요. 오... 여기에 레스토랑도 있군요. 이 장소는 정말로 믿을 수 없군요.

어휘

facility ***n.*** 시설, 기관 **renowned** ***a.*** 유명한 **amenities** ***n.*** 편의시설 **steam room** 한증실 **incredible** ***a.*** 믿을 수 없는

정답 ④

문제풀이

설계자(Pete Parker)와 건축 기간(about two years), 완공 시기(last spring), 포함된 내부 시설(an Olympic-sized swimming pool, a tennis court, a sauna, a steam room)은 언급되었지만 ④ '건축 비용'에 대한 언급은 없다.

총 어휘 수 149

11 내용 일치 · 불일치

소재 EcoBag 홍보

듣기 대본 해석

남: 오늘 아침, 저는 환경을 위한 위대한 새 발명품에 대해 말하겠습니다. 그것은 EcoBag이라 불립니다. 여러분께서 추측하시듯이, 그것은 환경 친화적인 가방입니다. 교수의 딸인 Amanda Stevens은 전 세계 학교에 사회적 인식을 불러일으키고자 이 위대한 가방을 만들었습니다. EcoBag은 전체가 재활용된 플라스틱으로 만들어졌습니다. 심지어 지퍼조차 이런 방식으로 만들어졌습니다. 가방의 끈과 손잡이는 재활용된 천과 플라스틱을 혼합하여 만들어져서 튼튼할 뿐만 아니라 편안하고 가볍습니다. 여러분이나 여러분의 자녀가 그것에 맞지 않게 자랐을 때, 그것은 재활용될 수 있습니다. 더 나아가 만약에 여러분이 온라인으로 그것을 구매하면, 회사는 어려움에 처한 학생에게 가방을 하나 기부할 것입니다. 보시다시피, EcoBag은 환경과 어려운 사람들을 도움으로써 여러분의 역할을 할 수 있는 훌륭한 방법입니다.

어휘

invention ***n.*** 발명 **awareness** ***n.*** 의식 **entirely** ***ad.*** 완전히, 전부
blend ***n.*** 혼합 ***v.*** 섞다, 혼합하다 **lightweight** ***a.*** 가벼운
outgrow ***v.*** ~보다 더 커지다, (옷 등에 비해 사람이) 자라서 맞지 않게 되다
purchase ***v.*** 구매하다 **the needy** 어려운 사람들

정답 ②

문제풀이

가방의 모든 부분을 재활용 플라스틱으로 만들었다고 강조하면서 지퍼까지도 그러한 방식으로 만들었다고 했으므로 내용과 일치하지 않는 것은 ② '지퍼를 제외한 가방 전체가 재활용된 플라스틱으로 만들어졌다.'이다.

총 어휘 수 135

12 도표

소재 동물들을 돕는 기부 프로그램 선택

듣기 대본 해석

남: 여보, 뭐 보고 있어?
여: Guardian's 자선단체에 대한 안내 책자야. 동물들을 돕기 위한 기부를 받는대.
남: 그래. 좋은 프로그램이네. 기부할 생각인 거야?
여: 글쎄, 당신은 어떻게 생각해? 동물 도와주는 거 좋아하지?
남: 당연하지. 작년에 지역 동물 보호소에 일회적으로 기부했었던 것 기억나? 올해는 다른 것을 해보자.
여: 그래. 최근에 나는 야생 동물 보호구역과 어떻게 이 보호구역들이 학대 당하고 다친 동물들을 자연 서식지로 돌려보내는지에 관한 기사를 읽었어.
남: 흥미롭네. 동물 보호구역에 매월 기부를 하는 게 좋을 것 같아.
여: 좋은 생각이야. 달마다 기부를 하는 게 더 비용이 알맞고 뜻깊어. 얼마를 기부할까?
남: 10달러 이상인 건 무리야.
여: 알겠어. 그럼 이 선택이 제일 좋겠다.

어휘

brochure ***n.*** 책자 **charity** ***n.*** 자선단체 **abused** ***a.*** 학대당한 **injured** ***a.*** 다친, 부상을 입은 **habitat** ***n.*** 서식지 **sanctuary** ***n.*** 보호구역

정답 ③

문제풀이

올해는 야생 동물 보호구역에 기부를 하자고 했으므로 ③~⑤중에 고르면 되고, 매월 하자고 했으므로 ③번과 ④번이 남게 된다. 한 달에 10달러 이상은 무리라고 했으므로 정답은 ③번이다.

총 어휘 수 146

13 긴 대화의 응답

소재 팬이 직접 마스코트를 정하는 이벤트

듣기 대본 해석

여: 야, 좋은 소식 있어! 우리 팀 사이트에서 재미있는 이벤트를 하고 있어.
남: 진짜? 뭔데?
여: 사람들이 "여러분의 마스코트를 선택하세요"라고 부르는 이벤트인데 다음 경기에서 할 거래.
남: 잘 이해가 안 가. 무슨 마스코트를 쓸지 팬들이 정할 수 있게 해준다는 거야?
여: 그렇지. 팬들이 팀의 마스코트가 뭐가 될지 고를 수 있다는 거야.
남: 그리고 그 마스코트는 팬들이 투표해서 고르는 그 어떤 것도 된단 말이야?
여: 응. 팬들이 투표해서 고르는 그 어떤 것이든 말이야.
남: 특별하네. 이벤트에 누구든 참여할 수 있는 거야?
여: 아니. 다음 경기를 보러 오는 팬들만 참여할 수 있대.
남: 재미있네. 나도 다음 마스코트 정하는 것에 참여하고 싶어.
여: 그럼 토요일에 하는 경기 표를 구해야 될 거야.
남: ⑤ 알았어. 지금 하나 살 거야.

어휘

mascot ***n.*** 마스코트 **vote** ***n.*** 투표 ***v.*** 투표하다 **participate** ***v.*** 참여하다 **attend** ***v.*** 참석하다

정답 ⑤

문제풀이

여자는 남자가 마스코트 정하는 이벤트에 참여하려면 토요일에 있을 다음 경기를 봐야 한다고 하였다. 이에 대한 남자의 응답으로 가장 적절한 것은 ⑤ '알았어. 지금 하나 살 거야.'이다.

오답 보기 해석

① 미안하지만 팬들만 투표할 수 있어.
② 이것들이 우리가 고를 수 있는 마스코트들이야.
③ 아니. 넌 이벤트에 참가할 수 없어.
④ 이벤트에 참여하려면 빨리 신청해야 돼.

총 어휘 수 132

14 긴 대화의 응답

소재 토론팀에서의 활동

듣기 대본 해석

남: 우리 견학 계획 바뀐 것 들었어?
여: 아니. 아무것도 못 들었는데.
남: 응. 금요일에 비가 와서 놀이공원에 가지 못하거든. 대신 과학 박물관에 갈 거야.
여: 아쉽네. 하지만 넌 좋겠다. 너 지난주에 가족하고 놀이공원에 간 거 맞지?
남: 응. 그리고 나는 과학 박물관이 열었을 때부터 정말 가고 싶었거든. 우리 과학동아리 구성원들에게 좋은 경험이 될 거야.
여: 음. 사실 난 이번 주 금요일에 견학을 못 가.
남: 정말? 왜 못 가는데?
여: 토론팀에서 해야 할 일이 있거든.
남: 정말? 금요일에 토론이 있는 줄은 몰랐어.
여: 그건 아닌데 다음 주 토론을 준비해야 하거든.
남: 알겠어. 넌 정말 팀에 헌신적이구나.
여: ⑤ 팀의 구성원이 되려면 열심히 해야 돼.

어휘

be supposed to V ~하기로 되어 있다 **amusement park** 놀이공원 **obligation** ***n.*** 의무, 해야 할 일 **dedicated** ***a.*** 전념하는, 헌신적인

정답 ⑤

문제풀이

토론 준비로 견학을 못 가는 여자에게 남자가 팀에 헌신적이라고 말했으므로 이에 대한 여자의 응답으로 가장 적절한 것은 ⑤ '팀의 구성원이 되려면 열심히 해야 돼.'이다.

오답 보기 해석

① 과학 박물관에서 기념품 사다 줄게.
② 이 견학을 정말 기다려 왔어.
③ 나는 과학 박물관이 열었을 때 방문했어.
④ 토론팀은 금요일에 겨뤄야 해.

총 어휘 수 160

15 상황에 적절한 말

소재 날씨에 대한 걱정으로 밖에서 뛰는 것 미루기

듣기 대본 해석

여: Bill이 그의 친구 Martin으로부터 전화를 받았을 때 그는 집에서 TV를 보고 있습니다. 그 두 친구는 보통 때 꽤 활동적이지만 날씨가 좋지 않아서 몇 주 동안 같이 놀지 못했습니다. 오늘 저녁 Martin은 뛰러 나가자고 제안합니다. Bill은 정말 뛰러 나가고 싶고 밖에서 운동하고 싶지만 그는 여전히 날씨에 대해 걱정하고 있습니다. 지난 여름, 그는 도시에서 꽤 멀리 자전거를 타러 나갔고 강한 뇌우를 만났습니다. 그 나쁜 기억 때문에, 그는 Martin의 제안을 거절하기로 결정합니다. 이런 상황에서 Bill이 Martin에게 할 말로 가장 적절한 것은 무엇일까요?
Bill: Martin, ③ 비가 오지 않을 것이 확실할 때 뛰러 가자.

어휘

catch ***v.*** (폭풍우 등이) 엄습하다, 급습하다 **thunderstorm** ***n.*** 뇌우 **decline** ***v.*** 거절하다

정답 ③

문제풀이

Bill은 작년 여름에 멀리 나가서 자전거를 타다가 강한 뇌우를 만났던 나쁜 기억 때문에 밖에서 뛰어 놀자는 Martin의 제안을 거절하기로 한다. 따라서 Bill이 Martin에게 할 말은 ③ '비가 오지 않을 것이 확실할 때 뛰러 가자.'이다.

오답 보기 해석

① 네가 길을 안내하면 내가 너를 따라갈게.
② 비가 올지 안 올지 나는 언제든 알 수 있어.
④ 운동 장비를 사용한 후 항상 잘 말려야 돼.
⑤ 안 좋은 날씨에 자전거를 탈 때는 항상 주의해.

총 어휘 수 123

16 담화 목적 / 17 세부 내용 파악

소재 목적에 맞게 고친 제품

듣기 대본 해석

남: 모든 사람들은 다른 목적에 맞게 고친 제품을 사용하는 것이 환경에 좋다고 알고 있지만 새로운 것을 사는 것만큼이나 품질이 좋을까요? 당신이 Greenbacks로부터 구매할 때, 그 대답은 항상 "네."입니다. 우리는 버려진 물건들을 수집하고 그것들을 흥미롭고 품질이 높은 새로운 물건으로 다른 용도에 맞게 만듭니다. 또한 가격도 매우 합리적입니다. 우리의 상품 목록에는 100달러가 넘는 것이 없습니다. 우리는 버려진 상업 나무로 만든 가구, 낡은 옷으로 만든 전등 갓, 오래된 사다리로 만든 책장을 팝니다. 만약에 봄에 새로운 화분이 필요하다면, 다른 곳 말고 Greenbacks를 찾으세요. 우리는 상자, 부츠, 항아리 같은 많은 것들을 당신의 정원에 멋지고 새로운 모습을 선사하기 위해서 재정비했습니다. 우리의 물품 모두가 독특해서 구매를 하시면 멋진 화제거리가 될 것입니다. 목적에 맞게 바꾸기 운동의 다른 많은 것들에 참여하기 위해서는 우리의 홈페이지 www.greenbacksrepurpose.com을 확인해 주세요. Greenbacks와 함께 현명하고 세련된 삶을 시작하세요.

어휘

repurpose ***v.*** 다른 목적에 맞게 만들다(바꾸다) **discarded** ***a.*** 버려진
reasonable ***a.*** 합리적인, 비싸지 않은 **inventory** ***n.*** 재고품, 상품 목록
lamp shade 전등 따위의 갓 **planter** ***n.*** (분재용) 장식 용기, 화분
crate ***n.*** 상자 **conversation piece** 화제거리

정답 16 ② 17 ①

문제풀이

16 폐품을 이용해서 목적에 맞게 고친 제품을 파는 회사를 홍보하는 내용이므로 정답은 ② '재활용 제품을 판매하는 회사를 홍보하려고'이다.

17 가구, 전등갓, 책장, 화분에 대한 언급은 있었지만 액자에 대한 언급은 하지 않았으므로 정답은 ① '액자'이다.

오답 보기 해석

17

② 가구 ③ 전등갓 ④ 책장 ⑤ 화분

총 어휘 수 150

DICTATION ANSWERS

01 confirm a reservation

02 Let's get outside

03 helps your body recover after injury / if eaten in excess / cause high blood pressure

04 The screen keeps flickering / every two years / new computers are so sleek and fast / there's nothing wrong with this one / take it to

05 made a decision / interesting and intense / be good at asking questions / join the school newspaper

06 is a little cheesy / the circle-shaped pillow is so ragged / commemorates our time here

07 going to go out for lunch / pick something up for you / I don't really have an appetite / that is so nice of you

08 going over my presentation / slipped my mind / doesn't solve my problem

09 look good on her / pay the rest / Would you help me choose one / This is one of our best sellers

10 designed by world-renowned trainer / What kinds of amenities are in / and the list goes on and on

11 made entirely out of recycled plastic / When you or your child outgrows it / purchase one online

12 made a one-time donation / abused and injured animals / monthly donation to a sanctuary

13 it's taking place / Fans will be allowed to choose / whatever mascot the fans vote on / that attend the next game

14 go to the amusement park / This will be a great experience for / I have an obligation / dedicated to your team

15 receives a call / suggests they go for a run / head out for a run / he was caught in a strong thunderstorm / decline Martin's offer

16-17 using repurposed products / repurpose them into new items / look no further than / Start living smart and stylish

09 수능영어듣기 실전모의고사

본문 p.56

01 ③	02 ③	03 ①	04 ④	05 ⑤	06 ⑤
07 ③	08 ④	09 ⑤	10 ②	11 ③	12 ③
13 ⑤	14 ①	15 ⑤	16 ③	17 ④	

01 짧은 대화의 응답

소재 스마트 워치 반품

듣기 대본 해석

남: 안녕하세요. 이 스마트 워치 반품하고 싶어요.
여: 알겠습니다. 언제 구매하셨죠?
남: 영수증 확인해 볼게요. *[잠시 후]* 한 달이 좀 넘은 것 같네요.
여: ③ 죄송합니다만 30일 이후로는 반품을 받지 않습니다.

어휘

purchase ***v.*** 구입하다 **receipt** ***n.*** 영수증 〈문제〉 **final** ***a.*** 변경할 수 없는, 최종적인 **refund** ***n.*** 환불

정답 ③

문제풀이

반품을 원하는 남자가 영수증 확인 후 한 달이 넘은 것 같다고 말하고 있으므로 그에 적절한 응답은 ③ '죄송합니다만 30일 이후로는 반품을 받지 않습니다.'이다.

오답 보기 해석

① 죄송하지만, 저희 매장에 있는 모든 제품은 반품이 안됩니다.
② 다음 주에 액정을 고칠 수 있을 겁니다.
④ 환불을 원하시면 영수증이 필요할 겁니다.
⑤ 이 제품에 문제가 많았어요.

총 어휘 수 42

02 짧은 대화의 응답

소재 비행기 도착 예정 시간

듣기 대본 해석

여: 실례합니다. 시애틀에는 언제 착륙하죠?
남: 저녁 7시쯤에 시애틀에 도착할 예정입니다.
여: 알겠습니다. 그럼 예정보다 약간 늦어지는 거군요.
남: ③ 네. 불편을 드려서 정말 죄송합니다.

어휘

behind schedule 예정보다 늦게 〈문제〉 **inconvenience** ***n.*** 불편

정답 ③

문제풀이

여자가 시애틀에 언제 도착하는지 묻고 남자는 예상 시간을 답해주는 것으로 보아 승객과 승무원의 대화임을 알 수 있다. 예정보다 늦어지는 거냐고 확인하는 여자의 말에 적절한 남자의 응답은 ③ '네. 불편을 드려서 정말 죄송합니다.'이다.

오답 보기 해석

① 문제없습니다. 저희는 금방 떠날 겁니다.
② 좋습니다. 정말 즐거운 비행이었습니다.
④ 맞습니다. 우린 공항에 정시에 도착할 겁니다.
⑤ 불편하게 해 드려서 죄송합니다. 금방 물을 가져다 드리겠습니다.

총 어휘 수 36

03 담화 목적

소재 체육관 보수공사로 인한 이용 통제

듣기 대본 해석

[벨이 울린다.]

여: 안녕하세요, 여러분. 주목해 주시겠습니까? 저는 교장인 Jones입니다. 날씨로부터 받은 피해로, 학교의 체육관이 앞으로 3주간 공사 때문에 문을 닫을 것입니다. 학생들은 체육관이 공사 중인 기간에 체육관을 이용할 수 없습니다. 이번 폐쇄로 인한 문제에 대해 사과드립니다만 이는 학생들의 안전을 위한 것입니다. 저는 보수된 체육관이 2월 22일 다시 문을 열었을 때 더 안전하고 훨씬 멋있을 거라고 여러분께 장담합니다. 체육관에서 실시하기로 계획되었던 모든 활동들은 길 아래 커뮤니티 센터로 옮겨갈 것입니다. 변경된 일정은 웹사이트에서 확인할 수 있습니다. 상황을 이해해줘서 고맙습니다.

어휘

principal ***n.*** 교장 ***a.*** 주요한 **damage** ***n.*** 피해, 훼손 **under construction** 공사 중 **apologize** ***v.*** 사과하다 **assure** ***v.*** 장담하다 **renovated** ***a.*** 개조된 **revised** ***a.*** 변경된

정답 ①

문제풀이

여자는 학생들에게 체육관 보수공사가 있어서 당분간 폐쇄된다는 것을 알리며 앞으로 3주간 체육관을 이용할 수 없다고 하였으므로, 정답은 ① '보수공사로 인한 이용 통제를 공지하려고'이다.

총 어휘 수 118

04 대화 주제

소재 음악 들으며 조깅하는 것의 위험성

듣기 대본 해석

여: 여보, 나 시내를 달릴 거예요.
남: 알겠어요. 근데 헤드폰을 가지고 가네요. 달리는 동안에 음악을 들을 거예요?
여: 물론이죠. 막 새로운 Maroon 5 앨범을 구했거든요. 이 앨범을 들어보길 기대하고 있어요.
남: 달리는 동안에 음악을 듣지 않는 게 좋겠어요.
여: 왜 안 돼요? 뛰는 것은 지루해요. 음악을 들으면 좀 더 견딜 만해요.
남: 헤드폰을 쓰면 지나가는 차량의 소리를 못 들을 거예요. 그건 매우 위험해요.
여: 흠... 그런 생각을 전혀 못했어요.
남: 네. 밖에 있을 때 주위 환경에 대해서 주의하는 것이 중요해요. 난 당신이 다치기를 원치 않아요.
여: 알았어요. 집에 왔을 때 이 앨범을 들어야겠어요.
남: 여보, 난 그저 당신이 조심하기를 바라요.

어휘

look forward to ~을 학수고대하다 **bearable** ***a.*** 견딜 수 있는 **be aware of** ~을 알아 차리다, ~을 알다

정답 ④

문제풀이

여자가 시내를 달리러 나가는데 헤드폰을 가지고 나가자 남자는 달릴 때 음악을 들으면 자동차 소리를 못 듣기 때문에 위험하다고 말해주고 있으므로 두 사람이 하는 말의 주제는 ④ '헤드폰 끼고 음악 들으며 뛰는 것의 위험성'이다.

총 어휘 수 130

05 대화자의 관계 파악

소재 뉴스 보도 방식

듣기 대본 해석

여: 안녕하세요, Sam. 손에 들고 있는 게 뭐예요?
남: 안녕, Erica. 사실 이건 우리가 최근에 받은 항의 편지들이에요.
여: 정말이요?
남: 네. 확실히 몇몇의 시청자들은 우리의 뉴스 내용을 좋아하지 않아요.
여: Sam, 당신은 지역 뉴스를 좀 더 가볍게 만들고 싶어하던 사람이잖아요.
남: 나도 알고 있지만, 우리가 시청자들을 실망시킨다면 그것은 소용이 없는 것 같아요.
여: 그럼 저는 더 진지한 뉴스를 보도하기 시작해야 하나요?
남: 그럴 것 같아요. 우리 회의를 소집해서 이 문제를 토론해보면 어떨까요?
여: 좋은 생각이에요. 저는 어떻게 해야 하죠?
남: 모든 스텝들에게 연락해서 점심 식사 후 회의실에서 모두 만나게 해줄래요?
여: 네, 알았어요. 그렇지만 저는 우리가 뉴스를 진행하고 있었던 방식이 정말 좋았다고 말하고 싶네요.
남: 네, 저도 그래요. 회의 때 모두 이야기해 봅시다.

어휘

audience ***n.*** 시청자, 청중 **light-hearted** ***a.*** 편안한 마음으로, 마음이 가벼운 **disappoint** ***v.*** 실망시키다 **serious** ***a.*** 진지한 **boardroom** ***n.*** 회의실

정답 ⑤

문제풀이

여자가 진지한 뉴스를 보도해야 하는지 물은 점이나 진행하고 있었던 방식이 좋았다고 말하는 것에서 여자는 뉴스 진행자임을 알 수 있고, 남자는 뉴스 보도를 위해 지시하고 회의를 소집하는 것으로 보아 프로듀서임을 알 수 있다. 그러므로 정답은 ⑤ '뉴스 진행자 — 프로듀서'이다.

총 어휘 수 138

06 그림의 세부 내용 파악

소재 누군가가 침입했던 방

듣기 대본 해석

여: 오, 이런! 너 아파트에 무슨 일이 있었니, Alvin?
남: 와! 누가 침입해서 집을 망가뜨려 놓은 것 같네.
여: 응. 여기 있던 사람이 너의 거울을 깨뜨렸네.
남: 내 테이블도 부서졌어. 끔찍하다.
여: 테이블 옆에 방망이가 있네. 아마도 그걸 사용해서 다 부쉈나 봐.
남: 그런 것 같아. 이런 적이 없었는데. 왜 누군가가 나한테 이런 일을 했을까?
여: 적어도 나무는 손상되지 않았는데.
남: 가져간 것은 없는 것 같아. 일단 없어진 건 없는 것 같은데. 책은 바닥에 내가 놓은 그대로 있어.
여: 그들이 어떻게 들어왔는지 궁금해.
남: 아마도 열려있는 창문으로 기어들어 왔을 거야.
여: 그랬을 수도 있겠다. 문을 사용한 것처럼 보이지는 않아.

어휘

destroy ***v.*** 파괴하다, 부수다 **crawl** ***v.*** (엎드려) 기다

정답 ⑤

문제풀이

대화의 마지막 부분에서 남자가 침입자는 열려 있는 창문으로 들어왔을 거라고 했는데 창문이 닫혀 있으므로 그림과 일치하지 않는 것은 ⑤번이다.

총 어휘 수 122

07 부탁한 일

소재 동아리 지도교사 섭외

듣기 대본 해석

여: 안녕, Daryl. 내가 뭐 도와줄까?
남: 네, Peterson 선생님, 선생님께 여쭤보고 싶은 게 있어요.
여: 그럼, 알다시피 어떤 것이든 물어봐도 좋아.
남: 몇몇 친구들과 저는 영화 만드는 데 정말 관심이 많고 우리가 영화 동아리를 시작한다면 어떨지 알고 싶어요.
여: 음, 내 생각에는 일단 너희들이 Stevenson 선생님과 이야기를 해야 할 것 같구나. 그는 동아리 활동을 담당하는 선생님이니까.
남: 네, 제가 Stevenson 선생님께 말씀드렸어요. Stevenson 선생님은 저희를 지도해 주실 선생님이 필요하다고 말씀하셨어요.
여: 그래, 그래서 너희가 생각하고 있는 사람은 누구니?
남: 저희는 선생님께서 비디오 제작에 계셨던 걸로 알고 있어요.
여: 오, 그걸 알고 있었니? 그래서 너희는 내가 너희 동아리를 지도해 주기를 원하는 거니?
남: 그러면 정말 좋을 것 같아요. 해주실 수 있으세요?
여: 물론 할 수 있지. 사실 아주 재미있을 것 같구나.
남: 정말 감사합니다, Peterson 선생님!

어휘

in charge of ~을 맡고 있는, 담당해서 **supervise** ***v.*** 지도하다, 감독하다

정답 ③

문제풀이

학생인 남자는 새로운 영화 동아리를 만들려 하는데 교사인 여자에게 그 동아리의 지도를 부탁하고 있다. 그러므로 남자의 부탁으로 가장 적절한 것은 ③ '새 동아리를 지도하는 것'이다.

오답 보기 해석

① Stevenson 선생님께 말하는 것
② 그녀의 강의에 등록하는 것
④ 그의 새로운 영화에 참여하는 것
⑤ 그에게 카메라 사용법을 보여주는 것

총 어휘 수 135

08 이유

소재 스페인어 시간에 있을 연설에 대한 걱정

듣기 대본 해석

남: 엄마, 커피 남은 게 있나요?
여: 있는 것 같은데. 왜 그러니?
남: 한 잔 마시고 싶어서요.
여: 커피를 마시기에는 너무 늦은 것 같은데. 커피에는 카페인이 많이 들어 있어서 마시면 잠잘 시간이 지나서도 잠이 오지 않을 거야.
남: 에너지가 좀 필요한 것 같아서요.
여: 왜 늦게까지 깨어있어야 하니?
남: 내일 스페인어 수업시간에 연설을 해야 해서 연습하고 싶어서요.
여: 지난주 내내 네 방에서 그것을 연습하는 것을 들었는데.
남: 네, 사실 지난 주부터 계속 연습했어요.
여: 그럼 이제 준비가 됐어야지.
남: 음, 제가 실수를 해서 모두가 절 비웃을까 봐 두려워요.
여: 그렇구나. 내 생각에는 네가 걱정할 필요가 없을 것 같구나. 만약 실수를 해서 모두가 웃는다면 그냥 같이 웃어 버리렴.
남: 네. 조언 감사해요 엄마.
여: 언제든. 자 이제 잘 준비를 하렴.

어휘
give a speech 연설하다 **make a mistake** 실수하다

정답 ④

문제풀이
여자가 왜 늦게까지 깨어있어야 하는지 물었을 때 남자는 스페인어 수업시간에 해야 할 연설을 연습하고 싶다고 했으므로 정답은 ④ '내일 할 연설을 연습하고 싶어서'이다.

총 어휘 수 149

09 숫자

소재 과학 센터 표 구매

듣기 대본 해석
남: Chester 과학 센터에 오신 것을 환영합니다. 어떻게 도와드릴까요?
여: 안녕하세요. 어른 두 명, 아이 한 명의 티켓이 필요해요.
남: 네. 어른은 30달러, 아이는 20달러예요.
여: 좋아요. 이 표로 박물관에 있는 모든 것을 이용할 수 있나요?
남: 음, 표는 직접 해보는 과학 쇼와 수족관을 포함해서 모든 쇼와 주요 명소를 포함하고 있어요.
여: 멋지네요. 천체 투영관은요? 그것도 표 가격에 포함되어 있나요?
남: 아니요. 하지만 천체 투영관과 레이저쇼뿐만 아니라 모든 쇼와 주요 명소를 포함하고 있는 Science Center Plus 표를 구매할 수 있어요.
여: 알았어요. 그 표는 얼마인가요?
남: 한 사람당 5달러를 추가하면 됩니다.
여: 좋아요. 그걸로 3장 주세요.
남: 네. 어른 두 명, 아이 한 명 맞죠?
여: 맞아요. 여기 제 카드요.

어휘
main attraction 주요 명소, 주요 명물 **hands-on** ***a.*** 직접 해보는 **aquarium** ***n.*** 수족관 **planetarium** ***n.*** 천체 투영관

정답 ⑤

문제풀이
어른 한 명당 30달러인데 두 명이므로 60달러, 아이는 한 명 당 20달러인데, Science Center Plus 표는 한 사람당 5달러로 세 명이면 15달러이다. 따라서 전체 지불할 금액은 95달러(=60달러+20달러+15달러)이므로 정답은 ⑤ '$95'이다.

총 어휘 수 132

10 언급 유무

소재 연례 마라톤에 대한 대화

듣기 대본 해석
남: Cathleen, 이번 달 27일에 연례 마라톤 열리는 거 알고 있었니?
여: 응 알고 있었어.
남: 너도 참가할 거야?
여: 그러고 싶지만, 26마일을 달리는 게 나한테는 너무 어려울 것 같아.
남: 응, 꽤나 멀지. 하지만 다 달릴 필요는 없어. 필요하면 걸어도 돼.
여: 정말? 나쁘지 않은데.
남: 올해는 뛰는 사람이 많아. 웹사이트에 따르면, 거의 2,000명이 등록을 했어.
여: 와! 정말 많다.
남: 너도 알다시피 좋은 목적을 위해서잖아. 참가비는 40달러인데, 수익금은 강변공원을 미화하는 데 사용될 거야.
여: 알았어.
남: 완주를 하면 티셔츠와 네 이름이 새겨진 상패도 받을 수 있어. 우리 같이 할 수 있어. 내가 끝내도록 도와줄게.
여: 좋아. 잠깐 생각할 시간을 줘. 다음 주가 되기 전에 참가할지 말지 알려줄게.

어휘
register ***v.*** 등록하다 **beautify** ***v.*** 아름답게 하다 **plaque** ***n.*** 명판

정답 ②

문제풀이
두 사람은 완주 거리, 현재 등록 인원, 수익금 사용처, 완주 기념품에 관한 언급은 했지만 ② '당일 복장'에 관한 언급은 하지 않았다.

총 어휘 수 173

11 내용 일치 · 불일치

소재 Miller Brody의 일생

듣기 대본 해석
여: 여러분, 좋은 아침이에요. 오늘 저는 여러분께 미국의 심리학자인 Miller Brody에 대해 이야기 하고 싶어요. 그는 1920년 Tennessee에서 태어났고, 열심히 일하는 사업가와 가정 주부 사이의 외아들이었어요. 그는 1945년 Minnesota 대학에서 심리학 박사가 되었고 다음 해에 Montana 대학에서 강의를 시작했어요. 그는 종종 동료 교수들과 충돌이 있었지만, 그가 잘 생겼고 재미있어서 학생들은 그를 많이 좋아했어요. 그의 경력 동안 그는 사회 계층과 지위가 사람들에게 끼치는 심리적 영향에 대해 많은 책을 펴냈습니다. 그는 결혼 후 유럽으로 갔고, 거기서 그는 미국에서 사회적 계층 체계의 기원을 발견하길 바라며 다른 나라에서 온 학자들을 만났습니다. Miller Brody는 2002년에 자연적 원인으로 사망했습니다.

어휘
psychologist ***n.*** 심리학자 **conflict** ***n.*** 충돌 **career** ***n.*** 사회생활, 경력 **publish** ***v.*** 출판하다 **pass away** 사망하다

정답 ③

문제풀이
그는 자주 그의 동료 교수들과 갈등을 겪었다고 했으므로 내용과 일치하지 않는 것은 ③ '동료 교수들과 충돌 없이 잘 지냈다.'이다.

총 어휘 수 140

12 도표

소재 Madison 관광 선택

듣기 대본 해석
여: 여보, 로비에서 이 팜플렛 찾았어. Madison 관광지에 대한 정보가 있더라.
남: 좋네. 내일 할 것을 찾아보자.
여: 그래. 일단 카누를 타고 싶은데 다섯 시간은 너무 길지 않아?
남: 맞아. 그리고 그건 너무 비싸. 좀 더 저렴한 걸 찾아보자.
여: 응. 우린 나비 정원을 보러 갈 수도 있어. 이맘때쯤 예쁘다고 들었어.
남: 갈 수도 있는데 호텔에서 가는 셔틀버스를 제공해 주지 않아.
여: 그렇네. 거기까지 가는 게 힘들겠다.
남: 맞아. 그럼 이제 선택지가 두 개 남았네. 어떤 게 더 재미 있을 것 같아?
여: 걸으면서 관광하기에는 내일 날씨가 너무 더울 것 같아.
남: 동감이야. 그럼 이걸로 하자.

어휘
pamphlet ***n.*** 팜플렛 **tourist attraction** 관광지 **canoeing** ***n.*** 카누 타기 **shuttle** ***n.*** 셔틀버스

정답 ③

문제풀이

카누는 시간도 길고 비싸서 제외되고, 남자가 70달러보다는 덜 비싼 활동을 찾자고 하였으므로 River Zipline도 제외된다. 나비 정원은 셔틀을 제공해 주지 않아서 제외된다. 따라서 남은 선택지는 ③번과 ④번인데 걷는 것은 너무 덥다고 했으므로 두 사람이 선택한 관광지는 ③ '와인 시음'이 된다.

총 어휘 수 137

13 긴 대화의 응답

소재 극장에서 생긴 일

듣기 대본 해석

여: 안녕, Tom! 어젯밤 그 연극 재미있었어?

남: 음, 연극 자체는 정말 좋았는데 나는 극장에서 그렇게 즐기지는 못했어.

여: 오, 나는 네가 그 연극을 보고 엄청 좋아할 거라고 생각했는데. 무슨 일이 있었는데?

남: 주연을 담당하는 배우를 좋아해서 정말 그 연극을 보고 싶었거든. 그런데 두어 사람과 말다툼을 했어.

여: 극장에서? 왜 말다툼 한 건데?

남: 그들이 내 자리에 앉아있었고 내가 지적한 후에도, 그 자리가 그들 것이라고 우기더라고.

여: 사람들이 그럴 때 정말 화가 나!

남: 그게 다가 아니야. 안내원이 그 상황을 해결하려고 왔고, 우리 표를 자세히 보더라고. 자세히 보니 직원이 나한테 잘못된 표를 인쇄해 준 것 같았어. 그래서 나는 훨씬 뒷자리에 앉아야 했어.

여: 너 정말 화가 났겠다. 결국 어떻게 했어?

남: ⑤ 연극을 본 후에, 극장에 항의했어.

어휘

argument ***n.*** 논쟁, 말다툼 **insist** ***v.*** 주장하다, 우기다 **annoy** ***v.*** 짜증나게 하다 **usher** ***n.*** 안내원 **handle** ***v.*** 다루다, 해결하다 **a close(r) look** 자세히 살핌

정답 ⑤

문제풀이

남자는 어제 연극을 보러 갔다가 잘못된 표를 받아서 뒤에서 연극을 봐야 했던 일을 여자에게 말해주었고 마지막에 여자는 그래서 어떻게 했는지를 물었다. 남자는 극장 측의 잘못으로 화가 났으므로 적절한 응답은 ⑤ '연극을 본 후에, 극장에 항의했어.'이다.

오답 보기 해석

① 그 안내원에게 그들을 조용히 시켜달라고 말했어.

② 그 주연을 담당하는 배우를 만났어.

③ 안내원에게 내가 화장실에 가도 되냐고 물었어.

④ 나는 그 훌륭한 공연을 절대 잊지 못할 거야.

총 어휘 수 166

14 긴 대화의 응답

소재 동물 실험 반대 캠페인

듣기 대본 해석

여: 이봐, Cameron. 너 피켓 표지에 뭐라고 한 거야? "동물 실험 반대?"

남: 오, 안녕, Ellie. 그래, 동물 실험 제품에 반대하는 캠페인이야.

여: 내가 아는 많은 사람들도 그것에 반대하고 있는데 나는 왜 그런지 잘 모르겠어.

남: 자, 사람들은 인간이 쓰기 위해 개발된 제품을 시험하기 위해 동물을 이용해선 안 돼. 이 사진들에 실험실에서 동물들에게 행해지는 모든 종류의 잔인한 행동들이 나와 있어.

여: 와, 정말 충격적이야. 난 사람들이 동물들을 그렇게 다루는지 몰랐어.

남: 사람들은 단지 제품 하나의 효과를 연구하기 위해 하루에 수백 마리의 동물들을 죽여!

여: 네가 이 캠페인에 그렇게 열정적인 게 대단하다고 생각해. 내가 기부를 할 수 있어?

남: 그거 좋겠다, Ellie. 우리 웹사이트에 가면 네가 필요한 정보가 있어.

여: ① 좋아. 나도 도울 수 있게 되어서 기뻐.

어휘

picket ***n.*** 피켓 **campaign** ***n.*** 캠페인, 사회 운동 **lab** ***n.*** 실험실 **passionate** ***a.*** 열정적인 **donation** ***n.*** 기부, 기부금 〈문제〉 **appreciate** ***v.*** 고맙게 여기다, 환영하다

정답 ①

문제풀이

동물 실험 반대 캠페인을 하는 친구를 만나서 기부가 가능한지 물었고 친구는 웹사이트에 들어가면 정보가 나와있다고 알려준다. 이에 대한 여자의 대답은 ① '좋아. 나도 도울 수 있게 되어서 기뻐.'가 가장 적절하다.

오답 보기 해석

② 우리는 너의 기부를 환영해. 너무 고마워.

③ 그 사진들을 안 보는 게 낫겠어. 너무 슬퍼.

④ 충고 고마워. 다시는 그렇게 하지 않도록 명심할게.

⑤ 여기에 이름 쓰고 사인만 하면 돼. 그게 우리가 필요한 전부야.

총 어휘 수 137

15 상황에 적절한 말

소재 고아원에서 자원봉사하자고 친구 설득하기

듣기 대본 해석

남: Kenny는 친구 Katie에게 같이 새 영화를 보러 가자고 합니다. Katie는 오늘 오후에 고아원에서 봉사를 해야 하기 때문에 거절을 합니다. Kenny는 Katie에게 왜 자원봉사를 하냐고 물어보자 Katie는 다른 사람들, 특히 어린이들을 도와주는 것은 무척 보람 있는 일이라고 답합니다. Kenny가 남을 도와주는 것을 좋아하기 때문에 자원봉사하는 것을 생각해 본 적이 있습니다. 그러나 어린이들과 잘 놀아주지 못하는 것 같아 고아원에서 봉사할 수는 없을 것 같다고 생각합니다. Katie는 Kenny가 자기와 함께 고아원에서 봉사활동을 했으면 좋겠고 그가 할 수 있도록 격려하고 싶어 합니다. 이러한 상황에서 Katie가 Kenny에게 할 말로 가장 적절한 것은 무엇일까요?

Katie: ⑤ 봉사는 매우 재미있고 아이들이 너를 좋아할 거라고 확신해.

어휘

decline ***v.*** 거절하다, 감소하다 **orphanage** ***n.*** 고아원 **volunteer** ***v.*** 자원봉사하다 **rewarding** ***a.*** 보람 있는 **encourage** ***v.*** 격려하다, 고무하다

정답 ⑤

문제풀이

Katie가 고아원에 봉사활동을 하러 간다는 것을 알게 된 Kenny는 이에 동참하고 싶어 하지만 자신이 아이들과 잘 놀지 못한다고 생각하여 주저하고 있다. Katie는 Kenny가 함께 자원봉사하기를 바라고 그를 격려하고자 하므로, 그녀가 할 말로 가장 적절한 것은 ⑤ '봉사는 매우 재미있고 아이들이 너를 좋아할 거라고 확신해.'이다.

오답 보기 해석

① 우리가 고를 수 있는 다른 영화들이 있어.

② 너는 자원봉사에 대한 보상은 받지 않을 거야.

③ 우리는 이미 자원봉사하는 사람들을 충분히 보유하고 있어.

④ 나는 고아원에서 일함으로써 돕고 싶어.

총 어휘 수 119

16 담화 목적 / 17 세부 내용 파악

소재 세계 최대의 호텔

듣기 대본 해석

남: Las Vegas에 있는 Venetian Hotel은 특별한 경험이 될 수 있습니다. 1999년에 문을 연 이래로 Venetian Hotel은 세계에서 가장 큰 호텔입니다. 7,000개 이상의 방을 갖추고 있으며, 호텔은 5개의 별개의 구역으로 나눠져 있습니다. 세계 곳곳의 다양한 음식을 제공하는 식당가는 A지역에 있는데, 그곳에는 피아노를 연주해주는 바도 있습니다. B지역에는 카지노가 있는데, 거기서 고객들이 매일 밤 크게 이깁니다. C지역에는 쇼핑몰이 있는데, 코치, 프라다, 루이비통과 같은 디자이너 브랜드가 다 모여있는 곳입니다. D지역은 Venetian 호텔의 오락구역이며, 그곳에서는 전세계의 유명 연극이 매일 밤낮으로 공연됩니다. 여러분은 서커스, 마술쇼를 보실 수 있고 Barbara Streisand 노래 혹은 많은 다른 Vegas풍의 쇼를 보실 수 있습니다. 마지막으로 E지역에는 로비와 무도회장이 있습니다. 이 지역에서는 보통 회의와 세미나가 개최됩니다. 만약 Las Vegas에 가시게 되면 꼭 세계에서 가장 큰 호텔인 Venetian Hotel을 방문하세요.

어휘

distinct ***a.*** 별개의, 뚜렷한 **variety of** 다양한 **patron** ***n.*** 고객, 후원자

정답 16 ③ 17 ④

문제풀이

16 남자는 라스베가스에 있는 세계 최대 호텔의 5개 구역을 설명해주고 있다. 따라서 남자가 하는 말의 목적은 ③ '세계 최대의 호텔을 소개하려고'이다.

17 오락구역인 D구역에서 매일 밤낮으로 공연을 한다고 했으므로 정답은 ④ 'Area D'이다.

총 어휘 수 181

DICTATION ANSWERS

01 return this smartwatch

02 behind schedule

03 Due to damage from the weather / while it is under construction / the renovated gym / revised schedule

04 go for a run / makes it more bearable / be aware of your surroundings / when I get home

05 complaint letters we've received recently / Why don't we call a meeting / Get in touch with

06 destroyed the place / My table is broken / crawled in through

07 interested in making movies / in charge of club activities / you used to be / sounds like a lot of fun

08 keep you up past your bedtime / stay up late / give a speech / you should be ready by now

09 include everything in the museum / Is it included / an additional five dollars per person

10 holding the annual marathon / too difficult for me to run / registration fee / Give me a while

11 a doctorate in psychology / in conflict with his fellow professors / social class and status / passed away

12 go canoeing / offer a shuttle / leaves us with two options / too hot tomorrow for a walking tour

13 played the main role / got into an argument / so annoying / I had to sit farther back

14 a campaign against testing products on animals / hundreds of animals / so passionate about this campaign

15 declines his offer / work at the orphanage / encourage him to volunteer

16-17 divided into five distinct areas / famous acts from around the world / be sure to visit the largest hotel

10 수능영어듣기 실전모의고사

본문 p.62

01 ①	02 ②	03 ⑤	04 ①	05 ②	06 ⑤
07 ③	08 ①	09 ④	10 ③	11 ⑤	12 ②
13 ②	14 ⑤	15 ④	16 ⑤	17 ③	

01 짧은 대화의 응답

소재 에어컨 고장

듣기 대본 해석
남: 와, 여기 정말 덥네. 에어컨 켜자, Amy.
여: 제대로 작동이 안 돼. 고칠 때까지 사용할 수 없어.
남: 자, 그럼 최대한 빨리 고쳐야지.
여: ① 좋아. 내가 지금 서비스 센터에 연락할게.

어휘
properly ***ad.*** 제대로 **fix** ***v.*** ~을 고치다

정답 ①

문제풀이
남자가 고장 난 에어컨을 빨리 고쳐야겠다고 말했으므로 여자의 응답은 서비스 센터에 연락한다는 ① '좋아. 내가 지금 서비스 센터에 연락할게.'가 가장 적절하다.

오답 보기 해석
② 내가 확실히 그것을 관리할게.
③ 우리는 같은 모델 제품을 사야 된다고 생각해.
④ 가능하다면 우리는 에너지를 절약하려고 해야 해.
⑤ 그가 가능한 빨리 와야 한다는 것을 반드시 알도록 해.

총 어휘 수 42

02 짧은 대화의 응답

소재 세차 가격

듣기 대본 해석
여: 오늘 날씨가 좋아.
남: 응, 세차를 해야겠어.
여: 세차하는 데에 얼마나 드니?
남: 보통 20달러 정도 들어.
여: 정말? 너무 비싸지 않아?
남: ② 별로 그렇지 않아. 그들이 일을 정말 잘해.

어휘
expensive ***a.*** 값비싼

정답 ②

문제풀이
세차 가격이 너무 비싸지 않냐는 말에 ② '별로 그렇지 않아. 그들이 일을 정말 잘해.'가 적절하다.

오답 보기 해석
① 사실, 세차를 할 필요가 있을지 모르겠어.
③ 나도 그렇게 생각해. 그들은 돈이 없어.
④ 내 차를 세차하지는 않아.
⑤ 그것은 내 차가 아니야.

총 어휘 수 40

03 담화 목적

소재 애완동물을 가진 아파트 주민들에 대한 협조 요청

듣기 대본 해석
남: 최근 몇 주간 동네 애완견들이 밤 늦게 짖는 것에 대한 항의가 많이 들어왔습니다. 이 애완견들은 특히 아침 일찍 출근해야 하는 주민들에게 골칫거리가 되었습니다. 상황은 어젯밤 주민 한 명이 경찰에 신고해 문제를 해결하기 위해 우리 동네로 경찰이 출동하는 지경까지 이르렀습니다. 이러한 소란에 더해져 애완동물 주인들이 애완동물들의 배설물을 치우지 않고 있다는 항의까지 들어왔습니다. 우리 Greenville 아파트는 주민들에게 동네의 청결과 조용함을 유지하기 위해 필요한 조치를 취하기를 권고합니다. 협조해주셔서 감사합니다.

어휘
nuisance ***n.*** 골칫거리, 성가신 일 **resident** ***n.*** 주민, 거주자
disturbance ***n.*** 소란, 방해

정답 ⑤

문제풀이
애완견이 밤늦게 짖거나 동물 주인이 배설물을 치우지 않아 아파트 주민들에게 피해를 끼치고 있다고 말하면서 적절한 조치를 취할 것을 요청하고 있으므로 정답은 ⑤ '애완동물이 이웃에 피해를 끼치지 않도록 요청하려고'이다.

총 어휘 수 107

04 의견

소재 산에서 쓰레기 다시 가져오기

듣기 대본 해석
여: Daniel, 여기 경치 좋다. 산 공기가 정말 맑고 경치가 굉장한데.
남: 맞아. 정말 멋지다. 그런데 우리 내려가는 게 좋을 것 같아.
여: 떠나기 싫지만 어두워지고 있어. 곧 가야 돼.
남: 우선, 이 쓰레기 어디에 버려야 되는 거지?
여: 쓰레기를 버릴 장소가 없어 보여. 우리가 그냥 가져가자.
남: 좋아. 그런데 여기 쓰레기통이 있으면 훨씬 더 편할 텐데.
여: 맞아. 그런데 그렇게 하면 쓰레기통을 비울 직원이 있어야 할 거야.
남: 글쎄, 사람들은 쓰레기통이 없으면 아무데나 쓰레기를 버리지.
여: 맞아. 그런데 쓰레기통이 있으면 금방 쓰레기가 가득 차고 넘쳐서 쓰레기가 쓰레기통 주변에 많이 쌓일 거야.
남: 네 말이 맞을 수도 있겠다.
여: 우리가 쓰레기를 다시 가져가는 것이 그리 힘든 일은 아니라고 생각해.
남: 그래, 힘든 일이 아니지.

어휘
amazing ***a.*** 놀라운, 굉장한 **fill up** 가득 차다 **build up** ~이 쌓이다
a big deal 큰일, 힘든 일

정답 ①

문제풀이
남자는 산 위에 쓰레기통이 있으면 더 편리할 것이라고 말했지만, 여자는 쓰레기통이 있으면 쓰레기통을 비울 사람이 필요하고 쓰레기통 주변에 쓰레기가 쌓이게 된다면서 쓰레기를 되가져가는 것은 그리 힘든 일이 아니라고 말했다. 따라서 정답은 ① '산에서 자신의 쓰레기를 다시 가지고 와야 한다.'이다.

총 어휘 수 155

05 대화자의 관계 파악

소재 연기 실수에 대한 사과

듣기 대본 해석

여: 실례합니다, Wise 선생님. 시간 있으신가요?
남: 물론이야, Shelly. 들어오렴. 뭘 도와줄까?
여: 지난밤 저의 연기에 대해 사과 드리고 싶어요. 제가 선생님과 다른 사람들을 실망 시켜드렸어요.
남: 그래, 네가 평소처럼 그 공연에 몰입하진 않았지. 너무 많은 실수를 했어.
여: 알아요. 좀 더 집중했었어야 했어요. 제가 최근 너무 좌절을 해서 제 연기에 영향을 끼쳤어요.
남: 무엇에 좌절했는데?
여: 음, 제가 수학시간에 너무 뒤떨어져 있어요. 그것에 스트레스를 받고 있어요.
남: 알았다. 학업에 집중할 수 있도록 공연 몇 개는 너 대신 다른 사람이 하게 할까?
여: 아니요, 괜찮아요. 저희 선생님께 말씀드렸어요. 그녀는 제가 지난 시험을 재시험 볼 수 있도록 동의했어요.
남: 좋아. 그러면, 지난밤에 대한 것은 잊으렴. 내일 공연에 집중하자.
여: 알겠습니다. 고맙습니다, Wise 선생님.

어휘

performance ***n.*** 공연, 연기 **let ~ down** ~을 실망시키다
stress out 스트레스를 받다

정답 ②

문제풀이

여자는 지난 공연에서 자신의 연기 실수에 대해 사과하고 있고, 남자는 문제점을 말해주면서 이제는 잊으라고 말하며 내일 공연에 집중하자고 하는 것으로 보아 두 사람의 관계는 ② '감독 ㅡ 배우'임을 유추할 수 있다.

총 어휘 수 150

06 그림의 세부 내용 파악

소재 시내 봄 축제

듣기 대본 해석

여: 나 봄 축제 보려고 시내에 나오는 게 정말 좋아, Carl. 진짜 재미있어!
남: 나도. 할 게 정말 많아.
여: 당연하지. 우선 뭐 좀 먹자.
남: 그래. 근데 ATM에서 현금 뽑아야 돼.
여: 시식 판매대가 은행 앞에 있으니까 딱 좋네.
남: 좋다! 먹은 다음에는 뭐 할래?
여: 음, 난 놀이기구 타는 게 좋아. 특히 저 큰 관람차.
남: 난 너랑 같이 못 탈 것 같아. 고소공포증이 있거든.
여: 아쉽네. 그럼, 저쪽에 있는 사람들처럼 나무 아래서 날 기다리면 되겠네. 그리고 밴드 음악을 들어도 되고.
남: 안타깝게도 지금은 연주하는 밴드가 없어.
여: 기다리는 동안 분명 뭔가 할 게 있을 거야.
남: 그래. 어쨌든, 이제 뭐 먹으러 가자!

어휘

food booth 시식 판매대

정답 ⑤

문제풀이

대화의 끝부분에서 지금은 연주하는 밴드가 없다고 했는데 그림에서는 밴드가 무대에서 공연을 하고 있으므로 정답은 ⑤번이다.

총 어휘 수 137

07 부탁한 일

소재 교통 검색 어플리케이션

듣기 대본 해석

여: 안녕하세요, Brown 선생님. 여기서 만나다니 반갑습니다. 버스 기다리세요?
남: 응. 어디 가는 거니, Laura?
여: 집에 가요. 저도 버스를 탈 거예요. 어떤 버스 기다리세요?
남: 52번. 거의 10분째 기다리고 있어. 아, 너 스마트폰 있니?
여: 네. 왜 물으세요?
남: 거기에 대중교통 검색 어플리케이션이 있다고 들었어. 내 버스가 언제 올지 알려줄 수 있니?
여: 물론이죠. 사실, 그 앱을 오늘 아침에 제 휴대폰에 설치했어요. 잠시만요. *[잠시 후]* 보세요. 여기, 52번 버스는 약 5분 뒤에 도착한대요.
남: 오, 그거 잘됐네. 고마워, Laura.
여: 천만에요. 오, 제 버스가 오네요. 내일 뵐게요, Brown 선생님.

어휘

public transportation 대중교통 **install** ***v.*** 설치하다

정답 ③

문제풀이

남자는 버스를 오래 기다려서 여자에게 대중교통 검색 어플리케이션을 이용해서 버스가 언제 오는지 봐달라고 부탁하고 있으므로 정답은 ③ '언제 그의 버스가 도착하는지 확인하기'이다.

오답 보기 해석

① 그를 어딘가로 데려다 주기
② 버스 요금 빌려주기
④ 버스 정류장 위치 알려주기
⑤ 어플리케이션 찾는 법 보여주기

총 어휘 수 123

08 이유

소재 조깅을 하지 않는 이유

듣기 대본 해석

여: 실례합니다. 우리 서로 아는 사이 아닌가요?
남: Cynthia! 저예요, Mason!
여: 오, 이런, 제가 너무 당황스럽네요. 잘 지내죠?
남: 나는 잘 지내요. 당신이 이사간 후로 우리가 이야기를 나누지 못한 것 같아요.
여: 맞는 것 같아요. 아직도 음악 연주를 해요? 당신은 드럼을 좋아했었잖아요.
남: 그래요. 여전히 연주하기를 좋아해요.
여: 조깅은 어때요? 당신이랑 조깅을 많이 했던 걸로 기억하는데.
남: 사실 오랫동안 조깅을 하지 않았어요.
여: 정말이요? 왜 안 했어요?
남: 제가 일 년 전쯤 음주 운전자한테 치였었어요. 저는 달릴 수가 없어요.
여: 끔찍하네요. 그 소식을 들으니 유감이에요. 그렇게 한 사람을 잡았길 바라요.
남: 네, 잡았어요. 사실 그는 멈춰서 경찰을 불러줬었어요. 어쨌든, 저는 가야 해요.
여: 네, 저도요. 연락하기로 해요!
남: 물론이죠.

어휘

embarrassed ***a.*** 쑥스러운, 당황스러운 **move away** 이사하다

정답 ①

문제풀이

남자는 일 년 전쯤에 교통사고를 당해서 그 뒤로 달릴 수가 없기 때문에 조깅을 하지 않는다고 말하고 있으므로 정답은 ① '교통사고 부상 때문에'이다.

총 어휘 수 139

09 숫자

소재 채소 구입

듣기 대본 해석

남: 안녕하세요, Smith씨.
여: 안녕하세요, Baron씨. 오늘은 모든 야채가 정말로 신선해 보이네요.
남: 네. 특히 양파와 당근을 추천해 드리고 싶습니다. 그것들은 막 도착했거든요.
여: 정말로 신선해 보이는군요. 얼마죠?
남: 양파는 한 개에 2달러이고 당근은 킬로그램 단위로 팔립니다. 당근 1킬로그램은 6달러입니다.
여: 그러면 당근 1킬로그램과 양파 2개 주세요.
남: 알겠습니다. 다른 것도 사실 건가요?
여: 네. 수프를 좀 만들기 위해 호박이랑 감자를 약간 사야 해요.
남: 호박 하나에 5달러이고 감자 1킬로그램은 4달러입니다.
여: 호박 2개와 감자 1킬로그램이면 충분합니다. 배달이 되나요?
남: 그럼요, 물론이지요. 사람을 시켜 약 2시간 내로 가져다 드리도록 하겠습니다.
여: 좋습니다. 여기 제 신용카드 받으세요.

어휘

fresh ***a.*** 신선한 **carrot** ***n.*** 당근 **by the kilogram** 킬로그램 단위로 **deliver** ***v.*** 배달하다

정답 ④

문제풀이

여자는 당근 1킬로그램(6달러), 양파 2개(4달러), 호박 2개(10달러)와 감자 1킬로그램(4달러)을 사기로 했으므로 지불해야 할 총 금액은 ④ '$24'이다.

총 어휘 수 128

10 언급 유무

소재 잘못 배송된 책

듣기 대본 해석

[전화벨이 울린다.]
남: Shine On Top 서점입니다. 무엇을 도와드릴까요?
여: 제가 온라인에서 2권의 책을 주문했고 오늘 아침에 받았는데요, 한 권의 책에 실수가 있네요.
남: 알겠습니다. 이름 좀 알려주시겠어요?
여: 네. 제 이름은 Rebecca Jackson입니다.
남: 구매내역을 확인해볼게요. *[키보드 치는 소리]* 수필 모음집 한 권과 과학 교과서 한 권을 주문하셨네요, 맞나요?
여: 네. 문제는 제가 받은 수필집이 제가 주문한 것이 아니라는 겁니다.
남: 아, 죄송합니다. 받은 책 제목이 뭐죠?
여: A Big Dream이에요. 제가 주문한 건 John Thomas의 Just a Dream이고요.
남: 실수에 대해 사과드립니다. 지금 바로 제대로 된 책을 보내겠습니다.
여: 제가 지금 가지고 있는 책은 어떻게 해야 하죠?
남: 우편으로 돌려 보내 주시겠어요? 우편요금은 저희가 낼게요.
여: 알겠습니다. 내일 보낼게요.

어휘

apologize ***v.*** 사과하다 **postage** ***n.*** 우편요금

정답 ③

문제풀이

여자가 책을 주문했는데 한 권이 잘못 배송되어 서점에 전화한 상황이다. 여자가 주문했던 책의 권 수, 여자가 주문했던 책의 종류, 잘못 배송된 책의 처리 방법, 운송료 지급에 관한 언급은 있었지만, 잘못 배송된 책의 작가에 대한 언급은 없었으므로 정답은 ③ '잘못 배송된 책의 작가'이다.

총 어휘 수 145

11 내용 일치 · 불일치

소재 가족 초대 행사

듣기 대본 해석

여: 여러분 안녕하세요. 저는 이곳 Maple's Academy의 아트 디렉터 Lilly Stevens입니다. 오늘 우리 학교의 특별한 학교공개 행사에 대해서 안내하고자 합니다. 이 이벤트는 학생 여러분이 가족들을 학교로 모셔와서 이번 학기 동안 여러분이 만든 작품들을 감상할 수 있게 합니다. 그리고 부모님뿐만 아니라 할아버지, 할머니, 형제자매, 그리고 다른 친척들도 모시고 와도 됩니다. 그리고 조각, 홀치기 염색과 같이 여러분이 여러분의 친척들과 함께 참여할 수 있는 여러 가지 행사들이 열릴 것입니다. 학교 공개 행사는 활동 센터에서 3월 26일, 수요일 오후 5시부터 9시까지 진행될 예정입니다. 공간에 100명만 들어갈 수 있기 때문에 인터넷으로 신청을 해주시기 바랍니다. 더 많은 정보를 보려면 우리 사이트를 방문 해 주세요.

어휘

announce ***v.*** 발표하다, 알리다 **open house** (학교 · 기숙사 등의) 공개일 **artwork** ***n.*** 미술품 **sibling** ***n.*** 형제자매 **relative** ***n.*** 친척 ***a.*** 연관 있는 **sculpt** ***v.*** 조각하다 **tie-dye** ***v.*** 홀치기 염색을 하다 **accommodate** ***v.*** 공간을 제공하다, 수용하다

정답 ⑤

문제풀이

100명만 수용할 수 있기 때문에 온라인상에서 등록해야 한다고 말했으므로 일치하지 않는 것은 ⑤ '선착순으로 입장한다.'이다.

총 어휘 수 126

12 도표

소재 배 타기와 스노클링 관광 스케줄 선택

듣기 대본 해석

여: 여보, 뭐 보고 있어?
남: 배 타기랑 스노클링 관광 스케줄이야. 집에 가기 전에 스노클링 좀 하면 좋을 것 같아.
여: 좋은 생각이야. 그 관광 가자. 애들한테 좋은 경험이 될 거야. 일곱 시간 프로그램은 어때?
남: 일곱 시간은 애들이랑 배에 타있기에는 너무 길어. 지겨워하거나 그대로 있기 힘들어하지 않을까?
여: 그럴 것 같아. 그럼 좀 더 짧은 것으로 하자.
남: 응. 점심을 제공해 주는 프로그램이 좋을까?
여: 별로 필요하진 않을 것 같은데. 여행 올 때 음식 많이 샀잖아. 내가 샌드위치 몇 개 만들게.
남: 알겠어. 우리가 따로 사고 싶지 않으면, 당연히 물안경 필요할 거야. 오리발은 어떡하지? 필요할까?
여: 당연하지. 스노클링은 오리발이 있으면 훨씬 재미있어.
남: 그래. 그럼 우릴 위한 안성맞춤의 관광 프로그램을 찾은 것 같아.

어휘

snorkeling ***n.*** 스노클링 **necessary** ***a.*** 필요한 **goggles** ***n.*** 고글, 물안경 **fin** ***n.*** 오리발

정답 ②

문제풀이

7시간은 너무 길다고 했고, 점심은 제공해 주지 않는 것으로 하자고 했으므로 ①, ③, ⑤번은 제외된다. ②, ④번 중에 물안경과 오리발은 필요하다고 했으므로 두 사람이 선택한 것은 ②번이다.

총 어휘 수 163

13 긴 대화의 응답

소재 아이스하키 경기 후 마중 약속

듣기 대본 해석
여: 너 오늘 Devils와 Rangers의 아이스하키 경기 볼 계획이니?
남: 물론이죠! 나는 이 경기가 정말 신이 나요.
여: 표는 샀어?
남: 물론이죠.
여: 경기가 몇 시에 끝나지?
남: 보통 저녁 9시 30분에서 10시 사이에 끝나요.
여: 아, 그래? 경기가 그렇게 늦게 끝나는 줄 몰랐네. 내가 차로 너를 데리러 갈게.
남: 그거 좋겠네요, 엄마. 우리 어디서 만나야 되죠?
여: 내가 경기장에 도착하면 너한테 전화할게.
남: 네, 좋아요. 반드시 휴대폰을 가지고 있도록 할게요.
여: 너 휴대폰 벨소리 들을 수 있겠니? 경기장은 매우 시끄럽잖니.
남: 전화가 오면 느낄 수 있도록 휴대폰을 진동 모드로 해 놓고 제 앞 주머니에 넣어둘게요.
여: ② 그래, 좋아. 그러면 내 전화를 놓치지 않겠구나.

어휘
stadium ***n.*** 경기장 **on vibrate** 진동으로

정답 ②

문제풀이
엄마는 아이스하키 경기가 끝날 때쯤 아들을 데리러 갈 예정인데, 엄마가 아들한테 전화했을 때 경기장이 시끄러워서 벨소리를 들을 수 있냐고 묻자 아들은 휴대폰을 진동으로 바꾸고 앞주머니에 넣겠다고 한다. 이에 대한 가장 적절한 엄마의 응답은 ② '그래, 좋아. 그러면 내 전화를 놓치지 않겠구나.'이다.

오답 보기 해석
① 통화할 때 항상 예의 바르게 행동해야 해.
③ 네가 집에 올 때 지하철을 타는 것이 좋겠어.
④ 휴대폰으로 통화할 때 꼭 부드럽게 말하도록 하렴.
⑤ 휴대폰을 꺼두어야 해.

총 어휘 수 138

14 긴 대화의 응답

소재 자녀의 취업에 관한 걱정

듣기 대본 해석
여: 여보, 친구들과 어땠어요?
남: 아주 좋았어요. 맛있는 점심을 먹고 공원에 갔어요.
여: 아주 즐거웠던 것 같네요.
남: 정말 그랬어요. 우리 모두 정말 좋은 시간 보냈고, 계속 좋은 시간을 보내고 싶어서 내가 친구들을 커피 마시러 초대했어요.
여: 훌륭한 생각이에요.
남: 오, Lauren이 내게 그녀의 딸이 Phoenix에 일자리를 얻었다고 하더군요.
여: 잘됐네요. 그녀가 부러워요? Alyssa가 일자리를 구하는 것에 대해 정말 걱정했었잖아요.
남: 아마 조금이요. 그렇지만 우리 Alyssa도 곧 일자리를 찾을 거라고 생각해요.
여: 당신 전보다 덜 걱정하는 것 같네요.
남: 글쎄요, 내가 그것에 대해 할 수 있는 것이 없다고 깨달았어요.
여: 맞아요, 걱정해보았자 바뀌는 건 아무것도 없어요.
남: ⑤ 네, 걱정은 상황을 더 좋지 않게 만들 뿐이라는 걸 이제 알아요.

어휘
land a job 일자리를 얻다 **envious** ***a.*** 부러워하는 **concerned** ***a.*** 걱정하는 **realization** ***n.*** 깨달음

정답 ⑤

문제풀이
여자는 걱정이 아무것도 해결해주지 않는다고 말하고 있고 남자도 이에 동조하는 맥락이므로 남자의 응답으로 가장 적절한 것은 ⑤ '네, 걱정은 상황을 더 좋지 않게 만들 뿐이라는 걸 이제 알아요.'이다.

오답 보기 해석
① 맞아요. 그녀가 괜찮은 직장을 찾을 방법은 없어요.
② 그래요. 난 늘 그녀의 딸이 좋은 직장을 갖기를 원했었죠.
③ 놀라워라! 난 파티에 그들을 초대하지 않았는데.
④ 걱정할 필요 없어요. Alyssa가 당신이 걱정한다는 것을 알았어요.

총 어휘 수 149

15 상황에 적절한 말

소재 어린아이의 믿음

듣기 대본 해석
여: Rachel과 그의 아버지는 십 분 동안 쇼핑몰 주차장을 차로 돌고 있습니다. 토요일이고 주차장은 거의 찼습니다. Rachel의 아버지는 눈에 띄게 답답해하고 있습니다. 그 때, Rachel은 인형을 꺼내고 인형한테 그들이 주차 공간 찾는 것을 도와달라고 말합니다. Rachel의 아버지는 그녀에게 무엇을 하고 있는지 물었습니다. 그녀는 그녀가 가장 좋아하는 만화에 나오는 인물 중 하나가 항상 말하기를 만약에 도움이 필요하면 친구한테 부탁해야 한다고 했다는 것을 이야기해줍니다. 그녀의 아버지는 이것은 만화에서 말하고 있는 도움의 종류가 아니라고 설명하려 하지만, Rachel은 주장합니다. 갑자기 그들은 그들 앞에 주차 공간이 나는 것을 봅니다. Rachel은 그녀의 아버지에게 무엇이라고 말할 것 같은가요?
Rachel: ④ 봐요, 나는 그녀가 우리를 도와줄 줄 알았어요!

어휘
visibly ***ad.*** 눈에 띄게, 분명히 **frustrated** ***a.*** 불만스러워 하는, 답답해하는 **insist** ***v.*** 주장하다 〈문제〉 **calm down** 진정하다

정답 ④

문제풀이
주차 공간이 없는 상황에서 Rachel은 만화에서 도움이 필요하면 친구한테 부탁해야 한다고 했다면서 가방에서 인형을 꺼내서 주차 공간 찾는 것을 도와달라고 말한다. 아버지는 그것은 도움이 안 되는 일이라고 설명해 주려 했지만 그 때 그들 앞에 주차 공간이 나타난다. 이 상황에서 Rachel이 할 수 있는 말은 ④ '봐요, 나는 그녀가 우리를 도와줄 줄 알았어요!'가 가장 적절하다.

오답 보기 해석
① 이 모든 것에 대해 죄송해요, 아빠.
② 진정해요, 아빠. 괜찮을 거예요.
③ 정말이요? 그녀에게 부탁하면 안 되나요?
⑤ 우리는 버스를 탔어야 했어요.

총 어휘 수 129

16 담화 목적 / 17 세부 내용 파악

소재 감시 카메라 남용의 문제점

듣기 대본 해석
남: 안녕하세요, 여러분. 저는 오늘 밤 폐쇄회로 또는 감시 카메라에 관해 간단히 이야기하는 시간을 가졌으면 합니다. 우리 나라에는, 어느 순간이든 3백만 대 이상의 감시 카메라가 작동하고 있습니다. 어떤 사람들은 이 카메라들이 범죄자들이 카메라 주변을 조심하기 때문에 범죄가 일어나는 것을 막아준다고 믿습니다. 그러나, 우리 대부분은 감시 카메라가 사생활을 침해할

수 있다고 느낍니다. 이러한 카메라들이 우리의 학교, 사무실, 상점, 그리고 우리 차에 이르기까지 모든 곳에 있습니다. 이 카메라들이 잠재적 범죄자들을 녹화할 수도 있는 반면에, 아무 죄가 없는 행인들도 녹화합니다. 사람들이 그들의 이웃이나 다른 사람들을 감시하기 위해 감시 카메라를 설치한다는 이야기도 있습니다. 이런 행동은 확실히 법에 어긋나지만, 거의 처벌받지 않습니다. 경찰들 또한 우리가 감시 카메라의 수를 줄이고 순찰 경찰관들의 수를 늘려야 한다는 것에 동의하는 것 같습니다. 우리는 사생활에 대한 우리의 권리를 보호하기 위해서 우리 도시에서 감시 카메라의 수를 줄이도록 같이 힘써야 합니다.

어휘

closed-circuit ***n.*** 폐쇄회로 **prevent A from -ing** A가 ~하는 것을 막다 **crime** ***n.*** 범죄 **commit** ***v.*** (일, 죄 등을) 저지르다 **criminal** ***n.*** 범죄자 ***a.*** 범죄의 **invade privacy** 사생활을 침해하다 **potential** ***a.*** 잠재적인, 가능성이 있는 **innocent** ***a.*** 아무 죄가 없는, 순진한 **passerby** ***n.*** 오가는 사람, 행인 **install** ***v.*** 설치하다 **punish** ***v.*** 처벌하다, 벌주다 〈문제〉 **demonstrate** ***v.*** 입증하다, 보여주다

정답 16 ⑤ 17 ③

문제풀이

16 남자는 감시 카메라가 사생활 침해의 소지가 있으니 그 수를 줄여야 한다고 말하고 있으므로 담화의 목적은 ⑤ '감시 카메라의 수를 줄일 것을 제안하기 위해서'이다.

17 남자가 감시 카메라가 설치된 곳으로 학교, 사무실, 상점, 자동차는 언급했지만 엘리베이터는 언급하지 않았다. 따라서 정답은 ③ '엘리베이터'이다.

오답 보기 해석

16

① 감시 카메라의 설치 방법을 알려주기 위해서
② 사람들이 감시 카메라를 구매하도록 설득하기 위해서
③ 감시 카메라가 어떻게 범죄를 막는지 설명하기 위해서
④ 감시 카메라의 효과를 입증하기 위해서

총 어휘 수 160

DICTATION ANSWERS

01 get it fixed

02 pay about twenty dollars

03 a nuisance to members of our community / gotten to the point where / On top of this disturbance / take the necessary action

04 we'd better start hiking back down / throw away all of this garbage / empty them / build up around it

05 do you have a minute / let you and the others down / having an effect on my performance / focus on your studies

06 The food booths are in front of / I'm afraid of heights / wait for me under the tree

07 taking a bus / public transportation application / will be arriving in / here comes my bus

08 I'm so embarrassed / remember jogging with you / I was hit by a drunk driver / keep in touch

09 look really fresh / How much are they / Anything else / have them delivered

10 ordered two books online / not the one I ordered / apologize for the error / pay for the postage

11 show off the artwork / grandparents, siblings, and other relatives / is scheduled to take place / register online

12 schedule of the boat and snorkeling tours / take a tour / they'll get bored or restless / more fun with fins

13 planning to watch the ice hockey game / pick you up / I'll give you a call / keep it on vibrate

14 had a great lunch / I invited them over for coffee / Are you feeling envious / came to the realization

15 is becoming visibly frustrated / asks her to make / All of a sudden

16-17 operating at any given moment / invade privacy / spy on their neighbors / reduce the number of surveillance cameras / protect our right to privacy

01 ⑤	02 ⑤	03 ④	04 ③	05 ①	06 ②
07 ①	08 ①	09 ②	10 ③	11 ③	12 ④
13 ④	14 ③	15 ⑤	16 ③	17 ②	

01 짧은 대화의 응답

소재 새 TV 구입

듣기 대본 해석

남: 자기, 이 새 TV 샀어?

여: 응. 우리가 선명한 화질의 더 좋은 것이 필요하다고 말했던 것 기억 안 나?

남: 기억 나. 그런데 왜 내게 알려주지도 않고 샀어?

여: ⑤ 난 당신이 새로운 TV 사는 걸 괜찮다고 말한 줄 알았어.

어휘

clear ***a.*** 선명한, 확실한 〈문제〉 **hang** ***v.*** 걸다 **regularly** ***ad.*** 정기적으로

정답 ⑤

문제풀이

왜 말해주지 않고 새 TV를 샀는지 묻는 남자의 말에 가장 적절한 대답은 ⑤ '난 당신이 새로운 TV 사는 걸 괜찮다고 말한 줄 알았어.'이다.

오답 보기 해석

① 아니, 이건 우리 집에는 너무 커.
② 그걸 사기 전에 네 조언이 필요했어.
③ 물론이지, 내가 그 TV를 벽에 걸게.
④ 당신은 거실을 주기적으로 청소해야 해.

총 어휘 수 46

02 짧은 대화의 응답

소재 친구의 생일파티

듣기 대본 해석

여: Robert, Helena의 17번째 생일이 얼마 남지 않았어.

남: 아, 깜박할 뻔 했어. 3월 23일이었지. 그녀를 위해 깜짝 파티를 해주는 게 어때?

여: 좋은 생각이야. 그렇다면 그녀가 가장 좋아하는 음식인 사과파이를 내가 준비할게.

남: ⑤ 좋아. 나는 음료를 가져올게.

어휘

just around the corner 임박하여 〈문제〉 **be proud of** ~을 자랑으로 여기다 **beverage** ***n.*** 음료

정답 ⑤

문제풀이

Helena의 생일 파티 준비에 관한 내용이다. 사과파이를 준비하겠다는 여자의 말에 적절한 응답은 ⑤ '좋아. 나는 음료를 가져올게.'이다.

오답 보기 해석

① 그녀는 틀림없이 네가 입상한 것이 자랑스러울 거야.
② 맞아, 그 빵집에서 맛있는 사과파이를 팔아.
③ 너의 생일에 특별한 케이크를 만들어줄게.
④ 나는 알코올 음료는 좋아하지 않아.

총 어휘 수 39

03 담화 목적

소재 연극 동아리 가입

듣기 대본 해석

여: 안녕하세요, 저는 언론학을 전공하는 3학년생인 Grace Stamos입니다. 여러분이 신입생으로 입학한 지 3개월이 되었군요. 대학 생활을 즐기고 계신가요? 모든 것이 여러분이 생각한 대로 되고 있습니까? 만약 여러분이 더 많은 것을 하기를 찾으신다면, 연극 동아리에 가입하는 것을 생각해 보십시오. 연극 동아리는 50년간 대학에서 큰 부분을 차지해 왔고 입학하는 많은 신입생들이 참여했습니다. 여러분이 동아리에 들어오면 새 친구를 사귀기가 쉽고, 여러분이 공연할 때 도시에 있는 모든 멋진 클럽과 극장에 가게 될 것입니다. 여러분이 동아리를 매우 즐기게 될 것이라고 저는 확신합니다. 만약 여러분이 새로운 사람을 만나고 싶고 이곳에서 여러분의 시간을 최대한으로 활용하고 싶다면 오늘 연극 동아리에 가입하세요!

어휘

involve ***v.*** 참여시키다, 관련시키다 **performance** ***n.*** 공연, 성과
positive ***a.*** 확신 있는, 적극적인

정답 ④

문제풀이

여자는 대학 생활에서 더 많은 것을 원한다면 연극 동아리에 가입할 것을 권유하면서, 동아리를 가입했을 때의 활동과 이점을 이야기하고 있으므로 정답은 ④ '연극 동아리 가입을 권유하려고'이다.

총 어휘 수 132

04 대화 주제

소재 탄산수의 이점

듣기 대본 해석

남: 와! 너무 덥다. 마실 것 좀 가져왔니, Katie?

여: 물론이지.

남: 고마워. *[잠시 후]* 잠깐만, 왜 소다를 가져왔어?

여: 그거 탄산수야.

남: 탄산수라고? 왜 일반 물이 아니지? 이건 맛이 좀 이상한데.

여: 음, 탄산수는 일반 물에서 얻을 수 없는 이점을 가지고 있어. 다이어트와 소화불량에 정말 좋아.

남: 그렇구나. 왜 그렇지?

여: 그것은 식욕을 억제해, 그래서 다이어트에 좋지. 내가 탄산수를 마신 이후로, 거의 4킬로그램이 빠졌어.

남: 믿을 수 없어.

여: 그것은 또한 이 지역 수돗물보다 훨씬 건강해. 여기 수돗물이 몇 달 동안 적절하게 여과되지 않고 있었다는 걸 뉴스에서 봤어.

남: 알았어. 나도 탄산수 마시기를 시작해야겠네.

어휘

indigestion ***n.*** 소화불량 **suppress** ***v.*** 참다, 억누르다
appetite ***n.*** 식욕 **tap water** 수돗물 **filtered** ***a.*** 여과된

정답 ③

문제풀이

여자가 탄산수를 가져와서 남자는 왜 탄산수를 마시는지 묻고 여자는 탄산수의 좋은 점을 말해주고 있으므로 두 사람 대화의 주제는 ③ '탄산수가 건강에 좋은 이유'이다.

총 어휘 수 121

05 대화자의 관계 파악

소재 집 계약

듣기 대본 해석

[휴대폰이 울린다.]

남: 안녕하세요, Tanner 부인. 저는 Joseph Lancaster입니다.

여: Lancaster씨, 연락이 와서 기쁘네요. 집은 결정하셨어요?

남: 네. 저와 제 아내는 Main Street의 집으로 결정했어요.

여: 아, 세 개의 화장실과 두 개의 침실이 있는 집이요. 정말 훌륭한 집이지요. 나와 있는 것 중에 최고예요.

남: 네. 우리는 마당에 탁 트인 공간이 너무 좋아요.

여: 아이들을 키우기에 완벽해요. 뛰어 놀 공간이 많을 거예요.

남: 네, 맞아요. 마당에 작은 정원을 만들어도 괜찮은지도 궁금해요.

여: 정원을 만들면 좋을 거라고 확신해요. 제가 집주인과 몇 년 동안 일해 왔어요.

남: 좋아요. 그럼 제가 언제 계약서를 볼 수 있어요?

여: 오늘 오후에 사무실에 들르실 수 있어요? 집주인도 여기로 올 거예요.

남: 물론이죠. 4시경에 갈게요.

어휘

property ***n.*** 부동산, 재산 **plenty of** 많은 **contract** ***n.*** 계약서

정답 ①

문제풀이

남자는 집을 구하고 있고, 여자는 집이 좋다고 말해주고 집주인이라는 말을 하는 것으로 보아 부동산 중개업자임을 알 수 있다. 따라서 정답은 ① '고객 — 부동산 중개업자'이다.

총 어휘 수 155

06 그림의 세부 내용 파악

소재 아빠가 만들어 주신 어린 시절의 놀이터

듣기 대본 해석

남: 여보 봐요, 내가 다락에서 이 오래된 사진을 발견했어요.

여: 어머나, 아주 오랫동안 이 사진을 못 봤는데. 저랑 제 남동생 Tim이 어렸을 때 아버지가 우리를 위해 만들어 주신 놀이터에요.

남: 그럼 이 작은 소녀는 당신이네요. 당신은 그네를 타고 있네요.

여: 맞아요. 저 귀엽지 않았나요?

남: 당신 손을 잡아주고 있는 사람이 당신 아버지고요. 그는 아주 젊어 보여요!

여: 음, 맞아요. 우리 모두 그래요!

남: 모래에서 놀고 있는 아이가 Tim, 맞죠?

여: 네. 그는 항상 더러워지는 걸 좋아했어요.

남: 저 미끄럼틀은 너무 재미있어 보이네요.

여: 정말 재미있었어요. 모든 이웃 아이들이 와서 타고 싶어 했죠.

남: 그럼 이 사진은 언제 찍은 거죠?

여: 언제 같아요?

남: 모든 것들이 매우 푸르른 것을 보니 아마 여름일 것 같은데요.

여: 네, 그래요. 우리가 학교에 갈 필요가 없기 때문에 여름은 항상 최고였죠.

남: 정말 멋진 정글짐이에요. 당신은 너무 좋은 여름을 보낸 것 같아요.

여: 정말 그래요. 아버지 덕분에요.

어휘

attic ***n.*** 다락(방) **awesome** ***a.*** 아주 좋은, 굉장한

정답 ②

문제풀이

아버지가 여자의 손을 잡고 있다고 했는데 그림에서 아버지는 여자의 그네를 밀어주고 있으므로 ②번이 그림과 일치하지 않는다.

총 어휘 수 175

07 할 일

소재 새로운 드러머 찾기

듣기 대본 해석

여: 오, 시내에 있는 재즈 카페에서 연주할 재즈밴드 오디션 공고를 보고 있구나. 관심 있니?

남: 난 없어. 내 여동생이 참가하는 것에 관심 있어해. 재즈밴드에서 기타를 치거든.

여: 그녀의 밴드가 이 오디션에 참여한대?

남: 그러고 싶대. 문제는 지난주에 드러머가 팔이 부러졌어.

여: 오, 이런! 그럼 그는 아직 드럼을 칠 수 없겠네.

남: 응. 그래서 밴드 리더가 새로운 드러머를 가능한 빨리 찾으려고 노력 중이야.

여: 흠... 내가 그를 만나볼 수 있을까?

남: 왜? 너 드럼 칠 줄 아니?

여: 응, 조금 칠 수 있어. 그리고 오랫동안 밴드에 참여하고 싶기도 했고.

남: 잘됐다! 내 여동생에게 그의 휴대폰 번호를 물어봐서 너에게 곧 알려줄게.

여: 고마워. 내가 그들과 함께 연주할 만큼 잘 하면 좋겠다.

어휘

notice ***n.*** 공고문, 안내문, 공지사항 ***v.*** 알아채다 **participate** ***v.*** 참가하다

정답 ①

문제풀이

남자는 여자에게 밴드 리더의 휴대폰 번호를 여동생에게 물어보고 알려주겠다고 했으므로 정답은 ① '밴드 리더의 전화번호 알려주기'이다.

총 어휘 수 140

08 이유

소재 작아져서 입을 수 없게 된 청바지

듣기 대본 해석

남: Stacy, 네 청바지가 바닥에 있어. 좀 치워주겠니?

여: 잠깐 그냥 거기에 두면 안 될까요, Brian? 오늘 중에 자선단체에 갖다 줄 거예요.

남: 정말? 그런데 새 것 같은데.

여: 네, 기본적으로는 새 거예요. 몇 번밖에 안 입었어요.

남: 왜 주려고 하는데? 정말 질이 좋아 보이는데.

여: 알아요. 그리고 그 청바지 좋아해요. 그런데 입을 수 없어요.

남: 무슨 말이야? 왜 안 돼?

여: 저에게 너무 작아요.

남: 좋아. 그런데, 꽉 낀 청바지는 유행인데. 요즘 애들이 정말 꽉 끼는 청바지 입고 다니는 것 줄곧 봤거든.

여: 네, 그런데 게다가 너무 짧기까지 해요.

남: 아하.

여: 그 청바지 지난 여름에 샀는데 그 이후로 키가 거의 2인치 자랐어요.

남: 음, 곧 너에게 새 청바지를 사줘야겠구나.

어휘

charity ***n.*** 자선단체 **in style** 유행인

정답 ①

문제풀이

여자가 그 청바지를 좋아하지만 사이즈가 작아지고 길이도 짧아져서 못 입겠다고 말했으므로 정답은 ① '키가 커지면서 바지가 맞지 않게 되어서'이다.

총 어휘 수 139

09 숫자

소재 헤드폰 구입하기

듣기 대본 해석

남: 안녕하세요. 새로운 헤드폰을 사려고 해요.
여: 네. 생각해 보신 특별한 브랜드나 스타일이 있으세요?
남: 글쎄요. 통근할 때 착용할 거라서 편한 것이었으면 좋겠어요.
여: 알겠어요. 제 생각엔 이것을 매우 좋아하실 것 같네요.
남: 어떤 특징들이 있나요?
여: 요즘에 굉장히 인기가 좋아요. 편안함을 위해서 조절 가능한 밴드가 있고요. 최적화된 소리를 위해 신기술을 사용했어요.
남: 좋아 보이네요. 얼마인가요?
여: 50달러에 팔리고 있지만 이번 주에 10퍼센트 할인이 돼요.
남: 좋네요! 그리고 웹사이트에서 10달러를 할인해주는 쿠폰을 찾았어요. 이 제품에 쿠폰을 사용할 수 있나요?
여: 물론이죠. 할인된 가격에 추가 10달러를 깎아 드릴게요.
남: 알겠어요. 현금으로 계산할게요.
여: 네. 문제없어요.

어휘

optimal ***a.*** 최적의 **retail** ***v.*** (특정 가격에) 팔리다

정답 ②

문제풀이

원래는 50달러지만 10퍼센트 할인을 받을 수 있고, 거기에 10달러 추가 할인을 받을 수 있는 쿠폰을 사용할 수 있다. 그러므로 남자가 지불할 금액은 ② '$35'이다.

총 어휘 수 131

10 언급 유무

소재 컴퓨터 게임 토너먼트

듣기 대본 해석

여: 자기야, 내일 Albert를 컴퓨터 게임 대회에 데려가는 건 어때?
남: 좋은 생각이야! PC Playground Arena에서 개최된다고 포스터에서 봤어.
여: 거기 맞아! 매달 마지막 토요일에 대회를 개최한대.
남: 근데 Albert가 그 대회에 관심을 가질까? 일인칭 슈팅 게임을 즐기기에는 너무 어린 것 같아.
여: 난 그렇게 생각하지 않아. 분명히 좋아할 거야. 가자는 건 사실 걔 생각이었어.
남: 알겠어. 뭘 싸가야 할까?
여: 점심 싸가고 간식이랑 음료수, 그리고 우리가 응원할 수 있게 Ryan이랑 Jason 티셔츠를 가져가는 게 좋을 것 같아.
남: 오후 행사인 것치고는 꽤 많이 챙겨야 되네. 일찍 출발해야 할까?
여: 너무 일찍 출발하는 건 별로일 것 같아. 열두 시에 시작하니까 열한 시쯤 출발하자.
남: 그래. 열한 시까지 다 준비해 놓을게.

어휘

tournament ***n.*** 토너먼트 **take place** 개최되다
first-person shooter 1인칭 슈팅 게임

정답 ③

문제풀이

두 사람은 장소(PC Playground Arena), 요일(토요일), 준비물(간식, 음료수, 티셔츠), 시작 시간(12시)은 언급하였으나 대상 연령에 대해서는 언급하지 않았으므로 정답은 ③ '대상 연령'이다.

총 어휘 수 146

11 내용 일치 · 불일치

소재 겨울 캠프 자원봉사자 모집

듣기 대본 해석

여: 주목해 주세요, 여러분. New Poets Society는 시와 예술에 관심 있는 새로운 학생들의 지원을 받고 있습니다. 겨울 방학 동안 시 캠프가 있을 예정인데 우리는 본 캠프에 자원봉사로 가능한 한 많은 학생들이 참여해 주었으면 합니다. 자원봉사 캠프 상담자들은 어린 학생들을 지켜봐 주시고 적절한 행동과 안전의 모델이 되어주실 책임이 있습니다. 겨울 캠프는 12월 23일에 그리고 1월 7일에 시작하며, 모든 수업은 Minneapolis에 있는 Walker Art Center에서 개최될 것입니다. 지원서는 8월 31일까지 제출되어야 합니다. 캠프 상담자들은 일주일에 3일, 최소 8시간 동안 일해야 합니다. 만약 겨울 캠프에 추가적인 정보를 원하시면 웹사이트 www.winterpoets.com을 방문해 주십시오.

어휘

volunteer ***n.*** 자원봉사자 **participate** ***v.*** 참가(참여)하다
appropriate ***a.*** 적절한 **submit** ***v.*** 제출하다 **additional** ***a.*** 추가의

정답 ③

문제풀이

캠프의 모든 수업은 Walker Art Center에서 진행된다고 말하였으므로 내용과 일치하지 않는 것은 ③ '수업마다 다른 장소에서 캠프를 진행한다.'이다.

총 어휘 수 127

12 도표

소재 CCTV 고르기

듣기 대본 해석

여: 저기, Samuel, 당신 집에 CCTV 시스템 사지 않았어요?
남: 샀어요. 왜요?
여: 아, 남편이랑 제가 하나 사려고 다니고 있는데, 제가 그것들에 대해 정말 많이 몰라서요. 저 좀 도와줄 수 있어요?
남: 물론이죠. 그 책자 좀 볼게요. *[잠시 후]* 네. 당신은 먼저 비디오 해상도를 고려하고 싶을 거예요.
여: 음, 어떤 것을 추천해 주시겠어요?
남: 제 생각엔 해상도가 높을수록 더 좋아요.
여: 좋아요. 높은 해상도로 할게요.
남: 어두운 데서 볼 수 있는 적외선이 필요할 거라고 생각해요?
여: 적외선이 달린 것은 훨씬 비싸네요. 그게 필요할 거라고 생각하지 않아요.
남: 좋아요. 다음으로 고려할 것은 저장 용량이에요.
여: 어, 제가 너무 많은 용량이 필요할 거라고 생각하진 않아요. 당신은 어떻게 생각해요?
남: 제 것도 많은 공간을 사용하지 않고 있어요. 32기가면 충분할 거라고 생각해요.
여: 좋아요. 이 제품이 저한테 좋을 것 같아요.

어휘

resolution ***n.*** 해상도, 해결 **recommend** ***v.*** 추천하다 **go with** ~로 하다 **infrared** ***a.*** 적외선의 **storage capacity** 저장 용량

정답 ④

문제풀이

해상도가 높고, 적외선이 포함되지 않은 것, 용량은 32기가라고 했으므로 정답은 ④번임을 알 수 있다.

총 어휘 수 149

13 긴 대화의 응답

소재 집에서 공룡영화를 보는 부녀의 대화

듣기 대본 해석

남: Debra, 영화 어떻게 생각해?
여: 좋았어요, 아빠! 다시 한 번 봐요.
남: 네가 좋아할 줄 알았다. 하지만 간식을 먹고 다른 것 보자.
여: 다른 건 보고 싶지 않아요. Before Time 다시 봐요!
남: 방금 봤잖니. 이제 다른 것을 넣자. 진심이야. Teddy Rex 어때? 좋은 영화라고 들었는데.
여: 알겠어요. 하지만 Before Time만큼 좋아야 할 거예요!
남: 훨씬 더 재미있을 거야. 네가 마음 바뀌기 전에 빨리 트는 게 좋겠다.
여: 안 바꿀 거예요. 이제 Teddy Rex 틀어줘요, 아빠.
남: 좀 놀랍구나 Debra. 우리가 Before Time을 보기 시작하기 직전에 공룡들이 무섭다고 말했잖아.
여: ④ 그러게요. 하지만 그것들이 그렇게 흥미로운지 몰랐어요.

어휘

snack ***n.*** 간식 **dinosaur** ***n.*** 공룡

정답 ④

문제풀이

남자는 여자가 영화 'Before Time'을 보기 전에는 공룡들이 무섭다고 하고서는 본 후에는 그것을 한 번 더 보자고 한 것에 놀라고 있다. 이에 대한 여자의 응답으로 가장 적절한 것은 ④ '그러게요. 하지만 그것들이 그렇게 흥미로운지 몰랐어요.'이다.

오답 보기 해석

① 놀랍지 않아요. 당신이 그 영화 좋아할 줄 알았어요.
② 난 왜 사람들이 공룡영화를 좋아하는지 모르겠어요.
③ 우리 쉬면서 간식을 좀 먹는 게 좋을 것 같아요.
⑤ 공룡영화를 한 편 더 보면 당신은 겁에 질릴 거예요.

총 어휘 수 127

14 긴 대화의 응답

소재 전공 선택

듣기 대본 해석

남: Lynn, 너 대학 전공 벌써 정했어?
여: 정했어. 난 최근에 온라인 저널리즘으로 결정했어. 너는 어때?
남: 나는 아직 결정 못 했어.
여: 나는 네가 회계학을 전공할 거라고 생각했는데. 너는 숫자와 돈 관리에 재주가 있잖아.
남: 맞아. 하지만 내가 숫자를 가지고 하는 일을 하고 싶은지 잘 모르겠어. 나는 예술이랑 예술 역사에도 관심이 있거든.
여: 그래서 무엇을 전공할지 확신하지 못하고 있구나?
남: 그래, 내가 무엇을 해야 할지 모르겠어.
여: 음, 너 상담 센터에 있는 Marshall 선생님을 찾아가 봤어?
남: 내가 왜 그녀를 찾아가야 해? 나는 어떤 행동적 문제가 없는데.
여: Marshall 선생님은 네가 무엇을 제일 잘하는지 볼 수 있는 적성검사를 해주실 수 있어. 내 생각엔 그것이 네가 결정하는 데 도움을 줄 것 같아.
남: ③ 정말? 당장 도움을 받으러 가야겠어.

어휘

major in ~을 전공하다 **figure** ***v.*** (~이라고) 생각하다, 중요하다
accounting ***n.*** 회계 **knack** ***n.*** 재주, 요령 **counseling** ***n.*** 상담
behavioral ***a.*** 행동의, 행동에 관한 **aptitude** ***n.*** 적성
make a decision 결정하다

정답 ③

문제풀이

자신의 전공을 정하지 못하고 있는 남자에게 여자는 학교 상담 센터의 Marshall 선생님을 찾아가면 적성검사를 해주신다고 말하며 그것이 도움이 될 거라고 했다. 거기에 대한 남자의 적절한 대답은 ③ '정말? 당장 도움을 받으러 가야겠어.'이다.

오답 보기 해석

① 나는 네가 너의 꿈을 좇아야 한다고 생각해.
② 난 회계학을 전공해야 할 것 같아.
④ 너는 전공을 곧 선택해야 해.
⑤ 예술에는 많은 직업들이 없어.

총 어휘 수 133

15 상황에 적절한 말

소재 인터넷으로 구매한 야구 카드

듣기 대본 해석

남: Morty는 물건들을 모으는 것을 좋아합니다. 야구 카드는 그가 모으기 가장 좋아하는 물건입니다. 몇 주전, Morty는 인터넷에서 개봉하지 않은 야구 카드 20팩을 20달러에 판다는 항목별 광고를 봤습니다. 그는 구매하기로 하고 즉시 카드 판매자에게 돈을 보냈습니다. 일주일 동안 기다리고 매일 우편함을 확인하지만 카드는 오지 않았습니다. 그는 일주일을 더 기다리기로 결심했지만 카드는 여전히 오지 않았습니다. 그는 더 이상 기다리지 못하고 오늘 카드 판매자에게 전화하기로 합니다. 신호가 세 번 가자 판매자는 전화를 받습니다. 이러한 상황에서 Morty가 카드 판매자에게 뭐라고 말할까요?
Morty: ⑤ 아직 카드를 못 받았습니다. 혹시 보내셨나요?

어휘

collect ***v.*** 수집하다 **classified ad** (신문의) 안내광고, 항목별 광고란
transfer ***v.*** 보내다, 이체하다 **dealer** ***n.*** 판매자, 밀매인 **impatient** ***a.*** 짜증난, 어서 ~하고 싶어 하는

정답 ⑤

문제풀이

인터넷으로 야구 카드를 구매했는데 이주일이 지나도 오지 않자 판매자에게 전화를 건 상황이다. 따라서 Morty가 할 말은 ⑤ '아직 카드를 못 받았습니다. 혹시 보내셨나요?'가 적절하다

오답 보기 해석

① 환불금을 저한테 벌써 보내셨나요?
② 카드 한 세트 더 구매할 수 있을까요?
③ 당신의 야구 카드 모음집은 얼마나 큰가요?
④ 당신이 다른 카드 판매자들을 알고 있나 궁금합니다.

총 어휘 수 124

16 담화 주제 / 17 세부 내용 파악

소재 여러 일들을 하기 위해 이용되는 동물들

듣기 대본 해석

남: 안녕하세요 여러분. 우리의 마지막 수업에서 동물들이 어떻게 오락을 위해서 학대되고 이용되는지 서커스에서의 코끼리와 곰을 예로 들어가며 이야기했습니다. 오늘 수업에서는 사람들이 교통수단 외의 여러 일들을 하기 위해 어떻게 동물들을 이용하는지에 대해서 이야기를 해 보겠습니다. 여러분은 쇼핑몰이나 거리를 걸을 때 첫 번째 동물을 보셨을 겁니다. 이것은 맹도견이며 맹인들이 일상생활을 하는 것을 도와줍니다. 맹도견은 보통 골든리트리버이며 주인이 길을 걷고 장애물을 피하는 것을 도와줍니다.

이런 개들은 동반자가 되어 주기도 하며 일반적으로 돌보는 일을 잘 하는 동물입니다. 다음으로 이야기할 동물은 송로돼지입니다. 북아메리카와 유럽 사람들은 돼지를 이용해서 송로라고 불리는 맛있고 비싼 버섯을 찾아냅니다. 돼지들은 땅 밑에 있는 음식을 찾는 것에 대한 본능적인 친화성이 있어서 이 임무에 완벽합니다.

어휘
mistreat *v.* 학대하다 **avoid** *v.* 피하다, 막다 **obstacle** *n.* 장애물
companionship *n.* 우정 **affinity** *n.* 친밀감, (~에 대한) 기호

정답 16 ③ 17 ②

문제풀이
16 남자는 이번 수업에서 사람들이 여러 일들을 하기 위해 어떻게 동물을 이용하는지에 대해 이야기하자면서 맹도견과 송로돼지의 예를 들었으므로 정답은 ③ '동물들이 사람을 돕는 방법들'이다.

17 남자는 학대 받는 동물로 코끼리와 곰을 언급했고, 사람을 도와주는 동물의 예로 맹도견과 송로돼지를 언급했지만 사슴에 관한 언급은 없으므로 정답은 ② '사슴'이다.

오답 보기 해석
16
① 학대 받는 동물들을 구조하는 방법
② 멸종위기에 처한 동물들을 구하기 위한 노력
④ 오락에서 동물들의 역할
⑤ 도움을 위해 동물들을 사용하는 것의 부정적 영향들

17
① 코끼리
③ 곰
④ 개
⑤ 돼지

총 어휘 수 170

DICTATION ANSWERS

01 without letting me know

02 just around the corner

03 as you thought it would be / joining the Drama Club / get involved / once you join the club / get the most out of your time

04 tastes a bit strange / good for dieting and indigestion / it hasn't been properly filtered / drinking sparkling water

05 one of the best on the market / plenty of room to play / take a look at the contract

06 playing on the swing / must be your father / loved to come over and play / What a great jungle gym

07 participate in the audition / as soon as possible / join a band / let you know

08 giving them to charity / What do you mean / tight jeans were in style / I have grown

09 during my commute / an adjustable band / use it on this item / pay for it in cash

10 computer game tournament / it's taking place / He seems a bit young to enjoy / What should we pack for the event / I'll have everything ready by

11 participate in these camps / all classes will be held / Applications should be submitted

12 consider the video resolution / the higher the resolution, the better / need infrared to see in the dark

13 What did you think of / get a snack / as good as / before you change your mind

14 I figured you'd major in / have a knack for / have you gone to / what you're best at

15 came across a classified ad / wait another week / He grew impatient

16-17 perform tasks other than transportation / helps blind people / avoid obstacles / search for delicious and expensive fungi / buried up to three feet underground

12 수능영어듣기 실전모의고사

본문 p.74

01 ⑤	02 ⑤	03 ⑤	04 ③	05 ④	06 ③
07 ④	08 ①	09 ④	10 ⑤	11 ④	12 ①
13 ②	14 ①	15 ⑤	16 ①	17 ①	

01 짧은 대화의 응답

소재 면접 일정

듣기 대본 해석

여: 안녕하세요. 제가 지원서를 다 작성했는데요. 제가 해야 할 다른 것이 있나요?
남: 아니요. 됐어요. 가셔도 됩니다.
여: 알겠어요. 면접 일정을 잡기 위해 언제 저에게 전화하실 거예요?
남: ⑤ 우리는 지금 당장은 바빠서 다음 주에 당신에게 연락할 거예요.

어휘

fill out 작성하다 **application** ***n.*** 지원(서)

정답 ⑤

문제풀이

면접 일정을 위해서 언제 전화를 줄 건지를 물었으므로 적절한 응답은 ⑤ '우리는 지금 당장은 바빠서 다음 주에 당신에게 전화할 거예요.'이다.

오답 보기 해석

① 당신은 건강 검진을 받아야 해요.
② 당신은 우선 지원서를 작성해야 해요.
③ 당연하죠. 면접관이 이제 당신을 만날 거예요.
④ 우리는 당신을 위해 어제 약속을 잡았어요.

총 어휘 수 44

02 짧은 대화의 응답

소재 전시회 티켓

듣기 대본 해석

남: Rosa, 널 위해 특별한 것을 준비했어. 뭔지 궁금하지?
여: 오, 그래 제발. 어서 말해줘.
남: 내가 Van Gogh 전시회 티켓 두 장을 예매했어!
여: ⑤ 믿을 수 없어! 내가 그의 작품을 좋아하는 것을 어떻게 알았어?

어휘

exhibition ***n.*** 전시회

정답 ⑤

문제풀이

Rosa를 위해 Van Gogh의 전시회 티켓 두 장을 예매했다는 남자의 말에 적절한 응답은 ⑤ '믿을 수 없어! 내가 그의 작품을 좋아하는 것을 어떻게 알았어?'이다.

오답 보기 해석

① 네 말이 맞아. 너무 비싸.
② 선물이 뭔지 알고 싶어.
③ 네 말이 맞아. 반 고흐는 최고의 예술가야.
④ 티켓이 고작 10달러라고? 정말 싸다.

총 어휘 수 43

03 담화 목적

소재 스포츠 음료 홍보

듣기 대본 해석

여: 안녕하세요, 선수 여러분. 여러분이 모두 알다시피 경기 중에 에너지 수준을 높게 유지하는 것은 쉽지 않습니다. 스포츠를 하는 것은 자연적으로 에너지를 소진시킵니다(체력을 저하시킵니다). 경쟁에서의 우위를 유지하는 것을 도와줄 방법이 있습니다. Rad CraCra를 마시세요. Rad CraCra는 당신이 경기를 계속하게 해줍니다. 비타민과 미네랄의 특수한 배합은 높은 수준의 에너지를 유지하도록 도와줍니다. 저렴하기도 합니다. Rad CraCra 한 캔이 약 1달러 정도 하는데 이것만으로도 경기 내내 활기차게 될 수 있습니다. 고품질 제품이지만 다른 스포츠 음료의 반값입니다. 더 비싼 다른 제품들보다 효과도 오랫동안 지속됩니다. 그러므로 더 많은 힘이 필요할 때는 Rad CraCra를 찾아주세요.

어휘

drain ***v.*** 빠지다, (체력이) 쇠진하다 **competitive edge** 경쟁 우위, 경쟁력

정답 ⑤

문제풀이

여자는 스포츠 음료 Rad CraCra가 운동 경기 중 체력 저하를 막고, 몸에 좋은 성분을 포함하고 있으며 가격도 저렴하다고 말하면서 그것을 홍보하고 있으므로 정답은 ⑤ '스포츠 음료를 홍보하려고'이다.

총 어휘 수 121

04 대화 주제

소재 시험으로 인한 긴장감 해소법

듣기 대본 해석

여: Joe, 무슨 일 있니? 표정이 안 좋아.
남: 엄마, 영어 시험 때문에 긴장돼요.
여: 진정해! 일주일 내내 공부했으니까 분명 잘 할 거야.
남: 그냥 너무 걱정돼요. 어떤 것에도 집중을 못하겠어요.
여: 요가를 좀 해보거나 친구와 이야기를 나눠봤니?
남: 전화로 Molly랑 이야기했는데, 별로 도움이 되지 않았어요. 엄마는 스트레스 받을 때 어떻게 진정해요?
여: 진정해야 할 때 엄마는 보통 조깅을 해.
남: 도움이 될까요? 조깅을 하면 피곤해질 것 같아요.
여: 운동은 뇌에 엔돌핀을 분비시켜서 머리를 맑게 해줘. 분명 네 기분도 나아지게 할 거야.
남: 그래요? 그럼 호수 전체를 한 바퀴 돌고 와야겠어요. 도와주셔서 감사해요, 엄마.

어휘

concentrate ***v.*** 집중하다 **release** ***v.*** 분비하다, 방출하다 **entire** ***a.*** 전체의

정답 ③

문제풀이

시험 때문에 긴장된다는 아들에게 엄마는 요가를 하거나 친구와의 수다를 제안하기도 하고, 조깅을 해서 기분을 전환할 것을 권하고 있으므로 이 대화의 주제는 ③ '시험으로 인한 긴장을 완화하는 방법'이다.

총 어휘 수 133

05 대화자의 관계 파악

소재 헌혈하기

듣기 대본 해석

여: 안녕하세요. 헌혈하러 오셨나요?
남: 네. 그런데 좀 긴장되네요. 헌혈은 처음이거든요.
여: 잘 오셨어요. 처음에 하셔야 하는 것은 이 양식을 작성하시는 겁니다.
남: 네. *[잠시 후]* 끝났어요. 다음에는 뭘 하죠?
여: 이제 혈액형을 확인하기 위해서 손가락을 찔러야 해요.
남: 네. 그런데 전 바늘이 좀 무서워요.
여: 약간만 아플 거에요. *[잠시 후]* 좋습니다. 현재 복용하고 있는 약이 있나요?
남: 음. 며칠 전에 알레르기 약을 좀 먹었어요. 괜찮을까요?
여: 문제가 될 것 같지는 않네요. 여기 앉으셔서 소매를 걷어 주세요.
남: 모임에 좀 늦을 것 같은데요. 오래 걸리진 않겠죠?
여: 헌혈하는 데 보통 20분 정도 걸립니다. 헌혈해 주셔서 정말 감사합니다.

어휘

donate ***v.*** 헌혈하다, 기부하다 **prick** ***v.*** 찌르다 **blood type** 혈액형 **be afraid of** ~을 두려워하다 **medication** ***n.*** 약 **donation** ***n.*** 기부, 기증

정답 ④

문제풀이

남자는 헌혈하러 처음 온 사람이고, 여자는 안내를 하며 헌혈을 도와주는 상황이므로 두 사람의 관계는 ④ '간호사 — 헌혈자'로 생각할 수 있다.

총 어휘 수 140

06 그림의 세부 내용 파악

소재 어릴 때 눈사람과 놀던 사진

듣기 대본 해석

남: 여보, 내 어린 시절 사진 좀 봐요.
여: 당신 그 때 정말 귀여웠네요. 야구 유니폼 입은 당신 좀 봐요.
남: 네, 전 야구를 정말 좋아했거든요. 겨울에도 유니폼을 입었는걸요. 저게 내 처음 글러브에요.
여: 정말이요? 왼손에는 눈 뭉치를 들고 있네요. 어렸을 때는 왼손잡이였어요?
남: 네. 어릴 땐 양손잡이였어요. 어떤 손을 써야 할지 모르겠더라고요.
여: 당신이 만든 눈사람 맘에 드는데요. 당신의 모자를 준 것 같은데요.
남: 맞아요. 내 Ravens 야구모자를 쓰고 있어요. 난 Lions 모자를 쓰고 있어요.
여: 그럼 당신은 투수고 눈사람은 타자네요? 눈사람이 당신의 배트를 가지고 있어요.
남: 네. 어릴 때 친구가 별로 없어서 겨울에는 스스로 만들곤 했어요.
여: 정말 사랑스럽네요, 여보.

어휘

childhood ***n.*** 어린 시절 **ambidextrous** ***a.*** 양손잡이의 **adorable** ***a.*** 사랑스러운, 귀여운

정답 ③

문제풀이

여자가 남자의 왼손에 눈 뭉치를 들고 있다고 말했는데 그림에서는 야구공을 들고 있으므로 정답은 ③번이다.

총 어휘 수 138

07 할 일

소재 인쇄물 출력

듣기 대본 해석

여: Bill, 수정 테이프 가지고 있나요?
남: 네. 수정 테이프가 왜 필요해요?
여: 오늘 제휴사 회의를 위한 인쇄물에 잘못된 게 있어요. 그걸 고쳐야 해요.
남: 제 생각에는 당신이 컴퓨터에서 잘못된 부분을 고치고 다시 프린트해야 할 것 같아요. 제휴사 회의는 중요해요.
여: 알아요. 하지만 우리 프린트가 작동하지 않고 회의는 30분 내에 있어요.
남: 네, 알아요. 당신은 인력관리부서로 내려가서 거기 프린터를 사용해야 할 거예요.
여: 그렇지만 저는 컬러 복사가 필요해요. 거기 프린터는 흑백만 돼요.
남: 그렇지 않으면 당신은 우리 것을 수리해줄 누군가가 올 때까지 기다려야 할 거예요.
여: 저는 그렇게 오래 기다릴 수 없어요. 길에 있는 인터넷 카페에 컬러 프린터가 있을 것 같아요?
남: 저도 잘 모르지만 제가 거기 전화번호를 찾아볼 테니 당신이 전화를 걸어 볼 수 있어요.
여: 그거 좋네요. Bill. 도와줘서 고마워요.
남: 천만에요.

어휘

human resources department 인력관리부 **repair** ***v.*** 수리하다 **look up** 찾아보다

정답 ④

문제풀이

남자가 인터넷 카페에 컬러 프린터가 있을지는 모르지만 카페 전화번호를 찾아줄 테니 전화해보라고 했으므로 여자가 할 일은 ④ '인터넷 카페에 전화하기'이다.

총 어휘 수 145

08 이유

소재 바쁜 대학 생활

듣기 대본 해석

남: 안녕, Sammie. 새 학교는 좀 어때?
여: 괜찮아. 시간표에 적응해 가고 있어.
남: 잘됐네. 아, Jeff 기억나? 주말에 같이 해변에 가기로 했어.
여: 좋네. 바르셀로나에서 학기 끝내고 돌아왔나 보네.
남: 맞아. 해변가로 가서 밀린 얘기도 하고 집으로 돌아온 거 축하해 줄 거야. 같이 가자.
여: 나도 그러고 싶은데 못 갈 것 같아. 과제가 엄청 많아.
남: 학교가 널 주말에도 바쁘게 하는 거야?
여: 가끔은. 이번 주말은 특히 더 바빠. 월요일까지 중요한 화학 리포트를 제출해야 되고 화요일에는 영어 시험이 있어.
남: 대학교 생활은 아주 힘든가 보다.
여: 맞아. 일주일 내내 너무 힘들었어.

어휘

beach ***n.*** 해변 **chemistry** ***n.*** 화학 **stressful** ***a.*** 스트레스가 많은, 힘든

정답 ①

문제풀이

남자는 오랜만에 집으로 돌아온 Jeff를 맞아주기 위해 주말에 해변에 같이 가자고 여자에게 제안하였으나 여자는 주말에 해야 할 과제가 많아서 갈 수 없다고 하였으므로 정답은 ① '과제를 해야 해서'이다.

총 어휘 수 129

09 숫자

소재 고속도로 개통으로 단축될 시간과 고속도로 이용 요금

듣기 대본 해석

여: 여보, 내일 Grove Beach에 가는 것이 어때요?
남: 여기에서 너무 멀지 않나요? 구불구불한 길로 산을 넘어가는 데 약 40분이 걸리잖아요.
여: 더 이상 그 길로 갈 필요가 없어요. 지난달에 개통된 새 고속도로로 가면 돼요.
남: 정말이요? 그러니까 우리가 그 구불구불하고 위험한 산길로 운전해 갈 필요가 없다는 말인가요?
여: 맞아요. 그 고속도로를 이용해서 거기에 도달하는 데 15분 정도밖에 걸리지 않아요.
남: 와, 굉장한데요.
여: 하지만 공짜가 아니에요. 사용료를 내야 해요.
남: 얼만데요?
여: 음, 정부의 원래 계획은 5달러를 부과하는 거였어요. 하지만 시민단체들이 정부에게 요금을 내려달라고 요청했어요.
남: 그래서 요금이 내렸나요?
여: 그래요. 정부는 결국 원래 계획했던 것 보다 2달러 적게 부과하게 되었어요.
남: 오, 그렇군요.

어휘

curvy ***a.*** 굽은 **fantastic** ***a.*** 멋진 **free** ***a.*** 무료의 **original** ***a.*** 원래의 **civil organization** 시민단체 **request** ***v.*** 요청하다 **lower** ***v.*** 낮추다

정답 ④

문제풀이

구불구불한 산길을 넘는 데 약 40분이 걸렸지만 고속도로를 이용하면 15분 정도밖에 걸리지 않으므로 약 25분이 단축될 것이고, 고속도로 요금은 원래 5달러였지만 시민단체의 요청으로 정부가 2달러 적게 청구하기로 하여 3달러가 되었으므로 정답은 ④ '약 25분 — $3'이다.

총 어휘 수 129

10 언급 유무

소재 캠핑 계획

듣기 대본 해석

남: 여보, 다음 주 토요일에 우리랑 캠핑 갈래요?
여: 모르겠어요. 거기에서 재미있을지 모르겠어요.
남: 재미있을 거예요. 호수가 정말 아름다워요. 내가 불 피우는 법과 텐트 치는 법을 알려줄게요.
여: 알았어요, 갈게요. 그런데 내가 지루해지지 않게 계속 참여시켜 줘야 해요.
남: 물론이죠, 여보. 우리가 가려는 곳은 아주 잘 알려져 있어요. 당신이 인터넷으로 찾아 볼 수도 있어요.
여: 거기까지 여기서 얼마나 걸려요?
남: 차로 3시간 30분 정도 걸리는데 가는 길의 경치가 너무 아름다워요.
여: 정말 기대가 되네요. 그런데 거기서 우리 뭘 먹을까요?
남: 물고기를 잡아 먹고 물론 핫도그나 햄버거 같은 다른 음식들도 먹을 거예요.
여: 알았어요. 짐 싸는 데 도울 일이 있나요?
남: 없어요! 내가 다 할 수 있어요. 당신은 그냥 친구가 되어주기만 하면 돼요.

어휘

build a fire 불을 피우다 **scenery** ***n.*** 경치 **pack** ***v.*** 짐을 싸다 **company** ***n.*** 친구

정답 ⑤

문제풀이

캠핑 가는 요일, 남자가 여자에게 알려줄 일, 캠핑 가는 데 걸리는 시간, 캠핑에서 먹을 음식은 언급되었지만 짐 싸야 할 항목에 대한 언급은 없으므로 정답은 ⑤ '짐을 싸야 할 항목'이다.

총 어휘 수 166

11 내용 일치 · 불일치

소재 Georgetown's Musical Mondays 행사

듣기 대본 해석

남: 여러분 안녕하세요. 여러분들도 아시다시피, 날씨가 따뜻해지고 있는데요, 이는 강가에서 Georgetown's Musical Mondays가 시작할 때라는 것을 의미합니다. 첫 번째 행사는 다음 주 월요일인 4월 22일 여섯 시에 개최될 예정입니다. 유명한 블루스 밴드인 Back Section Action이 Riverside Park에서 공연하러 올 예정이고요, 그 밴드의 리드보컬이 공연 후에 팬들과 만날 것입니다. 그 밴드는 6시에 무대에 오를 것이며 대략 8시에 끝날 예정입니다. 우리의 모든 행사와 마찬가지로, 이 공연도 모든 연령대를 위한 공연이므로 여러분의 친구와 가족 모두를 데리고 오세요. 모든 참석자는 5달러의 요금을 지불해야 하며, 수익금 전액은 Georgetown 예술문화 협회에 전달될 예정입니다. 시간 내주셔서 감사합니다.

어휘

kick off 시작하다 **take place** 일어나다, 개최되다 **entire** ***a.*** 전체의 **proceeds** ***n.*** 수익금

정답 ④

문제풀이

이 공연은 모든 연령대를 위한 공연이라고 언급했으므로 내용과 일치하지 않는 것은 ④ '초등학생 이상의 어린이부터 입장할 수 있다.'이다.

총 어휘 수 127

12 도표

소재 자전거 강좌 선택

듣기 대본 해석

남: 여보, 우리가 Adam한테 보조바퀴 없이 자전거 타는 법을 가르치기 시작해야 할 것 같아요.
여: 좋은 생각이긴 한데 여기 주변에서 하는 건 안전하지 않다고 생각해요. 거리가 항상 너무 북적이잖아요.
남: 그게, Freedom Park에서 하는 자전거 수업에 관한 이 전단지를 봤어요. 이 강사들은 아이들이 처음 자전거 타는 것을 가르치는 걸 전문으로 하고 있어요.
여: 정말 좋네요.
남: 나도 그렇게 생각해요. 우리가 남자선생님을 고용해야 할까요, 아니면 여자선생님을 고용해야 할까요?
여: 제 생각엔 여자선생님을 선택해야 할 것 같아요. 그 애는 학교에 여자선생님들을 좋아하는 것 같아 보여요.
남: 좋아요. 이 수업은 듣지 못하겠네요. 월요일에는 야구 연습이 있어요.
여: 남은 두 수업 중에서 좀 더 경험이 많은 분으로 해야 될 것 같아요.
남: 나도 동의해요. 우리에게 맞는 강사를 찾은 것 같네요.

어휘

flyer ***n.*** (광고 · 안내용) 전단 **instructor** ***n.*** 강사

정답 ①

문제풀이
아들에게 알맞은 자전거 강좌를 찾고 있는 두 사람은 여자선생님을 원하고, 월요일은 야구 연습 때문에 안 된다고 했으며 경력이 더 많은 선생님을 원하고 있다. 따라서 모든 조건을 만족시키는 강좌는 ①번이다.

총 어휘 수 141

13 긴 대화의 응답

소재 교내 장기자랑 참가 결정

듣기 대본 해석
여: 그래서 Larry, 너 올해 장기자랑에 나갈 거야?
남: 확실하지 않아요.
여: 왜 확실하지 않아? 너 저글링 정말 잘하고 무척 열심히 연습해 왔잖아.
남: 내가 실수하고 모든 사람들이 나보고 웃을까 걱정이 되거든요.
여: 넌 자신감을 갖고 너 자신을 믿을 필요가 있어, Larry. 많은 사람들이 사람들 앞에서 공연할 때 무대 공포증을 갖는단다.
남: 도와주시려 해서 감사해요, 엄마.
여: 그래, 한번 해볼 거지?
남: 음... 아직 모르겠어요.
여: 시도해봐! 자신감을 보여줘! 두려워하는 것은 너답지 않아!
남: 작년에 무대에서의 큰 실수 후에, 저한테 자신감이 있는지 확신을 못하겠어요.
여: 안심해. 누구도 완벽하지 않고 모든 사람은 실수를 한단다.
남: 그럼, 엄마는 제가 올해 더 잘할 거라고 생각하세요?
여: ② 물론이지, 너는 열심히 연습해 왔잖니.

어휘
take part in ~에 참가하다 **talent show** 장기자랑
make a mistake 실수하다 **stage fright** 무대 공포증
give ~ a shot ~을 시도해 보다 **confidence** ***n.*** 자신감
disaster ***n.*** 완전한 실패, 재해 **relax** ***v.*** 휴식을 취하다, 안심하다

정답 ②

문제풀이
장기자랑에 나가기를 망설이는 아들에게 엄마가 용기를 주고 있는 상황이다. 작년에 했던 실수 이후로 자신감을 잃은 아들이 이번에 나가면 잘할 수 있을지 물을 때 엄마가 할 수 있는 응답은 ② '물론이지, 너는 열심히 연습해 왔잖니.'가 적절하다.

오답 보기 해석
① 너는 전에 무대 공포증이 있었던 적이 없었어.
③ 네가 없었더라면 난 그걸 할 수 없었을 거야.
④ 아니, 나는 너무 긴장돼서 공연을 할 수 없어.
⑤ 그래, 내가 한번 시도해 봐야겠어.

총 어휘 수 139

14 긴 대화의 응답

소재 독일에 살다 온 이유

듣기 대본 해석
여: Nicholas, 제가 일전에 시내에서 당신을 본 것 같아요. 당신은 아주 매력적인 여성분과 이야기하고 있었어요.
남: 아, 기억나요. Clarice Heisenberg와 이야기하고 있었어요. 그녀는 저희 가족사업을 위해 일하고 있어요. 그녀가 저희의 모든 해외 계좌들을 관리하고 있죠.
여: 제가 들으려는 의도는 아니었는데 당신이 다른 언어로 이야기하는 것을 알아챌 수 밖에 없었어요.
남: 네, Clarice는 독일에서 왔어요. 그녀가 영어로 말할 수 있긴 하지만 그녀는 독일어로 말하는 게 더 쉽고, 저는 연습하는 것을 좋아해요.
여: 나는 당신이 독일어를 하는지 몰랐어요.
남: 네, 저는 사실 독일에서 태어나서 어릴 때 십 년 동안 살았어요.
여: 정말이요? 몰랐어요. 왜 독일에서 살았죠?
남: 저희 아버지의 사업이 거기에 근거지를 두고 있었어요.
여: 흥미롭네요. 언젠가 독일로 돌아갈 거예요?
남: ① 네, 저는 아이들이 조금 더 크면 돌아갈 거예요.

어휘
attractive ***a.*** 매력적인 **handle** ***v.*** 다루다, 관리하다 **overseas** ***a.*** 해외의 ***ad.*** 해외에서 **account** ***n.*** 계좌

정답 ①

문제풀이
남자는 어릴 때 독일에서 10년을 살았다고 말했고, 여자는 다시 돌아갈 것인지를 물었으므로 그에 적절한 남자의 대답은 ① '네, 저는 아이들이 조금 더 크면 돌아갈 거예요.'이다.

오답 보기 해석
② 사실은, 내가 어릴 때 미국을 떠나지 않았으면 좋았을 거예요.
③ 그래요, 해외에서 의사소통 하는 것은 힘들 거예요.
④ 맞아요, 열심히 하는 것은 모든 것을 가능하게 만들죠.
⑤ 나는 정말 외국에서 공부하고 싶었지만 여유가 없었어요.

총 어휘 수 143

15 상황에 적절한 말

소재 기부자들에게 감사 표하는 방법

듣기 대본 해석
남: 엄청난 토네이도가 최근에 근처 동네를 강타하자 Greg과 Henry는 피해를 입은 사람들에게 도움을 주기 위해 자선 행사를 열었습니다. 배려심 깊은 사람들이 돈과 통조림 식품과 생수 같은 기본적인 생필품을 기부해주어서 행사는 성공적이었습니다. Greg과 Henry는 기부에 감사해 하는 피해자들에게 이러한 물품들을 보내주었습니다. Greg과 Henry는 기부를 한 사람들에게 감사한 마음을 표현하기로 했습니다. Henry는 이메일을 보내는 것으로 충분할 것이라고 생각합니다. Greg은 이메일이 편리하다는 것에는 동의하지만 손글씨 편지가 더 사적이고 진심 어리기 때문에 손글씨 편지를 보내야 한다고 생각합니다. 이러한 상황에서 Greg은 Henry에게 뭐라고 말할까요?
Greg: ⑤ 감사한 마음을 보여주는 데에는 손글씨 감사 편지가 가장 좋은 방법이라고 생각해.

어휘
charity ***n.*** 자선 **necessities** ***n.*** 필수품 **suffice** ***v.*** 충분하다
convenient ***a.*** 편리한 **personal** ***a.*** 사적인, 개인적인 **sincere** ***a.*** 진심 어린

정답 ⑤

문제풀이
Greg과 Henry는 함께 자선 행사를 했고, 기부해준 사람들에게 고마움을 표하고자 한다. Greg은 이메일로도 충분하다고 생각하는 Henry에게 감사한 마음을 보여주는 데는 손으로 쓴 편지가 좋다고 말하려 하므로 ⑤ '감사한 마음을 보여주는 데에는 손글씨 감사 편지가 가장 좋은 방법이라고 생각해.'가 정답이다.

오답 보기 해석
① 이메일은 감사하는 마음을 보여주는 좋은 방법이야.
② 그들이 무엇을 기부했는지는 상관 없어. 마음이 중요한 거지.
③ 감사한 마음을 표현하기 위해 선물 바구니를 만드는 게 좋을 것 같아.
④ 감사 편지를 쓰는 데에 그렇게 많은 시간을 투자하면 안 된다고 생각해.

총 어휘 수 128

16 담화 주제 / 17 세부 내용 파악

소재 여름에 시원하게 지내는 법

듣기 대본 해석

남: 이번 여름은 좀 더웠습니다, 그렇지 않았나요? 사실, 전 지구가 지구 온난화로 점점 더 뜨거워지고 있습니다. 만약에 여러분께서 더위를 이기고 시원함을 유지하고 싶으시다면, 적절한 옷을 입으십시오. 밝은 색은 빛과 함께 열도 반사하지만 어두운 색은 그것을 흡수합니다. 그래서 더 밝은 색의 옷을 입는 것이 여러분을 더 시원하게 해줍니다. 또한 여러분은 열을 발생시키는 전자제품들을 사용하지 않을 때 꺼 두어야 합니다. 예를 들어, 전화기를 충전하고 있지 않을 때는 전화기 충전기의 선을 꽂아둘 필요가 없습니다. 또, 시원함을 유지하기 위해서 시계가 있는 것들의 플러그를 뽑는 것이 현명합니다. 전자레인지와 커피메이커가 열을 발생시키고 전기를 낭비하는 시계가 딸린 전자제품의 좋은 예들입니다. 컴퓨터 또한 많은 열을 발생시킵니다. 그래서 여러분이 컴퓨터를 쓰지 않을 때는 컴퓨터를 꺼야 합니다. 마지막으로, 가능한 아래층으로 내려오세요. 지하가 집의 다른 곳보다 항상 더 시원합니다. 보통 다른 층들보다 약 5-10도 더 시원합니다.

어휘

reflect *v.* 비추다, 반사하다 **absorb** *v.* 흡수하다 **generate** *v.* 발생시키다 **charger** *n.* 충전기 **unplug** *v.* 플러그를 뽑다

정답 16 ① 17 ①

문제풀이

16 남자는 지구 온난화로 점점 더워지는 지구에서 시원함을 유지할 수 있는 몇 가지 방법을 소개하고 있다. 따라서 남자가 하는 말의 주제는 ① '더운 날씨에 시원하게 지내는 것에 대한 조언'이 된다.

17 남자는 처음에 전화기 충전기를 언급했고 다음에 전자레인지와 커피메이커, 그리고 컴퓨터를 언급했으므로 언급되지 않은 것은 ① '냉장고'이다.

오답 보기 해석

16

② 비상 상황에 해야 하는 일

③ 환경을 위해 에너지를 절약하는 방법

④ 디지털 전자제품의 에너지 소비량

⑤ 전기 콘센트 과부하의 위험성

총 어휘 수 162

DICTATION ANSWERS

01 filling out the application

02 I reserved two tickets to

03 keep a competitive edge / maintain a high level of energy / stay energized for the entire game / last longer

04 You seem stressed out / concentrate on / go for a jog / around the entire lake

05 Are you here to donate / The first thing you need to do / took some medicine for my allergies

06 Were you left-handed / which hand to use / That's adorable

07 fix the mistake / our printer isn't working / someone comes to repair ours / look up their number

08 get used to my schedule / celebrate him coming home / keeping you busy / university life is stressful

09 It takes about forty minutes / those curvy, dangerous mountain roads / lower the fee / ended up charging

10 make sure to keep me involved / is very well known / the scenery on the way / I have it all under control

11 taking place / take the stage / an all-ages show / for all attendees

12 without training wheels / this flyer for bicycle lessons / with more experience

13 are you going to take part in / A lot of people get stage fright / give it a shot / No one is perfect

14 I didn't mean to / I wasn't aware / go back to Germany

15 benefit those who were affected / were very grateful for / sending emails would suffice

16-17 beat the heat and stay cool / turn off electronics that generate heat / it's wise to unplug anything / generate heat and waste electricity

13 수능영어듣기 실전모의고사

본문 p.80

01 ⑤	02 ①	03 ③	04 ②	05 ⑤	06 ⑤
07 ④	08 ⑤	09 ④	10 ⑤	11 ④	12 ②
13 ①	14 ①	15 ④	16 ③	17 ①	

01 짧은 대화의 응답

소재 저녁 식사

듣기 대본 해석

여: 영화 시작하기 전에 시간이 좀 있네. 저녁 먹자.
남: 좋아. 배고파 죽겠어. 뭐 먹고 싶어?
여: 일식이 먹고 싶어. 넌 어때?
남: ⑤ 좋은 생각이야. 근처에 괜찮은 식당을 알고 있어.

어휘

starve ***v.*** 굶주리다 **in the mood for** ~할 기분이 나서

정답 ⑤

문제풀이

여자가 일식이 먹고 싶다고 말하며 남자의 의견을 물었을 때 가장 적절한 대답은 ⑤ '좋은 생각이야. 근처에 괜찮은 식당을 알고 있어.'이다.

오답 보기 해석

① 나도. 중국 음식 엄청 좋아해.
② 좋은 생각이야. 팝콘 먹자.
③ 난 액션보다 로맨스 영화가 좋아.
④ 글쎄. 영화 끝나고 저녁을 먹고 싶어.

총 어휘 수 38

02 짧은 대화의 응답

소재 신입사원의 사무실 위치 찾기

듣기 대본 해석

남: 그게, 저 여기서 막 일하기 시작해서 제 사무실이 어딘지 모르겠어요.
여: 마케팅 부장님인 Sarah씨에게 물어보세요.
남: 그분이 어디 있는지 아세요? 전 그녀를 한 번도 못 만나봤거든요.
여: ① 그녀는 그녀의 사무실에 있을 겁니다. 제가 둘을 소개시켜 줄게요.

어휘

marketing manager 마케팅 책임자 〈문제〉 **fit** ***n.*** 어울림, 조화

정답 ①

문제풀이

남자는 자신의 사무실 위치를 알기 위해 마케팅 부장을 만나야 하는데 그녀를 만난 적조차 없으므로 이에 대한 여자의 응답으로 가장 적절한 것은 ① '그녀는 그녀의 사무실에 있을 겁니다. 제가 둘을 소개시켜 줄게요.'이다.

오답 보기 해석

② 만약 그러한 경우라면, 당신은 새로운 사무실을 찾아야 해요.
③ 제 사무실은 이 건물의 6층에 있어요.
④ 여긴 당신의 사무실이 아니에요. 당신의 사무실은 저기예요.
⑤ 새로운 팀 멤버가 아주 적합한 사람 같네요.

총 어휘 수 45

03 담화 목적

소재 채식주의자가 되는 이유

듣기 대본 해석

여: 지난 시간에 우리는 많은 종교, 특히 불교와 힌두교에서 고기를 먹지 않는 것이 일반적이라고 배웠습니다. 오늘 수업에서 저는 고기를 먹지 않고 채식주의자가 되는 여러 다른 이유들을 알아보고 싶습니다. 많은 사람들은 채식주의가 건강에 좋다고 믿기 때문에 채식주의를 선택합니다. 그들은 고기를 적게 먹고 섬유질을 많이 먹는 것이 심장병, 암, 당뇨병에 걸릴 위험을 낮출 것이라고 믿습니다. 채식주의자는 윤리적인 신념 또한 가지고 있습니다. 그들은 소나 닭 같은 특정 동물들을 크게 만들기 위해 다른 화학약품을 먹이는 것을 좋아하지 않습니다. 어떤 이유로든 동물을 죽이는 데에 반대하는 사람들도 있습니다. 채식주의자가 되고 싶은 어떤 다른 이유들이 있을까요? 우리와 함께 생각을 공유해 주세요.

어휘

Buddhism ***n.*** 불교 **Hinduism** ***n.*** 힌두교 **vegetarian** ***n.*** 채식주의자 **vegetarianism** ***n.*** 채식주의 **fiber** ***n.*** 섬유질 **diabetes** ***n.*** 당뇨병 **ethical** ***a.*** 윤리적인, 도덕상의 **chemical** ***n.*** 화학약품

정답 ③

문제풀이

사람들이 왜 채식주의자가 되는지를 알아보는 강의이다. 건강상의 이유, 윤리적인 신념 등으로 채식주의자가 된다고 말하고 있으므로 여자가 하는 말의 목적은 ③ '채식주의자가 되는 이유를 설명하려고'이다.

총 어휘 수 128

04 의견

소재 TV 자막을 이용한 영어 실력 향상

듣기 대본 해석

여: 저게 블루레이 재생기인가요? 조금 특이하게 생겼네요.
남: 청각 장애가 있는 사람들을 위한 자막이 제공돼요.
여: 정말이요? 아주 흥미로운 생각이네요. 그런 기술이 있는지 몰랐어요.
남: 모든 TV 프로그램에서 지원되는 것은 아니지만 대부분 지원이 되고 인터넷으로 더 주문할 수도 있어요.
여: 청각 장애가 없으신데 왜 이 기계를 갖고 계신가요?
남: 일년 동안 우리와 지내게 될 교환 학생이 있는데 이 재생기가 그녀의 영어 실력 향상에 도움이 될 것이라고 생각했어요.
여: 아주 사려 깊으시네요. 그런데 그녀가 TV 보는 것을 좋아하는지 어떻게 아세요?
남: 이메일로 물어봤어요. 미국 드라마 보는 것을 좋아하지만 대화 속도가 가끔은 너무 빨라서 알아듣기 어렵다네요.
여: 그렇다면 이 기기가 아주 도움이 되겠네요.
남: 그러면 좋겠어요. 기기가 싸지는 않았거든요.

어휘

subtitle ***n.*** 자막 **hearing disability** 청각 장애 **exchange student** 교환 학생 **thoughtful** ***a.*** 사려 깊은

정답 ②

문제풀이

남자의 집에서 지낼 교환 학생이 말하길 그녀는 미국 드라마 보는 것을 좋아하지만 빠른 대화 속도로 인해 어려움을 겪는다고 한다. 그런 교환 학생의 영어 실력 향상에 TV 자막이 도움이 될 것이라고 말한 것으로 보아 남자의 의견으로 적절한 것은 ② 'TV 자막을 활용하면 효과적으로 외국어를 학습할 수 있다.'이다.

총 어휘 수 143

05 장소 파악

소재 밴드 배틀 대회

듣기 대본 해석

여: 와, 이곳은 정말 붐비는 구나. 엄청 시끄럽네!
남: 응, 오늘이 대회 마지막 날이야. 최종 4개 밴드팀이 곧 공연할 거야.
여: 그렇구나. 난 이곳이 이렇게 붐비고 시끄러울 줄 몰랐어.
남: Clara, 이건 로큰롤 대회야. 당연히 시끄럽지.
여: 생각은 했었지. 하지만 이 정도일 줄은 몰랐어. 이건 정말 대단해.
남: 그래, 믿어지지 않을 정도지, 그렇지? 매년 열리는 밴드들의 배틀 대회가 지난 몇 년간 많은 인기를 누리고 있어.
여: 확실히 그랬지. 내 생각엔 모든 밴드들이 이 공연을 위해 최고의 노래들을 아껴두고 있었던 같아. 그렇지?
남: 응. 우리 형이 말하길 그의 밴드는 최종 결승을 위해 가장 시끄럽고 강력한 노래를 할 거라고 했어.
여: 정말 말 되네.
남: 난 그의 공연이 정말 기대가 돼.
여: 나도 그래.

어휘

competition ***n.*** 경쟁, 대회 **performance** ***n.*** 공연, 연주회

정답 ⑤

문제풀이

밴드 대회가 시작되기 전 남자와 여자가 나누고 있는 대화이므로 두 사람이 대화하고 있는 장소는 ⑤ '밴드 대회장'임을 알 수 있다.

총 어휘 수 134

06 그림의 세부 내용 파악

소재 고양이와 찍은 사진

듣기 대본 해석

남: 안녕, Maro. 뭐 보고 있어?
여: 내 고양이 Dubu랑 내 사진이야. 한번 봐.
남: *[잠시 후]* 이 사진에서 너 정말 어려 보인다. 언제 찍은 거야?
여: 분명 내가 Dubu를 받은 직후였을 거야. 나 안경을 썼었잖아.
남: 너 안경 쓴 거 본 적 없는데. Dubu의 색깔이 맘에 든다. 멋있게 완전한 회색이야.
여: 응. 이 셔츠 어떻게 생각해?
남: 내 생각에는 좀 저렴해 보이는 것 같은데. 난 물방울 무늬는 정말 별로거든. 목줄에 달려있는 건 하트 펜던트야?
여: 응. 귀여운 것 같아서 사줬지. 그는 또한 가장 좋아하는 장난감을 가지고 놀고 있어.
남: 공이네, 맞지?
여: 응. 나는 그에게 새로운 장난감을 항상 사주는데 여전히 저 공을 엄청 좋아해.
남: 멋지다. 좋은 고양이 같아.

어휘

solid ***a.*** 다른 색이 섞이지 않은(완전한) **cheesy** ***a.*** 싸구려의
polka dot 물방울무늬

정답 ⑤

문제풀이

대화의 마지막 부분에서 고양이가 가지고 있는 장난감은 공이라고 했는데 그림에서는 물고기를 가지고 있으므로 정답은 ⑤번이다.

총 어휘 수 138

07 부탁한 일

소재 집 안 대청소 후 외식

듣기 대본 해석

여: 이제야 집 청소를 마쳤어요.
남: 네, 쉽지 않았어요. 그렇게 힘들지 몰랐어요.
여: 오늘 날씨가 너무 더운 것도 도움이 되지 않았어요.
남: 그래도 결국, 우리가 해냈어요. 모든 게 훨씬 좋아 보이네요.
여: 맞아요. 오, 시간을 봐요. 우리가 저녁을 놓칠 뻔 했어요. 뭘 만들어야 할까요?
남: 아무것도 만들고 싶지 않아요. 나가서 저녁을 먹으러 갑시다. 우린 그럴 자격이 있어요.
여: 좋은 생각이에요. 우리가 이제 막 청소했는데 부엌을 어지럽히고 싶지 않아요.
남: 그래요. 나도 쉬고 싶고 남은 시간을 즐기고 싶어요.
여: 나가기 전에 개들한테 먹이 좀 줄래요? 저는 저녁 먹기 위해서 빨리 씻고 싶어요.
남: 물론이죠.
여: 고마워요, 여보.

어휘

miss ***v.*** 놓치다 **make a mess** 어지럽히다 **relax** ***v.*** 휴식을 취하다

정답 ④

문제풀이

청소를 마치고 저녁 식사를 하러 나가기로 했는데 여자는 나가기 전에 개들한테 먹이를 줄 것을 남자에게 부탁하고 있다. 따라서 정답은 ④ '저녁 전에 개들한테 먹이주기'이다.

오답 보기 해석

① 옷장 청소하기
② 저녁을 위한 음식 준비하기
③ 식당에 미리 전화하기
⑤ 집에 있는 모든 불 끄기

총 어휘 수 131

08 이유

소재 같이 오토바이 탈 시간 정하기

듣기 대본 해석

여: 안녕, Marcus. 너 오토바이 수리 끝났니?
남: 응, 오늘 아침에 직장에 타고 왔어. 마치 새 것 같았어. 오늘 일 끝나고 같이 타러 갈까?
여: 안 될 것 같은데. 내일 오후에 가자.
남: 토요일 오후? 오늘 밤은 왜 안 돼?
여: 음, 우리가 어떻게 다음 주에 그 중요한 출장을 가게 된 건지 너도 알잖아? 난 오늘 퇴근 전에 모든 준비를 마쳐야 해.
남: 오, 그런데 난 내일은 타러 못 갈 것 같은데.
여: 왜? 주말에 무슨 계획 있니?
남: 응. 내일 아침에 여동생을 만나기로 했어.
여: 뭐 할 건데?
남: 그녀는 새 아파트로 이사를 해서 내 도움이 필요해.
여: 힘들겠구나. 어쨌든, 여동생과 즐거운 시간이 되길 바라. 곧 같이 오토바이 탈 시간을 맞춰보자.
남: 좋아.

어휘

brand new 완전 새 것인 **exhausting** ***a.*** 힘든, 기진맥진하게 만드는

정답 ⑤

문제풀이
대화의 마지막 부분에서 여자가 내일 무슨 계획이 있는지 묻자 남자는 여동생의 이사를 도와줘야 한다고 했으므로 정답은 ⑤ '여동생 이사를 도와줘야 해서'이다.

총 어휘 수 144

09 숫자

소재 공항에 마중 가기

듣기 대본 해석
남: Marcia가 떠난 지 벌써 일 년이 되었다니 믿을 수가 없어요.
여: 알아요. 어서 그녀와 이야기를 나누고 싶어요.
남: 그녀가 탄 한국에서 오는 비행기는 언제 도착하죠?
여: 오후 6시요.
남: 좋아요. 그럼 5시쯤 여기서 출발하면 시간에 맞게 거기에 도착할 거예요.
여: 네. 근데 요즘 도로 공사 때문에 차가 많이 막혀요. 더 일찍 출발해야 될 거예요.
남: 좋아요. 30분 일찍은 어때요?
여: 좋은 생각이에요. 제가 지금 식료품점에 가서 오늘 저녁거리를 사올게요.
남: 출발할 수 있게 시간 맞춰 올 거죠?
여: 물론이죠. 그때 봐요.
남: 아주 좋아요. 절대 늦지 마요. 오늘은 정말 중요한 날이에요!
여: 알아요. 늦지 않을게요.

어휘
flight ***n.*** 항공기, 항공편 **road work** 도로 공사

정답 ④

문제풀이
원래는 5시쯤에 출발하려고 했지만 도로 공사 때문에 차가 막히므로 30분 더 일찍 출발하기로 했다. 그러므로 답은 ④ '4시 30분'이다.

총 어휘 수 130

10 언급 유무

소재 중고 판매점

듣기 대본 해석
여: Jason, 다음 달 대회를 위한 컴퓨터 게임 샀어?
남: 응, Big Panda's 중고 판매점에서 샀어. 새 것 같은데 15달러밖에 안 줬어.
여: 정말? 새 것 가격의 반이네. 그 가게는 얼마나 멀어?
남: 이 길 따라 쭉 내려가면 그 옛날 고등학교 근처에 있어.
여: 그럼 꽤 가깝네.
남: 응. 중고 책, 게임, 그리고 영화로 가득 차 있는 이층짜리 빌딩에 있어.
여: 우와! 꽤 크구나. 나도 거기 가서 게임을 좀 봐야겠다. 언제 문 닫아?
남: 밤 열 시에 닫는 것 같아. 근데 확실하게 전화해서 물어 보는 게 나을 거야.
여: 좋은 생각이야.
남: 아! 그리고 학생증 보여주면 10퍼센트 할인해 줘.
여: 좋다! 도와줘서 고마워.

어휘
resale ***n.*** 재판매, 중고 판매

정답 ⑤

문제풀이
남자가 여자에게 중고 판매점에 대해 말해주고 있는 상황이다. 매장의 위치, 규모, 문 닫는 시간, 할인 혜택은 언급되었지만 택배 서비스에 대한 언급은 하지 않았으므로 정답은 ⑤ '택배 서비스'이다.

총 어휘 수 147

11 내용 일치 · 불일치

소재 멜론 나무

듣기 대본 해석
여: 오늘 아침 저는 멜론 나무에 대해 말하려 합니다. 그것은 남아메리카의 남쪽 지역이 원산지이고, 그것의 오렌지색 꽃은 봄에 2주 동안 매일 밤 자정에 볼 수 있습니다. 멜론 나무는 그 지역에 사는 야생 꿀벌에 의해 수분됩니다. 수분될 때, 꽃들은 밤에 빛나는 것처럼 보입니다. 멜론 나무가 만드는 열매는 이 특정한 지역에서만 발견되는 특별한 종의 멜론입니다. 그 맛은 수박이나 칸탈루프와 비슷하며 매우 달콤하고 즙이 많습니다. 그러나 그 열매는 먹지는 못하는데 그 멜론 나무를 수분하는 벌들이 독성이 있고 식물에 그들 독의 강한 자취를 남기기 때문입니다. 과일은 먹을 수 없지만 씨는 햇볕으로 인한 심한 화상을 치료하기 위해 사용되는 효과 좋은 연고로 가공될 수 있습니다.

어휘
pollinate ***v.*** 수분하다 **inhabit** ***v.*** 살다, 거주하다 **glow** ***v.*** 빛나다 **poisonous** ***a.*** 독성이 있는 **trace** ***n.*** 자취, 흔적 **process** ***v.*** 가공(처리)하다 **ointment** ***n.*** 연고 **severe** ***a.*** 극심한, 심각한

정답 ④

문제풀이
멜론 나무의 열매는 달고 즙이 많지만 수분하는 벌들이 독성이 있고 식물에 그들 독의 강한 자취를 남기기 때문에 먹을 수 없다고 했으므로 내용과 일치하지 않는 것은 ④ '열매는 달고 즙이 많아 사람이 먹을 수 있다.'이다.

총 어휘 수 131

12 도표

소재 태블릿 선택

듣기 대본 해석
남: 여보, 새로운 태블릿을 살 때가 된 것 같아. 지금 우리가 갖고 있는 건 너무 오래됐고 느려.
여: 나도 그렇게 생각했어. 원하는 걸 찾았어?
남: 응. 우리가 살 수 있는 것들의 목록을 만들어봤어. 한번 봐봐.
여: *[잠시 후]* 이거 괜찮은 것 같아. 제일 싸기도 하고.
남: 응, 그게 싸. 그런데 별로 크지가 않아. 사실 우리가 지금 갖고 있는 것보다 작아.
여: 정말? 그럼 이게 화면이 제일 크네. 그리고 아주 인기 있는 브랜드 것이기도 하고.
남: 그걸 살까도 생각 했었어. 근데 태블릿에 250달러 이상을 쓰는 건 합리적인 것 같지 않아. 좀 더 저렴한 걸 찾아보자.
여: 그래. 그럼 이 두 개 중에서 골라야 된다는 거네. 이게 더 비싼데 보증 기간이 더 길어.
남: 그래. 보증 기간이 더 긴 게 중요한 것 같아. 고장 나면 비교적 쉽게 교체할 수 있잖아.
여: 좋아. 그럼 이걸로 하자.

어휘
tablet ***n.*** 태블릿 **justify** ***v.*** 정당화하다, 합리화하다 **warranty** ***n.*** 보증 기간, 품질 보증서

정답 ②

문제풀이
가장 저렴한 ①번은 너무 작다고 했고, 250달러 이상 쓰는 것은 합리적이지 않다고 했으므로 ②번과 ③번이 남는다. 그 중에 비싸지만 보증 기간이 긴 것으로 하자고 했으므로 정답은 ②번이다.

총 어휘 수 160

13 긴 대화의 응답

소재 생체공학적 다리

듣기 대본 해석

남: 안녕 Lana. 너 휠체어 어디 있어?
여: 오늘은 가져오지 않았어.
남: 그럼 이제 목발을 사용하는구나?
여: 아니, 난 목발도 필요 없어.
남: 그렇구나. 그럼 어떻게 돌아다니려고 해? 도움 없이 걷는 게 힘들잖아.
여: 이제는 휠체어나 목발 없이도 걸을 수 있어. 다시 사용할 필요가 없어.
남: 뭐? 말도 안돼! 평생 걸을 수 없었잖아!
여: 나 C-Braces를 맞췄어.
남: C-Braces가 뭐야?
여: 그건 내 다리에 붙여서 내가 다른 도움 없이 걸을 수 있는, 특별하고 컴퓨터로 조절되는 버팀대야. 새로운 기술이지.
남: 그럼 기본적으로 이제 네가 걸을 수 있다는 얘기야?
여: 맞아. 이제 내 생체공학적 다리로 돌아다닐 수 있어.
남: ① 대단하다. 기술이 참 놀랍지 않니?

어휘

crutch ***n.*** 목발 **brace** ***n.*** 버팀대 **bionic** ***a.*** 생체 공학적인

정답 ①

문제풀이

도움 없이는 걸을 수 없었던 여자가 갑자기 혼자 걷게 되자 남자는 이유를 물었고 여자는 C-Braces라는 생체공학적 다리를 맞췄다고 말해주고 있다. 남자의 마지막 반응은 ① '대단하다. 기술이 참 놀랍지 않니?'가 적절하다.

오답 보기 해석

② 너는 지금 당장 C-Braces를 맞춰야 해.
③ 충고 고마워. 새로운 목발을 살게.
④ 맞아. 난 곧 걸을 수 있게 될 거야.
⑤ 너와 같은 상태를 가진 사람들은 다시 걸을 수 있다고 들었어.

총 어휘 수 120

14 긴 대화의 응답

소재 아들의 컴퓨터 게임 시간 제한

듣기 대본 해석

여: 뭐하고 있어요, George?
남: 컴퓨터에 새로운 게임을 다운로드 받고 있어요.
여: 왜 다른 새로운 게임을 다운로드 받는 거예요?
남: 음, Teddy가 이런 교육용 게임을 좋아하고 무료라서 안 받을 이유가 없는 것 같아요.
여: 그에게 이미 게임이 충분히 있다고 생각하지 않아요?
남: 그렇게 생각하지 않아요. 그는 아주 빠르게 배우는 나이예요.
여: 알았어요. 그렇지만 만약에 당신이 너무 많은 게임을 다운로드 받으면, 그는 게임에 중독되고 밖에 나가서 놀고 싶어 하지 않을 수도 있어요.
남: 그것에 대해선 걱정하지 않아요. 우리는 그 애를 체조랑 야구에도 등록시켰잖아요.
여: 좋은 생각이지만 그런 활동들은 고작 일주일에 두 번인걸요. 게임은 매일 할 수 있잖아요.
남: 네, 당신의 요점을 알았어요. 아이가 컴퓨터에 쓰는 시간을 제한해야겠어요.
여: ① 당신이 균형 있는 해결책을 찾을 수 있을 거라고 생각해요.

어휘

addicted ***a.*** 중독된 **enroll** ***v.*** 등록하다 **gymnastics** ***n.*** 체조
see (one's) point ~의 요점을 알다

정답 ①

문제풀이

아들이 컴퓨터하는 시간을 제한해야겠다고 말하는 남자에게 여자가 해 줄 수 있는 말은 ① '당신이 균형 있는 해결책을 찾을 수 있을 거라고 생각해요.'가 적절하다.

오답 보기 해석

② 이 새 게임을 다운로드 하는 데에 도움이 필요해요.
③ 요즘은 아이들이 운동하는 게 너무 비싸요.
④ 그가 경기하는 야구팀의 이름을 나한테 말해줄 수 있어요?
⑤ 당신이 그 게임을 하기 위해서는 더 새로운 하드웨어가 필요한 것 같아요.

총 어휘 수 138

15 상황에 적절한 말

소재 집에 두고 온 보고서

듣기 대본 해석

여: Michael은 오늘 회사에 제출해야 할 중요한 보고서가 있습니다. 그는 독감에 걸려서 지난번의 보고서를 며칠 정도 늦게 제출했습니다. 그의 상사는 지연된 것에 대해 기분이 좋지 않았기 때문에 그는 이번 것은 제 시간에 제출하도록 의욕이 있는 상태입니다. 그가 회사에 도착했을 때, 그는 문서를 찾으려고 서류 가방을 열었고 거기에 그것들이 없다는 것을 알게 되었습니다. 그는 처음에 당황하고 어떻게 반응해야 할지 모릅니다. 그는 집에 있는 그의 아내에게 전화를 걸고 그녀는 그가 문서들을 주방 탁자 위에 놓고 갔다고 그에게 말합니다. 그는 보고서를 잃어버리지 않아 기뻐하지만 재빨리 제출해야만 합니다. 이 상황에서, Michael은 그의 아내에게 뭐라고 말하겠습니까?
Michael: ④ 내 사무실로 문서들을 갖다 줄래요?

어휘

turn in 제출하다 **flu** ***n.*** 독감 **delay** ***n.*** 지연, 지체 **briefcase** ***n.*** 서류 가방

정답 ④

문제풀이

Michael은 반드시 마감 전에 제출하려 했던 중요한 보고서를 집에 두고 왔음을 아내에게 전화해서 확인했는데, 그는 당장 그 보고서가 필요한 상황이다. 이런 상황에서 Michael이 아내에게 할 말로 가장 적절한 것은 ④ '내 사무실로 문서들을 갖다 줄래요?'이다.

오답 보기 해석

① 나는 지난주에 보고서를 제출했어요.
② 내가 도울 일이 있으면 알려주세요.
③ 문서들이 주방 탁자 위에 있어요.
⑤ 보고서 쓰는 것을 좀 도와줄래요?

총 어휘 수 131

16 담화 목적 / 17 세부 내용 파악

소재 코 호흡의 중요성

듣기 대본 해석

여: 안녕하세요, 여러분. 저는 오늘 적절한 호흡법이 여러분의 전반적인 건강에 얼마나 좋은 영향을 주는지 이야기하고 싶습니다. 먼저, 여러분은 코를 통해 숨을 쉬어야 합니다. 입으로 하는 호흡이 더 일반적이지만 코를 사용하면 사실 훨씬 더 자연스럽고 그래서 더 건강해집니다. 코는 우리가 숨을 쉴 때 공기 중에서 발견될 수 있는 모든 불순물에 대해 여과기로 작용합니다. 입으로 호흡하는 것은 공기를 전혀 정화시키지 못해서 먼지와 때가 걸러질

수 없습니다. 이는 여러분이 감기나 다른 공기로 전염되는 병을 더 쉽게 걸리게 만듭니다. 입으로 숨을 쉬면 찬 공기가 폐로 들어오도록 해서 호흡기에 염증이 생기게 합니다. 그러나 코를 통해 숨을 쉬면 여러분의 몸에 활력을 불어넣고 더 많은 에너지를 줍니다. 공기를 여과하고 따뜻하게 유지함으로써 코의 통로는 폐에 들어오기 적합한 공기만 들어오게 합니다. 이는 공기에 의존하는 모든 섬세한 기관들이 가장 잘 작동할 것이라는 것을 의미합니다.

어휘

breathing *n.* 호흡 **benefit** *n.* 이점, 혜택 *v.* 혜택을 주다 **overall** *a.* 전반적인 **impurity** *n.* 불순물 **airborne** *a.* 공기로 운반되는 **lung** *n.* 폐 **respiratory** *a.* 호흡의, 호흡성의 **organ** *n.* 장기(기관) **inflamed** *a.* 염증이 생긴 **vitalize** *v.* 활력을 불어넣다 **nasal** *a.* 코의 **passage** *n.* 통로 **fit** *a.* 적합한 **delicate** *a.* 섬세한 〈문제〉 **delicacy** *n.* 섬세함, 여림

정답 16 ③ 17 ①

문제풀이

16 여자는 입으로 하는 호흡과 코로 하는 호흡을 비교하면서 코로 하는 호흡의 중요성을 설명하고 있으므로 정답은 ③ '코로 하는 호흡의 중요성을 강조하려고'이다.

17 Mouth breathing의 단점으로 폐에 불순물 유입, 질병 감염에 대한 취약성, 폐에 찬 공기 유입, 호흡기 염증 유발 등이 언급되었으나 불면증 유발은 언급되어 있지 않으므로 정답은 ① '불면증 유발'이다.

오답 보기 해석

16

① 입으로 호흡하는 것을 효과적으로 피할 수 있는 방법을 설명하려고
② 호흡기관의 섬세함을 강조하려고
④ 여과된 공기를 마시는 것의 이점을 설명하려고
⑤ 호흡의 여러 가지 방법을 기술하려고

총 어휘 수 168

DICTATION ANSWERS

01 I'm starving

02 where my office is / You should probably ask

03 believe it to be good for their health / lower their chance of getting / people who are against the killing of animals

04 it doesn't work with / hearing disability / having an exchange student

05 jam-packed / has really taken off / perform their loudest, heaviest songs

06 When was it taken / he's wearing on his collar / he still loves that ball

07 It doesn't help that / almost missed dinner / make a mess / feed the dogs

08 It rides like it's brand new / I need to get everything prepared / Sounds exhausting

09 get there on time / Will you be back in time / I won't be late

10 half the price you would pay for / two-story building / give you an extra ten percent off

11 It's native to / They're pollinated by / leave behind strong traces of / can be processed into powerful ointment

12 a list of all our options / I don't think I can justify / it has a longer warranty

13 you're using crutches / You have trouble walking / get around on my bionic legs

14 I don't see why not / he might get addicted / have him enrolled in / I'll limit the amount of time

15 an important report to turn in / he was out with the flu / opens his briefcase / he needs to turn it in very soon

16-17 Your nose acts as a filter / make you more likely to catch a cold / cause the respiratory organs to become inflamed / vitalizes your body

14 수능영어듣기 실전모의고사

본문 p.86

01 ⑤	02 ⑤	03 ④	04 ④	05 ③	06 ⑤
07 ②	08 ④	09 ③	10 ③	11 ②	12 ⑤
13 ③	14 ②	15 ①	16 ⑤	17 ②	

01 짧은 대화의 응답

소재 테니스 경기 보러 가기

듣기 대본 해석

남: Mia, 테니스 경기 갈 준비 됐어?
여: 거의. 수학 숙제 마지막 문제 몇 개만 풀면 돼.
남: 얼마 정도 더 걸릴 것 같아?
여: ⑤ 15분 넘게 걸리진 않을 거야.

어휘

match ***n.*** 경기, 시합 〈문제〉 **turn in** ~을 제출하다

정답 ⑤

문제풀이

테니스 경기에 가기 전 수학 문제를 풀고 있는 여자에게 남자는 얼마나 더 걸릴 것인지 묻고 있으므로 정답은 ⑤ '15분 넘게 걸리진 않을 거야.'이다.

오답 보기 해석

① 경기 갈 준비 다 됐어.
② 대신 영화 보러 가자.
③ 우리 내일 아침에 출발해야 해.
④ 너 숙제 제출하는 것 까먹었어.

총 어휘 수 43

02 짧은 대화의 응답

소재 감기 기운

듣기 대본 해석

여: 얘, Kevin, 여기 좀 춥네. 창문을 좀 닫자.
남: 오늘 몸이 그다지 좋지 않네.
여: 무슨 일이야? 오늘 아침에 활기차게 보였는데.
남: ⑤ 내 생각엔 반 친구한테서 감기가 옮은 것 같아.

어휘

〈문제〉 **rewarding** ***a.*** 보람 있는 **catch a cold** 감기에 걸리다

정답 ⑤

문제풀이

오늘 아침에는 활기차 보였는데 왜 몸이 안 좋은 거냐고 묻는 여자의 말에 대한 남자의 응답으로 가장 적절한 것은 ⑤ '내 생각엔 반 친구한테서 감기가 옮은 것 같아.'이다.

오답 보기 해석

① 창문을 닫아줘서 고마워.
② 오늘 날씨가 훌륭해.
③ 맞아. 난 자주 운동을 해왔거든.
④ 다른 사람들을 돕는 것은 정말 보람 있는 일이야.

총 어휘 수 39

03 담화 목적

소재 공원 내 스포츠 광장 건립 반대

듣기 대본 해석

남: 여러분, 안녕하세요. 저는 Scott McGee이고, 저는 오늘 밤 Central Park에 스포츠 광장을 건립하려는 도시의 계획에 대해 말씀드리려 합니다. Central Park는 모두에게 휴식과 재미를 주는 공간이라는 것에 여러분 모두 동의하신다고 확신합니다. 우리는 그곳으로 봄, 여름에 소풍을 가고 일년 내내 운동과 건강관리를 위해 그곳을 이용합니다. 하지만, 우리가 만약 도시의 스포츠 광장 건립을 허락한다면 우리는 더 이상 그런 것들을 할 공간이 없을 것입니다. 스포츠 경기나 다른 이벤트를 보러 광장으로 가는 사람들 때문에 심한 교통 체증만 보게 될 것입니다. 이는 우리의 삶의 질을 낮출 거라고 저는 확신합니다! 저는 여기 여러분 모두가 저의 의견에 동감하시리라 생각합니다.

어휘

construct ***v.*** 건설하다 **relaxation** ***n.*** 휴식 **wellness** ***n.*** 건강, 건강관리 **opinion** ***n.*** 의견, 견해

정답 ④

문제풀이

남자는 시민들의 휴식과 운동의 공간인 Central Park에 스포츠 광장이 건립되면 어떻게 될지 설명하면서 도시의 스포츠 광장 건립 계획을 반대하고 있으므로 정답은 ④ '공원 내 스포츠 광장 건립 계획에 반대하려고'이다.

총 어휘 수 125

04 대화 주제

소재 바나나 껍질의 다양한 용도

듣기 대본 해석

여: Cody, 그거 버리지마.
남: 왜? 그냥 바나나 껍질이잖아.
여: 바나나 껍질은 쓸모가 아주 많아.
남: 응, 화단에 주려고 네가 껍질로 퇴비 만드는 걸 봤어. 그런 걸 말하는 거야?
여: 음, 응. 그렇긴 한데 그것 외에도 바나나 껍질은 여러 가지로 쓰여. 예를 들어 벌레가 문 곳이나 가려운 발진에 그걸 바르면 좋다는 거 알고 있었어?
남: 신기하다. 그래서 혹시 벌레한테 물릴 때에 대비해서 오래된 바나나 껍질을 모으겠다는 거야?
여: 그건 아냐. 사실 그 껍질로 내 가죽 신발 광내려고 했어.
남: 내 신발 광낼 때도 하나 써봐야지. 또 어디에 쓰여?
여: 창문 밖에다 놓으면 새들과 나비들이 모여들 거야.
남: 좋네. 왜 나보고 버리지 말라고 했는지 이제 알겠어.

어휘

peel ***n.*** 껍질 ***v.*** 껍질을 벗기다 **compost** ***n.*** 퇴비 **relieve** ***v.*** 없애다, 덜어주다 **rash** ***n.*** 발진 **polish** ***v.*** 광을 내다 **attract** ***v.*** 끌어들이다

정답 ④

문제풀이

여자는 바나나 껍질을 버리려는 남자에게 벌레 물림과 발진 완화, 신발 광 내기 등 다양한 쓸모를 이야기하고 있으므로 정답은 ④ '바나나 껍질의 다양한 용도'이다.

총 어휘 수 141

05 대화자의 관계 파악

소재 영화감독의 학교방문

듣기 대본 해석

[전화벨이 울린다.]

여: 여보세요?

남: 여보세요. 저는 Ryan James입니다. 저는 막 당신의 이메일을 받았고, 당신의 초대를 받아들이고 싶습니다.

여: 정말이에요? 잘 됐네요. 바쁜 스케줄 와중에도 우리 학교를 방문하기 위하여 시간을 내어 주셔서 정말 감사드립니다.

남: 괜찮습니다. 저는 사실 이 졸업식에서 연설하기를 무척 기대하고 있습니다.

여: 당신의 영화가 여기 Henderson County 고등학교의 많은 학생들에게 영감이 되었어요.

남: 오, 당신으로부터 그런 말을 듣다니 굉장히 기분이 좋네요.

여: 저희 학생들 몇 명이 당신과 직접 이야기하고 싶어해요. 졸업식 전에 팬미팅을 해주실 수 있나요?

남: 되고 말고요. 저는 저의 팬들을 존경하고 그들, 특히 어린 팬들의 얘기를 듣는 것을 좋아해요.

여: 학생들이 당신을 직접 만나게 돼서 무척 신나할 거예요.

어휘

appreciate *v.* 감사하다 **look forward to** ~을 기대하다
inspiration *n.* 영감, 영감을 주는 것 **ecstatic** *a.* 황홀해하는, 열광하는
in person 직접, 몸소 **meet-and-greet** *n.* 팬미팅

정답 ③

문제풀이

남자가 여자가 있는 학교에 와서 졸업식 때 연설을 해주기로 했고 여자는 그의 영화에 학생들이 영감을 받았다고 했으므로 두 사람의 관계는 ③ '영화감독 — 교사'로 유추할 수 있다.

총 어휘 수 132

06 그림의 세부 내용 파악

소재 기숙사 방

듣기 대본 해석

남: 네가 기숙사 방 꾸민 것 맘에 들어, Clara.

여: 고마워. 책상하고 침대 옮기느라 꽤 힘들었어.

남: 침대 위에 있는 건 봉제 인형이지?

여: 응. 내가 어릴 때부터 가지고 있었어. 이름은 Geoffrey인데 기린이야.

남: 멋지다. 오, 좋은 지도인데. 핀을 꽂아둔 곳은 모두 네가 가 본 곳이니?

여: 맞아. 난 그 옆에다 내 스케줄을 쓰기 위해 화이트보드를 놓았어. 너도 알지만 내가 건망증이 심하잖아.

남: 저 전등도 맘에 든다. 방을 잘 밝혀 주는구나.

여: 저건 할머니에게 받은 또 다른 선물이야.

남: 책상 위에 노트북 컴퓨터 좋은 거구나. 집에서 가져 온 거야?

여: 응. 아빠가 떠나는 선물로 나에게 주셨어.

남: 네 방은 내 방보다 훨씬 아늑해 보인다. 맘에 들어.

여: 오? 이제는 네 방이 궁금한걸.

어휘

dorm *n.* 기숙사 **forgetful** *a.* 잘 잊어 먹는, 건망증이 있는
light up 밝히다

정답 ⑤

문제풀이

책상 위에 노트북 컴퓨터가 있다고 했는데 책이 있으므로 정답은 ⑤번이다.

총 어휘 수 146

07 부탁한 일

소재 새집 만들기

듣기 대본 해석

여: 저는 이 길이 항상 좋았어요, 아빠.

남: 그렇다니 아빠도 기쁘구나. 아빠도 아주 좋아한단다.

여: 저는 예쁜 새들을 볼 수 있는 게 좋아요.

남: 그래, 새들이 여기 많이 나와 있구나.

여: 아빠, 새들은 어디서 자나요?

남: 새들은 나무에서 살지. 새들은 나뭇가지 저 위에 새집을 짓는데 둥지라고 부른단다.

여: 새들은 서로 둥지를 공유하나요?

남: 나도 그건 확실히 모르겠구나, 얘야. 그렇지만 집이 없는 새들도 있을 거야.

여: 정말이요? 그건 슬프네요. 우리가 새들을 위해 집을 만들어 줄 수 있어요?

남: 집이 없는 새들 때문에 네가 슬프다면, 물론 할 수 있지.

여: 정말 그래요, 아빠. 모든 새들이 멋진 집을 가지고 있었으면 해요.

남: 그래. 그럼 다음 주 주말에, 새집들을 만들어서 정원에 걸자꾸나.

여: 좋아요! 고마워요, 아빠.

어휘

trail *n.* 오솔길 **homeless** *a.* 집이 없는

정답 ②

문제풀이

아빠가 집이 없는 새들도 있을 거라고 하자 딸은 집이 없는 새들 때문에 슬프다며 새들을 위해 집을 만들어 주자고 한다. 따라서 딸이 아빠한테 부탁한 일은 ② '새집 만들어 주기'이다.

총 어휘 수 133

08 이유

소재 콘서트에 못 가게 된 이유

듣기 대본 해석

여: Jim, 오늘 왜 그렇게 우울해 보이니?

남: 내가 Eric Benet 콘서트 기다려 왔다는 것 알지? 내가 제일 좋아하는 가수잖아.

여: 물론이지. 너 아주 신나 있었잖아. 무슨 문제 있어?

남: 내가 콘서트에 갈 수 없게 되었거든.

여: 왜? 그거 취소됐어?

남: 아니. 회의 때문에 상하이에 가야만 해.

여: 사장님이 그 회의에 참석하기로 했던 거 아니었어?

남: 응, 그랬지. 그렇지만 사장님이 지난 주 일요일에 테니스를 치다가 팔이 부러지는 바람에 갈 수 없게 됐어.

여: 안타깝구나. 그럼 그 티켓은 어떻게 할 거니?

남: 이미 내 남동생한테 줬어.

여: 작년에 결혼한 그 남동생 말하는 거지?

남: 맞아. 티켓 받고 좋아하더라.

여: 그에게는 잘된 일이네. 언젠가 Eric Benet을 볼 기회가 있을 거야, Jim.

어휘

turn out ~인 것으로 드러나다 **cancel** *v.* 취소하다
be supposed to V ~하기로 되어 있다 **attend** *v.* 참석하다

정답 ④

문제풀이

남자는 원래 회의에 참석하기로 했던 상사의 팔이 부러져서 상사를 대신해서 상하이에서 열리는 회의에 참석해야 하기 때문에 콘서트에 가지 못하게 되었다고 말했으므로 정답은 ④ '상사 대신 출장을 가야 해서'이다.

총 어휘 수 129

09 숫자

소재 등산 용품 구매하기

듣기 대본 해석

남: 안녕하세요. 무엇을 도와드릴까요?
여: 등산화를 찾고 있어요. 저 가죽 등산화 좀 봐도 될까요?
남: 사실 그것들은 남성용 등산화예요.
여: 알아요. 십대인 제 아들 것을 사려고요. 얼마예요?
남: 원래 100달러였지만 이번에 20퍼센트 할인을 하게 됐어요. 저번 시즌에 굉장히 유행했죠. 그가 좋아할 거라고 확신해요.
여: 저도 그렇게 생각해요. 9 사이즈로 한 켤레 주세요. 아! 그리고 우리 둘이 쓸 등산 스틱도 필요해요.
남: 네. 분홍색, 보라색, 초록색, 그리고 파란색이 있습니다.
여: 보라색 하나랑 파란색 하나 살게요. 얼마예요?
남: 한 개당 20달러입니다.
여: 등산 스틱에도 20퍼센트 할인이 적용되나요?
남: 죄송하지만 할인은 등산화에만 적용됩니다.
여: 알겠어요. 여기 카드요.

어휘

apiece *ad.* 각각, 하나에 **apply to** ~에 적용되다

정답 ③

문제풀이

20퍼센트 할인 중인 100달러짜리 등산화 한 켤레와 정가로 판매 중인 20달러짜리 등산 스틱 2개이므로 80달러+40달러=120달러가 되어 정답은 ③ '$120'이다.

총 어휘 수 146

10 언급 유무

소재 여드름 관리

듣기 대본 해석

남: 오, 안돼! 내 얼굴에 뾰루지가 너무 많아요.
여: 작은 여드름이 났구나. 사춘기를 지날 때는 그게 조금 나는 것이 정상이란다. 네가 십대를 벗어날 때가 되면 그건 거의 완전히 없어질 거야.
남: 네, 그걸 전부 이해하긴 해요. 하지만 이런 여드름들을 보는게 정말 싫어요.
여: 그게 좋지 않다는 건 나도 알아.
남: 제가 그것에 대해 무엇을 할 수 있나요?
여: 피부를 깨끗하게 유지하고 여드름을 자극하지 말도록 해봐.
남: 네, 그렇게 할 수 있어요.
여: 네가 여드름을 봤을 때, 그것을 짜고 싶은 욕구를 참아야 해.
남: 정말이요? 그렇지만 저는 여드름을 즉시 없애고 싶어요.
여: 그래, 대부분의 사람들이 그렇지만, 그것들을 터트리는 건 더 악화시킬 뿐이야.
남: 어떤 음식이 여드름을 유발시킬까요?
여: 만약에 네가 여드름이 잘 난다면, 너는 기름기 있는 음식들은 피해야 한단다.

어휘

pimple *n.* 여드름, 뾰루지 **acne** *n.* 여드름 **puberty** *n.* 사춘기 **irritate** *v.* (피부 등을) 자극하다 **resist** *v.* 견디다, 저항하다 **squeeze** *v.* 짜다 **prone** *a.* ~하기 쉬운 **greasy** *a.* 기름진

정답 ③

문제풀이

여자는 여드름이 나기 시작한 사춘기 남자에게 깨끗한 피부를 유지할 것, 여드름을 자극하지 말 것, 여드름을 짜지 말 것, 기름진 음식을 피할 것을 조언으로 언급하였으나 ③ '여드름에 연고 바르기'는 언급하지 않았다.

총 어휘 수 140

11 내용 일치 · 불일치

소재 메이플 시럽

듣기 대본 해석

여: 오늘 저는 여러분께 우리가 메이플 시럽이라고 부르는 아주 달콤한 간식에 대해서 얘기해 드릴 겁니다. 유럽 식민지화되기 전에 북미의 원주민들은 메이플(단풍) 나무에 구멍을 뚫어 흘러 나오는 액체를 모아 그 시럽을 모았습니다. 그들은 메이플 시럽이 많은 요리에 쓰일 수 있는 자연 감미료임을 발견했습니다. 오늘날 캐나다의 퀘벡 주가 세계 최대의 메이플 시럽 생산지입니다. 그곳은 전체 메이플 시럽의 3/4을 생산합니다. 사탕 수수나 옥수수 시럽과 같은 다른 감미료들에 비해 메이플 시럽은 중요한 비타민과 영양분의 좋은 공급원입니다. 많은 의사들은 매일 메이플 시럽을 적당량 섭취하는 것이 심장병 예방에 도움이 되고 면역 체계를 강화시킬 수 있다고 생각합니다.

어휘

sweet treat 사탕, 과자 등의 단 음식 **colonization** *n.* 식민지화 **native** *a.* 토박이의 **tap** *v.* 가볍게 두드리다, (나무에 자국을 내고) 수액을 받다 **sap** *n.* 수액 **seep** *v.* 스미다 **sweetener** *n.* 감미료 **province** *n.* 주, 지방 **superior** *a.* 우수한 **source** *n.* 원천, 근원 **consume** *v.* 소모하다, 섭취하다 **moderate** *a.* 보통의, 적당한 **immune system** 면역 체계

정답 ②

문제풀이

원주민들은 메이플 시럽이 여러 요리에 쓰일 수 있는 자연 감미료임을 발견했다고 했으므로 일치하지 않는 것은 ② '주로 상처 치료에 널리 사용되었다.'이다.

총 어휘 수 130

12 도표

소재 전자레인지 선택

듣기 대본 해석

여: 안녕하세요. 뭐 찾는 것 있으세요?
남: 네. 새 전자레인지 사려고요. 추천하는 것 있으세요?
여: 네. 이거 한번 보세요.
남: 가격이 $100도 안 되는 걸로 봐서는 별로일 것 같네요.
여: 그럴지도 모르겠네요. 이건 어때요? 저번 주에 새로 들어온 모델이에요. 굉장히 인기 있는 것 같아요.
남: 겉모습은 괜찮은데 싼 제품의 전력량과 같아요. 좀 더 센 모델을 찾고 있어요.
여: 알겠습니다. 이것도 굉장히 잘 나가고, 거의 신상품이에요. 이것도 지난 주에 들어왔어요.
남: 이 모델의 장단점은 뭐예요?
여: 그건 회전을 하는데요, 근데 좀 작아요. 내부 크기가 0.9 세제곱 피트밖에 안돼요.
남: 우리는 좀 큰 요리들도 데워먹어서 더 큰 게 아마도 더 좋을 것 같네요.
여: 알겠습니다. 이건요?
남: 좋네요. 회전도 하고 내부 크기도 더 커 보여요. 오, 판넬 스티커에 1.2 세제곱 피트라고 써있네요. 이걸로 할게요.
여: 네. 카트에 싣는 것을 도와드릴게요. 앞쪽 계산대로 가져가세요.

어휘

microwave *n.* 전자레인지 **recommend** *v.* 추천하다 **visually** *ad.* 시각적으로 **appealing** *a.* 매력적인 **pros and cons** 장단점 **rotate** *v.* 회전하다 **interior** *n.* 내부

정답 ⑤

문제풀이

100달러가 안 되는 것은 별로일 것 같다고 했고, 전력이 센 것을 찾았으므로 ③~⑤번이 남는데 이 중 회전을 하고 내부가 1.2 세제곱 피트인 것은 ⑤번이다.

총 어휘 수 193

13 긴 대화의 응답

소재 언어의 정확성과 유창성

듣기 대본 해석

여: Issac, 우리 프랑스어 선생님 어때?
남: 내 생각엔 괜찮은데 너는 별로 좋아하지 않는 것처럼 보여.
여: 어학 실습은 많이 하지만 기초 문법은 충분하지 않은 것 같아.
남: 그게 맘에 들지 않아?
여: 나는 문법이 새로운 언어를 배우는 데 가장 중요한 부분이라고 생각하기 때문에 그게 좋지가 않아.
남: 너의 생각을 뒷받침할 만한 최근 연구가 있어?
여: 그렇진 않아.
남: 그럼, 너는 왜 그렇게 생각해?
여: 나는 만약에 문법적으로 옳은 문장을 사용해서 말하지 않는다면, 웃기게 들릴 거라고 생각해.
남: 나는 언어 교육의 많은 최근 이론들에 근거할 때 그렇게 생각하지 않아.
여: 정말? 그 이론들에서 뭐라고 주장하는데?
남: ③ 그들은 정확성보다 유창성이 더 중요하다고 말해.

어휘

on the basis of ~에 근거하여 〈문제〉 **theory** ***n.*** 이론 **fluency** ***n.*** 유창성 **accuracy** ***n.*** 정확도 **emphasize** ***v.*** 강조하다

정답 ③

문제풀이

남자가 문법을 중시하는 여자의 의견에 대해 최근 언어 교육 이론을 근거로 그렇지 않다고 반박하자 여자는 이론의 내용을 묻고 있으므로 응답으로 가장 적절한 것은 ③ '그들은 정확성보다 유창성이 더 중요하다고 말해.'이다.

오답 보기 해석

① 프랑스어가 영어보다 더 어려워.
② 우리는 이론에 의존해야 할 것 같아.
④ 그 이론들은 올바른 문법의 사용을 강조해.
⑤ 그들은 이론과 실제가 다르다고 지적해.

총 어휘 수 115

14 긴 대화의 응답

소재 친구를 위한 생일파티에 대한 상의

듣기 대본 해석

남: 안녕, Stacy. 이번 주말에 뭐해?
여: 아직 확실하지 않아. 왜 물어 보는 거야?
남: Bruno를 위해서 깜짝 생일 파티를 열려고 해. 그는 30살이 되잖아. 네가 온다면 그가 좋아할 거라 생각해.
여: 좋은 생각이야. 나는 그가 파티를 할지 궁금했었어. 난 가면 좋지.
남: 좋아. 음, 나는 모든 사람들이 5시에 나의 집에 왔으면 해.
여: 나에게 딱 좋네. 내가 파티 도와 줄까? 내가 간식거리 같은 것을 사갈 수 있어.
남: 내 생각에는 간식은 많을 것 같아. 너는 몸만 와.
여: 정말 내가 도울 수 있는 게 없을까? Bruno는 좋은 친구잖아. 그가 우리한테 얼마나 의미 있는지 그에게 보여주고 싶어.
남: 음, 그러면, 네가 파티를 위해 할 일이 있지.
여: 그게 뭔데?
남: Susie가 직장에서 우리 모두의 사진을 가지고 콜라주를 만들 거야. 그녀가 사진 고르는 걸 네가 도와주면 좋을 거라고 생각해.
여: ② 물론이지. 내가 그것을 할 수 있어. 도움이 될 수 있어서 기뻐.

어휘

surprise birthday party 깜짝 생일 파티 **bring yourself** 몸만 (빈 손으로) 와 **contribute** ***v.*** 기여하다 **collage** ***n.*** 콜라주

정답 ②

문제풀이

여자가 생일 파티를 위해 무언가를 돕고 싶다고 하자 남자가 사진을 찾아주면 좋을 것 같다고 했으므로 가장 적절한 여자의 응답은 ② '물론이지. 내가 그것을 할 수 있어. 도움이 될 수 있어서 기뻐.'이다.

오답 보기 해석

① 내가 반드시 그녀를 파티에 초대할게.
③ 좋아. 점심 후에 사진을 몇 장 찍을게.
④ 내가 콜라주를 만들었는데 진짜 멋져 보여.
⑤ 좋았어. 내가 꼭 간식을 좀 가져올게.

총 어휘 수 174

15 상황에 적절한 말

소재 퇴직 후 혼자 여행하기

듣기 대본 해석

남: Neil은 성공한 변호사이고 몇 년 동안 퇴직을 고대하고 있는 중이었습니다. 그가 마침내 퇴직했을 때, 그는 낚시, 카페에서 커피를 마시거나 운동으로 시간을 보냈습니다. 그는 그의 새로운 일상에 꽤 지루해져 갔고 그가 좀 더 흥미 있는 무언가를 해야만 한다고 결심했습니다. 그는 몇 달 동안 동남아시아를 쭉 여행하기를 원합니다. Neil이 그의 계획을 아내와 의논할 때, 그녀는 그렇게 오랜 여행을 감당하지 못할 것이라며 그와 함께 가는 것을 거절했습니다. Neil은 그의 아내에게 그가 다시는 여행할 기회를 갖지 못할 것이기 때문에 그가 혼자 갈 수 있도록 아내를 설득하고 싶어 합니다. 이 상황에서, Neil은 그의 아내에게 뭐라고 말할까요?
Neil: ① 나는 항상 이런 긴 여행을 하는 것을 원해왔어요.

어휘

look forward to ~을 고대하다 **retirement** ***n.*** 퇴직
handle ***v.*** 다루다, 감당하다 **convince** ***v.*** 납득시키다

정답 ①

문제풀이

퇴직 후의 일상에 지루함을 느낀 Neil은 동남아시아 여행을 하려고 한다. 하지만 아내가 동참을 거절하자 혼자라도 가겠노라고 아내를 설득하려는 상황이므로 Neil이 아내에게 할 말로 가장 적절한 것은 ① '나는 항상 이런 긴 여행을 하는 것을 원해왔어요.'이다.

오답 보기 해석

② 이제 내가 퇴직했으니, 나는 내가 원하는 언제든 낚시를 갈 수 있어요.
③ 나는 정말로 우리가 뭔가 흥미롭게 할 것을 찾길 바래요.
④ 나는 우리가 함께 배낭여행을 가야 한다고 생각해요.
⑤ 당신 말이 맞는 것 같아요. 그렇게 오랫동안 여행하는 것은 나한테 너무 어려워요.

총 어휘 수 123

16 담화 목적 / 17 세부 내용 파악

소재 아침에 먹기 좋은 과일 추천

듣기 대본 해석

남: 여러분은 얼마나 자주 아침을 드십니까? 너무 바빠서 하루의 가장 중요한 식사를 위해 시간을 낼 수 없는 자신을 발견하십니까? 다음 번에 급할 때는, 문을 나서는 길에 과일을 집으세요. 과일은 당신이 몹시 필요로 하는 아침 활력을 당신에게 줄 수 있는 훌륭한 방법입니다. 당신이 단 한 종류의 과일만 선택해야 한다면 사과를 고르십시오. 사과는 가장 건강한 과일입니다. 당신은 "하루에 사과 하나를 먹으면 의사가 필요 없다"는 옛 속담을 들은

기억이 있을 겁니다. 사과는 비타민C로 가득 차 있고 섬유질이라 우리가 체중을 관리하는 것을 도와줄 수 있습니다. 사과는 또한 뼈를 튼튼하게 하고 콜레스테롤을 낮추는 데도 좋습니다. 사과는 심장병과, 폐암, 유방암, 대장암 그리고 간암을 예방합니다. 사과는 영양적으로 이점을 가지고 있어서 당신을 건강한 삶으로 이끌어 줄 수 있습니다. 과일은 먹기 쉽고 아주 짧은 준비 시간을 필요로 합니다. 그러니 다음 번에 당신이 충분한 아침을 먹기에 너무 바쁘면, 사과를 집으세요.

어휘

in a hurry 바쁜, 서둘러 **grab** ***v.*** 붙잡다 **boost** ***n.*** 힘, 증가
proverb ***n.*** 속담 **packed with** ~로 가득 찬 **fibrous** ***a.*** 섬유질의
weight ***n.*** 체중 **strengthen** ***v.*** 강화하다, 더 튼튼하게 하다
prevent ***v.*** 예방하다, 막다 **lung** ***n.*** 폐, 허파 **breast** ***n.*** 가슴, 유방
colon ***n.*** 결장 **liver** ***n.*** 간 **cancer** ***n.*** 암 **preparation** ***n.*** 준비

정답 16 ⑤ 17 ②

문제풀이

16 남자는 바빠서 아침을 먹을 수 없다면 과일을 먹으라고 권한 후, 특히 사과의 좋은 점을 언급하며 추천하고 있다. 그러므로 남자가 하는 말의 목적은 ⑤ '건강에 도움이 되도록 아침에 과일 먹는 것을 제안하려고'이다.

17 남자는 사과의 건강상 이점으로 비타민C의 공급원이고, 체중 관리에 좋으며, 뼈를 튼튼하게 하고, 여러 가지 암을 예방한다고 언급했지만 소화를 촉진시킨다고는 언급하지 않았으므로 정답은 ② '소화를 촉진시킨다.'이다.

오답 보기 해석

16

① 과일을 신선하게 유지하는 비결을 제공하려고
② 아침 식사를 거르는 것의 위험에 대해 경고하려고
③ 하루 중 사과를 먹기에 가장 좋은 시간대를 추천하려고
④ 아침 식사를 즐길 새롭고 신나는 방법을 제안하려고

총 어휘 수 157

DICTATION ANSWERS

01 the last couple of questions / How much longer

02 not feeling so well / You were so full of energy

03 a place for relaxation and fun / use it for exercise and wellness / What we will have is a lot of car traffic / this will decrease our quality of life

04 many uses for banana peels / relieve bug bites / keep old banana peels around / didn't want me to throw it out

05 accept your invitation / I actually look forward to speaking / Your movies have been an inspiration / have a meet-and-greet before the ceremony / meet you in person

06 a stuffed animal / all of the places you've been / It really lights up / as a going away gift / looks a lot more homey

07 where do birds sleep / share their nests with each other / feel sad about the homeless birds / put them in our yard

08 looking so down / It turns out that / Was it canceled / your boss supposed to attend / You'll have another chance to

09 take a look at / they just went on sale / apply to the hiking poles

10 when you're going through puberty / try not to irritate it / the urge to squeeze it / you're prone to acne

11 Before European colonization / three-quarters of the world's supply / a superior source / consuming a moderate amount of maple syrup / strengthen the immune system

12 I doubt that one's any good / its pros and cons

13 there's too much language practice / learning a new language / grammatically correct sentences / I don't think so

14 what are you up to / throwing a surprise birthday party / need me to help with the party / contribute in some way

15 looking forward to retirement / He became quite bored with his new routine / she can't handle traveling / Neil wants to convince his wife

16-17 grab some fruit on the way out / An apple a day keeps the doctor away / are fibrous, so they can help you / strengthening your bones / grab an apple

15 수능영어듣기 실전모의고사

본문 p.92

01 ③	02 ⑤	03 ④	04 ②	05 ⑤	06 ③
07 ②	08 ①	09 ③	10 ③	11 ④	12 ④
13 ①	14 ⑤	15 ④	16 ⑤	17 ③	

01 짧은 대화의 응답

소재 선물 내용 알아 맞추기

듣기 대본 해석

여: 이 상자 안에 네게 줄 선물이 있어. 절대 맞힐 수 없을걸!
남: 맞혀 볼게. 음... 옷 같은 거 맞지?
여: 맞아! 도대체 어떻게 알았어?
남: ③ 내가 어떤 사이즈의 옷을 입는지 어제 네가 물었잖아.

어휘

how on earth 도대체 어떻게 〈문제〉 **eventually** ***ad.*** 결국

정답 ③

문제풀이

여자가 남자에게 선물을 주면서 절대 맞히지 못할 거라고 했는데, 남자가 맞혔고 여자는 어떻게 알았는지 묻고 있다. 이에 대한 응답으로는 ③ '내가 어떤 사이즈의 옷을 입는지 어제 네가 물어봤잖아.'가 가장 적절하다.

오답 보기 해석

① 그 가게가 결국 문을 닫을 줄 알았어.
② 그 옷들은 품질이 좋다는 걸 알았어.
④ 내가 그 상자를 탁자 위에 올려두지 말았어야 했어.
⑤ 너 그 날짜를 기억하려고 네 휴대폰에 입력해뒀잖아.

총 어휘 수 45

02 짧은 대화의 응답

소재 과학 보고서 도와주기

듣기 대본 해석

남: Helen, 학교 끝나고 내 과학 보고서 좀 도와줄 수 있니?
여: 물론이지. 도서관에서 만나는 게 어때?
남: 좋아. 계산기를 가져가야 할까?
여: ⑤ 내 생각엔 계산기를 쓰진 않을 것 같아. 그냥 교과서만 가져와.

어휘

calculator ***n.*** 계산기

정답 ⑤

문제풀이

계산기를 가져가야 하는지에 대한 대답이 와야 하므로 적절한 대답은 ⑤ '내 생각엔 계산기를 쓰진 않을 것 같아. 그냥 교과서만 가져와.'이다.

오답 보기 해석

① 고마워. 하지만 나 새 계산기를 샀어.
② 점심을 가져오지 않아도 돼. 무료야.
③ 올 때 내 과학 보고서 가지고 와줘.
④ 다른 데에서 만나자. 도서관이 지금 문을 닫았어.

총 어휘 수 41

03 담화 목적

소재 지하철 공사를 위한 기금 마련

듣기 대본 해석

남: 안녕하세요, 여러분. 지하철은 우리 시민들에게 가장 안전하고 시간 면에서 효율적인 교통수단입니다. 그런 이유에서 더 많은 사람들이 이용하고 도시 주변에 있는 더 많은 목적지로 데려다 주는 지하철 시스템이 필요합니다. 우리는 교통부와 접촉을 하였지만, 현재 그들은 우리 시민들의 대부분을 수용할 지하철 시스템을 만들기에 기금이 충분하지 않다고 생각합니다. 하지만 우리 사회에 최선의 것을 하는 것이 우리의 의무이기 때문에 우리는 앞으로 세 달 동안 기금을 마련할 방법에 대해 토론할 것입니다. 이는 다른 사회적 프로그램과 서비스를 포함할 수도 있습니다. 제 생각을 듣기 위해 시간을 내주신 여기 모든분들께 감사드립니다.

어휘

efficient ***a.*** 효율적인 **transportation** ***n.*** 교통수단, 수송 **citizen** ***n.*** 시민 **destination** ***n.*** 목적지, 도착지 **contact** ***v.*** 연락하다 **accommodate** ***v.*** 공간을 제공하다, 수용하다 **raise money** 돈을 마련하다

정답 ④

문제풀이

남자는 지하철이 가장 안전하고 시간을 효율적으로 사용할 수 있는 교통수단이므로 도시에 필요하지만 교통부에서 기금이 부족하여 더 만들 수 없다고 했기 때문에 앞으로 세 달 동안 기금 마련을 위한 토론을 하겠다고 알려주고 있다. 따라서 정답은 ④ '지하철 공사 기금 마련을 위한 토론을 알리려고'이다.

총 어휘 수 111

04 대화 주제

소재 국립 공원의 애완동물 입장 제한

듣기 대본 해석

남: 나 이번 주말에 Yosemite 국립 공원에 드라이브하러 갈 생각이야.
여: 정말? 멋진 여행이 될 것 같아.
남: 공원 내에 애완동물을 데려가는 데 대해 어떤 규정이 있는지 알고 있니?
여: 실제로 국립 공원은 애완동물에 대해 꽤 엄격한 규정이 있어.
남: 그래? 하지만 애완동물은 가장 좋은 여행의 동반자인 걸. 왜 그렇게 규정이 엄격하지?
여: 음, 애완동물은 국립 공원에 서식하는 더 작은 동물들을 해칠 수 있어.
남: 아, 네가 옳다고 생각되네. 나도 그런 것을 원하진 않아.
여: 너도 알다시피, 그 공원 규정은 너의 애완동물을 보호하기 위한 것이기도 해.
남: 어떻게 그렇지?
여: 사람들의 애완동물이 야생동물한테 공격받거나 때로는 죽임을 당하는 경우가 많이 있어 왔어.
남: 오, 이런! 그러면, 이번 여행에 내 애완동물은 반드시 집에 두고 가야 되겠다. 정보 고마워.

어휘

policy ***n.*** 정책, 방침 **companion** ***n.*** 동반자 **inhabit** ***v.*** 살다, 서식하다

정답 ②

문제풀이

남자는 주말에 국립 공원에 드라이브를 갈 예정이고, 여자가 애완동물 입장에 관한 엄격한 규정이 있다는 것과 그 이유를 설명해 주고 있다. 그러므로 ② '국립 공원에서 애완동물에 대한 규정이 엄격한 이유'가 두 사람이 하는 말의 주제로 가장 적절하다.

총 어휘 수 129

05 대화자의 관계 파악

소재 요리 경연 대회

듣기 대본 해석

여: 오늘 저녁 당신의 요리를 잘 먹었습니다. 굉장히 독특한 맛들을 낼 수 있으시군요.
남: 감사합니다. 여러 가지 조합으로 실험을 많이 해왔어요.
여: 이렇게 닭고기를 튀기는 것은 어디서 배웠나요? 이 기술을 쓰는 사람은 한 번도 본 적이 없어요.
남: 그게, 우리 할머니께서 저를 키우셨는데 저는 그녀가 주방에 있는 것을 보곤 했어요. 제가 아는 모든 것을 할머니에게서 배웠어요.
여: 훌륭한 선생님 같군요. 주요리를 만드는 데에는 어떤 영감이 있었나요?
남: 멕시코 남부에서 현지 맛을 2년 동안 공부했어요. 이 예술(요리)에 대한 제 관점을 완전히 바꾸었지요.
여: 자신의 일에 완전히 전념하시는 것 같군요. 여기 와 주셔서 감사합니다.
남: 기회를 주셔서 감사합니다.
여: 대회 다음 라운드에서도 저희와 함께 해주시기를 바랍니다.
남: 정말이요? 기회를 주셔서 감사합니다.

어휘

unique ***a.*** 독특한, 특별한 **combination** ***n.*** 조합 **inspiration** ***n.*** 영감 **perspective** ***n.*** 관점, 시각 **dedicated** ***a.*** 전념하는, 헌신하는

정답 ⑤

문제풀이

여자는 남자의 요리가 맛있었다며 남자의 요리에 대한 여러 가지 질문을 하고 있고 남자에게 다음 라운드에 가게 됐다고 말하고 있는 것으로 보아 두 사람의 관계는 ⑤ '심사위원 — 대회참가자'이다.

총 어휘 수 133

06 그림의 세부 내용 파악

소재 장애물을 들이받은 자동차 사고

듣기 대본 해석

여: 안녕, Spencer. 오늘 아침 회의에 왜 그렇게 늦었어?
남: 나에게 힘든 하루였어. 정말 많은 문제가 있었거든.
여: 정말? 무슨 일이었는데?
남: 응, 회의에 늦지 않으려고 집에서 정말 일찍 나갔는데 가는 길에 도로공사를 하고 있더라고.
여: 그렇구나. 그래서 도로를 막은 거야?
남: 맞아. 나는 그다지 주의를 기울이지 않았고 장애물을 들이받아서 내 차의 창문이 깨졌어.
여: 끔찍하다.
남: 그게 다가 아니야. 내 GPS가 우회경로를 찾아내지 못해서 일반 지도를 사용해야 했어.
여: 그런 지도는 난 몇 년 동안 보지 않았지.
남: 난 길을 잃어버려서 스마트폰을 가진 여자분에게 도와달라고 부탁해야 했어.
여: 처음 보는 사람의 친절함에 의지할 수 있다니 좋구나.
남: 네 말이 맞는 것 같아. 더 나쁜 상황이 되었을 수도 있었는데.

어휘

construction ***n.*** 공사, 건설 **detour** ***n.*** 우회길 **count on** 의지하다, 기대다

정답 ③

문제풀이

남자가 장애물을 들이받아서 창문이 깨졌다고 했는데 그림에서는 헤드라이트가 깨졌으므로 정답은 ③번이다.

총 어휘 수 141

07 할 일

소재 어머니의 크리스마스 방문

듣기 대본 해석

남: 여보, 나 왔어요. 무슨 일 있어요?
여: 방금 엄마한테 전화 받았어요. 엄마가 휴가를 보내기 위해 우리 집에 오신대요!
남: 그거 좋은데요!
여: 네, 나도 좋아요. 그런데 크리스마스는 겨우 이틀 뒤인데 난 엄마의 방문에 대해 계획을 하지 않았어요!
남: 여보, 괜찮아요. 걱정하지 말아요.
여: 집도 준비를 해야 하고 엄마께 드릴 선물도 사지 못했어요.
남: 내가 도와줄게요. 내가 집에서 일할까요, 아님 선물 사러 갈까요?
여: 음, 내가 당신보다 엄마의 취향을 좀 더 잘 아니까 내가 선물을 사야 된다고 생각해요.
남: 네, 그렇네요. 그러면 내가 집안을 조금 치울게요. 어머님은 언제 도착하실까요?
여: 엄마의 비행기는 오후 7시에 도착하니까 내가 내일 일 끝나고 공항에 모시러 갈게요.
남: 네, 좋은 생각이네요.

어휘

taste ***n.*** 기호, 취향 **make sense** 말이 되다, 이치에 맞다, 의미가 통하다 **pick up** ~을 (차에) 태우러 가다

정답 ②

문제풀이

어머니의 선물을 사는 일과 집안 일 중 여자는 자신이 어머니의 취향을 더 잘 알기 때문에 선물을 사겠다고 했고 남자는 집을 치우겠다고 했으므로 정답은 ② '집안 청소 하기'이다.

총 어휘 수 144

08 이유

소재 프레젠테이션 준비

듣기 대본 해석

여: 안녕하세요, Shepherd씨.
남: 안녕하세요, Paula. 오늘 저녁에 있을 회의 준비가 모두 되었나요?
여: 밤새 내내 준비해서 드디어 이제 프레젠테이션 준비가 끝났습니다.
남: 잘됐네요. 세탁소에서 제 정장을 찾았나요?
여: 네, 사무실 옷장에 있습니다.
남: 열심히 이 일을 해준 것에 대해 정말 고마워요. 이제 제 프레젠테이션을 좀 봐야겠군요.
여: 이메일로 보내드렸는데요, 수신함을 확인해보세요. 오, 그런데 회의가 1시로 일정이 변경되었습니다.
남: 뭐라고요? 그건 너무 이른데요. 회의 전에 먹을 시간이 없겠군요.
여: 걱정 마세요. 점심을 이미 주문했습니다. 사무실에서 드실 수 있어요.
남: 오, 잘됐군요. 고마워요.

어휘

closet ***n.*** 옷장, 벽장 **reschedule** ***v.*** 일정을 변경하다

정답 ①

문제풀이

여자가 회의 시간이 1시로 변경되었다고 말하자 남자가 너무 이르다며 회의 전에 점심 먹을 시간이 없겠다고 했고 여자는 미리 점심을 주문했으니 사무실에서 먹을 수 있다고 했으므로 정답은 ① '회의 시작 시간이 변경되어서'이다.

총 어휘 수 129

09 숫자

소재 숙박 요금 계산

듣기 대본 해석

남: 안녕하세요. 체크아웃 준비 되셨나요?

여: 네. 몇 분 늦어서 죄송해요.

남: 괜찮습니다.

여: 잘됐군요. 저번에 묵었던 곳은 5분 늦게 나왔다고 15달러를 연체료로 청구했거든요.

남: 걱정 마세요. 몇 분 늦으신다고 저희한테 피해가 가진 않아요. 카드로 내시겠어요?

여: 아니요. 여기 현금 있어요.

남: 알겠습니다. 금액이 세금 포함해서 120달러네요.

여: 네? 어제 왔을 때는 110달러라고 그러셨잖아요.

남: 그건 숙박료입니다. 하지만 여기 어젯밤에 영화를 주문하셨던 것으로 나타나는데요.

여: 그렇군요. 주문한 영화가 그렇게 비쌀 줄은 몰랐네요. 여기 150달러요.

남: 네. *[잠시 후]* 여기 거스름돈이요.

어휘

check out (호텔에서 비용을 지불하고) 나가다, 확인하다

inconvenience ***n.*** 불편, 피해 **change** ***n.*** 거스름돈, 변화 ***v.*** 바꾸다

정답 ③

문제풀이

여자가 낼 숙박료는 120달러인데 150달러를 냈다고 했으므로 거스름돈의 액수는 ③ '$30'이다.

총 어휘 수 147

10 언급 유무

소재 조건에 맞는 아파트

듣기 대본 해석

여: 여보, 아파트 안내 광고를 좀 봐요. 올해가 가기 전에 어느 아파트를 임대할지 결정해야 해요.

남: 맞아요. Demarest랑 Willington 중 어느 지역이 더 좋아요?

여: 사실 나는 Demarest가 더 좋지만 그 아파트들은 보통 훨씬 더 비싸요.

남: 그럼 Willington 지역을 봐요. 이 곳도 제법 살기 좋은 곳이에요.

여: 좋아요. 우리가 지불할 수 있는 최대 임대 비용은 한 달에 2,000달러 인 것 같아요.

남: 맞는 말이에요. 집의 크기는요? 우리가 적어도 세 개의 침실이 필요하다고 생각하지 않아요?

여: 그래요. 우리 아이들이 각자 자기 방을 쓰고 싶어하니까요.

남: 좋아요. 그들은 또한 7층 이상의 아파트에서 살고 싶어해요.

여: 동의해요. 아파트가 높을수록 경치가 더 좋아요.

남: 글쎄, 우리의 요구조건을 모두 만족시킬 아파트를 찾는 게 쉽지는 않을 거예요.

어휘

classified ad (항목별) 광고 **rent** ***v.*** 임대하다 ***n.***임대료

requirement ***n.*** 필요조건, 요구

정답 ③

문제풀이

위치는 Demarest와 Willington 중 하나로, 가격은 2,000달러 이하로, 침실의 개수는 3개로, 선호하는 층은 7층 이상으로 언급되었으나 편의시설에 관한 내용은 없으므로 정답은 ③ '편의시설'이다.

총 어휘 수 154

11 내용 일치 · 불일치

소재 Berry Delicious Day에 관한 안내

듣기 대본 해석

남: 안녕하세요 학생 여러분. 저는 Dustin Swift이고, Blue Mystic Berry Farm을 대표하여 말씀드리겠습니다. 저는 Berry Delicious Day에 대해서 소개해 드리고자 합니다. 딸기, 블루베리와 함께, 우리는 여러분이 직접 블랙베리, 라즈베리, 보이즌베리를 수확해볼 수 있는 Berry Delicious Day를 이번 토요일에 개최합니다. 행사는 오전 10시에 시작해서 오후 2시까지 계속됩니다. 무료이기 때문에 부모님께 말씀을 드려 온 가족을 모시고 오세요. 여러분이 따게 될 베리는 노숙자 쉼터를 돕기 위해 판매될 파이를 만드는 데 사용될 것입니다. 반드시 옷을 알맞게 입으시길 바랍니다. 소매가 긴 셔츠와 바지를 입으셔서 베리 덤불에 찔리지 않도록 하세요. 몇몇 베리들은 애완동물에게 해롭기 때문에 애완동물을 집에 두고 오시기를 요청합니다. 토요일에 여기 Blue Mystic Berry Farm에서 여러분들을 뵙기를 바랍니다.

어휘

announce ***v.*** 알리다, 발표하다 **harvest** ***v.*** 수확하다

free of charge 무료로 **benefit** ***v.*** ~에게 유익하다, 이롭다

appropriately ***ad.*** 알맞게 **bush** ***n.*** 덤불 **harmful** ***a.*** 해로운

정답 ④

문제풀이

베리 덤불에 찔리지 않도록 긴 셔츠와 바지를 입으라고 당부했으므로 내용과 일치하지 않는 것은 ④ '참가자는 활동을 위해 반바지를 입는 것이 좋다.'이다.

총 어휘 수 151

12 도표

소재 캠핑카 선택

듣기 대본 해석

남: 내가 이번 여름 우리 캠핑 여행을 위해서 레저용 자동차 대여를 찾아 봤어. 예약을 빨리 해야 될 것 같아.

여: 맞아, 그래야지. 너무 늦을 때까지 기다리면 안 되니까.

남: 음, 내가 다섯 가지 다른 옵션이 있는 회사를 찾았어.

여: 어디 보자. *[잠시 후]* 온 가족이 가는 거니까 최소한 네 명이 잘 수 있는 차가 필요해.

남: 맞아. 근데 좀 더 큰 걸 대여하는 게 좋을 것 같아. 적어도 다섯 명이 잘 수 있는 게 더 나을 것 같아.

여: 알겠어. 근데 물 연결 필요해?

남: 있으면 좋지. 그러면 샤워를 할 수 있으니까.

여: 알겠어. 스토브랑 냉장고는? 요리의 대부분은 야외에서 하잖아.

남: 이 옵션은 포함시키자. 음식 저장해 두려고 아이스박스 챙기는 건 정말 귀찮은 일이야.

여: 알겠어. 그럼 이제 선택지가 이 두 개로 좁혀졌네.

남: 굳이 돈을 더 낼 필요는 없는 것 같아. 더 싼 걸로 하자.
여: 좋아. 어서 예약해.

어휘
RV ***n.*** 레저용 자동차 **reservation** ***n.*** 예약 **hookup** ***n.*** 연결 **hassle** ***n.*** 번거로운 일, 귀찮은 일 **cooler** ***n.*** 아이스박스

정답 ④

문제풀이
먼저 적어도 다섯 명이 잘 수 있는 차로 하자고 했으므로 ②~⑤번 중에 고르게 되고 물 연결과 스토브, 냉장고도 포함시키면 ④번과 ⑤번이 남게 되는데 이 중에 싼 걸로 하자고 했으므로 정답은 ④번이다.

총 어휘 수 179

13 긴 대화의 응답

소재 티켓 챙기기

듣기 대본 해석
여: 여보, 우리 늦겠어요. 아직 준비 안 됐어요?
남: 서두르려고 하는데 휴대폰을 잃어버린 것 같아요.
여: 아까 소파에서 본 것 같은데요.
남: 아, 여기 있다. 좋아. 가기 전에 살펴야 할 게 있어요?
여: 오, 우리가 없는 동안 누가 물고기 먹이를 주죠?
남: 진정해요. Garcia 부인이 돌봐준댔어요.
여: 좋아요. 티켓을 꼭 가져가야 해요. 출력은 했죠?
남: 아니요. 하지만 휴대폰에 저장해 놨어요.
여: 휴대폰에 저장했다고요? 이젠 프린트로 출력할 필요가 없는 거예요?
남: 없어요. 바로 여기 전자 티켓이 있어요. 가판대에서 보여주기만 하면 돼요.
여: 전자 티켓이라. 꽤 편리해 보이는데 그래도 혹시 모르니까 출력하는 게 좋을 것 같아요.
남: ① 좋은 생각이에요. 내가 지금 그걸 할게요.

어휘
kiosk ***n.*** 매점, 가판대 **convenient** ***a.*** 편리한 **in case** (~할) 경우에 대비해서

정답 ①

문제풀이
만약에 사태에 대비해서 출력을 해가는 게 나을 것 같다고 말하는 여자의 말에 대한 남자의 대답으로 적절한 것은 ① '좋은 생각이에요. 내가 지금 그걸 할게요.'이다.

오답 보기 해석
② 내가 Garcia 부인에게 집 열쇠를 줬어요.
③ 우리는 충분한 물고기 먹이가 있어야 해요.
④ 알았어요. 그가 그것들을 우리한테 가져올 수 있는지 알아볼게요.
⑤ 알겠어요. 나는 이미 휴대폰을 켰어요.

총 어휘 수 151

14 긴 대화의 응답

소재 놓고 온 물건 가져다 줄 것 요청하기

듣기 대본 해석
[휴대폰이 울린다.]
남: 여보세요?
여: Charlie, 나 Riley야.
남: 안녕 Riley. 무슨 일이야?
여: 음, 지금 회의 때문에 EPL 본부로 가는 중이야.
남: 우리 새 경기장에 대해서 발표할 준비 돼 있어?
여: 응, 근데...
남: 근데 뭐? 무슨 문제 있어?
여: 그게, 발표 자료들을 다 사무실 책상에 두고 온 것 같아. 네가 어떻게 나에게 갖다 줄 수 있는 방법은 없을까?
남: 나도 도와주고 싶은데 내가 가져갈 수 있는 방법이 없어. 지금 사무실이 아니거든.
여: 근데 벌써 12시고 회의는 1시간 뒤에 시작해. 거기 다시 가서 자료들을 가져오면 시간 안에 도착할 수가 없어.
남: 정말 어떻게 할 수 없는 문제네. Kyle에게 전화해 봐. 아마 사무실에 있을 거야.
여: ⑤ 알았어. 그에게 전화해서 자료를 가져다 줄 수 있는지 물어볼게.

어휘
dilemma ***n.*** 진퇴양난, 궁지

정답 ⑤

문제풀이
여자는 발표에 필요한 자료들을 모두 사무실에 놓고 와서 난처한 상황이며 남자도 현재 사무실에 있지 않아 가져다 줄 수 없어 다른 사람에게 전화해볼 것을 제안했다. 이에 대해 가장 적절한 여자의 응답은 ⑤ '알았어. 그에게 전화해서 자료를 가져다 줄 수 있는지 물어볼게.'이다.

오답 보기 해석
① 그 경기장은 한 시까지 문을 열지 않아.
② 그래. 자료들을 최대한 빨리 가져다 줄게.
③ 내가 발표를 취소할 수 있을 거라고 생각하니?
④ 나쁘진 않네. 언제까지 발표가 준비돼야 하니?

총 어휘 수 149

15 상황에 적절한 말

소재 게임 결승전에서 우승하지 못한 친구 위로하기

듣기 대본 해석
남: Ryan과 Jason은 Counter Strike: GO라는 유명한 일인칭 슈팅 게임의 결승전에서 방금 패배했습니다. Ryan은 시합 초반부에 큰 실수를 몇 번 했으며, 이러한 실수들로 인해 그들은 경기에서 패배합니다. Jason은 경기 후에 Ryan이 밖에서 혼자 길에 앉아 있는 것을 발견합니다. 그는 Ryan이 속상하고 자신한테 실망한 듯 보이는 모습을 알게 됩니다. Jason은 속상하지 않고 오히려 결승전까지 간 것이 자랑스럽습니다. 그는 Ryan에게 그는 최선을 다했고 그의 노력 덕분에 결승전까지 올 수 있었음을 알고 있으며, Ryan에게 힘을 내라고 말하고 싶어합니다. 이러한 상황에서 Jason이 Ryan에게 할 말로 가장 적절한 것은 무엇일까요?
Jason: ④ 네가 없었더라면 우리는 결승까지 가지 못했을 거야.

어휘
upset ***a.*** 속상한 **disappointed** ***a.*** 실망한, 낙담한 〈문제〉 **cancel** ***v.*** 취소하다

정답 ④

문제풀이
게임 결승전에서 실수를 해서 낙담해 있는 친구에게 위로를 해주고 싶은 상황이다. 또 Jason은 Ryan덕분에 결승전까지 갈 수 있었다는 것을 말해주고 싶다고 했으므로 Jason이 할 말로 적절한 것은 ④ '네가 없었더라면 우리는 결승까지 가지 못했을 거야.'이다.

오답 보기 해석
① 나한테 친절하게 대해줘서 정말 고마워.
② 빨리 가서 경기에 최선을 다하자.
③ 챔피언전 이긴 걸 축하해.
⑤ 그들이 챔피언전을 취소해서 좋지 않아?

총 어휘 수 131

16 담화 주제 / 17 세부 내용 파악

소재 환경오염의 원인과 해결책

듣기 대본 해석
남: 요즘 인간은 오염의 영향으로부터 고통을 받기 시작하고 있습니다. 오염의 원인이 되는 많은 요인들이 있습니다. 그것들 중에 몇몇은 자연적이지만, 그것들의 대부분은 인간이 만들었고 예방이 가능합니다. 분명한 것부터 시작하면, 사람들은 종종 쓰레기로 거리와 수로를 오염시킵니다. 우리의 환경을 보호하고 아름답게 하는 데 도움을 주기 위해 스스로 뒤처리를 하는 것은 우리의 의무입니다. 재활용은 환경을 돕기 위한 좋은 방법인데 그것은 쓰레기 매립지로 가는 소비자의 폐기물의 양을 줄여주기 때문입니다. 개인 자동차는 또한 공기 오염에 상당히 기여합니다. 그러므로, 자전거 타기 또는 대중교통수단 이용이 우리 환경에 큰 도움을 줄 수 있습니다. 발전소 또한 공기를 오염시킬 수 있습니다. 만약 우리가 가정에서 에너지 사용을 줄인다면, 발전소로부터의 배기가스를 줄일 수 있습니다. 우리는 반드시 에너지 효율이 좋은 전구를 사용하고 에너지 효율이 좋은 가전제품에 투자를 해야 합니다. 이것은 공기 오염을 줄일 뿐만 아니라 우리로 하여금 돈을 절약하게 해 줄 것입니다.

어휘
man-made ***a.*** 인공의 **preventable** ***a.*** 예방 가능한
pick up after ~의 뒤처리를 하다 **landfill** ***n.*** 쓰레기 매립지
plant ***n.*** 공장 **emission** ***n.*** 배출가스 **efficient** ***a.*** 효율적인
appliance ***n.*** 가전제품

정답 16 ⑤ 17 ③

문제풀이
16 남자는 사람들의 어떤 행동이 환경을 오염시키는지 그리고 그를 막기 위한 해결책을 제시하고 있으므로 남자가 하는 말의 주제는 ⑤ '환경 오염에 대한 원인과 해결책'이다.
17 남자는 환경오염을 줄이기 위한 방법으로 쓰레기 줍기, 재활용과 대중교통수단의 이용, 에너지 아껴 쓰기를 제시했으므로 언급하지 않은 것은 ③ '태양 에너지 사용하기'이다.

오답 보기 해석
16
① 사람들이 오염에 기여하는 방법
② 공기 질 향상을 위해 해야 할 것들
③ 오염이 환경에 끼치는 영향
④ 에너지 절약 습관을 갖는 것의 이점
17
① 쓰레기 줍기
② 재활용 하기
④ 대중교통수단 사용하기
⑤ 에너지 아껴 쓰기

총 어휘 수 156

DICTATION ANSWERS

01 How on earth
02 How about we meet
03 the safest and most time-efficient method / accommodates most of our citizens / spending the next three months discussing
04 have rather strict rules / the best travel companions / to protect your pet / leave my pet at home
05 fry the chicken like that / the inspirations for the main dish / dedicated to your work / the next round of the competition
06 road construction on the way / paying attention / find a detour / count on the kindness of strangers
07 Christmas is only two days away / bought her a gift / that makes sense / pick her up at the airport
08 pick up my suit from the dry cleaners / hard work you put in here / has actually been rescheduled / ordered lunch
09 charged us a fifteen-dollar late fee / charge it to your card / includes sales tax / you ordered a movie
10 before the end of the year / a good area to live in / The higher the apartment is / meets all of our requirements
11 It's free of charge / dress appropriately / avoid getting pricked by / leave your pets at home
12 offers five different options / take showers / narrows it down
13 Aren't you ready yet / feed the fish / You printed them out / That sounds quite convenient
14 I'm on my way to / Is there any way you can / make it in time / quite a dilemma
15 it was due to these mistakes / disappointed in himself / did his best / thanks to his hard work
16-17 suffer from the effects of pollution / cuts down on the amount of consumer waste / using public transportation / invest in energy-efficient appliances

16 수능영어듣기 실전모의고사

본문 p.98

01 ④	02 ②	03 ②	04 ⑤	05 ⑤	06 ②
07 ⑤	08 ⑤	09 ①	10 ③	11 ②	12 ③
13 ②	14 ③	15 ⑤	16 ④	17 ⑤	

01 짧은 대화의 응답

소재 영화표 구입

듣기 대본 해석

남: Wrong Number 영화표 두 장 살 수 있나요?
여: 물론이죠. 몇 시 영화로 하시겠어요?
남: 저녁 7시요. 어른 2명 앞 쪽이요.
여: ④ 그 쇼는 발코니 자리밖에 남아있지 않네요.

어휘

〈문제〉 **available** ***a.*** 이용할 수 있는

정답 ④

문제풀이

남자는 극장에서 원하는 좌석을 말하고 있으므로 그에 대한 여자의 응답으로 ④ '그 쇼는 발코니 자리밖에 남아있지 않네요.'가 적절하다.

오답 보기 해석

① 예, 이쪽으로 저를 따라오세요.
② 죄송합니다. 줄 서서 기다리셔야 합니다.
③ Wrong Number는 더 이상 상영되지 않습니다.
⑤ 안 됩니다. 당신은 매니저와 이야기해야 해요.

총 어휘 수 36

02 짧은 대화의 응답

소재 머그잔 사용

듣기 대본 해석

여: 오, 너 커피 머그잔을 쓰고 있구나.
남: 응. 일회용 컵을 쓰는 것은 환경에 절대로 좋지 않아.
여: 전적으로 동의해. 나도 내 머그잔을 하나 사서 너와 함께 동참해야겠다.
남: ② 나에게 남는 머그잔들이 있어. 너한테 하나 줄 수 있어.

어휘

disposable ***a.*** 일회용의 〈문제〉 **prefer A to B** A를 B보다 선호하다
from now on 이제부터

정답 ②

문제풀이

머그잔을 사서 머그잔 사용하기에 동참하겠다는 여자의 말에 적절한 남자의 응답은 ② '나에게 남는 머그잔들이 있어. 너한테 하나 줄 수 있어.'이다.

오답 보기 해석

① 오늘 아침에 환경에 대한 뉴스를 들었어.
③ 종이컵을 쓰는 것은 참 편리해.
④ 틀렸어. 난 차를 커피보다 더 좋아해.
⑤ 이제부터 커피를 마시지 않겠어.

총 어휘 수 48

03 담화 목적

소재 교내 식당 시설 개선

듣기 대본 해석

여: 안녕하세요, 학생 여러분. 오늘 점심 식사 하실 계획이시죠? 아마 여러분이 "네."라고 말할 거라고 생각합니다. 그러면 여러분은 학교 식당에 대해 어떻게 생각하시나요? 시설이 좋다고 생각하시나요? 아마 아닐 겁니다. 최근 많은 학생들이 식당에 대해 꽤 불평을 하고 있습니다. 그들 중 몇몇은 학교 웹사이트에 글을 올리기도 했습니다. 저도 그 중 한 명입니다. 불행하게도, 학교는 저희의 얘기를 듣고 있는 것 같지 않습니다. 교내 식당은 우리 학교에 좋지 않은 평판만 주고 있습니다. 우리가 시설을 개선하지 않는다면 그런 평판은 계속 악화될 것입니다. 우리 모두 더 나은 학교 생활을 보장받기 위해 빨리 식당을 보수해야 합니다.

어휘

facility ***n.*** 시설, 설비 **complaint** ***n.*** 불평 **reputation** ***n.*** 평판, 명성 **renovate** ***v.*** 보수하다, 개조하다

정답 ②

문제풀이

여자는 교내 식당 시설에 대해 많은 학생들이 불만을 제기하고 있으며, 학교의 평판이 나빠지고 있으니 빨리 보수되어야 한다고 말하고 있다. 따라서 정답은 ② '교내 식당의 시설 개선을 요청하려고'이다.

총 어휘 수 118

04 대화 주제

소재 휴대폰과 건강

듣기 대본 해석

남: 와, 내 휴대폰이 정말 뜨거워졌어.
여: 너무 오랫동안 사용하면 안 돼.
남: 휴대폰이 건강에 좋지 않다는 것에 대해 어떻게 생각해?
여: 음, 지나친 장시간 휴대폰 사용이 뇌종양을 일으킬 수 있다고 보여준 많은 연구를 알고 있어.
남: 나도 전에 라디오에서 들었어.
여: 전자파는 우리 몸에 위험해. 그리고 이 사실이 많은 연구에서 밝혀져 왔지.
남: 나도 알아. 하지만 일 때문에 나는 상당히 자주 휴대폰을 사용해야 하거든.
여: 그럼, 네가 조심해서 사용할 수 있는 방법들이 있어. 예를 들어, 네가 이어폰을 사용하면 휴대폰 자체와 직접적인 접촉을 피하잖아.
남: 맞아. 나도 이어폰을 좀 더 자주 착용하기 시작해야겠어.
여: 다른 안전 예방책도 있어. 인터넷에서 찾아볼 수 있을 거야.

어휘

harmful ***a.*** 해로운 **excessive** ***a.*** 지나친, 과도한 **tumor** ***n.*** 종양
avoid ***v.*** 피하다, 막다

정답 ⑤

문제풀이

뇌종양 유발 및 전자파에 대한 노출 등 과도한 휴대폰 사용이 건강에 미치는 부정적인 영향에 대해 대화를 나누고 있으므로 정답은 ⑤ '휴대폰 사용이 건강에 미치는 영향'이다.

총 어휘 수 140

05 심정 파악

소재 코치 교체 후 연패

듣기 대본 해석

남: 안녕, Monica. 경기 어땠어?

여: 글쎄, 내가 너한테 이건 말할 수 있어. 당분간은 다른 경기를 보지 않을 거라고.

남: 왜? 나는 네가 미식축구를 정말 좋아한다고 생각했어. 너네 팀이 작년에 정말 잘하지 않았어?

여: 응, 그들은 수퍼볼에서 우승했지. 그런데 그 후에 코치가 은퇴했어. 새 코치가 왔고 팀이 전에 없이 형편없이 경기하고 있어!

남: 너는 이번 새 코치의 팬이 아닌 것처럼 들리네.

여: 그 코치 때문에 팀이 경기를 못하는 것 같아.

남: 그가 그렇게 별로야?

여: 글쎄, 그 팀의 기록을 봐. 올해 우리는 원정경기에서 한 번도 못 이겼어.

남: 진정해. 나는 그들이 이번 시즌에 경기가 차츰 좋아질 거라고 확신해.

여: 나는 그러길 바라지만 정말 그럴 것 같지가 않아. 지난주에도 그들보다 훨씬 약한 팀에 졌거든.

남: 오늘 경기는 어땠는데?

여: 그들은 리그에서 최고의 팀과 경기했고 물론 졌지.

어휘

retire ***v.*** 은퇴하다 **away game** 원정 경기 **league** ***n.*** (스포츠 경기의) 리그

정답 ⑤

문제풀이

여자가 좋아하는 미식축구팀이 코치가 교체된 후 계속 지고 있어서 여자는 그것이 새 코치 때문이라고 말하는 것으로 보아 여자의 심정은 ⑤ '스트레스를 받는'이 가장 적절하다.

오답 보기 해석

① 당황스러운
② 죄책감을 느끼는
③ 행복한
④ 느긋한

총 어휘 수 149

06 그림의 세부 내용 파악

소재 새 사무실 안내

듣기 대본 해석

여: 여기가 당신의 사무실이에요, Smith씨.

남: 와! 제가 상상했던 것보다 훨씬 좋아요. 창 밖을 봐요. 산의 경치가 얼마나 아름다운지!

여: 사랑스러워요, 그렇죠? 그것이 우리가 그 방향을 마주보게 의자를 놓은 이유예요.

남: 멋지네요. 그리고 저 책상 위에 있는 것이 저의 새 노트북 같군요.

여: 물론이죠. 지난주에 그걸 샀어요. 당신이 필요한 모든 것이 이미 노트북에 다 들어 있을 거예요.

남: 그런데 저 시계는 제가 어떻게 좀 해야 할 것 같아요.

여: 무슨 뜻이죠?

남: 얼마나 큰지 보세요. 너무 주의를 산만하게 하네요.

여: 당신이 원한다면 시계를 없애셔도 돼요.

남: 제가 커피를 좋아하는 것을 어떻게 알았어요?

여: 당신이 커피를 즐겨 마시게 보였어요, Smith씨. 농담이에요. 저희 모든 사무실마다 전기 커피포트가 있어요. 어쨌든, 저희 빌딩에 오신 것을 환영해요.

남: 정말 감사합니다.

어휘

distracting ***a.*** 주의집중을 방해하는 **get rid of** ~을 없애다

정답 ②

문제풀이

대화의 앞부분에서 창 밖 경치가 좋아서 의자를 그 방향으로 마주보게 놓았다고 했는데 그림에서는 반대 방향으로 놓여 있으므로 정답은 ②번이다.

총 어휘 수 141

07 부탁한 일

소재 아빠의 은퇴 파티 준비

듣기 대본 해석

남: Linda, 아빠 은퇴 기념파티 할 장소 정했니?

여: 두세 군데 생각해뒀어. 첫 번째는 새로 생긴 멕시칸 그릴이고 다른 한 곳은 그리스 식당이야.

남: 음, 너도 알다시피 아빠가 그리스 음식을 좋아하시니까 그리스 식당으로 가는 게 어떨까?

여: 그게 좋겠다.

남: 아빠 선물도 벌써 샀니?

여: 아니, 안 샀어. 너는?

남: 나도 안 샀어. 내 생각에 우리가 선물을 같이 사야 할 것 같아. 아마 아빠가 좋아하시는 비타민을 사드릴 수 있을 거야.

여: 그거 훌륭한 선물이겠다.

남: 좋았어. 내가 내일 일하면서 살게. 카드는 네가 살 수 있어?

여: 물론이지. 좋은 데 알아.

남: 완벽하네. 그럼 내일 보자.

여: 그래. 그때 봐.

어휘

retirement ***n.*** 퇴직, 은퇴

정답 ⑤

문제풀이

남자와 여자가 같이 아빠의 은퇴 기념파티를 준비하면서 식당을 정하고 선물을 준비하는 대화이다. 남자가 선물을 사겠다고 했고 여자에게 카드를 살 수 있는지 물었으므로 정답은 ⑤ '카드 사기'이다.

오답 보기 해석

① 예약하기
② 비타민 사기
③ 선물 추천하기
④ 저녁 준비하기

총 어휘 수 124

08 이유

소재 아빠에게 화가 난 엄마

듣기 대본 해석

여: 거실 청소해 주어서 고마워, Thomas.

남: 괜찮아요, 엄마.

여: 근데, 나의 USB 드라이브 봤니?

남: 못 본 것 같은데요. 왜요?

여: 음, 내 생각에는 탁자 위에 놓아둔 것 같은데 오늘은 찾을 수 없는 것 같아서.

남: 아, 맞아요. 아빠가 가지고 가시는 걸 봤어요.

여: 응? 아빠가 사무실에 가지고 가셨다고?

남: 네. 아빠가 함께 일하시는 분의 컴퓨터에서 파일을 꺼내는 데 그것이 필요하다고 말씀하셨어요.
여: 정말? 설마 그럴 리가. 그가 내 USB 드라이브를 먼저 물어보지 않고 가지고 갔다고?
남: 아빠가 엄마에게 물어보지 않으셨다는 거죠?
여: 절대로 안 물었지. 아빠는 거기에 우리 가족 사진 몇 장이 있다는 것을 알아. 그건 나에게 매우 중요해.
남: 아마 아빠가 묻는 것을 잊으셨나 봐요.
여: 때때로 나는 너의 아빠가 이해가 안 돼. 행동하기 전에 생각을 안 하셔.
남: 진정하세요, 엄마. 모두 잘 될 거라고 확신해요.

어휘
coworker ***n.*** 동료

정답 ⑤

문제풀이
엄마는 아빠가 자신의 허락을 받지 않고 가족 사진이 들어 있는 중요한 USB를 회사에 가져가서 화가 나 있다. 따라서 정답은 ⑤ '자신의 USB 드라이브를 허락 없이 가져가서'이다.

총 어휘 수 140

09 숫자

소재 옷 구매하기

듣기 대본 해석
여: 안녕하세요. 아들한테 줄 새 스웨터를 사려고 하는데요.
남: 도와드리겠습니다. 나이가 어떻게 되죠?
여: 15살이요. 보통 성인 중간사이즈로 입어요.
남: 좋습니다. 자, 고를 수 있는 몇 가지 소재가 있는데요. 면하고 울 중에서 어떤 게 좋으세요?
여: 가격 차이가 어떻게 되죠?
남: 면 스웨터는 55달러이고 울은 20달러 더 비싸요. 면으로 된 것이 요즘 정말 인기가 많아요.
여: 좋네요. 그럼 면으로 된 걸로 할게요. 청바지도 사고 싶은데요.
남: 네. 이 스키니 진이 스웨터하고 잘 어울려요. 정상가는 50달러지만 10퍼센트 세일하고 있습니다.
여: 스웨터도 할인이 적용되나요?
남: 죄송하지만 할인은 청바지에만 적용됩니다.
여: 괜찮습니다. 어쨌든 둘 다 주세요. 여기 카드 있습니다.
남: 감사합니다.

어휘
apply to ~에 적용되다

정답 ①

문제풀이
여자는 아들 옷으로 55달러짜리 면 스웨터와 10퍼센트 세일 중인 50달러짜리 스키니 진을 선택했다. 그러므로 55달러와 45달러를 합쳐 총 ① '$100'를 지불해야 한다.

총 어휘 수 143

10 언급 유무

소재 소설에 관한 대화

듣기 대본 해석
남: Amy, 벌써 다른 책을 읽고 있니?
여: 응. 지난번 책은 다 읽었고 오늘 아침 이 책을 읽기 시작했어. The Prized Prince라는 책이야.
남: 들어본 것 같은데. 최근 베스트셀러 목록에 있던 것 아니니?
여: 맞아. 200만 부가 넘게 팔렸지.
남: 정말 많이 팔렸구나! 그 책은 무엇 때문에 그렇게 인기가 많을까?
여: 무엇보다도 Steve Queen에 의해 쓰여졌잖아. 너도 알다시피 그는 정말 유명해.
남: Steve Queen? 그러면 그 책은 틀림없이 공포소설이겠구나.
여: 아니. 실은 이번에는 로맨스 소설이야.
남: 아. 난 로맨스 소설을 좋아하지는 않아. 그건 지루하거든.
여: 이것은 보통 로맨스 소설과는 약간 달라. 난 그것을 영화로 만들 계획이라고 온라인에서 읽었어.
남: 멋지네. 그런 경우면 한번 시도해 보고 싶은걸.
여: 그래. 내가 다 읽으면 너에게 빌려줄게.

어휘
horror novel 공포소설 **in that case** 그런 경우에는, 그렇다면
give it a shot ~을 시도하다

정답 ③

문제풀이
두 사람은 책의 판매 부수, 저자, 장르, 영화 제작 계획에 대해서는 언급했지만, 출판사에 대해서는 언급하지 않았으므로 정답은 ③ '출판사'이다.

총 어휘 수 146

11 내용 일치 · 불일치

소재 Science Fair 소개

듣기 대본 해석
여: 좋은 아침입니다, 여러분. 저는 올해의 Science Fair에 대해 말하려 합니다. 올해 모든 사람들은 팀이 되어 일할 것이고 여러분은 처음부터 끝까지 여러분의 프로젝트를 촬영할 것입니다. 팀은 서너 명의 학급친구들로 구성될 것입니다. 모든 팀은 올해의 과학 카탈로그에서 서로 다른 주제를 고를 것입니다. 올해의 주제는 수중 호흡, 경주용 차 디자인, 쓰레기 압축하는 과정, 로봇 가정부의 움직임을 포함하고 있습니다. 물론 프로젝트는 작동이 되는 모델을 만들 필요는 없고 개념의 입증만 있으면 됩니다. 모든 팀원의 이름과 여러분이 정한 주제를 지원서와 함께 5월 5일 오후 5시까지 제출해 주십시오. 질문이 있으면 과학 선생님께 이메일을 보내세요. 여러분 모두의 작업을 보는 것이 기대가 됩니다.

어휘
include ***v.*** 포함하다 **proof** ***n.*** 입증, 증거 **concept** ***n.*** 개념
application ***n.*** 지원서

정답 ②

문제풀이
주제는 올해의 과학 카탈로그에서 팀 별로 서로 다른 주제를 골라야 하므로 ② '주제는 제한 없이 자유롭게 선택하면 된다.'가 일치하지 않는다.

총 어휘 수 131

12 도표

소재 자동차 바퀴(휠) 구입

듣기 대본 해석
여: 무엇을 도와 드릴까요?
남: 제 차에 쓸 새로운 바퀴(휠)를 찾고 있어요. 제가 그것을 구입했을 때 딸려 나온 공장 것들은 맘에 들지 않아요.
여: 알겠습니다. 22 또는 24인치 휠이 손님의 차에 맞을 것 같네요.
남: 제가 좀 낮게 타는 것을 좋아해서 22인치 휠이 저한테 더 맞을 것 같군요.

여: 알겠습니다. 색상이 섞인 것이 좋으세요, 단색의 검은 가장자리가 좋으세요?
남: 색이 섞인 것은 나한테 너무 화려하고요. 검은색 휠이 좋아요. 더 스포티해요.
여: 네. 이 모델 좋아하실 것 같네요.
남: 멋지네요! 가격이 얼마예요?
여: 이번 주에 세일해서 1,200달러예요. 40퍼센트 할인가예요.
남: 나한테 여전히 너무 비싸네요. 1,000달러 미만으로 쓰려고 하거든요.
여: 좋아요. 그러면 이것이 손님이 찾고 있는 제품인 것 같네요.
남: 더 저렴한데 마찬가지로 좋아보이는군요. 그걸로 할게요.

어휘

rim ***n.*** 가장자리, 테

정답 ③

문제풀이

남자가 22인치 휠이 본인한테 더 알맞다고 했으므로 ①, ③, ⑤번 중에 선택해야 하는데 색은 검정이 좋다고 했으므로 ③, ⑤번이 남는다. 그런데 1,000달러 미만으로 하고 싶다고 했으므로 정답은 ③번이다.

총 어휘 수 150

13 긴 대화의 응답

소재 좋아하는 일과 잘하는 일 사이에서의 고민

듣기 대본 해석

남: Chloe, 뭐해?
여: 그냥 몇 주 전에 했던 군대 적성 검사 결과 보고 있었어.
남: 오, 나도 봐도 돼?
여: 그럼.
남: *[잠시 후]* 우와! 결과가 대단한데. 공간 추론 능력이랑 문제 해결 능력이 뛰어나다고 써있어. 건축가나 전략가가 되는 게 가장 좋을 거래.
여: 응, 근데 결과가 맘에 드는지는 모르겠어.
남: 진짜? 왜?
여: 음, 우리 부모님께서는 내가 군대에 들어가길 바라시지만 난 항상 작가가 되고 싶었어. 지금은 그렇게 잘 쓰는 작가는 아닌 것 같지만 연습하고 있었어.
남: 그렇구나. 네가 좋아하는 일이랑 네가 잘하는 일 사이에서 결정을 하는 건 항상 어려운 일이야.
여: 맞아. 네가 나라면 어떻게 하겠니?
남: ② 네가 열정을 갖고 있는 일을 하는 게 좋을 것 같아.

어휘

aptitude ***n.*** 적성 **spatial reasoning** 공간 추론 **strategist** ***n.*** 전략가

정답 ②

문제풀이

좋아하는 일과 잘하는 일 사이에서 고민하고 있는 여자에게 남자가 해줄 수 있는 적절한 조언은 ② '네가 열정을 갖고 있는 일을 하는 게 좋을 것 같아.'이다.

오답 보기 해석

① 내가 너라면 군대 적성 검사를 받아 볼 것 같아.
③ 아직 내가 하고 싶은 일을 결정하지 못했어.
④ 요즘 성공적인 건축가가 되는 것은 정말 어려운 일이야.
⑤ 넌 가능한 많은 군사 전략 책들을 모으는 편이 낫겠어.

총 어휘 수 142

14 긴 대화의 응답

소재 남편을 위한 스마트폰

듣기 대본 해석

남: 안녕하세요 Lewis 부인. 컴퓨터로 뭐하고 계세요?
여: 오, 안녕하세요, Chris. 저는 제 남편을 위한 새로운 스마트폰을 찾고 있어요.
남: 그렇군요. 그의 생일이 다가온다거나 하는 건가요?
여: 맞아요. 그는 다음 달에 47살이 돼요.
남: 그가 새로운 스마트폰을 가지게 되어 정말 기뻐하겠네요.
여: 그는 아직 몰라요. 그렇지만 그는 현재 그의 전화기가 정말 느리다고 항상 불평해요.
남: 전화기가 얼마나 오래 되었죠?
여: 약 4년 됐어요.
남: 네. 스마트폰이 요즘 매우 빨리 구식이 돼요.
여: 맞아요. 그는 현재의 전화기를 가지고 인터넷 검색을 하는 데 많은 어려움이 있고, 보다 최신 앱을 실행할 수 없어요.
남: 당신은 아마도 그에게 최신 모델 중에 하나를 사줘야겠네요. 그래야지 오래갈 거예요.
여: ③ 당신 말이 맞지만, 저는 어느 모델이 가장 좋은지 모르겠어요.

어휘

complain ***v.*** 불평하다 **outdated** ***a.*** 구식의 **browse** ***v.*** 인터넷을 돌아다니다

정답 ③

문제풀이

여자가 남자에게 남편의 전화기에 대한 얘기를 했고, 남자는 최신 모델 중 하나를 사줘야겠다고 했으므로 그에 적절한 응답은 ③ '당신 말이 맞지만, 저는 어느 모델이 가장 좋은지 모르겠어요.'이다.

오답 보기 해석

① 네. 구식 전화기로는 새로운 앱을 실행할 수 없어요.
② 그의 전화기는 잘 작동하지만 별로 세련되지는 않아요.
④ 맞아요. 저는 제가 어렸을 때 스마트폰을 결코 가지지 못했어요.
⑤ 네, 하지만 그는 평소에 그의 전화기가 얼마나 느린지 불평해요.

총 어휘 수 131

15 상황에 적절한 말

소재 건강한 음식의 선택

듣기 대본 해석

여: Nancy는 체중감량 클리닉에서 일하는 직원입니다. 그녀는 개인 트레이너는 아니지만 클리닉에서 5년 넘게 일해서 영양에 대해 그리고 어떻게 건강을 유지하는지에 대해 잘 압니다. 어느 오후에 그녀는 아파트 건물의 복도에서 친구인 Maya와 마주칩니다. 그녀는 식료품 가방을 나르고 있었습니다. 그녀가 Nancy를 봤을 때 그녀는 Nancy에게 자기가 산 음식에 대해 묻기 위해 멈춰 섰습니다. 그녀는 자기가 건강한 음식을 사려고 노력하지만 그녀 자신과, 남편, 아들을 위해 사야 하고 그녀의 선택에 대해 모두가 만족하기를 바랍니다. 이런 상황에서 Nancy는 Maya에게 뭐하고 말할 것 같은가요?
Nancy: ⑤ 너의 영양 목표에 맞는 음식들 몇 가지를 그들이 고르게 해 봐.

어휘

well-versed in ~에 정통한 **nutrition** ***n.*** 영양 〈문제〉 **pregnant** ***a.*** 임신한

정답 ⑤

문제풀이

Nancy의 친구 Maya는 건강한 음식을 사고 싶지만 자신과, 남편, 아들의 기호도 고려해야 한다며 조언을 구하고 있다. 이에 맞는 응답은 ⑤ '너의 영양 목표에 맞는 음식들 몇 가지를 그들이 고르게 해 봐.'이다.

오답 보기 해석
① 넌 체중감량 클리닉에 등록해야 해.
② 나는 체중감량과 영양에 대해 많이 알아.
③ 과식은 심각한 건강 문제를 일으키지.
④ 네가 임신 중이라면 자연히 더 많이 먹게 될 거야.

총 어휘 수 131

16 담화 목적 / 17 세부 내용 파악

소재 먼지를 줄이는 청소 방법

듣기 대본 해석

여: 여러분 안녕하세요. 제 이름은 Mary Anne Philips이고 저는 Big City 위생국의 수간호사입니다. 오늘 저는 알레르기 유발 항원, 특히 먼지에 대해서 얘기를 해보고 싶습니다. 먼지는 우리의 건강에 많은 악영향을 주기 때문에 우리는 집을 최대한 청결하게 유지하기 위해 노력해야 해야 합니다. 집에 있는 먼지의 양을 대폭 줄일 수 있는 몇 가지의 청소 방법이 있습니다. 먼저, 진공청소기를 얼마나 자주 쓰시나요? 최소한 일주일에 두 번은 사용해야 할 것 같습니다. 둘째, 베개와 소파 쿠션을 일주일에 한 번씩 밖에서 터는 것도 먼지를 제거합니다. 종종 바닥을 걸레로 닦는 것은 불편하겠지만 청소기를 쓰면서 놓쳤을 먼지와 흙을 치우기 위해서는 필수적으로 해야 하는 겁니다. 마지막으로 침구류를 자주 세탁하는 것이 좋은데 이는 본인이나 같이 사는 사람이 알레르기가 있을 때는 특히 더 중요합니다. 이런 도움이 되는 조언들을 명심한다면 깨끗하고 건강한 집을 유지할 수 있을 것입니다. 시간 내 주셔서 감사합니다.

어휘
briefly ***ad.*** 간략히 **allergen** ***n.*** 알레르겐(알레르기를 일으키는 항원)
strive ***v.*** 분투하다, 노력하다 **drastically** ***ad.*** 대폭, 과감하게
vacuum cleaner 진공청소기 **beat** ***v.*** 두드리다 **mop** ***v.*** 닦다

정답 16 ④ 17 ⑤

문제풀이
16 여자는 먼지를 줄일 수 있는 청소 방법들을 제시하고 있으므로 여자가 하는 말의 목적은 ④ '먼지를 줄이는 청소 요령을 알려주려고'이다.
17 여자는 진공청소기 사용하기, 베개와 쿠션 털기, 바닥 닦기, 침구 세탁하기에 대해서는 언급하였으나, 환기에 대한 언급은 하지 않았으므로 정답은 ⑤ '환기시키기'이다.

총 어휘 수 180

DICTATION ANSWERS

01 in the front section
02 a disposable cup / I couldn't agree more
03 planning on having lunch / a few complaints about the cafeteria / bad reputation / renovate the cafeteria
04 cell phones being harmful to your health / excessive or long-term cell phone use / dangerous to our health / you avoid direct contact with the phone itself
05 you're not a fan of / the team's record / I seriously doubt it
06 much nicer than I imagined / facing that direction / I might have to do something / free to get rid of it
07 have you decided where to eat / That works for me / get him some of the vitamins / Can you buy a card
08 by the way / left it on the coffee table / he didn't ask / He doesn't think before he does things
09 rather go with cotton or wool / costs twenty dollars more / are a great match with / applies to the jeans
10 Wasn't it on the best-seller list / a horror novel / I'm not a very big fan of / give it a shot
11 from start to finish / choose a different topic / submit your applications / email your science teacher
12 you'll be needing / will better suit me / They're sportier / spend less than one thousand dollars
13 Do you mind if I / spatial reasoning and problem solving / join the military / if you were me
14 turns forty-seven / his current phone is really slow / smartphones get outdated pretty quickly / browsing the Internet
15 has been working for over five years / runs into a friend of hers / stops to ask her a question / wants everyone to be happy with her choices
16-17 negative health effects / as clean as possible / at least twice a week / Keep these helpful tips in mind

17 수능영어듣기 실전모의고사

본문 p.104

01 ④	02 ③	03 ④	04 ②	05 ⑤	06 ①
07 ②	08 ⑤	09 ④	10 ③	11 ③	12 ③
13 ③	14 ①	15 ⑤	16 ②	17 ④	

01 짧은 대화의 응답

소재 물건 가격 흥정

듣기 대본 해석

여: 이 바지 정말 맘에 들어요. 얼마죠?

남: 100달러입니다. 디자이너 바지인데 최신 유행이에요.

여: 이런, 가격이 저한테 좀 비싸네요. 할인해 주실 수 있나요?

남: ④ 음, 오늘 10퍼센트 할인을 해드릴 수 있어요.

어휘

trendy ***a.*** 최신 유행의 〈문제〉 **sold out** 다 팔리고 없는 **tailor** ***v.*** 맞추다

정답 ④

문제풀이

남자는 바지가 좀 비싸다며 할인해 줄 수 있냐는 여자의 말에 맞는 대답을 해야 한다. 따라서 ④ '음, 오늘 10퍼센트 할인을 해드릴 수 있어요.'가 정답이다.

오답 보기 해석

① 죄송하지만 품절됐어요.

② 여기서 그것을 맞추실 수 있어요.

③ 저는 보통 디자이너 바지를 팔지 않아요.

⑤ 음, 전 다른 물건들을 보고 싶군요.

총 어휘 수 43

02 짧은 대화의 응답

소재 회사에 지각하지 않게 가기

듣기 대본 해석

남: 일어나, Annie! 열 시가 넘었어! 분명 회사에 지각할거야!

여: 진정해! 자동차로 이십 분밖에 안 걸려.

남: 잊었어? 네 자동차는 수리점에 있잖아.

여: ③ 그럼 택시를 잡아야겠네.

어휘

relax ***v.*** 진정하다, 휴식을 취하다 **repair shop** 수리점
〈문제〉 **flat tire** 바람이 빠진 타이어

정답 ③

문제풀이

여자의 차가 수리점에 있고, 차로 가야 늦지 않으므로 여자가 할 적절한 말은 ③ '그럼 택시를 잡아야겠네.'이다.

오답 보기 해석

① 괜찮아. 오늘은 내 차를 몰고 갈게.

② 혹시 이 주변에 수리점 있어?

④ 이런! 너 타이어 펑크 난 것 같아.

⑤ 난 식료품점에 먼저 들러야 돼.

총 어휘 수 41

03 담화 목적

소재 걷기의 중요성

듣기 대본 해석

여: 여러분은 건강을 어떻게 유지하십니까? 규칙적으로 운동을 하십니까? 걸으십니까? 여러분은 걷기가 건강에 주는 이점을 알고 계십니까? 간단히 말해서, 여러분이 더 많이 걸으면 여러분의 삶은 더 나아질 것입니다. 심장병으로 고생했던 Roger Williams라는 제 친구 이야기를 해 드릴게요. 그는 몇몇 의사들로부터 그의 병이 결코 완전히 치료되지 못할 것이라고 들었습니다. 의사들의 진단에도 불구하고 그는 더 이상 심장병을 조금도 앓고 있지 않습니다. 그를 도왔던 것은 걷기였습니다. 그는 걷기를 일상의 중요한 부분으로 만들었습니다. 많은 사람들이 걷기가 그들의 삶을 더 낫게 변화시킨다는 것을 보여줄 것입니다. 걷기는 특정한 유형의 사람들에게만 이로운 것이 아니라 모든 사람들에게 필수적입니다.

어휘

regularly ***ad.*** 규칙적으로 **aware of** ~을 인지하다, 알다 **suffer from** ~로 고통 받다 **cure** ***v.*** 치료하다, 고치다 **diagnosis** ***n.*** 진단, 진찰 **testify** ***v.*** 증언하다, 증명하다 **necessary** ***a.*** 필수의, 필연적인

정답 ④

문제풀이

걷기를 통해 자신의 병을 이겨낸 친구 이야기를 예로 들면서 걷기는 모든 사람들에게 필요하다고 말하며 걷기의 중요성을 강조하고 있으므로 정답은 ④ '걷기 운동의 중요성을 알려주려고'이다.

총 어휘 수 122

04 의견

소재 경고 표지판 세우기

듣기 대본 해석

여: 안녕하세요, Anderson씨.

남: 오늘 아침 저를 만나 주셔서 감사합니다. 제가 이 길을 당신께 보여드리고 싶었어요.

여: 네, 왜 그런지 알겠어요. 아주 위험해 보여요.

남: 정말 위험해요. 운전자에게 급커브에 대한 주의를 요하는 경고 표지판이나 전등이 충분하지 않아요.

여: 집에서 길이 보이나요?

남: 네, 보여요. 저는 차 사고를 많이 목격했어요.

여: 당신 생각에는 사람들이 너무 속력을 내서 사고가 일어난다고 생각하세요?

남: 정말이지 사람들이 너무 속도를 낸다고 생각해요. 저는 더 많은 경고 표지판이 사고 건수를 크게 줄여줄 거라고 믿어요.

여: 시에 항의를 한 적 있으신가요?

남: 제가 몇 번이나 했지만 아무도 신경 쓰지 않는 것 같은 게 저한테 전화나 이메일로 답변을 준 적이 한 번도 없어요.

여: 알았어요. 제가 사무실에 도착하자마자 담당하는 사람들과 연락을 해 볼게요.

남: 정말이요? 잘됐어요. 우리는 더 많은 경고 표지판이 필요하다고 꼭 말해 주세요.

어휘

warning sign 경고 표지판 **significantly** ***ad.*** 상당히, 크게
reduce ***v.*** 줄이다, 축소하다 **file a complaint** 항의를 제기하다
get in touch with ~와 연락하다 **in charge** 담당하고 있는

정답 ②

문제풀이
남자는 급커브 지역에 경고 표지판이나 전등이 없어서 사람들이 속력을 내고 그래서 사고가 많이 난다면서 급커브 지역에 경고 표지판이나 전등을 설치해야 한다고 말하고 있다. 따라서 정답은 ② '급커브 지역에 경고 표지판이나 전등을 설치해야 한다.'이다.

총 어휘 수 163

05 대화자의 관계 파악

소재 건물 세부정보 확인

듣기 대본 해석
[전화벨이 울린다.]
여: 여보세요. Brittney Smith입니다.
남: 안녕하세요, Smith씨. 저는 Dominic Antonoff입니다. 당신이 어제 저한테 건물 몇 개를 보여주셨는데 제가 몇 가지 질문을 해도 괜찮을지 모르겠네요.
여: 안녕하세요, Antonoff씨. 어떤 건물에 관심이 있으시죠?
남: Water Street에 있는 거요. 그 건물에 대형냉장고 있나요?
여: 제가 확인할 동안 잠깐 시간을 주세요. *[잠시 후]* 네, 있어요.
남: 좋아요. 그런데 중앙 난방과 냉방 시스템도 가지고 있나요?
여: 있어요. 문제 있나요?
남: 흠... 문제가 될 것 같아요. 6번가에 있는 건물은 어때요? 여전히 가능해요?
여: 네, 그것도 아직 가능합니다.
남: 제가 만약 가게 앞에 딸린 공간을 개조한다면 문제가 될까요?
여: 제 생각엔 괜찮을 것 같아요.
남: 좋습니다. 그리고 건물주에게 제가 식당 공간에 걸어놓는 등을 설치해도 되는지 물어봐 주셨나요?
여: 네, 제가 여쭤봤어요. 그분이 괜찮을 거라고 하셨어요.

어휘
wonder ***v.*** ~일지 모르겠다, 궁금하다 **walk-in freezer** 대형냉장고 **available** ***a.*** 이용할 수 있는

정답 ⑤

문제풀이
남자는 여자에게 건물의 시설과 개조 가능 여부에 관해 질문하고 있고 여자는 이에 답해주고 있으므로 두 사람의 관계는 ⑤ '부동산 중개인 – 고객'이다.

총 어휘 수 145

06 그림의 세부 내용 파악

소재 리조트에 놀러 갔던 가족 사진

듣기 대본 해석
여: 안녕 Jay. 휴가 어땠어?
남: 좋았어. 우리 가족은 머물렀던 리조트를 정말 좋아했어. 여기 사진이 있어.
여: *[잠시 후]* 멋지다. 벽에 있는 건 섬 지도니?
남: 맞아. 우리는 하와이의 Big Island에서 머물렀어.
여: 가족들 모두 경치를 정말 즐기고 있는 것 같네.
남: 맞아. 아내하고 나는 리조트에서 단지 휴식하는 걸 즐겼어. 그리고 저건 내가 가장 좋아하는 선글라스야.
여: 멋지네. 공을 가지고 노는 건 네 아이들이야?
남: 응. 내 아들 딸이야. 애들이 거기 날씨를 정말 좋아하더라.
여: 아내는 어떤 음료를 마시고 있어? 좋아 보이는데.
남: 저건 Blue Hawaiian이야. 하와이에서는 대중적인 음료야.
여: 그럼, 누가 이 사진을 찍었어?
남: 내 남동생이 찍었어. 난 내 스마트폰으로 찍고 싶었는데 그날 잃어버렸어.
여: 바닥에 있는 저거 아냐?
남: 응. 나 참 멍청하지.

어휘
vacation ***n.*** 휴가 **take a picture** 사진을 찍다

정답 ①

문제풀이
벽에 걸려 있는 것은 섬 지도라고 했는데, 그림에서는 화산이 그려져 있으므로 그림과 일치하지 않는 것은 ①번이다.

총 어휘 수 152

07 할 일

소재 Rain Valley Park 방문

듣기 대본 해석
여: 여보, 저기 Rain Valley Park 표지판이 보여요.
남: 저 사람들 좀 봐요! 여기가 틀림없어요.
여: 맞아요. 오, 주차장은 저기 있네요!
남: 아주 좋아요. 거기 주차하고 계곡까지 걸어갈 수 있어요. 거기까지 가는 데 오래 걸릴 거라고 생각해요?
여: 내가 생각하기엔 20분 정도 걸릴 거예요. 우리가 거기 도착하면 강가에 앉아있을 수 있을 거예요.
남: 와! 정말 차가 많군요.
여: 우리가 주차 공간을 찾을 수 있을까요?
남: 내가 찾을 거예요. 걱정 마세요. 당신은 차에서 내려서 입장권을 사세요. 저쪽에 줄이 있는 것 같은데.
여: 좋은 생각이에요. 내가 출력해 온 지도 가지고 있어요?
남: 네, 제가 가지고 있어요. 내가 반드시 가지고 갈게요.
여: 아주 좋아요. 공원 입구에서 만나요.

어휘
sign ***n.*** 표지판, 신호 **parking lot** 주차장 **parking space** 주차 공간 **entry permit** 입장권 **entrance** ***n.*** 입구

정답 ②

문제풀이
남자가 여자에게 차에서 내려서 입장권을 사라고 말했고 여자는 알았다고 대답했으므로 답은 ② '입장권 사기'이다.

총 어휘 수 149

08 이유

소재 친구 숙제 도와주기

듣기 대본 해석
[전화벨이 울린다.]
남: 여보세요?
여: 이봐, Mel, 나 Katie야.
남: 아, Katie. 요즘 어때?
여: 별 일 없어. 그런데 너, Levine 선생님께서 오늘 내주신 수학 문제 모두 다 했어?
남: 네가 전화하기 직전에 막 다했어.
여: 난 정말 수학을 이해 못 하겠어. 네가 그것들을 도와줄 어떤 방법이 있을까?
남: 물론, 문제 없어.
여: 좋아. 너 내일 학교에 일찍 올 생각이야? 그럼 우리가 만나서 네가 나에게 문제 푸는 것을 도와줄 수 있을 거야.

남: 음... 내가 내일 학교에 일찍 갈 수 있을 것 같지가 않아. 걸어서 남동생을 학교에 바래다 줘야 하거든.
여: 엄마가 동생을 왜 안 데려다 주셔?
남: 음, 엄마는 내일 아침에 바쁘실 거야. 지금 내가 널 도와줄 수 있어. 우리 Cup 카페에서 만나는 거 어때?
여: 좋은 생각이야. 너무 고마워.

어휘
assign ***v.*** 부과하다, 맡기다

정답 ⑤

문제풀이
남자는 내일 아침에 엄마가 바쁘셔서 동생을 학교까지 걸어서 바래다 줘야 하기 때문에 학교에 일찍 갈 수 없을 것 같다고 했으므로 정답은 ⑤ '걸어서 남동생을 학교에 바래다 줘야 하기 때문에'이다.

총 어휘 수 127

09 숫자

소재 전시회 티켓 구입

듣기 대본 해석
남: 서울 아트 센터에 오신 걸 환영합니다. 무엇을 도와 드릴까요?
여: 우리 가족의 오늘 전시회의 티켓을 사야 하거든요.
남: 네. 몇 장 필요하세요?
여: 음, 남편, 딸, 제 것이 필요한데요, 딸이 고등학생이에요. 그러니까 성인 두 명에 학생 한 명이 되겠네요.
남: 좋습니다. 성인표는 각각 60달러이고, 학생은 40달러입니다. 따님은 학생증 가지고 있나요?
여: 네, 여기 있어요.
남: 좋습니다. 그럼 성인 둘, 학생 한 명 맞죠?
여: 맞습니다. 아! 제가 딸이 학교에서 받은 쿠폰이 있는 걸 깜빡 했네요. 아직 사용할 수 있나요?
남: 아직 유효한지 확인해 볼게요.
여: 그럴 거예요. 지난주에 받았거든요.
남: *[잠시 후]* 맞습니다. 따님의 표는 반값에 사실 수 있어요.
여: 좋아요. 여기 카드 있어요.

어휘
exhibition ***n.*** 전시회 **valid** ***a.*** 유효한 **half price** 반값

정답 ④

문제풀이
성인 티켓은 60달러인데 2명이므로 120달러, 학생은 40달러이고 1명인데 할인쿠폰이 있어서 반값에 가능하다고 했으므로 20달러가 된다. 따라서 여자가 지불해야 할 금액은 ④ '$140'이다.

총 어휘 수 142

10 언급 유무

소재 학업 상담

듣기 대본 해석
남: 잠깐 이야기 할 수 있을까요, Whitman 선생님?
여: 그럼, 물론이지. 무엇을 도와줄까?
남: 전 공부를 아주 열심히 하는데 성적은 계속 좋지 않아요.
여: 문제점을 좀 찾아보자. 하루에 얼마나 오래 공부하니?
남: 저는 주중에 집에서 거의 자정까지 공부하니까 약 4시간 정도 되는 것 같아요. 하지만 제 동생들이 자주 집중을 못하게 해요.
여: 네가 밤에 늦게까지 공부할 때 방해받기 쉽겠구나. 도서관에서 공부하지 그러니?
남: 맞아요. 제 생각에도 저의 공부 습관을 바꿔야 할 것 같아요.
여: 그래. 너는 또 네가 사용하고 있는 교재들이 최고인지 확인해야 해.
남: 아, 알겠어요.
여: 너는 네가 왜 대학에 가고 싶어 하는지 알고 있니?
남: 그것에 대해서는 별로 생각해보지 않은 것 같아요.
여: 네가 무엇을 하고 싶은지에 대한 명확한 생각이 있다면, 네가 공부에서 더 많은 것을 얻을 거라고 믿어.
남: 네, 조언 감사합니다, Whitman 선생님.

어휘
distract ***v.*** 집중이 안 되게 하다 **sibling** ***n.*** 형제, 자매 **make sure** 확인하다, 확실히 하다

정답 ③

문제풀이
공부는 열심히 하고 있는데 성적이 좋지 않다는 남학생이 선생님께 조언을 구하고 있다. 하루에 공부하는 시간, 공부하는 장소, 사용하는 교재, 대학 진학을 원하는 이유는 언급했지만 수업을 듣는 태도에 대해서는 언급하지 않았으므로 정답은 ③ '수업을 듣는 태도'이다.

총 어휘 수 162

11 내용 일치 · 불일치

소재 파충류 박람회

듣기 대본 해석
남: 안녕하세요 학생 여러분. 코브라와 직접 맞닥뜨리고 싶습니까? 악어를 만져보고 먹이를 주고 싶습니까? 그렇다면 이번 주말 Mega Village 축제 마당에서 열리는 Reptile World 박람회에 오세요. 이번 박람회는 도마뱀과 이구아나부터 비단뱀과 악어까지 여러분이 가장 좋아하는 파충류를 모두 포함하고 있습니다. 이 박람회는 Mega Village 야생동물 협회에서 개최하는 것으로 관람객들이 독특한 야생동물들과 가까이 직접 다가가는 것을 허용합니다. 굉장히 많은 정보를 얻을 수 있고 교육적입니다. 무료 입장이지만 미리 표를 예약해 주시기 바랍니다. 더 많은 정보는 Mega Village 야생동물협회 홈페이지에서 확인해 주시기 바랍니다. 들어 주셔서 감사합니다.

어휘
crocodile ***n.*** 악어 **reptile** ***n.*** 파충류 **exhibit** ***n.*** 박람회
unique ***a.*** 독특한 **admission** ***n.*** 입장 **reserve** ***v.*** 예약하다

정답 ③

문제풀이
관람객들에게 독특한 야생동물들에게 가까이 직접 다가가는 것을 허용한다고 했으므로 내용과 일치하지 않는 것은 ③ '동물들에게 가까이 다가가서는 안 된다.'이다.

총 어휘 수 112

12 도표

소재 가족 여행용 렌터카 대여

듣기 대본 해석
여: 무엇을 도와드릴까요?
남: 가족 여행을 위한 차를 대여하고 싶어요. 한 대 추천해 주시겠습니까?
여: 네, 저희에게 이코노미, 패밀리, 럭셔리 차종이 있어요. 가족이 몇 분이신가요?
남: 저를 포함해서 네 명입니다.

여: 제 생각에는 패밀리 사이즈나 럭셔리 사이즈가 적당할 것 같군요.
남: 그것들과 이코노미 사이즈의 차이는 무엇인가요?
여: 대여 가격과 주행 마일 수의 차이 외에, 이코노미 차는 충분한 공간이 없어서 네 분이서 타시면 조금 불편하실 거예요.
남: 그렇군요. 그리고 저희는 짐을 위한 공간이 필요해서 대여할 차가 좀 넓어야 해요.
여: 그러면, 럭셔리 사이즈를 대여하시는 건 어떠세요? 일곱 명에게도 공간이 충분해서 가족들이 아주 편안하실 거예요.
남: 하지만 대여비가 저한테는 너무 비싸네요. 오, 여기 럭셔리 차와 같은 수용 인원수를 가진 패밀리 차가 있네요.
여: 죄송합니다, 손님. 이 모델은 지금 이용이 가능하지 않습니다. 모두 대여되었어요.
남: 그러면 다른 선택이 없네요. 저걸로 대여할게요.

어휘

include ***v.*** 포함하다 **suitable** ***a.*** 적당한 **besides** ***prep.*** ~외에 **gas mileage** 주행 마일 수, 연비 **spacious** ***a.*** 널찍한 **capacity** ***n.*** 용량, 수용력 **available** ***a.*** 이용 가능한

정답 ③

문제풀이

가족 4명과 짐을 위한 충분한 공간이 필요하므로, 좁은 이코노미는 제외된다. 직원이 럭셔리를 추천했지만, 남자가 너무 비싸다고 하였으므로 럭셔리도 제외된다. 럭셔리와 같은 수용 인원수를 가진 패밀리 타입이 있으나 이용 가능한 차가 없다. 그러므로 4명과 짐을 수용할 수 있으면서 럭셔리만큼 비싸지 않고, 현재 이용 가능한 차가 있는 차종은 ③번이다.

총 어휘 수 177

13 긴 대화의 응답

소재 사업에 대한 조언

듣기 대본 해석

여: 안녕, Rodrick.
남: 오, 안녕, Karen. 오랜만이야.
여: 그래 오랜만이야. 알다시피 내가 네 회사를 떠난 지 1년쯤 됐네. 거기에서 일했던 것이 그리워.
남: 우리도 너를 그리워해. 너 약간 달라 보여. 살이 좀 빠졌니?
여: 그래. 나는 보다 건강하게 먹고 이 강도 높은 규칙적인 운동을 하고 있어.
남: 멋진데. 너무 무리하게 하지는 마. 내 친구가 운동하다가 부상을 입었어.
여: 걱정하지 마. 나는 꽤 조심하고 있어.
남: 그렇구나. 너의 새로운 사업은 어때?
여: 음, 그거 정말 스트레스 받아. 할 일은 정말 많고 일 할 시간은 충분하지 않아.
남: 이해가 되네. 나도 처음 내 사업을 시작했을 때 힘든 시간을 보냈어.
여: 사업을 시작하는 것은 항상 어려운 것 같아. 나에게 조언 좀 해 줄래?
남: ③ 열심히 일은 하되 삶에서 중요한 것을 잊지 마.

어휘

lose weight 살을 빼다 **overdo** ***v.*** 무리하다, 지나치게 하다 **incredibly** ***ad.*** 믿을 수 없을 정도로, 엄청나게

정답 ③

문제풀이

여자가 사업에 관해 조언을 해달라고 했으므로 적절한 응답은 ③ '열심히 일은 하되 삶에서 중요한 것을 잊지 마.'이다.

오답 보기 해석

① 너의 새로운 사업에서 모든 것이 잘 되리라 확신해.
② 나의 이전 직원이 성공하는 것을 보면 항상 기분이 좋아.
④ 너를 만나서 반가웠어. 언젠가 너의 사무실에 들를게.
⑤ 너는 세 시간 이상 강도 높게 운동해서는 안 돼.

총 어휘 수 143

14 긴 대화의 응답

소재 야구 경기 응원

듣기 대본 해석

여: 너 지난밤에 야구 경기 봤니?
남: 봤어. 정말 훌륭한 경기였어! 나는 Los Angeles가 Detroit를 이겨서 너무 기뻤어.
여: 나는 사실 Detroit 팬이지만, Los Angeles 팀이 정말 잘 싸웠어.
남: LA의 투수가 대단했어. 정말 인상 깊었지.
여: 응, 그랬어. 그런데 경기가 끝날 무렵에 그가 팔을 다친 것 같던데.
남: 나도 봤어. 나는 구원투수를 보기 기대했는데 아무도 나오지 않았어.
여: 정말 긴 게임이었어. 선수들이 정말 지쳤을 거야.
남: 그래. 13회를 했잖아. 정말 긴 게임이지!
여: 맞아.
남: Detroit는 언제 다시 경기해?
여: 목요일 밤에.
남: 나는 너희 집에 가서 너랑 같이 그들을 응원할 거야.
여: ① 좋아. 그들이 이겼으면 좋겠어!

어휘

pitcher ***n.*** (야구에서) 투수 **impress** ***v.*** 깊은 인상을 주다 **relief pitcher** 구원투수

정답 ①

문제풀이

여자가 응원하는 Detroit팀의 다음 경기는 목요일 밤이고 남자는 여자와 같이 응원하고 싶다고 말했으므로 그에 대한 여자의 대답은 ① '좋아. 그들이 이겼으면 좋겠어!'가 적절하다.

오답 보기 해석

② 나도 너와 함께 너의 팀을 응원할게.
③ 물론이지. 7시쯤 갈게.
④ 대단한 걸. 그들 또한 응원하러 올 지도 몰라.
⑤ 사실은 이번 주말에 정말 바빠.

총 어휘 수 130

15 상황에 적절한 말

소재 전화기를 사용하며 걷다가 다른 사람과 부딪힌 상황

듣기 대본 해석

남: Candace는 바쁜 직장 여성입니다. 어느 날, 그녀는 중요한 업무 회의가 있어서 그녀의 전화기로 이메일을 작성하면서 버스 정류장으로 걸어가는 중입니다. 이름이 Larry인 한 중년의 남성이 아침 조깅을 위해 나옵니다. 그는 허우적대다가 Candace쪽으로 휘청거렸고, 그녀는 젖은 땅에 중요한 문서를 떨어뜨립니다. Larry는 그것들을 집어서 말리려고 애썼지만 엉망이 되었습니다. 그는 매우 미안해하고 그의 어설픔에 미안함을 느낍니다. Candace는 그녀도 사고 당시에 다른 데 정신이 팔려 있었기 때문에 그녀의 잘못도 있다고 생각합니다. 이 상황에서, Candace는 Larry에게 뭐라고 말하겠습니까?
Candace: ⑤ 저도 책임이 있어요. 전화기를 사용하지 말았어야 했어요.

어휘
business meeting 업무 회의 **struggle** *v.* 몸부림치다, 허우적거리다, 버둥거리다, 고투하다 **stumble** *v.* 발이 걸리다, 발을 헛디디다, 휘청거리다 **apologetic** *a.* 미안해하는 **clumsiness** *n.* 어색함, 서투름

정답 ⑤

문제풀이
Candace가 휴대폰으로 이메일을 작성하면서 걸어가다가 조깅하러 가던 Larry와 부딪혔고 그로 인해 Candace의 문서가 엉망이 된 상황에서 Larry가 사과했다. Candace는 본인에게도 책임이 있다고 생각하므로 그녀가 할 말로는 ⑤ '저도 책임이 있어요. 전화기를 사용하지 말았어야 했어요.'가 적절하다.

오답 보기 해석
① 당신에게 문제가 생기면, 꼭 저에게 알려주세요.
② 당신이 밖에서 달릴 때 좀 더 조심해야겠어요.
③ 이 문서들을 깨끗이 하기 위해 당신이 할 수 있는 것은 아무것도 없는 것 같아요.
④ 걱정 마세요. 몇 분 안에 또 다른 버스가 올 거예요.

총 어휘 수 120

16 담화 목적 / 17 세부 내용 파악

소재 해외 자원봉사 프로그램의 이점

듣기 대본 해석
남: 안녕하세요 학생 여러분. 오늘 여러분께 해외 자원봉사 여름 프로그램에 대해서 말씀 드리고자 합니다. 해외 자원봉사는 쉽지 않은 경험이 될 수 있습니다. 여러분들은 분명 어려움에 직면할 수 있고 적응하는 데 어려움을 겪을 것입니다. 하지만 그러한 경험은 놀랍도록 보람이 있으며 틀림없이 여러분이 세상을 바라보는 시각을 바꿔놓을 것입니다. 여러분들이 어려움에 처한 사람들을 도우면서 여러분의 우선순위가 무엇인지 알게 될 것입니다. 외국 땅에 사는 것이 당신을 바꿀 것이기 때문에 당신의 세계관이 넓어질 것입니다. 여러분은 새로운 풍습과 규범을 갖게 될 것입니다. 지금까지 꿈꿔보지도 못한 음식들을 먹어보게 되고 외국어로 의사소통을 하기 위해서 노력을 할 것입니다. 가장 중요한 것은, 도움이 필요한 사람들을 돕게 되는 것입니다. 여러분은 아프리카 사람들에게 어떻게 물을 정화하는지를 가르치고, 인도에서 아기들 밥을 먹이고, 미얀마에서 집을 짓고, 인도네시아에서 아픈 어린이들을 돌보고 있는 자신을 발견하게 될 것입니다. 해외 자원봉사는 정말 둘도 없는 기회이며, 여러분은 분명히 그로 인해 더 나은 사람이 될 것입니다.

어휘
adjust *v.* 적응하다 **rewarding** *a.* 보람이 있는 **perspective** *n.* 시각, 견지 **expand** *v.* 확대되다 **strain** *v.* 힘껏 노력하다, 안간힘을 쓰다

정답 16 ② 17 ④

문제풀이
16 남자는 해외 자원봉사를 했을 때 사람들이 얻을 수 있는 세계관의 확장과 다양한 경험 등 여러 가지 이점에 관해 이야기하였으므로 남자가 하는 말의 목적은 ② '해외 자원봉사의 이점을 알려주려고'이다.

17 남자는 물 정화방법 가르치기, 아기들 밥 먹이기, 집 짓기, 아픈 아이들 치료하기에 관한 언급은 했지만 영어 가르치기에 관한 언급은 하지 않았으므로 정답은 ④ '영어 가르치기'이다.

총 어휘 수 152

DICTATION ANSWERS

01 and they're really trendy / Can you give me a discount

02 be late for work / in the repair shop

03 health benefits of walking / suffered from heart disease / Despite their diagnosis / not beneficial for only certain types of people

04 to make the driver aware of all the really sharp turns / reduce the number of accidents / filed a complaint with the city / get in touch with the people in charge / we need more warning signs

05 Which building are you interested in / It might be an issue / it's still available / install hanging lights in the dining area

06 the resort we stayed at / a map of the islands on the wall / your kids playing with the ball / take a picture with my smartphone / How silly of me

07 This must be the right place / walk down to the valley / go buy our entry permits / It's with my things / at the entrance to the park

08 did you finish all of the math problems / Is there any way you could help me / walk my brother to school / she's going to be busy

09 How many do you need / got a coupon from her school / if it's still valid

10 How long do you study each day / I'm often distracted by / change my study habits

11 pet and feed a crocodile / include all of your favorite reptiles / allows visitors to get up close / We offer free admission

12 rent a car for my family trip / would be suitable for / the car we end up with should be a bit spacious / all rented out

13 been eating healthier / got injured while exercising / incredibly stressful / Do you have any tips

14 What a game / I was really impressed / towards the end of the game, though / cheer them on with you

15 He is struggling / they're ruined / feels sorry for his clumsiness

16-17 summer abroad volunteer programs / incredibly rewarding / help others in need / strain to communicate / feeding babies

18 수능영어듣기 실전모의고사

본문 p.110

01 ②	02 ④	03 ①	04 ②	05 ③	06 ③
07 ⑤	08 ①	09 ③	10 ④	11 ③	12 ③
13 ⑤	14 ④	15 ⑤	16 ④	17 ②	

01 짧은 대화의 응답

소재 새로 생긴 초밥집

듣기 대본 해석

남: 안녕 Pat. 너 초밥 Safari 식당에 가 봤니?
여: 가봤지. 나는 개업 첫 주말에 가봤어. 멋지던데.
남: 나는 내일 갈 예정이야. 여기서 가까워?
여: ② 응. 걸어서 5분 밖에 안 걸려.

어휘

opening ***n.*** 개막, 개통, 개업 **close** ***a.*** 가까운

정답 ②

문제풀이

새로 생긴 식당이 여기서 가까운지 물었으므로 그에 적절한 응답은 ② '응. 걸어서 5분밖에 안 걸려.'이다.

오답 보기 해석

① 물론. 나는 외국 음식을 먹는 것을 좋아해.
③ 아니. 난 요리를 잘 하지 못해.
④ 확실하지 않아. 나는 거기서 먹어 본 적이 없거든.
⑤ 그래. 내일은 문을 닫을 거야.

총 어휘 수 40

02 짧은 대화의 응답

소재 일기예보 확인하기

듣기 대본 해석

여: Wade, 너 흠뻑 젖었네. 무슨 일 있었어?
남: 밖에 비가 정말 많이 쏟아지고 있어. 내가 우산 가져가는 것을 생각하지 못했거든.
여: 그래, 안됐네. 매일 일기예보를 확인하지 않아?
남: ④ 평상시에는 그렇지만, 오늘 아침은 아주 바빴어.

어휘

soaked ***a.*** 흠뻑 젖은 **weather forecast** 일기예보

정답 ④

문제풀이

일기예보를 매일 확인하지 않느냐는 여자의 질문에 적절한 남자의 대답은 ④ '평상시에는 그렇지만, 오늘 아침은 아주 바빴어.'이다.

오답 보기 해석

① 고마워. 이런 날씨에 정말 하나 필요해.
② 응. 내일 날씨 확인해 봐.
③ 괜찮아. 내 우산 빌려도 돼.
⑤ 내일 날씨가 좋다니 기쁘네.

총 어휘 수 41

03 담화 목적

소재 야외 활동 시 뇌우 대처법

듣기 대본 해석

남: 대부분의 사람들은 날씨가 좋을 때 야외에서 노는 것을 즐깁니다. 그렇지만 날씨가 매우 빠르게 더 나쁜 상황으로 변할 수 있다는 것을 명심하는 것이 중요합니다. 여러분은 이런 일이 일어날 경우에 무엇을 해야 할지 알아야 합니다. 만약에 여러분이 뇌우를 만나면, 여러분은 빌딩 안이나 차 안에 대피처를 찾아야 합니다. 그런 것이 가능하지 않다면, 여러분 주변에서 가장 낮은 지역을 찾고 탁 트인 공간은 피해야 합니다. 만약 여러분이 탁 트인 공간에 있고 주변에 있는 모든 것보다 더 크다면, 여러분은 번개를 맞을 위험이 커집니다. 항상 나무와 전신주는 피하세요. 이런 조언을 따른다면 여러분은 다음에 나쁜 날씨가 덮쳤을 때 준비가 되어 있을 것입니다.

어휘

thunderstorm ***n.*** 뇌우 **shelter** ***n.*** 대피처 **avoid** ***v.*** 피하다
telephone pole 전신주

정답 ①

문제풀이

야외에서 갑자기 뇌우를 만나게 될 때 어떻게 행동하면 되는지를 알려주고 있다. 따라서 남자가 하는 말의 목적으로 적절한 것은 ① '야외 활동 시 뇌우에 대처하는 방법을 알려주려고'이다.

총 어휘 수 116

04 대화 주제

소재 나라마다 다른 개인 위생

듣기 대본 해석

남: 너 괜찮아? 걱정이 있어 보여.
여: 너 Dimitri 알지?
남: 물론이지. 그는 이탈리아 사람이잖아. 정말 친절한 친구야.
여: 응, 맞아. 나도 그를 좋아해. 그렇지만 그는 항상 입 냄새가 난다는 거 알고 있니?
남: 사실은 나도 알아. 그게 너를 화나게 해?
여: 그는 재미있고 같이 이야기를 나누면 재미있지만 입 냄새는 참을 수가 없어.
남: 편하게 생각해. 개인 위생의 기준은 나라마다 다르단다.
여: 그래? 다른 나라에 가본 적이 없어서 몰랐어.
남: 개인 위생에 대한 개념은 세계 여러 나라마다 다른 거야.
여: 이런 차이가 사회적 문제가 될 수도 있겠다, 그렇지?
남: 그래, 맞아. 나는 사람들이 모두 다르다는 것을 이해하려고 노력하는 것이 중요하다고 생각해.
여: 충고 고마워. 나는 Dimitri와 이제 더 잘 지낼 수 있을 것 같아.
남: 그렇게 말해주니 기쁘네.

어휘

bad breath 입 냄새 **unbearable** ***a.*** 참을 수 없는
personal hygiene 개인 위생 **get along** 사이 좋게 지내다

정답 ②

문제풀이

여자가 이탈리아에서 온 친구에게 입 냄새가 나서 참기 힘들다고 말하자 남자는 개인 위생에 대한 생각이 나라마다 다르므로 사람들이 서로 다름을 이해하도록 노력해야 한다고 말하고 있다. 따라서 두 사람의 대화 주제는 ② '나라마다 다른 개인 위생의 인식 차이'이다.

총 어휘 수 135

05 대화자의 관계 파악

소재 관광 중 입은 상처

듣기 대본 해석

여: 저기, 죄송한데요. 혹시 반창고 하나 있나요?

남: 물론입니다. 제가 인솔하는 모든 투어에 항상 구급상자를 들고 다녀요. 무슨 일이 있었나요?

여: 박물관 계단에서 넘어져서 무릎이 까졌어요.

남: 그럼 큰 게 필요하겠네요. 잠깐만요. *[잠시 후]* 여기 있어요.

여: 고마워요. 그리고 저와 제 남편 둘 다 여행을 굉장히 즐기고 있다고 말씀드리고 싶었어요.

남: 좋네요. 즐거운 시간을 보낼 수 있도록 최선을 다하고 있습니다.

여: 그럼 동굴 안에는 언제 들어가나요?

남: 1시쯤 거기 도착할 겁니다.

여: 별로 안 걸리네요. 그 동굴은 긴 역사를 갖고 있지 않나요?

남: 맞아요. 1800년대 중반에 Jesse James와 그의 노상강도 패거리의 은신처로도 쓰였어요.

여: 흥미롭네요. 이곳에는 재미있는 역사 이야기들이 많네요, 그렇죠?

남: 맞아요. 굉장히 역사가 깊은 곳이에요. 자연의 아름다움도 많이 담고 있고요.

어휘

bandage ***n.*** 밴드, 붕대 **first-aid kit** 구급상자 **scrape** ***v.*** 긁다, 긁히다 **ensure** ***v.*** 보장하다 **hideout** ***n.*** 은신처 **bandit** ***n.*** 노상강도

정답 ③

문제풀이

남자는 자신이 인솔하는 투어에 항상 구급상자를 가지고 다닌다고 하였고, 사람들이 즐거운 시간을 보낼 수 있도록 최선을 다 하고 있다고 하였다. 여자는 자신과 남편이 여행을 즐기고 있다고 말하고, 다음 관광 일정에 대해 묻는 것으로 보아 두 사람의 관계는 ③ '관광객 — 관광 가이드'임을 알 수 있다.

총 어휘 수 161

06 그림의 세부 내용 파악

소재 재즈 밴드에 관한 대화

듣기 대본 해석

여: 와! 이 밴드 정말 좋다, Joey!

남: 응. 내가 가장 좋아하는 재즈 밴드 중 하나야. Jazz Hands라고 불려.

여: 재미있는 이름인데. 여자 바이올리니스트가 있는 게 좋은데. 진짜 멋져.

남: 다들 재능이 엄청나지. 뒤에 기타리스트는 시에서 최고의 기타리스트 중 한 명이야.

여: 대단하다. 보컬이 노래하면서 기타를 치는 게 멋진데.

남: 응. 목소리가 정말 좋더라. 음역이 넓어.

여: 그런데 피아노 연주자는 어울리지 않는 것 같아. 나머지는 서 있는데 그만 앉아 있잖아.

남: 음, 그는 피아노를 치고 있잖아. 피아노 치면서 서 있을 수는 없어. 페달을 써야 하거든.

여: 오, 맞아. 어쨌든, 날 이 재즈 클럽에 데려와 줘서 정말 기뻐, Joey.

남: 네가 같이 와 줘서 내가 기쁘지.

어휘

awesome ***a.*** 멋진 **range** ***n.*** 범위(폭) **out of place** 어울리지 않는, 부적절한

정답 ③

문제풀이

대화의 중간 부분에서 여자가 보컬이 노래하면서 기타를 치는 게 멋있다고 했는데 그림에서 보컬은 기타가 없으므로 정답은 ③번이다.

총 어휘 수 137

07 할 일

소재 교환학생 다녀온 친구

듣기 대본 해석

[휴대폰이 울린다.]

남: 여보세요?

여: 안녕, Ted. 나 Grace야. 어떻게 지냈어?

남: Grace! 돌아왔어?

여: 응. 교환학생 프로그램이 끝나서 어젯밤에 비행기를 타고 돌아왔어.

남: 그랬어? Stone 선생님이 네가 다음 주 월요일에 학교로 돌아온다고 말씀하셨어. 중국은 어땠어?

여: 멋졌어. 중국어로 사람들에게 말하는 데 훨씬 더 자신감이 생겼어.

남: 훌륭해! 우리 모두 네가 중국에서 보낸 시간에 대해 이야기하길 기대하고 있어. 특히 선생님들이.

여: 나도 가능한 빨리 그들을 만나고 싶어. 하지만 수업의 처음 2주를 놓쳐서 조금 걱정이 돼.

남: 그래... 다음 주에 퀴즈가 2개 있어.

여: 정말? 난 퀴즈 준비가 안 됐는데.

남: 선생님들께서 주신 자료물이 나한테 있어. 네가 원하면 가져다 줄게.

여: 그래 줄래? 정말 잘됐다!

남: 친구 좋다는 게 뭐니?

어휘

exchange ***n.*** 교환 **since** ***conj.*** ~ 때문에 **prepare for** ~를 준비하다

정답 ⑤

문제풀이

선생님에게서 받은 자료물을 갖다 주겠다는 남자의 말로 미루어 보아 정답은 ⑤ '수업시간에 받은 자료 갖다 주기'이다.

총 어휘 수 137

08 이유

소재 우천으로 취소된 테니스 경기

듣기 대본 해석

여: Davis, 어디 가니?

남: 엄마의 꽃가게에 가고 있어. 엄마가 우체국에 볼 일이 있어서 내가 가게를 좀 봐야 하거든.

여: 정말 친절하구나. 오, 너 지난 일요일에 테니스 경기에 갔었지, 그렇지? 경기 어땠어?

남: 그 경기는 사실은 일요일이 아니라 토요일이었어.

여: 아, 어쨌든, 너 멋진 시간을 보냈음이 틀림없겠구나. 너 테니스 좋아하잖아.

남: 나는 경기장에 갔었는데 경기가 취소되었어.

여: 진짜? 왜?

남: 폭풍우(뇌우) 때문이야. 경기가 시작되기도 전에 우천으로 취소됐어.

여: 아, 맞아! 토요일에 날씨가 진짜 별로였지. 정말 안됐네.

남: 그래. 나는 정말 그 게임을 보러 가는 데 들떠 있었어. 내가 해야 하는 숙제와 공부 때문에 이번 시즌에 경기 볼 시간이 없었거든.

여: 그래. 네 심정 알겠어. 경기를 놓쳤다니 유감이야.

어휘

head ***v.*** 가다, 향하다 **run an errand** 심부름 하다 **rain out** 우천으로 경기가 취소되다

정답 ①

문제풀이
남자는 경기 전 시작된 폭풍우로 테니스 경기가 취소되었다고 했으므로 경기를 관람하지 못한 이유는 ① '폭우로 경기가 취소돼서'이다.

총 어휘 수 141

09 숫자

소재 골동품 구입

듣기 대본 해석
여: 와! 이 골동품들 진짜인가요?
남: 네. 몇 개는 저희 할머니가 저에게 주신 거예요.
여: 저기 있는 램프들은 비싼가요?
남: 황동 램프는 40달러이고 유리 램프는 60달러입니다.
여: 유리 램프가 정말 멋있긴 한데 제가 사기엔 비싼 것 같네요.
남: 정말 그게 맘에 드시면 황동 램프와 같은 가격으로 드릴게요.
여: 와, 정말이요? 좋아요, 그걸 살게요! 저 아름다운 접시들은 얼마예요?
남: 더 큰 접시들은 각각 10달러이고 작은 접시들은 각각 5달러예요.
여: 네, 제가 이 큰 접시 두 개 살게요.
남: 제가 손님께 권해드릴 만한 또 다른 품목이 있나요?
여: 저 의자가 아주 마음에 드네요.
남: 네, 아주 예쁜 의자이지 않나요? 사실 마지막 남은 겁니다. 다른 것들은 70달러에 팔렸지만 손님께는 50달러에 드릴게요.
여: 네, 좋아요. 고마워요!

어휘
antique ***n.*** 골동품 **brass** ***n.*** 놋쇠, 황동 **afford** ***v.*** (~을 살 금전적 · 시간적) 여유 · 형편이 되다 **item** ***n.*** 품목 **interest somebody in** (~을 사거나 먹도록) 권하다

정답 ③

문제풀이
유리 램프를 황동 램프 가격인 40달러에, 큰 접시 두 개는 20달러에, 그리고 의자를 50달러에 판다고 했으므로 합계는 110달러이다. 따라서 여자가 지불할 금액은 ③ '$110'이다.

총 어휘 수 154

10 언급 유무

소재 새로 산 컴퓨터

듣기 대본 해석
남: 여보, 오늘 택배 도착했어.
여: 좋다. 이 새 컴퓨터 빨리 설치하고 싶었어.
남: 우리 예전 컴퓨터보다 많이 커 보인다.
여: 맞아. 그리고 훨씬 빠르기도 해. 21인치 모니터랑 레이저 프린터가 포함된 세트로 샀어.
남: 꽤 복잡해 보인다. 내가 컴퓨터에 대해서 좀 더 유식했으면 좋겠어.
여: 굉장히 쉬워, 여보. 어떻게 쓰는지 가르쳐 줄게.
남: 좋네. 이 컴퓨터로 Cacao Chat 할 수 있어? 회사 동료들이 다 그 얘기 하더라고.
여: 당연하지. 또 영상통화도 무료로 즐길 수 있어.
남: 좋다. 보증기간도 있어?
여: 응. 2년 동안 무슨 일이 있으면 와서 고쳐준대.
남: 그럼 잃어버리지 않게 보증서를 안전한 곳에 보관하자.
여: 좋은 생각이야.

어휘
savvy ***n.*** 지식 ***a.*** 지식이 많은 **warranty** ***n.*** 보증서, 보증기간

정답 ④

문제풀이
두 사람은 21인치 모니터, 레이저 프린터, 무료 영상통화, 2년의 보증기간에 대해 언급했지만 백신에 대한 언급은 없었으므로 정답은 ④ '무료 백신'이다.

총 어휘 수 149

11 내용 일치 · 불일치

소재 자선 콘서트 소개하기

듣기 대본 해석
남: 여러분 안녕하세요. 저는 GBC 뉴스의 Ronnie Maroon입니다. 우리의 아름다운 도시에서 자선 음악회가 열린다는 사실을 알리게 되어 기쁩니다. 그 음악회는 The Great Tusk Concert라는 음악회이고 세상에서 가장 큰 동물 복지 단체인 Earth Wildlife Federation의 후원을 받고 있습니다. The Great Tusk Concert는 음악, 영화, TV 업계에서 유명한 인사들의 공연을 선보일 것이며, 그들은 화려한 저녁을 위해 지역사회를 하나로 화합시키기를 기대하고 있습니다. 행사는 7월 15일 Metropolitan Opera House에서 개최될 예정입니다. 이 행사의 수익금은 세계 각지에서 학대와 혹사를 당하고 있는 코끼리들의 복지에 쓰일 것입니다. 더 많은 정보와 표 구매를 위해서는 www.thegreattuskconcert.com라는 행사 사이트를 방문해 주십시오.

어휘
feature ***v.*** ~을 특징으로 하다 **proceeds** ***n.*** 수익금 **abuse** ***n.*** 학대, 남용 **mistreatment** ***n.*** 학대, 혹사

정답 ③

문제풀이
남자는 자선 음악회에 대해 소개하면서 행사 날짜는 7월 15일이라고 하였으므로 일치하지 않는 것은 ③ '행사 날짜는 6월 15일이다.'이다.

총 어휘 수 122

12 도표

소재 RV캠프장 선택

듣기 대본 해석
여: 여보, 뭐하고 있어요?
남: 다음 달에 있을 우리 RV(레크리에이션 차) 여행 옵션을 확인하고 있어요. 우리가 가려는 호수 주변에 5개의 캠핑장이 있어요.
여: 멋지네요. 선택하는 거 도와줄까요?
남: 물론이죠. 그런데, 우리의 선택에서 어떤 것들을 고려해야 하죠?
여: 음, 물을 쓸 수 있는 게 꽤 중요할 것 같아요.
남: 맞아요. 우리 차량은 샤워기를 가지고 있으니까 사용하려면 물을 연결할 수 있어야 하겠네요.
여: 그래요. 그러면 이 3개 중에서 하나를 골라야 해요.
남: 좋아요. 내 생각에는 애완동물은 금지라니까 이건 빼야겠어요.
여: 네. 난 정말 Baxter를 데리고 가고 싶어요. 정말 좋아 할거예요.
남: 그럼 이 2개로 좁혀지네요.
여: 당신 생각에 전기 없이 3일을 지낼 수 있을 것 같아요?
남: 가능하긴 한데, 필요할지도 모르니까 있는 게 나을 것 같아요.
여: 좋아요. 그럼 이 캠핑장으로 예약해야겠네요.

어휘
hookup ***n.*** (전기, 수도 등의 외부와의) 연결부 **prohibit** ***v.*** 금지하다
electricity ***n.*** 전기

정답 ③

문제풀이
처음에 물을 사용할 수 있어야 한다고 했으므로 A, C, E중에 골라야 하고, 애완동물을 데려가고 싶으므로 E는 제외된다. A, C중에서 전기가 되는 것으로 선택하자고 했으므로 정답은 ③번이다.

총 어휘 수 169

13 긴 대화의 응답

소재 옛 친구와의 만남

듣기 대본 해석
남: 지난밤에 내게 무슨 일이 일어났는지 아니, Maria?
여: 무슨 일이 일어났어?
남: 너 Dan이 누군지 아니?
여: 물론이지. 우리 고등학교 동안 라크로스 경기 같이 했었는데, 그가 졸업반 때 텍사스로 이사 갔잖아.
남: 맞아. 근데 그가 어젯밤에 나한테 Face Friend 메시지를 보냈어.
여: 정말? 그는 어떻게 지내?
남: 내 생각에 그는 다시 여기에 일하러 이사올 생각인 것 같고 그가 여기서 어울리던 사람들과 연락하고 싶었던 것 같아.
여: 그를 만나면 너무 좋을 것 같아. 많이 변했는지 궁금하다.
남: 음, 곧 그를 볼 수 있을 거야. 그는 2주 후에 아파트를 구하기 위해 여기에 올 거래.
여: 와! 좋은 소식이네!
남: 그래, 시내 어딘가에서 점심 먹을 거야. 너도 올래?
여: ⑤ 물론이야. 만날 일이 기대되네.

어휘
hang out 어울리다

정답 ⑤

문제풀이
남자는 예전에 살던 곳으로 다시 이사오기 전에 연락을 취한 Dan에 대해 여자에게 이야기해 주었고 여자도 고등학교 때 같이 경기 하던 친구라 어떻게 변했는지 궁금해하고 있다. 남자가 Dan과 점심 약속을 잡았다며 여자에게 합류 의향을 물었을 때 가장 적절한 여자의 대답은 ⑤ '물론이지. 만날 일이 기대되네.'이다.

오답 보기 해석
① 나는 그렇게 생각하지 않아. 그는 더 빨리 전화했어야 했어.
② 너한테 소식 듣는 건 항상 좋아. 몸 조심해.
③ 유감이지만 그 소식이 사실이기에는 너무나 좋아서 믿을 수 없구나.
④ 사실 나는 그 사람이 누군지 몰라.

총 어휘 수 135

14 긴 대화의 응답

소재 대학 선택

듣기 대본 해석
남: 안녕 Leah, 네가 원하는 대학에 들어갔니?
여: 응, Paul. 실은 두 군데 대학에서 입학 허가를 받았어.
남: 두 개 대학? 그럼, 어디로 갈지 벌써 정한 거야?
여: 두 학교 모두 좋은 학교야. 가장 큰 차이점은 Upstate 대학교는 주립대학이고, Lakeside는 사립이란 거지.
남: 두 학교 다 평판이 좋잖아.
여: 맞아. 그 둘 중에서 어떻게 한 군데를 골라야 할지 모르겠어.
남: 딜레마에 빠졌구나. 그렇지만 난 네가 어떻게 결정할 수 있을지 알고 있어.
여: 어떻게? 난 정말 조언이 필요해.
남: 동전을 던져봐. 동전이 공중에 있을 때, 넌 동전이 어느 쪽으로 떨어지길 바라는지 알게 될 거야.
여: 한번 해볼게. *[잠시 후]* 네 말이 맞았어. 그게 공중에 떠 있을 때, 난 Upstate 대학을 원했거든.
남: ④ 만약 그렇다면, 그곳이 네가 가야 하는 대학이야.

어휘
dilemma ***n.*** 딜레마 **flip** ***v.*** 톡(툭) 던지다

정답 ④

문제풀이
여자가 두 개의 대학으로부터 입학 허가를 받고 고민하자 남자가 조언을 해주고 있다. 남자는 동전을 던져서 동전이 공중에 있을 때 마음속으로 떨어지기를 바라는 면을 알아 보라고 조언하고, 여자는 그렇게 해서 정말로 자신이 원하는 대학을 알게 되었다. 이에 대한 남자의 대답으로 적절한 것은 ④ '만약 그렇다면, 그곳이 네가 가야 하는 대학이야.'이다.

오답 보기 해석
① 나는 내가 너에게 도움을 요청한 것이 정말 기뻐.
② 나는 네가 그 대학에 들어갔으면 좋겠어.
③ 정말로 너희 부모님께 조언을 구해야 해.
⑤ 대학에서 너 자신에 대해 많이 배워.

총 어휘 수 136

15 상황에 적절한 말

소재 동물 보호소 동물들의 식단 관리

듣기 대본 해석
여: Valerie는 최근에 자신의 동물 보호소를 시작하였고 그녀의 일에 매우 열정적입니다. 그녀는 동물들이 잘 관리되고 있다는 것을 확실히 하기 위해 자신의 직원들을 훈련시킵니다. 그녀는 각 종들이 다른 식단 요구를 갖고 있기 때문에 직원들이 동물들 먹이는 것을 특별히 신경쓰길 원합니다. 어느 날, 그녀는 몇몇 동물들이 아프기 시작한 것을 알아차립니다. 그녀가 철창 안을 들여다 보는데 구조된 너구리가 새 모이를 먹고 있는 것을 봅니다. 그녀는 동물들이 계속 잘못된 종류의 음식을 먹고 죽을까 봐 걱정합니다. 그녀는 이 문제를 다루기 위한 회의에 직원들을 불러들입니다. 이 상황에서, Valerie가 그녀의 직원들에게 할 말로 적절한 것은 무엇입니까?
Valerie: ⑤ 우리는 반드시 동물들이 적합한 음식을 먹도록 해야 합니다.

어휘
animal shelter 동물 보호소 **passionate** ***a.*** 열정적인
in good hands 안심할 수 있는, 잘 관리되는 **species** ***n.*** 종
dietary ***a.*** 음식물의

정답 ⑤

문제풀이
동물 보호소에 있는 동물들이 잘못된 음식을 먹고 죽을까 봐 걱정이 된 Valerie가 직원회의를 소집한 상황에서 직원들에게 할 말로 가장 적절한 것은 ⑤ '우리는 반드시 동물들이 적합한 음식을 먹도록 해야 합니다.'이다.

오답 보기 해석
① 어떤 방문자도 동물 보호소 내에 들어오지 못하도록 해주세요.
② 기금을 받기 위해 고군분투 하는 중이라 문을 닫아야 할 것 같아요.
③ 방문자들이 동물들에게 사람이 먹는 음식을 주지 못하도록 해야 합니다.
④ 동물들을 위해 더 신선한 음식을 사야 할 것입니다.

총 어휘 수 128

16 담화 주제 / 17 세부 내용 파악

소재 햇볕으로 인한 화상을 다루는 방법

듣기 대본 해석

여: 여러분, 좋은 아침입니다. 오랫동안 사람들은 햇빛이 우리의 피부에 줄 수 있는 손상에 대해 알고 있었지만 "애프터 썬 케어"와 같은 특정 제품들이 이 손상을 무효로 만들 수 있다고 믿게 했습니다. 사실, 애프터 썬 제품이라고 불리는 이런 제품들은 제품 속에 든 기름이 우리 피부 속에 열을 가두어 두기 때문에 사실 우리 몸이 가지고 있는 치유 과정을 방해할 수 있습니다. 그러면 우리가 우리 자신을 보호하기 위해 무엇을 할 수 있을까요? 우리가 일광 화상을 어떻게 다루어야 할까요? 단지 피부를 시원하게 두는 것이 방법입니다. 여러분은 시원한 물에 몸을 담그거나 식초를 사용할 수 있습니다. 수건을 식초에 담그고 그것을 일광 화상을 입은 자리에 두면 식초가 당신 피부의 열을 빼낼 겁니다. 놀랍지만 약간 냄새가 나죠. 여러분이 그 냄새를 맡길 원하지 않으시면, 알로에 베라 막이나 얇게 썬 오이도 같은 역할을 합니다.

어휘

damage ***n.*** 손상, 피해 **undo** ***v.*** 무효로 만들다, 원상태로 돌리다 **hinder** ***v.*** 저해하다, 막다 **trap** ***v.*** 가두다 **vinegar** ***n.*** 식초 **soak** ***v.*** 담그다 〈문제〉 **alternative** ***n.*** 대안

정답 16 ④ 17 ②

문제풀이

16 여자는 일광 화상을 입은 다음 제품을 바르는 것은 도움이 되지 않는다고 말하면서 다른 적당한 방법으로 시원한 물에 몸 담그기, 식초에 담근 수건 대고 있기 등을 알려주고 있다. 따라서 여자가 하는 말의 주제는 ④ '애프터 썬 제품의 대안'이다.

17 여자는 일광 화상을 입었을 때 찬물에 몸을 담그거나 식초, 알로에, 오이를 이용하라고 말했지만 우유에 대해서는 언급하지 않았으므로 정답은 ② '우유'이다.

오답 보기 해석

16

① 피부에 바르는 천연 재료의 효과

② 자외선 차단제를 항상 사용해야 하는 이유

③ 규칙적인 일광욕의 장점

⑤ 가장 좋은 애프터 썬 케어 제품

총 어휘 수 149

DICTATION ANSWERS

01 its opening weekend / I'm going to check it out

02 you're soaked / check the weather forecast

03 enjoys having fun outdoors / the weather can change for the worse / find yourself caught in a thunderstorm / getting struck by lightning

04 it's fun to talk with him / Personal hygiene is looked at differently / I appreciate the advice

05 carry a first-aid kit / having a great time on the trip / I'm doing my best

06 They're all super talented / That's awesome / He's got great range

07 student exchange program is finished / I'm not prepared for the quizzes / What are friends for

08 where are you headed / run some errands / It was rained out

09 the one made of glass / I don't think I can afford it / I can interest you in

10 I've been looking forward to / more computer-savvy / get a warranty on / let's be sure to keep the warranty papers

11 a benefit concert will be held / some of the biggest names in / experiencing abuse and mistreatment

12 What are you up to / water hookup / since it prohibits pets / That narrows it down to

13 during our senior year / used to hang out with / you might see him soon / we're going to set up a lunch

14 I got accepted to two universities / That's quite a dilemma / Flip a coin

15 her animals are in good hands / different dietary needs / calls her staff in for a meeting

16-17 we can undo this damage / hinder your body's own healing process / traps heat inside the skin / soak a towel in vinegar / pull the heat out of your skin

19 수능영어듣기 실전모의고사

본문 p.116

01 ②	02 ⑤	03 ③	04 ②	05 ②	06 ③
07 ③	08 ⑤	09 ⑤	10 ⑤	11 ②	12 ④
13 ③	14 ①	15 ③	16 ③	17 ④	

01 짧은 대화의 응답

소재 식사 주문

듣기 대본 해석

여: 저는 주문할 준비가 된 것 같은데, 주문 받아주실래요?
남: 물론이죠. 오늘 아침에 뭐가 좋으세요?
여: 베이컨과 계란 그리고 사이드 메뉴로 구운 감자를 주세요. 언제 될까요?
남: ② 그것은 15분 안에 준비될 것입니다.

어휘

〈문제〉 **waffle** ***n.*** 와플(밀가루 · 달걀 · 우유 등을 섞어 구운 것) **popular** ***a.*** 인기 있는

정답 ②

문제풀이

음식이 언제 준비되는지 물었으므로 남자의 응답으로 가장 적절한 것은 ② '그것은 15분 안에 준비될 것입니다.'이다.

오답 보기 해석

① 카페는 약 1시간 거리예요.
③ 애플 파이를 곁들인 와플은 인기 있는 메뉴입니다.
④ 사람들은 감자가 건강에 좋지 않다고 말해요.
⑤ 마트에서 며칠 전에 좀 사왔어요.

총 어휘 수 42

02 짧은 대화의 응답

소재 티켓 구하기

듣기 대본 해석

남: 이번 토요일에 올림픽 경기장에서 하는 Dragon Heart 콘서트를 정말 보고 싶어!
여: 응, 나도. 아직 티켓을 구할 수 있을까?
남: 잘 모르겠어. 하지만, 내 친구 Kevin이 티켓 판매소에서 일하고 있어.
여: ⑤ 네가 꼭 그에게 전화해서 물어봐야겠는데.

어휘

stadium ***n.*** 강당 〈문제〉 **definitely** ***ad.*** 분명히

정답 ⑤

문제풀이

남자의 친구 Kevin이 티켓 판매소에서 일하고 있다고 했으므로, 여자의 응답은 ⑤ '네가 꼭 그에게 전화해서 물어봐야겠는데.'가 알맞다.

오답 보기 해석

① 와, 나도 Dragon Heart 좋아해!
② 나는 이번 토요일에 정말로 바빠.
③ 유감스럽게도 매진됐다고 그가 말했어.
④ 나 그 콘서트 표를 두 장 가지고 있어.

총 어휘 수 43

03 담화 목적

소재 법률 분야 인턴십 모집 안내

듣기 대본 해석

여: 여러분 안녕하세요! 오늘 저는 여러분이 놓치고 싶어하지 않을 기회에 대해서 말씀 드리고자 합니다. 여러분 중에 로스쿨에 진학하고 싶으신 분이 계시다면, 제가 여러분과 공유하려는 인턴십은 직접 실무에 참여하는 경험을 얻을 수 있는 좋은 기회입니다. 그러나, 몇 가지 알아둘 점들이 있습니다. 이 인턴십 지원은 우리 학교에 현재 등록된 대학생과 대학원생에게 해당됩니다. 그러나, 이 기회를 얻을 수 있는 학부생들은 오로지 현재 졸업반 학생들임을 명심하십시오. 법대생들과 그 분야를 접해본 지원자가 선호될 것입니다. 마지막으로, 지원자들은 28세 이하여야 합니다. 법 분야에서 어렵지만 보람 있는 일을 시작하고 싶다면 오늘 지원하십시오.

어휘

hands-on ***a.*** 직접 해 보는, 직접 실무에 참여하는 **undergraduate** ***a.*** 학부의 ***n.*** 학부생 **be eligible for** ~에 자격이 있다 **senior** ***a.*** 졸업할 학년의 **candidate** ***n.*** 지원자, 후보자 **exposure** ***n.*** 노출, 접함 **preference** ***n.*** 선호 **career** ***n.*** 경력, 직업

정답 ③

문제풀이

법률 관련 분야에서 실무적인 경험을 쌓을 수 있는 인턴십에 지원할 수 있는 자격 조건으로 '등록된 학생인지 여부, 졸업반인 학부생, 지원가능 연령 등'을 말하고 있으므로 답은 ③ '인턴십에 지원할 수 있는 자격을 알리려고'이다.

총 어휘 수 131

04 대화 주제

소재 맨발로 뛰기의 장점

듣기 대본 해석

여: Cody, 뭐해?
남: 맨발로 뛰는 것의 장점에 대해 읽고 있어.
여: 요즘 사람들이 그거 많이 해보고 있다고 들었어.
남: 맞아. 어떤 연구자들은 맨발로 뛰는 게 건강에 굉장히 좋다고 생각해.
여: 어떤 이점이 있는데?
남: 일단 균형감각을 발달시켜 줄 수 있어.
여: 정말? 어떻게?
남: 신발을 신은 채로 뛰면 발이 (좁은) 신발 안에 밀어 넣어져 있어. 신발이 없으면 발가락을 펼 수 있어서 균형을 더 잘 잡을 수 있지.
여: 그렇구나. 다른 건 안 도와줘?
남: 다리 근육에도 좋아. 보통 운동화는 뒤꿈치에 굽이 있어서 아킬레스건이랑 종아리 근육이 많이 쓰이질 않아.
여: 왜 많은 사람들이 맨발로 뛰기 시작했는지 알겠어. 한번 해봐야겠다.
남: 나도 한번 해보려고.

어휘

benefit ***n.*** 이점 **balance** ***n.*** 균형 **cramped** ***a.*** 비좁게 있는 **tendon** ***n.*** 건, 힘줄 **calf** ***n.*** 종아리

정답 ②

문제풀이

두 사람은 맨발로 뛰었을 때의 균형감 향상과 다리 근육 단련 효과에 대해 이야기하고 있으므로 두 사람이 하는 말의 주제로 가장 적절한 것은 ② '맨발로 뛰기의 장점'이다.

총 어휘 수 139

05 대화자의 관계 파악

소재 자동차 수리 맡기기

듣기 대본 해석

남: 안녕하세요. 무엇을 도와드릴까요?

여: 그게, 최근에 사고가 났었어요. 그 이후로 계기판에 계속 빨간 불이 깜박거려요.

남: 한번 확인해 볼게요. 다른 문제는 없으신가요?

여: 있어요. 시속 70킬로미터 이상으로 달릴 때 차에서 딸깍거리는 소리가 나요.

남: 흠... 타이어의 문제 같네요.

여: 제 보험이 필요한 수리에 대한 모든 비용을 다 대줄 거예요. 그렇죠?

남: 유감스럽지만 저희는 그것에 관해서는 잘 모르겠습니다. 직접 보험사에 전화를 해보셔야 할 것 같습니다.

여: 점심 시간 후에 한 번 전화해 볼게요. 수리하는 데에 얼마나 걸릴까요?

남: 글쎄요. 차에 정확히 어떤 문제가 있느냐에 따라 다릅니다. 한번 점검한 다음에 알려드릴 수 있을 것 같습니다.

여: 이 주변에서 볼 일이 좀 있어요. 제가 나중에 와도 될까요?

남: 괜찮습니다. 전화번호를 남겨 주세요. 뭐가 문제인지 더 잘 알아내면 연락 드릴게요.

여: 알겠습니다.

어휘

dashboard ***n.*** 계기판 **errand** ***n.*** 일, 심부름

정답 ②

문제풀이

여자는 차에 문제가 있어 자동차 수리공인 남자에게 수리를 맡기고 있으므로 두 사람의 관계는 ② '자동차 수리공 — 고객'이다.

총 어휘 수 176

06 그림의 세부 내용 파악

소재 캠핑장 정리

듣기 대본 해석

여: 안녕, Peter. 늦어서 미안해. 나 너무 바빴어.

남: 괜찮아. 내가 캠핑장을 거의 다 설치했어. 내가 지금까지 해놓은 것 어때?

여: 아주 잘했어. 텐트를 강가에 친 것이 마음에 들어.

남: 응. 우리 그러면 수영도 낚시도 쉽게 할 수 있어. 강가에서 저녁을 즐기는 것도 멋질 거야.

여: 아, 그래서 테이블과 의자를 텐트와 강 사이에 놓았구나. 그런데 아이스박스는 어디에 뒀어? 그것은 그늘에 둬야 해.

남: 오, 깜빡했어. 지금 텐트 안에 있어. 내가 그걸 가지고 가서 나무 아래 둘게.

여: 그러면 그게 모닥불 옆에 놓일 거야. 게다가 나무 너무 가까이에 불을 피우는 것은 위험할 수도 있어.

남: 맞는 말이네. 그건 나중에 옮기도록 하고 강 근처에 새로 불을 만들자. 그건 그렇고, 나무 사이에 해먹을 걸었어. 어떻게 생각해?

여: 완벽해. 잘 했어!

어휘

campsite ***n.*** 캠핑장, 야영지 **set up** ~을 설치[설비]하다 **shade** ***n.*** 그늘 **make sense** 말이 되다, 이치에 닿다 **hang (-hung-hung)** ***v.*** 걸다

정답 ③

문제풀이

아이스박스는 텐트 안에 있다고 했는데 밖에 나와 있으므로 정답은 ③번이다.

총 어휘 수 168

07 부탁한 일

소재 친구에게 잠시 가방 맡기기

듣기 대본 해석

여: Jeff, 늦어서 진짜 미안해.

남: 진심으로 걱정했잖아. 네가 못 오는 줄 알았어. 전화도 해봤는데 네가 전화를 안 받더라고.

여: 그게, 택시를 타서 반쯤 왔을 때 휴대폰을 집에 놔두고 왔다는 걸 알아차려서 다시 가야 했어. 게다가 오는 도중에 차도 좀 막혔어.

남: 맞아, 금요일 저녁에는 항상 그런 식으로 막혀.

여: 몰랐어. 아, 버스 정류장 주변에 혹시 편의점 있어?

남: 저 쪽에 하나 있어. 왜?

여: 휴대폰 가지러 집에 다시 갔을 때 충전기를 깜박하고 안 가져왔어. 하나 사야 돼. 내 가방 좀 봐줄래?

남: 알겠어. 여기서 기다릴게.

여: 고마워. 몇 분 안 걸릴 거야.

어휘

traffic jam 교통 체증 **convenience store** 편의점 **charger** ***n.*** 충전기 〈문제〉 **keep an eye** 주시하다

정답 ③

문제풀이

여자는 집에서 휴대폰 충전기를 놓고 와서 편의점에서 하나 사려고 하는데 그 동안 잠시 남자에게 자신의 가방을 봐(맡아) 달라고 부탁하고 있으므로 정답은 ③ '가방 맡아주기'이다.

오답 보기 해석

① 휴대폰 가지러 가기

② 휴대폰 충전하기

④ 휴대폰 충전기 사주기

⑤ 버스 정류장에 데려다 주기

총 어휘 수 136

08 이유

소재 집에서 공부하려는 이유

듣기 대본 해석

남: 안녕, Kate. 내일 볼 시험 준비됐니?

여: 아닌 것 같아. 하루 종일 공부하고 있을 것 같아. 넌 어때?

남: 난 새로운 학생 센터에 있는 카페에서 계속 공부했어.

여: 아. 거기 어때?

남: 꽤 멋져. 거기에는 새로 연 레스토랑 몇 군데랑 탁구 테이블이 있는 레크레이션 룸 그리고 농구 코트가 있어.

여: 대단한 걸. 시험 끝나고 탁구 치러 가야겠다.

남: 거기에 생긴 새로운 피자가게도 정말 좋아.

여: 좋네. 그럼 거기서 점심 먹고 카페에서 같이 공부하는 건 어때?

남: 나도 점심 먹고 싶어. 하지만 거기서 공부하는 건 별로 좋은 생각이 아니야.

여: 정말? 왜 그런데?

남: 카페 테라스가 아직 공사 중이라 꽤 시끄러워.

여: 알았어. 그러면 나도 집에 가서 공부해야겠어.

어휘

recreation room 레크리에이션 룸, 오락실 **awesome** ***a.*** 굉장한, 엄청난 **under construction** 공사 중인

정답 ⑤

문제풀이
새로 생긴 학생 센터에 있는 카페에서 같이 공부하는 게 어떠냐는 여자의 말에 남자는 카페 테라스가 아직 공사 중이라 시끄러워서 거기서 공부하는 것은 좋은 생각이 아니라고 했다. 따라서 남자가 집에서 공부하려는 이유는 ⑤ '카페 외부 공사로 인한 소음이 시끄러워서'이다.

총 어휘 수 134

09 숫자

소재 토네이도 지역을 돕기 위한 기부

듣기 대본 해석
남: DeLaney 선생님, 안녕하세요. 바쁘신가요? 말씀드릴 게 좀 있어서요.
여: 아, Taylor. 들어오렴. 무엇이 필요하니?
남: 지난주에 Kentucky주에 닥친 토네이도에 관해서 들으셨을 거예요.
여: 들었지. 끔찍했어. 많은 집들이 완전히 파괴되었잖니.
남: 음, 많은 학생들이 피해자들에게 돈을 기부하기 위해 모였어요. 모든 학생들이 3달러를 냈어요.
여: 정말 잘한 일이구나. 도움이 될 거라고 확신해.
남: 저도 그러길 바라요. 모두들 도울 수 있어서 기뻐했어요.
여: 25명의 학생 모두가 기부했다고? 꽤 많은 돈일 텐데.
남: 네. 여기 저희가 모금한 돈이에요. 혹시 선생님께서 저희를 대신해서 돈을 보내 주실 수 있나 궁금해서요.
여: 물론이지. 나도 20달러를 기부할게.
남: 감사해요 DeLaney 선생님. 이 돈이 정말 도움이 되기를 바라요.
여: 확실히 도움이 될 거야, Taylor.

어휘
destroy ***v.*** 파괴하다 **donate** ***v.*** 기부하다 **pitch in** ~을 기부하다 **on one's behalf** ~을 대신(대표)하여

정답 ⑤

문제풀이
25명 학생 모두가 3달러를 기부했으므로 75달러이고, DeLaney 선생님이 20달러를 기부했으므로 여자가 토네이도 지역에 전달할 총 기부금은 ⑤ '$95'이다.

총 어휘 수 132

10 언급 유무

소재 브로콜리의 건강상 이점

듣기 대본 해석
남: 오늘 기분이 너무 좋아. 막 시작한 새로운 식단이 엄청나거든. 너는 어때? 어떻게 하고 있어?
여: 너만큼 좋지는 않아. 나도 네 식단을 시도해야겠어. 어떤 종류의 음식을 먹고 있어?
남: 나는 더 많은 야채를 먹고 있어. 너에게도 이걸 추천하고 싶어. 브로콜리가 너한테 좋아.
여: 정말? 브로콜리에 어떤 건강상 이점들이 있어?
남: 어, 우선, 브로콜리는 녹는 섬유질이 가득 차 있고, 그것이 콜레스테롤을 낮추는 데 좋아.
여: 알겠어. 또 다른 건?
남: 브로콜리는 비타민 C와 K가 가득한데, 그 비타민들은 뼈 건강을 증진시켜줘. 브로콜리는 또한 암을 예방하고 건강을 유지시켜주는 산화방지제의 훌륭한 원천이지.
여: 대단해. 나는 약간의 살도 좀 빼고 싶은데. 브로콜리가 그것을 도와줄 수 있을까?
남: 물론 그럴 거야. 브로콜리가 섬유질로 가득하다고 말했던 것 기억해? 이건 많은 칼로리를 먹지 않고도 네가 배부르게 느끼게끔 만들어주는 것을 의미해.
여: 와! 브로콜리는 정말 슈퍼푸드구나!

어휘
recommend ***v.*** 추천하다 **benefit** ***n.*** 이점 **soluble** ***a.*** 녹는 **fiber** ***n.*** 섬유질 **antioxidant** ***n.*** 산화방지제

정답 ⑤

문제풀이
브로콜리는 섬유질을 많이 함유해 콜레스테롤을 낮추고, 비타민 C와 K가 많아서 뼈 건강을 증진시키며 산화방지제가 있어 암을 예방하고 포만감을 주어서 체중 감소에도 도움을 수 있다고 언급하였다. 그러나 식욕증진에 대한 것은 언급되지 않았으므로 정답은 ⑤번이다.

총 어휘 수 162

11 내용 일치 · 불일치

소재 큰까마귀에 대한 설명

듣기 대본 해석
남: 북쪽 지방의 까마귀로 널리 알려진 큰까마귀는 북반구에서 주로 발견되는 크고 까만 새입니다. 이것은 까마귀 종류 중 가장 흔합니다. 사실, 진화론적 관점에서 이 종은 매우 성공적으로 발전해왔습니다. 큰까마귀는 수천 년 동안 인간과 공존해 왔고 어떤 지역에서는 너무 많아서 성가시게 여겨지기도 했습니다. 까마귀 생존 성공의 중요한 부분은 그것의 식습관에서 옵니다. 이 새들은 썩은 살, 곤충, 곡물 낟알들, 베리, 과일, 작은 동물과 음식물 쓰레기를 먹으면서 영양의 원천을 찾는 데 능하고 기회를 잘 잡습니다. 까마귀는 대단한 포식동물로 여겨져 왔고 전미 미식 축구 연맹의 Baltimore Ravens를 포함해서 다른 많은 스포츠팀의 마스코트로 사용되어 왔습니다.

어휘
widely ***ad.*** 널리 **Northern Hemisphere** 북반구 **numerous** ***a.*** 많은 **pest** ***n.*** 성가신 것, 해충 **crucial** ***a.*** 중요한 **versatile** ***a.*** 다재 다능한 **opportunistic** ***a.*** 기회주의적인 **nutrition** ***n.*** 영양 **grain** ***n.*** 곡물, 낟알 **predator** ***n.*** 포식자, 포식동물

정답 ②

문제풀이
큰까마귀는 수천 년 동안 인간과 공존해 왔다고 했으므로 내용과 일치하지 않는 것은 ② '인간과 공존한 지는 오래되지 않았다.'이다.

총 어휘 수 128

12 도표

소재 스포츠 센터 여름 프로그램 선택

듣기 대본 해석
여: Garrett, 스포츠 센터에서 이번 여름 프로그램 시간표 받았어. 그건 나를 이렇게 생각하게 만들었어. 이번 여름에 운동 좀 하자고, 하루 종일 안에서 아무것도 안 하는 건 너무 아쉬울 거야.
남: 맞아. 어떤 수업 보고 있어?
여: 수영 수업은 어때? 수영을 더 잘하고 싶어.
남: 사실 나 물 공포증이 있어.
여: 그럼 에어로빅은 어때? 재미있을 것 같아.
남: 괜찮을 것 같은데 수요일 밤에 독서 모임 있잖아.
여: 맞아. 그럼 이제 선택지가 두 개밖에 없네.

남: 수업이 저렴해서 좋네. 우리 부모님은 30달러보다 비싼 수업료는 내실 여유가 없으셔.
여: 그럼 너는 어느 게 좋아?
남: 일단 화요일이랑 목요일 수업은 우리가 들을 수 없네. 고학년 애들을 위한 거야.
여: 맞아. 그럼 이 수업 신청하자.
남: 좋은 생각이야.

어휘
afford ***v.*** 여유(형편)이 되다　**sign up** 등록하다　〈문제〉 **racquetball** ***n.*** 라켓볼

정답 ④

문제풀이
두 사람이 같이 수강할 프로그램을 고르고 있다. 남자가 수영은 싫다고 했고, 에어로빅은 독서 모임이 있는 수요일 밤이라 안 된다고 했으므로 ④번과 ⑤번이 남는다. 그런데 화요일과 목요일 수업은 연령이 더 높은 아이들을 위한 거라 듣지 못한다고 했으므로 두 사람이 수강할 강좌는 ④번이다.

총 어휘 수 148

13 긴 대화의 응답

소재 발을 다친 강아지

듣기 대본 해석
남: 여기 앉으세요. 당신의 강아지에게 무슨 문제가 있나요?
여: 글쎄요, 제대로 걷지를 못해요.
남: 발을 한번 보도록 할게요. *[잠시 후]* 아. 문제가 있네요. 왼쪽 발이 좀 부어 올랐네요. 왜 그런지 아세요?
여: 잘 모르겠는데요.
남: 다행히 그렇게 심각한 건 아니에요. 부기는 대략 일주일 내외로 가라 앉을 겁니다.
여: 일주일 내로요? 사실, 그는 다음 주에 Handsome Dog Contest에 참가해야 해요.
남: Dog-Lovers Club이 주최하는 대회 말씀이신가요?
여: 맞아요. 대회에 나가도 괜찮을까요? 참가하지 못 할까 봐 걱정되네요.
남: 걱정 마세요. 오, 그러면 9일 남았네요. 그때까지는 완전히 괜찮아질 겁니다.
여: 다행이네요. 정말 걱정 많이 했거든요.
남: ③ 아니에요, 그는 괜찮을 거예요. 대회에서 행운을 빌게요.

어휘
swollen ***a.*** 부어 오른, 부은　**take part in** ~에 참가하다　**host** ***v.*** 주최하다　**participate** ***v.*** 참가하다

정답 ③

문제풀이
강아지가 발이 부어서 대회에 참여하지 못 할까 봐 걱정을 많이 했다는 여자의 말에 남자는 걱정 말라며 그때까지는 완전히 나을 것이라고 했으므로 적절한 마지막 응답은 ③ '아니에요, 그는 괜찮을 거예요. 대회에서 행운을 빌게요.'이다.

오답 보기 해석
① 당신의 개는 매우 심각한 부상을 입었어요.
② 어디서 애완동물을 잃어버린 것 같아요?
④ 왜 애완동물을 기르기로 결심했는지 말해 줄 수 있어요?
⑤ 유감스럽게도 당신의 애완동물은 대회에 참가할 수 없을 거예요.

총 어휘 수 142

14 긴 대화의 응답

소재 경기 침체 극복하기

듣기 대본 해석
여: 안녕하세요, Goodman씨. 요즘 가게는 어떠세요?
남: 사실 요즘에 매출이 그리 좋지 않아요.
여: 유감이네요. 요즘 경기가 나쁘잖아요.
남: 네. 조만간 조치를 취해야겠어요.
여: 어떻게 경기를 바꾸시려 하세요?
남: 제가 경기를 바꿀 수는 없지만 제가 사업하는 방식을 바꿀 수는 있죠.
여: 말하자면 물건 가격을 낮추는 것 같은 건가요?
남: 음, 일간지에 쿠폰을 발행할까 생각 중이에요. 사람들에게 같은 돈으로 더 많은 혜택을 주고 싶어요.
여: 아주 인정이 많으시네요. 그런데 그렇게 하면 손해가 아닐까요?
남: 처음에는 그러겠죠. 그러나 힘든 시기에 제가 사람들을 돕는다고 사람들이 여길 것이고 그것이 단골 고객층을 만드는 데 도움이 될 거예요.
여: ① 당신이 그럴 여유가 있는 한 아주 좋은 생각이에요.

어휘
lately ***ad.*** 최근에　**economy** ***n.*** 경기　**lower** ***v.*** ~을 낮추다　**accommodate** ***v.*** ~을 수용하다　**in a time of need** 어려울(힘들) 때　**loyal customer base** 단골 고객층　〈문제〉 **loan** ***n.*** 대출, 대부

정답 ①

문제풀이
남자는 경기는 좋지 않지만 일간지에 쿠폰을 발행함으로써 고객들에게 더 많은 혜택을 주어 초반 손해를 감수하고서라도 단골층을 확보하겠다고 하므로 이에 대한 응답으로 가장 적절한 것은 ① '당신이 그럴 여유가 있는 한 아주 좋은 생각이에요.'이다.

오답 보기 해석
② 당신이 단골 고객층을 갖고 있어서 좋네요.
③ 제가 대출을 조금 받을 수 있을까요?
④ 그 판촉은 조금 도움이 됐다고 확신해요.
⑤ 광고는 대개 꽤 효과적이에요.

총 어휘 수 146

15 상황에 적절한 말

소재 그랜드캐니언 방문

듣기 대본 해석
여: Casey는 뉴욕시에 살지만, 그녀는 Arizona주의 Tucson에 사는 그녀의 친구 Danny의 집을 방문하기로 결심합니다. Casey는 긴 여행을 했고 Danny는 그녀를 보고 반가워합니다. 그는 그녀에게 그의 도시를 관광 시켜 줍니다. 모든 명소를 다 본 후, Casey는 Danny에게 그녀가 항상 그랜드 캐니언을 보길 원했다고 말합니다. 그들은 다음 날 그랜드캐니언으로 출발하고 그 관광지를 보기 위한 훌륭한 장소를 찾습니다. 그들은 그곳에 조금 있다가, Danny가 더 완벽한 경관을 보기 위해 헬리콥터를 타서 협곡을 돌 것을 제안합니다. 하지만 Casey는 높은 곳을 매우 두려워하고 헬리콥터를 타지 않기를 원합니다. 이 상황에서 Casey는 Danny에게 뭐라고 말할까요?
Casey: ③ 그거 재미있을 것 같아. 하지만 난 헬리콥터를 타지 않을래.

어휘
journey ***n.*** 여행　**be delighted** 반가워하다, 좋아하다　**sight** ***n.*** 명소, 관광지　**canyon** ***n.*** 협곡　**set out** 출발하다
〈문제〉 **check out** 나가다, 체크아웃 하다

정답 ③

문제풀이

Danny는 그랜드캐니언에서 더 좋은 경관을 보기 위해 Casey에게 헬리콥터를 타자고 제안하지만, Casey는 높은 곳에 대한 공포가 있어 헬리콥터를 타지 않길 원하는 상황이므로 Casey가 Danny에게 할 말로 가장 적절한 것은 ③ '그거 재미있을 것 같아. 하지만 난 헬리콥터를 타지 않을래.'이다.

오답 보기 해석

① 우리 뉴욕 헬리콥터 투어를 하자.
② 괜찮아. 나는 우리가 다음 헬리콥터를 탈 수 있을 것이라고 확신해.
④ 좋아. 나는 항상 위에서 그 협곡을 보길 원했어.
⑤ 그랜드캐니언 박물관에 가서 더 많은 정보를 얻자.

총 어휘 수 136

16 담화 주제 / 17 세부 내용 파악

소재 자신을 좀 더 정돈되게 하는 방법들

듣기 대본 해석

남: 당신은 자주 당신의 지저분한 책상 위에서 무언가를 미친 듯이 찾고 있는 자신을 발견하나요? 당신이 단지 너무 정리를 못해서 모임 또는 약속을 놓친 적이 있나요? 자, 저는 오늘 당신이 좀 더 독립적이고 정돈되도록 하는 방법에 약간의 조언을 드리기 위해 여기에 왔습니다. 첫째, 책상을 정돈하세요. 물건을 모아 두는 사람이 되지 마세요. 당신이 필요로 하지 않거나 중요하지 않은 것은 버리세요. 둘째, 당신의 업무를 기억하기 위해 달력, 일정 계획표 또는 스마트폰을 사용하세요. 달력과 일정 계획표는 약간 구식이지만 그것들은 당신을 정돈되게 해 줄 수 있습니다. 기술은 당신의 친구이고 당신의 일정을 체계화하는 데 도움을 줄 수 있는 많은 앱들이 있습니다. 셋째, 당신이 끝낼 필요가 있는 것들의 목록을 만드세요. 할 일 목록은 당신의 하루를 체계화할 좋은 방법이고 도움을 줄 수 있는 많은 멋진 스마트폰 앱들도 있습니다. 마지막으로 당신의 모든 계획을 완수하세요. 미루는 것을 멈추고 일정을 지키세요. 해야 할 일 목록에 그 항목을 위한 시간 범위를 정하세요. 시간을 절약하기 위해 항목들을 합치세요. 당신이 이러한 조언들을 따른다면, 저는 당신이 더 체계적이고 생산적인 삶을 영위하리라 확신합니다.

어휘

frantically ***ad.*** 미친 듯이 **hoarder** ***n.*** 축적가 **keep track of** ~을 계속 파악하다 **follow through** ~을 완수하다 **procrastinate** ***v.*** 미루다, 질질 끌다 **stick to** ~을 계속하다, 고수하다 **combine** ***v.*** 결합하다

정답 16 ③ 17 ④

문제풀이

16 남자는 체계적인 생활을 위해 책상을 정리정돈 하거나 시간 계획을 짜는 방법에 대해 조언하고 있으므로 남자가 하는 말의 주제는 ③ '보다 체계적인 생활을 하기 위한 조언들'이다.

17 달력, 일정 계획표, 스마트폰, 할 일 목록은 언급되었지만 시계에 대한 언급은 없으므로 정답은 ④ '시계'이다.

오답 보기 해석

16

① 할 일 목록의 필요성
② 자신의 책상을 정돈하는 방법
④ 달력과 일정 계획표를 사용하는 이유
⑤ 스마트폰 앱을 사용하는 것의 이점

총 어휘 수 175

DICTATION ANSWERS

01 Can you take my order / When will that be ready

02 Can we still get tickets / works at the ticket counter

03 to get hands-on experience / keep in mind that / are eligible for this opportunity / start a challenging, yet rewarding career

04 the benefits of running barefoot / improve your balance / your foot is cramped up inside / trying it out myself

05 check them out / starts making a clicking noise / what exactly is wrong with your car / errands I need to run

06 in the shade / I'll go get it / That makes sense

07 you were going to make it / got halfway here / a traffic jam / I forgot to grab my charger

08 are you ready for the exam / I'll be studying all day / is still under construction

09 were completely destroyed / donate money to the victims / on our behalf

10 broccoli is full of soluble fiber / promote great bone health / without actually eating many calories

11 found mostly in the Northern Hemisphere / has coexisted with humans / finding sources of nutrition / great predator

12 sit inside all day doing nothing / My parents can't afford anything / sign up for this one

13 His left foot is a bit swollen / he's supposed to take part in / participate in the contest

14 the way I do business / lowering your prices / in a time of need / build a loyal customer base

15 After seeing all the sights / great spot to view the landmark / to get a more complete view / is very afraid of heights

16-17 how you can become more independent and organized / keep track of your tasks / make lists of things you need to do / follow through on all your plans / Set time frames

20 수능영어듣기 실전모의고사

본문 p.122

01 ①	02 ②	03 ④	04 ①	05 ①	06 ②
07 ⑤	08 ④	09 ③	10 ④	11 ②	12 ④
13 ⑤	14 ③	15 ⑤	16 ③	17 ④	

01 짧은 대화의 응답

소재 농구 수업에서 집중 연습할 기술

듣기 대본 해석

남: Ava. 농구 연습에서 오늘은 뭐에 집중할 거야?
여: 패스와 슛 중에서 골라야 돼.
남: 슛 연습을 하는 게 좋을 것 같아. 그게 더 중요하다고 생각해.
여: ① 제안해줘서 고마워.

어휘

〈문제〉 **suggestion** ***n.*** 제안

정답 ①

문제풀이

여자가 슛과 패스 중 어떤 것에 더 집중해서 연습할지 정해야 된다고 하자 남자는 슛이 더 중요한 것 같다고 추천했으므로 그에 대한 여자의 대답은 ① '제안해줘서 고마워.'가 적절하다.

오답 보기 해석

② 응. 나는 슈팅을 잘해.
③ 괜찮아. 나 농구 별로 안 좋아해.
④ 넌 오늘 농구 연습에 가야 해.
⑤ 난 네가 농구에 관심 있는 줄 알았어.

총 어휘 수 35

02 짧은 대화의 응답

소재 악단에서 연주할 악기

듣기 대본 해석

여: 안녕, Max. 나 학교 악단에 시험 쳐 보기로 결심했어.
남: 좋은 생각이야! 어떤 악기를 연주할 건데?
여: 아마 금관악기를 연주할 건데 어떤 것을 할지는 확실치 않아.
남: ② 네가 가장 잘하는 악기를 연주해.

어휘

marching band 악단 **brass instrument** 금관악기
〈문제〉 **tryout** ***n.*** 오디션 **relieve** ***v.*** 없애주다, 덜어주다

정답 ②

문제풀이

여자가 악단 시험을 본다고 했는데 금관악기 중 어떤 악기로 할지 모르겠다고 말했으므로 적절한 응답은 ② '네가 가장 잘하는 악기를 연주해.'이다.

오답 보기 해석

① 내가 더 나은 연주자가 되도록 도와줘.
③ 너 오디션에서 드럼을 쳐서는 안 돼.
④ 악단 대회는 이번 주말이야.
⑤ 악기 연주는 스트레스를 해소하는 데 좋아.

총 어휘 수 41

03 담화 목적

소재 국제 영화제

듣기 대본 해석

남: 안녕하세요, 신사 숙녀 여러분. 이곳 역사적인 Wilma Theater에서 열리는 제 4회 국제 영화 축제에 와 주셔서 감사합니다. 찬사를 받고 있는 감독 Mark Young이 만든, 다음 상영작 Moonset Monarchy를 많은 분들께서 기대하고 계시리라 생각합니다. 하지만 저희는 현재 영사기에 기술적인 장애가 있는 상황입니다. 영화가 곧 시작하기로 되어 있었으나, 현재로서는 한 시간 동안 미루고자 합니다. 지연된 것에 대해 진심으로 사과 드리며, 이 특정 영화를 위해 구매하신 티켓은 환불을 해 드릴 준비가 되어있습니다. 양해해 주셔서 감사합니다.

어휘

acclaimed ***a.*** 칭찬(호평)을 받고 있는 **technical** ***a.*** 기술적인
film projector 영사기 **momentarily** ***ad.*** 곧, 금방, 잠깐 (동안)
as of now 현재로서는 **sincerely** ***ad.*** 진심으로

정답 ④

문제풀이

남자는 영사기에 문제가 생겨서 영화 상영 시간이 늦춰졌음을 알려주고 있으므로 정답은 ④ '영화 상영 시간의 변경을 알리려고'이다.

총 어휘 수 96

04 대화 주제

소재 몸과 마음을 건강하게 유지하는 방법

듣기 대본 해석

여: 안녕, Gilbert. 뭐하고 있어?
남: 안녕, Mary. 나 방금 건강과 관련 있는 새로운 오디오북을 듣기 시작했어.
여: 건강이라고? 식습관에 관한 거야?
남: 아니, 그건 어떻게 너의 몸과 마음을 건강하게 유지하느냐에 관한 거야.
여: 흥미롭게 들리네.
남: 우리는 장기적으로 중요한 영향을 끼치는 정말 단순한 일들을 매일 할 수 있어. 사람들은 효과를 바로 원해서 우리가 하는 것과 먹는 것들의 장기적인 효과를 무시하는 거야.
여: 그래서 건강한 마음과 건강한 몸을 향하는 바른 길로 가기 위해 네가 추천하려는 첫 번째 것은 뭐야?
남: 우리가 해야 할 첫 번째 일은 우리 생활에서의 목록을 만드는 거야. 우리가 가지고 있는 것을 파악한 다음에 그 중에서 우리가 얼마나 필요하고 나머지는 얼마나 없애야 하는지를 알아내야 해.
여: 그럼, 그 목록은 단지 물질적인 소유물이 아니라 음식, 사람, 일, 취미, 그리고 매일매일 우리가 다루는 꽤 많은 모든 것들을 포함해야 하는구나, 그렇지?
남: 그래, 정확해.

어휘

significant ***a.*** 중요한 **in the long run** 결국에는, 장기적으로는
ignore ***v.*** 무시하다 **long-term effect** 장기적 효과 **stuff** ***n.*** 물건, 물질 **recommend** ***v.*** 추천하다 **path** ***n.*** 길, 방향 **inventory** ***v.*** ~의 목록을 만들다 ***n.*** 목록, 재고 **figure out** 이해하다, 알아내다
deal with 다루다, 처리하다 **on a daily basis** 매일매일

정답 ①

문제풀이

남자는 여자에게 방금 읽기 시작한 오디오북의 내용을 얘기해주고 있다. 단순한 일들이 장기적으로 중요한 결과를 만들어낸다고 말하면서 건강한 마음과 몸을 유지할 수 있는 방법을 소개하고 있다. 따라서 두 사람 대화의 주제는 ① '몸과 마음을 건강하게 유지하는 방법'이다.

총 어휘 수 157

05 대화자의 관계 파악

소재 책자 사진 선택

듣기 대본 해석

[문을 두드리는 소리]

남: 들어오세요.

여: 안녕하세요. Anderson씨. 저를 만나고 싶어 하셨다고 들었어요.

남: 네. Stacy. 당신을 기다리고 있었어요. 앉아서 이 배치를 좀 살펴봐 주세요.

여: 오, 정말 좋은데요!

남: 잘됐네요. 이제 책자에 쓸 사진 두어 장을 고르는 데 당신의 도움이 필요해요.

여: 이 두 장이 정말 훌륭하네요. 이 사진들이 영화가 무엇에 관한 것인지를 가장 잘 포착해내는 것 같아요.

남: 기사가 당신의 연기에 초점을 맞추기 때문에 제 생각에 당신의 캐릭터를 가장 잘 표현하는 사진들을 찍었어요.

여: 당신과 일하는 것이 정말 신나요. 당신 사진들은 저를 멋지게 보이도록 만들어요.

남: 제 작품을 좋아해 주신다니 기뻐요. 감독에게 넘기기 전에 몇 장 더 찍어야 해요.

여: 좋은 생각이에요. 액션을 주제로 찍을까요?

남: 네. 스튜디오로 세 시까지 오세요.

여: 제가 네 시에 약속이 있으니 한 시간 더 일찍 만나도 될까요?

남: 물론이죠.

어휘

layout ***n.*** 배치, 설계 **shot** ***n.*** 촬영, 사진 **represent** ***v.*** 표현하다, 나타내다 **hand over** 넘겨주다 **appointment** ***n.*** 약속

정답 ①

문제풀이

남자가 기사에 쓸 여자의 사진을 찍었고 여자는 영화와 캐릭터를 이야기하는 것으로 보아 ① '사진작가 — 여배우'의 관계임을 알 수 있다.

오답 보기 해석

② 예술품 수집가 — 영화 감독
③ 기자 — 인터뷰 대상자
④ 광고인 — 편집자
⑤ 모델 — 교수

총 어휘 수 152

06 그림의 세부 내용 파악

소재 교사 휴게실 안내

듣기 대본 해석

여: 저희 학교에 오신 걸 환영합니다. Brown씨. 학교 안내를 해 드릴게요.

남: 감사합니다. 여기서 일하게 돼서 영광이에요. 이 방은 뭐죠?

여: 여기는 교사 휴게실이에요. 쉬는 시간에 휴식을 취하고 다른 선생님들과 이야기를 나누는 장소예요.

남: 우와, 꽤 좋아 보이네요. 저기 뒤에 있는 건 스낵 자판기인가요?

여: 맞아요. 왼쪽 벽에 인터넷에 접속할 수 있는 컴퓨터도 두 대 있어요.

남: 좋네요. 이 탁자에 있는 건 뭐죠?

여: 여기서 가끔 편하게 회의를 해서 의자 두 개와 필요할 때 전화 회담에 사용되는 전화기가 탁자 위에 있어요.

남: 좋네요. 자판기 옆의 게시판에는 뭐가 붙어 있는 거예요?

여: 조만간 있을 지구의 날 행사 포스터예요. 4월에 열려요.

남: 그럼 게시판은 다가오는 행사들을 홍보하는 건가요?

여: 맞아요. 가끔 다른 중요한 정보도 붙여 놓으니까 주기적으로 확인하는 게 좋아요.

남: 그렇군요. 다음은 어디로 가는 거죠?

여: 다음엔 체육관으로 갈 거예요.

어휘

lounge ***n.*** 휴게실 **relax** ***v.*** 쉬다, 휴식을 취하다 **snack machine** 스낵 자판기 **casual** ***a.*** 태평스러운, 편한 **bulletin board** 게시판 **announce** ***v.*** 발표하다, 알리다 **periodically** ***ad.*** 정기적으로, 주기적으로

정답 ②

문제풀이

여자가 인터넷에 접속할 수 있는 컴퓨터가 두 대 있다고 했는데 그림에는 한 대만 있으므로 정답은 ②번이다.

총 어휘 수 173

07 할 일

소재 주말 계획

듣기 대본 해석

여: 시험 어땠니, Donald?

남: 잘 모르겠어요. 다음 주 수요일까지는 결과가 나올 거예요.

여: 너는 공부를 열심히 했으니까, 좋은 점수 받을 거야.

남: 고마워요, 엄마. 그런데 이번 주 토요일에 친구들이랑 World Jazz Festival에 가도 될까요?

여: 오, 안돼. 아버지께서 하신 말씀 잊었니?

남: 무슨 말이요?

여: 우리는 집을 개조할 계획이야. 너의 도움이 정말 필요하단다.

남: 흠... 가면 안되겠네요. 그럼 대신에 일요일에 친구들이랑 영화 보러 가야겠어요.

여: 그래, 하지만 일요일 아침은 안돼. 그때는 할머니를 찾아 뵈어야 하거든. 편찮으시대.

남: 심각하신가요?

여: 아니야. 그저 독감이라고 말씀하시더구나.

남: 다행이네요! 걱정 마세요, 엄마. 할머니를 뵙고 나서 친구들을 만날게요.

여: 고맙다, Donald.

어휘

remodel ***v.*** 개조하다 **serious** ***a.*** 심각한 **relief** ***n.*** 안도, 안심

정답 ⑤

문제풀이

남자는 토요일에 World Jazz Festival에 가려고 했으나 집 수리를 돕기 위해 가지 않기로 했으므로 정답은 ⑤ '집 수리하는 것 돕기'이다. 할머니 방문하기는 일요일 아침이다.

총 어휘 수 138

08 이유

소재 스터디 그룹 모임

듣기 대본 해석

남: Claire, 괜찮니? 너 우울해 보여.

여: 내일 중요한 화학 시험이 있는데, 나는 자료를 이해 못하겠어. 내일 시험에 떨어질 것 같아.

남: 힘내. Ryan, Jason, Taylor와 나는 그룹 스터디를 시작했어. 너도 같이 하자.

여: 나도 하고 싶은데, 나는 성가시게 하고 싶진 않아. 나는 정말 뒤쳐져 있어.

남: 걱정 마. 나는 모든 사람들이 네가 있는 것을 좋아한다고 확신해.

여: 진짜로 고마워. 나는 내가 얻을 수 있는 모든 도움이 필요해.

남: 우리는 오늘 밤 6시에 모일 거야. 너도 올 수 있지?

여: 흠... 나 진짜 못 갈 것 같은데. 오늘 밤 부모님이랑 밖에 나가기로 되어 있어. 아버지 생신이거든.

남: 알았어. 그럼 네가 나중에 우리와 함께 하기를 원한다면 나에게 알려줘, 알았지?
여: 고마워. 정말 고마워.

어휘
down in the dumps 우울한 **material** ***n.*** 자료 **bother** ***n.*** 성가신 사람 **appreciate** ***v.*** 감사하다 **be supposed to V** ~하기로 되어 있다

정답 ④

문제풀이
6시 스터디 모임에 나올 수 있냐는 남자의 질문에 여자는 아버지 생신이라 부모님과 함께 나가야 해서 못 간다고 했다. 따라서 정답은 ④ '부모님과 함께 외출하기로 해서'이다.

총 어휘 수 137

09 숫자

소재 커피와 케이크 사기

듣기 대본 해석
여: 안녕하세요. 어떻게 도와드릴까요?
남: 안녕하세요. 아메리카노 한 잔에 얼마예요?
여: 5달러입니다. 그런데 이번 주는 판촉행사 진행 중이에요. 아메리카노를 한 잔 사시면 한 잔 공짜로 드려요. 그러니까 5달러에 두 잔을 드실 수 있어요.
남: 잘됐네요. 그럼 제가 네 잔을 두 잔 가격으로 살 수 있다는 말이죠. 그럼 아메리카노 네 잔 주세요.
여: 또 다른 필요한 것이 있나요?
남: 네. 실은 오늘이 제 동료의 생일이라서 그에게 케이크를 사 주려고요. 초콜릿 케이크는 얼마인가요?
여: 20달러예요. 사용할 수 있는 쿠폰이 있나요?
남: 없어요.
여: 음. 다음 번 구매 시 10퍼센트 할인쿠폰을 드릴 수 있어요.
남: 감사해요. 신용카드 사용해도 되나요?

어휘
run a promotion 판촉행사를 진행하다 **buy one, get one free** 한 개를 사면 한 개를 무료로 더 받다 **devil's food cake** 초콜릿 케이크 **purchase** ***n.*** 구매

정답 ③

문제풀이
한 잔에 5달러인 아메리카노가 한 잔 사면 한 잔이 공짜이므로 네 잔의 가격이 10달러이고, 20달러짜리 케이크를 산다고 했으므로 남자가 지불할 금액은 ③ '$30'이다.

총 어휘 수 119

10 언급 유무

소재 공연 에티켓

듣기 대본 해석
여: 여보, 우리가 제대로 된 좌석에 앉은 것 같지가 않아요.
남: 아니에요. 이 좌석 번호가 우리 티켓에 인쇄돼 있는 번호예요.
여: 그래요. 당신이 맞는 것 같아요. 연극이 곧 시작할 것 같아요. 휴대폰 무음으로 했어요?
남: 물론이죠.
여: 당신은 배려심이 있어서 다행이에요. 지난번 영화관에 갔을 때 기억나요? 우리 뒷좌석에 있던 커플이 많이 떠들었잖아요. 그들은 우리 자리를 계속 발로 차기도 했어요.
남: 네. 정말 매너가 없었죠. 안내 담당자가 세 번이나 와서 조용히 해달라고 요청했었지요.
여: 네. 정말 짜증났었어요. 공연을 제대로 즐기기가 어려웠어요. 당신이 온 바닥에 음료를 다 쏟아서 우리 앞줄에 있던 사람들 신발이 다 젖었고 끈적해진 것도 그 상황에 도움이 안됐죠.
남: 다시 상기시키지 말아요. 어쨌든. 이제 곧 공연이 시작할 것 같아요.
여: 좋아요. 지난번보다는 더 나은 경험이 되길 바라요.

어휘
considerate ***a.*** 배려하는, 사려 깊은 **usher** ***n.*** 좌석 안내원 **annoying** ***a.*** 짜증스러운 **spill** ***v.*** 쏟다, 흘리다

정답 ④

문제풀이
공연을 보러 온 두 사람은 휴대폰 무음으로 하기, 공연 중에 떠들지 않기, 앞좌석 발로 차지 않기, 음료수 쏟지 않기를 언급했지만 공연 시간을 지키는 것에 대한 언급은 하지 않았으므로 정답은 ④ '공연 시간 지키기'이다.

총 어휘 수 147

11 내용 일치 · 불일치

소재 학교 에세이 대회 공지

듣기 대본 해석
남: 안녕하세요, 학생과 교수단 여러분! 저는 해마다 열리는 제 20회 Maple 고등학교 에세이 대회를 발표하려고 합니다. 환경 문제가 요즘 점점 더 주요 뉴스가 되고 있어서 올해 저희는 우리가 환경을 보호할 수 있는 방법에 대한 여러분의 생각을 듣고 싶습니다. 에세이들은 1,000단어를 넘으면 안 되고, 학교 홈페이지를 통해 제출되어야만 합니다. 참가를 계획하시는 분들께서는 4월 20일까지 참가해 주세요. 제일 잘한 세 편을 이달 말에 발표하고 시상을 하겠습니다. 1등은 500달러를 받게 됩니다. 2등과 3등은 각각 200달러와 100달러를 받게 될 것입니다. 상금과 함께 1등 수상작은 도시 신문에 실리게 될 것입니다. 여러분 모두가 참여하시길 바랍니다. 더 많은 참가는 더 많은 아이디어를 의미하고, 더 많은 아이디어는 환경을 위한 더 많은 도움을 의미합니다!

어휘
faculty ***n.*** 교수단, 교수들 **announce** ***v.*** 발표하다, 알리다 **protect** ***v.*** 보호하다 **submit** ***v.*** 제출하다 **via** ***prep.*** 통하여 **award** ***v.*** (상을) 주다, 수여하다 **respectively** ***ad.*** 각각 **publish** ***v.*** 출판(발행)하다

정답 ②

문제풀이
제출은 학교 홈페이지를 통해서 하라고 했으므로 내용과 일치하지 않는 것은 ② '제출은 학교에 직접 와서 해야 한다.'이다.

총 어휘 수 147

12 도표

소재 피아노 레슨 선택

듣기 대본 해석
남: 여보, 뭐 하는 중이죠?
여: 아이를 위한 피아노 레슨 전단지를 보고 있어요. Susan은 피아노 치는 법을 배울 필요가 있다고 생각해요.

남: 맞는 말이에요. 그렇지만 Susan이 수업을 들을 수 있는 시간이 있어요? 그녀의 일정이 꽉 차 있잖아요.
여: 그건 걱정 마세요. 바이올린 수업이 3월 29일에 끝나니까 그 이후론 시간이 비어요.
남: 알았어요. 그렇다면 오후 6시 30분에 시작하는 수업 어때요?
여: 내 생각엔 그녀가 집에 너무 늦게 오지 않는 게 좋을 것 같아요.
남: 맞아요. 음, 오후 5시에 시작하는 수업이 몇 개 있어요. 어느 것이 좋을까요?
여: 목요일만 아니면 상관없어요. 매주 목요일엔 치과에 가야 하니까.
남: 좋아요. 그렇다면 그녀가 참여할 수 있는 수업이 딱 하나 있네요. 등록 마감일이 언제죠?
여: 전단지에 3월 10일이라고 적혀있어요. 수업이 다 차기 전에 서둘러야겠어요.
남: 오, 지금 당장 등록해요.

어휘

leaflet ***n.*** 광고용 전단지　**deadline** ***n.*** 기한, 마감시간　**register** ***v.*** 등록하다

정답 ④

문제풀이

Susan이 3월 30일부터 시간이 된다고 했으므로 ①번과 ②번은 제외된다. 또한 6시 30분에 시작하는 수업은 너무 늦다고 했으므로 ⑤번은 제외된다. 그리고 매주 목요일은 치과에 가야 한다고 했으므로 화요일, 목요일 수업인 ③번도 제외되므로 정답은 ④번이다.

총 어휘 수 162

13 긴 대화의 응답

소재 자전거 주차

듣기 대본 해석

남: 기분이 안 좋아 보여, Nora. 무슨 일이니?
여: 낮에 학교에서 내 자전거를 잃어버렸어. 나에게 아주 소중한 건데 대학교에 들어올 때 아버지께서 사 주셨거든.
남: 뭐? 네가 항상 타던 그 검은색 자전거?
여: 맞아.
남: 어떻게 된 거야?
여: 법학관 옆에 주차했어.
남: 너 자전거를 지정된 자전거 주차 구역에 둔 거니?
여: 지정된 자전거 주차 구역? 무슨 말이니?
남: 아, 너 새로운 규정에 대해 듣지 못했니? 캠퍼스 안에서 지정된 구역에만 자전거 주차가 허용돼.
여: 그러면 내가 잘못된 장소에 주차해서 견인된 거야?
남: 그럴 수도 있지.
여: 다시 찾으려면 어떡해야 하지?
남: ⑤ 먼저, 가서 네가 주차한 곳이 지정된 구역인지 확인해봐.

어휘

designated ***a.*** 지정된　**regulation** ***n.*** 규정

정답 ⑤

문제풀이

여자가 자전거를 잃어버렸다고 하자 남자는 지정된 구역을 제외하고는 자전거를 주차할 수 없다는 새로운 규정에 대해 말해주었고, 여자는 어떻게 자전거를 찾아야 되는지 물었다. 그러므로 주차했던 곳이 지정된 곳인지 알아보라고 말하는 ⑤ '먼저, 가서 네가 주차한 곳이 지정된 구역인지 확인해봐.'가 가장 적절하다.

오답 보기 해석

① 위층의 다른 주차 구역을 찾아보는 게 좋을 거야.
② 네 자전거 잠시만 써도 될까?
③ 자전거 탈 때 항상 헬멧을 써야 해.
④ 법학관에 가면 이 책 반납해줄래?

총 어휘 수 127

14 긴 대화의 응답

소재 X-Cross 운동 시작하기

듣기 대본 해석

여: 안녕, Louis! 너를 여기서 볼 것이라고 기대 못했는데. 무슨 일이야?
남: 안녕, Francis. 네가 너의 규칙적인 X-Cross 운동에 대해 얘기해서, 궁금해졌거든.
여: 그렇구나. 시작해보려고?
남: 그럴까 해. 네가 나에게 얼마나 기분이 좋은지 그리고 얼마나 더 행복한지 말했잖아. 나의 삶에 그런 종류의 변화가 필요하다고 생각해.
여: 음, X-Cross가 너를 훨씬 건강하게 해 줘. 또한 너의 정신에도 좋아.
남: 맞아. 좋은 몸 상태를 유지해야 한다고 생각해왔어. 나는 정말로 지난 몇 년 동안 내 마음대로 했거든.
여: 음, 이 프로그램이 너에게 딱 맞는 것 같아. 한번 해 보는 것이 어때?
남: 그래야겠어. 오늘 등록할 거야.
여: 멋져. 네가 시작하는 것을 도와 줄게.
남: 고마워. 하지만, 내가 말한 것처럼 나는 몸 상태가 좋지 않아. 수업에서 내가 잘 할거라 생각하니?
여: ③ 물론이지. 너는 쉬운 운동으로 시작할 수 있어.

어휘

exercise routine (규칙적인) 운동　**get in shape** 좋은 몸 상태(몸매)를 유지하다　**let oneself go** 자제력을 잃다　**give it a shot** 시도해 보다　**sign up** 등록하다

정답 ③

문제풀이

남자가 새로운 운동을 시작하려는데 자신 없어하고 있고, 여자는 도와준다고 말하고 있으므로 남자가 자신이 잘 할 수 있을지 물었을 때 적절한 여자의 응답은 ③ '물론이지. 너는 쉬운 운동으로 시작할 수 있어.'이다.

오답 보기 해석

① 균형 잡힌 식단이 네가 좋은 몸 상태를 유지하도록 도울 수 있어.
② 절대 아냐! 집에서 이 프로그램을 하는 것은 쉽지 않아.
④ 괜찮아. 초보자들을 위한 수업은 없어.
⑤ 문제 없어. 너는 훨씬 더 강해졌고, 건강해졌어.

총 어휘 수 152

15 상황에 적절한 말

소재 지진 피해자들을 위한 기부

듣기 대본 해석

여: 지난달, 거대한 지진이 일본을 강타했습니다. 사람들이 많이 죽었으며 집과 재산을 잃었습니다. Bella는 재난으로 영향을 받은 사람들을 도울 수 있는 돈과 다른 것들을 모으기 위해 모금행사를 열기로 결정했습니다. 그녀가 아는 거의 모든 사람들이 옷과 통조림 제품 그리고 돈을 기부하기 위해 그 행사에 참석했습니다. 그러나, 그의 가장 가까운 친구인 Nathaniel은 도움이 필요한 사람들을 돕는 것에 대해 관심이 없는 것 같았습니다. 나중에 Bella는 Nathaniel이 사실 지진의 피해자들을 돕기 위해 세워진 자선 단체에 그가 모은 돈을 전부 기부했다는 것을 친구로부터 들었습니다. 이는 그녀를 기분 좋게 만듭니다. Bella가 Nathaniel을 보면, 그녀는 그에게 뭐라고 말할까요?
Bella: Nathaniel, ⑤ 네가 그렇게 큰 기부를 했다니 대단해.

어휘

massive ***a.*** 거대한, 심각한　**property** ***n.*** 재산　**hold a fundraiser** 모금행사를 열다　**disaster** ***n.*** 재난, 재해　**donate** ***v.*** 기부하다　**canned goods** 통조림 제품　**charity** ***n.*** 자선단체　**victim** ***n.*** 피해자, 희생자　〈문제〉 **let down** 실망시키다　**cause** ***n.*** 대의명분, 취지　**contribution** ***n.*** 기부금, 성금

정답 ⑤

문제풀이

Bella는 친구인 Nathaniel이 기부에 관심이 없는 줄 알았다가 그가 모은 돈을 다 기부한 것을 알고 기쁨을 표하려 하므로 정답은 ⑤ '네가 그렇게 큰 기부를 했다니 대단해.'이다.

오답 보기 해석

① 자선기금 마련을 도와주겠니?
② 너는 정말 돈을 모으기 시작해야 돼.
③ 나는 가끔 나의 가장 친한 친구한테 실망을 해.
④ 왜 우리의 좋은 취지를 지지하지 않으려는 거니?

총 어휘 수 124

16 담화 주제 / 17 세부 내용 파악

소재 글램핑의 좋은 점

듣기 대본 해석

남: 여러분 안녕하세요. 오늘 저는 여러분에게 레크리에이션 캠핑에 대해서 이야기하려고 왔습니다. 처음에는 많은 사람들이 캠핑을 자연과 최대한 가까워지는 방법으로 사용했지요. 다른 사람들은 캠핑을 물이 새는 텐트, 축축한 침낭, 그리고 맛없는 음식이 연상되기 때문에 싫어합니다. 이러한 불편은 캠핑카와 레저용 자동차들의 출현을 낳았습니다. 요즘 새로운 캠핑 유행이 인기를 얻고 있습니다. 이름은 '글램핑'입니다. 이 단어는 '글래머'와 '캠핑'을 섞은 단어예요. 글램핑을 가면 텐트를 치거나 침낭을 풀 필요가 전혀 없습니다. 불을 피울 필요도 없습니다. 글램핑은 오두막이나 미리 세워진 텐트 또는 나무 위 오두막 안에서 자연을 느끼는 방법입니다. 글램핑을 가기 위해서 일상의 호화로움을 버릴 필요가 없는 것입니다. 이 취미는 캠핑의 불편함 없이 시골을 즐길 수 있게 해주기 때문에 인기를 끌고 있습니다. 글램핑은 전기, 샤워시설, 그리고 화장실까지 제공해 줍니다. 또, 글램핑을 할 때 제공되는 조리 기구들로 쉽게 요리를 할 수도 있습니다.

어휘

recreational ***a.*** 레크리에이션의, 오락의 **associate** ***v.*** 연상하다, 연관 짓다 **leaky** ***a.*** 새는, 구멍이 난 **damp** ***a.*** 축축한 **inconvenience** ***n.*** 불편 **glamour** ***n.*** 화려함 **assemble** ***v.*** 조립하다 **luxury** ***n.*** 호화로움, 사치 **equipment** ***n.*** 장비

정답 16 ③ 17 ④

문제풀이

16 기존 캠핑의 불편한 점을 보완한 새로운 형태의 캠핑인 글램핑을 소개하고 있으므로 남자가 하는 말의 주제는 ③ '글램핑이라는 새로운 캠핑 추세'가 된다.

17 글램핑은 미리 쳐진 텐트나 오두막에서 한다고 했고, 전기, 샤워시설, 화장실이 제공된다고 했으므로 언급되지 않은 것은 ④ '난방기기'이다.

오답 보기 해석

16

① 글램핑을 할 때의 안전의식
② 야외에서 휴식을 취하는 방법
④ 캠핑을 할 때 불편을 피하는 방법
⑤ 글램핑이 환경에 끼치는 긍정적 영향

총 어휘 수 186

DICTATION ANSWERS

01 choose between passing and shooting

02 I decided to try out / What instrument are you going to play

03 the next film to be screened / technical difficulties with our film projector / sincerely apologize for the delay

04 keep your body and mind healthy / the long-term effects / get rid of the rest

05 expecting you / represented your character / handing them over to the director / have an appointment

06 along the left wall / on the bulletin board / takes place in April / check it periodically

07 get a good grade / planning to remodel the house / visit your grandmother / That's a relief

08 You look down in the dumps / I'm really far behind / go out with my parents / let me know

09 running a promotion / four for the price of two / buying him a cake / Do you have any coupons

10 put your cell phone on silent / They kept kicking our seats / spilled your drink / Don't remind me

11 Environmental issues are making headlines / they must be submitted / please have your entries in by / Along with the prize money

12 Her schedule is full / not to come home so late / go to the dentist every Thursday

13 lost my bike on campus / in a designated bicycle parking area / my bike was picked up / get it back

14 how great you feel / make you a lot healthier / give it a shot / sign up

15 lost their homes and property / raise money / attended the event / did not seem to care / help the earthquake victims

16-17 as close as possible to nature / they associated it with / assemble a tent / without the discomfort of camping / cooking equipment that's provided for you

21 수능영어듣기 실전모의고사

본문 p.128

01 ④	02 ③	03 ④	04 ⑤	05 ⑤	06 ②
07 ③	08 ⑤	09 ②	10 ④	11 ⑤	12 ②
13 ⑤	14 ⑤	15 ③	16 ③	17 ③	

01 짧은 대화의 응답

소재 운동회 준비

듣기 대본 해석

남: Kate, 운동장에 운동회 날 행사를 위한 선을 그렸니?
여: 아니 아직. 그런데 일기 예보에서 그날 하루 종일 비가 심하게 올 거래.
남: 오, 안돼! 어떡하지?
여: ④ 내 생각엔 실내 활동만 할 수 있을 것 같아.

어휘

weather forecast 일기 예보 〈문제〉 **indoor** ***a.*** 실내의

정답 ④

문제풀이

여자가 운동회 날 비가 많이 올 거라는 예보를 말하자 남자는 어떻게 하냐고 물었으므로 여자의 대답으로 가장 적절한 말은 ④ '내 생각엔 실내 활동만 할 수 있을 것 같아.'이다.

오답 보기 해석

① 선을 그리고 다시 시작하자.
② 그릴 것 좀 가져다 줄 수 있니?
③ 오늘 우산을 가져왔어야 했는데.
⑤ 모든 행사는 저녁 6시 이후에 끝난다고 들었어.

총 어휘 수 46

02 짧은 대화의 응답

소재 박물관 내 사진 촬영 금지

듣기 대본 해석

여: 죄송하지만, 이 박물관에는 엄격한 "사진 촬영 금지" 방침이 있습니다.
남: 정말이요? 아무도 저에게 그것을 말해주지 않았고, 저는 입구에서 어떠한 표지판도 못 봤는데요.
여: 입구 근처에 "사진이나 비디오 촬영 금지"라는 표지판이 있어요.
남: ③ 정말로 죄송해요. 제가 들어올 때 알아채지 못했습니다.

어휘

strict ***a.*** 엄격한 **policy** ***n.*** 정책, 방침 **entrance** ***n.*** 입구
doorway ***n.*** 출입구

정답 ③

문제풀이

남자가 박물관 내 사진 촬영 금지에 대한 어떤 말이나 표지판이 없었다고 하자 여자는 입구에 표지판이 있다고 말했으므로 적절한 남자의 응답은 ③ '정말로 죄송해요. 제가 들어올 때 알아채지 못했습니다.'이다.

오답 보기 해석

① 그래서 전 늘 카메라를 가지고 다니죠.
② 이 박물관의 전시품이 별로 맘에 안 드네요.
④ 당신은 당신의 카메라를 가져왔어야 했어요.
⑤ 저는 사진 전시회가 있었는지 몰랐어요.

총 어휘 수 53

03 담화 목적

소재 다음 학기 수강 재신청 안내

듣기 대본 해석

여: 학생 여러분, 안녕하세요. 잠시 주목해 주시겠어요? 유감스럽게도 학생 여러분 모두 다음 학기에 들을 강의들을 다시 신청해야 한다는 사실을 알려드립니다. 어제 여러분 모두 스케줄을 완성한 것을 알고 있지만 수강신청 사이트의 문제로 신청 몇 개를 처리할 수 없었습니다. 기술적인 문제들은 모두 해결되어 차후에 이런 문제가 다시 발생할 일이 없길 바랍니다. 오늘까지 강의 신청을 해주시기 바랍니다. 협조해주셔서 감사드리고 불편을 끼쳐 죄송합니다. 감사합니다.

어휘

register ***v.*** 등록하다, 신청하다 **cooperation** ***n.*** 협조, 협력
inconvenience ***n.*** 불편

정답 ④

문제풀이

수강신청 사이트의 문제로 어제 했던 수강신청 몇 개가 처리되지 않았기 때문에 오늘까지 다시 신청을 해달라고 말하고 있으므로 여자가 하는 말의 목적은 ④ '다음 학기 수강신청을 다시 해줄 것을 안내하려고'이다.

총 어휘 수 98

04 대화 주제

소재 스포츠 음료 섭취를 통한 경쟁력 확보

듣기 대본 해석

여: Paul, 네가 이번에 FC APEC III 축구 캠프에 참여할 거라고 들었어. 축구 잘해?
남: 잘 못해.
여: 그럼 다른 참가자들과 어떻게 경쟁하려고 그래?
남: 큰 문제는 안 될 거야. 매일 Rad CraCra를 조금 마실 거야.
여: Rad CraCra가 어떻게 너의 축구 실력을 향상시켜?
남: 내가 필요한 힘을 그 특별한 혼합물(Rad CraCra)이 줄 수 있어. 내가 더 빨리 뛰고, 더 높이 뛰고, 더 오래 뛸 수 있게 도와줘.
여: 우와! 난 Rad CraCra가 그렇게 강력한지 몰랐어.
남: 맛도 좋고 FC APEC III의 공식 스포츠 음료야.
여: 최고네! Rad CraCra는 대단한 스포츠 음료야.
남: 맞아! 난 이거 없이는 절대 축구 안 해.

어휘

compete ***v.*** 경쟁하다 **mixture** ***n.*** 혼합물 **boost** ***n.*** 증가

정답 ⑤

문제풀이

여자는 축구를 잘하지 못하면서 축구 캠프에 참여하려는 남자에게 어떻게 경쟁할 것인지를 물었고, 남자는 축구 실력을 향상시키기 위해 스포츠 음료(Rad CraCra)를 섭취할 것이라고 이야기하고 있으므로, 정답은 ⑤ '축구 경기력 향상을 위한 음료 소개'이다.

총 어휘 수 120

05 대화자의 관계 파악

소재 이삿짐센터에 의뢰하는 대화

듣기 대본 해석

여: 안녕하세요. 들어오세요.
남: 우와. 여기를 봐요! 골동품인 꽃병들이 많네요. 수집가세요?

여: 맞아요. 그러니까 그쪽 회사는 부서지기 쉬운 물건들을 위해 특별한 서비스를 제공해 주시는 거죠?
남: 맞습니다. 조심히 다뤄야 할 물건들을 보호하기 위해 특별히 만들어진 용기가 있습니다. 다만, 추가로 150달러를 받습니다. 정확히 언제 이사 가시나요?
여: 다음 주 일요일이요. 근데 더 일찍 짐을 다 옮기려고요. 언제 시간 가능하시고 비용은 얼마 정도 드나요?
남: 금요일 오후까지 모든 짐을 옮겨드릴 수 있어요. 갖고 계신 것들을 보면 900달러가 적당한 것 같네요.
여: 좋네요. 미리 준비해둬야 할 것들 있나요?
남: 글쎄요, 귀중품은 따로 싸서 직접 챙겨가시기 바랍니다.
여: 네. 알겠습니다.

어휘
antique ***a.*** 골동품인, 고대의 ***n.*** 골동품 **fragile** ***a.*** 부서지기 쉬운, 섬세한
delicate ***a.*** 연약한, 다치기 쉬운 **ship** ***v.*** 싣다, 짐을 옮기다 ***n.*** 배
valuables ***n.*** 귀중품

정답 ⑤

문제풀이
두 사람의 대화에서 이사 가는 날짜와 부서지기 쉬운 물건에 대한 관리, 비용 등을 이야기 하는 것으로 보아 여자가 이삿짐센터에 의뢰하는 상황임을 알 수 있으므로 두 사람의 관계는 ⑤ '이삿짐센터 직원 — 고객'으로 볼 수 있다.

총 어휘 수 134

06 그림의 세부 내용 파악

소재 아이 방에 그릴 벽화

듣기 대본 해석
여: 여보, 드디어 Colin 방에 그릴 벽화 디자인을 완성한 것 같아.
남: 좋네. 나도 볼래.
여: 응. 어떤지 좀 말해 줘.
남: 일단 태양이 좀 흥미롭네. 멋진 선글라스도 쓰고 있어.
여: 맞아. 그리고 저 말은 땅에 있는 풀을 뜯어 먹고 있어.
남: 좋네. 저기 있는 건 사과나무겠네. 이거 그림 진짜 잘 그렸다.
여: 고마워. 나무 주변에 있는 토끼들은 어때?
남: 좀 더 쥐같이 생겼는데 벽에다가 그리면 훨씬 알아보기 쉬울 거야. 돼지가 진흙탕에서 노는 것도 맘에 들어.
여: 돼지들은 진흙을 진짜 좋아해. 당신도 알다시피, Colin이 독수리를 좋아해서 나무에도 한 마리 그려 놨어.
남: 예쁘네. Colin이 분명히 좋아할 거야.
여: 그럼 이제 미술 용품 가게에 가서 페인트 좀 사야겠다.
남: 음, 결과물이 어떻게 나올지 정말 기대된다.
여: 나도 여보.

어휘
mural ***n.*** 벽화 **art supply store** 미술 도구를 파는 가게
turn out 모습을 드러내다, 나타나다

정답 ②

문제풀이
말이 땅에 있는 풀을 뜯어 먹고 있다고 했는데, 그림에서는 나무에 있는 사과를 먹고 있으므로 정답은 ②번이다.

총 어휘 수 160

07 할 일

소재 휴식의 필요성

듣기 대본 해석
남: 괜찮니? 기분이 안 좋아 보이는구나.
여: 다음 주에 큰 시험이 있어서 제가 준비를 열심히 했었어야 했는데 공부 대신 친구들과 너무 어울려 놀았어요. 시험을 잘 못 볼까 걱정이 돼요.
남: 그거에 대해 너무 걱정하지 마. 만약 네가 오늘 공부를 시작한다면 시험을 잘 볼 거야.
여: 그렇게 말씀해 주셔서 감사해요. 기분이 좀 나아져요. 하지만 이 불안감이 저를 덥게 만드네요.
남: 이상하구나. 네가 열이 나지 않는지 보기 위해 체온을 재 보마. *[잠시 후]* 괜찮아.
여: 어쨌든 진통제를 좀 먹고 싶어요.
남: 아니, 진통제는 도움이 안 돼. 네가 정신을 차리고 공부를 하고 싶으면, 휴식을 취해야 해. 낮잠을 자야 한단다.
여: 지금 낮잠 잘 수는 없어요. 아직 이 숙제도 마치지 못했어요.
남: 너는 정말 잠이 필요한 것처럼 보이는구나. 올라가서 누우렴. 깼을 때 너는 더 정신이 맑아지고 숙제를 더 잘할 수 있을 거야.
여: 알람을 맞춰 주시겠어요? 만약 지금 낮잠을 자면 제가 너무 길게 잘까 걱정돼요.
남: 그래, 그럴게. 이제 쉬러 가렴.

어휘
hang out with ~와 시간을 보내다 **fever** ***n.*** 열 **medication** ***n.*** 약 **pain pill** 진통제 **alert** ***a.*** 정신을 바짝 차린 **assignment** ***n.*** 과제

정답 ③

문제풀이
남자는 두통이 있는 여자에게 일단 낮잠을 자면서 쉬고 일어나서 공부하기를 권하고 있다. 여자는 낮잠을 오래 잘까 걱정하며 알람을 맞춰달라고 부탁하고 있으므로 남자가 여자를 위해 할 일은 ③ '알람 맞춰주기'이다.

총 어휘 수 195

08 이유

소재 사무실 청소로 인해 미뤄진 이사

듣기 대본 해석
여: 안녕하세요 Staller 씨. 이번 주말에 새로운 사무실로 옮길 준비가 되었죠, 맞죠?
남: 못 들으셨어요? 다음 주 주말까지는 옮기지 않습니다.
여: 정말이요? 왜 갑자기 계획이 바뀌었죠?
남: 우리가 그곳에 옮겨 시작하기 전에 철저히 청소를 해놓는 것이 좋다고 생각했어요.
여: 이사 업체에 다시 스케줄을 잡아야 한다고 전화해 줬나요?
남: 그랬죠. 그들은 계획이 바뀐 것에 대해 좋아하지 않았어요. 사실 다음 주말에 이미 일정이 예약되어 있거든요.
여: 오, 이런. 우리가 만약 그들을 대체할 이사 업체를 찾지 못하면 어떻게 하죠?
남: 아직 확실하지는 않지만 토요일에 직원들이 모두 나와 짐을 빼주도록 생각하고 있어요.
여: 그들이 그 생각을 좋아할 것 같진 않군요.
남: 당신 말이 아마 맞을 거예요. 하지만 궁여지책이 필요한 절박한 시기거든요.

어휘
replace ***v.*** 교체하다, 대신하다 **desperate** ***a.*** 필사적인, 절박한
measure ***n.*** 조치

정답 ⑤

문제풀이
대화의 앞부분에서 여자가 왜 사무실 옮기는 계획이 바뀌었냐고 물었을 때 남자가 옮겨서 새로 시작하기 전에 철저히 청소하는 것이 좋다고 생각했다고 했으므로 정답은 ⑤ '이사 전에 사무실 청소를 해야 해서'이다.

총 어휘 수 138

09 숫자

소재 아들과 딸의 가방 구매하기

듣기 대본 해석
남: 안녕하세요. 어떻게 도와드릴까요?
여: 아들 가방 사려고요.
남: 아, 딱 좋을 때 오셨네요. 지금 개학 시즌이라 할인을 최대 40퍼센트까지 해드리고 있어요.
여: 좋네요! 요즘 제일 잘 나가는 가방이 뭐예요?
남: 음, 이 Spikey 상표 가방이 굉장히 잘 팔려요. 50달러로 가격이 책정되었지만 지금 20퍼센트 할인 중이에요.
여: 괜찮네요. 살게요.
남: 알겠습니다! 더 필요한 것 있으세요?
여: 우리 딸도 새 가방 하나 사주면 좋겠네요. 저 핑크색 가방은 얼마예요?
남: 그건 원래 60달러인데, 지금 10퍼센트 할인해 드려요.
여: 좀 비싸지만 딸 아이가 분명 좋아할 거예요. 살게요.
남: 알겠습니다. 원하시면 가방을 방수로 해드릴 수도 있어요.
여: 얼만데요?
남: 가방당 추가로 5달러가 들어요.
여: 괜찮아요. 그냥 이대로 가져갈게요.

어휘
back-to-school ***a.*** 신학기의, 개학의 **popular** ***a.*** 인기 많은
pricey ***a.*** 값비싼 **water-resistant** ***a.*** 방수의, 물이 잘 스며들지 않는

정답 ②

문제풀이
아들의 가방은 50달러인데 20퍼센트 할인하므로 40달러, 딸의 가방은 60달러인데 10퍼센트 할인되어 54달러이다. 방수 처리는 하지 않는다고 했으므로 총 40+54=94달러가 되어 정답은 ② '$94'이다.

총 어휘 수 153

10 언급 유무

소재 과수원으로의 현장학습

듣기 대본 해석
[전화벨이 울린다.]
남: 안녕하세요, Tafford 과수원입니다.
여: 여보세요, 저는 Paulson 고등학교에 있는 생물 선생님인 Fink예요. 제 학생들을 과수원으로 현장학습 데려가는 것에 대해 알아보려고 전화했습니다.
남: 그 말을 들으니 기쁘네요, Fink 선생님. 저희는 학생들을 위한 반나절 동안, 그리고 하루 종일 하는 프로그램이 있어요.
여: 반나절 프로그램이 더 적절할 것 같아요. 이런 프로그램에서 해주시는 활동들은 무엇인가요?
남: 날씨가 좋으면, 저희는 주로 학생들을 데리고 나가서 사과를 따고 사과주스를 만들어요.
여: 학생들이 좋아할 것 같네요. 저는 학생 약 25명을 데려가려고요. 9월 26일에 자리가 있나요?
남: 네, 저희 스케줄은 그 주 내내 비어 있어요.
여: 좋아요. 그러면 그때로 예약할게요.
남: 네. 9월 26일에 약 25명이라고 하셨죠?
여: 맞아요. 그리고 Paulson 고등학교예요.
남: 알겠어요. 학생들에게 점심을 제공하셔야 하고 학생들이 편한 복장을 입도록 말해주세요.
여: 그럴게요. 도와주셔서 감사해요.

어휘
orchard ***n.*** 과수원 **inquire** ***v.*** 묻다, 알아보다

정답 ④

문제풀이
대화에서 과수원에서의 활동 내용(사과 따서 주스 만들기), 인원(25명), 현장학습의 날짜(9월 26일), 당일 복장(편한 복장)에 관한 언급은 있지만 1인당 가격에 대한 언급은 없었으므로 정답은 ④ '1인당 가격'이다.

총 어휘 수 171

11 내용 일치 · 불일치

소재 유기농 농산물 시장에 대한 안내

듣기 대본 해석
남: 여름이 돌아왔고 Springfield 농산물 시장도 돌아왔습니다. 이 시장은 Springfield Square에 위치하고 있으며, 방문객들에게 주에서 가장 신선한 유기농 농산물을 기꺼이 제공해드립니다. 더 저렴한 가격에 지역 농부들로부터 직접 구매할 수 있는데 왜 굳이 돈을 더 내고 마트를 가나요? 수박이든, 줄기콩이든, 신선한 잼이든 우리 시장은 당신이 필요한 모든 것을 팔고 있습니다. 매주 토요일 정오부터 오후 7시, 일요일에는 정오부터 오후 5시까지 열려 있습니다. 가족 모두에게 즐거운 경험이 될 수 있습니다. 애완동물도 환영이므로, 이번 주말에 모두를 데리고 농산물 시장을 방문하세요.

어휘
produce ***n.*** 생산물, 농산물 **fraction** ***n.*** 부분, 일부

정답 ⑤

문제풀이
담화의 마지막 부분에서 애완동물도 환영이라고 말했으므로 내용과 일치하지 않는 것은 ⑤ '애완견은 데려올 수 없다.'이다.

총 어휘 수 112

12 도표

소재 정수기 선택하기

듣기 대본 해석
남: 안녕하세요. 무엇을 도와드릴까요?
여: 안녕하세요. 사무실에 놓을 정수기를 대여하려고요.
남: 맞게 찾아 오셨습니다. 지금 다섯 가지 모델 중에서 고를 수 있어요. 당신에게 꼭 맞는 정수기를 찾기 위해 질문을 몇 가지 할게요.
여: 네. 물어보세요.
남: 네. 먼저 이 정수기의 기능으로 어떤 것을 원하세요? 얼음을 만들길 원하세요?
여: 그러면 좋지만 꼭 그럴 필요는 없어요. 그렇지만, 뜨거운 물은 나왔으면 좋겠어요.
남: 알겠습니다. 자, 아시다시피 정수기가 다르면 쓰는 에너지의 양도 달라요. 에너지 효율 등급을 몇으로 찾고 계신가요?
여: 우리 회사는 친환경적인 회사라서 가장 좋은 등급이 좋을 것 같아요.
남: 알겠습니다. 낮은 숫자가 더 효율적인 것을 의미합니다. 자, 이제 마지막 질문입니다. 정수기에 한 달에 얼마 정도 쓰실 생각이신가요?
여: 한 달에 40달러가 우리가 지불하고자 하는 최대치인 것으로 결정했습니다.

남: 그러면 이 모델이 좋을 겁니다.
여: 좋네요. 살게요. 도와주셔서 감사합니다.

어휘
look for ~을 찾다 **water purifier** 정수기 **energy rating** 에너지 효율 등급

정답 ②

문제풀이
여자가 제빙 기능은 꼭 필요하지 않지만 뜨거운 물을 만드는 기능은 원한다고 했으므로 ③, ⑤번을 제외한 나머지 중 에너지 등급이 더 낮으면서 40달러 이하인 것을 고르면 정답은 ②번이다.

총 어휘 수 189

13 긴 대화의 응답

소재 원하는 전공 정하기

듣기 대본 해석
여: 안녕, 네가 전공으로 언론학을 공부할 거라고 들었어.
남: 응, 난 언론인이 되고 싶어.
여: 멋지다. 네가 글쓰기에 흥미가 있는 것 같은 걸?
남: 맞아. 어릴 적부터 글쓰기를 좋아했어. 아직도 인류학을 전공할 예정이니?
여: 아니, 사회학을 공부할까 생각 중이야.
남: 잠깐. 지난번 우리가 얘기했을 때는 네가 무엇을 전공할지 확실해 보였던 것 같은데.
여: 글쎄, 내가 사회학에도 정말 관심이 많다는 것을 깨달았어. 어떤 걸 더 공부하고 싶은지 모르겠어.
남: 졸업하면 어떤 직업을 갖고 싶은데?
여: 난 사회복지사가 정말 되고 싶은데 우리 아빠는 내가 인류학 교수가 되길 원하셔.
남: 아, 너의 아버지는 인류학 교수 아니셨니?
여: 맞아. 그러면 넌 내가 어떤 것을 선택해야 한다고 생각해?
남: ⑤ 내가 너라면, 내게 좀 더 흥미 있는 것을 전공할 거야.

어휘
journalism *n.* 언론학 **anthropology** *n.* 인류학 **sociology** *n.* 사회학 **social worker** 사회복지사

정답 ⑤

문제풀이
사회학과 인류학 중 어떤 것을 전공해야 할지 고민하는 여자에게 남자는 ⑤ '내가 너라면, 내게 좀 더 흥미 있는 것을 전공할 거야.'라고 응답하는 것이 가장 자연스럽다.

오답 보기 해석
① 난 정말 언론학 교수가 되고 싶어.
② 언론학이 좀 지루하지만, 난 여전히 좋아해.
③ 내 생각엔 높은 수준의 언론인이 요즘 드문 것 같아.
④ 난 전공을 바꾸고 싶은데 아빠가 허락하지 않으실 거야.

총 어휘 수 147

14 긴 대화의 응답

소재 과학 수업 과제 정리

듣기 대본 해석
[똑똑 두드리는 소리]
남: 거기 누구예요?
여: 나야, Kevin.
남: 아, 엄마. 어서 들어오세요. 요즘 어때요?
여: 나쁘지 않아. 뭐하고 있니?
남: 과학 시간을 위한 학습 과제를 하고 있어요. 내일이 마감이에요. 한번 보세요.
여: *[잠시 후]* 여기 내가 보고 있는 것이 뭔지 모르겠구나.
남: 감자로 만들어진 배터리에요. 꽤 훌륭하죠?
여: 음, 재미있긴 한데 좀 지저분한 것 같구나. 여기저기에 선들이 있구나. 좀 깔끔하게 할 수 있겠니?
남: 저도 조금 복잡한 거 알아요. 대신에 과정과 모든 것이 어떻게 작동하는지를 설명하기 위해서 이 포스터까지 만들었어요. 포스터에 대해 어떻게 생각하세요?
여: 음, 네가 무언가를 발표하고 다른 사람들을 이해시키려고 할 때는 가능한 단순하게 만드는 게 중요한 것 같구나.
남: 그럼 제가 어떻게 해야 할까요?
여: ⑤ 가장 중요한 메시지를 찾고 그것을 명확하게 하려고 노력하렴.

어휘
messy *a.* 지저분한 〈문제〉 **impressed** *a.* 감동을 받은

정답 ⑤

문제풀이
아들이 엄마에게 과학 과제인 감자 배터리를 보여주었고 엄마는 지저분해 보이니 조금 깔끔하게 만들 것을 조언했다. 이어서 설명 포스터에 대한 엄마의 생각은 단순하게 만드는 것이 중요하다고 했기 때문에 아들의 질문에는 ⑤ '가장 중요한 메시지를 찾고 그것을 명확하게 하려고 노력하렴.'으로 대답하는 것이 적절하다.

오답 보기 해석
① 모든 것을 학교에 있는 쓰레기통에 넣으렴.
② 네가 옳아. 나도 모든 사람들이 감동받을 거라고 생각해.
③ 아니야. 나는 그것을 좀 더 깔끔하게 만드는 것이 그렇게 중요하다고 생각하지 않아.
④ 선생님께 너의 프로젝트를 다 끝냈다고 말해도 좋아.

총 어휘 수 147

15 상황에 적절한 말

소재 방콕 여행 계획

듣기 대본 해석
여: Manny와 그의 여자친구인 Katie는 동남 아시아 배낭여행을 가려고 준비를 했습니다. 둘 다 이전에 해외로 여행을 간 적이 없어서, 그들은 여행사를 통해서 가기보다 직접 준비해서 가기로 결정했습니다. Katie가 준비를 위해 대부분의 일을 했습니다. 그녀는 값싼 숙박을 찾았고 모든 경로를 다 계획했습니다. 그녀는 현지인과 의사소통할 수 있도록 태국어 회화책도 샀습니다. 모든 준비 이후에, 그들은 마침내 방콕에 도착했고, Grand Palace 주위를 걷고 있습니다. 그러나 Katie는 여전히 그들의 여행 계획에 대해 강박감을 갖고, 새로 할 일을 생각해내고 있습니다. Manny는 Katie에게 계획 짜는 것을 걱정하지 말고 대신에 여행을 즐기라고 말하고 싶어 합니다. 이 상황에서 Manny가 Katie에게 할 말로 적절한 것은 무엇입니까?
Manny: ③ 모든 것이 괜찮을 거야. 재미있게 놀자.

어휘
make arrangements 준비하다 **accommodation** *n.* 숙박 **phrasebook** *n.* (여행객 등을 위한) 상용 회화집 **local** *n.* 현지인, 주민 **obsess** *v.* ~에 집착하게 하다, ~에 강박감을 갖다

정답 ③

문제풀이
방콕 여행 가기 전과 도착한 후에도 여행 계획에만 집착하는 여자친구 Katie에게 Manny가 할 말로 가장 적절한 것은 ③ '모든 것이 괜찮을 거야. 재미있게 놀자.'이다.

오답 보기 해석
① 내가 너의 안내책자를 봐도 될까?
② 모든 예약을 다시 한번 확인했니?
④ 오늘 밤에 우리가 어느 호텔에 머무를지 아니?
⑤ 우리가 방콕에 간다는 사실을 믿을 수 없어. 너무 신나.

총 어휘 수 138

16 담화 주제 / 17 세부 내용 파악

소재 효과적인 공부 습관

듣기 대본 해석

남: 여러분 안녕하세요. 기말고사가 다가오는 시점에서 효과적인 공부 습관에 대해서 좀 얘기해 보려고 합니다. 아마도 공부를 할 때 첫 번째로 고려해야 할 것은 집중할 수 있는 최적의 공간을 찾는 것입니다. 조용하고 편해야 하며 이는 교실, 자신의 방, 카페, 또는 도서관이 될 수 있습니다. 두 번째, 공부를 할 때는 목표를 세우는 것이 중요합니다. 목표를 세우는 것은 무언가를 향해 공부할 수 있게끔 도와줍니다. 그리고 자신이 세워놓은 목표들을 다 이뤘을 때 자기 자신한테 상을 줄 수도 있습니다. 제가 말하고 싶은 세 번째 습관은 방해를 받지 않으려고 하는 것입니다. 요즘에는 휴대폰이나 다른 전자기기로 인해 방해를 받기 쉬운데, 그러므로 공부를 할 때는 휴대폰, 텔레비전, 그리고 방해될 만한 다른 전자기기는 반드시 꺼놔야 합니다. 마지막으로 최근 연구 결과 어떤 소리들은 집중력 향상에 오히려 도움을 줄 수 있다고 합니다. 전등, 백색소음, 빗소리, 그리고 자연의 소리와 같이 단조로운 소리들은 정신을 맑게 하고 평온하게 해줍니다. 다음 주 기말고사 공부를 할 때 이러한 조언들을 기억하시길 바랍니다. 감사합니다.

어휘

effective ***a.*** 효과적인 **habit** ***n.*** 습관 **consider** ***v.*** 고려하다 **concentrate** ***v.*** 집중하다 **comfortable** ***a.*** 편한, 쾌적한 **reward** ***v.*** 상을 주다 ***n.*** 상 **treat** ***v.*** 다루다, 대하다 ***n.*** 특별한 것, 선물 **resist** ***v.*** 저항하다 **distraction** ***n.*** 집중을 방해하는 것 **electronics** ***n.*** 전자기기 **drone** ***v.*** 웅웅거리는 소리를 내다 ***n.*** 웅웅거리는 소리, 단조로운 소리

정답 16 ③ 17 ③

문제풀이

16 남자는 학습 최적의 공간, 목표 수립, 방해물을 멀리하는 것 등 효과적인 학습 방법에 대해 이야기하고 있으므로 정답은 ③ '공부를 더 효과적으로 할 수 있는 여러 가지 방법'이다.

17 조용하고 편한 최적의 학습 공간으로 교실, 자신의 방, 카페, 도서관은 언급되었지만 공원은 언급되지 않았으므로 정답은 ③ '공원'이다.

오답 보기 해석

16
① 주의 산만이 공부에 미치는 부정적 영향
② 주의 산만과 관련된 건강 문제
④ 목표를 세우고 스스로 보상하는 것의 이점
⑤ 편안한 환경에서 공부하는 것의 이점

총 어휘 수 188

DICTATION ANSWERS

01 rain heavily all day long

02 strict "no photography" policy

03 register for next semester's classes / technical difficulties / appreciate your cooperation

04 compete with other attendees / give me the energy boost / official sports drink

05 a special service for fragile items / get everything shipped / pack all of your valuables

06 Let me know what you think / I'm sure it'll look clearer on / how it turns out

07 I've been hanging out with my friends / have a fever / take a nap / Go upstairs and lie down / set an alarm for me

08 Why the sudden change of plans / They weren't happy with / call for desperate measures

09 offering discounts up to / That's kind of pricey / water-resistant

10 I'm calling to inquire about / A half-day program / for that entire week / remind them to wear comfortable clothes

11 enthusiastically provides visitors with / the freshest organic produce / open every Saturday / Pets are even welcome too

12 ask you a few questions / environmentally friendly company / we're willing to spend

13 major in journalism / you're interested in writing / Hold on

14 It's due tomorrow / made this poster to explain the process / make it as simple as possible

15 made arrangements to backpack / go through a travel agency / After all of the preparation / still obsessing over their travel plans

16-17 take a few minutes to talk about / set goals / get distracted / turn off your cell phone / Keep these tips in mind

22 수능영어듣기 실전모의고사

본문 p.134

01 ②	02 ②	03 ④	04 ⑤	05 ①	06 ⑤
07 ③	08 ⑤	09 ①	10 ③	11 ⑤	12 ③
13 ⑤	14 ①	15 ①	16 ⑤	17 ⑤	

01 짧은 대화의 응답

소재 환전하기

듣기 대본 해석
남: 안녕하세요. 환전하고 싶은 남은 돈이 있는데요. 환율이 어떻게 되죠?
여: 달러당 119엔입니다. 얼마나 환전하려고 하시죠?
남: 55,000엔 가지고 있어요. 여기 있습니다.
여: ② 고액권을 원하세요, 소액권을 원하세요?

어휘
leftover money 남은 돈 **exchange rate** 환율
〈문제〉 **large bill** 고액권 **small bill** 소액권

정답 ②

문제풀이
남자가 환전을 원하면서 돈을 내밀었을 때, 여자는 어떻게 바꾸길 원하는지 묻는 것이 적절하므로 정답은 ② '고액권을 원하세요, 소액권을 원하세요?'이다.

오답 보기 해석
① 100엔과 50엔짜리로 주세요.
③ 저는 은행에서 돈을 환전해야 해요.
④ 여기서 상품을 교환하실 수 없습니다.
⑤ 영수증 원본이 있으시면 교환해 드릴 수 있습니다.

총 어휘 수 43

02 짧은 대화의 응답

소재 다큐멘터리의 감상

듣기 대본 해석
여: Conan, HBO에서 방영하는 새 다큐멘터리 Our History 봤어?
남: 응, 어젯밤에 봤어. 인류의 역사에 관한 다른 관점을 보게 되어 정말 흥미로웠어.
여: 나도 그렇게 생각해. 어떤 역사가 진실인지 궁금하게 만들지.
남: ② 확실히 많은 생각이 들게 하더라.

어휘
perspective ***n.*** 관점 〈문제〉 **thought-provoking** ***a.*** 생각하게 하는, 시사하는 바가 많은

정답 ②

문제풀이
여자가 다큐멘터리를 보고 어떤 역사가 진실인지 궁금해졌다고 말했으므로 남자의 응답은 그에 동조하는 ② '확실히 많은 생각이 들게 하더라.'가 가장 적절하다.

오답 보기 해석
① 난 다큐멘터리를 본 적이 없어.
③ 내가 다 본 후에 빌릴 수 있어.
④ 너는 내가 그것을 아직 안 본 것 알잖아.
⑤ 나는 그가 쓴 책들 중 몇 권을 읽었어.

총 어휘 수 48

03 담화 주제

소재 일조량 부족으로 인한 우울증을 피하는 방법

듣기 대본 해석
남: 겨울철에 뚱해지거나 우울해진 적 있으신가요? 만약 있다면 당신은 전문가들이 말하는 '계절성 우울증'을 앓고 있을 지도 모릅니다. 이 질환은 사람의 몸이 햇빛으로부터 비타민을 받기 때문에 꽤나 흔합니다. 현재 전문가들이 말하기를 전 세계 사람들의 50퍼센트가 비타민D 결핍을 겪고 있다고 합니다. 충분한 양의 비타민D를 얻기 위해서 전문가들은 하루에 10분에서 15분을 야외에 있는 것을 추천합니다. 또, 집을 재배치해서 햇빛을 더 잘 들게 하는 방법도 있습니다. 이것이 가능하지 못하다면 밝은 빛 아래에서 시간을 보내는 것도 도움이 될 수 있습니다.

어휘
moody ***a.*** 뚱한, 기분 변화가 심한 **depression** ***n.*** 우울증
deficiency ***n.*** 결핍 **adequate** ***a.*** 충분한

정답 ④

문제풀이
겨울철에 일조량 부족으로 오는 우울증을 피하기 위한 방법을 설명해 주고 있으므로 남자가 하는 말의 주제는 ④ '일조량 부족으로 인한 우울증 대처법'이다.

총 어휘 수 95

04 의견

소재 자동차 경보장치 설치

듣기 대본 해석
남: Krista, 차에 경보장치 있어요?
여: 없어요. 왜 물었어요?
남: 어젯밤에 제가 나간 사이에 누군가 제 차에 침입했었어요.
여: 오, 저런. 무엇을 가져갔나요?
남: 다행히도 가져갈 것은 별로 없었어요. 하지만 그들이 칼로 내부를 잘라놨어요. 그들은 단지 재산을 파손하고 싶었던 것 같아요.
여: 당신 그것 때문에 굉장히 화났겠네요.
남: 네. 그래서 제가 경보장치 설치에 대해 생각하게 된 거예요.
여: 제 친한 친구가 하나 가지고 있었는데, 그것이 아무 때나 울려서 결국 떼어 버렸어요. 사람들이 당신의 물건을 파손하려 할 때 경보장치로는 그들을 멈추지 못할 거예요.
남: 네, 당신 말이 맞는 것 같아요. 그럼 저는 무엇을 해야 하죠?
여: 음, 항상 당신의 차를 밝은 곳이나 동네에서 좋은 지역에 주차하세요. 주차 공간이 가장 편리하지 않더라도 경보장치보다는 나을 거예요.
남: 그게 효과가 있을 거라고 생각해요?
여: 네, 저도 그렇게 하는데 한 번도 문제가 생기지 않았어요.
남: 좋아요. 이제부터 그렇게 할게요.

어휘
break into 침입하다, (차문을) 억지로 열다 **property** ***n.*** 재산
install ***v.*** 설치하다 **go off** (경보기 등이) 울리다
randomly ***ad.*** 닥치는 대로, 임의로 **wreck** ***v.*** 망가뜨리다, 파괴하다
convenient ***a.*** 편리한 **alternative** ***n.*** 대안, 선택 가능한 것

정답 ⑤

문제풀이
여자는 자동차 경보장치의 설치를 생각하고 있는 남자에게 경보장치를 설치했다가 제대로 작동하지 않아서 떼어버린 친구의 이야기를 해주면서 대신 밝고 좋은 곳에 주차를 해두라고 조언하고 있다. 따라서 정답은 ⑤ '경보장치보다는 밝고 좋은 곳에 주차하라.'이다.

총 어휘 수 174

05 대화자의 관계 파악

소재 작가와 성우의 만남

듣기 대본 해석

남: 안녕하세요. 당신이 Amelia Hawkins 씨군요.
여: 맞아요. 당신이 그 유명한 Jeffrey Martin 씨군요. 만나서 반갑습니다, Martin 씨.
남: 저야말로 만나서 반갑습니다. 편하게 Jeffrey라고 불러주세요.
여: 알겠습니다, Jeffrey. 이렇게 유명한 사람과 일할 수 있는 건 정말 영광이에요.
남: 감사합니다. 저도 얘기 많이 들었습니다, Amelia 씨. 이 분야에서 진정한 전문가시라고요.
여: 감사합니다. 이 자리에 오기까지 정말 많은 노력이 들었어요.
남: 이해합니다. 제 책을 읽어 본 적 있으신가요?
여: 다 읽어 봤어요. 정말 훌륭해요. 만나는 사람마다 추천해주고 있어요.
남: 과찬이세요. 근데 제 사랑스러운 아내 Lola 없이는 절대 그 어떤 책들도 쓰지 못했을 거예요. 그녀는 제가 그것들을 쓰도록 영감을 주었고 응원해 주었답니다. 제 이야기들을 녹음본으로 만들어 보라고 하기도 했고요.
여: 그걸 제가 하는 거군요?
남: 맞아요. 이렇게 훌륭하고 아름다운 목소리가 제 작품에 생명력을 불어 넣어 줄 것을 생각하니 기대됩니다.
여: 최선을 다 할게요, Jeffrey.

어휘

pleasure ***n.*** 기쁨, 즐거움 **professional** ***n.*** 전문가 ***a.*** 전문의
field ***n.*** 분야, 들판, 밭 **recommend** ***v.*** 추천하다
I'm flattered 과찬이세요, 영광이에요 **inspire** ***v.*** 영감을 주다
record ***v.*** 녹음하다 **talented** ***a.*** 재능이 있는, 훌륭한
bring ~ to life ~에 생기(활기)를 불어넣다

정답 ①

문제풀이

남자는 책을 썼다고 했으므로 작가임을 알 수 있고, 여자는 남자의 이야기를 녹음본으로 만드는 작업을 자신의 목소리로 한다고 했으므로 성우임을 알 수 있다. 따라서 정답은 ① '작가 — 성우'이다.

총 어휘 수 161

06 그림의 세부 내용 파악

소재 학교 장기자랑을 위한 무대

듣기 대본 해석

여: 아빠, 이 사진 좀 보실래요? 이게 학교 장기자랑을 위해 제가 작업하고 있는 무대예요.
남: 멋지구나. 어디 보자. 달력이 왜 있는 거지? 뒷벽에 있는 것 말이야.
여: 그건 시간의 흐름을 보여주기 위한 거예요.
남: 달력 옆에 창문은 뭐니?
여: 대부분의 등장인물들이 무대 밖에 있는 사람들과 말하기 위해 창문을 이용할 거예요.
남: 그래, 좋은 생각이구나. 무대의 오른쪽에 있는 소파와 커피 테이블이 정말 좋구나.
여: 고마워요. 저도 소파가 좋아요.
남: 꽤 자주 배우들이 거기에 앉아서 이야기할 것 같은데?
여: 네, 맞아요.
남: 무대의 다른 쪽에 쓰러진 나무가 보이네. 그 나무가 소파와 균형을 유지하지만, 그건 매력적이지 않게 보여.
여: 그게 제가 원하는 거예요, 아빠.
남: 네가 그것에 많은 공을 들인 것 같구나. 정말 잘했어.
여: 정말 감사해요, 아빠.

어휘

assume ***v.*** 추정하다, 가장하다 **inviting** ***a.*** 매력적인

정답 ⑤

문제풀이

무대의 오른쪽에 소파와 커피 테이블이 있고 다른 쪽에는 쓰러진 나무(a fallen tree)가 있다고 했는데 그림에서는 쓰러지지 않은 나무가 있으므로 정답은 ⑤번이다.

총 어휘 수 162

07 할 일

소재 수학여행 허가서

듣기 대본 해석

여: Peter, 버스 놓치겠다. 준비 다 안 됐어?
남: 금방 가요, 엄마. 금요일에 가는 수학여행 허가서 찾고 있어요.
여: 나한테 줬잖아. 자, 여기.
남: 이건 허가서가 아니에요!
여: 내가 원본을 잃어버린 것 같아서 그냥 쪽지로 썼어.
남: 이걸 받아줄지 모르겠어요, 엄마.
여: 괜찮아. Towns 선생님께 전화해서 설명할게.
남: 지금 전화해 줄 수 있어요?
여: 알겠어. 지금 전화할게. 너 지금 가야 되잖아. 좋은 하루 보내.

어휘

miss ***v.*** 놓치다 **permission slip** 허가서 **field trip** 수학여행
note ***n.*** 쪽지

정답 ③

문제풀이

대화의 마지막 부분에서 남자는 여자에게 전화해 줄 수 있는지를 물었고 여자는 지금 전화하겠다고 했으므로 정답은 ③ '선생님께 전화하기'이다.

총 어휘 수 95

08 이유

소재 오디션 프로그램의 방청

듣기 대본 해석

여: 어디 다녀왔니, Alan?
남: 책 몇 권을 사러 서점에 다녀왔어.
여: 그게 다야? 왜 그렇게 기뻐 보이니?
남: 실은, 서점에서 돌아오다가 몇 분 전에 전화 한 통을 받았어.
여: 오? 누가 전화했는데?
남: 이 소식을 들으려면 좀 앉는 게 좋겠어. 나 오디션 프로그램 Rising Star K를 서울에 있는 스튜디오에 가서 볼 기회가 생겼어.
여: 와, 네가 그거 정말 보고 싶어 했던 걸 내가 잘 아는데. 축하해!
남: 고마워, Beth. 대략 6개월 전에 그 방청권을 신청했는데, 아무런 응답이 없었거든. 그래서 거의 포기하고 전화가 올 거라고 기대하고 있지 않았었어.
여: 그것 참 놀랍다. 그 기회를 잡기가 얼마나 어려운지 알고 있어. 내 친구들 몇 명도 상당히 오래 전에 너랑 비슷하게 신청했었는데, 아무도 너처럼 전화를 받지 못했어. 그러면 언제 보러 가?
남: 다음 주 금요일. 세상에, 이건 정말로 엄청나. 아직도 믿을 수 없어!
여: 네가 너무 부럽다.

어휘

studio ***n.*** 스튜디오, 방송실, 촬영소 **apply to** ~에 신청하다, 지원하다
envy ***v.*** 부러워하다

정답 ⑤

문제풀이
남자는 6개월 전에 방청 신청을 했던 오디션 프로그램에서 연락이 와서 프로그램을 보러 가게 되었다고 기뻐하고 있으므로 정답은 ⑤ '오디션 프로그램을 방청하게 되어서'이다.

총 어휘 수 173

09 숫자

소재 영화 고르기

듣기 대본 해석
남: 여보, 무슨 영화 골랐어?
여: 좀 걸리긴 했는데 드디어 이걸로 골랐어.
남: Windsor's List? 그거 정말 우울하게 만드는 영화인데 최고 명작들 중 하나야.
여: 나도 그렇다고 들었어. 원래 가격은 30달러였는데 50퍼센트 할인 중이야.
남: 잘 골랐네. 당신이 들고 있는 다른 영화는 뭐야?
여: 아, 이거? 이건 Jake 거야. The Light Crystal이라는 영화야. 10달러 밖에 안 해.
남: 나 어렸을 때 그 영화 많이 좋아했는데. 오, 여기 만화책이랑 같이 있는 다른 버전이 있어.
여: 좋네. 그걸 사는 게 좋겠다. 그는 만화책 무척 좋아하잖아.
남: 응, 근데 이게 4달러 더 비싸. 14달러야.
여: 그래도 괜찮네. 당신 거는 안 사?
남: 원하는 게 없어.
여: 알겠어. 그럼 계산하고 집에 가자.

어휘
depressing ***a.*** 우울하게 만드는 **version** ***n.*** 버전, 판

정답 ①

문제풀이
처음 고른 Windsor's List는 30달러인데 50퍼센트 할인을 한다고 했으므로 15달러이고, 두 번째 고른 The Light Crystal은 만화책과 같이 있는 것이 14달러이므로 두 사람이 지불할 총액은 ① '$29'이다.

총 어휘 수 146

10 언급 유무

소재 신입사원

듣기 대본 해석
여: Anderson 씨, 가장 최근에 했던 사원 면접 때 있었던 Randal Kim을 기억하세요?
남: Randal Kim이요? 아, 여러 언어를 구사했던 사람이요?
여: 네, 그 사람이에요. 그에 대한 나의 첫인상은 매우 강했어요.
남: 그에게 가장 인상적인 것이 뭐였죠?
여: 언어 능력 외에 그는 팀 일원으로서의 능력에 매우 자신감이 있었어요.
남: 저도 그 점에 동의해요. 그를 인터뷰했을 때, 그는 자신감 있어 보이고 아주 동기 부여가 되어 있고 회사에 기여하는 데 열정적으로 보였어요.
여: 제가 그에 대해 좋았던 또 다른 한 가지는 그가 다양한 조직에서 자원봉사를 많이 해왔다는 거예요.
남: 저도 그것을 봤어요. 그는 중국과 폴란드에서 보낸 시간은 말할 것도 없고 아프리카에서 혼자 500시간 이상 자원봉사를 했더군요. 그가 말하길 그의 좌우명은 "뭔가를 하고 싶다면, 그것은 나에게 달려 있다."라고 했어요.
여: 제 생각에는 그가 우리 팀의 중요한 멤버가 될 것 같아요.
남: 저도 그렇게 생각해요.

어휘
initial ***a.*** 처음의, 초기의 **impression** ***n.*** 인상 **confident** ***a.*** 자신감 있는 **motivated** ***a.*** 동기가 부여된 **enthusiastic** ***a.*** 열정적인 **contribute** ***v.*** 기여하다 **not to mention** ~은 말할 것도 없고

정답 ③

문제풀이
남자와 여자는 채용 면접을 본 사람에 대해 이야기하고 있는데, 그의 외국어 능력, 첫인상, 자원봉사 이력, 좌우명에 대해서는 언급했지만 전공에 대한 언급은 하지 않았으므로 정답은 ③ '전공'이다.

총 어휘 수 156

11 내용 일치 · 불일치

소재 안경원숭이의 특징

듣기 대본 해석
여: 안녕하세요, 신사 숙녀 여러분. 오늘 저는 안경원숭이라고 불리는 특별한 작은 동물에 대해 조금 이야기하고 싶습니다. 이 작은 녀석은 필리핀 군도의 남쪽 부근 즉, 보홀섬과 민다나오섬에서 발견됩니다. 안경원숭이는 아주 작은 포유동물입니다. 다 자란 안경원숭이는 여러분의 손바닥에 딱 맞습니다. 안경원숭이를 유명하게 만드는 것은 그것의 커다란 눈입니다. 이 눈은 자리에 고정되어 있지만 안경원숭이는 머리를 양쪽 방향으로 180도 돌릴 수 있습니다. 더 놀라운 것은 안경원숭이의 눈은 믿을 수 없는 야간 시력을 가지고 있다는 것입니다. 최소한의 불빛이 있을 때, 한밤중에도 대낮처럼 잘 볼 수 있게 하기 위해 안경원숭이의 동공은 거의 눈의 크기만큼 확대됩니다. 정말 흥미롭지 않나요? 안경원숭이에 대해 더 알고 싶으시면 필리핀으로 가는 비행기를 타고 가셔서 직접 안경원숭이를 보시기를 제안합니다.

어휘
extraordinary ***a.*** 특별한, 보기 드문 **archipelago** ***n.*** 군도
namely ***ad.*** 즉, 다시 말해 **mammal** ***n.*** 포유동물 **palm** ***n.*** 손바닥
incredible ***a.*** 믿을 수 없는 **expand** ***v.*** 확장하다, 확대하다

정답 ⑤

문제풀이
안경원숭이의 눈은 최소한의 불빛만 있어도 동공이 크게 확대되어 한밤중에도 낮처럼 볼 수 있다고 했으므로 내용과 일치하지 않는 것은 ⑤ '낮에는 시력이 좋지만, 밤에는 잘 볼 수 없다.'이다.

총 어휘 수 152

12 도표

소재 아기 침대 고르기

듣기 대본 해석
남: 여보, 인터넷으로 뭐해?
여: 우리 아기를 위한 침대를 보고 있어. 알다시피 곧 태어나잖아.
남: 맞아. 아기 방에 놓을 것을 생각해 봐야겠어. 좋은 것 찾았어?
여: 음, 이 다섯 개 중에 고르는 게 좋을 거 같아. 이 회사가 질 좋은 침대를 많이 만들기 때문에 평이 좋아.
남: 어디 보자. *[잠시 후]* 낮은 것은 빼는 게 좋겠어. 그래야 아기가 커졌을 때 새로 안 사도 되니까.
여: 맞아. 매트리스도 포함하는 게 좋을 것 같아. 그럼 따로 안 사도 되잖아.
남: 동감이야.
여: 재질은 어떻게 할까? 어떤 것들은 나무로 만들어졌고 다른 건 플라스틱이야.
남: 나무로 하는 게 나을 것 같아. 방이랑 잘 어울릴 거야.
여: 응, 그럼 이 두 개로 선택이 좁혀졌어. 어떤 것이 나은 것 같아?

남: 예산이 좀 빠듯하니까 더 싼 걸로 하자.
여: 좋아. 바로 주문할게.

어휘
crib ***n.*** 아기 침대 **review** ***n.*** 논평, 평가 **mattress** ***n.*** 매트리스 **budget** ***n.*** 예산, 비용

정답 ③

문제풀이
남자와 여자가 아기 침대를 고르는 상황이다. 둘은 높이가 낮은 것은 빼자고 했으므로 ②~⑤번이 해당되는데 매트리스가 포함된 것으로 하자고 했으므로 ④번은 제외된다. 또한, 이들은 나무로 된 침대를 골랐으므로 ③, ⑤번이 남는데 그 중 더 싼 것으로 하자고 했으므로 두 사람이 선택한 침대는 ③번이다.

총 어휘 수 183

13 긴 대화의 응답

소재 유명 화가의 작품 전시회

듣기 대본 해석
남: 우리가 드디어 여기 있다는 게 믿어지지 않아. Banksy의 작품을 예전부터 정말 보고 싶었어.
남: 그가 우리 도시에서 이렇게 전시회를 한다는 게 믿겨지지가 않아.
여: 가자. 닫기 전에 충분히 둘러볼 시간이 있으면 좋겠어.
남: 먼저 표를 사야지.
여: 응. 근데 그가 만든 작품에 비해서 25달러는 좀 싼 것 같아.
남: 응. 분명히 그만큼의 값어치를 충분히 할 거야.
여: 어, 봐봐. 30분 후에 시작하는 투어 그룹이 있어. 기다려서 그 모임이랑 갈까?
남: 근데 그룹으로 가면 그들의 속도에 맞춰야 되잖아. 난 내가 원하는 대로 시간을 갖고 전시회를 즐기고 싶어.
여: 난 화가랑 작품들에 대해서 좀 더 배우는 게 재미있을 것 같아.
남: 그럼 오디오 안내 장치를 하나 빌리면 되겠네. 재미있겠다.
여: ⑤ 그렇게 하면 우리가 설명을 들을지 말지 선택할 수 있겠네.

어휘
exhibition ***n.*** 전시회 **pace** ***n.*** 속도, 걸음 **device** ***n.*** 장치
〈문제〉 **admission** ***n.*** 입장, 입장료

정답 ⑤

문제풀이
여자는 투어 그룹에 들어가서 설명을 듣고 싶어하지만 남자는 원하지 않는 상황에서 남자가 오디오 안내 장치를 빌리자고 제안했으므로 그에 적절한 여자의 대답은 ⑤ '그렇게 하면 우리가 설명을 들을지 말지 선택할 수 있겠네.'이다.

오답 보기 해석
① 그들은 입장료로 너무 많은 돈을 받아.
② 우리가 투어 그룹에 합류하게 돼서 기뻐.
③ 나는 왜 그렇게 많은 사람들이 Banksy의 작품을 사랑하는지 알겠어.
④ 전시회 투어 동안 오디오를 듣는 것은 예의 없는 거야.

총 어휘 수 153

14 긴 대화의 응답

소재 자신이 쓴 글에 대한 조언 부탁

듣기 대본 해석
여: Mike. 바빠? 시간 좀 있어?
남: 그렇게 바쁘지는 않아. 뭐 필요한 거 있어?
여: 학교 신문에 이 글을 실으려고 하고 있거든.
남: 난 네 글 읽는 거 좋아해.
여: 응. 난 쓰는 거 좋아해. 하여튼, 내 글을 읽고 어떤지 말해 줄 사람이 필요해. 건설적인 비판도 해주면 더 좋을 것 같아.
남: 근데 왜 나한테 봐달라고 하는 거야?
여: 실은, 너희 누나 말하는 거야. 그녀가 Kings and Queens 신문사에서 일한다고 하지 않았어?
남: 그렇긴 한데 다음 주까지 출장 가 있어.
여: 내 글을 너희 누나한테 이메일로 보내서 읽어봐 달라고 하면 안 될까?
남: ① 문제없어. 내가 누나한테 연락해서 그녀가 시간이 되는지 알아볼게.

어휘
article ***n.*** 글, 기사 **constructive** ***a.*** 건설적인, 적극적인
criticism ***n.*** 비판 **press** ***n.*** 신문사, 언론사

정답 ①

문제풀이
여자는 남자의 누나에게 자기 글을 이메일로 보내서 검토해주기를 부탁하고 있는 상황이므로 여자의 질문에 대한 남자의 적절한 답은 ① '문제없어. 내가 누나한테 연락해서 그녀가 시간이 되는지 알아볼게.'이다.

오답 보기 해석
② 물론이야. 내가 그것을 검토해서 내일 너한테 돌려줄게.
③ 괜찮긴 하지만 나는 이번 주말 전에 그것을 제출해야 해.
④ 네가 학교 신문과 관련된 일을 얻어서 잘됐어.
⑤ 아니, 그렇지만 내가 너한테 학교 신문 한 부를 꼭 줄게.

총 어휘 수 132

15 상황에 적절한 말

소재 졸업식 연설

듣기 대본 해석
여: Bill은 고등학교 3학년 학생이고 졸업반에서 가장 인기 있는 학생들 중 한 명입니다. 그는 굉장히 똑똑하고 외향적인 성격을 갖고 있습니다. 그의 많은 노력과 인기로 인해 학교의 교장인 Thomas 선생님은 Bill에게 졸업식 때 연설을 부탁했습니다. Bill은 기뻐하면서 이 제안을 받아들였고 연설에 많은 노력을 들여 왔습니다. Bill은 훌륭한 학생이고 여러모로 좋은 사람이지만 사람들 앞에서 말하는 것에 어려움을 겪습니다. 졸업식 전에 Thomas 선생님은 Bill이 긴장하고 있는 것을 발견하고 그에게 격려의 말 몇 마디를 하고 싶어 합니다. 이러한 상황에서 Thomas 선생님이 Bill에게 할 말로 가장 적절한 것은 무엇일까요?
Mr. Thomas: Bill, ① 숨을 깊이 들이쉬렴. 너는 잘할 거야.

어휘
senior ***n.*** 졸업반 학생, 상급생 **principal** ***n.*** 교장 선생님 **notice** ***v.*** 알아차리다 **encouragement** ***n.*** 격려 〈문제〉 **commencement** ***n.*** 졸업식, 학위 수여식, 시작

정답 ①

문제풀이
교장 선생님은 졸업식 연설을 앞두고 긴장하고 있는 Bill에게 격려의 말을 해주고 싶어하는 상황이므로 편안하게 긴장을 풀어주고 격려해 주는 내용인 ① '숨을 깊이 들이쉬렴. 너는 잘할 거야.'가 정답이다.

오답 보기 해석
② 나는 네가 졸업식 연설을 해주었으면 좋겠구나.
③ 나는 네가 연설 수업에서 잘할 거라고 확신해.
④ 고등학교 졸업을 축하해.
⑤ 네가 올해 졸업을 못 한다니 유감이구나.

총 어휘 수 118

16 담화 목적 / 17 세부 내용 파악

소재 휴가 가기 좋은 관광지 푸켓 소개

듣기 대본 해석

남: 매년 똑같은 해변가에 똑같은 여행을 가는 게 지겨우십니까? 올해는 새로운 것을 해보세요. 아름다운 푸켓으로 이국적인 여행을 해보세요. 푸켓은 태국 남쪽에 위치한 섬으로 여러분의 호기심뿐만 아니라 예산도 충족시켜주는 곳입니다. 이 섬에는 매년 푸켓의 문화, 훌륭한 해산물, 그리고 셀 수 없이 많은 해변가 활동들을 체험하는 수많은 관광객들이 찾아옵니다. 세상에서 가장 흰 모래를 갖고 있는 곳들 중 하나로 푸켓은 스쿠버 다이빙과 스노클링을 할 멋진 기회를 제공합니다. 채식 행사와 같은 수 많은 축제들이 여러분의 호기심을 충족하고 마음을 열어줄 것입니다. 파파야, 당근, 향신료, 그리고 다른 진미들을 사용하여 만든 유명한 요리 sum tam을 드셔보세요. 잊을 수 없는 맛일 겁니다. 좀 더 모험을 즐기는 사람이라면 무성한 화초와 고운 해변가로 유명한 Phi Phi섬에 가보세요. Blue Lagoon과 The Beach 같은 영화들을 촬영한 세트장에도 들러 보실 수 있습니다. 지금 바로 여행 계획 잡으시고 아름다운 푸켓으로 오세요!

어휘

exotic ***a.*** 이국적인 **cater** ***v.*** 음식을 공급하다, 충족시키다 **budget** ***n.*** 예산, 비용 **exquisite** ***a.*** 매우 아름다운, 정교한 **delicacy** ***n.*** 진미, 별미, 여림, 연약함 **adventurous** ***a.*** 대담한, 모험을 즐기는 **greenery** ***n.*** 화초 **powdered** ***a.*** 고운, 가루로 만든

정답 16 ⑤ 17 ⑤

문제풀이

16 푸켓에서 즐길 수 있는 다양한 즐길 거리와 먹거리, 볼거리들을 소개하며 여행을 하러 오라고 하는 것으로 보아 남자가 하는 말의 목적으로 가장 적절한 것은 ⑤ '좋은 휴양지를 홍보하려고'이다.

17 남자는 스노클링, 채식 행사(vegetarian festival), 음식 시식(sum tam), 유명한 Phi Phi섬 방문을 언급했으나, 기념품에 대해서는 언급하지 않았으므로 정답은 ⑤ '기념품 제작'이다.

총 어휘 수 180

DICTATION ANSWERS

01 What's the exchange rate

02 a different perspective / makes you wonder which history is true

03 seasonal depression / suffer from vitamin D deficiency / To get an adequate amount / If this is not a possibility

04 My car was broken into / getting an alarm installed / isn't going to stop them / park your car in a well-lit area

05 professional in this field / I'm flattered / record my stories / bring my work to life

06 let me take a look / window next to the calendar / a fallen tree on the other side / you put a lot of thought into this

07 miss the bus / find my permission slip / I just wrote a note / call her now / need to leave

08 got a phone call / won a chance to go / expecting to get the call / quite a while ago

09 That's a really depressing movie / that comes with a comic book / four dollars more expensive

10 spoke several languages / seemed very motivated and enthusiastic / not to mention his time in China and Poland

11 What makes the tarsier famous is / provide tarsiers with incredible night vision / see just as well in the middle of the night

12 they make high-quality cribs / rule out the low-height one / made of wood / kind of on a budget

13 putting on an exhibition / it'll be worth every penny / move at their pace / audio tour devices

14 constructive criticism / out of town on business / ask her to look it over

15 one of the most popular students in / accepted the offer / he struggles with public speaking / words of encouragement

16-17 caters to your curiosities / hundreds of thousands of visitors / satisfy your curiosities / you won't soon forget

23 수능영어듣기 실전모의고사

본문 p.140

01 ①	02 ⑤	03 ⑤	04 ③	05 ③	06 ④
07 ①	08 ①	09 ③	10 ④	11 ⑤	12 ⑤
13 ⑤	14 ②	15 ①	16 ③	17 ③	

01 짧은 대화의 응답

소재 휴대폰 분실

듣기 대본 해석

여: 아빠, 제 휴대폰 어디 있어요? 찾을 수가 없네요.

남: 학교에 가져가지 않았니? 가방 안에 있는지 먼저 보지 그래?

여: 오늘 학교에 가져가지 않았어요. 분명 여기 어딘가에 있어요.

남: ① 확실하니? 그렇다면, 같이 찾아보자꾸나.

어휘

〈문제〉 **guilty** ***a.*** 죄책감이 드는 **fault** ***n.*** 잘못, 책임

정답 ①

문제풀이

휴대폰을 찾고 있는 딸이 학교에 휴대폰을 가져가지 않았고 분명 여기 있을 거라고 말하는 데에 대한 아빠의 적절한 응답은 ① '확실하니? 그렇다면, 같이 찾아보자꾸나.'이다.

오답 보기 해석

② 미안해. 집 밖에서 네 휴대폰을 잃어버렸어.

③ 네가 죄책감을 느낄 필요는 없어. 다 내 잘못이야.

④ 걱정 마. 그것을 학교에서 찾을 수 있을 거야.

⑤ 내가 그것을 언제 마지막으로 갖고 있었는지 기억이 안 나.

총 어휘 수 45

02 짧은 대화의 응답

소재 보고서 준비

듣기 대본 해석

남: Ingrid, 제가 원하는 보고서 찾았어요?

여: 네. 제가 출력했어요. 여기 있어요.

남: 고마워요. *[잠시 후]* 잠시만요. 저는 직원 생산성에 관한 보고서는 필요하지 않아요. 저는 신입사원에 관한 보고서가 필요해요.

여: ⑤ 제가 실수했네요. 지금 당장 올바른 보고서를 출력할게요.

어휘

print out 인쇄하다, 출력하다 **employee** ***n.*** 종업원, 고용인

productivity ***n.*** 생산성 〈문제〉 **correct** ***a.*** 올바른, 적절한

정답 ⑤

문제풀이

남자가 다른 보고서가 필요하다고 말했으므로 그에 적절한 여자의 응답은 ⑤ '제가 실수했네요. 지금 당장 올바른 보고서를 출력할게요.'이다.

오답 보기 해석

① 문제없어요. 도와주게 되어서 항상 기뻐요.

② 물론이죠. 저는 여분의 보고서를 만들 거예요.

③ 제가 보고서를 끝냈고 지금 출력하는 중이에요.

④ 제가 신입사원에 관한 보고서가 필요하다고 당신한테 말했잖아요.

총 어휘 수 47

03 담화 목적

소재 전기 절약 방법

듣기 대본 해석

남: 여러분, 안녕하세요. 요즘 우리는 우리의 에너지 수요를 실컷 만족시키기 위해 너무 많은 석탄, 가스, 전기를 사용하고 있습니다. 이번 여름, 가장 중요한 주제는 전기입니다. 지구 온난화 때문에, 여름이 점점 더워지고 있어서 우리는 에어컨을 더 자주 켜는 경향이 있습니다. 그러나, 이는 문제를 가중시킬 뿐입니다. 우리는 시원함을 유지할 대안을 찾아 실천해야 합니다. 만약에 여러분이 자연광이 충분한 곳에서 일하고 있다면, 여러분은 머리 위의 불을 꺼야 합니다. 또한, 짧은 옷을 입으세요. 요즘 대부분의 회사들은 더 시원한 복장을 입을 수 있도록 복장 규정을 조절하고 있습니다. 마지막으로, 에어컨을 사용하는 대신에, 공기의 자연스러운 흐름을 조절하기 위해 창문을 이용하도록 노력하시고, 창문을 이용할 수 없다면 선풍기를 사용하도록 하세요. 우리 함께 환경에서 변화를 만들어서 시원함을 유지합시다!

어휘

satiate ***v.*** 실컷 만족시키다 **alternative** ***n.*** 대안, 선택 가능한 것

abundant ***a.*** 풍부한 **adjust** ***v.*** 조절하다 **attire** ***n.*** 의복, 복장

utilize ***v.*** 활용하다, 이용하다

정답 ⑤

문제풀이

남자는 요즘 에어컨의 잦은 사용이 문제가 됨을 지적하면서 시원함을 유지할 대안을 찾고 노력해야 한다고 말하며 전기 절약의 방법을 알려주고 있다. 따라서 남자가 말하는 목적으로 가장 적절한 것은 ⑤ '전기 절약을 위한 방법을 알려주려고'이다.

총 어휘 수 138

04 의견

소재 어린이 스페인어 교육

듣기 대본 해석

남: Hamilton 선생님, 좋은 스페인어 책 찾는 것을 도와주시겠어요?

여: 물론이죠. 그런데 왜요, Crowley 선생님? 선생님은 스페인어 교사가 아니잖아요.

남: 제 아들인 Alfred가 스페인어를 배우기 시작해서 제가 집에서 그 애 공부를 도와주고 싶어서요.

여: 좋아요. 그 애는 아마 수업시간에 듣기와 말하기를 연습하고 있을 거예요. 맞나요?

남: 네, 그래서 저는 그 애가 스페인어로 기본 교재 읽기를 배우는 걸 직접 도와주고 싶어요.

여: 제 생각에는 선생님께서 계속 그의 듣기와 말하기 실력에 집중하셔야 할 것 같아요.

남: 정말이요? 그렇지만 제 생각에는 읽기가 새로운 언어를 배우는 첫 번째 단계인 것 같은데요.

여: 읽기는 중요합니다. 하지만 선생님 아들이 영어로 말하기를 어떻게 배웠는지 생각해보세요. 그 애는 듣기와 말하기로 시작했잖아요.

남: 맞아요. 하지만 그 애는 더 나이가 들었고 언어의 기본을 이해하니까 그건 지금과는 다르다고 생각해요.

여: 사실, 모국어를 배우는 것과 같은 방법으로 공부한다면, 제 2언어 심지어 제 3언어조차 더 빨리 배우게 될 거예요.

남: 알겠어요. 조언 고마워요. 제가 조금 더 생각해 볼게요.

어휘

second language 제 2언어(모국어 외에 학교에서나 일을 위해 배워서 사용하는 언어) **native language** 모국어

정답 ③

문제풀이
여자는 영어를 어떻게 배웠는지 생각해보라며 다른 언어 습득도 모국어를 배우듯이 듣기와 말하기로 접근해야 한다고 말하고 있으므로 정답은 ③ '듣기와 말하기로 시작해야 한다.'이다.

총 어휘 수 166

05 심정 파악

소재 프레젠테이션을 앞둔 걱정

듣기 대본 해석
남: 안녕, Sandra. 내일 뉴욕으로 가는 출장 준비는 하고 있니?
여: 갈 준비는 됐지만, 솔직히 내가 가지 않아도 된다면 좋겠어.
남: 정말? 나는 네가 새로운 도시로 여행가게 되어서 정말 좋아할 거라고 생각했는데.
여: 응, 물론 뉴욕은 보고 싶지. 그런데 내가 거기에 도착하자마자 중요한 회의와 프레젠테이션을 하거든.
남: 너는 잘 할거야. 프레젠테이션 잘 하잖아.
여: 고마워. 하지만 고객들이 독일인이라 난 독일어를 써야 해. 내가 엉망으로 할까 봐 걱정돼.
남: 괜찮을 거야. 그들은 독일어가 너의 모국어가 아닌 것을 아니까 만약 네가 작은 실수를 하더라도 문제가 되지는 않을 거야.
여: 나도 그건 이해해. 이건 내 경력에 가장 중요한 프레젠테이션이라 걱정되네. 나 정말 잘해야 해.
남: 가장 중요한 건 긴장을 푸는 거야. 회의 준비가 되었으니 지금은 그것에 대해 잊으려고 해보고 네가 휴가를 위해 뉴욕으로 떠난다고 상상을 해봐.
여: 좋아. 해보겠지만 쉽지는 않을 것 같아.

어휘
mess up 엉망으로 만들다 **matter** ***v.*** 중요하다, 문제되다
〈문제〉 **elated** ***a.*** 신이 난 **anxious** ***a.*** 불안해하는, 염려하는
determined ***a.*** 단호한, 완강한 **envious** ***a.*** 부러워하는 **upset** ***a.*** 속상한, 마음이 상한

정답 ③

문제풀이
여자는 뉴욕으로 출장을 가는데 도착하자마자 아주 중요한 회의와 프레젠테이션이 있고, 그것을 독일어로 해야 해서 망치게 될까 봐 걱정하고 있다. 따라서 여자의 심정은 ③ '불안해하고 걱정하는'이 적절하다.

오답 보기 해석
① 조용하고 우아한
② 신이 나고 활기 넘치는
④ 의기양양하고 단호한
⑤ 부러워하고 화가 난

총 어휘 수 180

06 그림의 세부 내용 파악

소재 National Education Fund의 포스터

듣기 대본 해석
남: National Education Fund를 위해 만들어진 새 광고를 본 적 있습니까? 그 기금은 수입이 적은 성인이나 가족이 없는 아이들에게 대학까지 모든 교육을 위한 비용을 지불해 주기 위해 만든 것입니다. 포스터의 제목은, "모두를 위한 더 나은 미래"입니다. 그림의 중간에 공중으로 자신들의 모자를 던지는 대학 졸업생들이 있습니다. 포스터의 아랫부분에는 세 개의 그림이 더 있습니다. 왼쪽에는 유치원 교실에서 색칠을 하고 있는 행복한 아이가 있습니다. 중간에는 벤치에 앉아 함께 식사하고 있는 소녀들이 있습니다. 그리고 오른쪽에는 두 젊은 전문가들이 손을 맞잡고 있는 사진이 있습니다. 이 포스터는 National Education Fund로부터 혜택을 받을 수 있는 모든 다른 종류의 사람들을 보여주려 하고 있습니다.

어휘
income ***n.*** 소득, 수입 **graduate** ***n.*** 대학 졸업생 **benefit from** ~로부터 이익을 얻다

정답 ④

문제풀이
포스터의 중간 부분에는 모자를 공중으로 던지는 졸업생들이, 아랫부분에는 세 개의 그림이 있다고 했다. 세 그림 중 왼쪽에는 유치원 교실에서 색칠하는 아이가, 가운데는 벤치에 앉아 어떤 것을 먹고 있는 소녀들이, 오른쪽에는 두 젊은 전문가들이 손을 맞잡고 있는 사진이 있다고 했는데, 가운데 그림은 소녀들이 책을 읽고 있으므로 ④번이 내용과 일치하지 않는다.

총 어휘 수 134

07 부탁한 일

소재 교환학생 홈스테이

듣기 대본 해석
남: 좋은 아침이에요 여보. 당신, 뭐하고 있어요?
여: 이 지원서를 작성하고 있어요. Katie의 학교에서 하는 홈스테이 프로그램에 낼 거예요.
남: 홈스테이 프로그램이라고요? 외국 교환학생 같은 거 맞죠?
여: 맞아요. Katie네 학교가 다른 나라에서 온 몇몇 학생들을 초대할 예정이거든요.
남: 재미있겠는데요. 그리고 당신은 그 학생들 중 한 명을 여기에 머물게 하고 싶은 거죠?
여: 그러고 싶어요. Katie와 우리에게 멋진 경험이 될 거예요.
남: 맞아요. 그런데, 이 학생들은 어느 나라에서 오는 거예요?
여: 두 명은 한국에서 오고, 한 명은 대만에서 와요. Katie가 아시아의 생활 방식과 문화에 대해서 배울 기회를 가지게 돼서 좋을 거예요.
남: 나도 그 사람들의 문화에 대해서 더 많이 배우고 싶어요. 내가 도와줄 수 있는 게 뭐예요?
여: 음, 신청서와 함께 보낼 가족 사진이 필요할 거예요. 작년 크리스마스 때 찍은 사진 찾아줄 수 있어요?
남: 네. 어디 있는지 알 것 같아요.
여: 좋아요. 고마워요.

어휘
fill out 작성하다, 기입하다 **application** ***n.*** 지원(서), 신청(서) **host** ***v.*** 주최하다

정답 ①

문제풀이
대화의 끝부분에서 여자는 남자에게 작년 크리스마스 때 찍은 가족 사진을 찾아달라고 부탁했으므로 정답은 ① '가족 사진 찾아주기'이다.

총 어휘 수 157

08 이유

소재 버스 여행

듣기 대본 해석
여: Dylan, 이번 주에 Lilly랑 내가 함께 산으로 버스 여행가기로 했는데 너도 같이 갈 수 있는지 궁금해.
남: 좋을 것 같아. 이번 여름에 산으로 가고 싶었거든.
여: 근데 긴 여행일 거야. 너 차멀미 한 적 있어?
남: 어렸을 적엔 버스 탈 때 멀미를 하기도 했는데 지금은 괜찮아. 표가 얼마지?

여: 내 친구가 계획이 바뀌는 바람에 내가 표 세 장을 얻었어. 그래서 돈을 낼 필요가 없어.
남: 멋지다!
여: 응. 날씨 예보 때문에 걱정했었는데 날씨도 좋을 것 같아.
남: 잘됐다. 토요일 몇 시에 출발하니?
여: 토요일? 실은 금요일 정오에 출발해.
남: 정말? 오, 이런. 나 금요일에는 일해야 해.
여: 아, 아쉽다. Lilly가 너와 함께 가기를 정말로 원했는데.
남: 다음 번에 같이 갈 수 있겠지. 그래도 초대해줘서 고마워.

어휘
carsick *a.* 차멀미를 하는 **forecast** *n.* 예측, 예보 **depart** *v.* 떠나다, 출발하다

정답 ①

문제풀이
대화의 마지막 부분에서 여자가 금요일 정오에 출발한다고 하자 남자는 금요일에는 일을 해야 한다고 했으므로 남자가 여행에 가지 못하는 이유는 ① '일을 해야 해서'이다.

총 어휘 수 160

09 숫자

소재 야구 경기 표와 배너 구매

듣기 대본 해석
[전화벨이 울린다.]
남: 여보세요, 매표소입니다.
여: 안녕하세요. 곧 있을 경기의 표를 사는 것 때문에 전화드렸어요.
남: 그렇군요. LA Dodgers 경기의 표와 Chicago Cubs 경기의 표 중 어느 것을 사려고 하나요?
여: 사실 둘 다요. 근데 얼마죠?
남: LA Dodgers 표는 60달러이고 Chicago Cubs 표는 80달러입니다.
여: 제가 생각했던 것보다 비싸네요. 더 싼 표는 없나요?
남: 죄송해요. 이 경기들 표는 남은 게 이것들 밖에 없어요.
여: 그렇군요. LA Dodgers 표만 하나 살게요. 홈팀의 배너들을 파는 것도 봤는데, 표와 함께 무료로 오나요?
남: 배너는 20달러를 추가로 내셔야 합니다.
여: 네, 그럼 배너도 같이 살게요. 배송비는 가격에 포함된 건가요?
남: 죄송하지만 배송비로 5달러를 따로 내셔야 합니다.
여: 알겠어요. 돈은 최대한 빨리 입금해 드릴게요.

어휘
upcoming *a.* 다가오는, 곧 있을 **banner** *n.* 배너, 현수막
shipping *n.* 배송 **transfer** *v.* 옮기다, 이송하다

정답 ③

문제풀이
여자는 60달러짜리 LA Dodgers 표 한 장과 20달러짜리 현수막을 구매하였고, 배송비 5달러를 추가로 지불해야 하므로 총 송금할 금액은 ③ '$85'이다.

총 어휘 수 145

10 언급 유무

소재 북극의 빙하

듣기 대본 해석
여: Todd, 어젯밤에 환경에 대한 다큐멘터리 봤어요?
남: 아니요, 놓쳤어요. 무엇에 대한 거였죠?
여: 주요 주제 중 하나가 북극의 빙하가 녹고 있다는 거였어요.
남: 심각한 문제가 되고 있죠?
여: 그래요. 얼음이 태양 광선을 반사함으로써 지구가 과열되는 것을 막아 주는 거울과 같은 작용을 하거든요.
남: 정말이요? 나는 그런지 몰랐어요.
여: 네. 대부분의 사람들이 몰라요. 2009년 이후로, 사람들은 의식을 높이려 많이 노력했고 녹는 것을 막으려고 해왔어요.
남: 그건 정말 중요한 일인 것 같아요. 진전이 있었나요?
여: 조금씩이요. 그래도 갈 길이 멀어요.
남: 그래서 더 큰 문제가 녹는 것 때문에 생기는 거죠?
여: 네, 맞아요. 그것은 지구 기후에 큰 영향을 주지요. 이것이 전 세계 바다의 수면이 높아지게 만들어서 해변가의 도시들이 결국 물에 잠기게 될 위험에 처해 있다는 것도 문제의 일부예요.
남: 오, 이런. 세계 인구의 대부분이 해안이나 근처에 살고 있다고 들었어요.
여: 네. 하지만 그 변화가 자연스러운 순환의 한 부분이라고 믿는 몇몇 과학자들도 있어요. 누가 옳은지 말하는 것은 어려운 일이지만 어느 쪽이든 확실히 중요한 문제죠.

어휘
polar *a.* 극지의 **ice cap** 빙원(만년설) **reflect** *v.* 반사하다
make progress 진행하다, 전진하다 **coastal** *a.* 해안의
at risk 위험에 처한

정답 ④

문제풀이
지구에서 빙하의 역할, 해빙을 막기 위한 사람들의 노력, 해수면의 높이에 주는 영향, 다른 의견을 가진 과학자들에 대해서는 언급되었지만 빙하가 녹는 것을 막는 방법에 대한 언급은 없으므로 정답은 ④ '빙하가 녹는 것을 막는 방법'이다.

총 어휘 수 202

11 내용 일치 · 불일치

소재 가수 Brittany Spikes에 대한 소개

듣기 대본 해석
남: 안녕하세요, 여러분. 저는 우리 시대 가장 위대한 가수 중 한 명인 Brittany Spikes를 소개하려 합니다. 그녀는 전형적인 미국 가정에서 태어났고 Bertha Beatrice로 불렸습니다. 그녀가 7살이 되었을 때 노래와 춤을 훈련받기 시작했습니다. 그녀는 떠오르는 어린 가수와 댄서들을 위한 어린이 탤런트 쇼, Mickey Mouse Club에 처음 출연했습니다. 그녀는 16살이 될 때까지 쇼에서 공연했습니다. 그 동안 그녀는 화려한 댄스 동작과 애교 있는 미소로 많은 인기를 얻었습니다. 그녀는 겨우 20살이 되었을 때 Hollywood 영화감독 Albert Foster와 2001년 5월에 결혼했습니다. Foster는 그녀의 젊은 가수로서 밝은 미래를 보았고 음악 사업에 그녀를 투입시키기로 결정했습니다. 오늘날, Brittany는 여전히 차트 정상에 있고 전 세계의 팬들에게 기쁨을 주고 있습니다.

어휘
up-and-coming *a.* 전도유망한, 떠오르는 **gain popularity** 인기를 얻다 **flashy** *a.* 화려한 **winning** *a.* 애교 있는, 마음을 끄는
delight *v.* 기쁨을 주다

정답 ⑤

문제풀이
Brittany는 결혼을 한 후, 음악 사업에 투입되었고, 여전히 차트 정상에 있다고 했으므로 일치하지 않는 것은 ⑤ '지금은 가수 활동을 하지 않고 있다.'이다.

총 어휘 수 135

12 도표

소재 숙소 정하기

듣기 대본 해석

여: 학기가 거의 끝났네요. Amber가 여름 방학 때문에 대단히 들떠 있어요.

남: 사실 나도 그래요. 가까운 게스트 하우스에 머물면서 잠시 휴식을 취했으면 좋겠어요.

여: 좋을 것 같아요.

남: 좋아요. 내가 인터넷에서 찾아서 숙소 목록을 만들었어요. 우리가 하루 당 지출할 수 있는 금액이 얼마죠?

여: 가능하면 하루에 70달러가 넘지 않도록 노력해야 할 것 같아요.

남: 네. 이 지역 중에 당신은 어디서 묵었으면 좋겠어요?

여: 저는 가능하면 바다 옆에 묵었으면 좋겠어요. 우리가 신발을 벗어놓고 모래 해변을 걸을 수 있다면 멋있을 것 같아요.

남: 알았어요. 우리가 찾는 모든 것을 갖춘 것 같은 숙소가 두 개 있네요. 어디가 당신한테 제일 좋아 보여요?

여: 물론 아침 식사가 포함된 곳이죠. 아침엔 어떤 요리도 하지 싶지 않아요.

남: 좋아요. 내가 바로 전화해서 예약할게요.

어휘

guesthouse ***n.*** 여행자용 숙소　**sandy** ***a.*** 모래로 뒤덮인
make a reservation 예약하다

정답 ⑤

문제풀이

하루에 70달러가 넘지 않았으면 좋겠다고 했으므로 ②번이 제외되고, 바다 옆에 묵었으면 좋겠다고 했으므로 ①번과 ⑤번으로 좁혀지는데 아침 식사가 포함되었으면 좋겠다고 했으므로 정답은 ⑤번이다.

총 어휘 수 163

13 긴 대화의 응답

소재 졸업식에서의 인사

듣기 대본 해석

여: 졸업을 축하해, Dr. Nathan. 네가 자랑스러워.

남: 네가 와줘서 기뻐, Layla.

여: 남자친구 졸업식을 놓칠 리가 없잖아.

남: 어머니도 여기 오셨으면 정말 좋았을 텐데.

여: 어머님이 졸업식을 놓쳐서 정말 안 됐어.

남: 어쨌든 모든 의대 친구들이 모두 와줬어.

여: 그들을 빨리 만나보고 싶다.

남: 있잖아, Layla, 너를 안 만났더라면 난 지금 여기에 있지 못했을 거야.

여: 오, 아니야! 그렇게 많이 도와주지도 않았는걸.

남: 내가 최선을 다할 수 있도록 영감을 줬어.

여: 천만에, Nathan. 별로 대단한 것도 아니었는데.

남: ⑤ 난 진심으로 고마워. 그리고 네 도움에 대해 너한테 신세를 많이 졌어.

어휘

graduation ***n.*** 졸업식　**be proud of** ~을 자랑스러워하다
make it 해내다, 성공하다　**show up** 나타나다　**inspire** ***v.*** 영감을 주다　〈문제〉 **owe** ***v.*** ~덕분이다, 신세를 지다

정답 ⑤

문제풀이

남자가 여자에게 졸업하는 데 도움을 줬다며 고마움을 표하고 있는 상황이므로 남자의 응답은 ⑤ '난 진심으로 고마워. 그리고 네 모든 도움에 대해 너한테 신세를 많이 졌어.'가 적절하다.

오답 보기 해석

① 너는 열심히 했고 그 학위를 받았어.
② 나는 병원에서 인턴을 어떻게 하는지에 대한 조언이 좀 필요해.
③ 그는 우리 학교에서 가장 인기 있는 의사 선생님 중 한 분이셔.
④ 어머니는 외국에서 일하고 계셔서 오실 수가 없었어.

총 어휘 수 117

14 긴 대화의 응답

소재 저널리스트가 되고 싶은 학생

듣기 대본 해석

남: Collins 선생님, 시간 좀 있으세요?

여: 그래, Aron. 무슨 일이니?

남: 음, 지난 주에 내 주신 실화 문학 프로젝트 아시죠? 그걸 하면서 영감을 많이 얻었어요. 저는 저널리스트가 되고 싶어요.

여: 잘 됐네. 난 늘 너의 작품을 읽는 걸 좋아했단다.

남: 감사해요. 시나 단편소설 쓰는 건 별로인데 실화에 대해 쓰는 건 굉장히 흥미롭고 재미있어요. 그런데 제 실화 문학 프로젝트에 문제가 하나 있어요.

여: 오, 그게 뭔데?

남: 음, 그 글이 500자여야 되는 건 알지만 그 정도로 못 줄일 것 같아요.

여: 그럼 몇 자를 썼니?

남: 거의 1,000자 썼어요. 괜찮을까요?

여: ② 괜찮아. 네 글을 빨리 읽고 싶구나.

어휘

literary ***a.*** 문학의　**inspire** ***v.*** 영감을 주다　**journalist** ***n.*** 저널리스트, 기자　**be into** ~에 관심이 많다　**article** ***n.*** 글, 기사

정답 ②

문제풀이

여자가 내 준 과제가 500자여야 하는데 남자는 자신의 글이 1,000자가 되었다며 괜찮은지 물었으므로 그에 적절한 대답은 ② '괜찮아. 네 글을 빨리 읽고 싶구나.'이다.

오답 보기 해석

① 이 기사를 읽어봐. 내가 제일 좋아하는 것 중 하나야.
③ 내가 너에게 작가가 되도록 영감을 주었다니 기쁘구나.
④ 내가 너를 도와주고 싶지만 나는 저널리스트가 아니야.
⑤ 넌 내일 전에 그것을 꼭 마쳐야 해.

총 어휘 수 126

15 상황에 적절한 말

소재 자전거 타이어 교체

듣기 대본 해석

남: Craig은 자전거 정비공입니다. 그는 Tate 부인의 자전거를 손보고 있는데 그 자전거는 일 년 이상 손을 보지 않아서 부드럽게 나가지 않습니다. 그는 체인, 페달과 브레이크에 녹이 많이 슨 것을 알았습니다. 이 부분에 기름칠을 하자 이들이 좀 더 부드럽게 작동했습니다. 그는 또한 타이어의 접지면이 꽤 얇게 닳아서, 교체할 필요가 있다는 걸 발견했습니다. 만약에 Tate 부인이 이 바퀴들로 계속 탄다면 바퀴들이 닳아 구멍이 나고, 이는 사고를 유발할 수도 있습니다. Craig은 Tate 부인에게 해결책을 추천하고 싶습니다. 이런 상황에서, Craig은 Tate 부인에게 뭐하고 말할 것 같은가요?

Craig: ① 타이어가 너무 낡아서 즉시 교체하셔야 합니다.

어휘

rust ***n.*** 녹　**tread** ***n.*** (타이어의) 접지면　**wear** ***v.*** 닳다, 해어지다
〈문제〉 **properly** ***ad.*** 제대로, 적절히

정답 ①

문제풀이
자전거 정비공인 Craig은 Tate 부인의 자전거의 여러 부분을 손 본 후, 타이어 교체 시기가 지나서 너무 닳아 있음을 발견했고 해결책을 Tate 부인에게 추천하고자 하므로 정답은 ① '타이어가 너무 낡아서 즉시 교체하셔야 합니다.'이다.

오답 보기 해석
② 자전거를 제대로 관리하지 않으신 게 분명해요.
③ 브레이크가 제대로 작동하도록 확실히 할게요.
④ 작년에 타이어를 교체하신 것 같네요.
⑤ 당신 자전거가 상태가 좋아 보이네요.

총 어휘 수 118

16 담화 주제 / 17 세부 내용 파악

소재 스포츠 종류에 따른 신발 선택의 필요성

듣기 대본 해석
여: 매일 당신의 발은 스트레스를 많이 받습니다. 이러한 스트레스를 풀어주는 데에 신발이, 특히 운동 선수들에게, 매우 중요한 작용을 한다는 것은 놀랄 일도 아닙니다. 적절한 신발을 신는 것은 당신의 발목과 발을 지탱해 주면서 부상을 방지할 수 있습니다. 다른 운동들은 발에 다른 방식으로 긴장을 줍니다. 그러므로 당신이 참여하는 운동에 적절한 신발을 골라야 합니다. 예를 들어, 장거리 육상 선수는 발 뒤꿈치를 받쳐주면서 계속되는 쿵쿵거림에 쿠션을 제공해주는 신발을 골라야 합니다. 반면에 테니스와 배드민턴은 이쪽과 저쪽으로 많이 움직여야 합니다. 만약 당신이 이러한 스포츠를 한다면, 이런 활동을 도와줄 수 있는 신발을 찾아야 합니다. 농구에서는 점프하고, 코트에서 뛰고 방향 전환을 하기 위해 안정감이 요구됩니다. 그렇기 때문에 농구에는 하이탑 신발이 필요합니다. 보시다시피 신발은 종목에 따라 달라집니다. 다음 번에 운동화를 사려고 할 때 이 점을 기억해 두는 것이 좋을 것입니다.

어휘
factor *n.* 요인 **suitable** *a.* 적합한 **strain** *n.* 부담, 압박 *v.* (근육 등에) 무리를 주다 **sufficient** *a.* 충분한 **constant** *a.* 끊임없는, 거듭되는 **pound** *v.* 치다, 쿵쾅거리다 **in regards to** ~에 관해서 **stability** *n.* 안정, 안정성 **vary from ~ to** ~에서 ~까지 다양하다

정답 16 ③ 17 ③

문제풀이
16 여자는 운동에 따라 발에 다른 방식으로 긴장을 주기 때문에 각 운동에 맞게 다른 신발을 신어야 한다고 말하고 있으므로 여자가 하는 말의 주제는 ③ '다른 운동 종목에 다른 스타일의 신발이 필요한 이유'이다.
17 여자는 달리기, 테니스, 배드민턴, 농구는 언급했지만 축구는 언급하지 않았으므로 정답은 ③ '축구'이다.

오답 보기 해석
16
① 스포츠의 종류에 따라 어떻게 발에 긴장을 주는가
② 운동 전 스트레칭의 이점
④ 운동할 때 신발을 신는 것의 중요성
⑤ 하이탑 운동화의 장점과 단점

17
① 달리기
② 테니스
④ 배드민턴
⑤ 농구

총 어휘 수 183

DICTATION ANSWERS

01 bring it to school

02 the employee productivity reports

03 in order to satiate our energy needs / alternatives for staying cool / allow for cooler / try to utilize

04 continue to focus on his listening / the first step to learning any new language / understands the basics of language

05 honestly, I wish I didn't have to go / I might mess it up / try to forget about

06 adults with low incomes / in the air / The poster tries to show

07 filling out this application / foreign exchange students / get a chance to learn about

08 taking a bus trip to the mountains / Do you ever get carsick / work on Friday / get together some other time

09 ticket to an upcoming game / Is shipping included in the cost

10 melting of the polar ice caps / been working on raising awareness / effect on the global climate / an increase in the water levels

11 She was born / gained a lot of popularity / saw a bright future for / still tops the charts

12 we can afford per night / stay by the ocean / includes breakfast

13 on your graduation / I can't wait to / inspired me to try my hardest

14 really inspired me / I'm not so into poetry / Will that be okay

15 a lot of rust on the chain / need to be replaced / will likely wear through / recommend a solution

16-17 Wearing suitable shoes / providing support for your heels / require stability / Keep this in mind

24 수능영어듣기 실전모의고사

본문 p.146

01 ②	02 ④	03 ④	04 ②	05 ④	06 ⑤
07 ④	08 ③	09 ③	10 ③	11 ⑤	12 ③
13 ④	14 ④	15 ④	16 ①	17 ④	

01 짧은 대화의 응답

소재 잃어버린 전화기

듣기 대본 해석

남: Lucy, 내가 너한테 계속 전화 했었어. 우리 버스 함께 타기로 했었잖아.
여: 미안해. 나 전화기를 잃어버렸어. 어디에서도 그것을 찾을 수가 없어.
남: 나도 이전에 똑같은 문제가 있었어. 네가 마지막으로 전화기를 가지고 있었던 곳을 기억하니?
여: ② 음, 직장에서 사용한 건 확실해.

어휘

be supposed to V ~하기로 되어 있다 **anywhere** ***ad.*** 어디에서도

정답 ②

문제풀이

남자가 여자에게 전화기를 마지막으로 사용한 장소를 기억하는지를 물었으므로 적절한 응답은 ② '음, 직장에서 사용한 건 확실해.'이다.

오답 보기 해석

① 그것은 검정색 케이스가 있는 uPhone 6야.
③ 걱정하지 마. 나는 네가 그것을 집에 두고 왔다는 것을 확신해.
④ 나도 그렇게 생각했지만, 난 이미 버스를 확인했어.
⑤ 우리가 그것을 찾을 수 있는지 알아보기 위해 내가 다시 네 전화기에 전화해 볼게.

총 어휘 수 51

02 짧은 대화의 응답

소재 리포트 수정

듣기 대본 해석

여: Edward, 너의 리포트 검토를 끝냈단다.
남: 어떤가요? 리포트에 어떤 문제가 있나요, Jones 선생님?
여: 큰 실수는 없어. 하지만 이 예시는 삭제하는 게 좋겠다. 주제랑 관련이 없어.
남: ④ 맞아요. 바로 수정할게요.

어휘

eliminate ***v.*** 없애다, 제거하다 **irrelevant** ***a.*** 관련이 없는
〈문제〉 **fit well** 잘 어울리다, 잘 맞다

정답 ④

문제풀이

여자는 남자의 리포트 검토를 끝낸 후 예시를 삭제하는 것이 좋겠다는 충고를 하였다. 이에 대해 적절한 대답은 ④ '맞아요. 바로 수정할게요.'이다.

오답 보기 해석

① 전 그렇게 생각하지 않아요. 그건 유용한 예시가 아니에요.
② 그렇다면, 같은 예시를 사용할게요.
③ 동의해요. 그건 좋은 리포트예요.
⑤ 훌륭해요. 이곳에 딱 맞네요.

총 어휘 수 44

03 담화 목적

소재 안전한 뱃놀이를 위한 조언

듣기 대본 해석

여: 안녕하세요. 제 이름은 Jenny Brown이며 Minnesota주 수상 안전과의 관리자입니다. 오늘 저는 저희 호수와 강에서 안전하고 깨끗한 여름을 보내기 위해 모두가 명심해야 할 사항들을 공유하고자 합니다. 뱃놀이를 하는 동안, 배 위에 항상 있어야 하는 몇 가지 필수적인 물품들이 있습니다. 예를 들어, 배에 있는 구명조끼의 수는 배의 최대 승객 수용인원과 같아야 하고, 모든 배에는 제대로 작동하는 소화기, 경적이나 호각, 그리고 조명이 구비되어 있어야 합니다. 이러한 장비들을 배에 구비하는 것뿐만 아니라, 조명이 잘 작동하는지 항상 확인해야 합니다. 여러분이 물 위에 있을 때 이런 조언들을 잘 따르면 모두가 호수와 강에서 더 안전하고 재미있게 즐기실 수 있습니다. 수상 안전에 대해 더 많은 것을 알고 싶으시면 저희 웹사이트 www.MNwaterfun.gov를 방문하세요. 시간 내 주셔서 감사 드리며 멋진 여름 보내시기 바랍니다.

어휘

tip ***n.*** 조언 **ensure** ***v.*** 보장하다 **essential** ***a.*** 필수적인
on board 승선하여, 탑승하여 **life vest** 구명조끼 **vessel** ***n.*** 배
capacity ***n.*** 용량, 수용력 **be equipped with** ~을 구비하다
fire extinguisher 소화기 **horn** ***n.*** 경적, 뿔나팔 **spotlight** ***n.*** 조명

정답 ④

문제풀이

여름철 호수나 강에서 뱃놀이를 할 때 안전을 위해 점검하고 지켜야 할 사항들을 조언하고 있다. 따라서 여자가 하는 말의 목적은 ④ '안전한 뱃놀이를 위한 점검 항목들을 알려주려고'가 된다.

총 어휘 수 164

04 의견

소재 인간의 즐거움을 위한 동물의 사용

듣기 대본 해석

여: 이번 주말에 서커스 갈 생각이야. 같이 가자. 곰이랑 코끼리가 재주 부리는 거 보는 게 재미있어.
남: 물어봐 줘서 고마워. 근데 서커스가 그 동물들에게 하는 짓이 윤리적인지 모르겠어.
여: 무슨 말이야? 난 그게 사람들이 동물들의 지능과 노력에 감탄할 수 있는 방법이라고 생각하는데.
남: 서커스단에 있는 동물들이 당하는 학대에 대해서 요즘 많이 읽어왔어. 어떤 동물들은 처벌 받으면서 훈련을 받아.
여: 그게 사실일지 몰라도 동물들이 사육사랑 가깝고 긴밀한 관계를 갖고 있다고도 들었어.
남: 아마 그럴지도. 하지만 동물들은 작은 우리에 갇혀 있고 억지로 사람들을 즐겁게 해줘야 돼.
여: 그렇구나. 글쎄, 조건만 괜찮으면 서커스도 동물들에게 좋은 경험이 될 수 있다고 생각하지 않아?
남: 아니, 그렇게 생각하지 않아. 사람들을 즐겁게 해주기 위해서 동물들이 학대를 받는 것은 정말 잔인한 거라고 생각해.
여: 알겠어. 나도 서커스를 지지하는 걸 다시 생각해 봐야겠어.

어휘

ethical ***a.*** 윤리적인, 도덕적인 **abuse** ***v.*** 학대하다, 폭력을 가하다
victim ***n.*** 피해자, 희생자 **entertain** ***v.*** 즐겁게 해 주다

정답 ②

문제풀이
남자는 인간의 즐거움을 위해 동물을 훈련시키고 가두어 두는 것은 윤리적이지 않고 학대하는 것이라고 생각하고 있으므로 남자의 의견으로 적절한 것은 ② '인간의 즐거움을 위해 동물을 훈련시키는 것은 옳지 않다.'이다.

총 어휘 수 165

05 대화자의 관계 파악

소재 오토바이 사고를 당한 피해자와 구급대원의 대화

듣기 대본 해석
남: 안녕하세요. 당신이 사고가 나서 도움을 필요로 하시던 분인가요?
여: 네, 저 맞아요. 좀 심각한 것 같아요. 걸을 수가 없어요.
남: 알겠습니다. 일단 가만히 계시고 움직이지 마세요. 무슨 일이 있었나요?
여: 오토바이를 탄 어떤 사람이 인도로 와서 제가 걷고 있는데 치고 갔어요.
남: 정말 끔찍하네요. 어떻게 생겼는지 혹시 보셨나요?
여: 아뇨. 근데 헬멧과 가죽재킷을 입고 있었어요.
남: 경찰에는 연락하셨나요?
여: 아뇨. 정신이 없었어요.
남: 제가 경찰에 전화하도록 하겠습니다.
여: 감사합니다.
남: 그건 그렇고, 부상이 얼마나 심한지 알기 위해 몇 가지 테스트를 하겠습니다. 먼저 다리를 이렇게 뻗게 할겁니다. 아프세요?
여: 아야! 네, 아파요.
남: 저기, 아무래도 다리가 부러진 것 같습니다. 엑스레이를 찍기 위해 병원으로 이송해 드려야겠습니다.

어휘
assistance ***n.*** 도움 **still** ***a.*** 가만히 있는, 정지한 **leather** ***n.*** 가죽
contact ***v.*** 연락하다 **extent** ***n.*** 정도 **extend** ***v.*** 뻗다

정답 ④

문제풀이
여자는 오토바이 뺑소니를 당했고, 남자가 부상 정도를 확인하고 있는 것으로 보아 두 사람은 ④ '구급 대원 — 신고자' 관계임을 알 수 있다.

총 어휘 수 154

06 그림의 세부 내용 파악

소재 복도 안전 포스터

듣기 대본 해석
여: 아빠, 제가 만든 우리 학교 복도 안전 포스터를 좀 보세요.
남: 잘 그렸네. 왼쪽에 있는 아이들은 뭐 하고 있는 거야?
여: 세면대에서 놀고 있는데 그건 규칙에 위반되는 행동이에요. 저 물웅덩이에 누가 미끄러질지도 몰라요.
남: 띠를 두르고 있는 사람은 누구야?
여: 복도 감독관이에요. 규칙을 집행하는 데에 도움을 주고 학생들은 항상 그들의 말을 들어야 해요.
남: 그렇구나. 이 애들은 복도에서 뛰고 있는 거야?
여: 네, 맞아요. 사람들한테 학교에서 하면 안 되는 것들을 보여주려고요.
남: 맞아. 그리고 문을 열어 놓는 것도 위험한 거지?
여: 네. 사람들이 가다가 부딪혀서 다칠 수 있으니까 문을 항상 닫고 다녀야 돼요.
남: 뒤쪽에 있는 둥그런 시계가 맘에 들어. 추가적으로 잘 넣은 것 같아.
여: 고마워요, 아빠. 우리 학교에 있는 시계들은 다 저렇게 생겼어요.
남: 그러니? 하여튼 아주 잘 그렸네.

어휘
hallway ***n.*** 복도 **slip** ***v.*** 미끄러지다 **puddle** ***n.*** 웅덩이
monitor ***n.*** 감독관 **enforce** ***v.*** 집행하다, 강요하다

정답 ⑤

문제풀이
대화의 마지막 부분에서 남자가 둥그런 시계가 마음에 든다고 했는데, 그림에는 네모 모양의 시계가 걸려 있으므로 정답은 ⑤번이다.

총 어휘 수 149

07 할 일

소재 야외활동 장비 대 바겐세일

듣기 대본 해석
여: Charlie, Fat Panda Outfitters에서 야외활동 장비를 크게 세일하는 거 같던데.
남: 알아. 오늘 아침에 거기 잠시 들러서 새 하이킹화를 샀어. 좋은 제품들이 많아.
여: 나는 다음 주에 이틀 동안 하이킹을 갈 거라서, 캠핑 장비를 살까 생각 중이야.
남: 거기에 가능한 빨리 가야 해. 캠핑 장비 구역에는 많은 사람들이 있었어.
여: 그러면 서둘러야겠네. 오, 내가 캠프용 휴대 스토브를 사야 한다고 생각하니? 이번이 나의 첫 번째 여행이라서 말이야.
남: 글쎄, 네가 가지고 간 음식을 요리하기 위해서는 아마도 캠프용 휴대 스토브가 필요할 거야. 피크닉 가거나 산에 당일 여행 갈 때는 그게 또 꽤 유용하거든.
여: 알았어. 그렇다면 하나 사야겠네.
남: 거기에 어떻게 갈 거야? 너의 차는 정비소에 있잖아.
여: 좋은 지적이야. 거기에 어떻게 갈지 잘 모르겠네.
남: 내가 너를 태워 줄 수 있을 것 같은데. 오늘은 내가 쉬는 날이고, 하루 종일 별다른 계획이 없어.
여: 그렇게 하면 좋지. 정말로 고마워. 그런데 내가 지금 약간 바쁘거든. 우리 20분쯤 후에 갈까?
남: 좋아. 준비되면 알려줘.

어휘
pick up (싼값으로, 우연히) ~을 사다 **stock up** ~을 사서 비축하다
handy ***a.*** 유용한, 가까운 곳에 있는 **day trip** 당일여행 **day off** (근무, 일을) 쉬는 날

정답 ④

문제풀이
여자가 야외활동 장비를 세일하는 상점에 가려고 하는데 차가 수리소에 있다. 남자는 자신이 태워줄 수 있다고 했으므로 남자가 여자를 위해 할 일은 ④ '상점까지 차로 태워다 주기'이다.

총 어휘 수 200

08 이유

소재 육상 경기에 나갈 수 없는 이유

듣기 대본 해석
남: 안녕, Laura. 오늘의 용건은 뭐니?
여: 음, Baker 선생님. 이번 주말에 육상 경기에 나갈 수 없다는 것을 말씀 드리고 싶어서요.
남: 나갈 수 없다는 것이 무슨 말이니? 이틀 밖에 안 남았어. 지금은 대신할 사람도 구할 수 없어.
여: 정말로 죄송해요. 저를 필요로 하시는 것은 알지만 이번 주말에 저의 부모님께서 조부모님 댁에 가야 해요. 좀 긴급 상황이에요.
남: 알았어. 괜찮은 거니?
여: 제 할아버지께서 욕실에서 넘어져서 엉덩이를 다쳤어요. 할아버지께서는 수술을 받으셔서 얼마 동안은 집을 떠날 수가 없어요.
남: 안됐구나. 유감이야. 그럼 너도 조부모님 댁에 갈 거니?

여: 아니요. 부모님만 가셔요. 저는 부모님께서 안 계실 때 저의 어린 여동생을 돌봐야 해요.
남: 알았어. 정말로 안타깝네. 그렇지만 걱정하지는 마. 우리는 네가 분명히 그리울 거야. 할아버지께서 쾌차하시길 바라마.
여: 감사해요, Baker 선생님.

어휘
track meet 육상경기대회 **replacement** ***n.*** 교체, 대신할 사람 **emergency** ***n.*** 응급 상황, 비상 **have surgery** 수술 받다

정답 ③

문제풀이
여자는 부모님이 할아버지 댁에 가시는 동안 여동생을 돌봐야 해서 육상 경기에 나갈 수 없는 상황이다. 따라서 정답은 ③ '여동생을 돌봐야 해서'이다.

총 어휘 수 153

09 숫자

소재 리조트 숙박과 브런치 예약

듣기 대본 해석
[전화벨이 울린다.]
여: Beachwood Resort에 전화해 주셔서 감사합니다. 무엇을 도와드릴까요?
남: 네. 방을 예약하고 싶은데요. 하루 요금이 어떻게 되죠?
여: 주말에는 60달러이고, 주중에는 40달러예요.
남: 그러면 다음 주 토요일에 방을 예약하고 싶어요.
여: 네. 성함이 어떻게 되시나요?
남: Dennis Reynolds예요. 아, 그리고 식당에 브런치 예약을 두 명 하고 싶어요.
여: 네. 한 사람당 10달러를 추가하셔야 합니다.
남: 좋아요. 제가 여기 50퍼센트 할인 쿠폰도 있어요. 쿠폰 코드는 XT750이에요.
여: 제가 한번 확인해 볼게요. *[키보드 치는 소리]* 죄송하지만, 그 쿠폰은 방에는 사용 가능하지만 브런치에는 사용 가능하지 않네요.
남: 괜찮아요. 제가 카드로 돈을 지불하고 싶으면 지금 카드번호를 드려야 하나요, 아니면 토요일까지 기다려도 되나요?
여: 원하시면 토요일까지 기다리셔도 됩니다.
남: 좋아요. 그럼 토요일에 뵙겠습니다.

어휘
set up a reservation 예약하다 **rate** ***n.*** 요금 **apply** ***v.*** 적용되다, 해당되다

정답 ③

문제풀이
토요일에 방을 예약하므로 주말 요금이 적용되어 60달러이고, 브런치를 2명 예약하여 20달러가 추가된다. 남자는 숙박요금에만 50퍼센트 할인이 적용되는 쿠폰을 가지고 있으므로 총 지불할 금액은 숙박요금 30달러와 브런치 2인 20달러를 합한 ③ '$50'이다.

총 어휘 수 153

10 언급 유무

소재 이주 노동자들을 위해 집을 짓는 자원봉사

듣기 대본 해석
여: 안녕, Louie. 지금 시간이 괜찮으면 너의 여름 자원봉사에 대해서 내가 쓰고 있는 기사를 위해 몇 가지 질문을 해도 될까?
남: 물론이야, Stacy. 물어봐.
여: 좋아. 자원봉사자로서 무슨 일들을 했어?
남: 많은 일들을 했어. 이주 노동자들을 위해 집을 짓는 것을 도와주고 스태프진을 구성하는 것을 도왔어.
여: 알겠어. 얼마나 많은 집을 짓는 것을 도왔는데?
남: 우린 큰 팀을 가지고 있어서 2달 안에 32채의 집을 지을 수 있었어.
여: 멋지다. 이주 노동자들이 바로 집으로 들어갔어?
남: 응. 원래 낡은 판자집에서 살고 있었어서, 새 집으로 들어간다니 아주 신나 하더라고.
여: 분명 그랬을 거야. 이 일을 얼마나 오랫동안 한 거야?
남: 이 자원봉사 프로그램에서 대학교 1학년 때부터 일해 왔어.
여: 정말? 그러면 3년이 됐네. 좋아. 질문 하나만 더. 자원봉사를 해서 어떤 이점이 있어?
남: 많은 이점이 있는데, 무엇보다도, 난 다른 사람들을 도움으로써 생기는 감정이 좋아.
여: 잘됐구나. 시간 내줘서 고마워, Louie.

어휘
migrant ***n.*** 이주자 **organize** ***v.*** 조직하다, 정리하다 **originally** ***ad.*** 원래, 본래 **rickety** ***a.*** 곧 부서질 듯한 **shack** ***n.*** 판잣집

정답 ③

문제풀이
두 사람은 봉사활동에 관한 활동 내용, 봉사활동의 수혜자, 봉사해 온 기간, 봉사를 통해 얻는 이점에 관해 언급했지만 ③ '봉사 단체명'은 언급하지 않았다.

총 어휘 수 184

11 내용 일치 · 불일치

소재 미술관의 연간 행사 소개

듣기 대본 해석
남: 안녕하세요, 저희 미술관에 오신 것을 환영합니다. 저는 여러분께서 좋아하실 거라고 확신하는, 곧 있을 행사에 대해서 말씀드리고자 이 자리에 있습니다. 여기 미술관에 있는 저희들은 매년 열리는 8월의 예술인 행사에 여러분 모두를 초대하고자 합니다. 지난 16년간 매년 8월에 이 행사를 개최해 왔습니다. 저희는 지역 예술가들을 홍보하기 위해 이 행사를 개최하고, 미술관에 그들의 작품을 전시합니다. 우리 시의 예술가들은 창의성을 고무시킬 뿐만 아니라 공원 및 사업체들을 아름답게 가꾸도록 돕기 때문에 우리 지역사회에 중요합니다. 이 행사는 8월 17일에 시작하여 월말까지 계속됩니다. 본 행사의 입장료는 무료입니다. 하지만 저희는 지역 예술 프로그램을 지원하는 저희 재단에 소액의 기부를 해주시길 추천합니다. 올해 행사에 참여하셔서 이 지역 최고 수준의 회화, 소묘, 조각 작품들 일부를 관람하세요. 시간 내주셔서 감사합니다.

어휘
upcoming ***a.*** 다가오는, 곧 있을 **annual** ***a.*** 매년의, 연례의
promote ***v.*** 홍보하다 **beautify** ***v.*** 아름답게 하다, 꾸미다
modest ***a.*** 많지 않은, 수수한, 겸손한 **foundation** ***n.*** 재단

정답 ⑤

문제풀이
남자는 행사에 참여하여 이 지역의 회화, 소묘, 조각 작품들을 관람하라고 했으므로 내용과 일치하지 않는 것은 ⑤ '사진 작품을 볼 수 있다.'이다.

총 어휘 수 150

12 도표

소재 드럼 키트 구매

듣기 대본 해석
남: 안녕하세요, 부인. 무엇을 도와드릴까요?
여: 아들 생일 선물로 줄 드럼 키트를 찾고 있어요. 그는 로큰롤 밴드를 시작하고 싶어하거든요.

남: 좋습니다. 일단, 저희는 다섯 가지 키트가 있습니다.
여: 무엇이 그에게 가장 적합한지 모르겠네요. 도와주셨으면 하는데요.
남: 록음악을 한다면 3피스 키트는 충분하지 않아요. 5피스 아니면 7피스 키트를 원할 거예요.
여: 네. 깊은 베이스 사운드를 만들 수 있는 키트를 원하는 것 같던데요.
남: 그러면 아드님이 플로어 톰을 원할 것 같군요. 저희는 그것도 제공합니다. 이 두 세트 중에서 고르셔야 할 것 같은데요.
여: 네. 음... 800달러 이상은 쓰기를 원하지 않으니까, 그렇다면 이것을 선택해야겠네요.
남: 네. 집으로 가져가실 수 있게 준비하겠습니다.
여: 고맙습니다.

어휘

suitable ***a.*** 적합한

정답 ③

문제풀이

5피스 또는 7피스 키트를 원한다고 했으므로 ②~⑤번 중에 골라야 하는데 플로어 톰을 원한다고 했으므로 ③, ⑤번이 남게 된다. 그리고 800달러 이상은 쓰고 싶지 않다고 했으므로 정답은 ③번이다.

총 어휘 수 152

13 긴 대화의 응답

소재 퇴근 후 요가

듣기 대본 해석

남: 새로운 남자친구 또는 비슷한 관계가 생겼어요, Heather?
여: 하하! 아니요. 왜 그렇게 말한 거에요?
남: 요즘 훨씬 행복해 보이고 에너지가 충만해 보이는 것 같아서요.
여: 정말이요? 음, 제가 최근에 기분이 정말 좋지만, 제 삶에 새로운 사람이 있는 건 아니에요.
남: 그럼 어떤 다른 변화가 생겼어요?
여: 최근에 요가를 시작했어요. 일 끝나고 매일 밤 가거든요.
남: 요가를 연습한 지 얼마나 됐어요?
여: 겨우 3개월이요.
남: 당신한테 어렵진 않아요? 저는 제 발가락에조차 닿을 수가 없어요.
여: 저도 처음 시작했을 때는 어려웠지만, 몇 주 지나니 훨씬 더 유연해졌어요.
남: 요가가 코티솔 수준을 향상시켜, 병을 물리치는 것을 더 쉽게 해준다고 들었어요.
여: 저도 그렇게 들었어요. 어쨌든, 저는 매일 요가를 하는 것이 정말 좋아요. 요가는 퇴근 후에 기대할 만한 뭔가를 주거든요.
남: ④ 요즘 당신이 그렇게 행복해 보이는 이유가 그것인 것 같군요.

어휘

limber ***a.*** 유연한 **improve** ***v.*** 개선하다, 향상시키다
cortisol ***n.*** 코티솔 (부신 피질에서 생기는 스테로이드 호르몬의 일종)
look forward to ~을 기대하다

정답 ④

문제풀이

남자는 여자가 요즘 행복하고 에너지가 충만해 보이는 이유를 묻고 여자는 퇴근 후 하고 있는 요가 덕분이라고 말하고 있다. 요가가 퇴근 후 뭔가를 기대하게 만들어 준다는 여자의 말에 대한 적절한 응답은 ④ '요즘 당신이 그렇게 행복해 보이는 이유가 그것인 것 같군요.'이다.

오답 보기 해석

① 요가를 하기 위해 일찍 퇴근하면 안 돼요.
② 매일 요가를 가는 것은 할 가치가 없음이 분명해요.
③ 저는 오늘 밤 정말로 초과근무를 하고 싶지 않아요.
⑤ 그러면 우리 요가를 연습할 장소를 찾아야겠어요.

총 어휘 수 157

14 긴 대화의 응답

소재 프로젝트 실험 준비와 일기 예보

듣기 대본 해석

여: 여름 방학 때까지 기다릴 수 없어. 넌 어때, Henry?
남: 나도 정말 방학을 고대하고 있어. 하지만 난 우리가 그때까지 우리 과학 프로젝트를 마칠 수 없을까 봐 좀 걱정이 돼.
여: 안심해. 우리 할 일이 그렇게 많이 남지 않았어.
남: 네 말이 맞는 것 같아. 근데, 이번 주 날씨를 확인해 봤어?
여: 응, 이번 주 내내 비가 오고 바람이 불 예정이야.
남: 정말? 그러면 우리 프로젝트를 어떻게 마치지? 우리는 실험을 밖에서 해야 하는데.
여: 맞아! 음, 수요일에는 비 올 확률이 50퍼센트밖에 안 되는 것 같아.
남: 그럼, 우리 수요일에 비가 오지 않도록 행운을 빌어야겠어. 하지만 만약을 대비해서 예비 계획도 세워둬야 해.
여: 그래. 그런데 생각해 둔 거 있어?
남: 아마도 우리 실험을 하기 위해 체육관을 사용할 수 있을 거야. 그게 괜찮을지 Jones 선생님께 여쭤보자.
여: ④ 훌륭한 생각이야. 우리가 이 프로젝트의 파트너라서 좋아.

어휘

look forward to ~을 기대하다 **concerned** ***a.*** 걱정하는
be supposed to V ~하기로 되어 있다 **experiment** ***n.*** 실험
keep one's fingers crossed 행운을 빌다 **backup** ***n.*** 예비, 백업
just in case 만약을 대비해서, 혹시 모르니까 **gymnasium** ***n.*** 체육관
〈문제〉 **brilliant** ***a.*** 훌륭한, 멋진

정답 ④

문제풀이

두 사람은 과학 프로젝트에 관해 대화를 나누던 중 이번 주에 야외에서 실험을 해야 하는데 일주일 내내 비가 온다는 예보가 있다고 했다. 강수확률이 적은 수요일에 비가 오지 않도록 바라고, 예비 계획으로 체육관에서 실험을 할 수 있을지 알아보자는 남자의 말에 대한 여자의 응답은 ④ '훌륭한 생각이야. 우리가 이 프로젝트의 파트너라서 좋아.'가 가장 적절하다.

오답 보기 해석

① 걱정할 필요 없어. 그날 비가 오지 않을 거야.
② 우리 정말 서두를 필요가 있어. 일이 너무 많아.
③ 우리 여름 방학 전에 프로젝트를 끝낼 수 있어.
⑤ 우리가 왜 실험을 체육관에서 해야 하지? 우리는 밖에서 할 수 있어.

총 어휘 수 152

15 상황에 적절한 말

소재 수줍음이 많고 소극적인 딸

듣기 대본 해석

여: Pamela는 지난 밤에 학부모-교사 상담을 하러 학교에 갔고 그녀 딸의 선생님을 만났습니다. 그녀는 자신의 딸인 Malory가 매우 수줍음이 많고, 예민하다는 선생님의 말에 전혀 놀라지 않았습니다. 선생님은 Malory가 휴식 시간에 거의 뛰지 않고 걷기만 하는 조용한 아이라고 말했습니다. Malory의 선생님은 딸을 좀 더 활동적이고 에너지 넘치게 만들기 위해 몇 가지를 시도해 보라고 Pamela를 격려했습니다. 또한, 선생님은 Malory의 활동 수준을 올리기 위한 제안들이 많이 있는 웹사이트를 추천해주었습니다. Pamela는 선생님의 조언에 감사해하고 바로 집에 와서 웹사이트를 확인했습니다. 밤에, Pamela는 저녁을 준비하느라 바빴는데 전화가 울렸고, 그녀는 Malory에게 전화를 받으라고 부탁했습니다. Malory는 자신이 너무 부끄럼이 많기 때문에 전화 받기를 거절했습니다. 그녀의 딸이 언젠가 중요한 것을 놓칠까 걱정하면서 그녀는 딸에게 조언을 하기로 결심합니다. 이런 상황에서 Pamela가 Malory에게 어떤 말을 할 것 같은가요?
Pamela: ④ 좀 더 적극적이고 활동적인 것이 네 삶에 있어서 도움이 될 거야.

어휘

conference ***n.*** 의논, 회의 **at recess** 휴식 시간에 **active** ***a.*** 생기 있는, 활발한

정답 ④

문제풀이

수줍음이 많고 조용한 딸 Malory에게 Pamela는 좀 더 생기 있고 활동적으로 생활하라고 말해주고 싶어하므로 정답은 ④ '좀 더 적극적이고 활동적인 것이 네 삶에 있어서 도움이 될 거야.'이다.

오답 보기 해석

① 전화로 낯선 이와 이야기할 땐 주의하렴.
② 친구랑 밖에서 그렇게 자주 놀면 안돼.
③ 컴퓨터 게임을 하기 전에 네 숙제를 마치렴.
⑤ 네가 인터넷 하는 데 쓰는 시간을 좀 줄이는 게 어떠니?

총 어휘 수 172

16 담화 주제 / 17 세부 내용 파악

소재 축구 용품 구입 요령

듣기 대본 해석

남: 안녕하세요, 팀 여러분. 오늘 우리는 운동용품에 대해서 이야기를 나눌 것입니다. 운동용품점에 들어가면 살 수 있는 축구 용품이 너무 많아서 당황할 수 있습니다. 사람들은 항상 내게 가장 비싼 용품을 사야 하는지 물어봅니다. 저는 보통 아니라고 대답합니다. 예를 들어 평범하고 싼 양말들도 충분히 좋은데 굳이 돈을 더 들여서 특별하고 멋져 보이는(초현대적인) 양말을 살 필요는 없죠. 가장 중요한 용품은 물론 기본적인 용품입니다. 꽤 쓸만한 축구화, 정강이 보호대, 양말, 그리고 축구공이 필요할 것입니다. 저는 가장 중요한 용품을 좋은 축구화라고 생각합니다. 축구화가 잘 맞고 오래갈 수 있도록 내구성이 좋은지 확인하는 것이 좋을 것입니다. 또 다른 중요한 용품은 다리 부상을 막아주는 정강이 보호대입니다. 비싼 용품들이 멋져 보이고 남들에게 깊은 인상을 줄 수도 있지만 경기를 뛰는 데는 그렇게 필요하지 않다는 것을 기억하세요. 훈련 캠프에서 좋은 시간을 보내기 바랍니다.

어휘

equipment ***n.*** 장비, 용품 **overwhelmed** ***a.*** 압도된, 당황한 **massive** ***a.*** 거대한 **space-age** ***a.*** 초현대적인 **decent** ***a.*** 괜찮은, 제대로 된 **shin** ***n.*** 정강이 **durable** ***a.*** 내구성이 있는 **flashy** ***a.*** 호화로운, 멋진 **impress** ***v.*** 깊은 인상을 주다

정답 16 ① 17 ④

문제풀이

16 남자는 수많은 축구 용품 중에서 반드시 비싼 것을 살 필요가 없으며, 기본적인 용품들이 중요하다는 등 축구 용품 구매 시 요령에 대해 말하고 있으므로 주제로 가장 적절한 것은 ① '축구 용품을 사기 위한 조언'이다.

17 남자는 양말, 축구화, 정강이 보호대, 축구공을 가장 중요한 기본용품의 예로 언급하였으나 바지는 언급하지 않았으므로 정답은 ④ '반바지'이다.

오답 보기 해석

16
② 공원에서 축구 하는 것의 위험성
③ 비싼 물품 구입의 결과
④ 축구 캠프의 늘어가는 인기
⑤ 축구를 하는 것이 청소년에게 주는 다양한 이점들

총 어휘 수 181

DICTATION ANSWERS

01 were supposed to

02 It's irrelevant to

03 should always be kept on board / equal the vessel's maximum passenger capacity / are in working order

04 performing tricks / the animals in the circus are victim to / forced to entertain people

05 in need of assistance / Someone was riding their motorcycle / run a couple of tests

06 enforce the rules / what they shouldn't do at school / It's a great addition

07 stock up on camping gear / quite handy for picnics / Your car is in the shop / give you a ride

08 We can't find a replacement / It's kind of an emergency / had surgery / look after my little sister

09 set up a reservation for / What are your daily rates / I'd like to book a room for / coupon only applies

10 volunteering over the summer / build houses for migrant workers / originally living in rickety shacks

11 every August for the past sixteen years / promote area artists / Entry to the event / make a modest donation

12 the most suitable for / make some deep bass sounds / offer those as well

13 there's no new man in my life / took up yoga / I noticed I was much more limber / fight off sickness

14 I just can't wait until / keep our fingers crossed / should have a backup plan

15 not shocked at all / get her daughter to be more active / check out the websites

16-17 be overwhelmed by / protect your legs from injury

25 수능영어듣기 실전모의고사

본문 p.152

01 ②	02 ④	03 ①	04 ⑤	05 ⑤	06 ②
07 ⑤	08 ②	09 ③	10 ④	11 ②	12 ①
13 ④	14 ⑤	15 ④	16 ①	17 ④	

01 짧은 대화의 응답

소재 호텔 예약

듣기 대본 해석

여: 디즈니 호텔의 서비스에 정말 감동받았어요.

남: 사실 저도 이번 주말에 아이들을 데려갈까 생각 중이에요. 거기 예약 담당 전화번호 알아요?

여: 네, 물론이죠. 거기 가려는 특별한 이유라도 있나요?

남: ② 두 아이들 모두 생일이 이번 달이에요.

어휘

impressed ***a.*** 감동을 받은 〈문제〉 **typically** ***ad.*** 보통, 일반적으로

정답 ②

문제풀이

남자는 이번 주말에 디즈니 호텔에 갈까 한다며 여자에게 예약 전화번호를 알고 있는지 물었고, 여자는 안다고 대답하며 왜 가는지 이유를 물었다. 남자는 왜 가는지 대답해야 하는 상황이므로 ② '두 아이들 모두 생일이 이번 달이에요.'가 정답이다.

오답 보기 해석

① 전 아직 예약하고 싶지 않아요.
③ 전 디즈니 티켓을 할인 받길 바라요.
④ 그녀에게 휴가에 대해 이야기하려고 했어요.
⑤ 보통 우리는 오두막에 가서 낚시를 해요.

총 어휘 수 47

02 짧은 대화의 응답

소재 연극 관람하러 가는 길의 교통 정체

듣기 대본 해석

남: 오! 연극 제 시간에 못 갈 것 같은데.

여: 미안. 저녁 이 시간에 차가 이렇게 막힐 줄은 몰랐어.

남: 응. 도심지는 금요일 밤에 항상 막히지. 시작하려면 얼마나 남았어?

여: ④ 약 15분쯤.

어휘

on time 제 시간에, 늦지 않고

정답 ④

문제풀이

남자가 연극이 시작하려면 얼마나 남았는지 물었으므로 가장 적절한 여자의 대답은 ④ '약 15분쯤.'이다.

오답 보기 해석

① 약 2킬로미터 정도 떨어져 있어.
② 지하철 타고.
③ 장당 거의 100달러야.
⑤ 거의 9시 30분까지.

총 어휘 수 45

03 담화 주제

소재 블로그 방문자수 늘리는 방법

듣기 대본 해석

남: 기술은 요즘 빠르게 발전하고 있고 가장 빠르게 발전하고 있는 것들 중 하나가 블로깅입니다. 블로깅은 다른 사람들에게 자신의 생활과 관심사에 대해 알릴 수 있는 좋은 방법입니다. 또한 재미있기도 합니다. 그러나 수백만 개의 블로그들에서 여러분의 블로그가 돋보이기 위해 알아둬야 할 것들이 있습니다. 먼저 블로그가 흥미로워 보이도록 만들어야 합니다. 멋진 디자인과 색조를 고르세요. 두 번째, 블로그를 한 주제에 집중시키세요. 너무 많은 주제를 다루는 것은 집중력을 분산시키고 블로그 독자들을 잃게 할 것입니다. 마지막으로 독자들과 소통을 하세요. 블로그에 독자들이 남기는 댓글에 답을 하는 데 시간을 들이세요. 이러한 것들을 염두에 둔다면 당신의 블로그에 더 많은 사람들을 끌어들일 수 있습니다.

어휘

stand out 돋보이다 **attractive** ***a.*** 매혹적인, 멋진 **color scheme** 색조 **distracting** ***a.*** 집중력을 분산시키는 **respond to** ~에 응답하다

정답 ①

문제풀이

남자는 세 가지 방법을 제시하며 그렇게 하면 블로그에 더 많은 사람들을 끌어들일 수 있다고 했으므로 남자가 하는 말의 주제는 ① '블로그 활성화를 위한 팁'이다.

총 어휘 수 128

04 의견

소재 오락시설에서의 시간 제한 규정에 대한 불만

듣기 대본 해석

남: 안녕하세요, Cindy. 지난 토요일 당신 아들 생일 파티에서 아들이 즐거운 시간을 보냈나요?

여: 아니요, 끔찍했어요. 저는 오락시설에서 직원 때문에 너무 화났어요.

남: 이런! 무슨 일이 있었어요?

여: 우리가 도착했을 때 그들은 우리한테 30분을 기다려야 한다고 말했어요. 저는 예약을 했는데도 말이죠!

남: 음, 그들이 여름에는 매우 바쁘다는 건 확실해요.

여: 그렇긴 해요. 하지만 우리가 앉고 나서 그들이 우리한테 두 시간 제한이 있다고 말했어요!

남: 정말이요? 그리고 두 시간이 당신에게는 충분하지 않았나요?

여: 네, 확실히 충분치 않았죠. 우리는 15명의 아이들을 위해 음식을 주문하고, 음식을 받아서 아이들이 먹을 수 있도록 해야 했어요. 또한, 케이크를 먹고 선물을 열기 전에, 아이들이 모두 게임을 할 기회를 주기를 원했어요.

남: 음, 그들은 아마 가능한 많은 고객을 수용하려 했나 보네요.

여: 좋아요. 그렇지만 시간 제한은 고객이 데려간 아이들의 수가 몇 명인지에 기반을 두어야 한다고요.

남: 그래서, 관리팀에 이야기하셨어요?

여: 말했죠. 하지만 그들은 그것이 회사 방침이어서 그들이 해줄 수 있는 것은 아무것도 없다고 말했어요. 정말 무례했어요!

어휘

accommodate ***v.*** 수용하다 **based on** ~에 근거하여 **policy** ***n.*** 정책, 방침

정답 ⑤

문제풀이

여자는 아들의 생일 파티를 위해 간 오락시설에서 예약을 했는데도 30분을 기다렸다 들어갔고 자리에 앉자 두 시간의 시간 제한이 있다고 한 것에 불만을 표하면서 인원이 많은 만큼 시간이 길었어야 한다고 말했으므로 정답은 ⑤ '인원수에 따라 사용 시간을 다르게 줘야 한다.'이다.

총 어휘 수 180

05 대화자의 관계 파악

소재 배우와 의상 디자이너와의 대화

듣기 대본 해석
남: 안녕하세요, Marie. 여기서 다시 볼 줄 몰랐어요.
여: 안녕하세요, Paul. 방금 감독님과 이야기 좀 나눴어요.
남: 오, 저희와 다시 작업을 하실 것을 고려 중이신가요?
여: 네. LA에서의 일이 잘 풀리지 않았어요.
남: 그렇군요. 전에 현대극 해보신 적 있으신가요?
여: 아니요. 저는 고전극만 해봤어요. 그러면 당신은 The Shape of Things 공연에 참여하나요? 어떤 역을 맡고 계신가요?
남: Adam 역할을 맡았어요.
여: 와, 주연을 맡으셨네요. 정말 흥분되겠어요. 축하해요.
남: 고마워요. 하지만 일을 잘 해내기가 정말 어렵네요.
여: 이해해요. 저도 제 일에 대해 약간 긴장돼요. 전 셰익스피어 풍의 의상에 대해 많이 알고 있지만 현대 패션에 관해서는 잘 몰라요.
남: 음. 영화를 볼 수 있어요. 제 생각엔 영화를 통해 도움이 될만한 조언들을 얻을 수 있을 거예요.
여: 맞아요. 제가 할 수 있는 한 본래의 의상에 가장 가깝도록 유지할 거예요. 이번 주말에 작업하려고요. 그럼, 전 이제 가봐야 해요. 다음 드레스 리허설 때 봐요.
남: 잘 가요, Marie.

어휘
director ***n.*** 감독 **role** ***n.*** 역할, 배역 **costuming** ***n.*** 의상(재료)
dress rehearsal 총연습

정답 ⑤

문제풀이
여자가 어떤 역할을 맡았는지 물었을 때 남자는 Adam 역할을 맡았다고 하는 것으로 보아 배우임을 알 수 있고, 여자는 의상에 대해 공부하고 작업한다고 하는 것으로 보아 의상 디자이너임을 알 수 있다. 따라서 정답은 ⑤ '배우 — 의상 디자이너'이다.

총 어휘 수 163

06 그림의 세부 내용 파악

소재 가족들과 함께 갔던 캠핑

듣기 대본 해석
남: 안녕, Laura. 네가 핸드폰으로 보고 있는 것은 뭐야?
여: 작년 여름 방학에 우리 할아버지께서 찍어주신 사진이야.
남: 멋지다. 나도 보여줘.
여: 물론. 여기 있어.
남: 너희 캠핑 간 거구나, 그렇지? 난 저 산과 구름이 마음에 들어. 정말 평화롭고 편안해 보인다.
여: 맞아. 우리는 RV를 빌려서 Walker Mountain에 갔었어.
남: 그렇구나. 뒤에 있는 저 사람이 너지?
여: 응. 나는 야외에는 별로 관심이 없어서 뮤직 비디오를 보고 있었어.
남: RV 안에는 누구야?
여: 우리 삼촌이야. 삼촌은 책을 읽고 계셔.
남: 차 앞에 있는 저 여성은 누구셔?
여: 우리 엄마야. 엄마는 거미를 발견하고 도망치고 있어.
남: 그리고 개랑 놀고 있는 저 아이들은? 이 애들은 누구야?
여: 내 사촌들이야. 그들이 자기들 개를 여행에 데려왔어.
남: 그럼 RV에서 짐을 꺼내 옮기는 남자가 너희 아버지겠네.
여: 맞아. 그는 쉬기 위해 산에 가고 싶어하셨지만, 내 생각엔 우리가 아버지를 기분 좋지 않게 만들었던 것 같아.

어휘
RV ***n.*** 레저 차량 **RV=recreational vehicle, camping car라는 말은 잘 쓰지 않습니다.*
care for ~를 좋아하다 **miserable** ***a.*** 비참한, 기분이 좋지 않은

정답 ②

문제풀이
대화에서 차 안에 있는 사람은 삼촌이고 책을 읽고 계시다고 했는데 그림에서는 낮잠을 자고 있으므로 정답은 ②번이다.

총 어휘 수 174

07 할 일

소재 수돗물 필터 교체하기

듣기 대본 해석
여: 수돗물 맛이 이상해지는 것 같아, 그렇지 않아?
남: 그런 것 같아. 필터를 갈 때가 된 것 같아.
여: 다른 필터는 없어?
남: 있을 걸. 몇 달 전에 몇 개 사 놓은 것 같아.
여: 그럼 아무 때나 갈면 되겠네.
남: 지금 당장 가는 것이 좋을 것 같은데.
여: 알겠어. 지금 필터 갖고 올게.
남: 내가 갈게. 너 못 찾을 것 같아.
여: 도구 가져오는 것 잊지마.
남: 필요 없을 것 같은데.
여: 알겠어. 그럼 난 싱크대를 청소할게.
남: 그래. 금방 올게.

어휘
tap water 수돗물 **might as well** ~하는 편이 낫다

정답 ⑤

문제풀이
여자가 수돗물 필터를 가져오겠다고 하자 남자는 자신이 가져오겠다고 했으므로 남자가 할 일은 ⑤ '수돗물 필터 가져오기'이다.

총 어휘 수 108

08 이유

소재 등록을 놓쳐서 출전하지 못하게 된 육상경기대회

듣기 대본 해석
여: 안녕, Stan. 어깨 어때?
남: 훨씬 더 좋아졌어. 고마워.
여: 잘됐네! 그럼 다시 창 던질 수 있는 거야?
남: 응. 어제 좀 연습했어. 거의 부상 전만큼 좋아졌어.
여: 좋네. 이번 주말에 육상경기대회에서 네가 시합하는 게 정말 기대되네.
남: 불행하게도 나갈 수 없을 것 같아.
여: 왜 안 돼? 어깨 다친 동안 연습을 못해서?
남: 아니. 사실은 주말 경기에 등록하는 걸 깜빡 했어.
여: 저런! 바빠서 잊어버린 것 같은데.
남: 맞아. 중간고사 때문에 너무 스트레스를 받아서 까맣게 잊고 있었어.
여: 그랬구나. 난 여름 인턴십 프로그램에 등록하는 것 놓쳤어. 마감일이 저번 주였거든.
남: 안타깝네. 아마도 우리는 플래너를 사서 좀 더 계획성 있게 해야 할 것 같아.

어휘
javelin ***n.*** 창 **injury** ***n.*** 부상 **track meet** 육상경기대회
slip one's mind (깜빡) 잊어 버리다 **registration** ***n.*** 등록
organized ***a.*** 정리된, 계획성 있는

정답 ②

문제풀이
남자는 중간고사 때문에 스트레스를 받아서 주말 경기에 등록하는 것을 잊었다고 했으므로 남자가 육상경기에 나가지 못하는 이유는 ② '등록을 하지 못해서'이다.

총 어휘 수 139

09 숫자

소재 회사 소풍 간식 사기

듣기 대본 해석
남: 안녕하세요. 오늘은 무엇을 도와드릴까요?
여: 안녕하세요. 내일 오후에 갈 회사 소풍 간식 좀 사려고요. 이 쿠키들은 얼마예요?
남: 한 개당 2달러인데 곧 닫을 거라서 지금 가게에 있는 건 모두 20퍼센트 할인해 드려요.
여: 좋네요. 그러면 쿠키 20개 살게요. 그리고 파이도 남았나요?
남: 그럼요. 오후에 체스 파이를 좀 만들었어요. 소풍에 안성맞춤일 거예요.
여: 얼마 정도 하나요?
남: 하나 당 10달러입니다.
여: 좋네요. 두 개 살게요.
남: 다른 것 또 필요하세요?
여: 그게 다인 것 같아요. 10퍼센트 할인 쿠폰도 있는데 쓸게요.
남: 죄송하지만 이미 할인된 상품에 대해서는 쿠폰을 받지 않습니다.
여: 그렇군요. 그럼 다음 번에 쓸게요.
남: 알겠습니다. 그럼 쿠키 20개랑 파이 2개를 20퍼센트 할인된 가격으로 가져가시는 겁니다. 맞죠?
여: 맞아요. 여기 카드요.

어휘
apiece ***ad.*** 각각, 하나에 **batch** ***n.*** 한 회분 **discounted** ***a.*** 할인된

정답 ③

문제풀이
쿠키는 하나당 2달러이고 20개이므로 40달러, 체스 파이는 하나당 10달러인데 2개이므로 20달러로 합계는 60달러이고 여기서 20퍼센트 할인이 된다고 했으므로 정답은 ③ '$48'이다.

총 어휘 수 162

10 언급 유무

소재 새로 구입한 집에 대한 문의

듣기 대본 해석
여: 이것이 당신이 저에게 문의했던 집의 최근 사진이에요, Anderson 씨.
남: 좋네요. 저는 큰 뒷마당이 너무 마음에 들어요.
여: 네, 뒷마당이 정말 예뻐요. 방 세 개와 세 개의 화장실 그리고 앞에 아름다운 정원이 있어요.
남: 위치가 어디죠? 좋은 지역 내에 있나요?
여: 그래요. 근처가 아주 깨끗하고 안전해요. 교통량도 그리 많지 않아요.
남: 저는 중학생인 두 아들이 있어서 근처가 좋다고 들으니 기쁘네요. 근처에 학교가 있나요?
여: 네, 학교는 차로 5분 거리에 있습니다. 집도 학교버스의 노선에 있어요.
남: 훌륭해요. 시내버스나 지하철은 어때요? 지하철역이 걸어갈 수 있는 거리에 있나요?
여: 물론이죠. 지하철은 걸어서 십분 정도 거리에 있어요.
남: 집에 차고는 있나요? 차 한 대 아니면 두 대가 가능해요?
여: 두 대 세울 수 있는 차고가 붙어 있습니다.
남: 좋아요. 지금 집을 보러 갈 수 있을까요?
여: 문제 없을 거예요. 확실히 하기 위해 먼저 집주인한테 전화해 볼게요.

어휘
neighborhood ***n.*** 인근, 근처 **garage** ***n.*** 차고 **attach** ***v.*** 붙이다, 첨부하다

정답 ④

문제풀이
대화에서 침실과 화장실 개수, 인근 학교 유무, 대중교통, 차고 유무에 대한 언급은 있었지만 집이 언제 지어졌는지에 대해서는 언급한 적이 없으므로 정답은 ④ '건축연도'이다.

총 어휘 수 169

11 내용 일치 · 불일치

소재 파쇄

듣기 대본 해석
여: 학생 여러분, 하나가 더 있습니다. 가시기 전에 여러분에게 수압 파쇄, 줄여서 '파쇄'에 대해서 잠시 동안 이야기해보려고 합니다. 파쇄는 천연가스를 포함하고 있는 돌을 깨는 특정 화학물질을 이용하여 돌로부터 천연가스를 추출해 내는 방법입니다. 파쇄 방법은 굉장히 쉽고 비용 효율적입니다. 그러나 그 과정에서 환경에 끼치는 안 좋은 영향들이 있습니다. 예를 들어 파쇄는 지하수에 화학물을 넣는데 이는 인근 주민들의 수돗물을 오염시킬 수 있습니다. 파쇄는 지진이나 미진과 같은 지진 활동을 초래하는 것으로도 의심됩니다. 파쇄와 그 영향들을 다음 시간에 더 자세하게 얘기 나눠볼게요.

어휘
hydraulic fracking 수압 파쇄 **extract** ***v.*** 추출하다
chemical ***n.*** 화학물질 **cost-effective** ***a.*** 비용 효율이 높은
associated with ~와 관련된 **tap water** 수돗물
seismic activity 지진 활동 **tremor** ***n.*** 미진 **implication** ***n.*** 영향, 결과

정답 ②

문제풀이
파쇄는 천연가스를 갖고 있는 돌을 부수는 특정한 화학물을 이용한다고 했으므로 내용과 일치하지 않는 것은 ② '돌을 뭉쳐서 크게 만드는 방식을 이용한다.'이다.

총 어휘 수 103

12 도표

소재 자신에게 맞는 의사 선택하기

듣기 대본 해석
남: 오늘 눈이 너무 간지러워. 그 철이 다시 돌아왔나 봐.
여: 응, 나도 봄에 알레르기가 아주 심해. 알레르기 전문 의사에게 상담 받는 건 어때?
남: 사실 날 봐주는 알레르기 의사가 없어. 한 명 만나볼까?
여: 날 봐주는 의사는 굉장히 도움이 돼. 인터넷으로 빠르게 검색해서 너에게 맞는 의사를 찾자. 안과 의사는 필요 없는 거지?
남: 응, 알레르기 때문에 그런 거니까 안과 의사는 도움이 안 될 것 같아.
여: 알겠어. 이 사람이 알레르기 전문의로서 제일 경험이 많아. 전화해서 예약하지 그래?
남: 응, 잠깐! 이 의사는 Union County에 있잖아! 가는 데 45분이 걸릴 거야.
여: 그렇네. Henderson County에 있는 의사들로 선택지를 줄여보자. 이 둘밖에 안 남았네.
남: 그렇구나. 경험이 더 많은 사람으로 할래.

여: 그럼 이 사람이네. 예약할 수 있게 전화번호 줄게.
남: 좋아. 도와줘서 고마워.

어휘
itchy ***a.*** 간지러운 **allergy** ***n.*** 알레르기 **allergist** ***n.*** 알레르기 전문의사 **county** ***n.*** 군

정답 ①

문제풀이
안과 의사는 필요 없고 알레르기 의사로 해야 한다고 했고 Henderson County에 있는 의사로 한다고 했으므로 ①번과 ⑤번이 남는다. 그 중에 경험이 많은 의사로 하겠다고 했으므로 정답은 ①번이다.

총 어휘 수 180

13 긴 대화의 응답

소재 출판교실에서 제작한 애완동물에 관한 팜플렛

듣기 대본 해석
남: 안녕, Chloe. 네가 보고 있는 것이 뭐니?
여: 아, Greg. 이것은 우리 학교에 있는 모든 동물들의 안내책자야.
남: 동물 안내책자? 뭐 하려?
여: 음, 우리 학교는 사실 교실에서 키우는 애완동물이 많아. 이건 모든 애완동물과 애완동물이 어느 교실에 있는지를 보여줘. 한번 확인해봐.
남: 멋진데. 학교에 애완동물이 많이 있는지 몰랐네. 누가 이 안내책자를 만들었어?
여: Scott 선생님의 출판교실이 자료를 모으고 디자인하고 인쇄해서 만들었어. 꽤 깔끔해, 그렇지?
남: 그래. 그러니까 그들이 이 모든 일을 다 했다고? 그들은 애완동물 사진까지 다 찍었니?
여: 물론이지. 그들은 Bailey의 휴대폰을 사용했어. 사진이 정말 잘 나왔어, 그렇지?
남: 그래, 잘 나왔네. 우와, 6학년 과학 선생님의 교실에는 뱀이 있어? 나는 몰랐었어.
여: 나도 금시초문이었어. 그리고 너 Smith 선생님께서 이구아나를 애완동물로 기르시는 것 알아?
남: 진짜? 정말 멋지다. 어쨌든 출판교실이 이 팜플렛에 상당히 애쓴 것 같구나.
여: ④ 맞아. 그들이 팜플렛을 완성시키는 데 학기의 대부분이 걸렸어.

어휘
directory ***n.*** 안내책자 **assemble** ***v.*** 모으다, 조립하다
〈문제〉 **semester** ***n.*** 학기

정답 ④

문제풀이
남자와 여자는 출판교실에서 제작한 애완동물에 관한 팜플렛을 보면서 새로운 사실을 알게 되고 사진도 잘 나왔다고 말하면서 마지막에 이 팜플렛에 상당히 애를 쓴 것 같다고 했으므로 그에 적절한 대답은 ④ '맞아. 그들이 팜플렛을 완성시키는 데 학기의 대부분이 걸렸어.'이다.

오답 보기 해석
① 모든 사람들이 출판교실에 들어 갈 수 있는 것은 아니야.
② 나도. 나는 모든 학생들의 사진을 찍고 싶어.
③ 만약 네가 요청한다면 그는 네가 교실에서 애완동물 기르는 것을 허락하실 거라고 확신해.
⑤ 그래. 학생들은 그들의 학급 학생들에게 보여주기 위해 애완동물을 데려올 수도 있어.

총 어휘 수 177

14 긴 대화의 응답

소재 역사 성적 상담

듣기 대본 해석
남: 안녕하세요, Diaz 선생님. 선생님께서 저를 보기 원하신다고 들었는데요?
여: 그래. Tom, 내가 그랬어. 앉을래?
남: 네. *[잠시 후]* 무슨 일로 저를 보고 싶다고 하셨나요? 무슨 일이 있나요?
여: 음, 나는 너의 역사 성적이 점점 더 걱정이 된단다. *[마우스 클릭하는 소리]* 가장 최근의 시험 점수를 보렴.
남: 음... 네, 점수가 좋지 않네요.
여: 맞아. 그런데 3월까진 점수가 계속 올라갔어. 그러고 나서 그때부터 꾸준히 떨어졌구나.
남: 네, 그러네요.
여: 왜 그렇다고 생각하니? 집에 무슨 일 있니?
남: *[잠시 후]* 음, 사실대로 말하면, 저는 친구들과 충돌이 좀 있었는데 최근에는 저도 저 같이 느껴지지가 않았어요.
여: 자, Tom. 나는 지금부터 더 나은 점수를 기대하기 때문에 네가 친구들 사이에 일을 잘 해결하는 데 노력해야 해.
남: ⑤ 네, 상황이 나아지도록 최선을 다할게요.

어휘
steadily ***ad.*** 꾸준히 **figure ~ out** ~을 이해하다, 알아내다
〈문제〉 **improve** ***v.*** 개선하다, 향상시키다

정답 ⑤

문제풀이
남자의 역사 성적이 몇 달째 떨어진 것을 걱정하며 격려 및 조언을 해주는 여자에게 남자는 자신의 의지를 표현하는 것이 자연스럽다. 따라서 가장 적절한 대답으로는 ⑤ '네, 상황이 나아지도록 최선을 다할게요.'이다.

오답 보기 해석
① 특별한 건 없어요. 단지 제가 게을러서요.
② 좋아요. 제가 당신의 시험 공부를 도울게요.
③ 친구분들과 어떻게 지내세요?
④ 저도 동의해요. 사회과학은 제가 가장 좋아하는 과목이에요.

총 어휘 수 151

15 상황에 적절한 말

소재 오래된 스마트폰 처리

듣기 대본 해석
여: Betty는 친구인 John의 집에 갑니다. 그들이 거실에서 차를 마시며 앉아 있는 동안 Betty는 그가 새 스마트폰을 손에 쥐고 있고 예전 스마트폰은 탁자 위에 놓여있다는 것을 알아챕니다. 그는 그의 예전 스마트폰이 그다지 빠르지 않고 메모리가 충분하지 않아 새 스마트폰을 샀다고 말합니다. 그는 오래된 스마트폰을 쓰레기통에 버릴 것이라고 말합니다. Betty는 그렇게 하는 것은 말도 안 되는 일이고 그가 단지 새 폰을 원했다고 생각합니다. 어느 쪽이든, 그녀는 그가 그것을 그냥 버리면 안 된다고 생각합니다. Betty는 전자기기가 필요하지만 살 여유가 없는 사람들에게 주기 위해 필요하지 않은 전자기기를 모아 재디자인하는 지역 교회에 관한 기사를 읽은 것을 기억합니다. 그녀는 John에게 그가 자선단체에 폰을 주어야 한다고 말하고 싶습니다. 이 상황에서 Betty가 John에게 무슨 말을 할 것 같은가요?
Betty: ④ 그 폰을 나에게 주면 내가 그것을 기증하는 것은 어떠니?

어휘
notice ***v.*** 알아채다 **nonsense** ***n.*** 어처구니없는 말이나 글 **either way** 둘 중에 어느 쪽이든 **electronics** ***n.*** 전자기기 **can't afford something** ~을 살 여유가 없다 **charity** ***n.*** 자선, 자선단체
〈문제〉 **donate** ***v.*** 기부하다

정답 ④

문제풀이

Betty는 John이 쓰던 오래된 스마트폰을 버리는 것보다는 필요하지 않은 전자기기를 모아 개선해서 필요하지만 살 여유가 없는 사람들에게 주는 지역 교회에 기증하는 것이 낫다는 생각을 John에게 전하려 하므로 답은 ④ '그 폰을 나에게 주면 내가 그것을 기증하는 것은 어떠니?'이다.

오답 보기 해석

① 너는 내가 너의 오래된 폰을 고칠 수 있다는 것을 알았니?
② 근처 교회에 중고폰이 많다고 들었어.
③ 너는 오래 전에 새 폰을 샀어야 했어.
⑤ 저 오래된 폰을 좀 버려 줄래?

총 어휘 수 151

16 담화 목적 / 17 세부 내용 파악

소재 Arts Center Benefit 자선행사

듣기 대본 해석

남: 안녕하세요 학생, 학부모, 그리고 직원 여러분. 여러분을 우리 캠퍼스의 황홀한 저녁에 초대합니다. 열 번째 연례 Franklin 대학 Arts Center Benefit이 8월 15일 토요일 우리 캠퍼스 박람회 장소에서 개최됩니다. 언제나 그렇듯이 자선 행사의 목적은 예술 센터를 지원하고 우리 학생들뿐만 아니라 지역사회에도 혜택을 줄 수 있는 새로운 프로그램들을 만들기 위한 자금을 마련하기 위함입니다. 모두가 아시다시피, 예술은 지역사회에 중요한 요소입니다. 예술은 우리를 하나로 묶어주고 상상도 할 수 없는 방법으로 우리의 마음과 영혼을 길러줍니다. 자선 행사는 지역사회가 우리 프로그램에 받은 것을 갚을 수 있게 해줍니다. 이 행사에서 나온 모든 수익금은 FC 예술 센터의 자금에 도움을 줄 것입니다. 다양한 이벤트들이 계획되고 있는데요, 여느 때처럼 사진 전시회, 특별하게 여겨지는 작품들의 경매, 훌륭한 우리 학교 재즈 밴드의 공연, 그리고 당연히 많은 먹거리들이 준비되어 있습니다. 행사의 표를 예매하고 싶거나 행사에는 참여하지 못하지만 기부를 하고 싶은 분들은 우리 학교 홈페이지를 방문하여 자선 행사 링크를 눌러 주세요. 감사합니다.

어휘

incredible ***a.*** 믿을 수 없는 놀라운 **benefit** ***n.*** 이득, 자선 행사 **fund** ***n.*** 기금, 자금 ***v.*** 자금을 모으다 **vital** ***a.*** 필수적인 **cultivate** ***v.*** 경작하다, 기르다 **exhibition** ***n.*** 전시회 **auction** ***n.*** 경매 **donate** ***v.*** 기부하다

정답 16 ① 17 ④

문제풀이

16 담화의 중간 부분에서 행사의 목적이 FC 예술 센터 지원과 프로그램 개발을 위한 것이라고 했으므로 Arts Center Benefit의 목적은 ① '아트 센터에 도움을 줄 자금을 모으려고'이다.

17 이벤트로는 사진 전시회, 작품 경매, 재즈 밴드 공연, 그리고 많은 먹거리가 있다고 했으므로 언급되지 않은 것은 ④ '유명인사 초대'이다.

오답 보기 해석

16

② 아트 센터 경매를 위한 예술가들의 기부를 찾기 위해
③ Franklin 대학교 학생들의 작품을 전시하기 위해
④ 새로운 아트 센터의 건축을 위한 후원을 마련하기 위해
⑤ 예술 공동체 회원들에게 무료 캠퍼스 투어를 제공하기 위해

총 어휘 수 191

DICTATION ANSWERS

01 I was really impressed

02 make it to the play on time

03 to stand out from / attractive design and color scheme / take the time to respond to comments

04 had a reservation / there was a two-hour time limit / accommodate as many customers as possible / based on how many kids a customer brings

05 I'd ever see you here again / considering working with us / got the role / true to the original costuming

06 I really don't care for the outdoors much / getting the luggage out of the / made him miserable

07 taste a little strange / a couple of months back / Don't forget to bring your tools / I'll clean the sink out

08 you can throw a javelin / while your shoulder was injured / it slipped your mind / I can relate

09 I'm looking to buy some / baked a batch of chess pies / are they running for / save it for next time

10 There isn't much traffic, either / Are there any stations within walking distance / have an attached two-car garage / to be sure

11 extracting natural gas from rock / cost-effective / inserts chemicals / pollute nearby residents' tap water

12 it's that time of the year / I get bad allergies / Mine is a real help / set up an appointment

13 a directory of all of the animals / turned out really well / That was news to me

14 concerned about your grades / they've been steadily falling / felt like myself lately / from here on out

15 throw the old one in the garbage / thinks this is nonsense / remembers reading an article about / collects unwanted electronics and refurbishes them

16-17 invite each of you to / art is vital to a community / cultivates our minds and souls in / click the link for the benefit

26 수능영어듣기 실전모의고사

본문 p.158

01 ⑤	02 ③	03 ②	04 ④	05 ④	06 ②
07 ③	08 ②	09 ④	10 ③	11 ②	12 ④
13 ②	14 ①	15 ⑤	16 ②	17 ⑤	

01 짧은 대화의 응답

소재 야구경기 예매

듣기 대본 해석

남: 여보, 오늘 야구경기 티켓 예매했어?

여: 아, 맞다. 깜박했어. 지금 온라인으로 할게.

남: 너무 늦은 것 같은데. 온라인에서 표가 매진된 걸 봤어. 더 일찍 샀어야 했는데.

여: ⑤ 정말 미안해. 내일 경기 표 예매할게.

어휘

sold out (표가) 매진된, 다 팔린

정답 ⑤

문제풀이

예매하는 것을 깜박했는데 표가 매진되었다는 내용이다. 더 일찍 샀어야 했다는 남자의 말에 적절한 대답은 ⑤ '정말 미안해. 내일 경기 표 예매할게.'이다.

오답 보기 해석

① 나 이 표를 팔 생각이야.

② 안됐구나. 오늘 나중에 해보자.

③ 표를 어디다가 뒀는지 기억이 안 나.

④ 걱정하지 마. 벌써 표 샀어.

총 어휘 수 46

02 짧은 대화의 응답

소재 나비정원 방문

듣기 대본 해석

여: 여기가 안내책자에서 본 나비정원이 분명해요.

남: 맞아요. 우리 여행의 끝이기도 하죠. 즐거운 시간 보냈길 바라요, Conn 부인.

여: 네. 모든 것이 아름다웠어요. 정원에서 얼마나 있을 수 있죠?

남: ③ 공원이 해질 때 닫으니까 여유를 가지세요.

어휘

brochure ***n.*** 안내책자

정답 ③

문제풀이

여자가 정원에서 얼마나 있을 수 있냐고 물었으므로 남자의 적절한 대답은 ③ '공원이 해질 때 닫으니까 여유를 가지세요.'이다.

오답 보기 해석

① 우리가 박물관에서 더 많은 시간을 보냈으면 좋았을 것 같네요.

② 좋은 시간을 보냈는데 확실히 피곤하네요.

④ 여기가 여행에서 처음 멈추는 곳이니까 서둘러야 합니다.

⑤ 미안한데 그럴 수 없어요. 나비정원이 문을 닫았거든요.

총 어휘 수 52

03 담화 목적

소재 토크쇼 손님 소개

듣기 대본 해석

남: 안녕하세요, 여러분. 저는 Michael Johnson이고 오늘 아침 우리 프로그램인 Student Volunteers에 참여해 주셔서 감사합니다. 대학생들의 관점에서 우리 나라에서 가장 존경 받는 사람이 누구인지 알아보기 위해 우리가 실시한 조사에 여러분이 참여했거나 적어도 그것에 대해 알고 계시리라고 확신합니다. 거의 매년 선택된 사람은 성공한 사업가나 정치가 같은 힘 있는 사람이었습니다. 하지만 올해는 꽤 다릅니다. 학생들은 수년 동안 불우한 이웃을 도와준 사람인 Amelia Henderson에 투표했습니다. 그녀는 빈민 지역사회에서 불우한 이웃들이 기술을 배우도록 도와서 그들이 제대로 된 직장을 찾을 수 있게 해주었습니다. 그녀의 너그러움과 포부는 우리 학생들에게 강하고 긍정적인 영향을 주었습니다. 이 시점에서 저는 우리 모두와 이야기하기 위해 오늘 초대된 Henderson 씨를 소개하고자 합니다. 그녀는 왜 불우한 사람들을 돕는 것이 중요한지를 오늘 우리와 이야기를 나눌 것입니다. 안녕하세요, Henderson 씨. 오늘 우리가 당신과 함께하게 되어서 너무나 행운이라고 말하며 시작할게요.

어휘

survey ***n.*** 조사 **conduct** ***v.*** 수행하다 **in an attempt to V** ~하기 위하여, ~하려는 시도로 **entrepreneur** ***n.*** 사업가, 기업가 **decent** ***a.*** 괜찮은, 제대로 된 **generosity** ***n.*** 너그러움 **ambition** ***n.*** 야망, 포부 **in need** 어려움에 처한, 궁핍한

정답 ②

문제풀이

대학생들 사이에서 존경 받은 인물로 선정된 인물을 초청해 소개하고 있으므로 정답은 ② '오늘의 토크쇼 초대 손님을 소개하려고'이다.

총 어휘 수 180

04 대화 주제

소재 버스를 이용한 통학

듣기 대본 해석

남: 안녕, Rachel.

여: 좋은 아침이에요, Turner 선생님. 아침에 항상 학교에 버스를 타고 가시나요?

남: 매일 아침은 아니고 한 달에 두어 번 정도 타. 너는 어떠니?

여: 저는 매일 아침 타요. 엄마가 항상 차로 태워다 주신다고 하지만, 저는 버스가 더 좋아요.

남: 왜?

여: 저는 환경에 특별히 관심이 있어요. 게다가 비싼 기름값 때문에 그것이 더 싸기도 하고요.

남: 와. 참 훌륭하구나.

여: 음, 저는 버스를 타는 것보다 차를 타는 것이 열 배 더 비싸다고 읽었어요.

남: 정말? 큰 차이구나.

여: 또 스마트폰으로 뉴스를 읽고 제 LookBook 페이지를 확인할 수 있는 훌륭한 시간이죠.

남: 그렇구나. 음, 나는 조금 더 걸을 수 있는 기회가 생기기 때문에 보통 지하철을 타.

여: 무슨 말씀이신지 알겠어요. 저는 버스 정류장까지 짧게 걸어가는 것을 굉장히 즐겨요. 그것은 저에게 저의 하루에 대해 생각할 기회를 줘요. 그것은 또한 좋은 운동이에요.

남: 그렇게 생각하는 것도 좋네.

어휘

prefer ***v.*** 더 좋아하다 **environmentally** ***ad.*** 환경적으로 **conscious** ***a.*** 의식하는 **thoughtful** ***a.*** 사려 깊은

정답 ④

문제풀이
여자는 환경과 기름값, 시간 활용의 예를 들면서 버스로 통학할 때의 좋은 점을 말하고 있으므로 두 사람의 대화 주제는 ④ '버스로 통학하는 것의 장점'이다.

총 어휘 수 171

05 대화자의 관계 파악

소재 구직자와 직업 상담

듣기 대본 해석
여: Carter 씨군요. 어떻게 지내세요?
남: 음, 솔직히, 상황이 좋지는 않아요.
여: 유감이군요. 하지만 제가 당신의 상황이 호전되도록 도우러 왔어요. 당신과 관련된 소개를 좀 해주시겠어요?
남: 정식 훈련을 받지는 않았지만 오토바이를 고치는 것에 대해 많은 것을 알고 있어요.
여: 그렇군요. 여가시간에 무엇을 하시나요?
남: 컴퓨터 설계나 약간의 네트워킹을 하며 많은 시간을 보내요.
여: 알겠습니다. 컴퓨터를 좋아하시는군요?
남: 맞습니다. 저는 컴퓨터와 함께 자랐어요. 제가 어렸을 때 그것이 유일한 친구였거든요.
여: 좋습니다. 혼자 일하시길 원하시나요, 아니면 여러 명이 함께 하는 것이 좋으신가요?
남: 혼자 일하는 것이 낫겠군요. 약간 내성적이어서요.
여: 알겠습니다. Computers Plus에 기술자를 위한 자리가 있는 것 같군요. 당신 같은 분에게 잘 맞는 자리인 것 같아요.
남: 동의합니다. 도와주셔서 감사합니다.

어휘
relevant ***a.*** 관련 있는, 적절한 **introvert** ***n.*** 내향적인 사람
opening ***n.*** (사람을 쓸 수 있는) 빈자리(공석) **suitable** ***a.*** 적합한

정답 ④

문제풀이
여자는 남자에 대해 묻고, 남자는 자신의 능력과 기술, 원하는 일에 대해 대답해 주고 있다. 대화의 마지막 부분에서 여자가 남자에게 기술자를 위한 자리가 있다고 추천해주는 것으로 보아 두 사람의 관계는 ④ '취업 상담원 ― 구직자'가 가장 적절하다.

총 어휘 수 159

06 그림의 세부 내용 파악

소재 시계 구입

듣기 대본 해석
남: 안녕하세요. 뭘 도와드릴까요?
여: 부엌에 놓을 새 시계를 찾고 있어요. 어떤 것들이 있죠?
남: 현재는 이 다섯 개만 재고로 가지고 있습니다. 이 꽃 모양은 어떤가요? 부엌용으로 디자인된 건데요.
여: 저한테는 약간 싸구려같이 보이는데요. 제 부엌은 굉장히 현대식이거든요.
남: 알겠습니다. 그런 경우라면 이 사각형 모양은 어떤가요? 우아하고 단순하죠.
여: 전 이보다 더 단순한 게 좋은데요. 숫자가 12개 전부 있는 것 보다 4개만 있으면 좋겠어요.
남: 알겠습니다. 그럼 3개가 남았네요. 이건 맘에 안 들어 하실 것 같은데 별 모양이어서 손님의 부엌 장식용으로 아마도 어울리지 않을 것 같아요.
여: 네, 그리고 사각형 해 모양 시계는 저한테는 좀 요란한 것 같네요.
남: 네, 그럼 이게 가장 좋을 것 같네요.
여: 그런 것 같아요. 그걸로 할게요.
남: 좋습니다.

어휘
in stock 재고로 있는 **cheesy** ***a.*** 싸구려의, 값싼 **elegant** ***a.*** 우아한
fit ***v.*** 어울리다, 맞다 **loud** ***a.*** (색깔 · 무늬 등이) 야단스러운, 야한

정답 ②

문제풀이
꽃 모양은 싫다고 했고 숫자가 모두 써있는 것도 원하지 않는다고 했으므로 ②, ③, ⑤번이 남는데 별 모양과 해 모양도 안 어울릴 거라고 했으므로 정답은 ②번이다.

총 어휘 수 150

07 할 일

소재 손님이 찾는 책 가져다 주기

듣기 대본 해석
남: 안녕하세요. 무엇을 도와드릴까요?
여: *Chocalat*를 찾고 있어요.
남: 사탕 구역을 찾아보세요. 계산대 쪽에 있어요.
여: 아, 사탕을 말하는 게 아니에요. 그 이름으로 된 책을 찾고 있어요.
남: 아, 찾으시는 것 있는 것 같아요. 작가 이름 혹시 아세요?
여: 잘 모르겠어요. 프랑스에서 초콜릿 가게를 여는 여자에 관한 얘기란 것만 알아요.
남: 잠시만 기다려 주시면 제가 컴퓨터로 찾아 드릴게요. *[키보드 치는 소리]* 네, 재고에 한 권 있네요.
여: 좋네요. 얼마예요?
남: 13.99달러입니다. 저희 혜택 프로그램 회원이시면 10퍼센트 할인받으실 수 있으세요.
여: 안타깝게도 회원이 아니네요. 그래도 책 살게요.
남: 알겠습니다. 찾아서 갖고 올게요.

어휘
aisle ***n.*** 통로, 구역 **register** ***n.*** 계산대 **in stock** 재고로

정답 ③

문제풀이
남자는 여자가 찾는 책의 재고가 있는지 알아봐 주었고 여자가 책을 사겠다고 했으므로 남자는 책을 찾아서 가져오겠다고 했다. 따라서 남자가 할 일은 ③ '책 가져다 주기'이다.

총 어휘 수 129

08 이유

소재 경기에 참가 못하는 이유

듣기 대본 해석
[휴대폰이 울린다.]
여: 안녕, Leo. 너도 알다시피, 네가 오늘 연습에 빠져서 팀원들이 다 걱정하고 있어.
남: 응, 미안해. 연습에 갈 수 없었어. 사실 내가 전화한 건 내일 경기에 관해 얘기하기 위해서야.
여: 오, 무슨 일인데?
남: 그게 넌 내가 내일 못 뛸 걸 고려해야 할 것 같아.
여: 정말? 하지만 넌 우리의 가장 뛰어난 선수인걸. 우린 네가 필요해.
남: 나도 뛰고 싶은데 그럴 수가 없어.
여: 무슨 일이 있었는지 말해줄래?
남: 그게 좀 창피한 게, 내 차 타고 자랑하다가 자제력을 잃고 벽에 부딪혔어.
여: 큰일이네! 괜찮아?
남: 사고 때문에 멍이 좀 들긴 했는데 괜찮아. 근데 의사들이 엑스레이 찍고 오늘 하루는 병원에서 지내는 게 좋을 것 같대.

여: 큰일이네, 근데 어쩔 수 없지. 빨리 다 나았으면 좋겠다.
남: 고마워.

어휘
match ***n.*** 경기 **embarrassing** ***a.*** 난처한, 창피한 **show off** 과시하다, 자랑하다 **crash into** ~와 충돌하다 **bruised** ***a.*** 멍든, 타박상을 입은

정답 ②

문제풀이
남자는 차를 타고 자랑하다가 다친 나머지 하루 동안 병원에 입원할 처지에 놓여 내일 경기에 나갈 수 없게 되었다. 그러므로 정답은 ② '병원에 입원해야 해서'이다.

총 어휘 수 154

09 숫자

소재 피자 주문하기

듣기 대본 해석
남: 안녕하세요, 무엇을 도와드릴까요?
여: 배달 주문을 하고 싶어요.
남: 네, 어떤 것을 원하세요?
여: 슈프림 피자와 마늘빵 콤보와 디핑소스를 추가로 더 받고 싶어요.
남: 물론이죠, 그렇지만 추가 소스는 1달러를 더 내셔야 해요.
여: 좋아요. 닭고기도 있나요?
남: 네, 있어요. 후라이드 치킨과 버팔로윙이 있어요. 각각 5달러입니다.
여: 좋아요. 제가 주문한 것에 각각 하나씩 추가할게요.
남: 오늘은 그것이 전부인가요?
여: 네, 그게 전부예요. 모두 얼마죠?
남: 모두 합쳐서, 슈프림 피자와 마늘빵 콤보, 소스 추가와 치킨 두 개 추가해서 30달러입니다. 오늘 쿠폰을 사용하실 건가요?
여: 네, 30달러 이상 사용시 20퍼센트 할인되는 쿠폰이 있어요.
남: 네, 좋아요. 이 쿠폰은 손님께서 VISA 신용카드 혹은 직불카드로 결제하실 경우에만 가능합니다.
여: 네, 알아요. 전 VISA 직불카드를 가지고 있어요.

어휘
make an order 주문하다 **delivery** ***n.*** 배송, 배달 **valid** ***a.*** 유효한 **credit card** 신용카드 **debit card** 직불카드

정답 ④

문제풀이
여자가 주문한 전체 금액이 30달러라고 했는데, 30달러 이상 주문 시 사용 가능한 20퍼센트 할인 쿠폰이 있다고 했으므로 30달러에 20퍼센트 할인을 적용하면 24달러가 된다. 따라서 답은 ④ '$24'이다.

총 어휘 수 153

10 언급 유무

소재 노숙자 보호소를 위한 자선행사

듣기 대본 해석
여: 네가 보고 있는 그 전단지는 뭐야, Tommy?
남: 지역 노숙자 보호소에 도움을 주기 위한 자선행사에 관한 거야. 행사가 10월 13일야.
여: 다가오는 토요일이네, 맞지?
남: 맞아. 그들은 슬로건도 있어. 슬로건은 "생활필수품이 없는 사람들에게 그것들을 줍시다"야.
여: 그들은 좀 더 창의적인 뭔가를 생각해 낼 수 없었나 보다. 오, 이 전단지에 행사가 새로운 레크레이션 센터에서 열릴 거라고 써 있네. 거기가 어디지?
남: 길 바로 아래야. 너 법원 청사가 어디에 있는지 알지? 그것은 법원 청사로부터 바로 길 건너편에 있어.
여: 아, 그게 무슨 건물인지 궁금했었어. 우리도 참가해야 한다고 생각해.
남: 맞아. 난 불우한 사람들을 돕는 것을 언제나 좋아해.
여: 나도 그래. 그리고 광고에 참석자들을 위해 무료 다과를 준다고 나와 있네.
남: 그래. 가서 도와주자.

어휘
benefit ***v.*** ~에게 이익을 가져다 주다, 이익을 얻다
basic necessities 기본적 필수품 **come up with** 생각해 내다
courthouse ***n.*** 법원 청사 **advertisement** ***n.*** 광고
refreshments ***n.*** 다과, 음식 **attendee** ***n.*** 참석자

정답 ③

문제풀이
대화에서 자선행사의 날짜, 슬로건, 장소, 간식 제공 여부에 대한 언급은 있었지만 참가 방법에 관한 언급은 없으므로 정답은 ③ '참가 방법'이다.

총 어휘 수 131

11 내용 일치 · 불일치

소재 벚꽃 축제 안내

듣기 대본 해석
여: 좋은 아침입니다, 신사 숙녀 여러분. 드디어 봄이 다시 왔습니다. 벚꽃이 활짝 폈어요! 상쾌한 봄 공기를 깊이 들이마시고 여러분의 눈을 아름다운 꽃들에게 돌려보세요. 저희는 해마다 열리는 네 번째 벚꽃 축제의 개최를 발표하게 되어 더없이 기쁩니다! 축제 날짜는 해마다 바뀌는데 올해는 4월 20일부터 4월 27일까지입니다. 올해 축제에는 어린이들이 즐길만한 것들을 포함하여 새로운 활동들이 계획되어 있습니다! 그러니 가족 모두가 오셔서 멋진 축제를 즐겨주세요. 볼 것과 할 것이 너무 많아서 여러분은 시간이 더 있었으면 하실 겁니다! 만약 여러분이 축제 장소에 차를 주차하기 원하시면 요금은 15달러이지만 걸어서 오신다면 5달러입니다. 여러분 모두를 곧 뵙고 싶습니다!

어휘
announce ***v.*** 발표하다, 알리다 **blossom** ***n.*** 꽃 **in full bloom** 만발하여 **annual** ***a.*** 매년의, 연례의

정답 ②

문제풀이
벚꽃 축제의 날짜는 해마다 바뀐다고 되어 있으므로 내용과 일치하지 않는 것은 ② '축제는 매년 봄 같은 날짜에 열린다.'이다.

총 어휘 수 148

12 도표

소재 중고 오토바이 선택

듣기 대본 해석
남: 안녕하세요, 도와드릴까요?
여: 안녕하세요, 중고 오토바이를 찾고 있는데요.
남: 생각하고 계신 특정 모델이 있나요?
여: 네, S-35과 K-350이 가장 좋아하는 모델이에요.
남: 알겠습니다. *[마우스 클릭 소리]* 이 목록을 보세요. 그 모델 종류는 5종을 보유하고 있어요.
여: 음, 10년이 넘은 오토바이는 원하지 않아요.

남: 글쎄요, 하지만 이 K-350의 가격이 다섯 개 중 가장 저렴한데요.
여: 하지만 그래도 10년보다 오래되지 않았으면서 350cc보다 크지 않은 모델을 원해요.
남: 알겠습니다. 가격은 어느 정도 보고 계시는지 물어도 될까요?
여: 5,000달러 미만이요.
남: 그렇다면 두 가지 선택이 남는군요.
여: 흠, 비록 가격차가 약간 있지만 더 큰 엔진을 가진 오토바이를 원해요. 다른 것보다 더 빠를 테니까요.
남: 좋아요! 훌륭한 선택입니다!

어휘
available ***a.*** 이용할 수 있는

정답 ④

문제풀이
10년 넘은 기종은 원하지 않는다고 했으므로 ③번은 제외된다. 또한 350cc 이하가 아니기 때문에 ②번도 제외되고 가격이 5,000달러 이상인 ⑤번도 제외된다. 남아있는 ①번과 ④번 중 더 큰 엔진을 가진 것은 ④번이다.

총 어휘 수 129

13 긴 대화의 응답

소재 할아버지, 할머니와의 저녁 식사

듣기 대본 해석
[전화벨이 울린다.]
여: 아빠, 저예요.
남: 그래 Kaitlyn. 오는 중이야?
여: 아직이요, 근데 터미널에 도착했어요.
남: 그렇구나. 버스는 언제 출발해?
여: 3시 좀 지나서 출발 예정이에요. 기다리는 동안 카페에서 간식 사먹으려고요.
남: 그래. 할머니, 할아버지랑 저녁 먹으러 여기 6시까지 올 수 있겠어?
여: 아니요. 오늘 금요일이라 차가 많이 막혀서 도시 벗어나는 데 좀 걸릴 것 같아요.
남: 왜 좀 더 이른 시간의 버스를 타지 않았니?
여: 그러려고 했는데 터미널에 도착했을 때 표가 다 팔렸었어요.
남: 그래. 안됐구나. 그분들이 너 많이 보고 싶어 하셔.
여: 네, 저도 시간에 맞춰서 저녁 식사 같이 하고 싶은데 너무 늦게 도착할 것 같네요.
남: ② 그럼, 네가 도착할 때까지 우리가 저녁 식사를 미룰게.

어휘
in time 시간 맞춰 **traffic** ***n.*** 교통(량) **sold out** (표가) 매진된 〈문제〉 **postpone** ***v.*** 연기하다, 미루다

정답 ②

문제풀이
저녁 식사 약속 시간이 6시인데 여자가 너무 늦게 도착할 것 같다고 걱정하고 있으므로 아빠가 마지막에 할 말로 적절한 것은 ② '그럼, 네가 도착할 때까지 우리가 저녁 식사를 미룰게.'이다.

오답 보기 해석
① 나는 버스 정류장에서 차편이 필요할 거야.
③ 네가 더 이른 시간 버스표를 사야 할 것 같아.
④ 좋아. 나는 7시경에 역에 있을 거야.
⑤ 문제 없어. 내가 더 이른 시간의 버스 표를 예약해줄게.

총 어휘 수 142

14 긴 대화의 응답

소재 창 밖 가로등으로 인한 방 옮기기

듣기 대본 해석
[전화벨이 울린다.]
여: 안내 데스크입니다. 무엇을 도와드릴까요?
남: 안녕하세요. 3D 방의 Dennis Reynolds입니다.
여: 무엇을 도와드릴까요, Reynolds 씨?
남: 그게, 제 창 밖에 가로등이 있어요. 근데 너무 밝아요. 켜져 있는 채로는 잘 수가 없네요.
여: Reynolds 씨, 죄송하지만 그 가로등들은 안전상의 문제 때문에 켜져 있어야 합니다.
남: 아침 일찍 일어나야 하거든요. 전 잠을 자야 해요. 정말 거슬리네요.
여: 그럼 건물 반대편에 있는 방으로 옮겨 드릴게요. 괜찮을까요?
남: 그러면 되겠네요.
여: 알겠습니다. 2층의 4B방으로 옮겨 드릴게요.
남: 제 짐을 누군가가 같이 옮겨 줄 수 있을까요?
여: ① 물론이죠. 안내원이 곧 도우러 갈 겁니다.

어휘
purpose ***n.*** 목적 **nuisance** ***n.*** 성가신 것, 귀찮은 것 **belongings** ***n.*** 소유물

정답 ①

문제풀이
남자가 창 밖 가로등이 너무 밝아 잠을 잘 수 없다며 가로등을 꺼달라고 하자 방을 바꿔주는 상황인데, 마지막에 남자가 짐을 옮겨줄 수 있냐고 물었으므로 그에 적절한 대답은 ① '물론이죠. 안내원이 곧 도우러 갈 겁니다.'이다.

오답 보기 해석
② 문제 없어요. 손님은 방을 바꾸실 필요가 없습니다.
③ 체크아웃 때 추가 요금을 처리하실 수 있습니다, 손님.
④ 제가 반드시 창문 밖에 있는 등을 끄겠습니다, 손님.
⑤ 물론이죠. 안내 데스크에서 아침 7시에 모닝콜을 해드릴게요.

총 어휘 수 133

15 상황에 적절한 말

소재 효과적인 프레젠테이션 준비

듣기 대본 해석
여: Brody는 새로운 게임에 대해 컴퓨터 게임 회사에 홍보하기 위해 프레젠테이션의 마무리 작업을 합니다. 그는 좋은 친구인 Leah에게 건설적인 피드백뿐만 아니라 프리젠테이션에 대한 그녀의 의견을 얻기 위해 그녀와 프레젠테이션을 연습할 수 있는지 묻습니다. 그들은 카페에서 만나고, 거기서 그는 그의 프레젠테이션을 살펴봅니다. 그녀는 게임의 아이디어는 좋아하지만 그의 프레젠테이션에 문제가 좀 있다고 생각합니다. 게임의 스토리가 좀 복잡해 보이는 것 같고 스크린샷이 충분하지 않습니다. 그녀는 너무 많은 언어적 정보와 충분하지 않은 시각적 정보가 회사의 임원들을 지루하게 할 거라고 지적합니다. Brody는 프레젠테이션을 개선하기 위해 무엇을 해야 할지 궁금해서 Leah에게 조언을 구합니다. 이런 상황에서 Leah는 Brody에게 뭐라고 말할까요?
Leah: ⑤ 프레젠테이션에 더 많은 시각적 예들을 제공하는 것이 중요해.

어휘
constructive ***a.*** 건설적인 **go through** ~을 살펴보다, 조사하다 **complicated** ***a.*** 복잡한 **verbal** ***a.*** 언어의, 구두의 **executive** ***n.*** 경영진, 임원 〈문제〉 **in detail** 상세하게 **beta test** (신제품에 대한) 베타 테스트 **consult** ***v.*** 상담하다 **benefit** ***v.*** ~에게 이익을 가져다주다, 이익을 얻다

정답 ⑤

문제풀이

Leah는 Brody가 만든 프레젠테이션의 아이디어는 좋지만 언어적인 정보가 너무 많고 시각적 정보가 부족하다고 지적했으므로 프레젠테이션을 개선하기 위해 할 말로는 ⑤ '프레젠테이션에 더 많은 시각적 예들을 제공하는 것이 중요해.'가 가장 적절하다.

오답 보기 해석

① 스토리라인을 좀 더 자세하게 설명해야 해.
② 네가 발표하기 전에 게임의 베타테스트를 더 해야 해.
③ 매일 너의 프로그래밍 팀과 상담하는 것이 중요해.
④ 다른 사람이 게임을 발표하게 하는 것이 너한테 도움이 될 거야.

총 어휘 수 145

16 담화 주제 / 17 세부 내용 파악

소재 즐거운 캠핑을 위한 조언

듣기 대본 해석

남: 도시에서 살 때 밖으로 나와 자연을 즐기는 것이 쉽지 않습니다. 하지만 많은 사람들이 도시 생활에서 탈출하기 위해서 야외로 나갑니다. 특히 취미에 열심인 많은 사람들이 캠핑을 레저활동으로 선택하고 있습니다. 야외로 나가는 것은 정신적, 신체적 건강에 좋습니다. 하지만 캠핑을 갈 때 몇 가지 조심해야 할 것이 있습니다. 첫째로, 여러분은 여분의 옷을 꼭 챙기는 것이 좋을 것입니다. 기온이 갑자기 떨어지거나 원래 입고 간 옷이 젖었을 때 여러분을 따뜻하게 해 줄 것입니다. 둘째로, 여러분의 여행을 위해 충분한 음식을 가져가세요. 야영지 주변에서 하이킹을 하는 동안 만약 길을 잃어버릴 경우에 대비해 추가로 음식을 싸가는 것도 좋습니다. 셋째, 구급상자를 가져가세요. 다른 모든 야외활동과 마찬가지로, 캠핑은 위험할 수 있습니다. 또한, 야영지를 떠날 때는 뒷정리를 하세요. 우리의 환경을 깨끗하게 지키는 것이 중요합니다. 마지막으로, 즐거운 시간을 보내세요. 재미가 없다면 취미가 아닙니다. 이런 조언들을 염두에 둔다면 여러분께서는 다음 캠핑에서 안전하고 재미있는 시간을 보내실 수 있으실 겁니다.

어휘

outdoor ***a.*** 옥외의, 야외의 **precaution** ***n.*** 예방 조치
first-aid kit 구급상자

정답 16 ② 17 ⑤

문제풀이

16 안전하고 즐거운 캠핑을 위해 챙겨야 할 것들과 캠핑에 가서 그리고 캠핑이 끝난 후에 할 것들을 이야기하고 있으므로 정답은 ② '캠핑 동안 안전하고 즐겁게 놀기 위한 조언'이다.

17 캠핑 갈 때 가져가야 할 것으로 여분의 옷, 충분한 음식, 구급상자를 언급했고, 캠핑 후 뒷정리를 깨끗하게 청소해야 한다고 말했지만 랜턴에 관한 언급은 하지 않았으므로 정답은 ⑤ '랜턴'이다.

오답 보기 해석

16
① 야외 활동의 정신적, 신체적 장점들
③ 가족 캠핑 때 가져가야 할 것들
④ 캠핑하는 동안 길을 잃어버릴 위험성
⑤ 캠핑하는 동안 응급치료 하는 방법

총 어휘 수 204

DICTATION ANSWERS

01 they're all sold out

02 I hope you enjoyed yourself

03 that we conducted in an attempt to / had a strong positive impact on our students / to help those in need / how fortunate we are

04 always offers to take me in / I like to be environmentally conscious / it gives me the chance to walk

05 turn your life around / Do you prefer being alone / I'd much rather be alone

06 What do you have in stock / prefer one a little simpler / fit your kitchen's decor / I'll take that one

07 near the register / we probably have that / so we have one copy in stock

08 the best player we've got / showing off in my car / a little bruised up / we'll have to deal with it

09 make an order for delivery / this coupon is only valid

10 benefit the local homeless shelter / Give basic necessities / come up with / enjoy helping those less fortunate

11 are in full bloom / let your eyes take in / We couldn't be happier to announce that

12 have any particular model in mind / how much you're looking to pay / there's a little difference in price

13 you'll make it here in time / getting out of the city / tickets were sold out

14 I can't sleep with it on / stay on for safety purposes / It's really a nuisance

15 in order to get her opinion / too much verbal information / bore the executives of the company

16-17 get out and enjoy nature / several precautions you should take / if there's a sudden drop in temperature

27 수능영어듣기 실전모의고사

본문 p.164

01 ①	02 ②	03 ①	04 ③	05 ⑤	06 ④
07 ⑤	08 ④	09 ⑤	10 ③	11 ③	12 ⑤
13 ③	14 ①	15 ③	16 ④	17 ③	

01 짧은 대화의 응답

소재 옷 빌려주기

듣기 대본 해석

여: 와! 기온이 많이 떨어졌어. 얼어버릴 것 같아.
남: 좀 더 따뜻한 옷을 입었어야 했는데. 내 코트 입을래?
여: 아니, 괜찮아. 너도 코트가 없으면 추울 거야.
남: ① 난 차에 여분 코트가 있어.

어휘

freeze ***v.*** 얼다, 얼리다 〈문제〉 **bother** ***v.*** 귀찮게 하다

정답 ①

문제풀이

여자가 춥다고 하자 자기 코트를 입으라는 남자에게, 남자도 추울 테니 괜찮다고 말한다. 이때 남자의 응답으로 가장 적절한 것은 ① '난 차에 여분 코트가 있어.'이다.

오답 보기 해석

② 귀찮게 한 거 사과할게.
③ 내가 이해를 못한 것 같아.
④ 난 더 잘 준비해야 해.
⑤ 그래, 넌 틀림없이 그럴 거야.

총 어휘 수 39

02 짧은 대화의 응답

소재 배가 많이 고픈 딸

듣기 대본 해석

남: 안녕, Lisa. 너 얼굴빛이 안 좋아 보이네. 괜찮아?
여: 학교에서 오늘 정말 바빴어요, 아빠. 배고파 죽겠어요. 저녁은 뭐예요?
남: 음, 아직 어떤 것도 준비가 안 되었지만, 냉장고에 남은 피자가 있을 거야.
여: ② 남은 것이 없어요. 지난밤에 제가 다 먹었어요.

어휘

starve ***v.*** 굶주리다 **leftover** ***n.*** 남은 음식 ***a.*** 먹다 남은, 나머지의
refrigerator ***n.*** 냉장고

정답 ②

문제풀이

냉장고에 남은 피자가 있을 거라는 아빠의 말에 적절한 응답은 ② '남은 것이 없어요. 지난밤에 제가 다 먹었어요.'이다.

오답 보기 해석

① 괜찮아요. 이미 저녁 먹었어요.
③ 알았어요. 제가 좋은 이탈리아 식당을 알아요.
④ 남은 것을 냉장고에 넣어 주세요.
⑤ 저는 피자를 좋아하지만 여기서 팔지 않을 것 같은데요.

총 어휘 수 49

03 담화 주제

소재 식초를 이용한 블랙베리의 신선함 유지법

듣기 대본 해석

여: 봄이 왔습니다. 블랙베리와 같은 신선한 과일을 즐길 때가 온 겁니다. 저는 블랙베리를 신선하게 유지하는 것이 어려웠지만, 한 친구가 보존 기간을 최대화할 수 있는 쉬운 방법을 알려주었습니다. 간단하게 물과 식초로 된 용액을 사용함으로써, 여러분은 신선한 블랙베리의 기한을 크게 늘릴 수 있습니다. 과정은 아주 간단해서 누구라도 할 수 있습니다. 우선, 블랙베리를 식초와 물을 반반 섞은 것으로 씻으세요. 식초가 세균을 죽일 수 있도록 블랙베리를 약 5분 동안 담가주세요. 마지막으로 남아있는 식초를 제거하기 위해 싱크대에서 블랙베리를 헹구기만 하시면 됩니다. 그 비결은 블랙베리의 신선도를 해칠 수 있는 세균을 죽이는 것입니다. 식초의 산성은 세균을 죽이기에 충분히 강하지만, 식초는 가정에서 사용하기에 안전하며 먹어도 됩니다. 이 조언을 따르면, 여러분은 이렇게 하지 않았을 때보다 몇 주 더 오랫동안 신선한 블랙베리를 즐기실 수 있습니다.

어휘

maximize ***v.*** 극대화하다 **shelf life** (식품 등의) 보존 기간, 유통기한
solution ***n.*** 용액, 해결 **vinegar** ***n.*** 식초 **extend** ***v.*** 더 길게 늘이다
soak ***v.*** 담그다, 담기다 **rinse** ***v.*** 씻다 **acidity** ***n.*** 신맛, 산성

정답 ①

문제풀이

여자는 세균을 죽이는 식초를 물과 반반씩 섞은 용액에 블랙베리를 일정 시간 담근 후에 헹굼으로써 그냥 보관했을 때보다 장기간 신선하게 보관할 수 있다고 말하고 있다. 따라서 여자가 하는 말의 주제로 가장 적절한 것은 ① '식초를 이용한 블랙베리의 신선도 유지법'이다.

총 어휘 수 168

04 의견

소재 젊은 사람들의 은어 사용

듣기 대본 해석

남: May 선생님, 괜찮으세요? 화가 나 보이세요. 무슨 일 있으세요?
여: 제가 사는 도시에서 제가 이방인처럼 느껴져요.
남: 왜 그렇게 느끼세요?
여: 음, 오늘 아침에 여기에 올 때 지하철을 탔는데 제 건너편에 한 무리의 젊은이들이 앉아 있었어요. 전 그들이 하는 말 중에서 반은 이해할 수가 없었어요.
남: 그들이 은어를 사용하고 있었다는 거죠?
여: 확실히 그랬어요. 그 젊은 사람들이 무슨 말을 하는지 정확히는 모르겠지만 모두 너무 무례하게 들렸어요.
남: 네, 제가 생각하기에 많은 어른들이 젊은 사람들의 은어를 무례하게 생각하지만, 만약에 어른들이 그것을 사용하거나 이해한다면 젊은 사람들과 더 가까워 질 수 있을 거예요.
여: 나는 이해할 수 없어요.
남: 만약에 그들이 당신이 그들의 은어를 가끔 사용하는 것을 들으면 당신을 그들과 잘 어울리는 사람으로 볼 거예요.
여: 아, 네, 이제 알겠어요.
남: 가끔 저는 아이들에게 은어를 저한테 가르쳐 달라고 하거나 제가 TV에서 들은 것을 그들에게 물어봐요.
여: 저는 당신이 젊은 사람들과 가까워지는 것을 그렇게 중요하게 여기는 줄 몰랐어요.
남: 그렇게 하는 것이 그들과의 관계에 도움이 된다고 생각해요.

어휘

slang ***n.*** 은어, 속어 **impolite** ***a.*** 무례한 **fit in with someone** ~와 잘 어울리다 **once in a while** 가끔 **big deal** 대단한 일, 큰일

정답 ③

문제풀이
남자가 '젊은 사람들이 사용하는 은어를 자신이 가끔 사용하는 것을 그들이 들으면 그들과 잘 어울리는 사람으로 보일 것'이라는 말을 한 것으로 보아, 남자의 의견으로 가장 적절한 것은 ③ '은어 사용을 통해 젊은 사람들과 가까워질 수 있다.'이다.

총 어휘 수 188

05 대화자의 관계 파악

소재 부상당한 선수와 의사의 대화

듣기 대본 해석
여: Phillip, 내 말 들려요? 괜찮아요?
남: 그런 것 같은데요. 아, 내 목. 너무 아파요.
여: 그럴 거예요. 움직이지 마세요. 검사를 할 거예요. 그래서 무슨 일이 일어났는지 기억나요?
남: 제가 기억하는 마지막 일은 패스를 하려고 했는데 상대팀의 누군가가 뒤에서 태클을 걸었어요. 어깨로 넘어지면서 땅에 머리를 부딪쳤어요.
여: 그 이후에 어떤 것이라도 기억나는 것이 있나요?
남: 걸으려고 했는데 어지러웠던 게 기억나요. 제 생각에 제가 아마 다시 땅에 쓰러졌을 거예요. 제가 여기 탈의실에서 깨어날 때 까지 그 외에는 아무것도 기억이 나지 않아요
여: 뇌진탕인 것 같아요, Phillip.
남: 정말이요? 심각한 거예요?
여: 글쎄요, 좋지 않은 건 확실해요. 얼마나 심한지 보려면 검사를 몇 개 해야 돼요.
남: 감사합니다. 도와주셔서 정말 감사합니다.
여: 아니에요. 제 직업인 걸요.

어휘
tackle ***v.*** 태클을 걸다 **dizzy** ***a.*** 어지러운 **concussion** ***n.*** 뇌진탕 〈문제〉 **pedestrian** ***n.*** 보행자

정답 ⑤

문제풀이
남자는 아픈 곳을 말하며 패스하다가 태클을 당했다고 다친 상황을 설명하는 것으로 보아 운동선수임을 알 수 있고, 여자는 뇌진탕인 것 같은데 검사를 더 해보자고 했으므로 의사임을 알 수 있다. 따라서 정답은 ⑤ '의사 — 운동선수'이다.

오답 보기 해석
① 경찰 — 피해자 ② 택시 운전사 — 보행자
③ 기자 — 축구감독 ④ 보험 설계사 — 고객

총 어휘 수 145

06 그림의 세부 내용 파악

소재 소풍 상차림

듣기 대본 해석
남: 안녕 Carrie, 소풍 식사 준비 무척 잘했네.
여: 고마워, Bob. 근데 모두가 먹을 수 있을 정도로 음식이 많지 않을까 봐 걱정돼.
남: 충분할 거야. 어쨌든, 식탁 중간에 꽃으로 장식한 것 마음에 든다.
여: 정원에서 따왔어. 또, 채식주의자들을 위해 파스타를 만들었어. 그리고 그걸 식사하는 사람들에 제일 가깝게 놨어.
남: 진짜 맛있어 보인다. 우리처럼 고기 먹는 사람들을 위해 닭 요리도 했네.
여: 맞아. 옥수수가 너무 멀리 놓여 있나?
남: 응, 더 앞쪽에 놓는 게 좋을 것 같아. 근데, 음료들은 어디 있어?
여: 음료를 위한 테이블은 따로 있어.
남: 그렇구나. 음, 손님들을 위해 건강한 후식을 준비했구나.
여: 응. 과일은 여름에 하는 소풍에 좋고 컵케이크나 파이처럼 소화가 잘 안 되는 음식이 아니야.
남: 맞아. 그나저나 초대해줘서 고마워.
여: 아냐, Bob. 와줘서 기뻐.

어휘
decorate ***v.*** 장식하다 **vegetarian** ***n.*** 채식주의자 **diner** ***n.*** 식사하는 사람 **out of reach** 손이 닿지 않는 곳에

정답 ④

문제풀이
여자가 음료를 위한 테이블은 따로 준비했다고 했는데 그림에서는 꽃병 뒤에 위치해 있으므로 그림과 일치하지 않는다. 따라서 정답은 ④번이다.

총 어휘 수 162

07 할 일

소재 보고서를 위한 설문 도와주기

듣기 대본 해석
남: 안녕, Catherine. 나 이번 주 금요일 야구 경기 표가 두 장 있어. 같이 갈래?
여: 정말 그러고 싶지만 못 갈 것 같아. 다음 주 월요일까지 학기말 리포트 두 개를 내야 해.
남: 어떤 것들인데? 내가 그걸 끝내도록 도와주면 같이 갈 수 있어?
여: 당연하지. 하나는 소설에 대한 독서 리포트이고, 다른 하나는 스마트폰이 우리 생활을 어떻게 변화시켰는가에 대한 분석 리포트야.
남: 독서 리포트는 어떻게 되어 가?
여: 그건 내일이면 다 될 것 같아. 문제는 두 번째 리포트야.
남: 스마트폰의 영향에 대한 설문 질문은 만들었어?
여: 응. 그런데 그 짧은 시간에 충분한 사람들에게 설문지를 주긴 어려울 것 같아. 도와줄 수 있어?
남: 물론. 기꺼이 그럴게. 그러면 이번 금요일에 나랑 야구 경기에 가는 거야, 그렇지?
여: 응, 약속할게. 정말 고마워.

어휘
term paper 학기말 보고서 **effect** ***n.*** 효과 **be willing to V** 기꺼이 ~하다 **thanks a million** 대단히 고맙습니다

정답 ⑤

문제풀이
여자는 설문 질문은 만들었지만 짧은 시간에 혼자서 사람들에게 물어보기 어려울 것 같다면서 남자에게 도움을 청하고 있으므로 남자가 여자를 위해 할 일은 ⑤ '사람들에게 물어 설문 완성하기'이다.

오답 보기 해석
① 설문 조사 질문 만들기
② 두 장의 야구 경기 표 예매하기
③ 그녀의 두 개의 학기말 보고서 제출하기
④ 독서 리포트에 대한 조언 해주기

총 어휘 수 155

08 이유

소재 회의 일정 잡기

듣기 대본 해석
[전화벨이 울린다.]
남: 여보세요, Dan Brown입니다.
여: 안녕하세요, Brown 씨. Global Media의 Claudia입니다.

남: 안녕하세요, Claudia 씨. 무엇을 도와드릴까요?
여: 지난주 당신이 저희 회사와 일하는 것과 관련하여 이야기를 나눈 것에 대해 사장님께 말씀드렸습니다.
남: 그래서 자연 다큐멘터리를 허가받은 것을 이야기해주려고 전화하신 거군요, 맞죠?
여: 맞습니다. 당신이 아직도 그것을 제작해 주실 용의가 있으신지 궁금합니다.
남: 좋습니다. 그렇게 하겠습니다.
여: 감사합니다. 조만간 당신과 일하게 될 다른 프로듀서 분들과의 회의 일정을 정해야 하는데요. 목요일 저녁 7시 가능하신가요?
남: 그날은 안 되겠는데요. 그날은 제가 막 끝마친 저의 여행 다큐멘터리를 상영해야 하거든요. 금요일 낮 12시는 어떤가요?
여: 죄송하지만 금요일은 프로듀서 중 한 분이 출장을 가시고 14일이 돼서야 돌아오실 것 같아요.
남: 그렇다면 저 없이 회의하는 것이 가능할까요? 나중에 회의 내용을 간단히 알려주셔도 되니까요.
여: 그렇게 하면 될 것 같습니다. 제가 확인해 보겠습니다. 곧 다시 이야기 나누시죠, Brown 씨.

어휘

get the green light (착수) 허가를 받다 **screen** ***v.*** 상영하다
brief ***v.*** ~에게 (~에 대해) 알려주다(보고하다)

정답 ④

문제풀이

대화의 중간쯤에서 여자가 목요일 저녁에 회의가 가능한지 물었을 때 남자는 그 날은 여행 다큐멘터리를 상영해야 해서 안 된다고 말했으므로 남자가 회의에 참석할 수 없는 이유는 ④ '다른 다큐멘터리를 상영해야 해서'이다.

총 어휘 수 186

09 숫자

소재 조카들의 생일선물로 테니스 라켓 구입

듣기 대본 해석

남: 안녕하세요. 무엇을 도와드릴까요?
여: 안녕하세요. 제 조카들에게 줄 테니스 라켓 한 세트를 찾고 있어요. 아이들이 쌍둥이인데 생일이 곧 다가오거든요.
남: 네. 몇 살이 되는데요?
여: 이제 10살이 돼요. 그렇게 어린 아이들을 위한 것이 있나요?
남: 물론이죠. 이 검은색 라켓을 한번 보세요. 70달러예요.
여: 와! 좀 비싼데요.
남: 이건 티타늄 합금으로 만들어졌고요, 내구성이 좋도록 만들어졌어요. 그런데, 예산이 어느 정도 되세요?
여: 한 개에 대략 60달러씩 쓰려고요.
남: 알겠어요. 그보다 더 비싼 게 싫으시면 이 알루미늄 라켓은 어때요? 이 파란색 라켓은 제가 보여드렸던 검은색보다 20달러 더 싸답니다. 빨간 것은 40달러 밖에 안하고요.
여: 둘 다 파란색을 좋아해서요. 그걸로 할게요.
남: 잘 고르셨어요!
여: 신용카드로 계산 되죠?
남: 당연하죠. 계산대로 안내해 드릴게요.

어휘

alloy ***n.*** 합금 **budget** ***n.*** 예산, 비용 **register** ***n.*** 계산대

정답 ⑤

문제풀이

여자는 남자가 처음에 보여준 70달러짜리 검은색 라켓보다 20달러가 더 싼 파란색 라켓을 2개 샀으므로 총 지불할 금액은 ⑤ '$100'이다.

총 어휘 수 151

10 언급 유무

소재 마음에 드는 정장

듣기 대본 해석

남: 엄마, 졸업이 다가 오고 있어서 꽤 흥분돼요.
여: 그래, 아버지께서 오늘 아침에 그것에 관해 말씀하셨어. 아버지께서는 네가 새로운 정장을 찾고 있다고 말씀하시던데.
남: 그래요, 그리고 Bowtie Suits에서 멋진 정장을 찾았어요. 거기가 어디인지 아시죠, 그렇죠?
여: 물론이지. 내가 일하고 있는 Fourth Street 근처잖아. 어떤 종류의 정장을 찾았니?
남: 그 정장은 격식을 갖추었지만 너무 과하게 격식을 갖추지는 않았거든요. 재단도 멋져요. 제 생각에는 그 정장이 저에게 완벽하게 어울려요.
여: 그래, 정장은 검은색이니 짙은 남색이니?
남: 매우 진한 짙은 남색이에요. 거의 검은색처럼 보여요.
여: 가격은 얼마니?
남: 세일해서 300달러에요. 나쁘지 않죠, 그렇죠?
여: 그건 내가 예상한 것보다는 약간 더 비싸네. 오늘 매장에 가보자꾸나. 네가 한번 입어봤으면 좋겠구나.
남: 네. 언제 저를 데려가실 시간이 날까요?
여: 아버지께서 집에 오실 때까지 기다려 보자. 우리 모두가 함께 갈 수 있을 거야.

어휘

suit ***n.*** 정장 ***v.*** 어울리다, 잘 맞다 **formal** ***a.*** 격식을 차린, 형식을 갖춘

정답 ③

문제풀이

남자가 미리 찍어둔 정장에 대해 엄마와 이야기하는 상황이다. 매장 이름, 매장 위치, 색상, 가격에 대한 언급은 있었지만 사이즈에 대한 언급은 없었으므로 정답은 ③ '사이즈'이다.

총 어휘 수 156

11 내용 일치 · 불일치

소재 대학에서 열리는 겨울 캠프에 관한 안내

듣기 대본 해석

남: 여러분 안녕하세요. 올 겨울 Bellington University에서 제공하는 새로운 프로그램에 대해 말씀 드리고자 합니다. Bellington University는 연기와 연출을 중심으로 하는 일주일 간의 캠프를 제공할 것입니다. 그 캠프는 1월 2일부터 1월 8일까지 열릴 것이며 참가를 신청한 학생들은 캠프 기간 동안 캠퍼스 내에 머물게 될 것입니다. 참가비는 무료이나 참가할 수 있는 학생수는 제한되어 있습니다. 제한된 학생 수 때문에, 오직 최소한 평균 B학점을 보유한 고등학교 2학년과 3학년생에게만 참가 자격이 주어집니다. 또한, 관심이 있고 참가 자격이 있는 학생들은 미술이나 정보 통신 교사로부터 추천서를 받아야 합니다. 학교 홈페이지에 있는 신청서를 작성해서 지원하실 수 있습니다.

어휘

acting and directing 연기와 연출 **sign up for** ~에 지원하다, ~에 참가를 신청하다 **duration** ***n.*** 기간 **participate** ***v.*** 참가하다 **be eligible for** ~을 위한 자격이 있다 **letter of recommendation** 추천서 **application** ***n.*** 지원(서), 신청(서)

정답 ③

문제풀이

최소한 평균 B학점을 보유한 고등학교 2학년과 3학년생에게만 참가 자격이 주어진다고 언급되어 있으므로 내용과 일치하지 않는 것은 ③ '캠프 참가비는 무료이고 고등학생 누구나 참가 가능하다.'이다.

총 어휘 수 133

12 도표

소재 평면 TV 선택

듣기 대본 해석

남: 안녕하세요. 무엇을 도와드릴까요?

여: 안녕하세요. 새 텔레비전 사려고요. 지금 것은 굉장히 오래됐어요. 브라운관이에요.

남: 와. 한동안 그 스타일을 보지 못했네요. 음, 저희는 다양한 평면 텔레비전들이 있어요. 예산이 어떻게 되시죠?

여: 600달러 이상 쓰고 싶진 않아요.

남: 특별히 생각하고 계신 브랜드가 있나요?

여: 인터넷에서 후기를 여러 개 읽어봤는데 Solo 제품이 좋은 것 같더라고요.

남: 맞아요. 여기 지점은 Solo 제품을 팔아요. 3D 기능 있는 것, 아니면 없는 것 중 어느 것이 더 좋으세요?

여: 후기에서는 3D 기능이 훌륭하다고 했어요. 그런 걸로 제 가격 범위에 있는 걸로 주세요.

남: 조건에 맞는 게 두 개 있네요. 검은색과 은색으로 나와요.

여: 검은색으로 주세요. 그래야 제 케이블 박스랑 어울리거든요.

남: 알겠습니다. 여기 기다리시면 창고에서 하나 가져 올게요.

여: 알겠습니다. 도와주셔서 감사합니다.

어휘

outdated ***a.*** 구식의 **specific** ***a.*** 구체적인, 분명한 **criterion** ***n.*** 표준, 기준 (복수형 criteria) **stockroom** ***n.*** 창고

정답 ⑤

문제풀이

600달러 이하인 Solo 제품은 ③, ④, ⑤번이고 3D기능이 있는 검정색을 원했으므로 여자가 선택한 것은 ⑤번이다.

총 어휘 수 175

13 긴 대화의 응답

소재 알레르기 증상에 대한 대처

듣기 대본 해석

남: 여보, Mike 병원 데려 갔어?

여: 응. 위에 좀 심각한 문제가 있는 것 같아.

남: 그래? 밥 먹은 다음에 계속 배가 아프다고 한 건 알고 있어.

여: 응, 의사가 Mike한테 음식 알레르기가 있을 수 있다고 했어. 이 알레르기가 배탈을 일으킬 수 있대.

남: 아! 어렸을 땐 안 그랬던 것 같은데.

여: 음, 어떤 사람들은 나중에 크고 나서 알레르기가 생길 수 있다고 의사가 그랬어.

남: 그럼 어떻게 해야 돼?

여: 걔가 뭘 먹는 지를 봐야 돼. 당분간은 쌀이나 콩 같은 단순한 음식들만 먹어야 돼.

남: 그럼 평생 동안 그렇게 먹어야 된다는 거야?

여: 아니, 알레르기 검사를 받을 때까지만. 의사가 주사 맞는 것도 추천했어.

남: ③ <u>그가 그걸 좋아할 것 같지는 않지만, 결국엔 도움이 될 거야.</u>

어휘

serious ***a.*** 심각한, 진지한 **upset stomach** 배탈 **bother** ***v.*** 신경 쓰이게 하다 **stick to** ~을 고수하다, 계속하다

정답 ③

문제풀이

의사가 아들에게 알레르기 주사 맞기를 추천했다고 말하는 것에 대한 응답으로 ③ '그가 그걸 좋아할 것 같지는 않지만, 결국엔 도움이 될 거야.'가 적절하다.

오답 보기 해석

① 나는 알레르기 주사 정말 맞고 싶지 않아.

② 응. 그가 좋아질 때까지 학교에 못 갈 거야.

④ 나는 우리가 검진을 위해 그를 의사에게 데려가야 한다고 생각해.

⑤ 나는 네가 퇴원해서 집으로 돌아와서 기뻐.

총 어휘 수 142

14 긴 대화의 응답

소재 작은 물고기는 풀어주기

듣기 대본 해석

여: 아빠, 왜 그 물고기들을 풀어주는 거예요?

남: 음, 작은 거는 잡고 싶지 않잖아.

여: 왜요? 그래도 먹을 수는 있잖아요.

남: 작은 물고기들은 아직 더 커야 돼. 우리가 다 잡아가면 이 호수에 물고기가 없을 거야.

여: 도와드릴까요? 저 물고기랑 노는 거 좋아해요.

남: 그래. 물고기를 들고 이 자로 길이를 재봐.

여: 얼마나 길어야 해요?

남: 25센티미터가 안 되면 다시 호수에 던져. 사실 그 길이보다 작은 애들을 잡아 가는 건 이 공원 규칙에도 위반돼.

여: 정말이요? 그럼 작은 물고기들을 잡아 가져 가면 우리가 곤란해질 수 있겠네요.

남: 맞아. 아, 그건 풀어줘야 될 거야. 너무 작아.

여: ① <u>알았어요. 이 물고기한테 행운의 날인 것 같아요.</u>

어휘

ruler ***n.*** 자 **measure** ***v.*** 재다 **trouble** ***n.*** 곤란, 문제

정답 ①

문제풀이

남자가 그 물고기는 너무 작으니까 풀어주라고 말했으므로 여자의 적절한 답은 ① '알았어요. 이 물고기한테 행운의 날인 것 같아요.'이다.

오답 보기 해석

② 우리 토요일에 같이 낚시하러 가요.

③ 물이 너무 오염되면 물고기가 죽을 거예요.

④ 엄마가 이것을 저녁 만드는 데 사용하시면 좋을 것 같아요.

⑤ 맞아요. 더 큰 물고기는 재기가 훨씬 힘들어요.

총 어휘 수 129

15 상황에 적절한 말

소재 공대 대회에서의 우승

듣기 대본 해석

남: Peter는 물리학을 전공하고 있습니다. 그의 대학교는 학생들을 위한 공학 대회를 열었는데 Peter는 대회에 참여하기 위해 롤러코스터 모델을 만들기로 합니다. 몇 주간 전 세계에서 유명한 롤러코스터들을 연구하고 나서야 Peter는 마침내 아이디어를 떠올려 작업을 끝냈습니다. 이제 그 대회에서 그의 롤러코스터 모델은 뛰어난 성능을 보여줬고 관객들을 열광시켰습니다. 그 과의 학과장인 Goldberg 교수님은 특히 깊은 인상을 받고 Peter의 노력에 칭찬을 했습니다. 그는 Peter에게 다른 교수님들도 똑같이 생각했으며 Peter가 공학 대회 우승을 하게 될 것이라고 알려주었습니다. Peter는 Goldberg 교수님의 말을 듣고 기뻤고 자신이 뽑혔다는 사실이 믿어지지가 않습니다. 이러한 상황에서 Peter가 Goldberg 교수님에게 뭐라고 말할까요?

Peter: ③ <u>전 정말 제가 공학 대회에서 우승할 줄은 몰랐어요.</u>

어휘

physics *n.* 물리학 **major** *n.* 전공 **engineering** *n.* 공학, 공학 기술 **dean** *n.* 학과장, 주임 사제 **commend** *v.* 칭찬하다 〈문제〉 **flaw** *n.* 결점, 결함, 흠

정답 ③

문제풀이

Peter는 공학 대회에서 우승할 거라는 소식을 듣고 기쁘면서도 이 사실이 믿기지 않는다는 것을 표현하는 말을 해야 하므로 적절한 것은 ③ '전 정말 제가 공학 대회에서 우승할 줄은 몰랐어요.'이다.

오답 보기 해석

① 더 큰 롤러코스터는 못 만들 것 같아요.
② 설계상 결함들을 다시 작업해야 할 것 같아요.
④ 이 대학에서 공학 기술을 공부하는 것은 즐거워요.
⑤ 공학 대회에 우승한 것을 축하드립니다.

총 어휘 수 149

16 담화 주제 / 17 세부 내용 파악

소재 세계 곳곳에서 사용되는 영어의 차이점

듣기 대본 해석

여: 안녕하세요, 여러분. 오늘 우리는 영어에 대해 말하고자 합니다. 런던에 기반을 둔 높이 평가되는 소식통에 따르면, 영어를 말할 수 있는 사람이 세계에 20억 명이 넘습니다. 사실, 영어를 모국어로 하는 사람보다 영어를 모국어로 하지 않는 영어 사용자들이 4배나 더 많습니다. 모국어로 영어를 말하는 사람들에게도 영어는 다양한 종류가 있습니다. 예를 들어, 미국식 영어, 캐나다식 영어, 영국식 영어 그리고 호주식 영어가 있습니다. 이들 사이에 차이점은 보통 발음, 억양, 그리고 어휘에 있습니다. 종종 종류에 따라 철자의 차이도 있는데, 특히 미국식 영어와 영국식 영어 사이에 차이가 있습니다. Color와 colour, favorite과 favourite 같은 단어가 이 두 영어권 영어 차이의 보편적인 예입니다. 캐나다식 영어는 미국식 영어와 영국식 영어의 조합이지만 확실히 미국 쪽에서 더 많이 빌려왔습니다. 이런 영어를 모국어로 사용하는 나라에서의 차이점에 대한 더 많은 정보를 얻으시려면 제가 준비한 자료를 보십시오. *[잠시 후]* 이제 휴식시간 동안 여러분 각자 서로 같은 언어를 말하는 다른 나라에 대해 생각해보고 그들 사이에 차이점을 리스트로 만들어보세요. 여러분 들어주셔서 감사합니다. 휴식 후에 다시 봅시다.

어휘

respected *a.* 훌륭한, 높이 평가되는 **authority** *n.* 권한, 권위, 인가 **billion** *n.* 10억 **variety** *n.* 종류, 다양성 **pronunciation** *n.* 발음 **intonation** *n.* 억양 **combination** *n.* 조합 **handout** *n.* 인쇄물, 유인물

정답 16 ④ 17 ③

문제풀이

16 영국식 영어와 미국식 영어의 차이를 예로 들고 캐나다식 영어의 특징을 언급하면서 영어가 모국어인 나라에서 쓰는 영어의 차이점을 말하고 있으므로 정답은 ④ '영어 원어민들이 사용하는 영어의 차이점'이 된다.

17 발음, 억양, 어휘, 철자에서 차이가 있다고는 언급했지만 강세에 대한 언급은 하지 않았으므로 정답은 ③ '강세'이다.

오답 보기 해석

16

① 국제 영어를 규정하는 특징들
② 역사를 통해 일어난 영어의 변화
③ 어떻게 영어가 국제적인 언어가 되고 있는가
⑤ 미국 영어와 영국 영어에서 발음상의 차이점

총 어휘 수 205

DICTATION ANSWERS

01 It's freezing out here

02 I'm starving / leftover pizza

03 keeping my blackberries fresh / extend the life / rinse the berries off / The acidity of vinegar

04 it all sounded very impolite / if adults used it or understood it / who fits in with them / getting closer to young people

05 get you checked out / tackled me from behind / felt dizzy

06 we won't have enough food / a little out of reach / There's a separate table / as heavy as cupcakes

07 term papers due next Monday / changed the way we live / made survey questions / I'm more than willing to do that

08 got the green light / schedule a meeting / I'm screening a travel documentary

09 Have a look / it's built to last / cheaper than the black one / to the register to check out

10 It's near where I work / it suits me perfectly / looks black / expensive than I expected / try it on

11 stay on campus for the duration / are eligible for this camp / get a letter of recommendation / filling out the application

12 What's your budget / spend more than six hundred dollars / fit your criteria / like it in black

13 his stomach hurting after meals / cause upset stomachs / stick to simple foods / suggested shots

14 letting those fish go / use this ruler to measure it / against park rules / we can get in trouble

15 build a model roller coaster / is particularly impressed / receive the top prize

16-17 talk about the English language / different varieties of English / spelling differences between the varieties / a combination of

28 수능영어듣기 실전모의고사

본문 p.170

01 ③	02 ③	03 ①	04 ③	05 ⑤	06 ④
07 ④	08 ⑤	09 ③	10 ⑤	11 ③	12 ③
13 ④	14 ①	15 ②	16 ①	17 ④	

01 짧은 대화의 응답

소재 춤 대회

듣기 대본 해석

여: Aiden, 나 정말 긴장 돼. 내가 해낼 수 있을지 모르겠어.
남: 물론 너는 할 수 있어! 너는 모든 동작을 알고 있고 정말 열심히 노력해왔잖아.
여: 맞아. 그런데 다른 모든 댄서들은 정말 훌륭하게 춤 동작들을 해냈어.
남: ③ 다른 사람들과 비교해서 너의 능력을 판단하지 마.

어휘

dedicated ***a.*** 전념하는, 헌신적인 **awesome** ***a.*** 훌륭한
〈문제〉 **based on other people** 다른 사람들과 비교해서
compared to ~와 비교하여

정답 ③

문제풀이

여자가 다른 댄서들의 훌륭한 모습에 위축되는 모습을 보이자 남자가 여자에게 용기를 불어넣는 응답이 가장 적절하므로 답은 ③ '다른 사람들과 비교해서 너의 능력을 판단하지 마.'이다.

오답 보기 해석

① 네가 이미 공연을 했다는 것에 대해 정말 감사해야 해.
② 나의 춤 동작은 다른 사람들의 동작보다 낫다고 생각했어.
④ 내 춤 동작은 너의 것에 비해 정말 좋았어.
⑤ 공연은 1시간 안에 시작할 거야.

총 어휘 수 45

02 짧은 대화의 응답

소재 해변의 조개

듣기 대본 해석

남: Lillian! 해변에 있는 조개들 놔둬. 가져가면 안 돼.
여: 하지만 정말 많은데. 왜 제가 몇 개 가져가면 안 돼요?
남: 이 해변에 오는 모든 사람들이 "몇 개씩만" 가져간다고 생각해 봐.
여: ③ 아, 이제 알겠어요. 즉시 도로 갖다 놓을게요.

어휘

〈문제〉 **right away** 당장, 즉시

정답 ③

문제풀이

남자가 여자에게 해변의 조개를 단 몇 개라도 가져가서는 안 된다며 이유를 말하였으므로 여자의 응답은 그에 동조하는 ③ '아, 이제 알겠어요. 즉시 도로 갖다 놓을게요.'가 가장 적절하다.

오답 보기 해석

① 알았어요. 조개껍데기 조금만 가져갈게요.
② 그 곳을 기억해 내려고 애쓰고 있어요.
④ 멋져요! 저는 집에 더 많이 가져갈 거예요.
⑤ 우리 조만간 여기 다시 왔으면 좋겠어요.

총 어휘 수 51

03 담화 주제

소재 친환경적인 생활 습관의 예

듣기 대본 해석

남: 친환경적인 생활 습관을 갖는 것이 굉장히 중요해졌습니다. 에너지 비용의 문제 외에도, 최근 오염으로 인한 환경문제가 전국의 사람들로 하여금 더 새롭고 성실한 생활 방식을 갖게 만들었습니다. 도울 수 있는 방법이 여러 가지 있습니다. 예를 들어 승용차 이용은 꼭 필요할 때만 하는 게 좋습니다. 그렇지 않을 경우에는 자전거, 버스, 기차와 같이 더 친환경적인 교통수단을 이용하세요. 전자기기는 사용하지 않을 때 플러그를 뽑으세요. 켜져 있지 않아도 플러그가 꽂혀 있으면 텔레비전과 컴퓨터는 전기를 소모합니다. 차가운 물을 사용하면 세탁을 할 때 쓰는 에너지를 반으로 줄일 수 있습니다. 마트를 갈 때 매립 쓰레기를 줄이기 위해 가방을 챙겨 가시고 종이 컵과 접시 같은 일회용 쓰레기의 사용을 피하세요. 이렇게 솔선하셔서 친환경을 지지하는 수만 명과 함께 하세요.

어휘

conscientious ***a.*** 양심적인, 성실한 **opt for** ~을 선택하다
halve ***v.*** 반으로 줄이다(줄다) **disposable** ***a.*** 일회용의
initiative ***n.*** 계획, 주도(권)

정답 ①

문제풀이

남자는 친화경적인 생활 습관으로 대중교통 이용, 안 쓰는 가전제품 코드 뽑기, 일회용품 사용 줄이기 등을 말하고 있으므로 주제로 가장 적절한 것은 ①번이다.

총 어휘 수 161

04 의견

소재 도서관 신축

듣기 대본 해석

여: Tom, 오래된 도서관을 허물 것이라는 시의 계획에 대해 들었어요?
남: 네, 들었어요. 하지만 시에서 그 자리에 새로운 도서관을 지을 계획이라고 들었어요.
여: 정말 유감이네요. 현재 건물은 역사적인 건축물이거든요.
남: 그렇긴 하지만 새로운 자료들을 위한 공간이 충분하지 않은 게 사실이긴 해요.
여: 맞아요. 새로운 도서관이 필요하죠. 예전 도서관은 너무 불편하니까요.
남: 확실히 그래요. 거긴 여름엔 너무 덥고 겨울엔 얼 것 같이 추워요.
여: 새 건물이 그런 문제들은 확실히 해결하겠지만 적어도 원래 건물의 전면부는 살려야 해요.
남: 정말 좋은 생각이네요. 건물의 전면부는 너무 아름다워요.
여: 네, 그러면 우리는 외관은 고풍스러운 모습이고 내부는 현대적인 건물을 갖게 될 거예요.
남: 맞아요. 그것이 우리가 미래 세대를 위해 역사를 보존하는 방법이죠.

어휘

tear down (건물, 담 등을) 허물다, 헐다 **inconvenient** ***a.*** 불편한
definitely ***ad.*** 분명히, 틀림없이 **antique** ***a.*** 고풍스러운, (귀중한) 골동품인 **preserve** ***v.*** 지키다, 보존하다

정답 ③

문제풀이

여자는 새로운 도서관을 짓되 도서관의 전면부는 살려야 한다고 말하고 있다. 따라서 정답은 ③ '현 도서관의 전면부를 살려서 새로 지어야 한다.'이다.

총 어휘 수 148

05 대화자의 관계 파악

소재 새 자동차에 대한 설명

듣기 대본 해석

남: 구매해 주셔서 감사합니다, Allen 씨. 열쇠 여기 있습니다.
여: 감사합니다. 잠깐... 이건 그냥 리모컨이잖아요. 진짜 열쇠는 어디 있어요?
남: Mondo의 최신 승용차들은 모두 스마트 열쇠로 나옵니다. 이게 주머니에 있기만 하면 손잡이에 있는 버튼을 눌러서 문을 열 수 있습니다.
여: 한번 해볼게요. *[잠시 후]* 굉장히 좋네요. 그런데 시동은 어떻게 거나요?
남: 스마트 열쇠가 차에 있는 한, 출발 버튼을 누르시기만 하면 됩니다.
여: 우와! 굉장히 편리하네요. 무척 세련돼 보여요.
남: 맞아요! 또한, 열쇠를 절대 차에 두고 내릴 수가 없어요. 열쇠가 차에 있으면, 문이 잠기지 않거든요.
여: 제가 칠칠맞지 못하고 잘 잊어버리는데 너무 좋네요. 더 알아야 할 게 있나요?
남: 다 됐을 겁니다. 다시 한 번 저희 차를 구매해 주셔서 감사합니다. 문제가 있다면 언제든지 전화해 주세요.
여: 감사합니다.

어휘

as long as ~하는 동안은, ~하는 한은 **give it a try** 시도하다, 한번 해보다 **futuristic *a.*** 초현대적인, 세련된 **clumsy *a.*** 어설픈, 칠칠맞지 못한 **hesitate *v.*** 망설이다, 주저하다

정답 ⑤

문제풀이

남자는 여자에게 새로운 자동차의 스마트 열쇠의 사용법에 대해 설명해주고 있고, 마지막에 구매해 주셔서 감사하다고 인사했으므로 두 사람의 관계는 ⑤ '자동차 판매원 — 자동차 구매자'임을 알 수 있다.

총 어휘 수 160

06 그림의 세부 내용 파악

소재 과일 가게 포스터

듣기 대본 해석

남: Beth, 내가 농산물 직매장 과일 가게 포스터를 만들어 봤는데 한번 봐봐.
여: 잘 만들었다, Jerry. "Hungry for apples?"라는 슬로건 맘에 든다.
남: 내가 생각해 낸 거야.
여: 네가 이렇게 창의적일 줄은 몰랐어. 왼쪽에 있는 사과는 그림이야? 진짜 같이 생겼어.
남: 그거 그리는 데 오래 걸렸어. 우리 과일 가게 이름은 어떻게 생각해? 너무 진부하지는 않지?
여: 글쎄, 난 괜찮은 것 같은데.
남: 근데 "Jerry's Fruit Stand"는 너무 평범한 것 같아. 더 창의적인 걸 생각해 내야겠어.
여: 괜찮아. 근데 글씨 크기가 좀 더 크면 좋을 것 같아. 슬로건이 포스터를 너무 많이 차지해.
남: 동감이야. 인쇄하기 전에 글씨 크기를 수정할게. 우리 아들이 사과를 몇 개 들고 있는 것도 그려봤어.
여: 너무 귀엽다. 그리고, 네가 사과로 가득 찬 바구니 들고 있는 그림 역시 잘 나왔네.
남: 정말? 내 머리가 너무 크게 나온 것 같아.
여: 전혀 그렇지 않아. 과일 가게에 딱 일 거야.

어휘

farmers' market 농산물 직매장 **slogan *n.*** 문구, 구호, 슬로건 **plain *a.*** 평범한, 소박한 **take up** 차지하다 **basket *n.*** 바구니

정답 ④

문제풀이

남자가 아들이 사과를 몇 개 들고 있는 것도 그렸다고 했는데 그림에서는 아들이 사과를 한 개 들고 있으므로 그림과 일치하지 않는 것은 ④번이다.

총 어휘 수 181

07 할 일

소재 등산하기 전의 준비

듣기 대본 해석

남: Lucy, 나 왔어.
여: 안녕 Bobby. 일찍 와줘서 고마워. 등산하기 좋은 날씨지, 그렇지?
남: 맞아. 등산화 예쁘다.
여: 고마워, 근데 내 것이 아니야. 사촌한테 빌렸어.
남: 좋네. 갈 준비 다 된 거야?
여: 난 준비됐는데 너한테 미리 말해 둘게. 나 등산한지 꽤 됐어.
남: 괜찮아. 천천히 가자. 출발하기 전에 다 챙겼는지 보자.
여: 필요한 건 다 있는 것 같은데, 물을 너무 많이 챙겨 온 것 같아.
남: 괜찮아. 그 정도는 필요할지도 몰라. 등산스틱 가져왔어?
여: 아, 차에 두고 왔나 봐. 금방 갔다 올게.
남: 그래. 여기서 기다릴게.

어휘

hike *v.* 등산하다 **borrow *v.*** 빌리다 **warn *v.*** 경고하다 **pack *v.*** 챙기다

정답 ④

문제풀이

남자가 등산스틱을 가져왔는지 물었고 여자는 차에 두고 온 것 같다며 갖고 오겠다고 했으므로 정답은 ④ '등산스틱 가져오기'이다.

총 어휘 수 121

08 이유

소재 인터넷 연결을 끊은 이유

듣기 대본 해석

남: 너 새로운 Gamebox PC 봤니? 완전 멋져 보여.
여: 와! 정말 멋진데! 그래픽 좀 봐!
남: 사고는 싶은데, 작년에 새 컴퓨터를 샀어. 아직 비용을 다 갚지 못했어.
여: 그래, 네가 가지고 있는 컴퓨터가 여전히 잘 작동하는데 뭐 하러 새로운 PC를 사려고 해?
남: 네 말이 맞긴 한데, 이 새로운 컴퓨터가 그냥 세련되고 멋지잖아. 이 컴퓨터는 모든 최신 게임을 다 구동시킬 수 있어.
여: 너 아마도 몇몇의 수업에 낙제할 지도 모르겠어. 네가 너무 산만하게 될 거야.
남: 하하. 아마 네 말이 맞을지도. 그게 네가 너의 컴퓨터를 오랫동안 업그레이드 하지 않은 이유니?
여: 실은 난 인터넷 연결을 아예 끊었어. 내 명의를 도용당할까 봐 걱정돼서 말이야.
남: 나는 컴퓨터 사용하는 것이 점점 더 위험해진다는 것을 들었어. 그러나 나는 떨어져 있을 수는(컴퓨터를 안 쓸 수는) 없어. 나는 게임을 좋아하거든.
여: 그래, 그렇지만 나는 나의 사생활 보호가 오락보다 더 소중하다고 생각해.
남: 네가 무슨 말을 하는 건지 이해하겠어.

어휘

sleek *a.* 세련된, 윤기 있는 **distracted *a.*** 산만해진 **get rid of** ~을 처리하다, 없애다 **identity *n.*** 신분, 신원

정답 ⑤

문제풀이

여자는 컴퓨터를 오랫동안 업그레이드 하지 않은 이유가 수업에 낙제할까 봐서 그런 거냐는 남자의 질문에 사실은 명의를 도용당할까 봐 걱정돼서 인터넷을 끊었다고 답했으므로 정답은 ⑤ '명의 도용이 걱정되어서'이다.

총 어휘 수 149

09 숫자

소재 세탁기 구매

듣기 대본 해석

여: 안녕하세요. Frank's 가전 제품점입니다. 무엇을 도와드릴까요?
남: 그게, 세탁기가 고장 나서 새 것을 사려고 하고 있어요.
여: 알겠어요. 세탁기 종류가 정말 다양해요. 얼마 정도를 예상하고 계신가요?
남: 400달러 아래로 생각하고 있어요.
여: 그렇군요. 세일 상품에 어떤 것이 있는지 보도록 하지요. 이거 좋아요. 원래 500달러였는데 작은 흠집이 나 있어서 350달러에 판매하고 있어요.
남: 좋네요. 그걸로 살게요.
여: 아! 저희 매장으로부터 광고책자를 받으셨으면, 추가로 20퍼센트 할인받을 수 있는 쿠폰이 있을 거예요.
남: 네, 그거 보고 쿠폰 오려 왔어요. 여기요. 배송해주나요?
여: 그럼요. 배송비는 무료인데 설치 비용은 따로 받습니다. 추가비용은 40달러입니다.
남: 설치해주시는 게 좋을 것 같아요. 제가 할 수 있을지 모르겠네요.
여: 알겠습니다.

어휘

appliance ***n.*** (가정용) 기기 **clearance** ***n.*** (불필요한 것) 없애기(정리)
cosmetic ***n.*** 화장품 ***a.*** 겉치레에 불과한 **installation fee** 설치 비용

정답 ③

문제풀이

원래 500달러인 세탁기에 작은 흠집이 있어서 350달러에 파는 중이라고 했고, 쿠폰을 가져오면 20퍼센트를 추가 할인해준다고 했으므로 280달러이다. 배송비는 무료이지만 설치비가 40달러라고 했으므로 280+40=320달러가 되어 정답은 ③ '$320'이다.

총 어휘 수 156

10 언급 유무

소재 신혼부부를 위한 재정적 조언

듣기 대본 해석

여: Jiho, 너랑 Kate가 곧 결혼하니까, 너희 둘 모두 재정적인 것에 주의를 기울여야 해.
남: 그래, 나도 알아. 우리는 서로에 대한 책임을 져야 하고 우리의 모든 결정이 우리한테만 영향을 주는 게 아닐 거야.
여: 맞아. 너희는 분명 돈이 필요할 것이기 때문에 둘 다 저축을 더 하고 적게 쓰기 시작해야 해.
남: 좋은 조언이야. 나 당장 저축 계좌를 만들 거야.
여: 좋아. 그리고 그녀도 계좌를 만들어야 해. 일단 네가 결혼을 하면 너의 계좌는 공유될 거야.
남: 그녀는 지금 학생이라 파트타임으로만 일해서 계좌에 넣을 만한 많은 돈은 없을 거야.
여: 그녀는 지불해야 될 대출이 있니? 아니면 집세?
남: 아니, 없어.
여: 그러면 너희 둘이 편안해질 때까지 적어도 잠시 동안은 그녀가 버는 것의 대부분을 저축할 수 있을 거야.
남: 맞아. 그녀한테 말해보고, 이것에 대해 어떻게 생각하는지 봐야겠어.
여: 좋은 생각이야. 그 말을 들으니 기쁘다.

어휘

financially ***ad.*** 재정적으로 **impact** ***v.*** 영향을 주다
savings account 저축 예금 (계좌)

정답 ⑤

문제풀이

여자가 이제 막 결혼할 남자에게 해주는 조언으로 더 많이 저축하고, 적게 쓰고, 본인과 배우자의 계좌를 개설하라고 권했지만 보험 가입에 대한 언급은 하지 않았으므로 정답은 ⑤ '보험 가입하기'이다.

총 어휘 수 162

11 내용 일치 · 불일치

소재 Fantasy Film Festival

듣기 대본 해석

여: 안녕하세요, 여러분. 해마다 열리는 Fantasy Film Festival에 계속 성원해 주셔서 감사합니다. Fantasy Film Festival은 2012년부터 성장해 왔습니다. 지난해 저희는 장소가 크지 않아서 축제로 들어오는 많은 방문자의 출입을 막아야만 했습니다. 운 좋게도, 저희는 좀 더 크지만 지난 수년간 사용했던 위치의 친밀감과 개성은 여전히 가지고 있는 새로운 장소를 찾았습니다. 여러분의 친구와 가족들을 돌려보내지 않을 것이고, 훨씬 더 많은 관객들이 여러분의 영화를 볼 것이라고 장담합니다. 작년보다 더 많은 방문객을 예상하기 때문에 저희는 티켓 판매를 온라인으로 옮겼습니다. 여러분들은 여전히 박스 오피스에서 구매하실 수 있지만 웹사이트 www.fantasyfilms.com에서 구매하시는 것이 더 편리하실 겁니다. 1인 입장 가격은 60달러이고, 10명 이상의 단체는 할인이 있습니다.

어휘

deny ***v.*** 받아들이지 않다, 부인하다 **maintain** ***v.*** 유지하다
intimacy ***n.*** 친밀감 **personality** ***n.*** 개성, 성격 **assure** ***v.*** 장담하다, 확언하다 **turn somebody away** ~을 돌려보내다 **audience** ***n.*** 관람객, 청중

정답 ③

문제풀이

티켓 판매를 온라인으로 옮겼지만 박스 오피스에서도 구매는 가능하다고 했으므로 내용과 일치하지 않는 것은 ③ '입장권은 온라인으로만 구매 가능하다.'이다.

총 어휘 수 149

12 도표

소재 호텔 내의 활동 프로그램

듣기 대본 해석

남: 안내 데스크입니다. 무엇을 도와드릴까요?
여: 안녕하세요. 오늘 비가 와서 몹시 실망했어요. 해변가로 놀러 가고 싶었는데 실내에 있을 것 같아요. 이 호텔에 우리를 즐겁게 할 수 있는 활동들이 있다고 들었어요.
남: 그렇습니다. 하루 종일 제공해 드릴 수 있는 게 많아요.
여: 일단 옆방에서 오전 11시에 영화를 볼 거예요. 한 시간 반 정도 하는 것 같아요.
남: 그렇군요. 요리 교실은 어떠세요? 오늘은 크루아상 만드는 법을 배울 거예요.
여: 재미있을 것 같은데 제 딸이 재미있어 할지 모르겠네요. 좀 쉽게 지루해 해요.
남: 그럼 오후에 어린이 그림 프로그램 두 개를 추천해드려요. 따님이 좋아할 것 같아요.
여: 그럴 수 있겠지만 그건 어린이만을 위한 거죠? 온 가족이 즐길 수 있는 걸 찾고 있어요.

남: 알겠습니다. 다른 선택지가 몇 개 더 있네요. 활동 비용은 상관있으세요?
여: 오늘이 휴가 마지막 날이라서 돈이 좀 부족해요. 제 남편, 저, 그리고 제 딸을 합해서 15달러 이상 쓰고 싶진 않아요.
남: 알겠습니다. 가족 분들을 위한 안성맞춤의 활동을 찾았습니다.

어휘
hit the beach 해변으로 가다 **croissant** ***n.*** 크루아상 **look for** ~을 찾다 **option** ***n.*** 선택권

정답 ③

문제풀이
오전 11시부터는 한 시간 반 동안 영화를 볼 것이라고 했으므로 ④번 요가는 시간이 안 맞아서 제외된다. 요리 프로그램은 아이가 지루해 할 것 같다고 했고, 그림 프로그램은 어린이만을 위한 것이라서 다른 것을 찾고 있으므로 ①번과 ⑤번도 제외된다. 비용은 세 명이 15달러를 넘지 않아야 하므로 두 사람이 선택할 프로그램은 ③번이다.

총 어휘 수 209

13 긴 대화의 응답

소재 상대방 골키퍼의 약점

듣기 대본 해석
여: 주장, 뭐해?
남: FC Barcelona 비디오 좀 보고 있었어. 토요일에 얘네를 이길 수 있을지 잘 모르겠어.
여: 아! 근데 너희 팀이 제일 잘하는 축구 팀이잖아. 이길 수 있을 거야.
남: 그 쪽 골키퍼가 너무 잘해. 그는 자기한테 날아오는 공은 거의 다 막을 수 있어.
여: 그럴지 몰라도 약점을 찾으면, 너도 골을 넣을 수 있을 거야.
남: 하! 그럼 그의 약점이 뭔데?
여: 자세히 보면 골대 어느 부분을 막는 데 애를 먹는지 알 수 있어.
남: *[잠시 후]* 음, 그래도 아무것도 안 보이는데.
여: 그가 몸을 어떻게 움직이는지 봐봐. 왼쪽에 체중을 싣고 오른쪽으로 뛰고 있잖아.
남: 그렇네!
여: 그리고 다시 봐봐. 왼발로 밀어내면서 비슷한 행동을 하고 있어. 내가 너라면 왼쪽 코너에 슛을 할 거야.
남: ④ 네가 무슨 말 하는지 알겠어. 내가 그를 상대로 골을 넣을 수 있는 방법을 찾을 수 있을 것 같아.

어휘
goalie ***n.*** 골키퍼 **score on** 득점하다 **defend** ***v.*** 막다, 수비하다 **shift** ***v.*** 옮기다

정답 ④

문제풀이
여자가 상대방 골키퍼의 움직임을 보고 어디로 슛을 하면 될지 알려줬으므로 그에 적절한 남자의 응답은 ④ '네가 무슨 말 하는지 알겠어. 내가 그를 상대로 골을 넣을 수 있는 방법을 찾을 수 있을 것 같아.'이다.

오답 보기 해석
① 그는 오른발로 높이 점프해야 해.
② 그가 너를 향해 슛하는 거의 모든 방향을 막을 수 있을 거라고 생각해.
③ 걱정 마. 네가 열심히 하면, 그를 상대로 골을 넣을 수 있어.
⑤ 난 네가 토요일 시합에서 이길 수 없을 것 같아서 유감이야.

총 어휘 수 164

14 긴 대화의 응답

소재 손을 잡는 것이 결혼한 부부들에게 주는 효과

듣기 대본 해석
여: 여보, 뭘 읽고 있어요?
남: 인간의 신체 접촉에 관한 정말 재미있는 연구요.
여: 최근 것인가요?
남: 그래요.
여: 어떤 종류의 접촉이요?
남: 이를 테면, 손을 잡는 것과 그것이 결혼한 부부 사이에 주는 영향 같은 거죠.
여: 정말 재미있어 보이네요. 더 말해 주세요.
남: 그 연구는 두 집단의 결혼한 부부들을 살펴본 거예요. 한 집단에서, 부부들은 서로 손을 잡은 채로 산책을 하게 해요.
여: 그럼, 다른 집단은 서로 손을 잡지 않은 채로 산책을 하게 하나요?
남: 맞아요. 산책 후에 부부들은 연구자들과 앉아서 그들이 결혼한 이후 함께 겪었던 스트레스 받은 일을 상의하도록 하죠.
여: 결과가 어땠어요?
남: 부부들이 그들의 스트레스 받은 이야기를 말하는 동안, 손을 잡고 그날 오후를 보낸 부부들은 다른 그룹의 부부들보다 훨씬 더 혈압이 낮음을 보여줬어요.
여: ① 그러니까 손을 잡는 것은 부부간의 스트레스를 낮추게 하는 것 같군요.

어휘
significantly ***ad.*** 상당히 **blood pressure** 혈압

정답 ①

문제풀이
두 집단의 부부들에게 한 집단은 손을 잡고, 다른 집단은 손을 잡지 않고 산책을 하도록 해서 스트레스 받는 일들을 기억나게 했을 때, 손을 잡고 산책한 집단의 혈압이 훨씬 낮았다고 한다. 이러한 연구 결과를 알려준 남자의 말에 대한 가장 적절한 여자의 대답은 ① '그러니까 손을 잡는 것은 부부간의 스트레스를 낮추게 하는 것 같군요.'이다.

오답 보기 해석
② 그들이 사람들 있는 곳에서 애정표현을 해서는 안 된다고 생각해요.
③ 우리가 손 잡을 때 내가 스트레스 받는 건 당연하군요.
④ 그들은 좋은 오후를 보낸 것처럼 들리네요.
⑤ 그들은 아주 최근에 결혼했어요.

총 어휘 수 133

15 상황에 적절한 말

소재 룸메이트와 생활 중 생긴 소음 문제

듣기 대본 해석
여: 주요 FPS 토너먼트 경기에서 우승한 후로 Jason은 마침내 집을 살 수 있는 돈을 마련했습니다. 그는 2개의 침실이 있는 곳을 찾았고, 친구 Ryan에게 룸메이트가 되어 줄 것을 부탁했습니다. 처음엔 모든 것이 순조로웠습니다. Jason은 컴퓨터 게임을 같이 할 사람이 있어 즐거웠고, Ryan은 부모님과 떨어져 사는 것에 만족했습니다. 하지만, Jason이 대학에서 공부하기 시작한 후로, 재미있는 생활은 끝이 났습니다. 이제 Ryan은 게임을 하면서 늦게까지 깨어 있고, 종종 평일에 시끄러운 파티도 엽니다. 그건 매일 밤 공부를 해야 하고, 매일 아침 일찍 일어나 수업에 가야 하는 Jason에게 매우 골칫거리입니다. Jason은 이 소음 문제에 대해 Ryan과 이야기를 하고자 합니다. 이 상황에서 Jason이 Ryan에게 할 말로 가장 적절한 것은 무엇일까요?
Jason: Ryan, ② 주중에는 좀 더 조용히 해 줄래?

어휘
nuisance ***n.*** 성가신 일, 골칫거리, 소란 행위

정답 ②

문제풀이
Jason과 Ryan은 함께 사는 생활을 즐기다가 Jason이 학업에 열중하게 되면서 Ryan과 소음 문제로 마찰이 생기게 되었는데 이 때 Jason이 Ryan에게 할 말로 가장 적절한 것은 ② '주중에는 좀 더 조용히 해 줄래?'이다.

오답 보기 해석
① 내 룸메이트가 되어 주겠니?
③ 언제 내가 파티에 함께해도 될까?
④ 그 컴퓨터 게임 어떻게 하는지 가르쳐 줄래?
⑤ 컴퓨터 게임 토너먼트 하는 것은 어때?

총 어휘 수 132

16 담화 주제 / 17 세부 내용 파악

소재 코골이를 줄일 수 있는 방법

듣기 대본 해석
남: 청취자 여러분, 안녕하세요. 코골이로 인해 여러분이나 여러분의 배우자가 잠을 설친 경험을 하신 적이 있으십니까? 저는 코골이가 잠 설침, 낮 동안의 피곤함, 건강상의 문제, 그리고 배우자와의 문제를 야기할 수 있다는 얘기를 해드리기 위해 이 자리에 왔습니다. 코골이는 제가 삼십 대였을 때 많은 문제를 일으켰죠. 제 아내는 저의 코골이로 인해 잠을 자지 못했다고 불평을 했습니다. 저는 코골이에 대해 찾아보기 시작했고 인터넷에서 제가 멈출 수 있게 도와준 정보들을 찾았습니다. 제가 가장 먼저 따른 조언은 살을 빼는 것이었습니다. 비만은 목구멍 뒤쪽에 지방이 많은 조직을 만들어 코골이를 크고 자주하게 할 수 있습니다. 수면제를 먹는 것도 피해야 합니다. 이는 목에 있는 근육들이 이완되게 만들어서 호흡 곤란을 일으킬 수 있습니다. 카페인, 유제품, 그리고 밤 늦게 식사하는 것은 잠을 자기 전에는 피해야 합니다. 마지막으로 등을 대고 자는 대신 옆으로 누워서 자 보세요. 등을 대고 자면 혀가 떨어져서 기도를 막습니다. 옆으로 누워서 자면 그렇지 않습니다. 이런 모든 조언들을 따르면 당신은 분명 당신의 배우자 그리고 당신 자신을 더 행복하게 만들 수 있습니다.

어휘
snore ***v.*** 코를 골다 **quality** ***n.*** 질 **tissue** ***n.*** 조직 **supplement** ***n.*** 보충(물) **interfere with** ~을 방해하다 **airway** ***n.*** 기도 〈문제〉 **physiological** ***a.*** 생리적인 **insomnia** ***n.*** 불면증

정답 16 ① 17 ④

문제풀이
16 남자는 코골이가 많은 문제를 일으킨다면서 코골이를 줄일 수 있는 정보를 제공하고 있으므로 정답은 ① '코골이를 줄일 수 있는 방법'이다.
17 코골이를 줄일 수 있는 방법으로 살 빼기, 수면제 안 먹기, 카페인이나 유제품 및 수면 전 식사 피하기를 언급했지만 흡연에 대한 언급은 없으므로 정답은 ④ '흡연'이다.

오답 보기 해석
16
② 코골이를 하는 생리적인 원인
③ 불면증을 없애는 자연적인 방법
④ 코골이가 일상생활에 미치는 영향
⑤ 가장 잘 맞는 취침 자세 찾기

총 어휘 수 186

DICTATION ANSWERS

01 you've been really dedicated
02 take them with you
03 adopt a green lifestyle / opt for a more environmentally friendly means / You can halve the amount / Take the initiative
04 historical landmark / there just isn't enough space / preserve history for future generations
05 We appreciate your business / It seems so futuristic / pretty clumsy and forgetful
06 think of something more original / takes up so much space / turned out nice
07 are we good to go / We'll take our time / I might've even packed too much water
08 so sleek and cool / You'll be too distracted / I value my privacy over entertainment / where you're coming from
09 wide variety of washing machines / charge an installation fee
10 saving more and spending less / she's only working part-time / Does she have loans
11 Thank you for your continued support / maintains the intimacy and personality of / there are discounts for groups
12 We're pretty disappointed / wanted to hit the beach / have plenty to offer throughout / She gets bored pretty easily
13 the best soccer team around / get in front of / kicked toward / be able to score on him / pushing off his left foot
14 about human contact / the effect that has on / a stressful event they had been through / showed significantly lower blood pressure
15 had enough money to / fine in the beginning / fun came to an end / a huge nuisance to
16-17 a bad night's sleep / I'm here to tell you that / avoid taking sleeping supplements / your tongue drops and blocks your airways

29 수능영어듣기 실전모의고사

본문 p.176

01 ②	02 ⑤	03 ⑤	04 ⑤	05 ④	06 ⑤
07 ②	08 ①	09 ③	10 ③	11 ④	12 ②
13 ④	14 ①	15 ⑤	16 ④	17 ④	

01 짧은 대화의 응답

소재 보고서 작성

듣기 대본 해석

남: Stacy, 시간이 늦었어. 가볍게 뭐라도 먹고 집에 가자.
여: 오늘 밤은 안 돼, Tyler. 내일 아침 전까지 이 보고서를 꼭 끝내야 하거든.
남: 거의 다 끝났으면 기다릴게.
여: ② 끝내려면 시간이 좀 걸릴 거야.

어휘

grab a bite 가볍게 먹다 〈문제〉 **a while** 잠시, 잠깐

정답 ②

문제풀이

보고서 작성이 거의 끝났으면 기다리겠다는 남자의 말에 적절한 응답은 ② '끝내려면 시간이 좀 걸릴 거야.'이다.

오답 보기 해석

① 난 집에서 먹는 걸 좋아하지 않아.
③ 물론. 내가 보고서 끝내는 거 도와줄게.
④ 괜찮아. 네가 끝낼 때까지 기다릴게.
⑤ 배달원이 음식을 빨리 가져다 줬어.

총 어휘 수 44

02 짧은 대화의 응답

소재 농구 경기 티켓

듣기 대본 해석

여: 안녕, George. 나의 상사가 나에게 오늘 밤 농구 경기 티켓을 두 장 주었어. 너도 같이 가자.
남: 물론이지. 재미있겠는데. 자리는 좋니?
여: 팬 구역이라서 어디든지 앉을 수 있어.
남: ⑤ 앞쪽 근처에 앉을 수 있게 일찍 가자.

어휘

〈문제〉 **assigned** *a.* 할당된, 배정된

정답 ⑤

문제풀이

농구 경기 티켓이 어느 자리든 앉을 수 있는 것이라고 이야기했을 때 이어지는 적절한 응답은 ⑤ '앞쪽 근처에 앉을 수 있게 일찍 가자.'이다.

오답 보기 해석

① 우리는 배정된 좌석에 앉아야 해.
② 미안하지만, 나는 오늘 밤에 다른 계획이 있어.
③ 매진되어서 남은 티켓이 없어.
④ 문제 없어. 너는 이 두 장의 티켓을 가져도 돼.

총 어휘 수 47

03 요지

소재 재택근무 제도 개발

듣기 대본 해석

남: 여러분, 안녕하십니까. 오늘 저는 여러분의 사업체 생산성을 증가시키는 것에 대해 얘기하고 싶습니다. 과거에는 보통의 일상이란 직원들이 아침에 와서 관리자의 감독 하에 하루 종일 일하는 것으로 이루어져 있었습니다. 그러나 매일 아침 통근에 낭비되는 시간을 생각해 보셨습니까? 아니면 직원들이 일하러 도착하기도 전에 통근 스트레스가 그들의 에너지를 얼마나 감소시킬지 생각해 보셨나요? 저는 고용주인 여러분이 직원들의 전부 혹은 일부가 집에서 일할 수 있는 시스템을 개발했으면 합니다. 매일 통근이 주는 스트레스를 줄임으로써 여러분은 직원들이 그들의 일에 더 많은 에너지를 쏟게 할 수 있습니다. 직원들이 집에서 일하도록 허락하는 것은 결국에는 여러분에게 이익이 될 것입니다.

어휘

productivity *n.* 생산성 **consist of** ~로 구성되다 **supervisor** *n.* 감독관, 관리자 **commute** *v.* 통근하다 **diminish** *v.* 줄이다 **eliminate** *v.* 없애다, 제거하다 **end up** 결국 (어떤 처지에) 처하게 되다

정답 ⑤

문제풀이

남자는 직원들이 통근에서 오는 스트레스를 줄여서 일에 더 에너지를 쏟을 수 있도록 재택근무 제도를 개발하도록 권유하고 있으므로 정답은 ⑤ '생산성을 증가시키는 재택근무 제도를 개발해야 한다.'이다.

총 어휘 수 142

04 대화 주제

소재 소셜 네트워킹 사이트의 사생활 침해

듣기 대본 해석

남: 어제 Scott이 LookBook에 올린 Daryl 사진 봤어?
여: 그래, 봤어.
남: 그 사진 웃기다 생각했지?
여: 맞아, 꽤 웃겨. 근데 내가 생각하기에 Scott이 그 사진 올려서 Daryl이 화가 났을 것 같아.
남: 무슨 말이야?
여: 그 사진에서 Daryl이 너무 멍청해 보여.
남: 무슨 말인지 알겠어. 너는 Daryl이 그 사진을 보고, 다른 사람들이 그걸 봤다는 걸 알면 화가 날 수도 있다고 생각하는구나. 나도 그럴 경우 화날 것 같아.
여: 정말 그래. Scott이 Daryl에게 사진을 올려도 되는지 물어봤어야 했다고 생각해.
남: 나도 그렇게 생각해. LookBook 같은 소셜 네트워킹 사이트들은 네트워킹과 친구들과 지속적인 연락에는 유용하긴 한데, 사람들의 사생활이 침해되기도 해.
여: 맞아. 나는 처음에 그런 사이트들을 즐겨 이용했는데 곧 내 사생활이 얼마나 쉽게 사라질 수 있는지 깨달았어.
남: 맞아. 소셜 네트워킹 사이트에 무언가를 올릴 때는 더 주의를 기울여야 해.

어휘

post *v.* (글, 사진 따위를 어느 곳에) 게시하다 **social networking** 인맥 관리하기 **keep in touch with** ~과 접촉을 가지다, 연락을 취하다 **compromise** *v.* ~을 위태롭게 만들다 **privacy** *n.* 사생활 **cautious** *a.* 조심스러운, 신중한

정답 ⑤

문제풀이
소셜 네트워킹 사이트에 동의 없이 올린 사진이 사생활 침해가 될 수 있기 때문에 주의를 기울여야 한다는 내용이므로 답은 ⑤ '소셜 네트워킹 사이트 이용 시 서로의 사생활 보호에 주의해야 한다.'이다.

총 어휘 수 158

05 대화자의 관계 파악

소재 Alaska에 온 관광객

듣기 대본 해석
여: 안녕하세요. 저는 Lilly Jones에요. 늦어서 미안해요. 비행기가 몇 시간 늦어졌어요.
남: 괜찮아요, Jones 부인. Alaska에 오신 것을 환영해요. 저는 Joseph이에요. 하지만 내 친구들은 나를 Joey라고 불러요. 제가 당신의 가이드입니다.
여: 만나서 반가워요, Joey. 다른 사람들은 모두 이미 도착했나요?
남: 네. 그룹의 나머지 사람들은 이미 도착했어요. 그들은 라운지에서 기다리고 있어요. 당신은 아마도 화장실에서 더 따뜻한 옷으로 갈아입어야 할거예요. Alaska는 Florida만큼 따뜻하지 않아요.
여: 호텔에 도착하고 나서 옷을 갈아입으면 안 되나요?
남: 저는 지금 그것을 하는 것을 정말 추천해요. 우리가 호텔에 가기 전에 전통적인 Inuit 어시장에 들를 예정이니까요. 거기는 꽤 춥거든요.
여: 알았어요. 그러면 옷을 갈아 입어야겠네요.
남: 그리고 계획에 변경이 있어요. 일기예보에서 스키 리조트에 많은 눈이 온다고 하니, 우리는 대신 Denali 국립 공원에 갈 거예요.
여: 안됐지만, 괜찮아요. 그 공원은 아름답다고 들었어요.
남: 그렇더라도 제가 사과드립니다. 이해해주셔서 감사합니다.

어휘
weather forecast 일기예보 **that's a shame** 안됐군요, 유감이에요

정답 ④

문제풀이
남자는 여자에게 자신을 가이드라고 소개하고 Alaska에 온 것을 환영한다고 말하면서, 날씨가 추우니 옷을 갈아입을 것을 권했고 일정에 대해 말해주고 있으므로 두 사람의 관계는 ④ '여행 가이드 — 관광객'임을 알 수 있다.

총 어휘 수 176

06 그림의 세부 내용 파악

소재 생일 파티 사진

듣기 대본 해석
남: 아, 이거 네 생일 파티 사진 아니니?
여: 그래, 이건 나의 일곱 번째 생일 파티였어. 내가 케이크 위에 일곱 개의 양초를 전부 불어서 끄려고 했었기 때문에 기억이 나.
남: 사진에 네 옆에 있는 애네들은 네 친구들이니?
여: 응, Jessica와 Tim이야. 그들은 당시에 나의 가장 친한 친구들이었어. 지금 그들이 무엇을 하고 있는지 궁금해.
남: 생일 모자가 마음에 드네. 너희 모두 사랑스럽구나.
여: 그건 너무 귀여운 사진이지. 모자가 모두 조금씩 다른 것을 볼 수 있어. 내 친구들은 줄무늬 모자를 썼고 나는 물방울무늬 모자를 썼어.
남: 맞아. 너는 뒤에 풍선도 3개 가지고 있어.
여: 응, 우리 부모님이 방을 꾸미기 위해 풍선을 사용하셨어.
남: 멋지다. Tim 앞에 있는 네 개의 머핀들도 맛있어 보여.
여: 사실은, Tim이 우리가 사진을 찍기 전에 머핀 하나를 먹어 버렸어. 내가 무척 화났던 게 기억나네.
남: 정말? 사진에서는 너희 모두 무척 행복해 보여.

어휘
adorable ***a.*** 사랑스러운 **stripe** ***n.*** 줄무늬 **polka dot** 물방울무늬
decorate ***v.*** 장식하다, 꾸미다 **muffin** ***n.*** 머핀(컵 모양의 빵)

정답 ⑤

문제풀이
대화에서는 머핀이 4개라고 하였는데 그림에서는 5개이므로 대화의 내용과 일치하지 않는 것은 ⑤번이다.

총 어휘 수 158

07 할 일

소재 비타민제와 영양제 주고 영화 보러 가기

듣기 대본 해석
여: Larry, 잠시 시간 있어?
남: 사실 지금 헬스클럽에 가고 있었어. 정오에 PT 약속이 있어.
여: 오, 맞다. 잊어버렸네. 너 매주 월요일과 수요일에 개인 훈련이 있잖아, 맞지? 맘에 들어?
남: 정말 좋아. 내 트레이너가 아는 게 정말 많고 내가 열심히 하도록 동기 부여를 해주지.
여: 굉장한데. 오늘 운동 끝나고 바빠? 시간 있으면 우리 새로 나온 Iron Man 영화 보러 가자.
남: 글쎄, 건강식품점에 가서 비타민과 영양보충제를 좀 사려 했는데.
여: 오, 집에 많아. 사실, 어떤 종류가 필요한지에 달렸지만 나한테 여분이 있어. 우리 집에 와서 살펴 봐. 그리고 네가 필요한 걸 줄게.
남: 정말? 와, 굉장한데. 그럼 그래, 영화 보러 가자.
여: 좋아. 사실 나 어제 사무실에서 공짜 티켓 두 장 얻었거든.
남: 딱 이네. 우리 영화 보고 나서 영양보충제를 확인하러 가면 되겠다. 그러고 나서 내가 커피 살게.

어휘
knowledgeable ***a.*** 아는 것이 많은 **motivate** ***v.*** 동기를 부여하다
workout ***n.*** 운동 **supplement** ***n.*** (영양)보충제

정답 ②

문제풀이
운동을 마친 후 건강식품점에 비타민과 영양보충제를 사러 간다는 남자의 말을 들은 여자가 집에 비타민제과 영양보충제가 많다며 남자에게 조금 주겠다고 제안했다. 그러므로 답은 ② '비타민과 영양보충제 주기'이다.

총 어휘 수 173

08 이유

소재 고등학교 동창끼리의 근황

듣기 대본 해석
여: Paul, 나야, Lori Townsend. 우리 Markwell 고등학교 같이 다녔었잖아. 나 기억하니?
남: 맞아. 그렇구나. 어떻게 지냈어?
여: 나는 잘 지내. 나는 Green Tree financial에서 회계사 일을 시작했어. 넌 어때?
남: 난 아직 학교에 있어. Transylvania 대학에서 석사과정 중이야.
여: 그래? 무슨 공부를 하니? 고등학교에서 모두가 네가 대단한 가수가 될 거라고 생각했었어.
남: 그 이후로 내 흥미가 좀 바뀌었어. 지금은 정치학을 공부하고 있어.
여: 멋지다. 왜 정치학을 선택했니?
남: 지난 선거 이후로 정치에 사로잡혔어. 넌 어때? 왜 회계사가 되었어?
여: 너 고등학교 경제학 선생님이었던 Lee 선생님 기억나지?

남: 응. 그녀는 정말 멋졌지. 카리스마도 있고 재미도 있으셨지.
여: 난 언제나 그녀를 동경했어. 고등학교 졸업 후 선생님과 나는 좋은 친구가 되었고 그녀가 내가 회계학을 공부하도록 독려하셨지.
남: 정말? 멋지다.

어휘
accountant *n.* 회계사 **master's** *n.* 석사 학위 **charismatic** *a.* 카리스마가 있는 **adore** *v.* 존경하다, 사모하다 **accounting** *n.* 회계

정답 ①

문제풀이
대화의 마지막 부분에서 여자는 고등학교 때 경제학 선생님을 동경했고, 졸업 후 선생님과 좋은 친구가 되어 자신이 회계학을 공부하도록 독려해 주셨다고 했으므로 정답은 ① '학창 시절 매우 좋아했던 경제 선생님 때문에'이다.

총 어휘 수 162

09 숫자

소재 엄마 선물로 목걸이 사기

듣기 대본 해석
여: 야, 나 엄마 생일이 이번 주말인 거 방금 알았어.
남: 난 완전히 까먹고 있었어! 엄마한테 뭘 사다 드려야 되지?
여: 글쎄, 아까 백화점에 있었는데 엄마가 분명히 좋아하실 만한 목걸이를 봤어.
남: 정말? 비싸?
여: 그렇게 비싸지는 않아. 60달러 밖에 안하고 20퍼센트 할인을 해주고 있어.
남: 나한테는 너무 비싸. 나 22달러 밖에 없거든. 그 목걸이보다 더 싼 것은 없을까?
여: 글쎄, 귀걸이도 봤는데 내 생각엔 목걸이를 좋아하실 것 같아.
남: 근데 48달러잖아, 맞지? 반씩 낸다 해도 돈이 모자라.
여: 그럼 네가 나한테 22달러 주고 내가 나머지 낼게.
남: 좋네, 고마워.

어휘
mall *n.* 백화점 **discount** *v.* 할인하다 *n.* 할인 **split** *v.* 분담하다

정답 ③

문제풀이
목걸이가 60달러에 20퍼센트 할인을 해서 48달러인데 남자가 22달러 밖에 없다고 하자 여자는 나머지는 자기가 내겠다고 했으므로 여자가 부담할 금액은 ③ '$26'이다.

총 어휘 수 117

10 언급 유무

소재 코끼리 입양과 후원

듣기 대본 해석
여: 안녕 Max. 뭐해?
남: 내가 입양한 아프리카에 있는 코끼리에 대해서 읽고 있었어. 이 사진 좀 봐.
여: 코끼리라고? 정말 멋지다. 이름이 뭐야?
남: Chang이야.
여: 그럼, 자선 프로그램 같은 걸 통해서 입양한 거야?
남: 맞아. 내가 최근에 아프리카에서의 밀렵과 코끼리 학대에 관한 다큐멘터리를 봤거든. 너무 인상 깊어서 내가 도움이 될 수 있는 걸 하기로 결정했어.
여: 정말 잘했구나. Chang을 돕기 위해서 뭘 하고 있는 거야?
남: 음, 난 이러한 동물들을 돌보는 야생동물 보호구역을 찾았어. 그리고 그곳이 그가 사는 곳이야. 그 사람들에게 매달 돈을 보내고 있어.
여: 얼마나 많이 보내는데?
남: 음. 내가 원하는 만큼 보낼 수 있는데, 보통 한 달에 30달러를 넘지는 않아. 너도 그 프로그램에 참가하고 싶어?
여: 그거 멋지겠는데, 지금 당장은 그럴만한 형편이 안돼.
남: 괜찮아. 나중에 돈이 생기면 도와줄 수 있을 거야.

어휘
adopt *v.* 입양하다 **charity** *n.* 자선, 자선단체 **poach** *v.* 밀렵하다 **abuse** *n.* 학대 **sanctuary** *n.* 보호구역 **take part in** ~에 참여하다 **afford** *v.* 여유가 되다 **spare** *v.* 할애하다

정답 ③

문제풀이
동물을 입양한 지역, 입양한 동물의 이름, 입양하게 된 계기, 후원하는 방법에 대한 언급은 있지만, 동물을 후원해온 기간에 대해서는 언급하지 않았으므로 정답은 ③ '후원해 온 기간'이다.

총 어휘 수 166

11 내용 일치 · 불일치

소재 토네이도 대처법

듣기 대본 해석
남: 여러분 안녕하세요. 시청 회의에 참석해주셔서 감사합니다. 제 이름은 Jerry Mills로 Milford 소방서장입니다. 아시다시피 곧 토네이도가 닥쳐올 시기입니다. 토네이도가 올 때 여러분을 안전하게 해 줄 수 있는 조언을 몇 가지 하려고 합니다. 먼저 토네이도 경보가 울리면 바로 지하실로 대피하세요. 지하실이 없으면 화장실에 들어가 수건, 이불, 아니면 매트리스로 자신을 덮으세요. 창문과 날카로운 물건 주변은 피하세요. 날씨가 심하게 안 좋으면 밖에 나가지 마세요. 정전에 대비해서 배터리를 사용하는 라디오를 챙기는 것도 현명한 생각입니다. 그러면 날씨 상황에 대한 정보를 바로 받을 수 있습니다. 토네이도 중에 이러한 조언들을 들으면 안전할 수 있습니다. 감사합니다.

어휘
approach *v.* 다가오다 **siren** *n.* 사이렌, 경보 **severe** *a.* 극심한 **handy** *a.* 유용한, 가까운 곳에 있는 **in case of** ~이 발생할 시에는 **power outage** 정전

정답 ④

문제풀이
정전을 대비해서 건전지로 작동하는 라디오를 챙기라고 했으므로 내용과 일치하지 않는 것은 ④ '정전을 대비해서 휴대폰을 챙긴다.'이다.

총 어휘 수 142

12 도표

소재 버스 관광 코스

듣기 대본 해석
남: 오, 이런. 우리 9시 정원 관광 버스를 놓쳤어!
여: 너무 아쉽다. 다음 것은 몇 시야?
남: 버스 관광 스케줄에 따르면, 그건 4시간 간격으로 운행해. 그렇게 오래 기다릴 수 없어.
여: 여기 매 시간마다 운행하는 투어가 있네. 이 투어는 어때?
남: Christine, 우리 그 투어 다녀온 거 벌써 잊었어?
여: 아, 그렇지. 그러면 10시에 출발하는 이 투어는 어때? 지금이 9시 10분이니까 그 버스 타기에 충분한 시간이 있어.
남: 비용이 너무 비싸. 한 사람에 50 달러가 넘는 돈은 쓸 수가 없어.
여: 좋아. 여기 20분 뒤에 출발하는 투어가 있네. 그걸로 하자.

남: 그건 West Terminal에서 출발해. 여기에서 West Terminal까지 가는 데 적어도 30분은 걸려.
여: 그러면 우리는 한 가지 선택밖에 없어 보이네. 다음 버스까지 얼마 동안은 기다려야겠어.
남: Central Station을 돌아다니면서 시간을 좀 때울 수 있지.
여: 괜찮은 계획 같아.

어휘

run every hour 매 시간 운행하다 **plenty of** 많은 **afford to V** ~할 여유가 있다 **depart *v.*** 떠나다, 출발하다 **kill time** 시간을 때우다

정답 ②

문제풀이

처음에 Garden Tour를 놓쳤고 다음 출발 시간은 1시라서 그때까지 오랫동안 기다릴 수 없다고 하였다. 매 시간 출발하는 투어(City Tour)는 이미 다녀왔다고 했고, 10시에 출발하는 Castle Tour는 50달러가 넘어서 비싸다고 하였다. 다음으로 20분 안에 출발하는 투어(Shopping Tour)는 현재 위치에서 West 터미널까지 가는 시간 때문에 선택할 수 없으므로 마지막으로 조건에 맞는 투어는 ② 'Museum Tour'이다.

총 어휘 수 164

13 긴 대화의 응답

소재 학교 과학 축제 행사

듣기 대본 해석

여: 이봐 Luke, 너 Space Shooters 대회에 대해 들었어?
남: 못 들었어. 그게 뭔데?
여: 그건 해마다 하는 학교 과학 축제를 위한 행사야.
남: 그래서 네가 나한테 그것에 대해 말해줄 수 있는 게 어떤 거야?
여: 학생들은 하늘로 날려보낼 작동하는 미니어처 로켓을 만들기 위해 같이 작업해야 해. 네가 관심 있을 것 같아서.
남: 네 말이 맞아! 나 모형 로켓 만드는 거 좋아해. 내가 어렸을 때 아빠랑 나랑 항상 모형 로켓을 만들었었어.
여: 그러면 너 그것을 잘하겠구나! 너 내 파트너 할래?
남: 좋을 것 같지만 내가 참가하고 싶은지 아닌지 잘 모르겠어. 내가 다른 학생들과 경쟁하고 싶은지 아닌지 잘 모르겠거든.
여: 넌 잘할 거야! 같이 하자.
남: 음... 좋아. 우리는 팀이야. 우리가 뭐부터 시작해야 한다고 생각해?
여: 로켓 디자인들을 찾아보는 게 어떨까?
남: ④ <u>아이디어를 좀 얻기 위해서 인터넷을 이용하자.</u>

어휘

annual *a.* 매년의, 연례의 **miniature *a.*** 아주 작은, 축소된 **compete *v.*** 경쟁하다 **research *v.*** 조사하다 〈문제〉 **supply *n.*** 공급, 보급품

정답 ④

문제풀이

두 사람은 같이 학교 과학 축제에 나가기로 했고 먼저 로켓 디자인들을 찾아보자고 했으므로 남자의 적절한 응답은 ④ '아이디어를 좀 얻기 위해서 인터넷을 이용하자.'이다.

오답 보기 해석

① 지금 바로 우리 로켓을 시험해 보자!
② 미안해. 너는 새로운 파트너를 찾아야 해.
③ 우리 충분한 물품을 가지고 있지 않아.
⑤ 로켓을 가지고 노는 것은 위험한 것 같아.

총 어휘 수 148

14 긴 대화의 응답

소재 병문안

듣기 대본 해석

여: Owen, 당신이 병원에 있다고 들어서 놀랐어요. 괜찮아요?
남: 괜찮아요. 테니스 치다가 무릎을 다쳤을 뿐이에요. 보러 와줘서 고마워요, Nora.
여: 내가 당신이 여기 있다는 걸 들었을 때, 당신이 좋아할 만한 노래들을 다운받아 왔어요. 당신 휴대폰에 전송해 줄게요. 당신을 지루하지 않게 해 줄 거예요.
남: 당신은 정말 배려심이 있네요.
여: 그런데 어쩌다 무릎을 다쳤어요?
남: 오늘 아침에 연습하다가요. 공을 보고 뛰어올랐는데 내려올 때 무릎이 꺾였어요.
여: 오! 심각한가요?
남: 아뇨. 의사 선생님이 살짝 삔 거라고 했지만 이삼 일 정도는 쓰면 안 된대요.
여: 그러면 의사 선생님 말을 듣고 얼마 동안 쉬어요.
남: 그렇지만 저는 오는 가을에 토너먼트에 참가하려면 훈련을 계속해야 해요.
여: 그건 좋은 생각이 아닌 것 같아요. 만약 당신이 더 다치면 당신은 다시는 테니스를 칠 수 없을지도 몰라요.
남: 의사도 같은 말을 했어요. 그렇지만 저는 토너먼트에서 정말 이기고 싶어요.
여: ① <u>아마 당신은 우승할 수 있겠지만 지금은 쉬어야 해요.</u>

어휘

thoughtful *a.* 배려심 있는, 친절한 **sprain *n.*** 염좌 ***v.*** (손목, 발목 등을) 삐다 **stay off** 삼가다, 멀리하다 **compete *v.*** (시합 등에) 참가하다, 경쟁하다 〈문제〉 **consult *v.*** 상담하다

정답 ①

문제풀이

부상을 당해 입원해 있으면서도 테니스 대회 우승을 위해 연습을 하고 싶다는 남자에게 지금은 쉬어야 한다고 충고하는 것이 적절하므로 답은 ① '아마 당신은 우승할 수 있겠지만 지금은 쉬어야 해요.'이다.

오답 보기 해석

② 나도 동의해요. 당신이 당신의 몸을 다른 누구보다 더 잘 알겠죠.
③ 네, 나는 당신이 다른 의사와 상담해야 한다고 생각해요.
④ 와! 나는 당신이 그렇게 테니스를 잘 치는지 몰랐어요.
⑤ 서둘러요. 그렇지 않으면 당신은 놓칠 거예요.

총 어휘 수 193

15 상황에 적절한 말

소재 분실한 DVD 대체

듣기 대본 해석

여: Andrew는 Hudson 공공 도서관에서 DVD를 빌렸습니다. 그러나, 그가 일주일 후에 그것을 반납할 준비가 되었을 때 그는 DVD가 없어진 것을 알았습니다. 그는 누군가가 DVD를 훔쳐간 것이 틀림없다고 믿습니다. 하지만 도서관 규정에는 그가 잃어버린 것을 대체하기 위해서 새로운 것을 사야 한다고 명시되어 있습니다. Andrew는 새로운 DVD를 백화점에서 사서 그것을 도서관으로 가지고 갔습니다. 사서는 그 DVD에 도서관 스티커가 없다는 것을 알아차립니다. 그녀는 그 DVD를 반납 처리할 수 없고 Andrew가 실수를 했음이 틀림없다고 말합니다. Andrew는 자신의 입장을 해명하기를 원합니다. 이러한 상황에서, Andrew가 사서에게 무슨 말을 할까요?
Andrew: ⑤ <u>누군가가 제 원래 DVD를 훔쳐가서 제가 대체물을 샀어요.</u>

어휘

must have p.p. ~임이 틀림없다 **policy *n.*** 정책, 방침 **state *v.*** 말하다, 진술하다 **replace *v.*** 교체하다, 대신하다 **librarian *n.*** 사서 〈문제〉 **check something out** 대출하다 **replacement *n.*** 교체, 대신할 사람

정답 ⑤

문제풀이
Andrew는 일주일 전 DVD를 빌렸고, 그것이 없어져서 규정대로 새것으로 사갔으나, 사서는 도서관 스티커가 없다며 실수했다고 말하는 상황이므로 Andrew가 자신의 상황을 설명한 가장 적절한 응답은 ⑤ '누군가가 제 원래 DVD를 훔쳐가서 제가 대체물을 샀어요.'이다.

오답 보기 해석
① 제가 DVD를 제때 돌려줄 것을 약속할게요.
② 제가 DVD를 못 찾아서 늦었어요.
③ 제가 이 DVD를 좀 더 오래 대출하고 싶어요.
④ 저는 미래에 사서가 되고 싶어요. 저를 도와주시겠어요?

총 어휘 수 127

16 담화 목적 / 17 세부 내용 파악

소재 해외 근무의 이점

듣기 대본 해석
남: 안녕하세요, 신사 숙녀 여러분. 제 이름은 George Wondell이고 오늘 여기 San Jose State 취업박람회에서의 제 세미나에 여러분이 참가하게 되어 기쁩니다. 저는 해외 근무에 대해 얘기하고 싶습니다. 여러분은 다른 나라에서 일하는 기회에 대해 생각해 본 적이 있습니까? 제 이야기를 해보겠습니다. 저는 고등학교를 졸업한 후에 이 박람회와 매우 유사한 취업 박람회에 갔었습니다. 한 국제 선적회사가 저를 갑판원으로 고용했습니다. 이것이 제가 세계를 보고 제 관점을 넓히는 기회가 되었습니다. 저는 많은 아름답고 흥미로운 장소들을 여행했습니다. 저는 에펠탑, 피사의 사탑, 그리고 많은 다른 유명한 랜드마크들을 보았습니다. 저는 또한 여정 중에 많은 흥미로운 사람들을 만났고 어디를 가든 친구들을 만들었습니다. 어느 날, 저는 다양한 분야에서 일할 전 세계 사람들을 고용하는 회사를 소유한 한 남자를 만났습니다. 우리는 점심을 먹었고 저는 그에게 제 여행에 대해 들려주었습니다. 그는 제 이야기에 흥미로워하며 이와 같은 세미나와 취업 박람회에서 그의 회사를 대신하여 말할 수 있는 일자리를 저에게 제공했습니다. 해외 근무는 인생의 경험이었습니다. 그것은 문을 열어주고 당신이 다른 어느 곳에서도 찾을 수 없는 기회를 제공해 주었습니다. 만약 당신이 더 많은 정보를 원한다면 우리 부스를 방문해 주세요. 들어주셔서 감사합니다.

어휘
deckhand ***n.*** 갑판원 **perspective** ***n.*** 관점 **recruit** ***v.*** 모집하다, 뽑다 **in a variety of** 여러 가지의 ~으로 **on behalf of** ~을 대신하여

정답 16 ④ 17 ④

문제풀이
16 자신의 경험을 예로 들면서 해외 근무의 장점을 알리고 권유하는 내용이므로 남자 말의 목적은 ④ '해외 근무의 이점에 대해 말하기 위해'이다.
17 여행을 다니면서 현지에서 친구들을 사귀었다는 언급만 있으므로 정답은 ④ '그는 그의 친구들과 세계를 여행했다.'이다.

오답 보기 해석
16
① 기부금을 내도록 사람들을 설득하기 위해
② 채용 회사에서 새로운 직업을 찾기 위해
③ 선적 경험을 가진 사람들을 채용하기 위해
⑤ 해외 근무의 어려운 점을 논의하기 위해

17
① 그는 선적회사에서 일했다.
② 그는 피사의 사탑을 보았다.
③ 그는 많은 흥미로운 사람들을 만났다.
⑤ 그는 회사 소유주와 점심을 먹었다.

총 어휘 수 233

DICTATION ANSWERS

01 Let's grab a bite to eat

02 You should come with me / Are they good seats

03 increasing your business's productivity / the normal routine consisted of / work from their own homes / end up being beneficial

04 posted on / should have asked / keeping in touch with your friends / my privacy was evaporating / People should be extra cautious

05 My flight was delayed / change into warmer clothing / The weather forecast is calling for

06 I tried to blow out / used balloons to decorate / Those four muffins in front of

07 motivates me to work hard / Are you busy after your workout today / pick up some vitamins and supplements / I have extra

08 studying for my master's / I've been obsessed with / I always adored her / she pushed me to study accounting

09 That's too much for me / even if we split it / I'll take care of the rest

10 through a charity program / I was very touched by it / take part in the program / I can't really afford it

11 tornado season is quickly approaching / get to the basement immediately / in case of a power outage

12 a tour that runs every hour / we have plenty of time / We can't afford to spend / We can kill some time

13 the school's annual science fair / send up into the air / I don't know if I want to join / I'd like competing against

14 That's so thoughtful of you / it's just a minor sprain / take it easy for a while

15 it was missing / someone must have stolen it / made a mistake

16-17 working overseas / broaden my perspective / in a variety of settings / on behalf of his company

30 수능영어듣기 실전모의고사

본문 p.182

01 ②	02 ⑤	03 ④	04 ④	05 ②	06 ③
07 ①	08 ⑤	09 ③	10 ②	11 ④	12 ④
13 ①	14 ⑤	15 ④	16 ③	17 ①	

01 짧은 대화의 응답

소재 헤드라이트를 켜놓은 차주인에게 이를 알려주기

듣기 대본 해석

여: 저거 봐요, 아빠. 누가 헤드라이트를 켜 놓고 갔어요. 차 주변에 다른 사람은 안 보여요.

남: 끄는 걸 깜박했나 봐. 문 잠겨 있어?

여: 네. 근데 여기 전화번호가 있어요.

남: ② 지금 당장 전화해줘야 할 것 같구나.

어휘

turn ~ off ~을 끄다

정답 ②

문제풀이

헤드라이트가 켜져 있고, 차에 사람이 없는 대신 전화번호가 남겨진 것을 발견한 여자에게 남자가 할 말로 적합한 것은 ② '지금 당장 전화해줘야 할 것 같구나.'이다.

오답 보기 해석

① 헤드라이트 끄려고 해봤니?

③ 그런가 봐. 전화 받아 봐.

④ 네 전화번호를 남기면 그들이 나중에 전화할 거야.

⑤ 네 말이 맞아. 헤드라이트 바꿀 때가 된 것 같아.

총 어휘 수 42

02 짧은 대화의 응답

소재 함부로 버려진 쓰레기

듣기 대본 해석

남: Mary, 만약에 더우면 신발 벗고 물에 발을 담그는 게 어때요? 시원하고 좋아요.

여: 좋을 것 같아요. *[잠시 후]* 아우! 물에 떠다니는 게 쓰레기예요?

남: 네. 사람들이 어떻게 그렇게 사려 깊지 못한지 이해할 수가 없어요. 너무 쉽게 쓰레기를 버리네요.

여: ⑤ 어떤 사람들은 환경을 전혀 신경 쓰지 않아요.

어휘

take off (옷, 신발 등을) 벗다 **float** ***v.*** 떠다니다 **inconsiderate** ***a.*** 사려 깊지 못한 〈문제〉 **trash bin** 쓰레기통

정답 ⑤

문제풀이

사람들이 쓰레기를 함부로 버린다는 남자의 말에 여자도 환경을 언급하며 동조하는 것이 자연스러우므로 정답은 ⑤ '어떤 사람들은 환경을 전혀 신경 쓰지 않아요.'이다.

오답 보기 해석

① 우리는 쓰레기통을 하나 더 사는 게 좋겠어요.

② 나는 괜찮아요. 물이 아직 너무 차요.

③ 당신이 우리를 위해 해준 모든 것에 감사해요.

④ 쓰레기를 줍는 데 한 시간밖에 안 걸려요.

총 어휘 수 60

03 담화 목적

소재 예술 축제 행사 설문

듣기 대본 해석

남: 오늘 밤 후원자의 모임에 와주셔서 감사합니다. 후원자 위원회는 2016년 봄 예술 축제를 계획하였으며 이를 성공적인 행사로 만들기 위해 여러분의 도움을 원합니다. 예술 축제는 지금까지 우리 학교에서 아주 큰 행사였고, 우리는 올해가 이제까지 중 가장 성공적인 행사가 되었으면 합니다. 우리는 여러분 모두로부터 가능한 한 많은 의견을 기다리고 있습니다. 이 축제를 캠퍼스 혹은 다른 곳에서 개최해야 할까요? 라이브 음악을 해야 할까요? 우리가 다른 지역의 학교가 참가하도록 초대하기를 원하십니까, 안 하기를 원하십니까? 지금 돌리는 설문지에 있는 이러한 질문들 및 다른 몇 가지에 대해 답해주시면 감사하겠습니다. 작성하는 데 오래 걸리지 않을 것이고 여러분의 모든 대답과 선택은 매우 유용할 것입니다. 이것은 지역사회 행사이므로 우리는 여러분의 의견을 듣고 싶습니다. 작성이 끝나시면, 설문지를 공중으로 들어 주시기 바랍니다.

어휘

booster ***n.*** 후원자 **board** ***n.*** 위원회 **host** ***v.*** 개최하다 **district** ***n.*** 지역 **questionnaire** ***n.*** 설문지

정답 ④

문제풀이

학교의 예술 축제 행사의 개최를 위해 축제의 장소나 내용에 관한 설문지를 작성해 줄 것을 부탁하고 있으므로, 정답은 ④ '예술 축제 개최를 위한 설문 참여를 부탁하려고'이다.

총 어휘 수 171

04 대화 주제

소재 학생들의 운동량을 늘리기 위한 방안

듣기 대본 해석

여: Baker 씨, 제 생각에는 우리 학교 학생들이 적당한 양의 운동을 하지 않는 것 같아요.

남: 저도 그것에 동의하지만, 우리가 돕기 위해 뭘 할 수 있을까요?

여: 우리가 추가 운동 프로그램을 제공하는 게 좋을 것 같아요.

남: 방과후 교실 같은 것 말씀이세요?

여: 음, 저는 사실 우리가 그것을 아침에 할 수도 있을 거라고 생각하고 있었어요.

남: 우리가 그것을 어떻게 관리할 수 있을까요?

여: 아침에 학교가 시작하기 전에, 학생들에게 마당에서 간단한 운동을 하게 할 수 있어요.

남: 그거 꽤 괜찮은 생각 같은데요, 하지만 저는 당신이 학교가 시작하기도 전에 학생들을 지치게 만들길 원한다고 생각하지 않아요.

여: 저는 아침운동이 실제로 반대 효과를 갖는다고 읽었어요. 그것은 학생들의 주의 집중에 도움을 줄 수 있어요.

남: 그런가요? 어쨌든, 저는 몇몇 학교가 학생들이 더욱 활동적이도록 격려하기 위해 방과후 프로그램을 제공하고 있다고 들었어요.

여: 그것도 좋은 생각이네요.

남: 그럼, 이것들을 시도해보고 효과가 있는지 없는지 보죠.

어휘

after-school class 방과후 교실 **manage** ***v.*** 처리하다, 관리하다 **courtyard** ***n.*** 뜰, 마당 **opposite** ***a.*** 반대의 **concentration** ***n.*** 집중 **give it a try** 시도하다

정답 ④

문제풀이

남자와 여자는 학생들의 운동량을 늘려야 한다면서 그 방안에 대해 이야기하고 있으므로 정답은 ④ '학생들의 운동량을 늘리기 위한 방안'이다.

총 어휘 수 158

05 대화자의 관계 파악

소재 주방장과의 인터뷰

듣기 대본 해석
여: 만나주셔서 감사합니다. Gaines 선생님.
남: 저와 함께해주셔서 감사합니다.
여: Gaines' Eatery가 2015년 Austin의 최고 레스토랑으로 선정된 것을 먼저 축하드리고 싶습니다.
남: 감사합니다. 정말 감사드려요. 그러나 혼자서는 그것을 못했을 수도 있어요. 제 팀의 멤버들이 진정한 영웅들입니다.
여: Gaines 선생님, 제가 드리고 싶은 몇 가지 질문이 있어요. 먼저, 언제 처음으로 레스토랑 사업에 뛰어들기로 결정하셨죠?
남: 음, 제가 어렸을 때, 아버지께서 Second Street에 작은 빵집을 가지고 계셨어요. 제가 진정으로 제 사업에 대한 이해를 키워온 곳이 바로 그곳입니다.
여: 훌륭하네요. 당신의 일에서 가장 어려운 부분은 무엇인가요?
남: 저는 저녁의 혼잡한 시간대에 고객들이 만족하도록 유지하는 것이 때때로 어려워요. 그것은 스트레스 받는 일이지만 저희 팀은 혼란을 덜 수 있도록 도와줍니다.
여: 자유시간에는 무엇을 하시죠?
남: 저한테는 일이 끝나지 않습니다. 제가 일하지 않고 있을 때, 저는 항상 새로운 조리법을 찾고 새로운 방법을 시험합니다.
여: 당신은 일을 아주 진지하게 받아들이시는 것 같아요. 저희가 잡지에 사용하기 위한 당신 사진을 몇 장 찍어도 괜찮으시겠어요?
남: 물론이죠. 괜찮습니다.

어휘
appreciate ***v.*** 고마워하다, 인정하다 **crew** ***n.*** 팀, 반, 승무원 **appreciation** ***n.*** 감상, 공감 **rush** ***n.*** 혼잡, 북적거림 **ease** ***v.*** 덜어 주다, 덜해지다 **chaos** ***n.*** 혼란, 혼돈

정답 ②

문제풀이
2015년 최고의 레스토랑에 선정되었다고 했고 레스토랑 사업과 조리법 연구 등에 대해 말하는 것으로 보아 남자는 주방장임을 알 수 있고, 여자는 남자를 인터뷰하면서 잡지에 실을 사진을 찍고 싶다고 했으므로 기자임을 알 수 있다. 따라서 정답은 ② '기자 — 주방장'이다.

오답 보기 해석
① 고객 — 점원　　③ 기자 — 편집자
④ 사진작가 — 모델　　⑤ 면접관 — 지원자

총 어휘 수 189

06 그림의 세부 내용 파악

소재 Rad CraCra 광고

듣기 대본 해석
여: 광고는 어떻게 되고 있어, Patrick?
남: 거의 다 된 것 같아. 한번 봐줘.
여: 인상적이네. 위쪽에 'Need Energy?'라는 슬로건이 눈에 잘 띄네. 진한 대문자 글자들이 밝고 에너지가 차 있어.
남: 그게 내가 원하던 바야. 나는 또 앞으로 움직이는 것을 보여주기 위해 오른쪽을 향하는 화살표도 넣었어.
여: 좋은 생각인데.
남: 그리고, 사람들의 이목을 끌기 위해서, 손이 달린 Rad CraCra 캔도 넣었어. 그리고 그건 양손을 공중에 흔들고 있어.
여: 잘했어. 나는 공을 차고 있는 축구 선수도 좋아.
남: 그건 Phil Phillips야. 이 음료의 광고모델이지.
여: 아래에 영양상의 정보를 넣은 것도 너무 좋아. 그건 요즘 일부 사람들에게는 정말 중요하거든.

어휘
stick out 눈에 띄다, 잘 보이다 **arrow** ***n.*** 화살표 **include** ***v.*** 포함하다 **spokesmodel** ***n.*** 광고모델 **nutritional** ***a.*** 영양상의

정답 ③

문제풀이
남자가 Rad CraCra 캔이 공중에서 양손을 든 채로 흔들고 있다고 했는데 그림에서는 한 손만 흔들고 있으므로 정답은 ③번이다.

총 어휘 수 124

07 할 일

소재 유리병 구입

듣기 대본 해석
[전화벨이 울린다.]
남: 여보세요?
여: 안녕, Bill. 저예요.
남: 여보, 무슨 일 있어요?
여: 당신이 아직 사무실에 있는지 궁금해서요.
남: 네, 아직 사무실이에요. 하지만 곧 출발할 거예요.
여: 좋아요. 집에 오는 길에 슈퍼마켓에 들를 수 있어요?
남: 물론이죠. 내가 사왔으면 하는 게 있어요?
여: 음, 제가 어제 친구 Rachel이 해야 하는 심부름을 도와줬잖아요.
남: 맞아요. 당신이 그것에 대해 말했던 거 기억해요.
여: 그녀가 저한테 여러 가지 차와 향신료가 든 상자를 줘서 그것들을 담을 예쁜 병이 필요해요.
남: 당신에게 선물을 주다니 그녀는 정말 친절하군요. 그리고 그것들을 병에 담는 것도 멋진 생각이에요. 당신은 어떤 형태의 병을 생각하고 있어요?
여: 돌려서 닫는 뚜껑이 있는 작은 유리병이요. 구식으로 보이는 그 병 알잖아요.
남: 알겠어요. 내가 슈퍼마켓에 도착하면 다시 전화할게요.

어휘
stop by ~에 들르다 **assorted** ***a.*** 여러 가지의 **spice** ***n.*** 향신료, 양념 **screw-on** ***a.*** 돌려서 닫는 **lid** ***n.*** 뚜껑 **old-fashioned** ***a.*** 구식의, 유행이 지난, 고풍의

정답 ①

문제풀이
여자는 친구에게 여러 가지 차와 향신료를 선물로 받아서 그것들을 담을 병을 사고 싶어 한다. 남자에게 집에 오는 길에 슈퍼마켓에 들러서 병을 사올 것을 부탁했고 남자는 그러겠다고 했으므로 남자가 여자를 위해 할 일은 ① '유리병 사기'이다.

총 어휘 수 160

08 이유

소재 아내의 사고

듣기 대본 해석
남: Amanda, 여기 차 가져왔어.
여: Nathan, 정말 고마워. 어제 어디 있었니? 회의에 안 왔던데.
남: 아내가 사고가 나서 회사에 늦게 도착했어.
여: 이런! 별 문제 없어?
남: 어, 괜찮아. 아내가 그냥 욕실에서 미끄러져 넘어졌어.
여: 큰일났구나. 네가 왜 늦었는지 알겠다.
남: 음, 그게 다가 아니야. 시간을 줄일 수 있을 것이라고 생각해서 회사에 차로 운전해서 오기로 결정했지.
여: 오, 너 보통 회사까지 지하철 타고 오잖아. 그렇지?

남: 맞아. 운전해서 오면 더 빨리 도착할 수 있을 것 같았어. 그런데 교통체증과 주차 때문에 더 오래 걸렸어.
여: 알아. 나는 여기까지 오는 데 너무 오래 걸려서 절대 운전하지 않아.
남: 음, 나는 이 지역이 처음이라 교통 상황을 몰랐어. 누군가에게 물어봤어야 했는데.
여: 괜찮아. 그래서 아내는 괜찮아?
남: 응, 발목을 좀 다쳤어. 더 심각하지 않아서 정말 다행이야.

어휘
slip ***v.*** 미끄러지다 **turn out** ~임이 드러나다 **be aware of** ~을 알다 **traffic conditions** 교통 상황

정답 ⑤

문제풀이
남자는 아내의 사고로 인해 늦어서 차를 가지고 출근하다가 교통체증과 주차 때문에 늦었다고 말하고 있으므로 정답은 ⑤ '교통체증과 주차 때문에'이다.

총 어휘 수 169

09 숫자

소재 체리 케이크 만들 재료 구매하기

듣기 대본 해석
남: 안녕하세요, Crocker 부인. 오늘은 무엇을 도와드릴까요?
여: 음, 오늘 오후에 가족 모임이 있어서 제 유명한 체리 케이크를 만들려고요.
남: 알겠습니다. 필요하신 게 다 있습니다. 오늘 아침에 워싱턴에서 이 체리들이 들어왔어요. 1파운드당 6달러예요.
여: 좋네요. 2파운드 살게요. 모임에 파인애플도 있으면 좋을 것 같네요. 얼마 하나요?
남: 하나당 10달러예요.
여: 좀 비싸네요. 반만 살 수는 없나요?
남: 네, 문제 없어요.
여: 원래 파인애플 하나 가격의 반이죠?
남: 그게, 원래 파인애플 반 개에 6달러인데 저희 단골 손님이시니까 5달러에 드릴게요.
여: 고마워요. 레모네이드 1갤런도 주세요.
남: 레모네이드는 1갤런에 4달러예요. 하지만 25달러 이상 사시면 레모네이드는 공짜로 가져가실 수 있어요.
여: 괜찮아요. 체리 2파운드, 파인애플 반 개, 그리고 레모네이드 1갤런만 주세요. 나중에 청구서 보내주실 수 있죠?
남: 그럼요. 감사합니다, Crocker 부인.

어휘
reunion ***n.*** 재회, 모임 **regular customer** 단골, 단골손님
bill ***v.*** 청구서를 보내다 ***n.*** 청구서

정답 ③

문제풀이
체리는 2파운드 샀으므로 12달러, 파인애플 반 통은 5달러이고, 레모네이드는 4달러이므로 정답은 ③ '$21'이다.

총 어휘 수 178

10 언급 유무

소재 사진 대회를 위한 전시회 개최

듣기 대본 해석
여: 안녕하세요, Wise 선생님. 우리가 이번 봄에 사진 대회를 위한 전시회를 개최하는 것이 어떨지 생각을 해왔습니다.
남: 좋은 생각이에요. 우리 학생들의 노고를 우리 동네에 있는 사람들에게 보여줄 수 있겠네요.
여: 맞아요. 하지만 우리는 올해의 대회의 주제를 생각해야 해요. 자연 사진에 관해서 어떻게 생각하세요?
남: 저는 좋아요. 저, 제 생각에는 우리가 시내 도서관에 있는 전시실에 공간을 좀 확보할 수 있을 것 같은데요.
여: 그렇게 생각하세요? 비용은 얼마나 드나요?
남: 글쎄요, 제가 도서관 위원회에 계신 몇몇 분들을 알아요. 저는 우리가 공간을 무료로 예약할 수 있다고 생각해요. 제가 이용 가능한지 확인해 볼게요.
여: 좋아요. 우리가 전시회를 마을에 홍보하기 위해 제가 학생들에게 포스터를 만들게 할게요.
남: 좋은 생각이에요. 부모님들을 위한 정식 초대장은 어떻게 생각하세요?
여: 그건 필요하지 않다고 생각해요. 포스터와 입소문으로 충분해요.
남: 알았어요. 음, 우리가 일에 착수해야겠군요.

어휘
exhibition ***n.*** 전시회 **competition** ***n.*** 대회, 경쟁 **reserve** ***v.*** 확보하다, 예약하다 **formal invitation** 정식 초대장
word of mouth 입소문, 구전 **get to work** 일에 착수하다

정답 ②

문제풀이
두 사람은 전시회 주제, 장소 대여 비용, 홍보 포스터와 정식 초대장에 관한 언급은 했지만 전시회 기간에 대한 언급은 하지 않았으므로 정답은 ② '전시회 기간'이다.

총 어휘 수 170

11 내용 일치 · 불일치

소재 새로 문을 여는 식당 홍보

듣기 대본 해석
남: 올 가을, 저희는 여러분들에게 이 도시가 제공할 수 있는 가장 최고의 식사 경험을 가져다 드리려 합니다. Ricardo's on the Boardwalk은 어떤 식사 상황에도 완벽한 식당입니다. Scales Lake에 있으며, 시내에서 약 5분 정도 떨어진 곳에 자리하고 있습니다. 저희의 웅장한 식당 건축은 거의 2년이 걸렸지만 마침내 문을 열 준비가 되었답니다. 옥외 식사 공간은 놀라운 호수 전망을 제공하며, 위층의 라운지는 재즈에 재능이 있는 지역 사람들을 주말과 일부 평일 저녁에 제공합니다. 여러분은 이 지역에서 선사하는 최고의 재즈를 들으며 식사와 음료를 즐길 수 있습니다. 또한 저희는 여러분의 어린 자녀들에게 맞추어진 좀 더 가족 친화적인 식사 공간을 갖추고 있습니다. 저희 식당은 오직 최고의 요리사들만을 채용하고 있으며, 식품은 모두 현지에서 재배됩니다. 기억에 남을 만한 식사 경험을 찾고 계시다면, 올 가을에 문을 여는 Ricardo's on the Boardwalk 이외에 다른 곳은 더 알아보지 않으셔도 됩니다.

어휘
open-air ***a.*** 야외의, 옥외의 **house** ***v.*** 수용하다 **cater to** ~의 구미에 맞추다, ~을 충족시키다 **locally** ***ad.*** 근처에, 현지에서

정답 ④

문제풀이
남자는 주말과 일부 평일 저녁에 지역 재즈 음악가들에게 장소가 제공되어 재즈를 들으며 식사를 할 수 있다고 말했으므로 내용과 일치하지 않는 것은 ④ '매일 평일 저녁에 재즈 공연이 있다.'이다.

총 어휘 수 146

12 도표

소재 알맞은 축구화 선택

듣기 대본 해석
여: 어서 오세요, Owen 스포츠 용품 가게입니다. 무엇을 도와드릴까요?

남: 축구화를 새로 사려고 합니다. 추천해 줄 만한 것이 있나요?
여: 여기 저희 제품 목록이 있습니다. 수비수로 활동하나요, 공격수로 활동하나요?
남: 사실 아들 주려고 사는 건데 걔는 두 포지션 모두 뛰는 것을 좋아해요.
여: 그렇군요. 그럼 다용도 축구화가 아드님께 맞을 것 같네요.
남: 그럴 것 같아요. 플라스틱과 천 중에서 어느 것을 추천해 주시겠어요?
여: 플라스틱을 추천해드립니다. 플라스틱이 훨씬 내구성이 좋아서 오래가요.
남: 알겠습니다. 플라스틱으로 살게요. 그럼 이제 두 제품만 남았네요. 저렴한 것과 비싼 것.
여: 이것은 이번 시즌 신상품이라서 더 비싸요.
남: 신상품이든 아니든 제 아들은 별로 신경 쓸 것 같지 않네요. 더 저렴한 것 5 사이즈로 살게요.
여: 선택 잘하신 것 같아요. 카운터에서 계산 도와드릴게요.
남: 좋아요. 도와주셔서 감사합니다.

어휘

soccer cleat 축구화 **suit *v.*** 어울리다 **durable *a.*** 내구성 있는, 오래가는 〈문제〉 **offensive *a.*** 공격의 **defensive *a.*** 수비의

정답 ④

문제풀이

남자는 수비수와 공격수 모두에게 적합한 다목적이면서 재질은 내구성이 좋은 플라스틱, 가격은 더 저렴한 축구화를 선택하였으므로 정답은 ④번이다.

총 어휘 수 156

13 긴 대화의 응답

소재 태국 여행을 위한 조언

듣기 대본 해석

여: 안녕 Stan. 잘 지내니?
남: 음, 나는 이번 여름에 태국을 방문할 계획을 마무리 지으려고 하고 있어.
여: 정말? 태국 어디를 가려고 해? 알다시피 나는 지난 겨울에 거기에 갔잖아.
남: 그래, 나는 네가 태국에 대해 말했던 것 때문에 거기에 가려고 해. 너 방콕에 있었니 아니면 해안가로 갔었니?
여: 나는 며칠 동안 방콕에 있었고 그 다음에 Phi Phi 섬에 갔어. 너는 해변에 가봐야 해. 정말 끝내줘.
남: 그래, 내가 큰 도시는 그렇게 좋아할 것 같지가 않아. 거기에서 여행하는 것에 관한 조언 좀 해 줄래?
여: 음, 너는 어디에 가더라도 가격 흥정을 해야 해.
남: 정말? 거기에는 모든 것이 비싸니?
여: 아니, 모든 것이 꽤 싸지만, 처음 가격에 절대 동의하지 마. 거의 항상 흥정을 할 수 있어.
남: 그렇구나. 내가 항상 가격에 대해 언쟁을 해야겠네.
여: 그래. 대체로, 너는 그들이 처음 너에게 말한 가격의 1/3 가격에 기념품을 살 수 있어.
남: ① 조언 고마워. 많은 도움이 되었어.

어휘

finalize *v.* 마무리 짓다, 완결하다 **make it to** ~에 이르다, 도착하다 **incredible *a.*** 믿을 수 없는, 엄청난 **haggle *v.*** 흥정을 하다 **initial *a.*** 처음의, 초기의 **bargain *v.***협상(흥정)하다 **souvenir *n.*** 기념품 **quote *v.*** 값을 부르다, 인용하다 〈문제〉 **confirmation *n.*** 확인

정답 ①

문제풀이

여자가 남자에게 태국 여행에서 항상 가격 흥정을 하라는 조언을 해주고 있으므로 남자의 마지막 응답은 ① '조언 고마워. 많은 도움이 되었어.'가 적절하다.

오답 보기 해석

② 이번이 태국으로 첫 여행이야.
③ 나는 마침내 방콕으로 가는 비행기편의 확인을 받았어.
④ 내가 거기서 훨씬 더 싼 가격으로 이 기념품들을 살 수 있어.
⑤ 그거 좋은 생각이야. 나는 여기서 많은 돈을 썼어.

총 어휘 수 174

14 긴 대화의 응답

소재 F1(자동차경주) 관람 전 간식 사기

듣기 대본 해석

남: 처음으로 F1 보려니까 신나지?
여: 정말 기대 돼. 앉기 전에 매점에서 간식 좀 사자.
남: 그래. 단 게 좀 끌리네. 어, 봐봐, 솜사탕 판다.
여: 솜사탕 좋아해? 애들 간식이잖아.
남: 그럴 수도 있지만 이건 F1이고 솜사탕은 즐거운 간식이 되지.
여: 그럴 수도 있지. 다 큰 남자가 솜사탕 먹는 게 좀 웃겨 보일 것 같아서.
남: 알겠어. 츄러스는 어때? 나 츄러스도 진짜 좋아해.
여: 장난치지 마. 츄러스는 너무 달아. 평범한 사람들처럼 그냥 핫도그 몇 개랑 햄버거 사면 안 될까?
남: 오, 어서! 츄러스 먹자.
여: ⑤ 고맙지만 괜찮아. 나는 너무 단 것을 먹고 싶지 않아.

어휘

concession stand 매점 **in the mood for** ~할 기분이 나서 **cotton candy** 솜사탕 **foolish *a.*** 어리석은, 바보 같은

정답 ⑤

문제풀이

여자는 솜사탕과 츄러스를 사오려는 남자에게 너무 달다면서 핫도그나 햄버거를 사오면 안 되냐고 하고 있다. 다시 한번 츄러스를 권하는 남자의 말에 대한 대답으로 적절한 것은 ⑤ '고맙지만 괜찮아. 나는 너무 단 것을 먹고 싶지 않아.'이다.

오답 보기 해석

① 네가 틀렸어. 나는 디저트 먹는 것 정말 좋아해.
② 모든 사람들이 F1에서 츄러스 먹는 걸 좋아해.
③ 나는 매점에서는 원하는 게 아무것도 없어.
④ 나는 우리가 이번 주말에 F1 보러 가야 한다고 생각해.

총 어휘 수 126

15 상황에 적절한 말

소재 폭풍우 예보로 인한 등산 연기하기

듣기 대본 해석

여: Kristen과 가족들은 토요일에 산으로 등산을 갈 계획을 하고 있습니다. 그녀의 아들 Gavin은 야외를 굉장히 좋아하기 때문에 특히나 더 들떠 있습니다. Kristen은 일주일 내내 등산 갈 준비를 했고 Gavin이 제일 좋아하는 간식도 몇 개 준비했습니다. 그러나 Kristen이 금요일 밤에 일기예보를 확인하자 강수확률이 80%라는 것을 알게 됩니다. 사실 일기예보에서는 주말 내내 폭풍우가 연속적으로 그 지역에 있을 것이라고 예상하였습니다. 안 좋은 날씨로 인해 기상청은 사람들이 실내에 있기를 권고하고 있습니다. Kristen은 등산을 다음 주 토요일로 미루는 것이 좋을 것이라고 생각합니다. 이러한 상황에서 Kristen이 Gavin에게 어떤 말을 할까요?
Kristen: Gavin, ④ 우리 등산을 다음 주말로 일정을 변경해야 할 것 같아.

어휘

weather forecast 일기예보 **predict *v.*** 예측하다, 예견하다 **severe *a.*** 심각한, 안 좋은 **urge *v.*** 충고하다, 권고하다 **postpone *v.*** 연기하다, 미루다

정답 ④

문제풀이

Kristen은 주말의 일기예보를 보고 등산을 연기하자고 아들에게 말하려고 하므로 적절한 말은 ④ '우리 등산을 다음 주말로 일정을 변경해야 할 것 같아.'이다.

오답 보기 해석

① 내일 날씨가 등산 하기에 완벽할 거야.
② 등산을 위해 마른 옷 몇 벌이 필요할 거야.
③ 내가 우리 등산을 위해 네가 가장 좋아하는 간식을 좀 준비했어.
⑤ 빗속에서 산꼭대기까지 가려면 시간이 더 걸릴 거야.

총 어휘 수 137

16 담화 주제 / 17 세부 내용 파악

소재 음식에 돈을 절약할 수 있는 몇 가지 조언

듣기 대본 해석

남: 매일 요리를 하는 것은 비용이 많이 들고 시간이 많이 소요됩니다. 요즘 사람들은 항상 정신 없이 바쁘고 스스로 요리할 시간이 없습니다. 제가 여러분들에게 음식에 돈과 시간을 절약하는 요령들을 제공하기 위해 여기에 왔습니다. 첫째, 음식물을 대량으로 구매하세요. 음식물을 개별적으로 구매하는 것보다 대량으로 사는 것이 더 저렴합니다. 둘째, 유명 브랜드를 피하고 자가 브랜드 상품을 구매하세요. 유명 브랜드 상품은 종종 자가 브랜드의 제품과 같은 종류의 재료를 포함하고 있으면서 훨씬 더 비쌉니다. 셋째, 농산물이 제철일 때에만 농산물을 구매하세요. 농산물이 제철이 아니고 그 때문에 비쌀 때는 통조림이나 냉동된 음식이 대체물이 될 수 있습니다. 또한, 제품 판촉이나 세일에 관심을 가지세요. 여러분들은 쿠폰과 세일을 이용함으로써 많은 돈을 절약할 수 있습니다. 마지막으로, 대량으로 요리 하세요. 그것이 지루하다는 것을 저도 알지만, 여러분들이 직장에 매일 점심을 싸가면 많은 돈을 절약할 수 있습니다. 예를 들면, 여러분들이 일요일 밤에 약간의 시간을 그 주의 점심을 위한 요리를 하는 데 바칠 수 있습니다. 스파게티는 다시 데워서 그 주 내내 먹을 수 있는 훌륭하고 비용 효율적인 음식입니다. 돈을 절약하기 위해 여러분들의 생활 방식을 바꾸는 것은 힘들 수 있겠지만, 그것은 확실히 가치가 있습니다.

어휘

costly ***a.*** 많은 돈이 드는, 비용이 드는 **time-consuming** ***a.*** 시간 소비가 큰 **be on the go** 정신 없이 바쁘다 **in bulk** 대량으로 **store-brand** ***a.*** 자가 브랜드 상품의 **produce** ***n.*** 농산물 **in season** 제철인, 한창인 **take advantage of** ~을 이용하다 **dedicate** ***v.*** 전념하다, 바치다 **worthwhile** ***a.*** ~할 가치가 있는

정답 16 ③ 17 ①

문제풀이

16 남자는 음식에 돈을 절약하는 방법들을 몇 가지 알려주고 있다. 따라서 남자가 하는 말의 주제는 ③ '음식에 돈을 절약하는 방법에 대한 조언'이다.

17 제철 농산물, 통조림, 냉동식품, 스파게티에 대한 언급은 있었지만 즉석 요리 제품에 대한 언급은 없었으므로 정답은 ① '즉석 요리 제품'이다.

오답 보기 해석

16
① 집에서 식사를 요리하는 것의 이점
② 가장 신선한 농산물을 선택하는 방법
④ 맛있고 건강에 좋은 식사를 만드는 법
⑤ 바쁜 사람들을 위한 싸고 손쉬운 요리법

총 어휘 수 196

DICTATION ANSWERS

01 forgot to turn them off

02 take off your shoes / people can be so inconsiderate

03 input from all of you / host the festival on campus / fill out the form / hold your questionnaire in the air

04 getting the proper amount of exercise / How could we manage that / offering after-school programs / I say we give these a try

05 have done it alone / have difficulty keeping the customers happy / researching new recipes / to use in the magazine

06 at the top really sticks out / pointing to the right / both of them in the air / nutritional information at the bottom

07 I was wondering if / on your way home / some nice jars to put them in / the ones that look old-fashioned

08 missed the meeting / take the train to work / it turns out / traffic and bad parking / wasn't aware of the traffic conditions

09 Is there any way I can / It'll be half the cost / get the lemonade for free / You can bill me later

10 held an exhibition / a theme for this year's competition / reserve the room for free / have my students make posters / word of mouth will be enough

11 about five minutes from downtown / on the weekends and some weeknights / our food is all grown locally

12 play both positions / much more durable / take the cheaper ones

13 finalize my plans / Do you have any tips / never agree to the initial price / a third of the price

14 concession stand / in the mood for something sweet / eating cotton candy looks foolish / too sweet

15 go hiking in the mountains / checks the weather forecast / Due to the severe weather / postpone the hike until next Saturday

16-17 it's in season / pay attention to promotions / taking advantage of sales

31 수능영어듣기 실전모의고사

본문 p.188

01 ④	02 ①	03 ①	04 ④	05 ④	06 ②
07 ④	08 ③	09 ②	10 ④	11 ③	12 ⑤
13 ①	14 ②	15 ⑤	16 ③	17 ③	

01 짧은 대화의 응답

소재 회의에 늦은 이유

듣기 대본 해석

여: 안녕하세요. 무엇을 도와드릴까요?
남: 안녕하세요. 저는 Thomas Moore입니다. 저는 3시에 예정된 회의가 있는데요. 늦어서 죄송합니다.
여: 괜찮아요. Moore 씨. 우리 사무실을 찾는 것이 어려웠나요?
남: ④ 아니요. 제가 단지 지하철역을 잘못 내렸어요.

어휘

scheduled ***a.*** 예정된 〈문제〉 **direction** ***n.*** 방향, 지시

정답 ④

문제풀이

남자가 회의에 늦어서 여자는 사무실을 찾는 것이 어려웠냐고 묻고 있으므로 적절한 응답은 ④ '아니요. 제가 단지 지하철역을 잘못 내렸어요.'이다.

오답 보기 해석

① 물론이죠. 이제 저는 회의 준비가 되었습니다.
② 죄송하지만, 저는 거기에 어떻게 가는지 잘 몰라요.
③ 네. 당신 사무실로 가는 길을 저에게 알려주세요.
⑤ 그 사무실은 길 건너편 큰 건물에 있어요.

총 어휘 수 46

02 짧은 대화의 응답

소재 시력 관리

듣기 대본 해석

남: 칠판의 글씨를 선명하게 보기가 어려워.
여: 정말이야? 시력 좋았잖아. 무슨 일이야?
남: 최근에 컴퓨터 게임을 너무 많이 하는 안 좋은 습관이 생겼어.
여: ① 네 눈을 더 잘 관리해야겠다.

어휘

used to V ~하곤 했다 〈문제〉 **consider** ***v.*** 고려하다

정답 ①

문제풀이

최근에 컴퓨터 게임을 너무 많이 하는 안 좋은 습관이 생겼다는 남자에게 여자가 해줄 말은 ① '네 눈을 더 잘 관리해야겠다.'가 가장 적절하다.

오답 보기 해석

② 지금 시력 검사를 하진 않아도 돼.
③ 그런 방식으로는 습관을 고칠 수 없을 거야.
④ 책 읽기 전에 잠시 기다려야 해.
⑤ 컴퓨터를 좀 더 자주 사용할 것을 고려해 봐.

총 어휘 수 44

03 담화 주제

소재 온라인 쇼핑의 부정적인 면

듣기 대본 해석

여: 온라인으로 식품 구매를 할 수 있다는 것을 알고 있었나요? 온라인 식품 구매는 최근 몇 년 동안 꽤 대중화되었습니다. 온라인 구매는 소비자가 스마트폰, 태블릿 혹은 컴퓨터로 쇼핑을 할 수 있게 하며, 그들이 마트에 가는 시간을 절약해 줍니다. 온라인 쇼핑은 돈을 절약할 수도 있습니다. 하지만 몇 가지 부정적인 면도 있다는 것을 주의하세요. 대부분의 물건들이 상점 대신 창고에 대량으로 저장되기 때문에 더 싸지만, 이 창고들이 종종 방치되고 그래서 제품의 관리가 거의 되지 않는다는 것이 문제입니다. 이 때문에 벌레의 침입이나 부적절한 저장 방법으로 인해 제품이 손상될 수도 있습니다. 어떤 소비자들은 그들의 집으로 썩은 과일이 배송된 것을 신고했습니다. 항의를 하고자 할 때, 그들이 할 수 있는 것은 오직 이메일을 보내고 답변을 기다리는 것뿐입니다. 온라인 구매는 시간과 돈을 절약할 수 있는 좋은 방법이지만, 온라인으로 구매하는 물건들은 그것들이 방치되었을 때 부정적인 결과를 겪지 않을 물건들로 제한해야 합니다.

어휘

beware ***v.*** 조심하다, 주의하다 **aspect** ***n.*** 측면 **in bulk** 대량으로 **warehouse** ***n.*** 창고 **supervision** ***n.*** 감독, 관리 **goods** ***n.*** 제품 **lead to** ~로 이어지다 **infestation** ***n.*** (벌레의) 침입, 침략 **improper** ***a.*** 부당한, 부적절한 **file a complaint** 항의를 제기하다 **restrict** ***v.*** 제한하다 **neglect** ***v.*** 방치하다

정답 ①

문제풀이

여자는 온라인 쇼핑이 시간과 돈을 절약할 수 있는 좋은 방법이지만 부정적인 면도 있음을 알려주고 있다. 따라서 정답은 ① '온라인 쇼핑의 부정적인 측면'이다.

총 어휘 수 174

04 의견

소재 헌 샌들 기부

듣기 대본 해석

남: 어디 가고 있니, Amy?
여: 새 샌들을 사려고 쇼핑몰에 가.
남: 지금 신은 샌들도 괜찮아 보이는데.
여: 사실, 밑창이 너무 엉망이야(닳았어).
남: 새 신발 사면 그거 버릴 거니?
여: 아마도. 왜?
남: 그것들을 버리는 대신에 Good Will 재단에 주는 걸 고려할 수 있기 때문이야. 그들은 샌들이 필요한 누군가에게 그걸 줄 거야.
여: 정말? 그렇지만 나는 Good Will 재단이 어디에 있는지 모르는데.
남: 그건 걱정하지 마. 웹 사이트에 가서 가장 가까운 기부 센터를 찾아보면 돼.
여: 내가 기부하기 전에 내 신발을 수선해야 해?
남: 아니. 그들이 모든 것을 처리해. 그들이 밑창 수리까지 할 거야.
여: 정말 멋지구나. 그러면 새 신발 사고 나서 헌 것은 꼭 기부할래.
남: 좋아! 그러겠다니 나도 기뻐!

어휘

sole ***n.*** (신발의) 밑창 **foundation** ***n.*** 재단 **donate** ***v.*** 기부하다 **definitely** ***ad.*** 분명히

정답 ④

문제풀이

신던 샌들의 밑창이 닳아서 새 샌들을 사러 가는 여자에게 남자는 여자의 헌 샌들을 버리지 말고 Good Will 재단에 기부할 것을 제안하고 있다. 따라서 ④ '헌 신발을 버리지 말고 자선 단체에 기부하라.'가 정답이다.

총 어휘 수 143

05 대화자의 관계 파악

소재 태양광 에너지에 관한 인터뷰

듣기 대본 해석

여: 저희 프로그램에 함께해 주셔서 감사합니다, Marsh 교수님.
남: 초대해 주셔서 감사합니다.
여: 좋습니다. 바로 본론으로 들어가지요. 우선 다음 획기적인 기술이 무엇일 것이라고 생각하십니까?
남: 음, 아시겠지만 에너지가 우리나라에선 큰 문제입니다. 현재 에너지 기반시설이 비효율적일뿐더러 공기와 토지, 수질을 오염시키고 있습니다.
여: 맞습니다. 뉴스에서 항상 오염 이슈에 관한 소식을 듣죠. 그것은 덜 발달된 국가들에서는 훨씬 더 심각하지요.
남: 맞습니다. 우리는 대체에너지 자원을 개발할 필요가 있고 전통적인 방식은 버려야 합니다.
여: 어떠한 기술이 가장 탄력을 받을 것이라고 생각하십니까?
남: 태양전지입니다. 그게 바로 미래지요.
여: 그것이 풍력이나 수력과 같은 다른 재생 가능 에너지원들보다 더 나은 이점이 있나요?
남: 확실히 그렇죠. 대부분의 선진국은 태양광에 접근할 수 있지만 모두가 강에 가까이 있는 것도 아니고 바람을 이용할 수 있는 것도 아니지요. 태양광 에너지는 가격도 훨씬 싸지고 있습니다.
여: 바로 그거군요. 태양 에너지가 바로 미래군요. 함께해주셔서 감사합니다 Marsh 교수님.
남: 천만에요. 시청자분들께 이야기를 나누는 것은 언제나 좋습니다.

어휘

breakthrough ***n.*** 돌파구 **inefficient** ***a.*** 비효율적인 **pollute** ***v.*** 오염시키다 **alternative** ***a.*** 대체 가능한 **abandon** ***v.*** 버리다 **momentum** ***n.*** 탄력, 가속도 **renewable** ***a.*** 재생 가능한 **hydroelectric** ***a.*** 수력 전기의 **harness** ***v.*** 이용하다, 활용하다 **folks** ***n.*** 여러분, 얘들아(두 사람 이상의 사람들을 친근하게 부르는 말)

정답 ④

문제풀이

남자가 처음에 초대해줘서 고맙다고 인사했고, 여자는 남자에게 질문을 하고 남자는 태양광 에너지에 대해 이야기해주고 있다. 마지막 부분에서 viewers (시청자)가 나오는 것으로 보아 둘의 관계는 ④ '사회자 – 출연자'임을 알 수 있다.

총 어휘 수 180

06 그림의 세부 내용 파악

소재 새로 오픈하는 카페 전단지

듣기 대본 해석

남: Rose, 너 뭐 보고 있어?
여: 이거? 아, 스타디움의 새로운 카페를 위한 홍보용 전단지야. 한번 봐.
남: 재미있어 보이네. 왼쪽 뒤에 저건 빵집이야?
여: 응. 그리고 빵집 옆은 스낵바야.
남: 저 피자가 맛있어 보여. 그리고 저 사람이 카페에 있는 DJ야?
여: 응, 맞아. 그런데 카페에 DJ가 있어서 약간 이상해 보이는 것 같아. 그렇게 생각하지 않니?
남: 맞아. 이건 확실히 일반적인 카페는 아닌 것 같아.
여: 응. 카페 바깥에 어린이들을 위한 놀 거리도 좀 있어.
남: 보여. 저거 광대지?
여: 그런 것 같아. 그가 거기서 어린이들에게 동물 풍선을 만들어 주고 있어.
남: 그래, 그가 풍선을 준비하도록 돕고 있는 스태프도 보여. 이상한 카페이긴 하지만 성공할 것 같아.
여: 그랬으면 좋겠어. 개점은 이번 일요일 콘서트 전이야.

어휘

promotional ***a.*** 홍보의 **flyer** ***n.*** 전단지 **normal** ***a.*** 보통의, 평범한 **entertainment** ***n.*** 오락 **clown** ***n.*** 광대

정답 ②

문제풀이

빵집 옆에는 스낵바가 있다며 피자가 맛있겠다고 했는데 그림에서는 요리사가 햄버거를 팔고 있으므로 일치하지 않는 것은 ②번이다.

총 어휘 수 150

07 할 일

소재 리포트 작성을 위한 DVD 찾기

듣기 대본 해석

남: Rachel, 나 좀 도와줄 수 있어?
여: 그래, Peter. 무슨 일인데?
남: 그게, 이미 알고 있겠지만, 내가 목요일에 수업을 못 갔어.
여: 맞아. 야구 시 대회 나갔잖아. 어떻게 됐어?
남: 잘 했어. 다음 회로 넘어 갈 수 있게 됐어.
여: 잘 됐다. 올해 너희 팀 진짜 잘하더라. 모두가 열심히 연습했잖아. 분명 너희 팀이 우승할 거야.
남: 그럴 수 있었으면 좋겠다. 하여튼 Smith 선생님 수업의 지구 온난화 보고서 끝냈어?
여: 응. 너는 끝냈어?
남: 그게, 하고 싶은데 우리가 기초로 해야 할 영화를 못 찾겠더라.
여: 그렇구나. A Troublesome Fact 말하는 거지?
남: 그거 맞아.
여: 도서관 확인해 봤어? 거기 분명히 있을 거야.
남: 도서관 확인해 볼 생각을 못했네. 지금 가서 확인할게.

어휘

global warming 지구 온난화 **be supposed to V** ~하기로 되어 있다 **troublesome** ***a.*** 골칫거리인, 고질적인

정답 ④

문제풀이

남자는 숙제를 위해 영화를 찾고 있는데 여자가 도서관에 가면 있을 거라고 말하자 가서 확인해 보겠다고 했으므로 남자가 할 일은 ④ '도서관에 가서 영화 DVD 찾아보기'이다.

총 어휘 수 148

08 이유

소재 일일 캠프 관리자

듣기 대본 해석

여: 너 이번 여름에 뭐할 거야?
남: 나는 학교에서 일일 캠프 관리자로 일할 생각이야.
여: 재미있겠는걸.
남: 사실 나 지난 5년 동안 매 여름마다 캠프 관리자로 일해 왔었어.
여: 와, 몰랐어. 그 일은 어때?
남: 일은 꽤 쉬워. 나는 아이들을 가르치고 그날 우리가 계획한 재미있는 것들을 하게 하면 돼.
여: 상당히 편안한 환경이야?
남: 음, 사실 그래. 활동에 따라 날마다 달라질 수는 있지만, 모든 사람들이 늦게까지 일하거나 일찍 오는 데 대해서 신경 쓰지 않아. 스트레스가 거의 없지.
여: 보수는 어때?
남: 캠프 관리자로서는 보통이지만 다른 직업들보단 확실히 낮아. 그렇지만 나는 정말 돈에 별로 신경 쓰지 않아.
여: 너는 왜 그렇게 거기서 오랫동안 일해온 거니?

남: 그건 정말 나에게 이상적인 직업이야. 매일 자연을 즐기기 위해 밖으로 나가고 모든 일들을 직접 하거든.

어휘

supervisor ***n.*** 관리자 **fairly** ***ad.*** 상당히, 꽤 **vary** ***v.*** 다르다, 달라지다 **depending on** ~에 따라 **average** ***a.*** 보통의, 평균의 **hands-on** ***a.*** 직접 참여하는

정답 ③

문제풀이

대화의 마지막 부분에서 남자가 캠프 관리자로 일해 온 이유는 보수는 다른 일보다 적지만 매일 자연을 즐기기 위해 밖으로 나가고 모든 일들을 직접 하기 때문이라 말했다. 따라서 정답은 ③ '자연을 즐기며 일할 수 있어서'이다.

총 어휘 수 163

09 숫자

소재 커트 후 계산

듣기 대본 해석

여: 음, 다 됐어요. 가셔도 돼요.

남: 고마워요. 머리가 훨씬 보기 좋아요. 오늘 밤 회사 파티에서 멋지게 보일 것 같네요.

여: 제 일에 자부심이 있어요.

남: 훌륭해요. 제 친구들 모두에게 당신을 반드시 추천할게요.

여: 감사해요. 헤어 커트는 25달러가 될 겁니다. 오늘 다른 헤어 케어 제품을 구매하실 건가요?

남: 그럼요. 스타일링 왁스를 좀 살 거예요. 얼마죠?

여: 왁스는 20달러에요. 샴푸는 어떠세요? 알로에가 함유된 샴푸가 고객님의 머리 타입에 좋아요.

남: 그것도 한 병 살게요.

여: 좋아요. 그것은 한 병에 15달러예요. 다 되신 거죠?

남: 네. 저기요. 이 미용실에 첫 방문객들을 위한 어떤 할인이 있다고 언급하지 않으셨나요?

여: 맞아요. 고객님은 첫 방문 고객이시기 때문에 전체 가격에서 10퍼센트 할인을 받으십니다.

남: 좋네요. 카드 여기 있습니다.

어휘

take pride in ~을 자랑하다 **would like to V** ~하고 싶다 **infuse** ***v.*** 불어넣다

정답 ②

문제풀이

커트가 25달러, 왁스는 20달러, 샴푸는 15달러로 총 60달러에서 10퍼센트 할인이 적용되므로 남자는 ② '$54'를 지불해야 한다.

총 어휘 수 145

10 언급 유무

소재 여행지로 갈만한 곳 소개

듣기 대본 해석

남: 안녕, Sally. 이번 겨울에 좀 더 따뜻한 곳으로 여행을 갈까 생각 중이야. 제안할 만한 데 있니?

여: 물론이지. 내가 늘 가곤 했던 Tybee Island라고 불리는 곳이 있어. 분명히 네가 좋아할 거야.

남: Tybee Island라고? 한 번도 들어본 적 없는데. 어디에 있어?

여: Savannah 근처, Georgia에 있어.

남: 알겠어. 어떤 점이 그렇게 좋아?

여: 글쎄, 그 나라의 그 지역은 정말 아름다워. 식민지 시대 양식의 집들이 예쁘고, 해변가도 꽤 멋져.

남: 그때쯤 그곳 날씨는 어떨까?

여: 많이 덥지는 않지만, 수영을 하기에는 많이 추울 수도 있어.

남: 좋네. 그런데 난 수영을 별로 안 해서. 그곳 호텔들은 보통 얼마 정도니?

여: 글쎄, 일주일에 대략 700달러로 해변가 콘도를 빌릴 수 있어. 침실이 세 개 있는 방이면 너희 가족에게 딱 알맞을 것 같아.

남: 적당한 것 같네. 좀 더 역사적인 곳들을 꼭 관광하고 싶은데. 투어도 제공하겠지?

여: 당연하지. 네가 참여할 만한 몇 가지 역사 투어가 있어. 저녁에 할 수 있는 유령 투어들도 있고.

남: 정말 재미있어 보인다. 바로 Tybee Island를 알아 봐야겠어.

어휘

colonial ***a.*** 식민지의, 식민지 시대의 **beachfront** ***a.*** 해안지대의, 해변가의 **historic** ***a.*** 역사적인, 역사적으로 중요한

정답 ④

문제풀이

위치(Savannah 근처), 날씨(많이 덥지는 않지만 수영하기에는 추움), 숙박 비용(일주일에 약 700달러), 할 만한 것들(역사 투어, 유령 투어)은 언급되었지만 '현지 가이드'는 언급되지 않았으므로 정답은 ④ '현지 가이드'이다.

총 어휘 수 192

11 내용 일치 · 불일치

소재 무선 단말기 사진전

듣기 대본 해석

남: 저희는 세계적으로 유명한 Mobile Device Photo Contest(무선 단말기 사진전)를 위한 참가 날짜를 발표하게 되어서 자랑스럽습니다. 이는 젊은 사람들에게 그들의 스마트폰과 태블릿을 이용한 창의적인 사용권을 주기 위한 것입니다. 참가자들은 16세 이하여야 합니다. 자격이 있고 참가를 희망하는 사람들은 다음 주제 즉, 건축, 자연 또는 상업 중 하나에 해당하는 사진을 제출해야 합니다. 각각의 주제에서 한 장씩 우승 사진을 뽑을 것이고 우승자는 500달러의 상금을 받게 될 것입니다. 기억하세요, 각 참가자는 대회에 참가하기 위해서 부모님의 동의를 받아야만 합니다. 온라인 등록은 저희 웹사이트 www.mdphoto.com에서 이번 목요일 정오부터 시작될 것입니다. 출품작은 2016년 10월 15일까지 제출되어야 합니다.

어휘

announce ***v.*** 알리다, 발표하다 **entry** ***n.*** 참가, 출품작 **contestant** ***n.*** 참가자 **eligible** ***a.*** 자격이 있는 **submit** ***v.*** 제출하다 **architecture** ***n.*** 건축(양식) **commerce** ***n.*** 무역, 상업 **winning** ***a.*** 이긴, 우승한 **consent** ***n.*** 동의, 허락 **registration** ***n.*** 등록

정답 ③

문제풀이

우승자는 각 주제별로 한 명씩 뽑는다고 했으므로 내용과 일치하지 않는 것은 ③ '우승자는 각 분야를 합쳐서 단 한 명이다.'이다.

총 어휘 수 115

12 도표

소재 공룡 장난감 고르기

듣기 대본 해석

남: 여보, 뭐 보고 있어?

여: Jake에게 줄 선물을 인터넷에서 찾아 보고 있었어. 좀 있으면 걔 생일인 거 알지?

남: 당연하지. 뭐 사줄 생각인데?

여: 글쎄, 요즘 공룡을 많이 좋아하고 있으니까 장난감 트리케라톱스 사주려고. 이거 봐봐. 엄청 귀여워.
남: 그것도 좋을 것 같기는 한데 나한테 자기가 제일 좋아하는 공룡이 티라노사우루스라고 했어.
여: 그렇구나. 일단 이 사이트의 제일 인기 있는 공룡 장난감 목록을 찾아봤어. 얼마 정도 쓰려고 생각하고 있어?
남: 200달러 넘는 건 좀 무리인 것 같아.
여: 알았어. 재질은? 나무로 사는 게 좋을 것 같아. 플라스틱은 내구성이 떨어져.
남: 나도 그렇게 생각해. 어떤 크기로 살까?
여: 음, 2피트는 너무 큰 것 같아. 당신도 그렇게 생각하지 않아?
남: 동감이야. 그럼 우리가 살 게 정해졌네. 어서 주문해.
여: 알겠어. 생일 전에 배송되면 좋겠다.

어휘
browse ***v.*** 둘러보다, 훑어보다 **be into** ~에 관심이 많다 **figure** ***v.*** 생각하다, 판단하다 **durable** ***a.*** 내구성이 있는, 오래가는 **place an order** 주문하다

정답 ⑤

문제풀이
공룡은 티라노사우루스를 선택했으므로 ①, ③, ⑤번 중에 고르면 되는데 200달러가 넘지 않는 것으로 하자고 했으므로 ①번은 제외된다. 크기가 2피트는 너무 크다고 했으므로 두 사람이 선택한 것은 ⑤번이 된다.

총 어휘 수 167

13 긴 대화의 응답

소재 다른 사람들과 함께 하는 X-Fit 운동 프로그램

듣기 대본 해석
남: Laura, 오랜만이네. 잘 지내?
여: 잘 지내지. 너 저번에 봤을 때랑 좀 변한 것 같아.
남: 응, 요즘 다이어트하고 운동하면서 살이 많이 빠졌어.
여: 좋네. 어떤 운동하는데?
남: 축구 조금 하긴 하는데, 일주일에 네 번 X-Fit 프로그램도 해.
여: X-Fit? 나는 집에서 Lunacy 프로그램을 했는데 별로 좋지는 않았어.
남: 집에서 보는 비디오 프로그램 같은 거지? 그런 거 한 번 해봤어. 3일 후에 그만뒀어.
여: 그럼 X-Fit은 뭐가 달라?
남: 음, X-Fit은 다른 사람들과 함께하는 운동 방법이야. 헬스장에서 만나서 일련의 운동을 해.
여: 그렇구나. 혼자 운동하는 건 별로 동기부여가 안 되는 것 같아.
남: 맞아. 여러 사람과 같이 하면 서로가 더 열심히 할 수 있도록 격려해 줄 수 있어. 정말 재미있어.
여: 다시 운동을 해야겠어. 근데 혼자 하는 건 싫어.
남: ① 우리 X-Fit 운동 클럽에 들어오는 건 어때?

어휘
quit ***v.*** 그만두다 **routine** ***n.*** 규칙적 순서, 방법 **motivate** ***v.*** 동기를 부여하다

정답 ①

문제풀이
여자는 다시 운동을 시작하려 하지만 혼자 하는 것은 싫다고 했으므로 이에 대한 남자의 가장 적절한 응답은 같이 하자는 ① '우리 X-Fit 운동 클럽에 들어오는 건 어때?'이다.

오답 보기 해석
② 내가 갈 만한 체육관 혹시 아니?
③ 너도 살 좀 빠진 것 같은데.
④ 네가 혼자 운동하는 게 훨씬 나을 것 같아.
⑤ 혼자 운동할 때 조심해야 해.

총 어휘 수 166

14 긴 대화의 응답

소재 마음에 들지 않는 전공

듣기 대본 해석
남: 나의 전공은 너무 지루해, Sabrina. 난 무엇을 해야 할지 모르겠어.
여: 정말? 나는 너의 전공이 대학교에서 다른 어떤 전공들보다 훨씬 더 재미있다고 생각해.
남: 나는 매일 똑같은 것을 해. 나는 별로 많이 배우지 않아. 컴퓨터 공학은 나한테 맞지 않는 것 같아.
여: 너의 지도 교수님과 그것에 관해 이야기해 보았니?
남: 아니. 예전에 그녀와 얘기했을 때 별로 도움이 되지 않았거든. 게다가 학기 초라서 그녀는 신입생들과 이야기하느라 너무 바빠.
여: 그게 사실일 수도 있지만, 네가 그녀와 이야기하지 않는다면 넌 남은 일생 동안 네가 좋아하지 않는 것을 꼼짝없이 하게 될 거야.
남: 나는 그녀의 시간을 허비하고 싶지는 않아. 다른 어떤 전공을 내가 좋아할지도 확실하지 않아.
여: 나는 그것이 너의 지도 교수님께서 네가 결정하는 것을 도와 줄 수 있는 점이라고 생각해. 난 내가 뭘 하고 싶은지 확실하지 않았는데 내 지도 교수님께서 그 모든 것을 바꿔주셨어.
남: 정말? 그녀가 널 위해 무엇을 했길래?
여: ② 그녀는 내가 다른 무언가를 시도해 보는 것을 제안하셨어.

어휘
major ***n.*** 전공 **academic advisor** 지도 교수 **semester** ***n.*** 학기 **be stuck** 꼼짝도 못 하다

정답 ②

문제풀이
여자는 남자에게 마음에 들지 않는 전공에 대해 지도 교수님과 상의하라고 조언하면서 자신의 경험을 말해주었다. 마지막에 남자가 교수님이 무엇을 해주셨는지 물었으므로 여자의 적절한 응답은 ② '그녀는 내가 다른 무언가를 시도해 보는 것을 제안하셨어.'이다.

오답 보기 해석
① 그녀는 네가 잘 결정하도록 도와주었음이 틀림없어.
③ 그녀는 모든 학생의 흥미를 고려해.
④ 그녀는 내가 새로운 전공을 찾는 것을 도와주기를 거절했어.
⑤ 그녀는 학생들이 전공을 선택하는 것을 도와주곤 했어.

총 어휘 수 169

15 상황에 적절한 말

소재 친구가 장기자랑에 참여하도록 설득하기

듣기 대본 해석
남: Joseph은 학년 말에 열리는 교내 장기자랑을 기획하고 있습니다. 마술, 춤, 저글링 공연이 있긴 하지만 그는 공연에서 연주를 할 음악가를 정말 찾고 싶어 합니다. 그는 Katie가 작년에 주(state) 합창 대회에서 결승 진출자였던 것을 기억하고 있습니다. Joseph은 Katie에게 전화해서 그녀에게 참여해 줄 것을 부탁합니다. 그녀는 시험 공부를 하느라 너무 바빠 연습할 수 없기 때문에 그의 요청을 거절합니다. 하지만 Joseph은 끈질기게 Katie를 장기자랑에 합류시키려고 계속 설득합니다. 그는 그녀만이 공연의 균형을 맞춰 줄 수 있는 유일한 사람이라고 말합니다. 이제 Katie는 참여하는 것을 고려 중이지만 결정을 내리지 못하고 있습니다. 이러한 상황에서, Katie가 Joseph에게 할 말로 가장 적절한 것은 무엇일까요?
Katie: ⑤ 그것에 대해 생각할 시간을 좀 줄래?

어휘
finalist ***n.*** 결승 진출자 **choir** ***n.*** 합창단, 성가대 **participate** ***v.*** 참가하다 **persistent** ***a.*** 집요한, 끈질긴 **persuade** ***v.*** 설득하다 **talent show** 장기자랑 〈문제〉 **all-state** ***a.*** 주 대표의

정답 ⑤

문제풀이
Joseph은 Katie가 교내 장기자랑에서 음악 공연을 해 줄 유일한 사람이라고 생각하고 계속해서 설득을 하고 있으며, 이에 대해 Katie는 쉽게 결정을 하지 못하고 있으므로 이러한 상황에 그녀가 할 말로 가장 적절한 것은 ⑤ '그것에 대해 생각할 시간을 좀 줄래?'이다.

오답 보기 해석
① 네가 도와줄 수 있는 다른 사람이 있지 않니?
② 난 주 대표 합창대회에 참여할 수 없었어.
③ 장기자랑에 참여하게 돼서 너무 신난다.
④ 음악 공연을 포함시키려는 생각은 잊어버려.

총 어휘 수 138

16 담화 목적 / 17 세부 내용 파악

소재 부부간의 대화 시간

듣기 대본 해석
여: 안녕하세요, Sunday Evening Classics의 사회자 Lauren Bell입니다. 오늘 밤 시작하기 전에, 결혼한 부부와 의사소통에 관해 잠깐 말씀 드리고 싶어요. 남편과 아내 간의 대화의 양을 계산하기 위한 실험이 최근에 행해졌는데 여러분은 결과에 놀라실 거예요. 보통 사람들은 부부가 서로 꽤 자주 이야기를 나눈다고 생각할 거예요. 그런데 한 심리학자가 밝힌 것은 일반적인 부부가 사람들이 상상하는 것보다 훨씬 적게 이야기를 나눈다는 것을 보여 줍니다. 제가 지금 여러분께 알려드리고자 하는 숫자는 하루가 아니라 일주일 동안 대화를 나눈 시간입니다. 16분입니다! 충격적이지 않나요? 여러분 자신을 보통의 부부라고 생각한다면, 대화양이 총 30분이 될 수 있게 일주일에 14분 더 배우자와 이야기하도록 해 보세요. 그러고 나서 매일 30분 대화하도록 노력해보세요. 그것이 여러분의 관계에 도움이 될까요? 저희는 그렇게 생각해요. 생각과 감정을 공유하거나 심지어 사소한 대화도 부부에게 매우 중요합니다. 저 밖에 모든 부부들을 위해 Scotty McGee의 The Modern Love Song을 들려 드리겠습니다. 감상하세요!

어휘
host ***n.*** (TV · 라디오 프로의) 진행자 **conduct** ***v.*** 수행하다 **calculate** ***v.*** 계산하다 **assume** ***v.*** 추정하다 **psychologist** ***n.*** 심리학자 **spouse** ***n.*** 배우자 **trivial** ***a.*** 사소한 **in the interest of** ~을 위하여 〈문제〉 **promote** ***v.*** 촉진하다, 고취하다 **marital** ***a.*** 결혼의

정답 16 ③ 17 ③

문제풀이
16 음악 프로의 사회자가 부부간의 대화 시간에 관한 실험 결과를 공개하면서 부부간의 대화 시간을 늘릴 것을 장려하고 있으므로 정답은 ③ '남편과 아내 간의 대화를 장려하려고'이다.

17 여자의 말 중간 부분에서 일반적인 부부가 일주일 동안 서로 이야기를 나누는 시간은 16분이라고 했으므로 정답은 ③ '16분'이다.

오답 보기 해석
16
① 음악을 통해 부부 관계를 개선하려고
② 음악 프로그램에 부부들을 초대하려고
④ 건강한 부부 관계의 중요성을 가르쳐주려고
⑤ 결혼한 커플 간의 대화 주제를 소개하려고

총 어휘 수 194

DICTATION ANSWERS

01 have a meeting scheduled for three o'clock

02 Your eyesight used to be good

03 allows consumers to shop from their smartphones / a few negative aspects / goods being damaged / file a complaint / save time and money

04 Where are you headed / in really bad shape / throw them away / take care of all of that

05 get right into it / pollution issues in the news / gaining the most momentum / renewable energy sources

06 promotional flyer / pizzas look delicious / making balloon animals for children

07 as you might have noticed / moving on to the next round / we're supposed to base it on / have a copy of it

08 as a day camp supervisor / for the past five years / can vary from day to day depending on / lower than most other jobs / enjoy nature

09 You're all ready to go / take pride in my work / Will that be all / a first-time customer

10 a place I used to go to / What makes it so nice / rent a beachfront condo / even have ghost tours

11 Those who are eligible / submit pictures / a winning photo from each category / consent from their parents

12 he's really into / we can afford anything over / less durable / I hope it gets delivered

13 since I last saw you / lost a lot of / four times a week / you can push one another

14 My major is so terribly boring / talked to your academic advisor / beginning of the semester / for the rest of your life / what I wanted to do

15 organizing the school talent show / asks her to participate / persuade Katie to join the talent show / is now considering joining

16-17 amount of communication / anyone would have imagined / talking to your spouse / Sharing thoughts and feelings

32 수능영어듣기 실전모의고사

본문 p.194

01 ②	02 ①	03 ③	04 ⑤	05 ②	06 ③
07 ②	08 ④	09 ②	10 ③	11 ①	12 ②
13 ③	14 ④	15 ③	16 ③	17 ⑤	

01 짧은 대화의 응답

소재 Elvis 전시회 장소

듣기 대본 해석

남: 너 Elvis의 팬 아니니? 도시로 오는 새로운 Elvis 전시회가 있다는 것 봤어?
여: 응! 오늘 아침에 막 읽었어. 나 정말 기대돼.
남: 응, 나도 그래. 정확히 어디서 열리는데?
여: ② 그건 주립 극장에서 열릴 거야.

어휘

exhibition ***n.*** 전시회 **exactly** ***ad.*** 정확하게 〈문제〉 **inspiring** ***a.*** 고무적인, 감격적인 **take a picture** 사진을 찍다

정답 ②

문제풀이

남자가 전시회가 정확히 어디서 열리냐고 물었으므로 장소에 대한 대답이 나와야 한다. 따라서 정답은 ② '그건 주립 극장에서 열릴 거야.'이다.

오답 보기 해석

① 그의 음악은 전부 너무 감동적이야.
③ 충고해줘서 고마워.
④ 오, 그럼 난 못 갈 것 같아.
⑤ 사진 많이 찍는 것 잊지 마.

총 어휘 수 50

02 짧은 대화의 응답

소재 목적지까지 걸리는 시간과 비용

듣기 대본 해석

여: 안녕하세요. 제가 도심에 있는 미술관에 가야 하거든요. 시간이 얼마나 걸릴까요?
남: 음, 이 시간이면 차가 그렇게 막히지 않아요. 30분 정도 걸릴 거예요.
여: 나쁘지 않네요. 택시타면 얼마 나오는지 알아요?
남: ① 20달러보다 적게 나올 거예요.

어휘

downtown ***a.*** 중심가에, 도심지에 **traffic** ***n.*** 교통(량) **congested** ***a.*** 붐비는, 혼잡한 〈문제〉 **admission** ***n.*** 입장

정답 ①

문제풀이

여자가 택시비가 얼마나 나올지 아는지 물었으므로 가장 적절한 남자의 응답은 ① '20달러보다 적게 나올 거예요.'이다.

오답 보기 해석

② 입장료는 10달러예요.
③ 당신은 나에게 빨리 돈을 갚아야 해요.
④ 미술관이 저녁 9시에 닫는 것 같아요.
⑤ 저는 차가 막혀서 늦을지도 몰라요.

총 어휘 수 53

03 담화 주제

소재 기분과 창의성 간의 상관관계

듣기 대본 해석

남: 안녕하세요 여러분, 좋은 아침입니다. 저는 오늘 Minnesota 대학에서 얼마 전에 나온 흥미로운 연구에 대해 여러분께 말씀드리고 싶습니다. 연구는 행복과 창의성 간의 상관관계에 대한 것입니다. 연구자들은 사람들을 세 그룹으로 나누고 다른 상황에 두었습니다. 첫 번째 그룹은 놀이공원으로 보냈습니다. 두 번째 그룹은 공포 영화를 보러 극장에 보냈고, 세 번째 그룹은 도자기 박물관으로 보냈습니다. 각 그룹이 돌아온 후에 연구자들은 창의성 테스트를 했습니다. 놀이공원에 갔던 그룹이 다른 그룹보다 훨씬 더 좋은 결과를 낸 것으로 드러났습니다. 이 결과는 연구자들로 하여금 우리가 행복할 때 우리의 뇌가 이전에 얻은 지식에 더 잘 접근할 수 있고 이 지식을 (새로운 생각으로) 만들어내는 데 활용할 수 있다고 믿게 합니다. 그래서 행복한 사람들은 쉽게 다른 생각들을 합치고 그것으로부터 새로운 것을 만들어 내는 그들의 능력 때문에 더 창의적이게 됩니다.

어휘

correlation ***n.*** 상관관계 **horror** ***n.*** 공포물 **pottery** ***n.*** 도자기 **conduct** ***v.*** 수행하다 **access** ***v.*** 접근하다 **previously** ***ad.*** 이전에, 미리 **various** ***a.*** 여러 가지의

정답 ③

문제풀이

남자는 행복한 경험을 한 사람들이 창의력 검사에서 더 좋은 결과를 냈다고 말하고 있다. 따라서 남자가 하는 말의 주제는 ③ '기분과 창의성의 상관관계'이다.

총 어휘 수 166

04 의견

소재 너무 많은 장난감의 부정적 효과

듣기 대본 해석

여: Tommy의 놀이방을 봐요. 그의 부모가 정말 장난감을 많이 사줬나 봐요.
남: 네. 그리고 그의 침실도 봐야 해요. 거긴 장난감이 천장까지 쌓여있어요.
여: 전 더 적은 장난감이 아이들에게 다른 능력을 발달시켜준다는 것에 관한 기사를 읽었어요.
남: 정말이요? 저는 그런 건 들어본 적이 없어요. 더 많은 장난감이 더 좋다고 알고 있었어요.
여: 음, 약간의 장난감은 아이들이 자라고 배우는 데 좋지만 너무 많은 장난감은 실제로 해로울 수 있어요.
남: 흠... 왜 그런지 궁금해요.
여: 기사에선 너무 많은 장난감은 아이들의 상상력을 방해할 수 있다고 했어요.
남: 오? 어떻게요?
여: 더 적은 장난감을 가진 아이들은 더 많은 장난감을 가진 아이들보다 그들의 상상력을 더 많이 사용해야만 해요. 그들은 놀 때 창의력을 더 써야만 하죠.
남: 일리가 있네요. 저는 자랄 때 장난감이 별로 없었어요. 대신 저는 저만의 장난감을 만들거나 게임을 발명해야만 했죠.

어휘

stack ***v.*** 쌓다, 포개다 **ceiling** ***n.*** 천장 **article** ***n.*** 기사 **figure** ***v.*** (~일 거라고) 생각하다 **harmful** ***a.*** 해로운 **hinder** ***v.*** 방해(저해)하다 **imagination** ***n.*** 상상력 **make sense** 이해가 되다, 말이 되다

정답 ⑤

문제풀이

여자는 너무 많은 장난감은 아이들에게 해로울 수 있으며, 더 적은 장난감을 가진 아이들이 상상력을 더 많이 사용한다고 말하고 있다. 따라서 여자의 의견으로 가장 적절한 것은 ⑤ '너무 많은 장난감은 아이들의 상상력에 방해가 된다.'이다.

총 어휘 수 145

05 대화자의 관계 파악

소재 축구감독과의 인터뷰

듣기 대본 해석

여: 토요일에 Liverpool이랑 Manchester City 경기 보셨나요?
남: 네, 봤었어요.
여: Liverpool은 어땠나요?
남: 정말 잘 했어요. 골 찬스가 여러 번 있었는데 결국 이기지는 못했어요.
여: 네, 막상막하였어요. 골 하나 차이로 졌잖아요.
남: Manchester City가 그들을 잘 막았어요. 골키퍼가 아주 훌륭했어요.
여: 맞아요. 그래서 다음 주에 Liverpool이랑 경기할 때 어떤 전략을 쓸 건가요?
남: 그 슛들을 막으려면 수비를 강화해야 할 겁니다. 우리는 또한 공격을 재정비하고 있는데 그만큼 결과가 좋기를 바라야지요.
여: 경기가 기대됩니다. 이 인터뷰를 시청하고 있는 축구 팬들께 할 말 있나요?
남: 열렬한 성원과 우리가 리그에서 성장하는 것을 지켜봐 주셔서 감사합니다. 다음 경기 꼭 이기도록 하겠습니다.
여: Charlie, 인터뷰를 위해 시간을 내주셔서 감사합니다. BCC 뉴스의 Susan Peters였습니다.

어휘

shot ***n.*** (슛을 하기 위한) 시도 **pull off** (힘든 것을) 해내다 **goalie** ***n.*** 골키퍼 **amazing** ***a.*** 놀라운 **strengthen** ***v.*** 강화하다 **defense** ***n.*** 수비 **rework** ***v.*** 고치다 **offensive** ***n.*** 공격 ***a.*** 공격의 **appreciate** ***v.*** 고마워하다

정답 ②

문제풀이

여자는 전략이나 팬들에게 하고 싶은 말 등을 묻고 있으므로 기자이고 남자는 다음 경기의 전략을 말하며 자신들의 경기를 지켜봐 달라고 했으므로 축구감독임을 유추할 수 있다. 따라서 정답은 ② '기자 ㅡ 축구감독'이다.

총 어휘 수 180

06 그림의 세부 내용 파악

소재 중고차 팔기

듣기 대본 해석

[휴대폰이 울린다.]
남: 안녕, Megan.
여: Sam? 네가 나 좀 도와줄 수 있는지 알고 싶어.
남: 물론이지. 뭔데?
여: 음, 내 차를 팔려고 하는데 Twitter와 같은 소셜 미디어를 활용하는 것이 말을 퍼트리는 데 도움이 될 것 같아.
남: 그래, 좋은 생각이야. 난 Twitter에 팔로워가 많아. 내가 네 차에 대한 간략한 설명을 올려주길 바라니?
여: 그럼 너무 좋지. 차는 Wasp 2015 스페셜 에디션이고, 약 20,000 마일 정도 탔어.
남: 선루프는 있어?
여: 응, 스페셜 에디션은 선루프가 있는 게 기본으로 나오거든.
남: 그렇구나. 그리고 스페셜 에디션에 추가된 다른 특징들은 없는 거야?
여: 응, 옆면을 따라서 가는 세로줄 무늬가 있어.
남: 그게 다야?
여: 별 모양 휠도 있어.
남: 알았어. 차에 어떤 흠집은 없어?
여: 앞 범퍼에 작은 스크래치(긁힌 자국)가 있지만 난 그 점을 원하는 가격 결정하는 데 고려했어. 그거 말고는 내가 차를 잘 관리해 왔고, 모든 서비스 기록을 보관하고 있어.
남: 그래, 알았어. 내가 바로 Twitter에 설명을 올릴게.
여: 고마워, Sam.

어휘

description ***n.*** 서술, 묘사 **feature** ***n.*** 특징 **pinstripe** ***n.*** 가는 세로줄 무늬 **damage** ***n.*** 손상, 훼손 **factor something into** ~을 고려 요인으로 포함하다 **other than** ~외에

정답 ③

문제풀이

여자는 자신의 차를 팔려고 하는데 트위터의 팔로어가 많은 남자에게 내용을 올려달라고 부탁하면서 차의 세부사항을 알려주고 있다. 여자의 차는 스페셜 에디션으로 차의 옆면에 세로줄 무늬가 있다고 했으나, 그림에서는 차의 후드(보닛) 부분에만 줄무늬가 있으므로 정답은 ③번이다.

총 어휘 수 186

07 부탁한 일

소재 졸업 연설자 선정

듣기 대본 해석

남: 안녕하세요, Amanda.
여: 안녕하세요, John. 들어오세요.
남: 올해 졸업 연설자를 선정하는 데 도움이 필요하신지 궁금해서요.
여: 네, 도움 주시면 고맙죠. 제가 후보를 15명으로 추렸어요.
남: 좋아요. 그럼 제가 이 학생들과 무엇을 해야 하나요?
여: 저는 당신이 학생들을 개별로 만나서 대화를 하셨으면 해요. 학생 각자가 무엇을 강하게 느끼는지와 기회가 있다면 급우들과 어떤 메시지를 공유하고 싶은지 알아내 주셨으면 좋겠어요.
남: 제가 학생들과 만난 후엔 무엇을 해야 하나요?
여: 저와 다시 만나 각 학생들이 했던 이야기를 당신이 받은 전반적인 인상과 함께 자세히 알려주세요.
남: 알겠습니다. 그렇게 할게요. 그런데 학생 각자 일정이 달라서 모두와 만나기 어려울 수 있어요.
여: 당신이 일을 처리할 수 있을 거라 생각해요, John.
남: 저를 믿어주셔서 감사합니다. 좋아요, 해볼게요.
여: 고마워요, John. 이야기를 할 수 있게 끝나면 알려주세요.

어휘

graduation speech 졸업 연설 **candidate** ***n.*** 후보자 **handle** ***v.*** 다루다, 처리하다 **appreciate** ***v.*** 고마워하다

정답 ②

문제풀이

여자가 남자에게 자신이 추린 졸업 연설 후보자들과 만나 대화를 나누고 그 세부 내용을 알려줄 것을 부탁하고 있으므로 정답은 ② '졸업 연설 후보자들과 대화하기'이다.

총 어휘 수 185

08 이유

소재 놀이공원에 못 가는 이유

듣기 대본 해석

여: Joe, 어디로 가는 거예요?
남: 딸과 함께 박물관 가는 중이에요. 여름방학 동안에 고대 이집트에 관해 해야 할 숙제가 있거든요.
여: 방학 동안에 숙제라고요? 힘들겠네요. 자, 그녀는 이번 여름 방학 때 또 뭘 해요?
남: 음, Lake Totanka에서 하는 여름캠프에 그녀를 등록시켰어요. 왜요?
여: 제 상사가 Holidayland 놀이공원 티켓 8장을 주셨거든요. 저도 가족이랑 갈 건데 당신도 우리와 함께 가고 싶으신지 궁금해서요.
남: 그거 멋지겠는걸요. 언제 갈 건데요?
여: 다음 주 일요일 20일에요.

남: 다음 주 일요일이요? 음, 가고는 싶은데 갈 수 없어요. 다음 주에 부모님 댁에 가거든요.
여: 안됐군요.
남: 네. 일정을 변경할 수는 없어서요. 왜냐하면 가족 모임이 있거든요. 꽤 성대한 파티가 될 거예요.
여: 알았어요. 그럼 다음 기회에 가요.
남: 물론이죠. 초대해 줘서 고마워요.

어휘
assignment ***n.*** 과제 **rough** ***a.*** 힘든, 골치 아픈 **sign up for** ~에 신청하다, 등록하다 **reschedule** ***v.*** 일정을 변경하다 **reunion** ***n.*** 모임, 동창회

정답 ④

문제풀이
남자는 놀이공원에 가고 싶지만 그날 가족 모임이 있어서 부모님 댁에 가야 한다고 했으므로 정답은 ④ '가족 모임이 있어서'이다.

총 어휘 수 147

09 숫자

소재 모니터 구입

듣기 대본 해석
남: 무엇을 도와드릴까요?
여: 저는 어떤 모니터를 사야 할지 결정하려고 해요.
남: 전문가용 모니터를 원하세요, 일반용 모니터를 원하세요?
여: 음, 다른 점이 뭐죠?
남: 네, 전문가용은 비디오 편집과 그래픽 디자인과 같은 기능을 위해서 최고 해상도의 화면을 사용합니다.
여: 그렇군요. 일반용 모니터는 어때요? 그나저나, 일반용 목적은 뭔가요?
남: 일반용은 이메일 사용, 워드 프로세싱, 컴퓨터로 가끔 영화 보기가 가능해요.
여: 좋아요. 저는 그래픽 디자인이나 비디오 제작에는 관심이 없지만 화질은 좋았으면 해요.
남: 물론이죠. 모든 모니터가 정말 화질이 좋지만 일반용 모니터로 하시면 돈이 절약될 겁니다.
여: 좋아요. 얼마죠?
남: 원래 가격은 500달러이지만 현재 할인하고 있어서 10퍼센트 할인을 받으실 거예요.
여: 와, 가격 괜찮네요. 제가 웹사이트에서 가져온 쿠폰과 함께 쓸 수 있어요?
남: 물론이죠. 그래서 쿠폰이 있는걸요.
여: 좋아요. 그럼 제가 세일 가격에서 추가로 10퍼센트를 받는 거죠?
남: 맞아요. 모니터를 가지고 다시 올게요.

어휘
purpose ***n.*** 목적, 용도 **definition** ***n.*** 해상도, 선명도 **occasional** ***a.*** 가끔의 **on sale** 할인 판매 중인 **combine** ***v.*** 결합하다 **absolutely** ***ad.*** 틀림없이, 물론이죠, 그럼요 **additional** ***a.*** 추가의

정답 ②

문제풀이
모니터의 원래 가격은 500달러인데 남자가 현재 10퍼센트 할인을 받을 수 있다고 했으므로 450달러이고, 여자가 웹사이트에서 가져온 쿠폰으로 세일 가격에서 추가 10퍼센트 할인을 받을 수 있다고 했으므로 405달러에 구입할 수 있게 된다. 따라서 답은 ② '$405'이다.

총 어휘 수 176

10 언급 유무

소재 헌혈 자격 조건

듣기 대본 해석
남: 안녕하세요. 헌혈을 하기로 결정했어요. 처음이라 좀 긴장되네요.
여: 괜찮아요. 안 아프게 할게요. 그런데 몇 가지 질문을 좀 할게요. 먼저, 몇 살이세요?
남: 저 17살이에요. 문제가 되나요?
여: 음, 나이 제한이 있기는 한데 16세부터 69세까지여서 괜찮아요.
남: 그렇군요. 다른 필요조건은요?
여: 남성은 몸무게가 50킬로그램 이상이어야 하고 여성은 45킬로그램을 넘어야 해요. 당신은 괜찮을 것 같네요.
남: 당연하죠. 다른 거는요?
여: 맥박이 항상 안정적으로 분당 50비트에서 100비트 사이여야 해요. 또한, 최근에 아팠던 적 있으세요?
남: 아니요. 아프면 헌혈 못하나요?
여: 네. 체온이 섭씨 37.5도가 넘으면 헌혈을 못해요.
남: 그렇군요. 헌혈을 하려면 좋은 건강 상태여야 하는 것이 정말 중요한 것 같네요.

어휘
donate ***v.*** 기부하다, 헌혈하다 **nervous** ***a.*** 불안해 하는 **make it easy** 편하게 해 주다 **requirement** ***n.*** 필요, 필요조건 **pulse** ***n.*** 맥박, 맥

정답 ③

문제풀이
두 사람은 헌혈의 나이제한(16~69세), 체중(남성 50킬로그램 이상, 여성 45킬로그램 이상), 맥박(50~100비트), 체온(37.5도 이하)은 언급하였지만 혈액형에 관해서는 언급하지 않았으므로 정답은 ③ '혈액형'이다.

총 어휘 수 168

11 내용 일치 · 불일치

소재 행진 악단 오디션

듣기 대본 해석
남: 안녕하세요 학생 여러분. Franklin 대학교 행진 악단 오디션이 곧 다가오고 있습니다. 실제 오디션은 9월 25일에서 30일까지로 신청은 9월 10일에서 15일까지 받고 있습니다. 오디션에 참가하고 싶은 음악가는 누구나 자신이 작곡한 곡이나 다른 사람이 작곡한 곡을 연주하여 오디션을 볼 수 있습니다. 각 참가자 당 최소 10분 간 연주를 해 주시기 바랍니다. 신청을 할 때 자신의 경험에 대한 짧은 자기소개서와 연주할 곡 악보도 첨부해 주시기 바랍니다. 우리 전문가 심사위원들이 누가 합류할 자격이 있는지 판단할 것입니다. 악단 정원은 100명입니다. 수상까지 한 저희 행진 악단에 관심 있는 분들은 신청을 하고 오디션을 보시기 바랍니다. 감사합니다.

어휘
marching band 행진 악단 **tryout** ***n.*** 오디션 **take place** 개최되다, 일어나다 **biography** ***n.*** 전기, 자기소개서 **permit** ***v.*** 허락하다 **award-winning** ***a.*** 상을 받은

정답 ①

문제풀이
담화의 처음 부분에서 오디션의 접수 날짜는 9월 10일에서 15일까지이고 오디션 날짜가 9월 25일에서 30일까지라고 했으므로 내용과 일치하지 않는 것은 ① '접수 날짜는 9월 25일에서 30일까지이다.'이다.

총 어휘 수 138

12 도표

소재 파티룸 예약

듣기 대본 해석
여: 안녕하세요, 선생님. 무엇을 도와드릴까요?

남: 안녕하세요. 아들의 야구팀을 위한 파티를 계획하려고 합니다. 토요일 오후에 빈자리가 있을까요?
여: 물론이죠. 오후 2시에 이용 가능한 장소가 있을 것 같아요. 여러 다른 패키지를 제안합니다. 안내책자를 봐 주세요.
남: 음, 팀은 어린이 15명입니다. 모든 패키지에 피자가 제공됩니까?
여: 그렇습니다. 얼마나 오랫동안 파티룸을 예약하고 싶으신지요? 세 가지 선택권이 있어요.
남: 이것이 그들이 서로 볼 수 있는 마지막 시간이라 좀 더 긴 파티가 좋을 거라고 생각해요.
여: 그러면 90분이나 100분으로 방을 예약하셔야 하겠네요.
남: 좋을 것 같아요. 그런데 저는 200달러 이상은 쓰고 싶지 않아요.
여: 그러면, 손님의 요구에 맞는 두 가지 다른 패키지가 있습니다. 하나는 큰 피자 두 개와 음료가 포함되어 있습니다. 다른 하나는 큰 피자 한 개와 음료가 따라옵니다.
남: 두 개의 피자가 있는 것이 적당할 것 같아요.
여: 좋아요. 토요일 2시에 파티룸을 예약하겠습니다.

어휘
opening ***n.*** 빈자리, 결원 **available** ***a.*** 이용할 수 있는 **reserve** ***v.*** 예약하다 **put down for** ~의 예약자로서 이름을 적어 두다

정답 ②

문제풀이
남자는 참석할 어린이가 15명이라고 했으므로 ⑤번이 제외되고, 시간은 90분이나 100분이라 했으므로 ④번도 제외된다. 가격은 200달러를 넘지 않기를 바란다고 했으므로 ①번이 제외되고, 피자가 2개 나오는 패키지를 선택했으므로 정답은 ②번이다.

총 어휘 수 181

13 긴 대화의 응답

소재 9시 이후 소등에 관한 문제

듣기 대본 해석
[전화벨이 울린다.]
남: 안녕하세요. 세인트폴 고등학교입니다. 저는 교감 Jones입니다.
여: 안녕하세요. Jones 선생님. Raymond 엄마 되는 Grace Conroy입니다. 캠퍼스 내의 문제로 말씀드릴 게 있습니다.
남: 네. 뭐가 문제인가요?
여: 그게, 제가 어젯밤에 제 아들을 데리러 도서관에 갔는데 주차장·주변이 굉장히 어두운 걸 봤습니다.
남: 죄송하지만 9시 이후에 캠퍼스 내의 모든 불들을 끕니다. 전기를 절약하는 데에 도움이 돼요.
여: 이해해요. 전기 절약도 중요하죠. 그런데 안전상의 문제가 있지 않나요? 누가 넘어져서 다칠 수도 있습니다.
남: 그렇게 큰 문제일 줄은 몰랐네요.
여: 그리고 불을 켜는 게 나쁜 사람들이 오지 못하게 할 수도 있습니다.
남: ③ 불을 계속 켜놓는 것에 대해 제가 무엇을 할 수 있을지 볼게요.

어휘
vice principal 교감 선생님 **electricity** ***n.*** 전기 **conserve** ***v.*** 절약하다 **concern** ***n.*** 걱정, 관심, 문제 **undesirable** ***a.*** 원하지 않는, 달갑지 않은

정답 ③

문제풀이
여자가 남자에게 9시 이후로 캠퍼스에 불을 끄는 것에 대한 문제점을 이야기하며 남자를 계속 설득하고 있으므로 적절한 응답은 ③ '불을 계속 켜놓는 것에 대해 제가 무엇을 할 수 있을지 볼게요.'이다.

오답 보기 해석
① 어머님께서 아들을 더 빨리 데리러 오셨어야 해요.
② 학생들이 공부하기에 너무 어두울 거에요.
④ 걱정 마세요. 내일 등이 수리되도록 할게요.
⑤ Raymond가 더 주의를 기울여야 다치지 않아요.

총 어휘 수 132

14 긴 대화의 응답

소재 낡은 물건 리폼

듣기 대본 해석
남: 안녕 Amelia. 널 위해 내가 뭘 만들었어.
여: 핸드백? 나 새 것 정말 갖고 싶었는데. 네가 정말 직접 만든 거 아니지, 그렇지?
남: 글쎄, 내가 대부분의 작업을 했지만 우리 미술 선생님이 조금 도와 주셨어. 오래된 스웨터로 만든 거야.
여: 재미있네. 네가 스스로 생각해 낸 아이디어야?
남: 실은 학교에 있는 Greenback Club에 가입했어. 오래된 것들을 다른 목적에 맞게 만드는 걸 배워.
여: 정말 멋진데. "다른 목적에 맞게 만든다"는 게 무슨 뜻이니?
남: 우리는 낡고, 사용 안 하는 것들을 가지고 네 핸드백처럼 새로운 물건을 만들어.
여: 흥미로운 클럽이다. 이 핸드백 만들기 어려워 보이는데.
남: 별로. 사실 우리 프로젝트 대부분이 정말 쉬워. 다음 모임에서 우리는 낡은 병을 가지고 음료수 잔을 만드는 걸 배울 거야.
여: 재미있겠다. 어떻게 그것들을 만들지?
남: 선생님이 다음 모임에서 우리에게 보여주실 거야. 너도 같이 가자.
여: ④ 나도 그러고 싶지만 난 손으로 만드는 것에 서툴러.

어휘
come up with 생각해내다, 떠올리다 **repurpose** ***v.*** 다른 목적에 맞게 만들다 **instructor** ***n.*** 강사, 교사 〈문제〉 **woodworking** ***n.*** 목세공

정답 ④

문제풀이
남자는 여자에게 낡은 물건들을 리폼하는 클럽 활동의 흥미로운 프로젝트들을 이야기하면서 다음에 같이 가자고 제안한다. 이에 대한 여자의 응답으로 가장 적절한 것은 ④ '나도 그러고 싶지만 난 손으로 만드는 것에 서툴러.'이다.

오답 보기 해석
① 이 핸드백 얼마야?
② 낡은 물건들을 낭비해서는 안돼.
③ 난 핸드백 어떻게 만드는지 몰라.
⑤ 우리 미술 선생님은 취미로 목공예를 즐기셔.

총 어휘 수 166

15 상황에 적절한 말

소재 할아버지한테 선물 받은 셔츠를 동생에게 주기

듣기 대본 해석
남: Stella의 택배가 방금 도착했습니다. Stella가 자주 뵙지 못하는 할아버지로부터 온 것입니다. 포장을 열고 감동적인 편지를 읽고 나서 Stella는 할아버지께서 Taylor Swift 티셔츠를 보내주신 것을 보고 좋아합니다. 그러나 입어보니까 Stella는 셔츠가 좀 작다는 것을 알게 됩니다. 할아버지께 다시 보내 할아버지께 말씀드려서 더 큰 사이즈로 교환하는 것을 고려해 봅니다. 그러나 심사숙고 후 그녀는 할아버지께서 셔츠를 교환하고 다시 보내시는 게 쉬운 일이 아니라는 것을 깨닫습니다. 대신에 그녀는 여동생

Clara에게 셔츠를 줍니다. Clara도 Taylor Swift를 굉장히 좋아하고 선물에 대해 고마워하지만 Stella는 할아버지께서 자신이 여동생에게 그것을 준 것을 아시는 걸 원치 않습니다. 이러한 상황에서 Stella가 Clara에게 뭐라고 말할까요?

Stella: ③ 할아버지께 내가 너에게 이 셔츠 줬다고 말하지 마.

어휘

touching ***a.*** 감동적인 **deliberation** ***n.*** 숙고, 신중함 **grateful** ***a.*** 고마워하는, 감사하는

정답 ③

문제풀이

할아버지께서 Stella에게 보내주신 티셔츠가 작아서 동생에게 주기로 했다. 그러나 할아버지께는 이 사실을 알리고 싶지 않으므로 Stella가 동생에게 할 말로 적절한 것은 ③ '할아버지께 내가 너에게 이 셔츠 줬다고 말하지 마.'이다.

오답 보기 해석

① 할아버지께 그의 선물이 마음에 안 든다고 말씀 드리지 마.
② 우리 조만간 할아버지 뵈러 가는 게 좋을 것 같아.
④ 이 셔츠 너무 작아. 할아버지께 다시 보내드려 줘.
⑤ 이 셔츠를 교환하러 할아버지를 가게에 모시고 가 줄래?

총 어휘 수 161

16 담화 목적 / 17 세부 내용 파악

소재 일상생활에서 돈을 절약하는 방법

듣기 대본 해석

여: 여러분 안녕하세요. 저는 Baker Financial에서 일하는 Mary Anne Baker입니다. 오늘 저는 여러분들에게 일상생활에서 돈을 절약할 수 있는 방법들에 관해 이야기하고 싶습니다. 우선 교통수단이 비쌀 수 있습니다. 만약 여러분들이 매일 택시를 타고 직장에 가는 습관이 있다면, 대신 버스나 지하철을 탐으로써 많은 돈을 절약할 수 있습니다. 좀 더 일찍 일어나도록 수면 패턴을 바꿔 보세요. 둘째, 상점의 평면도(배치)는 여러분들이 사려는 것을 극대화하기 위해 만들어졌습니다. 여러분들은 왜 달걀과 우유 같은 가장 필요한 일상 용품들이 가게의 뒤편에 배치되어 있는지 궁금해 한 적 있나요? 그것은 가게를 걸으면서 세일 중인 모든 다른 상품을 보게 하기 위해서 입니다. 이러한 전략들을 의식하고 충동 구매를 억제하세요. 셋째, 온라인 쇼핑을 이용하세요. 온라인 상에서 쇼핑을 하는 것이 여러분에게 가격을 매우 쉽게 비교할 수 있게 하고 최고의 거래를 찾을 수 있게 하므로 돈을 절약하게 해줍니다. 마지막으로 생수를 사지 않도록 노력하세요. 매일 1달러나 2달러를 쓰는 대신에 물 여과기에 투자를 하고 집을 떠나기 전에 병을 채우세요. 여러분들이 이러한 간단한 조언들을 따른다면, 저는 여러분들이 돈을 절약하고 좀 더 성취감을 주는 삶을 영위하리라고 확신합니다. 들어 주셔서 감사합니다.

어휘

transportation ***n.*** 수송 수단, 교통 기관 **in the habit of** ~하는 버릇이 있는 **floor plan** 평면도 **resist** ***v.*** 저항하다, 반대하다 **impulse purchase** 충동 구매 **take advantage of** ~을 이용하다 **fulfilling** ***a.*** 성취감을 주는

정답 16 ③ 17 ⑤

문제풀이

16 여자는 일상생활에서 어떻게 하면 돈을 절약할 수 있는지를 말해주고 있으므로 여자가 하는 말의 목적은 ③ '돈을 절약하는 방법을 알려주려고'이다.

17 여자는 대중교통 이용, 상점 평면도 의식, 온라인 쇼핑 이용, 물 여과기 사용에 대해서는 언급했지만 ⑤ '가계부 작성'에 대해서는 언급하지 않았다.

총 어휘 수 219

DICTATION ANSWERS

01 Where is it going to be held

02 at this time of day

03 focused on the correlation between / conducted a creativity test / easily combine various ideas

04 They're stacked to the ceiling / the more toys, the better / hinder a child's imagination / I guess that makes sense

05 great shots on goal / couldn't pull off the win / They only lost by one goal / strengthen our defense

06 put up a short description / a small scratch on the front bumper / I have factored that into

07 who would give the graduation speeches / what they feel strongly about / you can handle the task / I'll do it

08 I'm heading over to / signed up for summer camp / That's a shame / we're having a family reunion

09 for professional or general purposes / I'm not into / they're currently on sale / ten percent off the sale price

10 make it easy on you / weigh more than fifty kilograms / have you been sick lately / if you're donating blood

11 with the actual tryouts taking place / submit a short biography / who will be permitted to join

12 organize a party for / reserve the party room / spend more than two hundred dollars / suit your needs / I'll put you down for

13 very dark in the parking lot / It helps us save on electricity / keep undesirable people away

14 It's made of old sweaters / come up with the idea / out of old bottles

15 trying it on / exchange it for a bigger size / offers the shirt to her younger sister / is grateful for the gift

16-17 are in the habit of / take advantage of online shopping / avoid buying bottled water

33 수능영어듣기 실전모의고사

본문 p.200

01 ①	02 ⑤	03 ③	04 ⑤	05 ③	06 ④
07 ④	08 ⑤	09 ④	10 ②	11 ②	12 ③
13 ①	14 ③	15 ③	16 ③	17 ④	

01 짧은 대화의 응답

소재 호텔 객실 불만

듣기 대본 해석

여: 좋은 아침입니다, 손님. 무엇을 도와드릴까요?
남: 음, 제 방에 문제가 있는 것 같아요.
여: 알겠습니다. 정확히 무슨 문제이신가요?
남: ① 침대 매트리스가 너무 딱딱해서 불편해요.

어휘

〈문제〉 **stiff** ***a.*** 딱딱한 **connect** ***v.*** 연결하다

정답 ①

문제풀이

남자가 호텔 객실에 문제가 있는 것 같다고 말하고 여자는 정확히 어떤 문제인지 물었으므로 남자는 ① '침대 매트리스가 너무 딱딱하고 불편해요.'라고 대답하는 것이 가장 적절하다.

오답 보기 해석

② 사실 저희는 이용 가능한 방이 없습니다.
③ 당신의 방 번호를 기억 못하겠어요.
④ 저는 305호와 연락하고 싶습니다.
⑤ 당신 짐을 저희에게 맡겨두세요.

총 어휘 수 33

02 짧은 대화의 응답

소재 친구를 위한 깜짝 마중

듣기 대본 해석

남: Julia, 소식 들었어? Owen이 다음 주에 홍콩에서 돌아올 거래.
여: 들었어. 거기서 그가 지낸 이야기를 듣고 싶어서 아주 흥분돼.
남: 그가 도착할 때 공항에 그를 만나러 가자.
여: ⑤ 좋은 생각이야. 그가 그 깜짝 마중을 좋아할 거라고 생각해.

어휘

〈문제〉 **appreciate** ***v.*** 고마워하다

정답 ⑤

문제풀이

남자가 다음 주에 홍콩에서 돌아오는 친구를 마중 나가자고 제안했으므로 그에 적절한 여자의 대답은 ⑤ '좋은 생각이야. 그가 그 깜짝 마중을 좋아할 거라고 생각해.'이다.

오답 보기 해석

① 너 언제 떠날 거야?
② 맞아. 축제는 토요일이야.
③ 너무 고마워. 나 그것이 정말 기대돼.
④ 우리 서둘러야 해. 파티가 10분 안에 시작할 거야.

총 어휘 수 48

03 담화 목적

소재 지식의 공유

듣기 대본 해석

남: 안녕하십니까, 여러분! 저희 학교에 계속 많은 관심 가져 주셔서 감사합니다. 저희가 집중하고 있는 것 중 하나는 여러분의 자녀들이 책임감 있는 사회 구성원이 되도록 준비시키고 장려하는 것입니다. 이제 여러분 모두에게 저희의 의미 있는 새 프로그램 중 하나를 소개해드리고자 합니다. 여러분 중 대부분이 "아는 것이 힘이다."라는 속담을 아실 것입니다. 그러나 지식이 공유되지 않으면 지식을 가지는 것이 무슨 소용이 있을까요? 여러분 중에 몇몇 분들은 중요한 결정에 영향을 미칠 수 있는 분들입니다. 여러분들의 지식과 전문 기술을 저희 학생들과 공유하셨으면 합니다. 참여해서 저희와 공유하고 싶으시면 다음 주 수요일에 학교로 오시면 됩니다. 여러분이 아는 것을 조금만 나눈다면 학생들의 삶에 큰 변화를 만들 수 있습니다.

어휘

meaningful ***a.*** 의미 있는, 중요한 **saying** ***n.*** 격언, 속담 **influence** ***v.*** 영향을 주다 **crucial** ***a.*** 중요한 **expertise** ***n.*** 전문 지식

정답 ③

문제풀이

전문 분야의 지식을 가진 학부모들이 그것을 학생들과 공유하도록 촉구하는 내용이므로 남자가 하는 말의 목적은 ③ '전문 분야의 지식을 공유하도록 요청하려고'이다.

총 어휘 수 131

04 대화 주제

소재 식료품 영양성분 표시제

듣기 대본 해석

여: 너 다이어트 중인 줄 알았는데, Roy.
남: 맞아. 왜 물어보니?
여: 음, 너 방금 치즈와 랜치드레싱을 곁들인 치킨샐러드를 주문했잖아. 만약 네가 다이어트 중이라면, 아시안 샐러드가 더 나은 선택일거야.
남: 정말? 뭐가 다른데?
여: 영양 정보를 봐.
남: 아, 알겠어. 치킨샐러드는 아시안 샐러드보다 칼로리가 더 많구나. 사실, 치킨 샐러드는 치즈버거 콤보만큼 많은 칼로리를 갖고 있네.
여: 맞아. 그건 샐러드라 건강해 보일지 몰라도, 사실 기름투성이의 샌드위치만큼 나빠.
남: 알겠어. 그런 정보를 볼 수 있게 되어 있는 건 참 좋다. 그들은 모든 식료품에 영양 정보를 담아야 돼. 그렇게 하면 우리는 더 좋고, 더 건강한 선택을 할 수 있어.
여: 동의해. 몇몇 나라에서는 영양상의 표시가 모든 음식과 음료에 요구되고 있어.
남: 정말? 나는 몰랐어.
여: 응. 예를 들어, 미국에서는 고기에 자세한 정보를 포함해야 해. 그들은 심지어 지방 비율까지도 포함해야만 돼.
남: 나는 우리나라가 같은 정책을 채택했으면 좋겠어. 그것은 나 같은 사람들이 건강하게 먹는 것을 더 쉽게 만들어줄 거야.
여: 맞아. 구매자들은 서로 다른 상품들이 어떤 게 더 많은 지방, 칼로리, 나트륨을 포함되어 있는지 보고 비교할 수 있어.

어휘

nutritional ***a.*** 영양상의 **greasy** ***a.*** 기름투성이의 **adopt** ***v.*** 채택하다 **contained** ***a.*** 포함된 **sodium** ***n.*** 나트륨

정답 ⑤

문제풀이
여자와 남자는 영양성분 표시로 구매자들이 더 쉽게 건강한 음식을 선택할 수 있다고 말하면서 음식의 영양 정보를 필수적으로 표시하는 정책을 받아들이길 바란다고 이야기하고 있다. 따라서 두 사람이 하는 대화의 주제는 ⑤ '식료품 영양성분 표시제의 필요성'이다.

총 어휘 수 207

05 대화자의 관계 파악

소재 학생과 선생님의 대화

듣기 대본 해석
남: Tomlin 선생님, 저에게 하실 말씀이 있다고 들었습니다.
여: 맞아, Alex. 들어와서 앉거라. 맹장 수술을 받았다고 막 들었어.
남: 몇 주 전에 수술을 받았어요. 갑작스러운 일이었어요.
여: 보통 꽤 갑작스럽게 그런 일이 일어나지. 지금은 괜찮니?
남: 이제 훨씬 나아졌어요. 그 일이 일어났을 때 약간 무서웠어요.
여: 네 체육 선생님께 그 일에 대해 말씀드렸니?
남: 네, 말씀드렸어요. 선생님께서 저에게 1~2주간 쉬라고 말씀하셨어요.
여: 네가 해결할 다른 문제는 없니?
남: 특별한 건 없어요. 수술 이후로 복부 쪽이 신경이 쓰여서요.
여: 그럴 만도 하지. 내가 생각하기에 그런 느낌은 곧 사라질 거야. 그런데 그 동안 안정을 취하고 편히 쉬어야 해.
남: 조언 주셔서 감사합니다. 당분간 저는 확실히 공부를 더 많이 하고 덜 놀아야 겠어요.
여: 좋아. 아마도 그렇게 하는 게 좋을 거야. 곧 밖에서 놀 수 있게 될 거야. 걱정 마.
남: 감사합니다. 이제 교실로 가봐야겠어요.

어휘
appendix ***n.*** 맹장 **operation** ***n.*** 수술 **sudden** ***a.*** 갑작스러운
P.E. teacher 체육 선생님 **fade** ***v.*** ~이 사라지다
in the meantime 그 동안에 **take it easy** 안정을 취하다
in no time 당장에, 곧

정답 ③

문제풀이
여자는 남자가 최근 맹장 수술을 받았다는 것을 듣고 남자를 불러서 상태가 어떤지 묻는 내용이다. 그리고 남자가 대화를 마치고 교실로 돌아가야겠다고 말했으므로 둘의 관계는 ③ '학생 ― 보건 교사'임을 알 수 있다.

총 어휘 수 165

06 그림의 세부 내용 파악

소재 Soccer Hall of Fame 방문

듣기 대본 해석
남: Katie, 지난주에 Soccer Hall of Fame 갔었어?
여: 갔었어. 내가 거기서 찍은 이 사진을 봐.
남: 와! 정말 인상적인걸. 벽에 있는 저 포스터들이 흥미롭네. 왜 왼쪽에 있는 사람은 장갑을 끼고 다른 유니폼을 입고 있지?
여: 음, 골키퍼는 다른 선수들과 구별되도록 항상 다른 유니폼을 입고 있어.
남: 포스터에서 그 옆에 있는 선수는 누구야? 그는 아주 진지해 보여.
여: 그는 팀의 CF, 그러니까 센터 포워드인 Conor James야.
남: 스마트폰으로 셀카를 찍고 있는 저 남자는 누구야?
여: 우리 아빠셔. 아빠 본인을 찍는 것에 아주 신나셨어. 그의 뒤에는 유명한 감독의 동상이 있어.
남: 멋지다. 오른쪽에는 너의 남동생과 엄마임에 틀림없는 것 같아.
여: 맞아. 내 남동생이 화장실을 가야 했어. 그는 여행을 그다지 즐기지 않았어.
남: 음, 적어도 너희 아버지는 즐거운 시간을 보내신 것 같아.

어휘
impressive ***a.*** 인상적인 **tell A apart from B** A를 B로부터 구별하다
statue ***n.*** 조각상

정답 ④

문제풀이
아빠 뒤에는 유명한 감독의 동상이 있다고 했는데 트로피가 있으므로 정답은 ④번이다.

총 어휘 수 165

07 할 일

소재 웹사이트 알려주기

듣기 대본 해석
여: 안녕 Aaron, 발표에 필요한 파일들 갖고 있어?
남: 응. 지금 플래시 드라이브 갖고 있으면, 내가 거기에 파일들을 전송해 줄 수 있어.
여: 나 하나 샀어. 자 여기 있어.
남: 이게 정말 플래시 드라이브야? 이거 좀 큰데, 그렇지 않아?
여: 응, 새 거야. 한쪽 끝에는 일반적인 USB 플러그가 있고, 다른 한쪽 끝에는 소형 USB 플러그가 있어.
남: 멋지다. 그러면 네가 꽤나 쉽게 파일들을 네 스마트폰에 전송할 수 있겠는걸.
여: 맞아. 근데 나도 이걸 처음 써 보는 거야.
남: 아주 잘 작동하는 것 같아. 모든 파일들을 엄청 빠르게 전송했어. 발표에 필요한 다른 건 없어?
여: 우리가 필요한 건 모두 있어. 내일 준비가 된 것 같아.
남: 알았어. 아, 그런데 그 플래시 드라이브 어디서 샀어? 나도 내 거 하나 사고 싶어서.
여: 온라인으로 샀어. 그 사이트 주소 적어 줄게.
남: 그럼 좋지. 고마워.

어휘
handy ***a.*** 유용한, 가까운 곳에 있는 **transfer** ***v.*** 옮기다, 이송하다

정답 ④

문제풀이
남자는 여자의 성능 좋은 플래시 드라이브를 보고 자신도 같은 것을 구매하고 싶어 한다. 어디서 샀냐는 남자의 질문에 여자는 온라인에서 샀다며 그 사이트 주소를 적어주겠다고 하였으므로 여자가 남자를 위해 할 일은 ④ '사이트 주소 알려주기'이다.

총 어휘 수 169

08 이유

소재 독서 클럽에 못 가는 이유

듣기 대본 해석
남: Susan, 독서 클럽 모임이 내일이야. 책 다 읽었니?
여: 다 못 읽었어. 너는?
남: 나는 주말 동안에 다 읽었어. 책에서 손을 뗄 수가 없었지. 너무 매혹적이고 흥미진진했어. 나는 네가 진짜 결말을 즐길 거라고 생각해.
여: 내가 그것을 다 읽을 수 있을 거라 생각되지가 않아. 어제 기차에 두고 내린 것 같아.
남: 네가 괜찮다면 내 책 빌려 줄게.
여: 그렇게 해 주면 좋겠네. 모임이 내일 8시지, 그렇지?
남: 아니, 사실 이번 주는 6시에 시작해.
여: 진짜로? 그러면 나는 못 갈 것 같은데.
남: 왜 못 와? 페이지가 많지 않은 책이야. 그때까지 다 읽을 수 있을 거야.

여: 그게 아니야. 내일 우리 아들 영어 선생님과 만나기로 했거든.
남: 네 남편이 갈 수는 없니?
여: 그는 (기꺼이) 가려 하겠지만 이번 주 내내 늦게까지 일해야 해. 금요일에 중요한 발표가 있거든.
남: 알았어. 음, 내가 모든 사람들에게 너의 안부를 전할게.
여: 고마워.

어휘
captivating ***a.*** 매혹적인 **say hello** 안부를 전하다

정답 ⑤

문제풀이
대화의 마지막 부분에서 여자는 아들의 영어 선생님과의 약속이 있어서 못 간다고 했으므로 정답은 ⑤ '아들의 영어 선생님과 만나야 해서'이다.

총 어휘 수 161

09 숫자

소재 기념품 가게에서 물건 구매하기

듣기 대본 해석
남: 기념품 가게에 오신 것을 환영합니다. 경기를 즐겁게 관람하셨기를 바랍니다.
여: 네. 마지막이 환상적이었어요!
남: 맞아요. 무엇을 도와드릴까요?
여: 기념품 좀 사려고요.
남: 기념품이 아주 많아요. 티셔츠, 저지, 모자, 범퍼 스티커도 있어요.
여: 저지는 얼마예요?
남: 음, 성인용 저지는 30달러이고 아동용 저지는 25달러예요.
여: 그렇군요. 그럼 성인용 두 개랑 아동용 두 개 주세요.
남: 알겠습니다. 다른 것 필요하세요?
여: 모자도 사려고요. 얼마 정도 하나요?
남: 하나당 20달러예요.
여: 네. 모자 두 개 살게요.
남: 알겠습니다. 표 아직도 갖고 계시면 추가로 10퍼센트 할인해 드려요.
여: 네. 여기 있어요.
남: 그럼, 성인용 저지 두 개, 아동용 저지 두 개, 모자 두 개 합한 금액에서 10퍼센트 할인해 드리면 되는 거죠.
여: 맞아요. 여기 카드요.

어휘
souvenir ***n.*** 기념품 **jersey** ***n.*** 저지, (운동 경기용) 셔츠 **bumper** ***n.*** 자동차 범퍼 **apiece** ***ad.*** 각각, 하나에 **stub** ***n.*** (표 등에서 한 쪽을 떼어 주고) 남은 부분, 토막 **additional** ***a.*** 추가의

정답 ④

문제풀이
성인용 저지 두 개 60달러, 아동용 저지 두 개 50달러, 모자 두 개에 40달러이므로 60+50+40=150달러인데 총 금액에서 10퍼센트를 할인해준다고 했으므로 정답은 ④ '$135'이다.

총 어휘 수 147

10 언급 유무

소재 컴퓨터 회사에서 실시하는 여름 인턴 프로그램

듣기 대본 해석
여: 안녕. 너 Pear Computers에서 여름 인턴 프로그램 등록 받기 시작한 것 봤어?
남: 정말? 거기에서 인턴을 구하는 건 몰랐어.
여: 응. 네가 컴퓨터 공학을 공부하고 싶어 하니까 관심 있을 거라고 생각했어. 너한테 좋은 기회가 될 거야.
남: 물론이지. 인턴이 뭐 해야 하는지 알아?
여: 그 회사에 있는 실험실에서 일하게 될 거야. 그럼 California에서 여름을 보내게 되는 거지.
남: 멋지다. 나를 받아줄 것 같아?
여: 그럴 것 같아. 너 컴퓨터로 일해본 경험이 많잖아. 그러니까 너는 적절한 자격을 가지고 있는 거지.
남: 좋은데! 인턴십은 얼마나 오랫동안 하는데?
여: 2달 프로그램이라고 하던데.
남: 좋다. 이번 인턴십으로 돈을 받지는 않겠지?
여: 응. 네가 모든 생활비와 여행 경비 또한 내야 할 거야.
남: 음, 그게 문제구나. 어쨌든 난 흥미가 있어. 집에 가면 바로 등록할게.

어휘
registration ***n.*** 등록 **awesome** ***a.*** 멋진, 근사한 **qualification** ***n.*** 자격 **living expenses** 생활비 **drawback** ***n.*** 문제점, 결점

정답 ②

문제풀이
두 사람은 인턴 프로그램의 근무 장소, 지원 자격, 근무 기간, 경비 지급에 관한 언급은 했지만 ② '지원 기한'에 관한 언급은 하지 않았다.

총 어휘 수 158

11 내용 일치 · 불일치

소재 사진대회 출품 안내

듣기 대본 해석
여: 학생 여러분 안녕하세요. Environmental Edge Photography Contest에 관하여 말할 시간을 좀 가지고 싶어요. 이 대회는 매년 개최되고 전국에 있는 모든 학생들이 참여하도록 장려합니다. 올해 대회의 주제는 환경적인 인식입니다. 사진 출품작은 환경 문제를 강조할 수 있는 사진이어야 합니다. 사진은 풀 컬러여야 하며, 가로 방향 포맷이어야 합니다. 모든 출품작은 Lopez 선생님에게 5월 15일전에 제출되어야 합니다. 이메일 출품작은 받지 않습니다. Environmental Edge는 6월 1일 대회의 우승자를 발표할 것입니다. 전국에서 가장 훌륭한 세 편의 사진 작품을 (선정하여) 시상할 것입니다. 우리 학교에는 많은 재능을 가진 학생들이 있다는 것을 알고 있기에 여러분의 많은 참여를 장려합니다. 더 많은 정보는 학교 홈페이지에서 찾을 수가 있습니다. 경청해 주셔서 감사합니다.

어휘
take place 개최되다, 일어나다 **entry** ***n.*** 출품작
make an attempt 시도하다 **landscape orientation** 가로 방향 포맷 **announce** ***v.*** 발표하다, 알리다 **talent** ***n.*** 재주, 재능있는 사람

정답 ②

문제풀이
여자는 출품사진은 모두 컬러여야 한다고 했으므로 일치하지 않는 것은 ② '컬러 또는 흑백사진으로 제출 가능하다.'이다.

총 어휘 수 129

12 도표

소재 냉장고 구매하기

듣기 대본 해석
남: 여보, 이 전단지 좀 봐요. 이번 주에 냉장고 파격 할인 행사가 있네요.
여: 정말이요? 우리 새 거 필요한데 잘 됐네요.
남: 전단지에 몇 가지 모델이 있어요. 돈은 얼마 정도 쓸 수 있다고 생각해요?
여: 글쎄요. 1,000달러 이상 쓰길 원하진 않아요.
남: 알겠어요. 그럼 이 모델들은 어때요?

여: 음... 저장 공간이 적어도 700리터인 거면 좋겠어요.
남: 나도 그렇게 생각해요. 700리터 이상이면 좋겠군요. 그럼 우리가 갖고 있는 음식들이 쉽게 들어가겠죠. 문이 두 개인 거랑 네 개인 것 중에 어느 걸 할까요?
여: 문이 두 개인 건 싫어요. 네 개짜리 문이 있는 냉장고가 물건들을 정리하기 쉬운 듯 해서요.
남: 그럼 우리가 고를 수 있는 모델이 두 개 남네요.
여: 오, 보증기간도 꽤 중요해요. 특히 가전제품은요.
남: 알았어요. 그럼 보증기간이 더 긴 걸로 사죠.
여: 좋았어요!

어휘

flyer ***n.*** 전단지 **storage** ***n.*** 저장, 보관 **appliance** ***n.*** (가정용) 기기 **warranty** ***n.*** 보증기간, 품질 보증서

정답 ③

문제풀이

남자와 여자는 1,000달러가 넘지 않으면서, 저장 공간은 700리터 이상, 문이 네 개, 더 긴 보증기간을 제공하는 냉장고를 선택하였으므로 두 사람이 구매할 냉장고 모델은 ③번이다.

총 어휘 수 142

13 긴 대화의 응답

소재 자신의 버전으로 결말 써보기

듣기 대본 해석

남: Rachel, The Babbit 다 봤니?
여: 네, 아빠, 다 봤어요. 왜 저보고 보라고 하신 거예요?
남: 재미있지 않았어?
여: 괜찮았어요. 저한텐 너무 행복하게 끝나는 할리우드식 결말이긴 했지만요.
남: 책과는 꽤 다르지?
여: 네. 책은 굉장히 어둡고 우울하게 만드는 결말이었잖아요. 영화도 똑같을 줄 알았어요.
남: 나도 그렇게 생각했어. 그래서 책이 더 나아, 아니면 영화가 더 나아?
여: 둘 다 별로예요. 원작은 너무 어둡고 영화는 너무 비현실적이고 밝기만 해요.
남: 그럼 무엇을 하면 이야기가 더 좋아질까?
여: 전반적으로 좀 더 밝으면서도 너무 비현실적이지 않으면 좋을 것 같아요.
남: 그럼 너의 버전으로 써보는 게 좋겠어.
여: 무슨 말씀이세요? 이야기를 재구성해서 쓰라는 거예요?
남: ① 물론이지. 나는 네 버전으로 쓴 이야기를 읽고 싶구나.

어휘

depressing ***a.*** 우울하게 만드는 **care for** ~를 좋아하다 **unrealistic** ***a.*** 비현실적인 〈문제〉 **review** ***n.*** 논평, 평가

정답 ①

문제풀이

책의 결말은 너무 어둡고 영화는 비현실적으로 밝다고 말하는 여자에게 남자는 자신의 버전으로 이야기를 써보라고 권하고 있는 상황이다. 이야기를 재구성해보라는 의미인지 되묻는 여자에게 해줄 적절한 응답은 ① '물론이지. 나는 네 버전으로 쓴 이야기를 읽고 싶구나.'이다.

오답 보기 해석

② 주제를 생각하지 마. 내용에 초점을 맞추렴.
③ 너는 정말 원작 읽기를 즐길 것 같구나.
④ 나는 작가의 허락이 먼저 필요할 거야.
⑤ 아니, 끝난 후에 너는 논평을 써야 해.

총 어휘 수 151

14 긴 대화의 응답

소재 건조한 방에 대나무 들여 놓기

듣기 대본 해석

여: Lenny, 무슨 일이야?
남: 안녕, Sam. 괜찮아? 너 꽤 피곤해 보여.
여: 괜찮아. 근데 지난 몇 주간 잠을 잘 못 자겠더라고. 날씨 때문에 내 방 공기가 너무 건조하거든.
남: 그렇구나. 그럼 네가 가습기를 사면 되잖아. 그리고 식물을 방에 두면 공기가 좀 습해진다고 들었어.
여: 내가 좀 무책임해서 그 식물들에게 물 주는 걸 깜박하고 다 시들어 죽을 거야.
남: 뭐, 그렇게 많은 관심을 안 줘도 되는 식물들도 있어. 그런 걸 키우면 되잖아.
여: 정말? 어떤 게 있는데?
남: 대나무를 물통에 넣으면 알아서 자랄 거야.
여: 아주 쉬워 보이는데.
남: 응, 나도 방에 대나무 몇 개 키우는데 물은 보통 한 달에 한 번, 통이 비어 있을 때 물을 주면 돼.
여: 대나무는 생김새도 마음에 들어.
남: 대나무가 네 방 공기를 좀 습하게 만들 것 같아. 한번 해봐.
여: ③ 오늘 꽃집에 가서 좀 사놓아야겠다.

어휘

humidifier ***n.*** 가습기 **humid** ***a.*** 습한 **irresponsible** ***a.*** 무책임한 **water** ***v.*** (화초 등에) 물을 주다 **wither** ***v.*** 시들다 **attention** ***n.*** 관심, 집중 **bamboo** ***n.*** 대나무

정답 ③

문제풀이

남자는 여자에게 건조한 방에 대나무를 놓을 것을 제안하고 있으므로 이에 대한 여자의 응답으로 가장 적절한 것은 ③ '오늘 꽃집에 가서 좀 사놓아야겠다.'이다.

오답 보기 해석

① 병원에 가봐야겠다.
② 우리 바깥에 대나무 좀 심어야겠어.
④ 매일 대나무에 물을 줘야 해.
⑤ 매일 8잔씩 물을 마셔야 해.

총 어휘 수 175

15 상황에 적절한 말

소재 과제 중 끊긴 인터넷에 대한 수리 요청

듣기 대본 해석

남: Paul은 역사 수업의 중요한 과제를 하고 있습니다. 하지만 컴퓨터로 조사를 하는 와중에 인터넷이 나갔습니다. 그는 인터넷을 제공하는 회사의 고객센터에 문제를 알리려고 전화를 겁니다. 늦은 시간인데다 고객 서비스 직원이 없어 대기 중입니다. 15분간의 대기 후에 상담원과 연결이 되었고, 상담원은 Paul에게 모뎀을 뽑았다가 다시 꽂아보라고 말합니다. 그는 상담원의 지시를 따랐지만 문제를 해결하지는 못했습니다. 그는 과제가 내일까지이므로 반드시 인터넷이 고쳐져야 합니다. 이런 상황에서 Paul이 고객센터 상담원에게 할 말로 가장 적절한 것은 무엇일까요?
Paul: ③ 최대한 빨리 인터넷을 손볼 사람을 보내주세요.

어휘

go out (불 등이) 꺼지다, 나가다 **customer service representative** 고객 서비스 상담원 **instruction** ***n.*** 설명, 지시 **desperately** ***ad.*** 필사적으로, 몹시

정답 ③

문제풀이
Paul은 기한이 내일까지인 역사 과제를 하던 중 인터넷이 끊겨 과제를 할 수 없는 처지에 놓여 있다. 이런 상황에서 그가 인터넷 서비스 제공업체의 고객 서비스 상담원에게 할 말로 가장 적절한 것은 ③ '최대한 빨리 인터넷을 손볼 사람을 보내주세요.'이다.

오답 보기 해석
① 문제가 해결되었어요. 도와주셔서 감사해요.
② 감사합니다만, 전 이미 (인터넷을 제공하는) 인터넷서비스 회사가 있어요.
④ 제가 어떻게 하면 고객 서비스 상담원이 될 수 있는지 알고 싶어요.
⑤ 문제가 생겨서 유감입니다. 문제를 살펴볼 사람을 보내겠습니다.

총 어휘 수 127

16 담화 주제 / 17 세부 내용 파악

소재 야외 활동이 아동에게 좋은 점들

듣기 대본 해석
남: 학부모 여러분 안녕하세요. 아이들의 건강에 대한 세미나에 오신 것을 환영합니다. 제 이름은 Dr. Jeffrey Day이고요 저는 거의 30년 동안 소아과 의사를 해 왔습니다. 우선 3세에서 12세 사이의 어린이들에 대해서 얘기를 해보도록 합시다. 이 나이대가 어린이들의 성장에 굉장히 중대한 시기입니다. 이 시기에 아이들은 자신감을 키우고, 더 활동적이게 되고, 문제해결 능력을 키우고, 평생 동안 갖고 갈 건강한 습관들을 확립하는 시기입니다. 이 때문에 저는 모든 부모가 자녀에게 최대한 많이 나가 놀도록 권고할 것을 추천합니다. 나가 노는 것은 놀라운 이점들을 갖고 있습니다. 아이들은 새로운 친구를 만날 기회를 갖게 되고 평생 갈 소꿉친구를 만들 수 있습니다. 그들은 또한 모험을 하고 야외 놀이를 함으로써 자신감도 키울 것입니다. 밖에서 노는 것이 항상 안전한 것은 아니지만, 아이가 위험을 감수하고 모험적인 행동을 하려는 의지를 키우는 것은 아이에게 새로운 능력들을 배우고 자신의 잠재력을 끝까지 끌어올릴 수 있는 기회를 줍니다. 마지막으로 나가 노는 것은 건강한 성장에 필수적인 비타민 D를 아이들에게 제공해 줍니다. 이 비타민은 아이들이 우울증, 심장병, 당뇨병 그리고 비만과 싸우는 데에 도움을 줍니다. 그래서 저는 학부모 여러분에게 아이들이 바깥에 나가 놀 수 있게 하기를 부탁드립니다. 이는 여러분에게도 도움이 될 것입니다.

어휘
pediatrician ***n.*** 소아과 의사 **critical** ***a.*** 중대한, 중요한
development ***n.*** 발달, 성장 **confidence** ***n.*** 자신감
establish ***v.*** 세우다, 확립하다 **willingness** ***n.*** 기꺼이 하는 마음, 의지
potential ***n.*** 잠재력 **depression** ***n.*** 우울증 **obesity** ***n.*** 비만

정답 16 ③ 17 ④

문제풀이
16 남자는 3세 ~ 12세의 아동들에게 가능한 한 많이 바깥에서 노는 것을 권하면서 어떠한 점이 좋은지에 대해 '새로운 친구 사귀기, 자신감과 위험을 무릅쓰려는 자세 기르기, 비타민 D공급 등'을 이야기 하고 있으므로 남자가 하는 말의 주제로 가장 적절한 것은 ③ '아이들에게 야외에서 노는 것의 장점'이다.
17 우울증(depression), 심장병(heart disease), 당뇨병(diabetes), 비만(obesity)에 비타민 D가 좋다고 언급되었지만 '피부병'은 언급되지 않았으므로 정답은 ④번이다.

오답 보기 해석
16
① 어린이의 건강관리에 있어 부모의 역할
② 아동기 습관의 지속적인 영향
④ 친밀한 부모-자식 관계의 중요성
⑤ 아이들이 기꺼이 모험을 해보려는 마음을 발달시킬 수 있는 활동들

총 어휘 수 216

DICTATION ANSWERS

01 there seems to be a problem with

02 coming back from

03 to be responsible members of the community / influence crucial decisions / share your knowledge and expertise with our students

04 you were on a diet / They should put nutritional information / nutrition labels are required / Shoppers would be able to compare different products

05 I had the operation / I take it easy / that feeling will fade soon

06 It looks really impressive / you can tell him apart from / take a picture of himself

07 the files for the presentation / transfer things to your smartphone / write down the web address

08 captivating and exciting / I'll get a chance to finish it / to be able to make it / he has to work late

09 I hope you enjoyed the game / I'm looking to buy some souvenirs / I'll take two for adults / get an additional ten percent off

10 what the interns' duties are / experienced in working with computers / I won't get paid for / pay for all living expenses

11 This contest takes place every year / make an attempt to / Photos should be in full color / Email entries will not be accepted / on the school's website

12 spend more than one thousand dollars / More than seven hundred liters / organize stuff / get the one with a longer warranty

13 dark and depressing ending / didn't care for either of them / write your own version / rewrite the story

14 make the air more humid / they'll wither and die / it'll grow on its own / the air in your room more humid

15 is put on hold / a representative gets on the line / desperately needs to

16-17 children build their confidence / establish healthy habits / play outside as much as possible / reach their full potential

34 수능영어듣기 실전모의고사

본문 p.206

01 ⑤	02 ⑤	03 ③	04 ①	05 ④	06 ⑤
07 ④	08 ③	09 ⑤	10 ②	11 ③	12 ②
13 ②	14 ①	15 ⑤	16 ②	17 ⑤	

01 짧은 대화의 응답

소재 과다한 전기요금

듣기 대본 해석

남: 우와! 이번 달 전기요금 청구서 좀 봐. 거의 500달러야.
여: 와! 너무 비싸다. 전기회사에 전화해 볼게. 분명 실수가 있었을 거야.
남: 그 사람들이 실수한 것 같진 않아. 이번 여름에 우리가 에어컨을 많이 튼 것 알잖아.
여: ⑤ 맞아. 우리가 집을 나설 때 그걸 꺼야겠어.

어휘

bill ***n.*** 청구서 **doubt** ***v.*** 확신하지 못하다, 의심하다
〈문제〉 **appliance** ***n.*** (가정용) 기기

정답 ⑤

문제풀이

여자는 전기회사에서 실수한 것 같다고 했는데, 남자는 여름에 에어컨을 많이 켰다고 말하고 있으므로 적절한 여자의 응답은 ⑤ '맞아. 우리가 집을 나설 때 그걸 꺼야겠어.'이다.

오답 보기 해석

① 전기회사에 전화해서 청구서에 대해서 물어볼게.
② 내가 수리하시는 분에게 우리 에어컨을 봐달라고 부탁할게.
③ 물론. 안이 더울 때는 에어컨을 켜.
④ 네가 가전제품을 사용할 때 플러그를 뽑아선 안 돼.

총 어휘 수 58

02 짧은 대화의 응답

소재 책에 대한 대화

듣기 대본 해석

여: Liam, 뭐하고 있니? 뭔가에 매우 몰두한 것처럼 보이는데.
남: Yann Martel의 Life of Pi 읽는 중이야. 너무 재미있어서 멈출 수가 없네.
여: 영화 먼저 봤어? 좋은 영화야.
남: ⑤ 아니야. 일단 이 책을 다 읽으면, 영화를 볼 거야.

어휘

immersed in ~에 깊이 빠진, 몰두한

정답 ⑤

문제풀이

Life of Pi라는 책을 읽고 있는 남자에게 여자가 영화를 먼저 봤냐고 물었다. 이에 적절한 대답은 ⑤ '아니야. 일단 이 책을 다 읽으면, 영화를 볼 거야.'이다.

오답 보기 해석

① 동의해. 온라인으로 그 책 주문하자.
② 알아. 그게 그 책이 읽기 쉬운 이유지.
③ 도서관에 가서 그 책을 대출하자.
④ 내 영화 DVD를 빌려줄게. 무척 재미있어.

총 어휘 수 48

03 담화 주제

소재 인간관계에서의 유사성

듣기 대본 해석

여: 안녕하세요 여러분. 저번 시간에 관계를 만들고 유지하는 것의 중요성과 그것이 우리의 성공에 어떤 영향을 미치는지에 대해서 토론했습니다. 오늘 수업에서는 '유유상종(같은 무리끼리 서로 사귐)'이란 옛말에 있는 진실에 대해 이야기할 겁니다. 인간으로서, 우리는 비슷한 사람들끼리 모이는 경향이 있습니다. 대부분의 사람들은 자신과 같은 나이, 인종, 그리고 성별을 가진 사람과 친구를 합니다. 학우들을 예로 들어볼게요. 여러분은 여러분 자신과 비슷한 특징을 가진 학우들과 친해지기 마련입니다. 이러한 특징들에는 관심사와 취미들이 포함됩니다. 물론 모두가 그런 것은 아닙니다. 어떤 사람들은 자신과 다른 인종의 사람과 연애하거나 결혼도 합니다. 그러나 이런 관계들은 일반적으로 공통된 가치관이나 교육으로부터 형성됩니다.

어휘

maintain ***v.*** 유지하다 **birds of a feather flock together** 유유상종 **be likely to** ~할 것 같다 **across the board** 전체에 걸쳐, 전체에 미치는 **typically** ***ad.*** 보통, 일반적으로 **value** ***n.*** 가치, 가치관

정답 ③

문제풀이

사람들은 유사성을 토대로 서로 관계를 맺어간다는 것을 이야기하고 있으므로 여자가 하는 말의 주제는 ③ '인간관계에 유사성이 미치는 영향'이다.

총 어휘 수 128

04 의견

소재 회전문 설치

듣기 대본 해석

남: Sarah, 무슨 일 있어요? 괜찮아요?
여: 두통이 있고 코가 막혔어요. 아픈 것 같아요.
남: 더 따뜻한 옷을 입어야 되겠어요.
여: 맞아요. 그래야 할 것 같아요. 여기 꽤 추워지네요.
남: 이해해요. 저도 전에 프런트 데스크에서 일했었어요. 전 항상 추위가 싫었어요.
여: 네. 사람들이 건물에 들어올 때 차가운 공기가 사람들을 따라 들어와요.
남: 아마 문을 바꾸면 찬 공기가 들어오는 것을 막을 수 있을 거예요.
여: 제 생각엔 새로운 문이 필요하진 않을 것 같아요. 추가적인 난방기를 사는 게 더 낫지 않겠어요?
남: 아니요, 새로운 문이 더 효율적일 거예요. 회전문을 설치하면 건물로 들어오는 차가운 공기를 많이 줄일 수 있을 거예요.
여: 정말요? 어떻게 그게 돼요?
남: 공기가 문에 갇혀서 문이 돌기 때문에 안으로 들어올 수가 없어요.
여: 그거 좋겠네요! 효과가 있으면 좋겠어요.

어휘

stuffy nose 코막힘 **effective** ***a.*** 효과적인 **revolving door** 회전문 **reduce** ***v.*** 줄이다, 낮추다 **trap** ***v.*** 가두다

정답 ①

문제풀이

남자는 외부의 찬 공기가 들어오는 것을 막기 위해 회전문을 설치해야 한다고 말하고 있으므로 남자의 의견으로 가장 적절한 것은 ① '출입문을 회전문으로 바꿔야 한다.'이다.

총 어휘 수 151

05 장소 파악

소재 간단한 아침식사 제안

듣기 대본 해석

남: Delgado 선생님, 다시 오신 것을 환영합니다.

여: 초대해주셔서 감사합니다. 저도 여기에 오게 되어 기뻐요.
남: 좋습니다. 프로그램을 시작해 보죠. 먼저, 관객분들에게 건강에 관한 간단한 조언 부탁드립니다.
여: 물론이죠. 요즘에는 모든 사람들이 정신 없이 바쁘죠. 그것은 여러분의 건강에 나쁠 수 있습니다.
남: 맞습니다. 그러면 늘 바쁜 사람이 건강하게 지내기 위해서는 무엇을 할 수 있을까요?
여: 좋은 아침식사가 건강 유지의 핵심입니다. 아침은 다른 끼니보다 거르기 쉽죠. 누구도 아침을 만들 시간이 없어요. 그러나 몇 가지 기본 재료들만 있다면 당신은 적절한 아침을 드실 수 있을 겁니다.
남: 어떤 종류의 재료에 관해 이야기할까요?
여: 단백질 쉐이크로 하루를 시작하는 것은 정말 좋은 방법입니다. 필요한 것은 단백질 파우더와 우유뿐이지요.
남: 과일이나 다른 재료는 어떤가요?
여: 좋은 의견이네요. 쉐이크를 좀 더 맛있게 하기 위해 바나나 혹은 딸기 등의 과일을 첨가할 수 있습니다. 제 것에는 영양가를 위해 시금치를 넣는 것을 좋아합니다.
남: 쉐이크 속에 시금치요? 맛있게 들리진 않는데요. 영양이 중요한 점이네요, 그렇지요? 감사합니다. Delgado 선생님. 잠시 광고 시간 후 돌아오겠습니다.

어휘
be on the go 정신 없이 바쁘다 **decent** ***a.*** 괜찮은, 제대로 된 **ingredient** ***n.*** 재료, 성분 **spinach** ***n.*** 시금치 **nutritional value** 영양가

정답 ④

문제풀이
대화의 시작 부분에서 프로그램을 시작하기 전에 청중들에게 말하라고 했고, 광고 시간 후 돌아온다고 한 것으로 보아 두 사람이 대화하고 있는 장소는 ④ 'TV 스튜디오'임을 추측할 수 있다.

오답 보기 해석
① 병원 ② 식당 ③ 교실 ⑤ 식료품점

총 어휘 수 192

06 그림의 세부 내용 파악

소재 FPS World Championship 포스터

듣기 대본 해석
여: Ryan, 나 방금 FPS World Championship의 포스터를 끝냈어. 어떤 것 같아?
남: 너 정말 잘했구나! 난 네가 위에 있는 제목을 꾸민 게 맘에 들어. 배너 같아 보여.
여: 고마워. 그리고 시간과 날짜를 왼쪽에 놓았어.
남: 봤어. 우리 날짜와 시간에 대해 확인을 받은 거야?
여: 받았어. 게임 협회가 오늘 아침에 확인해 줬어.
남: 좋아. 그럼 우리한테 준비할 시간이 많겠구나. 아래에 장소를 표시한 박스는 빈칸으로 둔 게 보여.
여: 그래. 우리가 스타디움에서 이벤트를 하도록 허가증을 받으려고 계속 노력 중이라 아직 정확하게 정해지지 않았어. 오른쪽에 너랑 Jason의 사진은 어때?
남: 내가 제일 잘 나온 사진은 아니지만, 네가 그것을 같이 놓은 것은 좋아.
여: (웃음)
남: 나는 아래쪽에 마스코트인 공룡 그림도 좋아. 그게 뭐라고 말하고 있어?
여: 그것은 "음식과 음료 제공!"이라고 말해.

어휘
outdo ***v.*** 능가하다 **confirmation** ***n.*** 확인 **association** ***n.*** 협회 **confirm** ***v.*** 확인해 주다 **blank** ***a.*** 빈 **permit** ***n.*** 허가증 ***v.*** 허락하다, 허용하다

정답 ⑤

문제풀이
아래쪽에 공룡 마스코트가 말하고 있다고 했는데 여자 안내원이 말하고 있으므로 정답은 ⑤번이다.

총 어휘 수 158

07 할 일

소재 학교에 셔츠 갖다 주기

듣기 대본 해석
[전화벨이 울린다.]
여: 여보세요?
남: 아, 엄마. 집에 계셔서 다행이에요. 도움이 필요한 일이 있어요.
여: 무슨 일이니, Andrew?
남: 오늘 밤에 큰 야구경기가 있는 것 알고 계시리라 생각해요.
여: 물론이지. 아빠랑 내가 보러 가기로 했잖아.
남: 좋아요. 그런데 제가 오늘 아침에 집에서 제 셔츠를 깜빡했어요.
여: 오, Andrew. 너는 왜 그렇게 잘 잊어버리니? 학교 끝나고 그걸 가지러 올 시간이 있니?
남: 없어요. 수업 후에 경기 전 저녁식사를 하고 바로 필드로 가야 해요.
여: 집에 잠깐 들러서 그걸 너한테 갖다 줄 사람은 없니?
남: 제가 알기론 없어요. 금요일 하교 후엔 모두 꽤 바빠요. 엄마가 학교에 갖다 주실 수 있을까요?
여: 그래. 내가 할 수 있을 것 같구나.
남: 너무 감사해요, 엄마.
여: 천만에, 얘야. 곧 보자.

어휘
forgetful ***a.*** 잘 잊어 먹는, 건망증이 있는 **swing by** 잠깐 들르다

정답 ④

문제풀이
남자는 오늘 큰 야구경기가 있는데 경기 때 입을 셔츠를 집에 두고 와서 엄마에게 갖다 줄 것을 부탁했고 엄마는 그렇게 하겠다고 했으므로 여자가 남자를 위해 할 일은 ④ '학교로 셔츠 가져다 주기'이다.

총 어휘 수 145

08 이유

소재 화가 난 이유

듣기 대본 해석
여: Daniel, 너 화나 보인다. 무슨 일이야?
남: 신경 쓰지마. 별거 아냐. 조금 피곤할 뿐이야.
여: 어서. 마음에 있는 것을 말해봐. 그럼 한결 나을 거야.
남: 음, Jeremy와 Jane, Selena, 그리고 나는 오늘 아침 영어 수업 발표 준비를 위해 만나기로 되어 있었어.
여: 그래, 맞아. 우리 조는 발표 파트를 나누기 위해 어제 모였어.
남: 우리도 발표를 나누고 그에 대한 자료를 수집하기로 되어있었어.
여: 그래서, 그 회의에서 무슨 일이 있었어?
남: Jeremy랑 Selena가 나타나지 않았어.
여: 와, 음, 아마도 그들도 나름의 이유가 있을 거야.
남: 아니, 둘 다 그냥 회의를 까먹었다고 말했어. 나는 화가 나. 어떻게 그들은 이렇게 무책임할 수 있지?
여: 음, 진정해. 발표를 준비할 시간은 아직 많잖아. 그들은 분명히 미안해하고 있을 거야.
남: 글쎄, 잘 모르겠다. 어쨌든 난 집에 가서 좀 쉬어야겠어.

어휘
presentation ***n.*** 발표 **divide** ***v.*** 나누다 **collect** ***v.*** 수집하다, 모으다 **material** ***n.*** 자료 **show up** 나타나다 **irresponsible** ***a.*** 책임감 없는

정답 ③

문제풀이
남자는 같이 발표 준비를 해야 하는 조원인 Jeremy와 Selena가 회의에 나오지 않아 화가 났으므로 정답은 ③ '조원들이 모임에 나오지 않아서'이다.

총 어휘 수 149

09 숫자

소재 캠핑장 예약

듣기 대본 해석
[전화벨이 울린다.]
남: Walker Mountain 캠핑장입니다. 오늘은 무엇을 도와드릴까요?
여: 안녕하세요. 다음 달 방학 동안에 우리 가족이 당신의 캠핑장에 갈 예정입니다. 하룻밤에 얼마죠?
남: 차량 한 대를 위한 자리를 포함해서 35달러입니다.
여: 음, 차량 두 대로 갈 예정이에요.
남: 그러한 경우에는 하룻밤에 10달러가 추가됩니다.
남: 알았어요. 8월 14일과 15일 이틀 밤을 예약하고 싶어요. 제 이름은 Minnie Martin이에요.
남: 알겠습니다. Martin 부인. 제가 도와드릴 다른 게 있나요?
여: 오, 야영장에서 물과 전기를 제공하나요?
남: 네, 제공합니다. 그러나, 물과 전기에 추가적인 비용을 청구합니다. 물이 나오는 야영지는 하룻밤에 5달러를 추가해야 하고 전기가 연결된 야영지는 하룻밤에 10달러를 추가해야 합니다.
여: 알겠어요. 물은 필요하지 않을 것 같은데 전기는 연결해주세요.
남: 네, 전기가 들어오는 자동차 2대용 캠프장 2일, 예약되었습니다. 다음 달에 뵙겠습니다.

어휘
nightly ***a.*** 야간의 **vehicle** ***n.*** 차량 **spot** ***n.*** 곳, 자리
additional ***a.*** 추가의 **reservation** ***n.*** 예약 **electricity** ***n.*** 전기
campsite ***n.*** 야영지 **hookup** ***n.*** 접속, 연결

정답 ⑤

문제풀이
차량 한 대를 포함한 자리는 하루에 35달러이고 차가 추가로 한 대 더 있으므로 10달러가 추가되어 하루에 45달러인데 이틀이므로 90달러이다. 그리고 전기가 있는 야영지는 하루에 10달러가 추가되므로 이틀에 20달러가 추가된다. 따라서 여자가 지불할 금액은 (35+10)x2+20=110달러이므로 정답은 ⑤ '$110'이다.

총 어휘 수 157

10 언급 유무

소재 게임 회사 인턴

듣기 대본 해석
여: Johnny, 너 내 이메일 받았어?
남: 아직 확인 안 했는데. 무엇에 관한 건데?
여: RD Games에서의 여름 인턴사원 근무 프로그램에 관한 거야.
남: 멋진데. 그들은 멋진 게임을 몇 개 만들었지.
여: 맞아. 그들은 Counterclockwise와 Super Doctor Brothers를 출시했어.
남: 그래, 나는 그 게임들을 좋아해.
여: 그래 멋있지. 어쨌든 프로그래밍, 캐릭터 디자인, 베타 테스팅에 관한 인턴직에 자리가 났어.
남: 잘됐다! 나는 프로그래밍에 대해서 조금 알지만, 캐릭터 디자인을 한번 해보고 싶어. 지원 자격이 어떻게 되니?
여: 음, 그들은 몇 개의 게임 디자인 수업을 들었고, 재미있고 흥미로운 게임을 만드는 것에 대한 애정을 가지고 있는 사람을 찾고 있어.
남: 나는 어느 정도 게임 디자인 수업을 들었고, 너도 알다시피 게임 하는 것을 정말 좋아해.
여: 그들이 너를 채용할 것 같은데. 너 게임 커뮤니티에서 꽤 인기 있잖아.
남: 당장 지원해야겠어. 이걸 알려줘서 고마워.

어휘
release ***v.*** 출시하다 **qualification** ***n.*** 자격, 필요조건 **take on** ~를 채용(고용)하다

정답 ②

문제풀이
인턴사원을 모집하는 게임회사에서 출시된 게임으로 Counterclockwise와 Super Doctor Brothers가 언급되었고, 모집 분야(프로그래밍, 캐릭터 디자인, 베타 테스팅), 남자의 지원 분야(캐릭터 디자인), 지원 자격(게임 디자인 수업 수강, 게임에 대한 애정)은 언급이 되었지만 모집 인원에 대해서는 언급되지 않았으므로 정답은 ② '모집 인원'이다.

총 어휘 수 149

11 내용 일치 · 불일치

소재 캠퍼스 투어의 내용과 일정 안내

듣기 대본 해석
여: 여러분 안녕하세요. 저는 Williams Academy의 교감인 Jones이고 여러분이 저희 일류 학교에 오신 것을 환영합니다. 오늘 저희는 예비 학생들에게 우리 캠퍼스를 방문하고 시설을 구경할 기회를 줄 것입니다. 여러분의 가이드는 저희 시설에서의 생활에 대해 직접적인 경험을 들려드릴 학교 학생들일 것입니다. 그들은 또한 교육 프로그램에 대한 상세한 얘기와 우리 캠퍼스의 역사에 대한 얘기를 해 줄 것입니다. 투어의 첫 부분은 12시까지 진행될 것입니다. 12시에 점심을 위해 학교 식당에서 만나도록 하겠습니다. 그런 다음 한 시에 강당으로 이동하며 거기서 학생회가 연극을 공연할 것입니다. 이후 짧은 프레젠테이션을 보도록 하겠습니다. 프레젠테이션 후에 저희 학교에 대한 여러분의 질문을 학생회가 받도록 하겠습니다. 즐거운 하루를 보내시길 바라며 방문해 주셔서 감사합니다.

어휘
prestigious ***a.*** 일류의, 명망 있는 **potential** ***a.*** 가능성이 있는, 잠재적인
facility ***n.*** 기관, 시설 **first-hand** ***a.*** 직접적인, 직접 얻은
auditorium ***n.*** 강당

정답 ③

문제풀이
여자는 학교 생활에 대해 학교 학생들이 안내해 줄 것이며, 정오까지 투어의 첫 부분이 끝나면 12시에 점심을 학교 식당에서 먹고, 1시까지 강당으로 이동하여 학생들의 연극, 발표, 질의응답 시간을 갖는다고 하였으므로 정답은 ③ '투어의 첫 부분은 1시에 시작한다.'이다.

총 어휘 수 156

12 도표

소재 원예관련 프로그램 선택

듣기 대본 해석
남: Brittney, 올해 정원을 시작하는 것에 관심이 있다고 그러지 않았니?
여: 응, 채식주의자가 될 거야. 왜?
남: 음, 이번 여름에 커뮤니티 칼리지에서 제공하는 몇몇 수업에 대한 전단지를 받았거든. 하나 가져.
여: 정말? 좋다. *[잠시 후]* 유기농 원예 수업이 재미있어 보여.
남: 그럼 채식주의 음식 요리하는 법도 배우고 싶어?
여: 정말 재미있어 보이네. 수업 시간 때 내가 직접 요리할 수 있는 거지, 맞지?
남: 맞아. 네가 만든 걸 집에 가져 와서 내가 먹어볼 수도 있어.
여: 좋다. 그럼 그 수업도 들어야지.
남: 그래. 그럼 이제 선택할 수 있는 두 프로그램으로 좁혀졌네. 수업에서 점심 제공해 주는 걸 원해?

여: 거기서 요리할 거니까 굳이 그럴 필요는 없을 것 같아. 내가 만든 것 먹으면 되지, 맞지? 그리고 10달러 더 싸잖아.
남: 알겠어. 그럼 너한테 딱 알맞은 프로그램을 찾은 것 같아.

어휘
organic ***a.*** 유기농의 **vegan** ***n.*** 채식주의자 〈문제〉 **sustainable** ***a.*** 지속 가능한

정답 ②

문제풀이
유기농 원예 수업과 채식주의 음식 요리를 한다고 했으므로 ①번과 ②번으로 좁혀지는데 점심은 제공되지 않은 것으로 한다고 했으므로 정답은 ②번이다.

총 어휘 수 160

13 긴 대화의 응답

소재 추천서 파일 부탁하기

듣기 대본 해석
여: 안녕하세요, Wilson 선생님.
남: 안녕, Margaret. 무슨 일이야?
여: 별일 아니에요. 저는 단지 선생님께서 저의 추천서를 끝내셨는지 궁금해서요. 제가 이번 주 말까지 저의 대학 지원서를 제출해야 해서요.
남: 맞아. 나는 월요일에 그것을 다 마쳤어. 여기 어딘가에 있을 거야. 잠깐만 기다려.
여: 천천히 찾으세요.
남: *[잠시 후]* 아, 여기 있네. 나는 추천서 쓰는 데 많은 시간을 보냈어. 너도 알다시피 너는 내가 가장 좋아하는 학생들 중 한 명이었지.
여: 감사해요. 추천서가 좋아 보이네요, Wilson 선생님. 제가 파일 가져가도 되나요?
남: 당연하지. 백업용이나 그런 것을 위해 필요한 거니?
여: 음, 요즘 모든 대학교 지원서가 온라인으로 제출되어서요. 그래서 제가 그것들을 이메일로 보내야 해요.
남: 내가 나의 서명이 들어간 이것을 스캔해줄게.
여: 좋아요. 스캔한 후에 저에게 이메일로 보내주실 수 있나요?
남: 그럼. 여기 종이에 너의 이메일 주소를 적어두기만 하렴.
여: 알겠습니다. 도와주셔서 감사합니다, Wilson 선생님.
남: ② 괜찮아. 준비되자마자 이 파일을 보내줄게.

어휘
letter of recommendation 추천장 **turn in** 제출하다 **backup** ***n.*** 예비, 백업 **application** ***n.*** 지원(서), 신청(서) **submit** ***v.*** 제출하다 **signature** ***n.*** 서명 〈문제〉 **misplace** ***v.*** 잘못 두다, 제자리에 두지 않다

정답 ②

문제풀이
여자는 남자에게 추천서를 파일로 보내달라고 부탁하고 있고, 남자는 흔쾌히 허락하는 분위기이므로 남자의 마지막 대답은 ② '괜찮아. 준비되자마자 이 파일을 보내줄게.'가 적절하다.

오답 보기 해석
① 네가 나한테 이메일을 보내게 하는 이유를 확신할 수 없구나.
③ 천만에. 오늘 밤에 반드시 편지 쓸게.
④ 정말로 미안한데, 내가 서류를 잘못 놓아둔 것 같구나.
⑤ 그럼. 나의 이메일 주소는 gwilson@northwestacademy.edu야.

총 어휘 수 181

14 긴 대화의 응답

소재 아이들을 돌보는 자원봉사

듣기 대본 해석
남: Hailey, 오늘 봉사하는 거 재미있었어?
여: 즐거웠어. 아이들이랑 게임도 하고 노래도 불렀어.
남: 좋네. 근데 어떻게 그렇게 많은 아이들을 감당할 수 있는지 모르겠어.
여: 사실 쉬워. 아이들이랑 노는 거 재미있어.
남: 다음 번에 너랑 같이 하고 싶은데 그래야 할지 모르겠다.
여: 왜 못해?
남: 글쎄, 애들이 날 별로 안 좋아할 것 같아.
여: 왜 그렇게 생각해? 너 보통 아주 친절하고 에너지 넘치잖아.
남: 난 노래도 못하고 걔네랑 게임을 하면서 놀 인내심도 없는 것 같아. 점심 만들어 주는 것 외에는 할 수 있는 게 없을 거야.
여: 음, 네가 그 자원봉사에 지원해도 될 것 같아. 다음 번에 같이 가자.
남: 진짜 내가 도와줄 수 있을까?
여: ① 물론이지. 우리는 받을 수 있는 모든 도움이 필요해.

어휘
energetic ***a.*** 정력적인 **patience** ***n.*** 참을성, 인내력
〈문제〉 **volunteer work** 자원봉사

정답 ①

문제풀이
남자가 아이들에게 자원봉사하는 것에 자신이 없어하면서 도움이 될 수 있을지 물었는데 여자는 할 수 있다고 용기를 주고 있으므로 적절한 대답은 ① '물론이지. 우리는 받을 수 있는 모든 도움이 필요해.'이다.

오답 보기 해석
② 네가 원한다면 우리가 다른 자원봉사를 찾을 수 있어.
③ 네가 나한테 아이들과 어떻게 잘 지내는지 가르쳐 주면 되겠네.
④ 네가 아이들과 노래 부르는 건 그들에게 중요해.
⑤ 게임하는 거랑 노래 부르기는 그들이 더 사교적이 되게 도와줘.

총 어휘 수 148

15 상황에 적절한 말

소재 직장 선택

듣기 대본 해석
남: Uptown 대학에서 저널리즘을 공부하는 학생인 Ryan은 이번 학기 말에 졸업할 것입니다. 그는 졸업 후 직업을 찾기 위해 열심히 일해왔고 높이 평가되는 신문사들로부터 두 개의 일자리 제안을 받았습니다. 첫 번째 제안은 Courier Crossing에서 온 것인데 대도시에 있는 큰 신문사입니다. 다른 제안은 작은 타블로이드 신문인 Hush-Hush에서 받았습니다. Courier Crossing은 그에게 높은 봉급과 직업 안정성을 제공하지만 그의 고향으로부터 멀리 떨어져서 가야만 합니다. Hush-Hush는 훨씬 적은 봉급이지만 그는 그의 가족과 친구들로부터 떠날 필요가 없을 겁니다. 많은 숙고 끝에, Ryan은 마침내 Hush-Hush의 제안을 받아들이기로 결정합니다. 그는 복도에서 그의 친구인 Sarah를 만났고 그녀에게 그가 결정한 것을 이야기합니다. Sarah는 왜 Ryan이 이런 결정을 했는지 이해하고 격려의 말을 해주고 싶습니다. 이런 상황에서, Sarah는 Ryan에게 뭐라고 말할까요?
Sarah: ⑤ 좋은 선택이야. 인생에서 어떤 것들은 돈보다 더 중요하니까.

어휘
semester ***n.*** 학기 **graduation** ***n.*** 졸업 **well-respected** ***a.*** 존경을 받는, 높이 평가되는 **tabloid** ***n.*** 타블로이드판 (보통 신문 크기의 절반) **security** ***n.*** 보장, 안심 **deliberation** ***n.*** 숙고 **hallway** ***n.*** 복도 **encouragement** ***n.*** 격려

정답 ⑤

문제풀이
Ryan은 가족, 친구들을 떠나고 싶지 않아서 높은 급여와 안정성이 보장되는 큰 신문사를 포기하고 작은 신문사를 선택한 상황을 친구인 Sarah에게 말했고, Sarah는 Ryan에게 격려와 지지의 말을 해주려 한다. 따라서 Sarah가 Ryan에게 해 줄 수 있는 적절한 말은 ⑤ '좋은 선택이야. 인생에서 어떤 것들은 돈보다 더 중요하니까.'이다.

오답 보기 해석
① 요즘 언론계에서 직장을 찾는 것은 쉬운 일이 아니야.
② 나는 네 꿈이 Hush-Hush에서 일하는 거였다고 생각했어.
③ 너는 Courier Crossing의 제안을 받아 들여서는 안 됐어.
④ 나는 돈을 위해 이 일을 하는 게 아냐. 내가 그것을 좋아하기 때문에 하고 있어.

총 어휘 수 156

16 담화 목적 / 17 세부 내용 파악

소재 어버이날 선물세트에 관한 홍보

듣기 대본 해석

남: 부모님들 안녕하세요. Franklin 대학교의 매년 열리는 어버이날 행사에 오신 것을 환영합니다. 여러분께서는 이러한 명문 대학생들의 학부모님들이시기에 우리는 여러분들께 1927년에 이 대학교가 설립된 이후로 여기 대학교의 전통인 우리의 어버이날 선물세트를 구매할 기회를 제공합니다. 이 선물세트에서 여러분들은 여러분들과 여러분의 사랑하는 사람들을 위한 범퍼 스티커, 펜, 열쇠고리를 보실 수 있을 것입니다. 학생 자치회의 회원들은 또한 올해의 축제 동안 여러분들이 즐길 수 있는 수제 쿠키를 구웠습니다. 우리의 어버이날 선물세트는 학생단체와 커뮤니티 사업에 의해 만들어졌습니다. 이러한 선물세트들을 만드는 것을 돕는 것 이외에, 이 사업은 또한 200달러 상당의 쿠폰 책자도 준비했습니다. 이 소책자에서 여러분은 Franklin City 카페, Rainbow 제과점, Echo Lanes 볼링장, 그리고 The Downtown 식당의 유용한 쿠폰을 찾을 수 있을 것입니다. 어버이날 선물세트의 모든 수익금은 Spring Fest (축제)와 해마다 열리는 재능 대회 같은 캠퍼스 전역의 이벤트에 유익하게 사용됩니다. 만약 여러분들이 어버이날 선물세트 중 하나를 구매하고 싶다면, 방문객 센터의 안내 데스크로 오세요. 우리의 멋진 캠퍼스에서 어버이날 행사에 참여해 주셔서 감사합니다.

어휘
annual *a.* 매년의, 연례의 **kit** *n.* 선물세트 **on top of** ~외에, ~뿐만 아니라 **booklet** *n.* 소책자 **proceeds** *n.* 돈(수익금)
〈문제〉 **faculty** *n.* 교수단 **upcoming** *a.* 다가오는, 곧 있을

정답 16 ② 17 ⑤

문제풀이
16 남자는 어버이날 행사에 참여한 학부모들에게 어버이날 선물세트를 판매하기 위해 홍보하고 있다. 따라서 남자가 하는 말의 목적은 ② '어버이날 선물세트 판매를 홍보하려고'이다.
17 쿠폰이 있는 곳으로 카페, 제과점, 볼링장, 식당은 언급되었지만 수영장은 언급되지 않았으므로 정답은 ⑤ '수영장'이다.

오답 보기 해석
16
① 지역사회 사업들을 광고하기 위해
③ 부모님들을 교수단 멤버들에게 소개하려고
④ 다가오는 대학교 이벤트를 부모님께 알리기 위하여
⑤ 환영 선물세트를 부모님들께 판매할 자원봉사자를 모집하려고

총 어휘 수 195

DICTATION ANSWERS

01 running the air conditioner
02 You look very immersed in something
03 maintain relationships / stick with our own kind / more likely to become friends / outside of their race
04 I have a headache / change the door / make more sense / install a revolving door / The air gets trapped
05 to stay healthy / you can have a decent breakfast / make the shake a little tastier / for its nutritional value
06 You've really outdone yourself / plenty of time to prepare / working on getting a permit / Food and Drinks Provided
07 you're aware / planned on coming down to watch / swing by the house / drop it off at school
08 It's no big deal / what's on your mind / what happened at the meeting
09 What's your nightly rate / be coming in two cars / we charge more for / take the electricity hookup
10 summer internship program / opened up internship positions for programming / try out character design
11 explore its facilities / give you their first-hand experience / will run until noon / perform a play
12 were interested in starting a garden / try to cook my own food
13 letter of recommendation / by the end of the week / are submitted online / email it to me
14 Did you have fun volunteering / deal with all those children / join you next time / have the patience / The only thing I could do
15 two job offers from well-respected newspapers / a small tabloid newspaper / After much deliberation / wants to offer words of encouragement
16-17 since it was founded in / valuable coupons from / pick up one of the Parents' Day kits

35 수능영어듣기 실전모의고사

본문 p.212

01 ②	02 ②	03 ③	04 ①	05 ③	06 ④
07 ②	08 ②	09 ③	10 ③	11 ①	12 ⑤
13 ①	14 ⑤	15 ④	16 ②	17 ③	

01 짧은 대화의 응답

소재 연회 준비

듣기 대본 해석

여: 안녕, Evan. 오늘 저녁 연회 준비하는 거 끝났어?
남: 대부분의 준비는 끝났는데 어떤 케이크를 만들지 정하지 못했어.
여: Jane한테 물어보지 그래? 자기가 도와줄 수 있다고 하던데.
남: ② 그거 좋은 생각이다. Jane은 정말 훌륭한 제빵사야.

어휘

banquet ***n.*** 연회 **preparation** ***n.*** 준비

정답 ②

문제풀이

연회 케이크를 결정하지 못한 남자에게 여자가 Jane에게 물어보지 그러냐고 했을 때 적절한 응답은 ② '그거 좋은 생각이다. Jane은 정말 훌륭한 제빵사야.'이다.

오답 보기 해석

① 좋아. 그렇게 주문을 취소하면 되겠다.
③ 내가 케이크를 구우면 문제가 되지 않을 거야.
④ 그거 좋은 생각인데 난 이미 케이크를 골랐어.
⑤ 그녀가 연회에 못 온다니 정말 안타깝네.

총 어휘 수 49

02 짧은 대화의 응답

소재 스키장 가기 전 물건 챙기기

듣기 대본 해석

남: 엄마, 저 오늘 밤 Walker 산에 친구들이랑 스키 타러 가요.
여: 오늘 밤에 정말 춥대. 목도리랑 비니 꼭 챙겨.
남: 알겠어요. 제 Southback 외투를 못 찾겠어요. 혹시 보셨어요?
여: ② 방금 세탁해서 지금 (말리느라) 걸려있어.

어휘

be supposed to V ~하기로 되어 있다 〈문제〉 **extra** ***a.*** 여분의 **just in case** 만일에 대비하여

정답 ②

문제풀이

남자는 스키장에서 입을 외투를 못 찾고 있어 엄마에게 물어보고 있으므로 여자의 응답으로 가장 적절한 것은 ② '방금 세탁해서 지금 (말리느라) 걸려 있어.'이다.

오답 보기 해석

① 미안한데 Southback 외투는 너무 비싸.
③ 혹시 모르니까 여분 장갑도 챙겨갈게.
④ 아빠의 스키바지 빌려 입고 가.
⑤ 아니, 거기로는 스키 타러 가면 안돼.

총 어휘 수 48

03 담화 주제

소재 일상생활에서 운동하기

듣기 대본 해석

남: 오늘 운동을 하셨나요? 모든 사람들이 운동은 건강에 좋다고 알고 있습니다. 그러나 아마 여러분은 너무 바쁘다고 그리고 단지 헬스장에 갈 시간이나 힘이 없다고 느낄 것입니다. 그러면 여러분과 같은 사람들은 무엇을 해야 할까요? 여러분의 일상의 환경을 체육관으로 바꾸도록 해보세요. 예를 들어, 가능하면 여러분은 우체국이나 식품점에 차로 가는 대신 걸어가거나 잔디를 깎기 위해 미는 잔디 깎기 기계를 사용해야 합니다. 최근의 연구는 하루의 대부분을 활동적으로 지내는 사람들이 매일 60분 체육관에서 운동하고 다른 때는 활동적이지 않게 지내는 사람들보다 10퍼센트 더 많은 에너지를 사용한다고 보여주었습니다. 하루종일 활동적으로 지내는 것이 더 쉽고 건강에 더 좋습니다. 이것은 체중감소라는 목표에 더 쉽게 도달하게 도와주기도 합니다. 여러분의 일상 생활에서 어떤 종류의 활동들이 운동이 될 수 있을까요?

어휘

surroundings ***n.*** 환경 **grocery store** 식료품점 **lawn mower** 잔디 깎는 기계 **indicate** ***v.*** 나타내다, 보여주다 **gym** ***n.*** (학교 등의) 체육관 (=gymnasium) **meet** ***v.*** 충족시키다

정답 ③

문제풀이

남자는 체육관에서 한 시간 운동하고 움직이지 않는 사람들보다 일상 생활에서 활동적으로 움직이는 것이 더 운동이 된다고 이야기하고 있으므로, 강의의 주제는 ③ '일상 생활에서 운동할 수 있는 방법을 찾아라.'이다.

오답 보기 해석

① 너무 많은 운동은 건강에 안 좋을 수 있다.
② 영양사에게 식이요법에 대해 말해라.
④ 식이요법과 운동을 같이 하라.
⑤ 매일 운동할 시간을 만들어라.

총 어휘 수 150

04 의견

소재 장난감이 가지고 있는 성 고정관념

듣기 대본 해석

남: 안녕, Katie. 너 크리스마스 쇼핑 했니?
여: 물론이지. 아버지 드릴 콘서트 DVD하고, 어머니 드릴 화분, 그리고 사촌한테 줄 캐릭터 인형을 샀어.
남: 멋지다. 난 어렸을 때 캐릭터 인형 좋아했는데. 분명 그 남자아이가 아주 좋아할 거야.
여: 왜 내 사촌이 남자애라고 생각하는데?
남: 그럼 여자 사촌 주려고 캐릭터 인형을 샀다는 얘기야?
여: 그렇지. 실제로 그 여자애가 캐릭터 인형 가지고 노는 걸 좋아하거든.
남: 음... 난 남자 애들만 가지고 노는 줄 알았지. 여자 애들은 인형을 가지고 놀잖아.
여: 나도 그렇게 생각했거든. 처음에는 좀 당황스러웠는데 그 아이가 얼마나 좋아하는지 알게 되니까 성에 대한 고정관념에 대해서 마음을 열게 됐지.
남: "성에 대한 고정관념"이 뭐야?
여: 그건 사회가 남자와 여자에 대해서 정상적이라고 여기는 것들이야. 내 생각에는 남자 애들이 여자아이 장난감을 가지고 놀거나 그 반대도 괜찮아.
남: 난 여태까지 그런 생각을 전혀 해본 적이 없어.
여: 나도 그래. 하지만 내 사촌이 그걸 생각해 보게 한 거지.

어휘

action figure (영화나 만화 등에 나온) 영웅이나 캐릭터 인형 **confuse** ***v.*** 혼란시키다 **gender stereotype** 성 고정관념 **perceive** ***v.*** 인지하다 **vice versa** 거꾸로, 반대로

정답 ①

문제풀이
여자는 캐릭터 인형을 좋아하는 여자 사촌을 통해서 성에 대한 고정관념에 대해 마음을 열게 되었다고 했으므로 정답은 ① '장난감에 대해 가지고 있는 성 고정관념을 없애야 한다.'이다.

총 어휘 수 166

05 장소 파악

소재 오래된 스파게티 집

듣기 대본 해석
여: 우와! 여기 되게 붐빈다. 누구 유명한 사람 왔어? 촬영 기사들 봐봐.
남: 지역 방송국에서 왔나 봐.
여: 여기가 뭐가 그렇게 특별한데?
남: 여기 스파게티가 아주 유명해. 주인 집안의 비밀 조리법을 쓴대. 증조할머니로부터 전승된 거야.
여: 와! 그럼 여기 꽤 오래 됐나 보네?
남: 응, 4대 동안 있었으니까. 거의 100년 됐다고 들었어.
여: 굉장하다. 저 스파게티 먹어봐야겠다.
남: 여기에 대해서 좋은 소문 많이 들었어. 봐! 저기 주인이 인터뷰하는 것 같아.
여: 땀 흘리는 것 봐. 엄청 긴장했나 봐.
여: 너도 인터뷰하면 긴장되지 않겠어?

어휘
recipe ***n.*** 요리법, 레시피 **pass down** ~에게 물려주다, 전해주다
generation ***n.*** 세대 **incredible** ***a.*** 믿을 수 없는, 믿기 힘든

정답 ③

문제풀이
오래되고 유명한 스파게티 집에 기자들이 촬영하러 와 있는 상황이므로 두 사람이 대화하고 있는 장소는 ③ '음식점'이다.

총 어휘 수 123

06 그림의 세부 내용 파악

소재 파티룸 꾸미기

듣기 대본 해석
여: 이봐, Taylor, 네가 보고 있는 게 뭐야?
남: 우리 기관으로 오는 Ryan과 Sarah를 환영해 주기 위한 파티룸 사진이야. 이제 막 장식을 마쳤어.
여: 멋지네. 좋은 시간이 될 거야.
남: 물론이지. 그런데 이 룸에 대해 어떻게 생각해?
여: 근사해 보여. 뒤 벽에 있는 배너가 엄청 크다!
남: 그래, 나는 좀 더 작을 거라고 생각했지만, 저것도 멋있는 것 같아. 오른쪽 코너에 있는 풍선은 어떻게 생각해?
여: 멋진 솜씨인 것 같아. 난 거기에 '환영합니다'라고 쓰인 게 마음에 들어. 음식을 위해서 왼쪽에 세 개의 테이블이 있는 거니?
남: 아니야. 우리는 뷔페를 하지 않아. 저것들은 손님이랑 Sarah의 지지자들을 위한 것들이야.
여: 와인병이 있는 중앙 테이블은 Sarah와 Ryan을 위한 것이 틀림없군.
남: 맞아. 난 그것들을 방 가운데 두면 좋을 거라고 생각했어.
여: 분명 좋아할 거야. 풍선 아래 단은 뭐야?
남: 그건 손님 발표자들을 위한 거야. Sarah의 친구와 가족들 몇몇이 그들의 지지를 보여주기 위해 말하고 싶어 해.
여: 좋을 것 같아.

어휘
facility ***n.*** 기관, 시설 **decorate** ***v.*** 장식하다 **podium** ***n.*** 단, 지휘대

정답 ④

문제풀이
여자가 중앙 테이블에 와인병이 있다고 했는데 그림에서는 꽃병이 있으므로 정답은 ④번이다.

총 어휘 수 191

07 할 일

소재 대학 합격 소식과 집 구하기

듣기 대본 해석
[휴대폰이 울린다.]
여: 여보세요?
남: 네, Alice. 나누고 싶은 좋은 소식이 있어서 전화했어요.
여: 좋은 소식? 네가 원하는 대학에 합격한 거니?
남: 맞아요! 막 집에 왔는데 우편함에 Princeton에서 온 입학 허가서가 있었어요.
여: 정말 훌륭하구나. 나는 네가 합격할 것이라는 것을 잠시도 의심한 적이 없단다. 축하해!
남: 정말 감사해요. Alice, 저를 도와주실 수 있으신지 궁금해요.
여: 물론이지. 내가 어떻게 도와줄까?
남: 학기가 시작하기 전에 시간은 많지 않고 해야 할 일은 많아서 제가 머물 곳을 찾지 못할 것 같아요.
여: 내가 아파트를 찾아주길 바라는 거니?
남: 그러면 좋을 것 같아요. 그 근처에 오래 사셨으니 당신의 판단을 신뢰할 수 있어요.
여: 좋아. 사실 좀 재미있을 것 같구나. 어떤 종류의 집을 원하니?
남: 침실 하나 딸린 아파트를 원해요. 저는 너무 큰 곳을 찾지는 않지만, 원룸보다는 넓은 공간이면 좋겠어요.
여: 그래, 내가 몇 군데 좋은 곳을 찾는 대로 다시 연락할게.
남: 최고예요. 도와주셔서 다시 한 번 감사드려요.
여: 나도 기쁘단다.

어휘
acceptance letter 합격통지서 **wonder** ***v.*** 궁금해하다
judgment ***n.*** 판단, 심사 **studio** ***n.*** 원룸 (아파트) **option** ***n.*** 선택권
〈문제〉 **college application** 대학 지원서

정답 ②

문제풀이
남자는 여자에게 대학 합격 소식을 알리고 대학교 근처에 자신의 아파트를 알아봐 달라고 부탁하고 있으므로 여자가 남자를 위해 할 일은 ② '그가 아파트 찾는 것을 도와주기'이다.

오답 보기 해석
① 도시를 구경시켜 주기
③ 기숙사에 대해 물어보기
④ 파티 전에 집 청소하기
⑤ 대학 지원서 작성 도와주기

총 어휘 수 203

08 이유

소재 일찍 일어난 이유

듣기 대본 해석
남: 누나, 좋은 아침이야. 무슨 요리해?
여: 오믈렛을 요리하고 있어. 일찍 일어났네. 어젯밤에 늦게까지 밖에 있어서 자고 있을 줄 알았는데.
남: 응. 친구들과 함께 학년 말을 축하하러 나갔었지.
여: 피곤하겠구나. 좀 더 자지 그러니. 여름방학 첫 날이잖아.

남: 그러고 싶지만, 오늘 아빠와 산에 하이킹 가기로 했거든.
여: 아, 그래서 일찍 일어났구나.
남: 우리랑 같이 가자. 아빠와 단둘이 가는 건 좀 어색해. 둘이 무슨 이야기를 해야 할지 모르겠어.
여: 나도 도와주고 싶지만 이미 계획이 있어. Brandon과 함께 영화를 보러 가기로 했거든.
남: 오, 아냐, 괜찮아. 엄마 어디 계신지 알아? 엄마한테 등산용 지팡이를 빌려야 하는데.
여: 식료품점에 가셨어. 곧 오실 거야.
남: 알았어. 내가 찾아보는 것 보다 엄마를 기다리는 게 나을 것 같아.

어휘
celebrate ***v.*** 기념하다, 축하하다 **awkward** ***a.*** 어색한 **borrow** ***v.*** 빌리다

정답 ②

문제풀이
여자가 어제 늦게 잤으니 더 자라고 권유했는데, 남자는 아빠와 산에 하이킹을 가기로 해서 일찍 일어났다고 말하고 있으므로 정답은 ② '아빠와 하이킹을 가기 위해서'이다.

총 어휘 수 164

09 숫자

소재 여자친구를 위한 기념품 구입

듣기 대본 해석
여: 오, 안녕하세요. 무엇을 도와드릴까요?
남: 글쎄요, 제 여자친구를 위한 기념품을 사려고 하는데요. 저랑 이번 여행을 같이 못 와서 매우 속상해 했거든요.
여: 그렇군요. 어떤 것을 생각하고 계신가요?
남: 전 그녀가 매일 사용할 수 있으면서도 그녀가 소중히 느낄 수 있는 것을 원해요.
여: 태국 전통 등은 어때요? 20달러밖에 안 한답니다.
남: 좋긴 한데, 이건 조금 작지 않나요? 더 큰 건 얼마예요?
여: 그건 40달러예요. 태국 북부의 부족민에 의해 수작업으로 만들어진 것이랍니다.
남: 아름답군요. 더 큰 랜턴으로 할게요.
여: 네. 어머니나 할머니에게 줄 선물은 어때요? 이 전통 부채들을 좋아할 텐데요. 각각 5달러 밖에 안 해요. 그리고 45달러 넘게 사시면 전체 금액에서 10퍼센트를 할인해드려요.
남: 좋네요. 2개 주세요. 이것들을 선물용 포장해주실 수 있나요?
여: 죄송하지만 여기서 그 서비스를 제공하지는 않아요.
남: 괜찮아요.

어휘
treasure ***v.*** 소중히 여기다 **handcraft** ***v.*** 손으로 만들다
tribesman ***n.*** 부족(종족) 구성원 **giftwrap** ***v.*** 선물용으로 포장하다

정답 ③

문제풀이
남자는 여자친구에게 줄 선물로 40달러짜리 전통 등과 5달러짜리 부채 두 개를 사서 총 금액은 50달러이다. 여자는 구매액이 45달러를 넘으면 10퍼센트 할인을 해준다고 하였으므로 남자가 지불할 금액은 ③ '$45'이다.

총 어휘 수 166

10 언급 유무

소재 네팔에서의 자원봉사

듣기 대본 해석
여: Kyle, 여름방학 어땠니?
남: 정말 좋았어. 네팔에서 봉사자로 시간을 보냈어.
여: 멋지다. 얼마나 오래 있었니?
남: 27일.
여: 와! 거기서 방학의 절반 이상을 보냈구나.
남: 응. 네팔에서 더 지냈으면 좋았을 텐데.
여: 거기서 무엇을 했니?
남: 너도 알다시피, 그곳은 몇 달 전 일어난 큰 지진으로 고통을 겪고 있어. 나는 병원에서 부상당한 사람들을 돌봐 줬고 변두리에 음식과 물을 전달해 줬어.
여: 멋지다. 스스로 보람을 느꼈겠구나. 다른 자원봉사자들은 모두 미국에서 왔니?
남: 아니, 우리 그룹에는 다른 미국인 한 명만 있었고, 나머지는 세계 여러 나라에서 왔어.
여: 나도 겨울방학 때는 자원봉사를 하고 싶은데. 그것을 어떻게 신청하지?
남: 내가 이메일로 관련 정보를 보내줄게. 먼저 웹사이트에 등록하고 네가 어떤 종류의 일에 자원봉사하고 싶은지 선택하면 돼.
여: 쉬워 보이네. 고마워.

어휘
volunteer ***n.*** 자원봉사, 자원봉사자 **suffer** ***v.*** 고통 받다 **outskirts** ***n.*** 변두리, 교외 **participate** ***v.*** 참가하다

정답 ③

문제풀이
두 사람은 자원봉사의 장소, 기간, 활동 내용, 신청 방법에 관해 언급했지만 주최 기관에 대한 언급은 하지 않았으므로 정답은 ③ '주최 기관'이다.

총 어휘 수 165

11 내용 일치 · 불일치

소재 필드하키 소개

듣기 대본 해석
남: 독특한 스포츠에 관심이 있으신가요? 그렇다면 필드하키를 알아보세요. 필드하키는 전 세계에서 하고 있지만 아이스 하키가 우위인 캐나다와 미국에서는 인기가 덜합니다. 그러나, 필드하키는 전 세계적으로 훨씬 더 유명합니다. 사실, 인도와 파키스탄 두 나라에서는 국민 스포츠입니다. 필드하키는 마른 땅에서 경기하는 것을 제외하면 아이스하키와 거의 비슷합니다. 경기하는 동안, 골키퍼는 몸의 어떤 부분으로든 공을 만질 수 있도록 허락되는 유일한 선수이고, 반면에 필드선수들은 스틱의 평평한 부분으로 공을 쳐야 합니다. 이 스포츠는 시작하는 데 그렇게 비싸지 않고 경기 할 스케이트장이 필요 없어서 세계 대부분의 지역에서 더 이용하기 쉽기 때문에 아이스하키의 훌륭한 대안입니다. 만약에 당신이 새로운 뭔가에 도전하고 싶으시다면, 당신의 지역에서 필드하키 클럽을 찾아보세요!

어휘
unique ***a.*** 독특한, 특별한 **dominate** ***v.*** 지배하다, 우세하다
identical ***a.*** 동일한, 똑같은 **alternative** ***n.*** 대안, 선택 가능한 것
accessible ***a.*** 이용 가능한, 접근 가능한

정답 ①

문제풀이
필드하키는 전 세계적으로 인기가 있지만, 캐나다와 미국에서는 인기가 덜하다고 했으므로 정답은 ① '캐나다와 미국에서 가장 인기 있는 운동이다.'이다.

총 어휘 수 162

12 도표

소재 가족여행을 위한 차 대여

듣기 대본 해석
남: Bird 자동차 대여 센터에 오신 것을 환영합니다. 제 이름은 Gabe입니다. 무엇을 도와드릴까요?
여: 안녕하세요. 차를 대여하고 싶습니다.

남: 알겠습니다. 어떤 기종을 대여하고 싶으신가요?
여: 음, 가족여행을 갈 거라서 좀 큰 게 필요할 거예요. 다섯 명이 여행을 가요.
남: 알겠습니다. 그런 경우에는 값싸고 편리한 사이즈의 차보다 큰 차를 선택하는 게 좋습니다.
여: 짐도 아주 많아요. 그래서 좀 큰 게 필요할 거예요.
남: 그럼 미니밴을 대여하는 것을 추천하고 싶네요. 자리도 충분하고 장거리 여행을 갈 때도 아주 편안해요.
여: 미니밴은 좀 비싸네요. Raven은요? 크기는 같은데 더 싸요.
남: 죄송하지만 이 기종은 지금 대여하실 수 있는 차가 없어요.
여: 그렇군요. 그럼 어쩔 수 없이 돈 좀 더 내서 이걸로 해야겠네요.
남: 잘 생각하셨습니다.

어휘

rent ***v.*** 대여하다 **economy-sized** ***a.*** 값싸고 편리한 사이즈의 **luggage** ***n.*** 짐 **ample** ***a.*** 충분한 **pricey** ***a.*** 값비싼 **capacity** ***n.*** 용량

정답 ⑤

문제풀이

다섯 명이 여행을 간다고 했으므로 ①번과 ②번은 제외되고 짐도 많아서 큰 차를 원한다고 했으므로 ④번과 ⑤번으로 좁혀진다. 남자가 미니밴을 추천하자 여자는 좀 비싸다고 ④번에 관심을 가졌지만 이용 가능한 차가 없어서 결국 미니밴을 선택하게 됐으므로 정답은 ⑤번이다.

총 어휘 수 154

13 긴 대화의 응답

소재 과제 주제 정하는 데 도움 받기

듣기 대본 해석

남: Lucy, Miller 선생님이 내 준 과제 끝냈어?
여: 어젯밤에는 할 기회가 없었어. 큰 과제인데 어디서부터 시작해야 할지 모르겠어.
남: 빨리 시작하는 게 좋을 거야. 목요일이 마감인 것 알잖아.
여: 응. 주제로 뭘 선택해야 할 지 모르겠어.
남: 내 보고서 좀 봐. 끝나지는 않았지만 아마 결정하는 데 도움이 될 거야.
여: *[잠시 후]* 이거 정말 재미있다. 미국 인구가 그렇게 빨리 늘어났는지 몰랐어.
남: 응. 시각화하기 쉽도록 선 그래프를 사용했어.
여: 정말 잘했네. 자료 정리하느라 시간 좀 걸렸겠는데.
남: 응. 주제를 정하느라 작업을 좀 했는데, 일단 결정하고 나니까 훨씬 쉬웠어.
여: 주제를 선택하고 나서 뭘 했어?
남: 가능한 많은 자료를 찾는 데 집중했어.
여: ① 도움이 많이 됐어. 이제 주제에 대한 아이디어가 떠올랐어.

어휘

assignment ***n.*** 과제 **be due on** ~까지 마감이다 **expand** ***v.*** 확대되다, 확장시키다 〈문제〉 **misinterpret** ***v.*** 잘못 이해하다

정답 ①

문제풀이

남자는 과제 주제를 정하지 못하고 있는 여자에게 자신의 과제를 보여주며 주제 결정, 자료 정리, 절차 등을 말해주고 있다. 이에 대한 여자의 응답으로 가장 적절한 것은 ① '도움이 많이 됐어. 이제 주제에 대한 아이디어가 떠올랐어.'이다.

오답 보기 해석

② 내 생각에 너는 그래프를 완성하는 데 집중해야 돼.
③ 네가 분명 과제를 잘못 이해한 거 같아.
④ 네 보고서가 무엇에 관한 것인지 이해가 안 가.
⑤ 물론. 네 프로젝트 도와줄게.

총 어휘 수 176

14 긴 대화의 응답

소재 가습기 구입에 관한 의논

듣기 대본 해석

남: 여보, 기침하는 거 들었어. 괜찮아?
여: 목이 좀 건조하네. 날씨 탓인가 봐.
남: 응, 나도 코가 좀 막혀. 우리 아파트가 너무 건조한 것 같아.
여: 가습기를 사는 게 좋을 것 같아.
남: 나도 그렇게 생각해. 지난 몇 주간 하나 살까 생각하고 있었어.
여: 전에 가게에 갔을 때 몇 개를 봤어. 맘에 드는 것을 찾았어.
남: 정말? 사지 그랬어.
여: 이렇게 필요할 줄은 몰랐지.
남: 지금 가게에 가서 하나 사올게.
여: 지금은 닫았을 거야. 인터넷에서 꽤 괜찮은 것을 찾을 수 있을 거야.
남: 그렇긴 한데 인터넷으로 주문하면 올 때까지 며칠 걸릴 거잖아. 그냥 내일 가게에 가서 하나 살게.
여: 근데 우리 지금 힘들어하고 있잖아. 그때까지 어떡하지?
남: ⑤ 우리가 잠시 동안 화장실에서 샤워기를 틀어놓을 수 있어.

어휘

stuffy ***a.*** 답답한, 막힌 **humidifier** ***n.*** 가습기 **suffer** ***v.*** 시달리다, 고통 받다

정답 ⑤

문제풀이

지금 당장의 건조함을 해결하기 위해서 어떡하면 좋을지 묻는 여자의 말에 대한 대답으로 적절한 것은 ⑤ '우리가 잠시 동안 화장실에서 샤워기를 틀어놓을 수 있어.'이다.

오답 보기 해석

① 가습기를 트는 게 어떨까?
② 당신은 코가 막혀서 의사한테 가야 해.
③ 당신이 원하는 것을 온라인에서 못 찾겠어.
④ 맞아. 건조한 공기는 피부에도 너무 안 좋아.

총 어휘 수 161

15 상황에 적절한 말

소재 자신감을 잃은 골키퍼 친구에게 조언해주기

듣기 대본 해석

여: Charles와 Jack은 JLA 축구단의 공동주장으로 뽑혔습니다. 첫 경기가 조만간 있을 예정이고 축구팀은 하루에 두 시간씩 훈련합니다. Charles는 팀의 골키퍼인데 요즘 따라 훈련 중에 골을 먹히는 일이 빈번해졌습니다. 그의 팀과 학교는 그가 상대편 팀이 점수 내는 것을 막아줄 것을 기대하고 있습니다. Charles는 팀원들로부터 많은 부담을 느끼게 되고 Jack에게 팀을 탈퇴하고 싶다고 말을 합니다. Jack은 Charles에게 그가 잘할 수 있고 그 누구도 완벽하지 않다는 것을 말해주고 싶어합니다. 이러한 상황에서 Jack은 Charles에게 어떤 말을 할까요?
Jack: ④ 우리 모두는 실수를 해. 넌 이번 게임에서 잘 할 거야.

어휘

goalie ***n.*** 골키퍼 **lately** ***ad.*** 최근에, 얼마 전에 **count on** ~를 믿다 **pressure** ***n.*** 압력, 부담 **reassure** ***v.*** 안심시키다

정답 ④

문제풀이

Jack은 연습 중 자꾸 골을 먹어서 팀을 탈퇴하고 싶어하는 Charles에게 잘할 수 있다고 말하려 하므로 적절한 말은 ④ '우리 모두는 실수를 해. 넌 이번 게임에서 잘 할 거야.'이다

오답 보기 해석
① 오늘 우리가 정말로 이겼다는 게 믿어지지가 않아!
② 너 도대체 왜 그래? 또 그들에게 점수를 내줬잖아!
③ 넌 더 열심히 할 필요가 있어. 우리는 이번 게임에서 질 거야.
⑤ 시즌이 거의 끝났어. 한 게임만 더 열심히 하자.

총 어휘 수 119

16 담화 주제 / 17 세부 내용 파악

소재 인간에게는 없는 동물의 여러 가지 감각들

듣기 대본 해석

남: West Town 동물원에 오신 여러분 모두를 환영합니다. 제 이름은 Frank Berger이고 저는 동물학자입니다. 저는 오늘 자연에 존재하는 감각들에 대해서 여러분들께 말씀드리고자 합니다. 누구든지 인간은 기본적으로 5가지의 감각인 시각, 후각, 촉각, 미각, 청각을 가지고 있다는 것을 압니다. 동물은 어떻습니까? 그들도 인간처럼 똑같은 감각을 가졌나요? 몇몇 동물은 인간보다 더 강력한 감각을 지니고 있고 몇몇은 인간이 지니고 있지 않은 감각을 가지고 있습니다. 비둘기를 예를 들어 보겠습니다. 비둘기는 지구의 자기장과 조화되어 있습니다. 그들은 비록 그들이 수백 마일 떨어진 곳으로 옮겨지더라도 그들의 집으로 가는 길을 찾을 수 있습니다. 그것이 전서구가 과거에 메시지를 보내는 데 사용된 이유입니다. 연어도 마찬가지로 알을 낳기 위해 그들의 출생지로 다시 돌아오는 길을 찾기 위해 지구의 자기장을 이용합니다. 바다거북도 그들이 태어난 해안가로 돌아오기 위해 비슷한 기법을 사용합니다. 몇몇의 뱀들 특히 독사는 적외선 시력을 가지고 있는데, 그들은 그들의 먹이를 식별하기 위해 적외선 시력을 사용합니다. 상어는 먹이의 근육 수축으로부터 나오는 전기를 감지할 수 있습니다. 동물계는 정말로 장대합니다. 이러한 놀라운 동물들 중 몇몇을 살펴보도록 하겠습니다.

어휘
zoologist ***n.*** 동물학자 **be in tune with** ~와 리듬이 맞다 **magnetic field** 자기장 **homing** ***a.*** 귀소성이 있는, 제 집에 돌아오는 **lay eggs** 알을 낳다 **vision** ***n.*** 시력 **prey** ***n.*** 먹이 **contraction** ***n.*** 수축, 축소 **animal kingdom** 동물계 **magnificent** ***a.*** 장대한, 훌륭한

정답 16 ② 17 ③

문제풀이
16 남자는 인간에게는 없는 여러 가지 감각을 가진 동물들의 예를 들면서 이야기를 하고 있으므로 정답은 ② '인간들에게서 발견되지 않는 동물의 감각들'이다.
17 비둘기, 연어, 바다거북, 뱀, 상어에 대한 언급은 했지만 박쥐에 대한 언급은 없으므로 정답은 ③ '박쥐'이다.

오답 보기 해석
16
① 동물들이 집으로 다시 돌아가는 길을 찾는 방법
③ 동물들이 먹이를 식별하기 위해 사용하는 방법들
④ 동물들에 관한 과학적 연구를 하는 것의 이점
⑤ 항해를 위해 전자기장을 이용하는 동물들

총 어휘 수 185

DICTATION ANSWERS

01 finished preparing for / what kind of cake to make
02 going skiing / It's supposed to be really cold
03 Try turning your everyday surroundings into / Recent studies indicate that / your health to stay active all day
04 likes playing with action figures / about gender stereotypes / perceives as normal for males and females
05 It was passed down from / Look how much he's sweating / Wouldn't you be nervous
06 We just finished decorating it / in the right corner / it would be nice to put them
07 there was an acceptance letter / I can trust your judgment / What type of place are you looking for
08 you stayed out so late / hike the mountain / Going alone with Dad is a bit awkward
09 what do you have in mind / she can treasure / How much for the bigger one / we don't offer that service
10 That's more than half of the vacation / they suffered a major earthquake / care of the injured / do some volunteering during winter vacation
11 where ice hockey dominates / it's played on a field of grass / with the flat side of their stick / making it more accessible to
12 an economy-sized car / It has the same capacity / available at the moment
13 where to begin / the population of the United States expanded so quickly / make it easier to visualize
14 my nose is feeling stuffy / we should buy a humidifier / a great deal on the Internet
15 has been allowing a lot of goals / to keep the other team from scoring / under a lot of pressure
16-17 people have five basic senses / even if they're taken hundreds of miles away / Earth's magnetic fields / identify their prey

대학수학능력시험 대비 모의평가 1회

01 ③	02 ⑤	03 ①	04 ③	05 ③	06 ④
07 ④	08 ③	09 ②	10 ③	11 ③	12 ⑤
13 ④	14 ⑤	15 ④	16 ①	17 ④	

01 짧은 대화의 응답

소재 DVD 더 늦게 돌려주기

듣기 대본 해석

여: Dylan, 지난주에 네가 나에게 빌려준 DVD 필요하니?
남: 글쎄, 지금은 필요 없는데 이번 주말에 볼 계획이야.
여: 나는 아직 볼 기회가 없었어. 목요일에 너에게 돌려줘도 되겠니?
남: ③ 문제 없어. 토요일까지 그것을 볼 시간이 없거든.

어휘

〈문제〉 **highly** ***ad.*** 매우, 대단히 **recommend** ***v.*** 추천하다

정답 ③

문제풀이

여자는 남자로부터 지난주에 빌린 DVD를 아직 못 봐서 목요일에 돌려줘도 되는지 남자에게 묻고 있으므로 이에 대한 가장 적절한 남자의 응답은 ③ '문제 없어. 토요일까지 그것을 볼 시간이 없거든.'이다.

오답 보기 해석

① 나는 진짜 그 영화를 재미있게 봤어. 그 영화를 강력히 추천해.
② 도서관에서 빌릴 수 있는지 알아봐야 할 거야.
④ 너 벌써 봤구나. 이렇게 빨리 돌려받을지는 예상하지 못했는걸.
⑤ 정말 미안한데, 며칠 더 DVD를 가지고 있어야 할 것 같아.

총 어휘 수 59

02 짧은 대화의 응답

소재 조언 부탁하기

듣기 대본 해석

남: Wilson 선생님, 제가 사회 과목 프로젝트에 대해 조언을 부탁드려도 괜찮을까요?
여: Tim, 정말 그러고 싶지만, 나는 지금은 너무 중요한 일을 하는 중이란다.
남: 그럼 제가 이따가 다시 올까요?
여: ⑤ 그래, 오후 3시경에 다시 오렴.

어휘

social studies (학교 교과로서의) 사회 〈문제〉 **give ~ a hand** ~를 도와주다

정답 ⑤

문제풀이

사회 과목 프로젝트에 대한 조언을 구하는 남자에게 여자는 지금은 중요한 일을 하는 중이라 했다. 남자가 이따가 다시 오면 되는지 묻는 데 대한 적절한 응답은 ⑤ '그래, 오후 3시경에 다시 오렴.'이다.

오답 보기 해석

① 이것 좀 도와주겠니?
② 나는 사실 지금 회의를 가야 해.
③ 나는 사회 과목을 전혀 잘하지 않았어.
④ 너는 항상 좋은 충고를 해주는구나.

총 어휘 수 46

03 담화 목적

소재 천문대 관측 프로그램 안내

듣기 대본 해석

남: 여러분은 은하계와 여러분이 가장 좋아하는 별자리를 보고 싶으십니까? 그렇다면 여러분의 다음 주말 여행 목적지를 Lone Star 천문대로 잡아 보십시오. 저희 천문대는 올해 5월 31일부터 10월 1일까지 수요일부터 일요일까지, 오후 1시부터 오후 8시 30분까지 개관합니다. Lone Star 천문대에서 제공하는 모든 프로그램은 일반인들에게 개방되어 있고 완전히 무료로 참여할 수 있으며 예약을 하실 필요도 없습니다. 오후에는 태양을 관측하실 수 있고 여러 종류의 망원경 전시도 보실 수 있습니다. 저녁 시간에 방문객들은 밤하늘과 모든 별, 먼 곳에 있는 은하수를 보실 수 있는 기회를 갖습니다. 보다 즐거운 방문이 되시도록 여러분들께 천문대를 안내해 드리는 천문학자들이 항상 상주해 있습니다. 이번 여름에 여러분들을 보기를 희망합니다!

어휘

constellation ***n.*** 별자리, 성좌 **observatory** ***n.*** 천문대 **destination** ***n.*** 목적지, 도착지 **reservation** ***n.*** 예약 **telescope** ***n.*** 망원경 **display** ***n.*** 전시 **galaxy** ***n.*** 은하계, 은하수 **astronomer** ***n.*** 천문학자

정답 ①

문제풀이

남자는 천문대의 운영 시간과 프로그램 소개 및 이용 방법 등을 언급하며 천문대 관측 프로그램에 대해 안내하고 있으므로 정답은 ① '천문대의 관측 프로그램에 대해 안내하려고'이다.

총 어휘 수 136

04 대화 주제

소재 생체 리듬

듣기 대본 해석

여: Bill, 너는 오후보다 아침에 더 에너지가 넘쳐 보여.
남: 그래. 오늘 오후는 정말 힘들었어. Field 선생님의 수학 수업 시간에 집중을 할 수가 없었어.
여: 정말? 나는 네가 그분 수업을 굉장히 좋아한다고 생각했어.
남: 그래. 하지만 나는 오후에는 힘이 하나도 없어. 어떤 것에도 집중할 수가 없어.
여: 그건 생체 리듬의 문제라고 생각해. 나는 오후에 집중이 잘되고 아침에는 힘이 하나도 없어.
남: 우리 둘은 다른 리듬을 가지고 있구나.
여: 맞아. 너는 아침형 인간이야.
남: 그럼 너는 오후형 인간이겠구나.
여: 그래. 모든 사람의 생체 시계는 조금씩 달라.
남: 대단한 걸!
여: 응, 나도 그렇게 생각해. 우리 모두 자신들이 공부한 것에서 최대의 것을 얻기 위해서는 자신의 생체 시계에 맞춰서 공부를 해야 해.
남: 나도 동의해. 나는 아침에 더 많이 공부하도록 노력해야겠다.

어휘

struggle ***v.*** 고투하다 **concentrate** ***v.*** 집중하다 **biological rhythm** 생체 리듬, 바이오리듬 **according to** ~에 따르면 **benefit** ***v.*** ~에게 이익을 가져다 주다, 이익을 얻다

정답 ③

문제풀이

남자는 오후보다 아침에 집중이 잘되고 반대로 여자는 오후에 집중이 잘된다고 하면서 그 이유가 각자 다른 생체 리듬 때문이라고 말하고 있다. 마지막에 생체 리듬에 맞춰 공부하면 최대의 것을 얻을 수 있다는 말이 있으므로 두 사람이 하는 대화의 주제로 가장 적절한 것은 ③ '생체 리듬에 따른 학습 능률'이다.

총 어휘 수 145

05 대화자의 관계 파악

소재 럭비팀 주장의 비행 여행

듣기 대본 해석

남: 안녕하세요. 마실 것 좀 드릴까요?
남: 물 한 잔만 주세요.
여: 네. *[잠시 후]* 여기 있습니다. 오! 당신은 럭비선수 아니신가요?
남: 맞아요. 저는 국가대표팀의 주장입니다.
여: 그렇게 생각했어요. 만나서 반가워요. 저는 정말 팬이에요.
남: 그래요? 지지해주셔서 감사해요.
여: 제가 당신에게 서비스를 제공하게 되다니 놀라워요. 저희는 아주 많은 유명인사 승객들을 만나진 않거든요. 저는 당신이 토너먼트에서 경기하기 위해 미국으로 가신다고 들었어요. 이게 그 여행이군요, 맞죠?
남: 맞아요. 저희는 미국에서 한 달 조금 넘게 머물 겁니다.
여: TV에서 경기를 꼭 보고 싶어요. 뭔가가 필요하시면 주저하지 말고 부르세요.
남: 감사합니다. 그런데 Los Angeles에 도착하려면 얼마나 남았나요?
여: 벌써 다섯 시니까, 약 네 시간 후에 도착할 거예요.
남: 그렇군요. 저, 만약 땅콩 있으면 좀 주셨으면 합니다.
여: 물론이죠. 여기 있습니다. 즐거운 비행 되시길 바랍니다.

어휘

captain ***n.*** 주장, 선장 **celebrity** ***n.*** 유명인사 **look forward to** ~을 기대하다 **match** ***n.*** 경기, 시합 **hesitate** ***v.*** 주저하다 **touch down** 착륙하다 **flight** ***n.*** 비행

정답 ③

문제풀이

여자는 남자에게 물을 갖다 주고 비행 시간도 알려주는 것으로 보아 비행기 승무원이고, 남자는 비행기에 탄 승객으로서 국가대표팀의 주장이므로 정답은 ③ '승무원 — 승객'이다.

총 어휘 수 169

06 그림의 세부 내용 파악

소재 공원으로 간 소풍

듣기 대본 해석

여: 너 지금 뭐 보고 있어, Jeff?
남: 그냥 지난주에 찍은 사진들을 보고 있었어. 나 소풍 갔었거든.
여: 정말 재미 있었겠다. 사진에 있는 게 너희 가족이지?
남: 물론이지.
여: 나무 아래 자고 있는 저 사람들은 누구야?
남: 잘 모르겠어. 그냥 공원에 있던 모르는 사람들이야. 벤치에서 책을 읽고 있는 분이 우리 엄마야.
여: 그렇구나. 너한테 원반을 던지는 분이 네 아버지시겠구나.
남: 맞아. 아빠랑 나는 공원에서 게임 하는 것을 좋아해.
여: 아버지랑 너랑 둘이 정말 많이 닮았어.
남: 그런 소리 많이 들었어.
여: 왼쪽에 바비큐를 담당하고 있는 사람은 누구야?
남: 우리 할아버지셔. 할아버지께서는 생선을 요리하고 계셔.
여: 또 여기 있는 사람은 누구야? 자전거를 타고 있는 네 여동생 Emma는 알겠는데 그녀를 쫓아가고 있는 게 누구지?
남: 그녀는 내 사촌이야. 그녀와 내 여동생은 서로 친해서 항상 붙어 다녀.
여: 사랑스럽다.
남: 정말 그래. 나는 소풍이 좋아. 다음 주에 또 가고 싶어.

어휘

go on a picnic 소풍가다 **alike** ***a.*** (아주) 비슷한 **man** ***v.*** 일하다, 담당하다 **hang out** (~에서) 많은 시간을 보내다 **adorable** ***a.*** 사랑스러운

정답 ④

문제풀이

대화에서는 왼쪽에 할아버지께서 바비큐를 하고 있다고 했는데 낚시를 하고 있으므로 그림과 일치하지 않는다. 따라서 정답은 ④번이다.

총 어휘 수 179

07 부탁한 일

소재 부모님의 결혼기념일 이벤트 준비

듣기 대본 해석

여: Nate, 이번 주말에 엄마 아빠 결혼 기념일인 거 알지?
남: 완전히 잊고 있었어. 알려줘서 고마워.
여: 좀 큰 기념일이야. 결혼하신 지 30년 될 거거든. 뭔가 좀 큰 걸 해야 할 것 같아.
남: 나 선물 같은 것 잘 못 골라. 같이 가서 좀 특별하고 큰 걸 사다 드리면 되겠다.
여: 깜짝 파티가 더 나을 것 같아.
남: 그거 좋다. 레스토랑에서 하자. 파티 하기에 좋은 레스토랑 알아?
여: 글쎄, 엄마 아빠가 가장 좋아하는 데는 Turoni's Pasta야.
남: 나 거기 정말 좋아해. 네가 토요일에 파티룸 예약할래?
여: 알아볼게. 또 다른 것도 하면 좋을 것 같지 않아?
남: 지금까지 같이 찍어 온 사진으로 콜라주 만드는 건 어때?
여: 좋은 생각이야. 굉장히 좋아하실 거야.

어휘

anniversary ***n.*** 기념일 **reminder** ***n.*** (이미 잊었거나 잊고 싶은 것을) 상기시키는(생각나게 하는) 것 **collage** ***n.*** 콜라주(색종이나 사진 등의 조각들을 붙여 그림을 만드는 미술 기법)

정답 ④

문제풀이

남자는 선물보다 깜짝 파티가 더 낫겠다는 여자의 의견에 동의하며 여자에게 부모님 결혼 기념일에 파티룸 예약을 부탁하였으므로 정답은 ④ '파티룸 예약하기'이다.

오답 보기 해석

① 휴일 기념하기
② 콜라주 만들기
③ 새 디지털 카메라 사기
⑤ 특별한 것 사기

총 어휘 수 145

08 이유

소재 아빠의 심부름

듣기 대본 해석

여: Logan, 정말 미안하지만 도서관에 같이 못 갈 것 같아.
남: 정말? 우리 거의 다 왔는데. 무슨 일 있어?
여: 응, 아빠가 방금 전화하셨는데 내가 오늘 내 동생을 돌봐줬으면 하셔.
남: 그럼 너 지금 집으로 가야 돼?
여: 곧. 집에 가기 전에 동생을 위해서 몇 가지를 사야 돼.
남: ABC 슈퍼마켓은 어때? 가는 길에 있어.
여: 거기가 편하긴 한데 내 동생이 Jojo's 피자를 정말 좋아해. 거기서 벌써 주문해서 나는 그걸 가져가기만 하면 돼.
남: 거기 피자 정말 훌륭하지. 나도 너랑 거기로 가야겠어. 나도 페퍼로니 한 조각 먹고 싶다.
여: 잘됐다. 너랑 같이 가면 좋지.
남: 난 음료수 몇 개도 사야 해.
여: Jojo's 피자 바로 옆집에 편의점이 있어. 거기에 네가 찾는 것이 있을 거야.
남: 그럴 것 같아. 가자.

어휘
look after ~을 돌보다 **convenient** ***a.*** 편리한, 간편한
pick something up ~을 사다, ~을 찾아오다 **amazing** ***a.*** 놀라운

정답 ③

문제풀이
여자는 전화를 받고 아빠가 동생을 돌봐줬으면 한다며 필요한 것 몇 가지를 사서 집으로 가야 한다고 말하고 있다. 그러므로 정답은 ③ '아빠의 부탁으로 동생을 돌보기 위해'이다.

총 어휘 수 149

09 숫자

소재 의자 구매

듣기 대본 해석
남: 안녕하세요. 무엇을 도와드릴까요?
여: 안녕하세요. 접이식 의자를 사려고요.
남: 그렇군요. 근데 탁자 세트를 구매하시는 게 훨씬 저렴해요. 이 탁자는 의자 두 개랑 같이 나와요. 보통 500달러인데 40퍼센트 할인해 드릴 수 있어요.
여: 좀 비싸네요. 좀 더 할인해 줄 순 없나요?
남: 그게 제일 싼 가격입니다.
여: 전 의자만 필요하거든요. 저기 있는 것들은 얼마예요?
남: 각각 150달러이에요. 그런데 네 개를 사시면 30퍼센트 할인해 드려요.
여: 의자 두 개만 사려고요.
남: 그래도 원래 가격의 20퍼센트를 할인해 드려요.
여: 좋네요! 그러면 그걸로 하겠습니다. 배송 서비스도 해주나요?
남: 그럼요. 그런데 배송비는 20달러가 추가됩니다.
여: 괜찮네요. 토요일 오후에 배송해 주세요.

어휘
original ***a.*** 원래의 **delivery** ***n.*** 배달, 배송 **additional** ***a.*** 추가의

정답 ②

문제풀이
여자가 각 150달러인 의자를 2개 구매하는데 원래 가격의 20퍼센트를 할인해준다고 했으므로 240달러가 된다. 여기에 배송비가 20달러 추가된다고 했으므로 여자가 지불할 총 금액은 ② '$260'이다.

총 어휘 수 152

10 언급 유무

소재 컨벤션 일정

듣기 대본 해석
여: 안녕하세요, Stan. 총회가 오늘이라니 믿어지지가 않아요.
남: 네. 시간이 정말 빨리 가네요. 여러 달 준비했어도 여전히 걱정돼요.
여: 긴장을 풀어요. 모든 것이 다 잘될 거예요.
남: 알아요. 하지만 다시 한번 준비사항들을 점검 해보고 싶어요.
여: 네. 부의장님이 제일 먼저 발언하시는 거죠?
남: 맞아요. 그가 첫 발언자예요. 그 다음 바로 제가 프레젠테이션을 할 차례죠.
여: 네. 프레젠테이션 이후 Paul Stevenson과 회담할 거예요, 맞죠?
남: 맞아요. 그의 비서와 이 모든 준비사항에 대해 확인했나요?
여: 그럼요. 아, 잊을 뻔 했네요. 오늘 아침에 Mary와 얘기해봤는데 그녀가 당신의 프레젠테이션에서 몇 가지를 수정하길 원했어요. 그녀가 리스트를 적어서 줬어요. 어떻게 생각하세요?
남: Mary는 정말 일을 잘하죠. 그래서 난 그녀를 믿어요.
여: 알겠어요. 이제 컨벤션 센터에 점심을 먹으러 가요.

어휘
preparation ***n.*** 준비, 대비 **go over** 점검하다, 검토하다
vice president 부의장, 부통령 **make an arrangement (with)** ~와 합의에 이르다

정답 ③

문제풀이
두 사람은 오늘 남자의 일정에 대해 확인하고 있다. 부의장님의 연설, 남자의 발표, Paul Stevenson과의 회의, 점심식사에 대한 언급은 했지만 청중과의 대화는 없으므로 정답은 ③ '청중과의 대화'이다.

총 어휘 수 147

11 내용 일치 · 불일치

소재 강좌 소개

듣기 대본 해석
여: DIY Science Museum에 오신 것을 환영합니다. 이번 여름 My Little Organics라는 새롭고 신나는 프로그램을 소개하고자 합니다. 유기농 과일과 야채를 비싸지 않은 기술과 최소한의 공간을 이용해 재배하는 방법을 참가자들에게 가르쳐줄 숙련된 강사들을 초빙할 것입니다. 강좌에 필요한 모든 재료를 제공할 것입니다. 그러나 본인의 장갑은 가져오셔야 합니다. 강좌는 월요일, 수요일, 금요일 저녁 7시 그리고 일요일 오후 2시 이렇게 일주일에 네 번 열릴 겁니다. 이 프로그램은 모든 연령대에 제공되고 또한 10명이 넘는 단체는 강좌 시간을 예약해드립니다. My Little Organics 프로그램에 참가하시기 위한 수업료는 한 회당 15달러이고 단체 강좌들은 20퍼센트 할인됩니다. My Little Organics 강좌에 대해 더 궁금한 것이 있으시면 홈페이지를 참조하시거나 555-251-8956으로 전화 주십시오.

어휘
skilled instructor 숙련된 강사 **on hand** 구할 수 있는, 도움을 줄 수 있는 **organic** ***a.*** 유기농의 **minimal** ***a.*** 최소한의

정답 ③

문제풀이
전 연령에게 강좌를 제공한다고 언급되었으므로 정답은 ③ '수강할 수 있는 연령에 제한이 있다.'이다.

총 어휘 수 160

12 도표

소재 청소대행 서비스 선정

듣기 대본 해석
여: Jeff, 뭐 보고 있어?
남: 여러 사무실 청소 서비스 가격을 보고 있어. 이곳 너무 더러워졌더라.
여: 맞아. 그래서 괜찮은 데 찾았어?
남: 음, 이게 가격도 제일 괜찮고 보증도 잘 되는 것 같아.
여: 어디 보자. *[잠시 후]* 아, 창문도 닦고 바닥도 왁싱 하려고 하는구나.
남: 글쎄, 잘 모르겠어. 넌 어떻게 생각해?
여: 창문은 꼭 닦아야 해.
남: 당연하지. 바닥은 어때? 왁싱 해야겠지?
여: 우리가 이 사무실로 옮긴 이후로 한 번도 한 적 없는 것 같으니까 왁싱을 해야 한다고 생각해.
남: 그럼 이제 이 두 개 중에서 고르면 되네.
여: 철저한 서비스와 신속한 서비스는 무슨 차이야?
남: 철저한 서비스는 청소를 조심스럽게 하고 청소의 질이 좋다는 거야. 예를 들어 이 서비스는 바닥을 보호하는 특별한 처리를 해줘.

여: 그렇구나. 근데 신속한 서비스보다 좀 비싸다.
남: 맞아. 음, 여기 온 이후로 한 번도 창문이나 바닥을 청소한 적 없으니까 좀 더 비싼 걸로 하는 게 좋을 것 같아.
여: 동감이야.
남: 좋아. 전화해서 날짜를 잡을게.

어휘
guarantee ***n.*** 보증, 보장 **thorough** ***a.*** 철저한, 빈틈없는
express ***a.*** 급행의, 신속한

정답 ⑤

문제풀이
남자와 여자는 유리창 청소와 바닥 왁싱을 하기로 동의했으므로 C, E 중에서 고르면 되는데 철저한 서비스인 더 비싼 것으로 하자고 했으므로 정답은 ⑤번이다.

총 어휘 수 201

13 긴 대화의 응답

소재 24시간 여는 레스토랑

듣기 대본 해석
여: 우와! 시간 봐봐! 그만 퇴근해야 될 거 같다.
남: 나도 그 생각하고 있었어. 뭐 먹으러 가자.
여: 좋은 생각이야. 뭐 먹고 싶은 기분이야?
남: Johnny 버거는 어때?
여: 지금 별로 버거가 먹고 싶은 기분은 아니야.
남: 글쎄, 꽤 늦어서 먹을 수 있는 데가 많지가 않아.
여: 그럼 멕시코 음식은? 이 주변에 늦게까지 하는 맛있는 멕시칸 식당 알아.
남: Walking Taco's 말하는 거지?
여: 맞아. 24시간 여는 것 같아.
남: 오, 그런데 오늘 거기 지나갔는데 닫혀 있더라.
여: 정말? 왜?
남: ④ 레스토랑을 보수하고 있는 것 같아.

어휘
grab a bite 간단히 먹다 **in a mood for** ~에 마음이 내켜서, ~할 기분이 되어 〈문제〉 **renovate** ***v.*** 개조(보수)하다

정답 ④

문제풀이
24시간 여는 레스토랑인데 문이 닫혀있는 이유로 적합한 대답을 골라야 하므로 정답은 ④ '레스토랑을 보수하고 있는 것 같아.'이다.

오답 보기 해석
① 거기 곧 문 닫을 거라 우리가 서둘러야 한다고 생각해.
② 우리가 먹기 전에 일을 끝내야 해.
③ 나는 오후 8시 이후에는 아무것도 먹지 않으려고 노력하고 있어.
⑤ 거기는 도시에서 최고의 생선 타코를 팔아.

총 어휘 수 111

14 긴 대화의 응답

소재 심리학에 대한 대화

듣기 대본 해석
여: 안녕 Blake. 옆에 앉아도 될까?
남: 응. 앉아.
여: 고마워. 뭐하고 있는 거야?
남: 어제 Malcolm George의 Ed Talk에 관한 심리학 수업 보고서를 쓰고 있어. 너 그거 봤어?
여: 응. 나 거기 있었어. 선택에 관한 정말 놀라운 강의였어, 그렇지?
남: 맞아. 그의 통찰력은 정말 흥미로웠어.
여: 응. 강의를 들으니 Barry Schwartz가 생각나던데.
남: 그 사람 The Right Choice 쓴 사람 맞지?
여: 맞아. 너 심리학자 정말 많이 아는구나, Blake.
남: 응. 나는 의사결정 뒤에 숨겨진 힘들에 대해서 정말 관심이 있거든. 그것이 내가 깊게 공부한 분야야.
여: 우리 공통점이 꽤 있네. Malcolm George하고 Barry Schwartz를 아는 사람은 많지 않은데.
남: 나는 그들이 심리학에 있어서 아주 중요하다고 생각하는데 왜냐하면 그들은 왜 사람들이 그와 같은 결정을 하는가를 이해하기 위해서 많은 시간을 바쳐왔기 때문이지.
여: ⑤ 나도 완전히 동의해. 나는 더 많은 사람들이 그들이 하는 헌신을 하면 좋겠어.

어휘
psychology ***n.*** 심리학 **insight** ***n.*** 통찰력
decision-making ***n.*** 의사결정 **in common** 공통으로
〈문제〉 **put yourself in somebody's shoes** 입장 바꿔 생각해보다
dedication ***n.*** 전념, 헌신

정답 ⑤

문제풀이
두 사람은 심리학에 대해 이야기 나누고 있다. 남자가 마지막에 그들이 언급했던 심리학자들이 왜 중요하다고 생각하는지에 대해 이야기했을 때 적절한 여자의 응답은 ⑤ '나도 완전히 동의해. 나는 더 많은 사람들이 그들이 하는 헌신을 하면 좋겠어.'이다.

오답 보기 해석
① 네가 판단을 하기 전에 그들하고 입장을 바꿔서 생각해 봐.
② 나는 의사결정의 뒤에 있는 힘들에는 별로 관심이 없어.
③ 완전히 실망이야. 그 사람 강의는 절대 다시 안 들을 거야.
④ 난 주제는 별로 마음에 들지 않았는데 강연자가 흥미로웠어.

총 어휘 수 164

15 상황에 적절한 말

소재 축제를 위한 음악 연습 도움 요청

듣기 대본 해석
여: Mike는 최근에 Charlestown으로 이사 가서 Jefferson Academy에 다니기 시작했습니다. 그는 Charlestown에 사는 것이 좋고 학교 친구들 모두와 잘 지내지만 곤경에 처하게 됩니다. 학교는 일 년마다 하는 Spring Sprung 행사를 이번에 개최하는데 반에서 유일하게 Mike만 음악 곡을 연습하지 못한 것입니다. 나머지 학생들은 몇 달 간 연습을 했지만 Mike는 학교에 새로 전학 왔기 때문에 연습을 몇 주밖에 못했습니다. 그는 방과 후에 연습을 하고 싶지만 도움이 필요합니다. Mike는 공연의 총 책임자인 Smith 선생님께 도움을 요청하고 싶어 합니다. 이러한 상황에서 Mike는 Smith 선생님께 뭐라고 말할까요?
Mike: Smith 선생님, ④ 음악 곡 연습하는 것을 도와주실 수 있으세요?

어휘
predicament ***n.*** 곤경 **annual** ***a.*** 매년의, 연례의

정답 ④

문제풀이
Mike는 새로 전학 온 학교에서 열리는 축제의 음악 공연 연습을 충분히 하지 못해 Smith 선생님께 도움을 요청하려고 하므로 이에 대해 할 말로 가장 적절한 것은 ④ '음악 곡 연습하는 것을 도와주실 수 있으세요?'이다.

오답 보기 해석
① Jefferson Academy에서 잘 지내고 계신가요?
② 행사에서 저희는 어떤 곡을 연주할 건가요?
③ 저는 행사에 있을 공연을 위한 준비가 되어 있어요.
⑤ 제가 공연의 책임자가 되고 싶어요.

총 어휘 수 137

16 담화 목적 / 17 세부 내용 파악

소재 대입 추천서 작성 관련 안내

듣기 대본 해석

남: 좋은 아침입니다, Middle Brook 고등학교 학생 여러분. 저는 학업 상담자 Michael Manson입니다. 여러분 중 많은 수가 졸업반이어서 대학 입학 시험 준비와 에세이 쓰기에 여러분 대부분의 자유시간을 사용할 것입니다. 여러분이 여러분의 모든 서류를 취합할 때 여러분의 현재 선생님들 중 한 분이나 그 이상으로부터 받는 추천서를 포함할 것을 잊지 마십시오. 이 추천서들은 작성하는 데 시간이 걸리고 아마도 당신의 선생님께서 당신 것만을 작성하는 것이 아니라는 것을 명심하십시오. 따라서 당신의 선생님께 요청드리러 가기 전에 여러분 자신에 대한 세부 정보를 준비하십시오. 우리는 이 작업을 빠르고 쉽게 하기 위해 웹 페이지를 개설했습니다. 단지 우리 학교 웹사이트에 들어가셔서 웹 페이지의 오른편 상단에 있는 "Academic Guidance" 링크를 클릭하기만 하면 됩니다. 거기서 여러분이 자기 소개서와 다른 정보를 등록할 수 있게 단계별로 안내를 해줄 것입니다. 그 정보들은 선생님께서 여러분의 추천서를 작성하시는 일을 훨씬 쉽게 만들어 줍니다. 여러분이 온라인 절차를 끝낸 후 여러분의 선생님께서 추천서를 작성하는 작업을 시작하실 것입니다. 당신의 정보를 올리는 것뿐만 아니라, 추천서와 쓰기 과정에 관해 여러분이 가질 수 있는 다른 질문들에 관해 상의하기 위해 선생님과 일대일 약속을 잡는 데에 웹사이트를 이용하실 수도 있습니다. 여러분의 자기소개서 작성과 관련된 도움이 필요하시다면 샘플 자기소개서를 보실 수 있습니다. 다른 필요한 서류에 관한 정보도 또한 얻으실 수 있습니다. 더 도움이 필요하시다면, 망설이지 말고 저를 찾아 주세요.

어휘

academic advisor 학업 상담자 **current** ***a.*** 현재의 **approach** ***v.*** 다가가다, 접촉하다 **specific** ***a.*** 구체적인 **process** ***n.*** 절차 **upload** ***v.*** (정보를 네트워크상에) 올리다 **personal statement** 자기소개서 **letter of recommendation** 추천서 **regarding** ***prep.*** ~에 관한 **assistance** ***n.*** 도움 **hesitate** ***v.*** 주저하다

정답 16 ① 17 ④

문제풀이

16 대학 입시에 필요한 추천서와 자기소개서 작성을 도와주는 웹사이트가 생겼음을 알리고 어떻게 이용하면 되는지를 설명해주고 있으므로 남자가 하는 말의 목적은 ① '대입 추천서 작성을 위한 웹사이트 개통을 알리려고'이다.

17 웹사이트에서 할 수 있는 일로 학생의 자기소개서 등록, 선생님과 상담 예약, 자기소개서 샘플 참조, 필요한 서류에 관한 정보 수집은 언급되었으나, ④ '지원 대학의 경쟁률 확인'은 언급되지 않았다.

총 어휘 수 262

대학수학능력시험 대비 모의평가 2회

01 ①	02 ②	03 ①	04 ④	05 ②	06 ⑤
07 ②	08 ③	09 ②	10 ⑤	11 ③	12 ③
13 ④	14 ⑤	15 ④	16 ③	17 ③	

01 짧은 대화의 응답

소재 과제 미리 받기

듣기 대본 해석

여: 안녕하세요, Nelson 선생님. 죄송하지만, 월요일에 수업에 못 올 것 같습니다.

남: 괜찮아. 네가 토론 팀 선수권 대회에 나가는 것을 알고 있단다.

여: 맞아요. 월요일 과제를 오늘 제가 받아갈 수 있나요?

남: ① 물론이지. 내가 지금 준비해 줄게.

어휘

debate ***n.*** 토론 **assignment** ***n.*** 과제 〈문제〉 **turn in** 제출하다

정답 ①

문제풀이

남자에게 과제를 먼저 받아갈 수 있는지 물었으므로 적절한 응답은 ① '물론이지. 내가 지금 준비해 줄게.'이다.

오답 보기 해석

② 좋아. 그것들을 월요일에 너에게 줄게.
③ 아직 토론 주제를 선택하지 못했어.
④ 나는 토론에 관해서 그다지 많이 알지 못해. 미안해.
⑤ 문제없어. 먼저 오늘 그것을 제출 할 수 있어.

총 어휘 수 49

02 짧은 대화의 응답

소재 플라스틱 병 재활용

듣기 대본 해석

남: 저 오래된 플라스틱 병들 가지고 뭐 할거니?

여: 내가 생각해온 작은 프로젝트를 위해 병들을 전부 살펴봐서 재사용하고 싶은 것들을 고르고 있어.

남: 멋지다! 네가 생각했던 게 무슨 프로젝트인데?

여: ② 나는 그것들을 새 모이통을 만드는 데 쓸 거야.

어휘

go through ~을 살펴보다 〈문제〉 **bird feeder** 새 모이통

정답 ②

문제풀이

플라스틱 병을 재활용해서 무엇을 할 것인지에 대한 남자의 질문에 가장 적절한 여자의 응답은 ② '나는 그것들을 새 모이통을 만드는 데 쓸 거야.'이다.

오답 보기 해석

① 네가 왜 이 프로젝트를 그렇게 흥미로워하는지 알겠다.
③ 너의 과학 프로젝트에 그것들을 사용하자.
④ 이 오래된 병들 전부 갖다 버릴 거야.
⑤ 넌 항상 헌 병들을 재활용을 해야 해.

총 어휘 수 51

03 담화 목적

소재 학생회장 선거의 투표 참여

듣기 대본 해석

남: 안녕하세요, 여러분. 저는 학생회 대표인 Tony Brown이고, Fine Arts 학교의 3학년입니다. 여러분께서 짐작하시듯이, 저는 다가오는 학생회장 선거에 대해 여러분과 이야기를 나누고자 여기 있습니다. 먼저 저는 제가 가장 관심 있는 것을 말하려 하는데요, 그것은 바로 유권자 투표율입니다. 지난해의 투표율은 고작 28%였습니다. 믿어지십니까? 그렇게 낮은 투표율 때문에 캠퍼스에서의 생활은 결코 만족스럽지 못했습니다. 여러분께서는 학교 도서관이 최신식 시설로 보수되기를 바라십니까? 학교 식당에서 좀 더 다양한 음식을 선택하고 싶으십니까? 만약에 그렇다면 그리고 많은 다른 변화들이 일어나기 바라신다면 여러분의 권리를 행사하여 투표하십시오. 모두의 한 표 한 표가 중요하고 우리 모두가 학교를 더 나은 곳으로 만들 수 있다는 것을 항상 기억하십시오.

어휘

representative ***n.*** 대표 **election** ***n.*** 선거 **voter** ***n.*** 투표자, 유권자 **turnout** ***n.*** 투표율 **satisfactory** ***a.*** 만족스러운, 충분한 **outfit** ***v.*** 채비하다, 준비하다 **up-to-date** ***a.*** 최신의 **take place** 개최되다, 일어나다

정답 ①

문제풀이

남자는 작년 학생회장 선거의 낮은 투표율 때문에 학교 생활이 만족스럽지 않았다고 말하며 학교 도서관, 학교 식당의 개선을 원한다면 투표를 해달라고 말하고 있으므로 정답은 ① '학생들의 학생회장 선거 투표를 촉구하려고'이다.

총 어휘 수 137

04 대화 주제

소재 등산을 취미로 시작한 친구에게 필요한 조언해주기

듣기 대본 해석

여: 이번 주말에 Steven's Peak로 등산 갈 생각이야.

남: Laura, 네가 등산을 좋아하는지 몰랐어.

여: 내 새로운 취미라서 조언을 구하려고 해. 조언해 줄 것 있니?

남: 물론이지. 첫 번째로 안전이 최우선이야. 그게 가장 중요한 고려 사항이지. 예를 들어 어두워지기 전에 산을 하산할 수 있도록 항상 주의해야 해.

여: 그건 알고 있었어.

남: 그렇지. 그리고 만약 네가 길을 잃어서 돌아올 수 없을 때를 대비해서 손전등이랑 라이터, 아니면 성냥을 갖고 다니는 게 좋아.

여: 아하. 내가 길을 잃었을 때 그것들로 불을 피워서 따뜻하게 있을 수 있겠구나.

남: 불은 네가 길을 잃었을 때 다른 사람들에게 신호 보낼 때도 사용할 수 있어.

여: 그건 한 번도 생각해 본 적이 없어. 다른 조언은 없어?

남: 구급상자도 하나 갖고 다니는 게 좋아. 옛말에 "나중에 후회하는 것보다 조심하는 것이 낫다"는 말이 있잖아.

여: 알겠어. 출발하기 전에 하나 꼭 챙길게. 도와줘서 고마워.

남: 아냐. 등산 즐겁게 하고 와. 이때쯤 Steven's Peak는 경치가 정말 아름다워.

어휘

daylight ***n.*** 햇빛, 일광 **first-aid kit** 구급상자
better safe than sorry [속담] 나중에 후회하는 것보다 조심하는 것이 낫다

정답 ④

문제풀이

등산을 취미로 시작한 여자가 남자에게 조언을 구하고, 남자는 이에 대해 안전한 등산을 위해 필요한 물품들과 유의 사항을 말해주고 있으므로 대화의 주제는 ④ '안전한 등산을 위한 유의 사항'이다.

총 어휘 수 186

05 대화자의 관계 파악

소재 배심원들에 의해 유죄가 아닌 것으로 난 판결

듣기 대본 해석

여: Clinton Town 법원 청사에서 속보가 있습니다. 현장에 있는 우리의 특파원 Ron Berger에게 들어보도록 하겠습니다. 안녕하세요, Ron!
남: 안녕하세요, Stacy. 저는 지금 공무원들에게 뇌물을 준 혐의로 기소된 백만장자 기업가 Pat Parker의 재판에 대해 배심원들이 마침내 판결을 내린 Clinton Town 법원 청사에 나와있습니다.
여: 시민들이 결과에 대해 궁금해 합니다. 배심원들이 결론을 어떻게 냈습니까, Ron?
남: 뜻밖에 사태의 전환으로 Pat Parker는 뇌물 혐의에 대해 유죄가 아니라고 판결이 났습니다. 우리 모두에게 충격입니다.
여: 와! 놀랍네요. 그렇다면 배심원들이 모든 점에서 유죄가 아니라고 판결한 건가요?
남: 맞습니다. 배심원들은 검찰 측에서 제시한 증거들이 Parker의 유죄를 입증하는데 충분하지 않다고 결정 내린 겁니다.
여: 검찰 측의 반응이 있나요?
남: 네. 검찰 측에서 항소하겠다고 했습니다.
여: 흥미롭군요. 앞으로 어떻게 진행될지 지켜보고 있겠습니다. 보도에 감사합니다. Ron. *[잠시 후]* Clinton Town 법원 청사에서 배심원들이 Pat Parker의 여러 뇌물 혐의에 대해 유죄가 아니라는 판결을 내린 내용을 보도한 Channel 2의 Ron Berger였습니다. 광고 후에 이 충격적인 소식에 관한 분석과 함께 돌아오도록 하겠습니다.

어휘

breaking news 뉴스 속보 **jury** ***n.*** 배심원단 **trial** ***n.*** 재판, 공판 **guilty** ***a.*** 유죄의 **bribery** ***n.*** 뇌물수수 **prosecution** ***n.*** 기소, 고발, 검찰 측 **convict** ***v.*** 유죄를 선고하다 **file** ***v.*** (소송을) 제기하다 **appeal** ***n.*** 항소 **commercial** ***n.*** 광고 ***a.*** 상업적인

정답 ②

문제풀이

여자가 속보가 있다고 전하면서 Ron에게 들어보겠다고 했고 남자에게 질문하고 있는 것으로 보아 앵커임을 알 수 있고, 남자는 법원에서 소식을 전해주고 있으므로 기자라고 추측할 수 있다. 따라서 정답은 ② '앵커 — 기자'이다.

총 어휘 수 197

06 그림의 세부 내용 파악

소재 도서관 상황 묻기

듣기 대본 해석

여: Nolan, 도서관에 갔었니?
남: 응, 갔었어. Meagan을 찾는 거야? 내가 들어갔을 때 Meagan이 책을 읽고 있던데.
여: 도서관에 다른 사람도 있었니, 아니면 Meagan만 있었니?
남: Meagan외에 다른 사람들도 좀 있었어. Gianna도 거기서 책을 반납하고 있더라.
여: 내가 30분 전에 Kathy가 도서관으로 향하는 걸 본 것 같아. 그녀가 거기 있었어?
남: 맞아. 나도 그녀를 봤어. Kathy는 반납된 책을 정리하고 있어서, 난 그녀가 자원봉사를 하거나 거기서 아르바이트를 하는 것으로 생각했지.
여: 음. 그녀는 현장 실습을 해야 해서 거기서 일하고 있어.
남: 경험을 얻기 위한 좋은 방법이 되겠네.
여: Nancy는 어때? 걔 봤니? 나는 Nancy가 도서관에서 공부를 하고 있었으면 했어. 왜냐하면 그녀의 성적이 요즘 별로 좋지 않거든.
남: Nancy도 봤어. 그녀는 책상에서 공부하고 있었어.
여: 알게 돼서 정말 좋네.
남: 그리고 William도 컴퓨터로 뭔가를 읽고 있었어.
여: 그래. 사실, 나는 프로젝트를 위한 조사를 좀 해야 하거든. 사용 가능한 또 다른 컴퓨터가 있었으면 좋겠다.
남: 내 생각에는 거기 있었어.

어휘

arrange ***v.*** 정리하다 **available** ***a.*** 이용할 수 있는

정답 ⑤

문제풀이

William은 컴퓨터로 뭔가를 읽고 있다고 했는데 그냥 모니터 위에 손을 대고 있는 모습이므로 ⑤번이 그림과 일치하지 않는다.

총 어휘 수 176

07 할 일

소재 영어캠프를 위한 준비

듣기 대본 해석

남: 안녕, Emma! 어디 가는 길이야?
여: 어, 안녕 Ian! 나 서점에 가고 있었어.
남: 정말? 나도 그래! 다음 주에 영어캠프를 위한 책을 좀 찾아야 해.
여: 좋겠다. 네가 찾고 있는 게 무슨 레벨이야?
남: 대부분 학생들이 상급인데 중급도 몇몇 섞여 있어.
여: 네 일이 너한테 잘 맞을 것 같구나. 두 레벨을 가르치기 어렵지 않을까?
남: 응, 그럴 것 같아. 나는 학습 안내서로 책을 이용해서 두 레벨에 동시에 유용한 활동들에 대한 생각을 얻고 싶어.
여: 그건 멋진 생각이네. 캠프를 정말 재미있고 독창적으로 만들어 줄 거야.
남: 나도 그러길 바라. 나는 학생들이 내 캠프에서 특별한 무언가를 배워가길 정말로 원해.
여: 네가 잘 준비했는지 그리고 계획대로 되지 않을 경우에 대체할 방안들이 있는지 확인해봐. 나는 네가 정말 잘할 거라고 확신해!
남: 그렇게 말해줘서 고마워.

어휘

advanced ***a.*** 상급의, 고급의 **cut out for** ~에 적합하여 **at the same time** 동시에, 함께 **original** ***a.*** 독창적인 **definitely** ***ad.*** 분명히, 확실히 **backup** ***n.*** 예비, 백업 ***a.*** 예비의

정답 ②

문제풀이

남자는 영어캠프에서 두 레벨의 학생들을 같이 지도하기 위해 필요한 책을 찾아보러 서점에 간다고 했으므로 남자가 할 일은 ② '캠프 활동을 위한 책 찾아보기'가 정답이다.

총 어휘 수 158

08 이유

소재 관심 진로가 바뀐 이유

듣기 대본 해석

남: 안녕, Patty. 네가 학교의 새로운 토론 우승자라는 소식을 방금 들었어. 축하해!
여: 고마워 Tommy.
남: 결승 토론 주제가 뭐였니?
여: 유럽연합이 회원국들에게 유익한지에 대한 논쟁에서 찬성 입장 쪽이었어. 그것을 위해 열심히 공부했어.
남: 그러면 너는 꽤 주제에 대해 잘 알고 있겠구나. 너는 그러면 정말 유럽연합이 회원국들에게 혜택을 줄 거라 생각하니?
여: 응. 국경을 개방하고, 자국의 거주민을 다른 나라에서 자유롭게 일하도록 허용함으로써 유럽의 보다 가난한 국가들을 돕게 되지. 그러면 이들은 가족들에게 돈을 보내고, 이 외부에서 온 돈은 그 나라에서 순환될 수 있게 돼.
남: 그렇구나. 그럼 너는 너의 토론 기술들을 미래에 이용할 수 있을 것이라고 생각해?
여: 그럼. 난 크면 변호사가 되고 싶어.
남: 정말?
여: 응. 난 언제나 변호사와 관련된 TV쇼를 좋아했거든. 너도 법에 대해 관심이 있잖아, 맞지?

남: 그랬었지. 하지만 최근에는 은행원이 되는 공부를 하고 있어. 약간 연관이 있긴 한 것 같은데.
여: 돈과 법은 협력관계이지. 무엇이 네 생각을 바꾸게 했니?
남: 주식거래로 큰 돈을 번 은행원에 관한 책을 읽었어. 그는 그의 꿈을 쫓았고 흥미로운 삶을 살았어. 난 그게 너무 좋아서 그의 삶을 모델 삼기로 결정했어.
여: 멋지다, Tommy.

어휘
pro side 찬성 쪽 **argument** ***n.*** 논쟁, 언쟁 **beneficial** ***a.*** 유익한, 이로운 **border** ***n.*** 경계, 국경 **related** ***a.*** 관련된 **hand-in-hand** ***a.*** 친밀한, 협력한 **trade stock** 주식을 거래하다

정답 ③

문제풀이
대화의 마지막 부분에서 여자가 무엇이 진로를 바꾸게 했냐고 물었고, 남자는 주식거래로 큰 돈을 번 은행원에 관한 책을 읽고 삶의 모델로 삼게 되었다고 했으므로 남자의 관심 진로 분야가 바뀐 이유는 ③ '인상 깊게 읽은 책 때문에'이다.

총 어휘 수 226

09 숫자

소재 과수원 견학 예약

듣기 대본 해석
[전화벨이 울린다.]
여: 안녕하세요. Backwoods 과수원입니다.
남: 안녕하세요. 저는 Vanguard 고등학교의 Lewis 선생님입니다. 우리 학생들을 위한 체험 학습 예약을 하고 싶습니다.
여: 네. Lewis 선생님. 반나절 견학과 종일 견학 중 어느 것을 원하시나요?
남: 가격 차이가 얼마인가요?
여: 음, 반나절 견학은 학생당 20달러이고 종일 견학은 학생당 30달러입니다.
남: 10월 13일에 종일 견학으로 20명을 예약할 것 같습니다.
여: 네. 그날 자리가 있는지 확인해 볼게요. *[클릭하는 소리]* 네, 저희가 학생들을 수용할 수 있을 것 같네요.
남: 좋아요.
여: 20명 이상의 그룹은 전체 입장료의 10퍼센트 할인을 받아요.
남: 선생님도 요금을 내나요?
여: 성인은 40달러이지만, 15명 이상의 학생을 데리고 오시는 선생님은 무료예요.
남: 좋네요. 지금 제 신용카드 정보를 원하시나요, 아니면 제가 거기에 갔을 때 드리면 되나요?
여: 여기에 왔을 때 지불하시면 돼요.
남: 좋아요. 감사해요.

어휘
field trip 체험 학습 **accommodate** ***v.*** 수용하다 **admission** ***n.*** 입장(료) **charge** ***v.*** (요금, 값을) 청구하다

정답 ②

문제풀이
남자는 종일 견학으로 20명 예약하고 싶다고 했으므로 30x20=600달러이고, 20명 이상이라 전체 금액의 10퍼센트 할인이 되며, 15명 이상의 학생을 데리고 가서 선생님은 무료이므로, 남자가 지불할 금액은 ② '$540'이다.

총 어휘 수 166

10 언급 유무

소재 구직 인터뷰

듣기 대본 해석
여: 안녕하세요. 저는 Nora Stenson이에요. 만나서 반갑습니다.
남: 저는 John Ramstad입니다. 저도 만나서 반갑습니다.
여: 몇 가지 질문으로 시작해 볼까 해요. 먼저, 왜 어린이를 위한 주간캠프에서 일하는 데 관심이 있으신가요?
남: 음... 저는 여름에 아이들과 야외 활동 하는 것을 좋아하고, 본 주간캠프는 이 주변에서 가장 인기 있는 캠프입니다. 훌륭한 기관이라고 생각하고 있으며, 저는 정말 이곳의 일원이 되고 싶습니다.
여: 그렇다니 좋군요. 좋습니다. 그러면 언제 CPR과 일반 치료 자격증을 받았죠?
남: 둘 다 9달 전에 받았습니다.
여: 경험은 얼마나 되시나요?
남: 캠프 상담자로 3년의 경력이 있습니다. 일 년 동안은 Little Acorns Day 캠프에서 일했고, 지난 2년은 Young Explorers 주간캠프에서 일했습니다.
여: 당신은 Young Explorers 주간캠프에서 왜 그만두기로 결심했습니까?
남: 그곳의 커리큘럼에 동의하지 않았고 직원들이 너무 무책임하다는 것을 알게 됐습니다.
여: 좋아요, 시간 내 주셔서 감사해요. 2주 후에 연락 드릴게요.

어휘
CPR ***n.*** 심폐소생술 **certificate** ***n.*** 자격증, 면허 **counselor** ***n.*** 상담자 **quit** ***v.*** 그만두다, 중지하다 **irresponsible** ***a.*** 무책임한

정답 ⑤

문제풀이
지원동기(Why are you interested in working at our day camp for kids?), 자격증 취득 시기(When did you receive your CPR and general care certificates?), 근무 경력(How much experience do you have?), 전 직장을 그만 둔 이유(Why did you decide to quit your job at Young Explorers Day Camp?)는 물었지만 희망 보수에 관한 언급은 하지 않았으므로 정답은 ⑤ '희망 보수'이다.

총 어휘 수 186

11 내용 일치 · 불일치

소재 역사공원에서 주관하는 두 가지 행사

듣기 대본 해석
여: 안녕하세요. 제 이름은 Eston Cotton이고 저는 Angel Mounds 역사공원의 큐레이터입니다. 이번 봄 저희는 두 가지 특별 행사를 개최할 것입니다. 첫 번째 행사는 3월의 마지막 주에 진행됩니다. 해마다 열리는 미국 원주민의 날 행사가 그것이지요. 이 행사에서 우리는 미국 원주민들이 어떻게 살았는지, 도구들과 집을 어떻게 만들고, 사냥을 어떻게 했는지 배웁니다. 투어 전체가 약 네 시간 소요되니 미리 예약을 하시고 일찍 오시기 바랍니다. 4월 17일에 개최되는 다른 행사는 어린이날 행사입니다. 이 행사에서 어린이들은 미국 원주민 춤을 배우고 페이스페인팅도 받고 미국 원주민들의 전통 음식을 맛볼 수 있습니다. 또한 이날 가족 전체가 즐길 수 있는 여러 가지 행사도 있습니다. 올해 행사에 꼭 오시길 바랍니다. 감사합니다.

어휘
curator ***n.*** 큐레이터 **reservation** ***n.*** 예약 **traditional** ***a.*** 전통적인

정답 ③

문제풀이
원주민의 날 행사에서는 원주민들이 도구들과 집을 어떻게 만들고 사냥을 했는지 배운다고 했다. 전통적인 원주민 음식을 먹는 것은 '원주민의 날 행사'가 아니라 '어린이날 행사' 내용이므로 일치하지 않는 것은 ③ '원주민의 날 행사에서는 원주민 전통 음식을 먹어볼 수 있다.'이다.

총 어휘 수 134

12 도표

소재 영화 편집 강좌 선택하기

듣기 대본 해석
남: 안녕하세요. 어떻게 도와드릴까요?
여: 영화 편집 강좌를 수강하고 싶은데요.

남: 제가 도와드릴게요. 저희 강좌를 수강하시는 것은 처음이신가요?
여: 실은 아니에요. 전에 여기 프로그램에 있는 다른 강좌들도 수강했어요.
남: 영화 편집에 관한 강좌였나요?
여: 아니요. 하지만 같은 분야의 강좌요. 영화 제작과 연출을 수강했어요.
남: 알았어요. 그렇다면 영화 편집 분야의 상급자 강좌 중 하나를 수강하시는 게 좋겠네요. 괜찮을 것 같으세요?
여: 네, 그럴 것 같아요.
남: 좋아요. 몇 가지 중 선택하실 수 있어요.
여: Michael의 강좌 중 하나를 수강하는 것은 가능한가요? Michael이 굉장히 좋은 강사라고 들었어요.
남: Michael이 당신의 수준에 맞는 강좌 세 개를 가르쳐요. 두 개는 학생 수가 10명으로 제한되어있고, 나머지 하나는 15명으로 제한되어있어요. 아침 강좌와 저녁 강좌 중에 선택하실 수 있어요.
여: 좋아요. 학생 수가 더 적은 강좌로 할게요.
남: 아침 강좌와 저녁 강좌 중에 선택하세요.
여: 아침 강좌로 할게요.
남: 아주 좋아요. 이제 등록되셨습니다.

어휘
sign up for ~을 신청하다 **film editing** 영화 편집
film production and directing 영화 제작과 연출

정답 ③

문제풀이
영화 관련 강좌를 들어본 적이 있는 여자는 상급반 강좌를 듣기로 했고, Michael의 강좌를 들으려 하므로 ②, ③, ④번이 남는다. 세 개의 Michael의 강좌 중에서도 여자는 학생 수가 적고 아침 시간대 강좌를 원했으므로 모든 조건이 맞는 것은 ③ 'Advanced B'이다.

총 어휘 수 171

13 긴 대화의 응답

소재 직원의 업무태도에 대한 상의

듣기 대본 해석
여: 안녕하세요, Green 씨, 시간 좀 있으세요?
남: 네. 무슨 일이에요?
여: 음, 제가 Karen에 관해 당신에게 말해야 할 것 같아서요.
남: 좋아요. Karen에 관한 어떤 거요?
여: 오해는 하지 마세요. 저는 그녀가 좋은 직원이라고 생각하지만, 요즘 그녀가 일에 집중을 못하는 것 같아요.
남: 무슨 말씀인지 잘 모르겠네요.
여: 나는 그녀가 당신에게 말했는지는 모르겠지만, 그녀는 실제로 꽤 유명한 소설가예요.
남: 그래요? 저는 몰랐어요. 그래서 무엇이 문제인가요?
여: 저는 그녀가 직장에서 그녀의 글쓰기에 공을 들이고 사무실에서의 임무는 소홀히 하는 것 같아요. 그녀는 이곳 일에서 뒤쳐져 있어요.
남: 확실히 문제네요. 그녀가 사무실에 있을 땐 일에 집중해야 해요.
여: 동의해요. 우리가 어떻게 해야 한다고 생각하세요?
남: ④ 제가 그녀가 이것에 관심을 가지도록 하고 그녀에게 경고를 할게요.

어휘
distracted ***a.*** (정신이) 산만해진 **work on** ~에 공을 들이다, 애쓰다
get behind (일이) 밀리다
〈문제〉 **bring something to somebody's attention** ~에 ~가 주목하게 하다

정답 ④

문제풀이
남자와 여자는 Karen의 업무태도에 문제가 있다는 생각을 가지고 대화하고 있으므로 남자의 마지막 응답은 ④ '제가 그녀가 이것에 관심을 가지도록 하고 그녀에게 경고를 할게요.'가 적절하다.

오답 보기 해석
① 그녀는 당신이 당신의 소설 쓰는 것을 도와 줄 수 있어서 기뻐할 거예요.
② 당신이 옳아요. 그녀는 제 시간에 직장에 도착해야 해요.
③ 음, 저는 그렇게 생각지 않아요. 저는 그녀의 소설을 그다지 좋아하지 않아요.
⑤ 잘 모르겠어요. 저는 소설 쓰는 것이 매우 시간이 많이 걸리는 일이라고 생각해요.

총 어휘 수 143

14 긴 대화의 응답

소재 축구 경기 티켓 구매

듣기 대본 해석
여: Devin, 너 컴퓨터로 하고 있는 게 뭐니?
남: 축구 경기 티켓을 판매할 때까지 기다리고 있어.
여: 약간 긴장되어 보이는데.
남: 나는 정말로 스탠딩 구역 티켓이 필요한데, 그들이 판매를 하자마자 버튼을 눌러야 해.
여: 정말? 무슨 경기인데?
남: FC Barcelona가 Real Madrid와 경기를 해. 멋진 경기가 될 거야.
여: 내 생각에는 그 티켓이 너를 위한 게 아닌 것 같아, 그렇지?
남: 맞아. 티켓은 나의 아버지를 위한 것이야. 그는 FC Barcelona의 열렬한 팬이고 그의 생신날에 그 경기가 있어.
여: 너의 아버지를 위한 멋진 선물이구나.
남: 그래. 아버지께서 이 축구 경기에 대해서 수개월 동안 말씀하셨어. 그는 그 경기에 대해서 정말 흥분해 계셔.
여: 작년 생각이 좀 나네. 나는 Real Madrid와 경기에 대해 정말 들떠 있었는데, 부모님께서 내가 가는 것을 허락하지 않으셨어.
남: 안 됐구나. 네가 그거 때문에 화가 났겠다.
여: ⑤ 그래. 우리 아버지께서 너희 아버지처럼 축구에 관심이 있으셨으면 좋겠어.

어휘
remind A of B A에게 B를 상기시키다 **that's a shame** 안됐군요, 유감이에요

정답 ⑤

문제풀이
남자가 축구의 열렬한 팬인 아버지를 위해 표를 산다고 하자 여자는 작년에 부모님께서 자신을 축구 경기에 못 가게 하셨던 게 생각난다고 했다. 그래서 화가 났겠다고 말하는 남자에게 할 수 있는 여자의 적절한 대답은 ⑤ '그래. 우리 아버지께서 너희 아버지처럼 축구에 관심이 있으셨으면 좋겠어.'이다.

오답 보기 해석
① 걱정 마. 네가 다음 경기에는 갈 수 있을 거라 확신해.
② 문제 없어. 내가 너의 아버지를 경기에 모시고 갈 수 있어.
③ 아니. 나는 그들이 얼마나 잘 했는지 정말 깜짝 놀랐어.
④ 우리 아버지가 내가 경기에 가는 것을 허락하지 않을까 봐 걱정돼.

총 어휘 수 168

15 상황에 적절한 말

소재 최근 들어 달라진 James의 학습 및 생활 태도

듣기 대본 해석
여: James는 인기가 많은 외향적인 학생입니다. 그는 항상 특별 활동에 활발하게 참여하고 평균 학점도 높습니다. 그는 친구가 많고 대부분의 학생들과 선생님들이 그를 칭찬합니다. 그러나 최근에 James는 다른 학생들이 식당 가서 점심을 먹으러 가는 동안 교실에 있습니다. 그의 선생님들도 그가 수업 시간에 집중을 하지 않는다는 것을 알아챕니다. 학교 상담 교사 Towns 선생님은 James의 이상한 행동에 대해 듣게 됩니다. Towns 선생님은 James의 문제가 더 심각해지는 것이 우려되어 James와 그의 문제에 대해 이야기를 나누기로 결심합니다. 이러한 상황에서 Towns 선생님은 James에게 뭐라고 말할까요?
Mrs. Towns: ④ 난 너의 행동이 걱정돼. 괜찮니?

어휘

outgoing ***a.*** 외향적인 **extracurricular event** 특별 활동
grade point average 평균 학점 **admire** ***v.*** 존경하다
counselor ***n.*** 상담자 **bizarre** ***a.*** 이상한, 기이한

정답 ④

문제풀이

최근 들어 달라진 James의 학교에서의 태도가 걱정된 Mrs. Towns는 James와 그의 문제에 대해 얘기해보고자 하고 있으므로 적절한 말은 ④ '난 너의 행동이 걱정돼. 괜찮니?'이다.

오답 보기 해석

① 네가 학교에서 인기가 많다고 들었어.
② 친구들과 너의 문제에 대해서 상의를 해봐.
③ 요즘 왜 이렇게 자주 수업에 빠지는 거니?
⑤ 이 학교 특별 활동에 대해 궁금했었어.

총 어휘 수 122

16 담화 주제 / 17 세부 내용 파악

소재 모기에 의해 전염되는 질병

듣기 대본 해석

남: 지난 수업시간에 우리는 어떻게 일부 곤충들이 질병의 매개체가 되는지 논의했었죠. 오늘은 여러분 모두가 친숙할거라고 자신하는 곤충, 바로 모기에 대해서 이야기할 겁니다. 모기 물림은 일시적인 간지러움보다 더 심각한 문제를 일으킬 수 있어요. 사실 모기는 세계적으로 다른 어떤 동물들을 합친 것보다도 더 많은 사람들을 죽게 합니다. 모기들은 이 사람 저 사람에게 질병을 옮김으로써 그렇게 합니다. 뎅기열과 말라리아 같은 이러한 질병들의 일부는 치명적일 수 있습니다. 뎅기열은 아이들과 노약자에게 매우 위험하고, 극단적인 경우 죽음에 이르게 합니다. 말라리아는 매년 전 세계적으로 약 2억 명에게 발병하는데 약물로 치료될 수 있습니다. 이러한 질병들은 모기들이 많이 서식하는 열대 지역에서 특히 흔하게 볼 수 있습니다. 여러분이 열대 지역으로 여행한다면 ABCD 접근법을 고려해보세요. A는 말라리아 감염의 위험성을 인식하는 것입니다. B는 물림을 예방하고, 모기 물림을 피하기 위해 예방조치를 취하는 것입니다. C는 말라리아 약을 복용해야 하는지를 점검하는 것입니다. 그리고 D는 진단입니다. 말라리아나 뎅기열과 같은 증상을 보이기 시작한다면 곧바로 치료를 강구해야 합니다.

어휘

carrier ***n.*** 보균자, (병원체의) 매개체 **fatal** ***a.*** 치명적인 **affect** ***v.*** 영향을 미치다, (병이) 발생하다, 병이 나게 하다 **worldwide** ***ad.*** 전 세계에
tropical ***a.*** 열대 지방의, 열대의 **prevention** ***n.*** 예방
take precautions 예방 조치를 취하다 **diagnosis** ***n.*** 진단
symptom ***n.*** 증상, 징후 〈문제〉 **infestation** ***n.*** 체내 침입

정답 16 ③ 17 ③

문제풀이

16 남자는 모기에 의해 전염되는 질병의 위험성, 질병의 예, 대처 방법(ABCD 접근법) 등에 이야기하고 있으므로 남자가 하는 말의 주제로 가장 적절한 것은 ③ '모기에 의해 전염되는 질병'이다.

17 ABCD의 접근법은 A가 감염의 위험성을 인식하는 것, B는 물림 예방, C는 약 복용이 필요한지 확인하기, D는 증상 발견 시 진단받기이다. '위험 지역은 방문하지 않기'는 언급되지 않았으므로 정답은 ③번이다.

오답 보기 해석

① 말라리아 감염자들의 증상
② 열대 지역의 곤충 문제
④ 말라리아 치료에 쓰이는 약물
⑤ 모기 습격을 예방하는 방법

총 어휘 수 192

대학수학능력시험 대비 모의평가 3회

01 ②	02 ③	03 ③	04 ⑤	05 ②	06 ①
07 ④	08 ④	09 ③	10 ⑤	11 ⑤	12 ②
13 ①	14 ②	15 ③	16 ④	17 ⑤	

01 짧은 대화의 응답

소재 글쓰기 클럽 가입

듣기 대본 해석

여: 안녕 Austin, 네가 글쓰기 클럽에 가입했다고 들었어. 너 글을 많이 쓰니?
남: 음, 나는 더 많이 쓰고 싶은데, 지금 당장은 1주일에 대략 한 시간 정도만 글을 써.
여: 얼마나 오랫동안 글 쓰는 것에 관심이 있었니?
남: ② 내가 4학년 이래로 줄곧 관심이 있었어.

어휘

join ***v.*** 가입하다 〈문제〉 **be better at** ~을 더 잘하다

정답 ②

문제풀이

여자가 얼마나 오랫동안 글쓰기에 관심 있었는지 물었으므로 적절한 남자의 대답은 ② '내가 4학년 이래로 줄곧 관심이 있었어.'이다.

오답 보기 해석

① 나는 학교에서 클럽 가입하는 것을 즐겼어.
③ 나는 너의 글쓰기 클럽에 가입하고 싶어.
④ 나는 1주일에 대략 2시간 동안 글을 쓰곤 했어.
⑤ 나는 초등학교 때 글을 더 잘 썼어.

총 어휘 수 50

02 짧은 대화의 응답

소재 잃어버린 휴대폰 찾기

듣기 대본 해석

남: 엄마, 제 휴대폰 어디 놓여 있는지 못 보셨죠?
여: 못 봤는데 방금 부엌을 청소했어. 잃어버린 것 같니?
남: 그런 것 같아요. 모든 곳을 찾아봤는데 아직 못 찾았어요.
여: ③ 전화해서 벨소리를 듣는 게 좋겠어.

어휘

search ***v.*** 수색하다, 뒤지다

정답 ③

문제풀이

휴대폰을 잃어버려서 찾고 있는 아들에게 엄마가 할 말은 ③ '전화해서 벨소리를 듣는 게 좋겠어.'이다.

오답 보기 해석

① 내 휴대폰 좀 찾아줄래?
② 하루 종일 집 청소 했어.
④ 어떤 종류의 휴대폰을 찾고 있어?
⑤ 오늘 휴대폰으로 누구에게도 전화하지 않았어.

총 어휘 수 49

03 요지

소재 환경을 위한 구매 습관

듣기 대본 해석

남: 지난 몇 년간 여러분과 같은 젊은이들이 그전보다 더 많이 스스로 물건을 구입하고 있습니다. 하지만 여러분이 하는 모든 구매가 여러분 주변의 세상에 영향을 주고 있다는 것을 상기시키고 싶습니다. 여러분이 사는 것이 무엇이든 모든 제품이 지구에서 오는 것이기 때문에 환경에 부정적인 영향을 줄 수 있습니다. 여러분의 멋진 새 uPhone조차 직접 땅에서 나오는 물질로 만들어집니다. 여러분이 도울 수 있는 일은 구매 습관을 통제하는 것입니다. 여러분이 원하는 것을 사는 대신에 여러분이 필요한 것을 사십시오. 여러분이 무엇을 사든지 그것이 환경친화적인지 생각할 시간을 가져야 합니다. 이런 약간의 조사는 현재와 그리고 다가올 세대를 위한 지구를 보호하는 데 도움을 줄 것입니다. 이는 쉽지만 현명한 일이고 여러분은 우리가 살고 있는 세상을 모두를 위한 더 나은 세상으로 만들 것입니다.

어휘

purchase ***n.*** 구매 **have an effect on** ~에 영향을 미치다 **material** ***n.*** 물질, 재료 **instead of** ~ 대신에 **friendly** ***a.*** 친화적인 **protect** ***v.*** 보호하다, 지키다

정답 ③

문제풀이

남자는 구매가 환경에 영향을 미칠 수 있으니 물건을 살 때 필요한 것만 사고 그 물건이 환경친화적인지 생각해 보라고 말하고 있다. 그러므로 정답은 ③ '환경친화적인 물건을 구입해야 한다.'이다.

총 어휘 수 146

04 대화 주제

소재 인터뷰 숙제에 대한 조언

듣기 대본 해석

남: Smith 선생님 수업은 어때, Katie?
여: 글쎄, 학기 초반에는 많은 학업량에 익숙해지는 데 정말 어려웠어.
남: 이해해. 나도 아주 힘들었어.
여: 그렇지만 이제는 모든 추가 과제들이 출판과 저널리즘에 관해 배우는 데 좋은 방법이라고 생각해.
남: 응, 그것은 흥미로운 방식의 수업이긴 하지만 나는 그것이 나한테는 매우 효과적이라고 생각하지 않아. 난 숙제에 흥미를 유지하기가 힘들어.
여: 나는 네가 과제를 잘 해오지 않고 있다는 걸 알아차렸어. 학교 신문에 너의 기사들을 많이 못 봤거든.
남: 음, 나는 학교에서 다른 학생들과 교수님들을 인터뷰하는 게 너무 부끄러워.
여: 나도 처음엔 똑같았어. 하지만 다른 사람에게 말하는 두려움을 극복한 뒤에는 내 사교 기술이 정말 향상되었어.
남: 알아. 내가 가진 두려움에 맞서서 인터뷰 요청을 시작해야 할 것 같아.
여: 그래야만 해. 나는 그것이 정말로 네가 수업을 더 즐기는 걸 도와줄 것이라고 생각해.

어휘

semester ***n.*** 학기 **get used to** ~에 익숙해지다 **workload** ***n.*** 업무량, 작업량 **struggle** ***v.*** 고투하다 **publishing** ***n.*** 출판 **journalism** ***n.*** 언론 **faculty** ***n.*** 교수단 **social skill** 사교 기술 **improve** ***v.*** 개선하다, 향상시키다

정답 ⑤

문제풀이

남자는 인터뷰 과제가 자신에게 힘들다고 말하고 여자는 자신도 처음에는 어려웠지만 두려움을 극복해야 한다고 말해준다. 따라서 두 사람의 대화의 주제는 ⑤ '인터뷰 숙제에 대한 조언'이다.

총 어휘 수 171

05 대화자의 관계 파악

소재 옷 수선하기

듣기 대본 해석

남: 안녕하세요.

여: 안녕하세요. 무엇을 도와드릴까요?

남: 그게, 제가 지난 주말에 이 정장 바지를 샀는데 저한테 좀 길어서 수선이 필요할 것 같아요.

여: 알겠습니다. 그러면 수선할 수 있도록 치수를 잴게요. 조금 짧게, 아니면 신발에 닿게 수선되기를 원해요?

남: 보통 바지를 좀 위로 해서 입어요.

여: 알겠습니다. 문제 없습니다.

남: 그리고 이 티셔츠를 한번 봐주세요.

여: 뭐가 문제인가요?

남: 그게, 저번 주에 이탈리안 식당에서 식사를 했는데 셔츠에 스파게티 소스를 흘렸어요.

여: 지우는 데 어렵지 않을 거예요.

남: 그게, 스파게티 소스를 흘린 다음에 와인도 흘렸어요. 두 자국을 없애는 방법은 없을까요?

여: 레드 와인 자국은 빼기 어려운데 할 수 있을 것 같습니다.

남: 고맙습니다. 언제 가지러 오면 될까요? 토요일에 중요한 저녁 약속에 입고 가고 싶어요.

여: 그때까지 다 될 수 있도록 최선을 다 할게요. 목요일에 전화 주시면 제가 다 됐는지 알려드리는 건 어떤가요?

남: 좋네요. 감사합니다.

어휘

hem ***v.*** 단을 만들다, 올리다 **measurement** ***n.*** 치수 **alter** ***v.*** 바꾸다 **spill** ***v.*** 엎지르다 **stain** ***n.*** 얼룩 **formal** ***a.*** 격식을 차린, 정중한

정답 ②

문제풀이

남자가 정장 바지를 줄이고 싶다고 하자 여자가 어디까지 줄일지 봐주고 있고, 남자가 다시 셔츠에 묻은 스파게티와 와인 얼룩을 제거할 수 있는지를 묻고 여자가 가능하다고 대답하고 있으므로, 두 사람의 관계는 ② '세탁소 주인 ─ 고객'임을 알 수 있다.

총 어휘 수 206

06 그림의 세부 내용 파악

소재 해변에서의 휴가

듣기 대본 해석

남: 마침내 휴가에서 돌아왔군요.

여: 네, 돌아와서 기쁘지만 벌써 해변이 그리워요.

남: 이해해요. 어느 해변에 갔었어요?

여: St. Petersburg 해변이요. 정말 좋았어요. 사진 찍었어요. 한번 보세요.

남: *[잠시 후]* 와, 사랑스러워 보여요. 나는 당신이 쓰고 있는 모자가 정말 맘에 들어요.

여: 고마워요. 저희 엄마가 저를 위해 사주셨죠. 그런데 제가 누구를 향해 손을 흔들고 있는지 모르겠어요.

남: 저 사람이 당신 남편인가요?

여: 네, 그는 파라솔 아래서 낮잠을 자고 있었어요. 휴가 대부분의 시간을 쉬면서 보냈죠.

남: 모래성을 만들고 있는 사람이 당신의 아들 Billy임이 틀림없어요.

여: 그는 꽤 창의적이에요. 그는 나를 매일 놀라게 해요.

남: 물에서 고무보트 위에 있는 사람은 누구죠?

여: 그분은 저의 시아버님인 William이에요. 아버님과 어머님은 사실 저희가 머물렀던 콘도를 가지고 계세요.

남: 배경에 있는 것이 콘도인 것 같군요.

여: 맞아요. 우리는 중간 건물의 7층에 머물렀어요.

남: 음, 저는 당신의 휴가가 정말 부럽네요. 저도 곧 가야겠어요.

여: 저도 다시 가고 싶어요.

어휘

take a nap 낮잠을 자다 **amaze** ***v.*** 놀라게 하다 **raft** ***n.*** 고무보트 **father-in-law** ***n.*** 장인, 시아버지 **envious** ***a.*** 부러워하는

정답 ①

문제풀이

대화에서 손을 흔들고 있는 여자 자신이 모자를 썼다고 했는데 그림에서는 모자가 없으므로 정답은 ①번이다.

총 어휘 수 163

07 할 일

소재 스포츠 활동 선택

듣기 대본 해석

여: 안녕하세요. 무엇을 도와드릴까요?

남: 안녕하세요. 전 스포츠 활동에 참여하는 것을 생각하고 있어요.

여: 아, 좋아요. 현재 저희한테 가입되어 계신가요?

남: 아니요, 되어 있지 않아요.

여: 괜찮아요. 생각하고 계신 특정 활동이 있으신가요?

남: 딱히 없어요. 저한테 무엇이 제일 좋을지 모르겠어요.

여: 알겠습니다. 음, 여기에 저희가 이번 여름을 위해 계획한 모든 스포츠 활동의 목록이 있어요. 저희가 실내와 실외 활동들을 모두 제공한다는 것을 보실 수 있어요.

남: 와, 선택할 수 있는 활동이 정말 많네요.

여: 네. 그러면 모든 활동을 검토하시고 손님께 맞는 활동을 선택하기 위해 시간을 좀 가지세요.

남: 도움을 좀 주실 수 있으신가요?

여: 활동을 선택하는 것에서요?

남: 네. 저는 적어도 두 가지 활동에 가입하고 싶은데 어떤 것을 선택해야 할지 모르겠어요.

여: 그럼 같이 목록을 보죠. 제가 도와드릴게요.

남: 그거 좋겠어요. 대단히 감사해요.

어휘

currently ***ad.*** 현재, 지금 **enroll** ***v.*** 등록하다 **specific** ***a.*** 특정한, 구체적인 **go over** 검토하다 〈문제〉 **assist** ***v.*** 돕다

정답 ④

문제풀이

남자는 스포츠 활동을 등록하고 싶은데 스포츠 활동의 종류가 많고 자기한테 어떤 것이 제일 좋을지 몰라서 선택을 못하고 있다. 그래서 남자는 여자에게 스포츠 활동 선택을 도와달라고 부탁하는 중이므로 정답은 ④ '활동을 선택하는 데 그를 도와주기'이다.

오답 보기 해석

① 강사 만나기
② 멤버십을 위해 돈을 지불하기
③ 개인 트레이닝에 등록하기
⑤ 연례 스포츠 행사에 대해 묻기

총 어휘 수 151

08 이유

소재 해외 자원봉사를 위한 휴학

듣기 대본 해석

여: 교수님 안녕하세요?

남: Amelia, 들어와서 앉으렴. 무엇을 도와줄까?

여: 교수님과 상의할 중요한 것이 있어서요.

남: 그렇구나. 그것이 무엇이지?

여: 말씀드리기 어려운데 한 학기 휴학할까 해요.

남: 정말? 왜지? 넌 정말 좋은 학생이었잖아.

여: 감사합니다. 제 시간을 바깥에서 좀 더 의미 있는 일을 하면서 보낼까 해서요.

남: 어떤 것 말이니?
여: 봉사활동 같은 거요. 해외에 나가서 도움이 필요한 사람들에게 도움을 주고 싶어요.
남: 훌륭하구나. 어느 나라로 가는 것을 생각하고 있니?
여: 최근 네팔에 큰 지진이 있어서요. 그곳에 가서 돕고 싶습니다.
남: 너한테 좋을 것 같구나. 일이 끝나면 언제든지 돌아와서 공부해도 된단다. 행운을 빌어, Amelia.
여: 이해해 주셔서 감사합니다, 교수님.

어휘
meaningful ***a.*** 의미 있는, 중요한 **volunteer** ***v.*** 자원하다, 자원봉사하다 ***n.*** 자원봉사, 자원봉사자 **recently** ***ad.*** 최근에

정답 ④

문제풀이
여자는 해외에 나가서 도움이 필요한 사람들에게 도움을 주고 싶어서 휴학을 하고 싶다고 했으므로 정답은 ④ '해외로 봉사활동을 가기 위해'이다.

총 어휘 수 145

09 숫자

소재 팝콘 구매 시 할인

듣기 대본 해석
남: Poptastic's Gourmet Popcorn에 오신 것을 환영합니다. 무엇을 도와 드릴까요?
여: 카라멜 팝콘 큰 봉지 얼마예요?
남: 한 봉지에 10달러입니다.
여: 적당한 가격이네요. 4봉지 살게요.
남: 네. 만약 손님께서 저희 메일 리스트에 등록을 하시면, 10퍼센트 할인을 해 드립니다. 서식을 작성하는 데 몇 분밖에 안 걸립니다.
여: 그래요? 좋아요. 등록할게요. *[잠시 후]* 다 했어요. 여기 있어요.
남: 잠깐 볼게요. 좋아요. 손님의 이메일 주소는 mashimaro@leemail.com 이죠?
여: 맞아요. 다른 할인도 있나요?
남: 물론이죠. 저희는 고객의 생일인 달에 20퍼센트 할인을 해드려요. 아! 방금 작성하신 신청서를 보면, 고객님의 생일이 내일이네요!
여: 맞아요. 제 신분증을 보시겠어요?
남: 괜찮아요. 고객님을 믿습니다. 두 가지 할인을 동시해 적용해드릴 수는 없으니 더 큰 할인율을 적용해드릴게요.
여: 좋아요. 신용카드 받으시죠?

어휘
reasonable ***a.*** 합리적인, 적당한 **sign up** 등록하다 **complete** ***v.*** 기입하다, 완료하다 **trust** ***v.*** 신뢰하다, 믿다

정답 ③

문제풀이
여자는 한 봉지당 10달러인 팝콘을 4봉지 산다고 했고, 메일 리스트에 등록해서 10퍼센트, 생일 할인으로 20퍼센트를 할인받게 되었다. 그러나 남자가 두 할인을 동시에 받을 수 없으며, 더 큰 할인율을 적용해주겠다고 하였으므로 여자는 전체 금액의 20퍼센트를 할인받게 된다. 따라서 40달러에서 20퍼센트 할인을 받는 것이므로 여자가 지불할 금액은 ③ '$32'이다.

총 어휘 수 158

10 언급 유무

소재 Speech contest 참가

듣기 대본 해석
여: 안녕, Andrew. 복도에 있는 게시판에서 이 전단지를 봤는데 네가 관심이 있을 거라 생각했어.
남: 오, 웅변대회에 관해서구나. 전단지를 봐도 될까?
여: 그래. 자, 너 9월 22일까지 준비할 수 있을 거라 생각해?
남: 준비할 수 있을 거라 생각하지만, 약간 걱정돼. 너도 그 대회가 모든 학생들이 참여할 수 있다는 걸 알잖아. 심지어 졸업반도 참가할 수 있어. 너 등록할 계획이니?
여: 등록할 생각은 하고 있어. 내가 아주 잘할 것이라고 생각하지는 않지만 나의 발표력을 향상시키는 데 그것을 이용하려고.
남: 그건 확실해. 너 유명한 연설에 관심이 많잖아, 그렇지 않니?
여: 당연하지. 그게 바로 그 대회가 나한테 유익한 좋은 이유야. 언젠가 나는 정치가가 되고 싶어. 너는 등록할거니?
남: 그럼. 웅변대회는 Walker 강당에서 개최될 거야. 꽤 가깝지.
여: 그래. 우리는 거기에 자전거를 타고 갈 수 있어. 그런데 우리 빨리 등록해야 해. 마감일이 이번 금요일이거든.
남: 우리 집에 가서 내 컴퓨터로 등록하자.
여: 좋은 생각이야.

어휘
flyer ***n.*** 전단지 **billboard** ***n.*** 게시판, 광고판 **compete** ***v.*** 참여하다, 경쟁하다 **senior** ***n.*** 졸업반, 최상급생 **deadline** ***n.*** 마감 기한 **register** ***v.*** 등록하다, 신청하다

정답 ⑤

문제풀이
두 사람은 speech contest의 개최 일자, 참가 자격, 개최 장소, 신청 마감일에 관한 언급은 했지만 연설 제한시간에 관한 언급은 하지 않았으므로 정답은 ⑤ '연설 제한시간'이다.

총 어휘 수 165

11 내용 일치 · 불일치

소재 미술관 견학을 위한 안내

듣기 대본 해석
여: 안녕하세요, 여러분. Center City Art Museum에 오신 것을 환영합니다. 저는 여러분의 자녀가 미술관 방문에서 최대한의 것을 얻기 위한 좋은 방법을 조언해 드리려 합니다. 먼저, 여러분께서는 자녀들과 항상 함께 다니세요. 아이들이 혼자 돌아다니면 그들은 쉽게 길을 잃을 수 있고 무서워합니다. 그러나 아이들이 그들 스스로 미술 작품을 즐기게 해 주세요. 아이들에게 문제를 내거나 작품을 해석해 주는 것은 좋은 생각이 아닙니다. 그들이 자유롭게 생각하게 두고 가장 좋아하는 작품이 무엇인지, 왜 그런지를 물어보세요. 아이들에게 미술관의 지도와 작품 목록을 주고 그들에게 당신을 위한 투어 가이드처럼 행동해보라고 하세요. 이는 아이들에게 전체 미술관을 보게 하고 그들이 책임자인 것처럼 느끼게 합니다. 한 번의 방문으로 모든 작품을 보는 것은 그렇게 중요하지 않습니다. 우리는 일년 내내 열려 있으니 여러 번 방문할 기회가 많습니다.

어휘
make sure 확실하게 하다 **wander off** 거닐다, 돌아다니다 **interpret** ***v.*** 해석하다 **artwork** ***n.*** 미술품 **in charge** ~을 맡은, 담당인 **multiple** ***a.*** 많은, 다수의

정답 ⑤

문제풀이
담화의 마지막 부분에서 한 번의 방문으로 모든 작품을 보는 것을 중요하지 않다고 했으므로 정답은 ⑤ '방문했을 때 최대한 많은 작품을 보여 주어라.'이다.

총 어휘 수 164

12 도표

소재 토스터 고르기

듣기 대본 해석
여: 여보, 곧 크리스마스야. 당신 부모님께는 뭘 선물해 드릴까?
남: 글쎄, 토스트기가 요즘 말썽이라고 엄마가 그러셨어. 토스트기 하나 찾아보자.
여: 알았어. 근데 140달러 넘게 쓰는 건 좀 아닌 것 같아.
남: 나도 그렇게 생각해. 다른 선물들도 사야 되니까.

여: 맞아. 어쨌든 어떤 크기를 사는 게 좋을 것 같아?
남: 두 조각 토스트기는 너무 작은 것 같아. 엄마는 분명히 더 큰 걸 원할 거야.
여: 당연하지. 네 조각이나 여섯 조각 토스트기로 하자. 디지털 화면은 뭐에 쓰이는 건지 알아?
남: 타이머를 써서 빵을 다 굽는 데 얼마나 시간이 남았는지 보여줘. 하지만 별로 필요하지는 않을 것 같아. 엄마가 쓰시기에는 너무 복잡할지도 몰라.
여: 맞아. 이 검은 것 봐봐. 아주 매끈하고 세련되어 보인다.
남: 우리 부엌에는 잘 어울릴 것 같은데 우리 부모님 부엌 용품은 다 하얗잖아.
여: 응. 그럼 그 색깔로 하자.
남: 이게 가장 좋을 것 같아. 주문하자.

어휘
act up 말을 안 듣다, 애를 먹이다 **slice** ***n.*** 조각 **digital display** 디지털 화면, 디지털 표시 장치 **complicated** ***a.*** 복잡한 **sleek** ***a.*** 윤이 나는, 매끈한 **modern** ***a.*** 세련된 **appliance** ***n.*** (가정용) 기기

정답 ②

문제풀이
남자와 여자는 토스터를 고르고 있다. 처음에 140달러는 넘지 않는 게 좋다고 했고, 네 조각이나 여섯 조각 토스터로 하자고 했으므로 ②, ③, ④번으로 압축된다. 그리고 디지털 표시는 없는 것이 낫다고 했으므로 ②, ④번이 가능하고 그 중에 흰색으로 하자고 했으므로 남자와 여자가 선택한 것은 ②번이 된다.

총 어휘 수 180

13 긴 대화의 응답

소재 갓 채용된 원어민 교사

듣기 대본 해석
남: JLA에 오신 것을 환영합니다. 저희는 강사 경험이 많은 영어 원어민과 일하게 되어 설레어요.
여: 고마워요. 저도 JLA 팀의 일원이 되어서 정말 기뻐요.
남: 저는 당신이 거의 4년 동안 여기 한국에서 ESL 강사를 해온 것을 봤어요.
여: 네. 저는 항상 가르치는 것을 즐겼고, 여기 서울에 있는 것이 놀라운 경험이었어요.
남: 전에 영어 학습 교재에 관해 작업해 본 적 있으세요?
여: 해보지는 않았지만 저는 새로운 프로젝트를 시작하는 데 대해 열정적이에요.
남: 그렇게 말씀하시니 기뻐요. 사실, 저희와 일하고 있는 다른 원어민이 있어요. 그는 아주 재능이 있어요.
여: 정말이요? 그를 만나보고 싶어요. 저는 우리가 공통점이 많을 거라고 확신해요.
남: 저도 그럴 것 같아요. 그가 곧 올 겁니다. 그럼 그를 만나실 수 있어요.
여: 지금까지 당신이 출판한 책은 몇 권인가요?
남: 지금까지 저희는 다섯 권만 출판했고, ESL BEST와 몇 가지 새로운 프로젝트를 함께 작업 중에 있습니다.
여: ① 대단해요. 저도 여기서 일할 것이 너무 기대돼요.

어휘
instructor ***n.*** 강사 **enthusiastic** ***a.*** 열정적인, 열렬한 **talented** ***a.*** 재능이 있는 **have something in common** (특징 등을) 공통적으로 지니다 **shortly** ***ad.*** 얼마 안 되어, 곧

정답 ①

문제풀이
여자가 JLA에서 새로 일하게 되어 남자와 대화를 나누는 상황이다. 남자가 JLA에서 출간한 교재가 몇 권 있고 지금도 진행 중이라고 말했을 때 적절한 여자의 응답은 ① '대단해요. 저도 여기서 일할 것이 너무 기대돼요.'이다.

오답 보기 해석
② 당신이 대학에서 언론학을 공부했다는 걸 알아봤어요.
③ 우린 당신이 이 회사와 아주 잘 맞을 거라 생각해요.
④ 전에 ESL BEST에서 책을 출판했었어요.
⑤ 전 늘 ESL 선생님이 되고 싶었어요.

총 어휘 수 158

14 긴 대화의 응답

소재 여가 시간에 TV 보기

듣기 대본 해석
남: Stephanie, 일주일에 TV 몇 시간 봐?
여: 보통 일주일에 TV 20시간 봐.
남: 정말? 우와, 너 TV를 많이 보는구나!
여: 응, 보통 하루에 TV를 서너 시간씩 봐.
남: 하루에 네 시간? 나는 그렇게 많이 볼 시간이 없어. 학교 끝나면 공부하고 피아노 치는 걸 연습해야 하거든.
여: 나도 할 게 많아, Steve. 난 그냥 내 시간을 다르게 할애할 뿐이야.
남: 어떻게 허비할 수 있는 시간이 그렇게 많을 수 있지?
여: 음, 내가 좋아하는 TV 프로그램만 봐. 숙제랑 다른 거는 그 프로그램들 사이사이에 해.
남: 그것도 하나의 방법이긴 하겠다. 그래도 시간을 너무 많이 낭비하는 것 같아.
여: 즐기는 시간은 버리는 시간이 아냐.
남: 그렇기는 해. 근데 아직도 네가 어떻게 네가 할 일을 다 해 놓는 건지 모르겠어.
여: 보통 다른 활동들은 내 TV 스케줄에 따라 계획해. 항상 오늘 해야 할 일들 목록을 만들고 TV 보는 시간 전에 해야 할 일들에 우선순위를 매겨.
남: ② 나도 한번 해볼까. 보고 싶은 TV 프로그램들이 아주 많아.

어휘
manage ***v.*** 관리하다 **to-do list** 해야 할 일을 적은 목록 **prioritize** ***v.*** 우선순위를 매기다 〈문제〉 **catch up on** ~을 따라잡다

정답 ②

문제풀이
남자가 여자에게 하루에 TV 보는 시간이 너무 많다고 하자 여자는 계획을 세워서 할 일들을 중간에 하면서 본다고 말해주고 있다. 여자가 어떻게 계획하는지에 대해 말하는 마지막 말에 대한 남자의 응답은 ② '나도 한번 해볼까. 보고 싶은 TV 프로그램들이 아주 많아.'가 적절하다.

오답 보기 해석
① 어젯밤에 숙제하는 걸 깜빡했어. 그래서 피아노 연습을 못했어.
③ 내가 보는 TV 프로그램들 최신편을 다 챙겨보는 게 나한테 제일 중요해.
④ 난 요즘 TV 프로그램 때문에 운동을 별로 안 해.
⑤ 네가 원한다면 우리 TV 같이 보자.

총 어휘 수 194

15 상황에 적절한 말

소재 친구 관계에 대한 어머니의 조언

듣기 대본 해석
여: Jane과 Olivia는 정말 가까운 친구였고 모든 것을 함께 합니다. 불행하게도, 그들은 최근에 특정한 그룹이나 클럽에 들어갈지 말지 같은 아주 단순한 일로 말다툼을 해 왔습니다. Jane은 말다툼을 피하고 싶었지만 그들은 계속 다투었고, 그래서 Jane은 그녀의 어머니에게 이런 상황을 이야기했습니다. Jane의 어머니는 Jane과 Olivia가 너무 오랜 시간을 함께 보내서 다툼이 일어났다고 생각합니다. 그녀는 그들이 서로 일정 기간 떨어져 있어야 한다고 생각하고, Jane의 어머니는 Jane에게 그녀와 Olivia의 우정에 휴식 시간을 가져야 한다고 말하려 합니다. 이와 같은 상황에서 Jane의 어머니는 뭐라고 말할 것 같은가요?
Jane's mother: Jane ③ 몇 주 만이라도 Olivia와 어울리는 것을 그만하는 건 어떠니?

어휘
argue ***v.*** 언쟁을 하다, 다투다 **apart** ***ad.*** 떨어져 〈문제〉 **hang out** (~에서) 많은 시간을 보내다

정답 ③

문제풀이

Jane과 Olivia가 너무 붙어 다녔기 때문에 서로 떨어져 지낼 시간이 필요하다고 생각한 어머니의 조언으로 가장 적절한 것은 ③ '몇 주 만이라도 Olivia와 어울리는 것을 그만하는 건 어떠니?'이다.

오답 보기 해석

① 당사자가 없을 때 험담 당하는 것은 누구도 좋아하지 않아.
② 너는 학교에서 만나는 모두에게 왜 그렇게 부정적이니?
④ 클럽을 고르기 전에 모든 선택을 살펴볼 필요가 있어.
⑤ 새로운 학교로 전학 가는 것이 너를 외롭게 만들 수 있어.

총 어휘 수 120

16 담화 주제 / 17 세부 내용 파악

소재 아이들에게 건강에 좋은 음식 먹이는 방법

듣기 대본 해석

여: 여러분의 가족 중에서 식성이 까다로운 사람이 있나요? 여러분의 아이가 채소나 다른 건강에 좋은 음식을 먹으려고 하지 않기 때문에 저녁식사 시간에 매일 싸움이 벌어집니까? 자, 아이들이 싫어하는 음식을 억지로 먹이는 것은 감정적으로 부정적인 영향을 미칠 수 있습니다. 현명한 부모는 아이들을 건강한 식습관으로 이끄는 데 인내심이 있습니다. 제 아이들의 습관을 바꾸는 데 도움을 주었던 몇 가지 비법을 여러분들께 알려드리고자 합니다. 첫째로, 아이의 음식을 더 매력적으로 보이도록 장식을 하세요. 예를 들면, 아이들의 접시 위에다 채소들을 웃는 얼굴처럼 보이도록 만드세요. 브로콜리는 멋진 코가 되고, 당근을 얇게 썬 것은 멋진 눈처럼 보이고, 감자를 썬 것은 여러분의 아이에게 미소를 던져줄 수 있습니다. 둘째로, 식용색소는 단조로운 음식을 재미있게 만들 수 있습니다. 파란색, 빨간색 식용색소 몇 방울을 아이들의 오트밀에다 넣어서 생기 넘치는 모습으로 만들어 보세요. 셋째, 여러분은 별 모양, 하트 모양, 글자 모양으로 아이들이 먹는 과일이나 채소들을 자를 수 있습니다. 아이들의 이름을 쓸 수도 있습니다. 마지막으로, 저는 가끔 아이들이 좋아하는 음식에 건강에 좋은 음식을 숨길 수 있다는 걸 알았습니다. 예를 들면 시금치는 영양분이 풍부하고 피자 또는 심지어 과자나 브라우니에도 숨기기가 쉽습니다. 여러분의 생각과 약간의 창의력을 사용하면 여러분의 아이들은 곧 건강하게 식사를 할 것입니다.

어휘

fussy eater 편식가, 식성이 까다로운 사람 **emotional *a.*** 감정의 **impact *n.*** 영향, 충격 **sensible *a.*** 합리적인 **appealing *a.*** 흥미로운 **vibrant *a.*** 활기찬 **appearance *n.*** 모습, 외모 **nutrient *n.*** 영양소 〈문제〉 **benefit *n.*** 혜택, 이득 **regularly *ad.*** 규칙적으로 **processed food** 가공된 식품 **spruce *v.*** 단장하다

정답 16 ④ 17 ⑤

문제풀이

16 아이들이 채소나 다른 건강에 좋은 음식을 안 먹으려고 할 때, 그 습관을 바꿔줄 수 있는 방법을 알려주고 있으므로 이 글의 주제는 ④ '아이들의 먹는 습관을 바꾸기 위한 조언'이다.

17 브로콜리, 당근, 오트밀, 시금치는 언급했지만 토마토에 대한 언급은 없으므로 정답은 ⑤ '토마토'이다.

오답 보기 해석

16
① 규칙적으로 야채를 먹는 것의 이점
② 가공된 식품을 먹는 것의 위험
③ 아이들 건강에 해로운 음식들
⑤ 아이들의 파티를 꾸미는 창의적인 방법

17
① 브로콜리 ② 당근 ③ 오트밀 ④ 시금치

총 어휘 수 232

대학수학능력시험 대비 모의평가 4회

01 ③	02 ⑤	03 ②	04 ④	05 ①	06 ⑤
07 ⑤	08 ③	09 ④	10 ②	11 ③	12 ③
13 ②	14 ④	15 ④	16 ⑤	17 ④	

01 짧은 대화의 응답

소재 예상 밖의 경기 결과

듣기 대본 해석

여: 지난밤에 경기 봤니? 정말 좋았어! 무슨 일이 일어났는지 알고 싶지, Steven?

남: North Stars팀이 이겼을 거라고 생각 되는데. 우리 팀은 항상 그 팀에 지거든.

여: 아니! 어젯밤엔 우리가 이겼어.

남: ③ 와, 최곤데! 믿을 수 없어!

어휘

〈문제〉 **assignment** ***n.*** 과제

정답 ③

문제풀이

남자의 추측과는 달리 우리 팀이 이겼다고 여자가 말했을 때 적절한 대답은 놀라움의 표시이므로 ③ '와, 최곤데! 믿을 수 없어!'가 적절하다.

오답 보기 해석

① 다른 기회가 있을 거야.
② 네가 그걸 봤으면 좋았을 텐데.
④ 문제 없어. 좀 더 연습하면 돼.
⑤ 네 과제를 잊지 마.

총 어휘 수 43

02 짧은 대화의 응답

소재 오페라 티켓 예매

듣기 대본 해석

남: 안녕, Linda. 이번 주말 오페라 티켓 남아있는지 확인해 줄 수 있어?

여: 잠깐만. *[잠시 후]* 다 팔린 것 같은데.

남: 정말? 지난주에 사 놓을 걸. 아내가 엄청 화낼 텐데.

여: ⑤ 아직 다음 주말 티켓은 예약할 수 있는 것 같은데.

어휘

sold out (표가) 매진된 **furious** ***a.*** 몹시 화가 난
〈문제〉 **book a ticket** 티켓을 예매하다

정답 ⑤

문제풀이

이번 주말 티켓이 없다는 말에 남자는 지난주에 사놓을 걸 그랬다며 후회하고 있다. 이에 적절한 여자의 응답은 ⑤ '아직 다음 주말 티켓은 예약할 수 있는 것 같은데.'이다.

오답 보기 해석

① 그러고 싶은데 할 수 없어. 이번 주말에 계획이 있거든.
② 응. 오페라 티켓을 구하는 게 쉽지 않았어.
③ 너와 네 아내가 오페라 본다니 멋진데.
④ 걱정 마. 극장에 어떻게 가는지 알아.

총 어휘 수 56

03 담화 목적

소재 휘트니스 센터 홍보

듣기 대본 해석

여: 오늘 여러분의 기분은 어떠신가요? 여러분은 오늘 사무실에서 특별히 에너지가 넘치는 사람들을 봤을 수도 있습니다. 여러분은 또한 특별한 이유 없이 기분이 좋지 않고 우울해하는 사람들도 봤을 것입니다. 여러분께서는 어느 그룹에 속하십니까? 만약 여러분이 두 번째 그룹에 속하신다면, Heavenly Fitness에 무료 상담을 받으러 들러 보시면 어떨까요? Heavenly Fitness는 기능적인 근력 운동과 전반적인 건강관리를 위한 최첨단 휘트니스 센터입니다. 여러분 개개인의 요구에 맞는 구체적인 운동 프로그램을 짤 수 있게 도와드릴 자격증을 가진 15명의 개인 트레이너가 있습니다. 더 좋은 것은, 사물함과 화장실을 포함한 모든 시설물들이 새 것이며 운동 장비들도 모두 최고입니다. 여러분의 삶에서 더 많은 것을 얻고 싶으시다면 오늘 Heavenly Fitness에 들러주십시오.

어휘

energetic ***a.*** 에너지가 넘치는 **depressed** ***a.*** 의기소침한, 우울한 **stop by** 잠시 들르다 **consultation** ***n.*** 상담, 회의 **state-of-the-art** ***a.*** 최신식의, 최첨단의 **functional** ***a.*** 기능성의, 작동하는 **certified** ***a.*** 공인의, 자격증을 가진 **specific to** ~에 특유한, 고유한 **facility** ***n.*** 기관, 시설 **equipment** ***n.*** 장비, 설비

정답 ②

문제풀이

여자는 Heavenly Fitness가 최고의 시설과 개인 트레이너를 갖추고 있다고 홍보하고 있으므로 정답은 ② '휘트니스 센터를 홍보하려고'이다.

총 어휘 수 134

04 대화 주제

소재 소셜 미디어 사이트의 영향

듣기 대본 해석

여: 안녕, Joshua. 무엇을 듣고 있니? 재미있는 거 있어?

남: 안녕, Ann. 온라인상으로 Podcast 듣고 있어.

여: 그래? 무엇에 관한 거야?

남: 소셜 미디어에 관한 거야. 2018년까지 미국에 있는 거의 모든 8살 이상의 아이들이 일종의 소셜 미디어 프로필을 가지게 될 것이라고 말하고 있어. 어떻게 생각해?

여: 음, 나는 소셜 미디어 사이트가 좋은 교육적인 가치가 있을 수 있고 온라인 보안에 대해 아이들에게 알려줄 수 있다고 생각해.

남: 좋아. 그렇지만 소셜 미디어 사이트가 아이들을 여러 가지 면에서 위험하게 한다고 생각하진 않니?

여: 어떤 면에서 그런데?

남: 미성년자들과 인터넷으로 대화하려고 어린 척 하는 위험한 어른들에 관한 기사를 읽은 적이 있어. 또한, 휴대폰 번호와 주소 같은 개인정보를 얻기 위해 어린 사용자들을 이용하는 사람들도 있어.

여: 아, 그런 점은 꽤 무섭구나.

남: 게다가, 소셜 미디어 사이트가 교육적일 수 있지만 한편으론 숙제나 아이디어를 공유하는 대신 친구들과 대화하는 데 그것을 사용하는 학생들에게는 주의 집중을 매우 방해할 수도 있어.

어휘

security ***n.*** 보안, 경비 **pretend to** ~인 체하다 **minor** ***n.*** 미성년자 **take advantage of** ~을 이용하다 **distract** ***v.*** 산만하게 하다

정답 ④

문제풀이

여자는 소셜 미디어 사이트가 아이들에게 주는 긍정적인 면을 이야기했고 남자는 부정적인 면에 대해 언급하고 있으므로 주제로 적절한 것은 ④ '소셜 미디어 사이트가 학생들에게 끼치는 다양한 영향'이다.

총 어휘 수 164

05 대화자의 관계 파악

소재 인테리어 공사의 변경 사항

듣기 대본 해석

여: 선생님, 계약서 보셨나요?
남: 네. 근데 바꾸고 싶은 사항들이 몇 개 있더라고요.
여: 그래요? 어떤 것을 바꾸고 싶으세요?
남: 첫 번째로는 훈련 시설에 대한 것을 바꾸고 싶네요. 원래는 사우나와 온수 욕조 하나씩을 원했지만 이제는 온수 욕조 두 개를 원합니다.
여: 좋을 것 같지만 비용이 추가적으로 나올 거예요.
남: 비용은 상관 없어요. 완료되면 청구서를 보내 주세요.
여: 알겠습니다. 그리고 또 어떤 것을 바꾸고 싶으신가요?
남: 원래 체력단련실의 벽을 붉은 색으로 칠하고 싶다고 말했지만 하얀 색으로 하기로 했어요.
여: 문제 없어요. 붉은 페인트 주문을 취소하고 하얀 페인트를 주문할게요. 다른 게 또 있나요?
남: 아뇨. 그게 끝이에요. 완성된 모습이 기대되네요.
여: 아주 멋질 거예요. 그런데 언제까지 완성되어야 하나요?
남: 음. 훈련은 8월에 시작하니까 7월 말까지는 완성되었으면 좋겠네요.

어휘

contract ***n.*** 계약서 **tub** ***n.*** 욕조 **bill** ***n.*** 청구서 ***v.*** 청구서를 보내다
complete ***a.*** 완료된 **cancel an order** 주문을 취소하다

정답 ①

문제풀이

여자는 계약서를 봤는지 남자에게 물었고, 남자는 훈련시설의 온수 욕조 개수와 체력단련실 벽의 페인트 색 변경을 원한다고 말한 것으로 보아 두 사람의 관계는 ① '인테리어 업자 — 고객'임을 알 수 있다.

총 어휘 수 165

06 그림의 세부 내용 파악

소재 스포츠 용품 가게에서 선물 고르기

듣기 대본 해석

남: 이 스포츠 용품 가게 꽤 저렴하다.
여: 응. 맞다. 곧 Jesse 삼촌 생일이잖아. 여기서 삼촌 선물 사 가자.
남: 좋은 생각이야. 저기 선반 위에 있는 운동화는 어때? 요맘때쯤 농구 많이 하시잖아.
여: 꽤 괜찮은 생각인데 어떤 사이즈 신는지 모르잖아. 혹시 아니?
남: 아니.
여: 복싱 장갑은 어때? 저기 구석에 장갑들이 아주 많다.
남: 복싱 보는 건 좋아하시는 것 같은데, 직접 하시지는 않아.
여: 응, 네 말이 맞는 것 같아. 저 긴 스케이트 보드 멋있다. 아랫면에 있는 디자인 좀 봐.
남: 멋있다. 호랑이가 그려져 있네. 근데 우리가 사기에는 너무 비싼 것 같아.
여: 맞아. 저 구석에 있는 스노우 보드도 아마 우리가 생각한 가격 범위 밖일 거야.
남: 응. 아, 탁자 위에 봐봐! 저 농구 셔츠 하나 사 드리자.
여: 좋은 생각이야! Indiana Pacers가 삼촌이 제일 좋아하는 팀이야. 삼촌이 정말 좋아하실 거야.
남: 나도 그렇게 생각해.

어휘

deal ***n.*** 거래 **pricey** ***a.*** 값비싼 **range** ***n.*** 범위 **jersey** ***n.*** 셔츠

정답 ⑤

문제풀이

탁자 위에 있는 Indiana Pacers팀의 농구 셔츠를 사드리자고 했는데, 탁자 위에 겨울 재킷이 있으므로 정답은 ⑤번이다.

총 어휘 수 184

07 할 일

소재 사무실에서의 대화

듣기 대본 해석

남: 오늘 날씨가 정말 좋네요. Wally's Waterland에 갔으면 좋겠군요.
여: 그 이름이 제 추억을 불러일으키네요. 나 어렸을 때 거기 많이 갔었어요.
남: 맞아요. 나도요. 지칠 때까지 하루 종일 미끄럼을 탔었죠.
여: 나는 파도풀도 정말 좋아했었는데.
남: 항상 좋긴 했지만 항상 사람들이 너무 많기도 했어요.
여: 네. 하지만 아직도 너무 재미있고, 이런 사무실에 갇혀 있는 것보다 훨씬 재미있죠.
남: 당신 말이 맞아요. 하지만 우리 일하러 돌아가야죠.
여: 오늘 우리 일을 빨리 마칠 수 있을 것 같아요?
남: 확실하지 않아요. 왜요?
여: 제가 오늘 친구 집에 있는 아들을 데리고 다음 주 크루즈 여행을 위한 쇼핑을 하러 갈 예정인데 할 일이 너무 많은 것 같아요.
남: 음. 내 일을 곧 마칠 거니까 오늘 오후에 당신의 보고서를 도와줄게요.
여: 당신은 너무나 친절해요. Greg. 정말 감사해요.
남: 천만에요. 언젠가 나도 당신한테 부탁을 하겠죠.

어휘

ride ***v.*** (~을) 타다 **stuck** ***a.*** 갇힌, 꼼짝 못하는

정답 ⑤

문제풀이

여자는 오늘 친구 집에서 아들을 데리고 다음 주 크루즈 여행을 위한 쇼핑을 하고 싶은데 일이 너무 많다고 했고, 남자가 자기 일을 마치고 보고서를 도와주겠다고 말했으므로 남자가 여자를 위해 할 일은 ⑤ '보고서 작성 도와주기'이다.

총 어휘 수 173

08 이유

소재 도서관에 온 이유

듣기 대본 해석

남: Melissa, 안녕. 도서관에서 뭐해?
여: Norman, 안녕. 할 게 굉장히 많아. 넌 어때? 일요일에 여긴 어쩐 일이야?
남: 식물 번식에 관한 생물 리포트에 쓸 것들 좀 찾아보려고. 화요일까지야.
여: 그렇구나. 어려워 보이네. 근데 넌 무척 성실하니까 분명 잘할 거야.
남: 고마워. 아 참, 너 몸이 별로 안 좋아 보여. 괜찮아?
여: 응. 감기가 좀 있는 것 같아. 쉬어야 되는데 요 며칠 간 잠을 제대로 못 잤어.
남: 그렇구나. 다음 주 기말고사 때문에 스트레스를 많이 받고 있구나?
여: 맞아. 시험 주 전에 항상 아픈 것 같아. 심지어 성적의 40%나 되는 역사 시험도 있어.
남: 힘들겠다. 원한다면 공부하는 거 도와줄게.
여: 괜찮아. 그래도 고마워.
남: 응. 다 잘됐으면 좋겠다.

어휘

research ***n.*** 연구 **biology** ***n.*** 생물학 **reproduction** ***n.*** 생식, 번식
studious ***a.*** 공부를 열심히 하는 **under the weather** 몸이 안 좋은

정답 ③

문제풀이

여자가 다음 주에 있을 기말고사 때문에 스트레스를 받고 있고, 성적의 40%나 차지하는 역사 시험이 있다고 말한 것으로 미루어보아 도서관에 온 이유는 ③ '기말고사 공부를 하기 위해서'이다.

총 어휘 수 159

09 숫자

소재 세차 비용

듣기 대본 해석

남: 안녕하세요. 무엇을 도와드릴까요?
여: 제 차의 카펫을 청소하려고요.
남: 네. 일반 청소기 청소는 10달러이고 고급 샴푸 청소는 25달러입니다.
여: 어떤 것이 좋을까요? 카펫을 겨울 동안 청소하지 않았어요.
남: 샴푸 청소를 권해드리고 싶어요. 그래야 봄과 여름까지 상쾌하고 깨끗한 카펫이 될 거예요.
여: 좋아요. 그러면 고급 샴푸 청소로 할게요. 차의 외부도 세차하고 싶어요.
남: 물론이죠. 외부 세차는 15달러입니다.
여: 그래요. 좋네요. 아 그리고 바퀴도 닦아야 해요.
남: 문제 없어요. 바퀴 세차는 보통 30달러이지만 손님께서 외부 세차와 카펫 청소를 하시니 30퍼센트 할인해 드릴게요.
여: 와. 좋아요. 차를 가지러 언제 오면 되죠?
남: 차는 45분 후에 준비될 겁니다.

어휘

vacuum ***n.*** 진공 **deluxe** ***a.*** 고급 **exterior** ***n.*** 외부

정답 ④

문제풀이

카펫을 고급 샴푸 청소하는 데 25달러, 외부 세차에 15달러이고, 바퀴 세차는 30달러인데 30퍼센트 할인해준다고 했으므로 21달러이다. 그러므로 여자가 지불해야 하는 전체 금액은 ④ '$61'이다.

총 어휘 수 143

10 언급 유무

소재 팔라완 섬의 발견

듣기 대본 해석

여: Tom, 뭐해?
남: 여행 잡지에서 필리핀의 팔라완에 대해 읽고 있어.
여: 팔라완? 무엇에 대한 이야기야?
남: 그 섬이 어떻게 그렇게 인기 있는 관광지가 되었는지에 관한 거야.
여: 난 팔라완에 대해 한 번도 들어 본 적이 없어. 거기는 경험이 풍부한 여행자들만 즐기는 그런 여행지 같은데, 맞지?
남: 이 이야기에 따르면 그렇지 않아. "팔라완의 문화는 필리핀의 다른 지역이나 아시아의 문화와 매우 다르고 경관이 너무나 아름다워서 여러 곳에서 사람들이 섬으로 휴가를 즐기기 위해 모여들기 시작했다."라고 하는데.
여: 그런데 팔라완은 처음에 어떻게 대중화됐는데?
남: 그 섬은 몇 년 전에 다른 더 좋은 다이빙 지역을 찾는 다이버들을 위한 유명한 목적지였어.
여: 정말? 그럼 이젠 그 섬이 다이버들만을 위한 것이 아니란 거야?
남: 전혀. 모든 사람들이 할 만한 게 있지. El Nido 마을은 특히 커플이나 나이든 관광객들에게 인기가 많은데 매우 부드러운 분위기를 주기 때문이야.
여: 정말 멋질 것 같아. 나도 나중에 구글로 검색해서 확인해야겠다.
남: 해봐. 너의 생각은 어떤지 알려줘.

어휘

tourist destination 관광지 **experienced** ***a.*** 숙련된
flock ***v.*** 모이다, 떼 지어 가다 **mellow** ***a.*** 부드러운, 느긋한

정답 ②

문제풀이

대화에서 팔라완 섬의 문화(다른 필리핀 지역과 동남아시아의 문화와 매우 다름), 사람들이 팔라완 섬을 찾는 이유(아름다움), 팔라완 섬을 처음 대중화시킨 사람들(다이버들), 팔라완 섬에서 인기 있는 마을(El Nido)에 대해서는 언급되어 있지만, 팔라완 섬의 날씨에 대해서는 언급되어 있지 않으므로 정답은 ② '팔라완 섬의 날씨'이다.

총 어휘 수 177

11 내용 일치 · 불일치

소재 부산국제영화제 소개

듣기 대본 해석

여: 대한민국의 부산, 해운대 해변에서 해마다 열리는 부산국제영화제에 대해 아십니까? 그것은 아시아에서 가장 중요한 영화축제 중 하나입니다. 이 영화축제들 중 첫 번째 축제는 1996년 9월 13일부터 9월 21일에 열렸습니다. 그것은 한국에서의 첫 번째 국제 영화축제였습니다. 부산국제영화제의 초점은 특히 아시아 국가들의 새로운 영화와 신예 감독을 소개하는 것입니다. 다른 주목할 만한 특징은 영화제가 끌어들이는 많은 젊은 관객들 측면에서, 그리고 젊은 인재들을 발전시키고 알리려는 영화제의 노력 측면에서 젊은이들이 영화제에 느끼는 매력입니다. 1999년 부산 프로모션 플랜은 새로운 감독과 자금 출처를 이어주기 위해 설립되었습니다. 2011년 16번째 부산국제영화제는 새로운 영구적인 장소인 Busan Cinema Center로 옮겨졌습니다.

어휘

annually ***ad.*** 해마다, 일년에 한 번 **notable** ***a.*** 주목할 만한, 중요한
appeal ***n.*** 호소, 매력 **in terms of** ~면에서 **attract** ***v.*** 끌다
promote ***v.*** 촉진하다 **establish** ***v.*** 설립하다 **connect** ***v.*** 연결하다
permanent ***a.*** 영구적인

정답 ③

문제풀이

부산국제영화제는 저예산 유럽 영화가 아닌 주로 아시아 출신의 신예 감독을 소개하므로 정답은 ③ '주로 유럽의 저예산 영화들을 소개한다.'이다.

총 어휘 수 134

12 도표

소재 스캐너 대여

듣기 대본 해석

남: 안녕하세요. 오늘 오후 무엇을 도와드릴까요?
여: 컬러 스캐너를 빌리고 싶은데요. 이용할 수 있는 것이 있나요?
남: 네. 도와드릴 수 있어요. 선택 가능한 네 가지 모델이 있어요. 이 책자를 보세요. 모델들이 나와있어요. 지금 가장 인기 있는 모델은 D-7이에요.
여: 좋아요. 그것에 대해 말씀해 주실래요?
남: 네. 한 달에 40달러만 내시면 정말 높은 품질의 스캐닝을 하실 수 있습니다.
여: 사실, 40달러는 제 예산에 비해 너무 비싸요. 최대 한 달에 35달러를 쓰고 싶어요.
남: 좋아요. 그럼 D-5 모델을 추천해드릴게요. 한 달에 32달러로 훌륭한 스캐닝을 제공하죠.
여: 그래요. 그게 좋네요. 제가 알아야 할 다른 특징들이 있나요?
남: 물론이죠. D-5는 컴퓨터에 선 없이 연결해서 일반 프린터로도 사용하실 수 있어요.
여: 제 사무실에 프린터는 많은데요 제가 원하는 것은 팩스기예요.
남: 그렇다면 이 모델이 당신에게 맞겠네요.
여: 좋아요. 이것으로 할게요.

어휘

available ***a.*** 이용할 수 있는 **at the most** 최대한 **feature** ***n.*** 특색, 특징 **normal** ***a.*** 보통의, 평범한 **hook up** 연결하다
wirelessly ***ad.*** 무선으로

정답 ③

문제풀이

여자가 원하는 컬러 스캐너의 한달 대여료는 35달러 이하, 프린터의 기능보다는 팩스의 기능이 되는 것이다. 따라서 여자가 선택한 모델은 ③ 'D-3'이다.

총 어휘 수 180

13 긴 대화의 응답

소재 인턴십 지원에 필요한 추천서 부탁

듣기 대본 해석

남: Towns 선생님, 잠깐 시간 내 주실 수 있어요?
여: 물론이지, Richard. 무엇을 도와줄까?
남: Pear Computers의 여름 인턴십 프로그램에 지원하려고 해요. 제가 합격할 만한 자격이 있다고 생각하세요?
여: 그럼. 넌 올해 모든 수업과 방과후 활동에서 뛰어나게 잘 했잖아.
남: 예. 하지만 인턴십을 할 기회를 가질 수 있을지 확신이 없네요.
여: 지금 농담하는 거지? 넌 그들이 이 인턴십에서 찾고 있는 적임자야. 어쨌든 도전해봐서 손해 볼 거 없잖아.
남: 격려의 말 감사해요 Towns 선생님. 아 그런데 저한테 추천서를 써 주실 수 있으세요? 인턴십에서 요구하는 것들 중 하나거든요.
여: 나도 그러고 싶은데 더 자격을 갖춘 사람이 쓰는 게 나을 거 같은데.
남: ② 맞는 말 같아요. 제 컴퓨터 공학 교수님께 여쭤볼게요.

어휘

qualification ***n.*** 자격, 능력 **outdo** ***v.*** 능가하다 **extracurricular** ***a.*** 과외의 **reference letter** 추천서 〈문제〉 **application** ***n.*** 지원(서), 신청(서)

정답 ②

문제풀이

남자는 여자에게 여름 인턴십 지원에 필요한 추천서를 부탁하였는데 여자는 자신보다 더 적합한 사람이 써주는 것이 나을 것이라고 말하였다. 이에 대한 남자의 응답으로 가장 적절한 것은 ② '맞는 말 같아요. 제 컴퓨터 공학 교수님께 여쭤볼게요.'이다.

오답 보기 해석

① 좋아요. 그럼 바로 지원서 보낼게요.
③ 고마워요. 편지 다 쓰시면 저한테 알려주세요.
④ 신청서를 쓰는 데 시간을 내주셔서 정말 감사합니다.
⑤ 그건 문제없어요. 주말까지 쓰는 걸 끝낼게요.

총 어휘 수 154

14 긴 대화의 응답

소재 시골에서 자란 엄마

듣기 대본 해석

남: 엄마, 오늘 밤 달 봤어요? 매우 거대했어요!
여: 그래, 그렇더구나. 그것은 일년 중 가장 큰 보름달이란다. 그것은 추수 달이라고 불러.
남: 왜 그렇게 불리죠?
여: 음, 그건 추분에 가장 가까운 달이라서 그래. 그것은 농부들이 밤 늦게까지 곡식을 추수할 수 있을 정도로 충분히 밝아.
남: 이 모든 것을 어떻게 아세요?
여: 음, 내가 시골에서 자랐다는 것을 알지, 그렇지?
남: 네, 엄마가 나에게 그것에 대해 말씀하신 것을 기억해요.
여: 음, 내가 어렸을 때 가족 농장을 돕곤 했거든.
남: 오, 맞아요. 가족들이 여전히 그곳에 살고 계시나요?
여: 그럼, 많은 분들이 아직 살고 계셔.
남: 아직도 그들과 연락하세요?
여: 물론이지. 몇 달마다 나의 이모 Lucinda에게 편지를 써. 나는 지난주에 그녀로부터 편지를 받았어.
남: 엄마가 마지막으로 고향을 방문하러 간 건 언제인가요?
여: 약 10년 전에 크리스마스를 보내러 갔었지. 그들과 함께 시간을 보내는 것은 좋았어.
남: 흥미로운 곳인 것 같아요. 어렸을 때 사진 가지고 있나요?
여: ④ 당연하지. 우리가 농장에서 찍은 사진들을 보여줄게.

어휘

full moon 보름달 **harvest moon** 추분 무렵의(한가위) 보름달 **autumnal equinox** 추분 **keep in touch with** ~와 연락을 취하다

정답 ④

문제풀이

아들이 엄마에게 어렸을 때 사진을 가지고 있는지 물었으므로 이어질 적절한 응답은 ④ '당연하지. 우리가 농장에서 찍은 사진들을 보여줄게.'이다.

오답 보기 해석

① 음, 거기에서의 보낸 시간을 그다지 많이 기억은 못해.
② 나는 나의 고향에 있는 모든 친척들과 연락이 두절되었어.
③ 아니, 크리스마스를 보내러 거기 갔을 때 나는 어떤 사진도 찍지 않았어.
⑤ 물론이지. 나는 네가 아기였을 때부터의 네 사진을 많이 가지고 있어.

총 어휘 수 195

15 상황에 적절한 말

소재 부모님이 자신을 아이 취급한다고 생각하는 Mike의 고민

듣기 대본 해석

남: 17세 고등학생인 Mike는 그를 잘 대해주시는 아주 사랑하는 부모님이 계십니다. 그러나 최근에 Mike는 그의 부모님께 불만을 느끼기 시작했습니다. 그는 자신이 좋아하는 방식으로 그의 인생을 살 정도로 나이가 들었다고 느끼지만, 그의 부모님은 여전히 마치 그가 어린아이인 것처럼 그를 대합니다. 그의 친구들은 금요일에 나가서 컴퓨터 게임을 하며 인터넷 카페에서 어울리는 반면에, Mike는 그의 부모님과 보드 게임을 하거나 오래된 영화를 보며 집에 갇혀 있습니다. 지난 주말에, Mike는 몇몇 친구들과 콘서트에 가는 것에 대해 부모님에게 허락을 청했습니다. 물론 그들은 거절하셨습니다. 그러자 그는 아버지께 그를 왜 콘서트에 보내줄 수 없는지를 여쭤 보았고 그의 아버지께서는 콘서트가 너무 늦게 끝날 거라고 말씀하셨습니다. Mike는 그의 부모님이 너무 엄격하시고 그들이 자신을 어른으로서 존중하지 않는다고 믿습니다. 그는 아버지와 이에 관해 이야기하기로 결심했습니다. 이런 상황에서, Mike는 그의 아버지에게 뭐라고 말할까요?
Mike: 아빠, ④ 저를 어른처럼 대해주실 때에요. 저는 더 이상 어린아이가 아니에요.

어휘

treat ***v.*** 다루다, 대하다 **frustrated** ***a.*** 불만스러워 하는, 좌절감을 느끼는 **stuck** ***a.*** 갇힌, 꼼짝 못하는 **permission** ***n.*** 허락 **strict** ***a.*** 엄격한

정답 ④

문제풀이

주말에도 친구들과 밖에서 놀지 못하고 콘서트도 못 가게 하는 부모님께 불만이 생긴 Mike는 아버지께 자신을 더 이상 어린아이 취급하지 말라고 말씀드리려 한다. Mike가 할 말로 가장 적절한 것은 ④ '저를 어른처럼 대해주실 때에요. 저는 더 이상 어린아이가 아니에요.'이다.

오답 보기 해석

① 제가 아버지를 얼마나 걱정하는지 아버지는 모르시는 것 같아요.
② 제 친구들은 아버지께서 저를 그들과 가도록 해주셔서 정말 감사하고 있어요.
③ 저는 우리가 그렇게 많은 시간을 함께 보내게 돼서 너무 행복해요.
⑤ 주말에 엄마랑 같이 더 많은 시간을 보내시는 게 어때요?

총 어휘 수 181

16 담화 목적 / 17 세부 내용 파악

소재 소를 이용해 가난한 사람들을 돕는 방법

듣기 대본 해석

남: 안녕하세요, 저는 Animals for Joy의 설립자인 Noah Redman입니다. 제가 어렸을 때 아버지께서는 소를 가지고 계셨어요. 그는 소가 정말로 필요한 가족들에게 소들을 주었습니다. 여러분은 왜 아버지께서 소를 궁핍한 가정에 주었는지 궁금하실 텐데요. 가축을 소유하는 것은 자신의 사업체를 갖는 것과 같기 때문입니다. 소에서 나오는 우유, 치즈, 그리고 다른 제품들은 팔 수 있고 그 소득은 학교, 주택 개조, 부채 탕감, 즉 간단히 말해 더 나은 삶을 위해 사용될 수 있습니다. 소는 자연스럽게 미래 작물을 위한 비료도 생산할 수 있습니다. 소들은 사업이 성장하듯이 번식도 합니다. 만약에 당신이 도와주는 가족이 소의 새끼를 다른 가족에게 보내기로 하고 이러한 경향이 지역사회 안에서 계속된다면 여러분은 곧 지역사회의 빈곤이 감소하는 것을 발견할 수 있을 것입니다. 온라인 기부를 통해 Animals for Joy에 대한 여러분의 지원을 보여주세요. 그렇게 하기 위해 저희의 웹사이트 www.animals4joy.org를 방문하십시오. 여러분의 시간과 지원에 미리 감사 드립니다.

어휘

livestock *n.* 가축 **income** *n.* 수입, 소득 **home improvement** 주택 개조 **debt relief** 채무면제, 부채 탕감 **fertilizer** *n.* 비료 **offspring** *n.* 자식, 새끼 **poverty** *n.* 가난, 빈곤 〈문제〉 **caution** *v.* 주의를 주다, 경고하다 **domesticated animal** 가축

정답 16 ⑤ 17 ④

문제풀이

16 남자의 아버지가 도움이 필요한 가족들에게 소를 줌으로써 어떻게 도움이 되었는지 예를 들며 기부를 촉구하고 있다. 따라서 정답은 ⑤ '가난한 사람들을 도울 수 있는 방법을 사람들에게 알려주기 위해서'이다.

17 남자는 소가 제공하는 것으로 우유, 치즈, 비료, 새끼는 언급했지만 고기는 언급하지 않았으므로 정답은 ④ '고기'이다.

오답 보기 해석

16

① 화장품을 위한 동물 실험에 대항하기 위해서
② 빈곤의 영향을 대중에게 경고하기 위해서
③ 새로운 축산업 기술을 소개하기 위해서
④ 가축 사육의 이점을 설명하기 위해서

총 어휘 수 162

대학수학능력시험 대비 모의평가 5회

01 ④	02 ④	03 ④	04 ①	05 ③	06 ⑤
07 ①	08 ③	09 ②	10 ①	11 ④	12 ③
13 ⑤	14 ⑤	15 ④	16 ⑤	17 ②	

01 짧은 대화의 응답

소재 도서관 가는 날

듣기 대본 해석

여: Hunter, 일어나렴! 오늘 도서관 가기로 했잖니.
남: 엄마, 제가 도서관에 가야 하는 건 내일이에요. 오늘은 16일이라고요.
여: 너무 바빠서 날짜를 기억 못하는 거니? 오늘은 17일이란다.
남: ④ 정말이에요? 얼른 일어나서 바로 준비해야겠어요.

어휘

wake up 일어나다 **be supposed to V** ~하기로 되어 있다

정답 ④

문제풀이

남자는 오늘이 16일이라고 착각하고 있으나 사실은 오늘이 도서관을 가야 하는 17일이라고 엄마가 말해준 상황이다. 이에 적절한 대답은 ④ '정말이에요? 얼른 일어나서 바로 준비해야겠어요.'이다.

오답 보기 해석

① 제가 왜 일찍 일어나야 하죠?
② 알다시피, 도서관은 오늘 휴관이에요.
③ 오, 저를 일찍 깨우지 말았어야 했어요.
⑤ 믿을 수 없어요. 16살이면 거기 혼자 가도 충분한 나이라고 생각해요.

총 어휘 수 47

02 짧은 대화의 응답

소재 단풍놀이

듣기 대본 해석

남: 가을은 내가 가장 좋아하는 계절이야. 난 가을의 바람이 좋아.
여: 맞는 말이야. 덥지도 않고 춥지도 않지.
남: 가을의 다른 좋은 점은 바로 단풍이야. 오늘 나랑 같이 단풍놀이 가는 게 어때?
여: ④ 좋은 생각이야! 내가 하고 싶었던 말이야.

어휘

breeze ***n.*** 산들바람, 미풍

정답 ④

문제풀이

남자가 좋아하는 계절인 가을에 대해 이야기하면서 단풍놀이를 가자고 제안하였다. 이에 적절한 여자의 대답은 ④ '좋은 생각이야! 내가 하고 싶었던 말이야.'이다.

오답 보기 해석

① 나도야. 가을은 내가 가장 좋아하는 계절이야.
② 밖이 너무 추워서 걸을 수 없어.
③ 고마워. 하지만 나 다음 주에 바쁠 것 같아.
⑤ 초대해줘서 고맙지만 이미 저녁을 먹었어.

총 어휘 수 52

03 담화 목적

소재 수도관의 동파 방지

듣기 대본 해석

남: 실례지만, 모두 주목해주세요. 저는 여러분의 교장 선생님입니다. 지난 겨울 학교에 있는 수도관들이 동파된 것을 기억하실 것입니다. 저는 그런 일이 다시 일어날 것이라고는 생각하지 않지만, 만일을 위해 학생들과 교직원들께 특히 하루 일과를 마치고 교실을 나서면서 모든 창문을 닫을 것을 상기시켜 드립니다. 우리 학교는 자동 난방 시스템을 갖추고 있지만 창문이 열려 있다면 제대로 작동되지 않을 것입니다. 하룻밤 동안 창문이 열려 있으면 교실이 너무 추워질 것이고 난방 시스템은 파이프들이 어는 것을 막지 못할 것입니다. 파이프가 얼 경우에 물이 역류될 수 있으며 며칠 동안 학교에 아무도 없는 주말에 이 문제가 발생할 경우에 역류가 생긴 파이프가 터지고 큰 침수 피해를 일으키게 됩니다. 모든 분들께서 단순히 창문을 닫는 각자의 역할만 해 주셔도 이 상황은 쉽게 방지할 수 있습니다.

어휘

interruption ***n.*** 간섭, 중단 **principal** ***n.*** 교장 선생님 **freeze** ***v.*** ~이 얼다, ~을 얼리다 **faculty** ***n.*** 교수단 **heating system** 난방 시스템 **get backed up** ~이 밀리다, ~이 역류되다 **massive** ***a.*** 거대한, 엄청난 **preventable** ***a.*** 예방할 수 있는

정답 ④

문제풀이

하루 일과를 마치고 교실을 나서며 창문을 열어 놓으면 자동 난방 시스템이 제대로 작동하지 않아 그로 인해 동파로 인한 큰 문제들이 발생할 수 있음을 알려주고 있다. 따라서 창문을 잘 닫고 다닐 것을 강조하고 있으므로 정답은 ④ '동파 방지를 위해 창문을 닫고 다닐 것을 요청하려고'이다.

총 어휘 수 152

04 대화 주제

소재 인터넷 사기를 피하는 방법

듣기 대본 해석

여: Carl, Mark에 대해 들었니?
남: 아니, 무슨 일이 있었어?
여: 음, Mark는 중고 전화기를 찾고 있었대. 마침내 온라인에서 마음에 드는 aPhone 5를 좋은 가격에 발견했지. 그런데 판매자에게 돈을 보냈는데 상품을 못 받았대.
남: 흠, 그는 판매자에게 연락을 시도해보았대?
여: 물론 그랬지. 그런데 소위 "회사"라고 하는 곳에서 가짜 연락처를 올려 놓았대.
남: 글쎄, 그가 사기 당한 것 같아. 인터넷 사기는 점점 더 흔해지고 있어.
여: 나도 중고 노트북을 사려고 찾아보고 있는데 걱정된다.
남: 근데 회사가 신뢰할 수 있는지 아닌지 알아보는 건 꽤 쉬워.
여: 정말? 내가 어떻게 확인할 수 있을까?
남: 음, 만약 판매자가 회사라면, 간단한 온라인 검색이 판매자의 이력을 알려줄 거야.
여: 그것은 하기 쉽게 들리는데.
남: 맞아. 너는 또한 판매자에게 배송 날짜와 품질 보증서가 있는지 같은 구매에 관한 질문을 할 수도 있어.
여: 너의 조언을 받아들여야겠다. 고마워, Carl.

어휘

contact ***v.*** 연락하다 ***n.*** 연락 **fake** ***a.*** 가짜의, 거짓의 **scam** ***v.*** 속이다, 사기 치다 ***n.*** 사기, 속임수 **fraud** ***n.*** 사기 **trustworthy** ***a.*** 신뢰할 수 있는 **purchase** ***n.*** 구매 **delivery** ***n.*** 배달, 배송 **warranty** ***n.*** 보증기간, 품질 보증서

정답 ①

문제풀이
여자는 Mark가 온라인에서 중고 전화기를 사려고 돈을 보냈지만 물건을 받지 못했다는 이야기를 전하면서 자신도 중고 노트북을 사려고 하는데 걱정이 된다고 하자 남자는 인터넷 사기를 피하는 방법을 설명해 주고 있다. 따라서 두 사람이 하는 말의 주제는 ① '인터넷 사기를 피하는 방법'이다.

총 어휘 수 160

05 장소 파악

소재 인턴 주방장의 첫 출근

듣기 대본 해석
남: 안녕하세요. 저는 Larry입니다.
여: 안녕하세요, Larry. 저는 Tammy Smith예요. 새로 온 인턴인 것 같군요.
남: 만나게 되어서 기뻐요, Tammy.
여: 저도 당신을 만나서 기뻐요. 우리가 해야 할 일이 많기 때문에 시작해야 해요.
남: 그래요. 제가 어떻게 도와드리면 되죠?
여: 먼저, 피부를 보호하고 음식에 머리카락이 떨어지지 않게 고무장갑과 머리망을 쓰세요. 그리고 저장고에 가서 감자를 갖다 주세요.
남: 알겠습니다. *[잠시 후]* 자, 여기 있어요.
여: 네, 최대한 빨리 감자 껍질을 벗겨 주세요. 한 시간 후에 시작하는 연회가 있어요.
남: 그럴게요. 손님들이 몇 명이나 올 것 같아요?
여: 약 80~90명의 고객이 될 것 같아요.
남: 네, 수석 주방장님은 언제 오시는 거죠?
여: 그는 곧 오실 거예요. 그가 도착할 때까지 감자 껍질을 모두 벗겨놓도록 하세요.

어휘
make somebody's acquaintance ~를 알게 되다, 처음으로 만나다 **storage room** 저장고 **peel** ***v.*** 껍질을 벗기다 **banquet** ***n.*** 연회, 만찬 〈문제〉 **culinary** ***a.*** 음식의, 요리의 **commercial** ***a.*** 상업의, 상업적인

정답 ③

문제풀이
여자가 남자에게 피부를 보호하고 머리카락이 떨어지지 않게 고무장갑과 모자를 쓰라고 했고 감자 껍질을 벗겨달라고 했으며, 수석 주방장이 등장하는 것으로 보아 대화가 일어난 장소는 ③ '상업용 주방'이다.

오답 보기 해석
① 슈퍼마켓
② 요리 학교
④ 사무실용 건물
⑤ 커피숍

총 어휘 수 147

06 그림의 세부 내용 파악

소재 지구의 날 행사 포스터

듣기 대본 해석
남: 엄마, 제가 그린 우리 학교 지구의 날 행사 포스터 좀 보세요.
여: 잘 그렸네. 지구의 날 때 학교에서 뭐 하는데?
남: 환경에 대해서 이야기를 나누고 어떻게 도울 수 있는지에 대해서도 얘기할 거예요.
여: 오, 좋은데. 저 포스터 왼쪽 아래에 사람들처럼 나무를 심는 것에 관해 말하려고 하는 거니?
남: 맞아요. 우린 나무를 어떻게 심는지에 관한 시범을 보려고 해요. 또 저희에게 태양 에너지를 공급해 주니까 위에 태양을 그렸어요.
여: 과연 그렇구나. 그래서 길 옆에도 풍력 터빈을 그려 놓은 거구나.
남: 네. 바람도 우리에게 에너지를 공급해 줄 수 있어요. 원래 전 터빈에 날이 네 개인 줄 알았는데 인터넷에서 본 건 다 세 개밖에 없더라고요.
여: 자전거를 타고 있는 사람은 누구야?
남: 제 친구 Frank예요. 운전을 하는 대신에 자전거를 타는 것도 환경에 도움을 주는 좋은 방법이에요.
여: 맞아. 오른쪽 아래에 애들 두 명은 뭐하고 있는 거야?
남: 길가에 있는 쓰레기를 치우고 있어요.
여: 지구를 더 살기 좋은 곳으로 만들려면 우린 모두 우리의 역할에 충실해야 하는 것 같아.
남: 맞아요, 엄마. 아, 저희 집은 재활용을 좀 더 많이 했으면 좋겠어요.
여: 알겠어. 오늘부터 그렇게 하자.

어휘
environment ***n.*** 환경 **solar** ***a.*** 태양의 **wind turbine** 풍력 발전용 터빈 **blade** ***n.*** 날 **garbage** ***n.*** 쓰레기

정답 ⑤

문제풀이
오른쪽 아래에 애들 두 명은 길가에 있는 쓰레기를 치우고 있다고 했는데, 그림에서는 개를 데리고 산책을 하고 있으므로 정답은 ⑤번이다.

총 어휘 수 216

07 할 일

소재 시험공부 도와주기

듣기 대본 해석
여: Bill, Nancy한테 소식 들었어?
남: 아니. 그런데 Nancy가 오늘 아침 수업에 안 왔던데, 괜찮아?
여: Nancy는 어젯밤에 교통 사고가 나서 팔이 부러졌어.
남: 끔찍하구나. Nancy는 괜찮을까?
여: 응. 그녀는 좋아질 거야. 그런데 올해 수영 팀을 못할 거야.
남: 나쁜 소식이구나. Nancy는 아직 병원에 있어?
여: 응. 나랑 오후에 병원에 가볼래?
남: 오늘은 못 가. 다음 주 과학 시험 때문에 공부할 게 너무 많아. 내가 Nancy한테 전화해 볼게.
여: 내가 공부를 도와줄 수 있을 것 같아. 나는 작년에 시험을 잘 봤거든. 나는 괜찮으니까 그러면 함께할 시간을 더 가질 수 있을 거야.
남: 그거 좋구나. 정말 도움이 되겠어. 그럼 너 병원에 갔다가 도서관에 와서 나를 만나줄래?
여: 물론이지. 나는 가능해. 내가 Nancy 보고 나서 너한테 전화 할까?
남: 그럼. Nancy에게 내 안부도 전해줘.

어휘
hang out (~에서) 많은 시간을 보내다 **regards** ***n.*** 안부

정답 ①

문제풀이
같이 병문안을 갈 수 있는지 물어보는 여자에게 남자는 다음 주 과학 시험 때문에 시간이 없다고 했고 여자는 공부를 도와주겠다고 말했으므로 정답은 ① '시험공부 도와주기'이다.

총 어휘 수 173

08 이유

소재 아르바이트를 할 수 없는 이유

듣기 대본 해석
여: Arthur, 어젯밤 권투경기 봤어?
남: 그래, 챔피언이 타이틀을 방어했어. 정말 대단한 싸움이었어.
여: 그래, 정말 멋졌지. 너 권투 꽤 잘 하잖아. 학교 팀에 지원해 봐.

남: 나도 하고 싶은데, 그렇게 할 수 없어.
여: 왜 못해?
남: 나는 방과 후에 극장에서 아르바이트를 하거든.
여: 오, 어떤 목표가 있어서 돈을 모으고 있는 거야?
남: 그래. 여름 방학 동안에 스페인에 수학여행을 정말로 가고 싶어.
여: 그것 참 멋지네. 나도 아르바이트를 하고 싶은데 부모님께서 허락하시지 않아. 내 성적이 떨어질 거라고 생각하셔.
남: 음, 그럴 수도 있어. 요즘 공부할 시간이 별로 없거든. 나의 수학 성적이 떨어지기 시작했어.
여: 넌 아마도 일하는 것을 그만두고 학업에 더 집중해야 할 거야.
남: 맞아. 성적이 더 중요하다고 생각하거든. 게다가, 내가 나이가 더 들었을 때 일할 수 있으니까.
여: 그래. 네 말이 맞아.

어휘
defend *v.* 방어하다 **besides** *ad.* 게다가, 또한

정답 ③

문제풀이
남자의 스페인 수학여행을 위한 돈을 모으기 위해 극장에서 아르바이트를 한다는 말을 듣고, 여자는 자신도 하고 싶지만 부모님이 허락하지 않으신다고 했으므로 정답은 ③ '부모님이 허락하시지 않아서'이다.

총 어휘 수 157

09 숫자

소재 침대와 스탠드 구매

듣기 대본 해석
남: 안녕하세요. Big Al의 가구 할인점에 오신 것을 환영합니다. 오늘 제가 무엇을 도와드릴까요?
여: 안녕하세요. 제 남편과 저는 이 침대 세트를 보고 있어요. 이건 얼마죠?
남: 이것은 가장 좋은 침대 세트 중 하나예요. 침대 프레임, 화장대, 침실용 스탠드와 책상을 포함해서 900달러예요.
여: 가격이 괜찮네요. 저 제품이 정말 마음에 들어요.
남: 그것은 가장 잘 팔리는 것 중에 하나고, 정가인 1,000달러에서 마침 10퍼센트 할인을 했는데 운이 좋으시네요.
여: 좋아요. 이것으로 살게요. 침실용 스탠드를 추가할 수 있는 방법이 있나요?
남: 문제없어요. 세트와 어울리는 것을 원하시죠?
여: 당연하죠. 이것은 얼마예요?
남: 그건 보통 하나로는 150달러이지만, 세트를 사시기 때문에 20퍼센트 할인해 드릴게요.
여: 좋아요. 또한 우린 이 모든 걸 옮길 트럭이 없어요. 배달받을 수 있나요?
남: 물론이죠. 저희는 보통 80달러 배송비가 있지만 운이 좋으시네요. 1,000달러 이상의 구매에 관해서는 해당 사항이 없어요.
여: 좋아요. 그러면 침대 세트와 침실용 스탠드를 사겠어요.

어휘
frame *n.* 틀, 액자 **dresser** *n.* 화장대 **nightstand** *n.* 침실용 스탠드 **top seller** 가장 잘 팔리는 것 **mark down** ~의 가격을 인하하다 **delivery fee** 배송비

정답 ②

문제풀이
침대 프레임, 화장대, 침실용 스탠드와 책상을 포함한 침대 세트가 900달러라고 했고, 침실용 스탠드가 150달러인데 세트와 같이 구매하기 때문에 20퍼센트를 할인해준다고 했으므로 120달러라서 합계는 1,020이 된다. 구매액이 1,000달러를 넘어서 배송비는 지불할 필요가 없으므로 여자가 지불할 총 금액은 ② '$ 1,020'이다.

총 어휘 수 185

10 언급 유무

소재 전시회 주최자와의 인터뷰

듣기 대본 해석
여: 안녕하세요. 전 CBC의 Lori예요.
남: 만나서 반가워요, Lori. 전 Stan이고요. 행사에 관해 궁금해할 만한 사항에 답해드리려고 해요.
여: 감사합니다. 음, 일단 매우 아름다운 전시회를 개최하셨다고 말씀드리고 싶네요.
남: 고마워요. 이곳에는 15개국에서 온 예술가들이 그들의 작품을 전시하고 있어요. 150점 이상의 작품들이 있고요.
여: 와, 대단하네요. 이 전시회를 시작할 생각을 어떻게 하시게 되었나요?
남: 전 일생 동안 예술에 관심이 많았답니다. 특히 라틴 아메리카의 예술에요. 2~3년 전에 Boston에서 봤던 전시회를 본떠 이번 전시회를 만들었어요.
여: 이번 행사에서 기금을 모으는 목적이 무엇인지요?
남: 라틴 아메리카는 어려운 시기를 겪고 있어요. 이번 행사에서 모금된 돈은 도심 지역의 예술 프로그램을 지원하는데 도움을 줄 것입니다.
여: 알겠습니다. 전시회 기간이 어떻게 되나요?
남: 모든 예술 작품들은 이번 달 말까지 전시될 것입니다.
여: 잘 알겠습니다. 시간 내주셔서 감사합니다, Stan 씨.

어휘
put on 개최하다, 무대에 올리다 **display** *v.* 전시하다 **model A after B** B를 본떠서 A를 만들다 **fall on hard times** 어려운 시기를 겪다, 빈곤해지다 **inner city** 도심 지역 (대도시 중심부의 저소득층 거주 지역)

정답 ①

문제풀이
작품의 수(150점 이상), 시작하게 된 계기(평생 동안 관심이 있었고, 2~3년 전에 봤던 전시회를 계기로), 기금마련의 목적(라틴 아메리카의 도심 지역 예술 프로그램 지원), 전시 기간(이번 달 말까지)은 언급되었지만, 참가 예술가의 수는 언급되지 않았으므로 정답은 ① '참가 예술가 수'이다.

총 어휘 수 161

11 내용 일치 · 불일치

소재 글쓰기 여름 캠프에 관한 소개

듣기 대본 해석
여: 학생 여러분, 안녕하세요. Aspiring Writers 여름 캠프 신청에 관한 공지를 하려고 합니다. 일주일 간 지속되는 이 캠프는 미래의 작가들에게 다양한 프로그램에 참여할 기회를 제공합니다. 이 프로그램들은 창의적인 글쓰기부터 실화를 쓰는 것까지 학생들의 재능을 강화할 수 있도록 만들어졌습니다. 매년 초청 작가가 와서 학생들과 대화를 나누는데 올해는 George Martins께서 오셔서 이야기를 나누시고 참가자들의 질문을 받도록 하겠습니다. 지금 신청을 받고 있습니다. 금요일 전에 신청하시면 일찍 신청하는 할인을 받을 수 있습니다. 캠프 인원이 빨리 차니까 최대한 빨리 신청해 주세요. 신청서는 학교 홈페이지에 있습니다. 감사합니다.

어휘
registration *n.* 등록 **a variety of** 여러 가지의 **attendee** *n.* 참가자 **early-bird** *a.* 이른 아침의, 일찍 오는 사람을 위한

정답 ④

문제풀이
금요일 전에 신청하면 일찍 신청하는 할인을 받을 수 있다고 했으므로 내용과 일치하지 않는 것은 ④ '한 달 전에 신청하면 할인을 받을 수 있다.'이다.

총 어휘 수 118

12 도표

소재 가방 선택하기

듣기 대본 해석

여: Andrew, 이 전단지 봤어? Rickshaw 가방을 이번 주에 백화점에서 할인한대.
남: 좋아! 나 진짜 새 가방이 필요해. 가을에 대학 들어가잖아.
여: 그렇지. 이 중 하나가 너한테 좋을 것 같아. 어떤 게 맘에 들어?
남: 글쎄, 공간이 그렇게 많이 필요할 것 같진 않고 큰 가방은 별로 안 좋아하니까 작은 게 더 나을 것 같아.
여: 나도 눈치 챘어. 지금 가방도 그렇게 크진 않잖아.
남: 맞아. 근데 어떤 스타일을 골라야 할까?
여: 모르겠어. 어깨에 메고 다닐 거야, 아니면 크로스로 매고 다닐 거야?
남: 크로스로. 그럼 메신저 가방이 나한테 더 잘 맞겠어.
여: 그렇구나. 그럼 두 개 밖에 안 남았네. 가죽 가방이 나아, 아니면 캔버스 가방이 나아?
남: 글쎄, 유행을 따르고 싶으니까 캔버스보다는 가죽으로 살래.
여: 그게 좀 더 비싸. 괜찮아?
남: 응, 괜찮아. 지금 백화점 가서 하나 사야겠다.

어휘

flyer ***n.*** 전단지 **mall** ***n.*** 백화점 **bulky** ***a.*** 부피가 큰, 덩치가 큰 **leather** ***n.*** 가죽 **waxed canvas** 캔버스 〈문제〉 **satchel** ***n.*** (어깨에 매는) 책가방

정답 ③

문제풀이

작은 게 나을 것 같다고 했으므로 ①, ②, ③번 중에 고르면 되는데 메신저 가방이 좋고, 가죽으로 한다고 했으므로 남자가 선택할 가방은 ③번이다.

총 어휘 수 183

13 긴 대화의 응답

소재 장기자랑 수상자에게 줄 상품

듣기 대본 해석

여: 야, 이번 학기 끝날 때 학교에서 장기자랑 한대.
남: 맞아, 매년 한 번씩 해. 사실 내가 올해 장기자랑을 기획하고 있어.
여: 정말? 왜 자원했던 거야?
남: 난 새로운 거 시도하는 걸 좋아해. 그리고 이벤트 기획하는 걸 한 번도 해 본적이 없어.
여: 좋네. 그럼 넌 뭘 해야 되는 거야?
남: 음, 일단 장기자랑에 참가할 사람들을 찾아야 해. 그리고 수상자들한테 줄 상품도 골라야 돼.
여: 꽤 쉽네. 어떤 상품 생각하고 있어?
남: 음, 원래 트로피를 만들려고 했는데 생각보다 너무 비싸더라고.
여: 흠... 수상자한테 리본 주는 건 어때?
남: 사실 수상자들이 오랫동안 갖고 간직할 수 있게 좀 더 값진 걸 준비하고 싶어.
여: ⑤ <u>그런 거라면, 메달은 어때?</u>

어휘

talent show 장기자랑 **semester** ***n.*** 학기 **volunteer** ***v.*** 자원하다, 자원봉사하다 **treasure** ***v.*** 소중히 여기다 ***n.*** 보물

정답 ⑤

문제풀이

남자는 장기자랑 수상자에게 여자가 제안한 리본보다는 좀 더 값진 것을 주고 싶어한다. 이에 대한 여자의 응답으로 가장 적절한 것은 ⑤ '그런 거라면, 메달은 어때?'이다.

오답 보기 해석

① 우리 학교 장기자랑을 기획해야 해.
② 그들이 그렇게 하면 안 될 것 같아.
③ 넌 학교 장기자랑에 가면 안 돼.
④ 리본은 메달만큼 비싸진 않아.

총 어휘 수 148

14 긴 대화의 응답

소재 지나친 콜라 섭취에 대한 친구의 조언

듣기 대본 해석

남: 다이어트 콜라 한 컵 더 마실 거야?
여: 응, 부엌에 있는 김에 뭐라도 가져다 줄까?
남: 난 괜찮아. 오늘 콜라 얼마나 마셨어?
여: 이게 3잔째야. 왜?
남: 너 콜라를 너무 많이 마시는 것 같아. 너한테 나쁘다고 생각하지 않아?
여: 이건 다이어트 콜라여서 실제로 나한테 훨씬 더 건강에 좋아.
남: 그렇게 생각해?
여: 설탕이 전혀 없어서 일반 콜라보다 더 좋아.
남: 그건 맞아, 근데...
여: 근데 뭐? 다이어트 콜라를 마시는 게 안 좋다는 얘기야?
남: 일반 콜라보다 더 낫다는 건 사실일지도 모르지만, 너무 많이 마시는 것은 분명 몸에 안 좋을 거야. 네가 섭취하는 모든 카페인을 생각해 봐.
여: 네 말이 맞는 것 같다. "모든 것을 적당히"라는 옛날 속담처럼 말이야.
남: ⑤ <u>바로 그거야. 내 생각에 넌 콜라를 덜 마시고 물을 더 마셔야 돼.</u>

어휘

consume ***v.*** 소비하다, 마시다 **in moderation** 적당히, 알맞게 〈문제〉 **productive** ***a.*** 생산적인 **kick** ***v.*** (마약 · 습관 등을) 끊다, 극복하다 **addiction** ***n.*** 중독

정답 ⑤

문제풀이

남자는 다이어트 콜라를 너무 많이 마시는 여자에게 양을 줄이라고 제안하고 있다. 여자는 남자의 말에 동의하며 적당히 마셔야 하겠다고 했으므로 이에 대한 남자의 응답으로 가장 적절한 것은 ⑤ '바로 그거야. 내 생각에 넌 콜라를 덜 마시고 물을 더 마셔야 돼.'이다.

오답 보기 해석

① 맞아. 넌 보통 어떤 브랜드를 마셔?
② 맞아. 카페인은 널 더 생산적으로 만들어 줄 수 있어.
③ 응 기억해. 나가서 콜라 좀 마시자.
④ 응. 내가 카페인 중독을 끊는 건 정말 힘들어.

총 어휘 수 157

15 상황에 적절한 말

소재 친구에게 컴퓨터 빌려주기

듣기 대본 해석

남: Seha는 Jason Lee Academy에서 세미나에 참석하고 있습니다. 그는 어제 밤새도록 준비한 캘리포니아에 대한 발표 순서를 기다리고 있습니다. 기다리면서 Seha는 옆에 Laura가 앉아 있는 것을 봅니다. 그녀는 정신없이 가방에서 무언가를 찾고 있습니다. 그녀는 굉장히 걱정하는 것처럼 보입니다. Seha는 그녀에게 무슨 문제냐고 물어봅니다. 그녀는 자기 노트북 배터리를 다 썼는데 충전기를 집에 놔두고 왔다고 합니다. 다음이 그녀의 발표 순서인데 컴퓨터 없이 그녀는 발표를 할 수 없습니다. Seha는 그녀를 동정하여 도와주고 싶어합니다. 그는 Laura에게 자신의 컴퓨터를 빌려주고 싶습니다. 이러한 상황에서 Seha는 뭐라고 말할까요?
Seha: ④ <u>내 것을 사용해도 돼. 나는 지금 당장 사용하지 않아.</u>

어휘

presentation ***n.*** 발표 **frantically** ***ad.*** 정신 없이 **charger** ***n.*** 충전기 **sympathetic** ***a.*** 동정적인, 동정 어린

정답 ④

문제풀이

Seha는 바로 다음 발표 순서인 Laura에게 자신의 컴퓨터를 빌려주려고 하므로 ④ '내 것을 사용해도 돼. 나는 지금 당장 사용하지 않아.'라고 하는 것이 가장 적절하다.

오답 보기 해석

① 걱정하지 마. 다음 번엔 더 잘할 거야.
② 괜찮아. 내가 집에 가서 내 충전기를 가져올게.
③ 안됐다. 새로 하나 사는 게 어때?
⑤ 네 컴퓨터를 내가 쓰게 해줘서 고마워.

총 어휘 수 131

16 담화 주제 / 17 세부 내용 파악

소재 보도에 사용되는 대중 매체의 변화

듣기 대본 해석

남: 지난주 수업에서 우리는 사회에서 언론이 갖는 중요성에 대해 논의했습니다. 오늘은 대중에게 메시지를 전하는 데 쓰이는 다른 종류의 매체에 대해 이야기할 겁니다. 먼저 우리가 이야기해볼 것은 신문을 생기게 한 인쇄기입니다. 역사상 최초로 정보는 정기적으로 대중에게 전달되었습니다. 세계 주요 도시의 글을 읽고 쓸 줄 아는 사람들은 제때에 중요 사건들에 대해 들을 수 있었습니다. 신문은 최초의 라디오 뉴스가 방송되기 전까지 거의 300년 동안 뉴스의 주요 원천이었습니다. 갑자기 언론인들은 많은 청중에게 방송을 통해 즉각적으로 뉴스를 전할 기회를 얻게 되었습니다. 텔레비전이 곧 라디오의 뒤를 이었고, 언론에 훨씬 더 많은 시각적 매체를 제공했습니다. 마지막으로, 정보화 시대는 인터넷 언론이 생기게 하였고, 이는 빠르게 전 세계에 걸쳐 뉴스의 주요 원천이 되고 있습니다. 인터넷 사용자들은 이제 거의 즉각적으로 기사를 읽고, 짧은 음성 코멘트를 들으며 영상을 볼 수 있습니다. Twitter와 같은 소셜 미디어는 즉각적인 보도를 낳았습니다. 기자들은 이제 사건이 일어나는 중일 때 보도를 방송할 수 있게 되었습니다. 이제 저는 여러분들의 생애에서 일어났던 언론의 다른 변화들에 대해 이야기하고자 합니다.

어휘

on a regular basis 정기적으로 **literate** ***a.*** 글을 읽고 쓸 줄 아는, 교양 있는 **significant** ***a.*** 중요한 **primary** ***a.*** 주요한, 기본적인, 주된 **instantly** ***ad.*** 즉시, 즉각 **visual** ***a.*** 시각적인, 시각의 **sound bite** 짧은 코멘트, 인상적인 한마디 **instantaneously** ***ad.*** 순간적으로, 즉석으로, 동시에 **bring about** 야기하다, 초래하다 **immediate** ***a.*** 즉각적인

정답 16 ⑤ 17 ②

문제풀이

16 남자는 오늘의 토론 주제가 대중에게 메시지를 전달하는 데 사용되는 매체들임을 말하였고, 과거 신문에서부터 현재의 인터넷 매체까지 소개한 것으로 보아 남자가 하는 말의 주제로 가장 적절한 것은 ⑤ '보도에 사용되는 대중 매체의 변화'이다.

17 남자는 신문, 라디오, 텔레비전, 소셜 미디어는 언급하였으나, 포스터는 언급하지 않았으므로 정답은 ② '포스터'이다.

오답 보기 해석

17

① 신문 ③ 라디오 ④ 텔레비전 ⑤ 소셜 미디어

총 어휘 수 193

MEMO

MEMO

MEMO

MEMO